Perspectives from the Past

PRIMARY SOURCES

CIVILIZATI

VOLUME 2

From Early Modern Era through (

JAMES M. BROPHY · STEVEN EPSTEIN · CAT NILAN

JOHN ROBERTSON · THOMAS MAX SAFLEY

D1275143

W · W · NORTON & COMPANY NEW YORK · LONDON

Copyright © 1998 by W. W. Norton & Company, Inc.

All rights reserved
Printed in the United States of America
First Edition

The text of this book is composed in Minion
with the display set in Optima
Composition by PennSet, Inc.
Manufacturing by Courier
Book design by Jack Meserole

Library of Congress Cataloging-in-Publication Data
Perspectives from the past : primary sources in western civilizations
/ James M. Brophy [et al.].
    p.   cm.
    Contents: v. 1. From the ancient Near East through the age of absolutism
—v. 2. From early modern era through contemporary times.
    ISBN 0-393-95876-0 (pbk. : v. 1), — ISBN 0-393-95879-5 (pbk. : v. 2)
    1. Civilization, Western—History—Sources. I. Brophy, James M.
CB245.P45   1998
909'.09812—dc21   98-13551
                                                                CIP

ISBN 0-393-95879-5 (pbk.)

Every effort has been made to contact the copyright holders of each of the
selections. Rights holders of any selections not credited should contact W. W.
Norton & Company, Inc., in order for a correction to be made in the next
reprinting of our work.

W. W. Norton & Company, Inc., 500 Fifth Avenue, New York, N.Y. 10110
,http://www.wwnorton.com

W. W. Norton & Company Ltd., 10 Coptic Street, London WC1A 1PU

3 4 5 6 7 8 9 0

JAMES M. BROPHY is Associate Professor of modern European history at the University of Delaware. He received his B.A. from Vassar College and did his graduate training at the Universität Tübingen and Indiana University, where he specialized in the social and political history of nineteenth-century Europe. He is the author of *Capitalism, Politics, and Railroads in Prussia, 1830–1870* (1998) and has published articles on German history in the *Journal of Social History*, *Central European History*, and *History Today*. He regularly teaches the western civilization survey as well as specialized courses and seminars on historiography, modern European history, modern German history, and European nationalisms.

STEVEN EPSTEIN teaches history at the University of Colorado-Boulder. He was educated at Swarthmore College, St John's College Cambridge, and Harvard, where he developed his interests in medieval social and economic history. He is the author of *Genoa and the Genoese 958–1528* (1996), *Wage Labor and Guilds in Medieval Europe* (1991), and other works on medieval history. He has taught the first half of the western civilizations survey for fifteen years, and is still working on the course.

CAT NILAN is an assistant professor of history at Arizona State University-West. She earned her undergraduate degree in French Studies and Ph.D. in Western European History at Yale University, and also holds an M.A. in Women's History from Sarah Lawrence College. She has taught a wide range of survey courses in European and world history, as well as seminars in the history of women, the family, the working classes, and crime and the prison system. Her research and writing focuses on the social and cultural history of childhood in Romantic-era France, with an emphasis on the problems of juvenile delinquency and child abuse.

JOHN ROBERTSON received both his M.A. (1976) and his Ph.D. (1981) in Ancient History from the University of Pennsylvania. A specialist in the social and economic history of the Ancient Near East, Professor Robertson has published several articles in major scholarly journals and contributed articles to such major reference works as the *Anchor Bible Dictionary* and the recently published *Civilizations of the Ancient Near East*. He has also participated in archaeological excavations in Syria and Greece as well as the American Southwest. Since 1982, Professor Robertson has been a member of the faculty of the Department of History at Central Michigan University, where he has taught the history of Western Civilization for both the Department of History and the University Honors Program, as well as more specialized courses in the history of the Ancient Near East and the Islamic and modern Middle East.

THOMAS MAX SAFLEY is Associate Professor of History at the University of Pennsylvania. A specialist in the economic and social history of early modern Europe, his particular research interests include the history of the Reformation, of the family, of charity, of work, and of business. In addition to numerous articles and reviews, Professor Safley is the author of *Let No Man Put Asunder: The Control Of Marriage In The German Southwest, 1550–1620* (1984) and *Charity And Economy In The Orphanages Of Early Modern Augsburg* (1996). He is also co-editor of *The Workplace Before The Factory Artisans And Proletarians, 1500–1800* (1993) and serves on the editorial board of *The Sixteenth Century Journal*. At the University of Pennsylvania, Professor Safley regularly teaches the first part of the introductory survey of European history and advanced lecture courses on the Protestant and Catholic Reformations and on the early modern period. He also offers a broad array of undergraduate and gradute seminars.

CONTENTS

CHAPTER 16 ❧ THE AGE OF ABSOLUTISM
(1660–1789)   76

CHAPTER 17 ❧ THE SCIENTIFIC REVOLUTION
AND ENLIGHTENMENT   117

CHAPTER 18   THE FRENCH REVOLUTION   186

CHAPTER 19 ✑ THE INDUSTRIAL REVOLUTION 224

CHAPTER 20 ✑ CONSEQUENCES OF INDUSTRIALIZATION: URBANIZATION AND CLASS CONSCIOUSNESS 256

CHAPTER 23 ✑ THE PROGRESS OF INTERNATIONAL INDUSTRIALIZATION AND COMPETITION (1870–1914)   357

CHAPTER 24 ✑ THE MIDDLE CLASS CHALLENGED   386

CHAPTER 29 ⤫ NEW POWER RELATIONSHIPS AND THE NEW EUROPE   554

CHAPTER 30 ⤫ PROBLEMS OF WORLD CIVILIZATION   589

PREFACE FOR INSTRUCTORS

The authors of this text are very pleased to have been afforded the opportunity to design and compile this reader, which is the outgrowth of approximately sixty years of combined experience teaching the history of Western Civilization. In the course of acquiring that experience, each of the authors of this text has been frustrated by what we perceived as serious shortcomings in most of the available supplementary readers. Among the more notable deficiencies have been a frequent overemphasis on political and intellectual history and on elite culture at the expense of social and economic history; a concomitant under-inclusion of sources relating to the experiences of people of lesser socioeco-nomic station and, especially, of women; a similar underinclusion of sources representative of the experiences and perspectives of European societies east of what is today Germany; and a focus on "Western" Civilization that often has neglected to address the "West" 's important interactions with, and develop-ment of attitudes toward, "non-Western" peoples and civilizations. Some texts, in a laudable attempt to be more inclusive, have opted for incorporating more selections to serve up a veritable smorgasbord of thematically unlinked snip-pets, many of them so abbreviated or cited so disjointedly that the student can hardly gain a proper appreciation of their context or of the nature and structure of the documents from which they are derived. For ancient and medieval sources, this problem is all too often compounded by the use of translations that are either obsolete (from the standpoint of recent advances in philology) or rendered in an antiquated idiom that is hardly conducive to engaging stu-dents' interest. Finally, many readers are compiled by only one editor, who, whatever his or her experience and scholarly credentials, may under-standably be hard pressed to command adequately the range and variety of primary sources available for examining the diverse aspects of Western Civilization.

We by no means have the hubris to believe that what we have assembled will satisfy all the desiderata of every instructor. Nonetheless, to address the concerns noted above, and others, we have endeavored to produce a text that incorporates, as much as possible, the following features:

- selections that consist of complete texts or lengthy excerpts of primary-source documents, ranging from one to eight pages in length and rendered in authoritative, and eloquent, yet idiomatic, translations.

- an appropriate balance of primary sources from the western "canon," works that are illustrative of the origins and development of western political institutions, intellectual life, and "high culture" or that illustrate aspects of social and economic history as well as more mundane aspects of life in western societies. In other words, we strived to provide selections pertinent to the lives, roles, achievements, and contributions of elite and commoner, ruler and ruled, master and servant, man and woman.

- selections that reflect the experiences and perspectives of women and the dynamics of gender relations, including family and household structure.

- selections that attempt to place a focus on the "western European experience" within a broader, even global perspective, by including selections relating to eastern Europe, the ancient and Islamic Middle East, Africa, Asia, and the Western Hemisphere. Thus, interspersed among the works of western authors are to be found excerpts from ancient Egyptian and Babylonian folk tales, the Quran, and works of such figures as Ibn Khaldun, Ibn Battuta, Bernai Diaz de Castillo, Edward Morel, Mahatma Gandhi, Frantz Fanon, Chai Ling, and Ayatollah Rhollah Khomeini. Readings such as these are intended to help students trace the evolution of the concept of "the West" and its relations with the "non-West"—matters of immense significance as an increasingly global society stands at the brink of the twenty-first century.

- the incorporation of several unifying questions and issues to link documents both within and among chapters in a coherent, pedagogically useful internal framework. Thus, the documents in this text have been chosen with an overarching purpose of interweaving a number of thematic threads that compose vital elements in the colorful fabrics of Western Civilization: What are the status, responsibilities, and rights of the individual within the local community and broader society, and how have they changed over time? How have people defined their own communities, and how have they viewed outsiders? Who should have power within and over the community and society, and why? How have people responded to changes in the material world around them? Who or what controls the cosmos, and how have humankind's perceptions of its appropriate role and function within the cosmos changed?

The pedagogical and critical apparatus provided in this reader has been designed to guide the student to an appreciation of the sources, but without imparting too much in the way of historical interpretation. For each chapter we have supplied an introduction that provides historical context for the readings and alerts the student to the thematic threads that link them. Each reading is in turn introduced by a brief treatment that supplies even more specific context and alerts the student to issues of interpretation or biased perspective. Finally, each selection is accompanied by several questions intended to stimulate analysis and discussion. The placement of these questions after each selection is quite intentional, as it is our hope that students will engage each document without a preconceived or predetermined sense of why it may be important and will instead learn to trust their own critical capacities and discern the significance of a reading on their own.

Obviously, to organize a project as complex as a text of this kind and to bring it to successful and timely fruition require the skills, support, inspiration, and dedication of many people other than the authors. We wish to express our admiration and profound gratitude to the editorial and marketing staff of W. W. Norton, especially to Kate Nash, Sarah Caldwell, and Susan Upson, and, most especially, to Jon Durbin, who assembled the team, helped us to define and refine our tasks, organized the project, offered useful insight and judicious criticism, and kept all of us on task and on time. The credit for this text is surely as much his, and theirs, as ours.

PREFACE FOR STUDENTS

The purpose of this collection of documents is to provide the student with the raw materials of history, the sources, in the form of the written words that survive from the past. Your textbook relies on such documents, known as "primary" sources, as well as on the works of many past and present historians who have analyzed and interpreted these sources—the "secondary" literature. In some cases the historians were themselves sources, eyewitnesses to the events they recorded. Authors of textbooks select which facts and interpretations you should know, and so the textbook filters what you can think about the human past by limiting the information available to you. Textbooks are useful because they provide a coherent historical narrative for students of history, but it is important to remember that they are only an introduction to the rich complexity of human experience over time.

A collection of historical documents provides a vital supplement to the textbook, but it also has problems. First, the sources, mostly not intended for us to read and study, exist for the reasons that prompted someone to write them down, and others to preserve them. These reasons may include a measure of lies, self deception, or ignorance about what was really happening and being recorded. So we must ask the following questions about any document—a treaty, contract, poem, or newspaper article. Why does it exist? What specific purpose did it serve when it was written down? Who is its author? What motives prompted him or her to write down this material in this form?

The second major problem is that we, the editors of this collection, have selected, from millions of possible choices, these particular documents and not the others. Even in this process, because of the limitations of space and our own personal experiences, we present a necessarily partial and highly selective view of Western Civilization. Our purpose is not to repeat what you can find in the textbook, but to give you the opportunity to see and discuss how historians, now including yourselves, make history out of documents and their own understanding of why people behave the way they do.

Before exploring in more detail what documents are, we should be clear about what history is. Simply put, history is what we can say about the human past, in this case about the vast area of Western Civilization from its origins to the most recent past. We can say, or write, anything at all about the past because people left us their own words, in the form of documents, and we can, like detectives, question these sources and then try to understand what happened. Before the written word, there is no history in the strictest sense; instead there are preliterate societies and the tens of thousands of years for which we know only what the anthropologists and archeologists can tell us from the physical remains of bodies and objects made by human hands. And yet during this time profoundly important human institutions like language, the family, and religion first appeared. History begins with writing because that is when the documents start.

Although history cannot exist without written documents, we must remember that this evidence is complex and ambiguous. In the first place, it first appears in ancient languages, and the majority of documents in this book were not originally in English. The act of translating the documents into modern English raises another barrier or filter, and we must use our imaginations to recreate the past worlds in which modern words like "liberty," "race," or "sin" had different meanings. One job of the historian is to understand the language of the documents in their widest possible contexts. All the authors intended their documents to communicate something, but as time passes, languages and contexts change, and so it becomes more difficult for us to figure out what a document meant then, and may mean now. Language is an imperfect way to communicate, but we must make the best of what we have. If we recollect how difficult it is sometimes to understand the events we ourselves see and experience, then we can perhaps understand how careful we must be when we interpret someone else's report about an event in the past, especially when that past is far removed in space and time from our own experience.

The documents give us the language, or testimony, of witnesses, observers, or people with some point to make. This evidence, like any other, must be examined for flaws, contradictions, lies, and what it tells us that the writer did not necessarily intend to reveal. Like a patient detective, we must question our witnesses with a full awareness of their limited and often biased perception, piecing together our knowledge of their history with the aid of multiple testimonies and a broad context. Consider the document, whatever it is, as testimony, and a piece of a bigger puzzle, many of the remaining pieces of which are missing or broken. It is useful at the beginning to be clear about the simple issues—what type of document is this evidence? Who wrote it? Where and when was it written? Why does it exist? Try to understand the context of the document by relating it to the wider world—how do words by Plato or about the Nazi Party fit with what you already know about ancient Greece or twentieth-century Germany?

When the document, or witness, has been correctly identified and placed in some context, we may then interrogate it further by asking questions about the words before us. Not all documents suggest the same questions, but there are some general questions that apply to nearly every document. One place to begin is to ask, Who or what is left out? Once you see the main point, it is interesting to ask what the document tells us about people and subjects often left out of the records—women, children, religious and ethnic minorities, for example. Or, if the document is actually about a religious minority, we can ask what it tells us about the majority. Take the document and try to turn it inside out by determining the basic assumptions or biases of its author, and then explore what has been intentionally or unintentionally left out. Another way to ask a fresh question of an old witness is to look beneath the surface and see what else is there. For example, if the document in question seems mainly to offer evidence on religion, ask what it tells us about the economy, or contemporary eating habits, or whatever else might occur to you. Documents frequently reveal excellent information on topics far from their official subjects, if we remember to ask.

Every document in this collection is some kind of story, either long or short. The stories are almost all nonfiction, at least in theory, but they all have characters, a plot or story line, and above all a point to the story, the meaning. We have suggested some possible meanings in the sample questions at the end of each document, but these questions are just there to help your thinking, or get a discussion going, about the many possible meanings of the documents. You can ask what the meaning was in the document's own time, as well as what we might now see as a meaning that makes sense to us of some pieces of the past. The point of the story in a document may often concern a central issue in history, the process of change. If history is what we can say about the human past, then the most important words describe how change occurs, for example, rapidly, as in revolutions and wars, or more slowly, as in marriage or family life. Every document casts some light on human change, and the meaning of the story often relates to why something changed.

History is often at its dullest when a document simply describes a static situation, for example a law, or farming. However, even a good description reveals choices and emphasis. And if we ask, Why this law now? Why farm in this way? How did these activities influence human behavior? we can see that the real subject of nearly all documents is human change, on some level. You will find that people can and will strongly disagree about the meaning of a story, and they can use the same evidence from a document to draw radically different meanings. This is one of the challenges of history, and what makes it fun, for some explanations and meanings make more sense than others in the broader context of what we know about an episode or period of history. Argue about meaning, and you will learn not only something about your own biases and values, but also the process of sifting facts for good arguments and answers. These skills have a wide value beyond the study of history.

The documents in this collection, even the most general works of philosophy or social analysis, reveal the particular and contingent aspects of history. Even the most abstract of these documents comes from a specific time, place, and person, and sheds some light on a unique set of circumstances. When history is like the other social sciences (economics, sociology, political science, and others) it tries to deal with typical or average people, societies, or behavior. When history is like the other humanities (literature, religion, art, and others) it stresses individual people, their quirks and uniqueness. The documents also illustrate the contingent aspect of history, which unlike the social or natural sciences but like the humanities, appears to lack rules or laws. History depends on what people did, subject to the restrictions of their natures, resources, climate, and other natural factors, all with histories of their own! Rerunning this history is not like a movie, and it would never turn out the same way twice, for it is specific and contingent to the way it turned out this time. The documents do not tell a story of an orderly progression from simple to complex societies, or from bad to good ones. Instead, history continues, and people cope (or not) with the issues of religious faith, family life, making a living, and creating documents. These documents collectively provide perspectives on how experiments in living succeeded or failed. We invite you to use these documents to learn more about the people of the past than the textbooks can say, and to use your imaginations to get these witnesses to answer your questions about the process and meaning of human change.

WHERE TO BEGIN?

This checklist is a series of questions that can be used to analyze most of the documents in this reader.

> ✔ What type of document is this evidence?
>
> ✔ Why does the document exist? What motives prompted the author to write the material down in this form?
>
> ✔ Who wrote this document?
>
> ✔ Who or what is left out—women, children, other minorities, members of the majority?
>
> ✔ In addition to the main subject, what other kinds of information can be obtained?
>
> ✔ How do the subjects of the document relate to what we know about broader society?
>
> ✔ What was the meaning of the document in its own time? What is its meaning for the reader?
>
> ✔ What does the document tell us about change in society?

14 ∞ A CENTURY OF CRISIS FOR EARLY MODERN EUROPE (1560–1660)

The challenge to the authority of classical culture that the "new worlds" posed, combined with the fragmentation of the medieval Christian Church, the "body of all believers," laid the foundation in the second half of the sixteenth century for profound crises of political and social order, and of epistemology, the very foundations of human knowledge. In their efforts to describe what they saw in the Americas, European conquistadores and clergy were forced to adopt analogies: hundreds of species of plants and animals were not to be found in Pliny, the great and trusted botanist and zoologist of the ancient world, or in the Bible. The cultures of the Americas posed new models of social and political relations, opening new possibilities for the ordering of political relations and calling into question the very nature of political authority.

Within Europe, civil wars arose in the wake of the fragmentation of the Christian Church. The wars of religion in France, 1562–1598, led astute observers such as Montaigne to question the claim of each side to know the truth, and to question whether human reason was sufficient to discern the truth. In all the religious wars, beginning with the German Peasants' War of 1525 and culminating in the Thirty Years' War, 1618–1648, the social order was overthrown, as peasant killed lord, brother killed brother, son killed father, and neighbor killed neighbor. What was it to be human? To be savage? And where was God as Christian slaughtered Christian?

The crisis of the seventeenth century was not simply intellectual and spiritual, but had real material aspects. The expansion of Europe into new worlds changed patterns of consumption and production, thus contributing to the overthrow of traditional work processes and lifestyles. It created a tremendous influx of wealth that aided the rise of new economic and political powers, both social groups and nation states, and that contributed to chronic inflation. Changes in society, economy, and politics created tensions that found expression in the violence of the period. Religious wars were seldom entirely religious in cause or in consequence. The almost constant march and countermarch of armies not only destroyed life and property, but also disrupted agriculture and spread disease. The struggle for existence, difficult under the best of circumstances in the early modern period, became much more difficult in the age of crisis.

By 1660, peasants had risen in unprecedented numbers against their lords; common Englishmen had executed their king; Europeans had witnessed multiple incidents of cannibalism in their own villages; and the medieval epistemology, those very bases by which Europeans could be certain of the veracity of what they knew, had collapsed. New formulations were being tentatively put forward, but they did not yet replace the old certainties that had been irrecoverably lost.

JEAN BODIN

FROM *On Sovereignty*

Jean Bodin (1529–1596) was born a bourgeois in Angers. He entered a Carmelite monastery in 1545, apparently set on an ecclesiastical career, but obtained release from his vows around 1549. He pursued a course of study at the royal Collège de Quatre Langues in Paris. By 1550, he was well trained in humanist studies and went on to be one of the greatest scholars of his day. His continual search for religious truth placed him repeatedly under suspicion of heresy, but no clear evidence exists to support a conversion to Calvinism. Bodin continued his studies and attended the University of Toulouse, where he studied law during the 1550s. In 1561, he launched his public career by serving as an advocate before the parlement in Paris. Bodin soon rose to the attention of high officials and dignitaries and received special commissions from the king as early as 1570. In 1571, he entered the service of Francis, Duke of Alençon, a prince of the blood. During his service to Alençon, and in the aftermath of the St. Bartholomew's Day massacre, Bodin published his great work, Six livres de la république *(1576), a systematic exposition of public law. It included an absolutist theory of royal government, from which the following selection is drawn. Bodin's theory was based on the controversial notion, which proved highly influential in the development of royal absolutism, that sovereignty was indivisible and that high powers of government could not be shared by separate agents or agencies. His notion that all governmental powers were concentrated in the king of France, can be seen as a direct response to the anarchy of civil war that gripped the kingdom during the second half of the sixteenth century. In 1576, Bodin was chosen as a deputy for the Third Estate of the Estates-General of Blois. Though a royalist, Bodin opposed the civil wars that raged in France and became a leading spokesman against royal requests for increased taxation and religious uniformity. It cost him royal favor and high office. With the death in 1584 of his patron, the duke of Alençon, Bodin's career in high politics ended. He retired to Laon, where he died.*

Book I, Chapter 8

ON SOVEREIGNTY

Sovereignty is the absolute and perpetual power of a commonwealth, which the Latins call *maiestas*; the Greeks *akra exousia, kurion arche,* and *kurion politeuma*; and the Italians *segnioria*, a word they use for private persons as well as for those who have full control of the state, while the Hebrews call it *tomech shévet*—that is, the highest power of command. We must now formulate a definition of sovereignty because no jurist or political philosopher has defined it, even though it is the chief point, and the one that needs most to be explained, in a treatise on the commonwealth. Inasmuch as we have said that a commonwealth is a just government, with sovereign power, of several households and of that which they have in common, we need to clarify the meaning of sovereign power.

*   *   *

We shall conclude, then, that the sovereignty of the monarch is in no way altered by the presence of the Estates. On the contrary, his majesty is all the greater and more illustrious when all his people publicly acknowledge him as sovereign, even though, in an assembly like this, princes, not wishing to rebuff their subjects, grant and pass many things that they would not consent to had they not been overcome by the requests, petitions, and just complaints of a harassed and afflicted people which has most often been wronged without the knowledge of the prince, who sees and hears only through the eyes, ears, and reports of others.

We thus see that the main point of sovereign majesty and absolute power consists of giving the law to subjects in general without their consent. Not to go to other countries, we in this kingdom have often seen certain general customs repealed by edicts of our kings without hearing from the Estates when the injustice of the rules was obvious. Thus the custom concerning the inheritance by mothers of their children's goods, which was observed in this kingdom throughout the entire region governed by customary law, was changed without assembling either the general or local estates. Nor is this something new. In the time of King Philip the Fair, the general custom of the entire kingdom, by which the losing party in a case could not be required to pay expenses, was suppressed by an edict without assembling the Estates.

*   *   *

Book I, Chapter 10

ON THE TRUE MARKS OF SOVEREIGNTY

Since there is nothing greater on earth, after God, than sovereign princes, and since they have been established by Him as His lieutenants for commanding other men, we need to be precise about their status so that we may respect and revere their majesty in complete obedience, and do them honor in our thoughts and in our speech. Contempt for one's sovereign prince is contempt toward God, of whom he is the earthly image. That is why God, speaking to Samuel, from whom the people had demanded a different prince, said "It is me that they have wronged."

To be able to recognize such a person—that is, a sovereign—we have to know his attributes, which are properties not shared by subjects. For if they were shared, there would be no sovereign prince. Yet the best writers on this subject have not treated this point with the clarity it deserves, whether from flattery, fear, hatred, or forgetfulness.

We read that Samuel, after consecrating the king that God had designated, wrote a book about the rights of majesty. But the Hebrews have written that the kings suppressed his book so that they could tyrannize their subjects. Melanchthon thus went astray in thinking that the rights of majesty were the abuses and tyrannical practices that Samuel pointed out to the people in a speech. "Do you wish to know," said Samuel, "the ways of tyrants? It is to seize the goods of subjects to dispose of at his pleasure, and to seize their women and their children in order to abuse them and to make them slaves." The word *mishpotim* as it is used in this passage does not mean rights, but rather practices and ways of doing things. Otherwise this good prince, Samuel, would have contradicted himself. For when accounting to the people for the stewardship that God had given him, he said, "Is there anyone among you who can say that I ever took gold or silver from him, or any present whatsoever?" And thereupon the whole people loudly praised him for never having done a wrong or taken anything from anyone no matter who.

*   *   *

We may thus conclude that the first prerogative of a sovereign prince is to give law to all in general and each in particular. But this is not sufficient. We have to add "without the consent of any other, whether greater, equal, or below him." For if the prince is obligated to make no law without the consent of a superior, he is clearly a subject; if of an equal, he has an associate; if of subjects, such as the senate or the people, he is not sovereign. The names of grandees that one finds affixed to edicts are not put there to give the law its force, but to witness it and to add weight to it so that the enactment will be more acceptable. For there are very ancient edicts, extant at Saint Denys in France, issued by Philip I and Louis the Fat in 1060 and 1129 respectively, to which the seals of their queens Anne and Alix, and of

Robert and Hugh, were affixed. For Louis the Fat, it was year twelve of his reign; for Adelaide, year six.

When I say that the first prerogative of sovereignty is to give law to all in general and to each in particular, the latter part refers to privileges, which are in the jurisdiction of sovereign princes to the exclusion of all others. I call it a privilege when a law is made for one or a few private individuals, no matter whether it is for the profit or the loss of the person with respect to whom it is decreed. Thus Cicero said, *Privilegium de meo capite latum est.* "They have passed," he said, "a capital privilege against me." He is referring to the authorization to put him on trial decreed against him by the commoners at the request of the tribune Clodius. He calls this the *lex Clodia* in many places, and he bitterly protests that privileges could be decreed only by the great Estates of the people as it was laid down by the laws of the Twelve Tables in the words: *Privilegia, nisi comitiis centuriatis irroganto, qui secus faxit capital esto.*[1] And all those who have written of regalian rights agree that only the sovereign can grant privileges, exemptions, and immunities, and grant dispensations from edicts and ordinances. In monarchies, however, privileges last only for the lifetime of the monarchs, as the emperor Tiberius, Suetonius reports, informed all those who had received privileges from Augustus.

*   *   *

WHETHER IT IS LAWFUL TO MAKE AN ATTEMPT UPON THE TYRANT'S LIFE AND TO NULLIFY AND REPEAL HIS ORDINANCES AFTER HE IS DEAD

Ignorance of the exact meaning of the term "tyrant" has led many people astray, and has been the cause of many inconveniences. We have said that a tyrant is someone who makes himself into a sovereign prince by his own authority—without

---

[1] "Let no privileges be imposed except in the *comita centuriata*; let him who has done otherwise be put to death."

election, or right of succession, or lot, or a just war, or a special calling from God. This is what is understood by tyrant in the writings of the ancients and in the laws that would have him put to death. Indeed, the ancients established great prizes and rewards for those who killed tyrants, offering titles of nobility, prowess, and chivalry to them along with statues and honorific titles, and even all the tyrant's goods, because they were taken as true liberators of the fatherland, or of the motherland, as the Cretans say. In this they did not distinguish, between a good and virtuous prince and a bad and wicked one, for no one has the right to seize the sovereignty and make himself the master of those who had been his companions, no matter what pretenses of justice and virtue he may offer. In strictest law, furthermore, use of the prerogatives reserved to sovereignty is punishable by death. Hence if a subject seeks, by whatever means, to invade the state and steal it from his king or, in a democracy or aristocracy, to turn himself from a fellow-citizen into lord and master, he deserves to be put to death. In this respect our question does not pose any difficulty.

*   *   *

At this point there are many questions one may ask, such as whether a tyrant, who I said may be justly killed without form or shape of trial, becomes legitimate if, after having encroached upon sovereignty by force or fraud, he has himself elected by the Estates. For it seems that the solemn act of election is an authentic ratification of the tyranny, an indication that the people have found it to their liking. But I say that it is nevertheless permissible to kill him, and to do so by force unless the tyrant, stripping off his authority, has given up his arms and put power back into the hands of the people in order to have its judgment. What tyrants force upon a people stripped of power cannot be called consent. Sulla, for example, had himself made dictator for eighty years by the Valerian law, which he got published with a powerful army camped inside the city of Rome. But Cicero said that this was not a law. Another example is Caesar, who had himself made per-

manent dictator by the Servian law; and yet another is Cosimo de Medici who, having an army inside Florence, had himself elected duke. When objections were raised, he set off a volley of gunfire in front of the palace, which induced the lords and magistrates to get on with it more quickly.

*   *   *

So much then for the tyrant, whether virtuous or wicked, who makes himself a sovereign lord on his own authority. But the chief difficulty arising from our question is whether a sovereign prince who has come into possession of the state by way of election, or lot, or right of succession, or just war, or by a special calling from God, can be killed if he is cruel, oppressive, or excessively wicked. For that is the meaning given to the word tyrant. Many doctors and theologians, who have touched upon this question, have resolved that it is permissible to kill a tyrant without distinction, and some, putting two words together that are incompatible, have spoken of a king-tyrant (*roi tyran*), which has caused the ruin of some very fine and flourishing monarchies.

But to decide this question properly we need to distinguish between a prince who is absolutely sovereign and one who is not, and between subjects and foreigners. It makes a great difference whether we say that a tyrant can be lawfully killed by a foreign prince or by a subject. For just as it is glorious and becoming, when the gates of justice have been shut, for someone, whoever he may be, to use force in defense of the goods, honor, and life of those who have been unjustly oppressed— as Moses did when he saw his brother being beaten and mistreated and had no way of getting justice—so is it a most beautiful and magnificent thing for a prince to take up arms in order to avenge an entire people unjustly oppressed by a tyrant's cruelty, as did Hercules, who traveled all over the world exterminating tyrant-monsters and was deified for his great feats. The same was done by Dion, Timoleon, Aratus, and other generous princes, who obtained the title of chastisers and correctors of tyrants. This, furthermore, was the sole cause for which Tamerlane, prince of the Tar-

tars, declared war on Bajazet, who was then besieging Constantinople, Tamerlane saying that he had come to punish him for tyranny and to deliver the afflicted peoples. He defeated Bajazet in a battle fought on the plateau of Mount Stella, and after he had killed and routed three hundred thousand Turks, he had the tyrant chained inside a cage until he died. In this case it makes no difference whether this virtuous prince proceeds against a tyrant by force, deception, or judicial means. It is however true that if a virtuous prince has seized a tyrant, he will obtain more honor by putting him on trial and punishing him as a murderer, parricide, and thief, rather than acting against him by the common law of peoples (*droit des gens*).

But as for subjects, and what they may do, one has to know whether the prince is absolutely sovereign, or is properly speaking not a sovereign. For if he is not absolutely sovereign, it follows necessarily that sovereignty is in the people or the aristocracy. In this latter case there is no doubt that it is permissible to proceed against the tyrant either by way of law if one can prevail against him, or else by way of fact and open force, if one cannot otherwise have justice. Thus the Senate took the first way against Nero, the second against Maximinus inasmuch as the Roman emperors were no more than princes of the republic, in the sense of first persons and chief citizens, with sovereignty remaining in the people and the Senate.

*   *   *

But if the prince is sovereign absolutely, as are the genuine monarchs of France, Spain, England, Scotland, Ethiopia, Turkey, Persia, and Moscovy —whose power has never been called into question and whose sovereignty has never been shared with subjects—then it is not the part of any subject individually, or all of them in general, to make an attempt on the honor or the life of the monarch, either by way of force or by way of law, even if he has committed all the misdeeds, impieties, and cruelties that one could mention. As to the way of law, the subject has no right of jurisdiction over his prince, on whom all power and authority to command depends; he not only can revoke all the power of his magistrates, but in his presence, all the power and jurisdiction of all magistrates, guilds and corporations, Estates and communities, cease, as we have said and will say again even more elaborately in the proper place. And if it is not permissible for a subject to pass judgment on his prince, or a vassal on his lord, or a servant on his master—in short, if it is not permissible to proceed against one's king by way of law—how could it be licit to do so by way of force? For the question here is not to discover who is the strongest, but only whether it is permissible in law, and whether a subject has the power to condemn his sovereign prince.

A subject is guilty of treason in the first degree not only for having killed a sovereign prince, but also for attempting it, advising it, wishing it, or even thinking it. And the law finds this so monstrous [as to subject it to a special rule of sentencing]. Ordinarily, if someone who is accused, seized, and convicted dies before he has been sentenced, his personal status is not diminished, no matter what his crime, even if it was treason. But treason in the highest degree can never be purged by the death of the person accused of it, and even someone who was never accused is considered in law as having been already sentenced. And although evil thoughts are not subject to punishment, anyone who has thought of making an attempt on the life of his sovereign prince is held to be guilty of a capital crime, no matter whether he repented of it. In fact there was a gentleman from Normandy who confessed to a Franciscan friar that he had wanted to kill King Francis I but had repented of this evil wish. The Franciscan gave him absolution, but still told the king about it; he had the gentleman sent before the Parlement of Paris to stand trial, where he was condemned to death by its verdict and thereupon executed. And one cannot say that the court acted from fear, in view of the fact that it often refused to verify edicts and letters patent even when the king commanded it. And in Paris a man, named Caboche, who was completely mad and out of his senses, drew a sword against King Henry II without any effect or even attempt. He too was condemned to die without consideration of his insanity, which the law ordinarily excuses no matter what murder or crime the madman may have committed.

*   *   *

As for Calvin's remark that if there existed in these times magistrates especially constituted for the defense of the people and to restrain the licentiousness of kings, like the ephors in Sparta, the tribunes in Rome, and the demarchs in Athens, then those magistrates should resist, oppose, and prevent their licentiousness and cruelty—it clearly shows that it is never licit, in a proper monarchy, to attack a sovereign king, or defend one's self against him, or to make an attempt upon his life or honor, for he spoke only of democratic and aristocratic states. I have shown above that the kings of Sparta were but simple senators and captains. And when he speaks of the Estates, he says "possible," not daring to be definite. In any event there is an important difference between attacking the honor of one's prince and resisting his tyranny, between killing one's king and opposing his cruelty.

We thus read that the Protestant princes of Germany, before taking up arms against the emperor, asked Martin Luther if it were permissible. He frankly replied that it was not permissible no matter how great the charge of impiety or tyranny. But he was not heeded; and the outcome of the affair was miserable, bringing with it the ruin of some great and illustrious houses of Germany. *Quia nulla iusta causa videri potest,* said Cicero, *adversus patriam arma capiendi.*[2] Admittedly, it is quite certain that the sovereignty of the German Empire does not lie in the person of the emperor, as we shall explain in due course. But since he is the chief, they could have taken up arms against him only with the consent of the Estates or its majority, which was not obtained. It would have

been even less permissible against a sovereign prince.

I can give no better parallel than that of a son with respect to his father. The law of God says that he who speaks evil of his father or his mother shall be put to death. If the father be a murderer, a thief, a traitor to his country, a person who has committed incest or parricide, a blasphemer, an atheist, and anything else one wants to add, I confess that the entire gamut of penalties will not suffice for his punishment; but I say that it is not for his son to lay hands on him, *quia nulla tanta impietas, nullum tantum factum est quod sit parricidio vindicandum,*[3] as it was put by an orator of ancient times. And yet Cicero, taking up this question, says that love of country is even greater. Hence the prince of our country, being ordained and sent by God, is always more sacred and ought to be more inviolable than a father.

I conclude then that it is never permissible for a subject to attempt anything against a sovereign prince, no matter how wicked and cruel a tyrant he may be. It is certainly permissible not to obey him in anything that is against the law of God or nature—to flee, to hide, to evade his blows, to suffer death rather than make any attempt upon his life or honor. For oh, how many tyrants there would be if it were lawful to kill them! He who taxes too heavily would be a tyrant, as the vulgar understand it; he who gives commands that the people do not like would be a tyrant, as Aristotle defined a tyrant in the *Politics*; he who maintains guards for his security would be a tyrant; he who punishes conspirators against his rule would be a tyrant. How then should good princes be secure in their lives? I would not say that it is illicit for other princes to proceed against tyrants by force of arms, as I have stated, but it is not for subjects.

*   *   *

---

[2] "Because there can never be a just cause to take up arms against one's country."

[3] "Because there is no impiety so great, and no crime so great that it ought to be avenged by patricide."

REVIEW QUESTIONS

1. What, according to Bodin, is the definition of sovereignty?
2. In describing its prerogatives, would Bodin have agreed with Machiavelli?

3. Can sovereignty be mixed? Why?
4. Is it permissible to resist a tyrant?
5. Can a sovereign ruler be a tyrant?
6. May one resist a sovereign?

ON THE PLAGUE

FROM Instructions of the Health Board of Florence

In 1348, an epidemic of bubonic plague erupted in the city of Genoa and swept across Europe. The effects were catastrophic. Population dropped sharply, especially in crowded cities. Without the advantages of medical science or even the rudiments of public hygiene, nothing could be done to control or resist the contagion. In Florence, the number of inhabitants dropped from about 100,000 in 1348 to less than 50,000 by 1351. Population loss translated into lost production and lost consumption. Markets shrank, industries declined, and firms went bankrupt. Serious social upheavals accompanied economic decline. Antagonism and violence followed disease and deprivation. France was shaken by the peasant revolt known as the Jacquerie (1358). Recovery proved slow and sporadic. Plague recurred intermittently and remained a threat, especially to cities, until the seventeenth century, and contributed notably to the general crisis of that period. In 1630, when plague raged in Florence and the surrounding countryside once again, the administration of the Grand Duchy of Tuscany released the following "Instructions of the Health Board of Florence for the Justices of the Countryside in Case of Infectious Sicknesses that Might be Discovered in the Areas under Their Jurisdiction." These were guidelines for fighting the disease. They reflect the seriousness with which the authorities viewed epidemic disease, as a threat to the political, social, and economic order, and the altogether insufficient measures they took against it.

Instructions of the Magistracy of Health in Florence for Justices in the Countryside

'It being the task of all justices, criminal as well as civil, to watch over everything that concerns good government, they shall in particular, above all else, have an eye to good regulations regarding the interests of the Public Health, and for this purpose shall make shift to have notice of all cases of sickness believed to be infectious that should chance to occur in their jurisdictions and as soon as they come by news of any case whether of sickness or death, they shall observe the following and proceed to carry out the orders herein described against any persons whatsoever, even if they should be Florentine citizens or others in other ways privileged.

'First, they shall give orders to whomever is concerned that those dead of suspected plague are not to be buried in the churches but in the countryside far from the high roads, and a hundred armslengths from the houses, and in a grave at least three armslengths deep with the benediction that will seem fit to the priests of the parish church where such deaths may be, and if there are no gravediggers, have the corpse put on a ladder and handling it as little as possible, carried to the grave, and, where possible, put on the said corpse lime and then earth.

'As soon as the news arrives of the sickness being discovered in whatsoever house, the Justice shall give orders that the sick man be carried to the pesthouse, if it is near enough for him to be carried there.

'Then he will have orders given to the occupants of the house where the sickness has been, if they are tenants, that they must not leave the house and the fields where they are, that they must not associate with anybody, and must not give away anything from their house or fields under pain, as transgressors, of their lives and confiscation of their goods.

'If the sick of the said houses should be far from the pesthouses so that they could not with ease be carried thither, give in any case orders that none must leave home or fields, as above, being tenants.

'If the said sick are subtenants or live in houses without land the order must be given to all the occupants, with the said penalty, not to leave the house.

'As the said persons under orders need to be sustained with victuals, if they are tenants, give orders to the owners of the land that they supply the said victuals, giving them credit to repay at the harvests or in some other way.

'If they are farmworkers, or occupants of houses without land, or poor, give order to the Chamberlain of the Council that he supply them with the necessary victuals from some innkeeper or shopkeeper nearby to the amount of eight *soldi* a day per head.

'If the landlords of the said sick tenants should not live in the same jurisdiction so that the order cannot be given to them, then have the Chamberlain of the Council supply the said expenses for victuals for the said eight *soldi* a day for each one of those under orders as above.

'And they shall give orders that the victuals be brought to those under orders, not in money, but in bread and eatables by the nearest innkeepers or shopkeepers or others they deem suitable, and such things should be delivered through the windows or in some other way such that whoever brings them does not approach and does not converse with the suspect cases and those under orders, and for this debt they must be reimbursed by the owners of the land who in turn shall reimburse themselves from the peasants on whom the money is being spent.

'The said Justices will give order to the Health Deputies nearest the dwelling of the suspects, or to other of their officials, who will from time to time go and inspect the affected areas and ensure that victuals are supplied them as above and that they do not leave the house and land respectively assigned to them as the place of disinfection, which they must do, proceeding against transgressors with every rigour, having them isolated and the doors of their houses nailed up; and then after the usual disinfection have them put into prison and advise the Magistrate of the Health Board of Florence and await orders from him, which will be given.

'The quarantine and disinfection that are to be carried out in each house must be of twenty-two days at least from the day that the last person sick with the suspect sickness had died or recovered; after this period the said houses can be opened and freed.

'It must be noted that before the houses closed or under orders are opened even where none of the occupants is left, it is very fitting and necessary that first the said houses be perfumed and purified in the following manner and with the diligence described, to wit:

'First, whoever enters the house to perfume it should carry in his hand brushwood, or something like it, lighted and burning and should go upstairs with it and make fire with flames in the rooms. Then shut the windows tight and make smoke with sulphur all through the house.

'Sweep the floors, benches, and walls well, and if possible, whitewash the house or, at least, wash the walls down with alkaline solution using a whitewashing brush. The woodwork should also be washed down with alkaline solution. Put the linen cloths to soak in water and wash the mattresses and put other cloths where they can get air, and keep them aired for many, many days before they are used again. And those that were used directly by the infected person are to be burnt if they be woollens or linen. The room where the dead or sick person had been must, for three days after it has come empty, be washed out with vinegar, and have it swept thoroughly every day, and the first time, scatter lime around the room and throw vinegar over it until it has smoked and burnt itself out.

'And since it often chances that the sick are peasants far away from lands and castles and from the advantage of being able to have physicians and medicines, make very sure that they know of some easy medicines proposed to the Magistrates of the Health Board as being easy by their physicians, with which the occupants of the said houses under orders and the sick themselves may make their own medicines.

'And they shall do their utmost to save those, above all, who are healthy in the said closed houses; and for this purpose the latter, every morning, shall take some Venice treacle, oil themselves with oil against the poison, and other like preservatives, and if they have none of these, shall take nuts, and dried figs, and rue and, early in the morning, eat them or other things that are meant for the purpose.

'Every morning the sick shall take a five-ounce glass of very hot chick-pea or goat's-rue juice, and shall cover themselves well so as to sweat; they must be informed that sweating is an excellent remedy for the infectious sickness that is latent. That they strive to bring out this sweat, however, with fire or with putting cloths on or as best they can.

'Oil the swellings that appear with oil of white lilies or of camomile or flax seeds and place upon them a little wool soaked in one of these oils.

'If these swellings do not come out, go about to make them do so with a cupping glass or by putting on them white onion roasted on the embers and mixed with Venice treacle.

'If a blister or small carbuncle be found, put upon it devil's bit or scabious grass crushed between two stones, and, to remove the scab, put a little chicken fat on it and slit with a razor and then put a little Venice treacle on it. Around the small carbuncle put pomegranate juice together with the pomegranate seeds, well peeled and crushed together.

'The sick must take good care of themselves, eating meat, eggs, and good things; they must abstain from wine, and drink boiled water with the soft part of a loaf and a few coriander seeds in it.

'Note must be taken of these medicines for the use of those who cannot have, as above, the services of physicians or other medicines, those, that is, like the poor peasants who live in the countryside, etc.'

REVIEW QUESTIONS

1. Why should those concerned with good government pay particular attention to public health?
2. What might be the relation of civic order to health?
3. What effect do you suppose quarantining had upon civic order and public health?
4. What do you learn about the understanding of disease in early modern Europe?
5. How is illness a social issue?

GIANFRANCESCO MOROSINI

FROM A Venetian Ambassador's Report on Spain

The struggle for supremacy in northern Italy, which marked the last half of the fifteenth century, gave rise to a new form of diplomacy, structures and procedures that would be fundamental to relations among all modern states. Requiring continuous contact and communication, Renaissance states turned to permanent diplomacy, distinguished by the use of accredited resident ambassadors rather than ad hoc missions of medieval legates. The tasks of a permanent ambassador were to represent his government at state ceremonies, to gather information, and, occasionally, to enter into negotiations. Nowhere was this system more fully and expertly articulated than by the Republic of Venice in the late fifteenth and sixteenth centuries. Ambassadors were chosen with unusual care from the most prominent families of the city. They were highly educated, and their duties were carefully defined. Among the latter were weekly dispatches reporting all matters of any interest to Venice. These reports were regularly read and debated in the senate, which replied with questions, instructions, and information of its own. As a result, Venetian ambassadors were among the most skilled and respected in early modern Europe. Their reports remain a singularly important source for the history of that period. Gianfrancesco Morosini is, perhaps, not typical among Venetian ambassadors. He had a particularly sharp eye for social structures and details. His reports to his principals, therefore, are unusually rich in observations on the states, in this case Spain, to which he was posted. In this case, he documented the distribution of wealth in Spain, the wealth and feebleness of its aristocrats, and the poverty and incompetence of its commoners. By so doing, he offers a first-hand account of the Spanish paradox, its power and impotence.

From *Pursuit of Power: Venetian Ambassadors' Reports on Spain, Turkey and France in the Age of Philip II, 1560–1600*, by James C. Davis. English translation copyright © 1970 by James C. Davis. Reprinted by permission of HarperCollins Publishers, Inc.

Most of the men in this country are small in stature and dark in complexion, haughty if they belong to the upper classes or prudently humble if they are common people, and unsuited for any kind of work. As farmers they are the most lackadaisical in the world, and as artisans they are so lazy and slow that work that would be done anywhere else in one month in Spain requires four. They are such stupid craftsmen that in all their provinces you can hardly find a building or anything else of interest except for antiquities done in Roman times or works built by the Moorish kings. Most of the Spanish live in houses so ineptly built of inferior materials that it is remarkable if one lasts as long as the man who built it. The cities are badly run and dirty; they throw all their refuse into the public streets instead of having the conveniences in their houses which are used in Italy and other parts of the world. They give no thought to food supplies; as a result the common people often have to fight each other to get bread, not so much because there is a shortage of grain as because there is no official whose job it is to make sure that there is bread. . . .

*   *   *

Spain might be quick to rebel if there were a leader courageous enough to direct a revolt. All of the people are discontented with their king and his current ministers. The nobles are dissatisfied because they are virtually ignored, and everyone else because they pay such unbearably heavy taxes; no other people in the world carry such a tax burden as the Castilians. True, the Aragonese and Castilians have ended their quarrels and there have been no more of those rebellions of the cities against the kings which happened in the reign of the emperor Charles V, and earlier during the reign of King Ferdinand. But when the king dies —or if he should get into serious problems— these and even more unpleasant humors might recur in the body politic. There would be a special danger if the rebels used religion as a battle standard, since religious faith lends itself very well to subverting and destroying monarchies. Spain

would be particularly susceptible because there are so many there who are Moors at heart, many others who secretly remain Jews, and even some heretics. They are all very cautious because they fear the Inquisition, a high tribunal so powerful and harsh that everyone is terrified of it. Without the Inquisition Spain would be more lost than Germany and England, even though the Spanish look at first glance like the most devout Catholics in the world.

Most Spaniards are either very rich or very poor, and there would seem to be a cause-and-effect relationship between the wealth of some and the poverty of the rest. It is as if four men had to divide this chamber among them. If one man took three-quarters there would be very little to divide among the other three. The Spanish clergy is very rich; the church in Toledo alone has revenues of 400,000 ducats a year, and all the other fifty-seven bishoprics are also very wealthy. The incomes of the churches have been estimated at four million in gold per year. Then there are twenty-two dukes, forty-seven counts, and thirty-six marquises in those lands, and their incomes total nearly three million in gold a year. The richest of all is said to be the duke of Medina Sidonia, the governor-elect of Milan, whose income exceeds 150,000 ducats a year.

*   *   *

Because the king does not use them in his service, very few of the grandees know anything about running a government, nor do they know anything else. They consider it beneath them to leave their estates unless to take major government positions; on the other hand, they are not suited for life on their own estates. They do not read; they do not discuss anything of value; they simply live in ignorance. The only noteworthy thing about them is a certain loftiness and dignity which in Italy we call "Spanish composure" and which makes all foreigners hate them. They let it be understood that not only is there no other people which bears comparison with them, but that everyone should be grateful to be ruled by them. And they do not forget to use this haughtiness even among themselves. Before addressing a person as "*Señor*," "*Vuestra Merced*," "you", . . . or "*el*," they give the matter a great deal of thought, because they believe that any distinction they confer on someone else reduces their own importance.

Because they remain on their own lands they have seen and they know nothing about the world. Their lack of schooling makes them ignorant and their lack of contacts with others makes them arrogant. This arrogance is very common among the young people, especially those who are surrounded by great wealth. Revered and deferred to by their own domestic servants, they soon come to believe that everyone should behave that way toward them, and that no one is so important as they. The result is that they look down on others —indeed, they often despise them—and only late or never do they realize their error, when they have been damaged and shamed.

The Spanish grandees consider attending to business matters just as ridiculous as book reading; both pursuits are detestable, or at least completely at odds with the life of a knight. And yet they do not take much pleasure in horsemanship. Instead they pass the time idly, even depravedly. The reasons for this are that they have been poorly brought up and they believe that exercise in Spain is "unhealthy," and also that the king lives in great seclusion and has no interest in watching tournaments.

*   *   *

The nobles and other aristocrats are all tax exempt; they pay the king no head or property tax at all. Their only obligation is to serve in his army at their own expense, and even then only when it is a question of defending Spain from attack. They are very firm and determined about guarding their tax immunity, just as the Aragonese defend all of their liberties. Once when the government tried to impose a very light tax on them they raised such an uproar that the matter was dropped.

The nobles and grandees of Castile have so little legal authority in their own jurisdictions that

most of them have courts only of the first instance; and few of their courts may hear appeals. All appeals eventually go to the chancelleries and the royal council. Their own vassals can have them summoned to these higher courts on the slightest of grounds, and they are often treated worse there than the lowliest subjects. This happens both because such is the king's wish and because the judges usually come from the lower classes. The reason for this is that judges have to be university graduates; since the nobles consider it beneath them to study anything, the power of the courts goes by default into the hands of plebeians. Professional learning is the only route by which men from the lower classes can rise to important posts. This explains why not only the law courts but almost all of the bishoprics are also in the hands of commoners, who are enemies of the nobility. This in turn is another of the grudges the upper classes have against the present regime. At one time most of the bishoprics were given as a matter of course to younger sons of the grandees, as a way of compensating them for not being the heirs. Despite all I have said, however, the king still has ample means to gratify the nobles, since he has many knighthoods in the military orders to distribute, all of which may be conferred only on nobles. Some of these have incomes of up to twelve thousand ducats.

*   *   *

REVIEW QUESTIONS

1. What were the sources of Spain's declining power, according to Morosini?
2. How does Morosini depict the nobility?
3. What are their values?
4. What does Morosini suggest is significantly undervalued by the Spanish nobility? Why?
5. What do we learn about the distribution of authority in Spain?
6. How are political decisions made?

REGINALD SCOT

FROM *Discoverie of Witchcraft*

Reginald Scot (1538–1599) was a Kentish squire who witnessed a number of fraud-ulent accusations of witchcraft in the villages of his shire during the reign of Eliza-beth I. In 1584 he wrote his Discoverie of Witchcraft *which contains a remarkable exposition of magical elements in medieval Catholicism, and a protest against the persecution of harmless old women. Scot doubted that God could ever have allowed witches to exercise supernatural powers, much less demand that they be persecuted for it. In this regard, he deserves to be ranked among the skeptics on the question of witchcraft, although he never denied the existence of witches. According to Scot, all "witches" fell into one of four categories. First were the innocent, those falsely ac-cused. Second were the deluded, those convinced through their own misery that they were witches. Third were the malefactors, those who harmed people and damaged property, though not by supernatural means. Fourth were imposters, those who posed as witches and conjurers. Scot denied that any of these witches had access to supernatural powers. Malefactors and imposters were, in fact, the witches named in the Bible as not being suffered to live. They were the only witches Scot admitted. His work is said to have made a great impression in the magistracy and clergy of his day. Nonetheless, his remained a minority opinion. Most contemporaries under-stood as tantamount to atheism any denial of the reality of spirits or the possibility of the supernatural. The persecution of witches continued unabated into the eigh-teenth century; many thousands, mostly harmless old women, fell victim to the rage.*

From *Discoverie of Witchcraft, 1584,* edited by Hugh Ross Wilkinson, Carbondale, Illinois, 1962.

*   *   *

The inconvenience growing by mens credulitie herein, with a reproofe of some churchmen, which are inclined to the common conceived opinion of witches omnipotencie, and a familiar example thereof. But the world is now so bewitched and over-run with this fond error, that even where a man shuld seeke comfort and counsell, there shall hee be sent (in case of necessitie) from God to the divell; and from the Physician, to the coosening witch, who will not sticke to take upon hir, by wordes to heale the lame (which was proper onelie to Christ: and to them whom he assisted with his divine power) yea, with hir familiar & charmes she will take upon hir to cure the blind: though in the tenth of S. *Johns* Gospell it be written, that the divell cannot open the eies of the blind. And they attaine such credit as I have heard (to my greefe) some of the ministerie affirme, that they have had in their parish at one instant, xvii. or xviii. witches: meaning such as could worke miracles superna-turallie. Whereby they manifested as well their infidelitie and ignorance, in conceiving Gods word; as their negligence and error in instructing their flocks. For they themselves might understand, and also teach their parishoners, that God onelie worketh great woonders; and that it is he which sendeth such punishments to the wicked, and such trials to the elect: according to the saieng of the Prophet *Haggai*, I smote you with blasting and mildeaw, and with haile, in all the labours of your hands; and yet you turned not unto me, saith the Lord. And therefore saith the same Prophet in another place; You have sowen much, and bring in little. And both in *Joel* and *Leviticus*, the like phrases and proofes are used and made. But more shalbe said of this hereafter.

* * *

At the assises holden at *Rochester*, Anno 1581, one *Margaret Simons*, the wife of *John Simons*, of *Brenchlie* in *Kent*, was araigned for witchcraft, at the instigation and complaint of divers fond and malicious persons; and speciallie by the meanes of one *John Ferrall* vicar of that parish: with whom I talked about that matter, and found him both fondlie assotted in the cause, and enviouslie bent towards hir: and (which is worse) as unable to make a good account of his faith, as shee whom he accused. That which he, for his part, laid to the poore womans charge, was this.

His sonne (being an ungratious boie, and prentise to one *Robert Scotchford* clothier, dwelling in that parish of *Brenchlie*) passed on a daie by hir house; at whome by chance hir little dog barked. Which thing the boie taking in evill part, drewe his knife, & pursued him therewith even to hir doore: whom she rebuked with some such words as the boie disdained, & yet nevert, helesse would not be persuaded to depart in a long time. At the last he returned to his maisters house, and within five or sixe daies fell sicke. Then was called to mind the fraie betwixt the dog and the boie: insomuch as the vicar (who thought himselfe so privileged, as he little mistrusted that God would visit his children with sicknes) did so calculate; as he found, partlie through his owne judgement, and partlie (as he himselfe told me) by the relation of other witches, that his said sonne was by hir bewitched. Yea, he also told me, that this his sonne (being as it were past all cure) received perfect health at the hands of another witch.

He proceeded yet further against hir, affirming, that alwaies in his parish church, when he desired to read most plainelie, his voice so failed him, as he could scant be heard at all. Which hee could impute, he said, to nothing else, but to hir inchantment. When I advertised the poore woman hereof, as being desirous to heare what she could saie for hir selfe; she told me, that in verie deed his voice did much faile him, speciallie when he strained himselfe to speake lowdest. How beit, she said that at all times his voice was hoarse and lowe: which thing I perceived to be true. But sir, said she, you shall understand, that this our vicar is diseased with such a kind of hoarsenesse, as divers of our neighbors in this parish, not long since, doubted that he had the French pox; & in that respect utterly refused to communicate with him: untill such time as (being therunto injoined by M. D. *Lewen* the Ordinarie) he had brought frō *London* a certificat, under the hands of two physicians, that his hoarsenes proceeded from a disease in the lungs. Which certificat he published in the church, in the presence of the whole congregation: and by this meanes hee was cured, or rather excused of the shame of his disease. And this I knowe to be true by the relation of divers honest men of that parish. And truelie, if one of the Jurie had not beene wiser than the other, she had beene condemned thereupon, and upon other as ridiculous matters as this. For the name of a witch is so odious, and hir power so feared among the common people, that if the honestest bodie living chance to be arraigned thereupon, she shall hardlie escape condemnation.

A CONFUTATION OF THE COMMON CONCEIVED OPINION OF WITCHES AND WITCHCRAFT, AND HOW DETESTABLE A SINNE IT IS TO REPAIRE TO THEM FOR COUNSELL OR HELPE IN TIME OF AFFLICTION.

But whatsoever is reported or conceived of such manner of witchcrafts, I dare avow to be false and fabulous (coosinage, dotage, and poisoning excepted:) neither is there any mention made of these kind of witches in the Bible. If Christ had knowne them, he would not have pretermitted to invaie against their presumption, in taking upon them his office: as, to heale and cure diseases; and to worke such miraculous and supernaturall things, as whereby he himselfe was speciallie knowne, beleeved, and published to be God; his actions and cures consisting (in order and effect) according to the power of our witchmoongers imputed to witches. Howbeit, if there be any in these daies afflicted in such strange sort, as Christs cures and patients are described in the new testament to have beene: we flie from trusting in God to trusting in witches, who doo not onelie in their coosening art take on them the office of Christ in this behalfe; but use his verie phrase of speech to such idolators, as com to seeke divine assistance at their hands, saieng; Go thy waies, thy sonne or thy daughter, &c. shall doo well, and be whole.

*   *   *

In like manner I say, he that attributeth to a witch, such divine power, as dulie and onelie apperteineth unto GOD (which all witchmongers doo) is in hart a blasphemer, an idolater, and full of grosse impietie, although he neither go nor send to hir for assistance.

A FURTHER CONFUTATION OF WITCHES MIRACULOUS AND OMNIPOTENT POWER, BY INVINCIBLE REASONS AND AUTHORITIES, WITH DISSUASIONS FROM SUCH FOND CREDULITIE.

If witches could doo anie such miraculous things, as these and other which are imputed to them, they might doo them againe and againe, at anie time or place, or at anie mans desire: for the divell is as strong at one time as at another, as busie by daie as by night, and readie enough to doo all mischeefe, and careth not whom he abuseth. And

in so much as it is confessed, by the most part of witchmoongers themselves, that he knoweth not the cogitation of mans heart, he should (me thinks) sometimes appeere unto honest and credible persons, in such grosse and corporall forme, as it is said he dooth unto witches: which you shall never heare to be justified by one sufficient witnesse. For the divell indeed entreth into the mind, and that waie seeketh mans confusion.

The art alwaies presupposeth the power; so as, if they saie they can doo this or that, they must shew how and by what meanes they doo it; as neither the witches, nor the witchmoongers are able to doo. For to everie action is required the facultie and abilitie of the agent or dooer; the aptnes of the patient or subject; and a convenient and possible application. Now the witches are mortall, and their power dependeth upon the analogie and consonancie of their minds and bodies; but with their minds they can but will and understand; and with their bodies they can doo no more, but as the bounds and ends of terrene sense will suffer: and therefore their power extendeth not to doo such miracles, as surmounteth their owne sense, and the understanding of others which are wiser than they; so as here wanteth the vertue and power of the efficient. And in reason, there can be no more vertue in the thing caused, than in the cause, or that which proceedeth of or from the benefit of the cause. And we see, that ignorant and impotent women, or witches, are the causes of incantations and charmes; wherein we shall perceive there is none effect, if we will credit our owne experience and sense unabused, the rules of philosophie, or the word of God. For alas! What an unapt instrument is a toothles, old, impotent, and unweldie woman to flie in the aier? Truelie, the divell little needs such instruments to bring his purposes to passe.

It is strange, that we should suppose, that such persons can worke such feates: and it is more strange, that we will imagine that to be possible to be doone by a witch, which to nature and sense is impossible; speciallie when our neighbours life dependeth upon our credulitie therein; and when we may see the defect of abilitie, which alwaies is an impediment both to the act, and also to the presumption thereof. And bicause there is nothing possible in lawe, that in nature is impossible; therefore the judge dooth not attend or regard what the accused man saith; or yet would doo: but what is prooved to have beene committed, and naturallie falleth in mans power and will to doo. For the lawe saith, that To will a thing unpossible, is a signe of a mad man, or of a foole, upon whom no sentence or judgement taketh hold. Furthermore, what Jurie will condemne, or what Judge will give sentence or judgement against one for killing a man at *Berwicke*; when they themselves, and manie other sawe that man at *London*, that verie daie, wherein the murther was committed; yea though the partie confesse himself guiltie therein, and twentie witnesses depose the same? But in this case also I saie the judge is not to weigh their testimonie, which is weakened by lawe; and the judges authoritie is to supplie the imperfection of the case, and to mainteine the right and equitie of the same.

Seeing therefore that some other things might naturallie be the occasion and cause of such calamities as witches are supposed to bring; let not us that professe the Gospell and knowledge of Christ, be bewitched to beleeve that they doo such things, as are in nature impossible, and in sense and reason incredible. If they saie it is doone through the divels helpe, who can work miracles; whie doo not theeves bring their busines to passe miraculouslie, with whom the divell is as conversant as with the other? Such mischeefes as are imputed to witches, happen where no witches are; yea and continue when witches are hanged and burnt: whie then should we attribute such effect to that cause, which being taken awaie, happeneth neverthelesse?

*   *   *

WHAT TESTIMONIES AND WITNESSES ARE ALLOWED TO GIVE EVIDENCE AGAINST REPUTED WITCHES, BY THE REPORT & ALLOWANCE OF THE INQUISITORS THEMSELVES, AND SUCH AS ARE SPECIALL WRITERS HEEREIN.

Excommunicat persons, partakers of the falt, infants, wicked servants, and runnawaies are to be admitted to beare witnesse against their dames in this mater of witchcraft: bicause (saith *Bodin* the champion of witchmoongers) none that be honest are able to detect them. Heretikes also and witches shall be received to accuse, but not to excuse a witch. And finallie, the testimonie of all infamous persons in this case is good and allowed. Yea, one lewd person (saith *Bodin*) may be received to accuse and condemne a thousand suspected witches. And although by lawe, a capitall enimie may be challenged; yet *James Sprenger*, and *Henrie Institor*, (from whom *Bodin*, and all the writers that ever I have read, doo receive their light, authorities and arguments) saie (upon this point of lawe) that The poore frendlesse old woman must proove, that hir capitall enimie would have killed hir, and that hee hath both assalted & wounded hir; otherwise she pleadeth all in vaine. If the judge aske hir, whether she have anie capitall enimies; and she rehearse other, and forget hir accuser; or else answer that he was hir capital enimie, but now she hopeth he is not so: such a one is nevertheles admitted for a witnes. And though by lawe, single witnesses are not admittable; yet if one depose she hath bewitched hir cow; another, hir sow; and the third, hir butter: these saith (saith *M. Mal.* and *Bodin*) are no single witnesses; bicause they agree that she is a witch.

THE FIFTEENE CRIMES LAID TO THE CHARGE OF WITCHES, BY WITCHMONGERS, SPECIALLIE BY BODIN, IN DAEMONOMANIA.

They denie God, and all religion.

Answere. Then let them die therefore, or at the least be used like infidels, or apostataes.

They cursse, blaspheme, and provoke God with all despite.

Answere. Then let them have the law expressed in *Levit.* 24. and *Deut.* 13 & 17.

They give their faith to the divell, and they worship and offer sacrifice unto him.

Ans. Let such also be judged by the same lawe.

They doo solemnelie vow and promise all their progenie unto the divell.

Ans. This promise proceedeth from an unsound mind, and is not to be regarded; bicause they cannot performe it, neither will it be prooved true. Howbeit, if it be done by anie that is sound of mind, let the cursse of *Jeremie*, 32.36. light upon them, to wit, the sword, famine and pestilence.

They sacrifice their owne children to the divell before baptisme, holding them up in the aire unto him, and then thrust a needle into their braines.

Ans. If this be true, I maintaine them not herein: but there is a lawe to judge them by. Howbeit, it is so contrarie to sense and nature, that it were follie to beleeve it; either upon *Bodins* bare word, or else upon his presumptions; speciallie when so small commoditie and so great danger and inconvenience insueth to the witches thereby.

They burne their children when they have sacrificed them.

Ans. Then let them have such punishment, as they that offered their children unto *Moloch: Levit.* 20. But these be meere devises of witchmoongers and inquisitors, that with extreame tortures have wroong such confessions from them; or else with false reports have beelied them; or by flatterie & faire words and promises have woon it at their hands, at the length.

They sweare to the divell to bring as manie into that societie as they can.

Ans. This is false, and so prooved elsewhere.

They sweare by the name of the divell.

Ans. I never heard anie such oth, neither have we warrant to kill them that so doo sweare; though indeed it be verie lewd and impious.

They use incestuous adulterie with spirits.

Ans. This is a stale ridiculous lie, as is prooved apparentlie hereafter.

They boile infants (after they have murthered them unbaptised) untill their flesh be made potable.

Ans. This is untrue, incredible, and impossible.

They eate the flesh and drinke the bloud of men and children openlie.

Ans. Then are they kin to the *Anthropophagi* and *Canibals.* But I beleeve never an honest man in *England* nor in *France,* will affirme that he hath seene any of these persons, that are said to be witches, do so; if they shuld, I beleeve it would poison them.

They kill men with poison.

Ans. Let them be hanged for their labour.

They kill mens cattell.

Ans. Then let an action of trespasse be brought against them for so dooing.

They bewitch mens corne, and bring hunger and barrennes into the countrie; they ride and flie in the aire, bring stormes, make tempests, &c.

Ans. Then will I worship them as gods; for those be not the works of man nor yet of witch: as I have elsewhere prooved at large.

They use venerie with a divell called *Iucubus*, even when they lie in bed with their husbands, and have children by them, which become the best witches.

Ans. This is the last lie, verie ridiculous, and confuted by me elsewhere.

OF FOURE CAPITALL CRIMES OBJECTED AGAINST WITCHES, ALL FULLIE ANSWERED AND CONFUTED AS FRIVOLOUS.

First therefore they laie to their charge idolatrie. But alas without all reason: for such are properlie knowne to us to be idolaters, as doo externall worship to idols or strange gods. The furthest point that idolatrie can be stretched unto, is, that they, which are culpable therein, are such as hope for and seeke salvation at the hands of idols, or of anie other than God; or fixe their whole mind and love upon anie creature, so as the power of God be neglected and contemned thereby. But witches neither seeke nor beleeve to have salvation at the hands of divels, but by them they are onlie deceived; the instruments of their phantasie being corrupted, and so infatuated, that they suppose, confesse, and saie they can doo that, which is as farre beyond their power and nature to doo, as to kill a man at *Yorke* before noone, when they have beene seene at *London* in that morning, &c. But if these latter idolaters, whose idolatrie is spirituall, and committed onelie in mind, should be punished by death; then should everie covetous man, or other, that setteth his affection anie waie too much upon an earthlie creature, be executed, and yet perchance the witch might escape scotfree.

Secondlie, apostasie is laid to their charge, whereby it is inferred, that they are worthie to die. But apostasie is, where anie of sound judgement forsake the gospell, learned and well knowne unto them; and doo not onelie embrace impietie and infidelitie; but oppugne and resist the truth erstwhile by them professed. But alas these poore women go not about to defend anie impietie, but after good admonition repent.

Thirdlie, they would have them executed for seducing the people. But God knoweth they have small store of Rhetorike or art to seduce; except to tell a tale of Robin good-fellow be to deceive and seduce. Neither may their age or sex admit that opinion or accusation to be just: for they themselves are poore seduced soules. I for my part (as else-where I have said) have prooved this point to be false in most apparent sort.

Fourthlie, as touching the accusation, which all the writers use herein against them for their carnall copulation with *Incubus*: the follie of mens credulitie is as much to be woondered at and derided, as the others vaine and impossible confessions. For the divell is a spirit, and hath neither flesh nor bones, which were to be used in the performance of this action. And since he also lacketh all instruments, substance, and seed ingendred of bloud; it were follie to staie overlong in the confutation of that, which is not in the nature of things. And yet must I saie somewhat heerein, bicause the opinion hereof is so stronglie and universallie received, and the fables thereupon so innumerable; wherby *M. Mal. Bodin, Hemingius, Hyperius, Danaeus, Erastus*, and others that take upon them to write heerein, are so abused, or rather seeke to abuse others; as I woonder at their fond credulitie in this behalfe. For they affirme undoubtedlie, that the divell plaieth *Succubus* to the man, and carrieth from him the seed of generation, which he delivereth as *Incubus* to the woman, who manie times that waie is gotten with child; which will verie naturallie (they saie) become a witch, and such one they affirme *Merline* was.

*　　*　　*

BY WHAT MEANES THE COMMON PEOPLE HAVE BEENE MADE BELEEVE IN THE MIRACULOUS WORKS OF WITCHES, A DEFINITION OF WITCHCRAFT, AND A DESCRIPTION THEREOF.

The common people have beene so assotted and bewitched, with whatsoever poets have feigned of witchcraft, either in earnest, in jest, or else in derision; and with whatsoever lowd liers and couseners for their pleasures heerein have invented, and with whatsoever tales they have heard from old doting women, or from their mothers maids, and with whatsoever the grandfoole their ghostlie father, or anie other morrow masse preest had informed them; and finallie with whatsoever they have swallowed up through tract of time, or through their owne timerous nature or ignorant conceipt, concerning these matters of hagges and witches: as they have so settled their opinion and credit thereupon, that they thinke it heresie to doubt in anie part of the matter; speciallie bicause they find this word witchcraft expressed in the scriptures; which is as to defend praieng to saincts, bicause *Sanctus, Sanctus, Sanctus* is written in *Te Deum.*

And now to come to the definition of witch-craft, which hitherto I did deferre and put off pur-poselie: that you might perceive the true nature thereof, by the circumstances, and therefore the rather to allow of the same, seeing the varietie of other writers. Witchcraft is in truth a cousening art, wherin the name of God is abused, prophaned and blasphemed, and his power attributed to a vile creature. In estimation of the vulgar people, it is a supernaturall worke, contrived betweene a cor-porall old woman, and a spirituall divell. The ma-ner thereof is so secret, mysticall, and strange, that to this daie there hath never beene any credible witnes thereof. It is incomprehensible to the wise, learned or faithfull; a probable matter to children, fooles, melancholike persons and papists. The trade is thought to be impious. The effect and end thereof to be sometimes evill, as when thereby man or beast, grasse, trees, or corne, &c; is hurt: sometimes good, as whereby sicke folkes are healed, theeves bewraied, and true men come to their goods, &c. The matter and instruments, wherewith it is accomplished, are words, charmes, signes, images, characters, &c; the which words al-though any other creature do pronounce, in man-ner and forme as they doo, leaving out no circumstance requisite or usually for that action: yet none is said to have the grace or gift to per-forme the matter, except she be a witch, and so taken either by hir owne consent, or by others imputation.

REASONS TO PROOVE THAT WORDS AND CHAR-ACTERS ARE BUT BABLES, & THAT WITCHES CANNOT DOO SUCH THINGS AS THE MULTITUDE SUPPOSETH THEY CAN, THEIR GREATEST WOONDERS PROOVED TRIFLES, OF A YOONG GENTLEMAN COUSENED.

That words, characters, images, and such other trinkets, which are thought so necessarie instru-ments for witchcraft (as without the which no such thing can be accomplished) are but bables, devised by couseners, to abuse the people with-all; I trust I have sufficientlie prooved. And the same maie be further and more plainelie per-ceived by these short and compendious reasons following.

First, in that *Turkes* and infidels, in their witchcraft, use both other words, and other char-acters than our witches doo and also such as are most contrarie. In so much as, if ours be bad, in reason theirs should be good. If their witches can doo anie thing, ours can doo nothing. For as our witches are said to renounce Christ, and despise his sacraments: so doo the other forsake *Mahomet*, and his lawes, which is one large step to chris-tianitie.

It is also to be thought, that all witches are couseners; when mother *Bungie*, a principall witch, so reputed, tried, and condemned of all men, and continuing in that exercise and estima-tion manie yeares (having cousened & abused the whole realme, in so much as there came to hir, witchmongers from all the furthest parts of the land, she being in diverse bookes set out with au-thoritie, registred and chronicled by the name of the great witch of *Rochester*, and reputed among all men for the cheefe ringleader of all other witches) by good proofe is found to be a meere cousener; confessing in hir death bed freelie, without compulsion or inforcement, that hir cunning consisted onlie in deluding and de-ceiving the people: saying that she had (towards the maintenance of hir credit in that cousening trade) some sight in physicke and surgerie, and the assistance of a freend of hirs, called *Heron*, a professor thereof. And this I know, partlie of mine owne knowledge, and partlie by the testimonie of hir husband, and others of credit, to whome (I saie) in hir death bed, and at sundrie other times she protested these things; and also that she never had indeed anie materiall spirit or divell (as the voice went) nor yet knew how to worke anie su-pernaturall matter, as she in hir life time made men beleeve she had and could doo.

*   *   *

Againe, who will mainteine, that common witchcrafts are not cousenages, when the great and famous witchcrafts, which had stolne credit not onlie from all the common people, but from men of great wisdome and authoritie, are discovered to be beggerlie slights of cousening varlots? Which otherwise might and would have remained a perpetuall objection against me. Were there not three images of late yeeres found in a doonghill, to the terror & astonishment of manie thousands? In so much as great matters were thought to have beene pretended to be doone by witchcraft. But if the Lord preserve those persons (whose destruction was doubted to have beene intended thereby) from all other the lewd practises and attempts of their enimies; I feare not, but they shall easilie withstand these and such like devises, although they should indeed be practised against them. But no doubt, if such bables could have brought those matters of mischeefe to passe, by the hands of traitors, witches, or papists; we should long since have beene deprived of the most excellent jewell and comfort that we enjoy in this world. Howbeit, I confesse, that the feare, conceipt, and doubt of such mischeefous pretenses may breed inconvenience to them that stand in awe of the same. And I wish, that even for such practises, though they never can or doo take effect, the practisers be punished with all extremitie: bicause therein is manifested a traiterous heart to the Queene, and a presumption against God.

* * *

REVIEW QUESTIONS

1. What is witchcraft?
2. How does Scot depict it?
3. According to Scot, what characterizes witches and witchcraft?
4. How does Scot confound the very notion of witchcraft?
5. Where does he locate the source of all power to override the laws of nature?
6. What sort of power is left to witches?
7. What, according to Scot, is their relation to the natural world?

BLAISE PASCAL

FROM *Pensées*

Blaise Pascal (1623–1662) was born the son of a French official. During his life, he dabbled in many subjects, including science, religion, and literature. His conversion to Jansenism plunged him into controversy with the Jesuits, giving rise to his Lettres provinciales. *These, along with his* Pensées, *from which the current selection is drawn, established his literary fame. His thought contains a fascinating blend of confidence in human reason and consciousness of its limits. René Descartes viewed*

Pascal as the embodiment of a mentality of intellectual and spiritual crisis. Be that as it may, Pascal is also considered one of the great stylists of the French language.

From *Pensées* by Blaise Pascal, translated by A. J. Krailsheimer, pp. 58–64, 121–125. Copyright © A. J. Krailsheimer, 1966, 1995. Reproduced by permission of Penguin Books Ltd.

FROM The Wager

* * *

Infinity—nothing. Our soul is cast into the body where it finds number, time, dimensions; it reasons about these things and calls them natural, or necessary, and can believe nothing else.

Unity added to infinity does not increase it at all, any more than a foot added to an infinite measurement: the finite is annihilated in the presence of the infinite and becomes pure nothingness. So it is with our mind before God, with our justice before divine justice. There is not so great a disproportion between our justice and God's as between unity and infinity.

God's justice must be as vast as his mercy. Now his justice towards the damned is less vast and ought to be less startling to us than his mercy towards the elect.

We know that the infinite exists without knowing its nature, just as we know that it is untrue that numbers are finite. Thus it is true that there is an infinite number, but we do not know what it is. It is untrue that it is even, untrue that it is odd, for by adding a unit it does not change its nature. Yet it is a number, and every number is even or odd. (It is true that this applies to every finite number.)

Therefore we may well know that God exists without knowing what he is.

Is there no substantial truth, seeing that there are so many true things which are not truth itself?

Thus we know the existence and nature of the finite because we too are finite and extended in space.

We know the existence of the infinite without knowing its nature, because it too has extension but unlike us no limits.

But we do not know either the existence or the nature of God, because he has neither extension nor limits.

But by faith we know his existence, through glory we shall know his nature.

Now I have already proved that it is quite possible to know that something exists without knowing its nature.

Let us now speak according to our natural lights.

If there is a God, he is infinitely beyond our comprehension, since, being indivisible and without limits, he bears no relation to us. We are therefore incapable of knowing either what he is or whether he is. That being so, who would dare to attempt an answer to the question? Certainly not we, who bear no relation to him.

Who then will condemn Christians for being unable to give rational grounds for their belief, professing as they do a religion for which they cannot give rational grounds? They declare that it is a folly, *stultitiam*, in expounding it to the world, and then you complain that they do not prove it. If they did prove it they would not be keeping their word. It is by being without proof that they show they are not without sense. 'Yes, but although that excuses those who offer their religion as such, and absolves them from the criticism of producing it without rational grounds, it does not absolve those who accept it.' Let us then examine this point, and let us say: 'Either God is or he is not.' But to which view shall we be inclined? Reason cannot decide this question. Infinite chaos separates us. At the far end of this infinite distance a coin is being spun which will come down heads or tails. How will you wager? Reason cannot make you choose either, reason cannot prove either wrong.

Do not then condemn as wrong those who have made a choice, for you know nothing about it. 'No, but I will condemn them not for having made this particular choice, but any choice, for, although the one who calls heads and the other one are equally at fault, the fact is that they are both at fault: the right thing is not to wager at all.'

Yes, but you must wager. There is no choice, you are already committed. Which will you choose then? Let us see: since a choice must be made, let us see which offers you the least interest. You have two things to lose: the true and the good; and two things to stake: your reason and your will, your knowledge and your happiness; and your nature has two things to avoid: error and wretchedness. Since you must necessarily choose, your reason is no more affronted by choosing one rather than the other. That is one point cleared up. But your happiness? Let us weigh up the gain and the loss involved in calling heads that God exists. Let us assess the two cases: if you win you win everything, if you lose you lose nothing. Do not hesitate then; wager that he does exist. 'That is wonderful. Yes, I must wager, but perhaps I am wagering too much.' Let us see: since there is an equal chance of gain and loss, if you stood to win only two lives for one you could still wager, but supposing you stood to win three?

You would have to play (since you must necessarily play) and it would be unwise of you, once you are obliged to play, not to risk your life in order to win three lives at a game in which there is an equal chance of losing and winning. But there is an eternity of life and happiness. That being so, even though there were an infinite number of chances, of which only one were in your favour, you would still be right to wager one in order to win two; and you would be acting wrongly, being obliged to play, in refusing to stake one life against three in a game, where out of an infinite number of chances there is one in your favour, if there were an infinity of infinitely happy life to be won. But here there is an infinity of infinitely happy life to be won, one chance of winning against a finite number of chances of losing, and what you are staking is finite. That leaves no choice; wherever there is infinity, and where there are not infinite chances of losing against that of winning, there is no room for hesitation, you must give everything. And thus, since you are obliged to play, you must be renouncing reason if you hoard your life rather than risk it for an infinite gain, just as likely to occur as a loss amounting to nothing.

For it is no good saying that it is uncertain whether you will win, that it is certain that you are taking a risk, and that the infinite distance between the certainty of what you are risking and the uncertainty of what you may gain makes the finite good you are certainly risking equal to the infinite good that you are not certain to gain. This is not the case. Every gambler takes a certain risk for an uncertain gain, and yet he is taking a certain finite risk for an uncertain finite gain without sinning against reason. Here there is no infinite distance between the certain risk and the uncertain gain: that is not true. There is, indeed, an infinite distance between the certainty of winning and the certainty of losing, but the proportion between the uncertainty of winning and the certainty of what is being risked is in proportion to the chances of winning or losing. And hence if there are as many chances on one side as on the other you are playing for even odds. And in that case the certainty of what you are risking is equal to the uncertainty of what you may win; it is by no means infinitely distant from it. Thus our argument carries infinite weight, when the stakes are finite in a game where there are even chances of winning and losing and an infinite prize to be won.

This is conclusive and if men are capable of any truth this is it.

'I confess, I admit it, but is there really no way of seeing what the cards are?'—'Yes. Scripture and the rest, etc.'—'Yes, but my hands are tied and my lips are sealed; I am being forced to wager and I am not free; I am being held fast and I am so made that I cannot believe. What do you want me to do then?'—'That is true, but at least get it into your head that, if you are unable to believe, it is because of your passions, since reason impels you to believe and yet you cannot do so. Concentrate then not on convincing yourself by multiplying proofs of God's existence but by diminishing your passions. You want to find faith and you do not know the road. You want to be cured of unbelief and you ask for the remedy: learn from those who were once bound like you and who now wager all they have. These are people who know the road you wish to follow, who have been cured of the affliction of which you wish to be cured: follow the way by which they began. They behaved just as if they did believe, taking holy water, having masses said, and so on. That will make you believe quite naturally, and will make you more docile.' —'But that is what I am afraid of.'—'But why? What have you to lose? But to show you that this is the way, the fact is that this diminishes the passions which are your great obstacles. . . .'

End of this address.

'Now what harm will come to you from choosing this course? You will be faithful, honest, humble, grateful, full of good works, a sincere, true friend. . . . It is true you will not enjoy noxious pleasures, glory and good living, but will you not have others?

'I tell you that you will gain even in this life, and that at every step you take along this road you will see that your gain is so certain and your risk so negligible that in the end you will realize that you have wagered on something certain and infinite for which you have paid nothing.'

'How these words fill me with rapture and delight!—'

'If my words please you and seem cogent, you must know that they come from a man who went down upon his knees before and after to pray this infinite and indivisible being, to whom he submits his own, that he might bring your being also to submit to him for your own good and for his glory: and that strength might thus be reconciled with lowliness.'

*   *   *

REVIEW QUESTIONS

1. How does Pascal conceive of the human condition?
2. What does it mean for him to have a body?
3. How does he differ in this respect from Montaigne?
4. How does Pascal construct his proof for the existence of God?
5. Why does he begin with infinity, a mathematical concept?
6. What is he saying about the limits of human knowledge?
7. For whom might this essay have been written?
8. Why must we "wager"?

JOHN DONNE

FROM **The First Anniversarie**

John Donne (1572–1631) was esteemed by his contemporary, Ben Jonson, as "the first poet in the world in some things." He was born in London, the son of a prosperous merchant. His father died while Donne was still an infant, and he was raised by his mother, the daughter of the playwright John Heywood, and granddaughter of Sir Thomas More's sister. His family was devoutly Roman Catholic.

Donne matriculated at Hart Hall, Oxford, in 1584 but left without a degree because it was impossible for Catholics to take the oath of supremacy required at graduation. He entered Thavies Inn, London, as a law student in 1591 and transferred to Lincoln's Inn in 1592. At this point he began to write poetry. In 1596, he joined the Earl of Essex's Cadiz expedition and upon his return became secretary to Sir Thomas Egerton, the Lord Keeper of the Great Seal of England. Donne abjured his Catholic faith to join the Church of England and was about to embark on a diplomatic career when he secretly married Ann More, the niece of his employer's wife. He was imprisoned for marrying a minor without her guardian's consent, and the girl's father secured his dismissal from Egerton's service. Upon his release, Donne found himself without employment and his wife without a dowry. Years of poverty and dependence turned the poet toward religion and reflection, both of which found ready expression in his writing. His first published work, The Pseudo-Martyr *(1610), written to persuade Catholics to take the oath of allegiance, earned him an honorary Master of Arts degree from Oxford and the notice of the king. In 1614, he was elected to Parliament and, in 1615, became an Anglican priest. During these middle years, Donne wrote his* Anniversaries, *the first of which was published in 1611. The subject was Elizabeth Drury, who died in 1610 at the age of fourteen. The poem captures something of the weariness and insecurity that accompanied the crisis of the seventeenth century. His subsequent career was divided between the poet and the priest. When he died, as Dean of St. Paul's, Donne had earned another reputation as the greatest preacher of his age.*

From *The Complete English Poems of John Donne,* edited by C. A. Patrides, Everyman's Library, 1985.

An Anatomy of the World.
Wherein, By occasion of the untimely death of
   Mistris
Elizabeth Drury the frailty and the decay of his
   whole
World is represented.

To The Praise of the Dead, and the Anatomy.
[by Joseph Hall?]

Wel dy'de the world, that we might live to see
This world of wit, in his Anatomee:
No evill wants his good: so wilder heyres
Bedew their fathers Toombs with forced teares,
Whose state requites their los: whils thus we
   gain
Well may wee walk in blacks, but not complaine.

*   *   *

She, of whom th'Auncients seem'd to prophesie,
When they call'd vertues by the name of shee;
She in whom vertue was so much refin'd,
That for Allay unto so pure a minde
Shee tooke the weaker Sex, she that could drive
The poysonous tincture, and the stayne of *Eve,*
Out of her thoughts, and deeds; and purifie
All, by a true religious Alchimy;
Shee, shee is dead; shee's dead: when thou
   knowest this,
Thou knowest how poore a trifling thing man is.
And learn'st thus much by our Anatomee,
The heart being perish'd, no part can be free.
And that except thou feed (not banquet) on
The supernaturall food, Religion,

Thy better Grouth growes withered, and scant;
Be more then man, or thou'rt lesse then an Ant.
Then, as mankinde, so is the worlds whole frame
Quite out of joynt, almost created lame:
For, before God had made up all the rest,
Corruption entred, and deprav'd the best:
It seis'd the Angels, and then first of all
The world did in her Cradle take a fall,
And turn'd her braines, and tooke a generall
    maime
Wronging each joynt of th'universall frame.
The noblest part, man, felt it first; and than
Both beasts and plants, curst in the curse of
    man.
So did the world from the first houre decay,
The evening was beginning of the day,
And now the Springs and Sommers which we see,
Like sonnes of women after fifty bee.
And new Philosophy cals all in doubt,
The Element of fire is quite put out;
The Sun is lost, and th'earth, and no mans wit
Can well direct him, where to looke for it.
And freely men confesse, that this world's spent,
When in the Planets, and the Firmament
They seeke so many new; they see that this
Is crumbled out againe to his Atomis.
'Tis all in pieces, all cohærence gone;
All just supply, and all Relation:
Prince, Subject, Father, Sonne, are things forgot,
For every man alone thinkes he hath got
To be a Phœnix, and that there can bee
None of that kinde, of which he is, but hee.
This is the worlds condition now, and now
She that should all parts to reunion bow,
She that had all Magnetique force alone,
To draw, and fasten sundred parts in one;
She whom wise nature had invented then
When she observ'd that every sort of men
Did in their voyage in this worlds Sea stray,
And needed a new compasse for their way;
Shee that was best, and first originall
Of all faire copies; and the generall
Steward to Fate; shee whose rich eyes, and brest,
Guilt the West Indies, and perfum'd the East;
Whose having breath'd in this world, did bestow
Spice on those Isles, and bad them still smell so,

And that rich Indie which doth gold interre,
Is but as single money, coyn'd from her:
She to whom this world must it selfe refer,
As Suburbs, or the Microcosme of her,
Shee, shee is dead; shee's dead: when thou
    knowst this,
Thou knowst how lame a cripple this world is.
And learnst thus much by our Anatomy,
That this worlds generall sickenesse doth not lie
In any humour, or one certaine part;
But, as thou sawest it rotten at the hart,
Thou seest a Hectique fever hath got hold
Of the whole substance, not to be contrould,
And that thou hast but one way, not t'admit
The worlds infection, to be none of it.
For the worlds subtilst immateriall parts
Feele this consuming wound, and ages darts.
For the worlds beauty is decayd, or gone,
Beauty, that's colour, and proportion.
We thinke the heavens enjoy their Spherical
Their round proportion embracing all.
But yet their various and perplexed course,
Observ'd in divers ages doth enforce
Men to finde out so many Eccentrique parts,
Such divers downe-right lines, such overthwarts,
As disproportion that pure forme. It teares
The Firmament in eight and fortie sheeres,
And in those constellations there arise
New starres, and old do vanish from our eyes:
As though heav'n suffred earth-quakes, peace or
    war,
When new Townes rise, and olde demolish'd
    are.
They have empayld within a Zodiake
The free-borne Sunne, and keepe twelve signes
    awake
To watch his steps; the Goat and Crabbe
    controule,
And fright him backe, who els to eyther Pole,
(Did not these Tropiques fetter him) might
    runne:
For his course is not round; nor can the Sunne
Perfit a Circle, or maintaine his way
One inche direct; but where he rose to day
He comes no more, but with a cousening line,
Steales by that point, and so is Serpentine:

And seeming weary with his reeling thus,
He meanes to sleepe, being now falne nearer us.
So, of the stares which boast that they do runne
In Circle still, none ends where he begunne.
All their proportion's lame, it sinks, it swels.
For of Meridians, and Parallels,
Man hath weav'd out a net, and this net
    throwne
Upon the Heavens, and now they are his owne.
Loth to goe up the hill, or labor thus
To goe to heaven, we make heaven come to us.
We spur, we raine the stars, and in their race
They're diversly content t'obey our pace.
But keepes the earth her round proportion still?
Doth not a Tenarif, or higher Hill
Rise so high like a Rocke, that one might thinke
The floating Moone would shipwracke there, and
    sink?
Seas are so deepe, that Whales being strooke to
    day,
Perchance to morrow, scarse at middle way
Of their wish'd journeys end, the bottom, dye.
And men, to sound depths, so much line untie,
As one might justly thinke, that there would rise
At end thereof, one of th'Antipodies:
If under all, a Vault infernall be,

(Which sure is spacious, except that we
Invent another torment, that there must
Millions into a strait hote roome be thrust)
Then solidnes, and roundnes have no place.
Are these but warts, and pock-holes in the face
Of th'earth? Thinke so: But yet confesse, in this
The worlds proportion disfigured is,
That those two legges whereon it doth relie,
Reward and punishment are bent awrie.
And, Oh, it can no more be questioned,
That beauties best, proportion, is dead,
Since even griefe it selfe, which now alone
Is left us, is without proportion.

*   *   *

REVIEW QUESTIONS

1. Of the changes in the early modern period that Donne catalogues, which does he highlight?
2. Why do you suppose he chose these?
3. What has been lost, according to Donne?
4. How might he understand Pascal's notion of "infinity"?

HANS JAKOB CHRISTOPH VON GRIMMELSHAUSEN

FROM *Simplicissimus*

Hans Jakob Christoph von Grimmelshausen (1621–1676), author of Simplicissimus, *the greatest German novel of the seventeenth century, and one of the great works of German literature, was born at Gelnhausen, near Hanau in Hesse Kassel. The troubled times of the Thirty Years' War (1618–1648) that found eloquent consideration in his writing are reflected by his life. He lost his parents early, probably in the 1634 sack of Gelnhausen by troops under Ferdinand, General Infanta of Spain, and was himself kidnapped by marauding Hessian troops the following year. His experiences became the stuff of his novel. In 1636 he joined the Imperial army. In 1639 he became secretary to Reinhard von Schauenburg, the commandant at Offenburg, on whose staff he served until 1647. At the end of the war, he was commandant on the Inn. Soon after the war he became steward of the Schauenburg estates, married, and converted to Catholicism. In 1667, Grimmelshausen was appointed magistrate and tax collector at Renchen, a town belonging to the Bishopric of Strasbourg. His duties evidently left him free to write; he published his masterpiece,* Simplicissimus, *in 1669. Modeled on the Spanish picaresque romance,* Simplicissimus *sketched the development of a human soul measured against the background of a land riven by warfare. It gave free reign to its authors narrative gifts: his realist detail, course humor, and social criticism.* Simplicissimus *is widely considered a historical document for its vivid picture of seventeenth century Germany. Grimmelshausen's life ended as it began, in the shadow of war. In 1674, Rechen was occupied by French troops and his household was broken up. He died in 1676, once more in military service.*

From *Simplicissimus,* translated by S. Goodrich, Daedalus, 1995.

Book I

CHAP. I: TREATS OF SIMPLICISSIMUS'S RUSTIC DESCENT AND OF HIS UPBRINGING ANSWERING THERETO

There appeareth in these days of ours (of which many do believe that they be the last days) among the common folk, a certain disease which causeth those who do suffer from it (so soon as they have either scraped and higgled together so much that they can, besides a few pence in their pocket, wear a fool's coat of the new fashion with a thousand bits of silk ribbon upon it, or by some trick of fortune have become known as men of parts) forthwith to give themselves out gentlemen and nobles of ancient descent. Whereas it doth often happen that their ancestors were day-labourers, carters, and porters, their cousins donkey-drivers, their brothers turnkeys and catchpolls, their sisters harlots, their mothers bawds—yea, witches even: and in a word, their whole pedigree of thirty-two quarterings as full of dirt and stain as ever was the sugarbakers' guild of Prague. Yea, these new sprigs of nobility be often themselves as black as if they had been born and bred in Guinea.

With such foolish folk I desire not to even myself, though 'tis not untrue that I have often fancied I must have drawn my birth from some great lord or knight at least, as being by nature disposed

to follow the nobleman's trade had I but the means and the tools for it. 'Tis true, moreover, without jesting, that my birth and upbringing can be well compared to that of a prince if we overlook the one great difference in degree. How! did not my dad (for so they call fathers in the Spessart) have his own palace like any other, so fine as no king could build with his own hands, but must let that alone for ever. 'Twas painted with lime, and in place of unfruitful tiles, cold lead and red copper, was roofed with that straw whereupon the noble corn doth grow, and that he, my dad, might make a proper show of nobility and riches, he had his wall round his castle built, not of stone, which men do find upon the road or dig out of the earth in barren places, much less of miserable baked bricks that in a brief space can be made and burned (as other great lords be wont to do), but he did use oak, which noble and profitable tree, being such that smoked sausage and fat ham doth grow upon it, taketh for its full growth no less than a hundred years; and where is the monarch that can imitate him therein? His halls, his rooms, and his chambers did he have thoroughly blackened with smoke, and for this reason only, that 'tis the most lasting colour in the world, and doth take longer to reach to real perfection than an artist will spend on his most excellent paintings. The tapestries were of the most delicate web in the world, wove for us by her that of old did challenge

Minerva to a spinning match. His windows were dedicated to St. Papyrius for no other reason than that that same paper doth take longer to come to perfection, reckoning from the sowing of the hemp or flax whereof 'tis made, than doth the finest and clearest glass of Murano: for his trade made him apt to believe that whatever was produced with much paint was also more valuable and more costly; and what was most costly was best suited to nobility. Instead of pages, lackeys, and grooms, he had sheep, goats, and swine, which often waited upon me in the pastures till I drove them home. His armoury was well furnished with ploughs, mattocks, axes, hoes, shovels, pitchforks, and hayforks, with which weapons he daily exercised himself; for hoeing and digging he made his military discipline, as did the old Romans in time of peace. The yoking of oxen was his generalship, the piling of dung his fortification, tilling of the land his campaigning, and the cleaning out of stables his princely pastime and exercise. By this means did he conquer the whole round world so far as he could reach, and at every harvest did draw from it rich spoils. But all this I account nothing of, and am not puffed up thereby, lest any should have cause to jibe at me as at other newfangled nobility, for I esteem myself no higher than was my dad, which had his abode in a right merry land, to wit, in the Spessart, where the wolves do howl good-night to each other. But that I have as yet told you nought of my dad's family, race and name is for the sake of precious brevity, especially since there is here no question of a foundation for gentlefolks for me to swear myself into; 'tis enough if it be known that I was born in the Spessart.

Now as my dad's manner of living will be perceived to be truly noble, so any man of sense will easily understand that my upbringing was like and suitable thereto: and whoso thinks that is not deceived, for in my tenth year had I already learned the rudiments of my dad's princely exercises: yet as touching studies I might compare with the famous Amphistides, of whom Suidas reports that he could not count higher than five: for my dad had perchance too high a spirit, and therefore followed the use of these days, wherein many persons of quality trouble themselves not, as they say with bookworms' follies, but have their hirelings to do their inkslinging for them. Yet was I a fine performer on the bagpipe, whereon I could produce most dolorous strains. But as to knowledge of things divine, none shall ever persuade me that any lad of my age in all Christendom could there beat me, for I knew nought of God or man, of Heaven or hell, of angel or devil, nor could discern between good and evil. So may it be easily understood that I, with such knowledge of theology, lived like our first parents in Paradise, which in their innocence knew nought of sickness or death or dying, and still less of the Resurrection. O noble life! (or, as one might better say, O noodle's life!) in which none troubles himself about medicine. And by this measure ye can estimate my proficiency in the study of jurisprudence and all other arts and sciences. Yea, I was so perfected in ignorance that I knew not that I knew nothing. So say I again, O noble life that once I led! But my dad would not suffer me long to enjoy such bliss, but deemed it right that as being nobly born, I should nobly act and nobly live: and therefore began to train me up for higher things and gave me harder lessons.

*   *   *

CHAP. IV: HOW SIMPLICISSIMUS'S PALACE WAS STORMED, PLUNDERED, AND RUINATED, AND IN WHAT SORRY FASHION THE SOLDIERS KEPT HOUSE THERE

Although it was not my intention to take the peaceloving reader with these troopers to my dad's house and farm, seeing that matters will go ill therein, yet the course of my history demands that I should leave to kind posterity an account of what manner of cruelties were now and again practised in this our German war: yea, and moreover testify by my own example that such evils must often have been sent to us by the goodness of Almighty God for our profit. For, gentle reader, who would ever have taught me that there was a God in

Heaven if these soldiers had not destroyed my dad's house, and by such a deed driven me out among folk who gave me all fitting instruction thereupon? Only a little while before, I neither knew nor could fancy to myself that there were any people on earth save only my dad, my mother and me, and the rest of our household, nor did I know of any human habitation but that where I daily went out and in. But soon thereafter I understood the way of men's coming into this world, and how they must leave it again. I was only in shape a man and in name a Christian: for the rest I was but a beast. Yet the Almighty looked upon my innocence with a pitiful eye, and would bring me to a knowledge both of Himself and of myself. And although He had a thousand ways to lead me thereto, yet would He doubtless use that one only by which my dad and my mother should be punished: and that for an example to all others by reason of their heathenish upbringing of me.

The first thing these troopers did was, that they stabled their horses: thereafter each fell to his appointed task: which task was neither more nor less than ruin and destruction. For though some began to slaughter and to boil and to roast so that it looked as if there should be a merry banquet forward, yet others there were who did but storm through the house above and below stairs. Others stowed together great parcels of cloth and apparel and all manner of household stuff, as if they would set up a frippery market. All that they had no mind to take with them they cut in pieces. Some thrust their swords through the hay and straw as if they had not enough sheep and swine to slaughter: and some shook the feathers out of the beds and in their stead stuffed in bacon and other dried meat and provisions as if such were better and softer to sleep upon. Others broke the stove and the windows as if they had a never-ending summer to promise. Houseware of copper and tin they beat flat, and packed such vessels, all bent and spoiled, in with the rest. Bedsteads, tables, chairs, and benches they burned, though there lay many cords of dry wood in the yard. Pots and pipkins must all go to pieces, either because they would

eat none but roast flesh, or because their purpose was to make there but a single meal.

Our maid was so handled in the stable that she could not come out; which is a shame to tell of. Our man they laid bound upon the ground, thrust a gag into his mouth, and poured a pailful of filthy water into his body: and by this, which they called a Swedish draught, they forced him to lead a party of them to a another place where they captured men and beasts, and brought them back to our farm, in which company were my dad, my mother, and our Ursula.

And now they began: first to take the flints out of their pistols and in place of them to jam the peasants' thumbs in and so to torture the poor rogues as if they had been about the burning of witches: for one of them they had taken they thrust into the baking oven and there lit a fire under him, although he had as yet confessed no crime: as for another, they put a cord round his head and so twisted it tight with a piece of wood that the blood gushed from his mouth and nose and ears. In a word each had his own device to torture the peasants, and each peasant his several torture. But as it seemed to me then, my dad was the luckiest, for he with a laughing face confessed what others must out with in the midst of pains and miserable lamentations: and such honour without doubt fell to him because he was the householder. For they set him before a fire and bound him fast so that he could neither stir hand nor foot, and smeared the soles of his feet with wet salt, and this they made our old goat lick off, and so tickle him that he well nigh burst his sides with laughing. And this seemed to me so merry a thing that I must needs laugh with him for the sake of fellowship, or because I knew no better. In the midst of such laughter he must needs confess all that they would have of him, and indeed revealed to them a secret treasure, which proved far richer in pearls, gold, and trinkets than any would have looked for among peasants. Of the women, girls, and maidservants whom they took, I have not much to say in particular, for the soldiers would not have me see how they dealt with them. Yet this I know, that one heard some of them scream most piteously in divers corners of the house; and well I can judge it fared no better with my mother and our Ursel than with the rest. Yet in the midst of all this miserable ruin I helped to turn the spit, and in the afternoon to give the horses drink, in which employ I encountered our maid in the stable, who seemed to me wondrously tumbled, so that I knew her not, but with a weak voice she called to me, "O lad, run away, or the troopers will have thee away with them. Look to it well that thou get hence: thou seest in what plight . . ." And more she could not say.

*   *   *

CHAP. XV: HOW SIMPLICISSIMUS WAS PLUNDERED, AND HOW DE DREAMED OF THE PEASANTS AND HOW THEY FARED IN TIMES OF WAR

Now when I came home I found that my fireplace and all my poor furniture, together with my store of provisions, which I had grown during the summer in my garden and had kept for the coming winter, were all gone. "And whither now?" thought I. And then first did need teach me heartily to pray: and I must summon all my small wits together, to devise what I should do. But as my knowledge of the world was both small and evil, I could come to no proper conclusion, only that 'twas best to commend myself to God and to put my whole confidence in Him: for otherwise I must perish. And besides all this those things which I had heard and seen that day lay heavy on my mind: and I pondered not so much upon my food and my sustenance as upon the enmity which there is ever between soldiers and peasants. Yet could my foolish mind come to no other conclusion than this—that there must of a surety be two races of men in the world, and not one only, descended from Adam, but two, wild and tame, like other unreasoning beasts, and therefore pursuing one another so cruelly.

    With such thoughts I fell asleep, for mere misery and cold, with a hungry stomach. Then it seemed to me, as if in a dream, that all the trees which stood round my dwelling suddenly changed and took on another appearance: for on every treetop sat a trooper, and the trunks were garnished, in place of leaves, with all manner of folk. Of these, some had long lances, others musquets, hangers, halberts, flags, and some drums and fifes. Now this was merry to see, for all was neatly distributed and each according to his rank. The roots, moreover, were made up of folk of little worth, as mechanics and labourers, mostly, however, peasants and the like; and these nevertheless gave its strength to the tree and renewed the same when it was lost: yea more, they repaired the loss of any fallen leaves from among themselves to their own great damage: and all the time they lamented over them that sat on the tree, and that with good reason, for the whole weight of the tree lay upon them and pressed them so that all the money was squeezed out of their pockets, yea, though it was behind seven locks and keys: but if the money would not out, then did the commissaries so handle them with rods (which thing they call military execution) that sighs came from their heart, tears from their eyes, blood from their nails, and the marrow from their bones. Yet among these were some whom men call light o' heart; and these made but little ado, took all with a shrug, and in the midst of their torment had, in place of comfort, mockery for every turn.

CHAP. XVI: OF THE WAYS AND WORKS OF SOLDIERS NOWADAYS, AND HOW HARDLY A COMMON SOLDIER CAN GET PROMOTION

So must the roots of these trees suffer and endure toil and misery in the midst of trouble and complaint, and those upon the lower boughs in yet greater hardship: yet were these last mostly merrier than the first named, yea and moreover, insolent and swaggering, and for the most part godless folk, and for the roots a heavy unbearable burden at all times. And this was the rhyme upon them:

> "Hunger and thirst, and cold and heat, and work and
>   woe, and all we meet;
> And deeds of blood and deeds of shame, all may ye
>   put to the landsknecht's name."

Which rhymes were the less like to be lyingly invented in that they answered to the facts. For gluttony and drunkenness, hunger and thirst, wenching and dicing and playing, riot and roaring, murdering and being murdered, slaying and being slain, torturing and being tortured, hunting and being hunted, harrying and being harried, robbing and being robbed, frighting and being frighted, causing trouble and suffering trouble, beating and being beaten: in a word, hurting and harming, and in turn being hurt and harmed—this was their whole life. And in this career they let nothing hinder them: neither winter nor summer, snow nor ice, heat nor cold, rain nor wind, hill nor dale, wet nor dry; ditches, mountain-passes, ramparts and walls, fire and water, were all the same to them. Father nor mother, sister nor brother, no, nor the danger to their own bodies, souls, and consciences, nor even loss of life and of heaven itself, or aught else that can be named, will ever stand in their way, for ever they toil and moil at their own strange work, till at last, little by little, in battles, sieges, attacks, campaigns, yea, and in their winter quarters too (which are the soldiers' earthly paradise, if they can but happen upon fat peasants) they perish, they die, they rot and consume away, save but a few, who in their old age, unless they have been right thrifty rievers and robbers, do furnish us with the best of all beggars and vagabonds.

Next above these hard-worked folk sat old henroost-robbers, who, after some years and much peril of their lives, had climbed up the lowest branches and clung to them, and so far had had the luck to escape death. Now these looked more serious, and somewhat more dignified than the lowest, in that they were a degree higher ascended: yet above them were some yet higher, who had yet loftier imaginings because they had to command the very lowest. And these people did call coat-beaters, because they were wont to dust the jackets of the poor pikemen, and to give the musqueteers oil enough to grease their barrels with.

Just above these the trunk of the tree had an interval or stop, which was a smooth place without

branches, greased with all manner of ointments and curious soap of disfavour, so that no man save of noble birth could scale it, in spite of courage and skill and knowledge, God knows how clever he might be. For 'twas polished as smooth as a marble pillar or a steel mirror. Just over that smooth spot sat they with the flags: and of these some were young, some pretty well in years: the young folk their kinsmen had raised so far: the older people had either mounted on a silver ladder which is called the Bribery Backstairs or else on a step which Fortune, for want of a better client, had left for them. A little further up sat higher folk, and these had also their toil and care and annoyance: yet had they this advantage, that they could fill their pokes with the fattest slices which they could cut out of the roots, and that with a knife which they called "War-contribution." And these were at their best and happiest when there came a commissary-bird flying overhead, and shook out a whole panfull of gold over the tree to cheer them: for of that they caught as much as they could, and let but little or nothing at all fall to the lowest branches: and so of these last more died of hunger than of the enemy's attacks, from which danger those placed above seemed to be free. Therefore was there a perpetual climbing and swarming going on on those trees; for each would needs sit in those highest and happiest places: yet were there some idle, worthless rascals, not worth their commissariat-bread, who troubled themselves little about higher places, and only did their duty. So the lowest, being ambitious, hoped for the fall of the highest, that they might sit in their place, and if it happened to one among ten thousand of them that he got so far, yet would such good luck come to him only in his miserable old age when he was more fit to sit in the chimney-corner and roast apples than to meet the foe in the field. And if any man dealt honestly and carried himself well, yet was he ever envied by others, and perchance by reason of some unlucky chance of war deprived both of office and of life. And nowhere was this more grievous than at the before-mentioned smooth place on the tree: for there an officer who had had a good sergeant or

corporal under him must lose him, however un-
willingly, because he was now made an ensign.
And for that reason they would take, in place of
old soldiers, ink-slingers, footmen, overgrown
pages, poor noblemen, and at times poor relations,
tramps and vagabonds. And these took the very
bread out of the mouths of those that had deserved it, and forthwith were made Ensigns.

*   *   *

REVIEW QUESTIONS

1. Who is Simplicissimus?
2. What is his relation to nature?
3. What does he consider noble and base?
4. What does Grimmelshausen tell us about the conduct of the Thirty Years' War?
5. What happens to the character of Simplicissimus when he witnesses the violence of war?
6. What did the Thirty Years' War do to the land and its occupants?

THOMAS HOBBES

FROM *Leviathan*

Thomas Hobbes (1588–1679) was an English philosopher whose mechanistic and deterministic theories of political life were highly controversial in his own time. Born in Malmesbury, Hobbes attended Magdalen Hall, Oxford, and became tutor to William Cavendish, later Earl of Devonshire, in 1608. With his student, he undertook several tours of the continent where he met and spoke with leading intellectual lights of the day, including Galileo and Descartes. Around 1637, he became interested in the constitutional struggle between parliament and Charles I and set to work writing a "little treatise in English" in defense of the royal prerogative. Before its publication in 1650, the book circulated privately in 1640 under the title Elements of Law, Natural and Politic. *Fearing arrest by parliament, Hobbes fled to Paris, where he remained for the next eleven years. While in exile, he served as math tutor to the Prince of Wales, Charles II, from 1646–1648. His great work,* Leviathan *(1651), was a forceful argument for political absolutism. Its title, taken from the horrifying sea monster of the Old Testament, suggested the power and authority Hobbes thought necessary to compel obedience and order in human society. Strongly influenced by mechanical philosophy, he treated human beings as matter in motion, subject to certain physical, rational laws. People feared one another and lived in a state of constant competition and conflict. For this reason, they must submit to the absolute, supreme authority of the state, a social contract among selfish individuals moved by fear and necessity. Once delegated, that authority was irrevocable and indivisible. Ironically, these theories found favor neither with royalists nor with anti-royalists. Charles II believed that it was written in justification of the Commonwealth. The French feared its attacks on the papacy. After the Restoration, Parliament added* Leviathan *to a list of books to be investigated for atheistic ten-*

dencies. Despite frustrations over the reception of his political theories, Hobbes retained his intellectual vigor. At age eighty-four, he wrote an autobiography in Latin and translated the works of Homer into English. He died at age ninety-one.

From *Leviathan*, edited by E. Hershey Sneath, Ginn, 1898.

＊　　＊　　＊

Of the Causes, Generation, and Definition of a Commonwealth

The final cause, end, or design of men, who naturally love liberty and dominion over others, in the introduction of that restraint upon themselves in which we see them live in commonwealths is the foresight of their own preservation, and of a more contented life thereby; that is to say, of getting themselves out from that miserable condition of war which is necessarily consequent . . . to the natural passions of men when there is no visible power to keep them in awe and tie them by fear of punishment to the performance of their covenants, and observation of the laws of nature. . . .

For the laws of nature, as "justice," "equity," "modesty," "mercy," and, in sum, "doing to others as we would be done to," of themselves, without the terror of some power to cause them to be observed, are contrary to our natural passions, that carry us to partiality, pride, revenge, and the like. And covenants without the sword are but words, and of no strength to secure a man at all. Therefore, notwithstanding the laws of nature, which every one has then kept when he has the will to keep them, when he can do it safely, if there be no power erected, or not great enough for our security; every man will, and may lawfully rely on his own strength and art, for protection against all other men. And in all places where men have lived by small families, to rob and spoil one another has been a trade, and so far from being reputed against the law of nature that the greater spoils they gained, the greater was their honor; and men observed no other laws therein but the laws of honor; that is, to abstain from cruelty, leaving to men their lives and instruments of livelihood. And as small families did then, so now do cities and kingdoms, which are but greater families, for their own security enlarge their dominions upon all pretenses of danger and fear of invasion or assistance that may be given to invaders, and endeavor as much as they can to subdue or weaken their neighbors by open force and secret arts, for lack of other protection, justly; and are remembered for it in later ages with honor.

Nor is it the joining together of a small number of men that gives them this security, because in small numbers small additions on the one side or the other make the advantage of strength so great as is sufficient to carry the victory; and therefore gives encouragement to an invasion. The multitude sufficient to confide in for our security is not determined by any certain number but by comparison with the enemy we fear; and is then sufficient when the advantage of the enemy is not so visible and conspicuous to determine the event of war as to move him to attempt it.

And should there not be so great a multitude, even if their actions be directed according to their particular judgments and particular appetites, they can expect thereby no defense nor protection, neither against a common enemy nor against the injuries of one another. For being distracted in opinions concerning the best use and application of their strength, they do not help but hinder one another, and reduce their strength by mutual opposition to nothing; whereby they are easily not only subdued by a very few that agree together, but also, when there is no common enemy, they make war upon each other for their particular interests. For if we could suppose a great multitude of men to consent in the observation of justice and other laws of nature without a common power to keep them all in awe, we might as well suppose all mankind to do the same; and then there neither would be, nor need to be, any civil government or commonwealth at all, because there would be peace without subjection.

Nor is it enough for the security which men desire should last all the time of their life that they be governed and directed by one judgment for a limited time, as in one battle or one war. For though they obtain a victory by their unanimous endeavor against a foreign enemy, yet afterwards, when either they have no common enemy or he that by one group is held for an enemy is by another group held for a friend, they must needs, by the difference of their interests, dissolve, and fall again into a war among themselves.

It is true that certain living creatures, as bees and ants, live sociably one with another, which are therefore by Aristotle numbered among political creatures, and yet have no other direction, than their particular judgments and appetites; nor speech whereby one of them can signify to another what he thinks expedient for the common benefit; and therefore some man may perhaps desire to know why mankind cannot do the same. To which I answer:

First, that men are continually in competition for honor and dignity, which these creatures are not; and consequently among men there arises on the ground envy and hatred and finally war, but among these not so.

Secondly, that among these creatures the common good differ not from the private; and being by nature inclined to their private, they procure thereby the common benefit. But man, whose joy consists in comparing himself with other men, can relish nothing but what is eminent.

Thirdly, that these creatures, having not, as man, the use of reason, do not see nor think they see any fault, in the administration of their common business; whereas among men, there are very many that think themselves wiser and abler to govern the public better than the rest; and these strive to reform and innovate, one this way, another that way, and thereby bring it into distraction and civil war.

Fourthly, that these creatures, though they have some use of voice in making known to one another their desires and other affections, yet lack that art of words by which some men can represent to others that which is good in the likeness of evil; and evil in the likeness of good; and augment or diminish the apparent greatness of good and evil, making men discontented and troubling their peace at their pleasure.

Fifthly, irrational creatures cannot distinguish between "injury" and "damage"; and, therefore, as long as they be at ease they are not offended with their fellows; whereas man is then most troublesome when he is most at ease; for then it is that he loves to show his wisdom and control the actions of them that govern the commonwealth.

Lastly, the agreement of these creatures is natural, that of men is by covenant only, which is artificial; and therefore, it is no wonder if there be somewhat else required besides covenant to make their agreement constant and lasting, which is a common power to keep them in awe and to direct their actions to the common benefit.

The only way to erect such a common power which may be able to defend them from the invasion of foreigners and the injuries of one another, and thereby to secure them in such sort so that by their own industry and by the fruits of the earth they may nourish themselves and live contentedly, is to confer all their power and strength upon one man, or upon one assembly of men that may reduce all their wills, by plurality of voices, unto one will; which is as much as to say, to appoint one man or assembly of men to bear their person; and every one to accept and acknowledge himself to be author of whatsoever he that so bears their person shall act or cause to be acted in those things which concern the common peace and safety, and therein to submit their wills every one to his will, and their judgments to his judgment. This is more than consent or concord; it is a real unity of them all in one and the same person, made by covenant of every man with every man, in such manner as if every man should say to every man, "I authorize and give up my right of governing myself to this man, or to this assembly of men, on this condition, that you give up your right to him and authorize all his actions in like manner." This done, the multitude so united in one person is called a "commonwealth," in Latin *civitas*. This is the generation of that great "leviathan," or rather, to speak more reverently, of that "mortal god," to which we owe, under the "immortal God," our peace and defense. For by this authority, given him by every particular man in the commonwealth, he has the use of so much power and strength conferred on him that, by terror thereof, he is enabled to form the wills of them all to peace at home and mutual aid against their enemies abroad. And in him consists the essence of the commonwealth, which, to define it, is "one person, of whose acts a great multitude, by mutual covenants one with another, have made themselves the author, to the end he may use the strength and means of them all as he shall think expedient for their peace and common defense."

And he that carries this person is called "sovereign" and said to have "sovereign power"; and every one besides, his "subject."

The attaining to this sovereign power is by two ways. One, by natural force, as when a man makes his children to submit themselves and their children to his government, as being able to destroy them if they refuse; or by war subdues his enemies to his will, giving them their lives on that condition. The other is when men agree among themselves to submit to some man or assembly of men voluntarily, on confidence that they will be protected by him against all others. This latter, may be called a political commonwealth, or commonwealth by "institution," and the former, a commonwealth by "acquisition." . . .

Of the Office of the Sovereign Representative

The office of the sovereign, be it a monarch or an assembly, consists in the end for which he was trusted with the sovereign power, namely, the se-

curing of "the safety of the people"; to which he is obliged by the law of nature, and to render an account thereof to God, the author of that law, and to none but him. But by safety here is not meant a bare preservation but also all other contentments of life which every man by lawful industry, without danger or hurt to the commonwealth, shall acquire to himself.

And this is to be done, not by care applied to individuals further than their protection from injuries when they shall complain, but by a general provision contained in public instruction, both of doctrine and example, and in the making and executing of good laws to which individual persons may apply their own cases.

And because, if the essential rights of sovereignty . . . be taken away, the commonwealth is thereby dissolved and every man returns into the condition and calamity of a war with every other man, which is the greatest evil that can happen in this life; it is the office of the sovereign, to maintain those rights entire, and consequently against his duty, first, to transfer to another or to lay from himself any of them. For he that deserts the means deserts the ends; and he deserts the means when, being the sovereign, he acknowledges himself subject to the civil laws and renounces the power of supreme judicature, or of making war or peace by his own authority; or of judging of the necessities of the commonwealth; or of levying money and soldiers when and as much as in his own conscience he shall judge necessary; or of making officers and ministers both of war and peace; or of appointing teachers and examining what doctrines are conformable or contrary to the defense, peace, and good of the people. Secondly, it is against his duty to let the people be ignorant or misinformed of the grounds and reasons of those his essential rights, because thereby men are easy to be seduced and drawn to resist him when the commonwealth shall require their use and exercise.

And the grounds of these rights have the need to be diligently and truly taught, because they cannot be maintained by any civil law or terror of legal punishment. For a civil law that shall forbid rebellion (and such is all resistance to the essential rights of the sovereignty), is not, as a civil law, any obligation, but by virtue only of the law of nature that forbids the violation of faith; which natural obligation if men know not, they cannot know the right of any law the sovereign makes. And for the punishment, they take it but for an act of hostility which when they think they have strength enough, they will endeavor by acts of hostility, to avoid. . . .

To the care of the sovereign belongs the making of good laws. But what is a good law? By a good law I mean not a just law; for no law can be unjust. The law is made by the sovereign power, and all that is done by such power is warranted and owned by every one of the people; and that which every man will have so, no man can say is unjust. It is in the laws of a commonwealth as in the laws of gaming; whatsoever the gamesters all agree on is injustice to none of them. A good law is that which is "needed" for the "good of the people" and "perspicuous."

For the use of laws, which are but rules authorized, is not to bind the people from all voluntary actions but to direct and keep them in such a motion as not to hurt themselves by their own impetuous desires, rashness, or indiscretion; as hedges are set not to stop travellers, but to keep them in their way. And, therefore, a law that is not needed, having not the true end of a law, is not good. A law may be conceived to be good when it is for the benefit of the sovereign, though it be not necessary for the people, but it is not so. For the good of the sovereign and people cannot be separated. It is a weak sovereign, that has weak subjects, and a weak people, whose sovereign lacks power to rule them at his will. Unnecessary laws are not good laws but traps for money; which, where the right of sovereign power is acknowledged, are superfluous, and where it is not acknowledged, insufficient to defend the people. . . .

It belongs also to the office of the sovereign to make a right application of punishments and rewards. And seeing the end of punishing is not revenge and discharge of anger, but correction, either of the offender, or of others by his example; the severest punishments are to be inflicted for those crimes that are of most danger to the public; such as are those which proceed from malice to the government established; those that spring from contempt of justice; those that provoke indignation in the multitude; and those which, unpunished, seem authorized, as when they are committed by sons, servants, or favorites of men in authority. For indignation carries men not only against the actors and authors of injustice, but against all power that is likely to protect them; as in the case of Tarquin, when for the insolent act of one of his sons he was driven out of Rome and the monarchy itself dissolved. But crimes of infirmity, such as are those which proceed from great provocation, from great fear, great need, or from ignorance, whether the fact be a great crime or not, there is place many times for leniency without prejudice to the commonwealth; and leniency, when there is such place for it, is required by the law of nature. The punishment of the leaders and teachers in a commotion, not the poor seduced people, when they are punished, can profit the commonwealth by their example. To be severe to the people is to punish that ignorance which may in great part be imputed to the sovereign, whose fault it was that they were no better instructed.

In like manner it belongs to the office and duty of the sovereign, to apply his rewards so that there may arise from them benefit to the commonwealth, wherein consists their use, and end; and is then done when they that have well served the commonwealth are, with as little expense of the common treasure as is possible, so well recompensed as others thereby may be encouraged both to serve the same as faithfully as they can and to study the arts by which they may be enabled to do it better. To buy with money or preferment from a popular ambitious subject to be quiet and desist from making ill impressions in the minds of the people has nothing of the nature of reward (which is ordained not for disservice, but for service past), nor a sign of gratitude, but of fear; nor does it tend to the benefit but to the damage of the public. It is a contention with ambition like that of Hercules with the monster Hydra which, having many heads, for every one that was vanquished there grew up three. For in like manner, when the stubbornness of one popular man is overcome with reward there arise many more, by the example, that do the same mischief in hope of like benefit; and as all sorts of manufacture, so also malice increases by being salable. And though sometimes a civil war may be deferred by such ways as that, yet the danger grows still the greater and the public ruin more assured. It is therefore against the duty of the sovereign, to whom the public safety is committed, to reward those that aspire to greatness by disturbing the peace of their country, and not rather to oppose the beginnings of such men with a little danger than after a longer time with greater. . . .

When the sovereign himself is popular, that is, revered and beloved of his people, there is no danger at all from the popularity of a subject. For soldiers are never so generally unjust as to side with their captain though they love him, against their sovereign, when they love not only his person but also his cause. And therefore those who by violence have at any time suppressed the power of their lawful sovereign, before they could settle themselves in his place have been always put to the trouble of contriving their titles to save the people from the shame of receiving them. To have a known right to sovereign power is so popular a quality as he that has it needs no more, for his own part, to turn the hearts of his subjects to him but that they see him able absolutely to govern his own family; nor, on the part of his enemies, but a disbanding of their armies. For the greatest and most active part of mankind has never hitherto been well contented with the present.

Concerning the offices of one sovereign to another, which are comprehended in that law which is commonly called the "law of nations," I need not say anything in this place because the law of nations and the law of nature is the same thing. And every sovereign has the same right, in securing the safety of his people that any particular man can have in securing the safety of his own body. And the same law that dictates to men that have no civil government what they ought to do and what to avoid in regard of one another dictates the same to commonwealths, that is, to the consciences of sovereign princes and sovereign assemblies, there being no court of natural justice but in the conscience only; where not man but God reigns whose laws, such of them as oblige all mankind, in respect of God as he is the author of nature are "natural," and in respect of the same God as he is King of kings are "laws."

*   *   *

REVIEW QUESTIONS

1. What is Hobbes' view of human nature?
2. What motivates human beings?
3. What, according to Hobbes, is the purpose of the state?
4. Why do human beings come together to form a political society?
5. What are the responsibilities of the sovereign?
6. What is the sovereign's highest obligation?
7. Does Hobbes hold out any hope that the state can improve human nature?

MICHEL EYQUEM DE MONTAIGNE

FROM It is Folly to Measure the True and False by Our Own Capacity

Michel Eyquem de Montaigne (1533–1592) introduced the essay as a literary form. Born of a wealthy family in the Château de Montaigne, near Libourne, he was first educated by a tutor who spoke Latin but no French. Until he was six years old, Montaigne learned the classical language as his native tongue. He was further educated at the Collège du Guyenne, where his fluency intimidated some of the finest Latinists in France, and studied law at Toulouse. In 1554, his father purchased an office in the Cour des Aides of Périgeaux, a fiscal court later incorporated into the Parlement of Bordeaux, a position he soon resigned to his son. Montaigne spent thirteen years in office at work he found neither pleasant nor useful. In 1571, he retired to the family estate. Apart from brief visits to Paris and Rouen, periods of travel, and two terms as mayor of Bordeaux (1581–1585), Montaigne spent the rest of his life as a country gentleman. His life was not all leisure. He became gentleman-in-ordinary to the king's chamber and spent the period 1572–1576 trying to broker a peace between Catholics and Huguenots. His first two books of the Essais *appeared in 1580; the third and last volume appeared in 1588. These essays are known for their discursive, conversational style, in which Montaigne undertook explorations of custom, opinion, and institutions. They gave voice to his opposition to all forms of dogmatism that were without rational basis. He observed life with a degree of skepticism, emphasizing the limits of human knowledge and the contradictions in human behavior. Indeed, Montaigne's essays are often cited as examples of an epistemological crisis born of the new discoveries, theological debates, and social tensions that marked the early modern period.*

From *The Complete Essays of Montaigne*, translated by Donald M. Fame with the permission of the publishers, Stanford University Press. © 1958 by the Board of Trustees of the Leland Stanford Junior University.

Perhaps it is not without reason that we attribute facility in belief and conviction to simplicity and ignorance; for it seems to me I once learned that belief was a sort of impression made on our mind, and that the softer and less resistant the mind, the easier it was to imprint something on it. *As the scale of the balance must necessarily sink under the weight placed upon it, so must the mind yield to evident things.* The more a mind is empty and without counterpoise, the more easily it gives beneath the weight of the first persuasive argument. That is why children, common people, women, and sick people are most subject to being led by the ears. But then, on the other hand, it is foolish presumption to go around disdaining and condemning as false whatever does not seem likely to us; which is an ordinary vice in those who think they have more than common ability. I used to do so once; and if I heard of returning spirits, prognostications of future events, enchantments, sorcery, or some other story that I could not swallow,

Dreams, witches, miracles, magic alarms,
Nocturnal specters, and Thessalian charms,

HORACE

I felt compassion for the poor people who were taken in by these follies. And now I think that I was at least as much to be pitied myself. Not that experience has since shown me anything surpassing my first beliefs, and that through no fault of my curiosity; but reason has taught me that to condemn a thing thus, dogmatically, as false and impossible, is to assume the advantage of knowing the bounds and limits of God's will and of the power of our mother Nature; and that there is no more notable folly in the world than to reduce these things to the measure of our capacity and competence. If we call prodigies or miracles whatever our reason cannot reach, how many of these appear continually to our eyes! Let us consider through what clouds and how gropingly we are led to the knowledge of most of the things that are right in our hands; assuredly we shall find that it is rather familiarity than knowledge that takes away their strangeness,

But no one now, so tired of seeing are our eyes,
Deigns to look up at the bright temples of the
    skies,

LUCRETIUS

and that if those things were presented to us for the first time, we should find them as incredible as any others, or more so.

If they were here for the first time for men to see,
If they were set before us unexpectedly,
Nothing more marvelous than these things could
    be told,
Nothing more unbelievable for men of old.

LUCRETIUS

He who had never seen a river thought that the first one he came across was the ocean. And the things that are the greatest within our knowl-

edge we judge to be the utmost that nature can do in that category.

A fair-sized stream seems vast to one who until
    then
Has never seen a greater; so with trees, with men.
In every field each man regards as vast in size
The greatest objects that have come before his
    eyes.

LUCRETIUS

The mind becomes accustomed to things by the habitual sight of them, and neither wonders nor inquires about the reasons for the things it sees all the time.

The novelty of things incites us more than their greatness to seek their causes.

We must judge with more reverence the infinite power of nature, and with more consciousness of our ignorance and weakness. How many things of slight probability there are, testified to by trustworthy people, which, if we cannot be convinced of them, we should at least leave in suspense! For to condemn them as impossible is to pretend, with rash presumption, to know the limits of possibility. If people rightly understood the difference between the impossible and the unusual, and between what is contrary to the orderly course of nature and what is contrary to the common opinion of men, neither believing rashly nor disbelieving easily, they would observe the rule of "nothing too much," enjoined by Chilo.

When we find in Froissart that the count of Foix, in Béarn, learned of the defeat of King John of Castile at Juberoth the day after it happened, and the way he says he learned it, we can laugh at it; and also at the story our annals tell, that Pope Honorius performed public funeral rites for King Philip Augustus and commanded them to be performed throughout Italy on the very day he died at Mantes. For the authority of these witnesses has perhaps not enough rank to keep us in check. But if Plutarch, besides several examples that he cites from antiquity, says that he knows with certain knowledge that in the time of Domitian, the news of the battle lost by Antonius in Germany was published in Rome, several days' journey from there, and dispersed throughout the whole world, on the same day it was lost; and if Caesar maintains that it has often happened that the report has preceded the event—shall we say that these simple men let themselves be hoaxed like the common herd, because they were not clear-sighted like ourselves? Is there anything more delicate, clearer, and more alert than Pliny's judgment, when he sees fit to bring it into play, or anything farther from inanity? Leaving aside the excellence of his knowledge, which I count for less, in which of these qualities do we surpass him? However, there is no schoolboy so young but he will convict him of falsehood, and want to give him a lesson on the progress of nature's works.

When we read in Bouchet about the miracles done by the relics of Saint Hilary, let it go: his credit is not great enough to take away our right to contradict him. But to condemn wholesale all similar stories seems to me a singular impudence. The great Saint Augustine testifies that he saw a blind child recover his sight upon the relics of Saint Gervase and Saint Protasius at Milan; a woman at Carthage cured of a cancer by the sign of the cross that a newly baptized woman made over her; Hesperius, a close friend of his, cast out the spirits that infested his house with a little earth from the sepulcher of our Lord, and a paralytic promptly cured by this earth, later, when it had been carried to church; a woman in a procession, having touched Saint Stephen's shrine with a bouquet, and rubbed her eyes with this bouquet, recover her long-lost sight; and he reports many other miracles at which he says he himself was present. Of what shall we accuse both him and two holy bishops, Aurelius and Maximinus, whom he calls upon as his witnesses? Shall it be of ignorance, simplicity, and credulity, or of knavery and imposture? Is there any man in our time so impudent that he thinks himself comparable to them, either in virtue and piety, or in learning, judgment, and ability? *Who, though they brought forth no proof, might crush me by their mere authority.*

It is a dangerous and fateful presumption, besides the absurd temerity that it implies, to disdain what we do not comprehend. For after you have established, according to your fine understanding, the limits of truth and falsehood, and it turns out that you must necessarily believe things even stranger than those you deny, you are obliged from then on to abandon these limits. Now, what seems to me to bring as much disorder into our consciences as anything, in these religious troubles that we are in, is this partial surrender of their beliefs by Catholics. It seems to them that they are being very moderate and understanding when they yield to their opponents some of the articles in dispute. But, besides the fact that they do not see what an advantage it is to a man charging you for you to begin to give ground and withdraw, and how much that encourages him to pursue his point, those articles which they select as the most trivial are sometimes very important. We must either submit completely to the authority of our ecclesiastical government, or do without it completely. It is not for us to decide what portion of obedience we owe it.

Moreover, I can say this for having tried it. In other days I exercised this freedom of personal choice and selection, regarding with negligence certain points in the observance of our Church which seem more vain or strange than others; until, coming to discuss them with learned men, I found that these things have a massive and very solid foundation, and that it is only stupidity and ignorance that make us receive them with less reverence than the rest. Why do we not remember how much contradiction we sense even in our own judgment? How many things were articles of faith to us yesterday, which are fables to us today? Vainglory and curiosity are the two scourges of our soul. The latter leads us to thrust our noses into everything, and the former forbids us to leave anything unresolved and undecided.

REVIEW QUESTIONS

1. What are the limits of human knowledge?
2. What roles do authority and experience play in knowledge?

3. How does Montaigne's attitude toward "prodigies or miracles" compare to that of Reginald Scot?

4. How do their conceptions of nature differ?

5. How might Montaigne's reflection on knowledge indicate an intellectual crisis?

15 ✑ THE ECONOMY AND SOCIETY OF EARLY MODERN EUROPE

Transition best characterizes the economy and society of early modern Europe. While the forms of production and exchange remained corporatist and traditional, elements of individualism and capitalism exerted increasingly strong influence. Accordingly, a society that remained in large part hierarchical and patriarchal showed signs of an emergent class structure. Evidence for these changes remained largely regional, being more evident in certain places and times than in others. Nonetheless, the evidence for such a transition can be seen nearly everywhere in Europe, driven by forces that gripped the entire continent.

For much of the period, the population remained locked in a struggle to survive. Beset by periodic famine and disease, life seemed tenuous and expectancies were short. Given high and early mortality, marriages occurred relatively late in life and truncated families were commonplace. Beginning in the late seventeenth century, however, mortality began to decline. By the eighteenth century populations were expanding across Europe.

The principal cause for the change in demographic dynamics was an increase in food supply that may be attributed in turn to a gradual change in agricultural techniques. Throughout the early modern period, traditional agricultural practices gradually yielded to techniques known generally as scientific farming. Landowners who sought gain in the marketplaces of Europe needed more direct control over land use, an ability to respond flexibly to market conditions. As a result, they enclosed communal lands and turned to the kinds of husbandry that would increase harvests and profits. The result was an increased food supply the eventually freed Europe from its age-old cycle of feast and famine.

An increasing population put new pressures on industry by raising demand for manufactured goods and supplying a ready labor force to produce them. Rural manufacturing in the form of extensive production networks, known as the putting-out system, increased industrial productivity and captured surplus

population in industrial work processes. Those who could not find such employ-
ment fled to the cities, which also grew rapidly, from which proto-industry was
commanded. It is interesting that urban manufacturing remained largely tradi-
tional, that is, highly regulated and guild-based, throughout the early modern
period.

The greatest single force for change between 1500 and 1800 was the expan-
sion of long-distance commerce based on the development of overseas empires
and the consolidation of central states. Capitalistic practices had existed since the
late fourteenth century at least, but the possibility of large profits from direct
trade with Asia and the Americas offered new scope for their application. The
development of mercantilist theories that advocated the expansion of trade as a
source of political power combined with capitalistic ambitions to facilitate global
commerce. As a result, enterprises, such as charter companies, emerged on a new
scale. The supplies of goods they traded and their profitability promoted the re-
finement of commercial facilities such as commodity exchanges, stock markets,
and banking techniques. Moreover, their activities introduced new commodities
in such volumes that new tastes emerged and old patterns of consumption were
transformed.

Growing populations and expanding economies notwithstanding, the society
of early modern Europe remained traditional. It was hierarchical in structure,
each individual's place having been fixed by birthright. Authority was patriar-
chal in nature, modeled upon the supposedly absolute authority of the father
within his family. Yet, change is also evident here. Economic change created mo-
bility. New wealth encouraged social and political aspirations as bourgeois every-
where chaffed under the exclusivity of the aristocracy and sought admission to
their ranks. New poverty created a class of have-nots that challenged the estab-
lished order and threatened its security.

Observers and theorists viewed the transformation of Europe's economy and
society with some trepidation. In most instances, their responses were reaction-
ary. They returned to notions of fatherhood for a model of authority that could
withstand the changing times. As the period progressed, however, more and
more turned to philosophical reason to find general laws of human interaction
that might be applied to govern economic and social behavior.

LORENZO BERNARDO

FROM A Venetian Ambassador's Report on the Ottoman Empire

The struggle for supremacy in northern Italy, which marked the last half of the fifteenth century, gave rise to a new form of diplomacy, structures and procedures that would be fundamental to relations among all modern states. Requiring continuous contact and communication, Renaissance states turned to permanent diplomacy, distinguished by the use of accredited resident ambassadors rather than ad hoc missions of medieval legates. The tasks of a permanent ambassador were to represent his government at state ceremonies, to gather information, and, occasionally, to enter into negotiations. Nowhere was this system more fully and expertly articulated than by the Republic of Venice in the late fifteenth and sixteenth centuries. Ambassadors were chosen with unusual care from the most prominent families of the city. They were highly educated, and their duties were carefully defined. Among the latter were weekly dispatches reporting all matters of any interest to Venice. These reports were regularly read and debated in the senate, which replied with questions, instructions, and information of its own. As a result, Venetian ambassadors were among the most skilled and respected in early modern Europe. Their reports remain a singularly important source for the history of that period. Lorenzo Bernardo had the distinction of serving as Venetian ambassador to a non-European state, Venice's chief rival in trade to the Middle East and the great power of the Moslem world, the Ottoman Empire. Though his assignment to Constantinople was brief, (1591–1592) he offered the following analysis of the empire's strengths and weaknesses and why Venice might expect its imminent decline. It offers insights into the understanding of political power in early modern Europe as well as a western perspective on non-western states and civilizations.

From *Pursuit of Power: Venetian Ambassadors' Reports on Spain, Turkey and France in the Age of Philip II, 1560–1600*, by James C. Davis. English translation copyright © 1970 by James C. Davis. Reprinted by permission of HarperCollins Publishers, Inc.

*   *   *

Three basic qualities have enabled the Turks to make such remarkable conquests, and rise to such importance in a brief period: religion, frugality, and obedience.

From the beginning it was religion that made them zealous, frugality that made them satisfied with little, and obedience that produced men ready for any dangerous campaign.

In an earlier report I discussed at length these three qualities, which were then and always had been typical of the Turks. Now I plan to follow the same order, but to discuss whether any changes have taken place subsequently that might lead us to hope that empire will eventually decline.

For nothing is more certain than that every living thing (including kingdoms and empires) has a beginning, a middle, and an end, or, you might say, a growth, maturity, and decline.

In former times, Serene Prince, all Turks held to a single religion, whose major belief is that it is "written" when and how a man will die, and that if he dies for his God and his faith he will go directly to Paradise. It is not surprising, then, that one reads in histories about Turks who vied for the chance to fill a ditch with their bodies, or made a human bridge for others to use crossing a river, going to their deaths without the slightest hesitation. But now the Turks have not a single religion, but three of them. The Persians are among the Turks like the heretics among us, because some of them hold the beliefs of Ali, and others those of Omar, both of whom were followers of Mohammed, but held different doctrines. Then there are the Arabs and Moors, who claim they alone preserve the true, uncorrupted religion and that the "Greek Turks" (as they call these in Constantinople) are bastard Turks with a corrupted religion, which they blame on their being mostly descended from Christian renegades who did not understand the Muslim religion. As a matter of fact, I have known many of these renegades who had no religious beliefs, and said religions were invented by men for political reasons. They hold that when the body dies the soul dies, just as it does with brute beasts, which they are.

The belief that one's death is "written" and that one has no free will to escape dangers is declining in Turkey with each passing day. Experience teaches them the opposite when they see that a man who avoids plague victims saves his life while one who has stayed with them catches plague and dies. During my time there as *bailo* I even saw their mufti flee Constantinople for fear of plague and go to the garden to live, and the Grand Signor himself took care to avoid all contacts with his generals. Having learned they can escape from plagues, they now apply the same lesson to wars. Everybody shirks war service as long as he can, and when he does go he hangs back from the front lines and concentrates on saving

his own life. When the authorities announce a campaign in Persia there are outcries and revolts, and if the sultan wants to send janissaries there he creates new ones who are so glad to have the higher pay that they are willing to risk dangers which the regulars dread and flee. In short, nowadays they all look out for their own safety.

As for frugality, which I said was the second of the three sources of the Turks' great power, this used to be one of their marked characteristics. At one time the Turks had no interest in fine foods or, if they were rich, in splendid decorations in their houses. Each was happy with bread and rice, and a carpet and a cushion; he showed his importance only by having many slaves and horses with which he could better serve his ruler. No wonder then that they could put up with the terrible effort and physical discomfort involved in conquering and ruling. What a shameful lesson to our own state, where we equate military glory with sumptuous banquets and our men want to live in their camps and ships as if they were back home at weddings and feasts!

But now that the Turks have conquered vast, rich lands they too have fallen victims to the corruption of wealth. They are beginning to appreciate fine foods and game, and most of them drink wine. They furnish their houses beautifully and wear clothes of gold and silver with costly linings. Briefly, then, they become fonder every day of luxury, comfort, and display. They are happy to follow the example provided by the sultan, who cares nothing about winning glory on the battlefield and prefers to stay at home and enjoy the countless pleasures of the seraglio. Modeling themselves on him, all the splendid pashas, governors, and generals, and the ordinary soldiers too, want to stay in *their* homes and enjoy *their* pleasures and keep as far as possible from the dangers and discomforts of war. The pashas make use of their wives, who are related to the Grand Signor, to persuade him to keep their husbands at home. They do this not only to satisfy the men but also because they know that if they stay in Constantinople their husbands can win more favor by serving and fawning on the Grand Signor. If they go to war their rivals find it easier to slander them and they run a greater risk of losing the sultan's favor. And right behind the great men are all the lower ranks of soldiers, following in their footsteps, and trying to avoid being pulled away from the comforts of home.

Obedience was the third source of the great power of the Turkish empire. In the old days obedience made them united, union made them strong, and strength rendered their armies invincible. They are all slaves by nature, and the slaves of one single master; only from him can they hope to win power, honors, and wealth and only from him do they have to fear punishment and death. Why should it be surprising, then, that they used to compete with each other to perform stupendous feats in his presence? This is why it is said that the Turks' strict obedience to their master is the foundation of the empire's security and grandeur. But when the foundation weakens, when the brake is released, ruin could easily follow. The point is that with those other state-preserving qualities changing into state-corroding qualities, disobedience and disunion could be the agents which finally topple it.

This is all the more likely now that the chief officials have no other goal but to oppose each other bitterly. They have all the normal rivalries and ambitions of ministers of state, but they also have unusual opportunities for undercover competition with each other, because many of them have married daughters, sisters, and nieces of the Grand Signor. These women can speak with His Majesty whenever they want and they often sway him in favor of their husbands. This practice throws government affairs into confusion and is a real source of worry to the first vizier, who fears to take the smallest step without notifying the sultan. He knows that his rivals' wives might sometime find the Grand Signor in the right mood and bring about his ruin, something the *caiacadin* did to the first vizier Sinan when I was there.

*   *   *

REVIEW QUESTIONS

1. What were the causes of Ottoman success?
2. Why does Bernardo stress these particular strengths?
3. What caused the decline of the Ottoman Empire?
4. How does the ambassador define success and failure, rise and decline?

THOMAS MUN

FROM Discourse on England's Treasure by Forraign Trade

Thomas Mun (1571–1641) was the son of an English mercer and rose to become a noted writer on economics and the first to give a clear statement of the theory of balance of trade. He was a prominent figure in commercial circles as a member of the standing commission on trade and the committee of the East India Company. His most important publication, Discourse on England's Treasure by Forraign

Trade, published posthumously in 1664, developed his idea that the wealth of a nation could not decline significantly so long as the value of exports exceeded the value of imports. Both in its emphasis on trade, as opposed to agriculture or industry, as the source of wealth, and in its vision of economic systems as incapable of expansion, this theory became a cornerstone of mercantilist thinking.

From *Early English Tracts on Commerce*, edited by J. R. McCulloch, Cambridge University Press, 1954.

FROM ## Chap. II.

THE MEANS TO ENRICH THIS KINGDOM, AND TO ENCREASE OUR TREASURE.

Although a Kingdom may be enriched by gifts received, or by purchase taken from some other Nations, yet these are things uncertain and of small consideration when they happen. The ordinary means therefore to increase our wealth and treasure is by *Forraign Trade*, wherein wee must ever observe this rule; to sell more to strangers yearly than wee consume of theirs in value. For suppose that when this Kingdom is plentifully served with the Cloth, Lead, Tinn, Iron, Fish and other native commodities, we doe yearly export the overplus to forraign Countreys to the value of twenty two hundred thousand pounds; by which means we are enabled beyond the Seas to buy and bring in forraign wares for our use and Consumptions, to the value of twenty hundred thousand pounds: By this order duly kept in our trading, we may rest assured that the Kingdom shall be enriched yearly two hundred thousand pounds, which must be brought to us in so much Treasure; because that part of our stock which is not returned to us in wares must necessarily be brought home in treasure.

For in this case it cometh to pass in the stock of a Kingdom, as in the estate of a private man; who is supposed to have one thousand pounds yearly revenue and two thousand pounds of ready money in his Chest: If such a man through excess shall spend one thousand five hundred pounds *per annum*, all his ready mony will be gone in four years; and in the like time his said money will be doubled if he take a Frugal course to spend but five hundred pounds *per annum*, which rule never faileth likewise in the Commonwealth, but in some cases (of no great moment) which I will hereafter declare, when I shall shew by whom and in what manner this ballance of the Kingdoms account ought to be drawn up yearly, or so often as it shall please the State to discover how much we gain or lose by trade with forraign Nations. But first I will say something concerning those ways and means which will encrease our exportations and diminish our importations of wares; which being done, I will then set down some other arguments both affirmative and negative to strengthen that which is here declared, and thereby to show that all the other means which are commonly supposed to enrich the Kingdom with Treasure are altogether insufficient and meer fallacies.

Chap. III.

THE PARTICULAR WAYS AND MEANS TO ENCREASE THE EXPORTATION OF OUR COMMODITIES, AND TO DECREASE OUR CONSUMPTION OF FORRAIGN WARES.

The revenue or stock of a Kingdom by which it is provided of forraign wares is either *Natural* or *Artificial*. The Natural wealth is so much only as can be spared from our own use and necessities to be exported unto strangers. The Artificial consists in our manufactures and industrious trading with forraign commodities, concerning which I will set down such particulars as may serve for the cause we have in hand.

1. First, although this Realm be already exceeding rich by nature, yet might it be much encreased by laying the waste grounds (which are infinite) into such employments as should no way hinder the present revenues of other manured lands, but hereby to supply our selves and prevent the importations of Hemp, Flax, Cordage, Tobacco, and divers other things which now we fetch from strangers to our great impoverishing.

2. We may likewise diminish our importations, if we would soberly refrain from excessive consumption of forraign wares in our diet and rayment, with such often change of fashions as is used, so much the more to encrease the waste and charge; which vices at this present are more notorious amongst us than in former ages. Yet might they easily be amended by enforcing the observation of such good laws as are strictly practised in other Countries against the said excesses; where likewise by commanding their own manufactures to be used, they prevent the coming in of others, without prohibition, or offence to strangers in their mutual commerce.

3. In our exportations we must not only regard our own superfluities, but also we must consider our neighbours necessities, that so upon the wares which they cannot want, nor yet be furnished thereof elsewhere, we may (besides the vent of the Materials) gain so much of the manufacture as we can, and also endeavour to sell them dear, so far forth as the high price cause not a less vent in the quantity. But the superfluity of our commodities which strangers use, and may also have the same from other Nations, or may abate their vent by the use of some such like wares from other places, and with little inconvenience; we must in this case strive to sell as cheap as possible we can, rather than to lose the utterance of such wares. For we have found of late years by good experience, that being able to sell our Cloth cheap in Turkey, we have greatly encreased the vent thereof, and the *Venetians* have lost as much in the utterance of theirs in those Countreys, because it is dearer. And on the other side a few years past, when by the

excessive price of Wools our Cloth was exceeding dear, we lost at the least half our clothing for forraign parts, which since is no otherwise (well neer) recovered again than by the great fall of price for Wools and Cloth. We find that twenty five in the hundred less in the price of these and some other Wares, to the loss of private mens revenues, may raise above fifty upon the hundred in the quantity vented to the benefit of the publique. For when Cloth is dear, other Nations doe presently practice clothing, and we know they want neither art nor materials to this performance. But when by cheapness we drive them from this employment, and so in time obtain our dear price again, then do they also use their former remedy. So that by these alterations we learn, that it is in vain to expect a greater revenue of our wares than their condition will afford, but rather it concerns us to apply our endeavours to the times with care and diligence to help our selves the best we may, by making our cloth and other manufactures without deceit, which will encrease their estimation and use.

4. The value of our exportations likewise may be much advanced when we perform it our selves in our own Ships, for then we get only not the price of our wares as they are worth here, but also the Merchants gains, the charges of ensurance, and fraight to carry them beyond the seas. As for example, if the *Italian* Merchants should come hither in their own shipping to fetch our Corn, our red Herrings or the like, in this case the Kingdom should have ordinarily but 25s. for a quarter of Wheat, and 20s. for a barrel of red herrings, whereas if we carry these wares our selves into *Italy* upon the said rates, it is likely that wee shall obtain fifty shillings for the first, and forty shillings for the last, which is a great difference in the utterance or vent of the Kingdoms stock. And although it is true that the commerce ought to be free to strangers to bring in and carry out at their pleasure, yet nevertheless in many places the exportation of victuals and munition are either prohibited, or at least limited to be done onely by the people and Shipping of those places where they abound.

5. The frugal expending likewise of our own

natural wealth might advance much yearly to be exported unto strangers; and if in our rayment we will be prodigal, yet let this be done with our own materials and manufactures, as Cloth, Lace, Imbroderies, Cut-works and the like, where the excess of the rich may be the employment of the poor, whose labours notwithstanding of this kind, would be more profitable for the Commonwealth, if they were done to the use of strangers.

6. The Fishing in his Majesties seas of *England, Scotland*, and *Ireland* is our natural wealth, and would cost nothing but labour, which the *Dutch* bestow willingly, and thereby draw yearly a very great profit to themselves by serving many places of Christendom with our Fish, for which they return and supply their wants both of forraign Wares and Mony, besides the multitude of Mariners and Shipping, which hereby are maintain'd, whereof a long discourse might be made to show the particular manage of this important business. Our fishing plantation likewise in *New-England, Virginia, Groenland*, the *Summer Islands* and the *New-found-land*, are of the like nature, affording much wealth and employments to maintain a great number of poor, and to encrease our decaying trade.

7. A Staple or Magazin for forraign Corn, Indigo, Spices, Raw-silks, Cotton wool or any other commodity whatsoever, to be imported will encrease Shipping, Trade, Treasure, and the Kings customes, by exporting them again where need shall require, which course of Trading, hath been the chief means to raise *Venice, Genoa*, the *low-Countreys*, with some others; and for such a purpose *England* stands most commodiously, wanting nothing to this performance but our own diligence and endeavour.

8. Also wee ought to esteem and cherish those trades which we have in remote or far Countreys, for besides the encrease of Shipping and Mariners thereby, the wares also sent thither and receiv'd from thence are far more profitable unto the kingdom than by our trades neer at hand; As for example; suppose Pepper to be worth here two Shillings the pound constantly, if then it be brought from the *Dutch* at *Amsterdam*, the Merchant may give there twenty pence the pound, and gain well by the bargain; but if he fetch this Pepper from the *East-indies*, he must not give above three pence the pound at the most, which is a mighty advantage, not only in that part which serveth for our own use, but also for that great quantity which (from hence) we transport yearly unto divers other Nations to be sold at a higher price: whereby it is plain, that we make a far greater stock by gain upon these *Indian* Commodities, than those Nations doe where they grow, and to whom they properly appertain, being the natural wealth of their Countries. But for the better understanding of this particular, we must ever distinguish between the gain of the Kingdom, and the profit of the Merchant; for although the Kingdom payeth no more for this Pepper than is before supposed, nor for any other commodity bought in forraign parts more than the stranger receiveth from us for the same, yet the Merchant payeth not only that price, but also the fraight, ensurance, customes and other charges which are exceeding great in these long voyages; but yet all these in the Kingdoms accompt are but commutations among our selves, and no Privation of the Kingdoms stock, which being duly considered, together with the support also of our other trades in our best Shipping to *Italy, France, Turkey*, the *East Countreys* and other places, by transporting and venting the wares which we bring yearly from the *East Indies*; It may well stir up our utmost endeavours to maintain and enlarge this great and noble business, so much importing the Publique wealth, Strength, and Happiness. Neither is there less honour and judgment by growing rich (in this manner) upon the stock of other Nations, than by an industrious encrease of our own means, especially when this later is advanced by the benefit of the former, as we have found in the *East Indies* by sale of much of our Tin, Cloth, Lead and other Commodities, the vent whereof doth daily encrease in those Countreys which formerly had no use of our wares.

9. It would be very beneficial to export money as well as wares, being done in trade only, it would

encrease our Treasure; but of this I write more largely in the next Chapter to prove it plainly.

10. It were policie and profit for the State to suffer manufactures made of forraign Materials to be exported custome-free, as Velvets and all other wrought Silks, Fustians, thrown Silks and the like, it would employ very many poor people, and much encrease the value of our stock yearly issued into other Countreys, and it would (for this purpose) cause the more forraign Materials to be brought in, to the improvement of His Majesties Customes. I will here remember a notable increase in our manufacture of winding and twisting only of forraign raw Silk, which within 35. years to my knowledge did not employ more than 300. people in the City and suburbs of London, where at this present time it doth set on work above fourteen thousand souls, as upon diligent enquiry hath been credibly reported unto His Majesties Commissioners for Trade. And it is certain, that if the said forraign Commodities might be exported from hence, free of custome, this manufacture would yet encrease very much, and decrease as fast in *Italy* and in the *Netherlands*. But if any man allege the *Dutch* proverb, *Live and let others live;* I answer, that the Dutchmen notwithstanding their own Proverb, doe not onely in these Kingdoms, encroach upon our livings, but also in other forraign parts of our trade (where they have power) they do hinder and destroy us in our lawful course of living, hereby taking the bread out of our mouth, which we shall never prevent by plucking the pot from their nose, as of late years too many of us do practise to the great hurt and dishonour of this famous Nation; We ought rather to imitate former times in taking sober and worthy courses more pleasing to God and suitable to our ancient reputation.

11. It is needful also not to charge the native commodities with too great customes, lest by indearing them to the strangers use, it hinder their vent. And especially forraign wares brought in to be transported again should be favoured, for otherwise that manner of trading (so much importing the good of the Commonwealth) cannot prosper nor subsist. But the Consumption of such forraign wares in the Realm may be the more charged, which will turn to the profit of the kingdom in the *Ballance of the Trade*, and thereby also enable the King to lay up the more Treasure out of his yearly incomes, as of this particular I intend to write more fully in his proper place, where I shall shew how much money a Prince may conveniently lay up without the hurt of his subjects.

12. Lastly, in all things we must endeavour to make the most we can of our own, whether it be *Natural* or *Artificial;* And forasmuch as the people which live by the Arts are far more in number than they who are masters of the fruits, we ought the more carefully to maintain those endeavours of the multitude, in whom doth consist the greatest strength and riches both of King and Kingdom: for where the people are many, and the arts good, there the traffique must be great, and the Countrey rich. The *Italians* employ a greater number of people, and get more money by their industry and manufactures of the raw Silks of the Kingdom of *Cicilia*, than the King of *Spain* and his Subjects have by the revenue of this rich commodity. But what need we fetch the example so far, when we know that our own natural wares doe not yield us so much profit as our industry? For Iron oar in the Mines is of no great worth, when it is compared with the employment and advantage it yields being digged, tried, transported, bought, sold, cast into Ordnance, Muskets, and many other instruments of war for offence and defence, wrought into Anchors, bolts, spikes, nayles and the like, for the use of Ships, Houses, Carts, Coaches, Ploughs, and other instruments for Tillage. Compare our Fleece-wools with our Cloth, which requires shearing, washing, carding, spinning, Weaving, fulling, dying, dressing and other trimmings, and we shall find these Arts more profitable than the natural wealth, whereof I might instance other examples, but I will not be more tedious, for if I would amplify upon this and the other particulars before written, I might find matter sufficient to make a large volume, but my desire in all is only to prove what I propound with brevity and plainness.

REVIEW QUESTIONS

1. How does Mun understand trade? Of what does it consist?
2. What is his chief concern regarding trade?
3. What is the relation of trade to the nation?
4. What are the foundations of successful trade for Mun?
5. Why does he emphasize moral values in a treatise on economic policy?
6. What are the goods to be found in commerce?

JEAN BAPTISTE POQUELIN (MOLIÈRE)

FROM The Citizen Who Apes the Nobleman

Molière (1622–1673) was baptized Jean Baptiste Poquelin. His life might be considered unorthodox from a very early stage. Though educated at the Collège de Clermont, which would number among its alumni such illustrious literati as Voltaire, and clearly intended for a career in royal service, he broke with tradition and joined a traveling company of players in 1643. He adopted his stage name, Molière, the following year and devoted the rest of his life to the stage. His rise to prominence began in 1658, when, playing on an improvised stage in a guardroom of the Louvre, he performed Corneille's Nicomède *as well as a play of his own,* Le docteur amoureux, *before Louis XIV.* Le bourgeois gentilhomme *appeared at the royal palace at Chambord in 1670. It satirized the ambition of contemporary bourgeois to compete in magnificence with the aristocracy. Yet, it was a double edged satire. Though the theme must have pleased Molière's noble audience, the figure of Jourdain is no unpleasant, boorish climber, but rather a delightfully good-natured soul, foolish but naive, fatuous but genuine. An unwillingness to subordinate his art to his audience may help explain why Molière frequently struggled in his lifetime. His actors often abandoned his company. Pensions went unpaid. His best works were not always well received. His fame spread only slowly. Though considered one of the greatest French writers, Molière was no writer in the strict sense. Little of his work was published; his comedies were written to be performed. Publication occurred only after several texts were pirated by Jean Ribou, and several remained unpublished long after Molière's death. This occurred in 1672, when Molière was taken ill during a performance of* Le malade imaginaire. *He died that same night, without receiving the sacraments or renouncing his stage life, and was buried unceremoniously in a common grave.*

From *The Dramatic Words of Molière, Volume V,* George Barrie and Sons, n.d.

FROM **Act I.**

The overture is played by a great many instruments; and in the middle of the stage, the pupil of the music-master is busy composing a serenade, ordered by M. Jourdain)

SCENE I—A MUSIC-MASTER, A DANCING-MASTER, THREE MUSICIANS, TWO VIOLIN PLAYERS, FOUR DANCERS.

Mus.-Mas. (*To the Musicians*). Come, retire into that room, and rest yourselves until he comes.

Dan.-Mas. (*To the Dancers*). And you also, on that side.

Mus.-Mas. (*To his Pupil*). Is it done?

Pup. Yes.

Mus.-Mas. Let me look. . . . That is right.

Dan.-Mas. It is something new?

Mus.-Mas. Yes, it is an air for a serenade, which I made him compose here, while waiting till our gentleman is awake.

Dan.-Mas. May one have a look at it?

Mus.-Mas. You shall hear it by-and-by with the dialogue, when he comes; he will not be long.

Dan.-Mas. Our occupations, yours and mine, are no small matter just at present.

Mus.-Mas. True: we have both of us found here the very man whom we want. It is a nice little income for us this Mr. Jourdain, with his notions of nobility and gallantry, which he has taken into his head; and your dancing and my music might wish that everyone were like him.

Dan.-Mas. Not quite; and I should like him to be more of a judge than he is, of the things we provide for him.

Mus.-Mas. It is true that he knows little about them, but he pays well; and that is what our arts require just now above aught else.

Dan.-Mas. As for myself, I confess, I hunger somewhat after glory. I am fond of applause, and I think that, in all the fine arts, it is an annoying torture to have to exhibit before fools, to have one's compositions subjected to the barbarism of a stupid man. Do not argue; there is a delight in having to work for people who are capable of appreciating the delicacy of an art, who know how to give a sweet reception to the beauties of a work, and who, by approbations which tickle one's fancy, reward one for his labour. Yes, the most pleasant recompense one can receive for the things which one does, is to find them understood, and made much of by applause which does one honour, There is nothing in my opinion, that pays us better for all our troubles; and enlightened praises are exquisitely sweet.

Mus.-Mas. I quite agree with you, and I enjoy them as much as you do. Assuredly, there is nothing that tickles our fancy more than the applause you speak of; but such incense does not give us our livelihood. Praise pure and simple does not provide for a rainy day: there must be something solid mixed withal; and the best way to praise is to put one's hand in one's pocket. M. Jourdain is a man, it is true, whose knowledge is very small, who discourses at random upon all things, and never applauds but at the wrong time; but his money makes up for his bad judgment; he has discernment in his purse; his praises are minted, and this ignorant citizen is of more value to us, as you see, than the great lord who introduced us here.

Dan.-Mas. There is some truth in what you say; but I think you make a little too much of money; and the interest in it is something so grovelling, that no gentleman ought ever to show any attachment to it.

Mus.-Mas. You are glad enough, however, to receive the money which our gentleman gives you.

Dan.-Mas. Assuredly; but I do not make it my whole happiness; and I could wish that with all his wealth he had also some good taste.

Mus.-Mas. I could wish the same; and that is what we are aiming at both of us. But, in any case, he gives us the means of becoming known in the world; and he shall pay for others, and others shall applaud for him.

Dan.-Mas. Here he comes.

*   *   *

SCENE III. — MRS. JOURDAIN,
M. JOURDAIN, TWO LACQUEYS.

MRS. JOUR. Ha! ha! this is something new again! What is the meaning of this curious get-up, husband? Are you setting the world at nought to deck yourself out in this fashion? and do you wish to become a laughing-stock everywhere?

M. JOUR. None but he-fools and she-fools will make a laughing-stock of me, wife.

MRS. JOUR. In truth, they have not waited until now; and all the world has been laughing for a long while already at your vagaries.

M. JOUR. Who is all this world, pray?

MRS. JOUR. All this world is a world which is right, and which has more sense than you have. As for myself, I am disgusted with the life which you lead. I do not know whether this is our own house or not. One would think it is Shrove Tuesday every day; and from early morn, for fear of being too late, one hears nothing but the noise of fiddles and singers disturbing the whole neighbourhood.

NIC. The mistress is right. I shall never see the ship-shape again with this heap of people that you bring to your house. They have feet that pick up the mud in every quarter of the town to bring it in here afterwards; and poor Françoise is almost worked off her legs, with rubbing the floors which your pretty tutors come to dirty again regularly every day.

M. JOUR. Good gracious! Miss Nicole, your tongue is sharp enough for a country-lass!

MRS. JOUR. Nicole is right; and she has more sense than you have. I should much like to know what you want with a dancing-master, at your age.

NIC. And with a great hulking fencing-master, who shakes the whole house with his stamping, and uproots all the floor-tiles in our big room.

M. JOUR. Hold your tongues, you girl and my wife.

MRS. JOUR. Do you wish to learn dancing against the time when you shall have no longer any legs?

NIC. Do you want to kill any one?

M. JOUR. Hold your tongues, I tell you: you are ignorant women, both of you; and you do not know the benefits of all this.

MRS. JOUR. You ought rather to think of seeing your daughter married, who is of an age to be provided for.

M. JOUR. I shall think of seeing my daughter married when a suitable party shall present himself for her; but I shall also think of acquiring some polite learning.

NIC. I have also heard, Mistress, that for fear of shortcoming, he has taken a philosophy-master to-day.

M. JOUR. Very good. I wish to improve my mind, and to know how to argue about things amongst gentle-folks.

MRS. JOUR. Shall you not go, one of these days, to school, to get the birch, at your age?

M. JOUR. Why not? Would to heaven I could have the birch at this hour before everybody, and that I could know all that they teach at school!

NIC. Yes, indeed! that would improve your legs.

M. JOUR. No doubt it would.

MRS. JOUR. All this is highly necessary to manage your house!

M. JOUR. Assuredly. You both talk like fools, and I am ashamed at your ignorance. (*To Mrs. Jourdain.*) For instance, do you know what you are saying at this moment?

MRS. JOUR. Yes. I know that what I say is very well said, and that you ought to think of leading a different life.

M. JOUR. I am not speaking of that. I am asking you what these words are which you are speaking just now.

MRS. JOUR. They are very sensible words, and your conduct is scarcely so.

M. JOUR. I am not speaking of that, I tell you. I ask you, what I am speaking with you, what I am saying to you at this moment, what that is?

MRS. JOUR. Nonsense.

M. JOUR. He, no, that is not it. What we are saying both of us, the language we are speaking at this moment?

MRS. JOUR. Well?

M. JOUR. What is it called?

MRS. JOUR. It is called whatever you like.

M. JOUR. It is prose, you stupid.

MRS. JOUR. Prose?

M. JOUR. Yes, prose. Whatever is prose is not verse, and whatever is not verse is prose. Eh? that comes from studying. (*To Nicole.*) And do you know what you are to do to say U?

NIC. How?

M. JOUR. Yes. What do you do when you say U?

NIC. What?

M. JOUR. Say U, just to see.

NIC. Well! U.

M. JOUR. What do you do?

NIC. I say U.

M. JOUR. Yes; but when you say U what do you do?

NIC. I do what you tell me to do.

M. JOUR. Oh! what a strange thing to have to do with fools? You pout the lips outwards, and bring the upper jaw near the lower one; U, do you see? I make a mouth, U.

NIC. Yes: that is fine.

MRS. JOUR. That is admirable!

M. JOUR. It is quite another thing, if you had seen O, and DA, DA, and FA, FA.

MRS. JOUR. But what is all this gibberish?

NIC. What are we the better for all this?

M. JOUR. It drives me mad when I see ignorant women.

MRS. JOUR. Go, you should send all these people about their business, with their silly stuff.

NIC. And above all, this great lout of a fencing-master, who fills the whole of my place with dust.

M. JOUR. Lord! this fencing-master sticks strangely in your gizzard! I will let you see your impertinence directly. (*After having had the foils brought, and giving one of them to Nicole.*) Stay, reason demonstrative. The line of the body. When one thrusts in carte, one has but to do so, and when one thrusts in tierce, one has but to do so. This is the way never to be killed; and is it not very fine to be sure of one's game when one has to fight somebody? There, just thrust at me, to see.

(*Nicole thrusts several times at M. Jourdain.*)

NIC. Well, what!

M. JOUR. Gently! Hullo! ho! Softly! The devil take the hussy!

NIC. You tell me to thrust at you.

M. JOUR. Yes; but you thrust in tierce, before thrusting at me in carte, and you do not wait for me to parry.

MRS. JOUR. You are mad, husband, with all your fancies; and this has come to you only since you have taken it in your head to frequent the nobility.

M. JOUR. When I frequent the nobility, I show my judgment; and it is better than to frequent your citizens.

MRS. JOUR. Indeed! really there is much to gain by frequenting your nobles; and you have done a great deal of good with this beautiful count, with whom you are so smitten!

M. JOUR. Peace; take care what you say. Do you know, wife, that you do not know of whom you are speaking, when you speak of him? He is a personage of greater importance than you think, a nobleman who is held in great consideration at court, and who speaks to the King just as I speak to you. Is it not a great honour to me to see a person of such standing come so frequently to my house, who calls me his dear friend, and who treats me as if I were his equal? He has more kindness for me than one would ever imagine, and, before all the world, shows me such affection, that I am perfectly confused by it.

MRS. JOUR. Yes, he shows you kindness and affection; but he borrows your money.

M. JOUR. Well, is it not an honour to lend money to a man of that condition? and can I do less for a nobleman who calls me his dear friend?

MRS. JOUR. And this nobleman, what does he do for you?

M. JOUR. Things you would be astonished at, if you knew them.

MRS. JOUR. But what?

M. JOUR. That will do! I cannot explain myself. It is enough that if I have lent him money, he will return it to me, and before long.

MRS. JOUR. Yes, you had better wait for it.

M. JOUR. Assuredly. Has he not said so?

Mrs. Jour. Yes, yes, he will be sure not to fail in it.

M. Jour. He has given me his word as a nobleman.

Mrs. Jour. Stuff!

M. Jour. Good gracious, you are very obstinate, wife! I tell you that he will keep his word; I am sure of it.

Mrs. Jour. And I, I am sure that he will not, and that all the caresses he loads you with are only so much cajoling.

M. Jour. Hold your tongue. Here he comes.

Mrs. Jour. It wanted nothing but this. He comes perhaps to ask you for another loan; and the very sight of him spoils my dinner.

M. Jour. Hold your tongue, I tell you.

*   *   *

SCENE XII.—CLÉONTE, M. JOURDAIN, MRS. JOURDAIN, LUCILE, COVIELLE, NICOLE.

Cle. Sir, I did not wish to depute any one else to prefer a request which I have long meditated. It concerns me sufficiently to undertake it in person; and without farther ado, I will tell you that the honour of being your son-in-law is a glorious favour which I beg of you to grant me.

M. Jour. Before giving you your answer, Sir, I pray you to tell me whether you are a nobleman.

Cle. Sir, most people, on this question, do not hesitate much; the word is easily spoken. There is no scruple in assuming that name, and present custom seems to authorize the theft. As for me, I confess to you, my feelings on this point are rather more delicate. I think that all imposture is unworthy of an honest man, and that it is cowardice to disguise what Heaven has made us, to deck ourselves in the eyes of the world with a stolen title, and to wish to pass for what we are not. I am born of parents who, no doubt, have filled honourable offices; I have acquitted myself with honour in the army, where I served for six years; and I am sufficiently well to do to hold a middling rank in society; but with all this, I will not assume what others, in my position, might think they had

the right to pretend to; and I will tell you frankly that I am not a nobleman.

M. Jour. Your hand, Sir; my daughter is not for you.

Cle. How.

M. Jour. You are not a nobleman: you shall not have my daughter.

Mrs. Jour. What is it you mean by your nobleman? Is it that we ourselves are descended from Saint Louis?

M. Jour. Hold your tongue, wife; I see what you are driving at.

Mrs. Jour. Are we two descended from aught else than from plain citizens?

M. Jour. If that is not a slander?

Mrs. Jour. And was your father not a tradesman as well as mine?

M. Jour. Plague take the woman, she always harps upon that. If your father was a tradesman, so much the worse for him; but as for mine, they are impertinent fellows who say so. All that I have to say to you, is that I will have a nobleman for a son-in-law.

Mrs. Jour. Your daughter wants a husband who is suited to her; and it is much better for her that she should have a respectable man, rich and handsome, than a beggarly and deformed nobleman.

Nic. That is true; we have the son of our village squire, who is the greatest lout and the most stupid nincompoop that I have ever seen.

M. Jour. (*To Nicole*). Hold your tongue, Miss Impertinence; you always thrust yourself into the conversation. I have sufficient wealth to give my daughter; I wish only for honours, and I will make her a marchioness.

Mrs. Jour. Marchioness?

M. Jour. Yes, marchioness.

Mrs. Jour. Alas! Heaven preserve me from it!

M. Jour. It is a thing I am determined on.

Mrs. Jour. It is a thing to which I shall never consent. Matches with people above one's own position are always subject to the most grievous inconvenience. I do not wish a son-in-law of mine to be able to reproach my daughter with her parents, or that she should have children who would be ashamed to call me their grandmother. If she were to come and visit me with the equipage of a grand lady, and that, through inadvertency, she should miss curtseying to one of the neighbourhood, people would not fail to say a hundred silly things immediately. Do you see this lady marchioness, they would say, who is giving herself such airs? She is the daughter of M. Jourdain, who was only too glad, when she was a child, to play at ladyship with us. She has not always been so high up in the world, and her two grandfathers sold cloth near the St. Innocent gate. They amassed great wealth for their children, for which they are probably paying very dearly in the other world; for people can scarcely become so rich by remaining honest folks. I will not have all this tittle-tattle, and in one word, I wish for a man who shall be grateful to me for my daughter, and to whom I shall be able to say: Sit down there, son-in-law, and dine with me.

M. Jour. These are the sentiments of a narrow mind, to wish to remain for ever in a mean condition. Do not answer me any more: my daughter shall be a marchioness in spite of all the world; and, if you put me in a passion, I shall make her a duchess.

*   *   *

REVIEW QUESTIONS

1. How are servants and masters, who operated in separate worlds, interdependent in Molière's comedy?
2. What is the relation between nobility and judgment? Is judgment gendered?
3. Do women judge differently or according to different standards?

ROBERT FILMER

FROM *Patriarcha*

Robert Filmer (1588–1563), the English theorist of patriarchalism and absolutism, was born into the Kentish squirearchy. Filmer was educated at Trinity College, Cambridge, and at Lincoln's Inn, and was knighted by Charles I. Though he never fought for the king, his house was sacked during the Civil War, and he was imprisoned in the royalist cause. He wrote many political tracts, but his most important work, Patriarcha *(1680), was not well received at the time. Common opinion seemed to follow that of John Locke, who wrote in his* Two Treatises of Government: *"There was never so much glib nonsense put together in well-sounding English." Yet, Filmer remains interesting in his own right. He is the first English absolutist. Despite the publication date,* Patriarcha *was written before the Civil War and before publication of* Leviathan, *before the actions of Parliament prompted any defense of the monarchy and its prerogatives. Filmer believed that the state was a family, that the first king was a father, and that submission to patriarchal authority was the key to political obligation. Of particular interest is his interpretation of patriarchy, the social structure that characterized early modern Europe until the industrial revolution. Indeed, many scholars argue that Filmer's description of social relations is more realistic than the mechanical individualism put forward by Locke. His achievement notwithstanding, his historical significance rests solely on the fact that all of Locke's political thought was directed against him.*

Since the time that school divinity began to flourish, there hath been a common opinion maintained as well by divines as by divers other learned men which affirms: 'Mankind is naturally endowed and born with freedom from all subjection, and at liberty to choose what form of government it please, and that the power which any one man hath over others was at the first by human right bestowed according to the discretion of the multitude.'

This tenet was first hatched in the schools, and hath been fostered by all succeeding papists for good divinity. The divines also of the reformed churches have entertained it, and the common people everywhere tenderly embrace it as being most plausible to flesh and blood, for that it prodigally distributes a portion of liberty to the meanest of the multitude, who magnify liberty as if the height of human felicity were only to be found in it—never remembering that the desire of liberty was the cause of the fall of Adam.

But howsoever this vulgar opinion hath of late obtained great reputation, yet it is not to be found in the ancient Fathers and doctors of the primitive church. It contradicts the doctrine and history of the Holy Scriptures, the constant practice of all ancient monarchies, and the very principles of the law of nature. It is hard to say whether it be more erroneous in divinity or dangerous in policy.

Yet upon the grounds of this doctrine both Jesuits and some over zealous favourers of the Geneva discipline have built a perilous conclusion, which is 'that the people or multitude have power to punish or deprive the prince if he transgress the laws of the kingdom'. Witness Parsons and Buchanan. The first, under the name of Doleman, in the third chapter of his first book labours to prove that kings have been lawfully chastised by their commonwealths. The latter in his book *De Jure Regni apud Scotos* maintains a liberty of the people to depose their prince. Cardinal Bellarmine and Mr Calvin both look asquint this way.

This desperate assertion, whereby kings are made subject to the censures and deprivations of their subjects, follows . . . as a necessary consequence of that former position of the supposed natural equality and freedom of mankind, and liberty to choose what form of government it please.

*   *   *

The rebellious consequence which follows this prime article of the natural freedom of mankind may be my sufficient warrant for a modest examination of the original truth of it. Much hath been said, and by many, for the affirmative. Equity requires that an ear be reserved a little for the negative.

*   *   *

To make evident the grounds of this question about the natural liberty of mankind, I will lay down some passages of Cardinal Bellarmine, that may best unfold the state of this controversy. 'Secular or civil power', said he

is instituted by men. It is in the people unless they bestow it on a prince. This power is immediately in the whole multitude, as in the subject of it. For this power is by the divine law, but the divine law hath given this power to no particular man. If the positive law be taken away, there is left no reason why amongst a multitude (who are equal) one rather than another should bear rule over the rest. Power is given by the multitude to one man, or to more by the same law of nature, for the commonwealth of itself cannot exercise this power, therefore it is bound to bestow it upon some one man, or some few. It depends upon the consent of the multitude to ordain over themselves a king, or consul, or other magistrate; and if there be a lawful cause, the multitude may change the kingdom into an aristocracy or democracy.

Thus far Bellarmine, in which passages are comprised the strength of all that ever I have read or heard produced for the natural liberty of the subject.

*　　*　　*

I come now to examine that argument which is used by Bellarmine, and is the one and only argument I can find produced by any author for the proof of the natural liberty of the people. It is thus framed: that God hath given or ordained power is evident by Scripture; but God hath given it to no particular man, because by nature all men are equal; therefore he hath given power to the people or multitude.

To answer this reason, drawn from the equality of mankind by nature, I will first use the help of Bellarmine himself, whose very words are these: 'if many men had been together created out of the earth, all they ought to have been princes over their posterity'. In these words we have an evident confession that creation made man prince of his posterity. And indeed not only Adam but the succeeding patriarchs had, by right of fatherhood, royal authority over their children. Nor dares Bellarmine deny this also. 'That the patriarchs', saith he, 'were endowed with kingly power, their deeds do testify'. For as Adam was lord of his children, so his children under him had a command and power over their own children, but still with subordination to the first parent, who is lord paramount over his children's children to all generations, as being the grandfather of his people.

I see not then how the children of Adam, or of any man else, can be free from subjection to their parents. And this subjection of children is the only fountain of all regal authority, by the ordination of God himself. It follows that civil power not only in general is by divine institution, but even the assignment of it specifically to the eldest parent, which quite takes away that new and mon distinction which refers only power un as absolute to God, but power respective in of the special form of government to the of the people. Nor leaves it any place fo imaginary pactions between kings and their as many dream of.

This lordship which Adam by creati over the whole world, and by right dese from him the patriarchs did enjoy, was and ample as the absolutest dominion monarch which hath been since the creat power of life and death we find that Ju father, pronounced sentence of death agai mar, his daughter-in-law, for playing th 'Bring her forth', saith he, 'that she may b Touching war, we see that Abraham com an army of 318 soldiers of his own fam Esau met his brother Jacob with 400 men a For matter of peace, Abraham made a leagu Abimelech, and ratified the articles by an These acts of judging in capital causes, of m war, and concluding peace, are the chiefest m of sovereignty that are found in any monarch

Not only until the Flood, but after it, this triarchal power did continue—as the very na of patriarch doth in part prove. The three sons Noah had the whole world divided amongst ther by their father, for of them was the whole worlc overspread, according to the benediction given to him and his sons: 'Be fruitful and multiply and replenish the earth'. Most of the civillest nations in the world labour to fetch their original from some one of the sons or nephews of Noah, which were scattered abroad after the confusion of Babel. In this dispersion we must certainly find the establishment of regal power throughout the kingdoms of the world.

It is a common opinion that at the confusion of tongues there were seventy-two distinct nations erected. All which were not confused multitudes, without heads or governors, and at liberty to choose what governors or government they pleased, but they were distinct families, which had fathers for rulers over them. Whereby it appears that even in the confusion, God was careful to preserve the therly authority by distributing the diversity of languages according to the diversity of families.

*   *   *

In this division of the world, some are of opinion that Noah used lots for the distribution of it. Others affirm that he sailed about the Mediterranean sea in ten years and as he went about, pointed to each son his part, and so made the division of the then known world into Asia, Africa, and Europe, according to the number of his sons, the limits of which three parts are all found in that midland sea.

*   *   *

Some, perhaps, may think that these princes and dukes of families were but some pretty lords under some greater kings, because the number of them are so many that their particular territories could be but small, and not worthy the title of kingdoms. But they must consider that at first kings had no such large dominions as they have nowadays. We find in the time of Abraham, which was about 300 years after the Flood, that in a little corner of Asia nine kings at once met in battle, most of which were but kings of cities apiece, with the adjacent territories, as of Sodom, Gomorrha, Shinar, etc. In the same chapter is mention of Melchisedek, king of Salem, which was but the city of Jerusalem. And in the catalogue of the kings of Edom, the name of each king's city is recorded as the only mark to distinguish their dominions. In the land of Canaan, which was but of a small circuit, Joshua destroyed thirty-one kings, and about the same time Adonibezek had seventy kings whose fingers and toes he had cut off, and made them feed under his table. A few ages after this, thirty-two kings came to Benhadad, king of Syria, and about seventy kings of Greece went to the wars of Troy. Caesar found more kings in France than there be now provinces there, and at his sailing over into this island he found four kings in our county of Kent. These heaps of kings in each nation are an **argument that their territories were** but small, **and strongly confirm our assertion that** erection of **kingdoms** came at first **only by dis**tinction of **families.**

By manifest footsteps we may trace this paternal government unto the Israelites coming into Egypt, where the exercise of supreme patriarchal jurisdiction was intermitted because they were in subjection to a stronger prince. After the return of these Israelites out of bondage, God, out of a special care of them, chose Moses and Joshua successively to govern as princes in the place and stead of the supreme fathers, and after them likewise for a time He raised up Judges to defend His people in times of peril. But when God gave the Israelites kings, He re-established the ancient and prime right of lineal succession to paternal government. And whensoever He made choice of any special person to be king, He intended that the issue also should have benefit thereof, as being comprehended sufficiently in the person of the father—although the father only were named in the grant.

It may seem absurd to maintain that kings now are the fathers of their people, since experience shows the contrary. It is true, all kings be not the natural parents of their subjects, yet they all either are, or are to be reputed as the next heirs to those progenitors who were at first the natural parents of the whole people, and in their right succeed to the exercise of supreme jurisdiction. And such heirs are not only lords of their own children, but also of their brethren, and all others that were subject to their fathers.

And therefore we find that God told Cain of his brother Abel: 'His desires shall be subject unto thee, and thou shalt rule over him'. Accordingly, when Jacob had bought his brother's birthright, Isaac blessed him thus: 'Be lord over thy brethren, and let the sons of thy mother bow before thee'. As long as the first fathers of families lived, the name of patriarchs did aptly belong unto them. But after a few descents, when the true fatherhood itself was extinct and only the right of the father descended to the true heir, then the title of prince or king was more significant to express the power of him who succeeds only to the right of that fatherhood which his ancestors did naturally enjoy. By this means it comes to pass that many a child, by succeeding a king, hath the right of a father over many a grey-headed multitude, and hath the title of *pater patriae*.

*　　*　　*

In all kingdoms or commonwealths in the world, whether the prince be the supreme father of the people or but the true heir of such a father, or whether he come to the crown by usurpation, or by election of the nobles or of the people, or by any other way whatsoever, or whether some few or a multitude govern the commonwealth, yet still the authority that is in any one, or in many, or in all of these, is the only right and natural authority of a supreme father. There is, and always shall be continued to the end of the world, a natural right of a supreme father over every multitude, although, by the secret will of God, many at first do most unjustly obtain the exercise of it.

To confirm this natural right of regal power, we find in the decalogue that the law which enjoins obedience to kings is delivered in the terms of 'honour thy father' as if all power were originally in the father. If obedience to parents be immediately due by a natural law, and subjection to princes but by the mediation of an human ordinance, what reason is there that the law of nature should give place to the laws of men, as we see the power of the father over his child gives place and is subordinate to the power of the magistrate?

If we compare the natural duties of a father with those of a king, we find them to be all one, without any difference at all but only in the latitude or extent of them. As the father over one family, so the king, as father over many families, extends his care to preserve, feed, clothe, instruct and defend the whole commonwealth. His wars, his peace, his courts of justice and all his acts of sovereignty tend only to preserve and distribute to every subordinate and inferior father, and to their children, their rights and privileges, so that all the duties of a king are summed up in an universal fatherly care of his people.

*　　*　　*

REVIEW QUESTIONS

1. What is the relation between the authority of a father and the authority of a king?
2. Why does Filmer link political authority to domestic authority?
3. What is the relation between authority and nature for Filmer?
4. How does political authority come into being?
5. What are the implications of Filmer's rejection of the natural liberty of humankind?
6. What are its implications for his conception of human nature?
7. What are its implications for economic relations?
8. What are its implications for social status?

JEAN BAPTISTE COLBERT

A Memorandum, 1669 and A Memorandum, 1670

Jean-Baptiste Colbert (1619–1683), the son of a merchant of Reims, rose above his mercantile roots to become a statesman and minister of finance to Louis XIV. His chief concern was the economic reconstruction of France. He reorganized the fiscal administration of the state and made it more efficient. He also promoted commerce and industry in ways consistent with mercantilist theory. To improve exports, he promoted industries that produced high-quality goods, increased the merchant fleet, attracted foreign artisans, and limited foreign competition. Indeed, the system of state sponsorship and regulation that arose under Colbert and soon bore his name was widely resented by entrepreneurs anxious to innovate and expand. In his capacity of secretary of state for the king's household, from 1669, he was also concerned with the arts and education in France. He founded schools and learned societies to foster these endeavors, including the Academy of Science in 1666 to promote science. All these activities served to expand the power and magnificence of the French state, in the service of which he remained his entire life. That service proved profitable on a private level as well. He died a very wealthy man, whose estate had risen to that of an aristocrat by dint of loyal service. Yet, he was a disappointed man. Though the state had become stronger and more prosperous through his policies, he saw his ambition to reform and expand the French economy frustrated by wars that pursued the ends of the king he had served.

From "A Memorandum" by Colbert in *Colbert and a Century of French Mercantilism*, by Charles Woolsey Cole. Copyright © 1939 by Columbia University Press. Reprinted with permission of the publisher.

A MEMORANDUM, 1669

The commerce of all Europe is carried on by ships of every size to the number of 20,000, and it is perfectly clear that this number cannot be increased, since the number of people in all the states remains the same and consumption likewise remains the same. . . .

Commerce is a perpetual and peaceable war of wit and energy among all nations. Each nation works incessantly to have its legitimate share of commerce or to gain an advantage over another nation. The Dutch fight at present, in this war, with 15,000 to 16,000 ships, a government of merchants, all of whose maxims and power are directed solely toward the preservation and increase of their commerce, and much more care, energy, and thrift than any other nation.

The English with 3,000 to 4,000 ships, less energy and care, and more expenditures than the Dutch.

The French with 500 to 600.

Those two last cannot improve their com-

From *The Century of Louis XIV*, by O. Ranum and P. Ranum, Walker, 1972.

merce save by increasing the number of their vessels, and cannot increase this number save from the 20,000 which carry all the commerce and consequently by making inroads on the 15,000 to 16,000 of the Dutch.

A MEMORANDUM, 1670

Formerly the Dutch, English, Hamburgers, and other nations bringing into the realm a much greater quantity of merchandise than that which they carried away, withdrew the surplus in circulating money, which produced both their abundance and the poverty of the realm, and indisputably resulted in their power and our weakness.

We must next examine the means which were employed to change this destiny.

Firstly, in 1662 Your Majesty maintained his right to 50 sols per ton of freight from foreign vessels, which produced such great results that we have seen the number of French vessels increase yearly; and in seven or eight years the Dutch have been practically excluded from port-to-port commerce, which is carried on by the French. The advantages received by the state through the increase in the number of sailors and seamen, through the money which has remained in the realm by this means and an infinity of others, would be too long to enumerate.

At the same time, Your Majesty ordered work done to abolish all the tolls which had long been established on all the rivers of the kingdom, and he began from then on to have an examination made of the rivers which could be rendered navigable in order to facilitate the descent of commodities and merchandise from inside the realm toward the sea to be transported into foreign lands. Although everything that invites the universal admiration of men was still in disorder in these first years and although the recovery work was a sort of abyss, Your Majesty did not delay in beginning the examination of the tariffs of the *cinq grosses fermes* and scrutinized the fact that the regulation and levying of these sorts of duties concerning commerce had always been done with a great deal of ignorance on the basis of memoranda by tax farmers, who, being solely concerned with their own interests and the increase in the profits from their tax farms while they possessed them, had always overvalued the commodities, merchandise, and manufactured items of the realm which they saw leaving in abundance, and favored the entrance of foreign merchandise and manufactured items, in order to have a greater quantity of them enter, without being concerned about whether money was as a result leaving the realm, for they were indifferent to this as long as their tax farms produced gain for them during the period of their possession.

Finally, after having thoroughly studied this matter, Your Majesty ordered the tariff of 1664, in which the duties are regulated on a completely different principle, that is to say, that all merchandise and manufactured items of the realm were markedly favored and the foreign ones priced out of the market, though not completely; for having as yet no established manufacturers in the realm, this increase in duties, had it been excessive, would have been a great burden for the *peuple*, because of their need for the aforesaid foreign merchandise and manufactured items; but this change began to provide some means of establishing the same manufactures in the realm; and to this end:

The fabric manufacture of Sedan has been reestablished, and enlarged to 62 from the 12 looms there were then.

The new establishments of Abbeville, Dieppe, Fécamp, and Rouen have been built, in which there are presently more than 200 looms.

The factory for barracan was next established at La Ferré-sous-Jouarre, which is made up of 120 looms;

That of little damasks from Flanders, at Meaux, consisting of 80 looms;

That for carpeting, in the same city, made up of 20 looms . . .

That for tin, in Nivernois;

That for French lace, in 52 cities and towns, in which more than 20,000 workers toil;

The manufacture of brass, or yellow copper, set up in Champagne;

That for camlet of Brussels, in Paris, which will become large and extensive;

Brass wire, in Burgundy;

Gold thread of Milan, at Lyons . . .

And since Your Majesty has wanted to work diligently at reestablishing his naval forces, and since for that it has been necessary to make very great expenditures, since all merchandise, munitions and manufactured items formerly came from Holland and the countries of the North, it has been absolutely necessary to be especially concerned with finding within the realm, or with establishing in it, everything which might be necessary for this great plan.

To this end, the manufacture of tar was established in Médoc, Auvergne, Dauphiné, and Provence;

Iron cannons, in Burgundy, Nivernois, Saintonge, and Périgord;

Large anchors, in Dauphiné, Nivernois, Brittany, and Rochefort;

Sailcloth for the Levant, in Dauphiné;

Coarse muslin, in Auvergne;

All the implements for pilots and others, at Dieppe and La Rochelle;

The cutting of wood suitable for vessels, in Burgundy, Dauphiné, Brittany, Normandy, Poitou, Saintonge, Provence, Guyenne, and the Pyrenees;

Masts, of a sort once unknown in this realm, have been found in Provence, Languedoc, Auvergne, Dauphiné, and in the Pyrenees.

Iron, which was obtained from Sweden and Biscay, is currently manufactured in the realm.

Fine hemp for ropes, which came from Prussia and from Piedmont, is currently obtained in Burgundy, Mâconnais, Bresse, Dauphiné; and markets for it have since been established in Berry and in Auvergue, which always provides money in these provinces and keeps it within the realm.

In a word, everything serving for the construction of vessels is currently established in the realm, so that Your Majesty can get along without foreigners for the navy and will even, in a short time, be able to supply them and gain their money in this fashion. And it is with this same objective of having everything necessary to provide abundantly for his navy and that of his subjects that he is working at the general reform of all the forests in his realm, which, being as carefully preserved as they are at present, will abundantly produce all the wood necessary for this.

REVIEW QUESTIONS

1. How does Colbert speak of "commerce"?
2. What does it entail?
3. What causes its success?
4. Why is commerce a war?
5. What does Colbert see as the source of Dutch and English power?
6. What has strengthened French commerce?
7. What goods does Colbert describe?
8. Why do you suppose he pays particular attention to them?

ANNE ROBERT JACQUES TURGOT

FROM Reflections on the Accumulation and Distribution of Wealth

Anne Robert Jacques Turgot, Baron de l'Aulne (1727–1781), was born in Paris and educated at the Sorbonne. His entire career was spent in state service. After holding numerous posts, he was appointed intendant *(chief administrative officer) of the district of Limoges in 1761. Influenced by physiocratic economic ideas that advocated the expansion of agriculture as the basis of all wealth, he instituted a number of fiscal reforms in his district, including the substitution of monetary payments for* corvée *(forced labor) service. While holding office in Limoges, Turgot published his economic treatise,* Reflections on the Accumulation and Distribution of Wealth *(1766), which began with the physiocratic notions of land as the sole source of wealth and agriculture as the most important kind of production, but developed in its course a surprisingly modern notion of capital. It provides an interesting perspec-*

tive on rural labor, productivity, and wealth before industrialization. In 1774, Turgot was appointed comptroller-general of finance. In this capacity he undertook a series of reforms aimed at controlling expenditures and taxation. He delivered his Six Edicts, *which urged the abolition of forced labor, the suppression of monopolies, and the taxation of the nobility, to the royal council in 1776. These sweeping reforms provoked such resistance from the nobility that Turgot was forced into permanent retirement.*

I

IMPOSSIBILITY OF COMMERCE ON THE ASSUMPTION OF AN EQUAL DIVISION OF LAND, WHERE EACH MAN WOULD HAVE ONLY WHAT WAS NECESSARY FOR HIS OWN SUPPORT.

If the land were distributed among all the inhabitants of a country in such a way that each of them had precisely the quantity necessary for his support, and nothing more, it is evident that, all being equal, no one would be willing to work for others. Also no one would have the means of paying for the labour of another; for each man, having only as much land as was necessary to produce his own subsistence, would consume all that he had gathered in, and would have nothing which he could exchange for the labour of others.

II

THE ABOVE HYPOTHESIS HAS NEVER EXISTED, AND COULD NOT HAVE CONTINUED TO EXIST. THE DIVERSITY OF SOILS AND THE MULTIPLICITY OF NEEDS LEAD TO THE EXCHANGE OF THE PRODUCTS OF THE LAND FOR OTHER PRODUCTS.

This hypothesis could never have existed, because the lands were cultivated before being divided, cultivation itself having been the only motive for the division and for the law which secures to every man his property. The first men who engaged in cultivation probably cultivated as much land as their resources would permit, and consequently more than was necessary for their own support.

Even if this state of affairs could have existed, it could not have been a lasting one. If each man drew no more than his subsistence from his land, and did not have the means of paying for the labour of others, he would not be able to meet his other needs for housing, clothing, etc. except by means of his own labour, and this would be virtually impossible, since *all land falls far short of producing everything.*

The man whose land was suitable only for corn, and would produce neither cotton nor hemp, would lack cloth with which to clothe himself. Another man would have land suitable for cotton which would produce no corn. One would lack wood to keep himself warm, while another would lack corn to feed himself. Experience would soon teach each man the kind of product for which his land was most suitable; and he would confine himself to cultivating this, in order to procure for himself the things which he lacked by means of exchange with his neighbours, who, having in their turn reasoned in the same way, would have cultivated the produce best suited to their land and abandoned the cultivation of all others.

III

THE PRODUCTS OF THE LAND REQUIRE LONG AND DIFFICULT PREPARATIONS IN ORDER TO RENDER THEM SUITABLE TO MEET MEN'S NEEDS.

The produce which the land yields in order to satisfy the different needs of men cannot for the most part serve to do this in the state in which nature affords it; it must be subjected to various changes and be prepared by means of art. Wheat must be converted into flour and then into bread; hides must be tanned or dressed; wool and cotton must be spun; silk must be drawn from the cocoons; hemp and flax must be soaked, peeled, and spun; then different fabrics must be woven from them; and then they must be cut and sewn in order to make them into clothing, footwear, etc. If the same man who caused these different things to be produced from his land, and who used them to meet his needs, were also obliged to subject them to all these intermediate preparations, it is certain that the result would turn out very badly. The greater part of these preparations demand an amount of care, attention, and long experience which is acquired only by working continuously and on a great quantity of materials. Take for example the preparation of hides. Where is the husbandman who could attend to all the details involved in this operation, which goes on for several months and sometimes for several years? If he could, would he be able to do it for a single hide? What a loss of time, space, and materials, which could have served at the same time, or successively, to tan a great number of hides! And even if he did succeed in tanning one single hide, he needs only one pair of shoes: what would he make out of the remainder? Shall he kill an ox in order to have this pair of shoes? Shall he cut down a tree to make himself a pair of clogs? The same may be said of all the other needs of each man, who, if he were reduced to his own land and his own labour, would involve himself in a great deal of time and trouble in order to be very badly equipped in every respect, and would cultivate his land very badly.

IV

THE NECESSITY FOR THESE PREPARATIONS LEADS TO THE EXCHANGE OF PRODUCTS FOR LABOUR.

The same motive which brought about the exchange of one kind of produce for another as between the Cultivators of soils of different qualities was bound to lead also to the exchange of produce for labour as between the Cultivators and another part of society, which had come to prefer the occupation of preparing and working up the products of the land to that of growing them. Everyone gained as a result of this arrangement, for each man by devoting himself to a single kind of work succeeded much better in it. The Husbandman obtained from his land the greatest possible quantity of products, and by means of the exchange of his surplus procured for himself all the other things he needed much more easily than he would have done by means of his own labour. The Shoemaker, by making shoes for the Husbandman, appropriated to himself a portion of the latter's harvest. Each Workman worked to meet the needs of the Workmen of all the other kinds, who in their turn all worked for him.

V

PRE-EMINENCE OF THE HUSBANDMAN WHO PRODUCES OVER THE ARTISAN WHO PREPARES. THE HUSBANDMAN IS THE PRIME MOVER IN THE CIRCULATION OF MEN'S LABOUR; IT IS HE WHO CAUSES THE LAND TO PRODUCE THE WAGES OF ALL THE ARTISANS.

It must however be noted that the Husbandman, who supplies everyone with the most important and considerable objects of their consumption (I mean their food and also the materials of almost all manufactures), has the advantage of a greater degree of independence. His labour, among the various kinds of labour which are shared out between the different members of society, retains the same primacy and the same pre-eminence that the labour which provided for his subsistence possessed among the different kinds of labour which he was obliged, when he was in a solitary state, to devote to his needs of all kinds. What we have here is a primacy arising not from honour or dignity, but from *physical necessity*. The Husbandman, generally speaking, can get on without the labour of the other Workmen, but no Workman can labour if the Husbandman does not support him. In this circulation, which by means of the reciprocal exchange of needs renders men necessary to one another and constitutes the bond of society, it is therefore the labour of the Husbandman which is the prime mover. Whatever his labour causes the land to produce over and above his personal needs is the unique fund from which are paid the wages which all the other members of society receive in exchange for their labour. The latter, in making use of the consideration which they receive in this exchange to purchase in their turn the produce of the Husbandman, do no more than return to him exactly what they have received from him. Here we have a very basic difference between these two kinds of labour, and before we deal with the innumerable consequences which spring from it we must dwell upon it in order that we may be fully aware of how self-evident it is.

VI

THE WAGE OF THE WORKMAN IS LIMITED TO HIS SUBSISTENCE AS A RESULT OF COMPETITION BETWEEN WORKMEN. HE EARNS NO MORE THAN A LIVING.

The simple Workman, who possesses only his hands and his industry, has nothing except in so far as he succeeds in selling his toil to others. He sells it more or less dear; but this higher or lower price does not depend upon himself alone; it results from the agreement which he makes with the man who pays for his labour. The latter pays him as little as he is able; since he has a choice between a great number of Workmen he prefers the one who works most cheaply. Thus the Workmen are obliged to vie with one another and lower their price. In every kind of work it is bound to be the case, and in actual fact is the case, that the wage of the Workman is limited to what is necessary in order to enable him to procure his subsistence.

VII

THE HUSBANDMAN IS THE ONLY ONE WHOSE LABOUR PRODUCES ANYTHING OVER AND ABOVE THE WAGE OF THE LABOUR. HE IS THEREFORE THE UNIQUE SOURCE OF ALL WEALTH.

The position of the Husbandman is quite different. The land, independently of any other man and of any agreement, pays him directly the price of his labour. Nature never bargains with him in order to oblige him to content himself with what is absolutely necessary. What she grants is proportionate neither to his needs nor to a contractual evaluation of the price of his working day. It is the physical result of the fertility of the soil, and of the correctness, much more than of the difficulty, of the means he has employed to render it fruitful. As soon as the labour of the Husbandman produces something over and above his needs, he is able, with this surplus over and above the reward for his toil which nature affords him as a pure gift, to purchase the labour of other members of the society. The latter, when they sell to him, earn no more than their living; but the Husbandman obtains, besides his subsistence, an independent and disposable form of wealth, which he has never purchased but which he sells. He is therefore the unique source of all wealth, which, through its circulation, animates all the industry of society; because he is the only one whose labour produces anything over and above the wage of the labour.

VIII

PRIMARY DIVISION OF SOCIETY INTO TWO CLASSES: FIRST, THE PRODUCTIVE CLASS, OR THE CULTIVATORS; AND SECOND, THE STIPENDIARY CLASS, OR THE ARTISANS.

Here then we have the whole society divided, as the result of a necessity founded on the nature of things, into two classes, both of which are occupied in work. But one of these, through its labour, produces or rather extracts from the land wealth which is continually renascent, and which provides the whole of society with subsistence and the materials for all its needs. The other, engaged in preparing the produced materials and giving them forms which render them suitable for men's use, sells its labour to the first, and receives its subsistence from it in exchange. The first may be called the *productive* class, and the second the *stipendiary* class.

IX

IN THE EARLIEST TIMES THE PROPRIETOR COULD NOT HAVE BEEN DISTINGUISHED FROM THE CULTIVATOR.

Up to now we have made no distinction at all between the Husbandman and the Proprietor of the land; and in the beginning they were not in fact distinguished at all. It was as a result of the labour of those who first worked the fields, and who enclosed them, in order to make certain of securing the harvest, that all the land ceased to be common to all and that landed property was established. Until societies were consolidated, and until public power, or the law, having come to predominate over individual power, was able to guarantee everyone the peaceful possession of his property against all invasion from without, one

could maintain one's ownership of a piece of land only in the way that one had acquired it, and by continuing to cultivate it. It would not have been safe to have one's fields worked by another who, having undergone all the toil involved, would have had difficulty in understanding that the whole of the harvest did not belong to him. Moreover, in these early times every industrious man would be able to find as much land as he wanted, and could thus not be induced to till the soil for others. Every proprietor was obliged either to cultivate his fields or to abandon them completely.

X

PROGRESS OF SOCIETY; ALL LAND COMES TO HAVE AN OWNER.

But the land became populated, and was brought into cultivation to a greater and greater extent. In the course of time all the best land came to be occupied. There remained for the last comers only the infertile soils which had been rejected by the first. But in the end all land found its owner; and those who could not possess properties had at first no course open to them other than to exchange the labour of their hands in the occupations of the *stipendiary* class for the surplus produce of the cultivating Proprietor.

XI

IT BEGINS TO BE POSSIBLE FOR THE PROPRIETORS TO SHIFT THE LABOUR OF CULTIVATION ON TO PAID CULTIVATORS.

But since the land rendered the owner who cultivated it not only his subsistence, not only the means of procuring for himself by way of exchange the other things he needed, but also a large surplus, he was able with this surplus to pay men to cultivate his land. And for men who live on wages, it is just as good to earn them in this occupation as in any other. Thus ownership could be separated from the labour of cultivation, and soon it was.

XII

INEQUALITY IN THE DIVISION OF PROPERTY: CAUSES WHICH MAKE THIS INEVITABLE.

The original Proprietors, as has already been said, at first occupied as much land as their resources allowed them and their families to cultivate. A man of greater strength, more industrious, and more anxious about the future took more land than a man with the opposite character. He whose family was larger, having more needs and more hands, extended his possessions further; here was already a first form of inequality. All land is not equally fertile: two men with the same area of land and the same labour may obtain very different products from it: a second source of inequality. Properties, in passing from fathers to children, are divided up into portions which are more or less small according to whether the families are more or less numerous. As one generation succeeds another, the inheritances at one time are further subdivided, and at another time are brought together again through the dying out of branches of the family: a third source of inequality. The contrast between the intelligence, the activity, and above all the thrift of some with the indolence, inactivity, and extravagance of others, constituted a fourth cause of inequality, and the most powerful one of all. The negligent and improvident Proprietor, who cultivates badly, and who in abundant years consumes the whole of his surplus in frivolities, on the occurrence of the slightest accident finds himself reduced to asking for help from his more prudent neighbour, and to living on loans. If, as the result of new accidents or the continuation of his negligence, he finds that he is not in a position to pay, and if he is obliged to have recourse to new loans, there will in the end be nothing left for him to do but abandon a part or even the whole of his estate to his creditor, who will take it as an

equivalent; or to part with it to another in exchange for other assets with which he will discharge his obligation to his creditor.

XIII

CONSEQUENCE OF THIS INEQUALITY: THE CULTIVATOR DISTINGUISHED FROM THE PROPRIETOR.

So here we have landed estates as objects of commerce, being bought and sold. The portion of the Proprietor who is extravagant or unfortunate serves to increase that of the Proprietor who is luckier or more prudent; and in the midst of this infinitely varied inequality of possessions it is impossible that a great number of Proprietors should not possess more than they are able to cultivate. Moreover it is natural enough that a wealthy man should wish to enjoy his wealth in peace, and that instead of employing all his time in arduous labour he should prefer to give a part of his surplus to people who will work for him.

XIV

DIVISION OF THE PRODUCT BETWEEN THE CULTIVATOR AND THE PROPRIETOR. NET PRODUCT OR REVENUE.

According to this new arrangement, the product of the land is divided into two parts. One comprises the subsistence and profits of the Husbandman, which are the reward for his labour and the condition upon which he undertakes to cultivate the Proprietor's fields. What remains is that independent and disposable part which the land gives as a pure gift to the one who cultivates it, over and above his advances and the wages of his toil; and this is the share of the Proprietor, or the *revenue*, with which the latter is able to live without working and which he takes wherever he wishes.

XV

NEW DIVISION OF THE SOCIETY INTO THREE CLASSES, THE CULTIVATORS, THE ARTISANS, AND THE PROPRIETORS, OR THE 'PRODUCTIVE' CLASS, THE 'STIPENDIARY' CLASS, AND THE 'DISPOSABLE' CLASS.

So now we have the Society divided into three classes: the class of Husbandmen, for which we may keep the name *productive class*; the class of Artisans and other *stipendiaries* supported by the product of the land; and the class of *Proprietors*, the only one which, not being bound by the need for subsistence to one particular kind of work, may be employed to meet the general needs of the Society, for example in war and the administration of justice, whether through personal service, or through the payment of a part of its revenue with which the State or the Society may hire men to discharge these functions. The name which for this reason suits it best is the *disposable class*.

XVI

RESEMBLANCE BETWEEN THE TWO INDUSTRIOUS OR NON-DISPOSABLE CLASSES.

The two classes of Cultivators and Artisans resemble one another in many respects, and above all in the fact that those of whom they are composed do not possess any revenue and live equally on the wages which are paid to them out of the product of the land. Both also have this in common, that they earn nothing but the price of their labour and of their advances, and this price is almost the same in the two classes. The Proprietor beats down those who cultivate his land in order to give up to them the smallest possible portion of the product, in the same way as he haggles with his Shoemaker in order to buy his shoes as cheaply as possible. In a word, neither the Cultivator nor the Artisan receive more than a recompense for their labour.

XVII

ESSENTIAL DIFFERENCE BETWEEN THE TWO INDUSTRIOUS CLASSES.

But there is this difference between these two kinds of labour, that the Cultivator's labour produces his own wage, and in addition the revenue which serves to pay the whole class of Artisans and other stipendiaries, whereas the Artisans receive simply their wages, that is, their share of the product of the land, in exchange for their labour, and do not produce any revenue. The Proprietor enjoys nothing except through the labour of the Cultivator; he receives from him his subsistence and the means of paying for the work of the other stipendiaries. He has need of the Cultivator because of a necessity which arises from the physical order of things, by virtue of which the land produces nothing at all without labour; but the Cultivator has need of the Proprietor only by virtue of human conventions and the civil laws which guaranteed to the original Cultivators and their heirs the ownership of the land which they had occupied, even after they ceased to cultivate it. But these laws could guarantee to the man who took no part in the work himself only that part of the product which the land yields over and above the recompense due to the Cultivators. The Proprietor is forced to abandon the latter, on pain of losing the whole. The Cultivator, completely restricted though he is to the recompense for his labour, thus retains that natural and physical primacy which renders him the prime mover of the whole machine of Society, and which causes not only his own subsistence, but also the wealth of the Proprietor and the wages for all other kinds of work, to depend upon his labour alone. The Artisan, on the other hand, receives his wages, either from the Proprietor or from the Cultivator, and gives them, by the exchange of his labour, only the equivalent of these wages and nothing over and above this.

Thus, although neither the Cultivator nor the Artisan earn more than a recompense for their labour, the Cultivator generates over and above this recompense the revenue of the Proprietor, and the Artisan does not generate any revenue, either for himself or for others.

XVIII

THIS DIFFERENCE JUSTIFIES THEIR BEING DISTIN- GUISHED AS THE PRODUCTIVE CLASS AND THE STER- ILE CLASS.

Thus we may distinguish the two non-disposable classes as the *productive class*, which is that of the Cultivators, and the *sterile class*, which includes all the other stipendiary members of the Society.

REVIEW QUESTIONS

1. What is different about Turgot's economic thought?
2. Have we seen constant principles applied to land and its use?
3. What might be the principles Turgot applies?
4. Why is labor of central importance to Turgot?
5. How is labor measured?
6. By what criteria does Turgot evaluate labor?
7. What is the source of wealth, according to Turgot?
8. What constitutes progress?

WILLIAM GOUDGE

FROM Of Domesticall Duties

William Goudge was a Puritan clergyman best remembered for his tract on family life, a conduct book entitled Of Domesticall Duties *(1634). It captured the common attitude toward domestic governance in early modern Europe. All authority rested in the hands of a pater familias, the husband-father-master, who possessed absolute control over the family's property and labor and to whom all members of the household owed unflinching obedience and loyalty. Though observed most often in the breach, this pattern of discipline was universally prescribed in early modern Europe.*

From *Western Societies,* edited by Brian Tierney and Joan Scott, Alfred E. Knopf, 1984.

*   *   *

But what if a man of lewd and beastly conditions, as a drunkard, a glutton, a profane swaggerer, an impious swearer and blasphemer, be married to a wise, sober, religious matron, must she account him her superior and worthy of an husband's honor?

Surely she must. For the evil quality and disposition of his heart and life doth not deprive a man of that civil honor which God hath given unto him. Though an husband in regard of evil qualities may carry the image of the devil, yet in regard of his place and office; he beareth the Image of God: so do Magistrates in the Commonwealth, Ministers in the Church, Parents and Masters in the Family. Note for our present purpose, the exhortation of St Peter to Christian wives which have infidel husbands, 'Be in subjection to them: let your conversation be in fear'. If Infidels carry not the devil's image and are not, so long as they are Infidels, vassals of Satan, who are? Yet wives must be subject to them.

*   *   *

REVIEW QUESTIONS

1. What is the conflict between order and nature Goudge depicts?
2. Why should a wife stay with a brutal husband?
3. What sort of order does Goudge invoke?

Vauban and Platelle

Much of our knowledge about the economy and society of early modern Europe comes from contemporary accounts. For many reasons, individuals described the life and times of which they were part. Some, like Sébastien Le Prestre, Marquis de Vauban (1633–1707), labored in the service of the state. A French military engineer and genius in the construction of fortifications under Louis XIV, he studied the society and economy of the Kingdom of France to determine its military capacity, the human and material resources that could be mobilized for war in pursuit of royal policy. The result was a series of sober, accurate descriptions of the French population. Others, like Henri Platelle, an obscure parish priest in the village of Rumegies, chronicled their own experiences and observations. The chance survival of Platelle's 1693 journal provides us with a firsthand account of the starkness of daily life in early modern Europe and the struggles of poor peasants simply to survive.

From *Ancien Regime: French Society, 1600–1750*, by Pierre Goubert. Copyright © 1973 by George Weidenfeld & Nicholson, Ltd. Reprinted by permission of HarperCollins Publishers, Inc.

Marquis de Vauban

FROM **Description Geographique de l'Election de Vezelay**

*   *   *

. . . All the so-called *bas peuple* live on nothing but bread of mixed barley and oats, from which they do not even remove the bran, which means that bread can sometimes be lifted by the straw sticking out of it. They also eat poor fruits, mainly wild, and a few vegetables from their gardens, boiled up with a little rape- or nut-oil sometimes, but more often not, or with a pinch of salt. Only the most prosperous eat bread made of rye mixed with barley and wheat.

. . . The general run of people seldom drink, eat meat not three times a year, and use little salt . . . So it is no cause for surprise if people who are so ill-nourished have so little energy. Add to this what they suffer from exposure: winter and summer, three fourths of them are dressed in nothing but half-rotting tattered linen, and are shod throughout the year with *sabots*, and no other covering for the foot. If one of them does have shoes he only wears them on saints' days and Sundays: the extreme poverty to which they are reduced, owning as they do not one inch of land, rebounds against the more prosperous town and country bourgeois, and against the nobility and the clergy. They lease their lands out to *métayage*, and the owner who wants a new *métayer* must begin by settling his obligations, paying his debts, stocking the holding with beasts and feeding him and his family for the coming year at his own expense . . .

The poor people are ground down in another manner by the loans of grain and money they take from the wealthy in emergencies, by means of which a high rate of usury is enforced, under the guise of presents which must be made after the debts fall due, so as to avoid imprisonment. After the term has been extended by only three or four months, either another present must be produced when the time is up, or they face the *sergent* who is sure to strip the house bare. Many others of these poor people's afflictions remain at my quill's tip, so as not to offend anybody.

Since hardship can hardly go much further, its normal effects are a matter of course: firstly, it makes people weak and unhealthy, especially the children, many of whom die for want of good food; secondly, the men become idle and apathetic, being persuaded that only the least and worst part of the fruit of their labours will turn to their own profit; thirdly, there are liars, robbers, men of bad faith, always willing to perjure themselves provided that it pays, and to get drunk as soon as they lay hands on the wherewithal . . .

. . . It only remains to take stock of two million men all of whom I suppose to be day-labourers or simple artisans scattered throughout the towns, *bourgs* and villages of the realm.

What I have to say about all these workers . . . deserves serious attention, for although this sector may consist of what are unfairly called the dregs of the people, they are nonetheless worthy of high consideration in view of the services which they render to the State. For it is they who undertake all the great tasks in town and country without which neither themselves nor others could live. It is they who provide all the soldiers and sailors and all the servants and serving women; in a word, without them the State could not survive. It is for this reason that they ought to be spared in the matter of taxes, in order not to burden them beyond their strength.

Let us begin with the town-dwellers. . . .

Among the smaller fry, particularly in the countryside, there are any number of people who, while they lay no claim to any special craft, are continually plying several which are most necessary and indispensable. Of such a kind are those whom we call *manoeuvriers*, who, owning for the most part nothing but their strong arms or very little more, do day- or piece-work for whoever wants to employ them. It is they who do all the major jobs such as mowing, harvesting, threshing, woodcutting, working the soil and the vineyards, clearing land, ditching, carrying soil to vineyards or elsewhere, labouring for builders and several other tasks which are all hard and laborious. These men may well find this kind of employment for part of the year, and it is true that they can usually earn a fair day's wage at haymaking, harvesting and grape-picking time, but the rest of the year is a different story . . .

It will not be inappropriate to give some particulars about what the country day-labourer can earn.

I shall assume that of the three hundred and sixty-five days in the year, he may be gainfully employed for one hundred and eighty, and earn nine *sols* a day. This is a high figure, and it is certain that except at harvest- and grape-picking time most earn not more than eight *sols* a day on average, but supposing we allow the nine *sols*, that would amount to eighty-five *livres* and ten *sols*, call it ninety *livres*, from which we have to deduct his liabilities (taxes plus salt for a family of four say 14*l*. 16*s*) . . . leaving seventy-five *livres* four *sols*.

Since I am assuming that this family . . . consists of four people, it requires not less than ten *septiers* of grain, Paris measure, to feed them. This grain, half wheat, half rye . . . commonly selling at six *livres* per *septier* . . . will come to sixty *livres*, which leaves fifteen *livres* four *sols* out of the seventy-five *livres* four *sols*, out of which the labourer has to find the price of rent and upkeep for his house, a few chattels, if only some earthenware bowls, clothing and linen, and the needs of his entire family for one year.

But these fifteen *livres* four *sols* will not take him very far unless his industry or some particular business supervenes and his wife contributes to their income by means of her distaff, sewing, knitting hose or making small quantities of lace . . . also by keeping a small garden or rearing poultry and perhaps a calf, a pig or a goat for the better-off . . . ; by which means he might buy a piece of larding bacon and a little butter or oil for making soup. And if he does not additionally cultivate some small allotment, he will be hard pressed to subsist, or at least he will be reduced, together with his family, to the most wretched fare. And if instead of two children he has four, that will be worse still until they are old enough to earn their own living. Thus however we come at the matter, it is certain that he will always have the greatest difficulty in seeing the year out . . .

Henri Platelle

FROM *Journal of the Curé of Rumegies*

. . . the final misfortune was the utter failure of the ensuing harvest, which caused grain to reach a tremendous price. And since the poor people were exhausted in like measure by the frequent demands of His Majesty and by these exorbitant taxes, they fell into such poverty as might just as well be called famine. Happy the man who could lay hands on a measure of rye to mix with oats, peas and beans and make bread to half fill his belly. I speak of two thirds of this village, if not more . . .

Throughout this time, the talk was all of thieves, murders and people dying of starvation. I do not know if it is to the credit of the *curé* of Rumegies to refer here to a death which occurred in his parish during that time: a man named Pierre du Gauquier, who lived by the statue of the Virgin, towards la Howardries. This poor fellow was a widower; people thought that he was not as poor as he was; he was burdened with three children. He fell ill, or rather he grew worn-out and feeble, but nobody informed the *curé*, until one Sunday, upon the final bell for mass, one of his sisters came and told the *curé* that her brother was dying of starvation, and that was all she said. The pastor gave her some bread to take to him forthwith, but perhaps the sister had need of it for herself, as seems likely to be the case. She did not take it to him, and at the second bell for vespers the poor man died of starvation. He was the only one to drop dead for want of bread, but several others died of that cause a little at a time, both here and in other villages, for that year saw a great mortality. In our parish alone, more people died than in several ordinary years . . . Truly men wearied of being of this world. Men of goodwill had their hearts wrung at the sight of the poor people's sufferings, poor people, without money while a measure of corn cost nine to ten *livres* at the end of the year, with peas and beans corresponding . . .

The ordinance made by His Majesty for the relief of his poor people cannot be forgotten here . . . Every community *had to* feed its poor. The pastors, mayors and men of law taxed the wealthiest and the middling, each according to his capability, in order to succour the poor, whom it was also their duty to seek out. It was the right way to keep everybody provided . . . In this village, where there is no court and everybody is his own master, the *curé* read out and re-read that ordinance to no avail. The *mayeurs* and men of law, who were the richest and would therefore have to be taxed most, fought it with all their might. With much hardship, August was finally reached. A fortnight beforehand, people were harvesting the rye when it was still green, and putting it in ovens to dry it, and because this grain was unripe and unhealthy it caused several serious illnesses.

May the Lord in his fatherly Providence vouchsafe us to be preserved henceforward from a like dearth . . .

REVIEW QUESTIONS

1. What does Vauban tell us about the lives of the great majority of French people?
2. How might they measure wealth?
3. How might they view taxes?
4. Would they be Turgot's workmen or husbandmen?
5. Who are the people Vauban describes? What is their social place?
6. What is their economic function?
7. What services might they render to the state?
8. Who are the people Platelle describes as poor?
9. Do they cause their own poverty?
10. Does Platelle suggest any attributes that may have caused their poverty?
11. Whom do taxes serve in Platelle's parish?
12. What was the purpose of taxes?

16 ❦ THE AGE OF ABSOLUTISM
(1660–1789)

Absolutism refers to a particular conception of political authority that emerged in the wake of the crises of the later sixteenth century. It asserted order, where Europeans felt order had been undermined in political and social relations, by positing a vision of a society which had its apex in the person of a single ruler. At the center of all conceptions of absolutism was the will of the ruler: for all theorists, that will was absolute, not merely sovereign, but determinative of all political relations. The king stood at the peak of that pyramid, and the function of that pyramid was to realize his will. Theories of absolutism drew upon an understanding of the will that had its origins in the writings of Italian humanists in the fifteenth century and its fullest expression in the writings of theologians such as John Calvin and Martin Luther. By the end of the period, there would be calls for enlightened absolutism, in which reason guided the will of the sovereign, but the will of the monarch was still the agent of political life.

Such an understanding of the nature and operation of political power required a number of developments, not the least of which was a military and a bureaucracy to carry out the king's will. In France and in Spain, over the course of some three centuries, elaborate machineries of rule had evolved: chanceries for the collection, supervision, management, and disbursement of various incomes; judiciaries to decide such diverse issues as disputes over property, relations between lords and servants, and, in some kingdoms, private relations among families; and the emergence of diplomatic professionals, as well as secretaries of various kinds for record-keeping, which increased exponentially in this period. Finally, certain theories that posited a hierarchy of human nature, from natural slavery to natural monarchy, supported an understanding of that pyramid as not only rational, but natural.

These developments did not go unopposed. Among theorists there arose several who countered the notion of absolute monarchy with that of sovereignty placed in the hands of property owners. Moreover, they argued persuasively that the exercise of sovereignty was limited in accordance with the principles of natural law. In practice as in theory, social groups, especially the aristocracy, struggled to limit the expanding powers of the monarch, whom they viewed as one of their own, and to preserve their own political prerogatives.

No monarch in this period was truly absolute—such an effective expression of the will of the ruler requires greater technological and military support than any ruler prior to the nineteenth century could have. Many, however, were largely successful in representing themselves as the center of all political life in their states, nurturing courts and bureaucracies that reflected images of omniscient and powerful rulers. These same courts provided both a milieu and the financial support for philosophes such as Voltaire and scientists such as Galileo, even as those intellectuals were calling into question the ethics of and the social bases for absolutism.

Revocation of the Edict of Nantes:
Louis XIV and the Duc de Saint-Simon

The Edict of Nantes, signed by Henry IV in 1598, granted a measure of religious liberty to his Protestant subjects, the Huguenots. It granted them freedom of conscience and the right to hold public worship services anywhere they had done so in 1576, including two towns in every administrative unit of France, the houses of aristocrats, and within five kilometers of Paris. It also granted French Protestants full civil rights: to enter trade, inherit property, attend universities, and hold offices. The edict included one crucial political concession: the Huguenots were permitted to retain such fortified places as they held in 1597 as garrisoned strongholds at the expense of the crown. The edict also restored Catholicism in all areas where it had been disrupted. Nonetheless, French Catholics resented it as being too tolerant of heresy. The monarchy soon came to view its political clause as a danger to the state. Cardinal Richilieu reduced the Protestant strongholds by force of arms, and the Edict of Alès rescinded the political agreement in 1629 Louis XIV revoked the edict in 1685 and deprived the Huguenots of all civil and religious liberties. Their clergy were forced into exile. Thousands of religious refugees fled France for the Protestant states of Europe and America, where their commercial and artisanal skills contributed significantly to economic prosperity. The revocation provoked a storm of outraged protest against an arbitrary act of state. The proclamation, extracted below, offers the monarch's justification, based on his absolute authority and its religious underpinnings. Entries from the Memoirs of the Duc de Saint-Simon, *an eyewitness at the royal court,* The Declaration of the Gallican Church, *interested parties to the revocation, and from Louis' Letter to His Heir reflect upon the political context and consequences of the deed.*

From *Readings in European History,* translated by J. H. Robinson, Ginn and Company, 1906.

Louis XIV

FROM *Revocation of the Edict of Nantes*

1. Be it known that of our certain knowledge, full power, and royal authority, we have, by this present perpetual and irrevocable edict, suppressed and revoked, and do suppress and revoke, the edict of our said grandfather, given at Nantes in April 1598, in its whole extent. . . .

2. We forbid our subjects of the R.P.R. [Religion pretendue reformee, i.e., the so-called reformed religion] to meet any more for the exercise of the said religion in any place or private house, under any pretext whatever. . . .

3. We likewise forbid all noblemen, of what condition soever, to hold such religious exercises in their houses or fiefs, under penalty to be inflicted upon all our said subjects who shall engage in the said exercises, of imprisonment and confiscation.

4. We enjoin all ministers of the said R.P.R., who do not choose to become converts and to embrace the Catholic, apostolic, and Roman religion, to leave our kingdom and the territories subject to us within a fortnight of the publication of our present edict, without leave to reside therein beyond that period, or, during the said fortnight, to engage in any preaching, exhortation, or any other function, on pain of being sent to the galleys. . . .

7. We forbid private schools for the instruction of children of the said R.P.R., and in general all things whatever which can be regarded as a concession of any kind in favor of the said religion.

*   *   *

FROM *Memoirs of the Duke of Saint-Simon*

*   *   *

The first-fruits of this dreadful plot were the wanton revocation of the Edict of Nantes, without a shadow of a pretext, and the proscriptions which followed it; its ultimate results were the depopulation of a fourth part of the kingdom and the ruin of our commerce. For a long time the country was given over to the authorised ravages of dragoons, which caused the deaths of, literally, thousands of innocent people of all ages and both sexes. Families were torn asunder; men of all classes, often old and infirm, highly respected for their piety and learning, were sent to toil in the galleys under the lash of the overseer; multitudes were driven penniless from their homes to seek refuge in foreign countries, to which they carried our arts and manufactures, enriching them and causing their cities to flourish at the expense of France.

*   *   *

I reminded the Regent of the disturbances and civil wars caused by the Huguenots from the reign of Henry II to that of Louis XIII; pointing out that even when they were comparatively quiet they had formed a body apart within the State, having their own chiefs, courts of justice specially appointed to deal with their affairs, even when they concerned Catholics, with strong places and garrisons at their disposal; corresponding with foreign Powers; always complaining and ready to take up arms: subjects, in short, merely in name, and yielding just as much or as little allegiance to their Sovereign as they thought fit. I recapitulated the heroic struggles by which his grandfather, Louis XIII, had at last beaten down this Hydra; thereby enabling his successor to get rid of it once for all by the mere expression of his will, without the slightest opposition.

I begged the Regent to reflect that he was now reaping the benefit of these struggles in a profound domestic tranquility; and to consider whether it was worth while, in time of peace when no foreign Power was thinking about the question, to make a concession which the late King had rejected with indignation when reduced to the utmost extremities by a long and disastrous war. I said, in conclusion, that if Louis XIV had made a mistake in revoking the Edict of Nantes it was not so much in the act itself as in the mode of carrying it out.

*   *   *

FROM *Declaration of the Gallican Church*

We, the archbishops and bishops assembled at Paris by order of the King, with other ecclesiastical deputies who represent the Gallican Church, have judged it necessary to make the regulations and the declaration which follows:

That St. Peter and his successors, Vicars of Jesus Christ, and the whole Church herself, have received power of God only in things spiritual, and pertaining to eternal salvation, not in things civil or temporal, the Lord Himself having said, "My kingdom is not of this world," and also "Render unto Caesar the things that be Caesar's, and unto God the things that are God's"; as also firmly declareth the Apostle, "Let every soul be subject unto the higher powers; for there is no power but of God; the powers that be are ordained of God; whosoever therefore resisteth the power, resisteth the ordinance of God."

Therefore kings and princes are in no wise subjected by God's appointment to any ecclesiastical power in temporal things; neither can the authority of the Keys of the Church directly or indirectly depose them, or their subjects be dispensed from the obedience and fidelity of their oaths to the same; and this doctrine we affirm to be necessary for the maintenance of public peace, no less profitable to the Church than to the State, and to be everywhere and every way observed as agreeable to the Word of God, to the tradition of the Fathers and the example of the Saints. . . .

*   *   *

Louis XIV

FROM *Letter to His Heir*

*   *   *

I have never failed, when an occasion has presented itself, to impress upon you the great respect we should have for religion, and the deference we should show to its ministers in matters specially connected with their mission, that is to say, with the celebration of the Sacred Mysteries and the preaching of the doctrine of the Gospels. But because people connected with the Church are liable to presume a little too much on the advantages attaching to their profession, and are willing sometimes to make use of them in order to whittle down their most rightful duties, I feel obliged to explain to you certain points on this question which may be of importance.

The first is that Kings are absolute *seigneurs*, and from their nature have full and free disposal of all property both secular and ecclesiastical, to use it as wise dispensers, that is to say, in accordance with the requirements of their State.

The second is that those mysterious names, the Franchises and Liberties of the Church, with which perhaps people will endeavour to dazzle you, have equal reference to all the faithful whether they be laymen or tonsured, who are all equally sons of this common Mother; but that they exempt neither the one nor the other from subjection to Sovereigns, to whom the Gospel itself precisely enjoins that they should submit themselves.

*   *   *

REVIEW QUESTIONS

1. Why does Louis revoke the Edict of Nantes?
2. What does this tell us about his conception of royal authority?

3. Is there any aspect of life that is exempt from royal authority?
4. How does this contrast with the political theory of John Locke?
5. What, according the Duke of Saint-Simon, were the real consequences of the revocation?
6. How might Louis or his advisors have justified the act?
7. What benefits might have been expected in the first place?

JOHN LOCKE

FROM *Two Treatises on Government*

John Locke (1632–1704) was an English philosopher whose thought contributed to the Enlightenment. He grew up in a liberal Puritan family, the son of an attorney who fought in the civil war against Charles I, and attended Christ's Church College, Oxford. He received his Bachelor of Arts in 1656, lectured in classical languages while earning his Master of Arts, and entered Oxford medical school to avoid being forced to join the clergy. In 1666, Locke attached himself to the household of the Earl of Shaftesbury and his fortunes to the liberal Whig Party. Between 1675 and 1679, he lived in France, where he made contact with leading intellectuals of the late seventeenth century. Upon his return to England, he plunged into the controversy surrounding the succession of James II, an avowed Catholic with absolutist pretensions, to the throne of his brother, Charles II. Locke's patron, Shaftesbury, was imprisoned for his opposition, and Locke went into exile in 1683. Though he was involved to some extent in the "glorious revolution" of 1688, he returned to England in 1689, in the entourage of Mary, Princess of Orange, who would assume the throne with her husband William. The Two Treatises on Government (1690) were published anonymously, although readers commonly assumed Locke's authorship. More interesting is the point at time in which they were written. Most scholars assume that they were written immediately before publication, as a justification of the revolution just completed. Many scholars believe, however, that the treatises were written from exile as a call to revolution, a much more inflammatory and risky project. The first treatise comprises a long attack on Robert Filmer's Patriarcha, a denial of the patriarchal justification of the absolute monarch. The second treatise constructs in the place of patriarchy a theory of politics based on natural law, which provides the foundation of human freedom. The social contract creates a political structure by consent of the governed designed to preserve those freedoms established in natural law. Locke's treatises inspired the political theories of the Enlightenment.

From *First Treatises in Two Treatises on Government,* edited by Ernst Rhys, E. P. Dutton, 1993.

Chapter VI
Of Paternal Power

It may perhaps be censured an impertinent criticism in a discourse of this nature to find fault with words and names that have obtained in the world. And yet possibly it may not be amiss to offer new ones when the old are apt to lead men into mistakes, as this of paternal power probably has done, which seems so to place the power of parents over their children wholly in the father, as if the mother had no share in it; whereas if we consult reason or revelation, we shall find she has an equal title, which may give one reason to ask whether this might not be more properly called parental power? For whatever obligation Nature and the right of generation lays on children, it must certainly bind them equal to both the concurrent causes of it. And accordingly we see the positive law of God everywhere joins them together without distinction, when it commands the obedience of children: "Honour thy father and thy mother"; "Whosoever curseth his father or his mother"; "Ye shall fear every man his mother and his father"; "Children, obey your parents" etc., is the style of the Old and New Testament.

*   *   *

Though I have said above "That all men by nature are equal," I cannot be supposed to understand all sorts of "equality." Age or virtue may give men a just precedency. Excellency of parts and merit may place others above the common level. Birth may subject some, and alliance or benefits others, to pay an observance to those to whom Nature, gratitude, or other respects, may have made it due; and yet all this consists with the equality which all men are in in respect of juris-

diction or dominion one over another, which was the equality I there spoke of as proper to the business in hand, being that equal right that every man hath to his natural freedom, without being subjected to the will or authority of any other man.

Children, I confess, are not born in this full state of equality, though they are born to it. Their parents have a sort of rule and jurisdiction over them when they come into the world, and for some time after, but it is but a temporary one. The bonds of this subjection are like the swaddling clothes they are wrapt up in and supported by in the weakness of their infancy. Age and reason as they grow up loosen them, till at length they drop quite off, and leave a man at his own free disposal.

Adam was created a perfect man, his body and mind in full possession of their strength and reason, and so was capable from the first instance of his being to provide for his own support and preservation, and govern his actions according to the dictates of the law of reason God had implanted in him. From him the world is peopled with his descendants, who are all born infants, weak and helpless, without knowledge or understanding. But to supply the defects of this imperfect state till the improvement of growth and age had removed them, Adam and Eve, and after them all parents were, by the law of Nature, under an obligation to preserve, nourish and educate the children they had begotten, not as their own workmanship, but the workmanship of their own Maker, the Almighty, to whom they were to be accountable for them.

The law that was to govern Adam was the same that was to govern all his posterity, the law of reason. But his offspring having another way of entrance into the world, different from him, by a natural birth, that produced them ignorant, and without the use of reason, they were not presently under that law. For nobody can be under a law that is not promulgated to him; and this law being promulgated or made known by reason only, he that is not come to the use of his reason cannot be said to be under this law; and Adam's children being not presently as soon as born under this law of reason, were not presently free. For law, in its true notion, is not so much the limitation as the direction of a free and intelligent agent to his proper interest, and prescribes no farther than is for the general good of those under that law. Could they be happier without it, the law, as a useless thing, would of itself vanish; and that ill deserves the name of confinement which hedges us in only from bogs and precipices. So that however it may be mistaken, the end of law is not to abolish or restrain, but to preserve and enlarge freedom. For in all the states of created beings, capable of laws, where there is no law there is no freedom. For liberty is to be free from restraint and violence from others, which cannot be where there is no law; and is not, as we are told, "a liberty for every man to do what he lists." For who could be free, when every other man's humour might domineer over him? But a liberty to dispose and order freely as he lists his person, actions, possessions, and his whole property within the allowance of those laws under which he is, and therein not to be subject to the arbitrary will of another, but freely follow his own.

The power, then, that parents have over their children arises from that duty which is incumbent on them, to take care of their offspring during the imperfect state of childhood. To inform the mind, and govern the actions of their yet ignorant nonage, till reason shall take its place and ease them of that trouble, is what the children want, and the parents are bound to. For God having given man an understanding to direct his actions, has allowed him a freedom of will and liberty of acting, as properly belonging thereunto within the bounds of that law he is under. But whilst he is in an estate wherein he has no understanding of his own to direct his will, he is not to have any will of his own to follow. He that understands for him must

will for him too; he must prescribe to his will, and regulate his actions, but when he comes to the estate that made his father a free man, the son is a free man too.

This holds in all the laws a man is under, whether natural or civil. Is a man under the law of Nature? What made him free of that law? what gave him a free disposing of his property, according to his own will, within the compass of that law? I answer, an estate wherein he might be supposed capable to know that law, that so he might keep his actions within the bounds of it. When he has acquired that state, he is presumed to know how far that law is to be his guide, and how far he may make use of his freedom, and so comes to have it; till then, somebody else must guide him, who is presumed to know how far the law allows a liberty. If such a state of reason, such an age of discretion made him free, the same shall make his son free too. Is a man under the law of England? what made him free of that law—that is, to have the liberty to dispose of his actions and possessions, according to his own will, within the permission of that law? a capacity of knowing that law. Which is supposed, by that law, at the age of twenty-one, and in some cases sooner. If this made the father free, it shall make the son free too. Till then, we see the law allows the son to have no will, but he is to be guided by the will of his father or guardian, who is to understand for him. And if the father die and fail to substitute a deputy in this trust, if he hath not provided a tutor to govern his son during his minority, during his want of understanding, the law takes care to do it: some other must govern him and be a will to him till he hath attained to a state of freedom, and his understanding be fit to take the government of his will. But after that the father and son are equally free, as much as tutor and pupil, after nonage, equally subjects of the same law together, without any dominion left in the father over the life, liberty, or estate of his son, whether they be only in the state and under the law of Nature, or under the positive laws of an established government.

*   *   *

The freedom then of man, and liberty of acting according to his own will, is grounded on his having reason, which is able to instruct him in that law he is to govern himself by, and make him know how far he is left to the freedom of his own will. To turn him loose to an unrestrained liberty, before he has reason to guide him, is not the allowing him the privilege of his nature to be free, but to thrust him out amongst brutes, and abandon him to a state as wretched and as much beneath that of a man as theirs. This is that which puts the authority into the parents' hands to govern the minority of their children. God hath made it their business to employ this care on their offspring, and hath placed in them suitable inclinations of tenderness and concern to temper this power, to apply it as His wisdom designed it, to the children's good as long as they should need to be under it.

But what reason can hence advance this care of the parents due to their offspring into an absolute, arbitrary dominion of the father, whose power reaches no farther than by such a discipline as he finds most effectual to give such strength and health to their bodies, such vigour and rectitude to their minds, as may best fit his children to be most useful to themselves and others, and, if it be necessary to his condition, to make them work when they are able for their own subsistence; but in this power the mother, too, has her share with the father.

Nay, this power so little belongs to the father by any peculiar right of Nature, but only as he is guardian of his children, that when he quits his care of them he loses his power over them, which goes along with their nourishment and education, to which it is inseparably annexed, and belongs as much to the foster-father of an exposed child as to the natural father of another. So little power does the bare act of begetting give a man over his issue, if all his care ends there, and this be all the title he hath to the name and authority of a father. And what will become of this paternal power in that part of the world where one woman hath more than one husband at a time? or in those parts of America where, when the husband and wife part, which happens frequently, the children are all left to the mother, follow her, and are wholly under her care and provision? And if the father die whilst the children are young, do they not naturally everywhere owe the same obedience to their mother, during their minority, as to their father, were he alive? And will any one say that the mother hath a legislative power over her children that she can make standing rules which shall be of perpetual obligation, by which they ought to regulate all the concerns of their property, and bound their liberty all the course of their lives, and enforce the observation of them with capital punishments? For this is the proper power of the magistrate, of which the father hath not so much as the shadow. His command over his children is but temporary, and reaches not their life or property. It is but a help to the weakness and imperfection of their nonage, a discipline necessary to their education. And though a father may dispose of his own possessions as he pleases when his children are out of danger of perishing for want, yet his power extends not to the lives or goods which either their own industry, or another's bounty, has made theirs, nor to their liberty neither, when they are once arrived to the enfranchisement of the years of discretion. The father's empire then ceases, and he can from thenceforward no more dispose of the liberty of his son than that of any other man. And it must be far from an absolute or perpetual jurisdiction from which a man may withdraw himself, having licence from Divine authority to "leave father and mother and cleave to his wife."

*   *   *

Chapter VII
Of Political or Civil Society

God, having made man such a creature that, in His own judgment, it was not good for him to be alone, put him under strong obligations of necessity, convenience, and inclination, to drive him into society, as well as fitted him with understanding and language to continue and enjoy it. The first society was between man and wife, which gave beginning to that between parents and children, to which, in time, that between master and servant came to be added. And though all these might, and commonly did, meet together, and make up but one family, wherein the master or mistress of it had some sort of rule proper to a family, each of these, or all together, came short of "political society," as we shall see if we consider the different ends, ties, and bounds of each of these.

Conjugal society is made by a voluntary compact between man and woman, and though it consist chiefly in such a communion and right in one another's bodies as is necessary to its chief end, procreation, yet it draws with it mutual support and assistance, and a communion of interests too, as necessary not only to unite their care and affection, but also necessary to their common offspring, who have a right to be nourished and maintained by them till they are able to provide for themselves.

For the end of conjunction between male and female being not barely procreation, but the continuation of the species, this conjunction betwixt male and female ought to last, even after procreation, so long as is necessary to the nourishment and support of the young ones, who are to be sustained by those that got them till they are able to shift and provide for themselves. This rule, which the infinite wise Maker hath set to the works of His hands, we find the inferior creatures steadily obey. In those vivaporous animals which feed on grass the conjunction between male and female lasts no longer than the very act of copulation, because the teat of the dam being sufficient to nourish the young till it be able to feed on grass, the male only begets, but concerns not himself for the female or young, to whose sustenance he can contribute nothing. But in beasts of prey the conjunction lasts longer, because the dam, not being able well to subsist herself and nourish her numerous offspring by her own prey alone (a more laborious as well as more dangerous way of living than by feeding on grass), the assistance of the

male is necessary to the maintenance of their common family, which cannot subsist till they are able to prey for themselves, but by the joint care of male and female. The same is observed in all birds (except some domestic ones, where plenty of food excuses the cock from feeding and taking care of the young brood), whose young, needing food in the nest, the cock and hen continue mates till the young are able to use their wings and provide for themselves.

And herein, I think, lies the chief, if not the only reason, why the male and female in mankind are tied to a longer conjunction than other creatures—viz., because the female is capable of conceiving, and, *de facto*, is commonly with child again, and brings forth too a new birth, long before the former is out of a dependency for support on his parents' help and able to shift for himself, and has all the assistance due to him from his parents, whereby the father, who is bound to take care for those he hath begot, is under an obligation to continue in conjugal society with the same woman longer than other creatures, whose young, being able to subsist of themselves before the time of procreation returns again, the conjugal bond dissolves of itself, and they are at liberty till Hymen, at his usual anniversary season, summons them again to choose new mates. Wherein one cannot but admire the wisdom of the great Creator, who, having given to man an ability to lay up for the future as well as supply the present necessity, hath made it necessary that society of man and wife should be more lasting than of male and female amongst other creatures, that so their industry might be encouraged, and their interest better united, to make provision and lay up goods for their common issue, which uncertain mixture, or easy and frequent solutions of conjugal society, would mightily disturb.

But though these are ties upon mankind which make the conjugal bonds more firm and lasting in a man than the other species of animals, yet it would give one reason to inquire why this compact, where procreation and education are secured and inheritance taken care for, may not be made determinable, either by consent, or at a certain time, or upon certain conditions, as well as any other voluntary compacts, there being no necessity, in the nature of the thing, nor to the ends of it, that it should always be for life—I mean, to such as are under no restraint of any positive law which ordains all such contracts to be perpetual.

But the husband and wife, though they have but one common concern, yet having different understandings, will unavoidably sometimes have different wills too. It therefore being necessary that the last determination (*i.e.*, the rule) should be placed somewhere, it naturally falls to the man's share as the abler and the stronger. But this, reaching but to the things of their common interest and property, leaves the wife in the full and true possession of what by contract is her peculiar right, and at least gives the husband no more power over her than she has over his life; the power of the husband being so far from that of an absolute monarch that the wife has, in many cases, a liberty to separate from him where natural right or their contract allows it, whether that contract be made by themselves in the state of Nature or by the customs or laws of the country they live in, and the children, upon such separation, fall to the father or mother's lot as such contract does determine.

For all the ends of marriage being to be obtained under politic government, as well as in the state of Nature, the civil magistrate doth not abridge the right or power of either, naturally necessary to those ends—viz., procreation and mutual support and assistance whilst they are together, but only decides any controversy that may arise between man and wife about them. If it were otherwise, and that absolute sovereignty and power of life and death naturally belonged to the husband, and were necessary to the society between man and wife, there could be no matrimony in any of these countries where the husband is allowed no such absolute authority. But the ends of matrimony requiring no such power in the husband, it was not at all necessary to it. The condition of conjugal society put it not in him; but whatsoever might consist with procreation and support of the children till they could shift for themselves—mutual assistance, comfort, and maintenance—might be varied and regulated by that contract which first united them in that society, nothing being necessary to any society that is not necessary to the ends for which it is made.

*   *   *

Let us therefore consider a master of a family with all these subordinate relations of wife, children, servants and slaves, united under the domestic rule of a family, with what resemblance soever it may have in its order, offices, and number too, with a little commonwealth, yet is very far from it both in its constitution, power, and end; or if it must be thought a monarchy, and the paterfamilias the absolute monarch in it, absolute monarchy will have but a very shattered and short power, when it is plain by what has been said before, that the master of the family has a very distinct and differently limited power both as to time and extent over those several persons that are in it; for excepting the slave (and the family is as much a family, and his power as paterfamilias as great, whether there be any slaves in his family or no) he has no legislative power of life and death over any of them, and none too but what a mistress of a family may have as well as he. And he certainly can have no absolute power over the whole family who has but a very limited one over every individual in it. But how a family, or any other society of men, differ from that which is properly political society, we shall best see by considering wherein political society itself consists.

Man being born, as has been proved, with a title to perfect freedom and an uncontrolled enjoyment of all the rights and privileges of the law of Nature, equally with any other man, or number of men in the world, hath by nature a power not only to preserve his property—that is, his life, liberty, and estate, against the injuries and attempts of other men, but to judge of and punish the breaches of that law in others, as he is persuaded the offence deserves, even with death itself, in crimes where the heinousness of the fact, in his opinion, requires it. But because no political society can be, nor subsist, without having in itself the power to preserve the property, and in order thereunto punish the offences of all those of that society, there, and there only, is political society where every one of the members hath quitted this natural power, resigned it up into the hands of the community in all cases that exclude him not from appealing for protection to the law established by it. And thus all private judgment of every particular member being excluded, the community comes to be umpire, and by understanding indifferent rules and men authorised by the community for their execution, decides all the differences that may happen between any members of that society concerning any matter of right, and punishes those offences which any member hath committed against the society with such penalties as the law has established; whereby it is easy to discern who are, and are not, in political society together. Those who are united into one body, and have a common established law and judicature to appeal to, with authority to decide controversies between them and punish offenders, are in civil society one with another; but those who have no such common appeal, I mean on earth, are still in the state of Nature, each being where there is no other, judge for himself and executioner; which is, as I have before showed it, the perfect state of Nature.

And thus the commonwealth comes by a power to set down what punishment shall belong to the several transgressions they think worthy of it, committed amongst the members of that society (which is the power of making laws), as well as it has the power to punish any injury done unto any of its members by any one that is not of it (which is the power of war and peace); and all this for the preservation of the property of all the members of that society, as far as is possible. But though every man entered into society has quitted his power to punish offences against the law of Nature in prosecution of his own private judgment, yet with the judgment of offences which he has given up to the legislative, in all cases where he can appeal to the magistrate, he has given up a right to the commonwealth to employ his force for the execution of the judgments of the commonwealth whenever he shall be called to it, which, indeed, are his own judgments, they being made by himself or his representative. And herein we have the original of the legislative and executive power of civil society, which is to judge by standing laws how far offences are to be punished when committed within the commonwealth; and also by occasional judgments founded on the present circumstances of the fact, how far injuries from without are to be vindicated, and in both these to employ all the force of all the members when there shall be need.

Wherever, therefore, any number of men so unite into one society as to quit every one his executive power of the law of Nature, and to resign it to the public, there and there only is a political or civil society. And this is done wherever any number of men, in the state of Nature, enter into society to make one people one body politic under one supreme government: or else when any one joins himself to, and incorporates with any government already made. For hereby he authorises the society, or which is all one, the legislative thereof, to make laws for him as the public good of the society shall require, to the execution whereof his own assistance (as to his own decrees) is due. And this puts men out of a state of Nature into that of a commonwealth, by setting up a judge on earth with authority to determine all the controversies and redress the injuries that may happen to any member of the commonwealth, which judge is the legislative or magistrates appointed by it. And wherever there are any number of men, however associated, that have no such decisive power to appeal to, there they are still in the state of Nature.

And hence it is evident that absolute monarchy, which by some men is counted for the only government in the world, is indeed inconsistent with civil society, and so can be no form of civil government at all. For the end of civil society being to avoid and remedy those inconveniencies of the state of Nature which necessarily follow from every man's being judge in his own case, by setting up a known authority to which every one of that society may appeal upon any injury received, or controversy that may arise, and which every one of the society ought to obey. Wherever any persons are who have not such an authority to appeal to, and decide any difference between them there, those persons are still in the state of Nature. And so is every absolute prince in respect of those who are under his dominion.

For he being supposed to have all, both legislative and executive, power in himself alone, there is no judge to be found, no appeal lies open to any one, who may fairly and indifferently, and with authority decide, and from whence relief and redress may be expected of any injury or inconveniency that may be suffered from him, or by his order. So that such a man, however entitled, Czar, or Grand Signior, or how you please, is as much in the state of Nature, with all under his dominion, as he is with the rest of mankind. For wherever any two men are, who have no standing rule and common judge to appeal to on earth, for the determination of controversies of right betwixt them, there they are still in the state of Nature, and under all the inconveniencies of it, with only this woeful difference to the subject, or rather slave of an absolute prince. That whereas, in the ordinary state of Nature, he has a liberty to judge of his right, according to the best of his power to maintain it; but whenever his property is invaded by the will and order of his monarch, he has not only no appeal, as those in society ought to have, but, as if he were degraded from the common state of rational creatures, is denied a liberty to judge of, or defend his right, and so is exposed to all the misery and inconveniencies that a man can fear from one, who being in the unrestrained state of Nature, is yet corrupted with flattery and armed with power.

*   *   *

Chapter VIII
Of the Beginning of
Political Societies

Men being, as has been said, by nature all free, equal, and independent, no one can be put out of this estate and subjected to the political power of another without his own consent, which is done by agreeing with other men, to join and unite into a community for their comfortable, safe, and peaceable living, one amongst another, in a secure enjoyment of their properties, and a greater security against any that are not of it. This any number of men may do, because it injures not the freedom of the rest; they are left, as they were, in the liberty of the state of Nature. When any number of men have so consented to make one community or government, they are thereby presently incorporated, and make one body politic, wherein the majority have a right to act and conclude the rest.

For, when any number of men have, by the consent of every individual, made a community, they have thereby made that community one body, with a power to act as one body, which is only by the will and determination of the majority. For that which acts any community, being only the consent of the individuals of it, and it being one body, must move one way, it is necessary the body should move that way whither the greater force carries it, which is the consent of the majority, or else it is impossible it should act or continue one body, one community, which the consent of every individual that united into it agreed that it should; and so every one is bound by that consent to be concluded by the majority. And therefore we see that in assemblies empowered to act by positive laws where no number is set by that positive law which empowers them, the act of the majority passes for the act of the whole, and of course determines as having, by the law of Nature and reason, the power of the whole.

And thus every man, by consenting with others to make one body politic under one government, puts himself under an obligation to every one of that society to submit to the determination of the majority, and to be concluded by it; or else this original compact, whereby he with others incorporates into one society, would signify nothing, and be no compact if he be left free and under no other ties than he was in before in the state of Nature. For what appearance would there be of any compact? What new engagement if he were no farther tied by any decrees of the society than he himself thought fit and did actually consent to? This would be still as great a liberty as he himself had before his compact, or any one else in the state of Nature, who may submit himself and consent to any acts of it if he thinks fit.

*   *   *

Whosoever, therefore, out of a state of Nature unite into a community, must be understood to give up all the power necessary to the ends for which they unite into society to the majority of the community, unless they expressly agreed in any number greater than the majority. And this is done by barely agreeing to unite into one political society, which is all the compact that is, or needs be, between the individuals that enter into or make up a commonwealth. And thus, that which begins and actually constitutes any political society is nothing but the consent of any number of freemen capable of majority, to unite and incorporate into such a society. And this is that, and that only, which did or could give beginning to any lawful government in the world.

*   *   *

Every man being, as has been showed, naturally free, and nothing being able to put him into subjection to any earthly power, but only his own consent, it is to be considered what shall be understood to be a sufficient declaration of a man's consent to make him subject to the laws of any government. There is a common distinction of an express and a tacit consent, which will concern our present case. Nobody doubts but an express consent of any man, entering into any society,

makes him a perfect member of that society, a subject of that government. The difficulty is, what ought to be looked upon as a tacit consent, and how far it binds—*i.e.*, how far any one shall be looked on to have consented, and thereby submitted to any government, where he has made no expressions of it at all. And to this I say, that every man that hath any possession or enjoyment of any part of the dominions of any government doth hereby give his tacit consent, and is as far forth obliged to obedience to the laws of that government, during such enjoyment, as any one under it, whether this his possession be of land to him and his heirs for ever, or a lodging only for a week; or whether it be barely travelling freely on the highway; and, in effect, it reaches as far as the very being of any one within the territories of that government.

To understand this the better, it is fit to consider that every man when he at first incorporates himself into any commonwealth, he, by his uniting himself thereunto, annexes also, and submits to the community those possessions which he has, or shall acquire, that do not already belong to any other government. For it would be a direct contradiction for any one to enter into society with others for the securing and regulating of property, and yet to suppose his land, whose property is to be regulated by the laws of the society, should be exempt from the jurisdiction of that government to which he himself, and the property of the land, is a subject. By the same act, therefore, whereby any one unites his person, which was before free, to any commonwealth, by the same he unites his possessions, which were before free, to it also; and they become, both of them, person and possession, subject to the government and dominion of that commonwealth as long as it hath a being. Whoever therefore, from thenceforth, by inheritance, purchases permission, or otherwise enjoys any part of the land so annexed to, and under the government of that commonweal, must take it with the condition it is under—that is, of submitting to the government of the commonwealth, under whose jurisdiction it is, as far forth as any subject of it.

But since the government has a direct jurisdiction only over the land and reaches the possessor of it (before he has actually incorporated himself in the society) only as he dwells upon and enjoys that, the obligation any one is under by virtue of such enjoyment to submit to the government begins and ends with the enjoyment; so that whenever the owner, who has given nothing but such a tacit consent to the government will, by donation, sale or otherwise, quit the said possession, he is at liberty to go and incorporate himself into any other commonwealth, or agree with others to begin a new one *in vacuis locis*, in any part of the world they can find free and unpossessed; whereas he that has once, by actual agreement and any express declaration, given his consent to be of any commonweal, is perpetually and indispensably obliged to be, and remain unalterably a subject to it, and can never be again in the liberty of the state of Nature, unless by any calamity the government he was under comes to be dissolved.

But submitting to the laws of any country, living quietly and enjoying privileges and protection under them, makes not a man a member of that society; it is only a local protection and homage due to and from all those who, not being in a state of war, come within the territories belonging to any government, to all parts whereof the force of its law extends. But this no more makes a man a member of that society, a perpetual subject of that commonwealth, than it would make a man a subject to another in whose family he found it convenient to abide for some time, though, whilst he continued in it, he were obliged to comply with the laws and submit to the government he found there. And thus we see that foreigners, by living all their lives under another government, and enjoying the privileges and protection of it, though they are bound, even in conscience, to submit to its administration as far forth as any denizen, yet do not thereby come to be subjects or members of that commonwealth. Nothing can make any man so but his actually entering into it by positive engagement and express promise and compact. This is that which, I think, concerning the beginning of political societies, and that consent which makes any one a member of any commonwealth.

Chapter IX
Of the Ends of Political Society and Government

If man in the state of Nature be so free as has been said, if he be absolute lord of his own person and possessions, equal to the greatest and subject to nobody, why will he part with his freedom, this empire, and subject himself to the dominion and control of any other power? To which it is obvious to answer, that though in the state of Nature he hath such a right, yet the enjoyment of it is very uncertain and constantly exposed to the invasion of others; for all being kings as much as he, every man his equal, and the greater part no strict observers of equity and justice, the enjoyment of the property he has in this state is very unsafe, very insecure. This makes him willing to quit this condition which, however free, is full of fears and continual dangers; and it is not without reason that he seeks out and is willing to join in society with others who are already united, or have a mind to unite for the mutual preservation of their lives, liberties and estates, which I call by the general name—property.

The great and chief end, therefore, of men uniting into commonwealths, and putting themselves under government, is the preservation of their property; to which in the state of Nature there are many things wanting.

Firstly, there wants an established, settled, known law, received and allowed by common consent to be the standard of right and wrong, and the common measure to decide all controversies between them. For though the law of Nature be plain and intelligible to all rational creatures, yet men, being biased by their interest, as well as ignorant for want of study of it, are not apt to allow of it as a law binding to them in the application of it to their particular cases.

Secondly, in the state of Nature there wants a

known and indifferent judge, with authority to determine all differences according to the established law. For every one in that state being both judge and executioner of the law of Nature, men being partial to themselves, passion and revenge is very apt to carry them too far, and with too much heat in their own cases, as well as negligence and unconcernedness, make them too remiss in other men's.

Thirdly, in the state of Nature there often wants power to back and support the sentence when right, and to give it due execution. They who by any injustice offended will seldom fail where they are able by force to make good their injustice. Such resistance many times makes the punishment dangerous, and frequently destructive to those who attempt it.

*   *   *

REVIEW QUESTIONS

1. What is the nature of political society?
2. How does political society come into being?
3. How does Locke's notion of a social contract compare with that of Hobbes? Of Rousseau?
4. What are the ends of political society?
5. What are the implications of Locke's reasoning for early modern economic thinking?

JACQUES-BENIGNE BOSSUET

FROM *Politics Drawn from the Very Words of Holy Scripture*

Jacques-Benigne Bossuet (1627–1704) was a French Roman Catholic clergyman and writer, considered by some to be the greatest French preacher in history. He was born in Dijon, and was educated at Jesuit schools and at the Collège de Navarre in Paris. Ordained a priest in 1652, he served at court as tutor to the Dauphin, the son of Louis XIV, for whom he wrote his great Discourse on Universal History *(1681), in which he argued that all history is moved by providence. The same year he was elevated to Bishop of Meaux, a dignity he possessed until his death. Though best remembered for his* Funeral Orations *(1689), panegyrics on important national figures, history records his theory of absolutism as well. Bossuet's* Politics Drawn from the Very Words of Holy Scripture *was published posthumously in 1708. It argued that because God created kingship, kings were answerable only to God. By so reasoning, Bossuet offered one of the most explicit and extreme arguments for the divine right of kings.*

Second Book
On authority: that the royal and hereditary [type] is the most proper for government

FIRST ARTICLE

BY WHOM AUTHORITY HAS BEEN EXERCISED SINCE THE BEGINNING OF THE WORLD

1ST PROPOSITION

God is the true king

A great king recognized this, when he spoke thus in the presence of his whole people: "Blessed be thou, Lord God of Israel our father, for ever and ever. Thine, O Lord, is the greatness, and the power, and the glory, and the victory, and the majesty: for all that is in the heaven and in the earth is thine; thine is the kingdom, O Lord, and thou art exalted as head above all. Both riches and honor come of thee, and thou reignest over all; and in thine hand is power and might; and in thine hand it is to make great, and to give strength unto all.

The empire of God is eternal, and from that comes the fact that he is called the king of the centuries.

The empire of God is absolute: "Who will dare to say to you, O Lord: Why do you act thus? Or who will stand against your judgment?"

This absolute empire of God has, for its original title and foundation, the Creation. He has drawn everything out of nothingness, and that is why everything is in his hand: "The word which came to Jeremiah from the Lord, saying: Arise, and go down to the potter's house, and there I will cause thee to hear my words. Then I went down to the potter's house, and, behold, he wrought a work on the wheels. And the vessel that he made of clay was marred in the hands of the potter: so that he made it again another vessel, as seemed good to the potter to make it. Then the word of the Lord came to me, saying, O house of

Israel, cannot I do with you as this potter? saith the Lord. Behold, as the clay is in the potter's hand, so are ye in mine, O house of Israel."

*   *   *

3RD PROPOSITION

The first empire among men is the paternal empire

Jesus Christ, who always goes to the bottom of things, seems to have indicated it by these words: "Every kingdom divided against itself is brought to desolation; and every city or house divided against itself shall not stand." From kingdoms he passes to cities, from which kingdoms arise; and from cities he goes back to families—as to the model and principle of cities and of the whole of human society.

At the beginning of the world God said to Eve, and through her to all women: "You will be under the power of the man, and he will command you."

To the first child that Adam had, who was Cain, Eve said, "I have gotten a man from the Lord." See then, too, children under paternal power. For this child was even more in the possession of Adam, to whom the mother herself was subject by the order of God. Both held this child, and their empire over him, from God. "I have gotten a man, Eve said, but by the grace of God."

God having placed in our parents, as being in some fashion the authors of our life, an image of the power by which he made everything, he also transmitted to them an image of the power which he has over his works. That is why we see in the Decalogue that after having said, "Thou shalt adore the Lord thy God, and serve only him," he adds as well: "Honor thy father and thy mother, that thy days may be long upon the land which the Lord thy God giveth thee." This precept is a kind of consequence of the obedience which must be rendered to God, who is the true father.

From this we can judge that the first idea of command and of human authority, has come to men from paternal authority.

Men lived for a long time at the beginning of the world, as not only Scripture but all the ancient traditions attest: and human life began to decline only after the deluge, where such a great change was made in the whole of nature. A large number of families found themselves united under the authority of a single grandfather by this means; and this union of so many families had the look of a kingdom.

Assuredly during the time that Adam lived Seth, whom God gave him in place of Abel, rendered him (together with his whole family) an entire obedience.

Cain, who first violated human fraternity by a murder, was also the first to withdraw himself from the paternal empire: hated by all men and constrained to establish a refuge for himself, he built the first city, to which he gave the name of his son, Enoch.

All other men lived in the countryside in this first simplicity, having for law the will of their parents and the ancient customs.

Such, after the deluge, was the conduct of several families, above all among the children of Shem, who preserved for a long time the ancient traditions of the human race—in both the worship of God and in the manner of government.

Thus Abraham, Isaac and Jacob persisted in the observance of a simple and pastoral life. They, with their families, were free and independent, and treated as equals with kings. Abimelech, King of Gerar, came to find Abraham; "and both of them made a covenant."

There was made a similar covenant between another Abimelech, son of the former, and Isaac the son of Abraham. "We saw certainly, said Abimelech, that the Lord was with thee; and we said, Let there be now an oath betwixt us, betwixt us and thee, and let us make a covenant with thee."

Abraham himself personally made war on the kings who had pillaged Sodom, defeated them, and offered a tenth of the spoils to Melchisedech, King of Salem, most high priest of God.

This is why the children of Heth, with whom he made an agreement, called him lord, and treated him as a prince. "Hear us, my lord: thou art a mighty prince among us—that is to say they stood up again only through him.

He also passed for a king in profane histories. Nicholas Damascene, careful observer of ancient things, calls him a king; and his reputation in the whole East caused him to give his all to his country. But at bottom the life of Abraham was pastoral; his kingdom was his family, and he alone exercised a domestic and paternal empire, after the example of the first men.

*   *   *

7TH PROPOSITION
Monarchy is the most common, the most ancient, and also the most natural form of government

The people of Israel on its own reduced itself to a monarchy, as being the universally received government. "Now make us a king, to judge us like all the nations."

If God was angered, that is because up till then he had governed this people by himself, and was its true king. That is why he said to Samuel, "they have not rejected thee, but they have rejected me, that I should not reign over them."

This government, moreover, was incomparably the most natural which was first seen among all the peoples.

This we have seen in sacred history: but here a slight recourse to profane histories will show us that polities with a republican form lived at first under kings.

Rome began in this way, and finally came back to it, as if to her natural condition.

It was only late, and little by little, that the Greek cities formed their republics. The ancient opinion of Greece was that expressed by Homer in this celebrated sentence from the *Iliad*: "To have several princes is not a good thing; let there be only one prince and one king.

At present there is not a single republic which was not subject to monarchs in other times. The Swiss were the subjects of the princes of the house of Austria. The United Provinces simply got out from under the domination of Spain and that of the house of Burgundy. The free cities of Germany had their individual lords, in addition to the Emperor who was the common leader of the whole Germanic body. The cities of Italy which made themselves into republics at the time of the Emperor Rudolph, bought their liberty from him. Even Venice, which prides itself on having been a republic since its origin, was still subject to the emperors during the reign of Charlemagne and long thereafter; then she transformed herself into a popular state, from which she has arrived, rather late, at the condition in which we see her.

Thus the whole world began with monarchies; and almost the whole world has preserved itself in that state, as being the most natural.

We have also seen that it has its foundation and its model in the paternal empire, that is in nature herself.

Men are all born subjects: and the paternal empire, which accustoms them to obey, accustoms them at the same time to have only one leader.

*　*　*

9TH PROPOSITION
Of all monarchies the best is the successive or hereditary, above all when it passes from male to male and from eldest to eldest

It is this that God established among his people. "For he has chosen the princes from the tribes of Judah, and within the tribe of Judah he has chosen me (it is David who is speaking), and he has chosen me among all my brothers. And among my sons . . . he hath chosen Solomon my son, to sit upon the throne of the kingdom of the Lord over Israel. And he said to me . . . : I will establish his kingdom for ever, if he continues to keep my commandments and my judgments."

See, then, royalty by succession attached to the house of David and of Solomon. "And the throne of David shall be firm for ever."

In virtue of this law the eldest was to succeed to the prejudice of his brothers. That is why Adonias, who was the eldest son of David, said to Bethsabee, mother of Solomon: "Thou knowest that the kingdom was mine, and all Israel had preferred me to be their king; but the kingdom is transferred, and is become my brother's; for it was appointed him by the Lord."

He spoke truly, and Solomon was in agreement with him when he replied to his mother (who was asking for Adonias a favor of extreme consequence according to the *moeurs* of these peoples): "Ask for him also the kingdom; for he is my elder brother, and hath Abiathar the priest and Joab supporting his interests." He meant to say that one must not strengthen a prince who has a natural title, and a great party within the state.

At least, then, if something extraordinary does not happen, the eldest ought to succeed: and one will scarcely find two contrary examples in the house of David, except at the beginning.

*　*　*

Third Book
In which one begins to explain the nature and the properties of royal authority

FIRST ARTICLE
TAKING NOTICE OF THE ESSENTIAL CHARACTERISTICS

SOLE PROPOSITION
There are four characteristics or qualities essential to royal authority

First, royal authority is sacred;
Secondly, it is paternal;
Thirdly, it is absolute;
Fourthly, it is subject to reason.

All of this must be established, in order, in the following articles.

ARTICLE II
ROYAL AUTHORITY IS SACRED

1ST PROPOSITION

God establishes kings as his ministers, and reigns through them over the peoples

We have already seen that all power comes from God.

"The prince, St. Paul adds, is God's minister to thee for good. But if thou do that which is evil, fear: for he beareth not the sword in vain. For he is God's minister: an avenger to execute wrath upon him that doth evil."

Thus princes act as ministers of God, and his lieutenants on earth. It is through them that he exercises his Empire. "And now say you that you are able to withstand the kingdom of the Lord, which he possesseth by the sons of David?"

It is in this way that we have seen that the royal throne is not the throne of a man, but the throne of God himself. "God hath chosen Solomon my son, to sit upon the throne of the kingdom of the Lord over Israel." And again: "Solomon sat on the throne of the Lord."

And in order that no one believe that it was peculiar to the Israelites to have kings established by God, here is what Ecclesiasticus says: "Over every nation he set a ruler. And Israel was made the manifest portion of God."

Thus he governs all peoples, and gives them, all of them, their kings; though he governs Israel in a more particular and announced fashion.

*   *   *

3RD PROPOSITION

One must obey the prince by reason of religion and conscience

St. Paul, after having said that the prince is the minister of God, concludes thus: "wherefore be

subject of necessity, not only for wrath, but also for conscience' sake."

This is why "one must serve, not to the eye, as it were pleasing men, but, as the servants of Christ doing the will of God, from the heart."

And again: "Servants, obey in all things your temporal masters, not serving to the eye, as pleasing men, but in simplicity of heart, fearing God. Whatsoever you do, do it from the heart, as to the Lord, and not to men; knowing that you shall receive of the Lord the reward of inheritance. Serve ye the Lord Christ."

If the apostle speaks thus of slavery, a condition contrary to nature, what must we think of legitimate subjection to princes and to magistrates, the protectors of public liberty?

This is why St. Peter says: "Be ye subject therefore to every human creature for God's sake: whether it be to the king as excelling; Or to governors as sent by him for the punishment of evildoers, and for the praise of the good."

Even if rulers do not acquit themselves of this duty, one must respect in them their charge and their ministry. "Servants, be subject to your masters with all fear, not only to the good and gentle, but also to the angry and unjust."

There is thus something religious in the respect one gives to the prince. The service of God and respect for kings are inseparable things, and St. Peter places these two duties together: "Fear God, Honor the King."

God, moreover, has put something divine into kings. "I have said: You are Gods, and all of you the sons of the most High." It is God himself whom David makes speak in this way.

This accounts for the fact that the servants of God swear by the life and health of the king, as by a divine and sacred thing. Uriah spoke to David: "By thy welfare and by the welfare of thy soul I will not do this thing."

Even if the king should be an infidel, from the respect one should have for the ordination of God. "By the health of Pharaoh, you shall not depart hence."

Here one must listen to the first Christians, and to Tertullian, who speaks as follows in the name of all of them: "We shall swear, not by the genius of the Caesars, but by their life and by their health, which is the most august of all geniuses. Do you not know that geniuses are demons? But we, who see in the emperors the choice and judgment of God, who gave them the command over all peoples, respect in them what God has placed there, and we uphold that through a great oath."

He adds: "What more can I say about our religion and about our piety for the emperor, whom we must respect as he whom our God has chosen: such that I can say that Caesar is more to us than to you, because it is our God who has established him?"

Thus it is the spirit of Christianity to make kings respected in a kind of religious way—which Tertullian (again) calls very well "the religion of the second majesty."

This second majesty simply flows out of the first, that is to say the divine, which, for the good of human affairs, has lent some of its brilliance to kings.

*   *   *

ARTICLE III
ROYAL AUTHORITY IS PATERNAL, AND ITS PROPER CHARACTER IS GOODNESS

After the things which have been said, this truth has no further need of proofs.

We have seen that kings hold the place of God, who is the true Father of the human race.

We have also seen that the first idea of power that there was among men, is that of paternal power; and that kings were fashioned on the model of fathers.

Moreover, all the world agrees that obedience, which is due to public power, is only found (in the Decalogue) in the precept which obliges one to honor his parents.

From all of this it appears that the name "king" is a father's name, and that goodness is the most natural quality in kings.

Let us, nonetheless, reflect particularly on so important a truth.

1ST PROPOSITION
Goodness is a royal quality, and the true prerogative of greatness

"The Lord your God is the God of gods, and the Lord of lords, a great and mighty and terrible, who accepteth no person nor taketh bribes. He doth judgment to the fatherless, and the widow, loveth the stranger, and giveth him food and raiment."

Because God is great and self-sufficient, he turns (as it were) entirely to do good to men, in conformity to this word: "For according to his greatness, also is his mercy with him."

He places an image of his greatness in kings, in order to oblige them to imitate his goodness.

He raises them to a condition in which they have nothing more to desire for themselves. We have heard David saying: "What can David add more, seeing thou hast thus glorified thy servant, and known him?"

And at the same time he declares to them that he gives them this greatness for love of the nations. "Because the Lord hath loved his people, therefore, he hath made thee king over them." And again: "God, whom thou hast pleased, . . . hath set thee upon the throne of Israel, because the Lord hath loved Israel for ever, and hath appointed thee king, to do judgment and justice."

That is why, in those passages where we read that the kingdom of David was raised over the people, the Hebrew and the Greek use *for* the people. This shows that greatness has for its object the good of subject peoples.

Indeed God, who has made all men from the same earth, bodily, and has placed equally in their souls his image and resemblance, has not established between them so many distinctions as to make on one side the proud and on the other slaves and wretches. He made the great only to protect the small; he gave his power to kings only to procure the public good, and for the support of the people.

*   *   *

Fourth Book
On the characteristics of royalty (continuation)

FIRST ARTICLE
ROYAL AUTHORITY IS ABSOLUTE

In order to make this term odious and insupportable, many pretend to confuse absolute government and arbitrary government. But nothing is more distinct, as we shall make clear when we speak of justice.

1ST PROPOSITION
The prince need account to no one for what he ordains

"Observe the mouth of the king, and the commandments of the oath of God. Be not hasty to depart from his face, and do not continue in an evil work: for he will do all that pleaseth him. And his word is full of power: neither can any man say to him: Why dost thou so? He that keepeth the commandment, shall find no evil."

Without this absolute authority, he can neither do good nor suppress evil: his power must be such that no one can hope to escape him; and, in fine, the sole defense of individuals against the public power, must be their innocence.

This doctrine is in conformity with the saying of St. Paul: "Wilt thou then not be afraid of the power? Do that which is good."

2ND PROPOSITION
When the prince has decided, there can be no other decision

The judgments of sovereigns are attributed to God himself. When Josaphat established judges to judge the people, he said: "It is not in the name of man that you judge, but in the name of God."

This is what Ecclesiasticus is made to say: "Judge not against a judge." For still stronger reasons against the sovereign judge who is the king. And the reason which is given is that, "he judgeth according to that which is just." It is not that he is always so judging, but that he is assumed to be so judging; and that no one has the right to judge or to review after him.

One must, then, obey princes as if they were justice itself, without which there is neither order nor justice in affairs.

They are gods, and share in some way in divine independence. "I have said: You are gods, and all of you the sons of the most High."

Only God can judge their judgments and their persons. "God hath stood in the congregation of gods, and being in the midst of them he judgeth gods."

It is for that reason that St. Gregory, Bishop of Tours, said to King Chilperic in a council: "We speak to you, but you listen to us only if you want to. If you do not want to, who will condemn you other than he who has said that he was justice itself?"

It follows from this that he who does not want to obey the prince, is not sent to another tribunal; but he is condemned irremissibly to death as an enemy of public peace and of human society. "Whoever will be proud and will not obey the command of the pontiff and the ordinance of the judge will die, and you will thus eradicate the evil from among you." And again: "Whosoever shall refuse to obey all your orders, may he die." It is the people who speak thus to Joshua.

The prince can correct himself when he knows that he has done badly; but against his authority there can be no remedy except his authority.

This is why he must take care of what he orders. "Take heed what you do; and whatsoever you judge, it shall rebound to you. Let the fear of the Lord be with you, and do all things with great care."

It is thus that Joseph instructed the judges, to whom he was entrusting his authority: how much of this he recollected when he himself had to judge!

*   *   *

Fifth Book
Fourth and final characteristic of royal authority

FIRST ARTICLE
ROYAL AUTHORITY IS SUBJECT TO REASON

1ST PROPOSITION
Government is a work of reason and intelligence. — "Now, listen, O kings, and be instructed, judges of the earth"

All men are created capable of understanding. But principally you upon whom reposes an entire nation, you who should be the soul and intelligence of a state, in whom must be found the first reason for all its movements: the less it is necessary for you to justify yourself to others, the more you must have justification and intelligence within yourself.

The contrary of acting from reason is to act out of passion or anger. To act out of anger, as Saul acted against David, driven by his jealousy or possessed by his black melancholy, entails all kinds of irregularities, inconsistencies, inequalities, anomalies, injustice, and confusion in one's conduct.

Though one has only a horse to lead and a flock to guide, one cannot do it without reason. How much more is needed for the leadership of men and a rational flock!

"The Lord took David from the care of his sheep to have him conduct Jacob, his servant, and Israel, his inheritance. And he led them in the innocence of his heart with an able and intelligent hand."

Everything among men is accomplished through intelligence and through counsel. "Houses are built out of wisdom and become solid through prudence. Ability fills the granaries and amasses riches. The wise man is courageous. The able man is robust and strong because war is waged by strategy and by industry, and salvation is found where there is much counsel."

Wisdom herself says: "It is through me that kings rule and through me that legislators prescribe what is just."

She is so born to command that she gives the empire even to those born in servitude. "The wise servant will command the children of the house who lack wisdom, and he will apportion their lots." And furthermore: "Free people will subject themselves to a judicious servant."

God, upon installing Joshua, orders him to study the law of Moses, which was the law of the kingdom, "in order," he says, "that you should understand all that you do." And furthermore: "and then you will carry out your designs and you will understand what to do." David said as much to Solomon in the last instructions he gave to him upon dying. "Take care to observe the laws of God so that you may understand all that you do and to which side you are to turn.

"So that you may not be turned, turn yourself knowingly. Let reason direct all your movements. Know what you do and why you are doing it."

Solomon had learned from God himself how much wisdom is necessary to govern a great people. "God appeared to him in a dream during the night, and said to him: Ask what thou wilt that I should give thee. And Solomon said: Thou hast shown great mercy to thy servant David my father, even as he walked before thee in truth, and justice, and an upright heart with thee: and thou hast kept thy great mercy for him, and hast given him a son to sit on his throne, as it is this day. And now, O Lord God, thou hast made thy servant king instead of David my father: and I am but a child, and know not how to go out and come in (that is to say, I do not know how to conduct myself: where to begin or to end matters). And thy servant is in the midst of the people which thou hast chosen, an immense people, which cannot be numbered nor counted for multitude. Give therefore to thy servant an understanding heart, to judge thy people, and discern between good and evil. For who shall be able to judge this people, thy people which is so numerous? And the word was pleasing to the Lord that Solomon had asked such a thing. And the Lord said to Solomon: Because thou hast asked this thing, and hast not asked for thyself long life, or riches, nor the lives of thy enemies, but hast asked for thyself wisdom to discern judgment, Behold I have done for thee according to thy words, and have given thee a wise and understanding heart, insomuch that there hath been no one like thee before thee, nor shall arise after thee. Yea and the things also which thou didst not ask, I have given thee: to wit riches and glory, so that no one hath been like thee among the kings in all days heretofore."

This dream of Solomon's was an ecstasy in which the mind of this great king, separated from the senses and united to God, enjoyed true knowledge. He saw, while in this state, that wisdom is the sole grace that a prince should ask of God.

He saw the weightiness of the affairs and the immense multitude of the people whom he had to lead. So many temperaments, so many interests, so many artifices, so many passions, so many surprises to fear, so many things to consider, so many people from every side to hear and know: what mind could be equal to it?

I am young, he said, and I still do not know how to conduct myself. He was not lacking in spirit, any more than in resolution. For he had already spoken in a masterly tone to his brother Adonias: and from the beginning of his reign he had done his part at a decisive juncture, with as much prudence as could be desired: and all the same he trembled still, when he saw this immense chain of cares and of matters that accompany royalty: and he saw well that he could only find his way out through consummate wisdom.

He asked it of God, and God gave it to him: but at the same time he gave him all the rest which he had not asked, that is to say riches and glory.

He teaches kings that they will lack nothing when they have wisdom, and that she alone draws all other goods to them.

We find a fine commentary on Solomon's prayer in the book of Wisdom, which makes this wise king speak as follows: "Wherefore I wished, and understanding was given me: and I called upon God, and the spirit of wisdom came upon me. And I preferred her before kingdoms and thrones, and esteemed riches nothing in comparison of her. Neither did I compare unto her any precious stone: for all gold in comparison of her, is as a little sand, and silver in respect to her shall be counted as clay. I loved her above health and beauty, and chose to have her instead of light: for her light cannot be put out. Now all good things came to me together with her, and innumerable riches through her hands."

* * *

REVIEW QUESTIONS

1. Why does Bossuet begin his consideration of political authority with God?
2. What are the implications of this point of departure?
3. How is absolutism understood?
4. How does conscience relate to obedience?
5. How does Bossuet's discussion of paternal authority compare with Filmer's?
6. Why is monarchy "natural"?
7. How is Bossuet construing nature?

DUC DE SAINT-SIMON

FROM *Historical Memoirs of the Duc de Saint-Simon*

Louis de Rouvroy, Duc de Saint-Simon (1675–1755), was a French soldier and diplomat, best remembered for his memoirs of court life during the reign of Louis XIV. Born the son of an aged nobleman, a parvenu raised to the aristocracy by Louis XIII, he was a remarkable figure. Physically unattractive, Saint-Simon possessed a violent and vindictive temper as well as great wit and intelligence. His career at court can best be described as disappointing. As his memoirs make clear, he never achieved the rank he sought because of his open and tactless opposition to Louis XIV on minor points of precedence and ceremony. Saint-Simon managed to attach himself to Philippe, duc de Orléans in 1712 and so persevered on the edge of affairs until his patron's death in 1723. From that point until his death in 1755, Saint-Simon remained in private life and devoted himself to writing his memoirs. A composite narrative, drawn from his own memory and papers as well as witness testimony and manuscript sources, it offers a wealth of information on life at the court and a close analysis of state affairs under an absolute monarch.

From *Historical Memoirs of the Duc De Saint-Simon, Volume I,* translated by Lucy Norton. McGraw–Hill, 1967.

*   *   *

After ten days at Givry the two armies separated and marched away, and two days later the siege of Namur was proclaimed, the King having covered that journey in a five-day march. Monseigneur, Monsieur, Monsieur le Prince, and the Maréchal d'Humières, in order of rank, led the army under the King's command. The Maréchal de Luxembourg, in sole command of his army, covered the siege and took observations. Meantime the ladies removed to Dinant. On the third day of the King's march Monsieur le Prince was sent on ahead to invest Namur town, for Vauban, the famous organizer of the King's sieges, had insisted on there being separate attacks for the town and the fortress. Nothing very eventful happened during the ten days of the siege; on the eleventh day of open trenches they sounded for a parley

and a surrender was arranged on the defenders' terms. During all this time the King was living under canvas in very hot weather, for it had not rained since we left Paris. The army moved camp in order to besiege the fortress, and whilst that was taking place the King's own regiment of infantry found its new position held by a small detachment of the enemy digging trenches. There was a brisk engagement in which the royal troops greatly distinguished themselves, with very few losses, and the enemy were soon routed. The King was delighted by this, for he was particularly devoted to that regiment which he liked to think of as being his personal property.

The King's tents and those of his courtiers were pitched in a pleasant meadow five hundred paces from the monastery of Marlagne. By this time the weather had changed to abundant and continuous rain, such as no one in the army could remember and had thus greatly increased the reputation of St. Médard, whose feast-day is 8 June. It had poured on that day and, according to the saying, whatever the weather is then it will continue so for the next forty days, as it happened in that year. The soldiers were driven nearly to desperation by the floods, so that they cursed the saint heartily, breaking and burning his images wherever they could lay hands on them. The rain was indeed a perfect plague, and the King's tents could only be reached by laying down paths of brushwood which had daily to be renewed. The other tents were not more easily accessible and the trenches were soon full of muddy water. It sometimes took as much as three days to move a cannon from one battery to another. The waggons were unusable, and shells, cannon-balls, etc., had to be transported on mules and horses, which became the sole support of every service to the army and the Court. Without them nothing would have been possible. The flooding of the roads also prevented the army of M. de Luxembourg from using their waggons. They were near starvation for lack of fodder and would have died had not the King issued orders that detachments of his *maison* should ride each day carrying sacks of grain to a certain village where M. de Luxembourg's officers would receive and count them.

Although the *maison* had had little rest on account of carrying brushwood, mounting the various guards, and their other daily duties, they were given this additional fatigue because the cavalry also had been continuously on duty and were down to leaves for forage. That consideration aroused no sympathy in the hearts of the pampered *maison*, who were accustomed to special privileges. They complained. The King was obdurate. The task remained theirs. On the very first day, however, the lifeguards and light cavalry were openly murmuring when they reached the depot in the early morning, and they so worked upon one another that the men actually threw the sacks down and refused to pick them up again. Cresnay, my brigadier, had most courteously asked me whether I was willing to take a sack, saying that otherwise he would find me some different duty;

but I had consented, hoping thus to please the King, especially in view of all the grumbling. It so happened that I arrived on the scene with my troop of musketeers at the precise moment when the red-coats were about to mutiny, and I took up my sack before them all. Thereupon Marin, a cavalry-brigadier, who was supervising the loading by the King's orders and raging at the mutineers, called out my name, exclaiming that if I did not think myself too good for such work, lifeguardsmen and the light horse need not be ashamed to copy me. That argument and his stern eye had their effect; there was a rush to pick up the sacks, and never afterwards the smallest objection. Marin watched us go and then went to tell the King what had happened and the influence of my good example. That kind office resulted in the King saying some gracious things to me, and throughout the remainder of the siege he never saw me without saying something civil. I was all the more obliged to Marin because I had no acquaintance with him socially.

*   *   *

1700

The year began with an economy. The King announced that he would no longer pay for the changes made by courtiers in their lodgings, which had cost him more than sixty thousand livres since Fontainebleau. Mme de Mailly was thought to be the cause, for she had changed hers annually in the past three or four years. The new arrangement was better in that one could get alterations made as one wished without first obtaining the King's consent; on the other hand one had to pay for everything.

From Candlemas to Lent there was a continual succession of balls and entertainments at the Court. The King gave several at Versailles and Marly, with wonderfully ingenious masquerades and tableaux, a form of diversion that vastly pleased him under the guise of amusing Mme la Duchesse de Bourgogne. There were concerts and private theatricals at Mme de Maintenon's; Monseigneur gave balls, and the most distinguished persons took pride in offering entertainment to Mme la Duchesse de Bourgogne. Monsieur le Prince, though his rooms were few and small, contrived to astonish the Court with the most elegant party in the world, a full-evening-dress ball, masks, tableaux, booths with foreign merchandise, and a supper most exquisitely staged. No one at the Court was refused admittance to any part of it, and there was no crowding nor any other inconvenience.

One evening when there was no ball Mme de Pontchartrain gave one at the Chancellery, and it turned out to be the gayest of them all. The Chancellor received Monseigneur, the three princes, and Mme la Duchesse de Bourgogne at the front entrance at ten o'clock and then immediately went off to sleep at the Château. There were different rooms provided for a full-evening-dress ball, masks, a splendid supper, and booths for the merchants of various countries, China, Japan, etc., offering vast quantities of objects of beauty and virtue, all chosen with exquisite taste. No money was taken; all were presents offered to Mme la Duchesse de Bourgogne and the other ladies. There was also a concert in her honour, a play, and tableaux. Never was anything better conceived, more sumptuous, nor more perfectly organized, and Mme de Pontchartrain in the midst of it all was as gay, civil, and unruffled as though she had no responsibilities.

Everyone enjoyed themselves immensely, and we did not reach home until eight in the morning. Mme de Saint-Simon, who was always in Mme la Duchesse de Bourgogne's retinue (a great favour), and I never saw the light of day in the last three weeks before Lent. Certain dancers were not allowed to leave the ball-room before the princess, and once at Marly when I tried to escape early she sent orders for me to be confined within its doors. The same thing occurred to others also. I was truly thankful when Ash Wednesday came, and for a couple of days after felt quite stunned. As for Mme de Saint-Simon, she was worn out by Shrove Tuesday and did not manage to stay the full course. The King amused himself also in Mme de Maintenon's room with some selected ladies, playing *brelan, petite prime,* and *reversis* on the days when he had no ministers or little work to do, and those diversions continued well into Lent.

*   *   *

1702

*   *   *

When the promotion of generals was finally put into execution it proved to be very sweeping, comprising seventeen lieutenants-general, fifty brigadiers, forty-one colonels of infantry, and thirty-eight of cavalry. But before recounting the action which that promotion led me to take, I must first describe how during that winter I was received into the Parlement.

In dealing with his bastards the King always gave immediate effect to the honours which he granted them, without waiting for the usual warrants, letters patent, notifications, or decrees to be published. Yet, for many years past, he had made it a rule that peers might not be received into the Parlement without his consent. That he never refused, but he had lately begun to withhold permission if the peer were not yet twenty-five years old, thus gradually instituting a custom which might later become the general rule. I was aware of this and accordingly deferred my own reception until a year after my twenty-fifth birthday, on the plea of forgetfulness.

My first action was to call on President Harlay, who was overwhelmingly polite. I was then obliged to call on the princes of the blood and finally on the bastards. M. du Maine, when I visited him, asked me to repeat the date, then with a delight that appeared restrained only by modesty and good manners, he exclaimed, 'I shall be most careful not to forget. Such an honour! So gratifying that you desire my presence! You may be sure of me,' and so saying he escorted me as far as the gardens, for this was at a Marly, and I was of the house-party. The Comte de Toulouse and

M. de Vendôme replied less effusively but no less pleasantly, and were as polite as M. du Maine. Cardinal de Noailles had never once attended at the Parlement since he received the Roman crimson because his hat did not entitle him to a seat higher than that of his rank as count and peer. I elected to visit him at one of his public audiences. 'You are aware,' said he, 'that I no longer have a seat?' 'On the contrary,' I replied, 'I know that you have a most splendid place, and I beg you to take it at my reception.' He then smiled, and I smiled also, for we perfectly understood one another. Later he personally escorted me to the top of his staircase, both doors open wide, and we walked together side by side, I on his right hand. M. de Luxembourg was the only one not to hear from me on that occasion. I had never forgiven him those abominable warrants, but he was not my friend and I did him no wrong.

Dongeois was at that time acting as registrar of the Parlement. He was a man whose ability and constant attendance had made him very knowledgeable in the customs of that body. I knew him well, and therefore went to consult him about the correct procedure. Yet despite the honesty and kindness of his intentions the good man laid three traps for me, but luckily I was on the watch and fell into none of them. He said that out of respect for the Parlement I should make my first appearance there in a plain black coat unadorned with gold lace; that out of respect for the princes of the blood, whose short mantles were worn longer than their coats, I should not allow mine to come below the level of my jacket, and that out of respect for the premier président I should call to thank him on the morning after my reception, still wearing parliamentary dress. He did not bluntly make these suggestions but tactfully hinted at them. I made no issue of it, but I did the exact opposite, and having been alerted I took care to warn all those who were received after me, and they defended themselves likewise. It is by such ruses that many humiliations have come upon the dukes, one after another, in a constant stream that almost passes belief.

The reforming of the army after the Peace of Ryswick was on a very large scale but very haphazard. The quality of the various regiments, especially of the cavalry, and the merits of their commanding officers were ignored by Barbezieux, who was young and impulsive, and to whom the King gave a free hand. I myself had no acquaintance with him; my regiment was re-formed, and as it was very good parts of it were allocated to the Royals and the rest incorporated in the Duras regiment. My company was added to that of Barbezieux's brother-in-law the Comte d'Uzès, of whom he took particular care. It was small consolation to hear that others were being treated in the same way, and I was deeply disappointed. The colonels of regiments re-formed like mine were placed at the bottom of the list in their new regiments, and I was ordered to serve under Saint-Mauris, a gentleman of Franche-Comté and a complete stranger to me, although his brother was a lieutenant-general and well regarded. Shortly after this, the petty discipline that runs alongside active service demanded two months' service from officers at the tail of new regiments. That seemed monstrous to me. I went, of course, but I had been indisposed for some time past, and having been recommended the waters of Plombières I asked for leave of absence and for the next three years spent there the two months when I should have been exiled to a strange regiment, with no troops to command and no work to do. The King did not seem to mind. I often went to Marly; he spoke to me sometimes, a very good sign that was much remarked upon; in a word he treated me kindly, indeed better than most of my age and rank.

From time to time officers junior to myself were promoted; but they were veterans who had earned regiments by long and distinguished service, and I could understand the reason. Talk of a general promotion did not excite me, for birth and rank counted for nothing. I was too junior to be made a brigadier; my entire ambition was to command a regiment and fight at its head in the coming war, thus avoiding the humiliation of having to serve as a supernumerary aide-de-camp to Saint-Mauris. The King had distinguished me after the Neerwinden campaign by giving me a regiment; and I had brought it up to strength, and, dare I say so, commanded it with care and honour in four successive campaigns until the war ended.

The promotion was announced; everyone was astonished at the numbers, for there had never been so large a list. I eagerly scanned the names of new cavalry brigadiers, hoping to find my own, and was mortified to see five junior to me mentioned. My pride was most deeply hurt but I kept silent for fear of saying something rash in my vexation. The Maréchal de Lorges was most indignant and his brother-in-law not less so, and they both insisted that I ought to quit the service. I myself felt so angry that I was much inclined to do so; but my youth, the war beginning, the thought of renouncing my ambitions in my chosen career, the boredom of being idle, the tedious summers when conversation would all turn on war and partings, the advancement that could be earned by distinguished conduct, were all powerful deterrents, and I spent two months in mental agony, resigning every morning and every night reversing my decision.

At last, driven to extremes and harried by the two marshals, I resolved to take advice from men on whom I could rely, and to choose them from different walks of life. I finally decided upon the Maréchal de Choiseul, M. de Beauvilliers, the Chancellor, and M. de La Rochefoucauld. They knew how I was placed and were indignant on my behalf, and, moreover, the three last were courtiers. This was most desirable, for what I wished to discover was what the best people would think, particularly the solid men about the King. Above all I sought for advice that would not leave me a prey to indecision, rash impulses, or afterthoughts. Their verdict, given unanimously and most firmly, was that I should leave the service. They all agreed that it would be both a shame and most unsuitable for a man of my rank who had served with honour at the head of a good regiment to return to fight without regiment, troops, or even a company to command. They added that no duke and peer, especially not one with an establishment, wife and children, should consent to be left a mere soldier of fortune, whilst others of lesser degree received

employment and commands in a large-scale promotion.

I did not take them as my judges in order to ponder their advice. My course was clear; but though I knew they were right I still hesitated, and three months passed in a torment of doubt before I could bring myself to act. When I finally did so, I followed the advice of those same arbiters. I was very careful to display no hurt feelings, for I wished to leave public and especially military opinion to judge of my having been passed over. The King's anger was inevitable; my friends warned me of it, and I was fully prepared. Need I say how much I dreaded it? He invariably took offence when officers left the service, calling it desertion, especially where the nobility were concerned. What really nettled him, however, was that a man should leave him with a grudge, and anyone who did so felt his displeasure long afterwards, if not for ever. Yet my friends drew no comparison between the disadvantage of resigning, which, at my age, would soon cease to affect me, and the disgrace of continuing to serve under such humiliating conditions. At the same time they insisted on my taking all possible precautions.

I accordingly wrote a short letter to the King, in which without complaining, or any sign of discontent, or mention of regiments or promotion, I stated my distress at being obliged to leave his service for reasons of health. I added that my consolation would be to attend on him assiduously, with the honour of seeing and paying my court to him all the time. My advisers approved my letter and on Tuesday in Holy Week I presented it myself, at the door of his study, as he returned from mass. I went thence to Chamillart, with whom I had little acquaintance at that time. He was leaving to go to the council, but I told him my story by word of mouth, showing no sign of discontent, and immediately set out for Paris. I had already put many of my friends, both men and women, on the alert, to report anything, no matter how trivial, that the King might say on the subject of my letter. I stayed away for a week; returning on Easter Tuesday, I learned that the Chancellor had found the King in the act of reading it, and that he had exclaimed angrily, 'Here is another deserter!' and had thereupon read my letter aloud word for word. On that same evening I attended on him for the first time since he had heard from me.

After that, for three consecutive years I received no sign of favour from him, and he never missed the smallest opportunity (for want of greater ones) to make me feel how deeply I had offended. He never spoke to or looked at me except by accident. He never mentioned my letter or the circumstances of my leaving his service. I was no longer invited to Marly, and after the first few visits I no longer gave him the satisfaction of refusing me. I must end this sorry tale. Fourteen or fifteen months later he paid a visit to Trianon and supped with the Princesses. The custom on those occasions was for him to make a list, a very short one, of the ladies whom he wished invited. This particular visit was from a Wednesday to a Saturday, and Mme de Saint-Simon and I were doing what we usually did when he went to Marly, that is to say, dining at L'Etang with the Chamillarts on our way to sleep in Paris. We were just sitting down to table when Mme de Saint-Simon received a message to say that she was on the King's supper-list for that evening. We were astounded and returned at once to Versailles. She then discovered that she was to be the only lady of her age at the King's table; the rest were Mme de Chevreuse, Mme de Beauvilliers, the Comtesse de Gramont, three or four chaperones, the palace ladies, and no others. She was invited again on the Friday, and thereafter the King always nominated her on his rare excursions to Trianon. I soon learned the reason for this favour and it struck me as absurd. He never invited her to Marly, because husbands had the right to go there with their wives. His intention was to show me that his disfavour was towards me alone and did not extend to my wife.

We none the less persevered in waiting on him as usual, but we never sought for invitations to Marly. We lived a pleasant enough life among our friends, and Mme de Saint-Simon continued to enjoy all the pleasures to which the King and Mme la Duchesse de Bourgogne summoned her, even although she could not share them with me. I have dealt with this matter at length because it throws light upon the King's nature.

*   *   *

REVIEW QUESTIONS

1. What is the relation between political power and military power?
2. What is the relation between nature and political power?
3. What does Saint-Simon tell us about the king's social and fiscal relations with his nobility?
4. What is part of the royal obligation?
5. What do balls and other festivities have to do with political power?
6. Why would legitimacy be both an issue and not an issue at the French court?
7. What are the relations of lineage to political power?

FREDERICK II, THE GREAT

FROM Antimachiavell

Frederick II, the Great (1712–1786), king of Prussia, was the third son of Frederick William II of Prussia and Sophia Dorothea of Hanover, sister of George II of England. As a boy, Frederick showed little interest in the military matters that fascinated his father and, led by his tutor, the French Calvinist refugee Jacob E. Duhan de Jandun, discovered a world of art and literature instead. He mastered the flute, for which he composed a number of pieces, and adopted a free-thinking philosophy. His father's efforts at discipline had little effect on the young Frederick, who tried to evade his duties by escaping to England in 1730. The plan was discovered, Frederick imprisoned, and his best friend executed. This brutal encounter had its desired effect: Frederick threw himself on his father's mercy and dedicated himself to the arts of kingship. After a period of military service, in 1735. Frederick withdrew to the castle of Rheinsberg, where he undertook a systematic program of reading. He corresponded with Voltaire and, through French literature, read widely in the philosophical works of the Enlightenment. His ideal of government became enlightened but absolute, serving the people but limited only by the ruler's sensibilities. In this period Frederick wrote a number of treatises on politics, among which was the Antimachiavell (1740), published by Voltaire at The Hague. In it, he developed his ideal of the enlightened, absolute monarch in contrast to those of the Florentine statesman. The work was widely read in France and praised as a formula for enlightened rule. In the same year, Frederick succeeded his father and began a long and illustrious reign as king of Prussia. He distinguished himself as the greatest military genius of his day. In peacetime, he transformed Prussia into the model of an enlightened despotism. His policies expanded education, promoted industry, and reformed justice, all in the interest of state power.

Reprinted with the permission of The Free Press, a division of Simon & Schuster. From *Frederick the Great on the Art of War*, translated and edited by Jay Luvaas. Copyright © 1966 by The Free Press.

The Duty of Sovereigns

Since Machiavelli wrote his political *Prince*, the face of Europe has changed so much that it can no longer be recognized. If some great general in the age of Louis XII were to come back into the world he would find himself much at a loss. He would see war now carried on by bodies of men so numerous that they can hardly be subsisted in the field, yet are kept up in peace as well as war, whereas in his age, to execute great enterprises and strike decisive blows a handful of men sufficed, and these were disbanded as soon as the war was over. Instead of coats of mail, lances, and harquebusses with matches, he would find the army furnished with uniforms, firelocks, and bayonets. He would see new methods of encamping, besieging, and giving battle, and find the art of subsisting the troops as necessary now as that of conquering was before.

But what would Machiavelli himself say upon seeing this new political face of Europe, and so many princes who were scarcely known in his day now being ranked with the greatest monarchs? What would he say upon seeing the power and authority of sovereigns firmly established, the present manner of negotiating, and that balance settled in Europe by the alliance of many princes and states against the over-powerful and ambitious, a balance solely designed for securing the peace and tranquility of mankind?

All of these things have produced such universal change that Machiavelli's maxims cannot be applied to modern politics. . . . He assumes that a prince who has a large territory, a numerous army, and a full treasury may defend himself against his enemies without foreign supplies. I venture to contradict. . . . Let a sovereign be ever so formidable, he cannot defend himself against powerful enemies without the assistance of allies. If the most formidable prince in Europe, Louis XIV, was reduced to the greatest distress and was nearly ruined by the war of the Spanish Succession, if for want of foreign assistance he was unable to defend himself against the alliance of so many kings and princes, how should a sovereign who is less powerful be able to resist the joint attacks of his neighbors, to which he may often be exposed, without allies?

It is often said—and often repeated without much reflection—that treaties are useless because they are never observed in all points, and that the present age is no more scrupulous in keeping faith than any other. I answer that although many examples may be produced, ancient, modern, and some very recent of princes who have not fulfilled all their engagements, yet it is always prudent and necessary to make alliances. For your allies otherwise will be so many enemies; and if they refuse to send you supplies when you need them, you may at least expect them to observe an exact neutrality.

IT IS A KNOWN TRUTH in politics that the most natural and consequently the best allies are those who have common interests and who are not such close neighbors as to be involved in any dispute over frontiers. Sometimes it happens that strange accidents give birth to extraordinary alliances. In our own time we have seen nations that had always been rivals and even enemies united under the same banners. But these are events that rarely occur and that never can serve as examples, for such connections can only be momentary, whereas the other kind, which are contracted from a unity of interests, alone are capable of execution. In the present situation in Europe, when all her princes are armed and preponderating powers rise up capable of crushing the feeble, prudence requires that alliances should be formed with other powers, as much to secure aid in case of attack as to repress the dangerous plans of enemies, and to sustain all just pretensions by the help of such allies. . . .

Nor is this sufficient. We must have eyes and ears among our neighbors, especially among our enemies, which shall be open to receive and faithfully report what they have seen and heard. Men are wicked. Care must be taken especially not to suffer surprise, because surprises intimidate and terrify. This never happens when preparations are made, however vexatious the event anticipated. European politics are so fallacious that the wisest men may become dupes if they are not always alert and on their guard.

ALLIANCES may be broken in the following cases: (1) When the ally fails to fulfill his obligations; (2) when the ally meditates deceit and there is no other course except to deceive first; (3) when a superior force oppresses and makes it necessary to break a treaty; and finally, (4) when one lacks the means for continuing the war. That despicable thing called money, by I know not what fatality, influences all affairs. . . .

To me it appears evident that a private individual ought to keep his promise scrupulously even though he should have made it thoughtlessly. If injured, he can always resort to the protection of the laws, and whatever the outcome, it is an individual alone who suffers. But where is the tribunal that can redress a monarch's wrongs, should another monarch forfeit his engagement? The word of an individual can only involve an individual in misfortune, while that of a sovereign may draw down calamities on nations. The question then will be reduced to this: Must the people perish, or must the prince violate a treaty?

MACHIAVELLI speaks . . . of the *principini*, those diminutive sovereigns who, having only small dominions, cannot send an army into the field. He advises them chiefly to fortify their capitals in order to secure themselves and their troops in time of war. Those Italian princes discussed by Machiavelli are really a breed of mongrels, half sovereign and half subjects. They only appear as sovereigns by the number of their domestics. The best advice that one can give them would be . . . to lessen a little the opinion they entertain of their own grandeur, the extreme veneration they have for their ancient and illustrious pedigree, and their inviolable zeal for the scutcheons. Men of sense claim that they had better assume no rank in the world other than what is due a noblemen of easy fortunes; that they ought to climb down from the scaffold of their pride and maintain at most no more troops than would be necessary to guard their palaces against robbers, if indeed any robbers could be reduced to the starving condition of seeking a subsistence in those palaces; that they ought to raze and demolish their ramparts and walls and everything that gives their place of residence the appearance of strength. The reasons are these: most of those petty princes, especially in Germany, ruin themselves by spending excessive sums to maintain that grandeur with which they are intoxicated, and to support the honor of their family they reduce themselves to beggary and want. There is hardly a second son of a younger brother who does not believe himself to be something like Louis XIV. He builds his Versailles, keeps his mistresses, and maintains his armies. . . .

The reason these little monarchs do not need to fortify their capitals is very plain: they can hardly be besieged at any time by their equals, for their larger neighbors would presently intervene

and offer to mediate, an offer they are not at liberty to refuse. Thus instead of bloodshed, two or three dashes of a pen are enough to terminate their quarrels.

What can be the use of their fortified towns? If they were strong enough to endure a siege as long as that of Troy against their equals, they would not be able to hold out as long as Jericho against a powerful prince. Besides, if they lie between two mighty neighbors who are at war, they have no choice but to observe neutrality unless they would be totally ruined. And if they join with either belligerent, their capitals become the frontier towns of that Prince's dominions. . . .

In short, to make war, give battle, and attack and defend fortified places is the business only of powerful sovereigns, and those who effect to imitate them are no wiser than the man who counterfeited the noise of thunder and believed himself to be Jupiter.

THE MILITARY SYSTEM ought . . . to rest on good principles that experience has shown to be valid. The genius of the nation ought to be understood—what it is capable of, and how far its safety may be risked by leading it against the enemy. . . .

There are states which, from their situation and constitution, must be maritime powers: such are England, Holland, France, Spain, and Denmark. They are surrounded by the sea, and their distant colonies force them to keep a navy and to maintain communication and trade between the mother country and these detached members. There are other states such as Austria, Poland, Prussia, and even Russia, some of which may well do without shipping and others that would commit an unpardonable error in politics if they were to . . . employ a part of their troops at sea when they stand indispensably in need of their services on land.

The number of troops maintained by a state ought to be in proportion to the troops maintained by its enemies. Their forces should be equal, or the weakest is in danger of being oppressed. Perhaps it may be argued that a king ought to depend on the aid of his allies. This reasoning would be good if allies were what they ought to be, but their zeal is only lukewarm, and he who shall depend upon another as upon himself will most certainly be deceived. If frontiers can be defended by fortresses, there must be no neglect in building nor any expense spared in bringing them to perfection. France has provided an example of this, and she has realized its advantages on different occasions.

But neither politics nor the army can prosper if the finances are not kept in the greatest order and if the prince himself be not a prudent economist. Money is like the magician's wand, for by its aid miracles are performed. Great political views, the maintenance of the military, and the best conceived plans for the well-being of the people will all remain lethargic if not animated by money. The economy of the sovereign is useful to the public good because, if he does not have sufficient funds in reserve either to supply the expenses of war without burdening his people with extraordinary taxes or to give relief to citizens in times of public calamity, all these burdens will fall on the subject, who will be without the means he needs most in such unhappy times.

IT IS IMPORTANT for the King of Prussia to rule independently. If a political system does not emanate from a single head it can no more be established and maintained than Newton could have been able to discover the law of gravitation working in concert with Leibnitz and Descartes. . . . The prince must design his system and put it into operation himself. Because his own thoughts lie closer to his heart than do the ideas of others, he naturally will pursue his plans with the zeal necessary for their success. Thus, his self-esteem, which chains him to his work, will also redound to the needs of the fatherland.

All branches of the state administration are intimately tied together in one bundle: finances, politics, and military affairs are inseparable. Not one, but all of these departments must be uniformly well administered. They must be steered in a straight line, head to head, as the team of horses in the Olympic contest which, pulling with equal weight and speed, covered the course and brought victory to their driver. A prince who rules independently and has fashioned his political system himself will not find himself in difficulty when he must make a quick decision, for he directs everything toward his established goal.

Above all, he must have acquired the greatest knowledge conceivable in the details of military affairs. One produces poor campaign plans at the round table, and where do the best plans lead if they are wrecked through the ignorance of those entrusted with their execution? A King may be the most able man, the best economist, the most subtle statesman—he will still fail as commander in chief if he neither knows the needs of an army nor cares about the countless details of its maintenance, if he is unaware how an army is mobilized, remains ignorant of the rules of war, or understands nothing of training troops in the garrison and leading them in the field. . . . The King of Prussia must make war his particular study and encourage the zeal of those who have chosen the noble and dangerous profession of arms.

Prussia is surrounded by powerful neighbors. . . . You must therefore be prepared for frequent wars. Hence it follows that the military in Prussia must be given the foremost positions, just as they were with the Romans, conquerors of the world, in the period of their ascendancy, and as in Sweden when Gustavus Adolphus, Charles X, and Charles XII filled the world with their fame, and the glory of Swedish names penetrated to the most distant lands. Offices, honors, and rewards bestowed alternately spur and encourage talent. To shower praise upon merit arouses high-minded rivalry in the heart of the nobleman, drives him to enter the army and acquire knowledge, and provides him with fortune and distinction. It makes no sense to despise officers and at the same time to ask them to serve with honor. To encourage a profession that constitutes the power of the kingdom, to respect the pillars of the state (if I may call the army that), to prefer army officers to the breed of soft and insipid men good only for decorating an ante-chamber—that is to say, not to bestow favor too highly nor to act capriciously, but to give honor where honor is due—is really a small enough offering of incense on the altar to officers who stand ready at any moment to shed their blood for the fatherland.

I myself have waged war and observed that colonels sometimes have decided the fate of the state. War cannot be conducted without encountering decisive battles that determine the fate of the kingdom. To win a battle gives the victor gay courage; to lose one strikes the vanquished to the ground. As a result of the battle of Ramillies France lost all of Flanders. Höchstädt cost the Elector of Bavaria his Electorate and all of Swabia. The battle of Turin ejected the French from Lombardy, and Villaviciosa placed Philip V on the Spanish throne and forced Charles VI to renounce Spain. It is for this reason that Henry IV said "a battle has a long tail."

On important and decisive days such as these one learns to treasure the value of good officers and to love them, if he sees with what proud defiance of death, what indestructible endurance they put the enemy to flight and remain master of the victory and the battlefield. It is not enough, however, to pay them respect only when they are needed and their deeds win your applause. In peacetime they must also enjoy the respect that they have so rightly earned for themselves. Esteem and distinctions rightfully belong to those who have shed their blood for the honor and preservation of the state.

In monarchies everyone looks to the ruler. The public follows his inclinations and seems ready to follow every stimulus that he gives. It is for this reason that the Roman prelates were luxurious and fond of show under Leo X and apathetic and indifferent under Sixtus V; that England was inclined to cruelty under Cromwell and devoted to the gay life under Charles II; that the Netherlands, although a republic, became a warlike nation under the animated example of the Prince of Orange; that the Roman Empire under Titus and the Antonines was still heathen and under Constantine, who was the first to accept the new cult, was converted to Christianity.

So in Prussia the ruler must do that which is most useful for the good of the state and therefore he must place himself at the head of the army. In this way he gives esteem to the military profession and preserves our excellent discipline and the order introduced among the troops. . . . If he possesses no expert knowledge, how will the king judge order and discipline among the different regiments and units? How can he improve what he himself does not understand? How can he blame the colonels for their mistakes and indicate to them at once the way in which they have been wrong and instruct them how to put their regiments in good order? If the king himself understands nothing of regimental and company economy, of troop leading and the art of maneuver, will he be so imprudent as to interfere? In this event he would expose himself to ridicule just as much as he would through ordering false troop movements. All this knowledge demands constant exercise, which one can only acquire if he is a soldier and applies himself to military service with unbroken diligence.

Finally, I venture the assertion that only the ruler can introduce and maintain this admirable discipline in the army. For often he must summon his authority, strongly censure the individual without regard for person and rank, reward others generously, have the troops mustered whenever possible, and not overlook the slightest negligence. The king of Prussia therefore must of necessity be a soldier and commander in chief. This office, which is courted in all republics and monarchies with diligence and ambition, nevertheless is held in low regard by the kings of Europe, who believe that they lose some of their dignity if they lead their armies themselves. But the throne turns out to be a disgrace if effeminate and lazy princes abandon the leadership of their troops to generals, and thus implicitly avow their own cowardice or incapacity.

In Prussia it is certainly honorable to work

with the flower of the nobility and the elite of the nation in strengthening discipline. For it is discipline that preserves the fame of the fatherland, gives it respect in peace, and produces victory in war. One would have to be a completely pitiful human being, bogged down in inertia and unnerved by high living, if he wished to shrink from the trouble and work that the maintenance of discipline in the army demands. But in exchange for his efforts, the king certainly would find his reward in victories and fame, which is even more valuable than the highest peak of grandeur or the pinnacle of power.

THE ART OF WAR is just like any other art: used correctly it can be profitable; abused it is fatal. A prince who wages war from unrest, frivolity, or wanton ambition deserves to be punished just as much as a judge who murders an innocent man with the sword of justice. That war is virtuous which is waged in order to maintain the authority of the state, preserve its security, aid allies, or check an ambitious prince who plots conquests contrary to your interests. . . . There is no finer and more useful art than the art of war when practiced by decent men. Under the protection of the noble defenders of the fatherland the peasant tills his fields, courts uphold the law, commerce thrives, and all business is pursued peacefully.

THE AMBITIOUS ought never to forget that arms and military discipline are much the same throughout Europe, and that alliances have the general effect of producing equality between the forces of belligerents. In these times, therefore, all that princes may hope from the greatest advantages is to acquire, after accumulated success, some small frontier town or some suburb, neither of which will pay interest on the debts incurred by war or contain nearly as many people as the number who have perished in the field.

Since the art of war has been so well understood in Europe, and policy has established a certain balance of power between sovereigns, great enterprises but rarely produce such effects as might be expected. An equality of forces, alternate loss and success, cause the opponents to find themselves much in the same state of reciprocal

strength at the end of the most desperate war as at the beginning. Exhausted treasuries at length are productive of peace, which ought to be the work of humanity, not of necessity.

AS FOR THE MANNER in which a prince ought to make war, I agree entirely with Machiavelli. Indeed, a great king ought always to assume command of his troops and to regard the camp as his place of residence. This is what his interest, duty, and glory require. As he is the chief magistrate in distributing justice to his people in times of peace, so he ought to be their chief protector and defender in war. When a prince is his own general and present in the field, his orders are more easily suited to all sudden emergencies and are executed with greater dispatch. His presence prevents that misunderstanding among the generals which is so often prejudicial to the interests of the sovereign and fatal to the army. More care is taken of the magazines, ammunition, and provisions, without which Caesar himself at the head of 100,000 men would never be able to accomplish anything. As it is the prince himself who gives orders for the battle, it seems to be his province to direct the execution of these orders, and by his presence and example to inspire his troops with valor and confidence.

But it may be objected that every man is not born to be a soldier and that many princes have not the talents, experience, or courage necessary for commanding an army. This objection may be easily removed: a prince will always find generals skilful enough to advise him, and it is sufficient for him in this case to be directed by their advice. Besides, no war can be carried on with great success if the general is under the direction of a ministry which is not present in the camp and consequently is unable to judge of sudden occurrences and to give orders accordingly.

*   *   *

REVIEW QUESTIONS

1. Why does a state need allies?
2. What has the state become, according to Frederick?
3. How does a ruler choose allies?
4. What is their relation to the state?
5. How do they reflect the state? Why does the state need a military?
6. What is the purpose of the military?
7. How is Frederick's idea different from Machiavelli's view?

HUGO GROTIUS

FROM On the Law of War and Peace

Hugo Grotius (1583–1645) was a Dutch statesman, jurist, theologian, poet, philologist, and historian, a man of all-embracing knowledge, whose writings were of fundamental importance in the formulation of international law. He was born in Delft, the son of the Burgomaster and Curator at the University of Leiden. Grotius was precocious; he matriculated at the University of Leiden at age eleven. By age fifteen, he had edited the encyclopedia of Martianus Capella and accompanied a diplomatic mission to the king of France, who described Grotius as the "miracle of Holland." He earned his doctorate in law at the University of Orléans and became a distinguished jurist at The Hague. In 1601, he was appointed historiographer of the States of Holland. He wrote a number of minor but memorable legal treatises before publishing his great work, On the Law of War and Peace, *in 1625. Grotius argued that the entire law of humankind was based on four fundamental precepts: neither state nor individual may attack another state or individual; neither state nor individual may appropriate what belongs to another state or individual; neither state nor individual may disregard treaties or contracts; neither state nor individual may commit a crime. In the case of a violation of one of these precepts, compensation might be sought either by war or by individual action. These principles and the arguments that surrounded them significantly aided the development of a theory of state sovereignty and international relations in the early modern period. During the remainder of his life, Grotius remained involved in political as well as intellectual affairs of his day. Apart from the vast corpus of his written works, he participated in the government of the United Provinces of the Netherlands. He was eventually imprisoned for his support of Arminianism and managed to escape hidden in a trunk. He spent the rest of his life in exile, honored as one of the great intellectuals of the seventeenth century, but unacknowledged by his own country.*

From *The Rights of War and Peace*, M. Walter Dunn, 1901.

*   *   *

VII.

That power is called sovereign, whose actions are not subject to the controul of any other power, so as to be annulled at the pleasure of any other human will. The term ANY OTHER HUMAN WILL exempts the sovereign himself from this restriction, who may annul his own acts, as may also his successor, who enjoys the same right, having the same power and no other. We are to consider then what is the subject in which this sovereign power exists. Now the subject is in one respect common, and in another proper, as the body is the common subject of sight, the eye the proper, so the common subject of sovereign power is the state, which has already been said to be a perfect society of men.

Now those nations, who are in a state of subjugation to another power, as the Roman provinces were, are excluded from this definition. For those nations are not sovereign states of themselves, in the present acceptation of the word; but are subordinate members of a great state, as slaves are members of a household. Again it happens that many states, forming each an independent body, may have one head. For political are not like natural bodies, to only one of which the same head can belong. Whereas in the former, one person can exercise the function of the head to many distinct bodies. As a certain proof of which, when the reigning house has become extinct, the sovereign power returns to the hands of the nation. So it may happen, that many states may be connected together by the closest federal union, which Strabo, in more places than one calls a system, and yet each retain the condition of a perfect, individual state, which has been observed by Aristotle and others in different parts of their writings. Therefore the common subject of sovereign power is the state, taken in the sense already explained. The proper subject is one or more persons according to the laws and customs of each nation. This is called by Galen in the sixth book DE PLACITIS HIP-POCRAT ET PLATONIS, the first power of the state.

VIII.

And here is the proper place for refuting the opinion of those, who maintain that, every where and without exception, the sovereign power is vested in the people, so that they have a right to restrain and punish kings for an abuse of their power. However there is no man of sober wisdom, who does not see the incalculable mischiefs, which such opinions have occasioned, and may still occasion; and upon the following grounds they may be refuted.

From the Jewish, as well as the Roman Law, it appears that any one might engage himself in private servitude to whom he pleased. Now if an individual may do so, why may not a whole people, for the benefit of better government and more certain protection, completely transfer their sovereign rights to one or more persons, without reserving any portion to themselves? Neither can it be alledged that such a thing is not to be presumed, for the question is not, what is to be presumed in a doubtful case, but what may lawfully be done. Nor is it any more to the purpose to object to the inconveniences, which may, and actually do arise from a people's thus surrendering their rights. For it is not in the power of man to devise any form of government free from imperfections and dangers. As a dramatic writer says, "you must either take these advantages with those imperfections, or resign your pretensions to both."

Now as there are different ways of living, some of a worse, and some of a better kind, left to the choice of every individual; so a nation, "under certain circumstances, WHEN for instance, the succession to the throne is extinct, or the throne has by any other means become vacant," may choose what form of government she pleases. Nor is this right to be measured by the excellence of this or that form of government, on which there may be varieties of opinion, but by the will of the people.

There may be many reasons indeed why a people may entirely relinquish their rights, and surrender them to another: for instance, they may have no other means of securing themselves from the danger of immediate destruction, or under the pressure of famine it may be the only way, through which they can procure support. For if the Campanians, formerly, when reduced by necessity surrendered themselves to the Roman people in the following terms:—"Senators of Rome, we consign to your dominion the people of Campania, and the city of Capua, our lands, our temples, and all things both divine and human," and if another people as Appian relates, offered to submit to the Romans, and were refused, what is there to prevent any nation from submitting in the same manner to one powerful sovereign? It may also happen that a master of a family, having large possessions, will suffer no one to reside upon them on any other terms, or an owner, having many slaves, may give them their liberty upon condition of their doing certain services, and paying certain rents; of which examples may be produced. Thus Tacitus, speaking of the German slaves, says, "Each has his own separate habitation, and his own household to govern. The master considers him as a tenant, bound to pay a certain rent in corn, cattle, and wearing apparel. And this is the utmost extent of his servitude."

Aristotle, in describing the requisites, which fit men for servitude, says, that "those men, whose powers are chiefly confined to the body, and whose principal excellence consists in affording bodily service, are naturally slaves, because it is their interest to be so." In the same manner some nations are of such a disposition that they are more calculated to obey than to govern, which seems to have been the opinion which the Cappadocians held of themselves, who when the Romans offered them a popular government, refused to accept it, because the nation they said could not exist in safety without a king. Thus Philostratus in the life of Apollonius, says, that it was foolish to offer liberty to the Thracians, the Mysians, and the Getae, which they were not capable of enjoying. The example of nations, who have for many ages lived happily under a kingly government, has induced many to give the preference to that form. Livy says, that the cities under Eumenes would not have changed their condition for that of any free state whatsoever. And sometimes a state is so situated, that it seems impossible it can preserve its peace and existence, without submitting to the absolute government of a single person, which many wise men thought to be the case with the Roman Republic in the time of Augustus Cæsar. From these, and causes like these it not only may, but generally does happen, that men, as Cicero observes in the second book of his offices, willingly submit to the supreme authority of another.

Now as property may be acquired by what has been already styled just war, by the same means the rights of sovereignty may be acquired. Nor is the term sovereignty here meant to be applied to monarchy alone, but to government by nobles, from any share in which the people are excluded. For there never was any government so purely popular, as not to require the exclusion of the poor, of strangers, women, and minors from the public councils. Some states have other nations under them, no less dependent upon their will, than subjects upon that of their sovereign princes. From whence arose that question, Are the Collatine people in their own power? And the Campanians, when they submitted to the Romans, are said to have passed under a foreign dominion. In the same manner Acarnania and Amphilochia are said to have been under the dominion of the Aetolians; Peraea and Caunus under that of the Rhodians; and Pydna was ceded by Philip to the Olynthians. And those towns, that had been under the Spartans, when they were delivered from their dominion, received the name of the free Laconians. The city of Cotyora is said by Xenophon to have belonged to the people of Sinope. Nice in Italy, according to Strabo, was adjudged to the people of Marseilles; and the island of Pithecusa to the Neapolitans. We find in Frontinus, that the towns of Calati and Caudium with their territories were adjudged, the one to the colony of Capua, and the other to that of Beneventum. Otho, as Tacitus relates, gave the cities of the Moors to the Province of Baetia. None of these instances, any more than the cessions of other conquered countries could be admitted, if it were a received rule that the rights of sovereigns are under the controul and direction of subjects.

Now it is plain both from sacred and profane history, that there are kings, who are not subject to the controul of the people in their collective body; God addressing the people of Israel, says, if thou shalt say, "I will place a king over me"; and to Samuel "Shew them the manner of the king, who shall reign over them." Hence the King is said to be anointed over the people, over the inheritance of the Lord, over Israel. Solomon is styled King over all Israel. Thus David gives thanks to God, for subduing the people under him. And Christ says, "the Kings of the nations bear rule over them." There is a well known passage in Horace, "Powerful sovereigns reign over their own subjects, and the supreme being over sovereigns themselves." Seneca thus describes the three forms of government, "Sometimes the supreme power is lodged in the people, sometimes in a senate composed of the leading men of the state, sometimes this power of the people, and dominion over the people themselves is vested in a single person." Of the last description are those, who, as Plutarch says, exercise authority not according to the laws, but over the laws. And in Herodutus, Otanes describes a monarch as one whose acts are not subject to controul. Dion Prusaeensis also and Pausanias define a monarchy in the same terms.

Aristotle says there are some kings, who have the same right, which the nation elsewhere possesses over persons and property. Thus when the Roman Princes began to exercise regal power, the people it was said had transferred all their own personal sovereignty to them, which gave rise to the saying of Marcus Antoninus the Philosopher, that no one but God alone can be judge of the Prince. Dion. L. liii. speaking of such a prince, says, "he is perfectly master of his own actions, to do whatever he pleases, and cannot be obliged to do any thing against his will." Such anciently was the power of the Inachidae established at Argos in Greece. For in the Greek Tragedy of the Suppliants, Aeschylus has introduced the people thus addressing the King: "You are the state, you the people; you the court from which there is no appeal, you preside over the altars, and regulate all affairs by your supreme will." King Theseus himself in Euripides speaks in very different terms of the Athenian Republic; "The city is not governed by one man, but in a popular form, by an annual succession of magistrates." For according to Plutarch's explanation, Theseus was the general in war, and the guardian of the laws; but in other respects nothing more than a citizen. So that they who are limited by popular controul are improperly called kings. Thus after the time of Lycurgus, and more particularly after the institution of the Ephori, the Kings of the Lacedaemonians are said by Polybius, Plutarch, and Cornelius Nepos, to have been Kings more in name than in reality. An example which was followed by the rest of Greece. Thus Pausanias says of the Argives to the Corinthians, "The Argives from their love of equality have reduced their kingly power very low; so that they have left the posterity of Cisus nothing more than the shadow of Kings." Aristotle denies such to be proper forms of government, because they constitute only a part of an Aristocracy or Democracy.

Examples also may be found of nations, who have not been under a perpetual regal form, but only for a time under a government exempt from popular controul. Such was the power of the Amimonians among the Cnidians, and of the Dictators in the early periods of the Roman history, when there was no appeal to the people, from whence Livy says, the will of the Dictator was observed as a law. Indeed they found this submission the only remedy against imminent danger, and in the words of Cicero, the Dictatorship possessed all the strength of royal power.

It will not be difficult to refute the arguments brought in favour of the contrary opinion. For in the first place the assertion that the constituent always retains a controul over the sovereign power, which he has contributed to establish, is only true in those cases where the continuance and existence of that power depends upon the will and pleasure of the constituent: but not in cases where the power, though it might derive its origin from that constituent, becomes a necessary and fundamental part of the established law. Of this nature is that authority to which a woman submits when she gives herself to a husband. Valentinian the Emperor, when the soldiers who had raised him to the throne, made a demand of which he did not approve, replied; "Soldiers, your election of me for your emperor was your own voluntary choice; but since you have elected me, it depends upon my pleasure to grant your request. It becomes you to obey as subjects, and me to consider what is proper to be done."

Nor is the assumption true, that all kings are made by the people, as may be plainly seen from the instances adduced above, of an owner admitting strangers to reside upon his demesnes on condition of their obedience, and of nations submitting by right of conquest. Another argument is derived from a saying of the Philosophers, that all power is conferred for the benefit of the governed and not of the governing party. Hence from the nobleness of the end, it is supposed to follow, that subjects have a superiority over the sovereign. But it is not universally true, that all power is conferred for the benefit of the party governed. For some powers are conferred for the sake of the governor, as the right of a master over a slave, in which the advantage of the latter is only a contingent and adventitious circumstance. In the same manner the gain of a Physician is to reward him for his labour; and not merely to promote the good of his art. There are other kinds of authority established for the benefit of both parties, as for instance, the authority of a husband over his wife. Certain governments also, as those which are gained by right of conquest, may be established for the benefit of the sovereign; and yet convey no idea of tyranny, a word which in its original signification, implied nothing of arbitrary power or injustice, but only the government or authority of a Prince. Again, some governments may be formed for the advantage both of subjects and sovereign, as when a people, unable to defend themselves, put themselves under the protection and dominion of any powerful king. Yet it is not to be denied, but that in most governments the good of the subject is the chief object which is regarded: and that what Cicero has said after Herodotus, and Herodotus after Hesiod, is true, that

Kings were appointed in order that men might enjoy complete justice.

Now this admission by no means goes to establish the inference that kings are amenable to the people. For though guardianships were invented for the benefit of wards, yet the guardian has a right to authority over the ward. Nor, though a guardian may for mismanagement be removed from his trust, does it follow that a king may for the same reason be deposed. The cases are quite different, the guardian has a superior to judge him; but in governments, as there must be some dernier resort, it must be vested either in an individual, or in some public body, whose misconduct, as there is no superior tribunal before which they can be called, God declares that he himself will judge. He either punishes their offences, should he deem it necessary; or permits them for the chastisement of his people.

This is well expressed by Tacitus: he says, "you should bear with the rapacity or luxury of rulers, as you would bear with drought, or excessive rains, or any other calamities of nature. For as long as men exist there will be faults and imperfections; but these are not of uninterrupted continuance, and they are often repaired by the succession of better times." And Marcus Aurelius speaking of subordinate magistrates, said, that they were under the controul of the sovereign: but that the sovereign was amenable to God. There is a remarkable passage in Gregory of Tours, where that Bishop thus addresses the King of France, "If any of us, Sir, should transgress the bounds of justice, he may be punished by you. But if you exceed them, who can call you to account? For when we address you, you may hear us if you please; but if you will not, who can judge you, except him, who has declared himself to be righteousness?" Among the maxims of the Essenes, Porphyry cites a passage, that "no one can reign without the special appointment of divine providence." Irenaeus has expressed this well, "Kings are appointed by him at whose command men are created; and their appointment is suited to the condition of those, whom they are called to govern." There is the same thought in the Constitutions of Clement, "You shall fear the King, for he is of the Lord's appointment."

Nor is it an objection to what has been said, that some nations have been punished for the offences of their kings, for this does not happen, because they forbear to restrain their kings, but because they seem to give, at least a tacit consent to their vices, or perhaps, without respect to this, God may use that sovereign power which he has over the life and death of every man to inflict a punishment upon the king by depriving him of his subjects.

IX.

There are some who frame an imaginary kind of mutual subjection, by which the people are bound to obey the king, as long as he governs well; but his government is subject to their inspection and controul. If they were to say that his duty to the sovereign does not oblige any one to do an act manifestly unjust and repugnant to the law of God; they would say nothing but what is true and universally admitted, but this by no means includes a right to any controul over the Prince's conduct in his lawful government. But if any people had the opportunity of dividing the sovereign power with the king, the privileges of the one, and the prerogatives of the other ought to be defined by certain bounds, which might easily be known, according to the difference of places, persons, or circumstances.

Now the supposed good or evil of any act, especially in political matters which admit of great variety of opinions and much discussion, is not a sufficient mark to ascertain these bounds. From whence the greatest confusion must follow, if under pretence of promoting good or averting evil measures, the people might struggle for the Prince's jurisdiction: a turbulent state of affairs, which no sober minded people ever wished to experience.

*   *   *

REVIEW QUESTIONS

1. What is the relation between political power and will according to Grotius?
2. What is the state?
3. The sovereign state?
4. Where does Grotius locate sovereignty?
5. Does sovereignty have a moral component?
6. What is its relation to property? To the good of the people?

17 ✑ THE SCIENTIFIC REVOLUTION AND ENLIGHTENMENT

The Scientific Revolution and the Enlightenment make a logical grouping. The Enlightenment of the eighteenth century continued the work of the seventeenth century developments in science, and the Scientific Revolution created the basic intellectual milieu for enlightened thinking.

The term "Scientific Revolution" is commonly applied to the changes in scientific theory and practice that took root in the early seventeenth century and promoted the advance of science as we know it today. It grew initially out of changes in astronomy and physics, the creation of mechanical philosophy as a general theory of nature, and the adoption of mathematics as a basic language of science. Natural phenomena were conceived to be regular and rational. Given that nature was subject to reason, human beings could uncover its laws, which were assumed to be few in number and universal in application, by the right exercise of their own rational capacities. Among these were mechanics, which altered the scientific vision of the universe. It explained all physical phenomena in terms of matter and assumed that motion was the natural state of the world. Mechanical philosophy posited that all bodies were composed of a single, universal substance, matter. These natural phenomena, matter and motion, were so defined as to be measured and translated into numbers that could be manipulated in mathematical formulae. As a form of reason, therefore, mathematics could become the language of scientific inquiry. Reason and mathematics, it was believed, could teach reliable truths about nature.

The Enlightenment continued the work begun by the revolution in science by spreading its new ideas to the general reading public and extending them to new disciplines devoted to the study of human nature. As an intellectual and cultural movement of the eighteenth century, it was characterized by faith in the power of human reason to solve the basic problems of existence. Though centered in Paris, the Enlightenment was international in scope, manifesting itself

throughout Europe and North America. Enlightened intellectuals turned a criti-
cal reason on all received institutions and traditions with an eye to rebuilding
human society according to the natural order of things. This natural order was
born of three scientific cornerstones: mechanics, reason, and empiricism. Reason
provided both an analogy for the universe and a tool for its analysis. Nature
was assumed to be rational, to be ordered according to knowable, controllable
relations, fundamental laws that might be discovered through observation and
experimentation. Confidence in the existence of natural laws encouraged the
search for similar laws governing human relations. Knowledge of these laws
would serve humankind by making possible practical reforms at all levels of life.

By popularizing and extending the ideas of the Scientific Revolution, the
Enlightenment encouraged a secular view of the world. In this way, it helped
bring Europe into the modern era.

FRANCIS BACON

FROM The Great Instauration

With Francis Bacon (1561–1626) we enter the so-called Age of Reason, the era of
science and enlightenment. Son of Sir Nicholas Bacon, Lord Keeper of the Great
Seal of England, he attended Trinity College, Cambridge, and entered the legal pro-
fession in 1582. His public life was not that of a natural philosopher, but that of a
statesman. Beginning his career under Elizabeth I, he rose to the position of Lord
Chancellor and was created Viscount St. Albans in 1621 under James I. His Great
Instauration (1620) was published in the eve of his advancement. After the collapse
of his career in 1622, when he pleaded guilty to charges of bribery, Bacon withdrew
into enforced retirement and, like Machiavelli, pursued his intellectual passion. In
his writings, he envisioned the transformation of the human mind through the right
use of reason. He called for the close observation of nature and scientific collabora-
tion in the cause of human improvement. In this, Bacon was the prophet of the
revolution in science.

From *Works of Francis Bacon*, 1857–1874.

Preface

That the state of knowledge is not prosperous nor
greatly advancing; and that a way must be opened for
the human understanding entirely different from any
hitherto known, and other helps provided, in order
that the mind may exercise over the nature of things
the authority which properly belongs to it.

It seems to me that men do not rightly understand either their store or their strength, but overrate the one and underrate the other. Hence it follows, that either from an extravagant estimate of the value of the arts which they possess, they seek no further; or else from too mean an estimate of their own powers, they spend their strength in small matters and never put it fairly to the trial in those which go to the main. These are as the pillars of fate set in the path of knowledge; for men have neither desire nor hope to encourage them to penetrate further. And since opinion of store is one of the chief causes of want, and satisfaction with the present induces neglect of provision for the future, it becomes a thing not only useful, but absolutely necessary, that the excess of honour and admiration with which our existing stock of inventions is regarded be in the very entrance and threshold of the work, and that frankly and without circumlocution, stripped off, and men be duly warned not to exaggerate or make too much of them. For let a man look carefully into all that variety of books with which the arts and sciences abound, he will find everywhere endless repetitions of the same thing, varying in the method of treatment, but not new in substance, insomuch that the whole stock, numerous as it appears at first view, proves on examination to be but scanty. And for its value and utility it must be plainly avowed that that wisdom which we have derived principally from the Greeks is but like the boyhood of knowledge, and has the characteristic property of boys: it can talk, but it cannot generate; for it is fruitful of controversies but barren of works. So that the state of learning as it now is appears to be represented to the life in the old fable of Scylla, who had the head and face of a virgin, but her womb was hung round with barking monsters, from which she could not be delivered. For in like manner the sciences to which we are accustomed have certain general positions which are specious and flattering; but as soon as they come to particulars, which are as the parts of generation, when they should produce fruit and works, then arise contentions and barking disputations, which are the end of the matter and all

the issue they can yield. Observe also, that if sciences of this kind had any life in them, that could never have come to pass which has been the case now for many ages—that they stand almost at a stay, without receiving any augmentations worthy of the human race; insomuch that many times not only what was asserted once is asserted still, but what was a question once is a question still, and instead of being resolved by discussion is only fixed and fed; and all the tradition and succession of schools is still a succession of masters and scholars, not of inventors and those who bring to further perfection the things invented. In the mechanical arts we do not find it so; they, on the contrary, as having in them some breath of life, are continually growing and becoming more perfect. As originally invented they are commonly rude, clumsy, and shapeless; afterwards they acquire new powers and more commodious arrangements and constructions; in so far that men shall sooner leave the study and pursuit of them and turn to something else, than they arrive at the ultimate perfection of which they are capable. Philosophy and the intellectual sciences, on the contrary, stand like statues, worshipped and celebrated, but not moved or advanced. Nay, they sometimes flourish most in the hands of the first author, and afterwards degenerate. For when men have once made over their judgments to others' keeping, and (like those senators whom they called *Pedarii*) have agreed to support some one person's opinion, from that time they make no enlargement of the sciences themselves, but fall to the servile office of embellishing certain individual authors and increasing their retinue. And let it not be said that the sciences have been growing gradually till they have at last reached their full stature, and so (their course being completed) have settled in the works of a few writers; and that there being now no room for the invention of better, all that remains is to embellish and cultivate those things which have been invented already. Would it were so! But the truth is that this appropriating of the sciences had its origin in nothing better than the confidence of a few persons and the sloth and indolence of the rest. For after the sciences had been in several parts perhaps cultivated and handled diligently, there has risen up some man of bold disposition, and famous for methods and short ways which people like, who has in appearance reduced them to an art, while he has in fact only spoiled all that the others had done. And yet this is what posterity like, because it makes the work short and easy, and saves further inquiry, of which they are weary and impatient. And if any one take this general acquiescence and consent for an argument of weight, as being the judgment of Time, let me tell him that the reasoning on which he relies is most fallacious and weak. For, first, we are far from knowing all that in the matter of sciences and arts has in various ages and places been brought to light and published; much less, all that has been by private persons secretly attempted and stirred; so neither the births nor the miscarriages of Time are entered in our records. Nor, secondly, is the consent itself and the time it has continued a consideration of much worth. For however various are the forms of civil polities, there is but one form of polity in the sciences; and that always has been and always will be popular. Now the doctrines which find most favour with the populace are those which are either contentious and pugnacious, or specious and empty; such, I say, as either entangle assent or tickle it. And therefore no doubt the greatest wits in each successive age have been forced out of their own course; men of capacity and intellect above the vulgar having been fain, for reputation's sake, to bow to the judgment of the time and the multitude; and thus if any contemplations of a higher order took light anywhere, they were presently blown out by the winds of vulgar opinions. So that Time is like a river, which has brought down to us things light and puffed up, while those which are weighty and solid have sunk. Nay, those very authors who have usurped a kind of dictatorship in the sciences and taken upon them to lay down the law with such confidence, yet when from time to time they come to themselves again, they fall to complaints of the subtlety of nature, the hiding-places of truth, the obscurity of things, the entanglement of causes, the weakness of the human mind; wherein nevertheless they show themselves never the more modest, seeing that they will rather lay the blame upon the common condition of men and nature than upon themselves. And then whatever any art fails to attain, they ever set it down upon the authority of that art itself as impossible of attainment; and how can art be found guilty when it is judge in its own cause? So it is but a device for exempting ignorance from ignominy. Now for those things which are delivered and received, this is their condition: barren of works, full of questions; in point of enlargement slow and languid; carrying a show of perfection in the whole, but in the parts ill filled up; in selection popular, and unsatisfactory even to those who propound them; and therefore fenced round and set forth with sundry artifices. And if there be any who have determined to make trial for themselves, and put their own strength to the work of advancing the boundaries of the sciences, yet have they not ventured to cast themselves completely loose from received opinions or to seek their knowledge at the fountain; but they think they have done some great thing if they do but add and introduce into the existing sum of science something of their own; prudently considering with themselves that by making the addition they can assert their liberty, while they retain the credit of modesty by assenting to the rest. But these mediocrities and middle ways so much praised, in deferring to opinions and customs, turn to the great detriment of the sciences. For it is hardly possible at once to admire an author and to go beyond him; knowledge being as water, which will not rise above the level from which it fell. Men of this kind, therefore, amend some things, but advance little; and improve the condition of knowledge, but do not extend its range. Some, indeed, there have been who have gone more boldly to work, and taking it all for an open matter and giving their genius full play, have made a passage for themselves and their own opinions by pulling down and demolishing former ones; and yet all their stir has but little advanced the matter; since their aim has been not to extend philosophy and the arts in substance and value, but only to change doctrines and transfer the kingdom of opinions to themselves; whereby little has indeed been gained, for though the error be the opposite of the other, the causes of erring are the same in both. And if there have been any who, not binding themselves either to other men's opinions or to their own, but loving liberty, have desired to engage others along with themselves in search, these, though honest in intention, have been weak in endeavour. For they have been content to follow probable reasons, and are carried round in a whirl of arguments, and in the promiscuous liberty of search have relaxed the severity of inquiry. There is none who has dwelt upon experience and the facts of nature as long as is necessary. Some there are indeed who have committed themselves to the waves of experience, and almost turned mechanics; yet these again have in their very experiments pursued a kind of wandering inquiry, without any regular system of operations. And besides they have mostly proposed to themselves certain petty tasks, taking it for a great matter to work out some single discovery;— a course of proceeding at once poor in aim and unskilful in design. For no man can rightly and successfully investigate the nature of anything in the thing itself; let him vary his experiments as laboriously as he will, he never comes to a resting-place, but still finds something to seek beyond. And there is another thing to be remembered; namely, that all industry in experimenting has begun with proposing to itself certain definite works to be accomplished, and has pursued them with premature and unseasonable eagerness; it has sought, I say, experiments of Fruit, not experiments of Light; not imitating the divine procedure, which in its first day's work created light only and assigned to it one entire day; on which day it produced no material work, but proceeded to that on the days following. As for those who have given the first place to Logic, supposing that the surest helps to the sciences were to be found in that, they have indeed most truly and excellently perceived that the human intellect left to its own course is not to be trusted; but then the remedy is altogether too weak for the disease; nor is it without evil in itself. For the Logic which is re-

ceived, though it be very properly applied to civil business and to those arts which rest in discourse and opinion, is not nearly subtle enough to deal with nature; and in offering at what it cannot master, has done more to establish and perpetuate error than to open the way to truth.

Upon the whole therefore, it seems that men have not been happy hitherto either in the trust which they have placed in others or in their own industry with regard to the sciences; especially as neither the demonstrations nor the experiments as yet known are much to be relied upon. But the universe to the eye of the human understanding is framed like a labyrinth; presenting as it does on every side so many ambiguities of way, such deceitful resemblances of objects and signs, natures so irregular in their lines, and so knotted and entangled. And then the way is still to be made by the uncertain light of the sense, sometimes shining out, sometimes clouded over, through the woods of experience and particulars; while those who offer themselves for guides are (as was said) themselves also puzzled, and increase the number of errors and wanderers. In circumstances so difficult neither the natural force of man's judgment nor even any accidental felicity offers any chance of success. No excellence of wit, no repetition of chance experiments, can overcome such difficulties as these. Our steps must be guided by a clue, and the whole way from the very first perception of the senses must be laid out upon a sure plan. Not that I would be understood to mean that nothing whatever has been done in so many ages by so great labours. We have no reason to be ashamed of the discoveries which have been made, and no doubt the ancients proved themselves in everything that turns on wit and abstract meditation, wonderful men. But as in former ages when men sailed only by observation of the stars, they could indeed coast along the shores of the old continent or cross a few small and mediterranean seas; but before the ocean could be traversed and the new world discovered, the use of the mariner's needle, as a more faithful and certain guide, had to be found out; in like manner the discoveries which have been hitherto made in the arts and sciences are such as might be made by practice, meditation, observation, argumentation,—for they lay near to the senses, and immediately beneath common notions; but before we can reach the remoter and more hidden parts of nature, it is necessary that a more perfect use and application of the human mind and intellect be introduced.

For my own part at least, in obedience to the everlasting love of truth, I have committed myself to the uncertainties and difficulties and solitudes of the ways, and relying on the divine assistance have upheld my mind both against the shocks and embattled ranks of opinion, and against my own private and inward hesitations and scruples, and against the fogs and clouds of nature, and the phantoms flitting about on every side; in the hope of providing at last for the present and future generations guidance more faithful and secure. Wherein if I have made any progress, the way has been opened to me by no other means than the true and legitimate humiliation of the human spirit. For all those who before me have applied themselves to the invention of arts have but cast a glance or two upon facts and examples and experience, and straightway proceeded, as if invention were nothing more than an exercise of thought, to invoke their own spirits to give them oracles. I, on the contrary, dwelling purely and constantly among the facts of nature, withdraw my intellect from them no further than may suffice to let the images and rays of natural objects meet in a point, as they do in the sense of vision; whence it follows that the strength and excellency of the wit has but little to do in the matter. And the same humility which I use in inventing I employ likewise in teaching. For I do not endeavour either by triumphs of confutation, or pleadings of antiquity, or assumption of authority, or even by the veil of obscurity, to invest these inventions of mine with any majesty; which might easily be done by one who sought to give lustre to his own name rather than light to other men's minds. I have not sought (I say) nor do I seek either to force or ensnare men's judgments, but I lead them to things themselves and the concordances of things, that they

may see for themselves what they have, what they can dispute, what they can add and contribute to the common stock. And for myself, if in anything I have been either too credulous or too little awake and attentive, or if I have fallen off by the way and left the inquiry incomplete, nevertheless I so present these things naked and open that my errors can be marked and set aside before the mass of knowledge be further infected by them: and it will be easy also for others to continue and carry on my labours. And by these means I suppose that I have established for ever a true and lawful marriage between the empirical and the rational faculty, the unkind and ill-starred divorce and separation of which has thrown into confusion all the affairs of the human family.

Wherefore, seeing that these things do not depend upon myself, at the outset of the work I most humbly and fervently pray to God the Father, God the Son, and God the Holy Ghost, that remembering the sorrows of mankind and the pilgrimage of this our life wherein we wear out days few and evil, they will vouchsafe through my hands to endow the human family with new mercies. This likewise I humbly pray, that things human may not interfere with things divine, and that from the opening of the ways of sense and the increase of natural light there may arise in our minds no incredulity or darkness with regard to the divine mysteries; but rather that the understanding being thereby purified and purged of fancies and vanity, and yet not the less subject and entirely submissive to the divine oracles, may give to faith that which is faith's. Lastly, that knowledge being now discharged of that venom which the serpent infused into it, and which makes the mind of man to swell, we may not be wise above measure and sobriety, but cultivate truth in charity.

And now having said my prayers I turn to men; to whom I have certain salutary admonitions to offer and certain fair requests to make. My first admonition (which was also my prayer) is that men confine the sense within the limits of duty in respect of things divine: for the sense is like the sun, which reveals the face of earth, but seals and shuts up the face of heaven. My next, that in flying from this evil they fall not into the opposite error, which they will surely do if they think that the inquisition of nature is in any part interdicted or forbidden. For it was not that pure and uncorrupted natural knowledge whereby Adam gave names to the creatures according to their propriety, which gave occasion to the fall. It was the ambitious and proud desire of moral knowledge to judge of good and evil, to the end that man may revolt from God and give laws to himself, which was the form and manner of the temptation. Whereas of the sciences which regard nature, the divine philosopher declares that "it is the glory of God to conceal a thing, but it is the glory of the King to find a thing out." Even as though the divine nature took pleasure in the innocent and kindly sport of children playing at hide and seek, and vouchsafed of his kindness and goodness to admit the human spirit for his playfellow at that game. Lastly, I would address one general admonition to all; that they consider what are the true ends of knowledge, and that they seek it not either for pleasure of the mind, or for contention, or for superiority to others, or for profit, or fame, or power, or any of these inferior things; but for the benefit and use of life; and that they perfect and govern it in charity. For it was from lust of power that the angels fell, from lust of knowledge that man fell; but of charity there can be no excess, neither did angel or man ever come in danger by it.

The requests I have to make are these. Of myself I say nothing; but in behalf of the business which is in hand I entreat men to believe that it is not an opinion to be held, but a work to be done; and to be well assured that I am labouring to lay the foundation, not of any sect or doctrine, but of human utility and power. Next, I ask them to deal fairly by their own interests, and laying aside all emulations and prejudices in favour of this or that opinion, to join in consultation for the common good; and being now freed and guarded by the securities and helps which I offer from the errors and impediments of the way, to come forward themselves and take part in that which remains to be done. Moreover, to be of good hope, nor to imagine that this Instauration of mine is a thing infinite and beyond the power of man, when it is in fact the true end and termination of infinite error; and seeing also that it is by no means forgetful of the conditions of mortality and humanity, (for it does not suppose that the work can be altogether completed within one generation, but provides for its being taken up by another); and finally that it seeks for the sciences not arrogantly in the little cells of human wit, but with reverence in the greater world. But it is the empty things that are vast: things solid are most contracted and lie in little room. And now I have only one favour more to ask (else injustice to me may perhaps imperil the business itself)—that men will consider well how far, upon that which I must needs assert (if I am to be consistent with myself), they are entitled to judge and decide upon these doctrines of mine; inasmuch as all that premature human reasoning which anticipates inquiry, and is abstracted from the facts rashly and sooner than is fit, is by me rejected (so far as the inquisition of nature is concerned), as a thing uncertain, confused, and ill built up; and I cannot be fairly asked to abide by the decision of a tribunal which is itself on its trial.

*   *   *

REVIEW QUESTIONS

1. What does Bacon believe to be the wrong relation to the past and to past authors?
2. Why does he think so?
3. What relation to the past and to past authors does he think a true scientist should hold?
4. Why does Bacon propose the necessity of a "method," and what method does he propose?
5. What is invention, and what is its relation to experience and prior knowledge?

GALILEO GALILEI

FROM The Starry Messenger and The Assayer

Galileo Galilei (1564–1642), an Italian astronomer, mathematician, and physicist, was a major contributor to the shift in scientific practice commonly called the Scientific Revolution. Born the son of a musician, Vincenzo Galilei, Galileo received his primary education from a tutor in Pisa and later from the monks of Santa Maria at Vallambrosa in Florence. From 1581 to 1585, he studied medicine at the University of Pisa and supplemented his education with private lessons in mathematics. Without formal instruction in that field, Galileo occupied the chair in mathematics at the University of Pisa from 1589 to 1591 and at the University of Padua from 1592 until 1610, when he was appointed court philosopher and mathematician to the Grand Duke of Tuscany. During his tenure at court, he published The Starry Messenger *(1610) and* The Assayer *(1619). The former gave evidence to confirm the heliocentric theory of the solar system. The latter offered a strong defense of the empirical basis of scientific reasoning. It was his advocacy of the Copernican theory that led him into conflict with the Roman Catholic Inquisition. Galileo was forced to abjure his scientific findings, sentenced to perpetual house arrest, and his books were burned. His trial, no less than his discoveries, secured his fame, and his books continued to circulate clandestinely throughout Europe.*

FROM The Starry Messenger

FROM *Astronomical Message*

Which contains and explains recent observations made with the aid of a new spyglass concerning the surface of the moon, the Milky Way, nebulous stars, and innumerable fixed stars, as well as four planets never before seen, and now named The Medicean Stars

Great indeed are the things which in this brief treatise I propose for observation and considera-tion by all students of nature. I say great, because of the excellence of the subject itself, the entirely unexpected and novel character of these things, and finally because of the instrument by means of which they have been revealed to our senses.

Surely it is a great thing to increase the numerous host of fixed stars previously visible to the unaided vision, adding countless more which have never before been seen, exposing these plainly to the eye in numbers ten times exceeding the old and familiar stars.

It is a very beautiful thing, and most gratifying to the sight, to behold the body of the moon, distant from us almost sixty earthly radii, as if it were no farther away than two such measures—

its diameter appears almost thirty times larger, its so that surface nearly nine hundred times, and its volume twenty-seven thousand times as large as when viewed with the naked eye. In this way one may learn with all the certainty of sense evidence that the moon is not robed in a smooth and polished surface but is in fact rough and uneven, covered everywhere, just like the earth's surface, with huge prominences, deep valleys, and chasms.

Again, it seems to me a matter of no small importance to have ended the dispute about the Milky Way by making its nature manifest to the very senses as well as to the intellect. Similarly it will be a pleasant and elegant thing to demonstrate that the nature of those stars which astronomers have previously called "nebulous" is far different from what has been believed hitherto. But what surpasses all wonders by far, and what particularly moves us to seek the attention of all astronomers and philosophers, is the discovery of four wandering stars not known or observed by any man before us. Like Venus and Mercury, which have their own periods about the sun, these have theirs about a certain star that is conspicuous among those already known, which they sometimes precede and sometimes follow, without ever departing from it beyond certain limits. All these facts were discovered and observed by me not many days ago with the aid of a spyglass which I devised, after first being illuminated by divine grace. Perhaps other things, still more remarkable, will in time be discovered by me or by other observers with the aid of such an instrument, the form and construction of which I shall first briefly explain, as well as the occasion of its having been devised. Afterwards I shall relate the story of the observations I have made.

About ten months ago a report reached my ears that a certain Fleming had constructed a spyglass by means of which visible objects, though very distant from the eye of the observer, were distinctly seen as if nearby. Of this truly remarkable effect several experiences were related, to which some persons gave credence while others denied them. A few days later the report was con-firmed to me in a letter from a noble Frenchman at Paris, Jacques Badovere, which caused me to apply myself wholeheartedly to inquire into the means by which I might arrive at the invention of a similar instrument. This I did shortly afterwards, my basis being the theory of refraction. First I prepared a tube of lead, at the ends of which I fitted two glass lenses, both plane on one side while on the other side one was spherically convex and the other concave. Then placing my eye near the concave lens I perceived objects satisfactorily large and near, for they appeared three times closer and nine times larger than when seen with the naked eye alone. Next I constructed another one, more accurate, which represented objects as enlarged more than sixty times. Finally, sparing neither labor nor expense, I succeeded in constructing for myself so excellent an instrument that objects seen by means of it appeared nearly one thousand times larger and over thirty times closer than when regarded with our natural vision.

It would be superfluous to enumerate the number and importance of the advantages of such an instrument at sea as well as on land. But forsaking terrestrial observations, I turned to celestial ones, and first I saw the moon from as near at hand as if it were scarcely two terrestrial radii away. After that I observed often with wondering delight both the planets and the fixed stars, and since I saw these latter to be very crowded, I began to seek (and eventually found) a method by which I might measure their distances apart.

Here it is appropriate to convey certain cautions to all who intend to undertake observations of this sort, for in the first place it is necessary to prepare quite a perfect telescope, which will show all objects bright, distinct, and free from any haziness, while magnifying them at least four hundred times and thus showing them twenty times closer. Unless the instrument is of this kind it will be vain to attempt to observe all the things which I have seen in the heavens, and which will presently be set forth. Now in order to determine without much trouble the magnifying power of an instrument, trace on paper the contour of two circles or two squares of which one is four hundred times as large as the other, as it will be when the diameter of one is twenty times that of the other. Then, with both these figures attached to the same wall, observe them simultaneously from a distance, looking at the smaller one through the telescope and at the larger one with the other eye unaided. This may be done without inconvenience while holding both eyes open at the same time; the two figures will appear to be of the same size if the instrument magnifies objects in the desired proportion.

Such an instrument having been prepared, we seek a method of measuring distances apart. This we shall accomplish by the following contrivance.

Let ABCD be the tube and E be the eye of the observer. Then if there were no lenses in the tube, the rays would reach the object FG along the straight lines ECF and EDG. But when the lenses have been inserted, the rays go along the refracted lines ECH and EDI; thus they are brought closer together, and those which were previously directed freely to the object FG now include only the portion of it HI. The ratio of the distance EH to the line HI then being found, one may by means of a table of sines determine the size of the angle formed at the eye by the object HI, which we shall find to be but a few minutes of arc. Now, if to the lens CD we fit thin plates, some pierced with larger and some with smaller apertures, putting now one plate and now another over the lens as required, we may form at pleasure different angles subtending more or fewer minutes of arc, and by this means we may easily measure the intervals between stars which are but a few minutes apart, with no greater error than one or two minutes. And for the present let it suffice that we have touched lightly on these matters and scarcely more than mentioned them, as on some other occasion we shall explain the entire theory of this instrument.

*   *   *

Deserving of notice also is the difference between the appearances of the planets and of the fixed stars. The planets show their globes perfectly round and definitely bounded, looking like little moons, spherical and flooded all over with light; the fixed stars are never seen to be bounded by a circular periphery, but have rather the aspect of blazes whose rays vibrate about them and scintillate a great deal. Viewed with a telescope they appear of a shape similar to that which they present to the naked eye, but sufficiently enlarged so that a star of the fifth or sixth magnitude seems to equal the Dog Star, largest of all the fixed stars. Now, in addition to stars of the sixth magnitude, a host of other stars are perceived through the telescope which escape the naked eye; these are so numerous as almost to surpass belief. One may, in fact, see more of them than all the stars included among the first six magnitudes. The largest of these, which we may call stars of the seventh magnitude, or the first magnitude of invisible stars, appear through the telescope as larger and brighter than stars of the second magnitude when the latter are viewed with the naked eye. In order to give one or two proofs of their almost inconceivable number, I have adjoined pictures of two constellations. With these as samples, you may judge of all the others.

From The Assayer

*   *   *

In Sarsi I seem to discern the firm belief that in philosophizing one must support oneself upon the opinion of some celebrated author, as if our minds ought to remain completely sterile and barren unless wedded to the reasoning of some other person. Possibly he thinks that philosophy is a book of fiction by some writer, like the *Iliad* or *Orlando Furioso*, productions in which the least important thing is whether what is written there is true. Well, Sarsi, that is not how matters stand. Philosophy is written in this grand book, the universe, which stands continually open to our gaze. But the book cannot be understood unless one first learns to comprehend the language and read the letters in which it is composed. It is written in the language of mathematics, and its characters are triangles, circles, and other geometric figures without which it is humanly impossible to understand a single word of it; without these, one wanders about in a dark labyrinth.

Sarsi seems to think that our intellect should be enslaved to that of some other man. . . . But even on that assumption, I do not see why he selects Tycho. . . . Tycho could not extricate himself from his own explanation of diversity in the apparent motion of his comet; but now Sarsi expects my mind to be satisfied and set at rest by a little poetic flower that is not followed by any fruit at all. It is this that Guiducci rejected when he quite rightly said that nature takes no delight in poetry. That is a very true statement, even though Sarsi appears to disbelieve it and acts as if acquainted with neither nature nor poetry. He seems not to know that fables and fictions are in a way essential to poetry, which could not exist without them, while any sort of falsehood is so abhorrent to nature that it is as absent there as darkness is in light.

*   *   *

REVIEW QUESTIONS

1. How does a telescope work? What is its relation to human sight?
2. What does Galileo "see"? What does he "discern"?
3. What are the two books for Galileo?
4. What is the relation of one to the other?
5. What are the implications of Galileo's assertion, that understanding depends on how one reads the book of the universe?

BLAISE PASCAL

FROM *Pensées*

Blaise Pascal (1623–1662) was the son of a French official. During his life, he dabbled in many subjects, including science, religion, and literature. His conversion to Jansenism plunged him into controversy with the Jesuits, giving rise to his Lettres provinciales. *These, along with his* Pensées, *from which the following selection is drawn, established his literary fame. His thought contained a fascinating blend of confidence in human reason and consciousness of its limits. Descartes viewed Pascal as the embodiment of a mentality of intellectual and spiritual crisis. Be that as it may, Pascal is also considered one of the great stylists of the French language.*

From *Pensées* by Blaise Pascal, translated by A. J. Krailsheimer, translation copyright © 1966 by Penguin Books Ltd., pp. 58–64, 121–125. Reproduced by permission of Penguin Books Ltd.

*   *   *

XV. Transition from Knowledge of Man to Knowledge of God

Prejudice leading to error. It is deplorable to see everybody debating about the means, never the end. Everyone thinks about how he will get on in his career, but when it comes to choosing a career or a country it is fate that decides for us.

It is pitiful to see so many Turks, heretics, unbelievers follow in their fathers' footsteps, solely because they have all been brought up to believe that this is the best course. This is what makes each of us pick his particular career as locksmith, soldier, etc.

That is why savages do not care about Provence.

Why have limits been set upon my knowledge, my height, my life, making it a hundred rather than a thousand years? For what reason did nature make it so, and choose this rather than that mean from the whole of infinity, when there is no more reason to choose one rather than another, as none is more attractive than another?

Little of everything. As we cannot be universal by knowing everything there is to be known about everything, we must know a little about everything, because it is much better to know something about everything than everything about something. Such universality is the finest. It would be still better if we could have both together, but, if a choice must be made, this is the one to choose. The world knows this and does so, for the world is often a good judge.

Some fancy makes me dislike people who croak or who puff while eating. Fancy carries a lot of weight. What good will that do us? That we indulge it because it is natural? No, rather that we resist it.

There is no better proof of human vanity than to consider the causes and effects of love, because the whole universe can be changed by it. Cleopatra's nose.

When I see the blind and wretched state of man, when I survey the whole universe in its dumbness and man left to himself with no light, as though lost in this corner of the universe, without knowing who put him there, what he has come to do, what will become of him when he dies, incapable of knowing anything, I am moved to terror, like a man transported in his sleep to some terrifying desert island, who wakes up quite lost and with no means of escape. Then I marvel that so wretched a state does not drive people to despair. I see other people around me, made like myself. I ask them if they are any better informed than I, and they say they are not. Then these lost and wretched creatures look around and find some attractive objects to which they become addicted and attached. For my part I have never been able to form such attachments, and considering how very likely it is that there exists something besides what I can see, I have tried to find out whether God has left any traces of himself.

I see a number of religions in conflict, and therefore all false, except one. Each of them wishes to be believed on its own authority and threatens unbelievers. I do not believe them on that account. Anyone can say that. Anyone can call himself a prophet, but I see Christianity, and find its prophecies, which are not something that anyone can do.

Disproportion of man. This is where unaided knowledge brings us. If it is not true, there is no truth in man, and if it is true, he has good cause to feel humiliated; in either case he is obliged to humble himself.

And, since he cannot exist without believing this knowledge, before going on to a wider inquiry concerning nature, I want him to consider nature just once, seriously and at leisure, and to look at himself as well, and judge whether there is any proportion between himself and nature by comparing the two.

Let man then contemplate the whole of nature in her full and lofty majesty, let him turn his gaze away from the lowly objects around him; let him behold the dazzling light set like an eternal lamp to light up the universe, let him see the earth as a mere speck compared to the vast orbit described by this star, and let him marvel at finding this vast orbit itself to be no more than the tiniest point compared to that described by the stars revolving in the firmament. But if our eyes stop there, let our imagination proceed further; it will grow weary of conceiving things before nature tires of producing them. The whole visible world is only an imperceptible dot in nature's ample bosom. No idea comes near it; it is no good inflating our conceptions beyond imaginable space, we only bring forth atoms compared to the reality of things. Nature is an infinite sphere whose centre is everywhere and circumference nowhere. In short it is the greatest perceptible mark of God's omnipotence that our imagination should lose itself in that thought.

Let man, returning to himself, consider what he is in comparison with what exists; let him regard himself as lost, and from this little dungeon, in which he finds himself lodged, I mean the universe, let him learn to take the earth, its realms, its cities, its houses and himself at their proper value.

What is a man in the infinite?

But, to offer him another prodigy equally astounding, let him look into the tiniest things he knows. Let a mite show him in its minute body incomparably more minute parts, legs with joints, veins in its legs, blood in the veins, humours in the blood, drops in the humours, vapours in the drops: let him divide these things still further until he has exhausted his powers of imagination, and let the last thing he comes down to now be the subject of our discourse. He will perhaps think that this is the ultimate of minuteness in nature.

I want to show him a new abyss. I want to depict to him not only the visible universe, but all the conceivable immensity of nature enclosed in this miniature atom. Let him see there an infinity of universes, each with its firmament, its planets, its earth, in the same proportions as in the visible world, and on that earth animals, and finally mites, in which he will find again the same results as in the first; and finding the same thing yet again in the others without end or respite, he will be lost in such wonders, as astounding in their minuteness as the others in their amplitude. For who will not marvel that our body, a moment ago imperceptible in a universe, itself imperceptible in the bosom of the whole, should now be a colossus, a world, or rather a whole, compared to the nothingness beyond our reach? Anyone who considers himself in this way will be terrified at himself, and, seeing his mass, as given him by nature, supporting him between these two abysses of infinity and nothingness, will tremble at these marvels. I believe that with his curiosity changing into wonder he will be more disposed to contemplate them in silence than investigate them with presumption.

For, after all, what is man in nature? A nothing compared to the infinite, a whole compared to the nothing, a middle point between all and nothing, infinitely remote from an understanding of the extremes; the end of things and their principles are unattainably hidden from him in impenetrable secrecy.

Equally incapable of seeing the nothingness from which he emerges and the infinity in which he is engulfed.

What else can he do, then, but perceive some semblance of the middle of things, eternally hopeless of knowing either their principles or their end? All things have come out of nothingness and are carried onwards to infinity. Who can follow these astonishing processes? The author of these wonders understands them: no one else can.

Because they failed to contemplate these infinities, men have rashly undertaken to probe into nature as if there were some proportion between themselves and her.

Strangely enough they wanted to know the principles of things and go on from there to know everything, inspired by a presumption as infinite as their object. For there can be no doubt that such a plan could not be conceived without infinite presumption or a capacity as infinite as that of nature.

When we know better, we understand that, since nature has engraved her own image and that of her author on all things, they almost all share her double infinity. Thus we see that all the sciences are infinite in the range of their researches, for who can doubt that mathematics, for instance, has an infinity of infinities of propositions to expound? They are infinite also in the multiplicity and subtlety of their principles, for anyone can see that those which are supposed to be ultimate do not stand by themselves, but depend on others, which depend on others again, and thus never allow of any finality.

But we treat as ultimate those which seem so to our reason, as in material things we call a point indivisible when our senses can perceive nothing beyond it, although by its nature it is infinitely divisible.

Of these two infinites of science, that of greatness is much more obvious, and that is why it has occurred to few people to claim that they know everything. 'I am going to speak about everything,' Democritus used to say.

But the infinitely small is much harder to see. The philosophers have much more readily claimed to have reached it, and that is where they have all tripped up. This is the origin of such familiar titles as *Of the principles of things, Of the principles of philosophy*, and the like, which are really as pretentious, though they do not look it, as this blatant one: *Of all that can be known.*

We naturally believe we are more capable of reaching the centre of things than of embracing their circumference, and the visible extent of the world is visibly greater than we. But since we in our turn are greater than small things, we think we are more capable of mastering them, and yet it takes no less capacity to reach nothingness than the whole. In either case it takes an infinite capacity, and it seems to me that anyone who had understood the ultimate principles of things might also succeed in knowing infinity. One depends on

the other, and one leads to the other. These extremes touch and join by going in opposite directions, and they meet in God and God alone.

Let us then realize our limitations. We are something and we are not everything. Such being as we have conceals from us the knowledge of first principles, which arise from nothingness, and the smallness of our being hides infinity from our sight.

Our intelligence occupies the same rank in the order of intellect as our body in the whole range of nature.

Limited in every respect, we find this intermediate state between two extremes reflected in all our faculties. Our senses can perceive nothing extreme; too much noise deafens us, too much light dazzles; when we are too far or too close we cannot see properly; an argument is obscured by being too long or too short; too much truth bewilders us. I know people who cannot understand that 4 from 0 leaves 0. First principles are too obvious for us; too much pleasure causes discomfort; too much harmony in music is displeasing; too much kindness annoys us: we want to be able to pay back the debt with something over. *Kindness is welcome to the extent that it seems the debt can be paid back. When it goes too far gratitude turns into hatred.*

We feel neither extreme heat nor extreme cold. Qualities carried to excess are bad for us and cannot be perceived; we no longer feel them, we suffer them. Excessive youth and excessive age impair thought; so do too much and too little learning.

In a word, extremes are as if they did not exist for us nor we for them; they escape us or we escape them.

Such is our true state. That is what makes us incapable of certain knowledge or absolute ignorance. We are floating in a medium of vast extent, always drifting uncertainly, blown to and fro; whenever we think we have a fixed point to which we can cling and make fast, it shifts and leaves us behind; if we follow it, it eludes our grasp, slips away, and flees eternally before us. Nothing stands still for us. This is our natural state and yet the state most contrary to our inclinations. We burn with desire to find a firm footing, an ultimate, lasting base on which to build a tower rising up to infinity, but our whole foundation cracks and the earth opens up into the depth of the abyss.

Let us then seek neither assurance nor stability; our reason is always deceived by the inconsistency of appearances; nothing can fix the finite between the two infinites which enclose and evade it.

Once that is clearly understood, I think that each of us can stay quietly in the state in which nature has placed him. Since the middle station allotted to us is always far from the extremes, what does it matter if someone else has a slightly better understanding of things? If he has, and if he takes them a little further, is he not still infinitely remote from the goal? Is not our span of life equally infinitesimal in eternity, even if it is extended by ten years?

In the perspective of these infinites, all finites are equal and I see no reason to settle our imagination on one rather than another. Merely comparing ourselves with the finite is painful.

If man studied himself, he would see how incapable he is of going further. How could a part possibly know the whole? But perhaps he will aspire to know at least the parts to which he bears some proportion. But the parts of the world are all so related and linked together that I think it is impossible to know one without the other and without the whole.

There is, for example, a relationship between man and all he knows. He needs space to contain him, time to exist in, motion to be alive, elements to constitute him, warmth and food for nourishment, air to breathe. He sees light, he feels bodies, everything in short is related to him. To understand man therefore one must know why he needs air to live, and to understand air one must know how it comes to be thus related to the life of man, etc.

Flame cannot exist without air, so, to know one, one must know the other.

Thus, since all things are both caused or caus-

ing, assisted and assisting, mediate and immediate, providing mutual support in a chain linking together naturally and imperceptibly the most distant and different things, I consider it as impossible to know the parts without knowing the whole as to know the whole without knowing the individual parts.

The eternity of things in themselves or in God must still amaze our brief span of life.

The fixed and constant immobility of nature, compared to the continual changes going on in us, must produce the same effect.

And what makes our inability to know things absolute is that they are simple in themselves, while we are composed of two opposing natures of different kinds, soul and body. For it is impossible for the part of us which reasons to be anything but spiritual, and even if it were claimed that we are simply corporeal, that would still more preclude us from knowing things, since there is nothing so inconceivable as the idea that matter knows itself. We cannot possibly know how it could know itself.

Thus, if we are simply material, we can know nothing at all, and, if we are composed of mind and matter, we cannot have perfect knowledge of things which are simply spiritual or corporeal.

That is why nearly all philosophers confuse their ideas of things, and speak spiritually of corporeal things and corporeally of spiritual ones, for they boldly assert that bodies tend to fall, that they aspire towards their centre, that they flee from destruction, that they fear a void, that they have inclinations, sympathies, antipathies, all things pertaining only to things spiritual. And when they speak of minds, they consider them as being in a place, and attribute to them movement from one place to another, which are things pertaining only to bodies.

Instead of receiving ideas of these things in their purity, we colour them with our qualities and stamp our own composite being on all the simple things we contemplate.

Who would not think, to see us compounding everything of mind and matter, that such a mixture is perfectly intelligible to us? Yet this is the thing we understand least; man is to himself the greatest prodigy in nature, for he cannot conceive what body is, and still less what mind is, and least of all how a body can be joined to a mind. This is his supreme difficulty, and yet it is his very being. *The way in which minds are attached to bodies is beyond man's understanding, and yet this is what man is.*

*   *   *

REVIEW QUESTIONS

1. What is the relation between universality and infinity?
2. Why does Pascal advocate the former?
3. Why can humans not know everything? What does Pascal's contention that nature is an infinite sphere teach us about human knowledge?
4. Why does nature hold forth abysses to human knowledge?
5. How has Pascal's concept of infinity, used earlier as a concept by which human beings might approach knowledge of God, changed in this passage?

RENÉ DESCARTES

FROM *Discourse on Method and Meditations on First Philosophy*

René Descartes (1596–1650) was born of a family of the judicial nobility. He graduated in 1612 from the Collège La Flèche and received a law degree in 1616 from the University of Poitiers. From 1616 until 1624, he saw military service in the Thirty Years' War. During the winter of 1620, while quartered near Ulm, Descartes claimed to have achieved the philosophical insights that would form the basis of his entire system of rational thought. In 1628 he left France, for reasons that are not clear, and returned only for relatively brief periods of time. Until 1649, he lived in the United Provinces of the Netherlands. There, with the publication of the Discourse on Method in 1637, he began to make public the ideas first glimpsed in 1620, the systematic philosophy that would make him famous. His was one of the three great systems rationalism of the seventeenth century, along with those created by Spinoza and Liebniz. Reacting to the skepticism of the early seventeenth century, represented by the thought of philosophers like Pascal, Descartes decided to subject every idea to critical scrutiny and retain as true only those ideas that were "self-evident." The result was a geometric method of reasoning that consisted of four simple rules: to start only with clear and distinct ideas; to simplify any difficulty in thinking by dividing it into small parts; to think in an orderly process from simplest to most complex; and to make thorough evaluations that overlook no part of the problem. The Cartesian method gained enthusiastic popular support and served as an important stimulus for the science of the Enlightenment.

*   *   *

It is now three years since I completed the treatise containing all these things, and I was beginning to revise it so as to be able to put it into the hands of a printer when I learned that persons to whom I defer, and whose authority over my actions is hardly less influential than my own reason over my thoughts, had disapproved of an opinion in a matter of physics, published a little earlier by another person, of which opinion I would not say that I was, but that I had not observed anything in it, before their having censured it, that I could have imagined to be prejudicial either to religion or to the State, or which, consequently, might have stopped me from writing it if reason had persuaded me it was correct; and this made me fear that there might likewise be among my own opinions some one in which I had been mistaken, notwithstanding the great care I have always taken never to accept any new beliefs for which I had not most certain proofs and never to write about any which might be the occasion of disturbance for anyone. This has been sufficient to make me feel obliged in conscience to alter the resolution I had made to publish them. For, although the reasons I had for taking the decision to publish earlier were very strong, my natural inclination, which has always made me hate the business of writing books, made me immediately find sufficient other reasons for not publishing. And these reasons, both for and against, are such, that not only is it to some extent my interest to set them down here, but perhaps also that of the public to know them.

I have never set much store on the things which have come from my own mind, and so long as I reaped no other harvest from the method that I use, apart from satisfying myself about certain difficulties in the field of the speculative sciences, or trying to regulate my conduct according to the precepts which the method taught me, I never considered myself to be under an obligation to write anything about it. For, as far as behaviour is concerned, everyone is so sure that he knows best, that as many reformers as heads might be found, if it were permitted to any to undertake to make changes in it, apart from those whom God had established as rulers over his peoples, or to whom he has given sufficient grace and zeal to be prophets; and although I was very well pleased with my speculations, I believed that others had their own which perhaps pleased them even more. But, as soon as I had acquired some general ideas about physics, and, beginning to test them on various particular difficulties, I observed how far they can lead and how they differ from the principles which have been used up to now, I believed I could not keep them hidden without sinning considerably against the law which obliges us to procure, by as much as is in us, the general good of all men. For they have made me see that it is possible to arrive at knowledge which is most useful in life, and that, instead of the speculative philosophy taught in the Schools, a practical philosophy can be found by which, knowing the power and the effects of fire, water, air, the stars, the heavens and all the other bodies which surround us, as distinctly as we know the various trades of our craftsmen, we might put them in the same way to all the uses for which they are appropriate, and thereby make ourselves, as it were, masters and possessors of nature. Which aim is not only to be desired for the invention of an infinity of devices by which we might enjoy, without any effort, the fruits of the earth and all its commodities, but also principally for the preservation of health, which is undoubtedly the first good, and the foundation of all the other goods of this life; for even the mind depends so much on the temperament and on the disposition of the organs of the body, that if it is possible to find some means of rendering men as a whole wiser and more dexterous than they have been hitherto, I believe it must be sought in medicine. It is true that the medicine practised now contains little of notable use; but without intending to do it any dishonour, I am sure there is no one, even among those who practise it, who does not admit that what is known of it is almost nothing compared to what remains to be known, and that we could free ourselves of an infinity of illnesses, both of the body and of the mind, and even perhaps also of the decline of age, if we knew enough about their causes and about all the remedies with which nature has provided us. So, intending to devote my whole life in the search for so necessary a science, and having come across a path which seems to me such that, by following it, one must inevitably find one's goal, provided one is not prevented either by the shortness of life or by the lack of experiments, I judged that there was no better remedy against these two obstacles than faithfully to communicate to the public all the little I had found, and to urge good minds to try to go beyond this in contributing, each according to his inclination and his capacity, to the experiments which must be made, and communicating also to the public everything they learned; so that, the last beginning where their predecessors had left off, and thereby linking the lives and the labours of many, we might all together go much further than each man could individually.

Moreover I noticed, concerning experiments, that they are all the more necessary the more one is advanced in knowledge. For, to begin with, it is better to use only what presents itself spontaneously to our senses and of which we cannot remain ignorant provided we give it even a moment's reflection, than to seek out more rare and more abstruse phenomena; the reason for this is that these rarer ones are often misleading when one does not yet know the causes of the commoner ones, and that the circumstances on which

they depend are almost always so special and so minute that they are very difficult to detect. But the order that I have adhered to in this has been as follows: firstly, I have tried to find in general the principles or first causes of everything which is, or which may be, in the world, without considering to this end anything but God alone, who has created it, or taking them from any other source than from certain seeds of truths which are naturally in our minds. After that, I examined what were the first and most ordinary effects that could be deduced from these causes, and it seems to me that in this way I have found heavens, stars, an earth, and even on the earth water, air, fire, minerals and other similar things, which are the most common and simplest of all, and consequently the easiest to know. But, when I wanted to come down to those which were more particular, so many different ones presented themselves to me, that I did not believe it possible for the human mind to distinguish the forms or species of bodies which are on the earth, from an infinity of others which might have been there, if it had been the will of God to put them there, or, consequently, to apply them to our use, unless we reach for causes through effects and make use of many particular experiments. Following which, turning over in my mind all the objects which had ever been presented to my senses, I dare to state that I observed nothing that I could not easily enough explain by means of the principles I had found. But I must also admit that the power of nature is so ample and so vast, and that these principles are so simple and so general, that I observe almost no individual effect without immediately knowing that it can be deduced in many different ways, and that my greatest difficulty is ordinarily to find in which of these ways the effect depends upon them; for to this end I know no other expedient but then to seek certain experiments which are such that their result will not be the same if it is in one of these ways that the explanation lies as if it lies in another. Moreover, I have reached the point at which I see well enough, it seems to me, how to go about making most of those experiments which serve this purpose; but I see also that they are such and in so great a number, that neither my hands nor my income, even if I were to have a thousand times more than I have, would suffice for all of them; so that, according to the means I shall henceforth have of doing more or less of them, I shall advance to a greater or lesser degree in knowledge of nature. This is what I promised myself to make known by the treatise which I had written, and to show in it so clearly the use the public could derive from it, that I would oblige all those who wish for the general well-being of men, that is to say, all those who are truly virtuous and not simply in appearance or who merely profess to be so, both to communicate to me the experiments they have already made and to help me to investigate those which remain to be done.

But since then I have had other reasons to change my mind and to think that I ought indeed to continue to record everything I judged to be of some importance, as I discovered the truth about them, and to bring to the task the same care as if I wished to publish. This as much in order to have the greater opportunity of examining them thoroughly, for there is no doubt that one always looks more closely at what one thinks will be seen by many people than at what one does only for oneself—and often the things which have seemed true when I first conceived them have appeared false when I committed them to paper—as in order to lose no opportunity of being useful to the public, if I can, so that, if my writings are worth anything, those who have them after my death may use them as they think most appropriate. But I decided that I could in no way consent to their publication in my lifetime, so that neither the oppositions nor the controversies of which they might be the object, nor even whatever reputation they might gain for me, would give me any occasion to waste the time I intend to use in acquiring knowledge. For, although it is true that every man is obliged to promote the good of others, as far as it is in him to do so, and that to be no use to anyone is really to be worthless, it is none the less true also that our solicitude ought to extend beyond the present time, and that it is

good to omit doing things which might perhaps bring some profit to those who are living, when one aims to do other things which will be of greater benefit to posterity. And, in truth, I will not hide the fact that the little I have learned so far is almost nothing compared to what I do not know, and to what I do not despair of being able to learn; for it is almost the same with those who discover truth in the sciences little by little, as with those who, becoming rich, have less trouble in making great acquisitions, than they had earlier, when poorer, in making much smaller ones. Or they can be compared to leaders of armies, whose forces usually grow in proportion to their victories, and who need more skill to maintain themselves after losing a battle than they need, after a victory, to take towns and provinces. For he indeed fights battles who tries to overcome all the difficulties and errors which prevent him from arriving at the knowledge of truth, and he loses a battle when he accepts some false opinion in a subject which is of some generality and importance. It takes much more skill afterwards to recover one's former position than it takes to make great progress when one is already in possession of principles which are assured. For myself, if I have already found any truths in the sciences (and I hope the things contained in this volume will prove that I have found a few), I can say that they are only the results and consequences of five or six principal difficulties which I have overcome, and that I count as so many battles in which I had victory on my side. I will not even fear to say that I believe I need only to win two or three more like them in order to reach completely my goal, and that I am not so advanced in age that, according to the ordinary course of nature, I may not still have enough leisure to this end. But I consider myself all the more obliged to organize prudently the time which remains to me, the greater hope I have of being able to use it well, and no doubt I should have many opportunities of wasting time if I were to publish the principles of my physics. For although they are almost all so evident that one has only to understand them to accept them, and although there is not one among them which I do not think I could demonstrate, yet, as it is impossible that they should be in accord with all the various opinions of others, I foresee that I would frequently be distracted by the oppositions they would engender.

One may say that these oppositions would be useful both in making me aware of my errors, and, if I had something sound to say, in better acquainting others with it; and as many men can see more than one man, by beginning henceforth to use my principles, they might help me in turn with their own discoveries. But although I recognize my extreme liability to error, and almost never trust the first thoughts which come to me, nevertheless the experience I have had of objections which may be made to my views, prevents me from expecting any profit from them. For I have already often experienced the judgements, both of those I have taken to be my friends and of some others to whom I thought I was an object of indifference, and even also of some whose malice and envy would make them try to reveal what partiality hid from my friends; but it has rarely happened that any objection has been put forward that I had not altogether foreseen, unless it were far removed from my subject, so that I have hardly ever encountered any critic of my opinions who did not seem either less exacting or less equitable than myself. And, moreover, I have never noticed that, by the method of disputation practised in the Schools, any truth has been discovered of which one was ignorant before. For, while each strives after victory, he is much more preoccupied in making the best of verisimilitudes than in weighing the reasons on both sides; and those who have been good advocates for a long time are not, for all that, subsequently better judges.

As for the usefulness to others of the communication of my thoughts, it could not be very great, inasmuch as I have not yet taken them so far that much does not need to be added to them before they could be applied in practice. And I think I can say without vanity that, if there is anyone capable of bringing them to this point, it must be myself rather than any other; not that there may not be in the world many minds in-

comparably better than mine, but because one cannot so well grasp a thing and make it one's own when it is learnt from another person, as when one discovers it oneself. This is so true of this matter that, although I have often explained some of my opinions to people of good mind, and who, while I was speaking to them, seemed to understand most distinctly, yet, when they repeated these opinions, I have noticed that they almost always change them in such a way that I could no longer acknowledge them as mine; I am glad to take this opportunity to ask future generations never to believe that the things people tell them come from me, unless I myself have published them; and I am not in the least astonished at the extravagances attributed to all those ancient philosophers whose writings we do not have, neither do I judge on that account that their thoughts were extremely unreasonable, seeing that they were the best brains of their time, but only that they have been misrepresented to us. For one sees also that it has almost never happened that any one of their disciples has surpassed them; and I am convinced that the most devoted of those who now follow Aristotle would think themselves happy if they had as much knowledge of nature as he had, even if it were a condition that they would never have more. They are like the ivy which does not seek to climb higher than the trees which support it, and which even often comes down again after reaching the top; for it seems to me that those people come down again, that is to say, become in some way less learned than if they abstained from study, who, not content with knowing all that is intelligibly explained in their author, wish, in addition, to find in him the solution of many difficulties of which he says nothing and about which he perhaps never thought. However, their fashion of philosophizing is most convenient for those who have only very mediocre minds; for the obscurity of the distinctions and principles which they use enables them to speak about all things as boldly as if they really knew them, and to maintain everything they say against the subtlest and most skilful, without anyone being able to convince them of their error. In this they seem to me like a blind man who, in order to fight a person who can see, without disadvantage, brings him into the depths of a very dark cellar; and I may say that these people have an interest in my abstention from publishing the principles of the philosophy I use, for, as these principles are very simple and evident, I would be doing almost the same, in publishing them, as if I opened a few windows and let the light of day into this cellar into which they have descended in order to fight. But even the best minds have no reason to wish to know these principles, for, if they wish to be able to talk about all things, and to acquire the reputation of being learned, they will achieve this more easily by contenting themselves with verisimilitudes, which can be found without much trouble in all kinds of matters, than by seeking the truth, which is revealed only little by little and in a few matters, and which, when other matters arise, obliges one to confess frankly one's ignorance. If, however, they prefer knowledge of a handful of truths to the vanity of appearing to be ignorant of none, as is undoubtedly preferable, and if they agree to follow a course similar to mine, they do not need me to say anything more, for this purpose, than I have already said in this discourse. For, if they are capable of going further than I have, they will be capable also, *a fortiori*, of discovering for themselves all that I think I have found; especially as, never having examined anything except in order, it is certain that what remains for me to discover is in itself more difficult and more remote than what I have encountered up to now, and it would give them much less pleasure to learn it from me than for themselves. Besides, the habit they will acquire in seeking first easy things, and passing little by degrees to other more difficult things, will be of more use to them than all my instructions could be. As for me, I am persuaded that if I had been taught from youth all the truths of which I have since sought demonstrations, and had had no trouble in learning them, I might never have known any others; at least I should never have acquired the habit and facility which I think I have of ever discovering new truths, according as I ap-

ply myself to looking for them. And, in a word, if there is any task in the world which cannot be completed by any other person as well as it can by the person who began it, it is that at which I am working.

It is true that, concerning the experiments which may serve this purpose, one man alone could not suffice to perform them all; but equally he could not usefully employ other hands than his own, unless those of artisans or such people as he could pay, and whom the hope of gain, which is a very effective means, would cause to perform accurately all the things which he laid down for them. For, as for the volunteers who would perhaps offer to help him, out of curiosity or the wish to learn, apart from being usually more full of promises than they are effective, and having only fine ideas of which none ever comes to anything, they would inevitably wish to be recompensed by the explanation of certain difficulties, or at least by compliments and useless conversations which could not cost him so little of his time that he would not lose by it. And as for the experiments already made by others, even if these people wish to communicate them to him, which those who consider them as secrets would never do, they are for the most part made up of so many circumstances and superfluous considerations that it would cause him no small difficulty to disentangle what truth they contain; besides, he would find almost all of them so badly explained or even so false, because those who made them have attempted to make them appear in conformity with their principles, that, even if there were a few which he could make use of, they could not be worth the time he would have to employ in selecting them. So that, if there were someone in the world whom one knew certainly to be capable of discovering the greatest, and most useful discoveries, and if therefore other men made every effort to help him achieve his designs, I do not see that they could do anything for him except to contribute to the cost of the experiments he would need to do, and for the rest, to prevent his leisure from being taken away from him by the importunity of anyone. But, while not being so presumptuous as to be willing to promise anything extraordinary, or feeding myself on such vain fancies as to imagine that the public must be much interested in my plans, I do not, on the other hand, have so base a soul as to wish to accept from anyone whatsoever any favour that I might not be deemed to have merited.

All these considerations, added together, were the reason why, three years ago, I did not wish to publish the treatise which I had on hand, and why I even resolved not to reveal any other during my lifetime, which was so general, or from which the foundations of my physics might be understood. But there have been since then two other reasons which have compelled me to set down here some particular specimens and to give the public some account of my actions and my plans. The first of these is that, if I omitted to do so, many people who have known of my earlier intention to publish some writings might imagine that the reasons why I have not done so are more dishonourable to me than they are. For, although I have no excessive love of fame, or even, if I dare say so, though I hate it, in so far as I judge it to be contrary to repose which I value above everything, yet, at the same time, I have never tried to conceal my actions as if they were crimes, neither have I taken much precaution to be unknown; and this as much because I should have thought I would be doing myself an injustice, as because it would have given me some sort of disquiet, which would again have been contrary to the perfect peace of mind which I seek. And since, while being thus indifferent to being known or not, I have been unable to avoid acquiring some sort of reputation, I thought I ought to do my best at least to save myself from having a bad one. The other reason which has compelled me to put pen to paper is that, becoming daily more and more conscious of the delay which my plan of self-instruction is suffering, owing to the vast number of experiments which I need to make, and which it is impossible for me to do without help from others, although I do not flatter myself so much as to hope that the public will take a great share in my interests, I am yet unwilling to default so much in my own

cause, as to give those who will survive me reason to reproach me one day for not having left them many things in a much better state than I have done, if I had not too much neglected to acquaint them of the ways in which they could have contributed to my designs.

And I thought that it was easy for me to choose some matters which, without being too much open to controversy, or obliging me to make known more of my principles than I wished, would yet show clearly enough what I can or cannot do in the sciences. I cannot say whether I have succeeded in this or not, and I do not wish to prejudice anyone's judgement by speaking myself of my writings; but I would be very pleased if they were to be examined, and, so that people may feel all the more free to do so, I beg all those who have any objections to make to them, to take the trouble to send them to my publisher, and, on being advised of them by him, I shall try to publish at the same time both the objection and my reply; and, by this means, readers, seeing both together, may judge the truth all the more easily. For I do not promise ever to give long answers, but only to admit my mistakes most frankly, if I perceive them, or, if I cannot, to say simply what I believe to be necessary for the defence of what I have written, without introducing the explanation of any new matter so as to avoid engaging myself in endless discussion from one topic to another.

And if some of the matters of which I have spoken at the beginning of the *Dioptrics* and *Meteorics* shock the reader at first sight, because I call them hypotheses, and do not seem to want to prove them, I request him to read the whole patiently and attentively, and I hope that he will be satisfied; for it seems to me that my reasonings follow each other in such a way that, as the last are demonstrated by the first, which are their causes, the first are proved, reciprocally, by the last, which are their effects. And one must not imagine that in this matter I commit the fallacy which logicians call a circle, for, experience rendering most of these effects very certain, the causes from which I deduce them do not serve so much to prove as to explain them; on the contrary, it is the reality of the causes which is proved by the reality of the effects. And I have called them hypotheses only so that it may be known that, while I think I can deduce them from these first truths which I have explained above, I have expressly decided not to do so, in order to prevent certain minds who imagine that they know in a day all that it has taken another person twenty years to think out, as soon as he has told them two or three words about it, and who are all the more liable to err, and the less capable of the truth the more penetrating and lively they are, from taking the opportunity to build some extravagant philosophy on what they believe to be my principles, and to avoid my being blamed for it. For, as to the opinions which are entirely mine, I offer no apology for their being new, since, if their reasons be properly examined, I am convinced that they will be found so simple and so in conformity with common sense that they will seem less extraordinary and less strange than any others one might have on the same subjects. Neither do I boast of being the first discoverer of any of them, but only of having accepted them, neither because they had been expressed by others, nor because they had not been, but only because reason convinced me of their truth. And if artisans are unable immediately to execute the invention which is explained in the *Dioptrics*, I do not believe one can say on that account that it is bad; for, inasmuch as skill and practice are needed to make and to adjust the machines that I have described, so that no detail is overlooked, I would be no less astonished if they succeeded at the first attempt than if someone were to learn in one day to play the lute with accomplishment merely because he had been given a good score. And if I write in French, which is the language of my country, rather than in Latin, which is that of my teachers, it is because I hope that those who use only their pure natural reason will be better judges of my opinions than those who believe only in the books of the ancients; and, as for those who unite good sense with

study, whom alone I wish to have for my judges, they will not, I feel sure, be so partial to Latin that they will refuse to hear my reasons because I express them in the vulgar tongue.

In conclusion, I do not wish to speak here in detail of the progress I hope to make in the sciences in the future nor to make any promise to the public that I am not certain of being able to fulfil; but I will say simply that I have resolved to devote the time left to me to live to no other occupation than that of trying to acquire some knowledge of Nature, which may be such as to enable us to deduce from it rules in medicine which are more assured than those we have had up to now; and that my inclination turns me away so strongly from all other sorts of projects, and particularly from those which can only be useful to some while being harmful to others, that if any situation arose in which I was forced to engage in such matters, I do not think that I would be able to succeed. On this, I here make a public declaration which I know very well cannot serve to make me of consequence in the world, but then I have no wish to be so; and I shall always hold myself more obliged to those by whose favour I enjoy my leisure unhindered, than to those who might offer me the highest dignities on earth.

*   *   *

REVIEW QUESTIONS

1. Why does Descartes not trust his own mind as a reasoning instrument?
2. What "method" does he propose, and what relationship exists between experience and knowledge?
3. Why are so many experiments and so much experience necessary to establish knowledge?
4. How is Descartes reminiscent of Montaigne?

ISAAC NEWTON

FROM *Mathematical Principles of Natural Philosophy*

Isaac Newton (1642–1727) created the great reformulation of seventeenth-century mechanical philosophy. Born of yeoman stock, his intellectual gifts were recognized early by a teacher and an uncle, who urged that Newton be prepared for a university education. He entered Trinity College, Cambridge, in 1661 and received his Bachelor of Arts in 1665 and his Master of Arts in 1668. The next year, Newton was appointed Lucasian professor, a position he held until 1701. As a natural philosopher, Newton agreed with Bacon that empiricism, that is, the gathering of experimental data, was the starting point for scientific inquiry. Yet he reserved a role for Cartesian rationalism by demonstrating the theoretical utility of mathematics in mechanical philosophy. In Mathematical Principles of Natural Philosophy *Newton laid out the quantitative framework of his mechanical philosophy and showed how it was possible, experimentally, to work with invisible bodies. In the following rules of reason, he offered a methodological guide to the study of reality.*

From *Mathematical Principles of Natural Philosophy, Volume II*, I. Newton, translated by Andrew Motte, Sherwood, Neely and Jones, 1919.

Book III.

In the preceding books I have laid down the principles of philosophy; principles not philosophical, but mathematical; such, to wit, as we may build our reasonings upon in philosophical enquiries. These principles are the laws and conditions of certain motions, and powers or forces, which chiefly have respect to philosophy; but, lest they should have appeared of themselves dry and barren, I have illustrated them here and there with some philosophical scholiums, giving an account of such things as are of more general nature, and which philosophy seems chiefly to be founded on; such as the density and the resistance of bodies, spaces void of all bodies, and the motion of light and sounds. It remains that, from the same principles, I now demonstrate the frame of the System of the World. Upon this subject I had, indeed, composed the third book in a popular method, that it might be read by many; but afterwards, considering that such as had not sufficiently entered into the principles could not easily discern the strength of the consequences, nor lay aside the prejudices to which they had been many years accustomed, therefore, to prevent the disputes which might be raised upon such accounts, I chose to reduce the substance of this book into the form of propositions (in the mathematical way), which should be read by those only who had first made themselves masters of the principles established in the preceding books: not that I would advise any one to the previous study of every proposition of those books; for they abound with such as might cost too much time, even to readers of good mathematical learning. It is enough if one carefully reads the definitions, the laws of motions, and the first three sections of the first book. He may then pass on to this book, and consult such of the remaining propositions of the *first two books*, as the references in this, and his occasions, shall require.

Rules of Reasoning in Philosophy.

RULE I.

We are to admit no more causes of natural things than such as are both true and sufficient to explain their appearances.

To this purpose the philosophers say that Nature does nothing in vain, and more is in vain when less will serve; for Nature is pleased with simplicity, and affects not the pomp of superfluous causes.

RULE II.

Therefore to the same natural effects we must, as far as possible, assign the same causes.

As to respiration in a man and in a beast; the descent of stones in Europe and in America; the light of our culinary fire and of the sun; the reflection of light in the earth and in the planets.

RULE III.

The qualities of bodies, which admit neither intension or remission of degrees, and which are found to belong to all bodies within the reach of our experiments, are to be esteemed the universal qualities of all bodies whatsoever.

For since the qualities of bodies are only known to us by experiments, we are to hold for universal all such as universally agree with experiments; and such as are not liable to diminution can never be quite taken away. We are certainly not to relinquish the evidence of experiments for the sake of dreams and vain fictions of our own devising; nor are we to recede from the analogy of Nature, which is wont to be simple, and always consonant to itself. We no other way know the extension of bodies than by our senses, nor do these reach it in all bodies; but because we perceive extension in all that are sensible, therefore we ascribe it universally to all others also. That abundance of bodies are hard, we learn by experience; and because the hardness of the whole arises from the hardness of the parts, we therefore justly infer the hardness of the undivided particles not only of the bodies we feel but of all others. That all bodies are impenetrable, we gather not from reason, but from sensation. The bodies which we handle we find impenetrable, and thence conclude impenetrability to be an universal property of all bodies whatsoever. That all bodies are moveable, and endowed with certain powers (which we call *vires inertiæ*) of persevering in their motion, or in their rest, we only infer from the like properties observed in the bodies which we have seen. The extension, hardness, impenetrability, mobility, and *vis inertiæ* of the whole, result from the extension, hardness, impenetrability, mobility, and *vires inertiæ* of the parts; and thence we conclude the least particles of all bodies to be also all extended, and hard, and impenetrable, and moveable, and endowed with their proper *vires inertiæ*. And this is the foundation of all philosophy. Moreover, that the divided but continuous particles of bodies may be separated from one another, is matter of observation; and, in the particles that remain undivided, our minds are able to distinguish yet lesser parts, as is mathematically demonstrated. But whether the parts so distinguished, and not yet divided, may, by the powers of Nature, be actually divided and separated from one another, we cannot certainly determine. Yet, had we the proof of but one experiment that any undivided particle, in breaking a hard and solid body, suffered a division, we might by virtue of this rule conclude that the undivided as well as the divided particles may be divided and actually separated to infinity.

Lastly, if it universally appears, by experiments and astronomical observations, that all bodies about the earth gravitate towards the earth, and that in proportion to the quantity of matter which they severally contain; that the moon likewise, according to the quantity of its matter, gravitates towards the earth; that, on the other hand, our sea gravitates towards the moon; and all the planets mutually one towards another; and the comets in like manner towards the sun; we must, in consequence of this rule, universally allow that all bodies whatsoever are endowed with a principle of mutual gravitation. For the argument from the appearances concludes with more force for the universal gravitation of all bodies than for their impenetrability; of which, among those in the celestial regions, we have no experiments, nor any manner of observation. Not that I affirm gravity to be essential to bodies: by their *vis insita* I mean nothing but their *vis inertiæ*. This is immutable. Their gravity is diminished as they recede from the earth.

RULE IV.

In experimental philosophy we are to look upon propositions collected by general induction from phænomena as accurately or very nearly true, notwithstanding any contrary hypotheses that may be imagined, till such time as other phænomena occur, by which they may either be made more accurate, or liable to exceptions.

This rule we must follow, that the argument of induction may not be evaded by hypotheses.

*   *   *

REVIEW QUESTIONS

1. Why does Newton take mathematical principles as the principles of philosophy?
2. If nature, as Newton asserts, is "pleased with simplicity," what is the origin of "superfluous causes"?
3. What is the relation between cause and law?
4. How does Newton arrive at the universal?
5. How does his method differ from that of Pascal?

VOLTAIRE

FROM *Letters Concerning the English Nation*

François-Marie Arouet (1694–1778) was the son of a Parisian notary and royal official at the Cour des Comptes, and became one of the fathers of the Enlightenment in France. As a youngster, he attached himself to his godfather, the abbé de Chateauneuf, a freethinker who introduced him to progressive circles in the French capital. He attended the Jesuit Collège Louis-le-Grand, where he graduated in 1711 with a degree in philosophy. Though he enrolled in law school, he decided on a literary career and frequented the salons of Paris. His first success came in 1718 with the staging of Oedipus. *At this point, he adopted the pen name of Voltaire. Legal difficulties that followed a brawl with the servants of the chevalier de Rohan resulted in Voltaire's exile to England. From 1726 to 1729 he was brought into personal contact with English philosophy, science, politics, and culture. Voltaire considered English thought and institutions the highest in human history and devoted himself to their introduction upon his return to France. His* Letters Concerning the English Nation *(1734) brought fame and notoriety. A warrant for his arrest forced him to flee once again. In fact, his career was marked by a series of legal difficulties and exiles: to Circey in Champagne in 1734; to Berlin and the court of Frederick II in 1750, to Geneva in 1752; to Ferney in 1757. His lifelong commitments to freedom, toleration, reform, and empiricism made Voltaire one of the great figures of the Enlightenment.*

From *Letters Concerning the English Nation,* F. Arouet, edited by Nicholas Cronk, 1994, by permission of Oxford University Press.

Letter XIV.

On Des Cartes *and Sir* Isaac Newton.

A Frenchman who arrives in *London,* will find Philosophy, like every Thing else, very much chang'd there. He had left the World a *plenum,* and he now finds it a *vacuum.* At *Paris* the Universe is seen, compos'd of Vortices of subtile Matter; but nothing like it is seen in *London.* In *France,* 'tis the Pressure of the Moon that causes the Tides; but in *England* 'tis the Sea that gravitates towards the Moon; so that when you think that the Moon should make it Flood with us, those Gentlemen fancy it should be Ebb, which, very unluckily, cannot be prov'd. For to be able to do this, 'tis necessary the Moon and the Tides should have been enquir'd into, at the very instant of the Creation.

You'll observe farther, that the Sun, which in *France* is said to have nothing to do in the Affair, comes in here for very near a quarter of its Assistance. According to your *Cartesians,* every Thing is perform'd by an Impulsion, of which we have very little Notion; and according to Sir *Isaac Newton,* 'tis by an Attraction, the Cause of which is as much unknown to us. At *Paris* you imagine that the Earth is shap'd like a Melon, or of an oblique Figure; at *London* it has an oblate one. A *Cartesian* declares that Light exists in the Air; but a *Newtonian* asserts that it comes from the Sun in six Minutes and a half. The several Operations of your Chymistry are perform'd by Acids, Alkalies and subtile Matter; but Attraction prevails even in Chymistry among the *English.*

The very Essence of Things is totally chang'd. You neither are agreed upon the Definition of the Soul, nor on that of Matter. *Descartes,* as I observ'd in my last, maintains that the Soul is the same Thing with Thought, and Mr. *Locke* has given a pretty good Proof of the contrary.

Descartes asserts farther, that Extension alone constitutes Matter, but Sir *Isaac* adds Solidity to it.

How furiously contradictory are these Opinions!
Non nostrum inter vos tantas componere lites.
                    VIRGIL, Eclog. III.
'Tis not for us to end such great Disputes.

This famous *Newton,* this Destroyer of the *Cartesian* System, died in *March Anno* 1727. His Countrymen honour'd him in his Life-Time, and interr'd him as tho' he had been a King who had made his People happy.

The *English* read with the highest Satisfaction, and translated into their Tongue, the Elogium of Sir *Isaac Newton,* which Mr. *de Fontenelle,* spoke in the Academy of Sciences. Mr. *de Fontenelle* presides as Judge over Philosophers; and the *English* expected his Decision, as a solemn Declaration of the Superiority of the *English* Philosophy over that of the *French.* But when 'twas found that this Gentleman had compar'd *Des Cartes* to Sir *Isaac,* the whole Royal Society in *London* rose up in Arms. So far from acquiescing with Mr. *Fontenelle*'s Judgment, they criticis'd his Discourse. And even several (who however were not the ablest Philosophers in that Body) were offended at the Comparison; and for no other Reason but because *Des Cartes* was a *Frenchman.*

It must be confess'd that these two great Men differ'd very much in Conduct, in Fortune, and in Philosophy.

Nature had indulg'd *Des Cartes* a shining and

strong Imagination, whence he became a very singular Person both in private Life, and in his Manner of Reasoning. This Imagination could not conceal itself even in his philosophical Works, which are every where adorn'd with very shining, ingenious Metaphors and Figures. Nature had almost made him a Poet; and indeed he wrote a Piece of Poetry for the Entertainment of *Christina* Queen of *Sweden*, which however was suppress'd in Honour to his Memory.

He embrac'd a Military Life for some Time, and afterwards becoming a complete Philosopher, he did not think the Passion of Love derogatory to his Character. He had by his Mistress a Daughter call'd *Froncine*, who died young, and was very much regretted by him. Thus he experienc'd every Passion incident to Mankind.

He was a long Time of Opinion, that it would be necessary for him to fly from the Society of his Fellow Creatures, and especially from his native Country, in order to enjoy the Happiness of cultivating his philosophical Studies in full Liberty.

Des Cartes was very right, for his Cotemporaries were not knowing enough to improve and enlighten his Understanding, and were capable of little else than of giving him Uneasiness.

He left *France* purely to go in search of Truth, which was then persecuted by the wretched Philosophy of the Schools. However, he found that Reason was as much disguis'd and deprav'd in the Universities of *Holland*, into which he withdrew, as in his own Country. For at the Time that the *French* condemn'd the only Propositions of his Philosophy which were true, he was persecuted by the pretended Philosophers of *Holland*, who understood him no better; and who, having a nearer View of his Glory, hated his Person the more, so that he was oblig'd to leave *Utrecht*. *Des Cartes* was injuriously accus'd of being an Atheist, the last Refuge of religious Scandal: And he who had employ'd all the Sagacity and Penetration of his Genius, in searching for new Proofs of the Existence of a God, was suspected to believe there was no such Being.

Such a Persecution from all Sides, must necessarily suppose a most exalted Merit as well as a very distinguish'd Reputation, and indeed he possess'd both. Reason at that Time darted a Ray upon the World thro' the Gloom of the Schools, and the Prejudices of popular Superstition. At last his Name spread so universally, that the *French* were desirous of bringing him back into his native Country by Rewards, and accordingly offer'd him an annual Pension of a thousand Crowns. Upon these Hopes *Des Cartes* return'd to *France*; paid the Fees of his Patent, which was sold at that Time, but no Pension was settled upon him. Thus disappointed, he return'd to his Solitude in *North-Holland*, where he again pursued the Study of Philosophy, whilst the great *Galileo*, at fourscore Years of Age, was groaning in the Prisons of the Inquisition, only for having demonstrated the Earth's Motion.

At last *Des Cartes* was snatch'd from the World in the Flower of his Age at *Stockholm*. His Death was owing to a bad Regimen, and he expir'd in the Midst of some *Literati* who were his Enemies, and under the Hands of a Physician to whom he was odious.

The Progress of Sir *Isaac Newton*'s Life was quite different. He liv'd happy, and very much honour'd in his native Country, to the Age of fourscore and five Years.

'Twas his peculiar Felicity, not only to be born in a Country of Liberty, but in an Age when all scholastic Impertinencies were banish'd from the World. Reason alone was cultivated, and Mankind cou'd only be his Pupil, not his Enemy.

One very singular Difference in the Lives of these two great Men is, that Sir *Isaac*, during the long Course of Years he enjoy'd was never sensible to any Passion, was not subject to the common Frailties of Mankind, nor ever had any Commerce with Women; a Circumstance which was assur'd me by the Physician and Surgeon who attended him in his last Moments.

We may admire Sir *Isaac Newton* on this Occasion, but then we must not censure *Des Cartes*.

The Opinion that generally prevails in *England* with regard to these two Philosophers is, that the latter was a Dreamer, and the former a Sage.

Very few People in *England* read *Descartes*,

whose Works indeed are now useless. On the other Side, but a small Number peruse those of Sir *Isaac*, because to do this the Student must be deeply skill'd in the Mathematicks, otherwise those Works will be unintelligible to him. But notwithstanding this, these great Men are the Subject of every One's Discourse. Sir *Isaac Newton* is allow'd every Advantage, whilst *Des Cartes* is not indulg'd a single one. According to some, 'tis to the former that we owe the Discovery of a *Vacuum*, that the Air is a heavy Body, and the Invention of Telescopes. In a Word, Sir *Isaac Newton* is here as the *Hercules* of fabulous Story, to whom the Ignorant ascrib'd all the Feats of ancient Heroes.

In a Critique that was made in *London* on Mr. de *Fontenelle*'s Discourse, the Writer presum'd to assert that *Des Cartes* was not a great Geometrician. Those who make such a Declaration may justly be reproach'd with flying in their Master's Face. *Des Cartes* extended the Limits of Geometry as far beyond the Place where he found them, as Sir *Isaac* did after him. The former first taught the Method of expressing Curves by Equations. This Geometry which, Thanks to him for it, is now grown common, was so abstruse in his Time, that not so much as one Professor would undertake to explain it; and *Schotten* in *Holland*, and *Format** in *France*, were the only Men who understood it.

He applied this geometrical and inventive Genius to Dioptricks, which, when treated of by him, became a new Art. And if he was mistaken in some Things, the Reason of that is, a Man who discovers a new Tract of Land cannot at once know all the Properties of the Soil. Those who come after him, and make these Lands fruitful, are at least oblig'd to him for the Discovery. I will not deny but that there are innumerable Errors in the rest of *Des Cartes*'s Works.

Geometry was a Guide he himself had in some Measure fashion'd, which would have conducted him safely thro' the several Paths of natural Philosophy. Nevertheless he at last abandon'd this Guide, and gave entirely into the Humour of forming Hypotheses; and then Philosophy was no more than an ingenious Romance, fit only to

amuse the Ignorant. He was mistaken in the Nature of the Soul, in the Proofs of the Existence of a God, in Matter, in the Laws of Motion, and in the Nature of Light. He admitted innate Ideas, he invented new Elements, he created a World; he made Man according to his own Fancy; and 'tis justly said, that the Man of *Des Cartes* is in Fact that of *Des Cartes* only, very different from the real one.

He push'd his metaphysical Errors so far, as to declare that two and two make four, for no other Reason but because God would have it so. However, 'twill not be making him too great a Compliment if we affirm that he was valuable even in his Mistakes. He deceiv'd himself, but then it was at least in a methodical Way. He destroy'd all the absurd Chimæra's with which Youth had been infatuated for two thousand Years. He taught his Cotemporaries how to reason, and enabled them to employ his own Weapons against himself. If *Des Cartes* did not pay in good Money, he however did great Service in crying down that of a base Alloy.

I indeed believe, that very few will presume to compare his Philosophy in any respect with that of Sir *Isaac Newton*. The former is an Essay, the latter a Master-Piece: But then the Man who first brought us to the Path of Truth, was perhaps as great a Genius as he who afterwards conducted us through it.

Des Cartes gave Sight to the Blind. These saw the Errors of Antiquity and of the Sciences. The Path he struck out is since become boundless. *Rohault*'s little Work was during some Years a complete System of Physicks; but now all the Transactions of the several Academies in *Europe* put together do not form so much as the Beginning of a System. In fathoming this Abyss no Bottom has been found. We are now to examine what Discoveries Sir *Isaac Newton* has made in it.

*   *   *

REVIEW QUESTIONS

1. How does Voltaire describe the scientific revolution?
2. What are its consequences?
3. Why does Voltaire single out Descartes and Newton?
4. What differentiates their respective methods?
5. Why, according to Voltaire, was Descartes persecuted and Newton not?

BARON DE LA BREDE ET DE MONTESQUIEU

FROM *The Spirit of the Laws*

Charles-Louis de Secondat, Baron de La Brède et de Montesquieu (1689–1755), was a French philosopher, historian, and satirist. He was born at the family chateau of La Brède near Bordeaux. His great-grandfather, a Calvinist, had been rewarded with a title of nobility for his service to Henry IV. In the next generation, however, the family had converted to Catholicism and had entered the judicial nobility by purchasing offices in the Parlement of Bordeaux. Charles-Louis de Secondat inherited one of these offices, that of presiding judge of the criminal division, in 1712 and held it for eleven years. Montesquieu studied law at the University of Bordeaux, and married Jeanne de Lartique, a practicing Calvinist who risked persecution for her faith. This and his own background may explain Montesquieu's lifelong championship of religious toleration. He entered the literary world with the publication of his Persian Letters (1721). Shortly thereafter Montesquieu moved to Paris and joined the intellectual world of the salon. His most influential work, at least among his contemporaries, was The Spirit of the Laws (1748). By 1750, twenty-two editions had appeared, and it had been translated into every major European language. Montesquieu explored the role of law in shaping political society and sought theoretical and practical responses to the problem of despotism. He envisioned political order as a human body, possessed of a dynamic balance among its various parts. A healthy political order contained inner mechanisms to maintain its balance. An ideal example of such separation and balance of power was the English system of monarch and parliament. These ideas made Montesquieu one of the most widely read and influential figures of the Enlightenment.

From *The Spirit of Laws, Volume I*, Montesquieu, translated by Thomas Nugent, 1901.

Book XII

Of the Laws that Establish Political Liberty, in Relation to the Subject

I. It is not sufficient to have treated of political liberty in relation to the constitution; we must examine it likewise in the relation it bears to the subject.

We have observed that in the former case it arises from a certain distribution of the three powers; but in the latter we must consider it in another light. It consists in security, or in the opinion people have of their country.

The constitution may happen to be free, and the subject not. The subject may be free, and not the constitution. In those cases, the constitution will be free by right, and not in fact; the subject will be free in fact, and not by right.

It is the disposition only of the laws, and even of the fundamental laws, that constitutes liberty in relation to the constitution. But as it regards the subject: manners, customs, or received examples may give rise to it, and particular civil laws may encourage it, as we shall presently observe.

Further, as in most states liberty is more checked or depressed than their constitution requires, it is proper to treat of the particular laws that in each constitution are apt to assist or check the principle of liberty which each state is capable of receiving.

II. Philosophic liberty consists in the free exercise of the will; or at least, if we must speak agreeably to all systems, in an opinion that we have the free exercise of our will. Political liberty consists in securing, or, at least, in the opinion that we enjoy security.

This security is never more dangerously attacked than in public or private accusations. It is, therefore, on the goodness of criminal laws that the liberty of the subject principally depends.

Criminal laws did not receive their full perfection all at once. Even in places where liberty has been most sought after, it has not been always found. Aristotle informs us that at Cumae the parents of the accuser might be witnesses. So imperfect was the law under the kings of Rome, that Servius Tullius pronounced sentence against the children of Ancus Martius, who were charged with having assassinated the king, his father-in-law. Under the first kings of France, Clotarius made a law that nobody should be condemned without being heard, which shows that a contrary custom had prevailed in some particular case or among some barbarous people. It was Charondas that first established penalties against false witnesses. When the subject has no fence to secure his innocence, he has none for his liberty.

The knowledge already acquired in some countries, or that may be hereafter attained in others, concerning the surest rules to be observed in criminal judgments, is more interesting to mankind than any other thing in the world.

Liberty can be founded on the practice of this knowledge only; and supposing a state to have the best laws imaginable in this respect, a person tried under that state, and conto be hanged the next day, would have much more liberty than a pasha enjoys in Turkey.

Those laws which condemn a man to death on the deposition of a single witness are fatal to liberty. In reason there should be two, because a witness who affirms, and the accused who denies, make an equal balance, and a third must incline the scale.

The Greeks and Romans required one voice more to condemn; but our French laws insist upon two. The Greeks pretend that their custom was established by the gods; but this more justly may be said of ours.

III. Liberty is in perfection when criminal laws derive each punishment from the particular nature of the crime. There are then no arbitrary decisions; the punishment does not flow from the capriciousness of the legislator, but from the very nature of the thing; and man uses no violence to man.

There are four sorts of crimes. Those of the first species are prejudicial to religion, the second to morals, the third to the public tranquillity, and the fourth to the security of the subject. The punishments inflicted for these crimes ought to proceed from the nature of each of these species.

In the class of crimes that concern religion, I rank only those which attack it directly, such as all simple sacrileges. For as to crimes that disturb the exercise of it, they are of the nature of those which prejudice the tranquillity or security of the subject, and ought to be referred to those classes.

In order to derive the punishment of simple sacrileges from the nature of the thing, it should consist in depriving people of the advantages conferred by religion in expelling them out of the temples, in a temporary or perpetual exclusion from the society of the faithful, in shunning their presence, in execrations, comminations, and conjurations.

In things that prejudice the tranquillity or security of the state, secret actions are subject to human jurisdiction. But in those which offend the Deity, where there is no public act, there can be no criminal matter; the whole passes between man and God, who knows the measure and time of his vengeance. Now, if magistrates confounding things should inquire also into hidden sacrileges, this inquisition would be directed to a kind of action that does not at all require it; the liberty of the subject would be subverted by arming the zeal of timorous as well as of presumptuous consciences against him.

The mischief arises from a notion which some people have entertained of revenging the cause of the Deity. But we must honor the Deity and leave him to avenge his own cause. And, indeed, were we to be directed by such a notion, where would be the end of punishments? If human laws are to avenge the cause of an infinite Being, they will be directed by his infinity, and not by the weakness, ignorance, and caprice of man.

A historian of Provence relates a fact which furnishes us with an excellent description of the consequences that may arise in weak capacities from the notion of avenging the Deity's cause. A Jew was accused of having blasphemed against the

Virgin Mary, and upon conviction was condemned to be flayed alive. A strange spectacle was then exhibited: gentlemen masked, with knives in their hands, mounted the scaffold, and drove away the executioner, in order to be the avengers themselves of the honor of the blessed Virgin. I do not here choose to anticipate the reflections of the reader.

The second class consists of those crimes which are prejudicial to morals. Such is the violation of public or private continence—that is, of the police directing the manner in which the pleasure annexed to the conjunction of the sexes is to be enjoyed. The punishment of those crimes ought to be also derived from the nature of the thing; the privation of such advantages as society has attached to the purity of morals, fines, shame, necessity of concealment, public infamy, expulsion from home and society, and, in fine, all such punishments as belong to a corrective jurisdiction, are sufficient to repress the temerity of the two sexes. In effect these things are less founded on malice than on carelessness and self-neglect.

We speak here of none but crimes which relate merely to morals, for as to those that are also prejudicial to the public security, such as rapes, they belong to the fourth species.

The crimes of the third class are those which disturb the public tranquillity. The punishments ought therefore to be derived from the nature of the thing, and to be in relation to this tranquillity: such as imprisonment, exile, and other like chastisements, proper for reclaiming turbulent spirits, and obliging them to conform to the established order.

I confine those crimes that injure the public tranquillity to things which imply a bare offense against the police; for as to those which by disturbing the public peace attack at the same time the security of the subject, they ought to be ranked in the fourth class.

The punishments inflicted upon the latter crimes are such as are properly distinguished by that name. They are a kind of retaliation, by which the society refuses security to a member who has actually or intentionally deprived another of his security. These punishments are derived from the nature of the thing, founded on reason, and drawn from the very source of good and evil. A man deserves death when he has violated the security of the subject so far as to deprive, or attempt to deprive, another man of his life. This punishment of death is the remedy, as it were, of a sick society. When there is a breach of security with regard to property, there may be some reasons for inflicting a capital punishment; but it would be much better, and perhaps more natural, that crimes committed against the security of property should be punished with the loss of property; and this ought, indeed, to be the case if men's fortunes were common or equal. But as those who have no property of their own are generally the readiest to attack that of others, it has been found necessary, instead of a pecuniary, to substitute a corporal, punishment.

All that I have here advanced is founded in Nature, and extremely favorable to the liberty of the subject.

IV. It is an important maxim that we ought to be very circumspect in the prosecution of witchcraft and heresy. The accusation of these two crimes may be vastly injurious to liberty, and productive of infinite oppression, if the legislator knows not how to set bounds to it. For as it does not directly point at a person's actions, but at his character, it grows dangerous in proportion to the ignorance of the people; and then a man is sure to be always in danger, because the most exceptional conduct, the purest morals, and the constant practice of every duty in life are not a sufficient security against the suspicion of his being guilty of the like crimes.

Under Manuel Comnenus, the Protestator was accused of having conspired against the emperor, and of having employed for that purpose some secrets that render men invisible. It is mentioned in the life of this emperor that Aaron was detected as he was poring over a book of Solomon's, the reading of which was sufficient to conjure up whole legions of devils. Now, by supposing a power in witchcraft to rouse the infernal spirits to arms, people look upon a man whom they call a sorcerer as the person in the world most likely to disturb and subvert society, and of course they are disposed to punish him with the utmost severity.

But their indignation increases when witchcraft is supposed to have the power of subverting religion. The history of Constantinople informs us that in consequence of a revelation made to a bishop of a miracle having ceased because of the magic practices of a certain person, both that person and his son were put to death. On how many surprising things did not this single crime depend!—that revelations should not be uncommon, that the bishop should be favored with one, that it was real, that there had been a miracle in the case, that this miracle had ceased, that there was an art magic, that magic could subvert religion, that this particular person was a magician, and, in fine, that he had committed that magic act.

The Emperor Theodorus Lascarus attributed his illness to witchcraft. Those who were accused of this crime had no other resource left than to handle a red-hot iron without being hurt. Thus among the Greeks a person ought to have been a sorcerer to be able to clear himself of the imputation of witchcraft. Such was the excess of their stupidity that to the most dubious crime in the world they joined the most dubious proofs of innocence.

Under the reign of Philip the Long, the Jews were expelled from France, being accused of having poisoned the springs with their lepers. So absurd an accusation ought to make us doubt all those that are founded on public hatred.

I have not here asserted that heresy ought not to be punished; I said only that we ought to be extremely circumspect in punishing it.

V. God forbid that I should have the least inclination to diminish the public horror against a crime which religion, morality, and civil government equally condemn. It ought to be proscribed, were it only for its communicating to one sex the weaknesses of the other, and for leading people by a scandalous prostitution of their youth to an ig-nominious old age. What I shall say concerning it will in no way diminish its infamy, being leveled only against the tyranny that may abuse the very horror we ought to have against the vice.

As a natural circumstance of this crime is se-crecy, there are frequent instances of its having been punished by legislators upon the deposition of a child. This was opening a very wide door to calumny. "Justinian," says Procopius, "published a law against this crime; he ordered an inquiry to be made not only against those who were guilty of it, after the enacting of that law, but even be-fore. The deposition of a single witness, sometimes of a child, sometimes of a slave, was sufficient, especially against such as were rich, and against those of the green faction."

It is very odd that these three crimes—witch-craft, heresy, and that against Nature, of which the first might easily be proved not to exist, the second to be susceptible of an infinite number of distinc-tions, interpretations, and limitations, the third to be often obscure and uncertain—it is very odd, I say, that these three crimes should among us be punished with fire.

I may venture to affirm that the crime against Nature will never make any great progress in so-ciety, unless people are prompted to it by some particular custom, as among the Greeks, where the youths of that country performed all their exercises naked; as among us, where domestic education is disused; as among the Asiatics, where particular persons have a great number of women whom they despise, while others can have none at all. Let there be no customs preparatory to this crime; let it, like every other violation of morals, be severely proscribed by the civil magistrate; and Nature will soon defend or resume her rights. Na-ture, that fond, that indulgent parent, has strewed her pleasures with a bounteous hand, and while she fills us with delights she prepares us, by means of our issue, in whom we see ourselves, as it were, reproduced—she prepares us, I say, for future sat-isfactions of a more exquisite kind than those very delights.

VI. It is determined by the laws of China that whosoever shows any disrespect to the emperor is to be punished with death. As they do not men-tion in what this disrespect consists, everything may furnish a pretext to take away a man's life, and to exterminate any family whatsoever.

Two persons of that country who were em-ployed to write the court gazette, having inserted some circumstances relating to a certain fact that was not true, it was pretended that to tell a lie in the court gazette was a disrespect shown to the court, in consequence of which they were put to death. A prince of the blood having inadvertently made some mark on a memorial signed with the red pencil by the emperor, it was determined that he had behaved disrespectfully to the sovereign, which occasioned one of the most terrible perse-cutions against that family that ever was recorded in history.

If the crime of high treason be indeterminate, this alone is sufficient to make the government degenerate into arbitrary power. I shall descant more largely on this subject when I come to treat of the composition of laws.

VII. It is likewise a shocking abuse to give the appellation of high treason to an action that does not deserve it. By an imperial law it was decreed that those who called in question the prince's judgment, or doubted the merit of such as he had chosen for a public office, should be prosecuted as guilty of sacrilege. Surely it was the cabinet council and the prince's favorites who invented that crime. By another law it was determined that whosoever made any attempt to injure the min-isters and officers belonging to the sovereign should be deemed guilty of high treason, as if he had attempted to injure the sovereign himself. This law is owing to two princes remarkable for their weaknesses—princes who were led by their ministers as flocks by shepherds; princes who were slaves in the palace, children in the council, strangers to the army; princes, in fine, who pre-served their authority only by giving it away every day. Some of those favorites conspired against their sovereigns. Nay, they did more, they conspired against the empire—they called in barbarous nations; and when the emperors wanted to stop their progress the state was so enfeebled as to be under a necessity of infringing the law, and of exposing itself to the crime of high treason in order to punish those favorites.

And yet this is the very law which the judge of Monsieur de Cinq-Mars built upon when endeavoring to prove that the latter was guilty of the crime of high treason for attempting to remove Cardinal Richelieu from the ministry. He says: "Crimes that aim at the persons of ministers are deemed by the imperial constitutions of equal consequence with those which are leveled against the emperor's own person. A minister discharges his duty to his prince and to his country; to attempt, therefore, to remove him is endeavoring to deprive the former one of his arms, and the latter of part of its power." It is impossible for the meanest tools of power to express themselves in more servile language.

By another law of Valentinian, Theodosius, and Arcadius, false coiners are declared guilty of high treason. But is not this confounding the ideas of things? Is not the very horror of high treason diminished by giving that name to another crime?

Paulinus having written to the Emperor Alexander that "he was preparing to prosecute for high treason a judge who had decided contrary to his edict," the emperor answered that "under his reign there was no such thing as indirect high treason."

Faustinian wrote to the same emperor, that as he had sworn by the prince's life never to pardon his slave, he found himself thereby obliged to perpetuate his wrath, lest he should incur the guilt of *laesa majestas*. Upon which the emperor made answer, "Your fears are groundless, and you are a stranger to my principles."

It was determined by a senatus-consultum that whosoever melted down any of the emperor's statues which happened to be rejected should not be deemed guilty of high treason. The Emperors Severus and Antoninus wrote to Pontius that those who sold unconsecrated statues of the emperor should not be charged with high treason. The same princes wrote to Julius Cassianus that if a person in flinging a stone should by chance strike one of the emperor's statues he should not be liable to a prosecution for high treason. The Julian law requires this sort of limitations; for in virtue of this law the crime of high treason was charged not only upon those who melted down the emperor's statues, but likewise on those who committed any suchlike action, which made it an arbitrary crime. When a number of crimes of *laesa majestas* had been established, they were obliged to distinguish the several sorts. Hence Ulpian, the civilian, after saying that the accusation of *laesa majestas* did not die with the criminal, adds that this does not relate to all the treasonable acts established by the Julian law, but only to that which implies an attempt against the empire, or against the emperor's life.

There was a law passed in England under Henry VIII, by which whoever predicted the king's death was declared guilty of high treason. This law was extremely vague; the terror of despotic power is so great that it recoils upon those who exercise it. In this king's last illness, the physicians would not venture to say he was in danger; and surely they acted very right.

VIII. Marsyas dreamed that he had cut Dionysius' throat. Dionysius put him to death, pretending that he would never have dreamed of such a thing by night if he had not thought of it by day. This was a most tyrannical action, for though it had been the subject of his thoughts, yet he had made no attempt toward it. The laws do not take upon them to punish any other than overt acts.

IX. Nothing renders the crime of high treason more arbitrary than declaring people guilty of it for indiscreet speeches. Speech is so subject to interpretation; there is so great a difference between indiscretion and malice; and frequently so little is there of the latter in the freedom of expression, that the law can hardly subject people to a capital punishment for words unless it expressly declares what words they are.

Words do not constitute an overt act; they

remain only in idea. When considered by themselves, they have generally no determinate signification, for this depends on the tone in which they are uttered. It often happens that in repeating the same words they have not the same meaning; this depends on their connection with other things, and sometimes more is signified by silence than by any expression whatever. Since there can be nothing so equivocal and ambiguous as all this, how is it possible to convert it into a crime of high treason? Wherever this law is established, there is an end not only of liberty, but even of its very shadow.

In the manifesto of the late Czarina against the family of the Dolgorukis, one of these princes is condemned to death for having uttered some indecent words concerning her person; another, for having maliciously interpreted her imperial laws, and for having offended her sacred person by disrespectful expressions.

Not that I pretend to diminish the just indignation of the public against those who presume to stain the glory of their sovereign; what I mean is, that if despotic princes are willing to moderate their power, a milder chastisement would be more proper on those occasions than the charge of high treason—a thing always terrible even to innocence itself.

Overt acts do not happen every day; they are exposed to the eye of the public, and a false charge with regard to matters of fact may be easily detected. Words carried into action assume the nature of that action. Thus a man who goes into a public marketplace to incite the subject to revolt incurs the guilt of high treason, because the words are joined to the action, and partake of its nature.

It is not the words that are punished, but an action in which words are employed. They do not become criminal but when they are annexed to a criminal action; everything is confounded if words are construed into a capital crime, instead of considering them only as a mark of that crime.

The Emperors Theodosius, Arcadius, and Honorius wrote thus to Rufinus, who was *praefectus praetorio*: "Though a man should happen to speak amiss of our person or government, we do not intend to punish him. If he has spoken through levity, we must despise him; if through folly, we must pity him; and if he wrongs us, we must forgive him. Therefore, leaving things as they are, you are to inform us accordingly, that we may be able to judge of words by persons, and that we may duly consider whether we ought to punish or overlook them."

X. In writings there is something more permanent than in words, but when they are in no way preparative to high treason they cannot amount to that charge. . . .

*   *   *

REVIEW QUESTIONS

1. What kinds of liberty does Montesquieu distinguish?
2. On what basis does he make his distinctions?
3. What is the relation between liberty and reason?
4. What is the relation between crime and nature?
5. What role does a concept of nature play in Montesquieu's differentiation of crimes?

IMMANUEL KANT

What Is Enlightenment?

Immanuel Kant (1724–1804) was born, lived, and died in Königsberg, eastern Prussia, but wandered much more widely in his mind. A rationalist and disciple of Christian von Wolff, he set himself the task of working out the philosophical implications of Newtonian physics. Appointed to the chair of logic and metaphysics at the University of Königsberg in 1770, he began work on his great system of critical thought. His trilogy, Critique of Pure Reason *(1781),* Critique of Practical Reason *(1788), and* Critique of Judgment *(1790), provided the foundations for reliable human knowledge. In addition, he penned popular shorter essays that explained aspects of his thought. One of the most famous of these appears here. Publication of his last great work,* Religion in the Bounds of Reason *(1793), earned the censure of the Prussian government. Alone and silent, he died a decade later.*

From "What Is Enlightenment" translated by Peter Gay in *Introduction to Contemporary Civilization in the West, Volume 1*, Copyright © 1954 by Columbia University Press. Reprinted with permission of the publisher.

Enlightenment is man's emergence from his self-imposed nonage. Nonage is the inability to use one's own understanding without another's guidance. This nonage is self-imposed if its cause lies not in lack of understanding but in indecision and lack of courage to use one's own mind without another's guidance. *Dare to know!* "Have the courage to use your own understanding," is therefore the motto of the enlightenment.

Laziness and cowardice are the reasons why such a large part of mankind gladly remain minors all their lives, long after nature has freed them from external guidance. They are the reasons why it is so easy for others to set themselves up as guardians. It is so comfortable to be a minor. If I have a book that thinks for me, a pastor who acts as my conscience, a physician who prescribes my diet, and so on—then I have no need to exert myself. I have no need to think, if only I can pay; others will take care of that disagreeable business for me. Those guardians who have kindly taken supervision upon themselves see to it that the overwhelming majority of mankind—among them the entire fair sex—should consider the step to maturity not only as hard, but as extremely dangerous. First, these guardians make their domestic cattle stupid and carefully prevent the docile creatures from taking a single step without the leading-strings to which they have fastened them. Then they show them the danger that would threaten them if they should try to walk by themselves. Now, this danger is really not very great; after stumbling a few times they would, at last, learn to walk. However, examples of such failures intimidate and generally discourage all further attempts.

Thus it is very difficult for the individual to work himself out of the nonage which has become almost second nature to him. He has even grown to like it and is at first really incapable of using his own understanding, because he has never been permitted to try it. Dogmas and formulas, these mechanical tools designed for reasonable use—or rather abuse—of his natural gifts, are the fetters of an everlasting nonage. The man who casts them off would make an uncertain leap over the narrowest ditch, because he is not used to such free movement. That is why there are only a few men who walk firmly, and who have emerged from nonage by cultivating their own minds.

It is more nearly possible, however, for the public to enlighten itself; indeed, if it is only given freedom, enlightenment is almost inevitable. There will always be a few independent thinkers, even among the self-appointed guardians of the multitude. Once such men have thrown off the yoke of nonage, they will spread about them the spirit of a reasonable appreciation of man's value and of his duty to think for himself. It is especially to be noted that the public which was earlier brought under the yoke by these men afterward forces these very guardians to remain in submission, if it is so incited by some of its guardians who are themselves incapable of any enlightenment. That shows how pernicious it is to implant prejudices: they will eventually revenge themselves upon their authors or their authors' descendants. Therefore, a public can achieve enlightenment only slowly. A revolution may bring about the end of a personal despotism or of avaricious and tyrannical oppression, but never a true reform of modes of thought. New prejudices will serve, in place of the old, as guidelines for the unthinking multitude.

This enlightenment requires nothing but *freedom*—and the most innocent of all that may be called "freedom": freedom to make public use of one's reason in all matters. Now I hear the cry from all sides: "Do not argue!" The officer says: "Do not argue—drill!" The tax collector: "Do not argue—pay!" The pastor: "Do not argue—believe!" Only one ruler in the world says: "Argue as much as you please, and about what you please, but obey!" We find restrictions on freedom everywhere. But which restriction is harmful to enlightenment? Which restriction is innocent, and which advances enlightenment? I reply: the public use of one's reason must be free at all times, and this alone can bring enlightenment to mankind.

On the other hand, the private use of reason may frequently be narrowly restricted without especially hindering the progress of enlightenment. By "public use of one's reason" I mean that use which a man, as *scholar*, makes of it before the reading public. I call "private use" that use which a man makes of his reason in a civic post that has been entrusted to him. In some affairs affecting the interest of the community a certain governmental mechanism is necessary in which some members of the community remain passive. This creates an artificial unanimity which will serve the fulfillment of public objectives, or at least keep these objectives from being destroyed. Here arguing is not permitted: one must obey. Insofar as a part of this machine considers himself at the same time a member of a universal community— a world society of citizens—(let us say that he thinks of himself as a scholar rationally addressing his public through his writings) he may indeed argue, and the affairs with which he is associated in part as a passive member will not suffer. Thus, it would be very unfortunate if an officer on duty and under orders from his superiors should want to criticize the appropriateness or utility of his orders. He must obey. But as a scholar he could not rightfully be prevented from taking notice of the mistakes in the military service and from submitting his views to his public for its judgment. The citizen cannot refuse to pay the taxes levied upon him; indeed, impertinent censure of such taxes could be punished as a scandal that might cause general disobedience. Nevertheless, this man does not violate the duties of a citizen if, as a scholar, he publicly expresses his objections to the impropriety or possible injustice of such levies. A pastor too is bound to preach to his congregation in accord with the doctrines of the church which he serves, for he was ordained on that condition. But as a scholar he has full freedom, indeed the obligation, to communicate to his public all his carefully examined and constructive thoughts concerning errors in that doctrine and his proposals concerning improvement of religious dogma and church institutions. This is nothing that could burden his conscience. For what he teaches in pursuance of his office as representative of the church, he represents as something which he is not free to teach as he sees it. He speaks as one who is employed to speak in the name and under the orders of another. He will say: "Our church teaches this or that; these are the proofs which it employs." Thus he will benefit his congregation as much as possible by presenting doctrines to which he may not subscribe with full conviction. He can commit himself to teach them because it is not completely impossible that they may contain hidden truth. In any event, he has found nothing in the doctrines that contradicts the heart of religion. For if he believed that such contradictions existed he would not be able to administer his office with a clear conscience. He would have to resign it. Therefore the use which a scholar makes of his reason before the congregation that employs him is only a private use, for, no matter how sizable, this is only a domestic audience. In view of this he, as preacher, is not free and ought not to be free, since he is carrying out the orders of others. On the other hand, as the scholar who speaks to his own public (the world) through his writings, the minister in the public use of his reason enjoys unlimited freedom to use his own reason and to speak for himself. That the spiritual guardians of the people should themselves be treated as minors is an absurdity which would result in perpetuating absurdities.

But should a society of ministers, say a Church Council, . . . have the right to commit itself by oath to a certain unalterable doctrine, in order to secure perpetual guardianship over all its members and through them over the people? I say that this is quite impossible. Such a contract, concluded to keep all further enlightenment from humanity, is simply null and void even if it should be confirmed by the sovereign power, by parliaments, and by the most solemn treaties. An epoch cannot conclude a pact that will commit succeeding ages, prevent them from increasing their significant insights, purging themselves of errors, and generally progressing in enlightenment. That would be a crime against human nature, whose proper destiny lies precisely in such progress. Therefore, succeeding ages are fully entitled to repudiate such decisions as unauthorized and outrageous. The touchstone of all those decisions that may be made into law for a people lies in this question: Could a people impose such a law upon itself? Now, it might be possible to introduce a certain order for a definite short period of time in expectation of a better order. But while this provisional order continues, each citizen (above all, each pastor acting as a scholar) should be left free to publish his criticisms of the faults of existing institutions. This should continue until public understanding of these matters has gone so far that, by uniting the voices of many (although not necessarily all) scholars, reform proposals could be brought before the sovereign to protect those congregations which had decided according to their best lights upon an altered religious order, without, however, hindering those who want to remain true to the old institutions. But to agree to a perpetual religious constitution which is not to be publicly questioned by anyone would be, as it were, to annihilate a period of time in the progress of man's improvement. This must be absolutely forbidden.

A man may postpone his own enlightenment, but only for a limited period of time. And to give up enlightenment altogether, either for oneself or one's descendants, is to violate and to trample upon the sacred rights of man. What a people may not decide for itself may even less be decided for it by a monarch, for his reputation as a ruler consists precisely in the way in which he unites the will of the whole people within his own. If he only sees to it that all true or supposed improvement remains in step with the civic order, he can for the rest leave his subjects alone to do what they find necessary for the salvation of their souls. Salvation is none of his business; it *is* his business to prevent one man from forcibly keeping another from determining and promoting his salvation to the best of his ability. Indeed, it would be prejudicial to his majesty if he meddled in these matters and supervised the writings in which his subjects seek to bring their views into the open, even when he does this from his own highest insight, because then he exposes himself to the reproach: *Caesar non est supra grammaticos.*[1] It is worse when he debases his sovereign power so far as to support the spiritual despotism of a few tyrants in his state over the rest of his subjects.

When we ask, Are we now living in an enlightened age? the answer is, No, but we live in an age of enlightenment. As matters now stand it is still far from true that men are already capable of using their own reason in religious matters confidently and correctly without external guidance. Still, we have some obvious indications that the field of working toward the goal of religious truth is now being opened. What is more, the hindrances against general enlightenment or the emergence from self-imposed nonage are gradually diminishing. In this respect this is the age of the enlightenment and the century of Frederick.

A prince ought not to deem it beneath his dignity to state that he considers it his duty not to dictate anything to his subjects in religious matters, but to leave them complete freedom. If he repudiates the arrogant word *tolerant*, he is himself enlightened; he deserves to be praised by a grateful world and posterity as that man who was the first to liberate mankind from dependence, at least on the government, and let everybody use his own reason in matters of conscience. Under his reign, honorable pastors, acting as scholars and regardless of the duties of their office, can freely and openly publish their ideas to the world for inspection, although they deviate here and there from accepted doctrine. This is even more true of every other person not restrained by any oath of office. This spirit of freedom is spreading beyond the boundaries of Prussia, even where it has to struggle against the external hindrances established by a government that fails to grasp its true interest. Frederick's Prussia is a shining example that freedom need not cause the least worry concerning public order or the unity of the commu-

nity. When one does not deliberately attempt to keep men in barbarism, they will gradually work out of that condition by themselves.

I have emphasized the main point of the enlightenment—man's emergence from his self-imposed nonage—primarily in religious matters, because our rulers have no interest in playing the guardian to their subjects in the arts and sciences. Above all, nonage in religion is not only the most harmful but the most dishonorable. But the disposition of a sovereign ruler who favors freedom in the arts and sciences goes even further: he knows that there is no danger in permitting his subjects to make public use of their reason and to publish their ideas concerning a better constitution, as well as candid criticism of existing basic laws. We already have a striking example [of such freedom], and no monarch can match the one whom we venerate.

But only the man who is himself enlightened, who is not afraid of shadows, and who commands at the same time a well-disciplined and numerous army as guarantor of public peace—only he can say what a free state cannot dare to say: "Argue as much as you like, and about what you like, but obey!" Thus we observe here as elsewhere in human affairs, in which almost everything is paradoxical, a surprising and unexpected course of events: a large degree of civic freedom appears to be of advantage to the intellectual freedom of the people, yet at the same time it establishes insurmountable barriers. A lesser degree of civic freedom, however, creates room to let that free spirit expand to the limits of its capacity. Nature, then, has carefully cultivated the seed within the hard core—namely, the urge for and the vocation of free thought. And this free thought gradually reacts back on the modes of thought of the people, and men become more and more capable of acting in freedom. At last free thought acts even on the fundamentals of government, and the state finds it agreeable to treat man, who is now more than a machine, in accord with his dignity.

---

[1] Caesar is not above grammarians.

REVIEW QUESTIONS

1. What is enlightenment?
2. What is its relation to habit? To freedom? To revolution?
3. What is the relation of enlightenment to argument? Why?
4. Why should reasoning be public?
5. How does Kant define "public"?
6. Is the church public or private?

DAVID HUME

FROM *A Treatise of Human Nature*

David Hume (1711–1776) was born the younger son of a gentry family from Scotland. Though he attended the University of Edinburgh, he found formal education distasteful and applied himself instead to an intense program of reading. After a nervous breakdown in 1729 and an unsuccessful foray into business, Hume moved to France in 1734. During his stay there, which lasted until 1737, he devoted himself to studying and to writing the A Treatise of Human Nature 1739–1740). Though he later dismissed it as immature, it became his most influential work. Here he introduced his notion of skepticism that restricted human knowledge to experience of ideas and impression and denied the ability to verify their ultimate truth. Nonetheless, given the cautious, persistent exercise of reason, humankind could gather knowledge that was reliable and useful. As historian, economist, and essayist, Hume was one of the most influential figures of the middle years of the Enlightenment.

From *A Treatise of Human Nature*, edited by L. A. Selby-Biggs, 1888, p. xvii–xxiii.

Introduction

Nothing is more usual and more natural for those, who pretend to discover any thing new to the world in philosophy and the sciences, than to insinuate the praises of their own systems, by decrying all those, which have been advanced before them. And indeed were they content with lamenting that ignorance, which we still lie under in the most important questions, that can come before the tribunal of human reason, there are few, who have an acquaintance with the sciences, that would not readily agree with them. 'Tis easy for one of judgment and learning, to perceive the weak foundation even of those systems, which have obtained the greatest credit, and have carried their pretensions highest to accurate and profound reasoning. Principles taken upon trust, consequences lamely deduced from them, want of coherence in the parts, and of evidence in the whole, these are every where to be met with in the systems of the most eminent philosophers, and seem to have drawn disgrace upon philosophy itself.

Nor is there requir'd such profound knowledge to discover the present imperfect condition of the sciences, but even the rabble without doors may judge from the noise and clamour, which they hear, that all goes not well within. There is nothing which is not the subject of debate, and in which men of learning are not of contrary opinions. The most trivial question escapes not our controversy, and in the most momentous we are not able to give any certain decision. Disputes are multiplied, as if every thing was uncertain; and these disputes are managed with the greatest warmth, as if every thing was certain. Amidst all this bustle 'tis not reason, which carries the prize, but eloquence; and no man needs ever despair of gaining proselytes to the most extravagant hypothesis, who has art enough to represent it in any favourable colours. The victory is not gained by the men at arms, who manage the pike and the sword; but by the trumpeters, drummers, and musicians of the army.

From hence in my opinion arises that common prejudice against metaphysical reasonings of all kinds, even amongst those, who profess themselves scholars, and have a just value for every other part of literature. By metaphysical reasonings, they do not understand those on any particular branch of science, but every kind of argument, which is any way abstruse, and requires some attention to be comprehended. We have so often lost our labour in such researches, that we commonly reject them without hesitation, and resolve, if we must for ever be a prey to errors and delusions, that they shall at least be natural and entertaining. And indeed nothing but the most determined scepticism, along with a great degree of indolence, can justify this aversion to metaphysics. For if truth be at all within the reach of human capacity, 'tis certain it must lie very deep and abstruse; and to hope we shall arrive at it without pains, while the greatest geniuses have failed with the utmost pains, must certainly be esteemed sufficiently vain and presumptuous. I pretend to no such advantage in the philosophy I am going to unfold, and would esteem it a strong presumption against it, were it so very easy and obvious.

'Tis evident, that all the sciences have a relation, greater or less, to human nature; and that however wide any of them may seem to run from

it, they still return back by one passage or another. Even *Mathematics, Natural Philosophy, and Natural Religion*, are in some measure dependent on the science of Man; since they lie under the cognizance of men, and are judged of by their powers and faculties. 'Tis impossible to tell what changes and improvements we might make in these sciences were we thoroughly acquainted with the extent and force of human understanding, and cou'd explain the nature of the ideas we employ, and of the operations we perform in our reasonings. And these improvements are the more to be hoped for in natural religion, as it is not content with instructing us in the nature of superior powers, but carries its views farther, to their disposition towards us, and our duties towards them; and consequently we ourselves are not only the beings, that reason, but also one of the objects, concerning which we reason.

If therefore the sciences of Mathematics, Natural Philosophy, and Natural Religion, have such a dependence on the knowledge of man, what may be expected in the other sciences, whose connexion with human nature is more close and intimate? The sole end of logic is to explain the principles and operations of our reasoning faculty, and the nature of our ideas: morals and criticism regard our tastes and sentiments: and politics consider men as united in society, and dependent on each other. In these four sciences of *Logic, Morals, Criticism, and Politics*, is comprehended almost every thing, which it can any way import us to be acquainted with, or which can tend either to the improvement or ornament of the human mind.

Here then is the only expedient, from which we can hope for success in our philosophical researches, to leave the tedious ling'ring method, which we have hitherto followed, and instead of taking now and then a castle or village on the frontier, to march up directly to the capital or center of these sciences, to human nature itself; which being once masters of, we may every where else hope for an easy victory. From this station we may extend our conquests over all those sciences, which more intimately concern human life, and may afterwards proceed at leisure to discover more fully those, which are the objects of pure curiosity. There is no question of importance, whose decision is not compriz'd in the science of man; and there is none, which can be decided with any certainty, before we become acquainted with that science. In pretending therefore to explain the principles of human nature, we in effect propose a compleat system of the sciences, built on a foundation almost entirely new, and the only one upon which they can stand with any security.

And as the science of man is the only solid foundation for the other sciences, so the only solid foundation we can give to this science itself must be laid on experience and observation. 'Tis no astonishing reflection to consider, that the application of experimental philosophy to moral subjects should come after that to natural at the distance of above a whole century; since we find in fact, that there was about the same interval betwixt the origins of these sciences; and that reckoning from Thales to Socrates, the space of time is nearly equal to that betwixt my Lord Bacon and some late philosophers in *England*, who have begun to put the science of man on a new footing, and have engaged the attention, and excited the curiosity of the public. So true it is, that however other nations may rival us in poetry, and excel us in some other agreeable arts, the improvements in reason and philosophy can only be owing to a land of toleration and of liberty.

Nor ought we to think, that this latter improvement in the science of man will do less honour to our native country than the former in natural philosophy, but ought rather to esteem it a greater glory, upon account of the greater importance of that science, as well as the necessity it lay under of such a reformation. For to me it seems evident, that the essence of the mind being equally unknown to us with that of external bodies, it must be equally impossible to form any notion of its powers and qualities otherwise than from careful and exact experiments, and the observation of those particular effects, which result from its different circumstances and situations. And tho' we must endeavour to render all our principles as universal as possible, by tracing up

our experiments to the utmost, and explaining all effects from the simplest and fewest causes, 'tis still certain we cannot go beyond experience; and any hypothesis, that pretends to discover the ultimate original qualities of human nature, ought at first to be rejected as presumptuous and chimerical.

I do not think a philosopher, who would apply himself so earnestly to the explaining the ultimate principles of the soul, would show himself a great master in that very science of human nature, which he pretends to explain, or very knowing in what is naturally satisfactory to the mind of man. For nothing is more certain, than that despair has almost the same effect upon us with enjoyment, and that we are no sooner acquainted with the impossibility of satisfying any desire, than the desire itself vanishes. When we see, that we have arrived at the utmost extent of human reason, we sit down contented; tho' we be perfectly satisfied in the main of our ignorance, and perceive that we can give no reason for our most general and most refined principles, beside our experience of their reality; which is the reason of the mere vulgar, and what it required no study at first to have discovered for the most particular and most extraordinary phaenomenon. And as this impossibility of making any farther progress is enough to satisfy the reader, so the writer may derive a more delicate satisfaction from the free confession of his ignorance, and from his prudence in avoiding that error, into which so many have fallen, of imposing their conjectures and hypotheses on the world for the most certain principles. When this mutual contentment and satisfaction can be obtained betwixt the master and scholar, I know not what more we can require of our philosophy.

But if this impossibility of explaining ultimate principles should be esteemed a defect in the science of man, I will venture to affirm, that 'tis a defect common to it with all the sciences, and all the arts, in which we can employ ourselves, whether they be such as are cultivated in the schools of the philosophers, or practised in the shops of the meanest artizans. None of them can go beyond experience, or establish any principles which are not founded on that authority. Moral philosophy has, indeed, this peculiar disadvantage, which is not found in natural, that in collecting its experiments, it cannot make them purposely, with premeditation, and after such a manner as to satisfy itself concerning every particular difficulty which may arise. When I am at a loss to know the effects of one body upon another in any situation, I need only put them in that situation, and observe what results from it. But should I endeavour to clear up after the same manner any doubt in moral philosophy, by placing myself in the same case with that which I consider, 'tis evident this reflection and premeditation would so disturb the operation of my natural principles, as must render it impossible to form any just conclusion from the phaenomenon. We must therefore glean up our experiments in this science from a cautious observation of human life, and take them as they appear in the common course of the world, by men's behaviour in company, in affairs, and in their pleasures. Where experiments of this kind are judiciously collected and compared, we may hope to establish on them a science, which will not be inferior in certainty, and will be much superior in utility to any other of human comprehension.

* * *

REVIEW QUESTIONS

1. To what does Hume attribute all the disputes in the sciences?
2. What is the "science of man," and what are its methods and goals?
3. Why must one understand human reason first?

JEANNE MANON PHILIPON ROLAND DE LA PLATIÈRE

FROM *Memoirs*

Jeanne Manon Philipon Roland de la Platière (1754–1793), better known simply as Madame Roland, was a revolutionary and social figure of the late Enlightenment. Born in Paris, she married a government official, Jean Roland de la Platière. As the wife of a public figure, her intelligence, charm, and energy had a broader influence than might otherwise have been the case. With her husband, she became a member of the Girondist faction during the French Revolution, and her home became its headquarters. There she presided over a salon where the issues of the day were discussed. When the Girondists lost power to the more radical Jacobins, Madame Roland was arrested and condemned to death by a revolutionary tribunal for royalist sympathies. She wrote her Memoirs *(1795) while in prison awaiting execution. With the correspondence of other noteworthy salonnières, such as Julie de Lespinasse,* Memoirs *offers a perspective on the social and intellectual role of well-educated women during the Enlightenment. As hostesses in literary salons, where philosophes met to discuss philosophical issues, they facilitated discourse between schools and across classes.*

From *Private Memoirs of Madame Roland,* edited by E. Gilpin Johnson, McClurg, 1901.

*   *   *

The little library of my relations afforded me some resources. I found there the works of Puffendorf, tedious perhaps in his universal history, but interesting to me in his "Duties of the Man and the Citizen;" the "Maison Rustique," and other works of agriculture and economy, that I studied for want of better, because it was necessary that I should be always learning something; the pleasant and delicate rhymes that Berni wrote when he was not restrained by the Romish purple; a Life of Cromwell, and a medley of other productions.

I must here remind the reader of the fact that in mentioning casually the long list of books that chance or circumstances had caused to pass through my hands, I have as yet said nothing of Rousseau. The fact is I read him very late—and it was as well for me that I did so, since I might have been so completely engrossed with him as to have read no other author. Even as it is, he has but too much strengthened what I may venture to term my cardinal failing.

I have reason to believe that my mother had been solicitous to keep him out of my way; for, as his name was not unknown to me, I had sought after his works, but, previously to her death, had read only his "Letters from the Mountain," and his "Letter to Christopher de Beaumont;" whereas I had then read the whole of Voltaire and Boulanger and the Marquis d'Argens and Helvetius, besides many other philosophers and critics. Probably my worthy mother, who perceived the necessity of permitting me to exercise my head, was not averse to my studying philosophy even at the risk of a little incredulity; but she doubtless felt that my tender heart, already too impressible, needed no master in the school of sensibility. What a multitude of useless cares to avoid one's destiny! The same idea influenced her, when she interfered to prevent me from devoting myself to painting; and had made her also oppose my studying the harpsichord, though I had a most excellent opportunity for doing so. We had become acquainted in the neighborhood with an Abbé

Jeauket, a musical amateur, good-natured, but frightfully ugly, and fond of the pleasures of the table. He was born in the environs of Prague, had passed many years at Vienna, and had given some lessons there to Marie Antoinette. Led by circumstances to Lisbon, he had at last settled at Paris, where he lived in independence on the pensions that composed his little fortune. He was extremely desirous that my mother would permit him to teach me the harpsichord. He contended that with such fingers and such a head I must have made a great performer, and that I ought not to fail to apply myself to composition. "What a shame," he cried, "to be jingling a guitar, when one might be composing and executing the finest pieces on the greatest of instruments!" But with all his enthusiasm and his repeated entreaties he could not overcome my mother's opposition. For myself, always ready to profit by an opportunity of instruction, but accustomed nevertheless to bow to her decisions, I did not press the matter. Besides, study, in general, afforded me so vast a field of occupation, that I never knew the lassitude of idleness. I often said to myself: When I shall be a mother in my turn it will then be my business to make use of what I shall have acquired; I shall then have no leisure for further studies; and I was the more earnest to employ my time, fearful of losing a single moment. The Abbé Jeauket was now and then visited by persons of some note, and whenever he invited them to his house, he was anxious to include us in his party. Thus, among others not worth remembering, I became acquainted with the learned Roussier, and the polite d'Odiment; but I have not forgotten the impertinent Paradelle and Madame de Puisieux. This Paradelle was a great scamp in the gown of an abbé, and the greatest coxcomb and braggart I have ever met with. He pretended to have ridden in his carriage at Lyons for twenty years; and yet, that he might not starve at Paris, he was obliged to give lectures on the Italian language, of which he was wholly ignorant. Madame de Puisieux, posing as the author of the work entitled "Caractères," to which her name is prefixed, retained at the age of sixty, with a hunch back and a toothless mouth, the air and pretensions of which the affectation is scarcely pardon-able even in youth. I had conceived that a literary woman must be a very respectable character, es-pecially when morality was the subject of her writ-ings. The absurdities of Madame de Puisieux furnished me with a topic for reflection. Her con-versation was as little indicative of talent as her caprices were of sense. I began to perceive it was possible to store up reason for a public occasion, without making much use of it in one's own af-fairs; and I thought that perhaps the men who made a jest of female authors were not otherwise to blame than in applying exclusively to them what is equally true of themselves. Thus in a round of life very circumscribed did I find means to accumulate a fund of observations. I was placed in solitude, it is true, but yet on the confines of a world where I saw a variety of objects without be-ing encumbered by any. The concerts of Madame Lépine offered me a fresh point of view. I have already said that Lépine was a pupil of Pigale: he was, indeed, his right hand. At Rome he had mar-ried a woman who, as I presume, had been a can-tatrice, and whom his family had at first beheld with disfavor, but who proved by the propriety of her conduct that their disdain was ill-founded.

She had formed at her house a company of amateurs, skilled performers, to which none were admitted but those whom she called good com-pany. It met every Thursday, and my mother often conducted me thither. It was here I heard Jarnowich, St. George, Duport, Guérin, and many others. Here too I saw the wits of both sexes: Mad-emoiselle Morville, Madame Benoît, Sylvain Ma-réchal, etc., together with haughty baronesses, smart abbés, old chevaliers, and young fops. What a pleasant magic lantern! The apartments of Ma-dame Lépine, rue Neuve Saint Eustache, were not remarkably fine, nor was the concert room spa-cious; but it opened into another apartment, of which the folding-doors were kept open: there, placed in the circle, you had the combined advan-tage of hearing the music, seeing the authors, and conversing in the intervals. Seated close to my mother, and maintaining the silence that custom prescribes to young women, I was all eyes and

ears—unless we chanced for a moment to be in private with Madame Lépine, when I put a few questions to her, in order to illustrate to myself by her answers such observations as I had made.

One day this lady proposed to my mother to accompany her to a "charming" assembly, held at the house of a man of wit, whom we had some-times seen at Madame Lépine's. There was to be a feast of reason, a flow of soul, a reunion of the wits; there were to be readings "most delightful" —in short something "delicious" was promised. The proposal, however, was several times repeated before it was accepted. "Let us go," said I at last to my mother, "I begin to know enough of the world to presume that it must be either extremely agreeable or very absurd; and should the latter be the case, we shall be sure to find for once sufficient amusement in its novelty." The business is settled; and on the following Wednesday, which was the day of M. Vâse's literary assemblies, we set off with Madame Lépine for the *barrière* of the Tem-ple, where he resided. We mount to the third story, and arrive at a spacious room indifferently furnished, where were placed rows of rush-bottomed chairs, already partly occupied; dirty brass chandeliers, with tallow candles, illumined this resort of the Muses, the grotesque simplicity of which did not belie what I had heard of the philosophical rigor and poverty of an author. Some agreeable women, young girls, old dowagers, with a number of minor poets, virtuosos, and men of intrigue, composed this brilliant circle.

The master of ceremonies, seated before a ta-ble which formed a desk, opened the *séance* by reading a poetic effusion of his own, the subject of which was a pretty little lap-dog that the old Marchioness de Préville always carried in her muff, and which she now exhibited to the com-pany; for she was present, and thought herself obliged to gratify the auditors with a sight of the hero of the piece. The *bravos* and plaudits of the whole room paid homage to the fancy of M. Vâse, who, highly satisfied with himself, was to have yielded his seat to M. Delpêches, a poet who wrote little comic dramas for the theatre of Audinot, upon which he was accustomed to take the judgment of the society, or, in other words, the encouragement of its applause; but, either because of a sore throat, or the want of some verses in several of his scenes, or some other cause, he was prevented from attending. Imbert, author of the "Judgment of Paris," accordingly took the chair, and read an agreeable trifle, which was also extolled to the skies. A further distinction was in store for him. Mademoiselle de la Cossonnière succeeded him with a "Farewell to Colin," which, if not very ingenious, was at least meltingly tender. It was known that the lines were addressed to Imbert, who was about to undertake a journey; and compliments fell upon him in showers. Imbert acquitted his muse and himself by saluting all the females in the assembly. This brisk and gay ceremony, conducted however with decorum, was not at all pleasing to my mother, and appeared in so strange a light to me as to give me an air of embarrassment. After an epigram or couplet in which there was nothing remarkable, a pompous declaimer recited some verses in praise of Madame Benoît, who was present. Let me here say a word as to this lady, for the sake of those who have not read her romances, which were dead long before the Revolution, and upon which thick dust will have gathered long before these memoirs see the light.

*   *   *

JULIE DE LESPINASSE

FROM *Letters of Julie de Lespinasse*

FROM MEMOIR OF BARON DE GRIMM

*   *   *

Her circle met daily from five o'clock until nine in the evening. There we were sure to find choice

men of all orders in the State, the Church, the Court,—military men, foreigners, and the most distinguished men of letters. Every one agrees that though the name of M. d'Alembert may have drawn them thither, it was she alone who kept them there. Devoted wholly to the care of preserving that society, of which she was the soul and the charm, she subordinated to this purpose all her tastes and all her personal intimacies. She seldom went to the theatre or into the country, and when she did make an exception to this rule it was an event of which all Paris was notified in advance. . . . Politics, religion, philosophy, anecdotes, news, nothing was excluded from the conversation, and, thanks to her care, the most trivial little narrative gained, as naturally as possible, the place and notice it deserved. News of all kinds was gathered there in its first freshness.

*   *   *

FROM MEMOIR OF MARMONTEL

*   *   *

The circle was formed of persons who were not bound together. She had taken them here and there in society, but so well assorted were they that once there they fell into harmony like the strings of an instrument touched by an able hand. Following out that comparison, I may say that she played the instrument with an art that came of genius; she seemed to know what tone each string would yield before she touched it; I mean to say that our minds and our natures were so well known to her that in order to bring them into play she had but to say a word. Nowhere was conversation more lively, more brilliant, or better regulated than at her house. It was a rare phenomenon indeed, the degree of tempered, equable heat which she knew so well how to maintain, sometimes by moderating it, sometimes by quickening it. The continual activity of her soul was communicated to our souls, but measurably; her imagination was the mainspring, her reason the regulator. Remark that the brains she stirred at

---

From *Letters of Julie de Lespinasse,* translated by Katherine Wormley, Hardy, Pratt and Co., 1903.

will were neither feeble nor frivolous: the Coudil-lacs and Turgots were among them; d'Alembert was like a simple, docile child beside her. Her talent for casting out a thought and giving it for discussion to men of that class, her own talent in discussing it with precision, sometimes with eloquence, her talent for bringing forward new ideas and varying the topic—always with the facility and ease of a fairy, who, with one touch of her wand, can change the scene of her enchantment—these talents, I say, were not those of an ordinary woman. It was not with the follies of fashion and vanity that daily, during four hours of conversation, without languor and without vacuum, she knew how to make herself interesting to a wide circle of strong minds.

*   *   *

REVIEW QUESTIONS

1. Why did Madame Roland turn to the writings of Rousseau so late in her education?
2. What does this tell you about her attitude toward his opinions specifically and toward the education of women generally?
3. Were the salonnières more than simply hostesses at social gatherings?
4. What was their function in the salons?
5. Why do you suppose women rather than men fulfilled this role?
6. What larger purpose did the salons serve?
7. What does the fact that the salons were among the foremost institutions of Enlightenment tell you about the nature of Enlightenment as a historical phenomenon?

MARQUIS DE CONDORCET

FROM *Outline of a Historical View of the Progress of the Human Mind*

Marie-Jean-Antoine-Nicolas Caritat, Marquis de Condorcet (1734–1794) came from an old noble family of the principality of Orange. His ancestors had converted to Calvinism and settled in the Dauphiné. During the repression of French Protestantism under Louis XIV they reconverted to Roman Catholicism. He lost his father while still an infant and was raised by his mother in an atmosphere of intense Catholic piety. He was educated by Jesuits in Reims and the Collège de Navare. As an adult, Condorcet's thought showed strains of anticlericalism, and he opposed the Jesuit tradition of education. In 1758, he defied his family's wishes by traveling to Paris to pursue studies in mathematics. His work on integral calculus won him a seat in the French Academy of Sciences, where he advanced to assistant to the perpetual secretary in 1774 and to perpetual secretary in 1775. He retained this post until 1793, when his political enemies forced him into hiding. Condorcet espoused revolutionary ideas and was an early supporter of the goals of the French Revolution. Yet, he attacked the constitution proposed in the National Convention of 1793. This earned him the enmity of radicals, including a fellow academician, Chabot, who denounced him as an enemy of the revolution. He went into hiding and eventually fled Paris only to be caught and imprisoned. He committed suicide while in prison. Condorcet was a champion of the improvement of humankind through the proper use of reason. Rational laws governed human affairs just as they did nature. These laws could be discovered by reason and applied to improve the human condition. His Outline of a Historical View of the Progress of the Human Mind *(1795) was published posthumously, one year after Condorcet's death.*

From *Sketch for a Historical Picture on the Progress of the Human Mind,* Jean Antoine Nicolas Caritat Marquis de Condorcet, translated by June Barraclough, Weidenfeld and Nicolson, 1955. Reprinted by permission of the publisher.

The Tenth Stage

The Future Progress of the Human Mind

If man can, with almost complete assurance, predict phenomena when he knows their laws, and if, even when he does not, he can still, with great expectation of success, forecast the future on the basis of his experience of the past, why, then, should it be regarded as a fantastic undertaking to sketch, with some pretence to truth, the future destiny of man on the basis of his history? The sole foundation for belief in the natural sciences is this idea, that the general laws directing the phenomena of the universe, known or unknown, are necessary and constant. Why should this principle be any less true for the development of the intellectual and moral faculties of man than for the other operations of nature? Since beliefs founded on past experience of like conditions provide the only rule of conduct for the wisest of men, why should the philosopher be forbidden to base his conjectures on these same foundations, so long as he does not attribute to them a certainty superior to that warranted by the number, the constancy, and the accuracy of his observations?

Our hopes for the future condition of the human race can be subsumed under three important heads: the abolition of inequality between nations, the progress of equality within each nation, and the true perfection of mankind. Will all nations one day attain that state of civilization which the most enlightened, the freest and the least burdened by prejudices, such as the French and the Anglo-Americans, have attained already? Will the vast gulf that separates these peoples from the slavery of nations under the rule of monarchs, from the barbarism of African tribes, from the ignorance of savages, little by little disappear?

Is there on the face of the earth a nation whose inhabitants have been debarred by nature herself from the enjoyment of freedom and the exercise of reason?

Are those differences which have hitherto been seen in every civilized country in respect of the enlightenment, the resources, and the wealth enjoyed by the different classes into which it is divided, is that inequality between men which was aggravated or perhaps produced by the earliest progress of society, are these part of civilization itself, or are they due to the present imperfections of the social art? Will they necessarily decrease and ultimately make way for a real equality, the final end of the social art, in which even the effects of the natural differences between men will be mitigated and the only kind of inequality to persist will be that which is in the interests of all and which favours the progress of civilization, of education, and of industry, without entailing either poverty, humiliation, or dependence? In other words, will men approach a condition in which everyone will have the knowledge necessary to conduct himself in the ordinary affairs of life, according to the light of his own reason, to preserve his mind free from prejudice, to understand his rights and to exercise them in accordance with his conscience and his creed; in which everyone will become able, through the development of his faculties, to find the means of providing for his needs; and in which at last misery and folly will be the exception, and no longer the habitual lot of a section of society?

Is the human race to better itself, either by discoveries in the sciences and the arts, and so in the means to individual welfare and general prosperity; or by progress in the principles of conduct or practical morality; or by a true perfection of the intellectual, moral, or physical faculties of man, an improvement which may result from a perfection either of the instruments used to heighten the intensity of these faculties and to direct their use or of the natural constitution of man?

In answering these three questions we shall find in the experience of the past, in the observation of the progress that the sciences and civilization have already made, in the analysis of the progress of the human mind and of the development of its faculties, the strongest reasons for believing that nature has set no limit to the realization of our hopes.

If we glance at the state of the world today we see first of all that in Europe the principles of the French constitution are already those of all enlightened men. We see them too widely propagated, too seriously professed, for priests and despots to prevent their gradual penetration even into the hovels of their slaves; there they will soon awaken in these slaves the remnants of their common sense and inspire them with that smouldering indignation which not even constant humiliation and fear can smother in the soul of the oppressed.

As we move from nation to nation, we can see in each what special obstacles impede this revolution and what attitudes of mind favour it. We can distinguish the nations where we may expect it to be introduced gently by the perhaps belated wisdom of their governments, and those nations where its violence intensified by their resistance must involve all alike in a swift and terrible convulsion.

Can we doubt that either common sense or the senseless discords of European nations will add to the effects of the slow but inexorable progress of their colonies, and will soon bring about the independence of the New World? And then will not the European population in these colonies, spreading rapidly over that enormous land, either civilize or peacefully remove the savage nations who still inhabit vast tracts of its land?

Survey the history of our settlements and commercial undertakings in Africa or in Asia, and you will see how our trade monopolies, our treachery, our murderous contempt for men of another colour or creed, the insolence of our usurpations, the intrigues or the exaggerated proselytic zeal of our priests, have destroyed the respect and goodwill that the superiority of our knowledge and the benefits of our commerce at first won for us in the eyes of the inhabitants. But doubtless the moment approaches when, no longer presenting ourselves as always either tyrants or corrupters, we shall become for them the beneficent instruments of their freedom.

*   *   *

The time will therefore come when the sun will shine only on free men who know no other master but their reason; when tyrants and slaves, priests and their stupid or hypocritical instruments will exist only in works of history and on the stage; and when we shall think of them only to pity their victims and their dupes; to maintain ourselves in a state of vigilance by thinking on their excesses; and to learn how to recognize and so to destroy, by force of reason, the first seeds of tyranny and superstition, should they ever dare to reappear amongst us.

In looking at the history of societies we shall have had occasion to observe that there is often a great difference between the rights that the law allows its citizens and the rights that they actually enjoy, and, again, between the equality established by political codes and that which in fact exists amongst individuals: and we shall have noticed that these differences were one of the principal causes of the destruction of freedom in the Ancient republics, of the storms that troubled them, and of the weakness that delivered them over to foreign tyrants.

These differences have three main causes: inequality in wealth; inequality in status between the man whose means of subsistence are hereditary and the man whose means are dependent on the length of his life, or, rather, on that part of his life in which he is capable of work; and, finally, inequality in education.

We therefore need to show that these three sorts of real inequality must constantly diminish without however disappearing altogether: for they are the result of natural and necessary causes which it would be foolish and dangerous to wish to eradicate; and one could not even attempt to bring about the entire disappearance of their effects without introducing even more fecund sources of inequality, without striking more direct and more fatal blows at the rights of man.

It is easy to prove that wealth has a natural tendency to equality, and that any excessive disproportion could not exist or at least would rapidly disappear if civil laws did not provide artificial ways of perpetuating and uniting fortunes; if free trade and industry were allowed to remove the advantages that accrued wealth derives from any restrictive law or fiscal privilege; if taxes on covenants, the restrictions placed on their free employment, their subjection to tiresome formalities and the uncertainty and inevitable expense involved in implementing them did not hamper the activity of the poor man and swallow up his meagre capital; if the administration of the country did not afford some men ways of making their fortune that were closed to other citizens; if prejudice and avarice, so common in old age, did not preside over the making of marriages; and if, in a society enjoying simpler manners and more sensible institutions, wealth ceased to be a means of satisfying vanity and ambition, and if the equally misguided notions of austerity, which condemn

spending money in the cultivation of the more delicate pleasures, no longer insisted on the hoarding of all one's earnings.

Let us turn to the enlightened nations of Europe, and observe the size of their present populations in relation to the size of their territories. Let us consider, in agriculture and industry the proportion that holds between labour and the means of subsistence, and we shall see that it would be impossible for those means to be kept at their present level and consequently for the population to be kept at its present size if a great number of individuals were not almost entirely dependent for the maintenance of themselves and their family either on their own labour or on the interest from capital invested so as to make their labour more productive. Now both these sources of income depend on the life and even on the health of the head of the family. They provide what is rather like a life annuity, save that it is more dependent on chance; and in consequence there is a very real difference between people living like this and those whose resources are not at all subject to the same risks, who live either on revenue from land, or on the interest on capital which is almost independent of their own labour.

Here then is a necessary cause of inequality, of dependence and even of misery, which ceaselessly threatens the most numerous and most active class in our society.

We shall point out how it can be in great part eradicated by guaranteeing people in old age a means of livelihood produced partly by their own savings and partly by the savings of others who make the same outlay, but who die before they need to reap the reward; or, again, on the same principle of compensation, by securing for widows and orphans an income which is the same and costs the same for those families which suffer an early loss and for those which suffer it later; or again by providing all children with the capital necessary for the full use of their labour, available at the age when they start work and found a family, a capital which increases at the expense of those whom premature death prevents from reaching this age. It is to the application of the calculus to the probabilities of life and the investment of money that we owe the idea of these methods which have already been successful, although they have not been applied in a sufficiently comprehensive and exhaustive fashion to render them really useful, not merely to a few individuals, but to society as a whole, by making it possible to prevent those periodic disasters which strike at so many families and which are such a recurrent source of misery and suffering.

We shall point out that schemes of this nature, which can be organized in the name of the social authority and become one of its greatest benefits, can also be the work of private associations, which will be formed without any real risk, once the principles for the proper working of these schemes have been widely diffused and the mistakes which have been the undoing of a large number of these associations no longer hold terrors for us.

[We shall reveal other methods of ensuring this equality, either by seeing that credit is no longer the exclusive privilege of great wealth, but that it has another and no less sound foundation; or by making industrial progress and commercial activity more independent of the existence of the great capitalists. And once again, it is to the application of the calculus that we shall be indebted for such methods.]

The degree of equality in education that we can reasonably hope to attain, but that should be adequate, is that which excludes all dependence, either forced or voluntary. We shall show how this condition can be easily attained in the present state of human knowledge even by those who can study only for a small number of years in childhood, and then during the rest of their life in their few hours of leisure. We shall prove that, by a suitable choice of syllabus and of methods of education, we can teach the citizen everything that he needs to know in order to be able to manage his household, administer his affairs and employ his labour and his faculties in freedom; to know his rights and to be able to exercise them; to be acquainted with his duties and fulfil them satisfactorily; to judge his own and other men's

actions according to his own lights and to be a stranger to none of the high and delicate feelings which honour human nature; not to be in a state of blind dependence upon those to whom he must entrust his affairs or the exercise of his rights; to be in a proper condition to choose and supervise them; to be no longer the dupe of those popular errors which torment man with superstitious fears and chimerical hopes; to defend himself against prejudice by the strength of his reason alone; and, finally, to escape the deceits of charlatans who would lay snares for his fortune, his health, his freedom of thought and his conscience under the pretext of granting him health, wealth and salvation.

From such time onwards the inhabitants of a single country will no longer be distinguished by their use of a crude or refined language; they will be able to govern themselves according to their own knowledge; they will no longer be limited to a mechanical knowledge of the procedures of the arts or of professional routine; they will no longer depend for every trivial piece of business, every insignificant matter of instruction on clever men who rule over them in virtue of their necessary superiority; and so they will attain a real equality, since differences in enlightenment or talent can no longer raise a barrier between men who understand each other's feelings, ideas and language, some of whom may wish to be taught by others but, to do so, will have no need to be controlled by them, or who may wish to confide the care of government to the ablest of their number but will not be compelled to yield them absolute power in a spirit of blind confidence.

This kind of supervision has advantages even for those who do not exercise it, since it is employed for them and not against them. Natural differences of ability between men whose understanding has not been cultivated give rise, even in savage tribes, to charlatans and dupes, to clever men and men readily deceived. These same differences are truly universal, but now they are differences only between men of learning and upright men who know the value of learning without being dazzled by it; or between talent or genius and the common sense which can appreciate and benefit from them; so that even if these natural differences were greater, and more extensive than they are, they would be only the more influential in improving the relations between men and promoting what is advantageous for their independence and happiness.

These various causes of equality do not act in isolation; they unite, combine and support each other and so their cumulative effects are stronger, surer and more constant. With greater equality of education there will be greater equality in industry and so in wealth; equality in wealth necessarily leads to equality in education: and equality between the nations and equality within a single nation are mutually dependent.

So we might say that a well directed system of education rectifies natural inequality in ability instead of strengthening it, just as good laws remedy natural inequality in the means of subsistence, and just as in societies where laws have brought about this same equality, liberty, though subject to a regular constitution, will be more widespread, more complete than in the total independence of savage life. Then the social art will have fulfilled its aim, that of assuring and extending to all men enjoyment of the common rights to which they are called by nature.

The real advantages that should result from this progress, of which we can entertain a hope that is almost a certainty, can have no other term than that of the absolute perfection of the human race; since, as the various kinds of equality come to work in its favour by producing ampler sources of supply, more extensive education, more complete liberty, so equality will be more real and will embrace everything which is really of importance for the happiness of human beings.

It is therefore only by examining the progress and the laws of this perfection that we shall be able to understand the extent or the limits of our hopes.

*   *   *

The progress of the sciences ensures the progress of the art of education which in turn advances that of the sciences. This reciprocal influence, whose activity is ceaselessly renewed, deserves to be seen as one of the most powerful and active causes working for the perfection of mankind. At the present time a young man on leaving school may know more of the principles of mathematics than Newton ever learnt in years of study or discovered by dint of genius, and he may use the calculus with a facility then unknown. The same observation, with certain reservations, applies to all the sciences. As each advances, the methods of expressing a large number of proofs in a more economical fashion and so of making their comprehension an easier matter, advance with it. So, in spite of the progress of science, not only do men of the same ability find themselves at the same age on a level with the existing state of science, but with every generation, that which can be acquired in a certain time with a certain degree of intelligence and a certain amount of concentration will be permanently on the increase, and, as the elementary part of each science to which all men may attain grows and grows, it will more and more include all the knowledge necessary for each man to know for the conduct of the ordinary events of his life, and will support him in the free and independent exercise of his reason.

In the political sciences there are some truths that, with free people (that is to say, with certain generations in all countries) can be of use only if they are widely known and acknowledged. So the influence of these sciences upon the freedom and prosperity of nations must in some degree be measured by the number of truths that, as a result of elementary instruction, are common knowledge; the swelling progress of elementary instruction, connected with the necessary progress of these sciences promises us an improvement in the destiny of the human race, which may be regarded as indefinite, since it can have no other limits than that of this same progress.

We have still to consider two other general methods which will influence both the perfection of education and that of the sciences. One is the more extensive and less imperfect use of what we might call technical methods; the other is the setting up of a universal language.

I mean by technical methods the art of arranging a large number of subjects in a system so that we may straightway grasp their relations, quickly perceive their combinations, and readily form new combinations out of them.

We shall develop the principles and examine the utility of this art, which is still in its infancy, and which, as it improves, will enable us, within the compass of a small chart, to set out what could possibly not be expressed so well in a whole book, or, what is still more valuable, to present isolated facts in such a way as to allow us to deduce their general consequences. We shall see how by means of a small number of these charts, whose use can easily be learned, men who have not been sufficiently educated to be able to absorb details useful to them in ordinary life, may now be able to master them when the need arises; and how these methods may likewise be of benefit to elementary education itself in all those branches where it is concerned either with a regular system of truths or with a series of observations and facts.

A universal language is that which expresses by signs either real objects themselves, or well-defined collections composed of simple and general ideas, which are found to be the same or may arise in a similar form in the minds of all men, or the general relations holding between these ideas, the operations of the human mind, or the operations peculiar to the individual sciences, or the procedures of the arts. So people who become acquainted with these signs, the ways to combine them and the rules for forming them will understand what is written in this language and will be able to read it as easily as their own language.

It is obvious that this language might be used to set out the theory of a science or the rules of an art, to describe a new observation or experiment, the invention of a procedure, the discovery of a truth or a method; and that, as in algebra, when one has to make use of a new sign, those already known provide the means of explaining its import.

Such a language has not the disadvantages of a scientific idiom different from the vernacular. We have already observed that the use of such an idiom would necessarily divide society into two unequal classes, the one composed of men who, understanding this language, would possess the key to all the sciences, the other of men who, unable to acquire it, would therefore find themselves almost completely unable to acquire enlightenment. In contrast to this, a universal language would be learnt, like that of algebra, along with the science itself; the sign would be learnt at the same time as the object, idea or operation that it designates. He who, having mastered the elements of a science, would like to know more of it, would find in books not only truths he could understand by means of the signs whose import he has learnt, but also the explanation of such further signs as he needs in order to go on to other truths.

We shall show that the formation of such a language, if confined to the expression of those simple, precise propositions which form the system of a science or the practice of an art, is no chimerical scheme; that even at the present time it could be readily introduced to deal with a large number of objects; and that, indeed, the chief obstacle that would prevent its extension to others would be the humiliation of having to admit how very few precise ideas and accurate, unambiguous notions we actually possess.

We shall show that this language, ever improving and broadening its scope all the while, would be the means of giving to every subject embraced by the human intelligence, a precision and a rigour that would make knowledge of the truth easy and error almost impossible. Then the progress of every science would be as sure as that of mathematics, and the propositions that compose it would acquire a geometrical certainty, as far, that is, as is possible granted the nature of its aim and method.

All the causes that contribute to the perfection of the human race, all the means that ensure it must by their very nature exercise a perpetual influence and always increase their sphere of action. The proofs of this we have given and in the great work they will derive additional force from elaboration. We may conclude then that the perfectibility of man is indefinite. Meanwhile we have considered him as possessing the natural faculties and organization that he has at present. How much greater would be the certainty, how must vaster the scheme of our hopes if we could believe that these natural faculties themselves and this organization could also be improved? This is the last question that remains for us to ask ourselves.

Organic perfectibility or deterioration amongst the various strains in the vegetable and animal kingdom can be regarded as one of the general laws of nature. This law also applies to the human race. No-one can doubt that, as preventitive medicine improves and food and housing become healthier, as a way of life is established that develops our physical powers by exercise without ruining them by excess, as the two most virulent causes of deterioration, misery and excessive wealth, are eliminated, the average length of human life will be increased and a better health and a stronger physical constitution will be ensured. The improvement of medical practice, which will become more efficacious with the progress of reason and of the social order, will mean the end of infectious and hereditary diseases and illnesses brought on by climate, food, or working conditions. It is reasonable to hope that all other diseases may likewise disappear as their distant causes are discovered. Would it be absurd then to suppose that this perfection of the human species might be capable of indefinite progress; that the day will come when death will be due only to extraordinary accidents or to the decay of the vital forces, and that ultimately the average span between birth and decay will have no assignable value? Certainly man will not become immortal, but will not the interval between the first breath that he draws and the time when in the natural course of events, without disease or accident, he expires, increase indefinitely? Since we are now speaking of a progress that can be represented with some accuracy in figures or on a graph, we shall take this opportunity of explaining the two meanings that can be attached to the word *indefinite*.

In truth, this average span of life which we suppose will increase indefinitely as time passes, may grow in conformity either with a law such that it continually approaches a limitless length but without ever reaching it, or with a law such that through the centuries it reaches a length greater than any determinate quantity that we may assign to it as its limit. In the latter case such an increase is truly indefinite in the strictest sense of the word, since there is no term on this side of which it must of necessity stop. In the former case it is equally indefinite in relation to us, if we cannot fix the limit it always approaches without ever reaching, and particularly if, knowing only that it will never stop, we are ignorant in which of the two senses the term 'indefinite' can be applied to it. Such is the present condition of our knowledge as far as the perfectibility of the human race is concerned; such is the sense in which we may call it indefinite.

So, in the example under consideration, we are bound to believe that the average length of human life will for ever increase unless this is prevented by physical revolutions; we do not know what the limit is which it can never exceed. We cannot tell even whether the general laws of nature have determined such a limit or not.

But are not our physical faculties and the strength, dexterity and acuteness of our senses, to be numbered among the qualities whose perfection in the individual may be transmitted? Observation of the various breeds of domestic animals inclines us to believe that they are, and we can confirm this by direct observation of the human race.

Finally may we not extend such hopes to the intellectual and moral faculties? May not our parents, who transmit to us the benefits or disadvantages of their constitution, and from whom we receive our shape and features, as well as our tendencies to certain physical affections, hand on to us also that part of the physical organization which determines the intellect, the power of the brain, the ardour of the soul or the moral sensibility? Is it not probable that education, in perfecting these qualities, will at the same time influence, modify and perfect the organization itself? Analogy, investigation of the human faculties and the study of certain facts, all seem to give substance to such conjectures which would further push back the boundaries of our hopes.

These are the questions with which we shall conclude this final stage. How consoling for the philosopher who laments the errors, the crimes, the injustices which still pollute the earth and of which he is often the victim is this view of the human race, emancipated from its shackles, released from the empire of fate and from that of the enemies of its progress, advancing with a firm and sure step along the path of truth, virtue and happiness! It is the contemplation of this prospect that rewards him for all his efforts to assist the progress of reason and the defence of liberty. He dares to regard these strivings as part of the eternal chain of human destiny; and in this persuasion he is filled with the true delight of virtue and the pleasure of having done some lasting good which fate can never destroy by a sinister stroke of revenge, by calling back the reign of slavery and prejudice. Such contemplation is for him an asylum, in which the memory of his persecutors can-

not pursue him; there he lives in thought with man restored to his natural rights and dignity, forgets man tormented and corrupted by greed, fear or envy; there he lives with his peers in an Elysium created by reason and graced by the purest pleasures known to the love of mankind.

*   *   *

REVIEW QUESTIONS

1. On what does Condorcet found his ability to predict the future?
2. Would Newton agree "that nature has set no limit to the realization of one's hopes"?
3. In what areas of human endeavor does Condorcet measure progress?
4. What are the standards by which he measures it?
5. What does Condorcet see as the end point of Enlightenment?
6. What is the nature of freedom? Equality?
7. How does Condorcet measure equality?
8. What is its relation to a universal language?

JEAN-JACQUES ROUSSEAU

FROM *The Social Contract*

Jean-Jacques Rousseau (1712–1778) was one of the most original writers of the Enlightenment. A native of Geneva, he was raised by his father, a watchmaker. When he was sixteen, he left home and eventually settled in Paris. His first attempts to penetrate the world of philosophes and encyclopedists were difficult. In 1750, however, he won a literary award from the Academy of Dijon for an essay that contrasted the corruption of modern civilization with the natural goodness of simple, uncivilized human beings. Rousseau eventually settled in the town of Montmorency. His years there proved to be the most fruitful of his life. In a two-year span he wrote his most significant works: La nouvelle Héloise (1761), Émile (1761), and Le contrat social (1762). In The Social Contract, *as well as in his other works, Rousseau struggled with the freedom of the individual and the question of how to bal-*

ance it against the needs of the collectivity. He believed that the preservation of liberty depended on the creation of a new society by means of a social contract. The idea was not new, having been adopted by other enlightened thinkers from the political theory of John Locke. Rousseau's interpretation, however, was highly original. Locke believed that the social contract preserved freedom; Rousseau argued that the social contract preserved equality. Under Rousseau's social contract, people voluntarily relinquished certain rights and submitted to the general will, a vague entity that found expression in a set of positive laws under a virtuous legislator. These laws had absolute authority and would preserve absolute equality between people. Rousseau died before the French Revolution, the proponents of which adopted his thought, and his remains were transferred to the Panthéon in Paris.

From *The Social Contract,* J. Rousseau, translated by Henry J. Tozer, Scribner, 1898.

Book I

I mean to inquire if, in the civil order, there can be any sure and legitimate rule of administration, men being taken as they are and laws as they might be. In this inquiry I shall endeavour always to unite what right sanctions with what is prescribed by interest, in order that justice and utility may in no case be divided.

I enter upon my task without proving the importance of the subject. I shall be asked if I am a prince or a legislator, to write on politics. I answer that I am neither, and that is why I do so. If I were a prince or a legislator, I should not waste time in saying what wants doing; I should do it, or hold my peace.

As I was born a citizen of a free State, and a member of the Sovereign, I feel that, however feeble the influence my voice can have on public affairs, the right of voting on them makes it my duty to study them: and I am happy, when I reflect upon governments, to find my inquiries always furnish me with new reasons for loving that of my own country.

Chapter I

SUBJECT OF THE FIRST BOOK

Man is born free; and everywhere he is in chains. One thinks himself the master of others, and still remains a greater slave than they. How did this change come about? I do not know. What can make it legitimate? That question I think I can answer.

If I took into account only force, and the effects derived from it, I should say: "As long as a people is compelled to obey, and obeys, it does well; as soon as it can shake off the yoke, and shakes it off, it does still better; for, regaining its liberty by the same right as took it away, either it is justified in resuming it, or there was no justification for those who took it away." But the social order is a sacred right which is the basis of all rights. Nevertheless, this right does not come from nature, and must therefore be founded on conventions. Before coming to that, I have to prove what I have just asserted.

Chapter II

THE FIRST SOCIETIES

The most ancient of all societies, and the only one that is natural, is the family: and even so the children remain attached to the father only so long as they need him for their preservation. As soon as this need ceases, the natural bond is dissolved. The children, released from the obedience they owed to the father, and the father, released from the care he owed his children, return equally to independence. If they remain united, they continue so no longer naturally, but voluntarily; and the family itself is then maintained only by convention.

This common liberty results from the nature of man. His first law is to provide for his own preservation, his first cares are those which he owes to himself; and, as soon as he reaches years of discretion, he is the sole judge of the proper means of preserving himself, and consequently becomes his own master.

The family then may be called the first model of political societies: the ruler corresponds to the father, and the people to the children; and all, being born free and equal, alienate their liberty only for their own advantage. The whole difference is that, in the family, the love of the father for his children repays him for the care he takes of them, while, in the State, the pleasure of commanding takes the place of the love which the chief cannot have for the peoples under him.

Grotius denies that all human power is established in favour of the governed, and quotes slavery as an example. His usual method of reasoning is constantly to establish right by fact. It would be possible to employ a more logical method, but none could be more favourable to tyrants.

It is then, according to Grotius, doubtful whether the human race belongs to a hundred men, or that hundred men to the human race: and, throughout his book, he seems to incline to the former alternative, which is also the view of Hobbes. On this showing, the human species is divided into so many herds of cattle, each with its ruler, who keeps guard over them for the purpose of devouring them.

As a shepherd is of a nature superior to that of his flock, the shepherds of men, i.e. their rulers, are of a nature superior to that of the peoples under them. Thus, Philo tells us, the Emperor Caligula reasoned, concluding equally well either that kings were gods, or that men were beasts.

The reasoning of Caligula agrees with that of Hobbes and Grotius. Aristotle, before any of them, had said that men are by no means equal naturally, but that some are born for slavery, and others for dominion.

Aristotle was right; but he took the effect for the cause. Nothing can be more certain than that every man born in slavery is born for slavery. Slaves lose everything in their chains, even the desire of escaping from them: they love their servitude, as the comrades of Ulysses loved their brutish condition. If then there are slaves by nature, it is because there have been slaves against nature. Force made the first slaves, and their cowardice perpetuated the condition.

I have said nothing of King Adam, or Emperor Noah, father of the three great monarchs who shared out the universe, like the children of Saturn, whom some scholars have recognized in them. I trust to getting due thanks for my moderation; for, being a direct descendant of one of these princes, perhaps of the eldest branch, how do I know that a verification of titles might not leave me the legitimate king of the human race? In any case, there can be no doubt that Adam was sovereign of the world, as Robinson Crusoe was of his island, as long as he was its only inhabitant; and this empire had the advantage that the monarch, safe on his throne, had no rebellions, wars, or conspirators to fear.

Chapter III

THE RIGHT OF THE STRONGEST

The strongest is never strong enough to be always the master, unless he transforms strength into right, and obedience into duty. Hence the right of the strongest, which, though to all seeming meant ironically, is really laid down as a fundamental principle. But are we never to have an explanation of this phrase? Force is a physical power, and I fail to see what moral effect it can have. To yield to force is an act of necessity, not of will—at the most, an act of prudence. In what sense can it be a duty?

Suppose for a moment that this so-called "right" exists. I maintain that the sole result is a mass of inexplicable nonsense. For, if force creates right, the effect changes with the cause: every force that is greater than the first succeeds to its right. As soon as it is possible to disobey with impunity, disobedience is legitimate; and, the strongest being always in the right, the only thing that matters is to act so as to become the strongest. But what kind of right is that which perishes when force fails? If we must obey perforce, there is no need to obey because we ought; and if we are not forced to obey, we are under no obligation to do so. Clearly, the word "right" adds nothing to force: in this connection, it means absolutely nothing.

Obey the powers that be. If this means yield to force, it is a good precept, but superfluous: I can answer for its never being violated. All power comes from God, I admit; but so does all sickness: does that mean that we are forbidden to call in the doctor? A brigand surprises me at the edge of a wood: must I not merely surrender my purse on compulsion; but, even if I could withhold it, am I in conscience bound to give it up? For certainly the pistol he holds is also a power.

Let us then admit that force does not create right, and that we are obliged to obey only legitimate powers. In that case, my original question recurs.

Chapter IV

SLAVERY

Since no man has a natural authority over his fellow, and force creates no right, we must conclude that conventions form the basis of all legitimate authority among men.

If an individual, says Grotius, can alienate his liberty and make himself the slave of a master, why could not a whole people do the same and make itself subject to a king? There are in this passage plenty of ambiguous words which would need explaining; but let us confine ourselves to the word *alienate*. To alienate is to give or to sell. Now, a man who becomes the slave of another does not give himself; he sells himself, at the least for his subsistence: but for what does a people sell itself? A king is so far from furnishing his subjects

with their subsistence that he gets his own only from them; and, according to Rabelais, kings do not live on nothing. Do subjects then give their persons on condition that the king takes their goods also? I fail to see what they have left to preserve.

It will be said that the despot assures his subjects civil tranquillity. Granted; but what do they gain, if the wars his ambition brings down upon them, his insatiable avidity, and the vexatious conduct of his ministers press harder on them than their own dissensions would have done? What do they gain, if the very tranquillity they enjoy is one of their miseries? Tranquillity is found also in dungeons; but is that enough to make them desirable places to live in? The Greeks imprisoned in the cave of the Cyclops lived there very tranquilly, while they were awaiting their turn to be devoured.

To say that a man gives himself gratuitously, is to say what is absurd and inconceivable; such an act is null and illegitimate, from the mere fact that he who does it is out of his mind. To say the same of a whole people is to suppose a people of madmen; and madness creates no right.

Even if each man could alienate himself, he could not alienate his children: they are born men and free; their liberty belongs to them, and no one but they has the right to dispose of it. Before they come to years of discretion, the father can, in their name, lay down conditions for their preservation and well-being, but he cannot give them irrevocably and without conditions: such a gift is contrary to the ends of nature, and exceeds the rights of paternity. It would therefore be necessary, in order to legitimize an arbitrary government, that in every generation the people should be in a position to accept or reject it; but, were this so, the government would be no longer arbitrary.

To renounce liberty is to renounce being a man, to surrender the rights of humanity and even its duties. For him who renounces everything no indemnity is possible. Such a renunciation is incompatible with man's nature; to remove all liberty from his will is to remove all morality from his acts. Finally, it is an empty and contradictory convention that sets up, on the one side, absolute authority, and, on the other, unlimited obedience. Is it not clear that we can be under no obligation to a person from whom we have the right to exact everything? Does not this condition alone, in the absence of equivalence or exchange, in itself involve the nullity of the act? For what right can my slave have against me, when all that he has belongs to me, and, his right being mine, this right of mine against myself is a phrase devoid of meaning?

Grotius and the rest find in war another origin for the so-called right of slavery. The victor having, as they hold, the right of killing the vanquished, the latter can buy back his life at the price of his liberty; and this convention is the more legitimate because it is to the advantage of both parties.

But it is clear that this supposed right to kill the conquered is by no means deducible from the state of war. Men, from the mere fact that, while they are living in their primitive independence, they have no mutual relations stable enough to constitute either the state of peace or the state of war, cannot be naturally enemies. War is constituted by a relation between things, and not between persons; and, as the state of war cannot arise out of simple personal relations, but only out of real relations, private war, or war of man with man, can exist neither in the state of nature, where there is no constant property, nor in the social state, where everything is under the authority of the laws.

Individual combats, duels, and encounters, are acts which cannot constitute a state; while the private wars, authorized by the Establishments of Louis IX, King of France, and suspended by the Peace of God, are abuses of feudalism, in itself an absurd system if ever there was one, and contrary to the principles of natural right and to all good polity.

War then is a relation, not between man and man, but between State and State, and individuals are enemies only accidently, not as men, nor even as citizens, but as soldiers; not as members of their country, but as its defenders. Finally, each State can have for enemies only other States, and not men; for between things disparate in nature there can be no real relation.

Furthermore, this principle is in conformity with the established rules of all times and the constant practice of all civilized peoples. Declarations of war are intimations less to powers than to their subjects. The foreigner, whether king, individual, or people, who robs, kills, or detains the subjects, without declaring war on the prince, is not an enemy, but a brigand. Even in real war, a just prince, while laying hands, in the enemy's country, on all that belongs to the public, respects the lives and goods of individuals: he respects rights on which his own are founded. The object of the war being the destruction of the hostile State, the other side has a right to kill its defenders, while they are bearing arms; but as soon as they lay them down and surrender, they cease to be enemies or instruments of the enemy, and become once more merely men, whose life no one has any right to take. Sometimes it is possible to kill the State without killing a single one of its members; and war gives no right which is not necessary to the gaining of its object. These principles are not those of Grotius: they are not based on the authority of poets, but derived from the nature of reality and based on reason.

The right of conquest has no foundation other than the right of the strongest. If war does not give the conqueror the right to massacre the conquered peoples, the right to enslave them cannot be based upon a right which does not exist. No one has a right to kill an enemy except when he cannot make him a slave, and the right to enslave him cannot therefore be derived from the right to kill him. It is accordingly an unfair exchange to make him buy at the price of his liberty his life, over which the victor holds no right. Is it not clear that there is a vicious circle in founding the right of life and death on the right of slavery, and the right of slavery on the right of life and death?

Even if we assume this terrible right to kill everybody, I maintain that a slave made in war, or a conquered people, is under no obligation to a master, except to obey him as far as he is compelled to do so. By taking an equivalent for his life, the victor has not done him a favour; instead of killing him without profit, he has killed him usefully. So far then is he from acquiring over him any authority in addition to that of force, that the state of war continues to subsist between them: their mutual relation is the effect of it, and the usage of the right of war does not imply a treaty of peace. A convention has indeed been made; but this convention, so far from destroying the state of war, presupposes its continuance.

So, from whatever aspect we regard the question, the right of slavery is null and void, not only as being illegitimate, but also because it is absurd and meaningless. The words *slave* and *right* contradict each other, and are mutually exclusive. It will always be equally foolish for a man to say to a man or to a people: "I make with you a convention wholly at your expense and wholly to my advantage; I shall keep it as long as I like, and you will keep it as long as I like."

*   *   *

Chapter VI

THE SOCIAL COMPACT

I suppose men to have reached the point at which the obstacles in the way of their preservation in the state of nature show their power of resistance to be greater than the resources at the disposal of each individual for his maintenance in that state. That primitive condition can then subsist no longer; and the human race would perish unless it changed its manner of existence.

But, as men cannot engender new forces, but only unite and direct existing ones, they have no other means of preserving themselves than the formation, by aggregation, of a sum of forces great enough to overcome the resistance. These they have to bring into play by means of a single motive power, and cause to act in concert.

This sum of forces can arise only where several persons come together: but, as the force and liberty of each man are the chief instruments of his self-preservation, how can he pledge them without harming his own interests, and neglecting the care he owes to himself? This difficulty, in its bearing on my present subject, may be stated in the following terms:

"The problem is to find a form of association which will defend and protect with the whole common force the person and goods of each associate, and in which each, while uniting himself with all, may still obey himself alone, and remain as free as before." This is the fundamental problem of which the *Social Contract* provides the solution.

The clauses of this contract are so determined by the nature of the act that the slightest modification would make them vain and ineffective; so that, although they have perhaps never been formally set forth, they are everywhere the same and everywhere tacitly admitted and recognized, until, on the violation of the social compact, each regains his original rights and resumes his natural liberty, while losing the conventional liberty in favour of which he renounced it.

These clauses, properly understood, may be reduced to one—the total alienation of each associate, together with all his rights, to the whole community; for, in the first place, as each gives himself absolutely, the conditions are the same for all; and, this being so, no one has any interest in making them burdensome to others.

Moreover, the alienation being without reserve, the union is as perfect as it can be, and no associate has anything more to demand: for, if the individuals retained certain rights, as there would be no common superior to decide between them and the public, each, being on one point his own judge, would ask to be so on all; the state of nature would thus continue, and the association would necessarily become inoperative or tyrannical.

Finally, each man, in giving himself to all, gives himself to nobody; and as there is no associate over which he does not acquire the same right as he yields others over himself, he gains an equivalent for everything he loses, and an increase of force for the preservation of what he has.

If then we discard from the social compact

what is not of its essence, we shall find that it reduces itself to the following terms:

"Each of us puts his person and all his power in common under the supreme direction of the general will, and, in our corporate capacity, we receive each member as an indivisible part of the whole."

At once, in place of the individual personality of each contracting party, this act of association creates a moral and collective body, composed of as many members as the assembly contains voters, and receiving from this act its unity, its common identity, its life, and its will. This public person, so formed by the union of all other persons, formerly took the name of *city*, and now takes that of *Republic* or *body politic*; it is called by its members *State* when passive, *Sovereign* when active, and *Power* when compared with others like itself. Those who are associated in it take collectively the name of *people*, and severally are called *citizens*, as sharing in the sovereign power, and *subjects*, as being under the laws of the State. But these terms are often confused and taken one for another: it is enough to know how to distinguish them when they are being used with precision.

Chapter VII

THE SOVEREIGN

This formula shows us that the act of association comprises a mutual undertaking between the public and the individuals, and that each individual, in making a contract, as we may say, with himself, is bound in a double capacity; as a member of the Sovereign he is bound to the individuals, and as a member of the State to the Sovereign. But the maxim of civil right, that no one is bound by undertakings made to himself, does not apply in this case; for there is a great difference between incurring an obligation to yourself and incurring one to a whole of which you form a part.

Attention must further be called to the fact that public deliberation, while competent to bind all the subjects to the Sovereign, because of the two different capacities in which each of them may be regarded, cannot, for the opposite reason, bind the Sovereign to itself; and that it is consequently against the nature of the body politic for the Sovereign to impose on itself a law which it cannot infringe. Being able to regard itself in only one capacity, it is in the position of an individual who makes a contract with himself; and this makes it clear that there neither is nor can be any kind of fundamental law binding on the body of the people—not even the social contract itself. This does not mean that the body politic cannot enter into undertakings with others, provided the contract is not infringed by them; for in relation to what is external to it, it becomes a simple being, an individual.

But the body politic or the Sovereign, drawing its being wholly from the sanctity of the contract, can never bind itself, even to an outsider, to do anything derogatory to the original act, for instance, to alienate any part of itself, or to submit to another Sovereign. Violation of the act by which it exists would be self-annihilation; and that which is itself nothing can create nothing.

As soon as this multitude is so united in one body, it is impossible to offend against one of the members without attacking the body, and still more to offend against the body without the members resenting it. Duty and interest therefore equally oblige the two contracting parties to give each other help; and the same men should seek to combine, in their double capacity, all the advantages dependent upon that capacity.

Again, the Sovereign, being formed wholly of the individuals who compose it, neither has nor can have any interest contrary to theirs; and consequently the sovereign power need give no guarantee to its subjects, because it is impossible for the body to wish to hurt all its members. We shall also see later on that it cannot hurt any in particular. The Sovereign, merely by virtue of what it is, is always what it should be.

This, however, is not the case with the relation of the subjects to the Sovereign, which, despite the common interest, would have no security that they would fulfil their undertakings, unless it found means to assure itself of their fidelity.

In fact, each individual, as a man, may have a particular will contrary or dissimilar to the general will which he has as a citizen. His particular interest may speak to him quite differently from the common interest: his absolute and naturally independent existence may make him look upon what he owes to the common cause as a gratuitous contribution, the loss of which will do less harm to others than the payment of it is burdensome to himself; and, regarding the moral person which constitutes the State as a *persona ficta*, because not a man, he may wish to enjoy the rights of citizenship without being ready to fulfil the duties of a subject. The continuance of such an injustice could not but prove the undoing of the body politic.

In order then that the social compact may not be an empty formula, it tacitly includes the undertaking, which alone can give force to the rest, that whoever refuses to obey the general will shall be compelled to do so by the whole body. This means nothing less than that he will be forced to be free; for this is the condition which, by giving each citizen to his country, secures him against all personal dependence. In this lies the key to the working of the political machine; this alone legitimizes civil undertakings, which, without it, would be absurd, tyrannical, and liable to the most frightful abuses.

Chapter VIII

THE CIVIL STATE

The passage from the state of nature to the civil state produces a very remarkable change in man, by substituting justice for instinct in his conduct, and giving his actions the morality they had formerly lacked. Then only, when the voice of duty takes the place of physical impulses and right of appetite, does man, who so far had considered only himself, find that he is forced to act on different principles, and to consult his reason before listening to his inclinations. Although, in this state, he deprives himself of some advantages which he got from nature, he gains in return others so great, his faculties are so stimulated and developed, his ideas so extended, his feelings so ennobled, and his whole soul so uplifted, that, did not the abuses of this new condition often degrade him below that which he left, he would be bound to bless continually the happy moment which took him from it for ever, and, instead of a stupid and unimaginative animal, made him an intelligent being and a man.

Let us draw up the whole account in terms easily commensurable. What man loses by the social contract is his natural liberty and an unlimited right to everything he tries to get and succeeds in getting; what he gains is civil liberty and the proprietorship of all he possesses. If we are to avoid mistake in weighing one against the other, we must clearly distinguish natural liberty, which is bounded only by the strength of the individual, from civil liberty, which is limited by the general will; and possession, which is merely the effect of force or the right of the first occupier, from property, which can be founded only on a positive title.

We might, over and above all this, add, to what man acquires in the civil state, moral liberty, which alone makes him truly master of himself; for the mere impulse of appetite is slavery, while obedience to a law which we prescribe to ourselves is liberty. But I have already said too much on this head, and the philosophical meaning of the word liberty does not now concern us.

*   *   *

Book II

Chapter I

THAT SOVEREIGNTY IS INALIENABLE

The first and most important deduction from the principles we have so far laid down is that the general will alone can direct the State according to the object for which it was instituted, i.e. the common good: for if the clashing of particular interests made the establishment of societies necessary, the agreement of these very interests made it possible. The common element in these different interests is what forms the social tie; and, were there no point of agreement between them all, no society could exist. It is solely on the basis of this common interest that every society should be governed.

I hold then that Sovereignty, being nothing less than the exercise of the general will, can never be alienated, and that the Sovereign, who is no less than a collective being, cannot be represented except by himself: the power indeed may be transmitted, but not the will.

In reality, if it is not impossible for a particular will to agree on some point with the general will, it is at least impossible for the agreement to be lasting and constant; for the particular will tends, by its very nature, to partiality, while the general will tends to equality. It is even more impossible to have any guarantee of this agreement; for even if it should always exist, it would be the effect not of art, but of chance. The Sovereign may indeed say: "I now will actually what this man wills, or at least what he says he wills"; but it cannot say: "What he wills tomorrow, I too shall will" because it is absurd for the will to bind itself for the future, nor is it incumbent on any will to consent to anything that is not for the good of the being who wills. If then the people promises simply to obey, by that very act it dissolves itself and loses what makes it a people; the moment a master exists, there is no longer a Sovereign, and from that moment the body politic has ceased to exist.

This does not mean that the commands of the rulers cannot pass for general wills, so long as the Sovereign, being free to oppose them, offers no opposition. In such a case, universal silence is taken to imply the consent of the people. This will be explained later on.

Chapter II

THAT SOVEREIGNTY IS INDIVISIBLE

Sovereignty, for the same reason as makes it inalienable, is indivisible; for will either is, or is not, general; it is the will either of the body of the people, or only of a part of it. In the first case, the will, when declared, is an act of Sovereignty and constitutes law: in the second, it is merely a particular will, or act of magistracy—at the most a decree.

But our political theorists, unable to divide Sovereignty in principle, divide it according to its object: into force and will; into legislative power and executive power; into rights of taxation, justice, and war; into internal administration and power of foreign treaty. Sometimes they confuse all these sections, and sometimes they distinguish them; they turn the Sovereign into a fantastic being composed of several connected pieces: it is as if they were making man of several bodies, one with eyes, one with arms, another with feet, and each with nothing besides. We are told that the jugglers of Japan dismember a child before the eyes of the spectators; then they throw all the members into the air one after another, and the child falls down alive and whole. The conjuring tricks of our political theorists are very like that; they first dismember the body politic by an illusion worthy of a fair, and then join it together again we know not how.

This error is due to a lack of exact notions concerning the Sovereign authority, and to taking for parts of it what are only emanations from it. Thus, for example, the acts of declaring war and making peace have been regarded as acts of Sovereignty; but this is not the case, as these acts do not constitute law, but merely the application of a law, a particular act which decides how the law applies, as we shall see clearly when the idea attached to the word "law" has been defined.

If we examined the other divisions in the same

manner, we should find that, whenever Sovereignty seems to be divided, there is an illusion: the rights which are taken as being part of Sovereignty are really all subordinate, and always imply supreme wills of which they only sanction the execution.

It would be impossible to estimate the obscurity this lack of exactness has thrown over the decisions of writers who have dealt with political right, when they have used the principles laid down by them to pass judgment on the respective rights of kings and peoples. Every one can see, in Chapters III and IV of the first book of Grotius, how the learned man and his translator, Barbeyrac, entangle and tie themselves up in their own sophistries, for fear of saying too little or too much of what they think, and so offending the interests they have to conciliate. Grotius, a refugee in France, ill content with his own country, and desirous of paying his court to Louis XIII, to whom his book is dedicated, spares no pains to rob the peoples of all their rights and invest kings with them by every conceivable artifice. This would also have been much to the taste of Barbeyrac, who dedicated his translation to George I of England. But unfortunately the expulsion of James II, which he called his "abdication," compelled him to use all reserve, to shuffle and to tergiversate, in order to avoid making William out a usurper. If these two writers had adopted the true principles, all difficulties would have been removed, and they would have been always consistent; but it would have been a sad truth for them to tell, and would have paid court for them to no one save the people. Moreover, truth is no road to fortune, and the people dispenses neither ambassadorships, nor professorships, nor pensions.

Chapter III

WHETHER THE GENERAL WILL IS FALLIBLE

It follows from what has gone before that the general will is always right and tends to the public advantage; but it does not follow that the deliberations of the people are always equally correct. Our will is always for our own good, but we do not always see what that is; the people is never corrupted, but it is often deceived, and on such occasions only does it seem to will what is bad.

There is often a great deal of difference between the will of all and the general will; the latter considers only the common interest, while the former takes private interest into account, and is no more than a sum of particular wills: but take away from these same wills the pluses and minuses that cancel one another, and the general will remains as the sum of the differences.

If, when the people, being furnished with adequate information, held its deliberations, the citizens had no communication one with another, the grand total of the small differences would always give the general will, and the decision would always be good. But when factions arise, and partial associations are formed at the expense of the great association, the will of each of these associations becomes general in relation to its members, while it remains particular in relation to the State: it may then be said that there are no longer as many votes as there are men, but only as many as there are associations. The differences become less numerous and give a less general result. Lastly, when one of these associations is so great as to prevail over all the rest, the result is no longer a sum of small differences, but a single difference; in this case there is no longer a general will, and the opinion which prevails is purely particular.

It is therefore essential, if the general will is to be able to express itself, that there should be no partial society within the State, and that each citizen should think only his own thoughts: which was indeed the sublime and unique system established by the great Lycurgus. But if there are partial societies, it is best to have as many as possible and to prevent them from being unequal, as was done by Solon, Numa, and Servius. These precautions are the only ones that can guarantee that the general will shall be always enlightened, and that the people shall in no way deceive itself.

Chapter IV

THE LIMITS OF THE SOVEREIGN POWER

If the State is a moral person whose life is in the union of its members, and if the most important of its cares is the care for its own preservation, it must have a universal and compelling force, in order to move and dispose each part as may be most advantageous to the whole. As nature gives each man absolute power over all his members, the social compact gives the body politic absolute power over all its members also; and it is this power which, under the direction of the general will, bears, as I have said, the name of Sovereignty.

But, besides the public person, we have to consider the private persons composing it, whose life and liberty are naturally independent of it. We are bound then to distinguish clearly between the respective rights of the citizens and the Sovereign, and between the duties the former have to fulfil as subjects, and the natural rights they should enjoy as men.

Each man alienates, I admit, by the social compact, only such part of his powers, goods, and liberty as it is important for the community to control; but it must also be granted that the Sovereign is sole judge of what is important.

Every service a citizen can render the State he ought to render as soon as the Sovereign demands it; but the Sovereign, for its part, cannot impose upon its subjects any fetters that are useless to the community, nor can it even wish to do so; for no more by the law of reason than by the law of nature can anything occur without a cause.

The undertakings which bind us to the social body are obligatory only because they are mutual; and their nature is such that in fulfilling them we cannot work for others without working for ourselves. Why is it that the general will is always in the right, and that all continually will the happiness of each one, unless it is because there is not a man who does not think of "each" as meaning him, and consider himself in voting for all? This proves that equality of rights and the idea of jus-

tice which such equality creates originate in the preference each man gives to himself, and accordingly in the very nature of man. It proves that the general will, to be really such, must be general in its object as well as its essence; that it must both come from all and apply to all; and that it loses its natural rectitude when it is directed to some particular and determinate object, because in such a case we are judging of something foreign to us, and have no true principle of equity to guide us.

Indeed, as soon as a question of particular fact or right arises on a point not previously regulated by a general convention, the matter becomes contentious. It is a case in which the individuals concerned are one party, and the public the other, but in which I can see neither the law that ought to be followed nor the judge who ought to give the decision. In such a case, it would be absurd to propose to refer the question to an express decision of the general will, which can be only the conclusion reached by one of the parties and in consequence will be, for the other party, merely an external and particular will, inclined on this occasion to injustice and subject to error. Thus, just as a particular will cannot stand for the general will, the general will, in turn, changes its nature, when its object is particular, and, as general, cannot pronounce on a man or a fact. When, for instance, the people of Athens nominated or displaced its rulers, decreed honours to one, and imposed penalties on another, and, by a multitude of particular decrees, exercised all the functions of government indiscriminately, it had in such cases no longer a general will in the strict sense; it was acting no longer as Sovereign, but as magistrate. This will seem contrary to current views; but I must be given time to expound my own.

It should be seen from the foregoing that what makes the will general is less the number of voters than the common interest uniting them; for, under this system, each necessarily submits to the conditions he imposes on others: and this admirable agreement between interest and justice gives to the common deliberations an equitable character which at once vanishes when any particular question is discussed, in the absence of a common interest to unite and identify the ruling of the judge with that of the party.

From whatever side we approach our principle, we reach the same conclusion, that the social compact sets up among the citizens an equality of such a kind, that they all bind themselves to observe the same conditions and should therefore all enjoy the same rights. Thus, from the very nature of the compact, every act of Sovereignty, i.e. every authentic act of the general will, binds or favours all the citizens equally; so that the Sovereign recognizes only the body of the nation, and draws no distinctions between those of whom it is made up. What, then, strictly speaking, is an act of Sovereignty? It is not a convention between a superior and an inferior, but a convention between the body and each of its members. It is legitimate, because based on the social contract, and equitable, because common to all; useful, because it can have no other object than the general good, and stable, because guaranteed by the public force and the supreme power. So long as the subjects have to submit only to conventions of this sort, they obey no one but their own will; and to ask how far the respective rights of the Sovereign and the citizens extend, is to ask up to what point the latter can enter into undertakings with themselves, each with all, and all with each.

We can see from this that the sovereign power, absolute, sacred, and inviolable as it is, does not and cannot exceed the limits of general conventions, and that every man may dispose at will of such goods and liberty as these conventions leave him; so that the Sovereign never has a right to lay more charges on one subject than on another, because, in that case, the question becomes particular, and ceases to be within its competency.

When these distinctions have once been admitted, it is seen to be so untrue that there is, in the social contract, any real renunciation on the part of the individuals, that the position in which they find themselves as a result of the contract is really preferable to that in which they were before. Instead of a renunciation, they have made an advantageous exchange: instead of an uncertain and precarious way of living they have got one that is better and more secure; instead of natural independence they have got liberty, instead of the power to harm others security for themselves, and instead of their strength, which others might overcome, a right which social union makes invincible. Their very life, which they have devoted to the State, is by it constantly protected; and when they risk it in the State's defence, what more are they doing than giving back what they have received from it? What are they doing that they would not do more often and with greater danger in the state of nature, in which they would inevitably have to fight battles at the peril of their lives in defence of that which is the means of their preservation? All have indeed to fight when their country needs them; but then no one has ever to fight for himself. Do we not gain something by running, on behalf of what gives us our security, only some of the risks we should have to run for ourselves, as soon as we lost it?

*   *   *

Chapter VII

THE LEGISLATOR

In order to discover the rules of society best suited to nations, a superior intelligence beholding all the passions of men without experiencing any of them would be needed. This intelligence would have to be wholly unrelated to our nature, while knowing it through and through; its happiness would have to be independent of us, and yet ready to occupy itself with ours; and lastly, it would have, in the march of time, to look forward to a distant glory, and, working in one century, to be able to enjoy in the next. It would take gods to give men laws.

What Caligula argued from the facts, Plato, in the dialogue called the *Politicus*, argued in defining the civil or kingly man, on the basis of right. But if great princes are rare, how much more so are great legislators! The former have only to follow the pattern which the latter have to lay down. The legislator is the engineer who invents the machine, the prince merely the mechanic who sets it up and makes it go. "At the birth of societies," says Montesquieu, "the rulers of Republics establish institutions, and afterwards the institutions mould the rulers."

He who dares to undertake the making of a people's institutions ought to feel himself capable, so to speak, of changing human nature, of transforming each individual, who is by himself a complete and solitary whole, into part of a greater whole from which he in a manner receives his life and being; of altering man's constitution for the purpose of strengthening it; and of substituting a partial and moral existence for the physical and independent existence nature has conferred on us all. He must, in a word, take away from man his own resources and give him instead new ones alien to him, and incapable of being made use of without the help of other men. The more completely these natural resources are annihilated, the greater and the more lasting are those which he acquires, and the more stable and perfect the new institutions; so that if each citizen is nothing and can do nothing without the rest, and the resources acquired by the whole are equal or superior to the aggregate of the resources of all the individuals, it may be said that legislation is at the highest possible point of perfection.

The legislator occupies in every respect an extraordinary position in the State. If he should do so by reason of his genius, he does so no less by reason of his office, which is neither magistracy, nor Sovereignty. This office, which sets up the Republic, nowhere enters into its constitution; it is an individual and superior function, which has nothing in common with human empire; for if he who holds command over men ought not to have command over the laws, he who has command over the laws ought not any more to have it over men; or else his laws would be the ministers of his passions and would often merely serve to perpetuate his injustices: his private aims would inevitably mar the sanctity of his work.

*   *   *

Chapter VIII

THAT ALL FORMS OF GOVERNMENT DO NOT SUIT ALL COUNTRIES

Liberty, not being a fruit of all climates, is not within the reach of all peoples. The more this principle, laid down by Montesquieu, is considered, the more its truth is felt; the more it is combated, the more chance is given to confirm it by new proofs.

In all the governments that there are, the public person consumes without producing. Whence then does it get what it consumes? From the labour of its members. The necessities of the public are supplied out of the superfluities of individuals. It follows that the civil State can subsist only so long as men's labour brings them a return greater than their needs.

The amount of this excess is not the same in all countries. In some it is considerable, in others middling, in yet others nil, in some even negative. The relation of product to subsistence depends on the fertility of the climate, on the sort of labour the land demands, on the nature of its products, on the strength of its inhabitants, on the greater or less consumption they find necessary, and on several further considerations of which the whole relation is made up.

On the other side, all governments are not of the same nature: some are less voracious than others, and the differences between them are based on this second principle, that the further from their source the public contributions are removed, the more burdensome they become. The charge should be measured not by the amount of the impositions, but by the path they have to travel in order to get back to those from whom they came. When the circulation is prompt and well established, it does not matter whether much or little is paid; the people is always rich and, financially speaking, all is well. On the contrary, however little the people gives, if that little does not return to it, it is soon exhausted by giving continually: the State is then never rich, and the people is always a people of beggars.

It follows that, the more the distance between people and government increases, the more burdensome tribute becomes: thus, in a democracy, the people bears the least charge; in an aristocracy, a greater charge; and, in monarchy, the weight becomes heaviest. Monarchy therefore suits only wealthy nations; aristocracy, States of middling size and wealth; and democracy, States that are small and poor.

In fact, the more we reflect, the more we find the difference between free and monarchical States to be this: in the former, everything is used for the public advantage; in the latter, the public forces and those of individuals are affected by each other, and either increases as the others grows weak; finally, instead of governing subjects to make them happy, despotism makes them wretched in order to govern them.

We find then, in every climate, natural causes according to which the form of government which it requires can be assigned, and we can even say what sort of inhabitants it should have.

Unfriendly and barren lands, where the product does not repay the labour, should remain desert and uncultivated, or peopled only by savages; lands where men's labour brings in no more than the exact minimum necessary to subsistence should be inhabited by barbarous peoples: in such places all polity is impossible. Lands where the surplus of product over labour is only middling are suitable for free peoples; those in which the soil is abundant and fertile and gives a great product for a little labour call for monarchical government, in order that the surplus of superfluities among the subjects may be consumed by the luxury of the prince: for it is better for this excess to be absorbed by the government than dissipated among the individuals. I am aware that there are exceptions; but these exceptions themselves confirm the rule, in that sooner or later they produce revolutions which restore things to the natural order.

*   *   *

REVIEW QUESTIONS

1. How does Rousseau's conception of the origin of political society compare with those of Filmer and Locke?
2. What is the relation between human slavery and human nature?
3. How do relations of subject and ruler come into being?
4. What is the social contract?
5. What is its relation to nature? To reason? To will?

18 → THE FRENCH REVOLUTION

The French revolutionary and Napoleonic eras, 1789–1815, launched the modern period in European history. Europe had so irrevocably changed after 1815 that contemporaries distinguished the period before 1789 as the old regime. To be sure, many features of the old regime continued into the new era, but the sentiment of sudden rupture was largely valid. In various dimensions of public life, the radical transformations of the French Revolution rendered many prerevolutionary attitudes toward society and politics obsolete. Following the abolition of feudalism, the declaration of civic equality, and the subordination of monarchy to national political sovereignty, traditional authority became irretrievable.

The areas of French society (aristocrats, civil servants, professionals, merchants, artisans, urban workers, peasants) willing to reform, if not dismantle, absolutist monarchy established the revolution's legitimacy. The wide range of grievances that had accumulated in the French provinces and cities provided the broad social base for the upheaval of 1789, just as the prevailing emphasis of eighteenth-century letters on applying reason, natural law, and social utility to public affairs offered a general intellectual framework. To understand the revolution's development, however, one must recognize that, while the revolution inaugurated a new era of political rights and citizenship ideals, the specific content of "liberty, equality, brotherhood" remained contested. Consequently, the freshly constituted polity of France embarked on an uncharted course of political experimentation, the prominent milestones of which (dissolution of monarchy, regicide, radical republicanism, political terror, republican imperialism) subsequently defined the parameters of the modern political landscape.

The revolutionary impulses in Paris resonated throughout Europe. As the largest and most powerful continental state in Europe (one out of five Europeans lived in France), French politics affected all Europeans. The precedent of French constitutionalism and the Declaration of the Rights of Man and Citizen reconfigured the domestic political cultures of all European states. The level of political disputation intensified; contemporaries alternately celebrated or denounced the potential of widened political participation. Even Great Britain's stable political establishment of limited monarchy and parliamentary rule perceived French republicanism as a threat. The decision of Austria and Prussia to invade France in 1792 not only radicalized French politics but also expanded the revolutionary political sphere. Napoleon's military prowess further embedded French revolutionary influence abroad with the creation of new kingdoms, the appointment of new rulers, the institution of new laws, and the transmission of a new political outlook. Although the European great powers attempted to eradicate most of Napoleon's political reordering after 1815, the revolutionary challenge to traditional elites remained a permanent feature of European political life.

ARTHUR YOUNG

FROM *Travels in France During the Years 1787, 1788, 1789*

Arthur Young, an established author and one of the "improving landlords" of English agriculture, traveled through France prior to and during the French Revolution. His acute observations of the conditions of French society offer an invaluable contemporary testimony to the many problems that hindered both agricultural prosperity and political stability.

From *Travels in France During the Years 1787, 1788, 1789*, A. Young, edited by Constantia Maxwell, Cambridge University Press, 1950.

*　　*　　*

Of all the subjects of political economy, I know not one that has given rise to such a cloud of errors as this of population. It seems, for some centuries, to have been considered as the only sure test of national prosperity. I am clearly of opinion from the observations I made in every province of the Kingdom, that her population is so much beyond the proportion of her industry and labour, that she would be much more powerful, and infinitely more flourishing, if she had five or six millions less of inhabitants. From her too great population, she presents in every quarter such spectacles of wretchedness as are absolutely inconsistent with that degree of national felicity which she was capable of attaining even under her old government. A traveller much less attentive than I was to objects of this kind must see at every turn most unequivocal signs of distress. That these should exist, no one can wonder who considers the price of labour, and of provisions, and the misery into which a small rise in the price of wheat throws the lower classes. The causes of this great population were certainly not to be found in the benignity of the old government yielding a due protection to the lower classes, for, on the contrary, it abandoned them to the mercy of the privileged orders. This great populousness of France I attribute very much to the division of the lands into small properties, which takes place in that country to a degree of which we have in England but little conception. Whatever promises the appearance even of subsistence induces men to marry. The inheritance of 10 or 12 acres to be divided amongst the children of the proprietor will be looked to with the views of a permanent settlement, and either occasions a marriage, the infants of which die young for want of sufficient nourishment, or keeps children at home, distressing their relations, long after the time that they should have emigrated to towns.

*   *   *

V. MÉTAYERS is the tenure under which perhaps seven-eighths of the lands of France are held.

*   *   *

At the first blush, the great disadvantage of the *métayage* system is to landlords; but on a nearer examination, the tenants are found in the lowest state of poverty, and some of them in misery. At Vatan, in Berry, I was assured that the *métayers* almost every year borrowed their bread of the landlord before the harvest came round, yet hardly worth borrowing, for it was made of rye and barley mixed. I tasted enough of it to pity sincerely the poor people. In Limousin the *métayers* are considered as little better than menial servants, removable at pleasure, and obliged to conform in all things to the will of the landlords. It is commonly computed that half the tenantry are deeply in debt to the proprietor, so that he is often obliged to turn them off with the loss of these debts, in order to save his land from running waste.

In all the modes of occupying land, the great evil is the smallness of farms. There are large ones in Picardy, the Isle of France, the Pays de Beauce, Artois and Normandy; but in the rest of the kingdom such are not general. The division of the farms and population is so great, that the misery flowing from it is in many places extreme; the idleness of the people is seen the moment you enter a town on market day; the swarms of people are incredible. At Landivisiau in Bretagne, I saw a man who walked 7 miles to bring 2 chickens, which would not sell for 24 *sous* the couple, as he told me himself. At Avranches, men attending each a horse, with a pannier load of sea ooze, not more than 4 bushels. Near Isenheim in Alsace, a rich country, women, in the midst of harvest, where their labour is nearly as valuable as that of men, reaping grass by the road side to carry home to their cows.

*   *   *

In this most miserable of all the modes of letting land, after running the hazard of such losses, fatal in many instances, the defrauded landlord receives a contemptible rent; the farmer is in the lowest state of poverty; the land is miserably cultivated; and the nation suffers as severely as the parties themselves.

*   *   *

The abuses attending the levy of taxes were heavy and universal. The kingdom was parcelled into *généralités*, with an Intendant at the head of each, into whose hands the whole power of the Crown was delegated for everything except the military authority; but particularly for all affairs of finance. The *généralités* were sub-divided into *élections*, at the head of which was a *subdélégué*, appointed by the Intendant. The rolls of the *taille, capitation, vingtièmes*, and other taxes, were distributed among districts, parishes, and individuals, at the pleasure of the Intendant, who could exempt, change, add, or diminish, at pleasure. Such an enormous power, constantly acting, and from which no man was free, must, in the nature of things, degenerate in many cases into absolute tyranny. It must be obvious, that the friends, acquaintances, and dependents of the Intendant, and of all his *subdélégués*, and the friends of these friends, to a long chain of dependence, might be favoured in taxation at the expense of their miserable neighbours; and that noblemen, in favour at court, to whose protection the Intendant himself would naturally look up, could find little difficulty in throwing much of the weight of their taxes on others, without a similar support. Instances, and even gross ones, have been reported to me in many parts of the kingdom, that made me shudder at the oppression to which numbers must have been condemned, by the undue favours granted to such crooked influence.

* * *

The *corvées*, or police of the roads, were annually the ruin of many hundreds of farmers; more than 300 were reduced to beggary in filling up one vale in Lorraine. All these oppressions fell on the *tiers état* only; the nobility and clergy having been equally exempted from *tailles*, militia, and *corvées*.

The penal code of finance makes one shudder at the horrors of punishment inadequate to the crime. A few features will sufficiently characterize the old government of France.

1. Smugglers of salt, armed and assembled to the number of five, in Provence, a *fine of 500 livres and nine years galleys*; in all the rest of the kingdom, *death*.

2. Smugglers armed, assembled, but in number under five, *a fine of 300 livres and three years galleys*. Second offence, *death*.

3. Smugglers, without arms, but with horses, carts, or boats, *a fine of 300 livres; if not paid, three years galleys*. Second offence, *400 livres and nine years galleys*. In Dauphiné, second offence, *galleys for life*. In Provence, *five years galleys*.

4. Smugglers, who carry the salt on their backs, and without arms, *a fine of 200 livres, and, if not paid, are flogged and branded*. Second offence, *a fine of 300 livres and six years galleys*.

5. Women, married and single, smugglers, first offence, *a fine of 100 livres*. Second, *300 livres*.

Third, *flogged, and banished the kingdom for life. Husbands responsible both in fine and body*.

6. Children smugglers, the same as women. *Fathers and mothers responsible; and for defect of payment flogged*.

* * *

But these were not all the evils with which the people struggled. The administration of justice was partial, venal, infamous. I have, in conversation with many very sensible men, in different parts of the kingdom, met with something of content with their government, in all other respects than this; but upon the question of expecting justice to be really and fairly administered, everyone confessed there was no such thing to be looked for. The conduct of the parliaments was profligate and atrocious. Upon almost every cause that came before them, interest was openly made with the judges; and woe betided the man who, with a cause to support, had no means of conciliating favour, either by the beauty of a handsome wife, or by other methods. It has been said, by many writers, that property was as secure under the old government of France as it is in England; and the assertion might possibly be true, as far as any violence from the King, his ministers, or the great was concerned; but for all that mass of property, which comes in every country to be litigated in courts of justice, there was not even the shadow of security, unless the parties were totally and equally unknown, and totally and equally honest; in every other case, he who had the best interest with the judges was sure to be the winner. To reflecting minds, the cruelty and abominable practice attending such courts are sufficiently apparent.

* * *

The true judgment to be formed of the French revolution must surely be gained from an attentive consideration of the evils of the old government. When these are well understood, and when the extent and universality of the oppression under which the people groaned, oppression which bore upon them from every quarter, it will scarcely be attempted to be urged that a revolution was not absolutely necessary to the welfare of the kingdom. Not one opposing voice can, with reason, be raised against this assertion; abuses ought certainly to be corrected, and corrected effectually. This could not be done without the establishment of a new form of government; whether the form that has been adopted were the best, is another question absolutely distinct.

*   *   *

REVIEW QUESTIONS

1. For Arthur Young, what are the chief problems in the French countryside?
2. What are the specific problems imposed on the small farmer by the nobility, the legal system, and the government?
3. How are public affairs conducted?
4. How did these problems in the countryside contribute to the success of the revolution?

THOMAS JEFFERSON

The Declaration of Independence

The successful attempt of the original thirteen states of the union to break their colonial allegiance to Great Britain was an important antecedent to the French Revolution. Not only did France's financial support of the insurgent colonies precipitate the financial crisis that would compel Louis XVI to convene the Estates General, but the American war for independence also produced a political culture that celebrated principles of popular sovereignty and "unalienable" individual liberties. The Declaration of Independence, among the noblest of United States documents, arose out of the need to attach a preamble to a resolution by Congress moved June 1776 "that these United Colonies are, and of right ought to be, free and independent States." Congress appointed a committee of five representatives to write the preamble, but one member, Thomas Jefferson, actually drafted the document, which was adopted by Congress on 4 July 1776.

When in the course of human events, it becomes necessary for one people to dissolve the political bands which have connected them with another, and to assume the Powers of the earth, the separate and equal station to which the Laws of Nature and of Nature's God entitle them, a decent respect to the opinions of mankind requires that they should declare the causes which impel them to the separation.

We hold these truths to be self-evident, that all men are created equal, that they are endowed by their Creator with certain unalienable rights, that among these are Life, Liberty, and the pursuit of Happiness. That to secure these rights, Governments are instituted among Men, deriving their just powers from the consent of the governed. That whenever any Form of Government becomes destructive of these ends, it is the Right of the People to alter or to abolish it, and to institute new Government, laying its foundation on such principles and organizing its powers in such form, as to them shall seem most likely to effect their Safety and Happiness. Prudence, indeed, will dictate that Governments long established should not be changed for light and transient causes; and accordingly all experience hath shown, that mankind are more disposed to suffer, while evils are sufferable, than to right themselves by abolishing the forms to which they are accustomed. But when a long train of abuses and usurpations, pursuing invariably the same Object evinces a design to reduce them under absolute Despotism, it is their right, it is their duty, to throw off such Government, and to provide new Guards for their future security—Such has been the patient sufferance of these Colonies; and such is now the necessity which constrains them to alter their former Systems of Government. The history of the present King of Great Britain is a history of repeated injuries and usurpations, all having in direct object the establishment of an absolute Tyranny over these States. To prove this, let Facts be submitted to a candid world.

He has refused his Assent to Laws, the most wholesome and necessary for the public good.

He has forbidden his Governors to pass Laws of immediate and pressing importance, unless suspended in their operation till his Assent should be obtained; and when so suspended, he has utterly neglected to attend to them.

He has refused to pass other Laws for the accommodation of large districts of people, unless those people would relinquish the right of Representation in the Legislature, a right inestimable to them and formidable to tyrants only.

He has called together legislative bodies at places unusual, uncomfortable, and distant from the depository of their public Records, for the sole purpose of fatiguing them into compliance with his measures.

He has dissolved Representative Houses repeatedly, for opposing with manly firmness his invasions on the rights of the people.

He has refused for a long time, after such dissolutions, to cause others to be elected; whereby the Legislative powers, incapable of Annihilation, have returned to the People at large for their exercise; the State remaining in the mean time exposed to all dangers of invasion from without, and convulsions within.

He has endeavoured to prevent the population of these States; for that purpose obstructing the Laws of Naturalization of Foreigners; refusing to pass others to encourage their migrations hither, and raising the conditions of new Appropriations of Lands.

He has obstructed the Administration of Justice, by refusing his Assent to Laws for establishing Judiciary powers.

He has made Judges dependent on his Will alone, for the tenure of their offices, and the amount and payment of their salaries.

He has erected a multitude of New Offices, and sent hither swarms of Officers to harass our People, and eat out their substance.

He has kept among us, in times of peace, Standing Armies without the Consent of our legislature.

He has affected to render the Military independent of and superior to the Civil Power.

He has combined with others to subject us to a jurisdiction foreign to our constitution, and unacknowledged by our laws; giving his Assent to their Acts of pretended Legislation:

For quartering large bodies of armed troops among us:

For protecting them, by a mock Trial, from Punishment for any Murders which they should commit on the Inhabitants of these States:

For cutting off our Trade with all parts of the world:

For imposing taxes on us without our Consent:

For depriving us of many cases, of the benefits of Trial by jury:

For transporting us beyond Seas to be tried for pretended offences:

For abolishing the free System of English Laws in a neighbouring Province, establishing therein an Arbitrary government, and enlarging its Boundaries so as to render it at once an example and fit instrument for introducing the same absolute rule into these Colonies:

For taking away our Charters, abolishing our most valuable Laws, and altering fundamentally the Forms of our Governments:

For suspending our own Legislatures, and declaring themselves in vested with Power to legislate for us in all cases whatsoever.

He has abdicated Government here, by declaring us out of his Protection and waging War against us.

He has plundered our seas, ravaged our Coasts, burnt our towns, and destroyed the lives of our people.

He is at this time transporting large armies of foreign mercenaries to compleat the works of death, desolation, and tyranny, already begun with circumstances of Cruelty & perfidy scarcely paralleled in the most barbarous ages, and totally unworthy the Head of a civilized nation.

He has constrained our fellow Citizens taken Captive on the high Seas to bear Arms against their Country, to become the executioners of their friends and Brethren, or to fall themselves by their Hands.

He has excited domestic insurrections amongst us, and has endeavoured to bring on the inhabitants of our frontiers, the merciless Indian Savages, whose known rule of warfare, is an undistinguished destruction of all ages, sexes, and conditions.

In every stage of these Oppressions We have Petitioned for Redress in the most humble terms: Our repeated Petitions have been answered only by repeated injury. A Prince, whose character is thus marked by every act which may define a Tyrant, is unfit to be the ruler of a free people.

Nor have We been wanting in attention to our British brethren. We have warned them from time to time of attempts by their legislature to extend an unwarrantable jurisdiction over us. We have reminded them of the circumstances of our emigration and settlement here. We have appealed to their native justice and magnanimity, and we have conjured them by the ties of our common kindred to disavow these usurpations, which, would inev-

itably interrupt our connections and correspondence. They too must have been deaf to the voice of justice and of consanguinity. We must, therefore, acquiesce in the necessity, which denounces our Separation, and hold them, as we hold the rest of mankind, Enemies in War, in Peace Friends.

WE, THEREFORE, the Representatives of the UNITED STATES OF AMERICA, in General Congress, Assembled, appealing to the Supreme Judge of the world for the rectitude of our intentions, do, in the Name, and by Authority of the good People of these Colonies, solemnly publish and declare, That these United Colonies are, and of Right ought to be FREE AND INDEPENDENT STATES; that they are Absolved from all Allegiance to the British Crown, and that all political connection between them and the State of Great Britain, is and ought to be totally dissolved; and that as Free and Independent States, they have full Power to levy War, conclude Peace, contract Alliances, establish Commerce, and to do all other Acts and Things which Independent States may of right do. And for the support of this Declaration, with a firm reliance on the Protection of Divine Providence, we mutually pledge to each other our Lives, our Fortunes, and our sacred Honor.

The foregoing Declaration was, by order of Congress, engrossed, and signed by the following members:* * *

REVIEW QUESTIONS

1. Upon what grounds does the Declaration of Independence justify a break from Great Britain?
2. Why is this document often viewed as a prominent example of the Enlightenment's political outlook?
3. Compare your earlier reading of Locke with the Declaration of Independence: what Lockian influences can be detected?
4. Assess the influence of the Declaration of Independence on the Declaration of Rights of Man and Citizen, one of the following readings in this chapter.

ABBÉ EMMANUEL SIEYES

FROM *What Is the Third Estate?*

King Louis XVI's announcement in the summer of 1788 to convene the Estates General, compounded by bread riots and widespread economic hardship, heated up political debate about reform and the future of France. Because the Estates General had not met since 1614, members of the Third Estate protested against the custom that the estates meet separately and vote by order. They insisted that the estates should instead deliberate in united sessions and vote as individuals, not as corporate bodies. Equally important, the Third Estate demanded that its votes be doubled, so that it could counter the votes of the First and Second Estates. In January 1789 Abbé Emmanuel Sieyes, a radical clergyman, sought to mobilize public support for these causes with the pamphlet, "What Is the Third Estate?" Its influence was pervasive and contributed to the plan to transform the Estates General into the National Constituent Assembly.

From *A Documentary Survey of the French Revolution* by Stewart, John Hall, © 1951. Adapted by permission of Prentice-Hall, Inc., Upper Saddle River, NJ.

*   *   *

The plan of this pamphlet is very simple. We have three questions to ask:

1st. What is the third estate? Everything.

2nd. What has it been heretofore in the political order? Nothing.

3rd. What does it demand? To become something therein.

We shall see if the answers are correct. Then we shall examine the measures that have been tried and those which must be taken in order that the third estate may in fact become *something*. Thus we shall state:

4th. What the ministers have *attempted*, and what the privileged classes themselves *propose* in its favor.

5th. What *ought* to have been done.

6th. Finally, what *remains* to be done in order that the third estate may take its rightful place.

Chapter I
The Third Estate Is a Complete Nation

What are the essentials of national existence and prosperity? *Private* enterprise and *public* functions.

Private enterprise may be divided into four classes: 1st. Since earth and water furnish the raw material for man's needs, the first class will comprise all families engaged in agricultural pursuits. 2nd. Between the original sale of materials and their consumption or use, further workmanship, more or less manifold, adds to these materials a second value, more or less compounded. Human industry thus succeeds in perfecting the benefits of nature and in increasing the gross produce twofold, tenfold, one hundredfold in value. Such is the work of the second class. 3rd. Between production and consumption, as well as among the different degrees of production, a group of intermediate agents, useful to producers as well as to consumers, comes into being; these are the dealers and merchants. . . . 4th. In addition to these three classes of industrious and useful citizens concerned with goods for consumption and use, a society needs many private undertakings and endeavors which are *directly* useful or agreeable to the *individual*. This fourth class includes from the most distinguished scientific and liberal professions to the least esteemed domestic services. Such are the labors which sustain society. Who performs them? The third estate.

Public functions likewise under present circumstances may be classified under four well known headings: the Sword, the Robe, the Church, and the Administration. It is unnecessary to discuss them in detail in order to demonstrate that the third estate everywhere constitutes nineteen-twentieths of them, except that it is burdened with all that is really arduous, with all the tasks that the privileged order refuses to perform. Only the lucrative and honorary positions are held by members of the privileged order. . . . nevertheless they have dared lay the order of the third estate under an interdict. They have said to it: "Whatever be your services, whatever your talents, you shall go thus far and no farther. It is not fitting that you be honored." . . .

. . . .

It suffices here to have revealed that the alleged utility of a privileged order to public service is only a chimera; that without it, all that is arduous in such service is performed by the third estate; that without it, the higher positions would be infinitely better filled; that they naturally ought to be the lot of and reward for talents and recognized services; and that if the privileged classes have succeeded in usurping all the lucrative and honorary positions, it is both an odious injustice to the majority of citizens and a treason to the commonwealth.

Who, then, would dare to say that the third

estate has not within itself all that is necessary to constitute a complete nation? It is the strong and robust man whose one arm remains enchained. If the privileged order were abolished, the nation would be not something less but something more. Thus, what is the third estate? Everything; but an everything shackled and oppressed. What would it be without the privileged order? Everything; but an everything free and flourishing. Nothing can progress without it; everything would proceed infinitely better without the others. It is not sufficient to have demonstrated that the privileged classes, far from being useful to the nation, can only enfeeble and injure it; it is necessary, moreover, to prove that the nobility does not belong to the social organization at all; that, indeed, it may be a *burden* upon the nation, but that it would not know how to constitute a part thereof.

. . . .

What is a nation? a body of associates living under a *common* law and represented by the same *legislature*.

Is it not exceedingly clear that the noble order has privileges, exemptions, even rights separate from the rights of the majority of citizens? Thus it deviates from the common order, from the common law. Thus its civil rights already render it a people apart in a great nation. It is indeed *imperium in imperio*.

Also, it enjoys its political rights separately. It has its own representatives, who are by no means charged with representing the people. Its deputation sits apart; and when it is assembled in the same room with the deputies of ordinary citizens, it is equally true that its representation is essentially distinct and separate; it is foreign to the nation in principle, since its mandate does not emanate from the people, and in aim, since its purpose is to defend not the general but a special interest.

The third estate, then, comprises everything appertaining to the nation; and whatever is not the third estate may not be regarded as being of the nation. What is the third estate? Everything!

Chapter III
What Does the Third Estate Demand? To Become Something

. . . The true petitions of this order may be appreciated only through the authentic claims directed to the government by the large municipalities of the kingdom. What is indicated therein? That the people wishes to be *something*, and, in truth, the very least that is possible. It wishes to have real representatives in the Estates General, that is to say, deputies *drawn from its order*, who are competent to be interpreters of its will and defenders of its interests. But what will it avail it to be present at the Estates General if the predominating interest there is contrary to its own! Its presence would only consecrate the oppression of which it would be the eternal victim. Thus, it is indeed certain that it cannot come to vote at the Estates General unless it is to have in that body *an influence at least equal to that of the privileged classes*; and it demands a number of representatives equal to that of the first two orders together. Finally, this equality of representation would become completely illusory if every chamber voted separately. The third estate demands, then, that votes be taken *by head and not by order*. This is the essence of those claims so alarming to the privileged classes, because they believed that thereby the reform of abuses would become inevitable. The real intention of the third estate is to have an influence in the Estates General equal to that of the privileged classes. I repeat, can it ask less? And is it not clear that if its influence therein is less than equality, it cannot be expected to emerge from its political nullity and become *something*?

But what is indeed unfortunate is that the three articles constituting the demand of the third estate are insufficient to give it this equality of in-fluence which it cannot, in reality, do without. In vain will it obtain an equal number of representatives drawn from its order; the influence of the privileged classes will establish itself and dominate even in the sanctuary of the third estate. . . .

. . . .

Besides the influence of the aristocracy . . . there is the influence of property. This is natural. I do not proscribe it at all; but one must agree that it is still all to the advantage of the privileged classes . . .

. . . .

The more one considers this matter, the more obvious the insufficiency of the three demands of the third estate becomes. But finally, such as they are, they have been vigorously attacked. Let us examine the pretexts for this hostility.

*　　*　　*

I have only one observation to make. Obviously there are abuses in France; these abuses are profitable to someone; they are scarcely advantageous to the third estate—indeed, they are injurious to it in particular. Now I ask if, in this state of affairs, it is possible to destroy any abuse so long as those who profit therefrom control the *veto*? All justice would be powerless; it would be necessary to rely entirely on the sheer generosity of the privileged classes. Would that be your idea of what constitutes the social order?

*　　*　　*

REVIEW QUESTIONS

1. What is the author's tone of voice and how does it affect the argument?
2. What reasons does Sieyes provide for his claim that the Third Estate constitutes the nation?
3. What kind of political and social order does the pamphlet advocate?

THIRD ESTATE OF DOURDAN

FROM Grievance Petitions

After summoning the Estates General, the king charged each estate with the task of drawing up grievance petitions, which in turn acted as suggestions for reform. Local assemblies throughout France, which appointed the Third Estate's deputies for the Estates General, wrote the grievance petitions, which are among the most valuable documents for assessing the moods of France's many regions and social groups just prior to the revolution. This particular petition is from the Third Estate of Dourdan, a town north of Paris in the Pan's basin.

From *A Documentary Survey of the French Revolution* by Stewart, John Hall, © 1951. Adapted by permission of Prentice-Hall, Inc., Upper Saddle River, NJ.

*   *   *

The order of the third estate of the City, *Bailliage,* and County of Dourdan, imbued with gratitude prompted by the paternal kindness of the King, who deigns to restore its former rights and its former constitution, forgets at this moment its misfortunes and impotence, to harken only to its foremost sentiment and its foremost duty, that of sacrificing everything to the glory of the *Patrie* and the service of His Majesty. It supplicates him to accept the grievances, complaints, and remonstrances which it is permitted to bring to the foot of the throne, and to see therein only the expression of its zeal and the homage of its obedience.

It wishes:

1. That his subjects of the third estate, equal by such status to all other citizens, present themselves before the common father without other distinction which might degrade them.

2. That all the orders, already united by duty and a common desire to contribute equally to the needs of the State, also deliberate in common concerning its needs.

3. That no citizen lose his liberty except according to law; that, consequently, no one be ar-
rested by virtue of special orders, or, if imperative circumstances necessitate such orders, that the prisoner be handed over to the regular courts of justice within forty-eight hours at the latest.

4. That no letters or writings intercepted in the post be the cause of the detention of any citizen, or be produced in court against him, except in case of conspiracy or undertaking against the State.

5. That the property of all citizens be inviolable, and that no one be required to make sacrifice thereof for the public welfare, except upon assurance of indemnification based upon the statement of freely selected appraisers.

*   *   *

9. That the national debt be verified; that the payment of arrears of said debt be assured by such indirect taxes as may not be injurious to the husbandry, industry, commerce, liberty, or tranquillity of the citizens.

10. That an annual reimbursement fund be established to liquidate the capital of the debt.

11. That as one part of the debt is liquidated, a corresponding part of the indirect tax also be liquidated.

12. That every tax, direct or indirect, be granted only for a limited time, and that every collection beyond such term be regarded as peculation, and punished as such.

13. That no loan be contracted, under any pretext or any security whatsoever, without the consent of the Estates General.* * *

15. That every personal tax be abolished; that thus the *capitation* and the *taille* and its accessories be merged with the *vingtièmes* in a tax on land and real or nominal property.

16. That such tax be borne equally, without distinction, by all classes of citizens and by all kinds of property, even feudal and contingent rights.

17. That the tax substituted for the *corvée* be borne by all classes of citizens equally and without distinction. That said tax, at present beyond the capacity of those who pay it and the needs to which it is destined, be reduced by at least one-half.

18. That provincial Estates, subordinate to the Estates General, be established and charged with the assessment and levying of subsidies, with their deposit in the national treasury, with the administration of all public works, and with the examination of all projects conducive to the prosperity of lands situated within the limits of their jurisdiction.

19. That such Estates be composed of freely elected deputies of the three orders from the cities, boroughs, and parishes subject to their administration, and in the proportion established for the next session of the Estates General.

*　　*　　*

Justice

1. That the administration of justice be reformed, either by restoring strict execution of ordinances, or by reforming the sections thereof that are contrary to the dispatch and welfare of justice.

2. That every royal *bailliage* have such juris-diction that persons be not more than three or four leagues distant from their judges, and that these pass judgment in the last resort up to the value of 300 *livres*.

3. That seigneurial courts of justice created by purely gratuitous right be suppressed.

4. That seigneurial courts of justice separated from the jurisdiction of royal *bailliages* . . . be returned thereto.

5. That seigneurial courts of justice, the creation of which has not been gratuitous, or usurpation of which is not proved, be suppressed with reimbursement.

*　　*　　*

8. That the excessive number of offices in the necessary courts be reduced in just measure, and that no one be given an office of magistracy if he is not at least twenty-five years of age, and until after a substantial public examination has verified his morality, integrity, and ability.

*　　*　　*

10. That the study of law be reformed; that it be directed in a manner analogous to our legislation, and that candidates for degrees be subjected to rigorous tests which may not be evaded; that no dispensation of age or time be granted.

*　　*　　*

12. That deliberations of courts and companies of magistracy which tend to prevent entry of the third estate thereto be rescinded and annulled as injurious to the citizens of that order, in contempt of the authority of the King, whose choice they limit, and contrary to the welfare of justice, the administration of which would become the patrimony of those of noble birth instead of being entrusted to merit, enlightenment, and virtue.

13. That military ordinances which restrict entrance to the service to those possessing nobility be reformed.

*　　*　　*

Finances

1. That if the Estates General considers it necessary to preserve the fees of *aides*, such fees be made uniform throughout the entire kingdom and reduced to a single denomination; that, accordingly, all ordinances and declarations in force be revoked . . . ; that the odious tax of *trop-bu* especially, a source of constant annoyance in rural districts, be abolished forever.

2. That the tax of the *gabelle* be eliminated if possible, or that it be regulated among the several provinces of the kingdom . . .

*   *   *

Agriculture

1. That exchange fees, disastrous to husbandry, . . . be suppressed.

*   *   *

3. That the privilege of hunting be restricted within its just limits; that the decrees of the *parlement* of the years 1778 and 1779, which tend rather to obstruct the claims of the cultivator than to effect his indemnification, be rescinded and annulled; that after having declared the excessive amount of game and summoned the seignieur to provide therefor, the landowner and the cultivator be authorized to destroy said game on their own lands and in their own woods—without permission, however, to use firearms, the carrying of which is forbidden by ordinances; that, moreover, a simple and easy method be established whereby every cultivator may have the damage verified and obtain compensation therefor.

4. That the right to hunt may never affect the property of the citizen; that, accordingly, he may at all times travel over his lands, have injurious herbs uprooted, and cut *luzernes, sainfoins,* and other produce whenever it suits him; and that stubble may be freely raked immediately after the harvest.

5. That, in conformity with former ordinances, gamekeepers be forbidden to carry arms, even in the retinue of their masters.

6. That hunting offences be punished only by pecuniary fines.

7. That His Majesty be supplicated to have enclosed the parks and forests which are reserved for his enjoyment; also to authorize elsewhere the destruction of wild beasts which ruin the rural districts, and particularly that bordering on this forest of Dourdan.

8. That every individual who, without title or valid occupancy, has dovecotes or aviaries, be required to destroy them; that those who have title or valid occupancy be required to confine their pigeons at seedtime and harvest.

*   *   *

10. That no cultivator be permitted . . . several farms or farmings, if the total thereof necessitates the use of more than two ploughs.

*   *   *

15. That the militia, which devastates the country, takes workers away from husbandry, produces premature and ill-matched marriages, and imposes secret and arbitrary taxes upon those who are subject thereto, be suppressed and replaced by voluntary enlistment at the expense of the provinces.

*   *   *

17. That the ordinance and regulation concerning woods and forests be reformed so as to preserve property rights, encourage plantings, and prevent deforestation.

*   *   *

Commerce

1. That every regulation which tends to impede the business of citizens be revoked.

2. That the exportation and circulation of

grain be directed by the provincial Estates, which shall correspond among themselves in order to prevent sudden and artificial increases in the price of provisions.

3. That when wheat reaches the price of twenty-five *livres* per *septier* in the markets, all day laborers be forbidden to buy any, unless it be for their sustenance.

4. That if circumstances necessitate the revenue from certificates and letters of mastership in the arts and crafts, no member be admitted into corporations except upon condition of residing in the place of his establishment; that widows may carry on the profession of their husbands without new letters; that their children be admitted thereto at a moderate price; that all persons without an established and recognized domicile be forbidden to peddle.

5. That fraudulent bankruptcy be considered a public crime; that the public prosecutor be enjoined to prosecute it as such, and that privileged positions no longer serve as a refuge for bankrupts.

6. That all toll rights and other similar ones be suppressed throughout the interior of the kingdom, that customhouses be moved back to the frontiers, and that rights of *traite* be entirely abolished.

7. That, within a given time, weights and measures be rendered uniform throughout the entire kingdom.

REVIEW QUESTIONS

1. What are the principal targets of criticism?
2. What groups and institutions are cited as the recurring causes of hardship?
3. How extensive are the proposals for reform?
4. On the basis of this petition, how would you characterize the relationship between the French state and its people?

NATIONAL ASSEMBLY

The Tennis Court Oath

On 20 June 1789 the Third Estate, after refusing to meet separately and vote by order, was barred from its hall. Seeking a chamber, deputies reconvened on a nearby tennis court, where they deliberated and vowed to remain in session as the National Assembly until a French constitution was drafted. Toward this end, they swore an oath, which remains among the most important documents of the French Revolution.

The National Assembly, considering that it has been summoned to establish the constitution of the kingdom, to effect the regeneration of public order, and to maintain the true principles of monarchy; that nothing can prevent it from continuing its deliberations in whatever place it may be forced to establish itself; and, finally, that wheresoever its members are assembled, *there* is the National Assembly;

Decrees that all members of this Assembly shall immediately take a solemn oath not to separate, and to reassemble wherever circumstances require, until the constitution of the kingdom is established and consolidated upon firm foundations; and that, the said oath taken, all members and each one of them individually shall ratify this steadfast resolution by signature.

REVIEW QUESTIONS

1. What is the significance of the Third Estate calling itself the National Assembly?

2. What role does this document assign to the National Assembly?

3. How did this oath radically alter the nature of political sovereignty in eighteenth-century France?

FROM Declaration of the Rights of Man and Citizen

This declaration, adopted on 27 August 1789, was a revolutionary clarion call to the people of France. Its subsequent impact on European political culture cannot be underestimated.

From *A Documentary Survey of the French Revolution* by Stewart, John Hall, © 1951. Adapted by permission of Prentice-Hall, Inc., Upper Saddle River, N.J.

*   *   *

The representatives of the French people, organized in National Assembly, considering that ignorance, forgetfulness, or contempt of the rights of man are the sole causes of public misfortunes and of the corruption of governments, have resolved to set forth in a solemn declaration the natural, inalienable, and sacred rights of man, in order that such declaration, continually before all members of the social body, may be a perpetual reminder of their rights and duties; in order that the acts of the legislative power and those of the executive power may constantly be compared with the aim of every political institution and may accordingly be more respected; in order that the demands of the citizens, founded henceforth upon simple and incontestable principles, may always be directed towards the maintenance of the Constitution and the welfare of all.

Accordingly, the National Assembly recognizes and proclaims, in the presence and under the auspices of the Supreme Being, the following rights of man and citizen.

1. Men are born and remain free and equal in rights; social distinctions may be based only upon general usefulness.

2. The aim of every political association is the preservation of the natural and inalienable rights of man; these rights are liberty, property, security, and resistance to oppression.

3. The source of all sovereignty resides essentially in the nation; no group, no individual may exercise authority not emanating expressly therefrom.

4. Liberty consists of the power to do whatever is not injurious to others; thus the enjoyment of the natural rights of every man has for its limits only those that assure other members of society the enjoyment of those same rights; such limits may be determined only by law.

5. The law has the right to forbid only actions which are injurious to society. Whatever is not forbidden by law may not be prevented, and no one may be constrained to do what it does not prescribe.

6. Law is the expression of the general will; all citizens have the right to concur personally, or through their representatives, in its formation; it must be the same for all, whether it protects or punishes. All citizens, being equal before it, are equally admissible to all public offices, positions, and employments, according to their capacity, and without other distinction than that of virtues and talents.

7. No man may be accused, arrested, or detained except in the cases determined by law, and according to the forms prescribed thereby. Whoever solicit, expedite, or execute arbitrary orders, or have them executed, must be punished; but every citizen summoned or apprehended in pursuance of the law must obey immediately; he renders himself culpable by resistance.

8. The law is to establish only penalties that are absolutely and obviously necessary; and no one may be punished except by virtue of a law established and promulgated prior to the offence and legally applied.

9. Since every man is presumed innocent until declared guilty, if arrest be deemed indispensable, all unnecessary severity for securing the person of the accused must be severely repressed by law.

10. No one is to be disquieted because of his opinions, even religious, provided their manifestation does not disturb the public order established by law.

11. Free communication of ideas and opinions is one of the most precious of the rights of man. Consequently, every citizen may speak, write, and print freely, subject to responsibility for the abuse of such liberty in the cases determined by law.

12. The guarantee of the rights of man and citizen necessitates a public force; such a force, therefore, is instituted for the advantage of all and not for the particular benefit of those to whom it is entrusted.

13. For the maintenance of the public force and for the expenses of administration a common tax is indispensable; it must be assessed equally on all citizens in proportion to their means.

14. Citizens have the right to ascertain, by themselves or through their representatives, the necessity of the public tax, to consent to it freely, to supervise its use, and to determine its quota, assessment, payment, and duration.

15. Society has the right to require of every public agent an accounting of his administration.

16. Every society in which the guarantee of rights is not assured or the separation of powers not determined has no constitution at all.

17. Since property is a sacred and inviolable right, no one may be deprived thereof unless a legally established public necessity obviously requires it, and upon condition of a just and previous indemnity.

*   *   *

REVIEW QUESTIONS

1. What similarities in issues do you see in the grievance petitions and in this declaration?
2. What are the principal differences between this declaration and the American Declaration of Independence?
3. How does this document reconcile the rights of the individual with the rights of government?
4. What civil liberties are missing here?

NATIONAL CONVENTION

FROM The Law of Suspects

Amid the chaos wreaked by foreign invasion, internal rebellion, inflation, and intense political factionalism, the republican government, dominated by the Jacobin club, erected political machinery in the form of emergency committees to monitor and suppress antirepublican activity. In 1793–1794 the fear of enemies of the revolution reached a fever pitch, endowing the revolutionary tribunals with an almost religious fervor as they sent their victims to the guillotine. The following law of 17 December 1793 gave the government the necessary legal authorization to suspend certain civil liberties in order to proceed with the extraordinary "revolutionary" measures of rescuing the republic from its actual and perceived enemies.

From *A Documentary Survey of the French Revolution* by Stewart, John Hall, © 1951. Adapted by permission of Prentice-Hall, Inc., Upper Saddle River, NJ.

*   *   *

1. Immediately after the publication of the present decree, all suspected persons within the territory of the Republic and still at liberty shall be placed in custody.

2. The following are deemed suspected persons: 1st, those who, by their conduct, associations, talk, or writings have shown themselves partisans of tyranny or federalism and enemies of liberty; 2nd, those who are unable to justify, in the manner prescribed by the decree of 21 March last, their means of existence and the performance of their civic duties; 3rd, those to whom certificates of patriotism have been refused; 4th, public functionaries suspended or dismissed from their positions by the National Convention or by its commissioners, and not reinstated, especially those who have been or are to be dismissed by virtue of the decree of 14 August last; 5th, those former nobles, husbands, wives, fathers, mothers, sons or daughters, brothers or sisters, and agents of the *émigrés*, who have not steadily manfested their devotion to the Revolution; 6th, those who have emigrated during the interval between 1 July,

1789, and the publication of the decree of 30 March–8 April, 1792, even though they may have returned to France within the period established by said decree or prior thereto.

3. The Watch Committees established according to the decree of 21 March last, or those substituted therefor, either by orders of the representatives of the people dispatched to the armies and the departments, or by virtue of particular decrees of the National Convention, are charged with drafting, each in its own *arrondissement*, a list of suspected persons, with issuing warrants of arrest against them, and with having seals placed on their papers. Commanders of the public force to whom such warrants are remitted shall be required to put them into effect immediately, under penalty of dismissal.

4. The members of the committee may order the arrest of any individual only if seven are present, and only by absolute majority of votes.

5. Individuals arrested as suspects shall be taken first to the jails of the place of their detention; in default of jails, they shall be kept under surveillance in their respective dwellings.

6. Within the following week, they shall be

transferred to national buildings, which the departmental administrations shall be required to designate and to have prepared for such purpose immediately after the receipt of the present decree.

7. The prisoners may have their absolutely essential belongings brought into said buildings; they shall remain there under guard until the peace.

8. The expenses of custody shall be charged to the prisoners, and shall be divided among them equally: such custody shall be confided preferably to fathers of families and to the relatives of citizens who are at or may go to the frontiers. The salary therefor is established, for each man of the guard, at the value of one and one-half days of labor.

9. The Watch Committees shall dispatch to the Committee of General Security of the National Convention, without delay, the list of persons whom they have arrested, with the reasons for their arrest and with the papers they have seized in such connection.

10. If there is occasion, the civil and criminal courts may have detained, in custody, and dispatched to the jails above stated, those who are accused of offences with regard to which it has been declared that there was no occasion for indictment or who have been acquitted of charges brought against them.

*   *   *

REVIEW QUESTIONS

1. For which social groups is this law intended?
2. What was the correct procedure for arresting suspects?
3. Did the suspect have rights?
4. Are there checks against potential abuses in this law?
5. On the basis of this document, what kind of social and political atmosphere pervaded France during the Jacobin republic?

FROM Decree Establishing the French Era *and* FROM Decree Establishing the Worship of the Supreme Being

The emergence of a distinct revolutionary public culture during the radical phase of the Terror merits attention. The following documents are two manifestations of a genuine belief that the new republic represented the threshold of a new political order, a new era in Western Civilization. While a spontaneous revolutionary culture budded in such forms as liberty caps, liberty trees, and republican forms of speech and address, the government also initiated measures to display the new political consciousness and mark its break from the old regime. Two prominent examples of the latter are the decree establishing a new calendar system on 5 October 1793, and the law of 7 May 1794, which sought to replace traditional religion with a more rational, transparent, civic-minded spirituality.

From *A Documentary Survey of the French Revolution* by Stewart, John Hall, © 1951. Adapted by permission of Prentice-Hall, Inc., Upper Saddle River, NJ.

Decree Establishing the French Era

*   *   *

1. The French era shall date from the establishment of the Republic on 22 September, 1792, of the common era, the day when the sun reached the true autumnal equinox . . .

2. The common era is abolished for civil uses.

3. The beginning of every year is established at midnight, beginning the day on which the true autumnal equinox falls for the Paris Observatory.

4. The first year of the French Republic began at midnight, 22 September, 1792, and ended at midnight, separating 21 from 22 September, 1793.

5. The second year began on 22 September, 1793, at midnight . . .

6. The decree establishing the beginning of the second year at 1 January, 1793, is repealed. All documents enacted within the period from 1 January to 21 September exclusive, and dated the second year of the Republic shall be regarded as belonging to the first year of the Republic.

7. The year shall be divided into twelve equal months, of thirty days each, after which five days, not belonging to any month, follow to complete the ordinary year; such days shall be called *complementary days.*

8. Each and every month shall be divided into three equal parts, of ten days each, called *décades,* and distinguished from one another as first, second, and third.

9. The months, the days of the décade, and the complementary days shall be designated by the ordinal denominations *first, second, third,* etc., day of the décade; *first, second, third,* etc., complementary day.

10. In memory of the Revolution which, after four years, has brought republican government to France, the bisextile period of four years shall be called the *franciade.*

The intercalary day terminating the aforementioned period shall be called *the day of the Revolution.* Said day shall be placed after the five complementary days.

11. The day, from midnight to midnight, shall be divided into ten parts or hours, each part into ten others, and so on up to the smallest commensurable portion of its duration. The present article shall be effective for public documents only from the first day of the first month of the third year of the Republic.

12. The Committee on Public Instruction is charged with having the new calendar printed in several formats, with a simple instruction to explain its most familiar principles and uses.

13. The new calendar, as well as the instruction, shall be sent to the administrative bodies, municipalities, courts, justices of the peace, and all public officials, schoolmasters and professors, armies, and popular societies. The provisional Executive Council shall have it transmitted to the ministers, consuls, and other agents of France in foreign countries.

14. All public documents shall be dated according to the new organization of the year.

15. Professors, schoolmasters and schoolmistresses, fathers and mothers of families, and all who direct the education of children in the Republic shall hasten to explain the new calendar to them, in conformity with the instruction annexed thereto.

16. Every four years, or every *franciade,* upon the day of the Revolution, republican games shall be celebrated in memory of the French Revolution.

Decree Establishing the Worship of the Supreme Being

*   *   *

1. The French people recognize the existence of the Supreme Being and the immortality of the soul.

2. They recognize that the worship worthy of

the Supreme Being is the observance of the duties of man.

3. They place in the forefront of such duties detestation of bad faith and tyranny, punishment of tyrants and traitors, succoring of unfortunates, respect of weak persons, defence of the oppressed, doing to others all the good that one can, and being just towards everyone.

4. Festivals shall be instituted to remind man of the concept of the Divinity and of the dignity of his being.

5. They shall take their names from the glorious events of our Revolution, or from the virtues most dear and most useful to man, or from the greatest benefits of nature.

6. The French Republic shall celebrate annually the festivals of 14 July, 1789, 10 August, 1792, 21 January, 1793, and 31 May, 1793.

7. On the days of *décade* it shall celebrate the following festivals:

To the Supreme Being and to nature; to the human race; to the French people; to the benefactors of humanity; to the martyrs of liberty; to liberty and equality; to the Republic; to the liberty of the world; to the love of the *Patrie*; to the hatred of tyrants and traitors; to truth; to justice; to modesty; to glory and immortality; to friendship; to frugality; to courage; to good faith; to heroism; to disinterestedness; to stoicism; to love; to conjugal love; to paternal love; to maternal tenderness; to filial piety; to infancy; to youth; to manhood; to old age; to misfortune; to agriculture; to industry; to our forefathers; to posterity; to happiness.

8. The Committees of Public Safety and Public Instruction are responsible for presenting a plan of organization for said festivals.

9. The National Convention summons all talents worthy of serving the cause of humanity to the honor of concurring in their establishment by hymns and civic songs, and by every means which may contribute to their embellishment and utility.

10. The Committee of Public Safety shall designate the works which seem to it the most suitable to realize these objectives, and shall compensate their authors.

11. Liberty of worship is maintained, in conformity with the decree of 18 Frimaire.

12. Every assembly which is aristocratic and contrary to public order shall be repressed.

13. In case of disturbances occasioned or motivated by any worship whatsoever, those who instigate them by fanatical preachings or counter-revolutionary insinuations, or those who provoke them by unjust and gratuitous violence, likewise shall be punished according to the rigor of the law.

14. A special report shall be made concerning the arrangements of detail relative to the present decree.

15. A festival in honor of the Supreme Being shall be celebrated on 20 Prairial next.

David is charged with presenting a plan therefor to the National Convention.

REVIEW QUESTIONS

1. What assumptions about the revolution are evinced in these documents?
2. What is the role of reason in the reconceptualization of time and religion?
3. What is the practical importance of religion and calendar reform for the revolutionary government?
4. What function did the new calendar and religion assume in public life?
5. What is revered and what is detested in the new religion?
6. How did the government plan to assimilate these new institutions into French society?
7. Do you think that the new institutions were successful?

OLYMPE DE GOUGES

FROM Declaration of the Rights of Woman

The revolution politicized millions of French men by transforming their status from subjects to citizens, but revolutionaries of all political stripes displayed extreme reluctance to incorporate women into the national political body. Heeding the new political discourse of equality, inalienable rights, and universal liberties, Olympe de Gouges, the self-educated daughter of a butcher, pointed up the revolutionaries' patent contradiction of applying tenets of natural law philosophy to one-half of the human race but not to the other. This pamphlet, published in September 1791, documents an important discussion during the revolution over the public roles and duties of women in civil society. Olympe de Gouges engaged her critical pen over a number of issues, which led to her arrest as a counterrevolutionary and her execution in 1793.

Copyright © 1996 From *The French Revolution and Human Rights: A Brief Documentary History,* Hunt (ed.). Reprinted with permission from St. Martin's Press.

To be decreed by the National Assembly in its last sessions or by the next legislature.

Preamble

Mothers, daughters, sisters, female representatives of the nation ask to be constituted as a national assembly. Considering that ignorance, neglect, or contempt for the rights of woman are the sole causes of public misfortunes and governmental corruption, they have resolved to set forth in a solemn declaration the natural, inalienable, and sacred rights of woman: so that by being constantly present to all the members of the social body this declaration may always remind them of their rights and duties; so that by being liable at every moment to comparison with the aim of any and all political institutions the acts of women's and men's powers may be the more fully respected; and so that by being founded henceforward on simple and incontestable principles the demands of the citizenesses may always tend toward maintaining the constitution, good morals, and the general welfare.

In consequence, the sex that is superior in beauty as in courage, needed in maternal sufferings, recognizes and declares, in the presence and under the auspices of the Supreme Being, the following rights of woman and the citizeness.

1. Woman is born free and remains equal to man in rights. Social distinctions may be based only on common utility.

2. The purpose of all political association is the preservation of the natural and imprescriptible rights of woman and man. These rights are liberty, property, security, and especially resistance to oppression.

3. The principle of all sovereignty rests essentially in the nation, which is but the reuniting of woman and man. No body and no individual may exercise authority which does not emanate expressly from the nation.

4. Liberty and justice consist in restoring all that belongs to another; hence the exercise of the

natural rights of woman has no other limits than those that the perpetual tyranny of man opposes to them; these limits must be reformed according to the laws of nature and reason.

5. The laws of nature and reason prohibit all actions which are injurious to society. No hindrance should be put in the way of anything not prohibited by these wise and divine laws, nor may anyone be forced to do what they do not require.

6. The law should be the expression of the general will. All citizenesses and citizens should take part, in person or by their representatives, in its formation. It must be the same for everyone. All citizenesses and citizens, being equal in its eyes, should be equally admissible to all public dignities, offices, and employments, according to their ability, and with no other distinction than that of their virtues and talents.

7. No woman is exempted; she is indicted, arrested, and detained in the cases determined by the law. Women like men obey this rigorous law.

8. Only strictly and obviously necessary punishments should be established by the law, and no one may be punished except by virtue of a law established and promulgated before the time of the offense, and legally applied to women.

9. Any woman being declared guilty, all rigor is exercised by the law.

10. No one should be disturbed for his fundamental opinions; woman has the right to mount the scaffold, so she should have the right equally to mount the tribune, provided that these manifestations do not trouble public order as established by law.

11. The free communication of thoughts and opinions is one of the most precious of the rights of woman, since this liberty assures the recognition of children by their fathers. Every citizeness may therefore say freely, I am the mother of your child; a barbarous prejudice should not force her to hide the truth, so long as responsibility is accepted for any abuse of this liberty in cases determined by the law.

12. The safeguard of the rights of woman and citizeness requires public powers. These powers are instituted for the advantage of all and not for the private benefit of those to whom they are entrusted.

13. For maintenance of public authority and for expenses of administration, taxation of women and men is equal; she takes part in all forced labor service, in all painful tasks; she must therefore have the same proportion in the distribution of places, employments, offices, dignities, and in industry.

14. The citizenesses and citizens have the right, by themselves or through their representatives, to have demonstrated to them the necessity of public taxes. The citizenesses can only agree to them upon admission of an equal division, not only in wealth, but also in the public administration, and to determine the means of apportionment, assessment, and collection, and the duration of the taxes.

15. The mass of women, joining with men in paying taxes, have the right to hold accountable every public agent of the administration.

16. Any society in which the guarantee of rights is not assured or the separation of powers not settled has no constitution. The constitution is null and void if the majority of individuals composing the nation has not cooperated in its drafting.

17. Property belongs to both sexes whether united or separated; it is for each of them an inviolable and sacred right, and no one may be deprived of it as a true patrimony of nature, except when public necessity, certified by law, obviously requires it, and then on condition of a just compensation in advance.

Postscript

Women, wake up; the tocsin of reason sounds throughout the universe; recognize your rights. The powerful empire of nature is no longer surrounded by prejudice, fanaticism, superstition, and lies. The torch of truth has dispersed all the clouds of folly and usurpation. Enslaved man has multiplied his force and needs yours to break his chains. Having become free, he has become unjust toward his companion. Oh women! Women, when will you cease to be blind? What advantages have you gathered in the revolution? A scorn more marked, a disdain more conspicuous. During the centuries of corruption you only reigned over the weakness of men. Your empire is destroyed; what is left to you then? Firm belief in the injustices of men. The reclaiming of your patrimony founded on the wise decrees of nature; why should you fear such a beautiful enterprise? . . . Whatever the barriers set up against you, it is in your power to overcome them; you only have to want it. Let us pass now to the appalling account of what you have been in society; and since national education is an issue at this moment, let us see if our wise legislators will think sanely about the education of women.

*   *   *

If giving my sex an honorable and just consistency is considered to be at this time paradoxical on my part and an attempt at the impossible, I leave to future men the glory of dealing with this matter; but while waiting, we can prepare the way with national education, with the restoration of morals and with conjugal agreements.

Form for a Social Contract Between Man and Woman

We, _____ and _____, moved by our own will, unite for the length of our lives and for the duration of our mutual inclinations under the following conditions: We intend and wish to make our wealth communal property, while reserving the right to divide it in favor of our children and of those for whom we might have a special inclination, mutually recognizing that our goods belong directly to our children, from whatever bed they come, and that all of them without distinction have the right to bear the name of the fathers and mothers who have acknowledged them, and we impose on ourselves the obligation of subscribing to the law that punishes any rejection of one's own blood. We likewise obligate ourselves, in the case of a separation, to divide our fortune equally and to set aside the portion the law designates for our children. In the case of a perfect union, the one the one who dies first will give up half his property in favor of the children; and if there are no children, the survivor will inherit by right, unless the dying person has disposed of his half of the common property in favor of someone he judges appropriate.

*   *   *

REVIEW QUESTIONS

1. Compare de Gouges's declaration with the Declaration of the Rights of Man and Citizen and determine the parallel and divergent aspects of the two documents.
2. How does de Gouges envision women in civil society, and how does this projected role differ from the social realities of eighteenth-century France?
3. What traditional institutions and mores does de Gouges criticize, and what does she exhort women to do?

NATIONAL CONVENTION

FROM **The National Convention Outlaws Clubs and Popular Societies of Women**

The political clubs and associations that mushroomed in France after 1789 played a significant role in revolutionary political culture. Because women had participated in critical events in the early phases of the revolution (e.g., the October Days), it is not surprising that women formed associations and participated in the public life of the republic. When the Society of Revolutionary Republican Women, an association that was initially supportive of Jacobin republicanism, grew critical of Jacobin government in 1793, it fell out of favor with the Jacobin-dominated National Convention, the nation's legislature. When a delegation of market women issued a formal complaint to the Convention regarding the society's brusque insistence that they wear revolutionary garb (pantaloons and red bonnets), the Convention used the incident to dissolve all women's societies.

National Convention
Moise Bayle, Presiding
Session of 9 Brumaire

. . . Amar, for the Committee of General Security: Citizens, your Committee has been working without respite on means of warding off the consequences of disorders which broke out the day before yesterday in Paris at the Marché des Innocents, near Saint-Eustache. It spent the night receiving deputations, listening to various reports which were made to it, and taking measures to maintain public order. Several women, calling themselves Jacobines, from an allegedly revolutionary society, were going about in the morning, in the market and under the ossuaries of les Innocents, in pantaloons and red bonnets. They intended to force other *citoyennes* to wear the same costume; several testified that they had been insulted by them. A mob of nearly six thousand

women gathered. All the women were in agreement that violence and threats would not make them dress in a costume they respected but which they believed was intended for men; they would obey laws passed by the legislators and acts of the people's magistrates, but they would not give in to the wishes and caprices of a hundred lazy and suspect women. They all cried out, "*Vive la Republique, une et indivisible!*"

Municipal officers and members of the Revolutionary Committee of the Section du Contrat Social quieted people down and dispersed the mobs. In the evening the same disturbance broke out with greater violence. A brawl started. Several self-proclaimed Revolutionary Women were roughed up. Some members of the crowd indulged themselves in acts of violence towards them which decency ought to have proscribed. Several remarks reported to your Committee show that this disturbance can be attributed only to a plot by enemies of the state. Several of these self-proclaimed Revolutionary Women may have been led astray by an excess of patriotism, but others, doubtless, were motivated only by malevolence.

Right now, when Brissot and his accomplices are being judged, they want to work up some disorders in Paris, as was the case whenever you were about to consider some important matter and when it was a question of taking measures useful for the Fatherland.

The Section des Marchés, informed of these events, drew up a resolution in which it informs your Committee that it believes several malevolent persons have put on the mask of an exaggerated patriotism to foment disturbances in the Section and a kind of counterrevolution in Paris. This Section requests that it be illegal to hinder anyone's freedom of dress and that popular societies of women be strictly prohibited, at least during the revolution.

The Committee thought it should carry its investigation further. It raised the following questions: (1) Is it permissible for citizens or for an individual society to force other citizens to do what the law does not prescribe? (2) Should meetings of women gathered together in popular societies in Paris be allowed? Don't the disorders already occasioned by these societies argue against tolerating their existence any longer?

Naturally, these questions are complicated, and their resolution must be preceded by two more general questions, which are: (1) Can women exercise political rights and take an active part in affairs of government? (2) Can they deliberate together in political associations or popular societies?

With respect to these two questions, the Committee decided in the negative. Time does not allow for the full development to which these major questions—and the first, above all—lend themselves. We are going to put forward a few ideas which may shed light on them. In your wisdom you will know how to submit them to thorough examination.

1. Should women exercise political rights and meddle in affairs of government? To govern is to rule the commonwealth by laws, the preparation of which demands extensive knowledge, unlimited attention and devotion, a strict immovability, and self-abnegation; again, to govern is to direct and ceaselessly to correct the action of constituted authorities. Are women capable of these cares and of the qualities they call for? In general, we can answer, no. Very few examples would contradict this evaluation.

The citizen's political rights are to debate and to have resolutions drawn up, by means of comparative deliberations, that relate to the interest of the state, and to resist oppression. Do women have the moral and physical strength which the exercise of one and the other of these rights calls for? Universal opinion rejects this idea.

2. Should women meet in political associations? The goal of popular associations is this: to unveil the maneuvers of the enemies of the commonwealth; to exercise surveillance both over citizens as individuals and over public functionaries—even over the legislative body; to excite the zeal of one and the other by the example of republican virtues; to shed light by public and in-depth discussion concerning the lack or reform of political laws. Can women devote themselves to these useful and difficult functions? No, because they would be obliged to sacrifice the more important cares to which nature calls them. The private functions for which women are destined by their very nature are related to the general order of society; this social order results from the differences between man and woman. Each sex is called to the kind of occupation which is fitting for it; its action is circumscribed within this circle which it cannot break through, because nature, which has imposed these limits on man, commands imperiously and receives no law.

Man is strong, robust, born with great energy, audacity, and courage; he braves perils and the intemperance of seasons because of his constitution; he resists all the elements; he is fit for the arts, difficult labors; and as he is almost exclusively destined for agriculture, commerce, navigation, voyages, war—everything that calls for force, intelligence, capability, so in the same way, he alone seems to be equipped for profound and serious thinking which calls for great intellectual effort and long studies which it is not granted to women to pursue.

What character is suitable for woman? Morals and even nature have assigned her functions to her. To begin educating men, to prepare children's minds and hearts for public virtues, to direct them early in life towards the good, to elevate their souls, to educate them in the political cult of liberty: such are their functions, after household cares. Woman is naturally destined to make virtue loved. When they have fulfilled all these obligations, they will have deserved well of the Fatherland. Doubtless they must educate themselves in the principles of liberty in order to make their children cherish it; they can attend the deliberations of the Sections and discussions of the popular societies, but as they are made for softening the morals of man, should they take an active part in discussions the passion of which is incompatible with the softness and moderation which are the charm of their sex?

We must say that this question is related essentially to morals, and without morals, no republic. Does the honesty of woman allow her to display herself in public and to struggle against men? to argue in full view of a public about questions on which the salvation of the republic depends? In general, women are ill suited for elevated thoughts and serious meditations, and if, among ancient peoples, their natural timidity and modesty did not allow them to appear outside their families, then in the French Republic do you want them to be seen coming into the gallery to political assemblies as men do? abandoning both reserve—source of all the virtues of their sex— and the care of their family?

They have more than one alternative way of rendering service to the Fatherland; they can enlighten their husbands, communicating precious reflections, the fruit of the quiet of a sedentary life, and work to fortify their love of country by means of everything which intimate love gives them in

the way of empire. And the man, enlightened by peaceful family discussions in the midst of his household, will bring back into society the useful ideas imparted to him by an honest woman.

We believe, therefore, that a woman should not leave her family to meddle in affairs of government.

There is another sense in which women's associations seem dangerous. If we consider that the political education of men is at its beginning, that all its principles are not developed, and that we are still stammering the word liberty, then how much more reasonable is it for women, whose moral education is almost nil, to be less enlightened concerning principles? Their presence in popular societies, therefore, would give an active role in government to people more exposed to error and seduction. Let us add that women are disposed by their organization to an over-excitation which would be deadly in public affairs and that interests of state would soon be sacrificed to everything which ardor in passions can generate in the way of error and disorder. Delivered over to the heat of public debate, they would teach their children not love of country but hatreds and suspicions.

We believe, therefore, and without any doubt you will think as we do, that it is not possible for women to exercise political rights. You will destroy these alleged popular societies of women which the aristocracy would want to set up to put them at odds with men, to divide the latter by forcing them to take sides in these quarrels, and to stir up disorder.

Charlier. Notwithstanding the objections just cited, I do not know on what principle one could lean in taking away women's right to assemble peaceably. (Murmurs.) Unless you are going to question whether women are part of the human species, can you take away from them this right which is common to every thinking being? When a popular society is negligent with respect to general order, to laws, then the members, accused of the offense, or the entire association, if it has made itself guilty, will be pursued by the police. And you have examples of the dissolution of several societies which had been taken over by the aristocracy. But may fear of a few abuses to which an institution is susceptible not force you to destroy the institution itself? For what institution is exempt from inconveniences?

Bazire. There is not anyone who does not sense the danger of abandoning to the police the surveillance and the overseeing of the popular societies. Thus, this remedy, which is itself an abuse, should not be cited against the all too real drawbacks of women's societies. Here is how the suspension of these societies can be justified. You declared yourselves a revolutionary government; in this capacity you can take all measures dictated by the public safety. For a brief period you have thrown a veil over principles out of fear that they might be abused to lead us into counterrevolution. Therefore, it is only a question of knowing whether women's societies are dangerous. Experience has shown these past days how deadly they are to the public peace. That granted, let no one say anything more to me about principles. I ask that in a revolutionary spirit and by way of a measure of public security these associations be prohibited, at least during the revolution.

The decree proposed by Amar is adopted in these terms:

The National Convention, after having heard the report of its Committee of General Security, decrees:

Article 1: Clubs and popular societies of women, whatever name they are known under, are prohibited. 2: All sessions of popular societies must be public.

*   *   *

REVIEW QUESTIONS

1. How did the national convention justify the abolition of women's clubs, and why was it threatened by women's political activities?
2. How does this document portray the behavior of women in public life?
3. What distinctions are made between the "private functions" of women and the social order of male public life?
4. Why are the two incompatible?
5. In this document, what is the role of nature in constructing the boundaries of civil society?

Opposing Views of the Revolution: Edmund Burke and Thomas Paine

Although Edmund Burke, an Irish Whig member of parliament, had supported the American cause against Great Britain in the 1770s, he denounced the French Revolution with a sustained rhetorical elegance that has few, if any, rivals. The circumstances that provoked Burke's essay was a speech in 1789 by Dr. Richard Price, who posited a close affinity between England's Glorious Revolution of 1688 and the recent French Revolution. Burke's scathing attack on the premises and principles of the French Revolution in his Reflections on the Revolution in France *(1790) incited an equally engaging rejoinder by Thomas Paine, a committed English democrat, whose earlier* Common Sense *had become a central political tract supporting the American Revolution. His* Rights of Man *(1791), the response to Burke, as-*

sumed the status in Britain of a primer for democratic republicanism. The British government prohibited its publication and sale in vain.

FROM REFLECTIONS ON THE REVOLUTION IN FRANCE

*   *   *

No experience has taught us that in any other course or method than that of an *hereditary crown* our liberties can be regularly perpetuated and preserved sacred as our *hereditary right*. An irregular, convulsive movement may be necessary to throw off an irregular, convulsive disease. But the course of succession is the healthy habit of the British constitution. Was it that the legislature wanted, at the act for the limitation of the crown in the Hanoverian line, drawn through the female descendants of James the First, a due sense of the inconveniences of having two or three, or possibly more, foreigners in succession to the British throne? No!—they had a due sense of the evils which might happen from such foreign rule, and more than a due sense of them. But a more decisive proof cannot be given of the full conviction of the British nation that the principles of the Revolution did not authorize them to elect kings at their pleasure, and without any attention to the ancient fundamental principles of our government, than their continuing to adopt a plan of hereditary Protestant succession in the old line, with all the dangers and all the inconveniences of its being a foreign line full before their eyes and operating with the utmost force upon their minds.

A few years ago I should be ashamed to overload a matter so capable of supporting itself by the then unnecessary support of any argument; but this seditious, unconstitutional doctrine is now publicly taught, avowed, and printed. The dislike I feel to revolutions, the signals for which have so often been given from pulpits; the spirit of change that is gone abroad; the total contempt which prevails with you, and may come to prevail with us, of all ancient institutions when set in opposition to a present sense of convenience or to the bent of a present inclination: all these considerations make it not unadvisable, in my opinion, to call back our attention to the true principles of our own domestic laws; that you, my French friend, should begin to know, and that we should continue to cherish them. We ought not, on either side of the water, to suffer ourselves to be imposed upon by the counterfeit wares which some persons, by a double fraud, export to you in illicit bottoms as raw commodities of British growth, though wholly alien to our soil, in order afterwards to smuggle them back again into this country, manufactured after the newest Paris fashion of an improved liberty.

The people of England will not ape the fashions they have never tried, nor go back to those which they have found mischievous on trial. They look upon the legal hereditary succession of their crown as among their rights, not as among their wrongs; as a benefit, not as a grievance; as a security for their liberty, not as a badge of servitude. They look on the frame of their commonwealth, *such as it stands*, to be of inestimable value, and they conceive the undisturbed succession of the crown to be a pledge of the stability and perpetuity of all the other members of our constitution.

I shall beg leave, before I go any further, to take notice of some paltry artifices which the abettors of election, as the only lawful title to the crown, are ready to employ in order to render the support of the just principles of our constitution a task somewhat invidious. These sophisters substitute a fictitious cause and feigned personages, in whose favor they suppose you engaged whenever you defend the inheritable nature of the crown. It is common with them to dispute as if they were in a conflict with some of those exploded fanatics of slavery, who formerly maintained what I believe no creature now maintains, "that the crown is held by divine hereditary and indefeasible right".-

From *Reflections on the Revolution in France,* edited by J. G. A. Pocock, Hackett, 1987.

—These old fanatics of single arbitrary power dogmatized as if hereditary royalty was the only lawful government in the world, just as our new fanatics of popular arbitrary power maintain that a popular election is the sole lawful source of authority. The old prerogative enthusiasts, it is true, did speculate foolishly, and perhaps impiously too, as if monarchy had more of a divine sanction than any other mode of government; and as if a right to govern by inheritance were in strictness *indefeasible* in every person who should be found in the succession to a throne, and under every circumstance, which no civil or political right can be. But an absurd opinion concerning the king's hereditary right to the crown does not prejudice one that is rational and bottomed upon solid principles of law and policy. If all the absurd theories of lawyers and divines were to vitiate the objects in which they are conversant, we should have no law and no religion left in the world. But an absurd theory on one side of a question forms no justification for alleging a false fact or promulgating mischievous maxims on the other.

*   *   *

I almost venture to affirm that not one in a hundred amongst us participates in the "triumph" of the Revolution Society. If the king and queen of France, and their children, were to fall into our hands by the chance of war, in the most acrimonious of all hostilities (I deprecate such an event, I deprecate such hostility), they would be treated with another sort of triumphal entry into London. We formerly have had a king of France in that situation; you have read how he was treated by the victor in the field, and in what manner he was afterwards received in England. Four hundred years have gone over us, but I believe we are not materially changed since that period. Thanks to our sullen resistance to innovation, thanks to the cold sluggishness of our national character, we still bear the stamp of our forefathers. We have not (as I conceive) lost the generosity and dignity of thinking of the fourteenth century, nor as yet have we subtilized ourselves into savages. We are not the converts of Rousseau; we are not the disciples of Voltaire; Helvetius has made no progress amongst us. Atheists are not our preachers; madmen are not our lawgivers. We know that *we* have made no discoveries, and we think that no discoveries are to be made in morality, nor many in the great principles of government, nor in the ideas of liberty, which were understood long before we were born, altogether as well as they will be after the grace has heaped its mold upon our presumption and the silent tomb shall have imposed its law on our pert loquacity. In England we have not yet been completely embowelled of our natural entrails; we still feel within us, and we cherish and cultivate, those inbred sentiments which are the faithful guardians, the active monitors of our duty, the true supporters of all liberal and manly morals. We have not been drawn and trussed, in order that we may be filled, like stuffed birds in a museum, with chaff and rags and paltry blurred shreds of paper about the rights of men. We preserve the whole of our feelings still native and entire, unsophisticated by pedantry and infidelity. We have real hearts of flesh and blood beating in our bosoms. We fear God; we look up with awe to kings, with affection to parliaments, with duty to magistrates, with reverence to priests, and with respect to nobility. Why? Because when such ideas are brought before our minds, it is *natural* to be so affected; because all other feelings are false and spurious and tend to corrupt our minds, to vitiate our primary morals, to render us unfit for rational liberty, and, by teaching us a servile, licentious, and abandoned insolence, to be our low sport for a few holidays, to make us perfectly fit for, and justly deserving of, slavery through the whole course of our lives.

YOU see, Sir, that in this enlightened age I am bold enough to confess that we are generally men of untaught feelings, that, instead of casting away all our old prejudices, we cherish them to a very considerable degree, and, to take more shame to ourselves, we cherish them because they are prejudices; and the longer they have lasted and the more generally they have prevailed, the more we cherish them. We are afraid to put men to live and trade each on his own private stock of reason, because we suspect that this stock in each man is small, and that the individuals would do better to avail themselves of the general bank and capital of nations and of ages. Many of our men of speculation, instead of exploding general prejudices, employ their sagacity to discover the latent wisdom which prevails in them. If they find what they seek, and they seldom fail, they think it more wise to continue the prejudice, with the reason involved, than to cast away the coat of prejudice and to leave nothing but the naked reason; because prejudice, with its reason, has a motive to give action to that reason, and an affection which will give it permanence. Prejudice is of ready application in the emergency; it previously engages the mind in a steady course of wisdom and virtue and does not leave the man hesitating in the moment of decision skeptical, puzzled, and unresolved. Prejudice renders a man's virtue his habit, and not a series of unconnected acts. Through just prejudice, his duty becomes a part of his nature.

Your literary men and your politicians, and so do the whole clan of the enlightened among us, essentially differ in these points. They have no respect for the wisdom of others, but they pay it off by a very full measure of confidence in their own. With them it is a sufficient motive to destroy an old scheme of things because it is an old one. As to the new, they are in no sort of fear with regard to the duration of a building run up in haste, because duration is no object to those who think little or nothing has been done before their time, and who place all their hopes in discovery. They conceive, very systematically, that all things which give perpetuity are mischievous, and therefore they are at inexpiable war with all establishments. They think that government may vary like modes of dress, and with as little ill effect; that there needs no principle of attachment, except a sense of present convenience, to any constitution of the state. They always speak as if they were of opinion that there is a singular species of compact between them and their magistrates which binds the magistrate, but which has nothing reciprocal in it, but

that the majesty of the people has a right to dissolve it without any reason but its will. Their attachment to their country itself is only so far as it agrees with some of their fleeting projects; it begins and ends with that scheme of polity which falls in with their momentary opinion.

These doctrines, or rather sentiments, seem prevalent with your new statesmen. But they are wholly different from those on which we have always acted in this country.

*   *   *

FROM RIGHTS OF MAN

*   *   *

Mr Burke talks about what he calls an hereditary crown, as if it were some production of Nature; or as if, like Time, it had a power to operate, not only independently, but in spite of man; or as if it were a thing or a subject universally consented to. Alas! it has none of those properties, but is the reverse of them all. It is a thing in imagination, the propriety of which is more than doubted, and the legality of which in a few years will be denied.

But, to arrange this matter in a clearer view than what general expressions can convey, it will be necessary to state the distinct heads under which (what is called) an hereditary crown, or, more properly speaking, an hereditary succession to the Government of a Nation, can be considered; which are,

First, The right of a particular Family to establish itself.

Secondly, The right of a Nation to establish a particular Family.

With respect to the *first* of these heads, that of a Family establishing itself with hereditary powers on its own authority, and independent of the consent of a Nation, all men will concur in calling it despotism; and it would be trespassing on their understanding to attempt to prove it.

But the *second* head, that of a Nation establishing a particular Family with *hereditary powers*, does not present itself as despotism on the first reflection; but if men will permit a second reflection to take place, and carry that reflection forward but one remove out of their own persons to that of their offspring, they will then see that hereditary succession becomes in its consequences the same despotism to others, which they reprobated for themselves. It operates to preclude the consent of the succeeding generation; and the preclusion of consent is despotism. When the person who at any time shall be in possession of a Government, or those who stand in succession to him, shall say to a Nation, I hold this power in 'contempt' of you, it signifies not on what authority he pretends to say it. It is no relief, but an aggravation to a person in slavery, to reflect that he was sold by his parent; and as that which heightens the criminality of an act cannot be produced to prove the legality of it, hereditary succession cannot be established as a legal thing.

In order to arrive at a more perfect decision on this head, it will be proper to consider the generation which undertakes to establish a Family with *hereditary powers*, a-part and separate from the generations which are to follow; and also to consider the character in which the *first* generation acts with respect to succeeding generations.

The generation which first selects a person, and puts him at the head of its Government, either with the title of King, or any other distinction, acts its *own choice*, be it wise or foolish, as a free agent for itself. The person so set up is not hereditary, but selected and appointed; and the generation who sets him up, does not live under an hereditary government, but under a government of its own choice and establishment. Were the generation who sets him up, and the person so let up, to live for ever, it never could become hereditary succession; and of consequence, hereditary succession can only follow on the death of the first parties.

As therefore hereditary succession is out of the question with respect to the *first* generation, we have now to consider the character in which *that* generation acts with respect to the commencing generation, and to all succeeding ones.

It assumes a character, to which it has neither right nor title. It changes itself from a *Legislator* to a *Testator*, and affects to make its Will, which is to have operation after the demise of the makers, to bequeath the Government; and it not only attempts to bequeath, but to establish on the succeeding generation, a new and different form of government under which itself lived. Itself, as is already observed, lived not under an hereditary Government, but under a Government of its own choice and establishment; and it now attempts, by virtue of a will and testament, (and which it has not authority to make), to take from the commencing generation, and all future ones, the rights and free agency by which itself acted.

But, exclusive of the right which any generation has to act collectively as a testator, the objects to which it applies itself in this case, are not within the compass of any law, or of any will or testament.

The rights of men in society, are neither deviseable, nor transferable, nor annihilable, but are descendable only; and it is not in the power of any generation to intercept finally, and cut off the descent. If the present generation, or any other, are disposed to be slaves, it does not lessen the right of the succeeding generation to be free: wrongs cannot have a legal descent. When Mr Burke attempts to maintain, that the *English Nation did at the Revolution of 1688, most solemnly renounce and abdicate their rights for themselves, and for all their posterity for ever;* he speaks a language that merits not reply, and which can only excite contempt for his prostitute principles, or pity for his ignorance.

In whatever light hereditary succession, as growing out of the will and testament of some former generation, presents itself, it is an absurdity. A cannot make a will to take from B the property of B, and give it to C; yet this is the manner in which (what is called) hereditary succession by law operates. A certain former generation made a will, to take away the rights of the commencing generation, and all future ones, and convey those rights to a third person, who afterwards comes forward, and tells them, in Mr Burke's language, that they have *no rights*, that their rights are already bequeathed to him, and that he will govern in *contempt* of them. From such principles, and such ignorance, Good Lord deliver the world!

But, after all, what is this metaphor called a crown, or rather what is monarchy? Is it a thing, or is it a name, or is it a fraud? Is it 'a contrivance of human wisdom,' or of human craft to obtain money from a nation under specious pretences? Is it a thing necessary to a nation? If it is, in what does that necessity consist, what services does it perform, what is its business, and what are its merits?* * * It appears to be a something going much out of fashion, falling into ridicule, and rejected in some countries both as unnecessary and expensive. In America it is considered as an absurdity; and in France it has so far declined, that the goodness of the man, and the respect for his personal character, are the only things that preserve the appearance of its existence.

＊　　＊　　＊

If there is any thing in monarchy which we people of America do not understand, I wish Mr Burke would be so kind as to inform us. I see in America, a government extending over a country ten times as large as England, and conducted with regularity, for a fortieth part of the expence which government costs in England. If I ask a man in America, if he wants a King? he retorts, and asks me if I take him for an ideot? How is it that this difference happens? are we more or less wise than others? I see in America, the generality of people living in a stile of plenty unknown in monarchical countries; and I see that the principle of its government, which is that of the *equal Rights of Man*, is making a rapid progress in the world.

＊　　＊　　＊

REVIEW QUESTIONS

1. What is Burke's position on tradition and monarchy, and what is Paine's response to it?
2. What is Burke's response to the Enlightenment and its primacy of reason?
3. How does Paine characterize the use of reason in politics?
4. How did the issue of the French Revolution have a direct bearing on British domestic politics in the 1790s?

WILLIAM WORDSWORTH

FROM *The Prelude*

William Wordsworth, one of the outstanding voices of English Romantic poetry, exemplified the unbounded optimism with which he and many other European artists embraced the French Revolution. Although Wordsworth's enthusiasm for the revolution faded, this excerpt from The Prelude *(1805), an epic poem of his youth and development as a poet, recaptures the initial sublime hope that he projected on the revolution. Because Wordsworth was not alone among poets, writers, and artists in finding inspiration in the promise of justice and freedom, one must recognize the revolution as an all-embracing cultural event.*

*   *   *

But from these bitter truths I must return
To my own History. It hath been told
That I was led to take an eager part
In arguments of civil polity
Abruptly, and indeed before my time:
I had approach'd, like other Youth, the Shield
Of human nature from the golden side
And would have fought, even to the death, to
    attest
The quality of the metal which I saw.
What there is best in individual Man,
Of wise in passion, and sublime in power,
What there is strong and pure in household
    love,
Benevolent in small societies,
And great in large ones also, when call'd forth
By great occasions, these were things of which
I something knew, yet even these themselves,
Felt deeply, were not thoroughly understood
By Reason; nay, far from it, they were yet,
As cause was given me afterwards to learn,
Not proof against the injuries of the day,
Lodged only at the Sanctuary's door,
Not safe within its bosom. Thus prepared,
And with such general insight into evil,
And of the bounds which sever it from good,
As books and common intercourse with life
Must needs have given; to the noviciate mind,
When the world travels in a beaten road,
Guide faithful as is needed, I began
To think with fervour upon management
Of Nations, what it is and ought to be,
And how their worth depended on their
    Laws
And on the Constitution of the State.

O pleasant exercise of hope and joy!
For great were the auxiliars which then stood
Upon our side, we who were strong in love;
Bliss was it in that dawn to be alive,
But to be young was very heaven; O times,
In which the meagre, stale, forbidding ways
Of custom, law, and statute took at once
The attraction of a Country in Romance;

When Reason seem'd the most to assert her
    rights
When most intent on making of herself
A prime Enchanter to assist the work,
Which then was going forwards in her name,
Not favour'd spots alone, but the whole earth
The beauty wore of promise, that which sets,
To take an image which was felt, no doubt,
Among the bowers of paradise itself,
The budding rose above the rose full blown.
What temper at the prospect did not wake
To happiness unthought of? The inert
Were rouz'd, and lively natures rapt away:
They who had fed their childhood upon dreams,
The Play-fellows of Fancy, who had made
All powers of swiftness, subtlety, and strength
Their ministers, used to stir in lordly wise
Among the grandest objects of the sense,
And deal with whatsoever they found there
As if they had within some lurking right
To wield it; they too, who, of gentle mood
Had watch'd all gentle motions, and to these
Had fitted their own thoughts, schemers more
    mild,
And in the region of their peaceful selves,
Did now find helpers to their hearts' desire,
And stuff at hand, plastic as they could wish,
Were call'd upon to exercise their skill,
Not in Utopia, subterraneous Fields,
Or some secreted Island, Heaven knows where,
But in the very world which is the world
Of all of us, the place in which, in the end,
We find our happiness, or not at all.

Why should I not confess that earth was then
To me what an inheritance new-fallen
Seems, when the first time visited, to one
Who thither comes to find in it his home?
He walks about and looks upon the place
With cordial transport, moulds it, and remoulds,
And is half pleased with things that are amiss,
'Twill be such joy to see them disappear.

An active partisan, I thus convoked
From every object pleasant circumstance
To suit my ends; I moved among mankind

With genial feelings still predominant;
When erring, erring on the better part,
And in the kinder spirit; placable,
Indulgent oft-times to the worst desires
As on one side not uninform'd that men
See as it hath been taught them, and that time
Gives rights to error; on the other hand
That throwing off oppression must be work
As well of license as of liberty;
And above all, for this was more than all,
Not caring if the wind did now and then
Blow keen upon an eminence that gave
Prospect so large into futurity;
In brief, a child of nature, as at first,
Diffusing only those affections wider
That from the cradle had grown up with me,

And losing, in no other way than light
Is lost in light, the weak in the more strong.

*   *   *

REVIEW QUESTIONS

1. What were young Wordsworth's sentiments on civil polity?
2. Why did Wordsworth remember 1789 as "bliss"?
3. What positive characteristics did he ascribe to the revolution?
4. What are the implicit criticisms of the revolution and his own attitudes?

NAPOLEON BONAPARTE

FROM Letters

Ineffective government, abuse of power, and lack of popular support during the first decade of the French Revolution abetted the meteoric rise of Napoleon's political career. A military hero and shrewd political opportunist, Napoleon took part in a coup d'état in 1799 that dismantled popular sovereignty and political liberties. Blending national glory with efficient administration, Napoleon reaped the acclaims of the French and crowned himself emperor in 1804, asserting nonetheless that he remained a son of the Enlightenment and of the revolution. The excerpts here present Napoleon's own interpretation of his place in the revolution, his French chauvinism, and his gift for inspiring the new citizen-soldier of France.

*   *   *

[Dictation, 1816] The French Revolution was . . . a general mass movement of the nation against the privileged classes. The French nobility, like that of all Europe, dates from the barbarian in-vasions which broke up the Roman Empire. In France, the nobles represented the ancient Franks and Burgundians; the rest of the nation, the Gauls. The introduction of the feudal system established the principle that every landed property had a lord. All political rights were exercised by the priests and the nobles. The peasants were enslaved, partly by binding them to the soil.

The progress of civilization and knowledge liberated the people. This new state of affairs caused the prosperity of industry and trade. In the eighteenth century, the larger part of the land, of wealth, and of the fruits of civilization belonged to the people. The nobles, however, still formed a privileged class: they controlled the upper and intermediate courts, they held feudal rights under a great variety of names and forms, they were exempt from contributing to any of the taxes imposed by society, and they had exclusive access to the most honorable employments.

All these abuses stirred the citizens to protest. The chief aim of the Revolution was to destroy all privileges; to abolish manorial courts, justice being an inalienable attribute of the sovereign authority; to suppress all feudal rights as remnants of the people's former slavery; to subject all citizens and all property without distinction to taxation by the State. Finally, the Revolution proclaimed the equality of rights. All citizens could fill all employments, subject only to their talents and the vicissitudes of chance.

The monarchy was made up of provinces annexed to the Crown at various periods. . . . France was not a state but an unamalgamated collection of several states placed side by side. Chance and the events of past centuries had determined the whole. The Revolution, applying its guiding principle of equality to the citizens among themselves as well as to the various territories, destroyed all these petty nations and created a new great nation. There was no more Brittany, no more Normandy, Burgundy, Champagne, Provence, or Lorraine: there was a France. . . .

Whatever had been brought about in the sequence of events since the time of Clovis ceased to exist. These changes were all so favorable to the people that they took hold with the greatest ease: by 1800 there remained not a single memory of the old privileges. . . . In order to trace any existing institution to its origin all that was necessary was to look up the new law that had established it. Half of the land had changed ownership; the farm-

ers and the bourgeois had become rich. The progress of agriculture, manufactures, and industry passed all our hopes. France offered the spectacle of thirty million inhabitants living within natural limits, forming a single class of citizens governed by a single law, a single organization, a single order. All these changes accorded with the well-being of the nation, with its laws, with justice, and with the spirit of the century.

*   *   *

[Conversation, 1816] The counterrevolution, even if given a free course, must inevitably come to drown in revolution. . . . For henceforth nothing can destroy or efface the grand principles of our Revolution. These great and noble truths must remain forever, so inextricably are they linked to our splendor, our monuments, our prodigious deeds. We have drowned its earlier shame in floods of glory. These truths are henceforth immortal. . . . They live on in England, they illumine America, they are naturalized in France: from this tripod the light will burst upon the world.

These truths will rule the world. They will be the creed, the religion, the morality of all nations. And, no matter what has been said, this memorable era will be linked to my person, because, after all, I have carried its torch and consecrated its principles, and because persecution now has made me its Messiah.

*   *   *

[Letter, 1810] My axiom is: France before everything.

*   *   *

[Letter, 1797, in answer to criticism that Napoleon failed to introduce the principles of the French Revolution in Italy] At no time has the French Republic adopted the principle of waging war for the sake of other nations. I should like to know what philosophical or moral principle demands the sacrifice of forty thousand Frenchmen against the clearly expressed will of the nation and the enlightened self-interest of the Republic.

I know full well that there is a handful of idle

talkers—they might well be described as madmen—who want a universal republic. Their talk costs them nothing. I should like these gentlemen to come and take part in a winter campaign.

*   *   *

[Conversation with Roederer, 1809, on King Joseph] This is another thing I reproach him with: he has become a Spaniard. . . . The king must be French; Spain must be French. It is for France I have conquered Spain—conquered her with French blood, French limbs, French gold. I am wholly French by attachment as well as by duty. I do nothing except from duty and from love of France. I have dethroned the Bourbons only because it was in the interest of France to insure the future of my dynasty. I had no other aim but the glory and the power of France. My whole family must be French. When, last winter, in Mantua, Lucien dared speak to me as to a foreigner, I said to him, "Go away, you wretch, out of my sight! All is finished between us!" I have conquered Spain; I have conquered her so that she may be French.

*   *   *

[Proclamation to the Army of Italy, Albenga, April 10, 1796] Soldiers! You are ill-fed and almost naked. The government owes you a great deal, but it can do nothing for you. Your patience and courage do you honor but give you neither worldly goods nor glory. I shall lead you into the most fertile plains on earth. There you shall find great cities and rich provinces. There you shall find honor, glory, riches. Soldiers of the Army of Italy! Could courage and constancy possibly fail you?

*   *   *

[Proclamation, San Massimo, November 11, 1796] When the drum has beaten the charge, when you must march straight upon the foe, bayonets fixed, your gloomy silence pledging victory—soldiers, remember to be worthy of yourselves!

*   *   *

[Proclamation on his return from Elba, Gulf of Juan, March 1, 1815] Soldiers! Come and take your places under the flags of your leader! He has no existence except in your existence; he has no rights except your rights and those of the people; his interests, his honor, his glory are none other than your interests, your honor, your glory. Victory will march at a quickstep. The eagle and tricolor shall fly from steeple to steeple to the towers of Notre Dame. Then you can show your scars without dishonor, then you can pride yourselves on what you have accomplished: you will be the liberators of the fatherland! In your old age, surrounded and admired by your fellow citizens, who will listen with respect when you tell of your great deeds, you will be able to say with pride, "I, too, was part of that Grand Army which twice entered the walls of Vienna, which entered Rome, Berlin, Madrid, and Moscow, which cleansed Paris of the pollution that treason and the presence of the enemy had left in it."

*   *   *

REVIEW QUESTIONS

1. How did Napoleon interpret the legacy of the French Revolution and his place in it?
2. What was Napoleon's attitude about France, and what were the implications of this attitude for Europe?
3. How did Napoleon strive to inspire his soldiers?
4. What sentiments did he employ?

VICTOR HUGO

To the Napoleon Column

Napoleon's legacy reached mythic proportions after his death, which tangibly shaped French political culture for the remainder of the century. After a brief flirtation with royalism, Victor Hugo (1802–1885), a central figure in both French letters and politics, lionized Napoleon in speeches, prose, and verse. In spite of Napoleon's ambivalence toward popular sovereignty, Hugo, the champion of republicanism, nonetheless held up Napoleon as a lodestar for French politics. This ode to Napoleon, published in Hugo's volume Songs of Twilight *(1835), evokes the martial and imperial spirit that gripped the imagination of nineteenth-century French citizens.*

From *The Poetical Works of Victor Hugo*, George Bell and Sons, 1887.

WHEN with gigantic hand he placed,
For throne on vassal Europe based,
   That column's lofty height—
Pillar, in whose dread majesty,
In double immortality,
   Glory and bronze unite!

Aye, when he built it that, some day,
Discord or war their course might stay,
   Or here might break their car;
And in our streets to put to shame
Pigmies that bear the hero's name
   Of Greek and Roman war.

It was a glorious sight; the world
His hosts had trod, with flags unfurled,
   In veteran array;
Kings fled before him, forced to yield,
He, conqueror on each battlefield,
   Their cannon bore away.

Then, with his victors back he came;
All France with booty teemed, her name
   Was writ on sculptured stone;
And Paris cried with joy, as when
The parent bird comes home again
   To th' eaglets left alone.

Into the furnace flame, so fast,
Were heaps of war-won metal cast,
   The future monument!
His thought had formed the giant mould,
And piles of brass in the fire he rolled,
   From hostile cannon rent.

When to the battlefield he came,
He grasped the guns spite tongues of flame,
   And bore the spoil away.
This bronze to France's Rome he brought,
And to the founder said, "Is aught
   Wanting for our array?"

And when, beneath a radiant sun,
That man, his noble purpose done,
   With calm and tranquil mien,
Disclosed to view this glorious fane,
And did with peaceful hand contain
   The warlike eagle's sheen.

Round *thee*, when hundred thousands placed,
As some great Roman's triumph graced,
   The little Romans all;
We boys hung on the procession's flanks,
Seeking some father in thy ranks,
   And loud thy praise did call.

Who that survey'd thee, when that day
Thou deem'd that future glory ray
   Would here be ever bright;
Fear'd that, ere long, all France thy grave
From pettifoggers vain would crave
   Beneath that column's height?

REVIEW QUESTIONS

1. Why does Hugo employ allusions to antiquity, and how does this support the Napoleon myth?
2. What is the "glorious sight" in the third stanza, and what emotions does Hugo wish to arouse with this passage?
3. Judging from the final stanzas, what kind of status did Napoleon assume in contemporary politics?

19 ♋ THE INDUSTRIAL REVOLUTION

The economic transition from mercantile to industrial capitalism in Britain and Europe constitutes one of the momentous structural revolutions in modern civilization. Industrialization not only expanded the material culture of the West but also penetrated and transformed most spheres of economic activity. The industrial revolution unleashed an unprecedented dynamism of sustained economic growth. It introduced a new scale and scope of economic activity, and the resulting need for new markets, better infrastructure, greater capitalization, and technological innovation came to characterize the modern world.

Early industrialization is largely associated with laissez-faire political economy, a doctrine of economic liberalism that championed free trade, private enterprise, meritocratic individualism, and the sanctity of private property. Grounded in the writings of the political economist Adam Smith, this doctrine roundly attacked any interference with the "natural laws" of the marketplace and advocated separation of government and economy. Although Adam Smith was not the first to criticize mercantilism and advocate unrestricted trade, his treatise, by associating free trade with the "natural rights" of other individual liberties, provided the philosophical underpinnings for the political demands of Great Britain's capitalist classes, whose enfranchisement after 1832 exerted influence on state policy. By dint of the vast wealth accumulated through private enterprise, the middle classes espoused the notion that commerce and industry were the twin pillars of civil society. Liberals confidently embraced the belief that these two spheres of public life provided the material basis for progress and prosperity.

In spite of England's self-proclaimed status as the "workshop of the world," industrialism clearly moved in both positive and negative directions. Contemporaries dubbed the new discipline of political economy the "dismal science," for its studies on population growth and wage levels suggested the impossibility of general happiness and welfare. Little consensus existed on the extent to which laissez-faire principles should be applied and how industrial society should be organized. Consequently, the industrialization of Europe did not follow any single model. European governments, accustomed to directing economic activity, proved reluctant to surrender to the "invisible hand," Smith's tenet that individual self-interest promoted general welfare. In contrast to England, these European governments nurtured domestic industry with subventions and protective tariffs, mobilized state capital to assist in railroad construction, promoted economic development through technical education, and oversaw the management of large-scale industrial enterprises. Moreover, the majority of European society remained predominantly rural throughout most of the nineteenth century. Hence, while one speaks of an industrial revolution, one must envision small handicraft workshops alongside mechanized factories and vital rural economies serving dynamic urban centers.

The onset of early industrialization also generated an extraordinary range of criticism against the premise that captitalism would benefit the majority of society. St. Simon, Robert Owen, and Karl Marx are but three observers who acknowledged capitalism's material benefits but nonetheless emphasized its elemental flaws in its treatment of wage workers. Their concerns for the material, moral, and creative dimensions of workers' lives compelled them to offer alternative visions to the dominant principles of competition and individual self interest. Such critical voices sharpened the debate on ethics and social justice, thus exerting force over the next century—through rational argument and political struggle—on Europe's elite to incorporate the interests of unpropertied workers into their statecraft.

Adam Smith

FROM *An Inquiry into the Nature and Causes of the Wealth of Nations*

Adam Smith (1723–1790), a professor of logic and moral philosophy as well as rector of Glasgow University, wrote on moral philosophy, rhetoric, astronomy, and the formation of languages, but his reputation rests on his work of political economy, Inquiry into the Nature and Causes of the Wealth of Nations (1776). The treatise's wide-ranging discussions on wages, profit, capital, and industry influenced po-

litical economists for the next century, but the book's attack on mercantilism and its corresponding advocacy of free trade heralded a new economic age. The following selections center on the division of labor, the productive "orders" of society, the "invisible hand" of individual interest, and the role of the state in political economy.

From *An Inquiry into the Nature and Causes of the Wealth of Nations*, Adam Smith, Oxford University Press, 1993.

Book I

Of the Causes of Improvement in the productive Powers of Labour, and of the Order according to which its Produce is naturally distributed among the different Ranks of the People

Chapter I
Of the Division of Labour

THE greatest improvement in the productive powers of labour, and the greater part of the skill, dexterity, and judgment with which it is any where directed, or applied, seem to have been the effects of the division of labour.

*   *   *

To take an example, therefore, from a very trifling manufacture; but one in which the division of labour has been very often taken notice of, the trade of the pin-maker; a workman not educated to this business (which the division of labour has rendered a distinct trade), nor acquainted with the use of the machinery employed in it (to the invention of which the same division of labour has probably given occasion), could scarce, perhaps, with his utmost industry, make one pin in a day, and certainly could not make twenty. But in the way in which this business is now carried on, not only the whole work is a peculiar trade, but it is divided into a number of branches, of which the greater part are likewise peculiar trades. One man draws out the wire, another straights it, a third cuts it, a fourth points it, a fifth grinds it at the top for receiving the head; to make the head requires two or three distinct operations; to put it on, is a peculiar business, to whiten the pins is another; it is even a trade by itself to put them into the paper; and the important business of making a pin is, in this manner, divided into about eighteen distinct operations, which, in some manufactories, are all performed by distinct hands, though in others the same man will sometimes perform two or three of them. I have seen a small manufactory of this kind where ten men only were employed, and where some of them consequently performed two or three distinct operations. But though they were very poor, and therefore but indifferently accommodated with the necessary machinery, they could, when they exerted themselves, make among them about twelve pounds of pins in a day. There are in a pound upwards of four thousand pins of a middling size. Those ten persons, therefore, could make among them upwards of forty-eight thousand pins in a day. Each person, therefore, making a tenth part of forty-eight thousand pins, might be considered as making four thousand eight hundred pins in a day. But if they had all wrought separately and independently, and without any of them having been educated to this peculiar business, they certainly could not each of them have made twenty, perhaps not one pin in a day; that is, certainly, not the two hundred and fortieth, perhaps not the four thousand eight hundredth part of what they are at present capable of performing, in consequence of a proper division and combination of their different operations.

*   *   *

It is the great multiplication of the productions of all the different arts, in consequence of the division of labour, which occasions, in a well-governed society, that universal opulence which extends itself to the lowest ranks of the people. Every workman has a great quantity of his own work to dispose of beyond what he himself has occasion for; and every other workman being exactly in the same situation, he is enabled to exchange a great quantity of his own goods for a great quantity, or, what comes to the same thing, for the price of a great quantity of theirs. He supplies them abundantly with what they have occasion for, and they accommodate him as amply with what he has occasion for, and a general plenty diffuses itself through all the different ranks of the society.

*   *   *

. . . The whole annual produce of the land and labour of every country, or what comes to the same thing, the whole price of that annual produce, naturally divides itself, it has already been observed, into three parts; the rent of land, the wages of labour, and the profits of stock; and constitutes a revenue to three different orders of people; to those who live by rent, to those who live by wages, and to those who live by profit. These are the three great, original and constituent orders of every civilized society, from whose revenue that of every other order is ultimately derived.

The interest of the first of those three great orders, it appears from what has been just now said, is strictly and inseparably connected with the general interest of the society. Whatever either promotes or obstructs the one, necessarily promotes or obstructs the other. When the publick deliberates concerning any regulation of commerce or police, the proprietors of land never can mislead it, with a view to promote the interest of their own particular order; at least, if they have any tolerable knowledge of that interest. They are, indeed, too often defective in this tolerable knowledge. They are the only one of the three orders whose revenue costs them neither labour nor care, but comes to them, as it were, of its own accord, and independent of any plan or project of their own. That indolence, which is the natural effect of the ease and security of their situation, renders them too often, not only ignorant, but incapable of that application of mind which is necessary in order to foresee and understand the consequences of any publick regulation.

The interest of the second order, that of those who live by wages, is as strictly connected with the interest of the society as that of the first. The wages of the labourer, it has already been shewn, are never so high as when the demand for labour is continually rising, or when the quantity employed is every year increasing considerably. When this real wealth of the society becomes stationary, his wages are soon reduced to what is barely enough to enable him to bring up a family, or to continue the race of labourers. When the society declines, they fall even below this. The order of proprietors may, perhaps, gain more by the prosperity of the society, than that of labourers: but there is no order that suffers so cruelly from its decline. But though the interest of the labourer is strictly connected with that of the society, he is incapable either of comprehending that interest, or of understanding its connection with his own. His condition leaves him no time to receive the necessary information, and his education and habits are commonly such as to render him unfit to judge even though he was fully informed. In the publick deliberations, therefore, his voice is little heard and less regarded, except upon some particular occasions, when his clamour is animated, set on, and supported by his employers, not for his, but their own particular purposes.

His employers constitute the third order, that of those who live by profit. It is the stock that is employed for the sake of profit, which puts into motion the greater part of the useful labour of every society. The plans and projects of the employers of stock regulate and direct all the most important operations of labour, and profit is the end proposed by all those plans and projects. But the rate of profit does not, like rent and wages, rise with the prosperity, and fall with the declension of the society. On the contrary, it is naturally low in rich, and high in poor countries, and it is always highest in the countries which are going fastest to ruin. The interest of this third order therefore, has not the same connection with the general interest of the society as that of the other two. Merchants and master manufacturers are, in this order, the two classes of people who commonly employ the largest capitals, and who by their weakness draw to themselves the greatest share of the publick consideration. As during their whole lives they are engaged in plans and projects, they have frequently more acuteness of understanding than the greater part of country gentlemen. As their thoughts, however, are commonly exercised rather about the interest of their own particular branch of business, than about that of the society, their judgment, even when given with the greatest candour (which it has not been upon every occasion) is much more to be depended upon with regard to the former of those two objects, than with regard to the latter. Their superiority over the country gentleman is, not so much in their knowledge of the publick interest, as in their having a better knowledge of their own interest than he has of his. It is by this superior knowledge of their own interest that they have frequently imposed upon his generosity, and persuaded him to give up both his own interest and that of the publick, from a very simple but honest conviction, that their interest, and not his, was the interest of the publick. The interest of the dealers, however, in any particular branch of trade or manufactures, is always in some respects different from, and even opposite to, that of the publick. To widen the market and to narrow the competition, is always the interest of the dealers. To widen the market may frequently be agreeable enough to the interest of the publick; but to narrow the competition must always be against it, and can serve only to enable the dealers, by raising their profits above what they naturally would be, to levy, for their own benefit, an absurd tax upon the rest of their fellow-citizens. The proposal of any new law or regulation of commerce which comes from this order, ought always to be listened to with great precaution, and ought never to be adopted till after having been long and carefully examined, not only with the most scrupulous, but with the most suspicious attention. It comes from

an order of men, whose interest is never exactly the same with that of the publick, who have generally an interest to deceive and even to oppress the publick, and who accordingly have, upon many occasions, both deceived and oppressed it. . . .

*   *   *

But the annual revenue of every society is always precisely equal to the exchangeable value of the whole annual produce of its industry, or rather is precisely the same thing with that exchangeable value. As every individual, therefore, endeavours as much as he can both to employ his capital in the support of domestick industry, and so to direct that industry that its produce may be of the greatest value; every individual necessarily labours to render the annual revenue of the society as great as he can. He generally, indeed, neither intends to promote the publick interest, nor knows how much he is promoting it. By preferring the support of domestick to that of foreign industry, he intends only his own security; and by directing that industry in such a manner as its produce may be of the greatest value, he intends only his own gain, and he is in this, as in many other cases, led by an invisible hand to promote an end which was no part of his intention. Nor is it always the worse for the society that it was no part of it. By pursuing his own interest he frequently promotes that of the society more effectually than when he really intends to promote it. I have never known much good done by those who affected to trade for the publick good. It is an affectation, indeed, not very common among merchants, and very few words need be employed in dissuading them from it.

What is the species of domestick industry which his capital can employ, and of which the produce is likely to be of the greatest value, every individual, it is evident, can, in his local situation, judge much better than any statesman or lawgiver can do for him. The stateman, who should attempt to direct private people in what manner they ought to employ their capitals, would not only load himself with a most unnecessary attention, but assume an authority which could safely be trusted, not only to no single person, but to no council or senate whatever, and which would nowhere be so dangerous as in the hands of a man who had folly and presumption enough to fancy himself fit to exercise it.

To give the monopoly of the home-market to the produce of domestick industry, in any particular art or manufacture, is in some measure to direct private people in what manner they ought to employ their capitals, and must, in almost all cases, be either a useless or a hurtful regulation. If the produce of domestick can be brought there as cheap as that of foreign industry, the regulation is evidently useless. If it cannot, it must generally be hurtful. It is the maxim of every prudent master of a family, never to attempt to make at home what it will cost him more to make than to buy. The taylor does not attempt to make his own shoes, but buys them of the shoemaker. The shoemaker does not attempt to make his own cloaths, but employs a taylor. The farmer attempts to make neither the one nor the other, but employs those different artificers. All of them find it for their interest to employ their whole industry in a way in which they have some advantage over their neighbours, and to purchase with a part of its produce, or what is the same thing, with the price of a part of it, whatever else they have occasion for.

What is prudence in the conduct of every private family, can scarce be folly in that of a great kingdom.

*　　*　　*

The expence of defending the society, and that of supporting the dignity of the chief magistrate, are both laid out for the general benefit of the whole society. It is reasonable, therefore, that they should be defrayed by the general contribution of the whole society, all the different members contributing, as nearly as possible, in proportion to their respective abilities.

The expence of the administration of justice too, may, no doubt, be considered as laid out for the benefit of the whole society. There is no impropriety, therefore, in its being defrayed by the general contribution of the whole society. The per-sons, however, who give occasion to this expence are those who, by their injustice in one way or another, make it necessary to seek redress or protection from the courts of justice. The persons again most immediately benefited by this expence, are those whom the courts of justice either restore to their rights, or maintain in their rights. The expence of the administration of justice, therefore, may very properly be defrayed by the particular contribution of one or other, or both of those two different sets of persons, according as different occasions may require, that is, by the fees of court. It cannot be necessary to have recourse to the general contribution of the whole society, except for the conviction of those criminals who have not themselves any estate or fund sufficient for paying those fees.

Those local or provincial expences of which the benefit is local or provincial (what is laid out, for example, upon the police of a particular town or district) ought to be defrayed by a local or provincial revenue, and ought to be no burden upon the general revenue of the society. It is unjust that the whole society should contribute towards an expence of which the benefit is confined to a part of the society.

The expence of maintaining good roads and communications is, no doubt, beneficial to the whole society, and may, therefore, without any injustice, be defrayed by the general contribution of the whole society. This expence, however, is most immediately and directly beneficial to those who travel or carry goods from one place to another, and to those who consume such goods. The turnpike tolls in England, and the duties called peages in other countries, lay it altogether upon those two different sets of people, and thereby discharge the general revenue of the society from a very considerable burden.

The expence of the institutions for education and religious instruction, is likewise, no doubt, beneficial to the whole society, and may, therefore, without injustice, be defrayed by the general contribution of the whole society. This expence, however, might perhaps with equal propriety, and even with some advantage, be defrayed altogether by those who receive the immediate benefit of such education and instruction, or by the voluntary contribution of those who think they have occasion for either the one or the other.

When the institutions or publick works which are beneficial to the whole society, either cannot be maintained altogether, or are not maintained altogether by the contribution of such particular members of the society as are most immediately benefited by them, the deficiency must in most cases be made up by the general contribution of the whole society. The general revenue of the society, over and above defraying the expence of defending the society, and of supporting the dignity of the chief magistrate, must make up for the deficiency of many particular branches of revenue. The sources of this general or publick revenue, I shall endeavour to explain in the following chapter.

*   *   *

REVIEW QUESTIONS

1. What is the organizational innovation of the pin factory and what, according to Smith, is its significance for society?
2. What are Smith's three productive orders and what political roles does he assign these orders?
3. How is Smith both praiseworthy and suspicious of businessmen's ability to serve the public good?
4. Why did Smith's metaphor of the "invisible hand" grip the minds of nineteenth-century capitalists?
5. Why does it continue to exert force today?
6. What is, for Smith, the importance of government in civil society?
7. Who should maintain state costs?

ANDREW URE

FROM *The Philosophy of Manufactures*

A doctor by training, Andrew Ure gained fame by his speeches and writings that advocated the great benefits of industrial capitalism. His Philosophy of Manufactures *(1835) played an important role in molding a positive public opinion on the factory system amid critical debates on factory reform and new poor laws.*

From *The Philosophy of Manufactures*, A. Ure, Charles Knight, 1835.

*   *   *

This island is pre-eminent among civilized nations for the prodigious development of its factory wealth, and has been therefore long viewed with a jealous admiration by foreign powers. This very pre-eminence, however, has been contemplated in a very different light by many influential members of our own community, and has been even denounced by them as the certain origin of innumerable evils to the people, and of revolutionary convulsions to the state. If the affairs of the kingdom be wisely administered, I believe such allegations and fears will prove to be groundless, and to proceed more from the envy of one ancient and powerful order of the commonwealth, towards another suddenly grown into political importance than from the nature of things.

In the recent discussions concerning our factories, no circumstance is so deserving of remark, as the gross ignorance evinced by our leading legislators and economists, gentlemen well informed in other respects, relative to the nature of those stupendous manufactures which have so long provided the rulers of the kingdom with the resources of war, and a great body of the people with comfortable subsistence; which have, in fact, made this island the arbiter of many nations, and the benefactor of the globe itself. Till this ignorance be dispelled, no sound legislation need be expected on manufacturing subjects. To effect this purpose is a principal, but not the sole aim of the present volume, for it is intended also to convey specific information to the classes directly concerned in the manufactures, as well as general knowledge to the community at large, and particularly to young persons about to make the choice of a profession.

The blessings which physico-mechanical science has bestowed on society, and the means it has still in store for ameliorating the lot of mankind, have been too little dwelt upon; while, on the other hand, it has been accused of lending itself to the rich capitalists as an instrument for harassing the poor, and of exacting from the operative an accelerated rate of work. It has been said, for example, that the steam-engine now drives the power-looms with such velocity as to urge on their attendant weavers at the same rapid pace; but that the handweaver, not being subjected to this restless agent, can throw his shuttle and move his treddles at his convenience. There is, however, this difference in the two cases, that in the factory, every member of the loom is so adjusted, that the driving force leaves the attendant nearly nothing at all to do, certainly no muscular fatigue to sustain, while it procures for him good, unfailing wages, besides a healthy workshop *gratis*:

whereas the nonfactory weaver, having everything to execute by muscular exertion, finds the labour irksome, makes in consequence innumerable short pauses, separately of little account, but great when added together; earns therefore proportionally low wages, while he loses his health by poor diet and the dampness of his hovel.

*   *   *

In its precise acceptation, the Factory system is of recent origin, and may claim England for its birthplace.

*   *   *

When the first water-frames for spinning cotton were erected at Cromford, in the romantic valley of the Derwent, about sixty years ago, mankind were little aware of the mighty revolution which the new system of labour was destined by Providence to achieve, not only in the structure of British society, but in the fortunes of the world at large. Arkwright alone had the sagacity to discern, and the boldness to predict in glowing language, how vastly productive human industry would become, when no longer proportioned in its results to muscular effort, which is by its nature fitful and capricious, but when made to consist in the task of guiding the work of mechanical fingers and arms, regularly impelled with great velocity by some indefatigable physical power. What his judgment so clearly led him to perceive, his energy of will enabled him to realize with such rapidity and success, as would have done honour to the most influential individuals, but were truly wonderful in that obscure and indigent artisan. The main difficulty did not, to my apprehension, lie so much in the invention of a proper self-acting mechanism for drawing out and twisting cotton into a continuous thread, as in the distribution of the different members of the apparatus into one co-operative body, in impelling each organ with its appropriate delicacy and speed, and above all, in training human beings to renounce their desultory habits of work, and to identify themselves with the unvarying regularity of the complex automaton. To devise and administer a successful code of factory discipline, suited to the necessities of factory diligence, was the Herculean enterprise, the noble achievement of Arkwright. Even at the present day, when the system is perfectly organized, and its labour lightened to the utmost, it is found nearly impossible to convert persons past the age of puberty, whether drawn from rural or from handicraft occupations, into useful factory hands.

*   *   *

In my recent tour, continued during several months, through the manufacturing districts, I have seen tens of thousands of old, young, and middle-aged of both sexes, many of them too feeble to get their daily bread by any of the former modes of industry, earning abundant food, raiment, and domestic accommodation, without perspiring at a single pore, screened meanwhile from the summer's sun and the winter's frost, in apartments more airy and salubrious than those of the metropolis, in which our legislative and fashionable aristocracies assemble. In those spacious halls the benignant power of steam summons around him his myriads of willing menials, and assigns to each the regulated task, substituting for painful muscular effort on their part, the energies of his own gigantic arm, and demanding in return only attention and dexterity to correct such little aberrations as casually occur in his workmanship. The gentle docility of this moving force qualifies it for impelling the tiny bobbins of the lace-machine with a precision and speed inimitable by the most dexterous hands, directed by the sharpest eyes. Hence, under its auspices, and in obedience to Arkwright's polity, magnificent edifices, surpassing far in number, value, usefulness, and ingenuity of construction, the boasted monuments of Asiatic, Egyptian, and Roman despotism, have, within the short period of fifty years, risen up in this kingdom, to show to what extent, capital, industry, and science may augment the resources of a state, while they meliorate the condition of its citizens. Such is the factory system, replete with prodigies in mechanics and political economy.

*   *   *

The principle of the factory system then is, to substitute mechanical science for hand skill, and the partition of a process into its essential constituents, for the division or graduation of labour among artisans. On the handicraft plan, labour more or less skilled, was usually the most expensive element of production—*Materiam superabat opus;* but on the automatic plan, skilled labour gets progressively superseded, and will, eventually, be replaced by mere overlookers of machines.

By the infirmity of human nature it happens, that the more skilful the workman, the more self-willed and intractable he is apt to become, and, of course, the less fit a component of a mechanical system, in which, by occasional irregularities, he may do great damage to the whole. The grand object therefore of the modern manufacturer is, through the union of capital and science, to reduce the task of his work-people to the exercise of vigilance and dexterity,—faculties, when concentred to one process, speedily brought to perfection in the young. In the infancy of mechanical engineering, a machine-factory displayed the division of labour in manifold gradations—the file, the drill, the lathe, having each its different workmen in the order of skill: but the dexterous hands of the filer and driller are now superseded by the planing, the key-groove cutting, and the drilling-machines; and those of the iron and brass turners, by the self-acting slide-lathe. Mr. Anthony Strutt, who conducts the mechanical department of the great cotton factories of Belper and Milford, has so thoroughly departed from the old routine of the schools, that he will employ no man who has learned his craft by regular apprenticeship; but in contempt, as it were, of the division of labour principle, he sets a ploughboy to turn a shaft of perhaps several tons weight, and never has reason to repent his preference, because he infuses into the turning apparatus a precision of action, equal, if not superior, to the skill of the most experienced journeyman.

*   *   *

REVIEW QUESTIONS

1. How does Ure compare the tempo and rewards of factory work with those of traditional labor?
2. How are factory work conditions characterized and how is factory work different from traditional labor?
3. What kind of persons are better suited for factory discipline?
4. What were the implications of the factory system for English laborers?

THOMAS MALTHUS

FROM *Essay on the Principle of Population*

Thomas Malthus (1766–1834), a minister and an economist, published this essay in 1798, which challenged the Enlightenment's indomitable belief in the perfectibility of humankind. The essay raised much controversy in the early nineteenth century. It not only resigned some social groups to the inevitability of poverty, but also encouraged them to abandon traditional charity. The custom of indiscriminately aiding all indigent people with satisfactory relief, argued Malthusians, only exacerbated the problem. The following passage on food supply and population increase laid the foundation for his bleak argument.

From *An Essay on the Principle of Population,* Thomas Malthus, John Murray, 1826.

In an inquiry concerning the improvement of society, the mode of conducting the subject which naturally presents itself, is,

1. To investigate the causes that have hitherto impeded the progress of mankind towards happiness; and,

2. To examine the probability of the total or partial removal of these causes in future.

To enter fully into this question, and to enumerate all the causes that have hitherto influenced human improvement, would be much beyond the power of an individual. The principal object of the present essay is to examine the effects of one great cause intimately united with the very nature of man; which, though it has been constantly and powerfully operating since the commencement of society, has been little noticed by the writers who have treated this subject. The facts which establish the existence of this cause have, indeed, been repeatedly stated and acknowledged; but its natural and necessary effects have been almost totally overlooked; though probably among these effects may be reckoned a very considerable portion of that vice and misery, and of that unequal distribution of the bounties of nature, which it has been the unceasing object of the enlightened philanthropist in all ages to correct.

The cause to which I allude, is the constant tendency in all animated life to increase beyond the nourishment prepared for it.

It is observed by Dr. Franklin, that there is no bound to the prolific nature of plants or animals, but what is made by their crowding and interfering with each other's means of subsistence. Were the face of the earth, he says, vacant of other plants, it might be gradually sowed and overspread with one kind only, as for instance with fennel: and were it empty of other inhabitants, it might in a few ages be replenished from one nation only, as for instance with Englishmen.

This is incontrovertibly true. Through the animal and vegetable kingdoms Nature has scattered the seeds of life abroad with the most profuse and liberal hand; but has been comparatively sparing in the room and the nourishment necessary to rear them. The germs of existence contained in this earth, if they could freely develop themselves, would fill millions of worlds in the course of a few thousand years. Necessity, that imperious, all-pervading law of nature, restrains them within the prescribed bounds. The race of plants and the race of animals shrink under this great restrictive law; and man cannot by any efforts of reason escape from it.

In plants and irrational animals, the view of the subject is simple. They are all impelled by a powerful instinct to the increase of their species; and this instinct is interrupted by no doubts about providing for their offspring. Wherever therefore there is liberty, the power of increase is exerted; and the superabundant effects are repressed afterwards by want of room and nourishment.

The effects of this check on man are more complicated. Impelled to the increase of his species by an equally powerful instinct, reason interrupts his career, and asks him whether he may not bring beings into the world, for whom he cannot provide the means of support. If he attend to this natural suggestion, the restriction too frequently produces vice. If he hear it not, the human race will be constantly endeavouring to increase beyond the means of subsistence. But as, by that law of our nature which makes food necessary to the life of man, population can never actually increase beyond the lowest nourishment capable of supporting it, a strong check on population, from the difficulty of acquiring food, must be constantly in operation. This difficulty must fall somewhere, and must necessarily be severely felt in some or other of the various forms of misery, or the fear of misery, by a large portion of mankind.

That population has this constant tendency to increase beyond the means of subsistence, and that it is kept to its necessary level by these causes, will sufficiently appear from a review of the different states of society in which man has existed. But, before we proceed to this review, the subject will, perhaps, be seen in a clearer light, if we endeavour to ascertain what would be the natural increase of population, if left to exert itself with perfect freedom; and what might be expected to be the rate of increase in the productions of the earth, under the most favourable circumstances of human industry.

*   *   *

According to a table of Euler, calculated on a mortality of 1 in 36, if the births be to the deaths in the proportion of 3 to 1, the period of doubling will be only 12 years and 4-5ths. And this proportion is not only a possible supposition, but has actually occurred for short periods in more countries than one.

*   *   *

It may safely be pronounced, therefore, that population, when unchecked, goes on doubling itself every twenty-five years, or increases in a geometrical ratio.

The rate according to which the productions of the earth may be supposed to increase, it will not be so easy to determine. Of this, however, we may be perfectly certain, that the ratio of their increase in a limited territory must be of a totally different nature from the ratio of the increase of population. A thousand millions are just as easily doubled every twenty-five years by the power of population as a thousand. But the food to support the increase from the greater number will by no means be obtained with the same facility. Man is necessarily confined in room. When acre has been added to acre till all the fertile land is occupied, the yearly increase of food must depend upon the melioration of the land already in possession. This is a fund, which, from the nature of all soils, instead of increasing, must be gradually diminishing. But population, could it be supplied with food, would go on with unexhausted vigour; and the increase of one period would furnish the power of a greater increase the next, and this without any limit.

* * *

It may be fairly pronounced, therefore, that, considering the present average state of the earth, the means of subsistence, under circumstances the most favourable to human industry, could not possibly be made to increase faster than in an arithmetical ratio.

The necessary effects of these two different rates of increase, when brought together, will be very striking. Let us call the population of this island eleven millions; and suppose the present produce equal to the easy support of such a number. In the first twenty-five years the population would be twenty-two millions, and the food being also doubled, the means of subsistence would be equal to this increase. In the next twenty-five years, the population would be forty-four millions, and the means of subsistence only equal to the support of thirty-three millions. In the next period the population would be eighty-eight millions, and the means of subsistence just equal to the support of half that number. And, at the conclusion of the first century, the population would be a hundred and seventy-six millions, and the means of subsistence only equal to the support of fifty-five millions, leaving a population of a hundred and twenty-one millions totally unprovided for.

Taking the whole earth, instead of this island, emigration would of course be excluded; and, supposing the present population equal to a thousand millions, the human species would increase as the numbers, 1, 2, 4, 8, 16, 32, 64, 128, 256, and subsistence as 1, 2, 3, 4, 5, 6, 7, 8, 9. In two centuries the population would be to the means of subsistence as 256 to 9; in three centuries as 4096 to 13, and in two thousand years the difference would be almost incalculable.

In this supposition no limits whatever are placed to the produce of the earth. It may increase for ever and be greater than any assignable quantity; yet still the power of population being in every period so much superior, the increase of the human species can only be kept down to the level of the means of subsistence by the constant operation of the strong law of necessity, acting as a check upon the greater power.

* * *

REVIEW QUESTIONS

1. For Malthus, how does nature check the happiness of human society?
2. What are his assumptions regarding food supply and demography, and are they valid?
3. How might this argument affect discussions on public relief of the poor?
4. How does this essay contribute to the emerging laissez-faire philosophy of the early nineteenth century?

Rules of a Factory in Berlin

The transition for Europeans from agricultural and artisanal labor to factory work was by no means an easy change. The task-oriented world of traditional labor clashed radically with the time-oriented, strictly routinized world of industrial capitalism. The following set of rules from a Berlin foundry and engineering works in the 1840s denotes the new demands of industrial discipline.

From "Rules of a Factory in Berlin" from *Documents of Economic European History, Volume 1, The Process of Industrialization, 1750–1870,* edited by Sidney Pollard and C. Holmes. Copyright © 1968 Edward Arnold and Company, Ltd. Reprinted with permission of the publisher.

In every large works, and in the co-ordination of any large number of workmen, good order and harmony must be looked upon as the fundamentals of success, and therefore the following rules shall be strictly observed.

Every man employed in the concern named below shall receive a copy of these rules, so that no one can plead ignorance. Its acceptance shall be deemed to mean consent to submit to its regulations.

(1) The normal working day begins at all seasons at 6 a.m. precisely and ends, after the usual break of half an hour for breakfast, an hour for dinner and half an hour for tea, at 7 p.m., and it shall be strictly observed.

Five minutes before the beginning of the stated hours of work until their actual commencement, a bell shall ring and indicate that every worker employed in the concern has to proceed to his place of work, in order to start as soon as the bell stops.

The doorkeeper shall lock the door punctually at 6 a.m., 8.30 a.m., 1 p.m. and 4.30 p.m.

Workers arriving 2 minutes late shall lose half an hour's wages; whoever is more than 2 minutes late may not start work until after the next break, or at least shall lose his wages until then. Any disputes about the correct time shall be settled by the clock mounted above the gatekeeper's lodge.

These rules are valid both for time- and for piece-workers, and in cases of breaches of these rules, workmen shall be fined in proportion to their earnings. The deductions from the wage shall be entered in the wage-book of the gatekeeper whose duty they are; they shall be unconditionally accepted as it will not be possible to enter into any discussions about them.

(2) When the bell is rung to denote the end of the working day, every workman, both on piece- and on day-wage, shall leave his workshop and the yard, but is not allowed to make preparations for his departure before the bell rings. Every breach of this rule shall lead to a fine of five silver groschen to the sick fund. Only those who have obtained special permission by the overseer may stay on in the workshop in order to work.— If a workman has worked beyond the closing bell, he must give his name to the gatekeeper on leaving, on pain of losing his payment for the overtime.

(3) No workman, whether employed by time or piece, may leave before the end of the working day, without having first received permission from the overseer and having given his name to the gatekeeper. Omission of these two actions shall lead to a fine of ten silver groschen payable to the sick fund.

(4) Repeated irregular arrival at work shall lead to dismissal. This shall also apply to those

who are found idling by an official or overseer, and refuse to obey their order to resume work.

(5) Entry to the firm's property by any but the designated gateway, and exit by any prohibited route, e.g. by climbing fences or walls, or by crossing the Spree, shall be punished by a fine of fifteen silver groschen to the sick fund for the first offences, and dismissal for the second.

(6) No worker may leave his place of work otherwise than for reasons connected with his work.

(7) All conversation with fellow-workers is prohibited; if any worker requires information about his work, he must turn to the overseer, or to the particular fellow-worker designated for the purpose.

(8) Smoking in the workshops or in the yard is prohibited during working hours; anyone caught smoking shall be fined five silver groschen for the sick fund for every such offence.

(9) Every worker is responsible for cleaning up his space in the workshop, and if in doubt, he is to turn to his overseer.—All tools must always be kept in good condition, and must be cleaned after use. This applies particularly to the turner, regarding his lathe.

(10) Natural functions must be performed at the appropriate places, and whoever is found soiling walls, fences, squares, etc., and similarly, whoever is found washing his face and hands in the workshop and not in the places assigned for the purpose, shall be fined five silver groschen for the sick fund.

(11) On completion of his piece of work, every workman must hand it over at once to his foreman or superior, in order to receive a fresh piece of work. Pattern makers must on no account hand over their patterns to the foundry without express order of their supervisors. No workman may take over work from his fellow-workman without instruction to that effect by the foreman.

(12) It goes without saying that all overseers and officials of the firm shall be obeyed without question, and shall be treated with due deference. Disobedience will be punished by dismissal.

(13) Immediate dismissal shall also be the fate of anyone found drunk in any of the workshops.

(14) Untrue allegations against superiors or officials of the concern shall lead to stern reprimand, and may lead to dismissal. The same punishment shall be meted out to those who knowingly allow errors to slip through when supervising or stock-taking.

(15) Every workman is obliged to report to his superiors any acts of dishonesty or embezzlement on the part of his fellow workmen. If he omits to do so, and it is shown after subsequent discovery of a misdemeanour that he knew about it at the time, he shall be liable to be taken to court as an accessory after the fact and the wage due to him shall be retained as punishment. Conversely, anyone denouncing a theft in such a way as to allow conviction of the thief shall receive a reward of two Thaler, and, if necessary, his name shall be kept confidential.—Further, the gatekeeper and the watchman, as well as every official, are entitled to search the baskets, parcels, aprons etc. of the women and children who are taking the dinners into the works, on their departure, as well as search any worker suspected of stealing any article whatever. . . .

(18) Advances shall be granted only to the older workers, and even to them only in exceptional circumstances. As long as he is working by the piece, the workman is entitled merely to his fixed weekly wage as subsistence pay; the extra earnings shall be paid out only on completion of the whole piece contract. If a workman leaves before his piece contract is completed, either of his own free will, or on being dismissed as punishment, or because of illness, the partly completed work shall be valued by the general manager with the help of two overseers, and he will be paid accordingly. There is no appeal against the decision of these experts.

(19) A free copy of these rules is handed to every workman, but whoever loses it and requires a new one, or cannot produce it on leaving, shall be fined 2½ silver groschen, payable to the sick fund.

Moabit, August, 1844.

REVIEW QUESTIONS

1. What does the specificity of these regulations suggest about the social realities of early factory work?
2. Judging from the rules' injunctions and monetary fines, what areas of factory work are for newcomers the most difficult to learn?
3. What kind of relationship is established between factory hands and their superiors?
4. How do these regulations distinguish the work experience of factories from those of agriculture, domestic service, or the traditional crafts?
5. How does this document compare with Ure's discussion of factory work?

FRIEDRICH LIST

FROM Promotion of the Leipzig-Dresden Railway

Railroads played a preeminent role in the industrial revolution on the continent. They opened up new markets, linked industrial centers with mines and harbors, employed tens of thousands in construction and administration, stimulated heavy industry in its demand for coal, iron, and locomotives, and transformed the financial world by attracting and multiplying the flow of unprecedented sums of share capital. By the 1850s both entrepreneurs and statesmen viewed railroads as the undisputed key to national wealth in the "age of capital." Yet European governments were initially wary of the new form of transportation, especially when it would compete with state-funded turnpikes and canals. In the following passage from the early 1830s, Friedrich List, a political economist and one of Germany's pioneering advocates of railroads, soberly discussed the advantages of railroads for the kingdom of Saxony to convince the government to promote construction in the Leipzig area, which became one of the great railway hubs of central Europe.

From *Documents of Economic European History, Volume 1, The Process of Industrialization, 1750–1870*, Sidney Pollard and C. Holmes, Edward Arnold, 1968.

. . . I could not watch the astonishing effects of railways in England and North America without wishing that my German fatherland would partake of the same benefits, and. . . .

. . . having settled in Saxony for some years, I determined to devote my leisure time to exploring the relevant local conditions, as far as this is possible for a stranger, and although my researches were but superficial, their results were so impor-tant as to induce me to submit them to you for further examination.

Above all, the level and firm surface stretching in all directions from Leipzig, which seems to invite its inhabitants to put down rails without further preparation, makes this area particularly suitable for the building of railways. If the occasional sharp corners of the main roads, and their progress through the middle of villages and towns, had not formed an obstacle to railway building, it might even have been advisable to lay the rails directly on that part of the main roads at present obstructed by heaps of road-building materials, in which case a very strong railway of oak rails lined with iron would have cost scarcely more than 15,000 Taler per German mile. That nature herself has done the work here . . . our American company spent 40,000 dollars per German mile to level the ground in the way in which nature has provided it here, while the rest of the permanent way cost only 15,000 dollars . . .

All in all, I believe that the normal costs of a railway like our American one, calculated to transport annually 2–4 million cwt. coal for 7–10 years, after which it would cost 4,000 dollars per German mile to keep in repair, would come in our local terrain and with local Saxon wages to 50,000 Taler per German mile at the most, including all normal tunnels, embankments, bridges and compensation for land, but excluding all major bridges across the larger rivers, and major tunnels.

A second important consideration for this locality is its position as the heart of the German inland traffic, the printing and publishing trade, and the German factory industry.

The numbers of travellers inward and outward and in transit, including the visitors to the fair, is greater than in any other German city and would by itself justify the building of four railways of 20 miles length each. The present estimate, including those in transit, is 50,000 visitors. This would at least double to 100,000 if it were possible to make the 40 miles return journey to Leipzig for 5 Taler without spending more than 10 hours on the road; the gross revenue in that case would be 500,000 Taler, and the net revenue, after deduction of one third for costs, would be above 8% on a capital of 4 million Taler.

The quantity of freight inward and outward and in transit . . . should amount, including salt and other mining products, to at least 1½ million cwt., which would yield, on 20 miles at 10 Groschen per mile (half the present freight charges), 625,000 Taler, or, after deducting one third for costs, over 10% on the capital.

Finally there is the consumption of the city itself. All food-stuffs and fuels are more expensive than on the coast, and of worse quality. Timber is twice as expensive as in towns four or five miles away. While at these high prices the mass of the population can afford very little fuel, the hills eight miles to the South are full of coal. Factories using water or steam power are out of the question; the existing water mills are hardly sufficient for grinding the necessary flour; the black bread for the poorer part of the population is brought in from the countryside. One can see everywhere how the lack of a cheap means of transport keeps down population and industry. How otherwise are we to explain that the centre of German trade has only 40,000 inhabitants? Even if we take only the existing levels of consumption, c. 60,000 klafter of wood would have costs of transport of 150,000 Taler (at 2½ Taler a cord); other articles of consumption may be estimated at as much again.

Railways would carry wood, turf and coal at less than half the present costs. Coal from Zwickau would cost only 1½–2 Groschen a cwt. more than at the pithead and would raise the city to an important manufacturing centre. Bavaria, where flour, meat and other foodstuffs are 50–100% cheaper than in Leipzig, could export its surplus to the Erzgebirge, the Elbe and the Hansa cities. . . . Cheaper food and fuel would partly enhance the well-being of the working classes, and partly lower money wages, increase population and increase the extent of industry. Cheap building materials and low money wages would encourage building and lower the rents in the new and more distant parts of the city. On the other hand, increased population and industry would increase the rents, and thereby the value of the houses, in the centre of the city, well placed for trade and industry. In one word: population, the number of buildings, industry, trade, and the value of land and houses in Leipzig would be doubled in a short space of time, and I do not doubt for a minute that this increase in value in Leipzig alone would in a few years exceed the total capital costs of the new railways.

In an appendix I subjoin a plan for a Saxon

railway system, as well as I could make it without an actual survey. According to it, the line from Leipzig to Dresden would have branches to Zwickau, Chemnitz and Freiberg, and the line from Weimar to Gotha, to Frankfort on the Main and Bamberg; by the line to Halle, the Kingdom of Saxony would be linked with the salt mines and with the river Saale; by the line to Dessau, Wittenberg or Torgau, the Elbe would be reached at a point at which it is still easily navigable. This network, which would not exceed 50 miles altogether, would meet all the needs of the Kingdom of Saxony. . . .

*   *   *

REVIEW QUESTIONS

1. What are the advantageous geologic, demographic, and economic conditions for railroad construction in the Leipzig area?
2. According to List, how will the proposed railway stimulate economic growth?
3. What social benefits are to be derived from the railway?
4. To what degree will railroads affect the economic structures of this German region?

FRIEDRICH LIST

FROM National System of Political Economy

Whereas British political economy largely stressed individual enterprise and free trade, Friedrich List (1789–1846), the German political economist, recognized disadvantages for German states in aligning themselves completely with British trade policies. Instead he centered on the nation as an economic unit, emphasizing the need for protectionist measures to create domestic free trade within the German Confederation (a union of thirty-nine political states) before Germany could become a mature, internationally competitive economy. List's National System of Political Economy (1840) thus manifests the concerns of German politics of the 1840s, linking liberal nationalism with questions of economic unity and power. Friedrich List's liberalism forced him to emigrate to the United States between 1825 and 1832. Upon returning to Germany, his promotion of railroad and commercial reform was tireless, but not always heeded.

From *Metternich's Europe*, edited by Mack Walker, Harper & Row, 1968.

N O BRANCH of political economy presents a greater diversity of views between men of theory and men of practice, than that which treats of international commerce and commercial policy. There is, however, in the domain of this science no topic, which, in regard to the well-being and civilization of nations, as well as to their independence, power and duration, presents the same degree of importance. Poor, weak, and uncivilized countries have not unfrequently attained power and wealth by a judicious commercial system, whilst others have sunk from a high rank for want of such a system; nations have even lost their independence, and their political existence, because their commercial policy had not aided the development and the consolidation of their nationality.

In our day, more than at any former period, among all the questions which belong to political economy, that of international commerce has acquired a preponderant interest; for the more rapidly the genius of discovery and of industrial improvement, as well as that of social and political progress advances, the more rapidly is the distance between stationary nations and those which are progressive increased, and the greater is the peril of remaining behind. If in time past it required centuries to monopolize that important branch of industry, the manufacture of wool, some ten years have sufficed in our time to obtain ascendency in the much more considerable manufacture of cotton; and now the start of a few years may enable England to absorb all the flax industry of the continent of Europe.

At no other epoch has the world seen a manufacturing and commercial power possessing resources so immense as those in the control of the power which now holds sway, pursuing designedly a system so consistently selfish, absorbing with such untiring energy the manufacturing and commercial industry of the world, the important colonies, the domination of the seas, and subjecting so many people, as in the case of the Hindoos, to a manufacturing and commercial yoke.

Alarmed by the consequences of that policy, nay, constrained by the convulsions it has occasioned, we have seen in our century, Prussia, a continental nation, as yet imperfectly prepared for manufacturing industry, seeking her welfare in the prohibitory system so condemned by theorists. And what has been her reward? National prosperity.

On the other hand, encouraged by promises of theory, the United States of America, which had made a rapid growth under the protective system, have been induced to open their ports to the man-ufacturers of England; and what fruits has this competition borne? A periodical visitation of commercial disaster.

*   *   *

The author will begin, as theory does not begin, by interrogating History, and deducing from it his fundamental principles; this being done, an examination of former systems will follow, and his tendency being especially practical, he will, in conclusion, furnish a sketch of the later phases of commercial policy.

For greater clearness, we give here a cursory view of the principal results of his researches and meditations:

The association of individuals for the prosecution of a common end is the most efficacious mode towards ensuring the happiness of individuals. Alone, and separated from his fellow-creatures, man is feeble and destitute. The greater the number of those who are united, the more perfect is the association, and the greater and the more perfect is the result, which is the moral and material welfare of individuals.

The highest association of individuals now realized, is that of the state, the nation; and the highest imaginable, is that of the whole human race. Just as the individual is happier in the bosom of the state than in solitude, all nations would be more prosperous if they were united together by law, by perpetual peace, and by free interchange.

Nature leads nations gradually to the highest degree of association; inviting them to commerce by variety of climate, soil, and productions; and by overflowing population, by superabundance of capital and talents, it leads them to emigration and the founding of distant colonies. International trade, by rousing activity and energy, by the new wants it creates, by the propagation among nations of new ideas and discoveries, and by the diffusion of power, is one of the mightiest instruments of civilization and one of the most powerful agencies in promoting national prosperity.

The association of nations by means of trade is even yet very imperfect, for it is interrupted, or at least weakened, by war or selfish measures on the part sometimes of one and sometimes of another nation.

*   *   *

The elevation of an agricultural people to the condition of countries at once agricultural, manufacturing, and commercial, can only be accomplished under the law of free trade when the various nations engaged at the time in manufacturing industry shall be in the same degree of progress and civilization; when they shall place no obstacle in the way of the economical development of each other, and not impede their respective progress by war or adverse commercial legislation.

But some of them, favored by circumstances, having distanced others in manufactures, commerce, and navigation, and having early perceived that this advanced state was the surest mode of acquiring and keeping political supremacy, have adopted and still persevere in a policy so well adapted to give them the monopoly of manufactures, of industry and of commerce, and to impede the progress of less advanced nations or those in a lower degree of culture. The measures enforced by such nations, taken as a whole, the prohibitions, the duties on imports, the maritime restrictions, premiums upon exports, &c., are called the protective system.

The anterior progress of certain nations, foreign commercial legislation and war have compelled inferior countries to look for special means of effecting their transition from the agricultural to the manufacturing stage of industry, and as far as practicable, by a system of duties, to restrain their trade with more advanced nations aiming at manufacturing monopoly.

The system of import duties is consequently not, as has been said, an invention of speculative minds; it is a natural consequence of the tendency of nations to seek for guarantees of their existence and prosperity, and to establish and increase their weight in the scale of national influence.

Such a tendency is legitimate and reasonable only so far as it renders easy, instead of retarding, the economical development of a nation; and it is not in opposition to the higher objects of society, the universal confederation of the future.

*   *   *

No commercial policy is more dangerous and reprehensible than a sudden resort to absolute prohibition of foreign products. It may, however, be justified when a country, separated from others by a long war, finds itself almost in a compulsory state of prohibitions in regard to foreign products, and under the absolute necessity of offering a high premium to the industry which will enable it to supply its own wants.

The return from such a condition must be by gradual transition from the prohibitive to the protective system, and should be effected by means of duties fixed by anticipation and decreasing gradually. On the other hand, a nation which is to pass from free trade to the protective system should commence with low duties to be afterwards raised by degrees according to a suitable scale.

Duties thus fixed by anticipation must be strictly maintained by the government; it must be careful not to diminish them before the appointed time, and equally careful to raise them if they should prove insufficient.

Duties upon imports so high as absolutely to exclude foreign competition are prejudicial to the country which adopts them; for they suppress all rivalry between domestic and foreign manufactures, and encourage indolence among the former.

When, under the rule of suitable and progressive duties, the manufactures of a country do not thrive, it is an evidence that the country does not yet possess the conditions requisite to a manufacturing people.

Duties designed to favor an industry should never be put so low as to endanger the existence of the latter from foreign competition. It should be a rule to preserve what exists—to protect national industry in its trunk and in its roots.

Foreign competition should not have more than its share in the annual increase of consumption. Duties should be raised when foreign commodities supply the greatest part or the whole of the increased annual consumption.

A country like England, which is far in advance of all its competitors, cannot better maintain and extend its manufacturing and commercial industry than by a trade as free as possible from all restraints. For such a country, the cosmopolitan and the national principle are one and the same thing.

This explains the favor with which the most enlightened economists of England regard free trade, and the reluctance of the wise and prudent of other countries to adopt this principle in the actual state of the world.

A quarter of a century since, the prohibitive and protective system of England operated to her detriment and to the advantage of her rivals.

Nothing could be more prejudicial to England than her restrictions upon the importation of raw material and food.

Union of customs and commercial treaties are the most efficient means of facilitating national exchanges.

But treaties of commerce are legitimate and durable only when the advantages are reciprocal. They are fatal and illegitimate when they sacrifice one country to another;* * *

If protective duties enhance for a time the price of domestic manufactures, they secure afterwards lower prices by means of internal competition; for an industry that has reached its full development can safely reduce its prices far below those which were necessary to ensure its growth, and thus save to its consumers the whole expense of transportation and the whole profits of trade which are consequent upon imports of the same articles from other countries.

The loss occasioned by protective duties consists, after all, only in values; whilst the country thus acquires a power by which it is enabled to produce a great mass of values. This loss in values must be considered as the price of the industrial training of the country.

Protective duties upon manufactured products do not press heavily upon the agriculture of a country. By the development of manufacturing industry the wealth, population, consumption of agricultural products, rent, and exchangeable value of real estate are vastly increased, whilst the manufactured products consumed by farmers gradually fall in price. The gain thus realized exceeds, in the proportion of ten to one, the loss which agriculturalists incur by the transient rise of manufactured products.

Internal and external trade flourish alike under the protective system; these have no importance but among nations supplying their own wants by their own manufacturing industry, consuming their own agricultural products, and purchasing foreign raw materials and commodities with the surplus of their manufactured articles. Home and foreign trade are both insignificant in the merely agricultural countries of temperate climes, and their external commerce is usually in the hands of the manufacturing and trading nations in communication with them.

A good system of protection does not imply any monopoly in the manufacturers of a country; it only furnishes a guarantee against losses to those who devote their capital, their talents, and their exertions to new branches of industry.

There is no monopoly, because internal competition comes in the place of foreign competition, and every individual has the privilege of taking his share in the advantages offered by the country to its citizens; it is only an advantage to citizens as against foreigners, who enjoy in their own country a similar advantage.

But this protection is useful not only because it awakens the sleeping energies of a country and puts in motion its productive power, but because it attracts the productive power of foreign countries, including capital, both material and moral, and skilful masters as well as skilful men.

*   *   *

History is not without examples of entire nations having perished, because they knew not and seized not the critical moment for the solution of the great problem of securing their moral, economical, and political independence by the establishment of manufacturing industry and the formation of a powerful class of manufacturers and tradesmen.

REVIEW QUESTIONS

1. How does List characterize Britain's economic relationship to Europe, and what is his advice to German states?

2. What are the roles of nations in economic life for List?

3. What are List's views of trade barriers and how do they compare with those of Adam Smith?

4. How applicable are List's views to the economic conditions in western society today?

THOMAS BANFIELD

FROM *Industry on the Rhine*

In comparing British and continental industrialization, historians often emphasize state involvement, limited money supply, and the paucity of credit on the continent as salient differences. In 1848 Thomas Banfield, a British writer, published his observations of agricultural and manufacturing conditions in the Rhineland. The following passage offers Banfield's insights on statist economic intervention and Prussia's credit system.

From *Industry on the Rhine, Volume 2: Manufactures*, T. Banfield, Augustus M. Kelley, 1969. Reprinted with permission of the publisher.

*   *   *

At Dortmund, in Westphalia, the mining-board of this district has its seat, and any special information that may be required respecting the mines is there obligingly communicated to persons who are introduced to the authorities, or who, by showing either a scientific or commercial object, cause themselves to be regarded as claimants on the national hospitality. In this respect the government offices of Prussia are deserving of all praise. The spirit inculcated by the government, and kept up by the distinguished scientific men whom they train up, and who at last preside over them, is one which courts communion and shuns no pains to spread information. However high may be the rank of an official at these boards, he gratefully acknowledges information when original and well authenticated, and often conceals the value of what he imparts in the conventional phrase of conversation. In fact, the system of appointing men to these situations who have gone through the grades of students at universities, and have risen in a laborious official career, encouraged as they are at every step to communicate through the medium of journals and societies the knowledge they acquire, provides a number of candidates for the higher posts whose zeal has been tried, and on whose qualifications (like those of our leading men at the bar) public opinion has pronounced its judgment.

Yet the weak side of the Prussian system is forcibly illustrated in the mining department. All is there done under the control of the government officials, who, however, acknowledge no responsibility. An inexperienced youth as "Geschworner," or overseer, has the power of stopping all works if his suggestions are not attended to. It is true the embargo can be raised by an appeal to the next officer, the "Bergmeister" of the district, and from him the party aggrieved can go to the "Oberbergrath," or even to the mining-board assembled "in pleno." These appeals are attended with no expense and are quickly dispatched. But a more invidious interference arises out of the government claim to tithe of the gross produce of all minerals. The mode of securing this claim on the part of the crown strikes at the root of all economy in mining. The *captain* employed by adventurers, instead of being taken on contract as in England, must be engaged permanently, and he is sworn to the crown as an official personage. He is thus independent of his employers unless he commits any gross dereliction of duty, such as would incapacitate him from trust anywhere. But as the owners have generally only the device of getting rid of him by letting the mine drop, he has a strong and dangerous hold on them. The principle of competition by which so much has been done in Cornwall is by this regulation altogether rejected. A captain in Germany is therefore not a man to whom miners attach themselves through confidence, and he brings with him no gang for whom he is responsible. He is appointed as a foreman, and miners are engaged as they offer, with the sanction of the mining-board. From the Ruhr to the Lahn every male knows something of mining, so that there is no deficiency in point of number. Their business they generally understand, but the discipline, which is the element by which time is played off against money, and which allows high wages to co-exist with large profits, does not show itself. Without this element neither high wages nor large profits are practicable, as the history of Rhenish Prussia testifies.

*　　*　　*

Yet without some credit arrangements even the small transactions of this district could not be carried on. Were work to be paid for in cash advances, it would here soon be put a stop to. It is therefore especially interesting to stand in the middle of a scene which resistance to progress has kept stationary for centuries, and to contemplate the origin of manufactures, of which we have so much lost sight in England, that we have lately manifested a desire to turn our back upon, and even kick down, the lowly ladder by which we climbed to our present eminence. The fact is that the trade, such as it is, depends nearly altogether upon credit, but upon that timid trust which exists where there is great subdivision of enterprise, and no one trusts the other out of his sight. Manufacturing is here, as in the greater part of Germany, dependent on the land. the furnace-owner and forest-owner, as well as the miner, club their property together to make iron, living the while upon the produce of their little estates. This iron is sold to the hammer-master at six months' credit, and is then paid for by a two, three, or four months' bill on the cutler. The cutler's acceptance is met by the dealer's draft upon a shipping house, which, being paid, cancels the original bill, that in all probability went to a grocer in the mining-districts, and was sent up to Cologne to pay for colonial produce. Here, therefore, as in Lancashire and Yorkshire in the olden time, we can see how tea-dealers come in time to be bankers, for, according to recent accounts, such was the origin of the powerful bank of Messrs. Jones, Loyd, and Co. The profits of a retail trade carried on under circumstances of this kind are always large, and a clever dealer cannot fail to lay the foundation of a fortune in a short time, if he be surrounded by industrious and honest neighbours. But it is, again, a manifest injustice to tie down the exertions of such good neighbours to the ability and good-will of a chance tea-dealer who becomes the dispenser of credit. This is what takes place here, where government monopolises issues. The source of credit is the confidence which one man reposes in his fellow-man. Credit, to be genuine, must therefore be local; it must spring from positive knowledge of a man and his transactions. Since this knowledge cannot be possessed by the government at Berlin, this country is reduced to its own expedients. Out of a similar position the English manufacturer was helped by two circumstances. The country banks of issue made the manufacturer independent of the tea-dealer; and, while they shortened the advances of the latter, they cut something off his rate of profit, to the benefit of labourers and masters. Small as this gain may appear, it clearly had its effect, by inducing people to go into trade, and reducing the amount of labour locked up in agriculture. But it did more than that; the banker, having stimulated credit, began to use caution in trusting. The general trust for very small sums, which a bad state of credit induced, changed to limited and selected credit for large sums. This was a proper premium upon credit, which means nothing else than morality, punctuality, and tact. The history of all our large speculations of early date in England shows that credit was obtained by men of character, even when they had no property, and that trade prospered as long as character was honestly and fairly appreciated by the country banker.

The second advantage at the command of the English manufacturer consisted in the Bank of England's being a commercial, and not a government establishment. The country banker, or his correspondent in London, obtained by his indorsement credit for the trader and manufacturer at this central bank of issue; and often chose to rely upon his power of obtaining this credit in preference to issuing his own notes.

The people of this industrious part of Germany are altogether in want of these two advantages; and, by the means adopted to extend credit, have risked prolonging the want. We shall speak at a later period of the new constitution given to the Royal Bank of Berlin last year. By the new charter this bank is made a bank of issue; but the issues are to emanate from the crown, which began by declaring ten millions of dollars disposable in the new notes. This is so obviously reversing the order in which issues ought to spring out of credit created, that there was some difficulty experienced in getting the new notes into circulation at all. It was then suggested that the new circulation would be promoted by establishing branch-banks in the principal trading and manufacturing districts. An attempt was made to engage the principal traders in those districts to subscribe a fixed amount of capital, on which it was promised that a branch would be opened. Such proposals have

been entertained at Elberfeld and at Siegen. But the government cannot wonder if these traders are cautious in embarking in a venture over which the control they are to have is as yet doubtful. Their capital is now employed remuneratively; and if they are to risk it in a vast and new undertaking like this royal bank, which is not managed by merchants at Berlin, and whose branch-officers may do more harm than good in the provinces, they are at least right to·consider well what they are doing. A central bank in each of the provinces of the kingdom of Prussia would not be too much, and would be far from dispensing with the necessity for private local banks, which might be allowed to issue on their own responsibility. Their issues would in no case be large, from the frugal habits and disposition to economise means that prevail in Germany, and which are in themselves a capital in health and happiness.

The want of facilities in the shape of currency pressing against the demands of trade and a growing population, has produced a similar result to that observable in England soon after the turn of popular opinion against the country banks of issue. The truck-system has for several years prevailed to a large extent in this whole district. The payment in wares is so natural a consequence of a limit being set upon the circulating medium, that the invectives it has often drawn forth may be considered matter of surprise. It was publicly declared that at Solingen, a few years back, three-fourths of the large dealers paid the small tradesmen in goods, both of questionable quality and at enormous prices. Amongst the most active opponents of this system was M. Knecht, whose letters attracted great attention, and perhaps restricted the exercise of the practice. But it is easier to point out an evil than to suggest a remedy; and many poor people will own that half a loaf is better than no bread.

These evils, the results in part of condensing great surfaces of country under central governments, that cannot enter into the minutiæ of the local wants, are pressing upon other countries as well as Prussia . . .

*   *   *

REVIEW QUESTIONS

1. What are Banfield's praises and criticisms of Prussian state involvement in industry?

2. How does Banfield compare Prussia's banking and credit system with Britain's?

3. Where does he place Prussia, one of Europe's leading industrialized states, in relation to Britain's economic development?

CLAUDE HENRI DE ROUVROY, COMTE DE ST. SIMON

The Incoherence and Disorder of Industry

European observers of early industrialization were not always enamored with the spirit of rugged individualism and minimalist governmental control. Claude Henri de Rouvroy (1760–1825), Comte de Saint-Simon, roundly criticized laissez-faire political economy, advocating instead an industrialized state directed by science, and an enlightened class of industrialists to address the needs of the poor. St. Simon, who fought in the American Revolution, used a self-made fortune to promote numerous large-scale industrial enterprises which left him an impoverished man. His writings, especially The New Christianity, *had little impact during his lifetime but influenced subsequent generations of French social theorists. His most enduring legacy was perhaps his influence on Auguste Comte, who founded the doctrine of Positivism.*

From *Documents of Economic European History, Volume 1, The Process of Industrialization, 1750–1870,* edited by Sidney Pollard and C. Holmes. Copyright © 1968 Edward Arnold and Company, Ltd. Reprinted with permission of the publisher.

In industry, as in science, emphasis is centred entirely on individualism; the sole sentiment which dominates all thinking is egotism. The industrialist is very little concerned about society's interests. His family, his capital and the personal fortune he strives to attain, constitute his humanity, his universe, his god. All those pursuing the same career are inevitably enemies . . . and it is by ruining them that he attains personal happiness and glory.

Problems which are no less serious exist regarding the organisation of work. Industry possesses a theory, which it might be believed holds the key to the harmonisation of production and consumption. Now this theory itself is the principal cause of disorder; the economists seem to pose the following problem:

'If it is accepted that leaders of society are more ignorant than those they govern; if it is supposed, moreover, that far from favouring the development of industry, these leaders wished to hinder its development, and their representatives were the born enemies of the producers, what kind of industrial organisation is suited to society?'

Laissez-faire, laissez-passer! Such has been the inevitable solution; such has been the single, general principle which they have proclaimed. The economists have thought by this to resolve with a stroke of the pen all questions relating to the production and distribution of wealth; they have entrusted the realisation of their schemes to *personal interest*, without realising that the individual, irrespective of his insight, is incapable of assessing total situations. . . . Well then! what is the picture we see before us? Each industry, deprived of direction, without any guidance other than personal observation, which is always imperfect . . . strives to become informed about consumer needs. Rumour has it that a branch of production offers wonderful prospects; all endeavour and capital are directed towards it, everyone dashes blindly into it. . . . The economists immediately applaud the stampede because in it they recognise the principle of competition. . . . Alas! What results from this struggle to the death? Several fortunate individuals triumph . . . the price is the complete ruin of innumerable victims. A necessary consequence of this over-production in certain sectors, this uncoordinated activity, is that the equilibrium between production and consumption is always affected. Innumerable crises result, those commercial crises which terrify speculators and frustrate worthwhile projects. Honest and hard-working men are ruined and morale is injured by such events; such people come to believe that to succeed something more than honesty and hard work are needed.

They become cunning, shrewd and sly; they even boast about these characteristics; once they have assumed this position, they are lost to humanity.

Let us add now that the fundamental principle, *laissez-faire, laissez-passer,* assumes that personal and social interests always coincide, a supposition which is disproved by innumerable facts. To select only one example, is it not clear that if society sees its interest in the establishment of a steam engine, the worker who lives by his hands cannot share this sentiment? The reply to the workers' objection is well-known; for example, printing is cited, and it is true that today it occupies more men than there were transcribers before its invention, therefore it is concluded and stated that in the long run a new equilibrium is obtained. An admirable conclusion! And until then what will happen to the thousands of hungry men? Will our reasoning console them? Will they bear their misery patiently because statistical calculations prove that in future years they will have food to appease their hunger?

REVIEW QUESTIONS

1. How does St. Simon's view of individual interest differ from Adam Smith's notion of the "invisible hand"?
2. Why does St. Simon reject competitive capitalism?
3. What social interests should capitalists aspire to embrace?

ROBERT OWEN

A New View of Society

Robert Owen (1771–1858), a highly successful manager and partner of a cotton mill in Manchester, grew disenchanted early in his life with the deplorable material and moral standards of factory workers. Resolved to direct a capitalist enterprise that could ameliorate the lives of factory workers, Owen convinced his partners to buy

cotton mills in New Lanaark and set up a model community. Workers received sa-
lubrious housing, quality goods from low-cost cooperative stores, and education for
their children; in turn, Owen inculcated the moral virtues of cleanliness, order,
thrift, and sobriety. Because New Lanaark combined moral improvement with com-
mercial success, Owen's communitarian project achieved international fame, and it
still ranks among the most important examples of utopian socialism. In 1813, Owen
delineated his views on the importance of human capital in his A New View of
Society. *The following speech is included in this work.*

From *A New View of Society*, R. Owen, Friends of the New System, 1826.

An Address
To the Superintendants of Manufactories, and to those Individuals generally, who, by giving employment to an aggregated Population, may easily adopt the means to form the Sentiments and Manners of such a Population.

LIKE you, I am a manufacturer for pecuniary profit. But having for many years acted on principles the reverse in many respects of those in which you have been instructed, and having found my procedure beneficial to others and to myself, even in a pecuniary point of view, I am anxious to explain such valuable principles, that you and those under your influence may equally partake of their advantages.

In two Essays, already published, I have developed some of these principles, and in the following pages you will find still more of them explained, with some detail of their application to practice, under the particular local circumstances in which I undertook the direction of the New Lanark Mills and Establishment.

By those details you will find that from the commencement of my management I viewed the population, with the mechanism and every other part of the establishment, as a system composed of many parts, and which it was my duty and interest so to combine, as that every hand, as well as every spring, lever, and wheel, should effectually co-operate to produce the greatest pecuniary gain to the proprietors.

Many of you have long experienced in your manufacturing operations the advantages of substantial, well-contrived, and well-executed machinery.

Experience has also shewn you the difference of the results between mechanism which is neat, clean, well arranged, and always in a high state of repair; and that which is allowed to be dirty, in disorder, without the means of preventing unnecessary friction, and which therefore becomes, and works, much out of repair.

In the first case, the whole economy and management are good; every operation proceeds with ease, order, and success. In the last, the reverse must follow, and a scene be presented of counteraction, confusion, and dissatisfaction among all the agents and instruments interested or occupied in the general process, which cannot fail to create great loss.

If then due care as to the state of your inanimate machines can produce such beneficial results, what may not be expected if you devote equal attention to your vital machines, which are far more wonderfully constructed?

When you shall acquire a right knowledge of these, of their curious mechanism, of their self-adjusting powers; when the proper main spring shall be applied to their varied movements, you will become conscious of their real value, and you will be readily induced to turn your thoughts more frequently from your inanimate to your living machines; you will discover that the latter may be easily trained and directed to procure a large increase of pecuniary gain, while you may also derive from them high and substantial gratification.

Will you then continue to expend large sums of money to procure the best devised mechanism of wood, brass, or iron; to retain it in perfect repair; to provide the best substance for the prevention of unnecessary friction, and to save it from falling into premature decay? Will you also devote years of intense application to understand the connection of the various parts of these lifeless machines, to improve their effective powers, and to calculate with mathematical precision all their minute and combined movements? And when in these transactions you estimate time by minutes, and the money expended for the chance of increased gain by fractions, will you not afford some of your attention to consider whether a portion of your time and capital would not be more advantageously applied to improve your living machines?

From experience which cannot deceive me, I venture to assure you that your time and money, so applied, if directed by a true knowledge of the subject, would return you, not five, ten, or fifteen per cent. for your capital so expended, but often fifty, and in many cases a hundred per cent.

I have expended much time and capital upon improvements of the living machinery; and it will soon appear that the time and money so expended in the manufactory at New Lanark, even while such improvements are in progress only, and but half their beneficial effects attained, are now producing a return exceeding fifty per cent., and will shortly create profits equal to cent. per cent. on the original capital expended in them.

Indeed, after experience of the beneficial effects, from due care and attention to the mechanical implements, it became easy to a reflecting mind to conclude at once, that at least equal advantages would arise from the application of similar care and attention to the living instruments. And when it was perceived that inanimate mechanism was greatly improved by being made firm and substantial; that it was the essence of economy to keep it neat, clean, regularly supplied with the best substance to prevent unnecessary friction, and, by proper provision for the purpose, to preserve it in good repair; it was natural to conclude that the more delicate, complex, living mechanism, would be equally improved by being trained to strength and activity; and that it would also prove true economy to keep it neat and clean; to treat it with kindness, that its mental movements might not experience too much irritating friction; to endeavour by every means to make it more perfect; to supply it regularly with a sufficient quantity of wholesome food and other necessaries of life, that the body might be preserved in good working condition, and prevented from being out of repair, or falling prematurely to decay.

These anticipations are proved by experience to be just.

Since the general introduction of inanimate mechanism into British manufactories, man, with few exceptions, has been treated as a secondary and inferior machine; and far more attention has been given to perfect the raw materials of wood and metals than those of body and mind. Give but due reflection to the subject, and you will find that man, even as an instrument for the creation of wealth, may be still greatly improved.

But, my friends, a far more interesting and gratifying consideration remains. Adopt the means which ere long shall be rendered obvious to every understanding, and you may not only partially improve those living instruments, but learn how to impart to them such excellence as shall make them infinitely surpass those of the present and all former times.

Here then is an object which truly deserves your attention; and instead of devoting all your faculties to invent improved inanimate mechanism, let your thoughts be, at least in part, directed to discover how to combine the more excellent materials of body and mind, which, by a well devised experiment, will be found capable of progressive improvement.

Thus seeing with the clearness of noon-day light, thus convinced with the certainty of conviction itself, let us not perpetuate the really unnecessary evils which our present practices inflict on this large proportion of our fellow subjects.* * * But when you may have ocular demonstration, that, instead of any pecuniary loss, a well-directed attention to form the character and increase the comforts of those who are so entirely at your mercy, will essentially add to your gains, prosperity, and happiness, no reasons, except those founded on ignorance of your self-interest, can in future prevent you from bestowing your chief care on the living machines which you employ; and by so doing you will prevent an accumulation of human misery, of which it is now difficult to form an adequate conception.

That you may be convinced of this most val-uable truth, which due reflection will shew you is founded on the evidence of unerring facts, is the sincere wish of

THE AUTHOR

REVIEW QUESTIONS

1. Who is the intended audience, and why is Owen's analogy of workers as machines especially effective for this social group?
2. How does Owen reconcile social improvement with capitalist principles?
3. Why was Owen's argument largely dismissed by his peers as radical and unacceptable?

KARL MARX

FROM Estranged Labour

As an intellectual and a political activist, Karl Marx (1818–1883) represents a re-markable synthesis of European thought. Combining a rigorous philosophical train-ing in German idealism and Hegelian dialectics with the revolutionary spirit of French politics and the materialist concerns of British political economy, Karl Marx not only wrote the most formidable critique of capitalism in the nineteenth century (Das Kapital), but also established a socialist ideology that profoundly altered the course of modern world history. The following passage captures the concerns of the early Marx, exiled in Paris in 1844, seeking to understand why wage labor and commodity production devalued and ultimately alienated workers. These writings, sometimes referred to as the Paris Manuscripts, evoke Marx's concerns with the philosophical essence of work and how it constructs identity. Implicitly comparing nineteenth-century wage work with the craft traditions of the early modern era, Marx saw a dehumanizing process inherent in capitalist commodity production, thus provoking him to envision capitalism as merely a stage in human development which would be superseded by an economic system that would restore human integ-rity to labor.

We have proceeded from the premises of political economy. We have accepted its language and its laws. We presupposed private property, the separation of labour, capital and land, and of wages, profit of capital and rent of land—likewise division of labour, competition, the concept of exchange-value, etc. On the basis of political economy itself, in its own words, we have shown that the worker sinks to the level of a commodity and becomes indeed the most wretched of commodities; that the wretchedness of the worker is in inverse proportion to the power and magnitude of his production; that the necessary result of competition is the accumulation of capital in a few hands, and thus the restoration of monopoly in a more terrible form; that finally the distinction between capitalist and land-rentier, like that between the tiller of the soil and the factory-worker, disappears and that the whole of society must fall apart into the two classes—the property-*owners* and the propertyless *workers*.

Political economy proceeds from the fact of private property, but it does not explain it to us. It expresses in general, abstract formulae the *material* process through which private property actually passes, and these formulae it then takes for *laws*. It does not *comprehend* these laws—i.e., it does not demonstrate how they arise from the very nature of private property. Political economy does not disclose the source of the division between labour and capital, and between capital and land. When, for example, it defines the relationship of wages to profit, it takes the interest of the capitalists to be the ultimate cause; i.e., it takes for granted what it is supposed to evolve. Similarly, competition comes in everywhere. It is explained from external circumstances. As to how far these external and apparently fortuitous circumstances are but the expression of a necessary course of development, political economy teaches us nothing. We have seen how, to it, exchange itself appears to be a fortuitous fact. The only wheels which political economy sets in motion are *avarice* and the *war amongst the avaricious—competition.*

*   *   *

Do not let us go back to a fictitious primordial condition as the political economist does, when he tries to explain. Such a primordial condition explains nothing. He merely pushes the question away into a grey nebulous distance. He assumes in the form of fact, of an event, what he is supposed to deduce—namely, the necessary relationship between two things—between, for example, division of labour and exchange. Theology in the same way explains the origin of evil by the fall of man: that is, it assumes as a fact, in historical form, what has to be explained.

We proceed from an *actual* economic fact.

The worker becomes all the poorer the more wealth he produces, the more his production increases in power and range. The worker becomes an ever cheaper commodity the more commodities he creates. With the *increasing value* of the world of things proceeds in direct proportion the *devaluation* of the world of men. Labour produces not only commodities; it produces itself and the worker as a *commodity*—and does so in the proportion in which it produces commodities generally.

This fact expresses merely that the object which labour produces—labour's product—confronts it as *something alien*, as a *power independent* of the producer. The product of labour is labour which has been congealed in an object, which has become material: it is the *objectification* of labour. Labour's realization is its objectification. In the conditions dealt with by political economy this realization of labour appears as *loss of reality* for the workers; objectification as *loss of the object* and *object-bondage*; appropriation as *estrangement*, as *alienation*.

So much does labour's realization appear as loss of reality that the worker loses reality to the point of starving to death. So much does objectification appear as loss of the object that the worker is robbed of the objects most necessary not only for his life but for his work. Indeed, labour itself becomes an object which he can get hold of only with the greatest effort and with the most irregular interruptions. So much does the appropriation of the object appear as estrangement that the more objects the worker produces the fewer can he possess and the more he falls under the dominion of his product, capital.

All these consequences are contained in the definition that the worker is related to the *product of his labour* as to an *alien* object. For on this premise it is clear that the more the worker spends himself, the more powerful the alien objective world becomes which he creates over-against himself, the poorer he himself—his inner world—becomes, the less belongs to him as his own. It is the same in religion. The more man puts into God, the less he retains in himself. The worker puts his life into the object; but now his life no longer belongs to him but to the object. Hence, the greater this activity, the greater is the worker's lack of objects. Whatever the product of his labour is, he is not. Therefore the greater this product, the less is he himself. The *alienation* of the worker in his product means not only that his labour becomes an object, an *external* existence, but that it exists *outside him*, independently, as something alien to him, and that it becomes a power of its own confronting him; it means that the life which he has conferred on the object confronts him as something hostile and alien.

*   *   *

Political economy conceals the estrangement inherent in the nature of labour by not considering the direct relationship between the worker (labour) *and production.* It is true that labour produces for the rich wonderful things—but for the worker it produces privation. It produces palaces—but for the worker, hovels. It produces beauty—but for the worker, deformity. It replaces labour by machines—but some of the workers it throws back to a barbarous type of labour, and the other workers it turns into machines. It produces intelligence—but for the worker idiocy, cretinism.

The direct relationship of labour to its produce is the relationship of the worker to the objects of his

production. The relationship of the man of means to the objects of production and to production itself is only a *consequence* of this first relationship—and confirms it. We shall consider this other aspect later.

When we ask, then, what is the essential relationship of labour we are asking about the relationship of the *worker* to production.

Till now we have been considering the estrangement, the alienation of the worker only in one of its aspects, i.e., the worker's *relationship to the products of his labour*. But the estrangement is manifested not only in the result but in the *act of production*—within the *producing activity* itself. How would the worker come to face the product of his activity as a stranger, were it not that in the very act of production he was estranging himself from himself? The product is after all but the summary of the activity of production. If then the product of labour is alienation, production itself must be active alienation, the alienation of activity, the activity of alienation. In the estrangement of the object of labour is merely summarized the estrangement, the alienation, in the activity of labour itself.

What, then, constitutes the alienation of labour?

First, the fact that labour is *external* to the worker, i.e., it does not belong to his essential being; that in his work, therefore, he does not affirm himself but denies himself, does not feel content but unhappy, does not develop freely his physical and mental energy but mortifies his body and ruins his mind. The worker therefore only feels himself outside his work, and in his work feels outside himself. He is at home when he is not working, and when he is working he is not at home. His labour is therefore not voluntary, but coerced; it is *forced labour*. It is therefore not the satisfaction of a need; it is merely a *means* to satisfy needs external to it. Its alien character emerges clearly in the fact that as soon as no physical or other compulsion exists, labour is shunned like the plague. External labour, labour in which man alienates himself, is a labour of self-sacrifice, of mortification. Lastly, the external character of labour for the worker appears in the fact that it is not his own, but someone else's, that it does not belong to him, that in it he belongs, not to himself, but to another. Just as in religion the spontaneous activity of the human imagination, of the human brain and the human heart, operates independently of the individual—that is, operates on him as an alien, divine or diabolical activity—in the same way the worker's activity is not his spontaneous activity. It belongs to another; it is the loss of his self.

As a result, therefore, man (the worker) no longer feels himself to be freely active in any but his animal functions—eating, drinking, procreating, or at most in his dwelling and in dressing-up, etc.; and in his human functions he no longer feels himself to be anything but an animal. What is animal becomes human and what is human becomes animal.

Certainly eating, drinking, procreating, etc., are also genuinely human functions. But in the abstraction which separates them from the sphere of all other human activity and turns them into sole and ultimate ends, they are animal.

We have considered the act of estranging practical human activity, labour, in two of its aspects. (1) The relation of the worker to the *product of labour* as an alien object exercising power over him. This relation is at the same time the relation to the sensuous external world, to the objects of nature as an alien world antagonistically opposed to him. (2) The relation of labour to the *act of production* within the *labour* process. This relation is the relation of the worker to his own activity as an alien activity not belonging to him; it is activity as suffering, strength as weakness, begetting as emasculating, the worker's *own* physical and mental energy, his personal life or what is life other than activity—as an activity which is turned against him, neither depends on nor belongs to him. Here we have *self-estrangement*, as we had previously the estrangement of the *thing*.

We have yet a third aspect of *estranged labour* to deduce from the two already considered.

Man is a species being, not only because in practice and in theory he adopts the species as his object (his own as well as those of other things), but—and this is only another way of expressing it—but also because he treats himself as the actual, living species; because he treats himself as a *universal* and therefore a free being.

The life of the species, both in man and in animals, consists physically in the fact that man (like the animal) lives on inorganic nature; and the more universal man is compared with an animal, the more universal is the sphere of inorganic nature on which he lives. Just as plants, animals, stones, the air, light, etc., constitute a part of human consciousness in the realm of theory, partly as objects of natural science, partly as objects of art—his spiritual inorganic nature, spiritual nourishment which he must first prepare to make it palatable and digestible—so too in the realm of practice they constitute a part of human life and human activity. Physically man lives only on these products of nature, whether they appear in the form of food, heating, clothes, a dwelling, or whatever it may be. The universality of man is in practice manifested precisely in the universality which makes all nature his *inorganic* body—both inasmuch as nature is (1) his direct means of life, and (2) the material, the object, and the instrument of his life-activity. Nature is man's *inorganic body*—nature, that is, in so far as it is not itself the human body. Man *lives* on nature—means that nature is his *body*, with which he must remain in continuous intercourse if he is not to die. That man's physical and spiritual life is linked to nature means simply that nature is linked to itself, for man is a part of nature.

In estranging from man (1) nature, and (2) himself, his own active functions, his life-activity, estranged labour estranges the *species* from man. It turns for him the *life of the species* into a means of individual life. First it estranges the life of the species and individual life, and secondly it makes individual life in its abstract form the purpose of the life of the species, likewise in its abstract and estranged form.

For in the first place labour, *life-activity, productive life* itself, appears to man merely as a *means* of satisfying a need—the need to maintain the physical existence. Yet the productive life is the life of the species. It is life-engendering life. The whole character of a species—its species character—is contained in the character of its life-activity; and free, conscious activity is man's species character. Life itself appears only as *a means to life*.

The animal is immediately identical with its life-activity. It does not distinguish itself from it. It is *its life-activity*. Man makes his life-activity itself the object of his will and of his consciousness. He has conscious life-activity. It is not a determination with which he directly merges. Conscious life-activity directly distinguishes man from animal life-activity. It is just because of this that he is a species being. Or it is only because he is a species being that he is a Conscious Being, i.e., that his own life is an object for him. Only because of that is his activity free activity. Estranged labour reverses this relationship, so that it is just because

man is a conscious being that he makes his life-activity, his *essential* being, a mere means to his *existence*.

*   *   *

REVIEW QUESTIONS

1. What are, for Marx, the "actual" economic facts of labor and why are these so deleterious for the happiness of the worker?
2. When can labor free the "physical and mental energy" of a worker and why does this not occur under wage labor?
3. According to Marx, why is work an indispensable component of human freedom?
4. What are the social and political ramifications of estranged labor?

20 ～ CONSEQUENCES OF INDUSTRIALIZATION: URBANIZATION AND CLASS CONSCIOUSNESS

The legacy of revolutionary republicanism combined with the harsh economic conditions of early industrial capitalism produced a new era in social relations and political struggle. For many contemporary observers, industrial society had established an unbridgeable chasm between propertied classes and wage-earning workers, "two nations" deeply divided in their political, cultural, and social outlooks.

The transition from agricultural and handicraft economies to the new urban industrial society produced pervasive dislocation and suffering. In the countryside, the erosion of traditional authority and social stability preceded large-scale industrialization. The enclosure of common lands and the increasing demand for profitable harvests replaced the paternalistic ties that bound together lords and tenant farmers with the more callous contractual relationship of wages and rents. Reduced to the penury of day laborers, many farmers migrated to the young industrial towns offering work. Similarly, cottage weavers throughout Europe, a proud class of skilled artisans, faced ruin when mechanized spinning and weaving drove down rates to starvation levels.

Squalor and grueling factory work offered little solace in the city. Unencumbered by any legal restraints, employers imposed insufferable working conditions on men, women, and children. In the 1830s, reformers likened the circumstances in English mill towns to colonial slavery and ridiculed the blind spots of bourgeois society, which fervently proselytized for the abolition of slavery but could not see similar misery and exploitation in their own cities. Because of the pervasive wretchedness of English urban life, with its heightened problems of malnutrition, disease, alcohol, prostitution, and theft, engaged commentators questioned whether laissez-faire capitalism possessed a moral center.

The social question of early industrialization inexorably took on political dimensions. Privation and bitterness produced machine-breaking, hayrick burning, and violent confrontations with masters, all early manifestations of political ac-

tion. *Bloody interventions of governments against workers articulated the differences of class interests between political elites and workers, who gradually developed their own political organizations. Chartism emerged as one of the earliest independent working-class movements, a national network of committees in Britain that agitated for workers' enfranchisement through colossal petition drives. Although unsuccessful in its immediate goals (parliament rejected all demands), the movement alerted the nation to a mature, responsible working class, thus laying the groundwork for a subsequent liberal-labor alliance and eventual integration into Britain's political body. On the continent, however, unremitting state hostility toward workers' rights produced more resolute positions against bourgeois capitalism, most vividly expressed in the classic pamphlet,* The Communist Manifesto *(1848). Influenced by the widespread poverty of the 1840s and the growing concentration of capital, Karl Marx and Friedrich Engels asserted the axiomatic existence of class struggle and the eventual triumph of workers' socialism. The manifesto launched the political movement of Marxist socialism, which anchored class antagonism as a central issue in European political life.*

In spite of the growing "specter" of socialism, this period is still labeled the bourgeois century. The growth of industrial capitalism brought with it a confident, well-defined middle-class culture, whose values of thrift, meritocracy, and hard work looked askance on indolent aristocrats and improvident laborers. The credo of self-reliance loomed large in the crowded Victorian marketplace of ideas. In the hands of popular writers, the appealing tales of rags-to-riches success through personal discipline and moral improvement enshrined a fundamental bourgeois tenet: social mobility for the deserving. Equally central to bourgeois life was the sharpened division between home and work as gender roles grew more pronounced. Bourgeois society expected women to preside over the private sphere's social and material complexities, while raising children and providing husbands with domestic sanctuary from the rigors of public life.

The divisions between employers and wage earners and the separation of private and public spheres constitute two fundamental shifts caused by the industrial revolution. While industrialization reconfigured the roles of bourgeois women and domesticity, class determined the new framework of social relations. Political affinities became class-specific, and expectations in life depended on one's relationship to the market.

ANONYMOUS

An Address by a Journeyman Cotton Spinner

The factory system in northern England brought with it new social relations and political tensions. This anonymous address of 1818, published in the radical democratic newspaper The Black Dwarf, *highlights the growing political divide between the two principal classes of Manchester: employers, who owned factories and controlled the market for commissioned work from weavers working from their homes; and the workers, either factory hands or independent, reduced to accepting ever-lower rates for their skills. The article's sharp invective against the new moneyed class of Manchester points up the power of the public sphere to mobilize public opinion against wealth and political power.* The Black Dwarf, *one among a handful of prominent radical-democratic newspapers, boasted a circulation of more than twelve thousand in 1820, which, compared with the seven thousand of* The Times, *the newspaper of record, suggests a literate, informed working class capable of political organization.*

From *The Making of the English Working Class,* by E. P. Thompson, quoting *The Black Dwarf,* September 30, 1818.

"First, then, as to the employers: with very few exceptions, they are a set of men who have sprung from the cotton-shop without education or address, except so much as they have acquired by their intercourse with the little world of merchants on the exchange at Manchester; but to counterbalance that deficiency, they give you enough of appearances by an ostentatious display of elegant mansions, equipages, liveries, parks, hunters, hounds, &c. which they take care to shew off to the merchant stranger in the most pompous manner. Indeed their houses are gorgeous palaces, far surpassing in bulk and extent the neat charming retreats you see round London . . . but the chaste observer of the beauties of nature and art combined will observe a woeful deficiency of taste. They bring up their families at the most costly schools, determined to give their offspring a double portion of what they were so deficient in themselves. Thus with scarcely a second idea in their heads, they are literally petty monarchs, absolute

and despotic, in their own particular districts; and to support all this, their whole time is occupied in contriving how to get the greatest quantity of work turned off with the least expence. . . . In short, I will venture to say, without fear of contradiction, that there is a greater distance observed between the master there and the spinner, than there is between the first merchant in London and his lowest servant or the lowest artisan. Indeed there is no comparison. I know it to be a fact, that the greater part of the master spinners are anxious to keep wages low for the purpose of keeping the spinners indigent and spiritless . . . as for the purpose of taking the surplus to their own pockets.

"The master spinners are a class of men unlike all other master tradesmen in the kingdom. They are ignorant, proud, and tyrannical. What then must be the men or rather beings who are the instruments of such masters? Why, they have been for a series of years, with their wives and their families, patience itself—bondmen and bondwomen to their cruel taskmasters. It is in vain to insult our common understandings with the observation that such men are free; that the law protects the rich and poor alike, and that a spinner can leave his master if he does not like the wages. True; so he can: but where must he go? why to another, to be sure. Well: he goes; he is asked where did you work last: 'did he discharge you?' No; we could not agree about wages. Well I shall not employ you nor anyone who leaves his master in that manner. Why is this? Because there is an abominable *combination existing amongst the masters*, first established at Stockport in 1802, and it has since become so general, as to embrace all the great masters for a circuit of many miles round Manchester, though not the little masters: they are excluded. They are the most obnoxious beings to the great ones that can be imagined. . . . When the combination first took place, one of their first articles was, that no master should take on a man until he had first ascertained whether his last master had discharged him. What then is the man to do? If he goes to the parish, that grave of all independence, he is there told—We shall not relieve you; if you dispute with your master, and don't support your family, we will send you to prison; so that the man is bound, by a combination of circumstances, to submit to his master. He cannot travel and get work in any town like a shoe-maker, joiner, or taylor; he is confined to the district.

"The workmen in general are an inoffensive, unassuming, set of well-informed men, though how they acquire their information is almost a mystery to me. They are docile and tractable, if not goaded too much; but this is not to be wondered at, when we consider that they are trained to work from six years old, from five in a morning to eight and nine at night. Let one of the advocates for obedience to his master take his stand in an avenue leading to a factory a little before five o'clock in the morning, and observe the squalid appearance of the little infants and their parents taken from their beds at so early an hour in all kinds of weather; let him examine the miserable pittance of food, chiefly composed of water gruel and oatcake broken into it, a little salt, and some-times coloured with a little milk, together with a few potatoes, and a bit of bacon or fat for dinner; would a London mechanic eat this? There they are, (and if late a few minutes, a quarter of a day is stopped in wages) locked up until night in rooms heated above the hottest days we have had this summer, and allowed no time, except three-quarters of an hour at dinner in the whole day: whatever they eat at any other time must be as they are at work. The negro slave in the West Indies, if he works under a scorching sun, has probably a little breeze of air sometimes to fan him: he has a space of ground, and time allowed to cultivate it. The English spinner slave has no enjoyment of the open atmosphere and breezes of heaven. Locked up in factories eight stories high, he has no relaxation till the ponderous engine stops, and then he goes home to get refreshed for the next day; no time for sweet association with his family; they are all alike fatigued and exhausted. This is no over-drawn picture: it is literally true. I ask again, would the mechanics in the South of England submit to this?

"When the spinning of cotton was in its infancy, and before those terrible machines for superseding the necessity of human labour, called steam engines, came into use, there were a great number of what were then called *little masters*; men who with a small capital, could procure a few machines, and employ a few hands, men and boys (say to twenty or thirty), the produce of whose labour was all taken to Manchester central mart, and put into the hands of brokers. . . . The brokers sold it to the merchants, by which means the master spinner was enabled to stay at home and work and attend to his workmen. The cotton was then always given out in its raw state from the bale to the wives of the spinners at home, when they heat and cleansed it ready for the spinners in the factory. By this they could earn eight, ten, or twelve shillings a week, and cook and attend to their families. But none are thus employed now; for all the cotton is broke up by a machine, turned by the steam engine, called a devil: so that the spinners wives have no employment, except they go to work in the factory all day at what can be done by children for a few shillings, four or five per week. If a man then could not agree with his master, he left him, and could get employed elsewhere. A few years, however, changed the face of things. Steam engines came into use, to purchase which, and to erect buildings sufficient to contain them and six or seven hundred hands, required a great capital. The engine power produced a more marketable (though not a better) article than the little master could at the same price. The consequence was their ruin in a short time; and the overgrown capitalists triumphed in their fall; for they were the only obstacle that stood between them and the complete control of the workmen.

"Various disputes then originated between the workmen and masters as to the fineness of the work, the workmen being paid according to the number of hanks or yards of thread he produced from a given quantity of cotton, which was always to be proved by the overlooker, whose interest made it imperative on him to lean to his master, and call the material coarser than it was. If the workman would not submit *he must summon his employer before a magistrate;* the whole of the acting magistrates in that district, with the exception of two worthy clergymen, being gentlemen who have sprung from the *same* source with the master cotton spinners. The employer generally contented himself with sending his overlooker to answer any such summons, thinking it beneath him to meet his servant. The magistrate's decision was generally in favour of the master, though on the statement of the overlooker only. The workman dared not appeal to the sessions on account of the expense. . . .

"These evils to the men have arisen from that dreadful monopoly which exists in those districts where wealth and power are got into the hands of the few, who, in the pride of their hearts, think themselves the lords of the universe."

REVIEW QUESTIONS

1. Why are employers characterized as "petty monarchs, absolute and despotic"?
2. Why is this a new attitude among employers?
3. How does this address compare the lives of Manchester workers with prior times and with workers elsewhere in Britain?
4. What is the perceived attitude of the state in this conflict between employers and workers?

ANONYMOUS

FROM *The Life & History of Captain Swing, the Kent Rick Burner, written by Himself*

The mechanization of spinning and weaving and the introduction of threshing machines in the English countryside brought waves of machine breaking and barn burnings in the 1820s and 1830s. Although this violence is often characterized as the futile resistance to inevitable change, these uprisings are more accurately seen as highly organized, disciplined political events. Under such fictional leaders as Ned Ludd or Captain Swing, weavers, artisans, and sharecroppers organized themselves into bands and destroyed private property that they believed had stripped them of their livelihoods and dignity. The following story, which circulated as a popular political tract in the early 1830s, compresses the major political grievances of England's agricultural workers into the life of Swing, a hard-working tenant farmer driven to destitution and despair by social and political change in the early nineteenth century.

From *The Life & History of Captain Swing, the Kent Rick Burner, written by Himself,* Anonymous, W.P. Chubb, 1830.

I WAS born on the day William Pitt became Prime Minister of England. My father was one of the class of small farmers, then so numerous in England, but whom the system of large farms has now altogether extinguished in the country. My father had two sons, of whom I was the younger; and as the savings of his predecessors had rendered him wealthy in his way, he determined educating me for a profession, and sent me to a grammar school in the neighbourhood; from whence I was removed in due time to a public school, preparatory to my entering college. When I was about to enter college, my elder brother died,—in consequence of which my father changed his intention of bringing me up to a profession, and took me home to attend to the farm. As I considered my future path in life was now definitively marked out for me, I gave up my entire time and attention to acquire a thorough knowledge of agriculture, and soon became one of the best farmers in that part of the kingdom. Soon after my father died, and bequeathed to me the farm and greater part of his effects. Some time after this I became acquainted with the daughter of a neighbouring curate,* * * and after a short period I proposed marriage to her, and she became my wife. I, of course, got no fortune with her, but she had that which surpasseth riches,—a most kind and amiable disposition; and if industry and integrity on the one side, and virtue and humility on the other, were sufficient to render our union a happy one, never was there a couple bid fairer for it than we did.

A few years passed as happily as I could wish,

and three little ones added to my felicity. Although working hard all day, I at night forgot my toil and trouble when I returned to my fireside and family; and as soon as my children began to lisp, the first words I taught them to utter were the same I had myself learned when I was their age,—namely,, "To fear God and honour the King—to give every man his due, and behave uprightly to all." A short time after the birth of my fourth child, our old landlord died, and was succeeded by his son.

About two years after our young landlord returned home, (he had been on the Continent since the death of his father) I received a notice to quit,—the receipt of which astonished me beyond measure, as I owed no rent, and had always supported the character of being the best and most improving tenant on the estate.* * * As I found it impossible to see the lord, I called on the steward, and asked him what fault I had committed, or what crime I had been guilty of, that I should be turned out of the farm where my forefathers had lived for centuries, and which they and I had done so much to improve? "There is no fault to be found with you," replied the steward, "you have always paid your rent regularly, and conducted yourself correctly; but my lord wants your to make a fox-cover, and you must leave it next settling day."

"Good God!" exclaimed I, "are my wife and children to be turned out to make room for wild beasts?"—"There is no use in talking," said the steward, "your land is the best site on the estate for a fox-cover, and you must give it up."

The lord himself happened to pass by, and

with tears in my eyes, I beseeched him not to turn out my family, in order to replace them with foxes. "Every man," said the lord, "*can do what he pleases with his own,*" and he walked away and left me.

*   *   *

Time, which flies equally fast whether we are miserable or happy, soon brought about the settling day, and as I found all appeals to the landlord utterly useless, I was prepared to give him possession, I had not sufficient capital to take a large farm, and small ones were not to be had, so I was obliged to dispose of my horses, black cattle, and farming machinery; and as the period I sold them was one of unusual depression, I did not receive one half their value.

As soon as my first burst of grief for the loss of my farm was over, I again applied myself to labour in my garden, (which I had taken with a cottage in the neighbourhood) and by dint of industry and exertion supported my family, by supplying a neighbouring village with vegetables. Up to this period I had never attended a political meeting in my life, nor took any part whatever in politics; I thought our laws and legislators too good to require alteration or change; and if I hated one thing more than another, it was Radicalism, the abettors of which I considered no better than rebels and revolutionists, who wanted to destroy our glorious constitution, and cause anarchy in the country. I begun, however, now to think otherwise. I had seen all around me, my neighbours reduced from comfort to poverty, and from poverty to the poor-rates; and as, in the greater number of cases, it had arisen from no fault of their own, it occurred to me that some change was necessary; as had England been governed as it ought, those things could never have taken place. Reflections of this sort determined me to attend the great meeting at Manchester, then about to be held, and I accordingly went there. Every thing passed quietly off until noon, when, to my horror and surprise, a charge was made by the military and yeomanry on the peaceable and unarmed multitude that were assembled, and I, amongst

others, was wounded by a sabre-cut in the arm. Bleeding profusely, and with my arm hanging uselessly by my side, I went into Manchester and got it dressed; I was kept awake the entire night by the pain of my wound, but consoled myself with the reflection that immediate and condign punishment would be inflicted on the lawless soldiery who had dared to massacre a peaceable multitude assembled to petition Parliament. "The King," said I, "will certainly send down a commission to have the monsters tried for their blood-thirsty outrage." What was my astonishment and indignation, in ten days after, when I saw a letter from the Secretary of State, thanking in the King's name, the military and magistrates, for massacring the people at Manchester.

I no longer wanted a proof that our country was sadly misgoverned,—that a great change was necessary,—and that the Reformers were the only real friends of the people.

*   *   *

[Swing is wrongfully accused of poaching and serves eighteen months in prison] When I was permitted to leave prison, I again commenced working in my garden, hoping my troubles were now over, and that, for the rest of my life, though poor, I should be allowed to rear my children peaceably and without persecution. A new and unexpected misfortune, however, arose; the parson of the parish considered his tithes not sufficiently productive, and made a claim for small tithes, which none of his predecessors had done, and demanded of me not only tithes for the current year, but also for that of the preceding one. I was unable to pay it, and was served with a law process, and, in a few weeks after, my cow sold by auction for the parson's tithes. I was now no longer able to keep my cottage and garden, and gave it up to the landlord, and rented a smaller one, having half an acre of ground attached to it. My present holding, though situated in the same parish, was two miles farther in the country than the former one, and adjoining it was a slip of uncultivated land, containing about an acre. My present landlord proposed that I should take this piece of land, in addition to what I had already; and, as an encouragement to me to do so, told me that he would not ask rent for the two first years, as during that time, he was perfectly well aware, the land would produce nothing. As I considered his proposal a fair one, I accepted it, and became his tenant for the piece of land, which I immediately set about enclosing with a ditch: having no person to assist me in making it, it was a considerable time before I had it finished: and I then commenced digging it with a spade, as I had no money to pay for getting it ploughed. In this way I fallowed it for two successive seasons; and in the beginning of the third spring I contrived, by parting with a good deal of my furniture to purchase some manure, which I carried in a basket on my head to the land: thus prepared, I sowed a crop in it, and nothing could succeed better than it did. When the time nearly came for gathering it, I was one day standing admiring it, with a gratification proportionate to the immense labour and time I had expended in bringing it about. "Although it had cost me three years labour," said I, "to grow this crop, it will nevertheless amply remunerate me." I had scarcely uttered the words, when two men rode up to me, one of whom I found to be the parson, whom I had never before seen in the parish, and the other his tithe valuator. After the latter had examined the crop, the parson asked me whether I would pay in kind or money?

"How much is it parson?" asked I.—"Only the tenth of the crop," replied he; "you must be very ignorant to ask such a question."

"But," said I, "if your reverence takes the tenth of the crop, it will be three-tenths of the produce of my laud; for I have been three years bringing the land into cultivation before it could grow any thing."—"I don't understand you," said the parson; "I must have my tithe."

"Why surely," said I, "your reverence will not rob my poor little children, by taking two-tenths more than you have a right to?"—"Rob them!" roared out the parson; "I see, my good fellow, you are a Radical, but I'll make you pay me my right; you shall not defraud the church of its lawful dues."

The parson went away, and the overseers came and demanded the poor-rates; the churchwardens called for an applotment, made to repair and beautify the church, and the landlord took his rent,—and I was a ruined man. My whole three years' labour went amongst them, without leaving me one shilling for myself. I was now broken in purse and spirit, and could no longer bear up against the misfortunes that had fallen upon me. I gave up my land, and as I could procure no employment, I was obliged to apply to the parish. In order to lessen the poor-rates as much as possible, the overseers and farmers met each Sunday, and every able-bodied labourer was set up to auction, and the farmer who bid most for him had him to work for him during the ensuing week. One farmer bid three shillings a week for me, and I was ordered to work for him for that sum, and four shillings that the overseer gave me, making together seven shillings a week, to support my wife, five children, and myself. At the end of a week the farmer had no further occasion for my services, and I was on the following Monday, in company with some others, yoked to a cart, and made to draw gravel to the road. "Good God!" exclaimed I, when I found the harness upon me, "what is England reduced to, when, without any fault of my own, in the same parish that so many generations of my forefathers lived comfortable and happy, I am obliged to submit so be treated as a beast of burthen!" The work of drawing stones was so dreadfully severe, and so unlike what I had been accustomed to, that a few weeks' trial soon convinced me it would soon kill me; and I determined leaving my native parish, and seeking employment elsewhere; and with this intention I came into Kent.* * *

In Kent I found myself still worse off than at home, for I could procure no employment whatever, and as I had no claim on the poor-rates, I was in danger of starving, and felt myself compelled to return home; before, however, I could do so, my poor wife fell ill of fever, and in order to prevent her perishing from want, I was obliged to go and beg—downright hunger having conquered my reluctance to ask charity. I proceeded along the road in order to do so, and saw a fat man, dressed in black, approaching me, to whom I applied for something to prevent my wife and children dying of starvation.—"I cannot *afford* to give you any thing," replied he; "go to your parish." His manner was so repulsive, that I considered it useless to make a second application, and passed on: when I had walked a few yards, I began to think I had somewhere before seen the gentleman in black, and, after a few minutes recollection, remembered he was the Rev. Mr. Saint Paul, who had taken my cow in payment of his small tithes, and who afterwards took three-tenths of my crop for his tithe of my plot of ground: he was a pluralist; and, having five livings, seldom or never came to the parish I had lived in, except to receive his tithes, so that I did not at first recognise him. I walked on for some time longer, and not meeting any person, was obliged to return to the cottage that my wife was in, without any thing to give her; as I could not bring myself to enter the cottage and behold my wife dying for want, I sat down on the road, a little distance from the door, and soon beheld the parson returning from his walk. He had a cake in his hand, which, as he had no inclination to eat, he threw to a large pampered dog that walked beside him. The dog, having no better appetite than his master, took the cake in his mouth, played with it for a moment, then tossed it in the dirt and left it there, A little child of mine beheld the scene from the cottage door, and ran and picked the cake out of the gutter, when the parson demanded how dare she take it from his dog? "Oh, Sir!" said the little girl, "the dog will not eat it, and I wish to bring it to my poor mother, who is starving."—"Your mother and yourself ought to be in the workhouse," said the parson; "it is a shame for the parish officers to allow little naked vagabonds like you to be running about the roads."

"Can this man," thought I, "be a descendant of the Apostles, who carried nothing with them but scrip and staff, and who preached that we should consider every man as our brother, and relieve the necessities of our fellow-creatures?" Such an impression did his conduct make on me,

that I got a piece of paper, and wrote a few lines, cautioning him against the consequences of his cruelty, and having signed it with my real name, "Swing," I left it at his hall-door during the night, and the following day the village rung with the report of the parson's having received a threatening notice, and that if the author could be detected, he would certainly be transported.

When writing the notice, I had not the most distant intention of making myself the instrument of punishment to the parson; it was an ebullition of the moment, called forth by my suffering, and I though no more about it. In a few days after the serving of the notice my wife died, and I was obliged to procure a coffin from the parish to bury her; no person attended her remains to the grave but a man who helped me to carry the coffin, and my five motherless children; it was late in the afternoon when we reached the churchyard, and as the man was obliged to leave me before the grave was entirely covered in, it became quite dark ere I could finish it, and I was obliged to procure a lantern to enable me to do so. When I completed it, I beheld my five children starving and shivering with cold beside the grave of their poor mother, without the smallest prospect of obtaining any food for them before morning; and in this condition I returned towards the cottage from whence I had that day carried my wife to be buried; the idea of passing the night on the straw on which she had expired was so repugnant to me, that I determined not to do so, and as the parson's haggard was only a short distance from me, I brought my children to pass the night on some loose straw that was lying on the ground. I was too much overwhelmed with grief and misery to attend to any thing, and I forgot to extinguish the light in the lantern which was carried by one of my children; the child incautiously placed the candle close to a rick, which caught fire, and was in a few minutes in a blaze; frightened and confounded at the accident, I immediately left the place, and the next morning journeyed homewards, begging for subsistence along the road: every where I went I heard of fires and notices signed "Swing." "How happens this," thought I. "I am not the author of these burnings!—What can have caused them?" A few minutes' reflection on the history of my own life, which without any alteration may stand for that of thousands of others, enabled me to give myself a satisfactory answer. "Those fires," said I, "are caused by farmers having been turned out of their lands to make room for foxes,—peaceable people assembled to petition Parliament, massacred by the military,—peasants confined two years in prison for picking up a dead partridge, English labourers set up to auction like slaves, and treated as beasts of burthen,—and pluralist parsons taking a poor man's only cow for the tythe of his cabbage garden. These are the things that have caused the burnings, and not unfortunate 'SWING!'" I continued my route, reached home, and am again harnessed like a horse to a gravel cart. But I bear it with patience, under the conviction that, in a very short time, Reform or Revolution must release me from it.

REVIEW QUESTIONS

1. What change initially uprooted Swing from his prosperity, and what factors continue to cause him misfortune?
2. How had traditional authority changed in the countryside?
3. What are Swing's political sympathies at the story's beginning and how do they evolve?
4. How does this story blur the boundaries of criminality and social justice?

RICHARD OASTLER

Yorkshire Slavery

Richard Oastler (1789–1861), a conservative church-and-king Tory, became a prominent social reformer in the 1830s after a factory owner exposed him to the ills of child employment. His letter to the liberal Leeds Mercury *in October 1830, "Yorkshire Slavery," launched a long campaign agitating for factory reform, which resulted in the Ten Hours Bill. His stirring oratory and his efforts to fuse a Radical-Tory alliance for factory legislation earned him the title the "Factory King." Imprisoned in 1840 for debt, Oastler published from prison the weekly* Fleet Papers, *which renewed the effort for factory reform and criticized the government's treatment of the poor. In the following letter, Oastler compares his cause to the anti-slavery movement of the 1820s, a cause embraced by religious associations and many elements of bourgeois society.*

From *The Factory System, Volume II: The Factory System and Society,* edited by J. T. Ward, Barnes and Noble, 1970.

To the Editors of the Leeds Mercury

'It is the pride of Britain that a slave cannot exist on her soil; and if I read the genius of her constitution aright, I find that slavery is most abhorrent to it—that the air which Britons breathe is free—the ground on which they tread is sacred to liberty'. *Rev. R. W. Hamilton's Speech at the Meeting held in the Cloth-hall Yard, September 22d, 1830.*

Gentlemen,—No heart responded with truer accents to the sounds of liberty which were heard in the Leeds Cloth-hall Yard, on the 22d instant, than did mine, and from none could more sincere and earnest prayers arise to the throne of Heaven, that hereafter slavery might only be known to Britain in the pages of her history. One shade alone obscured my pleasure, arising not from any difference in principle, but from the want of application of the general principle *to the whole empire.* The pious and able champions of *negro* liberty and *colonial* rights should, if I mistake not, have gone farther than they did; or perhaps, to speak more correctly, before they had travelled so far as the West Indies, should, at least for a few moments, have sojourned in our own immediate neighbourhood, and have directed the attention of the meeting to scenes of misery, acts of oppression, and victims of slavery, even on the threshold of our homes.

Let truth speak out, appalling as the statement may appear. The fact is true. Thousands of our fellow-creatures and fellow-subjects, both male and female, the miserable inhabitants of a *Yorkshire town*, (Yorkshire now represented in Parliament by the giant of anti-slavery principles) are this very moment existing in a state of slavery, *more horrid* than are the victims of that hellish system 'colonial slavery'. These innocent creatures drawl out, unpitied, their short but miserable existence, in a place famed for its profession of religious zeal, whose inhabitants are ever foremost in *professing* 'temperance' and 'reformation', and are striving to outrun their neighbours in missionary exertions, and would fain send the Bible to the farthest corner of the globe—aye, in the very place where the anti-slavery fever rages most furiously, her *apparent charity* is not more admired on earth, than her *real cruelty* is abhorred in Heaven. The very streets which receive the droppings of an 'Anti-Slavery Society' are every morning wet by the tears of innocent victims at the accursed shrine of avarice, who are *compelled* (not by the cart-whip of the negro slave-driver) but by the dread of the equally appalling thong or strap of the over-looker, to hasten, half-dressed, *but not half-fed*, to those magazines of British infantile slavery—*the worsted mills in the town and neighbourhood of Bradford! ! !*

Would that I had Brougham's eloquence, that I might rouse the hearts of the nation, and make every Briton swear, 'These innocents shall be free!'

Thousands of little children, both male and female, *but principally female*, from seven to fourteen years of age, are daily *compelled* to *labour* from six o'clock in the morning to seven in the evening, with only—Britons, blush while you read it!—*with only thirty minutes allowed for eating and recreation.* Poor infants! ye are indeed sacrificed at the shrine of avarice, *without even the solace of the negro slave;* ye are no more than he is, *free agents;* ye are compelled to work as long as the *necessity* of your needy parents may require, or the cold-blooded avarice of your worse than barbarian masters *may demand!* Ye live in the boasted land of freedom, and *feel* and mourn that *ye are slaves,* and slaves without the only comfort which the negro has. He knows it is his sordid, mercenary master's interest that he should *live,* be *strong* and *healthy.* Not so with you. Ye are doomed to labour from morning to night for one who cares not how soon your weak and tender frames are stretched to breaking! You are not mercifully valued at so much per head; this would assure you at least (even with the worst and most cruel masters) of the mercy shown to their own labouring beasts. No, no! your soft and delicate limbs are tired and fagged, and jaded, at only *so much per week,* and when your joints can act no longer, your emaciated frames are cast aside, the boards on which you lately toiled and wasted life away, are instantly supplied with other victims, who in this boasted land of liberty are HIRED—not sold—as slaves and daily forced to hear that they are free. Oh! Duncombe! Thou hatest slavery—I know thou dost resolve that 'Yorkshire children shall no more be slaves!' And Morpeth! who justly glorieth in the Christian faith—Oh, Morpeth! listen to the cries and count the tears of these poor babes, and let St. Stephen's hear thee swear 'they shall no longer groan in slavery!' And Bethell, too! who swears eternal hatred to the name of slave, whene'er thy manly voice is heard in Britain's senate, assert the rights and liberty of Yorkshire youths. And Brougham! thou who are the chosen champion of liberty in every clime! oh bend thy giant's mind, and listen to the sorrowing accents of these poor Yorkshire little ones, and note their tears; then let thy voice rehearse their woes, and touch the chord thou only holdest—the chord that sounds above the silvery notes in praise of heavenly liberty, and down descending at thy will, groans in the horrid caverns of the deep in muttering sounds of misery accursed to hellish bondage; and as thou sound'st these notes, let Yorkshire hear thee swear, 'Her children shall be free!' Yes, all ye four protectors of our rights, chosen by freemen to destroy oppression's rod,

'Vow one by one, vow altogether, vow
With heart and voice, eternal enmity
Against oppression by your brethren's hands;
Till man nor woman under Britain's laws,

Nor son nor daughter born within her empire,
Shall buy, or sell, or HIRE, or BE A SLAVE!'

The nation is now most resolutely determined that negroes shall be free. Let them, however, not forget that Britons have common rights with Afric's sons.

The blacks may be fairly compared to beasts of burden, *kept for their master's use*; the whites, to those *which others keep and let for hire*. If I have succeeded in calling the attention of your readers to the horrid and abominable system on which the worsted mills in and near Bradford is conducted, I have done some good. Why should not children working in them be protected by legislative enactments, as well as those who work in cotton mills? Christians should feel and act for those whom Christ so eminently loved, and declared that 'of such is the Kingdom of Heaven'.—I remain, yours, etc.,

A Briton.

REVIEW QUESTIONS

1. In what ways does Oastler expose the hypocrisy of English politics?
2. How does he compare colonial and domestic politics?
3. What are the author's rhetorical devices and tone of voice that make the letter such a powerful text?

FLORA TRISTAN

FROM *London Journal*

Flora Tristan (1803–1844), one of the earliest French socialists, visited England in 1831, 1835, and 1839. Her journal London Journal *(1840), a vivid and partisan analysis of London's social life, is particularly powerful in its indictment of the wretched effects of industrialization on working-class life. Her chapter on St. Giles*

Parish, the large Irish slum in central London, captures the misery, squalor, and desperation of urban conditions that made the "social question" the burning issue of the 1840s.

From *The London Journal of Flora Tristan 1842,* edited by Jean Hawkes, Virago, 1982. Reprinted with permission of Little, Brown and Company.

*   *   *

There are more than two hundred thousand members of the Irish proletariat living in different parts of the metropolis; they work as porters, men who are given the heaviest tasks because they will work for the lowest wages. That they are poor, Heaven knows, but at least they are employed; they do not give a true picture of Irish poverty, covered in rags and disputing with stray dogs for potato peelings in the streets. The Irish poverty * * * is found in the very heart of one of London's wealthiest districts, and that is where we must go to see in all its horror the misery that exists in a rich and fertile country when it is governed by the aristocracy for the benefit of its members.

At its starting-point, the elegant, long thoroughfare of Oxford Street, with its throng of carriages, its wide pavements and splendid shops, is joined almost at right angles by Totenham Court Road; just off this street, facing Oxford Street there is a narrow alley nearly always obstructed by an enormous cart loaded with coal, which leaves hardly enough room for you to pass, even if you flatten yourself against the wall. This little alley, Bainbridge Street, is the entrance to the Irish quarter.

*   *   *

It is not without fear that the visitor ventures into the dark, narrow alley known as Bainbridge Street. Hardly have you gone ten paces when you are almost suffocated by the poisonous smell. The alley, completely blocked by the huge coal-yard, is impassable. We turned off to the right into another unpaved muddy alley with evil-smelling soapy water and other household slops even more fetid lying everywhere in stagnant pools. I had to struggle against my revulsion and summon up all my courage to go on through this veritable cesspool. In St Giles, the atmosphere is stifling; there is no fresh air to breathe nor daylight to guide your steps. The wretched inhabitants wash their tattered garments themselves and hang them on poles across the street, shutting out all pure air and sunshine. The slimy mud beneath your feet gives off all manner of noxious vapours, while the wretched rags above you drip their dirty rain upon your head. The fantasies of a fevered imagination could never match the horrifying reality! When I reached the end of the alley, which was not very long, my resolution faltered; my body is never quite as strong as my will, and now I felt my stomach heave, while a fierce pain gripped my head. I was wondering whether I could bear to go any further when it struck me that I was in the midst of human beings, my fellow men, my brothers and sisters who had mutely suffered for centuries the pains I had endured for barely ten minutes. I overcame my suffering; the inspiration of my soul came to my aid and I felt within me an energy equal to the task I had set myself—to examine one by one every sign of destitution. Then an indefinable compassion surged through my heart, and at the same time a sombre terror took possession of me.

Picture, if you can, barefoot men, women and children picking their way through the foul morass; some huddled against the wall for want of anywhere to sit, others squatting on the ground, children wallowing in the mud like pigs. But unless you have seen it for yourself, it is impossible to imagine such extreme poverty, such total degradation. I saw children *without a stitch of clothing,* barefoot girls and women with babies at their breast, wearing nothing but a torn shirt that revealed almost the whole of their bodies; I saw old men cowering on dunghills, young men covered in rags.

Inside and out, the tumbledown hovels are entirely in keeping with the ragged population who inhabit them. In most of them the doors and windows lack fastenings and the floor is unpaved; the only furniture is a rough old oak table, a wooden bench, a stool, a few tin plates and a sort of *kennel* where father, mother, sons, daughters, and friends all sleep together regardless; such is the 'comfort' of the Irish quarter! All this is horrifying enough, but it is nothing compared with the expressions of the people's faces. They are all fearfully thin, emaciated and sickly; their faces, necks and hands are covered with sores; their skin is so filthy and their hair so matted and dishevelled that they look like negroes; their sunken eyes express a stupid animal ferocity, but if you look at them with assurance they cringe and whine. I recognised in them the self same faces and expressions that I had observed when I visited the prisons. It must be a red-letter day for them when they enter Coldbath Fields; at least in prison they will have fresh linen, comfortable clothes, clean beds and pure air.

How do they all live? By prostitution and theft. From the age of nine or ten the boys begin to steal; at eleven or twelve the girls are sold to brothels. The adults of both sexes are all professional thieves and their sole passion is drinking. If I had seen this quarter before I visited Newgate I would not have been so surprised to learn that the prison takes in fifty or sixty children a month and as many prostitutes. Theft is the only logical consequence when people live in such destitution as, this.

In great distress I asked myself what remedy there could be for such evils; then I thought of the doctrines propounded by our friends the English economists, and their maxims seemed to be written in blood. . . .

*   *   *

REVIEW QUESTIONS

1. At what or whom is Tristan's moral outrage directed?
2. How does Tristan connect physical and moral degradation?
3. How does Swing's tale of rural poverty compare with urban destitution?

FRIEDRICH ENGELS

FROM *The Condition of the English Working Class*

Friedrich Engels (1820–1895), the son of a pietistic textile manufacturer from the Rhenish town of Elberfeld, completed his apprenticeship as a textile entrepreneur in Manchester in 1842–1844. Prior to this apprenticeship, Engels read critical philosophy as a student in Berlin and published articles in the oppositional Cologne paper, Rheinische Zeitung. *In 1842 in Cologne Engels met Karl Marx for the first time. Manchester nurtured Engel's radical political spirit: he joined the Chartists, the movement agitating for universal suffrage and workingmen's rights; published articles in the Owenite newspaper* The New Moral World; *and wrote "Outlines of a Critique of Political Economy," which Marx published in his new Paris-based jour-*

nal, Deutsch-Französische Jahrbücher. *In 1844 he gathered material for a social history of England's working class, which became the* Condition of the Working Class in England *(first published in German in 1845), a descriptive work of English industrial life that amounted to an empirical indictment of capitalism's immorality. The following passage examines Manchester, a city whose population increase of seventy thousand between 1831 and 1841 produced deplorable living conditions for the city's poor.*

Reprinted from the Oxford World's Classic Edition of *The Condition of the Working Class in England* by Friedrich Engels edited by David McLellan (1993) by permission of Oxford University Press.

*   *   *

The south bank of the Irk is here very steep and between 15 and 30, feet high. On this declivitous hillside there are planted three rows of houses, of which the lowest rise directly out of the river, while the front walls of the highest stand on the crest of the hill in Long Millgate. Among them are mills on the river, in short, the method of construction is as crowded and disorderly here as in the lower part of Long Millgate. Right and left a multitude of covered passages lead from the main street into numerous courts, and he who turns in thither gets into a filth and disgusting grime, the equal of which is not to be found—especially in the courts which lead down to the Irk, and which contain unqualifiedly the most horrible dwellings which I have yet beheld. In one of these courts there stands directly at the entrance, at the end of the covered passage, a privy without a door, so dirty that the inhabitants can pass into and out of the court only by passing through foul pools of stagnant urine and excrement. This is the first court on the Irk above Ducie Bridge—in case anyone should care to look into it. Below it on the river there are several tanneries which fill the whole neighbourhood with the stench of animal putrefaction. Below Ducie Bridge the only entrance to most of the houses is by means of narrow, dirty stairs and over heaps of refuse and filth. The first court below Ducie Bridge, known as Allen's Court, was in such a state at the time of the cholera that the sanitary police ordered it evacu-

ated, swept, and disinfected with chloride of lime. Dr Kay gives a terrible description of the state of this court at that time. Since then, it seems to have been partially torn away and rebuilt; at least looking down from Ducie Bridge, the passer-by sees several ruined walls and heaps of debris with some newer houses. The view from this bridge, mercifully concealed from mortals of small stature by a parapet as high as a man, is characteristic for the whole district. At the bottom flows, or rather stagnates, the Irk, a narrow, coal-black, foul-smelling stream, full of debris and refuse, which it deposits on the shallower right bank. In dry weather, a long string of the most disgusting, blackish-green, slime pools are left standing on this bank, from the depths of which bubbles of miasmatic gas constantly arise and give forth a stench unendurable even on the bridge 40 or 50 feet above the surface of the stream. But besides this, the stream itself is checked every few paces by high weirs, behind which slime and refuse accumulate and rot in thick masses. Above the bridge are tanneries, bonemills, and gasworks, from which all drains and refuse find their way into the Irk, which receives further the contents of all the neighbouring sewers and privies. It may be easily imagined, therefore, what sort of residue the stream deposits. Below the bridge you look upon the piles of debris, the refuse, filth, and offal from the courts on the steep left bank; here each house is packed close behind its neighbour and a piece of each is visible, all black, smoky, crumbling, ancient, with broken panes and window-frames. The background is fur-

been delegated by their comrades, and the twenty-two manufacturers whom the Chamber of Commerce designated as representatives.

M. Douvier Dumolard could have, and ought to have, fixed the tariff himself; he did not have the courage; he contented himself with putting the two parties together.

On 21 October a new meeting was convoked at the Prefecture. The 25th of October had been fixed as a date for the definitive discussion of the rates of pay.

Among the delegates of both parties discussion centred upon the crying abuses which had crept into the factories, but particularly on the reduction of wage rates; and such was the moderation of the workers that those whom twelve years before the manufacturers were pleased to pay 8 sous had their wages reduced by one eighth. . . . The agreement was signed . . . and the Conseil des Prud'hommes was charged with supervising its execution, and one day per week was fixed to listen to the complaints which might arise through bad faith.

Among the manufacturers there were men who were honest and enlightened; they regarded the tariff as a necessary brake on the cupidity of several large speculators, and as a sure method of moderating disastrous market fluctuations resulting from competition. But this was the sentiment of a minority, and the news of the establishment of a tariff was no sooner known than the anger of most of the manufacturers spilled over into recriminations and menaces.

Infractions of the tariff were increasingly numerous; the Conseil des Prud'hommes, retracting its former decisions, refused to take action against those who violated the agreement; in this extreme situation the unfortunate weavers resolved to cease all work for a week; during this period they were to walk around the town calmly and without creating any disturbance, and they agreed that they would greet all those manufacturers who had kept the agreement. But this very moderation inflated the pride of their enemies. . . .

On Sunday, 20 November, a review of the National Guard was to take place on the Place Bel-

lecour. This review brought out all the elements of the discord which existed deep within the Lyons population. . . .

Everything seemed then to announce a battle on the morrow. At the meeting held at the Prefecture . . . it was decided that the five gate-ways which led from Lyons to Croix-Rousse would be occupied from day-break; that a battalion of the National Guard of Croix-Rousse and 300 men of the line would meet at 7.00 in the morning to prevent the formation of any mobs; that four battalions of the National Guard of Lyons and one from La Guillotière would assemble at the same time in their respective positions.

On Monday, 21 November, at 7.00 or 8.00 in the morning, the workers in a body of about three or four thousand, gathered together at the Croix-Rousse.

At their head they had one of their leaders, and they were armed with sticks. Their aim was not in any sense to engage the manufacturers in battle. All they wanted was a cessation of work until the tariff was recognized, and some workers went through the workshops to bring out those of their mates who were still at work. In the meantime, fifty or sixty guards appeared, and the Commanding Officer having cried 'My friends, we must sweep away that *canaille*', they advanced with bayonets. The indignant workers dashed forward, surrounded the platoon, disarmed some of the guards, and caused some of the others to flee. Soon the groups became more numerous, but they were not hostile. They spoke only of recommencing the peaceful demonstration of 25 October. With this in mind, the weavers, joining arms and walking four abreast, descended the Grand'Côte. The Infantry of the First Legion, specially formed by the manufacturers, resolutely advanced to meet the columns. Their anger had reached its highest point and several drew their cartridges from their pouches. Towards the middle of the Grand'Côte the two groups met face to face; the Infantry fired and eight workers fell seriously wounded; immediately, the column of which they were members retreated in disorder, up the Grand'Cote and back

nished by old barrack-like factory buildings. On the lower right bank stands a long row of houses and mills; the second house being a ruin without a roof, piled with debris; the third stands so low that the lowest floor is uninhabitable, and therefore without windows or doors. Here the background embraces the pauper burial-ground, the station of the Liverpool and Leeds railway, and, in the rear of this, the Workhouse, the 'Poor-Law Bastille' of Manchester, which, like a citadel, looks threateningly down from behind its high walls and parapets on the hilltop, upon the working-people's quarter below.

Above Ducie Bridge, the left bank grows more flat and the right bank steeper, but the condition of the dwellings on both banks grows worse rather than better. He who turns to the left here from the main street, Long Millgate, is lost; he wanders from one court to another, turns countless corners, passes nothing but narrow, filthy nooks and alleys, until after a few minutes he has lost all clue, and knows not whither to turn. Everywhere half or wholly ruined buildings, some of them actually uninhabited, which means a great deal here; rarely a wooden or stone floor to be seen in the houses, almost uniformly broken, ill-fitting windows and doors, and a state of filth! Everywhere heaps of debris, refuse, and offal; standing pools for gutters, and a stench which alone would make it impossible for a human being in any degree civilized to live in such a district.

* * *

Enough! The whole side of the Irk is built in this way, a planless, knotted chaos of houses, more or less on the verge of uninhabitableness, whose unclean interiors fully correspond with their filthy external surroundings. And how could the people be clean with no proper opportunity for satisfying the most natural and ordinary wants? Privies are so rare here that they are either filled up every day, or are too remote for most of the inhabitants to use. How can people wash when they have only the dirty Irk water at hand, while pumps and water-pipes can be found in decent parts of the city alone? In truth, it cannot be charged to the

account of these helots of modern society if their dwellings are not more clean than the pigsties which are here and there to be seen among them. The landlords are not ashamed to let dwellings like the six or seven cellars on the quay directly below Scotland Bridge, the floors of which stand at least 2 feet below the low-water level of the Irk that flows not 6 feet away from them; or like the upper floor of the corner-house on the opposite shore directly above the bridge, where the ground floor, utterly uninhabitable, stands deprived of all fittings for doors and windows, a case by no means rare in this region, when this open ground floor is used as a privy by the whole neighbourhood for want of other facilities!

If we leave the Irk and penetrate once more on the opposite side from Long Millgate into the midst of the working-men's dwellings, we shall come into a somewhat newer quarter, which stretches from St Michael's Church to Withy Grove and Shude Hill. Here there is somewhat better order. In place of the chaos of buildings, we find at least long straight lanes and alleys or courts, built according to a plan and usually square. But if, in the former case, every house was built according to caprice, here each lane and court is so built, without reference to the situation of the adjoining ones. The lanes run now in this direction, now in that, while every two minutes the wanderer gets into a blind alley, or, on turning a corner, finds himself back where he started from; certainly no one who has not lived a considerable time in this labyrinth can find his way through it.

If I may use the word at all in speaking of this district, the ventilation of these streets and courts is, in consequence of this confusion, quite as imperfect as in the Irk region; and if this quarter may, nevertheless, be said to have some advantage over that of the Irk, the houses being newer and the streets occasionally having gutters, nearly every house has, on the other hand, a cellar dwelling, which is rarely found in the Irk district, by reason of the greater age and more careless construction of the houses. As for the rest, the filth, debris, and offal heaps, and the pools in the streets are common to both quarters, and in the district now under discussion, another feature most injurious to the cleanliness of the inhabitants is the multitude of pigs walking about in all the alleys, rooting into the offal heaps, or kept imprisoned in small pens. Here, as in most of the working-men's quarters of Manchester, the pork-raisers rent the courts and build pigpens in them. In almost every court one or even several such pens may be found, into which the inhabitants of the court throw all refuse and offal, whence the swine grow fat; and the atmosphere, confined on all four sides, is utterly corrupted by putrefying animal and vegetable substances. Through this quarter, a broad and measurably decent street has been cut, Millers Street, and the background has been pretty successfully concealed. But if anyone should be led by curiosity to pass through one of the numerous passages which lead into the courts, he will find this piggery repeated at every twenty paces.

Such is the Old Town of Manchester, and on rereading my description, I am forced to admit that instead of being exaggerated, it is far from black enough to convey a true impression of the filth, ruin, and uninhabitableness, the defiance of all considerations of cleanliness, ventilation, and health which characterize the construction of this single district, containing at least twenty to thirty thousand inhabitants. And such a district exists in the heart of the second city of England, the first manufacturing city of the world. If anyone wishes to see in how little space a human being can move, how little air—and *such* air!—he can breathe, how little of civilization he may share and yet live, it is only necessary to travel hither.

*   *   *

REVIEW QUESTIONS

1. How does Engels' account of slum life differ from Tristan's?
2. What factors contribute to the overall hazardous conditions of living?
3. What was Engels' purpose of writing this book for a German audience?

LOUIS BLANC

FROM History of Ten Years, 1830–1840

The uprising of Lyons silkworkers in 1831 marked a new era in workers' class consciousness on the continent. The French state's brutal suppression of silkweavers' demands for just wages transformed economic grievances into a violent political contest that pitted unpropertied French workers against the constitutional monarchy of Louis Philippe (ruled 1830–1848), whose liberal reforms unquestionably supported capitalist interests. The following passage comes from Louis Blanc's History of Ten Years, 1830–1840 *(1841), an attack on Louis Philippe's regime that ran through four editions in four years. Blanc's essay, "The Organization of Work" (1839), established him as an influential social theorist. It denounced competition and self-interest as economic principles, advocating instead "social workshops," the equal wages and cooperative production of which would ameliorate unemployment and privation. Blanc led the radical faction during the revolution of 1848 in Paris, de-*

manding a labor ministry and a plan for the permanent elimination of unemployment.

From *Documents of Economic European History, Volume 1, The Process of Industrialization, 1750–1870,* edited by Sidney Pollard and C. Holmes. Copyright © 1968 Edward Arnold and Company, Ltd. Reprinted with permission of the publisher.

To give a fair account of the bloody drama we are about to describe, it is essential to be informed about the organization of manufacturing in Lyons. It was just the same in 1831 as it is today. The silk industry employed 30–40,000 workers. Above this class, living from day to day, having neither capital, credit nor fixed residence, were the *chefs d'atelier* who numbered 8–10,000, who owned four or five machines, and employed workers whom they supplied with machines in return for half the wages paid by the manufacturer. The manufacturers, about 800 of them, formed a third class, placed between the *chefs d'atelier* and those called agents, who were concerned with supplying raw materials, and who were the parasites and blood-suckers of Lyons industry. Thus, the agents exploited the manufacturers, who in their turn oppressed the *chefs d'atelier,* and the latter were compelled to place their burden on the *compagnons.*

Nevertheless, the prosperity of Lyons had pushed any danger resulting from this situation into the background. As long as they had not been obliged to work in murderous conditions, the workers had been satisfied with their moderate wages. But circumstances which were foreign, and anterior, to the July revolution affected Lyons industry. Numerous silk establishments had been set up in Zurich, Basle, Berne and Cologne; and England, for its part, was gradually freeing itself from the industrial tribute which for a considerable time it had paid to Lyons. Another more important factor complicated the situation. Since 1824 the number of manufacturers in Lyons had grown at a rapid rate, and to the effects of foreign competition, which, after all, hardly mattered except in relation to plain material, were added the disastrous effects of internal competition, which was pushed to the most extreme limits. Some m[an]facturers continued to prosper, but most of th[em] seeing a fall in profits, passed on their losses the *chefs d'atelier,* who placed some of their ov[er] whelming burden on the *compagnons.* From 4 6 francs, the wages of the intelligent and har[d] working man fell gradually to 40, 36 and 25 sou[s] in November 1831 the worker employed in the manufacture of plain material earned only 18 sou[s] for an 18 hour day . . . complaint became general; *chefs d'atelier* and *compagnons* shared their troubles; and from the depths of the Croix Rouss[e] sector, which bore the misery, at first a confused clamour was heard, but this soon became solemn, formidable and immense.

For some time the Prefect in Lyons had been a man who was skilled in soothing and handling popular passions. M. Douvier Dumolard understood immediately that no solution was possible in such a state of affairs, other than that of exterminating the working population, or satisfying its legitimate grievances. He took the latter course. . . .

M. Douvier began work . . . and on 11 October 1831 the Conseil des Prud'hommes had issued the following declaration:

'Considering that it is public knowledge that many manufacturers pay too low wages, it is expedient to establish a minimum wage.'

M. Douvier Dumolard resolved to deal with this resolution, which fell perfectly within his province; and on the 15th, under his Chairmanship, the Chamber of Commerce, the Mayor of Lyons and mayors of the three town suburbs met to discuss the situation. It became clear at thi[s] meeting that the bases of the wage structure woul[d] be discussed in a contradictory fashion by th[e] twenty-two workers, twelve of whom had alrea[dy]

nished by old barrack-like factory buildings. On the lower right bank stands a long row of houses and mills; the second house being a ruin without a roof, piled with debris; the third stands so low that the lowest floor is uninhabitable, and therefore without windows or doors. Here the background embraces the pauper burial-ground, the station of the Liverpool and Leeds railway, and, in the rear of this, the Workhouse, the 'Poor-Law Bastille' of Manchester, which, like a citadel, looks threateningly down from behind its high walls and parapets on the hilltop, upon the working-people's quarter below.

Above Ducie Bridge, the left bank grows more flat and the right bank steeper, but the condition of the dwellings on both banks grows worse rather than better. He who turns to the left here from the main street, Long Millgate, is lost; he wanders from one court to another, turns countless corners, passes nothing but narrow, filthy nooks and alleys, until after a few minutes he has lost all clue, and knows not whither to turn. Everywhere half or wholly ruined buildings, some of them actually uninhabited, which means a great deal here; rarely a wooden or stone floor to be seen in the houses, almost uniformly broken, ill-fitting windows and doors, and a state of filth! Everywhere heaps of debris, refuse, and offal; standing pools for gutters, and a stench which alone would make it impossible for a human being in any degree civilized to live in such a district.

*   *   *

Enough! The whole side of the Irk is built in this way, a planless, knotted chaos of houses, more or less on the verge of uninhabitableness, whose unclean interiors fully correspond with their filthy external surroundings. And how could the people be clean with no proper opportunity for satisfying the most natural and ordinary wants? Privies are so rare here that they are either filled up every day, or are too remote for most of the inhabitants to use. How can people wash when they have only the dirty Irk water at hand, while pumps and water-pipes can be found in decent parts of the city alone? In truth, it cannot be charged to the

account of these helots of modern society if their dwellings are not more clean than the pigsties which are here and there to be seen among them. The landlords are not ashamed to let dwellings like the six or seven cellars on the quay directly below Scotland Bridge, the floors of which stand at least 2 feet below the low-water level of the Irk that flows not 6 feet away from them; or like the upper floor of the corner-house on the opposite shore directly above the bridge, where the ground floor, utterly uninhabitable, stands deprived of all fittings for doors and windows, a case by no means rare in this region, when this open ground floor is used as a privy by the whole neighbourhood for want of other facilities!

If we leave the Irk and penetrate once more on the opposite side from Long Millgate into the midst of the working-men's dwellings, we shall come into a somewhat newer quarter, which stretches from St Michael's Church to Withy Grove and Shude Hill. Here there is somewhat better order. In place of the chaos of buildings, we find at least long straight lanes and alleys or courts, built according to a plan and usually square. But if, in the former case, every house was built according to caprice, here each lane and court is so built, without reference to the situation of the adjoining ones. The lanes run now in this direction, now in that, while every two minutes the wanderer gets into a blind alley, or, on turning a corner, finds himself back where he started from; certainly no one who has not lived a considerable time in this labyrinth can find his way through it.

If I may use the word at all in speaking of this district, the ventilation of these streets and courts is, in consequence of this confusion, quite as imperfect as in the Irk region; and if this quarter may, nevertheless, be said to have some advantage over that of the Irk, the houses being newer and the streets occasionally having gutters, nearly every house has, on the other hand, a cellar dwelling, which is rarely found in the Irk district, by reason of the greater age and more careless construction of the houses. As for the rest, the filth, debris, and offal heaps, and the pools in the streets are common to both quarters, and in the district now under discussion, another feature most injurious to the cleanliness of the inhabitants is the multitude of pigs walking about in all the alleys, rooting into the offal heaps, or kept imprisoned in small pens. Here, as in most of the working-men's quarters of Manchester, the pork-raisers rent the courts and build pigpens in them. In almost every court one or even several such pens may be found, into which the inhabitants of the court throw all refuse and offal, whence the swine grow fat; and the atmosphere, confined on all four sides, is utterly corrupted by putrefying animal and vegetable substances. Through this quarter, a broad and measurably decent street has been cut, Millers Street, and the background has been pretty successfully concealed. But if anyone should be led by curiosity to pass through one of the numerous passages which lead into the courts, he will find this piggery repeated at every twenty paces.

Such is the Old Town of Manchester, and on rereading my description, I am forced to admit that instead of being exaggerated, it is far from black enough to convey a true impression of the filth, ruin, and uninhabitableness, the defiance of all considerations of cleanliness, ventilation, and health which characterize the construction of this single district, containing at least twenty to thirty thousand inhabitants. And such a district exists in the heart of the second city of England, the first manufacturing city of the world. If anyone wishes to see in how little space a human being can move, how little air—and *such* air!—he can breathe, how little of civilization he may share and yet live, it is only necessary to travel hither.

*   *   *

REVIEW QUESTIONS

1. How does Engels' account of slum life differ from Tristan's?
2. What factors contribute to the overall hazardous conditions of living?
3. What was Engels' purpose of writing this book for a German audience?

LOUIS BLANC

FROM History of Ten Years, 1830–1840

The uprising of Lyons silkworkers in 1831 marked a new era in workers' class consciousness on the continent. The French state's brutal suppression of silkweavers' demands for just wages transformed economic grievances into a violent political contest that pitted unpropertied French workers against the constitutional monarchy of Louis Philippe (ruled 1830–1848), whose liberal reforms unquestionably supported capitalist interests. The following passage comes from Louis Blanc's History of Ten Years, 1830–1840 *(1841), an attack on Louis Philippe's regime that ran through four editions in four years. Blanc's essay, "The Organization of Work" (1839), established him as an influential social theorist. It denounced competition and self-interest as economic principles, advocating instead "social workshops," the equal wages and cooperative production of which would ameliorate unemployment and privation. Blanc led the radical faction during the revolution of 1848 in Paris, de-*

manding a labor ministry and a plan for the permanent elimination of unemployment.

To give a fair account of the bloody drama we are about to describe, it is essential to be informed about the organization of manufacturing in Lyons. It was just the same in 1831 as it is today. The silk industry employed 30–40,000 workers. Above this class, living from day to day, having neither capital, credit nor fixed residence, were the *chefs d'atelier* who numbered 8–10,000, who owned four or five machines, and employed workers whom they supplied with machines in return for half the wages paid by the manufacturer. The manufacturers, about 800 of them, formed a third class, placed between the *chefs d'atelier* and those called agents, who were concerned with supplying raw materials, and who were the parasites and blood-suckers of Lyons industry. Thus, the agents exploited the manufacturers, who in their turn oppressed the *chefs d'atelier*, and the latter were compelled to place their burden on the *compagnons*.

Nevertheless, the prosperity of Lyons had pushed any danger resulting from this situation into the background. As long as they had not been obliged to work in murderous conditions, the workers had been satisfied with their moderate wages. But circumstances which were foreign, and anterior, to the July revolution affected Lyons industry. Numerous silk establishments had been set up in Zurich, Basle, Berne and Cologne; and England, for its part, was gradually freeing itself from the industrial tribute which for a considerable time it had paid to Lyons. Another more important factor complicated the situation. Since 1824 the number of manufacturers in Lyons had grown at a rapid rate, and to the effects of foreign competition, which, after all, hardly mattered except in relation to plain material, were added the disastrous effects of internal competition, which was pushed to the most extreme limits. Some manufacturers continued to prosper, but most of them, seeing a fall in profits, passed on their losses to the *chefs d'atelier*, who placed some of their overwhelming burden on the *compagnons*. From 4 or 6 francs, the wages of the intelligent and hardworking man fell gradually to 40, 36 and 25 sous; in November 1831 the worker employed in the manufacture of plain material earned only 18 sous for an 18 hour day . . . complaint became general; *chefs d'atelier* and *compagnons* shared their troubles; and from the depths of the Croix Rousse sector, which bore the misery, at first a confused clamour was heard, but this soon became solemn, formidable and immense.

For some time the Prefect in Lyons had been a man who was skilled in soothing and handling popular passions. M. Douvier Dumolard understood immediately that no solution was possible in such a state of affairs, other than that of exterminating the working population, or satisfying its legitimate grievances. He took the latter course. . . .

M. Douvier began work . . . and on 11 October 1831 the Conseil des Prud'hommes had issued the following declaration:

'Considering that it is public knowledge that many manufacturers pay too low wages, it is expedient to establish a minimum wage.'

M. Douvier Dumolard resolved to deal with this resolution, which fell perfectly within his province; and on the 15th, under his Chairmanship, the Chamber of Commerce, the Mayor of Lyons and mayors of the three town suburbs met to discuss the situation. It became clear at this meeting that the bases of the wage structure would be discussed in a contradictory fashion by the twenty-two workers, twelve of whom had already been delegated by their comrades, and the twenty-two manufacturers whom the Chamber of Commerce designated as representatives.

M. Douvier Dumolard could have, and ought to have, fixed the tariff himself; he did not have the courage; he contented himself with putting the two parties together.

On 21 October a new meeting was convoked at the Prefecture. The 25th of October had been fixed as a date for the definitive discussion of the rates of pay.

Among the delegates of both parties discussion centred upon the crying abuses which had crept into the factories, but particularly on the reduction of wage rates; and such was the moderation of the workers that those whom twelve years before the manufacturers were pleased to pay 8 sous had their wages reduced by one eighth. . . . The agreement was signed . . . and the Conseil des Prud'hommes was charged with supervising its execution, and one day per week was fixed to listen to the complaints which might arise through bad faith.

Among the manufacturers there were men who were honest and enlightened; they regarded the tariff as a necessary brake on the cupidity of several large speculators, and as a sure method of moderating disastrous market fluctuations resulting from competition. But this was the sentiment of a minority, and the news of the establishment of a tariff was no sooner known than the anger of most of the manufacturers spilled over into recriminations and menaces.

Infractions of the tariff were increasingly numerous; the Conseil des Prud'hommes, retracting its former decisions, refused to take action against those who violated the agreement; in this extreme situation the unfortunate weavers resolved to cease all work for a week; during this period they were to walk around the town calmly and without creating any disturbance, and they agreed that they would greet all those manufacturers who had kept the agreement. But this very moderation inflated the pride of their enemies. . . .

On Sunday, 20 November, a review of the National Guard was to take place on the Place Bel-

lecour. This review brought out all the elements of the discord which existed deep within the Lyons population. . . .

Everything seemed then to announce a battle on the morrow. At the meeting held at the Prefecture . . . it was decided that the five gate-ways which led from Lyons to Croix-Rousse would be occupied from day-break; that a battalion of the National Guard of Croix-Rousse and 300 men of the line would meet at 7.00 in the morning to prevent the formation of any mobs; that four battalions of the National Guard of Lyons and one from La Guillotière would assemble at the same time in their respective positions.

On Monday, 21 November, at 7.00 or 8.00 in the morning, the workers in a body of about three or four thousand, gathered together at the Croix-Rousse.

At their head they had one of their leaders, and they were armed with sticks. Their aim was not in any sense to engage the manufacturers in battle. All they wanted was a cessation of work until the tariff was recognized, and some workers went through the workshops to bring out those of their mates who were still at work. In the meantime, fifty or sixty guards appeared, and the Commanding Officer having cried 'My friends, we must sweep away that *canaille*', they advanced with bayonets. The indignant workers dashed forward, surrounded the platoon, disarmed some of the guards, and caused some of the others to flee. Soon the groups became more numerous, but they were not hostile. They spoke only of recommencing the peaceful demonstration of 25 October. With this in mind, the weavers, joining arms and walking four abreast, descended the Grand'Côte. The Infantry of the First Legion, specially formed by the manufacturers, resolutely advanced to meet the columns. Their anger had reached its highest point and several drew their cartridges from their pouches. Towards the middle of the Grand'Côte the two groups met face to face; the Infantry fired and eight workers fell seriously wounded; immediately, the column of which they were members retreated in disorder, up the Grand'Cote and back into the Croix-Rousse. In an instant the cry went up, combatants emerged from every house, armed with picks, shovels, stones, forks; some had rifles. Some individuals ran from side to side crying 'To arms! Our brothers are being killed!' Barricades were erected by women and children in every street; the insurgents, in possession of two cannons belonging to the National Guard of the Croix-Rousse, began to march on Lyons, preceded by drums, and waving in the air a black banner, bearing the inscription. 'Live by working or die by fighting!' It was eleven o'clock. . . .

REVIEW QUESTIONS

1. How does Blanc characterize the economic structure of Lyons' industry and the factors that produced the insurrection of 1831?
2. What were the procedures to mediate disputes between manufacturers and workers, and why did they break down?
3. What is the relationship of the state with the two disputing sides?
4. What does this account suggest about the place of workers in France's political structure?

FRANCIS PLACE

The People's Charter and National Petition

As the first movement that explicitly advocated the political rights of unpropertied laborers, Chartism is a watershed moment in European political history. Following the Reform Act of 1832, which enfranchised the upper echelons of the bourgeoisie, radical democrats broke allegiance with liberals and sought ways to renew the call for political reform. With unions outlawed in 1834, reformers turned to the strategy of petitioning parliament for reform. In 1838, Francis Place, a venerable figure in English radical politics, drew up a statement entitled the People's Charter, *a set of demands presented in the* National Petition *submitted to parliament in 1839. Committees throughout England and Wales circulated the charter as a petition, and collected millions of signatures. The charter was presented to parliament in 1839 and 1842, and rejected. In 1848, with revolution rampant on the continent, Chartists organized six million signatures for a final petition; its submission to Parliament was demonstratively attended by five-hundred thousand workers. England's political establishment did not bow to Chartism, but the dignity and discipline of most Chartist demonstrations commanded respected, paving the way for trade associations in 1855 and a second Reform Act in 1867.*

From *The People's Charter and National Petition*, F. Place, J. Quigley, 1839.

Unto the Honourable the Commons of the United Kingdom of Great Britain and Ireland, in Parliament as- *sembled, the Petition of the undersigned, their suffering Countrymen,*

HUMBLY SHEWETH,

That we, your Petitioners, dwell in a land whose merchants are noted for enterprise, whose manufacturers are very skilful, and whose workmen are proverbial for their industry.

The land itself is goodly, the soil rich, and the temperature wholesome; it is abundantly furnished with the materials of commerce and trade; it has numerous and convenient harbours; in facility of internal communication it exceeds all others.

For three-and-twenty years we have enjoyed a profound peace.

Yet, with all these elements of national prosperity, and with every disposition and capacity to take advantage of them, we find ourselves overwhelmed with public and private suffering.

We are bowed down under a load of taxes; which, notwithstanding, fall greatly short of the wants of our rulers; our traders are trembling on the verge of bankruptcy; our workmen are starving; capital brings no profit, and labour no remuneration; the home of the artificer is desolate, and the warehouse of the pawnbroker is full; the workhouse is crowded, and the manufactory is deserted.

We have looked on every side, we have searched diligently, in order to find out the causes of a distress so sore and so long continued.

We can discover none in nature, or in providence.

Heaven has dealt graciously by the people; but the foolishness of our rulers has made the goodness of God of none effect.

The energies of a mighty kingdom have been wasted in building up the power of selfish and ignorant men, and its resources squandered for their aggrandisement.

The good of a party has been advanced to the sacrifice of the good of the nation; the few have governed for the interest of the few, while the interest of the many has been neglected, or insolently and tyrannously trampled upon.

It was the fond expectation of the people that a remedy for the greater part, if not for the whole, of their grievances, would be found in the Reform Act of 1832.

They were taught to regard that Act as a wise means to a worthy end; as the machinery of an improved legislation, where the will of the masses would be at length potential.

They have been bitterly and basely deceived.

The fruit, which looked so fair to the eye, has turned to dust and ashes when gathered.

The Reform Act has effected a transfer of power from one domineering faction to another, and left the people as helpless as before.

Our slavery has been exchanged for an apprenticeship to liberty, which has aggravated the painful feeling of our social degradation, by adding to it the sickening of still deferred hope.

We come before your Honourable House to tell you, with all humility, that this state of things must not be permitted to continue, that it cannot long continue without very seriously endangering the stability of the throne, and the peace of the kingdom; that if, by God's help, and all lawful and constitutional appliances, an end can be put to it, we are fully resolved that it shall speedily come to an end.

We tell your Honourable House, that the capital of the master must no longer be deprived of its due profit; that the labour of the workman must no longer be deprived of its due reward; that the laws which make food dear, and those which, by making money scarce, make labour cheap, must be abolished; that taxation must be made to fall on property, not on industry; that the good of the many, as it is the only legitimate end, so must it be the sole study of the government.

As a preliminary essential to these and other requisite changes; as the means by which alone the interests of the people can be effectually vindicated and secured, we demand that those interests be confided to the keeping of the people.

When the State calls for defenders, when it calls for money, no consideration of poverty or ignorance can be pleaded in refusal or delay of the call.

Required as we are, universally, to support and to obey the laws, nature and reason entitle us to demand that, in the making of the laws, the universal voice shall be implicitly listened to.

We perform the duties of freemen: we must have the privileges.

We Demand Universal Suffrage.

The Suffrage, to be exempt from the corruption of the wealthy and the violence of the powerful, must be secret.

The assertion of our right necessarily involves the power of its uncontrolled exercise.

We ask for the reality of a good, not for its semblance.

We Demand the Ballot.

The connection between the representatives and the people, to be beneficial, must be intimate.

The legislative and constituent powers, for correction and for instruction, ought to be brought into frequent contact.

Errors, which are comparatively light when susceptible of a speedy popular remedy, may produce the most disastrous effect when permitted to grow inveterate through years of compulsory endurance.

To public safety, as well as public confidence, frequent elections are essential.

We Demand Annual Parliaments.

With power to choose, and freedom in choosing, the range of our choice must be unrestricted.

We are compelled by the existing law, to take for our representatives, men who are incapable of appreciating our difficulties, or who have little sympathy with them; merchants who have retired from trade, and no longer feel its harassings; proprietors of land, who are alike ignorant of its evils and their cures; lawyers, by whom the honours of the Senate are sought after only as a means of obtaining notice in the Courts.

The labours of a representative, who is sedulous in the discharge of his duty, are numerous and burdensome.

It is neither just, nor reasonable, nor safe, that they should continue to be gratuitously rendered.

We demand that, in the future election of Members of your Honourable House, the approbation of the constituency shall be the sole qualification; and that, to every representative so chosen, shall be assigned, out of the public taxes, a fair and adequate remuneration for the time which he is called upon to devote to the public service.

Finally, we would most earnestly impress on your Honourable House, that this petition has not been dictated by any idle love of change; that it springs out of no inconsiderate attachment to fanciful theories—but that it is the result of much and long deliberation, and of convictions, which the events of each succeeding year tend more and more to strengthen.

The management of this mighty kingdom has hitherto been a subject for contending factions, to try their selfish experiments upon.

We have felt the consequences, in our sorrowful experience—short glimmerings of uncertain enjoyment, swallowed up by long and dark seasons of suffering.

If the self-government of the people should not remove their distresses, it will at least remove their repinings.

Universal Suffrage will, and it alone can, bring true and lasting peace to the nation; we firmly believe that it will bring prosperity.

May it, therefore, please your Honourable House to take this our Petition into your most serious consideration; and to use your utmost endeavours, by all constitutional means, to have a law passed granting to every male of lawful age, sane mind, and unconvicted of crime, the right of voting for Members of Parliament; and directing all future elections of Members of Parliament to be in the way of secret ballot; and ordaining that the duration of Parliament so chosen shall in no case exceed one year; and abolishing all property qualifications in the Members: and providing for their due remuneration while in attendance on their Parliamentary duties.

And your Petitioners, &c.

REVIEW QUESTIONS

1. What are, according to the petition, the economic and political circumstances that occasioned this plea?

2. What are the specific points of the petition and what do these demands implicitly reveal about British political culture in the 1830s?
3. How radical are these demands and why were they unacceptable to Parliament?

HEINRICH HEINE

The Silesian Weavers

In the following poem of 1844, Heinrich Heine, an exiled German writer and poet, aimed his satiric scorn at the Prussian state, which showed little aptitude in handling the widespread economic desperation of its provinces in the "hungry forties." The poem immortalized the plight of a once-proud class of Silesian linen weavers reduced to starvation wages because of mechanized cotton weaving and a declining demand in linen. In June 1844 Silesian weavers assembled before prominent merchants' houses to protest starvation wages; government intervention left eleven protesters dead. The poem, which evokes the rhythm of a loom, exemplifies a body of politically engaged literature of the 1840s that adumbrated the social necessity of revolution.

From *The Norton Anthology of World Masterpieces,* edited by Mack *et al.,* [Aaron Kramer, trans.], W.W. Norton & Company, 1992.

In gloomy eyes there wells no tear.
Grinding their teeth, they are sitting here:
"Germany, your shroud's on our loom;
And in it we weave the threefold doom.
    We weave; we weave.

"Doomed be the God who was deaf to our prayer
In Winter's cold and hunger's despair.
All in vain we hoped and bided;
He only mocked us, hoaxed, derided—
    We weave; we weave.

"Doomed be the king, the rich man's king,
Who would not be moved by our suffering,
Who tore the last coin out of our hands,

And let us be shot by his blood-thirsty bands—
    We weave; we weave.

"Doomed be the fatherland, false name,
Where nothing thrives but disgrace and shame,
Where flowers are crushed before they unfold,
Where the worm is quickened by rot and mold—
    We weave; we weave.

"The loom is creaking, the shuttle flies;
Nor night nor day do we close our eyes.
Old Germany, your shroud's on our loom,
And in it we weave the threefold doom;
    We weave; we weave!"

REVIEW QUESTIONS

1. What is the "threefold doom," and how is the poem politically charged?

2. How does Heine evoke desperation and despair?
3. What does Heine mean by "Old Germany" in the last stanza?

KARL MARX AND FRIEDRICH ENGELS

FROM Manifesto of the Communist Party

Written in 1848 to proclaim the existence of a newly constituted—and miniscule—revolutionary party, the manifesto became the most popular, widely read political pamphlet in modern European history. Written by Karl Marx and Friedrich Engels, the manifesto's success is grounded in its dramatic, confident presentation of the socialist blueprint for social development and political emancipation. Divided into three sections, the pamphlet outlines the class struggle between the bourgeoisie and the proletariat, the final stage of history under communism, and, finally, the false promises of competing socialist doctrines. The passage below is an excerpt of the first section, which boldly lays out the economic process by which the bourgeoisie and the capitalist mode of production would falter and surrender to the next stage of history.

From *The Marx-Engels Reader, Second Edition* by Robert C. Tucker. Copyright © 1978 by W.W. Norton & Company, Inc. Reprinted by permission of W.W. Norton & Company, Inc.

A spectre is haunting Europe—the spectre of Communism. All the Powers of old Europe have entered into a holy alliance to exorcise this spectre: Pope and Czar, Metternich and Guizot, French Radicals and German police-spies.

To this end, Communists of various nationalities have assembled in London, and sketched the following Manifesto, to be published in the English, French, German, Italian, Flemish and Danish languages.

*   *   *

I. Bourgeois and Proletarians

The history of all hitherto existing society is the history of class struggles.

Freeman and slave, patrician and plebeian, lord and serf, guild-master and journeyman, in a word, oppressor and oppressed, stood in constant opposition to one another, carried on an uninterrupted, now hidden, now open fight, a fight that each time ended, either in a revolutionary reconstitution of society at large, or in the common ruin of the contending classes.

In the earlier epochs of history, we find almost everywhere a complicated arrangement of society into various orders, a manifold gradation of social rank. In ancient Rome we have patricians, knights, plebeians, slaves; in the Middle Ages, feudal lords, vassals, guild-masters, journeymen, apprentices, serfs; in almost all of these classes, again, subordinate gradations.

The modern bourgeois society that has sprouted from the ruins of feudal society has not done away with clash antagonisms. It has but established new classes, new conditions of oppression, new forms of struggle in place of the old ones.

Our epoch, the epoch of the bourgeoisie, possesses, however, this distinctive feature: it has simplified the class antagonisms: Society as a whole is more and more splitting up into two great hostile camps, into two great classes directly facing each other: Bourgeoisie and Proletariat.

* * *

The feudal system of industry, under which industrial production was monopolised by closed guilds, now no longer sufficed for the growing wants of the new markets. The manufacturing system took its place. The guild-masters were pushed on one side by the manufacturing middle class; division of labour between the different corporate guilds vanished in the face of division of labour in each single workshop.

* * *

Modern industry has established the world-market, for which the discovery of America paved the way. This market has given an immense development to commerce, to navigation, to communication by land. This development has, in its turn, reacted on the extension of industry; and in proportion as industry, commerce, navigation, railways extended, in the same proportion the bourgeoisie developed, increased its capital, and pushed into the background every class handed down from the Middle Ages.

* * *

The bourgeoisie, historically, has played a most revolutionary part.

The bourgeoisie, wherever it has got the upper hand, has put an end to all feudal, patriarchal, idyllic relations. It has pitilessly torn asunder the motley feudal ties that bound man to his "natural superiors," and has left remaining no other nexus between man and man than naked self-interest, than callous "cash payment." It has drowned the most heavenly ecstasies of religious fervour, of chivalrous enthusiasm, of philistine sentimentalism, in the icy water of egotistical calculation. It has resolved personal worth into exchange value, and in place of the numberless indefeasible chartered freedoms, has set up that single, unconscionable freedom—Free Trade. In one word, for exploitation, veiled by religious and political illusions, it has substituted naked, shameless, direct, brutal exploitation.

* * *

The bourgeoisie cannot exist without constantly revolutionising the instruments of production, and thereby the relations of production, and with them the whole relations of society. Conservation of the old modes of production in unaltered form, was, on the contrary, the first condition of existence for all earlier industrial classes. Constant revolutionising of production, uninterrupted disturbance of all social conditions, everlasting uncertainty and agitation distinguish the bourgeois epoch from all earlier ones. All fixed, fast-frozen relations, with their train of ancient and venerable prejudices and opinions, are swept away, all new-formed ones become antiquated before they can ossify. All that is solid melts into air, all that is holy is profaned, and man is at last compelled to face with sober senses, his real conditions of life, and his relations with his kind.

The need of a constantly expanding market for its products chases the bourgeoisie over the whole surface of the globe. It must nestle everywhere, settle everywhere, establish connexions everywhere.

* * *

The bourgeoisie, during its rule of scarce one hundred years, has created more massive and more colossal productive forces than have all preceding generations together. Subjection of Nature's forces to man, machinery, application of chemistry to industry and agriculture, steam-navigation, railways, electric telegraphs, clearing of whole continents for cultivation, canalisation of rivers, whole populations conjured out of the ground—what earlier century had even a presentiment that such productive forces slumbered in the lap of social labour?

We see then: the means of production and of exchange, on whose foundation the bourgeoisie built itself up, were generated in feudal society. At a certain stage in the development of these means of production and of exchange, the conditions under which feudal society produced and exchanged, the feudal organisation of agriculture and manufacturing industry, in one word, the feudal relations of property became no longer compatible with the already developed productive forces; they became so many fetters. They had to be burst asunder; they were burst asunder.

Into their place stepped free competition, accompanied by a social and political constitution adapted to it, and by the economical and political sway of the bourgeois class.

*   *   *

Modern bourgeois society with its relations of production, of exchange and of property, a society that has conjured up such gigantic means of production and of exchange, is like the sorcerer, who is no longer able to control the powers of the nether world whom he has called up by his spells. For many a decade past the history of industry and commerce is but the history of the revolt of modern productive forces against modern conditions of production, against the property relations that are the conditions for the existence of the bourgeoisie and of its rule. It is enough to mention the commercial crises that by their periodical return put on its trial, each time more threateningly, the existence of the entire bourgeois society. In these crises a great part not only of the existing products, but also of the previously created productive forces, are periodically destroyed. In these crises

there breaks out an epidemic that, in all earlier epochs, would have seemed an absurdity—the epidemic of over-production. Society suddenly finds itself put back into a state of momentary barbarism; it appears as if a famine, a universal war of devastation had cut off the supply of every means of subsistence; industry and commerce seem to be destroyed; and why? Because there is too much civilisation, too much means of subsistence, too much industry, too much commerce. The productive forces at the disposal of society no longer tend to further the development of the conditions of bourgeois property; on the contrary, they have become too powerful for these conditions, by which they are fettered, and so soon as they overcome these fetters, they bring disorder into the whole of bourgeois society, endanger the existence of bourgeois property. The conditions of bourgeois society are too narrow to comprise the wealth created by them. And how does the bourgeoisie get over these crises? On the one hand by enforced destruction of a mass of productive forces; on the other, by the conquest of new markets, and by the more thorough exploitation of the old ones. That is to say, by paving the way for more extensive and more destructive crises, and by diminishing the means whereby crises are prevented.

The weapons with which the bourgeoisie felled feudalism to the ground are now turned against the bourgeoisie itself.

But not only has the bourgeoisie forged the weapons that bring death to itself; it has also called into existence the men who are to wield those weapons—the modern working class—the proletarians.

In proportion as the bourgeoisie, *i.e.*, capital, is developed, in the same proportion is the proletariat, the modern working class, developed—a class of labourers, who live only so long as they find work, and who find work only so long as their labour increases capital. These labourers, who must sell themselves piece-meal, are a commodity, like every other article of commerce, and are consequently exposed to all the vicissitudes of competition, to all the fluctuations of the market.

*   *   *

The proletariat goes through various stages of development. With its birth begins its struggle with the bourgeoisie. At first the contest is carried on by individual labourers, then by the workpeople of a factory, then by the operatives of one trade, in one locality, against the individual bourgeois who directly exploits them. They direct their attacks not against the bourgeois conditions of production, but against the instruments of production themselves; they destroy imported wares that compete with their labour, they smash to pieces machinery, they set factories ablaze, they seek to restore by force the vanished status of the workman of the Middle Ages.

*   *   *

But with the development of industry the proletariat not only increases in number; it becomes concentrated in greater masses, its strength grows, and it feels that strength more. The various interests and conditions of life within the ranks of the proletariat are more and more equalised, in proportion as machinery obliterates all distinctions of labour, and nearly everywhere reduces wages to the same low level. The growing competition among the bourgeois, and the resulting commercial crises, make the wages of the workers ever more fluctuating. The unceasing improvement of machinery, ever more rapidly developing, makes their livelihood more and more precarious; the collisions between individual workmen and individual bourgeois take more and more the character of collisions between two classes. Thereupon the workers begin to form combinations (Trades Unions) against the bourgeois; they club together in order to keep up the rate of wages; they found permanent associations in order to make provision beforehand for these occasional revolts. Here and there the contest breaks out into riots.

*   *   *

This organisation of the proletarians into a class, and consequently into a political party, is

continually being upset again by the competition between the workers themselves. But it ever rises up again, stronger, firmer, mightier. It compels legislative recognition of particular interests of the workers, by taking advantage of the divisions among the bourgeoisie itself. Thus the ten-hours' bill in England was carried.

*   *   *

Of all the classes that stand face to face with the bourgeoisie today, the proletariat alone is a really revolutionary class. The other classes decay and finally disappear in the face of Modern Industry; the proletariat is its special and essential product.

*   *   *

All previous historical movements were movements of minorities, or in the interests of minorities. The proletarian movement is the self-conscious, independent movement of the immense majority, in the interests of the immense majority. The proletariat, the lowest stratum of our present society, cannot stir, cannot raise itself up, without the whole superincumbent strata of official society being sprung into the air.

Though not in substance, yet in form, the struggle of the proletariat with the bourgeoisie is at first a national struggle. The proletariat of each country must, of course, first of all settle matters with its own bourgeoisie.

In depicting the most general phases of the development of the proletariat, we traced the more or less veiled civil war, raging within existing society, up to the point where that war breaks out into open revolution, and where the violent overthrow of the bourgeoisie lays the foundation for the sway of the proletariat.

Hitherto, every form of society has been based, as we have already seen, on the antagonism of oppressing and oppressed classes. But in order to oppress a class, certain conditions must be assured to it under which it can, at least, continue its slavish existence. The serf, in the period of serfdom, raised himself to membership in the commune, just as the petty bourgeois, under the yoke of feudal absolutism, managed to develop into a bourgeois. The modern labourer, on the contrary, instead of rising with the progress of industry, sinks deeper and deeper below the conditions of existence of his own class. He becomes a pauper, and pauperism develops more rapidly than population and wealth. And here it becomes evident, that the bourgeoisie is unfit any longer to be the ruling class in society, and to impose its conditions of existence upon society as an over-riding law. It is unfit to rule because it is incompetent to assure an existence to its slave within his slavery, because it cannot help letting him sink into such a state, that it has to feed him, instead of being fed by him. Society can no longer live under this bourgeoisie, in other words, its existence is no longer compatible with society.

The essential condition for the existence, and for the sway of the bourgeois class, is the formation and augmentation of capital; the condition for capital is wage-labour. Wage-labour rests exclusively on competition between the labourers.

The advance of industry, whose involuntary promoter is the bourgeoisie, replaces the isolation of the labourers, due to competition, by their revolutionary combination, due to association. The development of Modern Industry, therefore, cuts from under its feet the very foundation on which the bourgeoisie produces and appropriates products. What the bourgeoisie, therefore, produces, above all, is its own grave-diggers. Its fall and the victory of the proletariat are equally inevitable.

*   *   *

REVIEW QUESTIONS

1. What is the role of the bourgeoisie in world history?
2. How does Marx characterize the evolution of working-class political consciousness?
3. What does Marx mean when calling the bourgeoisie its "own gravediggers"?

SAM SMILES

FROM *Thrift*

One of the most powerful ideological buttresses of the bourgeois social order was the doctrine of self-help. The Scottish author Sam Smiles (1812–1904) achieved enormous success in a number of books that presented the virtues of self-reliance and self-education in an appealing and accessible manner. His biography of George Stephenson, the self-made railroad engineer, was followed by Self-Help *(1859), a primer on individualism that was translated into seventeen languages. The book's success spawned similar works:* Character *(1871),* Thrift *(1875), and* Duty *(1880). The following section from* Thrift *is particularly characeristic of his avuncular style and his themes of sobriety and frugality.*

From *Thrift*, S. Smiles, John Murray, 1875.

Improvidence

*   *   *

ENGLAND is one of the richest countries in the world. Our merchants are enterprizing, our manufacturers are industrious, our labourers are hardworking. There is an accumulation of wealth in the country to which past times can offer no parallel. The Bank is gorged with gold. There never was more food in the empire; there never was more money. There is no end to our manufacturing productions, for the steam-engine never tires. And yet, notwithstanding all this wealth, there is an enormous mass of poverty. Close alongside the Wealth of Nations, there gloomily stalks the Misery of Nations,—luxurious ease resting upon a dark background of wretchedness.

Parliamentary reports have again and again revealed to us the miseries endured by certain portions of our working population. They have described the people employed in factories, workshops, mines, and brick-fields, as well as in the pursuits of country life. We have tried to grapple with the evils of their condition by legislation, but it seems to mock us. Those who sink into poverty are fed, but they remain paupers. Those who feed them, feel no compassion; and those who are fed, return no gratitude. There is no bond of sympathy between the givers and the receivers. Thus the Haves and the Have-nots, the opulent and the indigent, stand at the two extremes of the social scale, and a wide gulf is fixed between them.

*   *   *

With respect to the poorer classes,* * *

They work, eat, drink, and sleep: that constitutes their life. They think nothing of providing for to-morrow, or for next week, or for next year. They abandon themselves to their sensual appetites; and make no provision whatever for the future. The thought of adversity, or of coming sorrow, or of the helplessness that comes with years and sickness, never crosses their minds. In these respects, they resemble the savage tribes, who know no better, and do no worse. Like the North American Indians, they debase themselves by the vices which accompany civilization, but make no use whatever of its benefits and advantages.

*   *   *

No one can reproach the English workman with want of industry. He works harder and more skilfully than the workman of any other country; and he might be more comfortable and independent in his circumstances, were he as prudent as he is laborious. But improvidence is unhappily the defect of the class. Even the best-paid English workmen, though earning more money than the average of professional men, still for the most part belong to the poorer classes because of their thoughtlessness. In prosperous times they are not accustomed to make provision for adverse times; and when a period of social pressure occurs, they are rarely found more than a few weeks ahead of positive want.

*   *   *

Though trade has invariably its cycles of good and bad years, like the lean and fat kine in Pharaoh's dream—its bursts of prosperity, followed by glut, panic, and distress—the thoughtless and spendthrift take no heed of experience, and make no better provision for the future. Improvidence seems to be one of the most incorrigible of faults. "There are whole neighbourhoods in the manufacturing districts," says Mr. Baker in a recent Report, "where not only are there no savings worth mentioning, but where, within a fortnight of being out of work, the workers themselves are starving for want of the merest necessaries." Not a strike takes place, but immediately the workmen are plunged in destitution; their furniture and watches are sent to the pawnshop, whilst deplorable appeals are made to the charitable, and numerous families are cast upon the poor-rates.

This habitual improvidence—though of course there are many admirable exceptions—is the real cause of the social degradation of the artizan. This too is the prolific source of social misery. But the misery is entirely the result of human ignorance and self-indulgence. For though the

Creator has ordained poverty, the poor are not necessarily, nor as a matter of fact, the miserable. Misery is the result of moral causes,—most commonly of individual vice and improvidence.

*   *   *

We have certainly had numerous "Reforms." We have had household suffrage, and vote by ballot. We have relieved the working classes of the taxes on corn, cattle, coffee, sugar, and provisions generally; and imposed a considerable proportion of the taxes from which they have been relieved on the middle and upper ranks. Yet these measures have produced but little improvement in the condition of the working people. They have not applied the principle of Reform to themselves. They have not begun at home. Yet the end of all Reform is the improvement of the individual. Everything that is wrong in Society results from that which is wrong in the Individual. When men are bad, society is bad.

*   *   *

Complaining that the laws are bad, and that the taxes are heavy, will not mend matters. Aristocratic government, and the tyranny of masters, are nothing like so injurious as the tyranny of vicious appetites. Men are easily led away by the parade of their miseries, which are for the most part voluntary and self-imposed,—the results of idleness, thriftlessness, intemperance, and misconduct. To blame others for what we suffer, is always more agreeable to our self-pride, than to blame ourselves. But it is perfectly clear that people who live from day to day without plan, without rule, without forethought—who spend all their earnings, without saving anything for the future—are preparing beforehand for inevitable distress. To provide only for the present, is the sure means of sacrificing the future. What hope can there be for a people whose only maxim seems to be, "Let us eat and drink, for to-morrow we die"?

All this may seem very hopeless; yet it is not entirely so. The large earnings of the working classes is an important point to start with. The gradual diffusion of education will help them to use, and not abuse, their means of comfortable living. The more extended knowledge of the uses of economy, frugality, and thrift, will help them to spend their lives more soberly, virtuously, and religiously.

*   *   *

REVIEW QUESTIONS

1. What does Smiles attribute to most workers' impoverished condition?
2. What worth does Smile ascribe to reform laws for the worker and what is for him the genuine source of improvement?
3. How does Smiles' argument compare with Engels' or Tristan's account of workers' improvidence?

ISABELLA BEETON

FROM *The Book of Household Management*

First published in serial form in 1859–1861, The Book of Household Management *remained in print for the remainder of the century, establishing itself as a self-evident necessity for bourgeois Victorian households. Today the book serves as an excellent example of prescriptive literature: a source documenting how proper bourgeois families ought to have led their social and domestic lives. The book provided a broad window on Victorian tastes in food, bourgeois attitudes toward other classes, and proper comportment in and outside the home. The following section is taken from the book's first chapter, which sets rules of conduct for the mistress of the household.*

From *Mrs. Beeton's Book of Household Management*, Isabella Beeton, Chancellor Press, 1982.

The Mistress

*   *   *

1. AS WITH THE COMMANDER OF AN ARMY, or the leader of any enterprise, so is it with the mistress of a house. Her spirit will be seen through the whole establishment; and just in proportion as she performs her duties intelligently and thoroughly, so will her domestics follow in her path. Of all those acquirements, which more particularly belong to the feminine character, there are none which take a higher rank, in our estimation, than such as enter into a knowledge of household duties; for on these are perpetually dependent the happiness, comfort, and well-being of a family. In this opinion we are borne out by the author of "The Vicar of Wakefield," who says: "The modest virgin, the prudent wife, and the careful matron, are much more serviceable in life than petticoated philosophers, blustering heroines, or virago queens. She who makes her husband and her children happy, who reclaims the one from vice and trains up the other to virtue, is a much greater character than ladies described in romances, whose whole occupation is to murder mankind with shafts from their quiver, or their eyes."

2. PURSUING THIS PICTURE, we may add, that to be a good housewife does not necessarily imply an abandonment of proper pleasures or amusing recreation; and we think it the more necessary to express this, as the performance of the duties of a mistress may, to some minds, perhaps seem to be incompatible with the enjoyment of life. Let us, however, now proceed to describe some of those home qualities and virtues which are necessary to the proper management of a Household, and then point out the plan which may be the most profitably pursued for the daily regulation of its affairs.

3. EARLY RISING IS ONE OF THE MOST ESSENTIAL QUALITIES which enter into good Household Management, as it is not only the parent of health, but of innumerable other advantages. Indeed, when a mistress is an early riser, it is almost certain that her house will be orderly and well-managed. On the contrary, if she remain in bed till a late hour, then the domestics, who, as we have before observed, invariably partake somewhat of their mistress's character, will surely become sluggards. To self-indulgence all are more or less disposed, and it is not to be expected that servants are freer from this fault than the heads of houses. The great Lord Chatham thus gave his advice in reference to this subject:—"I would have inscribed on the curtains of your bed, and the walls of your chamber, 'If you do not rise early, you can make progress in nothing.' "

4. CLEANLINESS IS ALSO INDISPENSABLE TO HEALTH, and must be studied both in regard to the person and the house, and all that it contains. Cold or tepid baths should be employed every morning, unless, on account of illness or other circumstances, they should be deemed objectionable. The bathing of *children* will be treated of under the head of "MANAGEMENT OF CHILDREN."

5. FRUGALITY AND ECONOMY ARE HOME VIRTUES, without which no household can prosper. Dr. Johnson says: "Frugality may be termed the daughter of Prudence, the sister of Temperance,

and the parent of Liberty. He that is extravagant will quickly become poor, and poverty will enforce dependence and invite corruption." The necessity of practising economy should be evident to every one, whether in the possession of an income no more than sufficient for a family's requirements, or of a large fortune, which puts financial adversity out of the question. We must always remember that it is a great merit in housekeeping to manage a little well. "He is a good waggoner," says Bishop Hall, "that can turn in a little room. To live well in abundance is the praise of the estate, not of the person. I will study more how to give a good account of my little, than how to make it more." In this there is true wisdom, and it may be added, that those who can manage a little well, are most likely to succeed in their management of larger matters. Economy and frugality must never, however, be allowed to degenerate into parsimony and meanness.

*　*　*

13. THE DRESS OF THE MISTRESS should always be adapted to her circumstances, and be varied with different occasions. Thus, at breakfast she should be attired in a very neat and simple manner, wearing no ornaments. If this dress should decidedly pertain only to the breakfast-hour, and be specially suited for such domestic occupations as usually follow that meal, then it would be well to exchange it before the time for receiving visitors, if the mistress be in the habit of doing so. It is still to be remembered, however, that, in changing the dress, jewellery and ornaments are not to be worn until the full dress for dinner is assumed. Further information and hints on the subject of the toilet will appear under the department of the "LADY'S-MAID."

*　*　*

16. A HOUSEKEEPING ACCOUNT-BOOK should invariably be kept, and kept punctually and precisely. The plan for keeping household accounts, which we should recommend, would be to make an entry, that is, write down into a daily diary every amount paid on that particular day, be it ever so small; then, at the end of the month, let these various payments be ranged under their specific heads of Butcher, Baker, &c.; and thus will be seen the proportions paid to each tradesman, and any one month's expenses may be contrasted with another. The housekeeping accounts should be balanced not less than once a month; so that you may see that the money you have in hand tallies with your account of it in your diary. Judge Haliburton never wrote truer words than when he said, "No man is rich whose expenditure exceeds his means, and no one is poor whose incomings exceed his outgoings."

When, in a large establishment, a housekeeper is kept, it will be advisable for the mistress to examine her accounts regularly. Then any increase of expenditure which may be apparent, can easily be explained, and the housekeeper will have the satisfaction of knowing whether her efforts to manage her department well and economically, have been successful.

17. ENGAGING DOMESTICS is one of those duties in which the judgment of the mistress must be keenly exercised. There are some respectable registry-offices, where good servants may sometimes be hired; but the plan rather to be recommended is, for the mistress to make inquiry amongst her circle of friends and acquaintances, and her tradespeople. The latter generally know those in their neighbourhood, who are wanting situations, and will communicate with them, when a personal interview with some of them will enable the mistress to form some idea of the characters of the applicants, and to suit herself accordingly.

We would here point out an error—and a grave one it is—into which some mistresses fall. They do not, when engaging a servant, expressly tell her all the duties which she will be expected to perform. This is an act of omission severely to be reprehended. Every portion of work which the maid will have to do, should be plainly stated by the mistress, and understood by the servant. If this plan is not carefully adhered to, domestic contention is almost certain to ensue, and this may not be easily settled; so that a change of servants, which is so much to be deprecated, is continually occurring.

18. In obtaining a Servant's Character, it is not well to be guided by a written one from some unknown quarter; but it is better to have an interview, if at all possible, with the former mistress. By this means you will be assisted in your decision of the suitableness of the servant for your place, from the appearance of the lady and the state of her house. Negligence and want of cleanliness in her and her household generally, will naturally lead you to the conclusion, that her servant has suffered from the influence of the bad example.

The proper course to pursue in order to obtain a personal interview with the lady is this:—The servant in search of the situation must be desired to see her former mistress, and ask her to be kind enough to appoint a time, convenient to herself, when you may call on her; this proper observance of courtesy being necessary to prevent any unseasonable intrusion on the part of a stranger. Your first questions should be relative to the honesty and general morality of her former servant; and if no objection is stated in that respect, her other qualifications are then to be ascertained. Inquiries should be very minute, so that you may avoid disappointment and trouble, by knowing the weak points of your domestic.

19. The Treatment of Servants is of the highest possible moment, as well to the mistress as to the domestics themselves. On the head of the house the latter will naturally fix their attention; and if they perceive that the mistress's conduct is regulated by high and correct principles, they will not fail to respect her. If, also, a benevolent desire is shown to promote their comfort, at the same time that a steady performance of their duty is exacted, then their respect will not be unmingled with affection, and they will be still more solicitous to continue to deserve her favour.

*   *   *

REVIEW QUESTIONS

1. What are the duties and expectations of bourgeois women?
2. What virtues and attitudes are extolled?
3. What does this document reveal about the way bourgeois families lived?
4. What are the shortcomings of such prescriptive literature?

ELIZABETH POOLE SANFORD

FROM *Woman in her Social and Domestic Character*

The widened separation of domestic and public spheres in the nineteenth century brought with it fundamental changes in the economic and social roles of bourgeois women. No longer expected to work in the productive sphere, middle-class married women took on domestic, motherly, and religious duties. Not surprisingly, characterological assumptions accompanied this role of the "angel in the house." Alongside purity, delicacy, and virtue, subservience to husbands was foremost among the traits considered desirable for women. The following excerpt from Elizabeth Poole Sanford's book (1833) is an early example of the prescriptive literature aimed at middle-class women of the Victorian era.

From *Woman in her Social and Domestic Character,* Elizabeth Poole Sanford, Bowles, 1833.

* * *

Domestic comfort is the chief source of her influence, and the greatest debt society owes her; for happiness is almost an element of virtue, and nothing conduces more to improve the character of men than domestic peace. A woman may make a man's home delightful, and may thus increase his motives for virtuous exertion. She may refine and tranquillise his mind,—may turn away his anger or allay his grief. Her smile may be the happy influence to gladden his heart, and to disperse the cloud that gathers on his brow. And she will be loved in proportion as she makes those around her happy,—as she studies their tastes, and sympathises in their feelings. In social relations adaptation is therefore the true secret of her influence.

* * *

Domestic life is a woman's sphere, and it is there that she is most usefully as well as most appropriately employed. But society, too, feels her influence, and owes to her, in great measure, its balance and its tone. She may be here a corrective of what is wrong, a moderator of what is unruly, a restraint on what is indecorous. Her presence may be a pledge against impropriety and excess, a check on vice, and a protection to virtue.

And it is her delicacy which will secure to her such an influence, and enable her to maintain it. It is the policy of licentiousness to undermine where it cannot openly attack, and to weaken by stratagem what it may not rudely assail. But a delicate woman will be as much upon her guard against the insidious as against the direct assault, and will no more tolerate the innuendo than the avowal. She will shrink from the licentiousness which is couched in ambiguous phrase or veiled in covert allusion, and from the immorality which, though it may not offend the ear, is meant to corrupt the heart. And though a depraved taste may relish the condiments of vice, or an unscrupulous palate receive them without detection, her virtue will be too sensitive not to reject the poison, and to recoil spontaneously from the touch.

Delicacy is, indeed, the point of honor in woman. And her purity of manner will ensure to her deference, and repress, more effectually than any other influence, impropriety of every kind. A delicate woman, too, will be more loved, as well as more respected, than any other; for affection can scarcely be excited, and certainly cannot long subsist, unless it is founded on esteem.

Yet such delicacy is neither prudish nor insipid. Conversation, for instance, is one great source of a woman's influence; and it is her province, and her peculiar talent, to give zest to it. She is, and ought to be, the enlivener of society: if she restrains impropriety, she may promote cheerfulness; and it is not because her conversation is innocent that it need therefore be dull. The sentiment of woman contributes much to social interest: her feeling imparts life, and her gentleness a polish.

* * *

Again, to be agreeable, a woman must avoid egotism. It is no matter how superior she is, she will never be liked, if she talks chiefly of herself. The impression of her own importance can convey no pleasure to others: on the contrary, as a desire for distinction is always mutual, a sense of inferiority must be depressing.

If we would converse pleasingly, we must endeavor to set others at ease: and it is not by flattery that we can succeed in doing so, but by a courteous and kind address, which delicately avoids all needless irritation, and endeavors to infuse that good humor of which it is itself the result.

In woman this is a Christian duty. How often should they suppress their own claims rather than interfere with those of others! How often should they employ their talent in developing that of their associates, and not for its own display! How invariably should they discard pretension, and shun even the appearance of conceit; and seek to imbibe the spirit of that lovely religion, of which sympathy is the characteristic feature, and humility the pre-eminent grace!

* * *

It is seldom, indeed, that women are great proficients. The *chefs-d'œuvre* of the sculptress need the polish of the master chisel; and the female pencil has never yet limned the immortal forms of beauty. The mind of woman is, perhaps, incapable of the originality and strength requisite for the sublime. Even Saint Cecilia exists only in an elegant legend, and the poetry of music, if often felt and expressed, has seldom been conceived by a female adept. But the practical talents of women are far from contemptible; and they may be both the encouragers and the imitators of genius. They should not grasp at too much, nor be content with superficial attainment; they should not merely daub a few flowers, or hammer out a few tunes, or trifle away their time in inept efforts, which at best claim only indulgence; but they should do well what they do attempt, and do it without affectation or display.

*   *   *

REVIEW QUESTIONS

1. What are the character traits assigned to women, and for what goals should women strive?
2. What attributes constitute the domestic sphere of women?
3. What is the ideal relationship between husband and wife, and how is this justified?

21 ❧ THE RISE OF LIBERALISM

At the core of most discussions explaining change from the traditional to the modern world lies an evolving form of liberalism. After the Glorious Revolution in England, elements of a liberal social contract emerged, many of which have been accented in earlier chapters: individual liberties guaranteed by constitutional law; the sanctity of private property; unrestricted movement of individuals, ideas, and goods; and, finally, social advancement based on merit. Such beliefs irreparably undermined the social foundations of the old regime.

The principles of the Enlightenment and liberalism largely overlap. Liberalism, for example, inherited the Enlightenment's emphasis on reason, social utility, pragmatic reform, and aversion to arbitrary rule. Above all, both embraced the indomitable belief in progress. The French Revolution, however, significantly affected liberalism's development. Shaped by the experiences of the Terror and Napoleonic demagoguery, liberals reasserted the Lockian emphasis on the limits of power that public authority held over the individual. Governments based upon popular will, they argued, could be as despotic as absolutist monarchy, for they sacrificed individual liberties in the name of general welfare and collective happiness. For liberals, the whole could never be greater than the sum of its parts; the irreducible unit of a free civil society remained the individual, not the general will. Following classical economic theory, liberals averred that the "invisible hand" of individual self-interest best secured the greater good of society. Liberalism further distinguished itself from democracy by rejecting universal human suffrage, assigning those classes lacking property and education merely passive rights of citizenship. Consequently, liberalism evolved into a solidly bourgeois ideology.

For the traditional elite, liberalism remained a subversive threat. Its advocacy of constitutions, civil liberties, and centralized government challenged the post-Napoleonic restoration of dynastic legitimacy and aristocratic privilege. Because liberals in the Italian, German, and eastern European states coupled their ideals of constitutionalism with a unified nation-state, the doctrine was doubly alarming. In the first half of the nineteenth century, conservative statesmen and rulers vigorously strove to contain the spread of liberal-national ideals.

The economic and cultural dimensions of liberalism are particularly important in understanding the doctrine's impact on European society. Economically, Europeans largely associated liberalism as the promoter of laissez-faire capitalism. Liberals believed that society and government were compelled to acquiesce in the natural laws of the market. Between 1840 and 1870 the doctrine of free trade assumed the status of a moral imperative for British and European liberals, who associated material wealth with the advance of civilization. If governments minimized their presence in the marketplace, liberals argued, industry and commerce could expand markets, lower the costs of food and goods, and thus lift the diligent out of privation. Culturally, liberalism advocated a secular civil society in which religion played little or no role in public affairs. Liberals viewed the Catholic Church as "obscurantist," an outmoded institution that hindered the diffusion of rational, materialist knowledge. Education, the battle for childrens' minds, was a particularly devisive issue. Denying the church its traditional role as educator by instituting state-supervised school systems with national curricula and state-trained teachers became a central plank in the platform of many liberal parties.

In all its facets, liberalism was a critical agent of change in the first century of the modern era after 1789. By locating its role in such overarching themes as individualism, constitutional rights, capitalism, free trade, nationalism, and secular statebuilding, one sees liberalism as a preponderant force in nineteenth-century civil society.

Marquis de Condorcet

FROM A Sketch for the Historical Picture of the Progress of the Human Mind

Marie Jean Antoine Nicholas de Caritat, Marquis de Condorcet (1743–1794), linked the traditions of the Enlightenment and liberalism with his unshakable belief in the triumph of reason, civil liberties, the rights of the individual, and rational social organization to ensure progress and prosperity for humankind. Condorcet, a mathme-

tician and member of the Academy of Science, served as President of the Legislative Assembly in the first phase of constitutional monarchy after the French Revolution. His criticism of the republican constitution in 1793 provoked a warrant for his arrest; while in hiding he wrote the following treatise. He was discovered, arrested, and imprisoned, where he died in 1794.

The Ninth Stage

FROM *Descartes to the foundation of the French Republic*

. . . This sketch of the progress of philosophy and of the dissemination of enlightenment . . . brings us up to the stage when the influence of progress upon public opinion, of public opinion upon nations or their leaders, suddenly ceases to be a slow, imperceptible affair, and produces a revolution in the whole order of several nations, a certain earnest of the revolution that must one day include in its scope the whole of the human race.

After long periods of error, after being led astray by vague or incomplete theories, publicists have at last discovered the true rights of man and how they can all be deduced from the single truth, that *man is a sentient being, capable of reasoning and of acquiring moral ideas.*

They have seen that the maintenance of these rights was the sole object of men's coming together in political societies, and that the social art is the art of guaranteeing the preservation of these rights and their distribution in the most equal fashion over the largest area. It was felt that in every society the means of assuring the rights of the individual should be submitted to certain common rules, but that the authority to choose these means and to determine these rules could belong only to the majority of the members of the society itself; for in making this choice the individual cannot follow his own reason without subjecting others to it, and the will of the majority is the only mark of truth that can be accepted by all without loss of equality.

*   *   *

Thus, an understanding of the natural rights of man, the belief that these rights are inalienable and indefeasible, a strongly expressed desire for liberty of thought and letters, of trade and industry, and for the alleviation of the people's suffering, for the proscription of all penal laws against religious dissenters and the abolition of torture and barbarous punishments, the desire for a milder system of criminal legislation and jurisprudence which should give complete security to the innocent, and for a simpler civil code, more in conformance with reason and nature, indifference in all matters of religion which now were relegated to the status of superstitions and political impostures, a hatred of hypocrisy and fanaticism, a contempt for prejudice, zeal for the propagation of enlightenment: all these principles, gradually filtering down from philosophical works to every class of society whose education went beyond the catechism and the alphabet, became the common faith, the badges of all those who were neither Machiavellians nor fools. In some countries these principles formed a public opinion sufficiently widespread for even the mass of the people to show a willingness to be guided by it and to obey it. For a feeling of humanity, a tender and active compassion for all the misfortunes that afflict the human race and a horror of anything that in the actions of public institutions, or governments, or individuals, adds new pains to those that are natural and inevitable, were the natural consequences of those principles; and this feeling exhaled from all the writings and all the speeches of the time, and already its happy influence had been felt in the laws and the public institutions, even of those nations still subject to despotism.

*   *   *

Up to this stage, the sciences had been the birthright of very few; they were now becoming common property and the time was at hand when their elements, their principles, and their simpler methods would become truly popular. For it was then, at last, that their application to the arts and their influence on men's judgment would become of truly universal utility. . . .

We shall show how the printing press multiplies and spreads abroad even those works primarily intended to be performed or read aloud in public, and so allows them to reach incomparably more people as readers than they ever could as mere listeners; we shall show how, as a consequence of the way that any important decision taken in a large assembly is now determined by what the members of that assembly have learnt through the written word, a new art of persuasion has arisen amongst the moderns, different from that practised by the ancients, a difference that is analogous to the differences in the effects produced, in the means employed between this modern art and that of the ancients. . . .

Turning now our attention to the human race in general, we shall show how the discovery of the correct method of procedure in the sciences, the growth of scientific theories, their application to every part of the natural world, to the subject of every human need, the lines of communication established between one science and another, the great number of men who cultivate the sciences, and most important of all, the spread of printing, how together all these advances ensure that no science will ever fall below the point it has reached. We shall point out that the principles of philosophy, the slogans of liberty, the recognition of the true rights of man and his real interests, have

spread through far too great a number of nations, and now direct in each of them the opinions of far too great a number of enlightened men, for us to fear that they will ever be allowed to relapse into oblivion. And indeed what reason could we have for fear, when we consider that the languages most widely spoken are the languages of the two peoples who enjoy liberty to the fullest extent and who best understand its principles, and that no league of tyrants, no political intrigues, could prevent the resolute defence in these two languages, of the rights of reason and of liberty?

*   *   *

The Tenth Stage

The future progress of the human mind

*   *   *

If we glance at the state of the world today we see first of all that in Europe the principles of the French constitution are already those of all enlightened men. We see them too widely propagated, too seriously professed, for priests and despots to prevent their gradual penetration even into the hovels of their slaves; there they will soon awaken in these slaves the remnants of their common sense and inspire them with that smouldering indignation which not even constant humiliation and fear can smother in the soul of the oppressed. . . .

Can we doubt that either common sense or the senseless discords of European nations will add to the effects of the slow but inexorable progress of their colonies, and will soon bring about the independence of the New World? And then will not the European population in these colonies, spreading rapidly over that enormous land, either civilize or peacefully remove the savage nations who still inhabit vast tracts of its land? . . .

The time will therefore come when the sun

will shine only on free men who know no other master but their reason; when tyrants and slaves, priests and their stupid or hypocritical instruments will exist only in works of history and on the stage; and when we shall think of them only to pity their victims and their dupes; to maintain ourselves in a state of vigilance by thinking on their excesses; and to learn how to recognize and so to destroy, by force of reason, the first seeds of tyranny and superstition, should they ever dare to reappear amongst us.

In looking at the history of societies we shall have had occasion to observe that there is often a great difference between the rights that the law allows its citizens and the rights that they actually enjoy, and, again, between the equality established by political codes and that which in fact exists amongst individuals: and we shall have noticed that these differences were one of the principal causes of the destruction of freedom in the ancient republics, of the storms that troubled them, and of the weakness that delivered them over to foreign tyrants.

These differences have three main causes: inequality in wealth; inequality in status between the man whose means of subsistence are hereditary and the man whose means are dependent on the length of his life, or, rather, on that part of his life in which he is capable of work; and, finally, inequality in education.

. . . These three sorts of real inequality must constantly diminish without however disappearing altogether: for they are the result of natural and necessary causes which it would be foolish and dangerous to wish to eradicate; and one could not even attempt to bring about the entire disappearance of their effects without introducing even more fecund sources of inequality, without striking more direct and more fatal blows at the rights of man. . . .

* * *

REVIEW QUESTIONS

1. For Condorcet, what is the ideal political order?
2. How and why will civilization progress?
3. What is the place of the individual in society?

MARY WOLLSTONECRAFT

FROM *The Vindication of the Rights of Woman*

Mary Wollstonecraft (1759–1797), a teacher and writer, wrote this essay as a critical response to the French Revolution. An enthusiastic supporter of the revolution, she was nonetheless angered that the national assembly did not extend the same liberties to women as to men. Her essay, appealing to reason, utility, and natural law, exhorted both men and women to reform education for women and enable them to participate in civil society as useful members. Scorned as a radical francophile by contemporaries, her essay convincingly applies liberal reasoning to the cause of women at a critical juncture in European history.

From *The Vindication of the Rights of Woman*, M. Wollstonecraft, W.W. Norton & Company, 1970.

AFTER considering the historic page, and viewing the living world with anxious solicitude, the most melancholy emotions of sorrowful indignation have depressed my spirits, and I have sighed when obliged to confess that either Nature has made a great difference between man and man, or that the civilization which has hitherto taken place in the world has been very partial. I have turned over various books written on the subject of education, and patiently observed the conduct of parents and the management of schools; but what has been the result?— a profound conviction that the neglected education of my fellow-creatures is the grand source of the misery I deplore, and that women, in particular, are rendered weak and wretched by a variety of concurring causes, originating from one hasty conclusion. The conduct and manners of women, in fact, evidently prove that their minds are not in a healthy state; for, like the flowers which are planted in too rich a soil, strength and usefulness are sacrificed to beauty; and the flaunting leaves, after having pleased a fastidious eye, fade, disregarded on the stalk, long before the season when they ought to have arrived at maturity. One cause of this barren blooming I attribute to a false system of education, gathered from the books written on this subject by men who, considering females rather as women than human creatures, have been more anxious to make them alluring mistresses than affectionate wives and rational mothers; and the understanding of the sex has been so bubbled by this specious homage, that the civilized women of the present century, with a few exceptions, are only anxious to inspire love, when they ought to cherish a nobler ambition, and by their abilities and virtues exact respect.

In a treatise, therefore, on female rights and manners, the works which have been particularly written for their improvement must not be overlooked, especially when it is asserted, in direct terms, that the minds of women are enfeebled by false refinement; that the books of instruction, written by men of genius, have had the same tendency as more frivolous productions; and that, in the true style of Mahometanism, they are treated as a kind of subordinate beings, and not as a part of the human species, when improvable reason is allowed to be the dignified distinction which raises men above the brute creation, and puts a natural sceptre in a feeble hand.

Yet, because I am a woman, I would not lead my readers to suppose that I mean violently to agitate the contested question respecting the quality or inferiority of the sex; but as the subject lies in my way, and I cannot pass it over without subjecting the main tendency of my reasoning to misconstruction, I shall stop a moment to deliver, in a few words, my opinion. In the government of the physical world it is observable that the female in point of strength is, in general, inferior to the male. This is the law of Nature; and it does not appear to be suspended or abrogated in favour of woman. A degree of physical superiority cannot, therefore, be denied, and it is a noble prerogative! But not content with this natural pre-eminence, men endeavour to sink us still lower, merely to render us alluring objects for a moment; and women, intoxicated by the adoration which men, under the influence of their senses, pay them, do not seek to obtain a durable interest in their hearts, or to become the friends of the fellow-creatures who find amusement in their society.

I am aware of an obvious inference. From every quarter have I heard exclamations against masculine women, but where are they to be found? If by this appellation men mean to inveigh against their ardour in hunting, shooting, and gaming, I shall most cordially join in the cry; but if it be against the imitation of manly virtues, or, more properly speaking, the attainment of those talents and virtues, the exercise of which ennobles the human character, and which raises females in the scale of animal being, when they are comprehensively termed mankind, all those who view them with a philosophic eye must, I should think, wish with me, that they may every day grow more and more masculine.

This discussion naturally divides the subject. I shall first consider women in the grand light of human creatures, who, in common with men, are placed on this earth to unfold their faculties; and afterwards I shall more particularly point out their peculiar designation.

I wish also to steer clear of an error which many respectable writers have fallen into; for the instruction which has hitherto been addressed to women, has rather been applicable to *ladies*, if the little indirect advice that is scattered through 'Sandford and Merton' be excepted; but, addressing my sex in a firmer tone, I pay particular attention to those in the middle class, because they appear to be in the most natural state. Perhaps the seeds of false refinement, immorality, and vanity, have ever been shed by the great. Weak, artificial beings, raised above the common wants and affections of their race, in a premature unnatural manner, undermine the very foundation of virtue, and spread corruption through the whole mass of society! As a class of mankind they have the strongest claim to pity; the education of the rich tends to render them vain and helpless, and the unfolding mind is not strengthened by the practice of those duties which dignify the human character. They only live to amuse themselves, and by the same law which in Nature invariably produces certain effects, they soon only afford barren amusement.

But as I purpose taking a separate view of the different ranks of society, and of the moral character of women in each, this hint is for the present sufficient; and I have only alluded to the subject because it appears to me to be the very essence of an introduction to give a cursory account of the contents of the work it introduces.

My own sex, I hope, will excuse me, if I treat them like rational creatures, instead of flattering their *fascinating* graces, and viewing them as if they were in a state of perpetual childhood, unable to stand alone. I earnestly wish to point out in what true dignity and human happiness consists. I wish to persuade women to endeavour to acquire strength, both of mind and body, and to convince them that the soft phrases, susceptibility of heart, delicacy of sentiment, and refinement of taste, are almost synonymous with epithets of weakness, and that those beings who are only the objects of pity, and that kind of love which has been termed its sister, will soon become objects of contempt.

Dismissing, then, those pretty feminine phrases, which the men condescendingly use to soften our slavish dependence, and despising that weak elegancy of mind, exquisite sensibility, and sweet docility of manners, supposed to be the sexual characteristics of the weaker vessel, I wish to show that elegance is inferior to virtue, that the first object of laudable ambition is to obtain a character as a human being, regardless of the distinction of sex, and that secondary views should be brought to this simple touchstone.

This is a rough sketch of my plan; and should I express my conviction with the energetic emotions that I feel whenever I think of the subject, the dictates of experience and reflection will be felt by some of my readers. Animated by this important object, I shall disdain to cull my phrases or polish my style. I aim at being useful, and sincerity will render me unaffected; for wishing rather to persuade by the force of my arguments than dazzle by the elegance of my language, I shall not waste my time in rounding periods, or in fabricating the turgid bombast of artificial feelings, which, coming from the head, never reach the heart. I shall be employed about things, not words! and, anxious to render my sex more respectable members of society, I shall try to avoid that flowery diction which has slided from essays into novels, and from novels into familiar letters and conversations.

These pretty superlatives, dropping glibly from the tongue, vitiate the taste, and create a kind of sickly delicacy that turns away from simple unadorned truth; and a deluge of false sentiments and overstretched feelings, stifling the natural emotions of the heart, render the domestic pleasures insipid, that ought to sweeten the exercise of those severe duties, which educate a rational and immortal being for a nobler field of action.

The education of women has of late been more attended to than formerly; yet they are still reckoned a frivolous sex, and ridiculed or pitied by the writers who endeavour by satire or instruction to improve them. It is acknowledged that they spend many of the first years of their lives in acquiring a smattering of accomplishments; meanwhile strength of body and mind are sacrificed to libertine notions of beauty, to the desire of establishing themselves—the only way women can rise in the world—by marriage. And this desire making mere animals of them, when they marry they act as such children may be expected to act—they dress, they paint, and nickname God's creatures. Surely these weak beings are only fit for a seraglio! Can they be expected to govern a family with judgement, or take care of the poor babes, whom they bring into the world?

If, then, it can be fairly deduced from the present conduct of the sex, from the prevalent fondness for pleasure which takes place of ambition and those nobler passions that open and enlarge the soul, that the instruction which women have hitherto received has only tended, with the constitution of civil society, to render them insignificant objects of desire—mere propagators of fools!—if it can be proved that in aiming to accomplish them, without cultivating their understandings, they are taken out of their sphere of duties, and made ridiculous and useless when the short-lived bloom of beauty is over, I presume that *rational* men will excuse me for endeavouring to persuade them to become more masculine and respectable.

Indeed the word masculine is only a bugbear; there is little reason to fear that women will acquire too much courage or fortitude, for their apparent inferiority with respect to bodily strength must render them in some degree dependent on men in the various relations of life; but why should it be increased by prejudices that give a sex to virtue, and confound simple truths with sensual reveries?

Women are, in fact, so much degraded by mistaken notions of female excellence, that I do not mean to add a paradox when I assert that this artificial weakness produces a propensity to tyrannize, and gives birth to cunning, the natural opponent of strength, which leads them to play off those contemptible infantine airs that undermine esteem even whilst they excite desire. Let men become more chaste and modest, and if women do not grow wiser in the same ratio it will be clear that they have weaker understandings. It seems scarcely necessary to say that I now speak of the sex in general. Many individuals have more sense than their male relatives; and, as nothing preponderates where there is a constant struggle for an equilibrium without it has naturally more gravity, some women govern their husbands without degrading themselves, because intellect will always govern.

Review Questions

1. Why is Wollstonecraft's emphasis on education critical for her argument?
2. What are the similarities and differences between this essay and Olympe de Gouges's declaration?
3. At which social classes is this essay aimed, and what are Wollstonecraft's criticisms of the women from these classes?
4. What distinctions does Wollstonecraft make between men and women, and what is her point in drawing such distinctions?

BENJAMIN CONSTANT

FROM The Principles of Politics

The political writings of Benjamin Constant de Rebecque (1767–1830) addressed critical issues of popular sovereignty and individual liberty in the immediate post-revolutionary period. An advocate of parliamentary monarchy, Constant sought in his many essays to check the abuses of the general will against individual rights. The following passage, written weeks before Napoleon's final defeat at Waterloo, constitutes a classic liberal argument, distinguishing between sovereignty, authority, and individual freedom.

Of the Sovereignty of the People

The error of those who, sincere in their love of freedom, have attributed unlimited power to the sovereign people, comes of the manner in which their ideas about politics have been formed. They have seen in history a few men, or even one man alone, possessed of immense and very harmful power; and their anger has turned against the possessors of power and not against power itself. Instead of destroying it, they dreamt only of displacing it. It was a scourge, but they looked upon it as something to be conquered. They endowed society as a whole with it. And it passed perforce from the whole to the majority, and from the majority into the hands of a few men, and often of one man alone; and it has done as much harm as before. Manifold examples, objections, arguments and facts have been used to condemn all political institutions.

Certainly, in a society where the people's sovereignty is accepted as a basic principle, no man and no class may subject the others to his or their particular will; but it is not true that society as a whole possesses over its members an unlimited sovereignty.

The generality of citizens constitute the sovereign in the sense that no individual, no fraction, no partial association can assume the sovereignty unless it has been delegated to him or them. But it does not follow that the citizens generally, or those in whom they have vested the sovereignty, may dispose absolutely of the lives of individuals. On the contrary, there is a part of life which necessarily remains personal and independent, which of right is beyond the competence of society. Sovereignty can be only limited and relative. At the point where personal independence and life begin, the jurisdiction of the sovereign ceases. If society goes beyond this point, it is as guilty as the despot whose only title is the sword of the destroyer; society cannot pass beyond the sphere of its competence without usurpation, nor the majority without factiousness. The assent of the majority is not always enough to make its acts legitimate: there are some which nothing can justify. When authority commits such actions, it matters little from what source the authority is alleged to come, or whether it belongs to an individual or a nation; even when it is exercised by the whole nation, except for the citizen oppressed, it is not the more legitimate for that.

Rousseau failed to recognize this truth, and his error has made of his *Social Contract*, so often invoked in favour of liberty, the most terrible support of all kinds of despotism. He defines the contract made by society with its members as the complete and unreserved alienation of each individual with all his rights to the community. To reassure us about the consequences of so absolute a surrender of all aspects of our life to an abstract being, he tells us that the sovereign, that is to say the social body, cannot injure either its members in general or any one of them in particular; that, since each gives himself entire, the condition is the same for all, and none has an interest in making it burdensome to others; that each in giving himself to all gives himself to nobody, that each acquires over all his associates the rights which he grants to them, and gains the equivalent of all that he loses together with greater power to preserve what he has. But he forgets that all these preservative attributes which he confers on the abstract being he calls the sovereign derive from its including within it all individuals without exception. But, as soon as the sovereign has to make use of the power belonging to him—that is to say, as soon as authority has to be organized for practical purposes—the sovereign, since he cannot himself exercise it, must delegate it; and all these attributes disappear. Since the action taken in the name of all is willy nilly done by one person or by a few, it is not true that in giving oneself to all one gives oneself to no one; on the contrary, one gives oneself to those who act in the name of all. Whence it follows that, in giving oneself entire, one does not enter a condition which is equal for all, because there are some who alone benefit from the sacrifice of the others. It is not true that no one has an interest in making the condition a burden to others, since there are associates to whom the condition does not apply. It is not true that all the associates acquire over others the rights which they grant to them over themselves; they do not all gain the equivalent of what they lose, and what results from their sacrifice is, or may be, the es-

tablishment of a power which takes from them what they have.

Rousseau himself took fright at these consequences. Appalled by the immensity of the social power he had created, he did not know in what hands to place that monstrous power, and could find as a safeguard against the danger inseparable from sovereignty thus conceived only an expedient which made its exercise impossible. He declared that sovereignty could not be alienated or delegated or represented; which amounted to saying that it could not be exercised. This was to annihilate the principle he had just proclaimed. . . .

Where sovereignty is unlimited, there is no way of protecting the individual against the government. It is in vain that you claim to subject governments to the general will. It is they who give utterance to that will, and all precautions become illusory.

The people, says Rousseau, are sovereign in one respect, and subjects in another: but in practice these two respects merge into one another. Authority can easily oppress the people taken as subjects in order to compel them in their sovereign capacity to express a will prescribed to them by authority.

No political organization can remove this danger. It is in vain that you separate the powers: if the sum total of power is unlimited, the separate powers have only to make an alliance, and there is despotism without a remedy. What matters is not that our rights should be inviolable by one power without the approval of another, but that the violation be forbidden to all the powers. It is not enough that executive agents should have to invoke a grant of authority by the legislator; the legislator must be able to grant them authority to act only within a legitimate sphere. It is of little moment that the executive power should not have the right to act without the backing of the law, if limits are not set to that backing; if it is not laid down that there are matters about which the lawmaker may not make law—or, in other words, that sovereignty is limited, and there are decisions which neither the people nor their delegates have the right to make.

It is this that must be proclaimed; this, the important truth, the essential principle, to be established.

No authority on earth is unlimited; whether it resides in the people, or in the men who claim to be their representatives, or in kings, whatever their title to rule, or in the law, which, being only the expression of the people's or the prince's will (depending on the form of government), must be confined within the same limits as that will.

Citizens possess rights independently of all social or political authority, and every authority which violates these rights becomes illegitimate. These rights are freedom of person, of religious worship, and of opinion (including its publication), the enjoyment of property, and security against arbitrary power. No one in authority can infringe these rights without destroying his own title to authority. . . .

We owe to public tranquillity many sacrifices; and we should be morally to blame if, by holding inflexibly to our rights, we resisted all laws which appeared to us to impair them; but no duty binds us to those pretended laws whose corrupting influence threatens the noblest aspects of life, to the laws which not only restrict our legitimate rights but require of us actions contrary to the eternal principles of justice and compassion which man cannot cease to observe without degrading and belying his nature.

So long as a law, though a bad one, does not tend to deprave us, so long as the encroachments of authority require only sacrifices which do not make us vile or cruel, we can submit. We then make compromises which affect only ourselves. But if the law should require us to tread underfoot our affections or our duties; if, on the pretext of an extraordinary and factitious sacrifice, in favour either of the monarchy or the republic (as the case may be), it should forbid loyalty to friends in misfortune; if it should require us to betray our allies, or even to persecute vanquished enemies, anathema upon the promotion of injustices and crimes thus covered with the name of law!

Whenever a law appears unjust, it is a positive, general unrestricted duty not to become an executor of it. This force of inertia entails neither upheavals, nor revolutions, nor disorders.

Nothing justifies the man who gives his support to a law which he believes is iniquitous. . . .

*   *   *

REVIEW QUESTIONS

1. What are Constant's reservations about sovereignty of the people and what are his criticisms of Rousseau?
2. According to Constant, on what individual liberties may no authority trespass?
3. What justifications does Constant cite for obeying and breaking laws?

KLEMENS VON METTERNICH

Letter, 24 June 1832

Prince Klemens Lothar von Metternich (1773–1859), who served the Austrian Empire from 1809 to 1848, ranked as one of the most influential statesmen of his time. Following the defeat of Napoleon, Metternich, a staunch conservative, sought to restore aristocratic privilege and legitimate royal authority in Europe. His efforts to use laws, police surveillance, and military intervention to uncover and suppress movements advocating constitutional liberties and national unity were unsurpassed. In 1819, Metternich authorized the Carlsbad Decrees, laws in the German Confederation that clamped down on the liberal politics of students and secret political associations. In July 1832 these were reenforced with the Six Articles, which strengthened censorship and prohibited all associations, assemblies, and festivals with political character. Metternich wrote the following letter on the eve of the Six Article's promulgation. In this missive Metternich instructs his ambassador how to justify these laws to the British government, whose regard for civil liberties offered potential problems to Metternich's German policies.

From *Memoirs of Prince Metternich, Volume III, 1830–35,* translated by Gerard Smith, Harper and Bros., 1882

Metternich to Neumann in London, Vienna, June 24, 1832

The position of the German Governments has at all times deservedly engaged our anxious care and attention.

Germany has long suffered from the evil which is now spread over the whole of Europe. In some sense, the evil may be said to have been in existence there previous to the outbreak in France of 1789. The sect of the *Illuminati,* the first *Radical* association, owed its existence, long before that time, to the weakness of the Bavarian Government and the complicity of several men who were among its members from the first. This sect, in spite of all endeavors on the part of the same Government to put it down by the severest measures of repression, has never ceased to exist from that time forward, and has assumed in turn, according to circumstances and the requirements of the moment, the names of *Tugendbund, Burschenschaft,* etc.

Several Princes have committed the unpardonable error of giving their States institutions copied from those of France. This error they followed up by a second, in preserving, side by side with the new institutions, the *Dienst-Pragmatik* (Pragmatic of Service), an institution of great efficacy under the laws of the old German Empire, but absolutely incompatible with institutions of a different character. The modern representative system, which makes Ministers responsible *to the nation* for the acts of the Government, necessarily demands that the *employés* should be removable at will; in the German Constitutional States, the Ministers are *responsible* and the *employés* of all classes are *not removable.* Thence the Governments have no longer the means of enforcing obedience among their own agents, and experience shows that in these countries obedience still exists among the people, but that it has long since disappeared among those who form the intermediate class between the throne and the people. If to all this we add the extraordinary influence exercised by the Universities at all times in Germany, the respect which was paid to those learned bodies, and the extraordinary privileges which they never ceased to enjoy, it is evident that nothing more was needed than the liberty of the Press and the right of public discussion, to reduce the German States to the condition in which we now find them.

I have entered into these details with a view to presenting, in as brief a space as possible, a sketch which it may be well to bring before the English Cabinet. That Cabinet, engrossed by very different cares, has no means of forming an accurate judgment on the condition of things in Germany, and yet the fate which awaits this part of the Continent will decide that of the whole of Europe.

Our action upon the Confederation, as, in fact, any influence which the Emperor permits himself to exert on foreign political bodies, has consistently been confined within strictly lawful limits. Austria is a member of the Confederation. As such she holds the foremost place in it, and her representative acts as President of the Diet. Like Prussia, Bavaria, etc., she has only a single vote.

Our constant endeavor has been to maintain order in the proceedings of this central body, and to preach *Justice* and *Strength* to the German Courts. The evil which has been done and which has reached such a pitch of intensity, is none of our doing. It is the result of the grave errors into which the German Governments have fallen, and is partly owing to their want of judgment. When this defeat is aggravated by a vicious system of legislation, it becomes difficult to uphold and ensure public order. If this be the case at all times, what far greater proportions does the danger threaten to assume, in face of the examples which France continues to set before Germany, and an influence so potent as that of the Directing Committee has become since the Revolution of 1830! The affiliation between the German sectaries and those of Paris is no longer a mystery; it was celebrated by a public banquet, under the presidency of General Lafayette, on the same day that the Hambach scandal came upon the Governments like a final trump of warning. The question which the latter have to decide is, whether they shall continue to exist or yield to inevitable ruin. The German Princes who have been most blind hitherto have now opened their eyes to their true position, and are firmly resolved not to let themselves be beguiled into taking the course which foolish or perfidious advisers have marked out for them.

They applied to us. The Emperor, convinced as he had been for a long time of the existence of the danger, had foreseen this contingency. A full understanding had been come to with the King of Prussia, and the two monarchs have shown no hesitation as to the means to be employed. The complementary Act of 1820 contained all that was requisite. The German Governments have had their attention called to laws which already existed, and it is these which are about to be set in motion at Frankfort.

You will find, Baron, in the documents enclosed ample information as to the course affairs are about to take at the Diet. That course is clear and decided; in adopting it there will be no need to have recourse to exceptional laws or measures; there is nothing in it against which an objection could be raised, and its effects should be proportionably great.

Be pleased to put these facts before Lord Palmerston in a friendly way. I should be loath to take up his time, occupied as he is by other pressing cares, by inviting his attention to legislative details, to which, moreover, the fullest publicity will shortly be given. It is from a political point of view that the British Cabinet should be interested in the success of the undertaking. The question to be settled reduces itself to this: whether Germany is to remain an independent country, or whether she is to be absorbed into the French Revolution and so become dependent on France. If the members of the Confederation only know how to do their duty, their triumph is assured, for it will be at the same time the triumph of patriotism and true liberty.

REVIEW QUESTIONS

1. What is the "evil . . . spread over the whole of Europe" and why is Germany particularly beset with this "evil"?
2. What is Metternich's opinion of the press, public discussion, and the universities?
3. What political activities does Metternich find so threatening and why is this so?

W. J. FOX

FROM *Speech on Corn Laws*

*Following the enfranchisement of the British middle class in 1832, the greatest indi-
cator of bourgeois political influence was the repeal of the Corn Laws in 1846. In
1815, parliamentary landed interests levied tariffs on cheap imported wheat to ensure that domestic grain would not be undersold, thus promoting the continued
prosperity of England's landed elite. Businessmen, however, sharply criticized the
tariff. They argued that it kept bread prices artificially high and, in turn, raised the
cost level of a worker's sustenance, by which employers set wages. Claiming that
the Corn Laws blunted the competitive edge of British manufactured exports, business interests formed the Anti-Corn Law League in 1839. This pressure group tirelessly promoted free trade as a policy benefiting the entire nation. Bad harvests and
the specter of famine in the 1840s magnified the league's charge that cheap, plentiful
bread was a moral necessity. The following Anti-Corn Law speech from 1844 typifies the arguments of free traders.*

From *Speech on Corn Laws*, W. J. Fox, Augustus M. Kelley, 1903.

*　　*　　*

Who that lives by eating bread has not an interest
in the repeal of the bread tax? Who that is endeavouring to support himself and his family by commerce has not an interest in Free Trade? Who has
not an interest in what advances the general prosperity of the country, even though his pursuits are
artistical or intellectual, ministering to the spiritual
rather than the material portions of our nature? For
as one thrives will all thrive—they react the one
upon the other—the starving do not encourage literature and art—they are bound together by the
ties which Providence formed to uphold society;
and it is because they and we have an interest in this
matter that we are determined the question shall
not drop until it is satisfactorily settled.

I say all classes have an interest in this matter;
even they who are represented as the great opposing class—the landlord class. For what has

made England the paradise of landowners but its
being the workshop of the world? In the progress
of manufacture, if machinery has enabled one
man to do the work of two hundred, it has also
employed two hundred, and two thousand, where
one was employed; all bread eaters, coming to the
landowner for his produce. And while the manufacturers of this country have been thus advancing in the last century, its growth of wheat has
been tripled, and the rents of the farmers have
been in many cases quadrupled. The landlords
gain by railways enhancing the worth of their
property; they gain by the rich and flourishing
community arising around them; and if for a
while they should have to make some slight sacrifice—if at first their rents should fall in the
change—why, they will still be gaining that which
gold could never buy. By the graceful concession
they would be gaining the goodwill and gratitude
of their fellow-countrymen; they would gain for

themselves an exemption from the execration that pursues their class—from the infamy of their names in history—from the reprobation of their consciences, and the pollution of their souls.

* * *

Some affect to sneer at abstract principles; but abstract good is the real, practical good, after all; the exceptions made to it are some little, dirty contrivances of those who would have trade free for others, but would reserve the monopoly for themselves—would have free trade as to what they buy, but restrictions as to what they sell; and who tell us that those principles are sound and excellent things in reference to all other commodities whatever, but that there is some one exception left—the exception of that in which the exceptor deals; and each in turn will tell you that Free Trade is the noblest thing in the world, except for corn, except for sugar, except for coffee, and except for this, that, and the other, till once, even in the House of Commons, it came to an exception of second-hand glass bottles. I say this is a principle recognized by all—recognized even by the Government in its measures of last year, however paltry their nature and limited their operation; recognized in their Canada Corn Bill; recognized in the repeal of the laws against the exportation of machinery, the last rag of that form of monopoly; and the repeal of the duties on imports must follow that of restriction on exports. A principle thus practically recognized by foes, as well as by friends, is certain of success. Thus was it that the great principle of Negro liberty was recognized, and thus eventually carried. And did not the recognition of a principle emancipate the Roman Catholics of Ireland? Ask Sir Robert Peel and the Duke of Wellington whether this was not the secret of the success of that measure.

* * *

Why, the corn laws and the policy of our agricultural legislators hunt poverty and wretchedness from their own districts into ours. The landlord class call themselves feeders of the people. They speak of their ability, if properly encouraged and protected, to feed the nation. What feeds the people? Not the growing of corn, but the people being able to buy it. The people are no more fed, for all the wheat that is grown, than as if there were so many stones covering the rich valleys of the country. It is in the price required of the people who eat it; and if that is beyond the power of the multitude to give, the landlords become starvers instead of feeders of the people. Agriculture cannot support its own population; it is not in the course of nature that it should, for one man is vested with the ability to raise food for the many. Twenty-eight per cent of the population are amply sufficient to cultivate the ground so as to yield food for the remainder of the hundred. How are the rest to be fed? By opening markets for the products of their industry, that they may obtain the means.

* * *

Wisely has the Council appealed to the great towns, for there is the power. What can the poor farmer do? His money is in his landlord's ground, and the man who has money in another man's ground must needs be a slave. His freedom is buried there with it, not, like the grain, to germinate, but only to rot and dissolve in corruption. It is where great bodies are congregated that they can stand by one another; where not the importance of the individual, but the importance of the many, is the great thing for all. And how independent are such places, if they but knew their position, of all that aristocracy is, or can do! Landlords! They built not this magnificent metropolis; they covered not these forty square miles with the great mass of human dwellings that spread over them; they crowd not our ports with shipping; they filled not your city with its monuments of science and art, with its institutions of literature and its temples of religion; they poured not that stream of commercial prosperity into the country which during the last century has made the grandeur of London, quadrupling its population, and showing that it has one heart with the entire community.

* * *

The time is opportune for the appeal which has been made to the inhabitants of this metropolis, and for the appeal to those among you who enjoy the franchise of the city of London. There will, in a very short period, be an opportunity for you to show decidedly that the principle of Free Trade is consecrated in your hearts and guides your votes. I trust the contest will be by no means a personal one, but one wholly of principle, and that no ambiguous pretensions, no praise of Free Trade, with certain qualifications and accommodations necessary to the hustings, will be tolerated for an instant; but that the plain and simple test will be the complete, total, and immediate abolition of the monopoly of food.* * * Here, then, I hope, will one of the first great electoral experiments be tried, that not merely every member of the League, but every inhabitant of London, who can honourably influence the result of that election, should feel himself bound to do so, as amongst his earliest pledges of adherence to this great cause—the commencement of his answer to the appeal which has now been made to him for support. Other ways will soon open themselves; and I trust that its past backwardness will be amply redeemed by the metropolis in the readiness with which it will respond to the great call now made for its pecuniary liberality, and in the ardour which many will manifest in other modes of co-operating in this great work, showing that we look to yet higher principles and considerations than any that belong either to rural districts or to particular classes, and that we regard this as the common cause of humanity. And so it is; for Free-Trade principles are the dictates of Nature plainly written on the surface of land and ocean, so that the simplest may read them and imbibe their spirit. For that Power which stretched abroad the land, poured forth the ocean, and piled up the mountains; that Power which gave Western America its broad prairies, and reared the gigantic and boundless forests of the north; that Power which covered with rich vineyards the smiling hills of France, which wafts sweet odours from the 'spicy shores of Araby the blest,' which has endowed this country with its minerals and its insular advantages, and its people with their indomitable Saxon energy, with their skill, their hardihood, their perseverance, their enterprise;—that Power which doth all this, evidently designed it for the common good, for the reciprocal advantage of all; it intended that all should enrich all by the freest interchange, thus making the world no longer the patrimony of a class, but the heritage and the paradise of humanity.

REVIEW QUESTIONS

1. What are the principal criticisms raised against the landlord class?
2. What are the chief differences between the commercial and agriculture interests?
3. Why is free trade more than just an economic doctrine?
4. What attributes are projected onto this trade policy?
5. Why is London considered so important for the repeal?

ALEXANDER HERZEN

FROM *From the Other Shore*

Alexander Herzen (1812–1870), a Russian intellectual who lived in self-imposed exile for most of his adult life, followed in the political tradition of the ill-fated Decembrists, who in 1825 had sought to introduce constitutionalism and "westernization" to Russia. In From the Other Shore, *written in Paris in 1849, Herzen developed a political program that synthesized western principles of individualism and social democracy with the communitarian framework of the Russian peasant commune (Mir). Although Herzen criticized bourgeois capitalist society, he celebrated the West's tradition of civil liberties that conferred dignity on the individual. The following passage is taken from the book's introduction.*

From *From the Other Shore*, A. Herzen, translated by Richard Wollheim, Oxford University Press, 1979.

Our parting will last for a long time yet—perhaps for ever. At the present moment I do not wish to return—whether it will be possible later I do not know. You have been waiting for me, you are still waiting, so I must give you an explanation. If there is anyone to whom I am obliged to account for my absence, for my actions, it is certainly you, my friends.

An unconquerable revulsion and a strong inner voice of prophecy do not permit me to cross the frontier of Russia, especially now, when autocracy, infuriated and frightened by everything that is happening in Europe, strangles with redoubled severity every intellectual movement, and brutally cuts off sixty million souls from the rest of mankind which is gaining its freedom, deflecting the last light which falls feebly on a few of them with its black iron hand caked with the blood of Poland. No, my friends, I cannot cross the border of this kingdom of darkness, lawlessness, silent death, mysterious disappearances, gagged and tortured prisoners. I shall wait until that time when the weary rulers weakened by vain efforts and by the resistance that they have pro-voked, recognize *something* worthy of respect in the Russian man.

Do not, I beg you, make a mistake: it is not happiness, not distraction, not rest, not even personal safety that I have found here; indeed, I do not know who could find in Europe to-day happiness or rest, rest in the midst of an earthquake, happiness in the midst of a desperate struggle.

You saw sadness expressed in every line of my letters; life here is very hard, venomous malignity mingles with love, bile with tears, feverish anxiety infects the whole organism, the time of former illusions and hopes has passed. I believe in nothing here, except in a handful of people, a few ideas, and the fact that one cannot arrest movement; I see the inevitable doom of old Europe and feel no pity for anything that now exists, neither the peaks of its culture nor its institutions. . . . I love nothing in this world except that which it persecutes, I respect nothing except that which it kills—and I stay . . . stay to suffer doubly, to suffer my own personal anguish and that of this world; which will perish, perhaps, to the sound of thunder and destruction towards which it is racing at full steam. . . . Why then do I stay?

I stay because the struggle is *here*, because despite the blood and tears it is here that social problems are being decided, because it is here that suffering is painful, sharp, but *articulate*. The struggle is open, no one hides. Woe to the vanquished, but they are not vanquished without a struggle, nor deprived of speech before they can utter a word; the violence inflicted is great, but the protest is loud; the fighters often march to the galleys, chained hand and foot, but with heads uplifted, with free speech. Where the word has not perished, neither has the deed. For the sake of this open struggle, for this free speech, this right to be heard—I stay here; for its sake I give up everything; I give up you for it, a portion of my heritage and perhaps shall give my life in the ranks of an energetic minority of 'the persecuted but undefeated'.

For the sake of this freedom of speech, I have broken, or, better still, suppressed for a while my ties of blood with the people in whom I found so much response both to the bright and to the dark side of my soul, whose song and speech are my song and speech, and I stay among a people in whose life I am in deep sympathy only with the bitter tears of the proletariat and the desperate courage of its friends.

This decision has cost me dear . . . you know me . . . and you will believe me. I have stifled the inner pain; I have lived through the painful struggle and I have made my decision, not like an angry youth, but like a man who has thought over what he is doing . . . how much he has to lose . . . for months I have been calculating and pondering and vacillating, and have finally sacrificed everything to:

Human Dignity and Free Speech

The consequences are no affair of mine; they are not in my power, they are rather in the power of some arbitrary whim which has gone so far as to draw a capricious circle not only round our words but round our very steps. It was in my power not to obey—and I did not obey.

To obey against one's convictions when there is a possibility of not obeying—is immoral. Passive obedience becomes almost impossible. I have witnessed two upheavals, I have lived too long as a free man to allow myself to be chained again; I have lived through popular disturbances, I have become accustomed to free speech and I cannot accept serfdom again, not even for the sake of suffering with you. If it had been necessary to restrain oneself for the common cause, perhaps one might have found the strength to do so; but where at this moment is our common cause? At home you have no soil on which a free man can stand. How after this can you summon us? . . . If it were to battle—yes, then we would come: but to obscure martyrdom, to sterile silence, to obedience—no, under no circumstances. Demand anything of me, but do not demand duplicity, do not force me again to play at being a loyal subject; respect the free man in me.

The liberty of the individual is the greatest thing of all, it is *on this and on this alone* that the true will of the people can develop. Man must respect liberty in himself, and he must esteem it in himself no less than in his neighbour, than in the entire nation. If you are convinced of that, then you will agree that to remain here is my right, my duty; it is the only protest that an individual can make amongst us; he must offer up this sacrifice to his human dignity. If you call my withdrawal an escape and will forgive me only out of your love, this will mean that you yourselves are not wholly free.

I know all the answers that can be made from the point of view of romantic patriotism and formal civil responsibility, but I cannot allow these antiquated attitudes. I have outlived them, left them behind, and it is precisely against them that I am fighting. These *réchauffé* remnants of the Roman and Christian heritage are the greatest obstacles to the establishment of true ideas of freedom, ideas that are healthy, clear, mature. Fortunately, in Europe, custom and a long process of development partly counterbalance these absurd theories and absurd laws. The people who live here are living on a soil fertilized by two civilizations; the path traversed by their ancestors for the past two and a half thousand years was not in vain, many human virtues have developed independently of the external organization and the official order.

Even in the worst periods of European history, we encounter some respect for the individual, some recognition of independence, some rights conceded to talent and genius. Vile as were the German rulers of that time, Spinoza was not sentenced to transportation, Lessing was not flogged or conscripted. This respect not merely for material but also for moral force, this unquestioning recognition of the individual—is one of the great human principles in European life.

In Europe a man who lives abroad has never been considered a criminal, nor one who emigrates to America a traitor.

We have nothing similar. With us the individual has always been crushed, absorbed, he has never even tried to emerge. Free speech with us has always been considered insolence, independence, subversion; man was engulfed in the State, dissolved in the community. The revolution of Peter the Great replaced the obsolete squirearchy of Russia—with a European bureaucracy; everything that could be copied from the Swedish and German codes, everything that could be taken over from the free municipalities of Holland into our half-communal, half-absolutist country, was taken over; but the unwritten, the moral check on power, the instinctive recognition of the rights of man, of the rights of thought, of truth, could not be and were not imported.

*   *   *

REVIEW QUESTIONS

1. What reasons does Herzen cite for not returning to his beloved Russia?
2. Why is individual liberty so important for Herzen's political views?
3. How is Russia compared to the West?

JOHN STUART MILL

FROM *On Liberty*

In 1859 J. S. Mill (1806–1873) presented to Victorian society the now-classic statement on individual freedom, On Liberty. *Mill, however, should not be mistaken as a typical liberal. He not only abandoned classical economic theory early in his career, advocating certain forms of government regulation, but also foresaw the moral necessity of extending the vote to workers and women. Yet he continued to harbor distrust in state authority and in governments' inability to guarantee rights of minorities. His passages on individual liberty, the freedom of opinion, and the limits of authority over the individual are critical to the canon of liberal political philosophy.*

From *On Liberty*, by John Stuart Mill, edited by David Spitz, W.W. Norton & Company, 1975.

Chapter I

Introductory

The subject of this Essay is not the so-called Liberty of the Will so unfortunately opposed to the misnamed doctrine of Philosophical Necessity; but Civil, or Social Liberty: the nature and limits of the power which can be legitimately exercised by society over the individual. A question seldom stated, and hardly ever discussed, in general terms, but which profoundly influences the practical controversies of the age by its latent presence, and is likely soon to make itself recognised as the vital question of the future. It is so far from being new, that, in a certain sense, it has divided mankind, almost from the remotest ages; but in the stage of progress into which the more civilised portions of the species have now entered, it presents itself under new conditions, and requires a different and more fundamental treatment.

The struggle between Liberty and Authority is the most conspicuous feature in the portions of history with which we are earliest familiar, particularly in that of Greece, Rome, and England. But in old times this contest was between subjects, or some classes of subjects, and the Government. By liberty, was meant protection against the tyranny of the political rulers. The rulers were conceived (except in some of the popular governments of Greece) as in a necessarily antagonistic position to the people whom they ruled. They consisted of a governing One, or a governing tribe or caste, who derived their authority from inheritance or conquest, who, at all events, did not hold it at the pleasure of the governed, and whose supremacy men did not venture, perhaps did not desire, to contest, whatever precautions might be taken against its oppressive exercise. Their power was regarded as necessary, but also as highly dangerous; as a weapon which they would attempt to use against their subjects, no less than against external enemies. To prevent the weaker members of the community from being preyed upon by innumerable vultures, it was needful that there should be an animal of prey stronger than the rest, commissioned to keep them down. But as the king of the vultures would be no less bent upon preying on the flock than any of the minor harpies, it was indispensable to be in a perpetual attitude of defence against his beak and claws. The aim, therefore, of patriots was to set limits to the power which the ruler should be suffered to exercise over the community; and this limitation was what they meant by liberty. It was attempted in two ways. First, by obtaining a recognition of certain immunities, called political liberties or rights, which it was to be regarded as a breach of duty in the ruler to infringe, and which if he did infringe, specific resistance, or general rebellion, was held to be justifiable. A second, and generally a later expedient, was the establishment of constitutional checks, by which the consent of the community, or of a body of some sort, supposed to represent its interests, was made a necessary condition to some of the more important acts of the governing power. To the first of these modes of limitation, the ruling power, in most European countries, was compelled, more or less, to submit. It was not so with the second; and, to attain this, or when already in some degree possessed, to attain it more completely, became everywhere the principal object of the lovers of liberty. And so long as mankind were content to combat one enemy by another, and to be ruled by a master, on condition of being guaranteed more or less efficaciously against his tyranny, they did not carry their aspirations beyond this point.

A time, however, came, in the progress of human affairs, when men ceased to think it a necessity of nature that their governors should be an independent power, opposed in interest to themselves. It appeared to them much better that the various magistrates of the State should be their tenants or delegates, revocable at their pleasure. In that way alone, it seemed, could they have complete security that the powers of government would never be abused to their disadvantage. By degrees this new demand for elective and temporary rulers became the prominent object of the exertions of the popular party, wherever any such party existed; and superseded, to a considerable extent, the previous efforts to limit the power of rulers. As the struggle proceeded for making the ruling power emanate from the periodical choice of the ruled, some persons began to think that too much importance had been attached to the limitation of the power itself. *That* (it might seem) was a resource against rulers whose interests were habitually opposed to those of the people. What was now wanted was, that the rulers should be identified with the people; that their interest and will should be the interest and will of the nation. The nation did not need to be protected against its own will. There was no fear of its tyrannising over itself. Let the rulers be effectually responsible to it, promptly removable by it, and it could afford to trust them with power of which it could itself dictate the use to be made. Their power was but the nation's own power, concentrated, and in a form convenient for exercise. This mode of thought, or rather perhaps of feeling, was common among the last generation of European liberalism, in the Continental section of which it still apparently predominates. Those who admit any limit to what a government may do, except in the case of such governments as they think ought not to exist, stand out as brilliant exceptions among the political thinkers of the Continent. A similar tone of sentiment might by this time have been prevalent in our own country, if the circumstances which for a time encouraged it, had continued unaltered.

But, in political and philosophical theories, as well as in persons, success discloses faults and infirmities which failure might have concealed from observation. The notion, that the people have no need to limit their power over themselves, might seem axiomatic, when popular government was a thing only dreamed about, or read of as having existed at some distant period of the past. Neither was that notion necessarily disturbed by such temporary aberrations as those of the French Revolution, the worst of which were the work of a usurping few, and which, in any case, belonged, not to the permanent working of popular institutions, but to a sudden and convulsive outbreak against monarchical and aristocratic depotism. In time, however, a democratic republic came to occupy a large portion of the earth's surface, and made itself felt as one of the most powerful members of the community of nations; and elective and responsible government became subject to the observations and criticisms which wait upon a great existing fact. It was now perceived that such phrases as "self-government," and "the power of the people over themselves," do not express the true state of the case. The "people" who exercise the power are not always the same people with those over whom it is exercised; and the "self-government" spoken of is not the government of each by himself, but of each by all the rest. The will of the people, moreover, practically means the will of the most numerous or the most active *part* of the people; the majority, or those who succeed in making themselves accepted as the majority; the people, consequently, *may* desire to oppress a part of their number; and precautions are as much needed against this as against any other abuse of power. The limitation, therefore, of the power of government over individuals loses none of its importance when the holders of power are regularly accountable to the community, that is, to the strongest party therein. This view of things, recommending itself equally to the intelligence of thinkers and to the inclination of those important classes in European society to whose real or supposed interests democracy is adverse, has had no difficulty in establishing itself; and in political speculations "the tyranny of the majority" is now generally included among the evils against which society requires to be on its guard.

*   *   *

The object of this Essay is to assert one very simple principle, as entitled to govern absolutely the dealings of society with the individual in the way of compulsion and control, whether the means used be physical force in the form of legal penalties, or the moral coercion of public opinion. That principle is, that the sole end for which mankind are warranted, individually or collectively, in interfering with the liberty of action of any of their number, is self-protection. That the only purpose for which power can be rightfully exercised over any member of a civilised community, against his will, is to prevent harm to others. His own good, either physical or moral, is not a sufficient warrant. He cannot rightfully be compelled to do or forbear because it will be better for him to do so, because it will make him happier, because, in the opinions of others, to do so would be wise, or even right. These are good reasons for remonstrating with him, or reasoning with him, or persuading him, or entreating him, but not for compelling him, or visiting him with any evil in case he do otherwise. To justify that, the conduct from which it is desired to deter him must be calculated to produce evil to some one else. The only part of the conduct of any one, for which he is amenable to society, is that which concerns others. In the part which merely concerns himself, his independence is, of right, absolute. Over himself, over his own body and mind, the individual is sovereign.

*   *   *

We have now recognised the necessity to the mental well-being of mankind (on which all their other well-being depends) of freedom of opinion, and freedom of the expression of opinion, on four distinct grounds; which we will now briefly recapitulate.

First, if any opinion is compelled to silence, that opinion may, for aught we can certainly know, be true. To deny this is to assume our own infallibility.

Secondly, though the silenced opinion be an error, it may, and very commonly does, contain a portion of truth; and since the general or prevailing opinion on any subject is rarely or never the whole truth, it is only by the collision of adverse opinions that the remainder of the truth has any chance of being supplied.

Thirdly, even if the received opinion be not only true, but the whole truth; unless it is suffered to be, and actually is, vigorously and earnestly contested, it will, by most of those who receive it, be held in the manner of a prejudice, with little comprehension or feeling of its rational grounds. And not only this, but, fourthly, the meaning of the doctrine itself will be in danger of being lost, or enfeebled, and deprived of its vital effect on the character and conduct; the dogma becoming a mere formal profession, inefficacious for good, but cumbering the ground, and preventing the growth of any real and heartfelt conviction, from reason or personal experience.

*   *   *

Chapter IV

Of the Limits to the Authority of Society over the Individual

What, then, is the rightful limit to the sovereignty of the individual over himself? Where does the authority of society begin? How much of human life should be assigned to individuality, and how much to society?

Each will receive its proper share, if each has that which more particularly concerns it. To individuality should belong the part of life in which it is chiefly the individual that is interested; to society, the part which chiefly interests society.

Though society is not founded on a contract, and though no good purpose is answered by inventing a contract in order to deduce social obligations from it, every one who receives the protection of society owes a return for the benefit, and the fact of living in society renders it indispensable that each should be bound to observe a certain line of conduct towards the rest. This conduct consists, first, in not injuring the interests of one another; or rather certain interests, which, either by express legal provision, or by tacit understanding, ought to be considered as rights; and secondly, in each person's bearing his share (to be fixed on some equitable principle) of the labours and sacrifices incurred for defending the society or its members from injury and molestation. These conditions society is justified in enforcing, at all costs to those who endeavour to withhold fulfilment. Nor is this all that society may do. The acts of an individual may be hurtful to others, or wanting in due consideration for their welfare, without going to the length of violating any of their constituted rights. The offender may then be justly punished by opinion, though not by law. As soon as any part of a person's conduct affects prejudicially the interests of others, society has jurisdiction over it, and the question whether the general welfare will or will not be promoted by interfering with it, becomes open to discussion. But there is no room for entertaining any such question when a person's conduct affects the interests of no persons besides himself, or needs not affect them unless they like (all the persons concerned being of full age, and the ordinary amount of understanding). In all such cases, there should be perfect freedom, legal and social, to do the action and stand the consequences.

It would be a great misunderstanding of this doctrine to suppose that it is one of selfish indifference, which pretends that human beings have no business with each other's conduct in life, and that they should not concern themselves about the well-doing or well-being of one another, unless their own interest is involved. Instead of any diminution, there is need of a great increase of disinterested exertion to promote the good of others. But disinterested benevolence can find other instruments to persuade people to their good than whips and scourges, either of the literal or the metaphorical sort. I am the last person to undervalue the self-regarding virtues; they are only second in importance, if even second, to the social. It is equally the business of education to cultivate both. But even education works by conviction and persuasion as well as by compulsion, and it is by the former only that, when the period of education is passed, the self-regarding virtues should be inculcated. Human beings owe to each other help to distinguish the better from the worse, and encouragement to choose the former and avoid the latter. They should be forever stimulating each other to increased exercise of their higher faculties, and increased direction of their feelings and aims towards wise instead of foolish, elevating instead of degrading, objects and contemplations. But neither one person, nor any number of persons, is warranted in saying to another human creature of ripe years, that he shall not do with his life for his own benefit what he chooses to do with it. He is the person most interested in his own well-being: the interest which any other person, except in cases of strong personal attachment, can have in it, is trifling, compared with that which he himself has; the interest which society has in him individually (except as to his conduct to others) is fractional, and altogether indirect; while with respect to his own feelings and circumstances, the most ordinary man or woman has means of knowledge immeasurably surpassing those that can be possessed by any one else. The interference of society to overrule his judgment and purposes in what only regards himself must be grounded on general presumptions; which may be altogether wrong, and even if right, are as likely as not to be misapplied to individual cases, by persons no better acquainted with the circumstances of such cases than those are who look at them merely from without. In this department, therefore, of human affairs, Individuality has its proper field of action. In the conduct of human beings towards one another it is necessary that general rules should for the most part be observed, in order that people may know what they have to expect: but in each person's own concerns his individual spontaneity is entitled to free exercise.

*   *   *

REVIEW QUESTIONS

1. What are the liberties of the individual, and what is the relationship of these liberties to society?
2. What is the importance of freedom of opinion for society?
3. Why would Mill consider the "tyranny of the majority" one of the prominent ills of nineteenth-century society?

ALEXANDER II

FROM Manifesto Emancipating the Serfs

The emancipation of twenty-two million serfs in 1861 constitutes the most ambitious social reform of nineteenth-century Russia. Although Russia's socioeconomic structure did not undergo radical change after 1861, the abolition of serfdom inaugurated a series of judicial, military, and governmental reforms that liberalized Russian society. Extending basic civil liberties to Russians was the necessary first step in the effort to westernize Russia within the Tsarist autocratic tradition.

From Cracraft, James (editor), *Major Problems in the History of Imperialist Russia,* © 1994 by D. C. Heath and Company. Reprinted with permission of Houghton Mifflin Company.

Called by Divine Providence and the sacred law of succession to Our ancestral All-Russian Throne, in response to which call We vowed in Our heart to embrace in Our Royal love and Solicitude all Our faithful of every rank and estate . . . ; investigating the condition of [those] who comprise the State, We saw that State law, while actively promoting the welfare of the higher and middle estates defining their obligations, rights, and privileges, has not equally favored the bonded people, so called because as a matter partly of old laws and partly of current custom they have been hereditarily bound to the authority of landlords, who are obliged accordingly to see to their welfare. Hitherto the rights of the lords were broad and not precisely defined in law, wherefore tradition, custom, and the lord's good will prevailed. At best this [system] produced good patriarchal relations of sincere solicitude and benevolence on the part of the lords and good-natured submission from the peasants. But owing to the decline of morals, an increase in the variety of relationships, and a lessening of the lords' direct paternal relations with their peasants, whereupon landlord rights sometimes fell into the hands of persons seeking only their own advantage; good relations weakened, and the way was opened to an arbitrariness that has been burdensome for the peasants and not conducive to their welfare, whence they have shown indifference to any improvement in their lives.

Such was perceived by Our Predecessors of worthy memory, and they took steps to improve the condition of the peasantry. But these steps were only partly successful, depending as they did on the good will and voluntary action of landlords and applicable as they were only to certain localities, as required by special circumstances or by way of experiment. . . .

We were therefore convinced that the task of improving the condition of the bonded people is a legacy to Us from Our Predecessors, and a destiny conferred upon Us in the course of events by the hand of Providence.

We began this task by an act of trust in the Russian Nobility, knowing of its great proofs of loyalty to the Throne and of its readiness to make sacrifices for the good of the Fatherland. We left it to the Nobility Itself to assemble and consider a new arrangement of peasant affairs, whereupon it was proposed to the Nobles to limit their rights over peasants and to bear the difficulties of a transformation that would entail losses to themselves. And Our trust was justified. Through its representatives in the Provincial Committees chosen by the whole Nobility of every province, the

Nobility voluntarily renounced any rights to the person of the bonded ones. These Committees, after collecting the needed information, drew up proposals regarding a new order for people living in bondage and relations with lords.

* * *

Having called on God for assistance, We are resolved to complete this task.

Pursuant to these new Statutes, the bonded people are to receive in due course the full rights of free rural inhabitants.

The landlords, preserving their right of ownership of all lands belonging to them, are to grant to the peasants, in return for a certain obligation, perpetual use of their homestead as well as such quantity of plowland and other goods as is provided in the Statutes, so that they may be secure in their livelihood and fulfill their duties to the Government.

In taking advantage of this land allotment, the peasants are thereby required to fulfill the obligations to lords specified in the Statutes. In this condition, which is transitional, the peasants are temporarily obligated.

They are also to be given the right to buy their homestead; and with their lord's agreement they may acquire ownership of the plowland and other goods assigned to their perpetual use. On acquiring ownership of said land, the peasants are freed of any duties owed on it to the lord, and thus enter the well-defined estate of free peasant proprietors.

A Special Statute defines the transitional status of domestic folk, as appropriate to their duties and needs. Two years after publication of this Statute, they will receive complete freedom and certain temporary privileges.

* * *

Although these Statutes, the General, Local, and Supplementary Rules for certain special localities, for small landowners, and for peasants working in their lords' factories or industries, have been adapted as far as possible to local economic needs and practices; nevertheless, to preserve the customary order where it is mutually advantageous We leave it to the lords to reach voluntary understandings with peasants and to conclude agreements regarding the extent of the peasants' land allotments and corresponding obligations, observing therein the rules laid down for preserving the inviolability of such agreements.

As this new arrangement, given the inescapable complexity of the changes required by it, cannot be introduced at once, but rather needs time for that, meaning not less than two years: so in the course of this time, to avoid confusion, and to maintain the public and private good, the order hitherto existing on seigneurial estates should be preserved until, on completion of the necessary preparations, the new order will begin.

* * *

Considering the inescapable difficulties involved in this transformation, We place Our hope first of all in the surpassing goodness of Divine Providence, which protects Russia.

Then do We rely on the valiant zeal for the common good of the Well-born Noble estate, to whom We cannot fail to express, on behalf of Ourselves and the whole Fatherland, well-deserved recognition of unselfish execution of Our designs. Russia will not forget that, prompted only by respect for human dignity and Christian love of neighbor, they voluntarily renounced the law of bondage and laid the basis of a new economic future for peasants. We assuredly expect that with like nobility they will exhibit the utmost care in seeing that the new Statutes are carried out in good order, and in a spirit of peace and benevolence; that every landowner will complete, on his own land, the great civic act of his entire estate; and that, having arranged the affairs of the peasants settled on his land and of his domestic folk on terms advantageous to both sides, he will thus give a good example to the rural people and an incentive to exact and conscientious fulfillment of State regulations.

Mindful of examples of the landowners' generous solicitude for the good of peasants, and of the peasants' recognition of same, We are confirmed in Our hope that mutual voluntary agreements will resolve most of the difficulties that are unavoidable when general rules are applied to the varying circumstances of individual estate lands. In this way the transition from the old order to the new will be alleviated, and mutual trust, good accord, and a unanimous aspiration for the common good will be strengthened in the future.

* * *

And We place Our hope in the good sense of Our people.

When word of the Government's plan to abolish the law of bondage reached peasants unprepared for it, there arose a partial misunderstanding. Some thought about freedom and forgot about obligations. But the general good sense was not disturbed in the conviction that anyone freely enjoying the goods of society correspondingly owes it to the common good to fulfill certain obligations, both by natural reason and by Christian law, according to which "every soul must be subject to the governing authorities" and "pay all of them their dues," in particular "labor, tribute, fear, and honor" * * * rights legally acquired by the landlords cannot be taken from them without a decent return or voluntary concession; and that it would be contrary to all justice to make use of the lords' land without bearing the corresponding obligations.

And now We hopefully expect that the bonded people, as a new future opens before them, will understand and accept with gratitude the important sacrifice made by the Well-born Nobility for the improvement of their lives.

They will understand that, receiving the advantages of ownership and the freedom to conduct their own affairs, they owe it to society and to themselves to realize the beneficence of the new law by a loyal, judicious, and diligent exercise of the rights granted to them. The most beneficent law cannot make people happy if they do not themselves labor to build their happiness under the protection of the law. Prosperity is acquired and increased only by hard work, the judicious use of strength and resources, strict economy, and, overall, by an honest, God-fearing life.

* * *

Make the sign of the cross, Orthodox people, and invoke with Us God's blessing on thy free labor, the pledge of thine own prosperity and of the public good.

Given at St. Petersburg in the year of Our Lord one thousand eight hundred sixty-one, and of Our Reign the seventh.

Alexander

REVIEW QUESTIONS

1. What social changes provoked emancipation?
2. What role does the aristocracy play in the execution of emancipation and how realistic is this prescribed role?
3. How is religion invoked to unify Russian society in this period of change?

JULES FERRY

FROM The State Must Be Secular AND Letter to Teachers

The clash of views between clerics and liberals over the proper role of religion in civil society endured throughout the nineteenth century. Liberals associated progress with a secular state promoting rational, materialist knowledge and criticized the meddling of the Catholic Church in such temporal public affairs as government and education. In France liberals attacked the Catholic Church as a royalist institution that undermined the values of the republic. Clerics and others, however, averred that a society bereft of spirituality and Christian mores in public life tokened a cold, increasingly insensitive world. In 1882 Jules Ferry (1832–1893), the statesman of the French Third Republic, secured a law that made primary education obligatory, free, and non-clerical. In the following speech and letter, Ferry outlined the classic liberal position on secular society and education.

From *Nineteenth Century Europe: Liberalism and its Critics,* edited by Jan Goldstein and John W. Boyer, University of Chicago Press, 1988. Reprinted by permission of the publisher.

The State Must Be Secular

Given before the Chamber of Deputies, 3 June 1876

I pronounce the words *secular state* without any trepidation, even though, for some of our honorable colleagues they would seem to have a certain radical, anarchist, or revolutionary flavor. Yet I am not saying anything new, revolutionary, or anarchist when I maintain that the state must be secular, that the totality of society is necessarily represented by secular organizations.

What, exactly, is this principle? It is a doctrine that [the Catholic church] prides itself on having introduced into the world: the doctrine of the separation of temporal and spiritual power. Yes, Christianity introduced the doctrine of the separation of these two domains, the realm of the state and that of conscience, the temporal and the spiritual. It was successful, after centuries of struggle,

in the midst of full-blown paganism. However, there is one reproach we could make against the church in this matter. After taking four or five centuries to introduce this doctrine, the church has then spent seven or eight centuries vehemently attacking it.

Gentlemen, what was the key accomplishment, the major concern, the great passion and service of the French Revolution? To have built this secular state, to have succeeded in making the social organisms of society exclusively secular, to have taken away from the clergy its political organization and role as a cadre within the state—that, precisely, is the French Revolution in its full reality. Well now, we do not presume to convert the honorable members seated on this side of the Chamber [i.e., on the right] to the doctrines of the revolution. We only wish it to be well understood that we do not deviate from these doctrines. Convinced that the first concern, the first duty of a democratic government is to maintain incessant, powerful, vigilant and efficient control over public education, we insist that this control belong to no authority other than the state. We cannot admit, we will never admit, and this country of France will never admit that the State can be anything but a secular one.

*   *   *

Letter to Teachers (17 November 1883)

The law of 28 March[1] is marked by two tendencies that complement without contradicting each other: on the one hand, the law excludes the teaching of any particular dogma from the required program; on the other, it accords moral and civic education the highest rank. Religious instruction belongs to the home and the church; moral instruction belongs to the school. The legislator thus did not intend to undertake a purely negative project. Undoubtedly, his first goal was to separate school and church, to assure the freedom of conscience for both masters and pupils, to distinguish at last between two domains that have been for too long confused: that of beliefs, which are personal, free, and variable; and that of knowledge, which is common and indispensable to all, consensual. But there is something else in the law of 28 March. It is a declaration of our will to found our own national education and base it on those notions of duty and right that the lawmaker does not hesitate to place among the first truths no one can fail to know. For this keystone of education, it is upon you, gentlemen, that the public powers have counted.

By dispensing you from religious instruction, we have no thoughts of freeing you from the teaching of morals. That would be removing the dignity of your profession. On the contrary, it seemed completely natural that the teacher, while teaching children to read and write, teach them as

well the elementary rules of the moral life, which are no less universally accepted than those of grammar and mathematics.

. . . You do not, strictly speaking, have to teach anything new, anything that is not already as familiar to you as it is to all good people. And when we speak to you of your mission and apostolate, you should not misunderstand us. You are not the apostles of a new gospel. The legislator did not wish to transform you into philosophers or makeshift theologians. He asks of you what one may ask of any man of heart and sense. It is impossible for you to see all these children who gather around you every day to listen to your lessons, who observe your conduct and are inspired by your example, at the age when the mind awakens, the heart opens, the memory becomes enriched, without your having the idea of taking advantage of this docility and this confidence for purposes of moral instruction. You cannot help but give, along with what is strictly speaking, scholarly knowledge, the very principles of morality—by which I mean that good, simple, and ancient morality that we received from our parents and that in our relationships in life we all pride ourselves on following without troubling to examine its philosophical basis.

You are the auxiliary and, in some respects, the substitute for the father of the family. Speak then to his son as you would wish one to speak to your own: with force and authority every time it is a question of an incontestable truth, of a matter of common morality: with the greatest reserve the moment you risk touching upon a religious feeling of which you are not the judge.

If at times you are at a loss to know exactly how far you may go in your moral teaching, here is a practical rule for you to follow. The moment you are planning to propose any precept or maxim to your students, ask yourself if you know of any good man who could be offended by what you are going to say. Ask yourself if any family man present in your class and hearing you could with good faith refuse to assent to what you say. If the answer is yes, refrain from saying it. If not, speak boldly, for what you are going to commu-

---

[1] The law of 28 March 1882, often called the Ferry Law, made primary education in France free, nonclerical, and obligatory.

nicate to the child is not your own wisdom, but that of the human race. It is one of the ideas of a universal order that centuries of human civilization have bequeathed us. However narrow this circle of action may seem, make it a point of honor never to leave it. Remain within its boundaries rather than overstepping them. You can never be too scrupulous about touching that delicate and sacred thing that is a child's conscience. But, once you are thus loyally confined to the humble and secure role of everyday morality, what do we ask of you? Speeches? Wise explanations? Brilliant exposés, scholarly teaching? No! Family and society ask you to help raise their children, to make honest people of them. That is to say that they expect not words but acts, not another course added to the program but a completely practical service that you can render to the country more as a man than as a teacher.

REVIEW QUESTIONS

1. According to Ferry, what is the history of the secular state in Europe, and why does the secular state represent progress?
2. Why is a secular education so critical for Ferry?
3. What is Ferry's advice to teachers regarding morality and knowledge?

POPE LEO XIII

FROM *Rerum Novarum* (*About New Things*)

Throughout the modern era, the Catholic Church's position on modern science, secular civil society, and republican politics remained critical and oppositional. In 1864 Pope Pius IX issued the Syllabus of Errors, *an encyclical that reinforced the church's irresolvable differences on progress, liberalism, and modern civilization. A subsequent declaration of papal infallibility in 1870 inflamed anew the tension between church and state. Pope Leo XIII (1878–1903), however, took a different tack. He accepted the principal features of the modern age, but strove to offer moral leadership with constructive criticism of civil society's disregard for social justice and economic morals. His encyclical of 1896,* Rerum Novarum, *critiqued both capitalism and socialism, and its influence unintentionally spawned a wave of Christian socialist movments throughout Europe.*

From *Rerum Novarum, Encyclical Letter of Pope Leo XIII on the Condition of Labor,* © 1939, Paulist Press. Used by permission of Paulist Press.

It is not surprising that the spirit of revolutionary change, which has long been predominant in the nations of the world, should have passed beyond politics and made its influence felt in the cognate field of practical economy. The elements of a conflict are unmistakable: the growth of industry, and the surprising discoveries of science; the changed relations of masters and workmen; the enormous fortunes of individuals and the poverty of the masses; the increased self-reliance and the closer mutual combination of the working population; and, finally, a general moral deterioration. The momentous seriousness of the present state of things just now fills every mind with painful apprehension; wise men discuss it; practical men propose schemes; popular meetings, legislatures, and sovereign princes, all are occupied with it—and there is nothing which has a deeper hold on public attention.

Therefore, Venerable Brethren, as on former occasions, when it seemed opportune to refute false teaching, We have addressed you in the interests of the Church and of the commonwealth, and have issued Letters on Political Power, on Human Liberty, on the Christian Constitution of the State, and on similar subjects, so now We have thought it useful to speak on

The Condition of Labor

It is a matter on which we have touched once or twice already. But in this Letter the responsibility of the Apostolic office urges Us to treat the question expressly and at length, in order that there may be no mistake as to the principles which truth and justice dictate for its settlement. The discussion is not easy, nor is it free from danger. It is not easy to define the relative rights and the mutual duties of the wealthy and of the poor, of capital and of labor. And the danger lies in this, that crafty agitators constantly make use of these disputes to pervert men's judgments and to stir up the people to sedition.

But all agree, and there can be no question whatever, that some remedy must be found, and quickly found, for the misery and wretchedness which press so heavily at this moment on the large majority of the very poor. The ancient workmen's Guilds were destroyed in the last century, and no other organization took their place. Public institutions and the laws have repudiated the ancient religion. Hence by degrees it has come to pass that Working Men have been given over, isolated and defenceless, to the callousness of employers and the greed of unrestrained competition. The evil has been increased by rapacious Usury, which, although more than once condemned by the Church, is nevertheless, under a different form but with the same guilt, still practiced by avaricious and grasping men. And to this must be added the custom of working by contract, and the concentration of so many branches of trade in the hands of a few individuals, so that a small number of very rich men have been able to lay upon the masses of the poor a yoke little better than slavery itself.

To remedy these evils the *Socialists*, working on the poor man's envy of the rich, endeavor to destroy private property, and maintain that individual possessions should become the common property of all, to be administered by the State or by municipal bodies. They hold that, by thus transferring property from private persons to the community, the present evil state of things will be set to rights, because each citizen will then have his equal share of whatever there is to enjoy. But their proposals are so clearly futile for all practical purposes, that if they were carried out the working man himself would be among the first to suffer. Moreover they are emphatically unjust, because they would rob the lawful possessor, bring the State into a sphere that is not its own, and cause complete confusion in the community.

Private Ownership

It is surely undeniable that, when a man engages in remunerative labor, the very reason and motive of his work is to obtain property, and to hold it as his own private possession. If one man hires out to another his strength or his industry, he does this for the purpose of receiving in return what is necessary for food and living; he thereby expressly proposes to acquire a full and real right, not only to the remuneration, but also to the disposal of that remuneration as he pleases. Thus, if he lives sparingly, saves money, and invests his savings, for greater security, in land, the land in such a case is only his wages in another form; and, consequently, a working man's little estate thus purchased should be as completely at his own disposal as the wages he receives for his labor. But it is precisely in this power of disposal that ownership consists, whether the property be land or movable goods. The *Socialists*, therefore, in endeavoring to transfer the possessions of individuals to the community, strike at the interests of every wage earner, for they deprive him of the liberty of disposing of his wages, and thus of all hope and possibility of increasing his stock and of bettering his condition in life.

What is of still greater importance, however, is that the remedy they propose is manifestly against justice. For every man has by nature the right to possess property as his own. This is one of the *chief points of distinction* between man and the animal creation. For the brute has no power of self-direction, but is governed by two chief instincts, which keep his powers alert, move him to use his strength, and determine him to action without the power of choice. These instincts are self-preservation and the propagation of the species. Both can attain their purpose by means of things which are close at hand; beyond their surroundings the brute creation cannot go, for they are moved to action by sensibility alone, and by the things which sense perceives. But with man it is different indeed. He possesses, on the one hand, the full perfection of animal nature, and therefore he enjoys, at least, as much as the rest of the animal race, the fruition of the things of the body. But animality, however perfect, is far from being the whole of humanity, and is indeed humanity's humble handmaid, made to serve and obey. It is the mind, or the reason, which is the chief thing in us who are human beings; it is this which makes a human being human, and distinguishes him essentially and completely from the brute. And on this account—viz., that man alone among animals possesses reason—it must be within his right to have things not merely for temporary and momentary use, as other living beings have them, but in stable and permanent possession; he must have

not only things which perish in the using, but also those which, though used, remain for use in the future.

*   *   *

Socialism Rejected

The idea, then, that the civil government should, at its own discretion, penetrate and pervade the family and the household, is a great and pernicious mistake. True, if a family finds itself in great difficulty, utterly friendless, and without prospect of help, it is right that extreme necessity be met by public aid; for each family is a part of the commonwealth. In like manner, if within the walls of the household there occur grave disturbance of mutual rights, the public power must interfere to force each party to give the other what is due; for this is not to rob citizens of their rights, but justly and properly to safeguard and strengthen them. But the rulers of the State must go no further: nature bids them stop here. Paternal authority can neither be abolished by the State nor absorbed; for it has the same source as human life itself; "the child belongs to the father," and is, as it were, the continuation of the father's personality; and, to speak with strictness, the child takes its place in civil society not in its own right, but in its quality as a member of the family in which it is begotten. And it is for the very reason that "the child belongs to the father," that, as St. Thomas of Aquin says, "before it attains the use of free-will, it is in the power and care of its parents." The Socialists, therefore, in setting aside the parent and introducing the providence of the State, act *against natural justice*, and threaten the very existence of family life.

And such interference is not only unjust, but is quite certain to harass and disturb all classes of citizens, and to subject them to odious and intolerable slavery. It would open the door to envy, to evil speaking, and to quarrelling; the sources of wealth would themselves run dry, for no one would have any interest in exerting his talents or his industry; and that ideal equality of which so much is said would, in reality, be the leveling down of all to the same condition of misery and dishonor.

Thus it is clear *that the main tenet of Socialism, the community of goods, must be utterly rejected*; for it would injure those whom it is intended to benefit, it would be contrary to the natural rights of mankind, and it would introduce confusion, and disorder into the commonwealth. Our first and most fundamental principle, therefore, when we undertake to alleviate the condition of the masses, must be the inviolability of private property This laid down, We go on to show where we must find the remedy that we seek.

*   *   *

Employer and Employee

The great mistake that is made in the matter now under consideration, is to possess oneself of the idea that class is naturally hostile to class; that rich and poor are intended by nature to live at war with one another. So irrational and so false is this view, that the exact contrary is the truth. Just as the symmetry of the human body is the result of the disposition of the members of the body, so in a State it is ordained by nature that these two classes should exist in harmony and agreement, and should, as it were, fit into one another, so as to maintain the equilibrium of the body politic. Each requires the other; capital cannot do without labor, nor labor without capital. Mutual agreement results in pleasantness and good order; perpetual conflict necessarily produces confusion and outrage. Now, in preventing such strife as this, and in making it impossible, the efficacy of Christianity is marvelous and manifold. First of all, there is nothing more powerful than Religion (of which the Church is the interpreter and guardian) in drawing rich and poor together, by reminding each class of its duties to the other, and especially of the duties of justice. Thus Religion teaches the

laboring man and the workman to carry out honestly and well all equitable agreements freely made, never to injure capital, nor to outrage the person of an employer; never to employ violence in representing his own cause, nor to engage in riot and disorder; and to have nothing to do with men of evil principles, who work upon the people with artful promises, and raise foolish hopes which usually end in disaster and in repentance when too late. Religion teaches the rich man and the employer that their work people are not their slaves; that they must respect in every man his dignity as a man and as a Christian; that labor is nothing to be ashamed of, if we listen to right reason and to Christian philosophy, but is an honorable employment, enabling a man to sustain his life in an upright and creditable way, and that it is shameful and inhuman to treat men like chattels to make money by, or to look upon them merely as so much muscle or physical power.

*   *   *

The Right Use of Money

Therefore, those whom fortune favors are warned that freedom from sorrow and abundance of earthly riches, are no guarantee of that beatitude that shall never end, but rather the contrary; that the rich should tremble at the threatenings of Jesus Christ—threatenings so strange in the mouth of our Lord; and that a most strict account must be given to the Supreme Judge for all that we possess. The chiefest and most excellent rule for the right use of money is one which the heathen philosophers indicated, but which the Church has traced out clearly, and has not only made known to men's minds, but has impressed upon their lives. It rests on the principle that it is one thing to have a right to the possession of money, and another to have a right to use money as one pleases. Private ownership, as we have seen, is the natural right of man; and to exercise that right, especially as members of society, is not only lawful but absolutely necessary. "It is lawful," says

St. Thomas of Aquin, "for a man to hold private property; and it is also necessary for the carrying on of human life." But if the question be asked, How must one's possessions be used? the Church replies without hesitation in the words of the same holy Doctor: "Man should not consider his outward possessions as his own, but as common to all, so as to share them without difficulty when others are in need. Whence the Apostle saith, Command the rich of this world . . . to give with ease, to communicate." True, no one is commanded to distribute to others that which is required for his own necessities and those of his household; nor even to give away what is reasonably required to keep up becomingly his condition in life; "for no one ought to live unbecomingly." But when necessity has been supplied, and one's position fairly considered, it is a duty to give to the indigent out of that which is over. "That which remaineth give alms." It is a duty, not of justice (except in extreme cases), but of Christian Charity—a duty which is not enforced by human law.

*   *   *

Workmen's Associations

In the first place—employers and workmen may themselves effect much in the matter of which We treat, by means of those institutions and organizations which afford opportune assistance to those in need, and which draw the two orders more closely together. Among these may be enumerated: societies for mutual help; various foundations established by private persons for providing for the workman, and for his widow or his orphans, in sudden calamity, in sickness, and in the event of death; and what are called "patronages," or institutions for the care of boys and girls, for young people, and also for those of more mature age.

The most important of all are Workmen's Associations; for these virtually include all the rest. History attests what excellent results were affected

by the Artificer's Guilds of a former day. They were the means not only of many advantages to the workmen, but in no small degree of the advancement of art, as numerous monuments remain to prove. Such associations should be adapted to the requirements of the age in which we live—an age of greater instruction, of different customs, and of more numerous requirements in daily life. It is gratifying to know that there are actually in existence not a few societies of this nature, consisting either of workmen alone, or of workmen and employers together; but it were greatly to be desired that they should multiply and become more effective. We have spoken of them more than once; but it will be well to explain here how much they are needed, to show that they exist by their own right, and to enter into their organization and their work.

*   *   *

These lesser societies and the society which constitutes the State differ in many things, because their immediate purpose and end is different. Civil society exists for the common good, and, therefore, is concerned with the interests of all in general, and with the individual interests in their due place and proportion. Hence, it is called *public* society, because by its means, as St. Thomas of Aquin says, "Men communicate with one another in the setting up of a commonwealth." But the societies which are formed in the bosom of the State are called *private*, and justly so, because their immediate purpose is the private advantage of the associates. "Now, a private society," says St. Thomas again, "is one which is formed for the purpose of carrying out private business; as when two or three enter into partnership with the view of trading in conjunction." Particular societies, then, although they exist within the State, and are each a part of the State, nevertheless cannot be prohibited by the State absolutely and as such. For to enter into a "society" of this kind is the natural right of man; and the State must protect natural rights, not destroy them; and if it forbids its citizens to form associations, it contradicts the very principle of its own existence; for both they and it exist in virtue of the same principle, viz., the natural propensity of man to live in society.

*   *   *

Conclusion

We have now laid before you, Venerable Brethren, who are the persons, and what are the means, by which this most difficult question must be solved. Every one must put his hand to work which falls to his share, and that at once and immediately, lest the evil which is already so great may by delay become absolutely beyond remedy. Those who rule the State must use the law and the institutions of the country; masters and rich men must remember their duty; the poor, whose interests are at stake, must make every lawful and proper effort; since Religion alone, as We said at

the beginning, can destroy the evil at its root, all men must be persuaded that the primary thing needful is to return to real Christianity, in the absence of which all the plans and devices of the wisest will be of little avail.

*   *   *

REVIEW QUESTIONS

1. What is the position of the Catholic Church on the condition of labor?
2. What are Leo XIII's criticisms of capitalism and socialism?
3. How does the Catholic Church's view of civil society differ from these two doctrines?
4. What reforms of market economy does the encyclical propose, and how are these critical of liberalism?

22 ✑ NATIONALISM AND NATION-BUILDING

Nationalism is strictly a modern phenomenon. Arising as a cultural doctrine in the late eighteenth century, the sentiment of nationalism quickly became a widespread political force, constantly evolving over time and adapting to particular needs. Its impact was registered at all levels of public life. As one of the chief solvents of the old regime, the principle of national unity not only realigned the European state system, but also radically recast political culture with a new consciousness of citizenship. Political and economic change eroded older forms of local and regional loyalties, enabling the ideal of national citizenship to embed itself as a self-evident assumption for millions of Europeans.

The cultural dominance of the French Enlightenment, and its insistence on uniform standards, produced a wave of cultural resistance among European writers. In contrast to the Enlightenment's search for social and artistic norms applicable to all societies, select intellectuals celebrated instead the teeming heterogeneity of European language, customs, and culture. Each culture or people, they argued, embodied a national spirit: unique manifestations of geography, climate, and language that defied qualitative comparison. Humanitas, argued cultural nationalists, was not reducible to core characteristics, but rather was the aggregate of humankind's cultural diversity. By honoring all cultures and nations and conferring upon them the self-evident right to develop of their own accord, early forms of cultural nationalism perceived the nation within a tolerant, cosmopolitan world view.

The French Revolution converted this cultural sentiment into political strength. By endowing the nation with political sovereignty and transforming subjects into citizens, the French Revolution evinced the enormous potential of nationalism to wield political and military power. Reaffirmed in flags, anthems, emblems, festivals, and dress, the words "nation" and " 'Fatherland' (la patrie)" stirred the blood of patriots, enabling the revolutionary government to mobilize its citizenry to serve the nation-state with unprecedented engagement. Under the leadership of Napoleon, the massive revolutionary armies of citizen-soldiers stood out as a superior fighting force, compelling the great powers of Europe to adapt or perish.

Napoleonic occupation, in turn, awakened national consciousness in other European cultures. The traditional elite initially tapped patriotism to counter Napoleon's armies, but unwittingly set into motion popular movements whose ideals of national sovereignty, unified nation-states, and constitutional liberties challenged kingdoms, multinational empires, and conservative principles of social hierarchy. Emancipating peoples from the injustice of imposed foreign rule gripped the imagination of artists, writers, and poets, who depicted nationalist movements as romantic quests for liberty and freedom. In the first half of the nineteenth century, liberals, democrats, and nationalists formed strong bonds, for they saw a constitutional nation-state as the vehicle of progress for all social groups. The struggle to unify a people under modern principles of citizenship assumed an ethical, humanitarian character. Advocates of nationalism adopted rhetoric, imagery, and ceremonies once reserved exclusively for religions. The ideal of self-sacrifice further sanctified nationalist movements; bloodshed consecrated the nation as a higher purpose for which to die.

The principle of nationalism shaped the course of nineteenth-century state-building, but not in the manner envisioned by liberals. Statesmen reworked nationalism into a conservative mold, using patriotism and nationalist sentiment to support conservative monarchism and authoritarian government. Calculating that rural voters were inherently resistant to innovative change, conservative rulers shrewdly introduced constitutions and universal manhood suffrage to lend popular legitimacy to their conservative policies, thereby checking the reformist impulses of urban liberals. Yet nationalism did not remain the manipulative tool of conservative statesmen. Urbanization, improved communications, and the vote produced grassroots political movements that used nationalism to protect domestic industry, agitate for imperial expansion, and to brand socialists, Jews, and foreigners as pernicious influences on the nation's political body. The numerous hybrid forms of nationalisms circulating in Europe by the end of the nineteenth century contributed to the increasingly chauvinistic political culture that condoned aggressive militarism, xenophobia, and racial exclusion.

In the wake of the industrial and French revolutions, political consciousness underwent radical change. Traditional authority was either modified or replaced by political communities whose legitimacy and power hinged on their representation of the nation. Yet the meaning of nationalism never became fixed; it remained a protean ideology serving a wide array of political interests and social classes over the long period from 1789 to 1914.

JOHANN GOTTFRIED HERDER

FROM *Reflections on the Philosophy of the History of Mankind*

Johann Gottfried Herder (1744–1803), a theologian by training and profession, greatly influenced German letters with his literary criticism and his philosophy of history. In his later years, Herder resided in the Duchy of Weimar and his presence, along with J. W. Goethe and F. Schiller, made Weimar the seat of German neohumanism. His analogy of national cultures as organic beings had an enormous impact on modern historical consciousness. Nations, he argued, possessed not only the phases of youth, maturity, and decline but also singular, incomparable worth. His mixture of anthropology and history, as witnessed in the passage below, is characteristic of the age.

From *Reflections on the Philosophy of the History of Mankind*, J. G. Herder, edited by Frank E. Manuel, University of Chicago Press, 1970. Reprinted by permission of the publisher.

Chapter 1

Notwithstanding the Varieties of the human Form, there is but one and the same Species of Man throughout the Whole of our Earth

No two leaves of any one tree in nature are to be found perfectly alike; and still less do two human faces, or human frames, resemble each other. Of what endless variety is our artful structure susceptible! Our solids are decomposable into such minute and multifariously interwoven fibres, as no eye can trace; and these are connected by a gluten of such a delicate composition, as the utmost skill is insufficient to analyse. Yet these constitute the least part of us: they are nothing more than the containing vessels and conduits of the variously compounded, highly animated fluid, existing in much greater quantity, by means of which we live and enjoy life. "No man," says Haller, "is exactly similar to another in his internal structure: the courses of the nerves and blood vessels differ in millions and millions of cases, so that amid the variations of these delicate parts, we are scarcely able to discover in what they agree." But if the eye of the anatomist can perceive this infinite variety, how much greater must that be, which dwells in the invisible powers of such an artful organization! So that every man is ultimately a world, in external appearance indeed similar to others, but internally an individual being, with whom no other coincides.

And since man is no independent substance, but is connected with all the elements of nature; living by inspiration of the air, and deriving nutriment from the most opposite productions of the Earth, in his meats and drinks; consuming fire, while he absorbs light, and contaminates the air he breathes; awake or asleep, in motion or at rest, contributing to the change of the universe; shall not he also be changed by it? It is far too little, to compare him to the absorbing sponge, the sparkling tinder: he is a multitudinous harmony, a living self, on whom the harmony of all the powers that surround him operates.

The whole course of a man's life is change: the different periods of his life are tales of transformation, and the whole species is one continued metamorphosis. Flowers drop and wither; others sprout out and bud: the vast tree bears at once all the seasons on its head. If, from a calculation of the insensible perspiration alone, a man of eighty have renovated his whole body at least four and twenty times; who can trace the variations of matter and its forms through all the race of mankind upon the Earth, amid all the causes of change; when not one point on our complicated Globe, not one wave in the current of time, resembles another? A few centuries only have elapsed since the inhabitants of Germany were Patagonians: but they are so no longer, and the inhabitants of its future climates will not equal us. If now we go back to those times, when every thing upon Earth was apparently so different; the times for instance, when elephants lived in Siberia and North America, and those large animals existed, the bones of which are to be found on the Ohio; if men then lived in those regions, how different must they have been from those, who now inhabit them! Thus the history of man is ultimately a theatre of transformations, which He alone can review, who animates all these figures, and feels and enjoys in them all. He builds up and destroys, improves and alters forms, while he changes the World around them. The wanderer upon Earth, the transient ephemeron, can only admire the wonders of this great spirit in a narrow circle, enjoy the form that belongs to him in the general choir, adore, and disappear with this form. "I too was in Arcadia": is the monumental inscription of all living beings in the ever-changing, ever-renewing creation.

As the human intellect, however, seeks unity in every kind of variety, and the divine mind, its prototype, has stamped the most innumerable multiplicity upon the Earth with unity, we may venture from the vast realm of change to revert to the simplest position: *all mankind are only one and the same species.*

*   *   *

For each genus Nature has done enough, and to each has given its proper progeny. The ape she has divided into as many species and varieties as possible, and extended these as far as she could: but thou, O man, honour thyself: neither the pongo nor the gibbon is thy brother: the American and the Negro are: these therefore thou shouldst not oppress, or murder, or steal; for they are men, like thee: with the ape thou canst not enter into fraternity.

Lastly, I could wish the distinctions between the human species, that have been made from a laudable zeal for discriminating science, not carried beyond due bounds. Some for instance have thought fit, to employ the term of *races* for four or five divisions, originally made in consequence of country or complexion: but I see no reason for this appellation. Race refers to a difference of origin, which in this case either does not exist, or in each of these countries, and under each of these complexions, comprises the most different races. For every nation is one people, having its own national form, as well as its own language: the climate, it is true, stamps on each its mark, or spreads over it a slight veil, but not sufficient to destroy the original national character. This originality of character extends even to families, and its transitions are as variable as imperceptible. In short, there are neither four or five races, nor exclusive varieties, on this Earth. Complexions run into each other: forms follow the genetic character: and upon the whole, all are at last but shades of the same great picture, extending through all ages, and over all parts of the Earth. They belong not, therefore, so properly to systematic natural history, as to the physico-geographical history of man.

*   *   *

Now as mankind, both taken as a whole, and in its particular individuals, societies, and nations, is a permanent natural system of the most multifarious living powers; let us examine, wherein its stability consists; in what point its highest beauty, truth, and goodness, unite; and what course it takes, in order to reapproach its permanent condition, on every aberration from it, of which many are exhibited to us by history and experience.

1. The human species is such a copious scheme of energies and capacities, that, as every thing in nature rests on the most determinate individuality, its great and numerous capacities could not appear on our planet otherwise than *divided among millions*. Every thing has been born, that could be born upon it; and every thing has maintained itself, that could acquire a state of permanence according to the laws of Nature. Thus every individual bears within himself that symmetry, for which he is made, and to which he must mould himself, both in his bodily figure, and mental capacities. Human existence appears in every shape and kind, from the most sickly deformity, that can scarcely support life, to the superhuman form of a Grecian demigod; from the passionate ardour of the Negro brain, to the capacity for consummate wisdom. Through faults and errours, through education, necessity, and exercise, every mortal seeks the symmetry of his powers; as in this alone the most complete enjoyment of his existence lies: yet few are sufficiently fortunate, to attain it in the purest, happiest manner.

2. As an individual man can subsist of himself but very imperfectly, *a superiour maximum of co-operating powers* is formed with every society. These powers contend together in wild confusion, till, agreeably to the unfailing laws of nature, opposing regulations limit each other, and a kind of equilibrium and harmony of movement takes place. Thus nations modify themselves, according to time, place, and their internal character: each bears in itself the standard of its perfection, totally independent of all comparison with that of others. Now the more pure and fine the maximum on which a people hit, the more useful the objects to which it applied the exertions of its nobler powers, and, lastly, the more firm and exact the bond of union, which most intimately connected all the members of the state, and guided them to this good end; the more stable was the nation itself, and the more brilliant the figure it made in history. The course that we have hitherto taken through certain nations shows how different, according to place, time, and circumstances, was the object for which they strove. With the Chinese it was refined political morality; with the Hindoos, a kind of retired purity, quiet assiduity in labour, and endurance; with the Phoenicians, the spirit of navigation, and commercial industry. The culture of the Greeks, particularly at Athens, proceeded on the maximum of sensible beauty, both in arts and manners, in science and in political institutions. In Sparta, and in Rome, men emulated the virtues of the patriot and hero; in each, however, in a very different mode. Now as in all these most depended on time and place, the ancients will scarcely admit of being compared with each other in the most distinguished features of national fame.

3. In all, however, we see the operation of *one principle*, namely *human reason*, which endeavours to produce unity out of multiplicity, order out of disorder, and out of variety of powers and designs one symmetrical and durably beautiful whole. From the shapeless artificial rocks, with which the Chinese ornaments his garden, to the Egyptian pyramid, or the ideal beauty of Greece, the plan and design of a reflecting understanding is every where observable, though in very different degrees. The more refined the reflections of this understanding were, and the nearer it came to the point, which is the highest in its kind, and admits no deviation to the right or to the left; the more were its performances to be considered as models, for they contain eternal rules for the human understanding in all ages. Thus nothing of the kind can be conceived superiour to an Egyptian pyramid, or to several Greek and Roman works of art. They are simple solutions of certain problems of the understanding, which admit no arbitrary supposition, that the problems are perhaps not yet solved, or might be solved in a better way, for in them the simple idea of what they ought to be is displayed in the easiest, fullest, and most beautiful manner. Every deviation from them would be a

fault; and were they to be repeated and diversified in a thousand modes, we must still return to that single point, which is the highest of its kind.

4. Thus through all the polished nations, that we have hitherto considered, or shall hereafter consider, *a chain of cultivation* may be drawn, flying off in extremely divergent curves. In each it designates increasing and decreasing greatness, and has maximums of every kind. Many of these exclude or limit one another, till at length a certain symmetry takes place in the whole; so that were we to reason from one perfection of any nation concerning another, we should form very treacherous conclusions. Thus, because Athens had exquisite orators, it does not follow, that its form of government must likewise have been the best possible; or that, because the Chinese moralize so excellently, their state must be a pattern for all others. Forms of government refer to a very different maximum, from that of beautiful morals, or a pathetic oration; notwithstanding, at bottom, all things in any nation have a certain connexion, if it be only that of exclusion and limitation. No other maximum, but that of the most perfect bond of union, produces the most happy states; even supposing the people are in consequence obliged to dispense with many shining qualities.

5. But in one and the same nation every maximum of its commendable endeavours ought not and cannot endure for ever; since it is but one point in the progress of time. This incessantly moves on; and the more numerous the circumstances, on which the beautiful effect depends, the sooner is it liable to pass away. Happy if its master pieces remain as rules for future ages.

*　　*　　*

REVIEW QUESTIONS

1. What is Herder's argument regarding difference and similarity in the human race?
2. What is the role of time, place, and climate in Herder's view of civilizations?
3. How is Herder's presentation of cultural development different from that of the Enlightenment?

CLAUDE-JOSEPH ROUGET DE LISLE

La Marseillaise

The French national anthem originated in Strasbourg in April 1792 as a battle hymn of the Army of the Rhine; Claude-Joseph Rouget de Lisle, an army captain roused by the French declaration of war against Austria, composed the song. The song's synthesis of patriotism and martial spirit exemplifies not only the new power of an armed citizenry, but also the speed with which nationalist sentiment embedded itself in the popular culture of revolutionary France.

From *The Voice of Nations: European National Anthems and Their Authors*, edited by F. Gunther Eyck, Greenwood Press, 1995.

Arise, children of the native land,
The day of glory has arrived,
Tyranny is upon us
Its bloodstained banner raised.
Do you hear in the fields
Those ferocious soldiers roar?
They are coming right into our midst
To slaughter your sons, your companions,

     To arms, oh citizens,
     Form your battalions;
     March, March!
     So that their impure blood
     Will drench our furrows!

Sacred love of our native land,
Guide, sustain our avenging arms!

Liberty, oh dearest liberty,
Do fight along your defenders!
With our banners there lies victory
Flock to their virile appeal;
So that our dying enemies
Witness your triumph and our glory

REVIEW QUESTIONS

1. How is the call to arms justified?
2. What qualities does the song ascribe to the nation and its defenders?
3. What does this song suggest about French perceptions of the revolutionary era?

NATIONAL CONVENTION

FROM Levée en Masse Edict

This decree of 23 August 1793 mobilized the French nation for war, marking a new era in the modern history of warfare. Numerous setbacks of the French revolutionary army after its initial victories in 1792 compelled the government to pass a universal levy to repulse the enemy. The government's ability to conscript soldiers, requisition supplies, and organize the economy for war reveals the nationalist spirit that gripped France and provides one critical reason for success in the government's subsequent military campaigns.

Documentary Survey of the French Revolution, Stewart, John Hall. © 1951. Adapted by permission of Prentice-Hall Inc., Upper Saddle River, NJ.

*   *   *

1. Henceforth, until the enemies have been driven from the territory of the Republic, the French people are in permanent requisition for army service.

The young men shall go to battle; the married men shall forge arms and transport provisions; the women shall make tents and clothes, and shall serve in the hospitals; the children shall turn old linen into lint; the old men shall repair to the public places, to stimulate the courage of the warriors and preach the unity of the Republic and hatred of kings.

2. National buildings shall be converted into barracks; public places into armament workshops; the soil of cellars shall be washed in lye to extract saltpeter therefrom.

3. Arms of caliber shall be turned over exclusively to those who march against the enemy; the service of the interior shall be carried on with fowling pieces and sabers.

4. Saddle horses are called for to complete the cavalry corps; draught horses, other than those employed in agriculture, shall haul artillery and provisions.

5. The Committee of Public Safety is charged with taking all measures necessary for establishing, without delay, a special manufacture of arms of all kinds, in harmony with the *élan* and the energy of the French people. Accordingly, it is authorized to constitute all establishments, manufactories, workshops, and factories deemed necessary for the execution of such works, as well as to requisition for such purpose, throughout the entire extent of the Republic, the artists and workmen who may contribute to their success. For such purpose a sum of 30,000,000, taken from the 498,200,000 livres in *assignats* in reserve in the "Fund of the Three Keys," shall be placed at the disposal of the Minister of War. The central establishment of said special manufacture shall be established at Paris.

6. The representatives of the people dispatched for the execution of the present law shall have similar authority in their respective *arrondissements*, acting in concert with the Committee of Public Safety; they are invested with the unlimited powers attributed to the representatives of the people with the armies.

7. No one may obtain a substitute in the service to which he is summoned. The public functionaries shall remain at their posts.

8. The levy shall be general. Unmarried citizens or childless widowers, from eighteen to twenty-five years, shall go first; they shall meet, without delay, at the chief town of their districts, where they shall practice manual exercise daily, while awaiting the hour of departure.

9. The representatives of the people shall regulate the musters and marches so as to have armed citizens arrive at the points of assembling only in

so far as supplies, munitions, and all that constitutes the material part of the army exist in sufficient proportion.

10. The points of assembling shall be determined by circumstances, and designated by the representatives of the people dispatched for the execution of the present decree, upon the advice of the generals, in co-operation with the Committee of Public Safety and the provisional Executive Council.

11. The battalion organized in each district shall be united under a banner bearing the inscription: *The French people risen against tyrants.*

12. Such battalions shall be organized according to established decrees, and their pay shall be the same as that of the battalions at the frontiers.

13. In order to collect supplies in sufficient quantity, the farmers and managers of national property shall deposit the produce of such property, in the form of grain, in the chief town of their respective districts.

14. Owners, farmers, and others possessing grain shall be required to pay, in kind, arrears of taxes, even the two-thirds of those of 1793, on the rolls which have served to effect the last payment.

*   *   *

17. The Minister of War is responsible for taking all measures necessary for the prompt execution of the present decree; a sum of 50,000,000, from the 498,200,000 *livres* in *assignats* in the "Fund of the Three Keys," shall be placed at his disposal by the National Treasury.

18. The present decree shall be conveyed to the departments by special messengers.

REVIEW QUESTIONS

1. Which social groups and areas of the economy does this edict affect, and what roles are they assigned?
2. How is this organization for war different from warfare under the old regime?
3. How does this document evoke the sense of emergency and crisis that characterized the years of the republic?

JOHANN GOTTLIEB FICHTE

FROM *Speeches to the German Nation*

One of the most important ramifications of the revolutionary era was the awakening of nationalist sentiment in Europe. The origin of German national consciousness provides a good example. Following the stunning victories of France over Germany between 1802 and 1807, Napoleon redrew the map of Germany, reducing the great power status of Prussia, erecting a federation of satellite states, and creating new kingdoms. Faced with this humiliation, German rulers, statesmen, and intellectuals realized that reform from above was necessary so that the untapped energies of German citizenry could be summoned to defeat the French foe. In the occupied Prussian capital of Berlin in the winter of 1807–1808, the philosopher Johann Gottlieb Fichte held a series of lectures that called for the spiritual renewal of Germany through a program of reformed education that stressed the German nation's character and strength. It typified the idealism and romanticism of German patriotism in this era.

From *Address to the German Nation,* translated by R. F. Jones and G. H. Turnbull, Open Court Publishing, 1922.

Fourteenth Address

Conclusion

In the addresses which I conclude to-day, I have spoken aloud to you first of all, but I have had in view the whole German nation, and my intention has been to gather round me, in the room in which you are bodily present, everyone in the domain of the German language who is able to understand me. If I have succeeded in throwing into any heart which has beaten here in front of me a spark which will continue to glow there and to influence its life, it is not my intention that these hearts should remain apart and lonely; I want to gather to them from over the whole of our common soil men of similar sentiments and resolutions, and to link them together, so that at this central point a single, continuous, and unceasing flame of patriotic disposition may be kindled, which will spread over the whole soil of the fatherland to its utmost boundaries. These addresses have not been meant for the entertainment of indolent ears and eyes in the present age; on the contrary, I want to know once for all, and everyone of like disposition shall know it with me, whether there is anyone besides ourselves whose way of thinking is akin to ours. Every German who still believes himself to be a member of a nation, who thinks highly and nobly of that nation, hopes for it, ventures, endures, and suffers for it, shall at last have the uncertainty of his belief removed; he shall see clearly whether he is right or is only a fool and a dreamer; from now on he shall either pursue his way with the glad consciousness of certainty, or else firmly and vigorously renounce a fatherland here below, and find in the heavenly one his only consolation. To them, not as individuals in our everyday limited life, but as representatives of the nation, and so through their ears to the whole nation, these addresses make this appeal:—

Centuries have come and gone since you were last convoked as you are to-day; in such numbers; in a cause so great, so urgent, and of such concern to all and everyone; so entirely as a nation and as Germans. Never again will the offer come to you in this way. If you now take no heed and withdraw into yourselves, if you again let these addresses go by you as if they were meant merely to tickle your ears, or if you regard them as something strange and fabulous, then no human being will ever take you into account again. Hearken now at last; reflect now at last. Go not from your place this time at least without first making a firm resolution; and let everyone who hears my voice make this resolution by himself and for himself, just as if he were alone and had to do everything alone. If very many individuals think in this way, there will soon be formed a large community which will be fused into a single close-connected force. But if, on the contrary, each one, leaving himself out, puts his hope in the rest and leaves the matter to others, then there will be no others, and all together will remain as they were before. Make it on the spot, this resolution.

*　　*　　*

To all you Germans, whatever position you may occupy in society, these addresses solemnly appeal; let every one of you, who can think, think first of all about the subject here suggested, and let each do for it what lies nearest to him individually in the position he occupies.

Your forefathers unite themselves with these addresses, and make a solemn appeal to you. Think that in my voice there are mingled the voices of your ancestors of the hoary past, who with their own bodies stemmed the onrush of Roman world-dominion, who with their blood won the independence of those mountains, plains, and rivers which under you have fallen a prey to the foreigner. They call to you: "Act for us; let the memory of us which you hand on to posterity be just as honourable and without reproach as it was when it came to you, when you took pride in it and in your descent from us. Until now, the re-sistance we made has been regarded as great and wise and noble; we seemed the consecrated and the inspired in the divine world-purpose. If our race dies out with you, our honour will be turned to shame and our wisdom to foolishness. For if, indeed, the German stock is to be swallowed up in Roman civilization, it were better that it had fallen before the Rome of old than before a Rome of to-day. The former we resisted and conquered; by the latter you have been ground to dust. Seeing that this is so, you shall now not conquer them with temporal weapons; your spirit alone shall rise up against them and stand erect. To you has fallen the greater destiny, to found the empire of the spirit and of reason, and completely to annihilate the rule of brute physical force in the world. If you do this, then you are worthy of your descent from us."

Then, too, there mingle with these voices the spirits of your more recent forefathers, those who fell in the holy war for the freedom of belief and of religion. "Save our honour too," they cry to you. "To us it was not entirely clear what we fought for; besides the lawful resolve not to let ourselves be dictated to by external force in matters of conscience, there was another and a higher spirit driving us, which never fully revealed itself to us. To you it is revealed, this spirit, if you have the power of vision in the spiritual world; it beholds you with eyes clear and sublime. The varied and confused mixture of sensuous and spiritual motives that has hitherto ruled the world shall be displaced, and spirit alone, pure and freed from all sensuous motives, shall take the helm of human affairs. It was in order that this spirit might have freedom to develop and grow to independent existence—it was for this that we poured forth our blood. It is for you to justify and give meaning to our sacrifice, by setting this spirit to fulfil its purpose and to rule the world. If this does not come about as the final goal to which the whole previous development of our nation has been tending, then the battles we fought will turn out to be a vain and fleeting farce, and the freedom of conscience and of spirit that we won is a vain word, it from now onwards spirit and conscience are to be no more."

*   *   *

All ages, all wise and good men who have ever breathed upon this earth, all their thoughts and intuitions of something loftier, mingle with these voices and surround you and lift up imploring hands to you; even, if one may say so, providence and the divine plan in creating a race of men, a plan which exists only to be thought out by men and to be brought by men into the actual world —the divine plan, I say, solemnly appeals to you to save its honour and its existence. Whether those were right who believed that mankind must always grow better, and that thoughts of a true order and worth of man were no idle dreams, but the prophecy and pledge of the real world that is to be— whether they are to be proved right, or those who continue to slumber in an animal and vegetable existence and mock at every flight into higher worlds—to give a final and decisive judgment on this point is a work for you. The old world with its glory and its greatness, as well as its defects, has fallen by its own unworthiness and by the violence of your fathers. If there is truth in what has been expounded in these addresses, then are you of all modern peoples the one in whom the seed of human perfection most unmistakably lies, and to whom the lead in its development is committed. If you perish in this your essential nature, then there perishes together with you every hope of the whole human race for salvation from the depths of its miseries. Do not console yourselves with an opinion based on thin air and depending on the mere recurrence of cases that have already

happened; do not hope that when the old civilization has fallen a new one will arise once more out of a semi-barbarous nation on the ruins of the first. In ancient times there was such a people in existence, equipped with every requirement for such a destiny and quite well known to the civilized people, who have left us their description of it; and they themselves, if they had been able to imagine their own downfall, would have been able to discover in this people the means of reconstruction. To us also the whole surface of the globe is quite well known and all the peoples that dwell thereon. But do we know a people akin to the ancestral stock of the modern world, of whom we may have the same expectation? I think that everyone who does not merely base his hopes and beliefs on idle dreaming, but investigates thoroughly and thinks, will be bound to answer this question with a NO. There is, therefore, no way out; if you go under, all humanity goes under with you, without hope of any future restoration.

This it was, gentlemen, which at the end of these addresses I wanted and was bound to impress upon you, who to me are the representatives of the nation, and through you upon the whole nation.

REVIEW QUESTIONS

1. How does Fichte define the nation? What is the significance of Fichte's stress on continuity between contemporary Germans and their forefathers?
2. What is the relationship of Fichte's nationalism to humanity?

HEINRICH VON GAGERN

FROM Letter to His Father, 17 June 1818

In the years following the Congress of Vienna (1814–1815), German governments suppressed the ideals of constitutionalism and national unity that had arisen during the wars to liberate Germany from Napoleon. In spite of the reactionary policies of Metternich and German states, university students established fraternities, voluntary associations that promoted liberal nationalism. In 1817 these student fraternities organized the Wartburg Festival, mentioned in the letter below, which commemorated Martin Luther's Reformation, denounced official conservative policies, and called for a unified liberal nation-state. Heinrich von Gagern (1799–1880), who co-founded a fraternity as a student and later became one of the prominent liberal leaders during the revolution of 1848, typifies the romantic ideals and nationalist aspirations of German students in the first half of the nineteenth century.

From *Metternich's Europe,* edited by Mack Walker, Harper & Row, 1968.

It is very hard to explain the spirit of the student movement to you, but I shall try, even though I can only give you a few characteristics. At first glance the prudent and experienced man will find fault with the student spirit here, but with a closer view and better understanding he will come to expect the best of the same people when they reach a more mature age. It speaks to the better youth, the man of heart and spirit and love for all that is good, and gives him nourishment and being. For the average student of the past, the university years were a time to enjoy life, and to make a sharp break with his own background in defiance of the philistine world, which seemed to him somehow to foreshadow the tomb. Their pleasures, their organizations, and their talk were determined by their *status* as students, and their university obligation was only to avoid failing the examination and scraping by adequately—bread-and-butter learning. They were satisfied with themselves if they thought they could pass the examination. There are still many of those nowadays, indeed the majority over-all. But at several universities, and especially here, another group—in my eyes a bet-ter one—has managed to get the upper hand in the sense that it sets the mood. I prefer really not to call it a mood; rather, it is something that presses hard and tries to spread its ideas—ideas in the spirit of the Wartburg, as you yourself said; but in that case it was a bit exaggerated, perhaps through external circumstances: collective feelings, thoughts of the holiness of the festival, associated with that place and date, emotions raised by individual events. All these things may have led to overexcitement. But this much is sure, from all I have heard, that festival was undertaken in a noble spirit.

This is going to be a long letter again, for I am already beginning to tell long stories.—Those who share in this spirit have then quite another tendency in their student life, Love of Fatherland is their guiding principle. Their purpose is to make a better future for the Fatherland, each as best he can, to spread national consciousness, or to use the much ridiculed and maligned Germanic expression, more folkishness, and to work for better constitutions. Their student organizations, their self-development, and their whole way of life are means to these ends. They hold no particular bias as students that would lapse when they cease to be students; rather, they want to bring the ideals they have grasped as students into civic life with them and adapt their civic careers to their student ideals as best they can. They are accused of trying to express their German sentiments in an absurd way by wearing old-fashioned Germanic cloaks. But to this they answer: "We are not trying to make something special out of wearing Germanic cloaks, we only want Germany to have its own fashion. Let anybody who likes invent a native form of cloak in Germany, and we shall wear them as German cloaks; but until that happens we shall wear the cloak our forefathers wore, rather than let other peoples impose their fashions upon us and have us copy them."—People say to them: "How high and mighty do you think you are? How can you take it upon yourselves to create something new in the world?"—They answer: "Do we want to create something new? We only want to sustain it and always sustain it, wherever civic circumstances give us the chance to do so. If we stay true to this principle, and if those who come after us at the universities behave as we do, and if there are more and more such, then in civic life too there will be larger numbers of like-minded, who will also show it by their cloaks. We are not trying to be high and mighty at all. We are young people who act according to their convictions, though we willingly accept better advice when we hear it. But until we hear it we must be true to our convictions still. The prejudice that the world in general has against students will cease little by little when we engage in more regular activities, and when we try to overcome the sharp contradiction between ordinary civic life and the special status of student life—which is of course our aim. We shall not always remain students, either; many of the chief servants of the state will emerge from among us. Let us see whether we hold to the same principles then. At most they will have been led from the boiling torrent of youthful imagination into the quiet, peaceful channel of cooler intelligence and of reality. But we hope that these ideas will not suffer the fate of cham-

pagne, whose spirit flees when the effervescence does; the spirit rather will have settled into the wine."

As an informed observer you will say now, my dear Father: "That is all well and good, but what is the aim in practical fact? What do you want Germany to be? What are your political views? What is your purpose?"—This I have only briefly suggested so far, and now I shall make some additions. We want more sense of community among the several states of Germany, greater unity in their policies and in their principles of government; no separate policy for each state, but the nearest possible relations with one another; above all, we want Germany to be considered *one* land and the German people *one* people. In the forms of our student comradeship we show how we want to approach this as nearly as possible in the real world. Regional fraternities are forbidden, and we live in a German comradeship, one people in spirit, as we want it for all Germany in reality. We give our selves the freest of constitutions, just as we should like Germany to have the freest possible one, insofar as that is suitable for the German people. We want a constitution for the people that fits in with the spirit of the times and with the people's own level of enlightenment, rather than what each prince gives his people according to what he likes and what serves his private interest. Above all, we want the princes to understand and to follow the principle that they exist for the country and not the country for them. In fact, the prevailing view is that the constitution should not come from the individual states at all. The main principles of the German constitution should apply to all states in common, and should be expressed by the German federal assembly. This constitution should deal not only with the absolute necessities, like fiscal administration and justice, general administration and church and military affairs and so on; this constitution ought to be extended to the education of the young, at least at the upper age levels, and to many other such things.

There is a learned society here made up entirely of young people, or I should say it is just now really getting started, in which the members come together just as they like and choose, to work out certain things bearing on all kinds of subjects. One group works on historical subjects, another on constitutional law, where constitutions are made and existing ones criticized and so on. There are drafts of church statutes, others on education, and so on. Drafts and proposals are submitted first within the groups working on each subject, and then laid before larger meetings of the whole. Ideas are developed there, discussed, criticized, praised, accepted or rejected. Because this is a very good system and there is no compulsion, we can learn a great deal that way. Sometime I shall send you work that comes from this for your inspection and criticism. The state constitutions are examined very closely there; and that certainly has the value of making us very well acquainted with them.

*   *   *

REVIEW QUESTIONS

1. According to von Gagern, what is the spirit and purpose of the fraternities?
2. What explicit political purposes are expressed in this letter?
3. What is the significance of university students engaging in oppositional politics?
4. How does von Gagern's view of student fraternities compare to Metternich's perspective on student politics?

LORD BYRON

On This Day I Complete My Thirty-Sixth Year

George Gordon, Lord Byron (1788–1824), one of the prominent English Romantic poets, took up the cause of liberating Greece from the Ottoman empire, lending his money, time, and pen to the cause of independence. In 1823 he sailed to Greece, where he partook in preparation for the Greek uprising. Before he had the chance to fight and find "a soldier's grave," Byron fell ill and died. Just prior to his death, however, he composed the following poem, which immortalized the Greek nationalist movement. The engagement of such intellectuals as Byron for national freedom generated widespread support among western European bourgeois circles for nationalist movements.

From *The Best of Byron*, edited by Richard Ashley Rice, Ronald Press Co., 1942. 2nd edition.

'Tis time this heart should be unmoved,
    Since others it hath ceased to move:
Yet, though I cannot be beloved,
    Still let me love!

My days are in the yellow leaf;
    The flowers and fruits of love are gone;
The worm, the canker, and the grief
    Are mine alone!

The fire that on my bosom preys
 Is lone as some volcanic isle;
No torch is kindled at its blaze—
 A funeral pile.

The hope, the fear, the jealous care,
 The exalted portion of the pain
And power of love, I cannot share,
 But wear the chain.

But 'tis not *thus*—and 'tis not *here*—
 Such thoughts should shake my soul nor
  now,
Where glory decks the hero's bier,
 Or binds his brow.

The sword, the banner, and the field,
 Glory and Greece, around me see!
The Spartan, borne upon his shield,
 Was not more free.

Awake! (not Greece—she *is* awake!)
 Awake, my spirit! Think through *whom*
Thy life-blood tracks its parent lake,
 And then strike home!

Tread those reviving passions down,
 Unworthy manhood!—unto thee
Indifferent should the smile or frown
 Of beauty be.

If thou regrett'st thy youth, *why live?*
 The land of honourable death
Is here:—up to the field, and give
 Away thy breath!

Seek out—less often sought than found—
 A soldier's grave, for thee the best;
Then look around, and choose thy ground,
 And take thy rest.

REVIEW QUESTIONS

1. What does the poem exhort the reader to do?
2. How does the author romanticize the Greek cause?
3. How are immortality, manhood, and honor achieved in this poem, and how are these attributes related to nationalism?

ADAM MICKIEWICZ

FROM The Books of the Polish Nation

The Polish uprising of 1830–1831 against Russian imperial control produced an outpouring of sympathy in western Europe. Adam Mickiewicz (1798–1855), a Polish patriot living in Paris, wrote the following poem in 1832. The heroic epic typifies the histrionic nature of patriotic Romantic verse, but the poem is further significant in its attempt to breathe religious spirituality into the cause of Polish nationalism.

From *Metternich's Europe*, edited by Mack Walker, Harper & Row, 1968.

In the beginning there was belief in one God, and there was freedom in the world. And there were no laws, only the will of God, and there were no lords and slaves, only patriarchs and their children.

But later the people denied the one God, and made for themselves idols, and bowed themselves down to them, and slew in their honor bloody offerings, and waged war for the honor of their idols.

Therefore God sent upon the idolaters the greatest punishment, which is slavery.

*   *   *

Finally in idolatrous Europe there rose three rulers; the name of the first was *Frederick the Second* of Prussia, the name of the second was *Catherine the Second* of Russia, the name of the third was *Maria Theresa* of Austria.

And this was a Satanic trinity, contrary to the Divine Trinity, and was in the manner of a mock and a derision of all that is holy.

Frederick, whose name signifieth *friend of peace*, contrived wars and pillage throughout his whole life, and was like Satan eternally panting for war, who in derision should be called Christ, the God of peace.

*   *   *

Now *Catherine* signifieth in Greek pure, but she was the lewdest of women, and it was as though the shameless Venus had called herself a pure virgin.

And this Catherine assembled a council for the establishing of laws, that she might turn lawmaking into a mockery, for the rights of her neighbors she overthrew and destroyed.

And this Catherine proclaimed that she protected freedom of conscience or tolerance, that she might make a mock of freedom of conscience, for she forced millions of her neighbors to change their faith. And *Maria Theresa* bore the name of the most meek and immaculate Mother of the Savior, that she might make a mock of humility and holiness.

For she was a proud she-devil, and carried on war to make subject the lands of others.

*   *   *

Then this trinity, seeing that not yet were the people sufficiently foolish and corrupt, fashioned a new idol, the most abominable of all, and they called this idol *Interest*, and this idol was not known among the pagans of old.

*   *   *

But the Polish nation alone did not bow down to the new idol, and did not have in its language the expression for christening it in Polish, neither for christening its worshipers, whom it calls by the French word *egoists*.

The Polish nation worshiped God, knowing that he who honoreth God giveth honor to everything that is good.

The Polish nation then from the beginning to the end was true to the God of its ancestors.

Its kings and men of knightly rank never assaulted any believing nation, but defended Christendom from the pagans and barbarians who brought slavery.

And the Polish kings went to the defense of Christians in distant lands, King Wladislaw to Varna, and King Jan to Vienna, to the defense of the east and the west.

And never did their kings and men of knightly rank seize neighboring lands by force, but they received the nations into brotherhood, uniting them with themselves by the gracious gift of faith and freedom.

And God rewarded them, for a great nation, Lithuania, united itself with Poland, as husband with wife, two souls in one body. And there was never before this such a union of nations. But hereafter there shall be.

For that union and marriage of Lithuania and Poland is the symbol of the future union of all Christian peoples in the name of faith and freedom.

And God gave unto the Polish kings and knights freedom, that all might be called brothers, both the richest and the poorest. And such freedom never was before. But hereafter there shall be.

The king and the men of knightly rank received into their brotherhood still more people; they received whole armies and whole tribes. And the number of brothers became as great as a nation, and in no nation were there so many people free and calling each other brothers as in Poland.

And finally, on the Third of May, the king and the knightly body determined to make all Poles brothers, at first the burghers and later the peasants.

And they called the brothers the nobility, because they had become noble, that is had become brothers with the Lachs, who were men free and equal.

And they wished to bring it about that every Christian in Poland should be ennobled and called a Nobleman, for a token that he should have a noble soul and always be ready to die for freedom.

Just as of old they called each man accepting the gospel a Christian, for a token that he was ready to shed his blood for Christ.

Nobility then was to be the baptism of freedom, and every one who was ready to die for freedom was to be baptized of the law and of the sword.

And finally Poland said: "Whosoever will come to me shall be free and equal, for I am FREEDOM."

But the kings when they heard of this were terrified in their hearts and said: "We banished freedom from the earth; but lo, it returneth in the person of a just nation, that doth not bow down to our idols! Come, let us slay this nation." And they plotted treachery among themselves.

And the King of Prussia came and kissed the Polish Nation and greeted it, saying: "My ally," but already he had sold it for thirty cities of Great Poland, even as Judas for thirty pieces of silver.

And the two other rulers fell upon and bound the Polish Nation. And Gaul was judge and said: "Verily I find no fault in this nation, and France my wife, a timid woman, is tormented with evil dreams; nevertheless, take for yourselves and martyr this nation." And he washed his hands.

And the ruler of France said: "We cannot ransom this innocent nation by our blood or by our money, for my blood and my money belong to me, but the blood and money of my nation belong to my nation."

And this ruler uttered the last blasphemy against Christ, for Christ taught that the blood of the Son of Man belongeth to all our brother men.

And when the ruler had uttered these words, then the crosses fell from the towers of the godless capital, for the sign of Christ could no longer shine upon a people worshiping the idol *Interest.*

And this ruler was called Casimir-Périer, a Slavic first name and a Roman last name. His first name signifieth corrupter or annihilator of peace, and his last name signifieth, from the word *perire* or *périr*, destroyer or son of destruction. And these two names are anti-Christian. And they shall be alike accursed among the Slavic race and among the Roman race.

And this man rent the league of peoples as that Jewish priest rent his clothes upon hearing the voice of Christ.

And they martyred the Polish Nation and laid it in the grave, and the kings cried out: "We have slain and we have buried Freedom."

But they cried out foolishly, for in committing the last sin they filled up the measure of their iniquities, and their power was coming to an end at the time when they exulted most.

For the Polish Nation did not die: its body lieth in the grave, but its spirit hath descended from the earth, that is from public life, to the abyss, that is to the private life of people who suffer slavery in their country and outside of their country, that it may see their sufferings.

But on the third day the soul shall return to the body, and the Nation shall arise and free all the peoples of Europe from slavery.

And already two days have gone by. One day passed with the first capture of Warsaw, and the second day passed with the second capture of

Warsaw, and the third day shall begin, but shall not pass.

And as after the resurrection of Christ bloody offerings ceased in all the world, so after the resurrection of the Polish Nation wars shall cease in all Christendom.

REVIEW QUESTIONS

1. Why is the poem's biblical cadence significant?
2. How does Christianity serve the cause of Polish nationalism?
3. How does the poem recount Poland's plight in the history of eastern Europe?

ALEXEI STEPANOVICH KHOMYAKOV

FROM To the Serbs: An Epistle from Moscow

Alongside national consciousness arose two allied movements in eastern Europe: Panslavism and Slavophilism. The former explored the means for political and cultural unity of Europe's Slavic cultures; the Pan-Slav Congress in June 1848, for example, sought ways to unite Slav interests in the Austrian Empire. Slavophilism, however, was largely a Russian intellectual movement in the second half of the nineteenth century that sought to bring southern and western Slav cultures back into the orbit of Eastern Orthodox Church thinking. Alexei Khomyakov, one of the chief exponents of this doctrine, argued forcefully that the overarching religious influence of orthodoxy was more critical than national roots for the proper development of Slavic identity, whose cultural and political communities transcended national borders. The epistle below, written in 1860, captures the mood and substance of the Slavophilism movement.

From *A Documentary History of Russian Thought: From the Enlightenment to Marxism*, (eds.) W. J. Leatherbarrow and C. C. Offord, (Ardis, 1987.) Reprinted by permission.

*   *   *

. . . In truth, O Serbs, God has bestowed great favors upon you, greater, we think, than you yourselves know. A healthy body is one of man's greatest blessings, but he realizes this only when he loses it, or when he observes the illnesses of others and compares them with his own healthy state. In the same way you can come to know your advantages only through comparison with the shortcomings of other societies (and you have not yet attended to such a comparison), or through the frank confession of such other societies, who know from experience their sicknesses and their causes. Let this knowledge serve as a warning to you, so that you might avoid the errors which other nations have not been able to avoid, and so that, in adopting what is good and useful, you will not be infected by those malignant principles which often accompany good things, unnoticed by the inexperienced eye.

The first, most important and priceless blessing which you, the Serbs, possess is your unity in Orthodoxy, that highest wisdom and highest truth, the root of all spiritual and moral growth. Such is your unity in the faith that for the Turk the words "Serb" and "Orthodox" are synonymous. You must value this finest of all blessings above all others, and guard it as you would the pupil of your eye; after all, what is Orthodoxy if not the pupil of one's inner, spiritual eye?

Christianity was not sown by force in the world; nor did it develop through violence, but by overcoming all violence. Thus it must not be preserved by violence, and woe to him who seeks to protect the might of Christ with the feebleness of human weapons! Faith is a matter of spiritual freedom, and it tolerates no compulsion. True faith is conquering the world, but it does not seek the temporal sword for its triumph. Therefore, respect all freedom of conscience and faith, in order that no one should offend against the truth by saying that it fears falsehood and does not dare compete with falsehood armed only with thought and words. Defend God's honor, not with timidity and doubt as to its might, but boldly and with a calm confidence in its victory.

But, on the other hand, always bear in mind the significance and dignity of the faith. Those who think that it is simply a matter of creed, rituals, or even the direct communion of man with God, are quite wrong. No, faith penetrates man's whole being and all his relations with his neighbor. As if with invisible threads or roots it binds together all his feelings, all his convictions and all his aspirations. It is a sort of rarefied air, recreating and transforming within him every mundane principle, or a luminous light, illuminating all his moral conceptions and all his views on other people and the inner laws which bind him to them. Therefore, faith is also the highest social principle; for society itself is precisely the visible manifestation of our inner relations with other people and our union with them.

A healthy civil society is based on its citizens' understanding of brotherhood, truth, justice and mercy; but this understanding cannot be the same among men if their faiths are different. The Jew and the Mohammedan profess one God, just like the Christian, but is their understanding of truth and mercy the same as ours? Of course, it will be said that they know neither the Sacrament of the Holy and Ever-Worshipful Trinity, nor the love of God, which is our salvation through Christ, and that consequently the difference between them and us is too great. But we know that even Christians, apart from the true Orthodox Church, possess neither a totally clear understanding nor a totally sincere sense of brotherhood. Such an understanding and such a sense develop and strengthen only in Orthodoxy. It is no accident that the commune, the sanctity of the communal verdict and the unquestioning submission of each individual to the unanimous decision of his brethren are preserved only in Orthodox countries. The teachings of the faith cultivate the soul even in social life. The Papist seeks extraneous and personal authority, just as he is used to submitting to such authority in matters of faith; the Protestant takes personal freedom to the extreme of blind arrogance, just as in his sham worship. Such is the spirit of their teaching. Only the Orthodox Christian, preserving his freedom, yet humbly acknowledging his weakness, subordinates his freedom to the unanimous resolution of the collective conscience. It is for this reason that the local commune has not been able to preserve its laws outside Orthodox countries. And it is for this reason that the Slav cannot be fully a Slav without Orthodoxy. Even our brethren who have been led astray by the Western falsehood, be they Papists or Protestants, acknowledge this with grief. This principle applies to all matters of justice and truth, and to all conceptions about society; for at the root of it lies brotherhood.

*   *   *

REVIEW QUESTIONS

1. How is the Eastern Orthodox Church portrayed as the superior religion?
2. What are the cultural advantages for Serbs to

embrace the Eastern Orthodox religion and way of life?

3. What is promised?

4. How does this eastern doctrine undermine western notions of nationalism?

5. What are the implications of this doctrine for relations between the Austrian and Russian empires?

GIUSEPPE MAZZINI

FROM Duties of Man

Giuseppe Mazzini (1805–1872) was one of the most well known liberal-national revolutionaries of the nineteenth century. Mazzini achieved international renown for his founding of Young Italy in 1831, an organization that strove for an Italian republic, which spawned the parallel associations Young Poland, Young Germany, and Young Ireland. In 1849 he assisted Garibaldi in defending the Roman republic, and after its defeat was compelled to flee Italy. In exile he continued his efforts as a writer for a unified Italian republic. The eventual unification of Italy during the period 1859–1871 brought him little satisfaction, because it was realized under the conservative political settlement of a constitutional monarchy. His Duties of Man, first begun in weekly installments in 1840, best characterized Mazzini's liberal-democratic humanitarian spirit, which endowed the nationalism of this period with an ethical, moral core.

To the Italian Working Class

To you, sons and daughters of the people, I dedicate this little book, wherein I have pointed out the principles in the name and strength of which you may, if you so will, accomplish your mission in Italy; a mission of republican progress for all and of emancipation for yourselves. Let those who are specially favoured by circumstances or in understanding, and able to comprehend these principles more easily, explain and comment on them to the others, and may that spirit of love inspire them with which, as I wrote, I thought on your griefs and on your virgin aspirations towards the new life which—once the unjust inequality now stifling your faculties is overcome—you will kindle in the Italian country.

I loved you from my first years. The republican instincts of my mother taught me to seek out among my fellows the Man, not the merely rich and powerful individual; and the simple unconscious virtue of my father accustomed me to admire, rather than conceited and pretentious semi-knowledge, the silent and unnoticed virtue of self-sacrifice so often found in you. Later on I gathered from the history of our country that the true life of Italy is the life of the people, and that the slow work of the centuries has constantly tended, amid the shock of different races and the superficial transitory changes wrought by usurpations and conquests, to prepare the great democratic National Unity. . . .

Duties to Country

Your first Duties—first, at least, in importance—are, as I have told you, to Humanity. You are *men* before you are *citizens* or *fathers*. If you do not embrace the whole human family in your love, if you do not confess your faith in its unity —consequent on the unity of God—and in the brotherhood of the Peoples who are appointed to reduce that unity for fact—if wherever one of your fellowmen groans, wherever the dignity of human nature is violated by falsehood or tyranny, you are not prompt, being able, to succour that wretched one, or do not feel yourself called, being able, to fight for the purpose of relieving the deceived or oppressed—you disobey your law of life, or do not comprehend the religion which will bless the future.

But what can *each* of you, with his isolated powers, *do* for the moral improvement, for the progress of Humanity? . . . God gave you this means when he gave you a Country, when, like a wise overseer of labour, who distributes the different parts of the work according to the capacity of the workmen, he divided Humanity into distinct groups upon the face of our globe, and thus planted the seeds of nations. Bad governments have disfigured the design of God, which you may see clearly marked out, as far, at least, as regards Europe, by the courses of the great rivers, by the lines of the lofty mountains, and by other geographical conditions; they have disfigured it by conquest, by greed, by jealousy of the just sovereignty of others; disfigured it so much that today there is perhaps no nation except England and France whose confines correspond to this design. They did not, and they do not, recognise any country except their own families and dynasties, the egoism of caste. But the divine design will in-

fallibly be fulfilled. Natural divisions, the innate spontaneous tendencies of the people will replace the arbitrary divisions sanctioned by bad governments. The map of Europe will be remade. The Countries of the People will rise, defined by the voice of the free, upon the ruins of the Countries of Kings and privileged castes. Between these Countries there will be harmony and brotherhood. And then the work of Humanity for the general amelioration, for the discovery and application of the real law of life, carried on in association and distributed according to local capacities, will be accomplished by peaceful and progressive development; then each of you, strong in the affections and in the aid of many millions of men speaking the same language, endowed with the same tendencies, and educated by the same historic tradition, may hope by your personal effort to benefit the whole of Humanity.

To you, who have been born in Italy, God has allotted, as if favouring you specially, the best-defined country in Europe. In other lands, marked by more uncertain or more interrupted limits, questions may arise which the pacific vote of all will one day solve, but which have cost, and will yet perhaps cost, tears and blood; in yours, no. God has stretched round you sublime and indisputable boundaries; on one side the highest mountains of Europe, the Alps; on the other the sea, the immeasurable sea. Take a map of Europe and place one point of a pair of compasses in the north of Italy on Parma; point the other to the mouth of the Var, and describe a semicircle with it in the direction of the Alps; this point, which will fall, when the semicircle is completed, upon the mouth of the Isonzo, will have marked the frontier which God has given you. As far as this frontier your language is spoken and understood; beyond this you have no rights. Sicily, Sardinia, Corsica, and the smaller islands between them and the mainland of Italy belong undeniably to you. Brute force may for a little while contest these frontiers with you, but they have been recognised from of old by the tacit general consent of the peoples; and the day when, rising with one accord for the final trial, you plant your tricoloured flag upon that frontier, the whole of Europe will acclaim re-risen Italy, and receive her into the community of the nations. To this final trial all your efforts must be directed.

Without Country you have neither name, token, voice, nor rights, no admission as brothers into the fellowship of the Peoples. You are the bastards of Humanity. Soldiers without a banner, Israelites among the nations, you will find neither faith nor protection; none will be sureties for you. Do not beguile yourselves with the hope of emancipation from unjust social conditions if you do not first conquer a Country for yourselves; where there is no Country there is no common agreement to which you can appeal; the egoism of self-interest rules alone, and he who has the upper hand keeps it, since there is no common safeguard for the interests of all. Do not be led away by the idea of improving your material conditions without first solving the national question. You cannot do it. Your industrial associations and mutual help societies are useful as a means of educating and disciplining yourselves; as an economic fact they will remain barren until you have an Italy. The economic problem demands, first and foremost, an increase of capital and production; and while your Country is dismembered into separate fragments—while shut off by the barrier of customs and artificial difficulties of every sort, you have only restricted markets open to you—you cannot hope for this increase. Today—do not delude yourselves—you are not the working-class of Italy; you are only fractions of that class; powerless, unequal to the great task which you propose to yourselves. Your emancipation can have no practical beginning until a National Government, understanding the signs of the times, shall, seated in Rome, formulate a Declaration of Principles to be the guide for Italian progress, and shall insert into it these words, *Labour is sacred, and is the source of the wealth of Italy.*

Do not be led astray, then, by hopes of material progress which in your present conditions can only be illusions. Your Country alone, the vast and rich Italian Country, which stretches from the Alps to the farthest limit of Sicily, can fulfil these hopes. You cannot obtain your *rights* except by obeying the commands of *Duty*. Be worthy of them, and you will have them. O my Brothers! love your Country. Our Country is our home, the home which God has given us, placing therein a numerous family which we love and are loved by, and with which we have a more intimate and quicker communion of feeling and thought than with others; a family which by its concentration upon a given spot, and by the homogeneous nature of its elements, is destined for a special kind of activity. Our Country is our field of labour; the products of our activity must go forth from it for the benefit of the whole earth; but the instruments of labour which we can use best and most effectively exist in it, and we may not reject them without being unfaithful to God's purpose and diminishing our own strength. In labouring according to true principles for our Country we are labouring for Humanity; our Country is the fulcrum of the lever which we have to wield for the common good. If we give up this fulcrum we run the risk of becoming useless to our Country and to Humanity. Before *associating* ourselves with the Nations which compose Humanity we must exist as a Nation. There can be no association except among equals; and you have no recognised collective existence.

Humanity is a great army moving to the conquest of unknown lands, against powerful and wary enemies. The Peoples are the different corps and divisions of that army. Each has a post entrusted to it; each a special operation to perform; and the common victory depends on the exactness with which the different operations are carried out. Do not disturb the order of the battle. Do not abandon the banner which God has given you. Wherever you may be, into the midst of whatever people circumstances may have driven you, fight for the liberty of that people if the moment calls for it; but fight as Italians, so that the blood which you shed may win honour and love, not for you only, but for your Country. And may the constant thought of your soul be for Italy, may all the acts of your life be worthy of her, and may the standard beneath which you range yourselves to work for

Humanity be Italy's. Do not say *I*; say *we*. Be every one of you an incarnation of your Country, and feel himself and make himself responsible for his fellow-countrymen; let each one of you learn to act in such a way that in him men shall respect and love his Country.

Your Country is one and indivisible. As the members of a family cannot rejoice at the common table if one of their number is far away, snatched from the affection of his brothers, so you should have no joy or repose as long as a portion of the territory upon which your language is spoken is separated from the Nation.

*   *   *

A Country is a fellowship of free and equal men bound together in a brotherly concord of labour towards a single end. You must make it and maintain it such. A Country is not an aggregation, it is an *association*. There is no true Country without a uniform right. There is no true Country where the uniformity of that right is violated by the existence of caste, privilege, and inequality— where the powers and faculties of a large number of individuals are suppressed or dormant—where there is no common principle accepted, recognised, and developed by all. In such a state of things there can be no Nation, no People, but only a multitude, a fortuitous agglomeration of men whom circumstances have brought together and different circumstances will separate. In the name of your love of your Country you must combat without truce the existence of every privilege, every inequality, upon the soil which has given you birth.

*   *   *

The laws made by one fraction of the citizens only can never by the nature of things and men do otherwise than reflect the thoughts and aspirations and desires of that fraction; they represent, not the whole country, but a third, a fourth part, a class, a zone of the country. The law must express the general aspiration, promote the good of all, respond to a beat of the nation's heart. The whole nation therefore should be, directly or indirectly, the legislator. By yielding this mission to a few men, you put the egoism of one class in the place of the Country, which is the union of *all* the classes.

A Country is not a mere territory; the particular territory is only its foundation. The Country is the idea which rises upon that foundation; it is the sentiment of love, the sense of fellowship which binds together all the sons of that territory. So long as a single one of your brothers is not represented by his own vote in the development of the national life—so long as a single one vegetates uneducated among the educated—so long as a single one able and willing to work languishes in poverty for want of work—you have not got a Country such as it ought to be, the Country of all and for all. *Votes, education, work* are the three main pillars of the nation; do not rest until your hands have solidly erected them.

*   *   *

REVIEW QUESTIONS

1. How is Mazzini's nationalism related to the larger issue of humanity?
2. For Mazzini what is necessary to achieve progress in humanity?
3. How does Mazzini define a country?
4. Why might Mazzini's nationalism be termed utopian?

THOMAS DAVIS

FROM *Letters of a Protestant on Repeal*

England's closest and most unruly colony, Ireland, renewed its agitation for political independence in the 1840s. Daniel O'Connell's Catholic Association, which had been instrumental in wresting political rights from parliament in 1828, lobbied again in the 1840s for repeal from the union. During the 1840s, however, Young Ireland, a party that coalesced around the paper The Nation, *offered a more radical vision of a unified Irish republic. Thomas Osborne Davis (1814–1845), an Irish poet and politician, cofounded the paper, in which he published many ballads and expounded on the viability of Ireland as an independent republic.*

From *Letters of a Protestant on Repeal*, The Irish Confederation, 1847.

*   *   *

In my last letter I tried to prove, from the latest statistics, that "if liberty were the product of material forces, Ireland would be an independent nation." Throughout America, Asia, and Africa, there are but four independent nations exceeding us in revenue and fighting men, though these continents contain many hundreds of free—perfectly free nations.

*   *   *

The great majority of states in all ages have been inferior to Ireland in dimensions and numbers. Each of the clans and tribes, wherein the ruder nations lived, rarely equalled the population of our smallest county; and the coolest of all political philosophers—a statesman who had outlived revolutions, who had ordered a young nation, and prepared constitutions under which millions live and die—Thomas Jefferson—came to the conclusion, that village or clan government was the noblest and the happiest of any. I may differ from him, but his words demand respect; nor does he speak alone.

Take the next stage, and you find that the republics of Phoenicia, Etruria, Asia Minor, and Greece, created the arts which have most strengthened the hand of man—the sciences which have crowned his intellect—the poetry which has spiritualized his habits—the philosophy that judges his virtue—the history which subjects the past to his uses—and the examples which trouble the depths of his soul as with the hand of heaven.

Yet the largest of these was not a tenth of the size of Ireland. Most of them had not more territory than the liberties of one of our large towns.

*   *   *

Of the force of small states we have three striking instances before us at this present hour. After Russia had swept from her path the powers of Poland, Turkey, Persia, and a hundred more, she met her match—nay, praise be to God! her conqueror, in the scanty tribes of Circassia. France, the vast, the warlike, the renowned, after that she had overran Europe four times, and been ultimately beaten only by a world in combination—France, which since that dark day could traverse Spain in a summer, has been baffled by the heroic clans of northern Africa. And England, having put a hundred millions of Hindoos beneath her feet, and while dictating terms with a handful of men to three hundred and odd million Chinese, retreats with loss and difficulty from the shepherds of Affghanistan.

Ireland, then has the bulk of a nation and the physical power of independence; but the higher power—knowledge, and the highest power—resolve, she hath not. She has them not, or she would be free. Body hath she, but where—where is the soul?

What wants she to be a nation? Heavens! why is it that the commonplace chatter of these twenty years back is forgotten, or its first consequences overlooked? Men have talked, till the ear grew dull, of her harbours—they are a hundred—of her land—here so rich, there so stern, in all so goodly—of her climate—so varied, genial, and instructive—and of her position—out to sea, and fossed round by the deep guardian ocean. These things she has had always, and her people, 'tis added, are eight millions. Eight millions or more —they are owners of no mean heritage from nature. With riches at their feet, and beauty around them, and glory behind, before, and above them, the fame of illustrious ancestors, the inspiration of great endowments, the hope of a splendid future —why are they slaves? Slaves they are, for they do not govern themselves, speak for themselves, act, toil, fight, live, hope for themselves. They are taxed by the English, legislated for by England. Englishmen execute their laws, they are taught the language, history, policy, and prejudices of England; they live for England, die for England, are owned by England. Is not this slavery? What matter that with delusive laws she talks sometimes of Irish rights? What matter that she tolerates the existence of Irish Helots, and suffers their noise till her nerves get fretted, and she is forced to smite them into silence? They live impoverished, dishonoured, and obedient. They are slaves, they are things. Ireland has a body, but no soul.

Eight millions, good sooth! When Ulster had not 200,000 people, it maintained its independence for four centuries against the splendid Plantagenet and the fiery Tudor. In the 17th century, when Ireland had but a million and a quarter of disunited people, she supported a National Government, and carried on two great wars against England, one of twelve years' duration, from 1641 to 1653; and the other of four years, from 1688 to 1692. Yet, then, the Roman Catholics alone represented Ireland, and harassed by the Protestants of the North, and divided among themselves, they, that handful of Roman Catholics, held their own against England. They were not talking of numbers only; they computed the force of duty, and the greatness of resolve.

Again, in 1782, look at the Protestants, who then represented Ireland. After a struggle of twenty years, holding the fetters of the Catholic with one hand, and with the other grappling with England, they wrung their independence by the terror of arms. Let no man hasten to condemn them for not emancipating the Roman Catholics, Their ancestors, brutalized by the temptations of wealth and the pangs of bigotry, had enslaved the Roman Catholics; but fifty years gave the sons of the tyrants a *habit* of domination which nothing but the stormy virtue of a revolution could destroy, and had corrupted and debased the slave. Or, if they be condemned, condemn Leonidas, Brutus, and Washington—freemen, yet served by Helots—by Helots despised, because degraded— "wretches and cowards, because slaves."

But, be that as it may, heart and soul, knowledge and purpose, a well-selected opportunity, and a bold policy which did not shrink from the battle-field, enabled the million of Protestants, gazed on by three and a-half millions of Roman Catholics, to triumph in '82.

In '93 the partial union of four millions of Irishmen, led by Tone, Keogh, and such men, who hastened to avail themselves of French victories, extorted fresh liberties from England.

Again, in 1828, when the Roman Catholics once more represented Ireland, was it mere numbers effected Catholic Emancipation? No; opposed by England, Scotland, and the North, five million Roman Catholics did the deed, by union, firmness, and devotion. They resolved to succeed—they accepted and sought out the help of America, France, and of part of England, without asking whether the one held slaves, the other was orthodox in theology, or the third had a rag of private morals left. They sacrificed ease, time, and money. They were notoriously ready to sacrifice life, too. Their foes grew pale, and Emancipation was carried. Their numbers were almost as many for years before—they have been much greater for many years since; yet what was done save in that hour of stern and intelligent purpose?

'Tis needless for me to draw conclusions from this survey of past and present.

But, you will tell me, Ireland has now resumed her energy, and is resolved to be free, at any cost. If so, she will soon be independent. If so, she has *all* the elements of nationality,—size, place, strength, and purpose; she need only "pronounce her will"—"its very breath will rend her chains."

"For a nation to be free," says the French declaration, " 'tis sufficient that it wills it." The expressed will *is* enough, if the country has the soul as well as the body of a nation. A hundred millions of Hindoos *will* to be free, but they have no national soul, and they sob in vain.

I, too, believe Ireland is rapidly acquiring the high spirit, the political sagacity, and the stedfast purpose of a nation, That she may soon perfectly learn all the virtues which give and guard independence, is the sincere prayer of

AN IRISH PROTESTANT.

REVIEW QUESTIONS

1. What is the significance of the reference in the title to Protestantism?
2. What is Davis's intention with his discussion of small republics?
3. Why should Ireland become a national republic?
4. How does Davis periodize the Irish quest for independence?
5. Why does Davis characterize the Irish as slaves?

OTTO VON BISMARCK

FROM *The Memoirs*

Otto von Bismarck (1815–1898), a Prussian noble, served the Prussian crown as its premier statesmen from 1862 to 1890. Under his aegis, Prussia united Germany, creating the German Empire in 1871, a nation-state whose power and size significantly altered the European state system. Prussia's bid to unite Germany brought armed conflict with Austria in 1866. Yet Prussia's military victory was only partly successful, for Prussia's role as unifier could only become legitimate with popular support. On the eve of war with Austria, Bismarck promulgated a constitution that included a bicameral legislation and universal manhood suffrage, a political move that sought to shift public opinion in favor of Prussia. The move achieved the intended effect, enabling Bismarck to sever the once-indivisible bond between nationalism and liberalism. The following passage, written at the end of his life, throws light on a conservative's views of popular politics and nationalism.

From *The Memoirs*, O. Von Bismarck, translated by A. J. Butler, Howard Fertig, 1890.

*   *   *

Looking to the necessity, in a fight against an overwhelming foreign Power, of being able, in extreme need, to use even revolutionary means, I had had no hesitation whatever in throwing into the frying-pan, by means of the circular dispatch of June 10, 1866, the most powerful ingredient known at that time to liberty-mongers, namely, universal suffrage, so as to frighten off foreign monarchies from trying to stick a finger into our national omelette. I never doubted that the German people would be strong and clever enough to free themselves from the existing suffrage as soon as they realised that it was a harmful institution. If it cannot, then my saying that Germany can ride when once it has got into the saddle was erroneous. The acceptance of universal suffrage was a weapon in the war against Austria and other foreign countries, in the war for German Unity, as well as a threat to use the last weapons in a struggle against coalitions. In a war of this sort, when it becomes a matter of life and death, one does not look at the weapons that one seizes, nor the value of what one destroys in using them: one is guided at the moment by no other thought than the issue of the war, and the preservation of one's external independence; the settling of affairs and reparation of the damage has to take place after the peace. Moreover, I still hold that the principle of universal suffrage is a just one, not only in theory but also in practice, provided always that voting be not secret, for secrecy is a quality that is indeed incompatible with the best characteristics of German blood.

The influence and the dependence on others that the practical life of man brings in its train are God-given realities which we cannot and must not ignore. If we refuse to transfer them to political life, and base that life on a faith in the secret insight of everybody, we fall into a contradiction between public law and the realities of human life which practically leads to constant frictions, and finally to an explosion, and to which there is no theoretical solution except by way of the insanities of social-democracy, the support given to which

rests on the fact that the judgment of the masses is sufficiently stultified and undeveloped to allow them, with the assistance of their own greed, to be continually caught by the rhetoric of clever and ambitious leaders.

The counterpoise to this lies in the influence of the educated classes, which would be greatly strengthened if voting were public, as for the Prussian Diet. It may be that the greater discretion of the more intelligent classes rests on the material basis of the preservation of their possessions. The other motive, the struggle for gain, is equally justifiable; but a preponderance of those who represent property is more serviceable for the security and development of the state. A state, the control of which lies in the hands of the greedy, of the *novarum rerum cupidi,* and of orators who have in a higher degree than others the capacity for deceiving the unreasoning masses, will constantly be doomed to a restlessness of development, which so ponderous a mass as the commonwealth of the state cannot follow without injury to its organism. Ponderous masses, and among these the life and development of great nations must be reckoned, can only move with caution, since the road on which they travel to an unknown future has no smooth iron rails. Every great state-commonwealth that loses the prudent and restraining influence of the propertied class, whether that influence rests on material or moral grounds, will always end by being rushed along at a speed which must shatter the coach of state, as happened in the development of the French Revolution. The element of greed has the preponderance arising from large masses which in the long run must make its way. It is in the interests of the great mass itself to wish decision to take place without dangerous acceleration of the speed of the coach of state, and without its destruction. If this should happen, however, the wheel of history will revolve again, and always in a proportionately shorter time, to dictatorship, to despotism, to absolutism, because in the end the masses yield to the need of order; if they do not recognise this need *a priori,* they always realise it eventually after manifold arguments *ad hominem;* and in order to purchase order from a dictatorship and Caesarism they cheerfully sacrifice that justifiable amount of freedom which ought to be maintained, and which the political society of Europe can endure without ill-health.

I should regard it as a serious misfortune, and as an essential weakening of our security in the future, if we in Germany are driven into the vortex of this French cycle. Absolutism would be the ideal form of government for an European political structure were not the King and his officials ever as other men are to whom it is not given to reign with superhuman wisdom, insight and justice. The most experienced and well-meaning absolute rulers are subject to human imperfections, such as overestimation of their own wisdom, the influence and eloquence of favourites, not to mention petticoat influence, legitimate and illegitimate. Monarchy and the most ideal monarch, if in his idealism he is not to be a common danger, stand in need of criticism; the thorns of criticism set him right when he runs the risk of losing his way. Joseph II is a warning example of this.

Criticism can only be exercised through the medium of a free press and parliaments in the modern sense of the term. Both correctives may easily weaken, and finally lose their efficacy if they abuse their powers. To avert this is one of the tasks of a conservative policy, which cannot be accomplished without a struggle with parliament and press. The measuring of the limits within which such a struggle must be confined, if the control of the government, which is indispensable to the country, is neither to be checked nor allowed to gain a complete power, is a question of political tact and judgment.

It is a piece of good fortune for his country if a monarch possess the judgment requisite for this—a good fortune that is temporary, it is true, like all human fortune. The possibility of establishing ministers in power who possess adequate qualifications must always be granted in the constitutional organism; but also the possibility of maintaining in office ministers who satisfy these requirements in face of occasional votes of an adverse majority and of the influence of courts and camarillas. This aim, so far as human imperfections in general allow its attainment, was approximately reached under the government of William I.

*　　*　　*

REVIEW QUESTIONS

1. What is Bismarck's opinion of universal suffrage?
2. What political system and balance of social forces does Bismarck advocate?
3. Why is Bismarck often viewed as a conservative revolutionary?

MAURICE BARRÈS

The Nancy Program

The writer and vehement nationalist politician Maurice Barrès (1862–1923) provides a good example of late nineteenth-century radical nationalism. As a writer Barrès critiqued modern urban civilization, which he depicted as a society of decadent, uprooted individuals cut off from their native soil and ancestral customs. At the age of twenty-six he was elected to the Chamber of Deputies with the Boulan-

*gistes, a party of populist chauvinists who rallied around General Boulanger's prom-
ises of revenge against Germany for the French defeat in 1870–1871. In 1898,
Barrès ran again as a National Socialist in the city of Nancy, using the platform
below. Although he lost, the platform illustrates how the nationalism of right-wing
populist movements reconfigured political discourse with its xenophobia and
antisemitism.*

Electors,
The nationalist and social ideas which we brought to a joint triumph for the first time in 1889, had at that time alarmed certain minds because of the popularity of General Boulanger. Today, whether because they seem to be more matured, or whether circumstances now justify them more, they attract many adherents even among the antagonists of the previous campaign, disabused by a party which has done nothing since we left it with a free field.

The "Nationalist Socialist Republican Committee of Meurthe-et-Moselle" and a large number of independent electors have asked me to take up again the electoral battle.

To a policy having for its aim only animosities to satisfy, and for its driving force only lust for power, I come anew to oppose those *national* and *social* ideas which already you have acclaimed and which you will not today repudiate.

I. We Are Nationalists

In the top ranks of society, in the heart of the provinces, in the moral and in the material sphere, in commerce, industry, and agriculture, even in the shipyards where they are competing with French workers, foreigners are poisoning us like parasites.

One vital principle that should underlie the new French policy is to protect all its nationals against this invasion, and to beware of that brand of socialism that is so cosmopolitan, or rather so German, that it would weaken the country's defenses.

The Jewish problem is linked to the national problem. The Jews were assimilated to the native French by the Revolution, but have retained their peculiar characteristics and now, instead of being persecuted as they once were, are themselves the overlords. We believe in complete freedom of conscience; what is more, we should consider it highly dangerous to allow the Jews the chance of invoking (and so to appear to be defending) the principles of civil liberty promulgated by the Revolution. But they violate these principles by characteristically isolated behavior, by monopolies, speculation, and cosmopolitanism. There is, moreover, in the army, the magistracy, the ministries, in all branches of the administration, a far higher proportion of them than their numbers justify. They have been appointed prefects, judges, treasurers, officers—because they have money, which corrupts. We ought to destroy this dangerous disproportion, without even changing the law, by insisting on greater fairness on the part of those who govern, and so gain more consideration for our real nationals, the children of Gaul and not of Judea.

But the most urgent need is to make the process of naturalization more difficult. It is by this loophole that the worst Jews and many second-rate Frenchmen have slipped in.

Statistics show that 90 per cent of foreigners do not become naturalized until they have evaded active army service. We should insist that military service is a condition of nationality. What is more, a naturalized person (except those from Alsace-Lorraine) should be allowed just private rights, while only his descendants should be assimilated to French-born citizens and enjoy political rights.

The opportunist policy over the last twenty years has favored Jews, foreigners, cosmopolitans. The reason given by those who committed this criminal mistake was that these aliens would introduce a vigorous element into France. Fine elements these—Reinach, Cornelius Herz, Alfred Dreyfus, and the like—who have almost brought us to decay! This is the real position: French society does need vigorous new elements, it is true, but they can be found within that society, by encouraging the least privileged, the poorest, by raising their standard of living and improving their vocational training.

So nationalism leads inevitably to socialism. We define socialism as "the material and moral improvement of the largest and poorest classes."

It has taken some centuries for the French nation to give political security to its members. It must now protect them against that economic insecurity that prevails at all levels.

Let us define this insecurity.

II. We Demand Protection against Economic Insecurity

Insecurity of the worker—The elderly worker has not enough to eat. Even if he is able-bodied, he runs the risk of unemployment.

Wages are kept low by foreign competition.

Mechanization means that he is crowded into factories, subjected to military discipline under the arbitrary rule of the boss. In some districts he is reduced by certain economic organizations to real slavery.

He cannot get out. For one thing, you do not take your native earth with you on the soles of your boots, and for many of them exile is heartbreak. Again, materially speaking, if he goes, he and his family will probably starve to death for he

will have no savings. Besides, where could he find work?

Insecurity of the small trader—The small trader has the same economic insecurity as the worker. They are interdependent. It is, in fact, the lower working class, black-coated and manual workers, who keep the small trader going, for the middle classes go to the big stores. The small trader helps the black-coated or manual worker to survive periods of unemployment by allowing credit. But the credit that the worker gets from the small trader —baker, butcher, grocer, or landlord—lays him open to ruin if unemployment is prolonged or too frequent.

Another cause of insecurity is that prime costs for small industrialists and tradespeople fluctuate arbitrarily, at the bidding of speculators.

We should note in passing that these traders and industrialists did not gain from the lowering of the bank rate. They still pay 8 per cent (6 per cent for three months with four renewals that cost ½ per cent, making 8 per cent in all). Without going so far as a State bank, which could be held to ransom in wartime, we should like to have seen commerce profit by the renewal of the charter of the Bank of France. But the Government and the financial feudality thought otherwise.

Insecurity of the farmer—The price of wheat no longer depends solely on the French harvest. At one time the producer used to get compensation for a poor harvest in the higher prices charged to the consumer. Nowadays these prices depend on the harvests of India and the United States.

They have begun to remedy this situation by protection, which is basically a socialist measure, intervention by the State in the natural course of events. (Just as the same circumstances are sweeping away parties, like a flood tide!)

We are in full agreement with the major aspects of protection. It aims at guaranteeing a minimum price to the producer. But the big middlemen absorb the profits with their fluctuations and speculative maneuvers, which should be opposed with terrorist severity. . . .

Insecurity of the bourgeoisie—The bourgeoisie

is menaced by the international finance feudality, which turns financial securities into bits of paper.

I will not go back as far as Panama—I could find ten examples in the last twelve months. Take this one. The price of gold mines launched on the French market was raised to the point where their total value reached about 1.8 billion francs. Today they are worth no more than 615 million. This means that in less than two years national savings worth 1.2 billion was lost on securities held by small French investors.

No investigation followed.

ELECTORS

It is for the defense of the ideas that I have just explained that I propose for your approbation the following Program:

I. MEASURES TO BE TAKEN TO ENSURE THE UNION OF ALL FRENCHMEN

Against foreign produce: the work of protectionism must be maintained:

Against the foreign worker who, being dispensed from military service, draws every year a billion in wages from France and causes poverty and destitution, through unemployment, among the families of French workers. In particular public works, financed from taxes, must be carried out by national workers;

Against the international financial feudality which, through its joint-stock association, eliminates the worker from the country and replaces him by undercutting with foreign workers, paralyzes the action of protective measures taken in support of agriculture and industry, organizes monopoly and speculation in the basic essentials, falsifies prices, sending them up and down, and in the end ruins the real producers of wealth—our farmers, our traders, our workers;

Against the naturalized foreigner, who claims to play a role in politics and to whom we would allow only private rights, reserving political rights

for his descendants. This is the best way to get at the Jew, whose invasion of State functions the executive power would otherwise have to restrict.

II. INSTITUTION OF A SUPERANNUATION FUND for workers organized by the State.

The duties which must be levied on foreign workers and the customs duties levied on basic essential goods must be specifically allotted to this superannuation fund in order to simplify somewhat these taxes where strictly no levy should be imposed.

The matter of superannuation funds is one of the most important to settle for the sake of social peace. It is urgent. It forces itself upon us. But it is complicated by a grave financial problem which has to be solved. I shall give this all my attention and care. I declare myself in favor of the principle. I shall accept any solution likely to produce the quickest and most lasting results.

III. REFORM OF TAXATION TO PROMOTE DEMOCRATIC JUSTICE aiming at lowering taxes on consumer goods and charges which hit the small growers. The land tax is charged on an estimated income which often does not exist, on the basis of assessments which no longer correspond to reality. The tax on consumer goods is infinitely heavier on the poor than on the rich.

IV. ORGANIZATION OF AGRICULTURAL CREDIT, WHICH COULD INCLUDE THE FUNDS OF THE SAVINGS BANKS, today drained away from the whole province in order to BE CENTRALIZED and riskily used for the purchase of stocks.

V. FREEDOM OF ASSOCIATION. THIS IMPLIES EXTENSION OF THE CIVIL PERSONALITY OF THE TRADE UNIONS IN SUCH A WAY THAT WHETHER AGRICULTURAL OR INDUSTRIAL UNIONS, THEY CAN USE THE POWER OF CREDIT, BECOME ASSOCIATIONS OF PRODUCERS and own the premises and working tools needed in industrial, commercial, or agricultural production.

VI. EXTENSION OF THE INDEPENDENT FREEDOMS AND THE CIVIL PERSONALITY OF THE COMMUNES, so as to permit them to achieve in part certain kinds of social progress—always provided they do not infringe the rights of the State.

VII. DEVELOPMENT OF PUBLIC EDUCATION IN THE DIRECTION OF OCCUPATIONAL TRAINING in order to allow all national aptitudes, all forms of intelligence to be developed.

VIII. REVISION OF THE CONSTITUTION with the aim of giving universal suffrage its full and complete sovereignty, particularly by means of the *municipal referendum.*

ELECTORS,

It is useful that, in this region of Lorraine, where day by day they become more numerous, the workers in factories and in the fields should be able to express their wishes; it would be dangerous to suppress them into silence, as the old opportunists wished to do.

This program of the "National Socialist Republican Committee"—what generous and just mind would wish to misunderstand it?—corresponds to the needs of our population; IT IS IN TUNE WITH THE SPECIAL SPIRIT OF OUR LORRAINE and of our frontier.

Articles IV, V, VI, VII, which concern decentralization, strongly indicate the direction of our demands in our region, where the "School of Nancy" matches public feeling.

In all our Articles, as anyone can see who examines them in the light of our preliminary arguments, the path of the future is prepared, and at the same time immediate interests are guaranteed. I undertake to defend them with every means at my disposal, at the same time as I place myself completely at the service of the special interests of my compatriots.

REVIEW QUESTIONS

1. For Barrès, what are the defining characteristics of a nationalist?
2. Why are Jews and foreigners a problem for Barrès?
3. What social groups does Barrès hope to attract with his economic policy?
4. When comparing Herder or Mazzini with Barrès, how has nationalism evolved over the course of the nineteenth century?

23 ⟡ THE PROGRESS OF INTERNATIONAL INDUSTRIALIZATION AND COMPETITION (1870–1914)

The last third of the nineteenth century witnessed not only a new level of prosperity in Europe but also a greater measure of economic and political power that European states wielded over the world. Industrialization entered into a second, more mature stage that produced innovative technologies, a greater scale and scope of economy, and new economic competition that sharpened political rivalries.

While Britain remained the undisputed leader of the first industrial revolution, the emergence of such new leading sectors as steel, chemicals, and electrical engineering after 1870 enabled German companies to achieve explosive economic expansion and thus vie with England and France for a greater share of world markets. After 1890 Britain felt the sting of its free-trade policy when other countries, but especially Germany, could compete in her own colonies and in Britain. The ubiquitous label "made in Germany" vexed British industrialists, reminding them of their relative decline. Economic nationalism became an increasingly important component of political discussions.

The widening sphere of industrialization, which was accompanied by rapid population growth, also produced new levels and patterns of consumption. Department stores arose to meet the breadth and depth of urban consumer tastes, indicating the efflorescence of bourgeois consumer culture. Newly invented machinery, which sewed, cut, pressed, and molded with labor-saving efficiency, allowed entrepreneurs to meet demand at lower prices. Employers furthermore maximized profit margins with "scientific" time-work studies, producing more efficient, rationalized work regimens of laborers. Although hardly proportional to employers' gains, workers' living standards rose, demonstrating capitalism's ability, through innovation and adaptation, to offer better wages and yet still consolidate and expand. In this respect, the pending collapse of capitalism, as predicted by Marx, seemed far off. Socialist parties debated the utility of preaching imminent revolution when they might use their voting and striking power to wrest incremental political reforms and short-term economic gains for the working class.

Europe's dynamic economic expansion, when matched with both its military might and its cultural assumptions of superiority, combined to produce a feverish revival of formal imperialism after 1880. Colonies assumed a new status in European culture: economically, advocates promised cheap raw materials and markets for finished goods; culturally, they provided the points of entry for the spread of Christianity and European civilization; and politically, they signified great-power status and offered a glorious, nation-uniting mission to European publics seeking solace from contentious domestic political issues. Contemporaries, however, largely perceived the various justifications for imperialism as a totality: the civilizing effects of commerce and religion followed the glory of the flag. Thus arose the "friendly competition" among European nations to carve up Africa and penetrate the far east.

Prior to the First World War, Europe almost exclusively viewed the imperialism question in terms of its own interests and needs, presuming that non-western peoples benefited. Some contemporaries, however, criticized this assumption, pointing up the crushing "black man's burden" that had accumulated from the imperialist legacy. Indeed, the inheritance of imperial plantation economies and nationalist politics forever changed the social organization of indigenous cultures. Just as imperialism defined the national identities of European states in the nineteenth century, so too it shaped political and cultural revolt against the West in the twentieth century. It is difficult to understand the cultural perceptions and political identities of non-western peoples without first weighing the impact of the new imperialism between 1880 and 1914.

In retrospect, one sees that Europe was at the zenith of its power in world history. At home, Europe reveled in its belle époque *of rising living standards and a sustained economic expansion that appeared to fulfill the bourgeois ideal of progress. Abroad, never before had European finances, politics, and cultural views affected so many non-western peoples. But this global economy and imperial power was fraught with tension and instability. The conflation of economic and political issues, compounded by imperial pretensions, strained the European balance of power, producing an awesome build up of arms. The threat of war was best exemplified by the Anglo-German naval rivalry, a contest of battleship building that not only fanned the flames of jingoism, but signaled the resolve of governments to pursue a military course of action.*

E. D. HOWARD

FROM The Cause and Extent of the Recent Industrial Progress of Germany

The second industrial revolution (roughly 1870 to 1920) marked the rise of important new industries that stimulated a new wave of economic expansion. Electrical engineering provided expanding cities with streetcar lines; the chemical industry produced more dyes and synthetic materials for new consumer goods; and the machine-building industry developed the internal combustible engine, enabling countries without reserves of coal and iron ore to industrialize. In these industrial sectors Germany became the acknowledged leader, producing impressive growth during a period of general slackened production. The following passage, written in 1907, delineates some of the reasons for Germany's economic ascendancy.

From *Industrial Power and National Rivalry*, edited by Sidney Pollard and C. Holmes. Copyright © 1972 Edward Arnold and Company, Ltd. Reprinted with permission of the publisher.

*   *   *

It is in the electrical industry that Germany has made her greatest progress, one of the direct results, no doubt, of her excellent technical schools. In 1880 electricity was commercially employed only in telegraphy, and in 1882 the total number of persons employed in the industry was too small to be separately enumerated. In 1895 there were 15,000 people engaged in the industry, and the number at the present time is estimated at 50,000. The capital invested is estimated at two billion dollars. This tremendous and rapid growth, which has placed Germany second only to the United States in the industry, was extraordinarily stimulating to other branches, and accounts for not a little of the boom from 1896 to 1900.

One of the principal uses of electricity is in street railways. In 1902 over 100 German cities had electric street railways, with a length of 2,200 miles, and representing an investment of a billion dollars. Germany has over one third of all the elec-

tric street railways in Europe and over half of the total mileage. Ninety-one per cent of all the electric roads of Europe (excluding Great Britain) were built by German firms. The electric roads have not yet begun to compete with the steam roads for long-distance traffic, as in the United States.

The 6 largest electrical companies have an invested capital in stocks and bonds of over $80,000,000 which has increased since 1894 from $16,000,000.

The Allgemeine Elektrizitätsgesellschaft has three large factories employing 17,000 men. Their sales for the year 1899–1900 included 16,000 dynamos of 208,000 H.P. Up to that year, the company had built 250 electrical plants. Their field includes all Europe, and extends to countries beyond the seas. They have established a branch company, with $2,500,000 capital, to handle their business in Argentine and Chili.

The export of electrical machinery in 1903 was $5,000,000. Great Britain is by far the best customer, taking in that year over 25 per cent of the whole export. . . .

In the chemical industry Germany is easily the first nation of the world. This industry affords the best illustration of the recent progress, and reveals more clearly than any others, the causes which have made that country industrially great. The importance of the manufacture of chemicals can be appreciated when we learn that the total value of the annual product is over $300,000,000, which is more than the value of all the machinery manufactured.

This splendid industry is the direct produce of German technical education. The beginning was made when Professor Justus V. Liebig founded the first chemical laboratory in 1827, at the University of Giessen. The convincing success of this experiment led the several state governments to found and maintain advanced schools for scientific study. These technical schools and university laboratories may be regarded as the corner-stone of the nation's industrial greatness, and the whole foundation of its supremacy in the chemical industry.

For the manufacture of crude chemicals, Germany possesses an abundant supply of raw materials, salt, sulphur, and limestone, together with the coal necessary for heat and power.

The capital invested in this industry in 104 of the largest stock companies amounted in 1898 to 295,373,100 marks ($71,003,000), on which a dividend of 39,921,970 marks ($9,115,800) was paid, an average of 13.52 per cent which was slightly higher than the average for the previous 10 years.

The most interesting branch of the chemical industry is the manufacture of dye-stuffs from coal-tar. It is in this field that the most recent and brilliant achievements of the German chemists have been won. In 1860 all the dyes used were organic, and Germany was almost entirely dependent on foreign countries for her supply. The annual import of dyes at that time cost the country 50,000,000 marks ($12,150,000). By 1900 the conditions had so changed that the import had sunk to almost nothing, and the export, on the other hand, had risen to 100,000,000 marks

($24,300,000). Almost without exception, the discovery and production of coal-tar dyes has remained in the hands of the Germans. . . .

Four-fifths of all the world's products of dye-stuffs as well as a large proportion of the medical preparations derived from coal tar, are made in Germany. The annual production of these dyes amounted, according to the statement of the Reichsamt des Innern in Germany in the year 1897, to the value of 120,000,000 marks.

For centuries indigo had been one of the great items of import to the textile-producing countries. In 1892 the German Empire imported 3,556,740 pounds of natural or vegetable indigo, valued at $4,450,000. The discovery of a process for making artificial indigo, made by a Münchner chemist, Dr. Bayer, in 1897, has completely revolutionized this trade, for in 1902 the import of vegetable indigo had decreased to 833,000 pounds, while the export of artificial indigo amounted to 18,308,000 pounds in 1903.

Dr. Bayer's discovery, which had such an important effect on a great industry, consisted of a process for the making of artificial indigo, called alizarene, from a coal-tar product, anthracene. As the result of this one discovery, Germany is not only relieved from the necessity of importing this dye-stuff at a great expense, but she is also able to realize from its export a very considerable national profit.

This is but one instance of the advantage Germany has derived from the labours of her army of scientifically trained chemists. While it may be the most spectacular, it is by no means the most important. The sugar-beet industry owes a large debt to the agricultural chemists, who have been able to raise the percentage of saccharine content of sugar-beet from 5.7 per cent in 1840 to 13 per cent at the present time.

*   *   *

REVIEW QUESTIONS

2. What factors enabled Germany to surge ahead in the chemicals industry?
3. How are the industrial sectors of the second industrial revolution different from those of the classic industrial revolution?

1. What is the impact of the electrical industry on Germany's economy?

E. LEVASSEUR

The Paris Department Store

The rise of large department stores marked a new era in commercial retail, mechanized production for consumer goods, and the way in which men and women spent their leisure time. More than just a convenient emporium for purchasing a wide variety of goods, department stores strove to create a glamorous environment in monumental spaces that made shopping itself an experience. Department stores epitomized bourgeois consumerism. The following passage from 1907 examines the early history of department stores and the commercial strategies by which they revolutionized urban shopping.

From *Industrial Power and National Rivalry*, edited by Sidney Pollard and C. Holmes. Copyright © 1972 Edward Arnold and Company, Ltd. Reprinted with permission of the publisher.

It was in the reign of Louis-Philippe that department stores for fashion goods and dresses, extending to material and other clothing began to be distinguished. The type was already one of the notable developments of the Second Empire; it became one of the most important ones of the Third Republic. These stores have increased in number and several of them have become extremely large. Combining in their different departments all articles of clothing, toilet articles, furniture and many other ranges of goods, it is their special object so to combine all commodities as to attract and satisfy customers who will find conveniently together an assortment of a mass of articles corresponding to all their various needs. They attract customers by permanent display, by free entry into the shops, by periodic exhibitions, by special sales, by fixed prices, and by their ability to deliver the goods purchased to customers' homes, in Paris and to the provinces. Turning themselves into direct intermediaries between the producer and the consumer, even producing sometimes some of their articles in their own workshops, buying at lowest prices because of their large orders and because they are in a position to profit from bargains, working with large sums, and selling to most of their customers for cash only, they can transmit these benefits in lowered selling prices. They can even decide to sell at a loss, as an advertisement or to get rid of out-of-date fashions. Taking 5–6 per cent on 100 millions brings them in more than 20 per cent would bring to a firm doing a turnover of 50,000 francs.

The success of these department stores is only

possible thanks to the volume of their business and this volume needs considerable capital and a very large turnover. Now capital, having become abundant, is freely combined nowadays in large enterprises, although French capital has the reputation of being more wary of the risks of industry than of State or railway securities. On the other hand, the large urban agglomerations, the ease with which goods can be transported by the railways, the diffusion of some comforts to strata below the middle classes, have all favoured these developments.

As example we may cite some figures relating to these stores, since they were brought to the notice of the public in the *Revue des Deux-Mondes*.

The *Belle-Jardinière*, starting as a modest shop set up by Mr. Parissot near the Petit-Pont, was moved to the Cité in 1856 near the Pont-Neuf on a plot of 3,400 metres: in 1893 it did business of 38 millions, realizing a net gain of 6.3 per cent. *Le Louvre*, dating to the time of the extension of the rue de Rivoli under the Second Empire, did in 1893 a business of 120 million at a profit of 6.3 per cent. *Le Bon-Marché*, which was a small shop when Mr. Boucicaut entered it in 1852, already did a business of 20 million at the end of the Empire. During the republic its new buildings were erected; Mme. Boucicaut turned it by her will into a kind of co-operative society, with shares and an ingenious organization; turnover reached 150 million in 1893, leaving a profit of 5 per cent. *La Samaritaine*, which had its most modest beginnings in 1869, today occupies the third rank among department stores of this kind by the number of its employees; it seeks its customers principally among the small consumers and makes great use of credit coupons.

It is worthy of note that the creators of these great department stores have arisen from the ranks of small shop assistants; they have succeeded because of their ability. The commercial organism shaped by them runs true to one type: strongly concentrated general authority, division of labour by departments and responsibility by each departmental head, individual effort of each employee in buying and selling stimulated by profit sharing or commission, etc.

According to the tax records of 1891, these stores in Paris, numbering 12, employed 1,708 persons and were rated on their site values at 2,159,000 francs; the largest had then 542 employees. These same stores had, in 1901, 9,784 employees: one of them over 2,000 and another over 1,600, their site value was doubled (4,089,000 francs).

REVIEW QUESTIONS

1. What is critical for the economic success of department stores?
2. What innovations did the new stores introduce?
3. What is significant about the social origins of the store owners?
4. Why is the department store viewed as a quintessential bourgeois institution?

FREDERICK W. TAYLOR

FROM *The Principles of Scientific Management*

*In its later phase the second industrial revolution introduced innovative manage-
ment methods for increasing worker productivity, which would eventually culminate
in Henry Ford's assembly lines. But the new philosophy of "scientific management"
was often labeled Taylorism, named after F. W. Taylor, who presented his precepts
for greater discipline and worker efficiency in his* Principles of Scientific Management *(1912), which became an international model for large-scale businesses. The
following excerpt centers on the now-classic example of Schmidt the pig-iron worker.*

From *The Principles of Scientific Management*, F. W. Taylor, W. W. Norton, 1967.

*   *   *

Perhaps the most prominent single element in
modern scientific management is the task idea.
The work of every workman is fully planned out
by the management at least one day in advance,
and each man receives in most cases complete
written instructions, describing in detail the task
which he is to accomplish, as well as the means to
be used in doing the work. And the work planned
in advance in this way constitutes a task which is
to be solved, as explained above, not by the workman alone, but in almost all cases by the joint
effort of the workman and the management. This
task specifies not only what is to be done but how
it is to be done and the exact time allowed for
doing it. And whenever the workman succeeds in
doing his task right, and within the time limit
specified, he receives an addition of from 30 per
cent. to 100 per cent. to his ordinary wages. These
tasks are carefully planned, so that both good and
careful work are called for in their performance,
but it should be distinctly understood that in no
case is the workman called upon to work at a pace
which would be injurious to his health. The task
is always so regulated that the man who is well
suited to his job will thrive while working at this
rate during a long term of years and grow happier

and more prosperous, instead of being over-
worked. Scientific management consists very
largely in preparing for and carrying out these
tasks.

*   *   *

The first illustration is that of handling pig
iron, and this work is chosen because it is typical
of perhaps the crudest and most elementary form
of labor which is performed by man. This work is
done by men with no other implements than their
hands. The pig-iron handler stoops down, picks
up a pig weighing about 92 pounds, walks for a
few feet or yards and then drops it on to the
ground or upon a pile. This work is so crude and
elementary in its nature that the writer firmly believes that it would be possible to train an intelligent gorilla so as to become a more efficient
pig-iron handler than any man can be. Yet it will
be shown that the science of handling pig iron is
so great and amounts to so much that it is impossible for the man who is best suited to this type
of work to understand the principles of this science, or even to work in accordance with these
principles without the aid of a man better educated than he is. And the further illustrations to
be given will make it clear that in almost all of the
mechanic arts the science which underlies each

workman's act is so great and amounts to so much that the workman who is best suited actually to do the work is incapable (either through lack of education or through insufficient mental capacity) of understanding this science. This is announced as a general principle, the truth of which will become apparent as one illustration after another is given. After showing these four elements in the handling of pig iron, several illustrations will be given of their application to different kinds of work in the field of the mechanic arts, at intervals in a rising scale, beginning with the simplest and ending with the more intricate forms of labor.

One of the first pieces of work undertaken by us, when the writer started to introduce scientific management into the Bethlehem Steel Company, was to handle pig iron on task work. The opening of the Spanish War found some 80,000 tons of pig iron placed in small piles in an open field adjoining the works. Prices for pig iron had been so low that it could not be sold at a profit, and it therefore had been stored. With the opening of the Spanish War the price of pig iron rose, and this large accumulation of iron was sold. This gave us a good opportunity to show the workmen, as well as the owners and managers of the works, on a fairly large scale the advantages of task work over the old-fashioned day work and piece work, in doing a very elementary class of work.

The Bethlehem Steel Company had five blast furnaces, the product of which had been handled by a pig-iron gang for many years. This gang, at this time, consisted of about 75 men. They were good, average pig-iron handlers, were under an excellent foreman who himself had been a pig-iron handler, and the work was done, on the whole, about as fast and as cheaply as it was anywhere else at that time.

A railroad switch was run out into the field, right along the edge of the piles of pig iron. An inclined plank was placed against the side of a car, and each man picked up from his pile a pig of iron weighing about 92 pounds, walked up the inclined plank and dropped it on the end of the car.

We found that this gang were loading on the average about 12½ long tons per man per day. We were surprised to find, after studying the matter, that a first-class pig-iron handler ought to handle between 47 and 48 long tons per day, instead of 12½ tons. This task seemed to us so very large that we were obliged to go over our work several times before we were absolutely sure that we were right. Once we were sure, however, that 47 tons was a proper day's work for a first-class pig-iron handler, the task which faced us as managers under the modern scientific plan was clearly before us. It was our duty to see that the 80,000 tons of pig iron was loaded on to the cars at the rate of 47 tons per man per day, in place of 12½ tons, at which rate the work was then being done. And it was further our duty to see that this work was done without bringing on a strike among the men, without any quarrel with the men, and to see that the men were happier and better contented when loading at the new rate of 47 tons than they were when loading at the old rate of 12½ tons.

Our first step was the scientific selection of the workman. In dealing with workmen under this type of management, it is an inflexible rule to talk to and deal with only one man at a time, since each workman has his own special abilities and limitations, and since we are not dealing with men in masses, but are trying to develop each individual man to his highest state of efficiency and prosperity. Our first step was to find the proper workman to begin with. We therefore carefully watched and studied these 75 men for three or four days, at the end of which time we had picked out four men who appeared to be physically able to handle pig iron at the rate of 47 tons per day. A careful study was then made of each of these men. We looked up their history as far back as practicable and thorough inquiries were made as to the character, habits, and the ambition of each of them. Finally we selected one from among the four as the most likely man to start with. He was a little Pennsylvania Dutchman who had been observed to trot back home for a mile or so after his work in the evening about as fresh as he was when he came trotting down to work in the morning. We found that upon wages of $1.15 a day he had succeeded in buying a small plot of ground, and that he was engaged in putting up the walls of a little house for himself in the morning before starting to work and at night after leaving. He also had the reputation of being exceedingly "close," that is, of placing a very high value on a dollar. As one man whom we talked to about him said, "A penny looks about the size of a cart-wheel to him." This man we will call Schmidt.

The task before us, then, narrowed itself down to getting Schmidt to handle 47 tons of pig iron per day and making him glad to do it. This was done as follows. Schmidt was called out from among the gang of pig-iron handlers and talked to somewhat in this way:

"Schmidt, are you a high-priced man?"

"Vell, I don't know vat you mean."

"Oh yes, you do. What I want to know is whether you are a high-priced man or not."

"Vell, I don't know vat you mean."

"Oh, come now, you answer my questions. What I want to find out is whether you are a high-priced man or one of these cheap fellows here. What I want to find out is whether you want to earn $1.85 a day or whether you are satisfied with $1.15, just the same as all those cheap fellows are getting."

"Did I vant $1.85 a day? Vas dot a high-priced man? Vell, yes, I vas a high-priced man."

"Oh, you're aggravating me. Of course you want $1.85 a day—every one wants it! You know perfectly well that that has very little to do with your being a high-priced man. For goodness' sake answer my questions, and don't waste any more of my time. Now come over here. You see that pile of pig iron?"

"Yes."

"You see that car?"

"Yes."

"Well, if you are a high-priced man, you will load that pig iron on that car to-morrow for $1.85. Now do wake up and answer my question. Tell me whether you are a high-priced man or not."

"Vell—did I got $1.85 for loading dot pig iron on dot car to-morrow?"

"Yes, of course you do, and you get $1.85 for

loading a pile like that every day right through the year. That is what a high-priced man does, and you know it just as well as I do."

"Vell, dot's all right. I could load dot pig iron on the car to-morrow for $1.85, and I get it every day, don't I?"

"Certainly you do—certainly you do."

"Vell, den, I vas a high-priced man."

"Now, hold on, hold on. You know just as well as I do that a high-priced man has to do exactly as he's told from morning till night. You have seen this man here before, haven't you?"

"No, I never saw him."

"Well, if you are a high-priced man, you will do exactly as this man tells you to-morrow, from morning till night. When he tells you to pick up a pig and walk, you pick it up and you walk, and when he tells you to sit down and rest, you sit down. You do that right straight through the day. And what's more, no back talk. Now a high-priced man does just what he's told to do, and no back talk. Do you understand that? When this man tells you to walk, you walk; when he tells you to sit down, you sit down, and you don't talk back at him. Now you come on to work here to-morrow morning and I'll know before night whether you are really a high-priced man or not."

This seems to be rather rough talk. And indeed it would be if applied to an educated mechanic, or even an intelligent laborer. With a man of the mentally sluggish type of Schmidt it is appropriate and not unkind, since it is effective in fixing his attention on the high wages which he wants and away from what, if it were called to his attention, he probably would consider impossibly hard work.

What would Schmidt's answer be if he were talked to in a manner which is usual under the management of "initiative and incentive"? say, as follows:

"Now, Schmidt, you are a first-class pig-iron handler and know your business well. You have been handling at the rate of 12½ tons per day. I have given considerable study to handling pig iron, and feel sure that you could do a much larger day's work than you have been doing. Now don't you think that if you really tried you could handle

47 tons of pig iron per day, instead of 12½ tons?"

What do you think Schmidt's answer would be to this?

Schmidt started to work, and all day long, and at regular intervals, was told by the man who stood over him with a watch, "Now pick up a pig and walk. Now sit down and rest. Now walk— now rest," etc. He worked when he was told to work, and rested when he was told to rest, and at half-past five in the afternoon had his 47½ tons loaded on the car. And he practically never failed to work at this pace and do the task that was set him during the three years that the writer was at Bethlehem. And throughout this time he averaged a little more than $1.85 per day, whereas before he had never received over $1.15 per day, which was the ruling rate of wages at that time in Beth-lehem. That is, he received 60 per cent. higher wages than were paid to other men who were not working on task work. One man after another was picked out and trained to handle pig iron at the rate of 47½ tons per day until all of the pig iron

was handled at this rate, and the men were re-ceiving 60 per cent. more wages than other work-men around them.

*   *   *

REVIEW QUESTIONS

1. What are the management's objectives and how is it achieved?
2. Why is it "scientific"?
3. How is Schmidt the worker handled, and what are the advantages for both him and the man-agement?
4. What are Taylor's assumptions about workers?
5. How does Taylor's prescription for a new in-dustrial discipline compare with the "Rules of a Factory in Berlin" (chapter 19)?
6. What are the ramifications of this method for industrial production and industrial relations?

EDUARD BERNSTEIN

FROM *Evolutionary Socialism*

At the turn of the century, Eduard Bernstein (1850–1932) was a leading member of the Social Democratic Party of Germany (SPD), Europe's largest, best-organized Marxist party. In 1899 Bernstein published The Premises of Socialism and the Tasks of Social Democracy, *which called attention to the evolutionary changes in capitalism that rendered orthodox Marxist doctrine obsolete. In the book Bernstein argued for the need to revise tactics and goals for working-class constituencies. Bern-stein's treatise, which sparked an important debate among socialists, is a useful doc-ument, for it throws light not only on the revisionist political strategies of socialists but also on the changing nature of late nineteenth-century capitalist political economy.*

From *Evolutionary Socialism: A Criticism and Affirmation,* E. Bernstein, translated by Edith C. Harvey, Schocken Books, 1963. Reprinted with permission of the publisher.

*   *   *

It has been maintained in a certain quarter that the practical deductions from my treatises would be the abandonment of the conquest of political power by the proletariat organised politically and economically. That is quite an arbitrary deduction, the accuracy of which I altogether deny.

I set myself against the notion that we have to expect shortly a collapse of the bourgeois economy, and that social democracy should be induced by the prospect of such an imminent, great, social catastrophe to adapt its tactics to that assumption. That I maintain most emphatically.

The adherents of this theory of a catastrophe, base it especially on the conclusions of the *Communist Manifesto*. This is a mistake in every respect.

The theory which the *Communist Manifesto* sets forth of the evolution of modern society was correct as far as it characterised the general tendencies of that evolution. But it was mistaken in several special deductions, above all in the estimate of the *time* the evolution would take. The last has been unreservedly acknowledged by Friedrich Engels, the joint author with Marx of the *Manifesto*, in his preface to the *Class War in France*. But it is evident that if social evolution takes a much greater period of time than was assumed, it must also take upon itself *forms* and lead to forms that were not foreseen and could not be foreseen then.

Social conditions have not developed to such an acute opposition of things and classes as is depicted in the *Manifesto*. It is not only useless, it is the greatest folly to attempt to conceal this from ourselves. The number of members of the possessing classes is to-day not smaller but larger. The enormous increase of social wealth is not accompanied by a decreasing number of large capitalists but by an increasing number of capitalists of all degrees. The middle classes change their character but they do not disappear from the social scale.

The concentration in productive industry is not being accomplished even to day in all its departments with equal thoroughness and at an equal rate. In a great many branches of production it certainly justifies the forecasts of the socialist critic of society; but in other branches it lags even to-day behind them. The process of concentration in agriculture proceeds still more slowly. Trade statistics show an extraordinarily elaborated graduation of enterprises in regard to size. No rung of the ladder is disappearing from it. The significant changes in the inner structure of these enterprises and their interrelationship cannot do away with this fact.

In all advanced countries we see the privileges of the capitalist bourgeoisie yielding step by step to democratic organisations. Under the influence of this, and driven by the movement of the working classes which is daily becoming stronger, a social reaction has set in against the exploiting tendencies of capital, a counteraction which, although it still proceeds timidly and feebly, yet does exist, and is always drawing more departments of economic life under its influence. Factory legislation, the democratising of local government, and the extension of its area of work, the freeing of trade unions and systems of co-operative trading from legal restrictions, the consideration of standard conditions of labour in the work undertaken by public authorities—all these characterise this phase of the evolution.

But the more the political organisations of modern nations are democratised the more the needs and opportunities of great political catastrophes are diminished. He who holds firmly to the catastrophic theory of evolution must, with all his power, withstand and hinder the evolution described above, which, indeed, the logical defenders of that theory formerly did. But is the conquest of political power by the proletariat simply to be by a political catastrophe? Is it to be the appropriation and utilisation of the power of the State by the proletariat exclusively against the whole non-proletarian world?

He who replies in the affirmative must be reminded of two things. In 1872 Marx and Engels announced in the preface to the new edition of the *Communist Manifesto* that the Paris Commune had exhibited a proof that "the working classes cannot simply take possession of the ready-made

State machine and set it in motion for their own aims." And in 1895 Friedrich Engels stated in detail in the preface to *War of the Classes* that the time of political surprises, of the "revolutions of small conscious minorities at the head of unconscious masses" was to-day at an end, that a collision on a large scale with the military would be the means of checking the steady growth of social democracy and of even throwing it back for a time—in short, that social democracy would flourish far better by lawful than by unlawful means and by violent revolution. And he points out in conformity with this opinion that the next task of the party should be "to work for an uninterrupted increase of its votes" or to carry on a slow *propaganda of parliamentary activity*.

Thus Engels, who, nevertheless, as his numerical examples show, still somewhat overestimated the rate of process of the evolution! Shall we be told that he abandoned the conquest of political power by the working classes, because he wished to avoid the steady growth of social democracy secured by lawful means being interrupted by a political revolution?

If not, and if one subscribes to his conclusions, one cannot reasonably take any offence if it is declared that for a long time yet the task of social democracy is, instead of speculating on a great economic crash, "to organise the working classes politically and develop them as a democracy and to fight for all reforms in the State which are adapted to raise the working classes and transform the State in the direction of democracy."

That is what I have said in my impugned article and what I still maintain in its full import. As far as concerns the question propounded above it is equivalent to Engel's dictum, for democracy is, at any given time, as much government by the working classes as these are capable of practising according to their intellectual ripeness and the degree of social development they have attained. Engels, indeed, refers at the place just mentioned to the fact that the *Communist Manifesto* has "proclaimed the conquest of the democracy as one of the first and important tasks of the fighting proletariat."

In short, Engels is so thoroughly convinced that the tactics based on the presumption of a catastrophe have had their day, that he even considers a revision of them necessary in the Latin countries where tradition is much more favourable to them than in Germany. "If the conditions of war between nations have altered," he writes, "no less have those for the war between classes." Has this already been forgotten?

No one has questioned the necessity for the working classes to gain the control of government. The point at issue is between the theory of a social cataclysm and the question whether with the given social development in Germany and the present advanced state of its working classes in the towns and the country, a sudden catastrophe would be desirable in the interest of the social democracy. I have denied it and deny it again, because in my judgment a greater security for lasting success lies in a steady advance than in the possibilities offered by a catastrophic crash.

And as I am firmly convinced that important periods in the development of nations cannot be leapt over I lay the greatest value on the next tasks of social democracy, on the struggle for the political rights of the working man, on the political activity of working men in town and country for the interests of their class, as well as on the work of the industrial organisation of the workers.

In this sense I wrote the sentence that the movement means everything for me and that what is *usually* called "the final aim of socialism" is nothing; and in this sense I write it down again to-day. Even if the word "usually" had not shown that the proposition was only to be understood conditionally, it was obvious that it *could* not express indifference concerning the final carrying out of socialist principles, but only indifference— or, as it would be better expressed, carelessness— as to the form of the final arrangement of things. I have at no time had an excessive interest in the future, beyond general principles; I have not been able to read to the end any picture of the future. My thoughts and efforts are concerned with the duties of the present and the nearest future, and I only busy myself with the perspectives beyond so far as they give me a line of conduct for suitable action now.

The conquest of political power by the working classes, the expropriation of capitalists, are no ends in themselves but only means for the accomplishment of certain aims and endeavours. As such they are demands in the programme of social democracy and are not attacked by me. Nothing can be said beforehand as to the circumstances of their accomplishment; we can only fight for their realisation. But the conquest of political power necessitates the possession of political *rights*; and the most important problem of tactics which German social democracy has at the present time to solve, appears to me to be to devise the best ways for the extension of the political and economic rights of the German working classes.

*   *   *

That which concerns me, that which forms the chief aim of this work, is, by opposing what is left of the utopian mode of thought in the socialist theory, to strengthen equally the realistic and the idealistic element in the socialist movement.

REVIEW QUESTIONS

1. According to Bernstein, in what ways was the *Communist Manifesto* incorrect?
2. What aspects of political and economic life had alleviated class conflict?
3. What is Bernstein's solution, and how does it differ from orthodox Marxism?

FRIEDRICH FABRI

FROM Does Germany Need Colonies?

The small pamphlet "Does Germany Need Colonies?" by F. Fabri, a former inspector of the Rhenish Missionary Association, was published in 1879, and was one among many publications that generated a widespread public debate in Germany regarding its need for colonies. Fabri cited overpopulation as a motivating factor, and his emphasis on Germany's "cultural mission" infused imperialism with an idealism that enthused the general public. The domestic agitation for colonial expansion by pressure groups and grassroots associations radically affected domestic politics. Germany's decision in the 1880s to enter the race for colonial territories in Africa and Asia had, moreover, a profound impact on the European balance of power.

From *The Imperialism Reader*, edited by Louis L. Snyder, Van Nostrand, 1962.

*   *   *

Should not the German nation, so seaworthy, so industrially and commercially minded, more than other peoples geared to agricultural coloni-

zation, and possessing a rich and available supply of labor, all these to a greater extent than other modern culture-peoples, should not this nation-successfully hew a new path on the road of imperialism? We are convinced beyond doubt that the colonial question has become a matter of life or death for the development of Germany. Colonies will have a salutary effect on our economic situation as well as on our entire national progress.

Here is a solution for many of the problems that face us. In this new Reich of ours there is so much bitterness, so much unfruitful, sour, and poisoned political wrangling, that the opening of a new, promising road of national effort will act as a kind of liberating influence. Our national spirit will be renewed, a gratifying thing, a great asset. A people that have been led to a high level of power can maintain its historical position only as long as it understands and proves itself to be *the bearer of a culture mission*. At the same time, this is the only way to stability and to the growth of national welfare, the necessary foundation for a lasting expansion of power.

At one time Germany contributed only intellectual and literary activity to the tasks of our century. That era is now over. As a people we have become politically minded and powerful. But if political power becomes the primal goal of a nation, it will lead to harshness, even to barbarism. We must be ready to serve for the ideal, moral, and economic culture-tasks of our time. The French national-economist, Leroy Beaulieu, closed his words on colonization with these words: "That nation is the greatest in the world which colonizes most; if she does not achieve that rank today, she will make it tomorrow."

No one can deny that in this direction England has by far surpassed all other countries. Much has been said, even in Germany, during the last few decades about the "disintegrating power of England." Indeed, there seems to be something to it when we consider the Palmerston era and Gladstonian politics. It has been customary in our age of military power to evaluate the strength of a state in terms of its combat-ready troops. But anyone who looks at the globe and notes the steadily increasing colonial possessions of Great Britain, how she extracts strength from them, the skill with which she governs them, how the Anglo-Saxon strain occupies a dominant position in the overseas territories, he will begin to see the military argument as the reasoning of a philistine.

The fact is that England tenaciously holds on to its world-wide possessions with scarcely one-fourth the manpower of our continental military state. That is not only a great economic advantage but also a striking proof of the solid power and cultural fiber of England. Great Britain, of course, isolates herself far from the mass warfare of the continent, or only goes into action with dependable allies; hence, the insular state has suffered and will suffer no real damage. In any case, it would be wise for us Germans to learn about colonial skills from our Anglo-Saxon cousins and to begin a friendly competition with them. When the German Reich centuries ago stood at the pinnacle of the states of Europe, it was the Number One trade and sea power. If the New Germany wants to protect its newly won position of power for a long time, it must heed its *Kultur*-mission and, above all, delay no longer in the task of renewing the call for colonies.

*　　*　　*

REVIEW QUESTIONS

1. Why does Fabri consider the acquisition of colonies "a matter of life or death for the development of Germany"?
2. How does Fabri compare Germany's political status with England?
3. What political, economic, and cultural uses will, according to Fabri, be derived from colonies?

DAVID LIVINGSTONE

FROM Cambridge Speech of 1857

David Livingstone (1813–1873), the Scottish missionary and explorer of Africa, personified for Britain the higher cause of imperialism. Between 1840 and 1873, Livingstone traversed nearly a third of Africa, missionizing Christianity, opposing the persistent slave trade, and recording the geography and ethnographic customs of its peoples. His achievement and his self-effacing devotion to opening up Africa to commerce and Christianity provided inspiration to a nineteenth-century British public in search of a moral center to its imperialist policies in Africa.

From *Dr. Livingstone's Cambridge Lectures,* edited by William Monk, Deighton Bell, 1858.

*   *   *

My object in going into the country south of the desert was to instruct the natives in a knowledge of Christianity, but many circumstances prevented my living amongst them more than seven years, amongst which were considerations arising out of the slave system carried on by the Dutch Boers. I resolved to go into the country beyond, and soon found that, for the purposes of commerce, it was necessary to have a path to the sea. I might have gone on instructing the natives in religion, but as civilization and Christianity must go on together, I was obliged to find a path to the sea, in order that I should not sink to the level of the natives. The chief was overjoyed at the suggestion, and furnished me with twenty-seven men, and canoes, and provisions, and presents for the tribes through whose country we had to pass.

*   *   *

In a commercial point of view communication with this country is desirable. Angola is wonderfully fertile, producing every kind of tropical plant in rank luxuriance. Passing on to the valley of Quango, the stalk of the grass was as thick as a quill, and towered above my head, although I was mounted on my ox; cotton is produced in great abundance, though merely woven into common cloth; bananas and pine-apples grow in great luxuriance; but the people having no maritime communication, these advantages are almost lost. The country on the other side is not quite so fertile, but in addition to indigo, cotton, and sugarcane, produces a fibrous substance, which I am assured is stronger than flax.

The Zambesi has not been thought much of as a river by Europeans, not appearing very large at its mouth; but on going up it for about seventy miles, it is enormous. The first three hundred miles might be navigated without obstacle: then there is a rapid, and near it a coal-field of large extent. The elevated sides of the basin, which form the most important feature of the country, are far different in climate to the country nearer the sea, or even the centre. Here the grass is short, and the Angola goat, which could not live in the centre, had been seen on the east highland by Mr Moffat.

My desire is to open a path to this district, that civilization, commerce, and Christianity might find their way there. I consider that we made a great mistake, when we carried commerce into India, in being ashamed of our Christianity; as a matter of common sense and good policy, it is always best to appear in one's true character. In travelling through Africa, I might have imitated certain Portuguese, and have passed for a chief; but I never attempted anything of the sort, although endeavouring always to keep to the lessons of cleanliness rigidly instilled by my mother long ago; the consequence was that the natives respected me for that quality, though remaining dirty themselves.

I had a pass from the Portuguese consul, and on arriving at their settlement, I was asked what I was. I said, "A missionary, and a doctor too." They asked, "Are you a doctor of medicine?"— "Yes."—"Are you not a doctor of mathematics too?"—"No."—"And yet you can take longitudes and latitudes."—Then they asked me about my moustache; and I simply said I wore it, because men had moustaches to wear, and ladies had not. They could not understand either, why a sacerdote should have a wife and four children; and many a joke took place upon that subject. I used to say, "Is it not better to have children with than without a wife?" Englishmen of education always command respect, without any adventitious aid. A Portuguese governor left for Angola, giving out that he was going to keep a large establishment, and taking with him quantities of crockery, and about five hundred waistcoats; but when he arrived in Africa, he made a 'deal' of them. Educated Englishmen seldom descend to that sort of thing.

A prospect is now before us of opening Africa for commerce and the Gospel. Providence has been preparing the way, for even before I proceeded to the Central basin it had been conquered and rendered safe by a chief named Sebituane, and the language of the Bechuanas made the fashionable tongue, and that was one of the languages into which Mr Moffat had translated the Scriptures. Sebituane also discovered Lake Ngami some time previous to my explorations in that part. In going back to that country my object is to open up traffic along the banks of the Zambesi, and also to preach the Gospel. The natives of Central Africa are very desirous of trading, but their only traffic is at present in slaves, of which the poorer people have an unmitigated horror: it is therefore most desirable to encourage the former principle, and

thus open a way for the consumption of free productions, and the introduction of Christianity and commerce. By encouraging the native propensity for trade, the advantages that might be derived in a commercial point of view are incalculable; nor should we lose sight of the inestimable blessings it is in our power to bestow upon the unenlightened African, by giving him the light of Christianity. Those two pioneers of civilization— Christianity and commerce—should ever be inseparable; and Englishmen should be warned by the fruits of neglecting that principle as exemplified in the result of the management of Indian affairs. By trading with Africa, also, we should at length be independent of slave-labour, and thus discountenance practices so obnoxious to every Englishman.

Though the natives are not absolutely anxious to receive the Gospel, they are open to Christian influences. Among the Bechuanas the Gospel was well received. These people think it a crime to shed a tear, but I have seen some of them weep at the recollection of their sins when God had opened their hearts to Christianity and repentance. It is true that missionaries have difficulties to encounter; but what great enterprise was ever accomplished without difficulty? It is deplorable to think that one of the noblest of our missionary societies, the Church Missionary Society, is compelled to send to Germany for missionaries, whilst other societies are amply supplied. Let this stain be wiped off.—The sort of men who are wanted for missionaries are such as I see before me;— men of education, standing, enterprise, zeal, and piety. It is a mistake to suppose that *any one*, as long as he is pious, will do for this office. Pioneers in every thing should be the ablest and best qualified men, not those of small ability and education. This remark especially applies to the first teachers of Christian truth in regions which may never have before been blest with the name and Gospel of Jesus Christ. In the early ages the monasteries were the schools of Europe, and the monks were not ashamed to hold the plough. The missionaries now take the place of those noble men, and we should not hesitate to give up the small luxuries of life in order to carry knowledge and truth to them that are in darkness. I hope that many of those whom I now address will embrace that honourable career. Education has been given us from above for the purpose of bringing to the benighted the knowledge of a Saviour. If you knew the satisfaction of performing such a duty, as well as the gratitude to God which the missionary must always feel, in being chosen for so noble, so sacred a calling, you would have no hesitation in embracing it.

For my own part, I have never ceased to rejoice that God has appointed me to such an office. People talk of the sacrifice I have made in spending so much of my life in Africa. Can that be called a sacrifice which is simply paid back as a small part of a great debt owing to our God, which we can never repay?—Is that a sacrifice which brings its own blest reward in healthful activity, the consciousness of doing good, peace of mind, and a bright hope of a glorious destiny hereafter?—Away with the word in such a view, and with such a thought! It is emphatically no sacrifice.

Say rather it is a privilege. Anxiety, sickness, suffering, or danger, now and then, with a foregoing of the common conveniences and charities of this life, may make us pause, and cause the spirit to waver, and the soul to sink, but let this only be for a moment. All these are nothing when compared with the glory which shall hereafter be revealed in, and for, us. I never made a sacrifice. Of this we ought not to talk, when we remember the great sacrifice which HE made who left His Father's throne on high to give Himself for us.

*   *   *

REVIEW QUESTIONS

1. What is for Livingstone the relationship between commerce and missionary work?
2. What are Livingstone's perceptions of African culture?
3. Judging from this speech, how did Livingstone inspire a generation to enter into missionary work?

EDWARD D. MOREL

FROM *The Black Man's Burden*

Alongside the dominant ideological assertion that "moral responsibility" obliged the West to build empires, critics of imperialism also voiced their dissent. Although the most consistent denunciation came from socialists, liberals also criticized imperialism on a number of economical and political principles. E. D. Morel, a British journalist writing in the immediate aftermath of the First World War, offers here a stinging indictment of imperialism's fatal impact on Africa. Written in 1920, Morel's scathing criticism of Britain must be situated in the postwar debate concerning the future of the colonies and the question of African self-determination.

From *The Black Man's Burden*, E. D. Morel, Metro Books, 1972.

*   *   *

I⊤ is with the peoples of Africa, then, that our inquiry is concerned. It is they who carry the "Black man's" burden. They have not withered away before the white man's *occupation*. Indeed, if the scope of this volume permitted, there would be no difficulty in showing that Africa has ultimately absorbed within itself every Caucasian and, for that matter, every Semitic invader too. In hewing out for himself a fixed abode in Africa, the white man has massacred the African in heaps. The African has survived, and it is well for the white settlers that he has.

In the process of imposing his political dominion over the African, the white man has carved broad and bloody avenues from one end of Africa to the other. The African has resisted, and persisted.

For three centuries the white man seized and enslaved millions of Africans and transported them, with every circumstance of ferocious cruelty, across the seas. Still the African survived and, in his land of exile, multiplied exceedingly.

But what the partial occupation of his soil by the white man has failed to do; what the mapping out of European political "spheres of influence" has failed to do; what the maxim and the rifle, the slave gang, labour in the bowels of the earth and the lash, have failed to do; what imported measles, smallpox and syphilis have failed to do; what even the oversea slave trade failed to do, the power of modern capitalistic exploitation, assisted by modern engines of destruction, may yet succeed in accomplishing.

For from the evils of the latter, scientifically applied and enforced, there is no escape for the African. Its destructive effects are not spasmodic: they are permanent. In its permanence resides its fatal consequences. It kills not the body merely, but the soul. It breaks the spirit. It attacks the African at every turn, from every point of vantage. It wrecks his polity, uproots him from the land, invades his family life, destroys his natural pursuits and occupations, claims his whole time, enslaves him in his own home.

Economic bondage and wage slavery, the grinding pressure of a life of toil, the incessant demands of industrial capitalism—these things a landless European proletariat physically endures, though hardly.* * * The recuperative forces of a temperate climate are there to arrest the ravages, which alleviating influences in the shape of prophylactic and curative remedies will still further circumscribe. But in Africa, especially in tropical Africa, which a capitalistic imperialism threatens and has, in part, already devastated, man is incapable of reacting against unnatural conditions. In those regions man is engaged in a perpetual struggle against disease and an exhausting climate, which tells heavily upon child-bearing; and there is no scientific machinery for salving the weaker members of the community. The African of the tropics is capable of tremendous physical labours. But he cannot accommodate himself to the European system of monotonous, uninterrupted labour, with its long and regular hours, involving, moreover, as it frequently does, severance from natural surroundings and nostalgia, the condition of melancholy resulting from separation from home, a malady to which the African is specially prone. Climatic conditions forbid it. When the system is forced upon him, the tropical African droops and dies.

Nor is violent physical opposition to abuse and injustice henceforth possible for the African in any part of Africa. His chances of effective resistance have been steadily dwindling with the increasing perfectibility in the killing power of modern armament. Gunpowder broke the effectiveness of his resistance to the slave trade, although he continued to struggle. He has forced and, on rare occasions and in exceptional circumstances beaten, in turn the old-fashioned musket, the elephant gun, the seven-pounder, and even the repeating rifle and the gatling gun. He has been known to charge right down repeatedly, foot and horse, upon the square, swept on all sides with the pitiless and continuous hail of maxims. But against the latest inventions, physical bravery, though associated with a perfect knowledge of the country, can do nothing. The African cannot face the high-explosive shell and the bomb-dropping aeroplane. He has inflicted sanguinary reverses upon picked

European troops, hampered by the climate and by commissariat difficulties. He cannot successfully oppose members of his own race free from these impediments, employed by his white adversaries, and trained in all the diabolical devices of scientific massacre. And although the conscripting of African armies for use in Europe or in Africa as agencies for the liquidation of the white man's quarrels must bring in its train evils from which the white man will be the first to suffer, both in Africa and in Europe; the African himself must eventually disappear in the process. Winter in Europe, or even in Northern Africa, is fatal to the tropical or sub-tropical African, while in the very nature of the case anything approaching real European control in Africa, of hordes of African soldiery armed with weapons of precision is not a feasible proposition. The Black man converted by the European into a scientifically-equipped machine for the slaughter of his kind, is certainly not more merciful than the white man similarly equipped for like purposes in dealing with unarmed communities. And the experiences of the civilian population of Belgium, East Prussia, Galicia and Poland is indicative of the sort of visitation involved for peaceable and powerless African communities if the white man determines to add to his appalling catalogue of past misdeeds towards the African, the crowning wickedness of once again, as in the day of the slave trade, supplying him with the means of encompassing his own destruction.

Thus the African is really helpless against the material gods of the white man, as embodied in the trinity of imperialism, capitalistic-exploitation, and militarism. If the white man retains these gods and if he insists upon making the African worship them as assiduously as he has done himself, the African will go the way of the Red Indian, the Amerindian, the Carib, the Guanche, the aboriginal Australian, and many more. And this would be at once a crime of enormous magnitude, and a world disaster.

....

An endeavour will now be made to describe the nature, and the changing form, which the burden inflicted by the white man in modern times upon the black has assumed. It can only be sketched here in the broadest outline, but in such a way as will, it is hoped, explain the differing causes and motives which have inspired white activities in Africa and illustrate, by specific and notable examples, their resultant effects upon African peoples. It is important that these differing causes and motives should be understood, and that we should distinguish between them in order that we may hew our way later on through the jungle of error which impedes the pathway to reform. Diffused generalities and sweeping judgments generate confusion of thought and hamper the evolution of a constructive policy based upon clear apprehension of the problem to be solved.

The history of contact between the white and black peoples in modern times is divisible into two distinct and separate periods: the period of the slave trade and the period of invasion, political control, capitalistic exploitation, and, the latest development, militarism. Following the slave trade period and preceding the period of invasion, occurs the trade interlude which, indeed, had priority of both periods, as when the Carthagenians bartered salt and iron implements for gold dust on the West Coast. But this interlude concerns our investigations only when we pass from destructive exposure to constructive demonstration.

The first period needs recalling, in order to impress once more upon our memories the full extent of the African's claim upon us, the white imperial peoples, for tardy justice, for considerate and honest conduct.

Our examination of the second period will call for sectional treatment. The history of contact and its consequences during this period may be roughly sub-divided thus:

(a) The struggle for supremacy between European invading *Settlers* and resident African peoples in those portions of Africa where the climate and other circumstances permit of Europeans rearing families of white children.

(b) *Political action* by European Governments aiming at the assertion of sovereign rights over particular areas of African territory.

(c) *Administrative policy*, sanctioned by European Governments, and applied by their local representatives in particular areas, subsequent to the successful assertion of sovereign rights.

These sub-divisions are, perhaps, somewhat arbitrary. The distinctiveness here given to them cannot be absolutely preserved. There is, for instance, a natural tendency for both *a* and *b* to merge into *c* as, through efflux of time, the originating cause and motive of contact is obscured by developments to which contact has given rise.

Thus racial contention for actual possession of the soil, and political action often resulting in so-called treaties of Protectorate thoroughly unintelligible to the African signees, are both landmarks upon the road leading to eventual administrative policy: *i.e.*, to direct government of the black man by the white.

*   *   *

It is often argued that the agricultural and arboricultural methods of the African are capable of improvement. The statement is undoubtedly true. It applies with equal force to the land of Britain. There is no difference of opinion among British agricultural experts as to the capacities for improvement in the methods of British agriculture. As for British arboriculture it is still an almost entirely neglected field of British home enterprise. We can afford to be patient with the African if he has not yet attained perfection. Why, it is only since the beginning of the 18th century that the rotation of crops has been practised in England! But the Kano farmers in Northern Nigeria have understood rotation of crops and grass manuring for at least five hundred years.

To advance such truisms as an excuse for robbing the native communities of their land, degrading farmers in their own right to the level of hired labourers urged on by the lash, and conferring monopolistic rights over the land and its fruits to private corporations, is to make truth the stalking horse of oppression and injustice. The statement of fact may be accurate. The claim put forward on the strength of it is purely predatory.

Those who urge this and kindred arguments only do so to assist the realisation of their purpose. That purpose is clear. It is to make of Africans all over Africa a servile race; to exploit African labour, and through African labour, the soil of Africa for their own exclusive benefit. They are blind to the cost in human suffering. They are indifferent to the fact that in the long run their policy must defeat its own ends. They care only for the moment, and for the objects of the moment they are prepared to sacrifice the future. But since their purpose is selfish, short-sighted and immoral it must be striven against without pause or relaxation. There can be no honest or safe compromise with these people and their policy. A great moral issue is involved. But although that issue comes first, and must come first, it is not the only issue.

For a time it may be possible for the white man to maintain a white civilisation in the colonisable, or partly colonisable, areas of the African Continent based on servile or semi-servile labour: to build up a servile State. But even there the attempt can be no more than fleeting. The days of Roman imperialism are done with for ever. Education sooner or later breaks all chains, and knowledge cannot be kept from the African. The attempt will be defeated in the north by Islam, which confers power of combination in the political sphere, and a spiritual unity which Europe has long lost in the mounting tides of her materialism. It will fail in the south through the prolificness of the African, through the practical impossibility of arresting his intellectual advance and through race admixture, which is proceeding at a much more rapid rate than most people realise. In the great tropical regions the attempt must fail in the very nature of things, if for no other reason, because it can only be enforced by employing the black man, trained in the art of modern warfare as the medium through which to coerce his unarmed brother. The former will be well content to play that part for a period more or less prolonged, but when he becomes alive to his power the whole fabric of European domination will fall to pieces in shame and ruin. From these failures the people of Europe will suffer moral and material damage of a far-reaching kind.

And the criminal folly of it! The white imperial peoples have it in their power, if their rulers will cultivate vision and statesmanship enough to thrust aside the prompting of narrow, ephemeral interests—anti-national in the truest sense—to make of Africa the home of highly-trained and prosperous peoples enriching the universe as their prosperity waxes, dwelling in plains and valleys, in forests and on plateaux made fruitful by their labours, assisted by science; a country whose inhabitants will be enterprising and intelligent, loving their land, looking to it for inspiration, co-operating faithfully in the work of the world, developing their own culture, independent, free, self-respecting, attaining to higher mental growth as the outcome of internal evolutionary processes. Why cannot the white imperial peoples, acknowledging in some measure the injuries they have inflicted upon the African, turn a new leaf in their treatment of him? For nearly two thousand years they have professed to be governed by the teachings of Christ. Can they not begin in the closing century of that era, to practise what they profess

—and what their missionaries of religion teach the African? Can they not cease to regard the African as a producer of dividends for a selected few among their number, and begin to regard him as a human being with human rights? Have they made such a success of their own civilisation that they can contemplate with equanimity the forcing of all its social failures upon Africa—its hideous and devastating inequalities, its pauperisms, its senseless and destructive egoisms, its vulgar and soulless materialism? It is in their power to work such good to Africa—and such incalculable harm! Can they not make up their minds that their strength shall be used for noble ends? Africa demands at their hands, justice, and understanding sympathy—not ill-informed sentiment. And when these are dealt out to her she repays a thousandfold.

*   *   *

REVIEW QUESTIONS

1. How does Morel outline the history of gradual European domination over indigenous Africans?
2. What is the extent of blame that Morel lays at Europe's door?
3. List the range of abuse and exploitation that Morel ascribes to the western imperial powers.
4. What does Morel's criticism of Europe's use of industrial work habits in Africa suggest about European attitudes toward colonies?
5. Why does Morel call the preservation of colonies in Africa a "criminal folly"?

ERNEST EDWIN WILLIAMS

FROM *Made in Germany*

The dynamism of German economic growth after 1870 caused concern in England. Comparing the output of pig iron—a reliable index of industrial production—in Germany and England reveals the relative decline of England as an industrial power. Whereas German pig iron production increased from 1.56 million metric tons in 1871 to 14.8 in 1910, English pig iron rose in the same time period from 6.5 in 1871 to 10.1 in 1910. Germany also surpassed the United Kingdom in metallurgical and steel production, while developing a world reputation for its machines, tools, cutlery, optics, and precision instruments. Consequently, economic competition sharpened the edge of the political rivalry that developed between England and Germany after 1890. E. E. William's enormously popular book, which went through numerous editions in the 1890s, exemplifies the popular literature that fueled the economic nationalism of this period.

From *Made in Germany*, E. E. Williams, William Heinemann, London, 1896.

THE Industrial Supremacy of Great Britain has been long an axiomatic commonplace; and it is fast turning into a myth, as inappropriate to fact as the Chinese Emperor's computation of his own status. This is a strong statement. But it is neither wide nor short of the truth. The industrial glory of England is departing, and England does not know it. There are spasmodic outcries against foreign competition, but the impression they leave is fleeting and vague. The phrase, "Made in Germany," is raw material for a jape at the pantomime, or is made the text for a homily by the official guardians of some particular trade, in so far as the matter concerns themselves. British Consuls, too, send words of warning home, and the number of these is increasing with significant frequency. But the nation at large is yet as little alive to the impending danger as to the evil already wrought. The man in the shop or the factory has plenty to say about the Armenian Question and the House of Lords, but about commercial and industrial matters which concern him vitally he is generally much less el-

oquent. The amount of interest evinced by the amateur politician seems invariably to advance with the remoteness of the matter from his daily bread. It is time to disturb the fatal torpor: even though the moment be, in one sense, unhappily chosen. The pendulum between depression and prosperity has swung to the latter, and manufacturers and merchants are flushed with the joyful contemplation of their order-books. Slackness has given way to briskness; the lean years have been succeeded by a term of fat ones. The prophet of evil commands his most attentive audiences when the times are with him. When they are good— though the good be fleeting—his words are apt to fall unheeded.

*   *   *

As It Was

There was a time when our industrial Empire was unchallenged. It was England which first emerged from the Small-Industry stage. She produced the Industrial Revolution about the middle of the last century, and well-nigh until the middle of this she developed her multitude of mills, and factories, and mines, and warehouses, undisturbed by war at home, and profiting by wars abroad. The great struggles which drained the energies of the Continental nations, sealed her industrial supremacy, and made her absolute mistress of the world-market. Thanks to them, she became the Universal Provider. English machinery, English pottery, English hardware, guns, and cutlery, English rails and bridge-work, English manufactures of well-nigh every kind formed the material of civilisation all over the globe. She covered the dry land with a network of railways, and the seas were alive with her own ships freighted with her own merchandise. Between 1793 and 1815 the value of her exports had risen from £17,000,000 to £58,000,000. Her industrial dominion was immense, unquestioned, unprecedented in the history of the human race; and not unnaturally we have come to regard her rule as eternal. But careless self-confidence makes not for Empire. While she was throwing wide her gates to the world at large, her sisters were building barriers of protection against her; and, behind those barriers, and aided often by State subventions, during the middle and later years of the century, they have developed industries of their own. Of course, this was to a certain extent inevitable. England could not hope for an eternal monopoly of the world's manufactures; and industrial growths abroad do not of necessity sound the knell of her greatness. But she must discriminate in her equanimity. And most certainly she must discriminate against Germany. For Germany has entered into a deliberate and deadly rivalry with her, and is battling with might and main for the extinction of her supremacy.

In estimating England's industrial position, regard must also be had to her function as the world's middleman. Not only is she a manufacturer for other peoples: she is likewise their agent for distribution. There is scarce a nation—certainly not one of any importance—which does not come to England to buy goods sent in for sale from elsewhere. She sells those nations hams from her Colonies, coffee from Arabia, gloves from France, currants from Greece, cotton from America—in fact it would be hard to name an article produced abroad which is not on sale in those universal market-places, the Mersey and the Thames. In this retail business, also, the Germans are setting themselves to beat us; and South Americans are already buying their Irish linen through Hamburg houses. If there be an advance in this form of competition on the part of Germany, we shall lose the little benefit accruing from the German export trade, for in all other respects it is wholly baneful to us.

The German Revolution

Up to a couple of decades ago, Germany was an agricultural State. Her manufactures were new and unimportant; her industrial capital was small; her export trade was too insignificant to merit the attention of the official statistician; she imported largely for her own consumption. Now she has changed all that. Her youth has crowded into English houses, has wormed its way into English manufacturing secrets, and has enriched her establishments with the knowledge thus purloined. She has educated her people in a fashion which has made it in some branches of industry the superior, and in most the equal of the English. Her capitalists have been content with a simple style, which has enabled them to dispense with big immediate profits, and to feed their capital. They have toiled at their desks, and made their sons do likewise; they have kept a strict controlling hand on all the strings of their businesses; they have obtained State aid in several ways—as special rates to shipping ports; they have insinuated themselves into every part of the world—civilised, barbarian, savage—learning the languages, and patiently studying the wants and tastes of the several peoples. Not content with reaping the advantages of British colonisation—this was accomplished with alarming facility—Germany has "protected" the simple savage on her own account, and the

Imperial Eagle now floats on the breezes of the South Sea Islands, and droops in the thick air of the African littoral. Her diplomatists have negotiated innumerable commercial treaties. The population of her cities has been increasing in a manner not unworthy of England in the Thirties and Forties. Like England, too, she is draining her rural districts for the massing of her children in huge factory towns. Her yards (as well as those of England) too, are ringing with the sound of hammers upon ships being builded for the transport of German merchandise. Her agents and travellers swarm through Russia, and wherever else there is a chance of trade on any terms—are even supplying the foreigner with German goods *at a loss*, that they may achieve their purpose in the end. In a word, an industrial development, unparalleled, save in England a century ago, is now her portion. A gigantic commercial State is arising to menace our prosperity, and contend with us for the trade of the world. It is true that this mad rush towards industrialism does not meet with universal approval; and the Agrarian Party is energetic in its denunciation of the ruin wrought thereby to Germany as an agricultural State. But its protests have nothing availed it yet, nor are ever likely to avail it anything.

Made in Germany

The phrase is fluent in the mouth: how universally appropriate it is, probably no one who has not made a special study of the matter is aware. Take observations, Gentle Reader, in your own surroundings: the mental exercise is recommended as an antidote to that form of self-sufficiency which our candid friends regard as indigenous to the British climate. Your investigations will work out somewhat in this fashion. You will find that the material of some of your own clothes was probably woven in Germany. Still more probable is it that some of your wife's garments are German importations; while it is practically beyond a doubt that the magnificent mantles and jackets wherein her maids array

themselves on their Sundays out are German-made and German-sold, for only so could they be done at the figure. Your governess's *fiancé* is a clerk in the City; but he also was made in Germany. The toys, and the dolls, and the fairy books which your children maltreat in the nursery are made in Germany: nay, the material of your favourite (patriotic) newspaper had the same birthplace as like as not. Roam the house over, and the fateful mark will greet you at every turn, from the piano in your drawing-room to the mug on your kitchen dresser, blazoned though it be with the legend, *A Present from Margate*. Descend to your domestic depths, and you shall find your very drain-pipes German made. You pick out of the grate the paper wrappings from a book consignment, and they also are "Made in Germany." You stuff them into the fire, and reflect that the poker in your hand was forged in Germany. As you rise from your hearthrug you knock over an ornament on your mantlepiece; picking up the pieces you read, on the bit that formed the base, "Manufactured in Germany." And you jot your dismal reflections down with a pencil that was made in Germany. At midnight your wife comes home from an opera which was made in Germany, has been here enacted by singers and conductor and players made in Germany, with the aid of instruments and sheets of music made in Germany. You go to bed, and glare wrathfully at a text on the wall; it is illuminated with an English village church, and it was "Printed in Germany." If you are imaginative and dyspeptic, you drop off to sleep only to dream that St. Peter (with a duly stamped halo round his head and a bunch of keys from the Rhineland) has refused you admission into Paradise, because you bear not the Mark of the Beast upon your forehead, and are not of German make. But you console yourself with the thought that it was only a Bierhaus Paradise any way; and you are awakened in the morning by the sonorous brass of a German band.

Is the picture exaggerated? Bear with me, while I tabulate a few figures from the Official Returns of Her Majesty's Custom House, where, at any rate, fancy and exaggeration have no play. In '95

Germany sent us linen manufactures to the value of £91,257; cotton manufactures to the value of £536,471; embroidery and needlework to the value of £11,309; leather gloves to the value of £27,934 (six times the amount imported six years earlier); and woollen manufactures to the value of £1,016,694. Despite the exceeding cheapness of toys, the value of German-made playthings for English nurseries amounted, in '95, to £459,944. In the same year she sent us books to the value of £37,218, and paper to the value of £586,835. For musical instruments we paid her as much as £563,018; for china and earthenware £216,876; for prints, engravings, and photographs, £111,825. This recital of the moneys which *in one year* have come out of John Bull's pocket for the purchase of his German-made household goods is, I submit disproof enough of any charge of alarmism. For these articles, it must be remembered, are not like oranges and guano. They are not products which we must either import or lack:—*they all belong to the category of English manufactures,* the most important of them, indeed, being articles in the preparation of which Great Britain is held pre-eminent. The total value of manufactured goods imported into the United Kingdom by Germany rose from £16,629,987 in '83 to £21,632,614 in '93: an increase of 30·08 per cent.

A few figures more. I said that a little while since Germany was a large importer of manufactures needed for her own consumption. Take as a first example, the iron and steel industries. In '78 the make of pig-iron in Germany was 2,147,000 tons; in '95 it was 5,788,000 tons. Germany made in '78 492,512 tons of steel; in '94 3,617,000 tons. Her import and export statistics tell the same tale. In '80 her iron exports only totalled 1,301,000 tons; in '94 they stood at 2,008,000 tons. (In the same period England's exports of iron had decreased.) In the matter of cottons Germany exported 14,666,100 kilogs. in '83; in '93, 33,350,800 kilogs., an increase of more than 127 per cent. (England's increase in the same period was only about 2½ per cent.) Shipping returns are a pretty sure test of commercial prosperity: it is therefore significant that in '93 the total tonnage of the sea-going ships which touched at Hamburg for the first time left Liverpool behind, and in '94 Hamburg cut her record of the year before.

*   *   *

The Significance of these Facts

These are the sober—to believers in our eternal rule, the sobering—facts. They are picked almost at random from a mass of others of like import, and I think they are sufficient to prove that my general statements are neither untrue nor unduly emphatic. And yet the data needed for the purpose of showing the parlous condition into which our trade is drifting are still largely to seek. Germany is yet in her industrial infancy; and the healthiest infant can do but poor battle against a grown man. England, with her enormous capital, and the sway she has wielded for a century over the world-market, is as that strong man. Now, to tell a strong man, conscious of his strength to an over-weening degree, that he is in peril from a half-grown youngster, is to invite his derision; and yet if a strong man, as the years advance on him, neglect himself and abuse his strength, he may fall before an energetic stripling. Germany has already put our trade in a bad way; but the worst lies in the future, and it is hard to convince the average Englishman of this.

*   *   *

REVIEW QUESTIONS

1. In what stages of growth does Williams perceive both England and Germany?
2. Why have German products flooded Britain's domestic market?
3. Does Williams's economic argument have political ramifications?

EYRE CROWE

FROM Memorandum on the Present State of British Relations with France and Germany

Growing international tension and the rigidification of the alliance system during the 1890s compelled Britain to abandon its policy of "splendid isolation" in 1904 and establish the Entente Cordial with France. Britain's continental alliance was above all motivated by its sustained tension with Germany over a number of issues, but especially in regard to naval supremacy. In an influential memorandum of 1907, Sir Eyre Alexander Crowe (1864–1925) sketched the justifications for pursuing a vigilant and critical policy toward Germany. As a leading official in the foreign office, Crow's document is a telling indicator of the government's attitude toward Germany in the era just prior to the First World War.

From *British Documents on the Origins of the War, 1898–1914,* His Majesty's Stationary Office, 1928.

*   *   *

With the events of 1871 the spirit of Prussia passed into the new Germany. In no other country is there a conviction so deeply rooted in the very body and soul of all classes of the population that the preservation of national rights and the realization of national ideals rest absolutely on the readiness of every citizen in the last resort to stake himself and his State on their assertion and vindication. With "blood and iron" Prussia had forged her position in the councils of the Great Powers of Europe. In due course it came to pass that, with the impetus given to every branch of national activity by the newly-won unity, and more especially by the growing development of oversea trade flowing in ever-increasing volume through the now Imperial ports of the formerly "independent" but politically insignificant Hanse Towns, the young empire found opened to its energy a whole world outside Europe, of which it had previously hardly had the opportunity to become more than dimly conscious. Sailing across the ocean in German ships, German merchants began for the first time to divine the true position of countries such as England, the United States, France, and even the Netherlands, whose political influence extends to distant seas and continents. The colonies and foreign possessions of England more especially were seen to give to that country a recognized and enviable status in a world where the name of Germany, if mentioned at all, excited no particular interest. The effect of this discovery upon the German mind was curious and instructive. Here was a vast province of human activity to which the mere title and rank of a European Great Power were not in themselves a sufficient passport. Here in a field of portentous magnitude, dwarfing altogether the proportions of European countries, others, who had been perhaps rather looked down upon as comparatively smaller folk, were at home and commanded, whilst Germany was at best received but as an honoured guest. Here was distinct inequality, with a heavy bias in favour of the maritime and colonizing Powers.

Such a state of things was not welcome to German patriotic pride. Germany had won her place as one of the leading, if not, in fact, the foremost Power on the European continent. But over and beyond the European Great Powers there seemed to stand the "World Powers." It was at once clear that Germany must become a "World Power."

*　　*　　*

Meanwhile the dream of a Colonial Empire had taken deep hold on the German imagination. Emperor, statesmen, journalists, geographers, economists, commercial and shipping houses, and the whole mass of educated and uneducated public opinion continue with one voice to declare: We *must* have real Colonies, where German emigrants can settle and spread the national ideals of the Fatherland, and we *must* have a fleet and coaling stations to keep together the Colonies which we are bound to acquire. To the question, "Why *must*?" the ready answer is: "A healthy and powerful State like Germany, with its 60,000,000 inhabitants, must expand, it cannot stand still, it must have territories to which its overflowing population can emigrate without giving up its nationality." When it is objected that the world is now actually parcelled out among independent States, and that territory for colonization cannot be had except by taking it from the rightful possessor, the reply again is: "We cannot enter into such considerations. Necessity has no law. The world belongs to the strong. A vigorous nation cannot allow its growth to be hampered by blind adherence to the *status quo*. We have no designs on other people's possessions, but where States are too feeble to put their territory to the best possible use, it is the manifest destiny of those who can and will do so to take their places."

*　　*　　*

No modern German would plead guilty to a mere lust of conquest for the sake of conquest. But the vague and undefined schemes of Teutonic expansion ("die Ausbreitung des deutschen Volkstums") are but the expression of the deeply rooted feeling that Germany has by the strength and purity of her national purpose, the fervour of her patriotism, the depth of her religious feeling, the high standard of competency, and the perspicuous honesty of her administration, the successful pursuit of every branch of public and scientific activity, and the elevated character of her philosophy, art, and ethics, established for herself the right to assert the primacy of German national ideals. And as it is an axiom of her political faith that right, in order that it may prevail, must be backed by force, the transition is easy to the belief that the "good German sword," which plays so large a part in patriotic speech, is there to solve any difficulties that may be in the way of establishing the reign of those ideals in a Germanized world.

*　　*　　*

So long, then, as Germany competes for an intellectual and moral leadership of the world in reliance on her own national advantages and energies England can but admire, applaud, and join in the race. If, on the other hand, Germany believes that greater relative preponderance of material power, wider extent of territory, inviolable frontiers, and supremacy at sea are the necessary and preliminary possessions without which any aspirations to such leadership must end in failure, then England must expect that Germany will surely seek to diminish the power of any rivals, to enhance her own by extending her dominion, to hinder the co-operation of other States, and ultimately to break up and supplant the British Empire.

Now, it is quite possible that Germany does not, nor ever will, consciously cherish any schemes of so subversive a nature. Her statesmen have openly repudiated them with indignation. Their denial may be perfectly honest, and their indignation justified. If so, they will be most unlikely to come into any kind of armed conflict with England, because, as she knows of no causes of present dispute between the two countries, so she would have difficulty in imagining where, on the hypothesis stated, any such should arise in the future. England seeks no quarrels, and will never give Germany cause for legitimate offence.

*   *   *

For purposes of foreign policy the modern German Empire may be regarded as the heir, or descendant of Prussia. Of the history of Prussia, perhaps the most remarkable feature, next to the succession of talented Sovereigns and to the energy and love of honest work characteristic of their subjects, is the process by which on the narrow foundation of the modest Margraviate of Brandenburg there was erected, in the space of a comparatively short period, the solid fabric of a European Great Power. That process was one of systematic territorial aggrandizement achieved mainly at the point of the sword, the most important and decisive conquests being deliberately embarked upon by ambitious rulers or statesmen for the avowed object of securing for Prussia the size, the cohesion, the square miles and the population necessary to elevate her to the rank and influence of a first class State.

*   *   *

The immediate object of the present inquiry was to ascertain whether there is any real and natural ground for opposition between England and Germany. It has been shown that such opposition has, in fact, existed in an ample measure for a long period, but that it has been caused by an entirely one-sided aggressiveness, and that on the part of England the most conciliatory disposition has been coupled with never-failing readiness to purchase the resumption of friendly relations by concession after concession.

It might be deduced that the antagonism is too deeply rooted in the relative position of the two countries to allow of its being bridged over by the kind of temporary expedients to which England has so long and so patiently resorted. On this view of the case it would have to be assumed that

Germany is deliberately following a policy which is essentially opposed to vital British interests, and that an armed conflict cannot in the long run be averted, except by England either sacrificing those interests, with the result that she would lose her position as an independent Great Power, or making herself too strong to give Germany the chance of succeeding in a war. This is the opinion of those who see in the whole trend of Germany's policy conclusive evidence that she is consciously aiming at the establishment of a German hegemony, at first in Europe, and eventually in the world.

After all that has been said in the preceding paragraphs, it would be idle to deny that this may be the correct interpretation of the facts. There is this further seemingly corroborative evidence that such a conception of world-policy offers perhaps the only quite consistent explanation of the tenacity with which Germany pursues the construction of a powerful navy with the avowed object of creating slowly, but surely, a weapon fit to overawe any possible enemy, however formidable at sea.

*   *   *

There is then, perhaps, another way of looking at the problem: It might be suggested that the great German design is in reality no more than the expression of a vague, confused, and unpractical statesmanship, not fully realizing its own drift. A charitable critic might add, by way of explanation, that the well-known qualities of mind and temperament distinguishing for good or for evil the present Ruler of Germany may not improbably be largely responsible for the erratic, domineering, and often frankly aggressive spirit which is recognizable at present in every branch of German public life, not merely in the region of foreign policy; and that this spirit has called forth those manifestations of discontent and alarm both at home and abroad with which the world is becoming familiar; that, in fact, Germany does not really know what she is driving at, and that all her excursions and alarums, all her underhand intrigues do not contribute to the steady working out of a well conceived and relentlessly followed system of policy, because they do not really form part of any such system. This is an hypothesis not flattering to the German Government, and it must be admitted that much might be urged against its validity. But it remains true that on this hypothesis also most of the facts of the present situation could be explained.

*   *   *

REVIEW QUESTIONS

1. What kind of portrait does Crowe paint of Germany?
2. What are the salient issues that have driven a wedge between Germany and England?
3. Does Crowe deem conflict with Germany inevitable?
4. What does this document reveal about diplomatic relations before the First World War?

24 ❧ THE MIDDLE CLASS CHALLENGED

Middle-class liberalism posited that criticism, debate, and scientific change were necessary elements of a modern civil society. Yet in the last third of the nineteenth century, Europe's intellectuals, artists, and scientists shook the foundations of the bourgeois world, challenging the fundamental premises by which bourgeois values and norms organized society and politics. The richness of European letters defies simple generalization; indeed, intellectuals constituted a fragmented social group with varying interests and angles of vision on bourgeois society. Nonetheless, many of the enduring voices from this period were increasingly detached from the normative bourgeois assumptions, especially those grounded in rationality and progress.

The bourgeoisie's self-evident notion of public and private spheres, and their accompanying gender roles, was submitted to critical scrutiny in the last third of the nineteenth century. No longer content with the "natural" roles of reproduction and domesticity, women contested the power arrogated by men to deny them political citizenship and control over their property and legal affairs. The issue of emancipation brought politics inside the home, for many women perceived their principal role as helpmeet to husband fraught with inequality. Awakening to new identities, women demanded the vote, the right to a higher education, and overall respect for their intelligence and ability to serve society. The failure of the political establishment to initiate change for women abetted the rise of women's associations to agitate for the vote and overall access to public life. When peaceful petitioning failed to produce parliamentary debates, English women resorted to civil disobedience and militancy to drive home their point. Hunger strikes, destruction of property, and contentious demonstrations by women scandalized Europeans and disturbed ideals of peaceful, evolutionary change.

The redefinition of gender roles in the late nineteenth century constituted only one aspect of the overall waning political consensus. The rise of violent and irrational political ideologies in the late nineteenth century also undermined middle-class confidence in rationality and progress. Marxists, embracing the axiom of class conflict, preached the imminent collapse of bourgeois capitalism; syndicalists, centering on the need for direct political action, advocated the general strike to paralyze the state; and some anarchists, urging the abolition of the state, advocated random acts of violence as means to purify and rebuild. On the other side of politics, the new right peddled antisemitism as a political tool to garner larger conservative constituencies; pretentious treatises on racism asserted the putative superiority of Germanic and Anglo-Saxon peoples. With blood and soil marking the destiny of individuals and cultures, politics became more aggressive and exclusionary. Social theorists contorted scientific discoveries to justify imperial dominance. Charles Darwin's theory of natural selection, which explained how species of flora and fauna evolved, became especially susceptible to false analogies to social behavior. Popular writers distorted the Darwinian tenet that the stronger triumphed over the weaker, reducing it to jingoistic cant. In sum, the ideals of humanitarianism and perpetual peace, legacies of enlightened civil society, found little resonance.

Philosophy, literature, science, and art also produced little to uphold the values of the bourgeois establishment. Philosophers attacked Judeo-Christian values of social justice as spiritually enervating and culturally debilitating. Avant-garde literature, when not exposing the hypocrisy and avarice of bourgeois society, became fascinated with the darker forces of an indifferent universe as well as with the irrational, tormented behavior of humans. The fledgling science of psychoanalysis further challenged the bourgeoisie's belief in rational, purposive action by demonstrating that behavior was largely determined by the inner mechanisms of the unconscious. Artists rejected the convention of representational beauty and sought to strip art to its essence, experimenting with dimensionality, pure abstraction, the interpenetration of interior and exterior worlds, and new media to redefine the creative act.

Although abounding in material prosperity and technological progress, European political and intellectual life reflected little optimism in sustaining the bourgeois social order. From all quarters, the values that framed bourgeois civil society came under question. While some parties demanded more radical forms of political emancipation and social justice, others scorned the civic-minded premises of the Enlightenment. Science no longer endorsed the middle-class faith in a stable, ordered material world, and psychology asserted that rationality was not the dominant drive in humankind. In its multifaceted critique of the status quo, European letters of the late nineteenth century laid the intellectual seedbed of a new era.

HENRIK IBSEN

FROM A Doll's House

Henrik Ibsen (1828–1906) had a keen eye for the plight of individuals trapped in the conventions and institutions of bourgeois life. His drama A Doll's House *(1879) confronts the legal and financial restrictions that subordinated women to their husbands and how such limitations affected individual lives. The play was controversial in its time for its depiction of the bourgeois marriage as hypocritical and hollow. The scene below follows an epiphany of Nora, the wife of a respectable bourgeois banker, who slowly grasps that she does not genuinely know her husband. This realization grows out the complex set of events that produces the play's climax. Her husband, Torvald Helmer, learns that his wife is faced with the prospect of arrest for forging her father's signature for a loan. Nora took on this debt to save her husband's finances during his long illness and kept it a secret from him to preserve his sense of honor. Expecting gratitude and a chivalrous defense of her actions and motives, Nora received instead a severe rebuke for her moral turpitude. Yet when the threat of exposure, arrest, and public shame vanish, he forgives her and considers the matter forgotten. The incident, however, produces a profound change of heart for Nora.*

From *Plays: Two,* translated by Michael Meyer, Methuen, 1990. Used with permission of the publisher.

*   *   *

HELMER. No, don't go—(*Looks in.*) What are you doing there?

NORA (*offstage*). Taking off my fancy dress.

HELMER (*by the open door*). Yes, do that. Try to calm yourself and get your balance again, my frightened little songbird. Don't be afraid. I have broad wings to shield you. (*Begins to walk around near the door.*) How lovely and peaceful this little home of ours is, Nora. You are safe here; I shall watch over you like a hunted dove which I have snatched unharmed from the claws of the falcon. Your wildly beating little heart shall find peace with me. It will happen, Nora; it will take time, but it will happen, believe me. Tomorrow all this will seem quite different. Soon everything will be as it was before. I shall no longer need to remind you that I have forgiven you; your own heart will tell you that it is true. Do you really think I could ever bring myself to disown you, or even to reproach you? Ah, Nora, you don't understand what goes on in a husband's heart. There is something indescribably wonderful and satisfying for a husband in knowing that he has forgiven his wife —forgiven her unreservedly, from the bottom of his heart. It means that she has become his property in a double sense; he has, as it were, brought her into the world anew; she is now not only his wife but also his child. From now on that is what you shall be to me, my poor, helpless, bewildered little creature. Never be frightened of anything again, Nora. Just open your heart to me. I shall be both your will and your conscience. What's this? Not in bed? Have you changed?

NORA (*in her everyday dress*). Yes, Torvald. I've changed.

HELMER. But why now—so late—?

NORA. I shall not sleep tonight.

HELMER. But, my dear Nora—

NORA (*looks at her watch*). It isn't that late. Sit down there, Torvald. You and I have a lot to talk about.

She sits down on one side of the table.

HELMER. Nora, what does this mean? You look quite drawn—

NORA. Sit down. It's going to take a long time. I've a lot to say to you.

HELMER (*sits down on the other side of the table*). You alarm me, Nora. I don't understand you.

NORA. No, that's just it. You don't understand me. And I've never understood you—until this evening. No, don't interrupt me. Just listen to what I have to say. You and I have got to face facts, Torvald.

HELMER. What do you mean by that?

NORA (*after a short silence*). Doesn't anything strike you about the way we're sitting here?

HELMER. What?

NORA. We've been married for eight years. Does it occur to you that this is the first time we two, you and I, man and wife, have ever had a serious talk together?

HELMER. Serious? What do you mean, serious?

NORA. In eight whole years—no, longer—ever since we first met—we have never exchanged a serious word on a serious subject.

HELMER. Did you expect me to drag you into all my worries—worries you couldn't possibly have helped me with?

NORA. I'm not talking about worries. I'm simply saying that we have never sat down seriously to try to get to the bottom of anything.

HELMER. But, my dear Nora, what on earth has that got to do with you?

NORA. That's just the point. You have never understood me. A great wrong has been done to me, Torvald. First by papa, and then by you.

HELMER. What? But we two have loved you more than anyone in the world!

NORA (*shakes her head*). You have never loved me. You just thought it was fun to be in love with me.

HELMER. Nora, what kind of a way is this to talk?

NORA. It's the truth, Torvald. When I lived with papa, he used to tell me what he thought about everything, so that I never had any opinions but his. And if I did have any of my own, I kept them quiet, because he wouldn't have liked them. He called me his little doll, and he played with me just the way I played with my dolls. Then I came here to live in your house—

HELMER. What kind of a way is that to describe our marriage?

NORA (*undisturbed*). I mean, then I passed from papa's hands into yours. You arranged everything the way you wanted it, so that I simply took over your taste in everything—or pretended I did—I don't really know—I think it was a little of both—first one and then the other. Now I look back on it, it's as if I've been living here like a pauper, from hand to mouth. I performed tricks for you, and you gave me food and drink. But that was how you wanted it. You and papa have done me a great wrong. It's your fault that I have done nothing with my life.

HELMER. Nora, how can you be so unreasonable and ungrateful? Haven't you been happy here?

NORA. No; never. I used to think I was. But I haven't ever been happy.

HELMER. Not—not happy?

NORA. No. I've just had fun. You've always been very kind to me. But our home has never been anything but a playroom. I've been your doll-wife, just as I used to be papa's doll-child. And the children have been my dolls. I used to think it was fun when you came in and played with me, just as they think it's fun when I go in and play games with them. That's all our marriage has been, Torvald.

HELMER. There may be a little truth in what you

say, though you exaggerate and romanticize. But from now on it'll be different. Playtime is over. Now the time has come for education.

NORA. Whose education? Mine or the children's?

HELMER. Both yours and the children's, my dearest Nora.

NORA. Oh, Torvald, you're not the man to educate me into being the right wife for you.

HELMER. How can you say that?

NORA. And what about me? Am I fit to educate the children?

HELMER. Nora!

NORA. Didn't you say yourself a few minutes ago that you dare not leave them in my charge?

HELMER. In a moment of excitement. Surely you don't think I meant it seriously?

NORA. Yes. You were perfectly right. I'm not fitted to educate them. There's something else I must do first. I must educate myself. And you can't help me with that. It's something I must do by myself. That's why I'm leaving you.

HELMER (*jumps up*). What did you say?

NORA. I must stand on my own feet if I am to find out the truth about myself and about life. So I can't go on living here with you any longer.

HELMER. Nora, Nora!

NORA. I'm leaving you now, at once. Christine will put me up for tonight—

HELMER. You're out of your mind! You can't do this! I forbid you!

NORA. It's no use your trying to forbid me any more. I shall take with me nothing but what is mine. I don't want anything from you, now or ever.

HELMER. What kind of madness is this?

NORA. Tomorrow I shall go home—I mean, to where I was born. It'll be easiest for me to find some kind of a job there.

HELMER. But you're blind! You've no experience of the world—

NORA. I must try to get some, Torvald.

HELMER. But to leave your home, your husband, your children! Have you thought what people will say?

NORA. I can't help that. I only know that I must do this.

HELMER. But this is monstrous! Can you neglect your most sacred duties?

NORA. What do you call my most sacred duties?

HELMER. Do I have to tell you? Your duties towards your husband, and your children.

NORA. I have another duty which is equally sacred.

HELMER. You have not. What on earth could that be?

NORA. My duty towards myself.

HELMER. First and foremost you are a wife and mother.

NORA. I don't believe that any longer. I believe that I am first and foremost a human being, like you—or anyway, that I must try to become one. I know most people think as you do, Torvald, and I know there's something of the sort to be found in books. But I'm no longer prepared to accept what people say and what's written in books. I must think things out for myself, and try to find my own answer.

HELMER. Do you need to ask where your duty lies in your own home? Haven't you an infallible guide in such matters—your religion?

NORA. Oh, Torvald, I don't really know what religion means.

HELMER. What are you saying?

NORA. I only know what Pastor Hansen told me when I went to confirmation. He explained that religion meant this and that. When I get away from all this and can think things out on my own, that's one of the questions I want to look into. I want to find out whether what Pastor Hansen said was right—or anyway, whether it is right for me.

HELMER. But it's unheard of for so young a woman to behave like this! If religion cannot guide you, let me at least appeal to your conscience. I presume you have some moral feelings left? Or—perhaps you haven't? Well, answer me.

NORA. Oh, Torvald, that isn't an easy question to answer. I simply don't know. I don't know where I am in these matters. I only know that these things mean something quite different to me from what they do to you. I've learned now that certain laws are different from what I'd imagined them to be; but I can't accept that such laws can be right. Has a woman really not the right to spare her dying father pain, or save her husband's life? I can't believe that.

HELMER. You're talking like a child. You don't understand how society works.

NORA. No, I don't. But now I intend to learn. I must try to satisfy myself which is right, society or I.

HELMER. Nora, you're ill. You're feverish. I almost believe you're out of your mind.

NORA. I've never felt so sane and sure in my life.

*   *   *

REVIEW QUESTIONS

1. What are Helmer's assumptions about the relationship between husband and wife?
2. What disturbs Nora most about her relationship with Helmer?
3. What does Nora realize about herself and her life?
4. What social criticisms are embedded in this dialogue?

EMMELINE PANKHURST

FROM Why We Are Militant

In 1903, Emmeline Pankhurst (1858–1928) founded the Women's Social and Political Union, an organization that advocated militancy and direct action to promote the cause of female suffrage, which had become an international movement since the 1890s. Angered by the insouciance of the British political establishment, which remained unphased by the massive petitions and peaceful demonstrations of suffragettes, Pankhurst's association organized hunger strikes and assaults on private property to signify the gravity of the matter. In the following speech of 21 October 1913, delivered in New York, Pankhurst justified the tactics of the Women's Social and Political Union.

From *Suffrage and the Pankhursts*, edited by Jane Marcus, Routledge & Kegan and Paul, 1987.

I know that in your minds there are questions like these; you are saying, 'Woman Suffrage is sure to come; the emancipation of humanity is an evolutionary process, and how is it that some women, instead of trusting to that evolution, instead of educating the masses of people of their country, instead of educating their own sex to prepare them for citizenship, how is it that these militant women are using violence and upsetting the business arrangements of the country in their undue impatience to attain their end?'

Let me try to explain to you the situation.

Although we have a so-called democracy, and so called representative government there, England is the most conservative country on earth. Why, your forefathers found that out a great many years ago! If you had passed your life in England as I have, you would know that there are certain words which certainly, during the last two generations, certainly till about ten years ago, aroused a feeling of horror and fear in the minds of the mass of the people. The word revolution, for instance, was identified in England with all kind of horrible ideas. The idea of change, the idea of unsettling the established order of things was repugnant.

*   *   *

The extensions of the franchise to the men of my country have been preceded by very great violence, by something like a revolution, by something like civil war. In 1832, you know we were on the edge of a civil war and on the edge of revolution, and it was at the point of the sword —no, not at the point of the sword—it was after the practice of arson on so large a scale that half the city of Bristol was burned down in a single night, it was because more and greater violence and arson were feared that the Reform Bill of 1832 was allowed to pass into law. In 1867, John Bright urged the people of London to crowd the approaches to the Houses of Parliament in order to show their determination, and he said that if they did that no Parliament, however obdurate, could resist their just demands. Rioting went on all over the country, and as the result of that rioting, as the result of that unrest, which resulted in the pulling down of the Hyde Park railings, as a result of the fear of more rioting and violence the Reform Act of 1867 was put upon the statute books.

In 1884 came the turn of the agricultural labourer. Joseph Chamberlain, who afterwards became a very conservative person, threatened that, unless the vote was given to the agricultural labourer, he would march 100,000 men from Birmingham to know the reason why. Rioting was threatened and feared, and so the agricultural labourers got the vote.

Meanwhile, during the '80's, women, like men, were asking for the franchise. Appeals, larger and more numerous than for any other reform, were presented in support of Woman's Suffrage. Meet-

ings of the great corporations, great town councils, and city councils, passed resolutions asking that women should have the vote. More meetings were held, and larger, for Woman Suffrage than were held for votes for men, and yet the women did not get it. Men got the vote because they were and would be violent. The women did not get it because they were constitutional and law-abiding. Why, is it not evident to everyone that people who are patient where mis-government is concerned may go on being patient! Why should anyone trouble to help them? I take to myself some shame that through all those years, at any rate from the early '80's, when I first came into the Suffrage movement, I did not learn my political lessons.

I believed, as many women still in England believe, that women could get their way in some mysterious manner, by purely peaceful methods. We have been so accustomed, we women, to accept one standard for men and another standard for women, that we have even applied that variation of standard to the injury of our political welfare.

Having had better opportunities of education, and having had some training in politics, having in political life come so near to the 'superior' being as to see that he was not altogether such a fount of wisdom as they had supposed, that he had his human weaknesses as we had, the twentieth century women began to say to themselves. 'Is it not time, since our methods have failed and the men's have succeeded, that we should take a leaf out of their political book?'

We were led to that conclusion, we older women, by the advice of the young—you know there is a French proverb which says, 'If youth knew; if age could,' but I think that when you can bring together youth and age, as we have done, and get them to adopt the same methods and take the same point of view, then you are on the high road to success.

Well, we in Great Britain, on the eve of the General Election of 1905, a mere handful of us— why, you could almost count us on the fingers of both hands—set out on the wonderful adventure of forcing the strongest Government of modern times to give the women the vote. Only a few in number; we were not strong in influence, and we had hardly any money, and yet we quite gaily made our little banners with the words 'Votes for Women' upon them, and we set out to win the enfranchisement of the women of our country.

The Suffrage movement was almost dead. The women had lost heart. You could not get a Suffrage meeting that was attended by members of the general public. We used to have about 24 adherents in the front row. We carried our resolutions and heard no more about them.

Two women changed that in a twinkling of an eye at a great Liberal demonstration in Manchester, where a Liberal leader, Sir Edward Grey, was explaining the programme to be carried out during the Liberals' next turn of office. The two women put the fateful question, 'When are you going to give votes to women?' and refused to sit down until they had been answered. These two women were sent to gaol, and from that day to this the women's movement, both militant and constitutional, has never looked back. We had little more than one moribund society for Woman Suffrage in those days. Now we have nearly 50 societies for Woman Suffrage, and they are large in membership, they are rich in money, and their ranks are swelling every day that passes. That is how militancy has put back the clock of Woman Suffrage in Great Britain.

Now, some of you have said how wicked it is (the immigration commissioners told me that on Saturday afternoon), how wicked it is to attack the property of private individuals who have done us no harm. Well, you know there is a proverb which says that you cannot make omelettes without breaking eggs. I wish we could.

I want to say here and now that the only justification for violence, the only justification for damage to property, the only justification for risk to the comfort of other human beings is the fact that you have tried all other available means and have failed to secure justice, and as a law-abiding person—and I am by nature a law-abiding person, as one hating violence, hating disorder—I want to say that from the moment we began our militant agitation to this day I have felt absolutely guiltless in this matter.

I tell you that in Great Britain there is no other way. We can show intolerable grievances. The Chancellor of the Exchequer, Mr Lloyd George, who is no friend of the woman's movement, although a professed one, said a very true thing when speaking of the grievances of his own country, of Wales. He said that there comes a time in the life of human beings suffering from intolerable grievances when the only way to maintain their self respect is to revolt against that injustice.

Well, I say the time is long past when it became necessary for women to revolt in order to maintain their self respect in Great Britain. The women who are waging this war are women who would fight, if it were only for the idea of liberty —if it were only that they might be free citizens of a free country—I myself would fight for that idea alone. But we have, in addition to this love of freedom, intolerable grievances to redress.

*   *   *

All my life I have tried to understand why it is that men who value their citizenship as their dearest possession seem to think citizenship ridiculous when it is to be applied to the women of their race. And I find an explanation, and it is the only one I can think of. It came to me when I was in a prison cell, remembering how I had seen men laugh at the idea of women going to prison. Why they would confess they could not bear a cell door to be shut upon themselves for a single hour without asking to be let out. A thought came to me in my prison cell, and it was this: that to men women are not human beings like themselves. Some men think we are superhuman; they put us on pedestals; they revere us; they think we are too fine and too delicate to come down into the hurly-burly of life. Other men think us sub-human; they think we are a strange species unfortunately having to exist for the perpetuation of the race. They think that we are fit for drudgery, but that in some strange way our minds are not like theirs, our love for great things is not like theirs, and so we are a sort of sub-human species.

We are neither superhuman nor are we sub-human. We are just human beings like yourselves.

*   *   *

When we were patient, when we believed in argument and persuasion, they said, 'You don't really want it because, if you did, you would do something unmistakable to show you were determined to have it.' And then when we did something unmistakable they said, 'You are behaving so badly that you show you are not fit for it.'

Now, gentlemen, in your heart of hearts you do not believe that. You know perfectly well that there never was a thing worth having that was not worth fighting for. You know perfectly well that if the situation were reversed, if you had no constitutional rights and we had all of them, if you had the duty of paying and obeying and trying to look as pleasant, and we were the proud citizens who could decide our fate and yours, because we knew what was good for you better than you knew yourselves, you know perfectly well that you wouldn't stand it for a single day, and you would be perfectly justified in rebelling against such intolerable conditions.

Well, in Great Britain, we have tried persuasion, we have tried the plan of showing (by going upon public bodies, where they allowed us to do work they hadn't much time to do themselves) that we are capable people. We did it in the hope that we should convince them and persuade them to do the right and proper thing. But we had all our labour for our pains, and now we are fighting for our rights, and we are growing stronger and better women in the process. We are getting more fit to use our rights because we have such difficulty in getting them.

*   *   *

People have said that women could never vote, never share in the government, because government rests upon force. We have proved that is not true. Government rests not upon force; government rests upon the consent of the governed; and the weakest woman, the very poorest woman, if she withholds her consent cannot be governed.

They sent me to prison, to penal servitude for three years. I came out of prison at the end of nine days. I broke my prison bars. Four times they took me back again; four times I burst the prison door open again. And I left England openly to come and visit America, with only three or four weeks of the three years' sentence of penal servitude served. Have we not proved, then, that they cannot govern human beings who withhold their consent?

And so we are glad we have had the fighting experience, and we are glad to do all the fighting for all the women all over the world. All that we ask of you is to back us up. We ask you to show that although, perhaps, you may not mean to fight as we do, yet you understand the meaning of our fight; that you realise we are women fighting for a great idea; that we wish the betterment of the human race, and that we believe this betterment is coming through the emancipation and uplifting of women.

REVIEW QUESTIONS

1. What precedents in history does Pankurst cite to justify her cause and tactics?
2. According to Pankhurst, what is the catalyst of political reform?
3. Why were contemporaries outraged by the idea of women undertaking militant civil disobedience and going to prison for political beliefs?
4. Compare the positions and pleas of both Wollstonecraft and Pankhurst.
5. What had changed over the course of the century?

GEORGES SOREL

FROM *Reflections on Violence*

Although Marxist socialism was the dominant political ideology of workers, syndicalism was widely preferred in areas of France, Spain, and Italy. Syndicalism grew out of trade union associations that espoused the utopian vision of one day controlling their industries and, eventually, the political state. The strike became the central weapon of syndicalism, but it was the general strike that made syndicalism revolutionary. The thousands of strikes in Europe at the end of the century offered the potential of one mighty, total work stoppage that would ruin capitalism and dismantle the state. Georges Sorel (1847–1922) wrote his treatise on syndicalism in 1908. The following excerpt includes Sorel's important notion of the general strike as a mythic belief, the widespread acceptance of which would prompt collective action by workers as well as soften employers' resolve against concessions.

From *Reflections on Violence*, edited by T. E. Hulme, W.B. Huebsch, 1914.

*   *   *

Against this noisy, garrulous, and lying Socialism, which is exploited by ambitious people of every description, which amuses a few buffoons, and which is admired by decadents—revolutionary Syndicalism takes its stand, and endeavours, on the contrary, to leave nothing in a state of indecision; its ideas are honestly expressed, without trickery and without mental reservations; no attempt is made to dilute doctrines by a stream of confused commentaries. Syndicalism endeavours to employ methods of expression which throw a full light on things, which put them exactly in the place assigned to them by their nature, and which bring out the whole value of the forces in play. Oppositions, instead of being glozed over, must be thrown into sharp relief if we desire to obtain a clear idea of the Syndicalist movement; the groups which are struggling one against the other must be shown as separate and as compact as possible; in short, the movements of the revolted masses must be represented in such a way that the soul of the revolutionaries may receive a deep and lasting impression.

These results could not be produced in any very certain manner by the use of ordinary language; use must be made of a body of images which, *by intuition alone*, and before any considered analyses are made, is capable of evoking as an undivided whole the mass of sentiments which corresponds to the different manifestations of the war undertaken by Socialism against modern society. The Syndicalists solve this problem perfectly, by concentrating the whole of Socialism in the drama of the general strike; there is thus no longer any place for the reconciliation of contraries in the equivocations of the professors; everything is clearly mapped out, so that only one interpretation of Socialism is possible. This method has all the advantages which "integral" knowledge has over analysis, according to the doctrine of Bergson; and perhaps it would not be possible to cite another example which would so perfectly demonstrate the value of the famous professor's doctrines.

The possibility of the actual realisation of the general strike has been much discussed; it has been stated that the Socialist war could not be decided in one single battle. To the people who think themselves cautious, practical, and scientific the difficulty of setting great masses of the proletariat in motion at the same moment seems prodigious; they have analysed the difficulties of detail which such an enormous struggle would present. It is the opinion of the Socialist-sociologists, as also of the politicians, that the general strike is a popular dream, characteristic of the beginnings of a working-class movement; we have had quoted against us the authority of Sidney Webb, who has decreed that the general strike is an illusion of youth, of which the English workers—whom the monopolists of sociology have so often presented to us as the depositaries of the true conception of the working-class movement—soon rid themselves.

*   *   *

And yet without leaving the present, without reasoning about this future, which seems for ever condemned to escape our reason, we should be unable to act at all. Experience shows that the *framing of a future, in some indeterminate time, may*, when it is done in a certain way, be very effective, and have very few inconveniences; this happens when the anticipations of the future take the form of those myths, which enclose with them all the strongest inclinations of a people, of a party or of a class, inclinations which recur to the mind with the insistence of instincts in all the circumstances of life; and which give an aspect of complete reality to the hopes of immediate action by which, more easily than by any other method, men can reform their desires, passions, and mental activity. We know, moreover, that these social myths in no way prevent a man profiting by the observations which he makes in the course of his life, and form no obstacle to the pursuit of his normal occupations.

The truth of this may be shown by numerous examples.

The first Christians expected the return of Christ and the total ruin of the pagan world, with the inauguration of the kingdom of the saints, at the end of the first generation. The catastrophe did not come to pass, but Christian thought profited so greatly from the apocalyptic myth that certain contemporary scholars maintain that the whole preaching of Christ referred solely to this one point. The hopes which Luther and Calvin had formed of the religious exaltation of Europe were by no means realised; these fathers of the Reformation very soon seemed men of a past era; for present-day Protestants they belong rather to the Middle Ages than to modern times, and the problems which troubled them most occupy very little place in contemporary Protestantism. Must we for that reason deny the immense result which came from their dreams of Christian renovation?

*   *   *

In our own times Mazzini pursued what the wiseacres of his time called a mad chimera; but it can no longer be denied that, without Mazzini, Italy would never have become a great power, and that he did more for Italian unity than Cavour and all the politicians of his school.

*   *   *

The myth must be judged as a means of acting on the present; any attempt to discuss how far it can be taken literally as future history is devoid of sense. *It is the myth in its entirety which is alone important*: its parts are only of interest in so far as they bring out the main idea. No useful purpose is served, therefore, in arguing about the incidents which may occur in the course of a social war, and about the decisive conflicts which may give victory to the proletariat; even supposing the revolutionaries to have been wholly and entirely deluded in setting up this imaginary picture of the general strike, this picture may yet have been, in the course of the preparation for the Revolution, a great element of strength, if it has embraced all the aspirations of Socialism, and if it has given to the whole body of Revolutionary thought a precision and a rigidity which no other method of thought could have given.

To estimate, then, the significance of the idea of the general strike, all the methods of discussion which are current among politicians, sociologists, or people with pretensions to political science, must be abandoned. Everything which its opponents endeavour to establish may be conceded to them, without reducing in any way the value of the theory which they think they have refuted. The question whether the general strike is a partial reality, or only a product of popular imagination, is of little importance. All that it is necessary to know is, whether the general strike contains everything that the Socialist doctrine expects of the revolutionary proletariat.

To solve this question we are no longer compelled to argue learnedly about the future; we are not obliged to indulge in lofty reflections about philosophy, history, or economics; we are not on the plane of theories, and we can remain on the level of observable facts. We have to question men who take a very active part in the real revolutionary movement amidst the proletariat, men who do not aspire to climb into the middle class and whose mind is not dominated by corporative prejudices. These men may be deceived about an infinite number of political, economical, or moral questions; but their testimony is decisive, sovereign, and irrefutable when it is a question of knowing what are the ideas which most powerfully move them and their comrades, which most appeal to them as being identical with their socialistic conceptions, and thanks to which their reason, their hopes, and their way of looking at particular facts seem to make but one indivisible unity.

Thanks to these men, we know that the general strike is indeed what I have said: the *myth* in which Socialism is wholly comprised, *i.e.* a body of images capable of evoking instinctively all the sentiments which correspond to the different manifestations of the war undertaken by Socialism against modern society. Strikes have engendered in the proletariat the noblest, deepest, and most moving sentiments that they possess; the general strike groups them all in a co-ordinated picture, and, by bringing them together, gives to each one of them its maximum of intensity; appealing to their painful memories of particular conflicts, it colours with an intense life all the details of the composition presented to consciousness. We thus obtain that intuition of Socialism which language cannot give us with perfect clearness—and we obtain it as a whole, perceived instantaneously.

We may urge yet another piece of evidence to prove the power of the idea of the general strike. If that idea were a pure chimera, as is so frequently said, Parliamentary Socialists would not attack it with such heat; I do not remember that they ever attacked the senseless hopes which the Utopists have always held up before the dazzled eyes of the people.

*   *   *

They struggle against the conception of the general strike, because they recognise, in the course of their propagandist rounds, that this conception is so admirably adapted to the working-class mind that there is a possibility of its dominating the latter in the most absolute manner, thus leaving no place for the desires which the Parliamentarians are able to satisfy. They perceive that this idea is so effective as a motive force that once it has entered the minds of the people they can no longer be controlled by leaders, and that thus the power of the deputies would be reduced to nothing. In short, they feel in a vague way that the whole Socialist movement might easily be absorbed by the general strike, which would render useless all those compromises between political groups in view of which the Parliamentary régime has been built up.

The opposition it meets with from official Socialists, therefore, furnishes a confirmation of our first inquiry into the scope of the general strike.

*   *   *

REVIEW QUESTIONS

1. How does Sorel differentiate between socialism and syndicalism?
2. For Sorel, what is the real significance of the general strike?
3. How is syndicalism compared with Christianity and nationalism?
4. What is the importance of myth in political struggle?

HOUSTON STEWART CHAMBERLAIN

FROM *Foundations of the Nineteenth Century*

In 1890, Houston Stewart Chamberlain (1855–1926), an Englishman who lived and wrote in Germany, published Foundations of the Nineteenth Century, *which went through numerous German editions and earned him widespread notoriety in Germany. Although English contemporaries resented the anti-British tone of the book, more disturbing were the rambling arguments that ridiculed western humanitarianism and posited the superiority of the Teutonic race, which possessed the self-evident right to assert itself against lesser cultures. The book marks a watershed moment in the early discourse of pseudoscientific racial theory.*

From *Foundations of the Nineteenth Century,* edited by H. S. Chamberlain, translated by John Lees, The Bodley Head, 1913.

*   *   *

Historical Criterion

If we then free ourselves from the delusion of a progressive or retrogressive humanity, and content ourselves with the realisation of the fact that our culture is specifically North-European, *i.e.*, Teutonic, we shall at once gain a sure standard by which to judge our own past and our present, and at the same time a very useful standard to apply to a future which has yet to come. For nothing Individual is limitless. So long as we regard ourselves as the responsible representatives of all humanity, the more clear-seeing minds must be driven to despair by our poverty and obvious incapacity to pave the way for a golden age; at the same time, however, all shallow-brained phrasemakers turn us from those earnest aims which we might attain, and undermine what I should like to call historical morality, in that, shutting their eyes, blind to our universal limitation, and totally failing to realise the value of our specific talents, they dangle before our eyes the Impossible, the Absolute: natural rights, eternal peace, universal brotherhood, mutual fusion, &c. But if we know that we Northern Europeans are a definite individuality, responsible, not for humanity, but certainly for our own personality, we shall love and value our work as something individual, we shall recognise the fact that it is by no means complete, but still very defective, and, above all, far from being sufficiently independent; no vision of an "absolute" perfection will mislead us, but we shall, as Shakespeare wished, remain true to ourselves, and be satisfied with doing our very best within the limits of the Teuton's power of achievement; we shall deliberately defend ourselves against the un-Teutonic, and seek not only to extend our empire farther and farther over the surface of the globe and over the powers of nature, but above all unconditionally to subject the inner world to ourselves by mercilessly overthrowing and excluding those who are alien to us, and who, nevertheless, would fain gain the mastery over our thought. It is often said that politics can know no scruples; nothing at all can know scruples; scruples are a crime against self. Scruple is the soldier who in the battle takes to his heels, presenting his back as a target to the enemy. The most sacred duty of the Teuton is to serve the Teutonic cause. This fact supplies us with an historical standard of measurement. In all spheres that man and that deed will be glorified as greatest and most important which most successfully advance specific Teutonism or have most vigorously supported its supremacy. Thus and thus only do we acquire a limiting, organising, absolutely positive principle of judgment. To refer to a well-known instance; why is it that, in spite of the admiration which his genius inspires, the personality of the great Byron has something repulsive in it for every thorough Teuton? Treitschke has answered this question in his brilliant essay on Byron: it is "because nowhere in this rich life do we encounter the idea of duty." That is an unsympathetic, un-Teutonic feature.

*　　*　　*

Inner Contrasts

There is yet a word to be said, and one of great importance, if we would clearly recognise and distinguish what is thoroughly Teutonic. In the matters which I have just mentioned, as in a thousand others, we discover everywhere that specific characteristic of the Teuton, the close association—as though they were twin brothers, walking hand in hand—of the Practical and the Ideal* * * At all points we shall encounter similar contradictions in the Teuton, and shall learn to value them equally highly. For when we realise that we have to deal with something individual, we shall, in forming our judgment, refrain above all from taking into consideration the logical notions of abstract theories about Good and Evil, Higher and Lower, and direct our attention simply to the individuality; but an individuality is always best recognised from its inner contrasts; where it is uniform, it is also without shape, without individuality. Thus, for example, the Teutons are characterised by a power of expansion possessed by no race before them, and at the same time by an inclination to concentration which is equally new. We see the expansive power at work—in the practical sphere, in the gradual colonisation of the whole surface of the globe;—in the scientific sphere, in the revelation of the infinite Cosmos, in the search for ever remoter causes;—in the ideal sphere, in the conception of the Transcendent, in the boldness of hypotheses, and in sublime artistic flights which lead to more and more comprehensive means of expression. At the same time, however, we are inclined to return within more and more narrowly circumscribed limits, carefully cut off from everything external by ramparts and trenches; we return to the idea of blood-relationships of the Fatherland, of the native district, of the village of our birth, of the inviolable home (*my home is my castle,* as in Rome), of the closest family circle; finally we return to the innermost central point of the individual, who now, purified and elevated to consciousness of absolute isolation, faces the outer world as an invisible, independent being, a supreme lord of freedom, as was the case with the Indians; this is that concentration which in other spheres reveals itself as division of countries into small Principalities, as limitation to a special "field," whether in science or industry, as inclination to form sects and schools as in Greece, as poetical effects of the innermost nature, *e.g.,* the woodcut, engraving, chamber music. In character these contrasted qualities which are held in coherence by the higher individuality of the race, signify a spirit of enterprise allied to conscientiousness, or they lead—if misguided—to speculation (on the Stock Exchange or in philosophy, it is all the same), to narrow-minded pedantry and pusillanimity.

I cannot on this occasion be expected to attempt an exhaustive description of Teutonic individuality; everything individual—however manifest and recognisable beyond all doubt it may be—is inexhaustible. As Goethe says, "Words cannot clearly reveal the Best," and if personality is the highest gift which we children of earth receive, then truly the individuality of our definite race is one of those "best" things. It alone carries along all separate personalities, as the ship is borne by the flood, and without it (or when this flood is too shallow easily to float anything great) even the strongest character must lie helpless and impotent, like a barque stranded and capsized.

*   *   *

REVIEW QUESTIONS

1. What does Chamberlain mean by his term "retrogressive humanity"?
2. What attributes are ascribed to the Teutonic race?
3. What is the Teutonic race explicitly exhorted to do with its talents?
4. How do Chamberlain's views of races and peoples differ from those of Herder or Mazzini?

CHARLES DARWIN

FROM *The Origin of Species*

The impact of the work of Charles Darwin (1809–1882) cannot be underestimated. The theory of natural selection not only framed the modern view of evolution but also diminished the authority of the Bible in modern thinking. Darwin's theory of how species adapted and evolved over time grew out of his five-year journey on the H.M.S. Beagle (1831–1836) as the ship's naturalist. Published in 1859, The Origin of Species *was followed by* The Descent of Man *in 1871, which applied the theory of evolution to humans. Darwin's argument that humans descended from apes shocked a Victorian society teethed on Genesis, the biblical creation myth. The following selection comes from the conclusion of* The Origin of Species.

From *The Origin of Species* by Charles Darwin. Used by permission of Penguin Books, a division of Penguin Books Ltd.

Chapter XIV
Recapitulation and Conclusion

*   *   *

As this whole volume is one long argument, it may be convenient to the reader to have the leading facts and inferences briefly recapitulated.

That many and grave objections may be advanced against the theory of descent with modification through natural selection, I do not deny. I have endeavoured to give to them their full force. Nothing at first can appear more difficult to believe than that the more complex organs and instincts should have been perfected, not by means superior to, though analogous with, human reason, but by the accumulation of innumerable slight variations, each good for the individual possessor. Nevertheless, this difficulty, though appearing to our imagination insuperably great, cannot be considered real if we admit the following propositions, namely,—that gradations in the perfection of any organ or instinct, which we may consider, either do now exist or could have existed, each good of its kind,—that all organs and instincts are, in ever so slight a degree, variable, —and, lastly, that there is a struggle for existence leading to the preservation of each profitable deviation of structure or instinct. The truth of these propositions cannot, I think, be disputed.

It is, no doubt, extremely difficult even to conjecture by what gradations many structures have been perfected, more especially amongst broken and failing groups of organic beings; but we see so many strange gradations in nature, as is proclaimed by the canon, 'Natura non facit saltum,' that we ought to be extremely cautious in saying that any organ or instinct, or any whole being, could not have arrived at its present state by many graduated steps. There are, it must be admitted, cases of special difficulty on the theory of natural selection; and one of the most curious of these is the existence of two or three defined castes of workers or sterile females in the same community of ants; but I have attempted to show how this difficulty can be mastered.

*   *   *

As on the theory of natural selection an interminable number of intermediate forms must have existed, linking together all the species in each group by gradations as fine as our present varieties, it may be asked, Why do we not see these linking forms all around us? Why are not all organic beings blended together in an inextricable chaos? With respect to existing forms, we should remember that we have no right to expect (excepting in rare cases) to discover *directly* connecting links between them, but only between each and some extinct and supplanted form. Even on a wide area, which has during a long period remained continuous, and of which the climate and other conditions of life change insensibly in going from a district occupied by one species into another district occupied by a closely allied species, we have no just right to expect often to find intermediate varieties in the intermediate zone. For we have reason to believe that only a few species are undergoing change at any one period; and all changes are slowly effected. I have also shown that the intermediate varieties which will at first probably exist in the intermediate zones, will be liable to be supplanted by the allied forms on either hand; and the latter, from existing in greater numbers, will generally be modified and improved at a quicker rate than the intermediate varieties, which exist in lesser numbers; so that the intermediate varieties will, in the long run, be supplanted and exterminated.

*   *   *

As each species tends by its geometrical ratio of reproduction to increase inordinately in number; and as the modified descendants of each species will be enabled to increase by so much the more as they become more diversified in habits and structure, so as to be enabled to seize on many and widely different places in the economy of nature, there will be a constant tendency in natural selection to preserve the most divergent offspring of any one species. Hence during a long-continued course of modification, the slight differences, characteristic of varieties of the same species, tend to be augmented into the greater differences characteristic of species of the same genus. New and improved varieties will inevitably supplant and exterminate the older, less improved and intermediate varieties; and thus species are rendered to a large extent defined and distinct objects. Dominant species belonging to the larger groups tend to give birth to new and dominant forms; so that each large group tends to become still larger, and at the same time more divergent in character. But as all groups cannot thus succeed in increasing in size, for the world would not hold them, the more dominant groups beat the less dominant. This tendency in the large groups to go on increasing in size and diverging in character, together with the almost inevitable contingency of much extinction, explains the arrangement of all the forms of life, in groups subordinate to groups, all within a few great classes, which we now see everywhere around us, and which has prevailed throughout all time. This grand fact of the grouping of all organic beings seems to me utterly inexplicable on the theory of creation.

As natural selection acts solely by accumulating slight, successive, favourable variations, it can produce no great or sudden modification; it can act only by very short and slow steps. Hence the canon of 'Natura non facit saltum,' which every fresh addition to our knowledge tends to make more strictly correct, is on this theory simply intelligible. We can plainly see why nature is prodigal in variety, though niggard in innovation. But why this should be a law of nature if each species has been independently created, no man can explain.

Many other facts are, as it seems to me, explicable on this theory. How strange it is that a bird, under the form of woodpecker, should have been created to prey on insects on the ground; that upland geese, which never or rarely swim, should have been created with webbed feet; that a thrush should have been created to dive and feed on sub-aquatic insects; and that a petrel should have been created with habits and structure fitting it for the life of an auk or grebe! and so on in endless other cases. But on the view of each species constantly trying to increase in number, with natural selection always ready to adapt the slowly varying descendants of each to any unoccupied or ill-occupied place in nature, these facts cease to be strange, or perhaps might even have been anticipated.

As natural selection acts by competition, it adapts the inhabitants of each country only in relation to the degree of perfection of their associates; so that we need feel no surprise at the inhabitants of any one country, although on the ordinary view supposed to have been specially created and adapted for that country, being beaten and supplanted by the naturalised productions from another land. Nor ought we to marvel if all the contrivances in nature be not, as far as we can judge, absolutely perfect; and if some of them be abhorrent to our ideas of fitness. We need not marvel at the sting of the bee causing the bee's own death; at drones being produced in such vast numbers for one single act, and being then slaughtered by their sterile sisters; at the astonishing waste of pollen by our fir-trees; at the instinctive hatred of the queen bee for her own fertile daughters; at ichneumonidae feeding within the live bodies of caterpillars; and at other such cases. The wonder indeed is, on the theory of natural selection, that more cases of the want of absolute perfection have not been observed.

*   *   *

The fact, as we have seen, that all past and present organic beings constitute one grand natural system, with group subordinate to group, and with extinct groups often falling in between recent groups, is intelligible on the theory of natural selection with its contingencies of extinction and divergence of character. On these same principles we see how it is, that the mutual affinities of the species and genera within each class are so complex and circuitous. We see why certain characters are far more serviceable than others for classification;

—why adaptive characters, though of paramount importance to the being, are of hardly any importance in classification; why characters derived from rudimentary parts, though of no service to the being, are often of high classificatory value; and why embryological characters are the most valuable of all. The real affinities of all organic beings are due to inheritance or community of descent. The natural system is a genealogical arrangement, in which we have to discover the lines of descent by the most permanent characters, however slight their vital importance may be.

The framework of bones being the same in the hand of a man, wing of a bat, fin of the porpoise, and leg of the horse,—the same number of vertebrae forming the neck of the giraffe and of the elephant,—and innumerable other such facts, at once explain themselves on the theory of descent with slow and slight successive modifications. The similarity of pattern in the wing and leg of a bat, though used for such different purposes,—in the jaws and legs of a crab,—in the petals, stamens, and pistils of a flower, is likewise intelligible on the view of the gradual modification of parts or organs, which were alike in the early progenitor of each class. On the principle of successive variations not always supervening at an early age, and being inherited at a corresponding not early period of life, we can clearly see why the embryos of mammals, birds, reptiles, and fishes should be so closely alike, and should be so unlike the adult forms. We may cease marvelling at the embryo of an air-breathing mammal or bird having branchial slits and arteries running in loops, like those in a fish which has to breathe the air dissolved in water, by the aid of well-developed branchiae.

*   *   *

In the distant future I see open fields for far more important researches. Psychology will be based on a new foundation, that of the necessary acquirement of each mental power and capacity by gradation. Light will be thrown on the origin of man and his history.

Authors of the highest eminence seem to be fully satisfied with the view that each species has been independently created. To my mind it accords better with what we know of the laws impressed on matter by the Creator, that the production and extinction of the past and present inhabitants of the world should have been due to secondary causes, like those determining the birth and death of the individual. When I view all beings not as special creations, but as the lineal descendants of some few beings which lived long before the first bed of the Silurian system was deposited, they seem to me to become ennobled. Judging from the past, we may safely infer that not one living species will transmit its unaltered likeness to a distant futurity. And of the species now living very few will transmit progeny of any kind to a far distant futurity; for the manner in which all organic beings are grouped, shows that the greater number of species of each genus, and all the species of many genera, have left no descendants, but have become utterly extinct. We can so far take a prophetic glance into futurity as to fortell that it will be the common and widely-spread species, belonging to the larger and dominant groups, which will ultimately prevail and procreate new and dominant species. As all the living forms of life are the lineal descendants of those which lived long before the Silurian epoch, we may feel certain that the ordinary succession by generation has never once been broken, and that no cataclysm has desolated the whole world. Hence we may look with some confidence to a secure future of equally inappreciable length. And as natural selection works solely by and for the good of each being, all corporeal and mental endowments will tend to progress towards perfection.

It is interesting to contemplate an entangled bank, clothed with many plants of many kinds, with birds singing on the bushes, with various insects flitting about, and with worms crawling through the damp earth, and to reflect that these elaborately constructed forms, so different from each other, and dependent on each other in so complex a manner, have all been produced by laws acting around us. These laws, taken in the largest sense, being Growth with Reproduction; Inheritance which is almost implied by reproduction; Variability from the indirect and direct action of the external conditions of life, and from use and disuse; a Ratio of Increase so high as to lead to a Struggle for Life, and as a consequence to Natural Selection, entailing Divergence of Character and the Extinction of less-improved forms. Thus, from the war of nature, from famine and death, the most exalted object which we are capable of conceiving, namely, the production of the higher animals, directly follows. There is grandeur in this view of life, with its several powers, having been originally breathed into a few forms or into one; and that, whilst this planet has gone cycling on according to the fixed law of gravity, from so simple a beginning endless forms most beautiful and most wonderful have been, and are being, evolved.

Review Questions

1. According to Darwin, what are the driving forces of natural selection?
2. What is the relationship between heredity and environment?
3. Why is the last paragraph so successful in conveying the gist of his argument?
4. Why was the theory of natural selection so threatening to Christianity?

Thomas Henry Huxley

from Evolution and Ethics

In positing the theory of natural selection, Darwin rejected any parallel relevance to human society. Yet the notion of stronger species dominating over the weaker gripped the nineteenth-century political imagination, enabling various political interests to employ Social Darwinism to justify the use of raw power over ethics. In the era of imperialism and saber-rattling chauvinism, the phrase "survival of the fittest" (a term coined by the social theorist Herbert Spencer) circulated widely as a political belief grounded in scientific fact. T. H. Huxley (1825–1895), a philosopher who eloquently defended Darwin against his detractors, strongly objected to pseudoscientific Social Darwinism and sought to distinguish sharply between natural phenomena and human ethics. The following essay, written in 1893, addresses the contemporary fallacies stemming from Darwinian thought.

*   *   *

The propounders of what are called the 'ethics of evolution', when the 'evolution of ethics' would usually better express the object of their speculations, adduce a number of more or less interesting facts and more or less sound arguments, in favour of the origin of the moral sentiments, in the same way as other natural phenomena, by a process of evolution. I have little doubt, for my own part, that they are on the right track; but as the immoral sentiments have no less been evolved, there is, so far, as much natural sanction for the one as the other. The thief and the murderer follow nature just as much as the philanthropist. Cosmic evolution may teach us how the good and the evil tendencies of man may have come about; but, in itself, it is incompetent to furnish any better reason why what we call good is preferable to what we call evil than we had before. Some day, I doubt not, we shall arrive at an understanding of the evolution of the æsthetic faculty; but all the understanding in the world will neither increase nor diminish the force of the intuition that this is beautiful and that is ugly.

There is another fallacy which appears to me to pervade the so-called 'ethics of evolution'. It is the notion that because, on the whole, animals and plants have advanced in perfection of organization by means of the struggle for existence and the consequent 'survival of the fittest'; therefore men in society, men as ethical beings, must look to the same process to help them towards perfection. I suspect that this fallacy has arisen out of the unfortunate ambiguity of the phrase 'survival of the fittest'. 'Fittest' has a connotation of 'best'; and about 'best' there hangs a moral flavour. In cosmic nature, however, what is 'fittest' depends upon the conditions. Long since, I ventured to point out that if our hemisphere were to cool again, the survival of the fittest might bring about, in the vegetable kingdom, a population of more and more stunted and humbler and humbler organisms, until the 'fittest' that survived might be nothing but lichens, diatoms, and such microscopic organisms as those which give red snow its colour; while, if it became hotter, the pleasant valleys of the Thames and Isis might be uninhabitable by any animated beings save those that flourish in a tropical jungle. They, as the fittest, the best adapted to the changed conditions, would survive.

Men in society are undoubtedly subject to the cosmic process. As among other animals, multiplication goes on without cessation, and involves severe competition for the means of support. The struggle for existence tends to eliminate those less fitted to adapt themselves to the circumstances of their existence. The strongest, the most self-assertive, tend to tread down the weaker. But the influence of the cosmic process on the evolution of society is the greater the more rudimentary its civilization. Social progress means a checking of the cosmic process at every step and the substitution for it of another, which may be called the ethical process; the end of which is not the survival of those who may happen to be the fittest, in respect of the whole of the conditions which obtain, but of those who are ethically the best.

As I have already urged, the practice of that which is ethically best—what we call goodness or virtue—involves a course of conduct which, in all respects, is opposed to that which leads to success in the cosmic struggle for existence. In place of ruthless self-assertion it demands self-restraint; in place of thrusting aside, or treading down, all competitors, it requires that the individual shall not merely respect, but shall help his fellows; its influence is directed, not so much to the survival of the fittest, as to the fitting of as many as possible to survive. It repudiates the gladiatorial theory of existence. It demands that each man who enters into the enjoyment of the advantages of a polity shall be mindful of his debt to those who have laboriously constructed it; and shall take heed that no act of his weakens the fabric in which he has been permitted to live. Laws and moral precepts are directed to the end of curbing the cosmic process and reminding the individual of his duty to the community, to the protection and influence of which he owes, if not existence itself, at least the life of something better than a brutal savage.

It is from neglect of these plain considerations that the fanatical individualism of our time attempts to apply the analogy of cosmic nature to society. Once more we have a misapplication of the stoical injunction to follow nature; the duties of the individual to the State are forgotten, and his tendencies to self-assertion are dignified by the name of rights. It is seriously debated whether the members of a community are justified in using their combined strength to constrain one of their number to contribute his share to the maintenance of it; or even to prevent him from doing his best to destroy it. The struggle for existence, which has done such admirable work in cosmic nature, must, it appears, be equally beneficent in the ethical sphere. Yet if that which I have insisted upon is true; if the cosmic process has no sort of relation to moral ends; if the imitation of it by man is inconsistent with the first principles of ethics; what becomes of this surprising theory?

Let us understand, once for all, that the ethical progress of society depends, not on imitating the cosmic process, still less in running away from it, but in combating it. It may seem an audacious proposal thus to pit the microcosm against the macrocosm and to set man to subdue nature to his higher ends; but I venture to think that the great intellectual difference between the ancient times with which we have been occupied and our day, lies in the solid foundation we have acquired for the hope that such an enterprise may meet with a certain measure of success.

*   *   *

REVIEW QUESTIONS

1. For Huxley, what are the limitations of evolution theory?
2. What are the problems of applying the theory of natural selection to human society?
3. What are the essential differences between cosmic and human processes?
4. What code of ethics does Huxley suggest for individuals and states?

FRIEDRICH NIETZSCHE

FROM *The Genealogy of Morals*

Over the course of his numerous writings, the German philosopher Friedrich Nietzsche (1844–1900) leveled an impressively sustained attack on western values. Although his philosophical inquiries ranged over a wide area, his devastating criticisms of Judeo-Christian values of individual worth and social justice are probably the most disturbing of his literary corpus. Nietzsche countered his scorn for the "slave mentality" of Judeo-Christian ethics with a wholly different set of ethics that dismissed guilt and a moral conscience as corrosive to life-affirming creativity, what he called the "will to power." Written in a vivid aphoristic prose and organized loosely in detached paragraphs, Nietzsche's writings were frequently misunderstood and often abused in the twentieth century. He remains one of the influential writers of the modern era.

IX

—"But what is all this talk about nobler values? Let us face facts: the people have triumphed—or the slaves, the mob, the herd, whatever you wish to call them—and if the Jews brought it about, then no nation ever had a more universal mission on this earth. The lords are a thing of the past, and the ethics of the common man is completely triumphant. I don't deny that this triumph might be looked upon as a kind of blood poisoning, since it has resulted in a mingling of the races, but there can be no doubt that the intoxication has succeeded. The 'redemption' of the human race (from the lords, that is) is well under way; everything is rapidly becoming Judaized, or Christianized, or mob-ized—the word makes no difference. The progress of this poison throughout the body of mankind cannot be stayed;* * *

*   *   *

X

The slave revolt in morals begins by rancor turning creative and giving birth to values—the rancor of beings who, deprived of the direct outlet of action, compensate by an imaginary vengeance. All truly noble morality grows out of triumphant self-affirmation. Slave ethics, on the other hand, begins by saying *no* to an "outside," an "other," a non-self, and that *no* is its creative act. This reversal of direction of the evaluating look, this invariable looking outward instead of inward, is a fundamental feature of rancor. Slave ethics requires for its inception a sphere different from and hostile to its own. Physiologically speaking, it requires an outside stimulus in order to act at all; all its action is reaction. The opposite is true of aristocratic valuations: such values grow and act spontaneously, seeking out their contraries only in order to affirm themselves even more gratefully and delightedly. Here the negative concepts, *humble, base, bad*, are

late, pallid counterparts of the positive, intense and passionate credo, "We noble, good, beautiful, happy ones." Aristocratic valuations may go amiss and do violence to reality, but this happens only with regard to spheres which they do not know well, or from the knowledge of which they austerely guard themselves: the aristocrat will, on occasion, misjudge a sphere which he holds in contempt, the sphere of the common man, the people. On the other hand we should remember that the emotion of contempt, of looking down, provided that it falsifies at all, is as nothing compared with the falsification which suppressed hatred, impotent vindictiveness, effects upon its opponent, though only in effigy. There is in all contempt too much casualness and nonchalance, too much blinking of facts and impatience, and too much inborn gaiety for it ever to make of its object a downright caricature and monster. Hear the almost benevolent nuances the Greek aristocracy, for example, puts into all its terms for the commoner; how emotions of compassion, consideration, indulgence, sugar-coat these words until, in the end, almost all terms referring to the common man survive as expressions for "unhappy," "pitiable"* * *; how, on the other hand, the words *bad, base, unhappy* have continued to strike a similar note for the Greek ear, with the timbre "unhappy" preponderating. The "well-born" really felt that they were also the "happy." They did not have to construct their happiness factitiously by looking at their enemies, as all rancorous men are wont to do, and being fully active, energetic people they were incapable of divorcing happiness from action. They accounted activity a necessary part of happiness* * *.

All this stands in utter contrast to what is called happiness among the impotent and oppressed, who are full of bottled-up aggressions. Their happiness is purely passive and takes the form of drugged tranquillity, stretching and yawning, peace, "sabbath," emotional slackness. Whereas the noble lives before his own conscience with confidence and frankness* * *, the rancorous person is neither truthful nor ingenuous nor honest and forthright with himself. His soul squints; his mind loves hide-outs, secret paths, and back doors; everything that is hidden seems to him his own world, his security, his comfort; he is expert in silence, in long memory, in waiting, in provisional self-depreciation, and in self-humiliation. A race of such men will, in the end, inevitably be cleverer than a race of aristocrats, and it will honor sharp-wittedness to a much greater degree, i.e., as an absolutely vital condition for its existence. Among the noble, mental acuteness always tends slightly to suggest luxury and overrefinement. The fact is that with them it is much less important than is the perfect functioning of the ruling, unconscious instincts or even a certain temerity to follow sudden impulses, court danger, or indulge spurts of violent rage, love, worship, gratitude, or vengeance. When a noble man feels resentment, it is absorbed in his instantaneous reaction and therefore does not poison him. Moreover, in countless cases where we might expect it, it never arises, while with weak and impotent people it occurs without fail. It is a sign of strong, rich temperaments that they cannot for long take seriously their enemies, their misfortunes, their *misdeeds*; for such characters have in them an excess of plastic curative power, and also a power of oblivion. * * * Such a man simply shakes off vermin which would get beneath another's skin—and only here, if anywhere on earth, is it possible to speak of "loving one's enemy." The noble person will respect his enemy, and respect is already a bridge to love. . . . Indeed he requires his enemy for himself, as his mark of distinction, nor could he tolerate any other enemy than one in whom he finds nothing to despise and much to esteem. Imagine, on the other hand, the "enemy" as conceived by the rancorous man! For this is his true creative achievement: he has conceived the "evil enemy," the Evil One, as a fundamental idea, and then as a pendant he has conceived a Good One— himself.

*   *   *

XII

Here I want to give vent to a sigh and a last hope. Exactly what is it that I, especially, find intolerable; that I am unable to cope with; that asphyxiates me? A bad smell. The smell of failure, of a soul that has gone stale. God knows it is possible to endure all kinds of misery—vile weather, sickness, trouble, isolation. All this can be coped with, if one is born to a life of anonymity and battle. There will always be moments of re-emergence into the light, when one tastes the golden hour of victory and once again stands foursquare, unshakable, ready to face even harder things, like a bowstring drawn taut against new perils. But, you divine patronesses—if there are any such in the realm beyond good and evil—grant me now and again the sight of something perfect, wholly achieved, happy, magnificently triumphant, something still capable of inspiring fear! Of a man who will justify the existence of mankind, for whose sake one may continue to believe in mankind! . . . The leveling and diminution of European man is our greatest danger; because the sight of him makes us despond. . . . We no longer see anything these days that aspires to grow greater; instead, we have a suspicion that things will continue to go downhill, becoming ever thinner, more placid, smarter, cosier, more ordinary, more indifferent, more Chinese, more Christian— without doubt man is getting "better" all the time. . . . This is Europe's true predicament: together with the fear of man we have also lost the love of man, reverence for man, confidence in man, indeed the *will to man*. Now the sight of man makes us despond. What is nihilism today if not that?

*   *   *

XVI

Let us conclude. The two sets of valuations, good/bad and good/evil, have waged a terrible battle on this earth, lasting many millennia; and just as surely as the second set has for a long time now been in the ascendant, so surely are there still places where the battle goes on and the issue remains in suspension. It might even be claimed that by being raised to a higher plane the battle has become much more profound. Perhaps there is today not a single intellectual worth his salt who is not divided on that issue, a battleground for those opposites. The watchwords of the battle, written in characters which have remained legible throughout human history, read: "Rome vs. Israel, Israel vs. Rome." No battle has ever been more momentous than this one. Rome viewed Israel as a monstrosity; the Romans regarded the Jews as *convicted* of hatred against the whole of mankind —and rightly so if one is justified in associating the welfare of the human species with absolute supremacy of aristocratic values. But how did the Jews, on their part, feel about Rome? A thousand indications point to the answer. It is enough to read once more the Revelations of St. John, the most rabid outburst of vindictiveness in all recorded history. (We ought to acknowledge the profound consistency of the Christian instinct in assigning this book of hatred and the most extravagantly doting of the Gospels to the same disciple. There is a piece of truth hidden here, no matter how much literary skulduggery may have gone on.) The Romans were the strongest and most noble people who ever lived. Every vestige of them, every least inscription, is a sheer delight, provided we are able to read the spirit behind the writing. The Jews, on the contrary, were the priestly, rancorous nation *par excellence*, though possessed of an unequaled ethical genius; we need only compare with them nations of comparable endowments, such as the Chinese or the Germans, to sense which occupies the first rank. Has the victory so far been gained by the Romans or by the Jews? But this is really an idle question. Remember who it is before whom one bows down, in Rome itself, as before the essence of all supreme values—and not only in Rome but over half the globe, wherever man has grown tame or desires to grow tame: before three Jews and one Jewess (Je-

sus of Nazareth, the fisherman Peter, the rug weaver Paul, and Maria, the mother of that Jesus). This is very curious: Rome, without a doubt, has capitulated. It is true that during the Renaissance men witnessed a strange and splendid awakening of the classical ideal; like one buried alive, Rome stirred under the weight of a new Judaic Rome that looked like an ecumenical synagogue and was called the Church. But presently Israel triumphed once again, thanks to the plebeian rancor of the German and English Reformation, together with its natural corollary, the restoration of the Church—which also meant the restoration of ancient Rome to the quiet of the tomb. In an even more decisive sense did Israel triumph over the classical ideal through the French Revolution. For then the last political nobleness Europe had known, that of seventeenth- and eighteenth-century France, collapsed under the weight of vindictive popular instincts. A wilder enthusiasm was never seen. And yet, in the midst of it all, something tremendous, something wholly unexpected happened: the ancient classical ideal appeared incarnate and in unprecedented splendor before the eyes and conscience of mankind. Once again, stronger, simpler, more insistent than ever, over against the lying shibboleth of the rights of the majority, against the furious tendency toward leveling out and debasement, sounded the terrible yet exhilarating shibboleth of the "prerogative of the few." Like a last signpost to an *alternative* route Napoleon appeared, most isolated and anachronistic of men, the embodiment of the noble ideal. It might be well to ponder what exactly Napoleon, that synthesis of the brutish with the more than human, did represent. . . .

*   *   *

REVIEW QUESTIONS

1. What are slave morals and why is Nietzsche so critical of them?
2. In contrast, what are construed as "noble" values?

3. Is Nietzsche criticizing or endorsing the spirit of the Enlightenment?

4. What is Nietzsche's relationship with European society?

5. What does he not like about modern times?

6. Where is there room for abuse in such an argument?

FYODOR DOSTOYEVSKY

FROM *Notes from Underground*

Fyodor Dostoyevsky (1821–1881) ranks among Russia's great novelists of the nineteenth century. As a young man he was arrested, tried, and sentenced to four years in a penal camp for his participation in a circle that discussed political reform. At his trial, his judges delivered a bogus sentence of death; Dostoyevsky and his compatriots prepared themselves for death, and the actual sentence of deportation was read to them only when they expected the fateful volley. This incident and subsequent years profoundly altered his look on life, which is manifested in his dark view of humanity in his later works. His novels brought a new intensity of psychological imagination to fiction; his downtrodden, tormented characters often stressed the irrational and uncontrollable desires of the human psyche. The Notes from the Underground, written in 1864, offered withering criticism of bourgeois society from characters marginalized through tragedy and suffering.

VII

But these are all golden dreams. Oh, tell me who was first to announce, first to proclaim that man does nasty things simply because he doesn't know his own true interest; and that if he were to be enlightened, if his eyes were to be opened to his true, normal interests, he would stop doing nasty things at once and would immediately become good and noble, because, being so enlightened and understanding his real advantage, he would realize that his own advantage really did lie in the good; and that it's well known that there's not a single man capable of acting knowingly against his own interest; consequently, he would, so to speak, begin to do good out of necessity. Oh, the child! Oh, the pure, innocent babe! Well, in the first place, when was it during all these millennia, that man has ever acted only in his own self interest? What does one do with the millions of facts bearing witness to the one fact that people knowingly, that is, possessing full knowledge of their own true interests, have relegated them to the background and have rushed down a different path, that of risk and chance, compelled by no one and nothing, but merely as if they didn't want to follow the beaten track, and so they stubbornly, willfully forged another way, a difficult and absurd one, searching for it almost in the darkness? Why, then, this means that stubbornness and willfulness were really more pleasing to them than any kind of advantage. . . . Advantage! What is advantage? Will you take it upon yourself to define with absolute precision what constitutes man's advantage? And what if it turns out that man's advantage sometimes not only may, but even must in certain circumstances, consist precisely in his desiring something harmful to himself instead of something advantageous? And if this is so, if this can ever occur, then the whole theory falls to pieces. What do you think, can such a thing happen? You're laughing; laugh, gentlemen, but answer me: have man's advantages ever been calculated with absolute certainty? Aren't there some which don't fit, can't be made to fit into any classification? Why, as far as I know, you gentlemen have derived your list of human advantages from averages of statistical data and from scientific-economic formulas. But your advantages are prosperity, wealth, freedom, peace, and so on and so forth; so that a man who, for example, expressly and knowingly acts in opposition to this whole list, would be, in your opinion, and in mine, too, of course, either an obscurantist or a complete madman, wouldn't he? But now here's what's astonishing: why is it that when all these statisticians, sages, and lovers of humanity enumerate man's advantages, they invariably leave one out? They don't even take it into consideration in the form in which it should be considered, although the entire calculation depends upon it. There would be no great harm in considering it, this advantage, and adding it to the list. But the whole point is that this particular advantage doesn't fit into any classification and can't be found on any list. I have a friend, for instance. . . . But gentlemen! Why, he's your friend, too! In fact, he's everyone's friend! When he's preparing to do something, this gentleman straight away explains to you eloquently and clearly just how he must act according to the laws of nature and truth. And that's not all: with excitement and passion he'll tell you all about genuine, normal human interests;

with scorn he'll reproach the shortsighted fools who understand neither their own advantage nor the real meaning of virtue; and then—exactly a quarter of an hour later, without any sudden outside cause, but precisely because of something internal that's stronger than all his interests—he does a complete about-face; that is, he does something which clearly contradicts what he's been saying: it goes against the laws of reason and his own advantage, in a word, against everything. . . . I warn you that my friend is a collective personage; therefore it's rather difficult to blame only him. That's just it, gentlemen; in fact, isn't there something dearer to every man than his own best advantage, or (so as not to violate the rules of logic) isn't there one more advantageous advantage (exactly the one omitted, the one we mentioned before), which is more important and more advantageous than all others and, on behalf of which, a man will, if necessary, go against all laws, that is, against reason, honor, peace, and prosperity—in a word, against all those splendid and useful things, merely in order to attain this fundamental, most advantageous advantage which is dearer to him than everything else?

"Well, it's advantage all the same," you say, interrupting me. Be so kind as to allow me to explain further; besides, the point is not my pun, but the fact that this advantage is remarkable precisely because it destroys all our classifications and constantly demolishes all systems devised by lovers of humanity for the happiness of mankind. In a word, it interferes with everything. But, before I name this advantage, I want to compromise myself personally; therefore I boldly declare that all these splendid systems, all these theories to explain to mankind its real, normal interests so that, by necessarily striving to achieve them, it would immediately become good and noble—are, for the time being, in my opinion, nothing more than logical exercises! Yes, sir, logical exercises! Why, even to maintain a theory of mankind's regeneration through a system of its own advantages, why, in my opinion, that's almost the same as . . . well, claiming, for instance, following Buckle, that man has become kinder as a result of civilization; consequently, he's becoming less bloodthirsty and less inclined to war. Why, logically it all even seems to follow. But man is so partial to systems and abstract conclusions that he's ready to distort the truth intentionally, ready to deny everything that he himself has ever seen and heard, merely in order to justify his own logic. That's why I take this example, because it's such a glaring one. Just look around: rivers of blood are being spilt, and in the most cheerful way, as if it were champagne. Take this entire nineteenth century of ours during which even Buckle lived. Take Napoleon—both the great and the present one. Take North America—that eternal union. Take, finally, that ridiculous Schleswig-Holstein. . . . What is it that civilization makes kinder in us? Civilization merely promotes a wider variety of sensations in man and . . . absolutely nothing else. And through the development of this variety man may even reach the point where he takes pleasure in spilling blood. Why, that's even happened to him already. Haven't you noticed that the most refined blood-shedders are almost always the most civilized gentlemen to whom all these Attila the Huns and Stenka Razins are scarcely fit to hold a candle; and if they're not as conspicuous as Attila and Stenka Razin, it's precisely because they're too common and have become too familiar to us. At least if man hasn't become more bloodthirsty as a result of civilization, surely he's become bloodthirsty in a nastier, more repulsive way than before. Previously man saw justice in bloodshed and exterminated whomever he wished with a clear conscience; whereas now, though we consider bloodshed to be abominable, we nevertheless engage in this abomination even more than before. Which is worse? Decide for yourselves. They say that Cleopatra (forgive an example from Roman history) loved to stick gold pins into the breasts of her slave girls and take pleasure in their screams and writhing. You'll say that this took place, relatively speaking, in barbaric times; that these are barbaric times too, because (also comparatively speaking), gold pins are used even now; that even now, although man has learned on occasion to see more clearly than in barbaric times, *he's still far*

from having learned how to act in accordance with the dictates of reason and science. Nevertheless, you're still absolutely convinced that he will learn how to do so, as soon as he gets rid of some bad, old habits and as soon as common sense and science have completely re-educated human nature and have turned it in the proper direction. You're convinced that then man will voluntarily stop committing blunders, and that he will, so to speak, never willingly set his own will in opposition to his own normal interests. More than that: then, you say, science itself will teach man (though, in my opinion, that's already a luxury) that in fact he possesses neither a will nor any whim of his own, that he never did, and that he himself is nothing more than a kind of piano key or an organ stop; that, moreover, there still exist laws of nature, so that everything he's done has been not in accordance with his own desire, but in and of itself, according to the laws of nature. Consequently, we need only discover these laws of nature, and man will no longer have to answer for his own actions and will find it extremely easy to live. All human actions, it goes without saying, will then be tabulated according to these laws, mathematically, like tables of logarithms up to 108,000, and will be entered on a schedule; or even better, certain edifying works will be published, like our contemporary encyclopedic dictionaries, in which everything will be accurately calculated and specified so that there'll be no more actions or adventures left on earth.

At that time, it's still you speaking, new economic relations will be established, all ready-made, also calculated with mathematical precision, so that all possible questions will disappear in a single instant, simply because all possible answers will have been provided. Then the crystal palace will be built. And then . . . Well, in a word, those will be our halcyon days. Of course, there's no way to guarantee (now this is me talking) that it won't be, for instance, terribly boring then (because there won't be anything left to do, once everything has been calculated according to tables); on the other hand, everything will be extremely rational. Of course, what don't people think up out of boredom! Why, even gold pins get stuck into other people out of boredom, but that wouldn't matter. What's really bad (this is me talking again) is that for all I know, people might even be grateful for those gold pins. For man is stupid, phenomenally stupid. That is, although he's not really stupid at all, he's really so ungrateful that it's hard to find another being quite like him. Why, I, for example, wouldn't be surprised in the least, if, suddenly, for no reason at all, in the midst of this future, universal rationalism, some gentleman with an offensive, rather, a retrograde and derisive expression on his face were to stand up, put his hands on his hips, and declare to us all: "How about it, gentlemen, what if we knock over all this rationalism with one swift kick for the sole purpose of sending all these logarithms to hell, so that once again we can live according to our own stupid will!" But that wouldn't matter either; what's so annoying is that he would undoubtedly find some followers; such is the way man is made. And all because of the most foolish reason, which, it seems, is hardly worth mentioning: namely, that man, always and everywhere, whoever he is, has preferred to act as he wished, and not at all as reason and advantage have dictated; one might even desire something opposed to one's own advantage, and sometimes (this is now my idea) one *positively must do so.* One's very own free, unfettered desire, one's own whim, no

matter how wild, one's own fantasy, even though sometimes roused to the point of madness—all this constitutes precisely that previously omitted, most advantageous advantage which isn't included under any classification and because of which all systems and theories are constantly smashed to smithereens. Where did these sages ever get the idea that man needs any normal, virtuous desire? How did they ever imagine that man needs any kind of rational, advantageous desire? Man needs only one thing—his own *independent* desire, whatever that independence might cost and wherever it might lead. And as far as desire goes, the devil only knows. . . .

*   *   *

REVIEW QUESTIONS

1. What is the narrator's opinion of virtue, and why is this a scathing criticism of middle-class values?
2. What kinds of hypocrisy does the narrator see in society?
3. What is the narrator's point about Cleopatra's gold pins?
4. What is the narrator's opinion of rationalism and science?

SIGMUND FREUD

FROM *Five Lectures on Psychoanalysis*

Sigmund Freud (1856–1939), an Austrian doctor, is largely credited as the first scientist of psychoanalysis, a discipline that seeks to understand the mechanisms of the unconscious and to explain the role of suppressed desire in determining people's actions and dysfunctions. In doing so, Freud fundamentally changed the way humankind perceived itself, thus affecting numerous disciplines of knowledge and a wide range of literary and art movements. Perhaps it is impossible to interpret twentieth-

century culture without first weighing Freud's impact. Psychoanalysis first arose in 1895 when Freud and Josef Breuer, a physician friend, published a case study that posited the link between hysteria and sexual malfunctions and the need to uncover repressed memory for recovery. Freud outlined the early development of his understanding of resistance and repression in five lectures, excerpted below, presented at Clark University, Worcester, Massachussets, in 1912.

From *Five Lectures on Psychoanalysis*, S. Freud, translated by James Strachey, Hogarth Press, 1976.

*   *   *

When, later on, I set about continuing on my own account the investigations that had been begun by Breuer, I soon arrived at another view of the origin of hysterical dissociation (the splitting of consciousness). A divergence of this kind, which was to be decisive for everything that followed, was inevitable, since I did not start out, like Janet, from laboratory experiments, but with therapeutic aims in mind.

I was driven forward above all by practical necessity. The cathartic procedure, as carried out by Breuer, presupposed putting the patient into a state of deep hypnosis; for it was only in a state of hypnosis that he attained a knowledge of the pathogenic connections which escaped him in his normal state. But I soon came to dislike hypnosis, for it was a temperamental and, one might almost say, a mystical ally. When I found that, in spite of all my efforts, I could not succeed in bringing more than a fraction of my patients into a hypnotic state, I determined to give up hypnosis and to make the cathartic procedure independent of it. Since I was not able at will to alter the mental state of the majority of my patients, I set about working with them in their *normal* state. At first, I must confess, this seemed a senseless and hopeless undertaking. I was set the task of learning from the patient something that I did not know and that he did not know himself. How could one hope to elicit it? But there came to my help a recollection of a most remarkable and instructive experiment which I had witnessed when I was with Bernheim at Nancy. Bernheim showed us that

people whom he had put into a state of hypnotic somnambulism, and who had had all kinds of experiences while they were in that state, only *appeared* to have lost the memory of what they had experienced during somnambulism; it was possible to revive these memories in their normal state. It is true that, when he questioned them about their somnambulistic experiences, they began by maintaining that they knew nothing about them; but if he refused to give way, and insisted, and assured them that they *did* know about them, the forgotten experiences always reappeared.

So I did the same thing with my patients. When I reached a point with them at which they maintained that they knew nothing more, I assured them that they *did* know it all the same, and that they had only to say it; and I ventured to declare that the right memory would occur to them at the moment at which I laid my hand on their forehead. In that way I succeeded, without using hypnosis, in obtaining from the patients whatever was required for establishing the connection between the pathogenic scenes they had forgotten and the symptoms left over from those scenes. But it was a laborious procedure, and in the long run an exhausting one; and it was unsuited to serve as a permanent technique.

I did not abandon it, however, before the observations I made during my use of it afforded me decisive evidence. I found confirmation of the fact that the forgotten memories were not lost. They were in the patient's possession and were ready to emerge in association to what was still known by him; but there was some force that prevented them from becoming conscious and compelled them to remain unconscious. The existence of this force could be assumed with certainty, since one became aware of an effort corresponding to it if, in opposition to it, one tried to introduce the unconscious memories into the patient's consciousness. The force which was maintaining the pathological condition became apparent in the form of *resistance* on the part of the patient.

It was on this idea of resistance, then, that I based my view of the course of psychical events in hysteria. In order to effect a recovery, it had proved necessary to remove these resistances. Starting out from the mechanism of cure, it now became possible to construct quite definite ideas of the origin of the illness. The same forces which, in the form of resistance, were now offering opposition to the forgotten material's being made conscious, must formerly have brought about the forgetting and must have pushed the pathogenic experiences in question out of consciousness. I gave the name of '*repression*' to this hypothetical process, and I considered that it was proved by the undeniable existence of resistance.

The further question could then be raised as to what these forces were and what the determinants were of the repression in which we now recognized the pathogenic mechanism of hysteria. A comparative study of the pathogenic situations which we had come to know through the cathartic procedure made it possible to answer this question. All these experiences had involved the emergence of a wishful impulse which was in sharp contrast to the subject's other wishes and which proved incompatible with the ethical and aesthetic standards of his personality. There had been a short conflict, and the end of this internal struggle was that the idea which had appeared before consciousness as the vehicle of this irreconcilable wish fell a victim to repression, was pushed out of consciousness with all its attached memories, and was forgotten. Thus the incompatibility of the wish in question with the patient's ego was the motive for the repression; the subject's ethical and other standards were the repressing forces. An acceptance of the incompatible wishful impulse or a prolonga-tion of the conflict would have produced a high degree of unpleasure; this unpleasure was avoided by means of repression, which was thus revealed as one of the devices serving to protect the mental personality.

To take the place of a number of instances, I will relate a single one of my cases, in which the determinants and advantages of repression are sufficiently evident. For my present purpose I shall have once again to abridge the case history and omit some important underlying material. The patient was a girl, who had lost her beloved father after she had taken a share in nursing him—a situation analogous to that of Breuer's patient. Soon afterwards her elder sister married, and her new brother-in-law aroused in her a peculiar feeling of sympathy which was easily masked under a disguise of family affection. Not long afterwards her sister fell ill and died, in the absence of the patient and her mother. They were summoned in all haste without being given any definite information of the tragic event. When the girl reached the bedside of her dead sister, there came to her for a brief moment an idea that might be expressed in these words: 'Now he is free and can marry me.' We may assume with certainty that this idea, which betrayed to her consciousness the intense love for her brother-in-law of which she had not herself been conscious, was surrendered to repression a moment later, owing to the revolt of her feelings. The girl fell ill with severe hysterical symptoms; and while she was under my treatment it turned out that she had completely forgotten the scene by her sister's bedside and the odious egoistic impulse that had emerged in her. She remembered it during the treatment and reproduced the pathogenic moment with signs of the most violent emotion, and, as a result of the treatment, she became healthy once more.

Perhaps I may give you a more vivid picture of repression and of its necessary relation to resistance, by a rough analogy derived from our actual situation at the present moment. Let us suppose that in this lecture-room and among this audience, whose exemplary quiet and attentiveness I cannot sufficiently commend, there is nevertheless someone who is causing a disturbance and whose ill-mannered laughter, chattering and shuffling with his feet are distracting my attention from my task. I have to announce that I cannot proceed with my lecture; and thereupon three or four of you who are strong men stand up and, after a short struggle, put the interrupter outside the door. So now he is 'repressed', and I can continue my lecture. But in order that the interruption shall not be repeated, in case the individual who has been expelled should try to enter the room once more, the gentlemen who have put my will into effect place their chairs up against the door and thus establish a 'resistance' after the repression has been accomplished. If you will now translate the two localities concerned into psychical terms as the 'conscious' and the 'unconscious', you will have before you a fairly good picture of the process of repression.

You will now see in what it is that the difference lies between our view and Janet's. We do not derive the psychical splitting from an innate incapacity for synthesis on the part of the mental apparatus; we explain it dynamically, from the conflict of opposing mental forces and recognize it as the outcome of an active struggling on the part of the two psychical groupings against each other. But our view gives rise to a large number of fresh problems. Situations of mental conflict are, of course, exceedingly common; efforts by the ego to ward off painful memories are quite regularly to be observed without their producing the result of a mental split. The reflection cannot be escaped that further determinants must be present if the conflict is to lead to dissociation. I will also readily grant you that the hypothesis of repression leaves us not at the end but at the beginning of a psychological theory. We can only go forward step by step however, and complete knowledge must await the results of further and deeper researches.

*   *   *

To put the matter more directly. The investigation of hysterical patients and of other neurotics leads us to the conclusion that their repression of the idea to which the intolerable wish is attached has been a *failure*. It is true that they have driven it out of consciousness and out of memory and have apparently saved themselves a large amount of unpleasure. *But the repressed wishful impulse continues to exist in the unconscious.* It is on the look-out for an opportunity of being activated, and when that happens it succeeds in sending into consciousness a disguised and unrecognizable *substitute* for what had been repressed, and to this there soon become attached the same feelings of unpleasure which it was hoped had been saved by the repression. This substitute for the repressed idea—the *symptom*—is proof against further attacks from the defensive ego; and in place of the short conflict an ailment now appears which is not brought to an end by the passage of time. Alongside the indication of distortion in the symptom, we can trace in it the remains of some kind of indirect resemblance to the idea that was originally repressed. The paths along which the substitution was effected can be traced in the course of the patient's psychoanalytic treatment; and in order to bring about recovery, the symptom must be led back along the same paths and once more turned into the repressed idea. If what was repressed is brought back again into conscious mental activity—a process which presupposes the overcoming of considerable resistances—the resulting psychical conflict, which the patient had tried to avoid, can, under the physician's guidance, reach a better outcome than was offered by repression. There are a number of such opportune solutions, which may bring the conflict and the neurosis to a happy end, and which may in certain instances be combined. The patient's personality may be convinced that it has been wrong in rejecting the pathogenic wish and may be led into accepting it wholly or in part; or the wish itself may be directed to a higher and consequently unobjectionable aim (this is what we call its 'sublimation'); or the rejection of the wish may be recognized as a justifiable one, but the automatic and therefore inefficient mechanism of repression may be replaced by a condemning judgement with the help of the highest human mental functions—conscious control of the wish is attained.

*   *   *

REVIEW QUESTIONS

1. How does Freud view the pathology of hysteria and its solution?

2. What does the theory of repression imply for individuals' identities and actions?

3. What were the implications of Freud's theory of the unconscious for bourgeois culture?

GUILLAUME APOLLINAIRE

FROM On Painting

A critical break in the history of western art came in the late nineteenth century when artists ceased to ground their artistry in aesthetically pleasing representations of the world and began to move toward abstraction and expressions of internal emotion. In the following essay, Guillaume Apollinaire (1880–1918), an accredited poet and a friend to many avant-garde artists of Paris, described generally the new "truth" of modern art and examined specifically the cubist movement, one of the first major art movements of the twentieth century. The essay's open-ended, evocative language became typical of many subsequent manifestos announcing new movements.

From *Paths to the Present: Aspects of European Thought from Romanticism to Existentialism*, translated by Lionel Abel, edited by Eugene Weber, Dodd, Mead & Co., 1960.

The plastic virtues: purity, unity, and truth, keep nature in subjection.

The rainbow is bent, the seasons quiver, the crowds push on to death, science undoes and remakes what already exists, whole worlds disappear for ever from our understanding, our mobile images repeat themselves, or revive their vagueness, and the colors, the odours, and the sounds to which we are sensitive astonish us, then disappear from nature—all to no purpose.

This monster beauty is not eternal.

We know that our breath has had no beginning and will never cease, but our first conceptions are of the creation and the end of the world.

However too many painters still adore plants, stones, the sea, or men.

We quickly get used to the bondage of the mysterious. And servitude ends by creating real delights.

Workers are allowed to control the universe, yet gardeners have even less respect for nature than have artists.

The time has come for us to be the masters.

And good will is not enough to make victory certain.

* * *

Many new painters limit themselves to pictures which have no real subjects. And the titles which we find in the catalog are like proper names, which designate men without characterizing them.

There are men named Stout who are in fact quite thin, and others named White who are very dark; well now, I have seen pictures entitled *Solitude* containing many human figures.

In the cases in question, the artists even condescend at times to use vaguely explanatory words such as *Portrait, Landscape*, and *Still-life*; however, many young painters use as a title only the very general term *Painting*.

These painters, while they still look at nature, no longer imitate it, and carefully avoid any representation of natural scenes which they may have observed, and then reconstructed from preliminary studies.

Real resemblance no longer has any importance, since everything is sacrificed by the artist to truth, to the necessities of a higher nature whose existence he assumes but does not lay bare. The subject has little or no importance any more.

Generally speaking, modern art repudiates most of the techniques of pleasing devised by the great artists of the past.

While the goal of painting is today, as always, the pleasure of the eye, the art-lover is henceforth asked to expect delights other than those which looking at natural objects can easily provide.

Thus we are moving towards an entirely new art which will stand, with respect to painting as envisaged heretofore, as music stands to literature.

It will be pure painting, just as music is pure literature.

The music-lover experiences, in listening to a concert, a joy of a different order from the joy given by natural sounds, such as the murmur of the brook, uproar of a torrent, the whistling of the wind in a forest, or the harmonies of human speech based on reason rather than on esthetics.

In the same way, the new painters will provide their admirers with artistic sensations by concentrating exclusively on the problem of creating harmony with unequal lights.

* * *

The new school of painting is known as cubism, a name first applied to it in the fall of 1908 in a spirit of derision by Henri Matisse, who had just seen a picture of some houses whose cube-like appearance had greatly struck him.

The new esthetics was first elaborated in the mind of André Dérain, but the most important and audacious works the movement at once produced were those of a great artist, Pablo Picasso, who must also be considered one of the founders: his inventions, corroborated by the good sense of Georges Braque, who exhibited a cubist picture at the *Salon des Indépendants* as early as 1908, were envisaged in the study of Jean Metzinger, who exhibited the first cubist portrait (a portrait of myself) at the *Salon des Indépendants* in 1910, and who in the same year managed to induce the Jury of the *Salon d'Automne* to admit some cubist paintings. It was also in 1910 that pictures by Robert Delaunay, Marie Laurencin and Le Fauconnier, who all belonged to the same school, were exhibited at the *Indépendants*.

The first group exhibition of the cubists, who were becoming more numerous, took place in 1911 at the *Indépendants*. Room 41, which was devoted to their works, made a deep impression. There were the knowing and seductive works of Jean Metzinger; some landscapes, *Male Nude* and *Women with Phlox* by Albert Gleizes; *Portrait of Mme Fernande X* and *Young Girls* by Marie Laurencin; *The Tower*, by Robert Delaunay, *Abundance* by Le Fauconnier, and *Landscape with Nudes*, by Fernand Léger.

That same year the cubists made their first appearance outside France, in Brussels; and in the preface to the catalog of this exhibition, I accepted on behalf of the exhibitors the appellations: cubism and cubist.

Towards the end of 1911 the exhibition of the

cubists at the *Salon d'Automne* made a considerable stir, and Gleizes (*The Hunt, Portrait of Jacques Nayral*), Metzinger (*Woman with Spoon*), and Fernand Léger, were ridiculed without mercy. A new painter, Marcel Duchamp, had joined the group, as had the sculptor-architect Duchamp-Villon.

Other group exhibitions were held in November, 1911 (at the *Galérie d'Art Contemporain*, rue Tronchet, Paris), and in 1912 (at the *Salon des Indépendants;* this show was marked by the *début* of Juan Gris); in May of the same year another cubist exhibition was held in Spain (Barcelona welcomed the young Frenchmen with enthusiasm); finally in June, at Rouen, an exhibition was organized by the *Société des Artistes Normands* (important for presenting Francis Picabia, who had just joined the new school).

Cubism differs from the old schools of painting in that it aims, not at an art of imitation, but at an art of conception, which tends to rise to the height of creation.

In representing conceptualized reality or creative reality, the painter can give the effect of three dimensions. He can to a certain extent cube. But not by simply rendering reality as seen, unless he indulges in *trompe l'oeil*, in foreshortening, or in perspective, thus distorting the quality of the forms conceived or created.

I can discriminate four trends in cubism. Of these, two are pure, and along parallel lines.

Scientific cubism is one of the pure tendencies. It is the art of painting new structures out of elements borrowed not from the reality of sight, but from the reality of insight. All men have a sense of this interior reality. A man does not have to be cultivated in order to conceive, for example, of a round form.

The geometrical aspect which made such an impression on those who saw the first canvases of the scientific cubists, came from the fact that the essential reality was rendered with great purity, while visual accidents and anecdotes had been eliminated. The painters who follow this tendency are: Picasso, whose luminous art also belongs to the other pure tendency of cubism, Georges Braque, Albert Gleizes, Marie Laurencin, and Juan Gris.

Physical cubism is the art of painting new structures with elements borrowed, for the most part, from visual reality. This art, however, belongs in the cubist movement because of its constructive discipline. It has a great future as historical painting. Its social role is very clear. But it is not a pure art. It confuses what is properly the subject with images. The painter-physicist who created this trend is Le Fauconnier.

Orphic cubism is the other important trend of the new art school. It is the art of painting new structures out of elements which have not been borrowed from the visual sphere, but have been created entirely by the artist himself, and been endowed by him with fulness of reality. The work of the Orphic artist must simultaneously be a pure esthetic pleasure, a structure which is self-evident, and a sublime meaning, that is, a subject. This is pure art. The light in Picasso's paintings is based on this conception, to which Robert Delaunay's inventions have contributed much, and towards which Fernand Léger, Francis Picabia, and Marcel Duchamp are also addressing themselves.

Instinctive cubism, the art of painting new structures of elements which are not borrowed from visual reality, but are suggested to the artist by instinct and intuition, has long tended towards Orphism. The instinctive artist lacks lucidity and an esthetic doctrine; instinctive cubism includes a large number of artists. Born of French Impressionism, this movement has now spread all over Europe.

Cézanne's last paintings and his water colors belong to cubism, but Courbet is the father of the new painters; and André Derain, whom I propose to discuss some other time, was the eldest of his beloved sons, for we find him at the beginning of the fauvist movement, which was a kind of introduction to cubism, and also at the beginning of this great subjective movement; but it would be too difficult today to write discerningly of a man who so wilfully stands apart from everyone and everything.

The modern school of painting seems to me the most audacious that has ever appeared. It has posed the question of what is beautiful in itself.

It wants to visualize beauty disengaged from whatever charm man has for men, and until now, no European artist has dared attempt this. The new artists demand an ideal beauty, which will be, not merely the proud expression of the species, but the expression of the universe, to the degree that it has been humanized by light.

The new art clothes its creations with a grandiose and monumental appearance which surpasses anything else conceived by the artists of our time. Ardent in its search for beauty, it is noble and energetic, and the reality it brings us is marvellously clear. I love the art of today because above all else I love the light, for man loves light more than anything; it was he who invented fire.

REVIEW QUESTIONS

1. What distinguishes Apollinaire's new attitude toward art from conventional perspectives?
2. Why is the new art considered "pure"?
3. Who are the cubists and what unites them as a movement?
4. What does cubist art share with most modern art movements?

25 ∾ A DELICATE EQUILIBRIUM (1870–1914)

Europeans who lived through the First World War would later look back on the years between 1870 and 1914 as the "Belle Époque." But if the turn of the century seemed like "the good old days" in hindsight, it was in fact a time when European society was riven by deep divisions and haunted by a fear of impending cataclysm. Despite real and significant improvements in the general standard of living and substantial progress in science and technology, growing conflict between and within European nations produced a widespread belief that Western Civilization was in decline. In the international arena, diplomats nego-tiated alliance treaties, but these agreements only seemed to exacerbate interna-tional antagonisms. Ordinary people benefited from state-sponsored social welfare programs, but these reforms seemed to do little to ease sometimes-violent class conflict. Even the domestic sphere—idealized by nineteenth-century Euro-peans as a private world free from the cutthroat competition of the public arena—seemed threatened by a "war between the sexes" being waged over women's right to vote and to work.

The perceived failure of existing political regimes to respond adequately to the many crises of the era generated opposition from both ends of the political spectrum. On the left, socialists promoted the solidarity of European working men and women in the interest of overcoming class oppression, yet even within their ranks socialists remained divided over the means by which capitalism might be transformed. On the right, traditionalist conservatives continued to support the power of autocrats and the established churches, especially in the central and eastern European empires. However, conservatives were also divided between intransigent monarchists and those who were willing to promote conser-vative causes within existing parliamentary systems.

Acutely aware of the individual's isolation in the emerging mass society, late nineteenth-century Europeans became preoccupied with finding a home in a harmonious community, whether that community consisted of trade unionists, revolutionary workers, suffragettes, or simply those who shared a common religion, national origin, or ethnicity. However, if traumatic change inspired Europeans with the desire to unite with others in pursuit of shared goals, it also encouraged a hunt for enemies and the scapegoating of individuals or groups identified as a threat to the survival of the community.

CLARA ZETKIN

FROM Women's Work and the Organization of Trade Unions

The German socialist Clara Zetkin (1857–1933) was well known throughout Europe for her ardent support of working women. Unlike the many left wing activists who rejected feminism in the belief that the workers' revolution would inevitably bring gender equality in its wake, Zetkin argued that an active commitment to women's rights must go hand in hand with the socialist struggle against capitalism. Although Zetkin was a strong supporter of women's right to vote, as a socialist she rejected the liberal feminism of middle-class suffragettes such as the Pankhursts (see chapter 24) and instead focused her efforts on seeking solutions to the specific forms of economic oppression suffered by women as workers.

The following article appeared in Gleichheit ("Equality"), the highly successful German Socialist women's newspaper that Zetkin edited between 1892 and 1917. Responding to male labor organizers who saw low-paid women workers as competitors and who wished to exclude women from the industrial work force, Zetkin argues here that the socialist movement would benefit more if male workers sought to bring working women into trade union organizations.

From *Clara Zetkin: Selected Writings*, Clara Zetkin, edited by Philip S. Foner, translated by Kai Schoenhals, International Publishers, 1984.

*   *   *

In all capitalist countries, women's work in industry plays an ever larger role. The number of industrial branches in which women nowadays toil and drudge from morning till night increases with every year. Factories which have traditionally em- ployed women, employ more and more women workers. It is not only that the number of all industrially employed women is constantly growing, but their number in relation to the men who are working in industry and trade is also on the increase.

Some branches of industry (one has only to

think of clothing) are virtually dominated by women's labor which constantly reduces and replaces men's labor.

For understandable reasons, particularly during periods of recession (like the one we are experiencing right now), the number of women workers has increased in both relative and absolute terms whereas the number of employed male laborers has decreased.

*   *   *

The reasons for the constantly growing use of female laborers have been repeatedly pointed out: their cheapness and the improvement of the mechanical means and methods of production. The automatic machine, which in many cases does not even stand in need of having to be regulated, works with the powers of a giant, possesses unbelievable skill, speed and exactness and renders muscle power and acquired skills superfluous. The capitalist entrepreneur can employ only female labor at those places where he previously had to use male employees. And he just loves to hire women because female labor is cheap, much cheaper than male labor.

Even though the productive capacity of female workers does not lag behind that of male workers, the difference between men's and women's wages is very significant. The latter is often only half of the former and often only a third.

*   *   *

. . . the living conditions of these female workers correspond to their miserable earnings. It is easily understandable that these customary starvation wages for female laborers push thousands of them from the proletariat into the lumpenproletariat.[1] Their dire straits force some of them to take up part-time or temporary prostitution so that by selling their bodies, they may earn the piece of bread that they cannot secure by the sale of their labor.

But it is not just the women workers who suffer because of the miserable payment of their labor. The male workers, too, suffer because of it. As a consequence of their low wages, the women are transformed from mere competitors into unfair competitors who push down the wages of men. Cheap women's labor eliminates the work of men and if the men want to continue to earn their daily bread, they must put up with low wages. Thus women's work is not only a cheap form of labor, it also cheapens the work of men and for that reason it is doubly appreciated by the capitalist, who craves profits.

*   *   *

The transfer of hundreds of thousands of female laborers to the modernized means of production that increase productivity ten or even a hundredfold should have resulted (and did result in some cases) in a higher standard of living for the proletariat, given a rationally organized society. But as far as the proletariat is concerned, capitalism has changed blessing into curse and wealth into bitter poverty. The economic advantages of the industrial activity of proletarian women only aid the tiny minority of the sacrosanct guild of coupon clippers and extortionists of profit.

Frightened by the economic consequences of women's work and the abuses connected with it, organized labor demanded for a while the prohibition of female labor. It was viewing this question merely from the narrow viewpoint of the wage question. Thanks to Socialist propaganda, the class-conscious proletariat has learned to view this question from another angle, from the angle of its historical importance for the liberation of women and the liberation of the proletariat. It understands now how impossible it is to abolish the industrial labor of women. Thus it has dropped its former demand and it attempts to lessen the bad economic consequences of women's work within capitalist society (and only within it!) by two other means; by the legal protection of female workers and by their inclusion in trade union organiza-

---

[1] In Marxist terminology, the *lumpenproletariat* consists of the lowest ranks of the working class. It verges on being a criminal underclass and is disinclined to join with honest workers in the struggle against capitalism.

tions. We have already mentioned above the necessity and the advantageous effects of the legal protection of women workers.* * *

Given the fact that many thousands of female workers are active in industry, it is vital for the trade unions to incorporate them into their movement. In individual industries where female labor plays an important role, any movement advocating better wages, shorter working hours, etc., would be doomed from the start because of the attitude of those women workers who are not organized. Battles which began propitiously enough, ended up in failure because the employers were able to play off non-union female workers against those that are organized in unions. These non-union workers continued to work (or took up work) under any conditions, which transformed them from competitors in dirty work to scabs.

It is not only because of the successful economic battles of trade unions that women should be included in them. The improvement of the starvation wages of female workers and the limitation of competition among them requires their organization into unions.

The fact that the pay for female labor is so much lower than that of male labor has a variety of causes. Certainly one of the reasons for these poor wages for women is the circumstance that female workers are practically unorganized. They lack the strength which comes with unity. They lack the courage, the feeling of power, the spirit of resistance and the ability to resist which is produced by the strength of an organization in which the individual fights for everybody and everybody fights for the individual. Furthermore, they lack the enlightenment and the training which an organization provides. Without an understanding of modern economic life in whose machinery they are inextricably caught up, they will neither be able to take advantage of periods of boom through conscious, calculating and unified conduct nor will they be able to protect themselves against the disadvantages occurring during periods of economic recession. If, under the pressure of unbearable conditions they finally fight back, they usually do so at an inopportune moment and in a disorganized fashion.

This situation exercises a great influence upon the miserable state of women's work and is further reflected by the bitterness that male workers feel about women's competition. Thus in the interest of both men and women workers, it is urgently recommended that the latter be included in the trade unions. The larger the number of organized female workers who fight shoulder to shoulder with their comrades from the factory or workshop for better working conditions, the sooner and the greater will women's wages rise so that soon there may be the realization of the principle: Equal pay for equal work regardless of the difference in sex. The organized female worker who has become the equal of the male worker ceases to be his scab competitor.

The unionized male workers realize more and more just how important it is that the female workers are accepted into the ranks of their organization. During these past few years, there was no lack of effort on the part of the unions in regard to this endeavor. And yet how little has been accomplished and how incredibly much remains to be done in this respect.

*   *   *

Even in those industrial branches in which the trade union organization of women began, these organizations are still in their infancy.

*   *   *

As far as the percentage of female membership is concerned, the Tobacco Workers rank first, and yet these women workers do not even constitute a fourth of its entire membership. In 1882, 43.1% of all tobacco industry workers were women. In the other four trade unions which come next, as far as the percentage of women that work in the industries they represent are concerned, women workers do not even constitute 10% of the membership. The Organization of Gold and Silver Workers does not have a female membership of even 5% even though there are large numbers of

women workers who are employed by the gold and silver industry. In 1882, 60% of all laborers in spinning mills and 30% of all laborers in weaving mills happened to be women, yet the percentage of them who were unionized amounted to only 9½%. These numbers, in conjunction with the slave wages which generally prevail in the textile industry, speak whole volumes about the necessity of unionizing women.

In recognition of this necessity, the trade unions should use all of their energies to work for the inclusion of women in their organizations.

We certainly do not fail to recognize the difficulties raised by women workers which are detrimental to the solution of this problem. Stupid resignation, lack of a feeling of solidarity, shyness, prejudices of all kinds and fear of the factory tyrant keep many women from joining unions. Even more than the just mentioned factors, the lack of time on the part of female workers represents a major obstacle against their mass organization because women are house as well as factory slaves and are forced to bear a double workload. The economic developments, however, as well as the increasing acuteness of the class struggle, educate both male and female laborers and force them to overcome the above-mentioned difficulties.* * *

Theoretically, most male union members admit that the common unionization of both male and female workers of the same trade has become an unavoidable necessity. In practice, however, many of them do not make the effort that they could be making. Rather there are only a few unions and within them only certain individuals who pursue with energy and perseverance the organization of female workers. The majority of trade union members give them precious little support. They treat such endeavors as a hobby which should be tolerated but not supported "as long as there are still so many indifferent non-union male workers." This point of view is totally wrong.

The unionization of women workers will make significant progress only when it is no longer merely aided by the few, but by every single union member making every effort to enlist their female colleagues from factory and workshop. In order to fulfill this task, two things are necessary. The male workers must stop viewing the female worker primarily as a woman to be courted if she is young, beautiful, pleasant and cheerful (or not). They must stop (depending on their degree of culture or lack of it) molesting them with crude and fresh sexual advances. The workers must rather get accustomed to treat female laborers primarily as female proletarians, as working-class comrades fighting class slavery and as equal and indispensable co-fighters in the class struggle. The unions make such a big thing out of having all of the members and followers of the political party become members of the unions. It seems to us that it would be much more important to put the emphasis on enrolling the broad, amorphous masses in the labor movement. In our opinion, the main task of the unions is the enlightenment, disciplining and education of all workers for the class struggle. In view of the increasing use of female labor and the subsequent results, the labor movement will surely commit suicide if, in its effort to enroll the broad masses of the proletariat, it does not pay the same amount of attention to female workers as it does to male ones.

REVIEW QUESTIONS

1. To what extent does Zetkin's discussion of women's work reflect the changes in industrial work conditions brought about by the second industrial revolution?
2. According to Zetkin, what factors cause divisions between male and female workers?
3. How does Zetkin suggest that socialist workers build solidarity within their ranks?
4. What sort of socialist is Zetkin? What sort of feminist is she?

ÉDOUARD DRUMONT

FROM *Jewish France*

During the first half of the nineteenth century, European Jews won many new guarantees of legal and political equality, largely as a result of political liberalism and the growing secularization of European society. In western Europe especially, it almost seemed that centuries of anti-Semitism would be brought to an end through the quiet assimilation of Jews into mainstream national cultures. However, in the final quarter of the century, a new and very virulent form of anti-Semitism emerged, threatening Jewish communities' fragile political and social gains.

In France as elsewhere, Jews served as scapegoats for deep-seated cultural anxieties stimulated by the political instability of the Third Republic, as well as the massive social and economic changes generated by French industrialization. During the Dreyfus affair, French anti-Semites were rallied to the cause by Édouard Drumont (1844–1917), the editor of La Libre parole *("The Free Word"), a conservative anti-Semitic journal, and the founder of the French Anti-Semitic League. Drumont's* Jewish France, *published in 1885, enjoyed immense popularity: at least one-hundred and fifty thousand copies were sold within two years of its first appearance and it remained in print long into the twentieth century. As the following excerpt from his work demonstrates, Drumont's anti-Semitism took the form of an argument that "old France" was being "conquered" by an alien and parasitic Jewish culture.*

From *La France juive. Essai d'histoire contemporaine*, by Édouard Drumont, C. Marpon and E. Flammarion, 1885. (Translated by Cat Nilan, 1997.)

The only one who has benefitted from the Revolution [of 1789] is the Jew. Everything comes from the Jew; everything returns to the Jew.

We have here a veritable conquest, an entire nation returned to serfdom by a minute but cohesive minority, just as the Saxons were forced into serfdom by William the Conqueror's 60,000 Normans.

The methods are different, the result is the same. One can recognize all the characteristics of a conquest: an entire population working for another population, which appropriates, through a vast system of financial exploitation, all of the profits of the other. Immense Jewish fortunes, castles, Jewish townhouses, are not the fruit of any actual labor, of any production: they are the booty taken from an enslaved race by a dominant race.

It is certain, for example, that the Rothschild family, whose French branch alone possesses a declared fortune of three billion [francs], did not have that money when it arrived in France; it has invented nothing, it has discovered no mine, it has tilled no ground. It has therefore appropriated these three billion francs from the French without giving them anything in exchange.

*   *   *

All Jewish fortunes have been built up in the same manner, through an appropriation of the work of others.

*   *   *

Today, thanks to the Jew, money—to which the Christian world attached only a secondary importance and assigned only a subordinate role—has become all powerful. Capitalist power concentrated in a tiny number of hands governs at will the entire economic life of the people, enslaves their labor, and feasts on iniquitous profits acquired without labor.

These problems, familiar to all thinking Europeans, are all but unknown in France. The reason is simple. The Jew Lassalle himself has noted how slender are the intellectual foundations of the bourgeoisie, whose opinions are fabricated by the newspapers.* * *

Now, since almost all newspapers and all organs of publicity in France are in the hands of Jews or belong to them indirectly, it is not surprising that the significance and the scope of the immense anti-Semitic movement that has begun to organize itself everywhere is being carefully hidden from us.

*   *   *

In any case, it seems to me interesting and useful to describe the successive phases of this *Jewish Conquest*, to indicate how, little by little, as a result of Jewish activities, old France has been dissolved, broken up, how its unselfish, happy, loving people has been replaced by a hateful people, hungry for gold and soon to be dying of hunger.

*   *   *

Thanks to the Jews' cunning exploitation of the principles of '89, France was collapsing into dissolution. Jews had monopolized all of the public wealth, had invaded everything, except the army. The representatives of the old [French] families, whether noble or bourgeois, had divided themselves into two camps. Some gave themselves up to pleasure, and were corrupted by the Jewish prostitutes they had taken as mistresses or were ruined by the horse-sellers and money-lenders, also Jews, who aided the prostitutes. The others obeyed the attraction exercised over the Aryan

race by the infinite, the Hindu Nirvana, Odin's paradise. They became almost uninterested in contemporary life, they lost themselves in ecstasy, they barely had one foot still planted in the real world.

If the Semites could have been patient for a few years they would have achieved their goal. Jules Simon, one of the few truly wise men they count among their ranks* * *, told them exactly what they needed to do: quietly take over the earth and let the Aryans migrate up to heaven.

The Jews never wanted to listen to this message: they preferred the Semite Gambetta to the Semite Simon. * * *they believed that [Gambetta] was going to help them get rid of Christ, whom they still hated just as much as they had on the day they crucified him. Freemasonry made its contribution, Jewish journals stirred up public opinion, gold was freely distributed, police superintendents were richly paid off, although they refused to make themselves guilty of a crime up to the last minute.

What happened?* * *The Aryan—provoked, troubled, wounded in his innate feelings of nobility and generosity—felt his blood rise to his face when he saw unfortunate old [monks] dragged from their cells by the dregs of the police. He took a while to deliberate, to gather his thoughts, to reflect.

"In the name of what principle are you acting?," he asked.

"In the name of the principal of liberty," replied in unison the newspapers of Porgès, Reinach, Dreyfus, Eugène Mayer, Camille Sée, Naquet.

"And what does this principle consist of?"

"Of this: some Jew or another leaves Hamburg, Frankfurt, Vilna, or anyplace else, and he amasses a certain number of millions at the expense of the *goyim* [gentiles]. He can take his carriage out for a ride, his domicile is inviolable, unless a warrant is issued, and naturally it never is. On the other hand, a native Frenchman, a *natural Frenchman*, to use the words of Saint-Simon, gives away everything he owns to help the poor; he goes barefoot, he lives in a narrow, white-washed cell that the servant of Rothschild's servant wouldn't want. He is the outlaw. He can be thrown out in the street like a dog.

The Aryan, roused from his slumbers, decides, not without reason, that once this so precious tolerance—talked about so much for the last hundred years—is interpreted in this way, it is better to strike back than be struck. He decides that it is more than time to wrest the country from such impatient masters. "Since the monk's rough robe is so annoying to your frock-coat, we'll give you back the yellow rag, my old Shem." Such was the upshot of [the Aryan's] meditations. It is from that moment that one can date the establishment of the first anti-Semitic—or, to be more precise, anti-Jewish—committee.

* * *

* * *The fatherland, in the sense that we attach to that word, has no meaning for the Semite. The Jew, to use the energetic expression of the *Israelite Alliance*, is characterized by an *inexorable universalism*.

I can see no reason for reproaching the Jews for thinking this way. What does the word "Fatherland" mean? Land of the fathers. One's feelings for the Fatherland are engraved in one's heart in the same way that a name carved in a tree is driven deeper into the bark with each passing year, so that the tree and the name eventually become one. You can't become a patriot through improvization; you are a patriot in your blood, in your marrow.

Can the Semite, a perpetual nomad, ever experience such enduring impressions?

* * *the first requirement for adopting a new fatherland, is to renounce the old one. Now, the Jew has a fatherland he never renounces: Jerusalem, the holy and mysterious city Jerusalem. In triumph or persecution, joyous or sad, it serves as a link uniting all of those children who say every year at Rosh Hashanah: "next year in Jerusalem!"

Aside from Jerusalem, every other country, whether France, or Germany, or England, is only a residence for the Jew, any old place, a social agglomeration, in the midst of which he may find himself at home, whose interests he may even find

it profitable to serve for the moment, but which he joins only as a free agent, as a temporary member.

* * *

To succeed in their attack against Christian civilization, the Jews of France had to use deceit, to lie, to disguise themselves as freethinkers. If they had said frankly: "We want to destroy that France of old, so glorious, so beautiful, and replace it with domination by a fistful of Hebrews from many lands," our fathers, less soft than ourselves, would not have let this happen. For a long time [the Jews] kept things vague, working with Freemasonry, hiding behind sonorous words: emancipation, enfranchisement, the struggle against superstition and the prejudices of another age.

* * *

* * *among the Jews, religious persecution takes on a particularly bitter character. For them, nothing has changed: they hate Christ as much in 1885 as they hated him at the time of Tiberius Augustus, and they heap the same outrages upon him. Whipping the crucifix on Good Friday, profaning the host, besmirching sacred images: such was the great joy of the medieval Jew, and such is his great joy today. Then, he attacked the bodies of children; today, he tries to get at their souls through atheist education. Then, he bled them; today, he poisons their minds: which is worse?

* * *

Despite everything, it is difficult to escape the influence of what one hears from morning to night, from the impression of the artificial intellectual climate created by the Jewish press, and even the best sometimes are subject, despite themselves, to what we have already named the *prejudices of modernism*.

* * *

As for myself, I repeat that I claim to have done nothing more than to attempt a work of good will, to demonstrate by what an underhanded and crafty enemy France has been invaded, corrupted, and brutalized, to such a point that she has broken with her proper hands everything that once made her powerful, respected, and happy. Have I written our last will and testament? Have I laid the foundations for our rebirth? I do not know. I have done my duty, in any case, by responding with insults to the numberless insults that the Jewish press directs at Christians. In proclaiming the Truth, I have obeyed the imperious command of my conscience: *liberavi animam meam* [free my soul].* * *

*   *   *

REVIEW QUESTIONS

1. Of what "crimes" are the Jews of France guilty, according to Drumont?
2. How have they gotten away with these crimes?
3. What does Drumont mean by "tolerance"? Why does he reject it?
4. What are the "prejudices of modernism"?
5. Why does Drumont associate Jews with modernism?
6. On the basis of this reading, why do you think Drumont hates Jews?
7. Why do you think his arguments might have appealed to many late-nineteenth-century Europeans?

ELIZABETH ROBINS

FROM *The Convert*

Like the Dreyfus affair in France, the British Woman Suffrage campaign took on a cultural importance that went far beyond the specific political issues raised by the question of whether or not to extend the vote to women. Suffragettes' increasingly violent tactics struck deep at the heart of the Victorian consensus, unsettling established notions of femininity and social harmony. Women's demand for voting rights necessarily served as a critique of existing gender relations, but it also raised questions about class relations insofar as the woman suffrage campaign often pitted upper-class women activists against newly enfranchised male workers. At the same time, the suffrage movement became entangled in the realignments of political power occasioned by the emergence of the modern British Conservative, Liberal, and Labour parties.

In 1907, the novelist and suffrage activist Elizabeth Robins (1862–1952) published The Convert, *a fictional account of the suffrage movement closely modeled on the real-life activities of suffragettes such as the Pankhursts. In the novel, Miss Vida Levering, a young and affluent society woman, is gradually "converted" to the suffrage cause. In the following scene, Miss Levering, in the company of her scandalized maid, attends an outdoor suffrage meeting at London's Hyde Park. Robins' lively fiction offers a snapshot of British urban society, providing evidence of the complex interaction between the lived experiences of class, gender, and political allegiance.*

From *The Convert*, Elizabeth Robins, MacMillan Co., 1907.

*   *   *

Yes. There it was! a rectangle of red screaming across the vivid green of the park not a hundred yards from the Marble Arch, the denunciatory banner stretched above the side of an uncovered van. A little crowd of perhaps a hundred collected on one side of the cart—the loafers on the outermost fringe, lying on the grass. Never a sign of a Suffragette, and nearly three o'clock! Impossible for any passer-by to carry out the programme of pausing to ask idly, 'What are those women screeching about?'

Seeming to search in vain for some excuse to linger, Miss Levering's wandering eye fell upon a young mother wheeling a perambulator. She had glanced with mild curiosity at the flaunting ensign, and then turned from it to lean forward and straighten her baby's cap.

'I wonder what *she* thinks of the Woman Question,' Miss Levering observed, in a careless aside to her maid.

Before Gorringe could reply: 'Doddy's a boo-tiful angel, isn't Doddy?' said the young mother, with subdued rapture.

'Ah, she's found the solution,' said the lady, looking back.

Other pedestrians glanced at the little crowd about the cart, read demand and denunciation on the banner, laughed, and they, too, for the most part, went on.

An Eton boy, who looked as if he might be her grandson, came by with a white-haired lady of distinguished aspect, who held up her voluminous silken skirts and stared silently at the legend.

'Do you see what it says?' the Eton boy laughed as he looked back. ' "*We demand the vote.*" Fancy! They "demand" it. What awful cheek!' and he laughed again at the fatuity of the female creature.

Vida glanced at the dignified old dame as though with an uneasy new sense of the incongruity in the attitude of those two quite commonplace, everyday members of a world that was her world, and that yet could for a moment look quite strange. * * * Miss Levering stood a moment hesitating.

'I believe I'm a little tired,' she said to the discreet maid. 'We'll rest here a moment,' and she sat down with her back to the crowd.

A woman, apparently of the small shopkeeping class, was already established at one end of the only bench anywhere near the cart. Her child who was playing about, was neatly dressed, and to Vida's surprise wore sandals on her stockingless feet. This fashion for children, which had been growing for years among the upper classes, had found little imitation among tradesmen or working people. They presumably were still too near the difficulty of keeping their children in shoes and stockings, to be able to see anything but a confession of failure in going without. In the same way, the 'Simple Life,' when led by the rich, wears to the poverty-struck an aspect of masked meanness—a matter far less tolerable in the eyes of the pauper than the traditional splendour of extravagance in the upper class, an extravagance that feeds more than the famished stomach with the crumbs that it lets fall.

As Miss Levering sat watching the child, and wondering a little at the sandals, the woman caught her eye.

'Could you please tell me the time?' she asked.

Miss Levering took out her watch, and then spoke of the wisdom of that plan of sandals.

The woman answered with such self-possession and good sense, that the lady sent a half-amused glance over her shoulder as if relishing in advance the sturdy disapproval of this highly respectable young mother when she should come to realize how near she and the precious daughter were to the rostrum of the Shrieking Sisterhood. It might be worth prolonging the discussion upon health and education for the amusement there would be in seeing what form condemnation of the Suffragettes took among people of this kind. By turning her head to one side, out of the tail of her eye the lady could see that an excitement of some sort was agitating the crowd. The voices rose more shrill. People craned and pushed. A derisive cheer went up as a woman appeared on the cart.

The wearer of the tam-o'-shanter! Three others followed—all women. Miss Levering saw without seeming to look, still listening while the practical-minded mother talked on about her child, and what 'was good for it.' All life had resolved itself into pursuit of that.

An air of semi-abstraction came over the lady. It was as if in the presence of this excellent bourgeoise she felt an absurd constraint in showing an interest in the proceedings of these unsexed creatures behind them.

To her obvious astonishment the mother of the child was the first to jump up.

'Now they're going to begin!' she said briskly.

'Who?' asked Miss Levering.

'Why, the Suffrage people.'

'Oh! Are *you* going to listen to them?'

'Yes; that's what I've come all this way for.' And she and her bare-legged offspring melted into the growing crowd.

Vida turned to the maid and met her superior smile. 'That woman says she has come a long way to hear these people advocating Woman's Suffrage,' and slowly with an air of complete detachment she approached the edge of the crowd, followed by the supercilious maid. They were quickly hemmed in by people who seemed to spring up out of the ground. It was curious to look back over the vivid green expanse and see the dotted humanity running like ants from all directions to listen to this handful of dowdy women in a cart!

In finding her way through the crowd it would appear that the lady was not much sustained by the presence of a servant, however well-meaning. * * * The punctilious Gorringe was plainly horrified at the proximity to her mistress of these canaille, and the mistress was not so absorbed it would seem but what she felt the affront to seemliness in a servant's seeing her pushed and shoved aside—treated with slight regard or none. Necessary either to leave the scene with lofty disapproval, or else make light of the discomfort.

'It doesn't matter!' she assured the girl, who was trying to protect her mistress's dainty wrap from contact with a grimy tramp. And, again,

when half a dozen boys forced their way past, 'It's all right!' she nodded to the maid * * *

But it was much worse, and Gorringe knew it. 'The old man is standing on your gown, miss.'

'Oh, would you mind——' Miss Levering politely suggested another place for his feet.

But the old man had no mind left for a mere bystander—it was all absorbed in Suffragettes.

' 'is feet are filthy muddy, 'm,' whispered Gorringe.

It may have been in part the maid's genteel horror of such proximities that steeled Miss Levering to endure them. Under circumstances like these the observant are reminded that no section of the modern community is so scornfully aristocratic as our servants. Their horror of the meanly-apparelled and the humble is beyond the scorn of kings. The fine lady shares her shrinking with those inveterate enemies of democracy, the lackey who shuts the door in the shabby stranger's face, and the dog who barks a beggar from the gate.

And so while the maid drew her own skirts aside and held her nose high in the air, the gentlewoman stood faintly smiling at the queer scene.

Alas! no Mrs. Chisholm. It looked as if they must have been hard up for speakers to-day, for two of them were younger even than Miss Claxton of the tam-o'-shanter. One of them couldn't be more than nineteen.

'How dreadful to put such very young girls up there to be stared at by all these louts!'

'Oh, yes, 'm, quite 'orrid,' agreed the maid, but with the air of 'What can you expect of persons so low?'

'However, the young girls seem to have as much self-possession as the older ones!' pursued Miss Levering, as she looked in vain for any sign of flinching from the sallies of cockney impudence directed at the occupants of the cart.

They exhibited, too, what was perhaps even stranger—an utter absence of any flaunting of courage or the smallest show of defiance. What was this armour that looked like mere indifference? It couldn't be that those quiet-looking young girls *were* indifferent to the ordeal of standing up there before a crowd of jeering rowdies whose less objectionable utterances were: 'Where did you get that 'at?' 'The one in green is my girl!' 'Got yer dog-whip, miss?' and such-like utterances.

The person thus pointedly alluded to left her companions ranged along the side of the cart against the background of banner, while she, the famous Miss Claxton, took the meeting in charge. She wasted no time, this lady. Her opening remarks, which, in the face of a fire of interruption, took the form of an attack upon the Government, showed her an alert, competent, cut-and-thrust, imperturbably self-possessed politician, who knew every aspect of the history of the movement, as able to answer any intelligent question off-hand as to snub an impudent irrelevance, able to take up a point and drive it well in—to shrug and smile or frown and point her finger, all with most telling effect, and keep the majority of her audience with her every minute of the time.

As a mere exhibition of nerve it was a thing to make you open your eyes. Only a moment was she arrested by either booing or applause. When a knot of young men, who had pushed their way near the front, kept on shouting argument and abuse, she interrupted her harangue an instant. Pointing out the ringleader—

As a mere exhibition of nerve it was a thing to make you open your eyes. Only a moment was she arrested by either booing or applause. When a knot of young men, who had pushed their way near the front, kept on shouting argument and abuse, she interrupted her harangue an instant. Pointing out the ringleader—

'Now you be quiet, if you please,' she said. 'These people are here to listen to *me*.'

'No, they ain't. They come to see wot you look like.'

'That can't be so,' she said calmly, 'because after they've seen us they stay.' Then, as the interrupter began again, 'No, it's no use, my man' —she shook her head gently as if almost sorry for him—'you can't talk *me* down!'

'Now, ain't that just *like* a woman!' he complained to the crowd.

Just in front of where Miss Levering and her satellite first came to a standstill, was a cheerful, big, sandy man with long flowing moustachios, a polo cap, and a very dirty collar. At intervals he inquired of the men around him, in a great jovial voice, 'Are we down-'earted?' as though the meeting had been called, not for the purpose of rousing interest in the question of woman's share in the work of the world, but as though its object were to humiliate and disfranchise the men. But his exclamation, repeated at intervals, came in as a sort of refrain to the rest of the proceedings.

'The Conservatives,' said the speaker, 'had never pretended they favoured broadening the basis of the franchise. But here were these Liberals, for thirty years they'd been saying that the demand on the part of women for political recognition commanded their respect, and would have their support, and yet there were four hundred and odd members who had got into the House of Commons very largely through the efforts of women —oh, yes, we know all about that! We've been helping the men at elections for years.'

'What party?'

Adroitly she replied, 'We have members of every party in our ranks.'

'Are you a Conservative?'

'No, I myself am not a Conservative——'

'You work for the Labour men—I know!'

'It's child's play belonging to any party till we get the vote,' she dismissed it. 'In future we are neither for Liberal nor Conservative nor Labour. We are for Women. When we get the sex bar removed, it will be time for us to sort ourselves into parties. At present we are united against any Government that continues to ignore its duty to the women of the country. In the past we were so confiding that when a candidate said he was in favour of Woman's Suffrage (he was usually a Liberal), we worked like slaves to get that man elected, so that a voice might be raised for women's interests in the next Parliament. Again and again the man we worked for got in. But the voice that was to speak for us—that voice was mute. We had served his purpose in helping him to win his seat, and we found ourselves invariably forgotten or ignored. The Conservatives have never shown the abysmal hypocrisy of the Liberals. We can get on with our open enemies; it's these *cowards*' ('Boo!' and groans)—'these cowards, I say—who, in order to sneak into a place in the House, pretend to sympathize with this reform—who use us, and then betray us; it's these who are women's enemies!'

'Why are you always worrying the Liberals? Why don't you ask the Conservatives to give you the vote?'

'You don't go to a person for something he hasn't got unless you're a fool. The Liberals are in power; the Liberals were readiest with fair promises; and so we go to the Liberals. And we shall continue to go to them. We shall never leave off' (boos and groans) 'till they leave office. Then we'll begin on the Conservatives.' She ended in a chorus of laughter and cheers . . .

*　　*　　*

REVIEW QUESTIONS

1. What do you learn about British class and gender relations from Robins' description of a woman suffrage rally?
2. How does Robins portray the opponents of woman suffrage?
3. How does she portray its supporters?
4. What factors influence Miss Claxton's response to the political parties of the period?

KONSTANTIN POBEDONOSTSEV

FROM *Reflections of a Russian Statesman*

In late nineteenth-century Russia, the autocratic tsarist state and the traditionalist Eastern Orthodox Church were increasingly challenged by reformist liberals, revolutionary intellectuals, and a restive peasantry and industrial working class. After the assassination of Tsar Alexander II in 1881, the new government of Alexander III retreated from earlier reform initiatives and clamped down on political opposition. Those activists who escaped imprisonment in Siberia were forced into exile or driven underground, which only served to further reinforce their radicalism and commitment to an overthrow of the tsarist state.

The Russian statesman Konstantin Pobedonostsev (1827–1907) served as a vocal proponent of Russian conservatism throughout the second half of the nineteenth century. During the course of a long and illustrious career as a government official, Pobedonostsev lobbied tirelessly in support of the monarchy and the Eastern Orthodox Church. He was also an ardent supporter of Russification, refusing to recognize the independent rights of ethnic and religious minorities within the Russian empire. In Reflections of a Russian Statesman, *published in Russia in 1896 and read widely throughout Europe in translation, Pobedonostsev presented a summary of his conservative political and religious beliefs.*

From *Reflections of a Russian Statesman*, Konstantin Pobyedonostseff, translated by Robert Crozier Long, Grant Richards, 1898.

The New Democracy

What is this freedom by which so many minds are agitated, which inspires so many insensate actions, so many wild speeches, which leads the people so often to misfortune? In the democratic sense of the word, freedom is the right of political power, or, to express it otherwise, the right to participate in the government of the State. This universal aspiration for a share in government has no constant limitations, and seeks no definite issue, but incessantly extends * * * For ever extending its base, the new Democracy now aspires to universal suffrage—a fatal error, and one of the most remarkable in the history of mankind. By this means, the political power so passionately demanded by Democracy would be shattered into a number of infinitesimal bits, of which each citizen acquires a single one. What will he do with it, then? how will he employ it? In the result it has undoubtedly been shown that in the attainment of this aim Democracy violates its sacred formula of "Freedom indissolubly joined with Equality." It is shown that this apparently equal distribution of "freedom" among all involves the total destruction of equality. Each vote, representing an inconsiderable fragment of power, by itself signifies nothing; an aggregation of votes alone has a relative value. The result may be likened to the general meetings of shareholders in public companies. By themselves individuals are ineffective, but he who controls a number of these fragmentary forces is master of all power, and directs all decisions and dispositions. We may well ask in what consists the superiority of Democracy. Everywhere the strongest man becomes master of the State; sometimes a fortunate and resolute general, sometimes a monarch or administrator with knowledge, dexterity, a clear plan of action, and a determined will. In a Democracy, the real rulers are the dexterous manipulators of votes, with their placemen, the mechanics who so skilfully operate the hidden springs which move the puppets in the arena of democratic elections. Men of this kind are ever ready with loud speeches lauding equality; in reality, they rule the people as any despot or military dictator might rule it. The extension of the right to participate in elections is regarded as progress and as the conquest of freedom by democratic theorists, who hold that the more numerous the participants in political rights, the greater is the probability that all will employ this right in the interests of the public welfare, and for the increase of the freedom of the people. Experience proves a very different thing. The history of mankind bears witness that the most necessary and fruitful reforms—the most durable measures—emanated from the supreme will of statesmen, or from a minority enlightened by lofty ideas and deep knowledge, and that, on the contrary, the extension of the representative principle is accompanied by an abasement of political ideas and the vulgarisation of opinions in the mass of the electors. It shows also that this extension—in great States—was inspired by secret aims to the centralisation of power, or led directly to dictatorship. In France, universal suffrage was suppressed with the end of the Terror, and was re-established twice merely to affirm the autocracy of the two Napoleons. In Germany, the establishment of universal suffrage served merely to strengthen the high authority of a famous statesman who had acquired popularity by the success of his policy. What its ultimate consequences will be, Heaven only knows!

* * *

The Church

* * *

He who is truly Russian, heart and soul, knows what the Church of God means to the Russian people. Piety, experience, and respect for religious feelings are not enough in order to understand the import of the Church for the Russian people, or to love this Church as one's own. It is necessary to live the life of the people, to pray with it in congregation, to feel the heart beating in accord, penetrated by the same solemnity, inspired by the same words and the same chants. Thus, many who know the faith only from their private chapels, frequented by select congregations, have no true understanding of the Church, or of religious sentiment, and regard with indifference or repulsion those rites and customs which to the people are especially dear, and constitute the beauty of the Church.

The beauty of the Orthodox Church is its congregation. On entering, we feel that all are united, all is the work of the people, and all is maintained by them. In the Catholic Church, all seems empty, cold, and artificial to the Orthodox worshipper. The priest officiates and reads alone, as if he were above the people, and independent of them. He prays alone from his book, the members of the congregation from theirs; having prayed, and attended one or another part of the service, the congregation departs. On the altar the mass is performed, the worshippers, while present, do not seem to participate by common prayer. The service is addressed to sentiment, and its beauty, if beauty there be, is strange to us, and not our own. The actions of the service, mechanically performed, to us seem strange, cold, and inexpressive; the sacred vesture is unsightly; the recitative inharmonious and uninspired; the chants—in a strange tongue which we do not understand—are not the hymns of the whole congregation, not a cry coming from the soul, but an artificial concert which conceals the service, but never unites with it. Our hearts yearn for our own Church, as we yearn for our homes, among strangers. How different with us: in our service there is an indescribable beauty which every Russian understands, a beauty he loves so much that he is ready to give up his soul for it. As our national songs, the chants of our service flow in wide, free streams from the breasts of the people—the freer they are the more they appeal to our hearts. Our religious melodies are the same as among the Greeks, but they are sung otherwise by our peoples, who place in them their whole souls. He who would hear the true voice of this soul must not go where famous choirs sing the music of new composers; he should

hear the singing in some great convent or parish church: there he will hear in what wide, free streams flows the hymn from the Russian breast, with what solemn poetry is sung the dogmatic, what inspiration sings in the canticles of Easter and Christmas. We hear the word of our chants echoed by the congregation, it illumines upturned faces, it is borne over bowed heads, borne everywhere, for to all the congregation the words and melodies are known from childhood, till the very soul seems to give forth song. This true, harmonious service is a festival for the Russian worshipper; even outside his church he preserves its deep impressions, and is thrilled at the recollection of some solemn moment: he is exalted with the harmony, when in his soul echoes again the song of the Easter or Christmas canticle.

In him to whom these words and sounds have been known from childhood, how many recollections and images arise out of that great poem of the past which each has lived, and each still carried in himself! Happy is he who has known these words and sounds and images; who from childhood has found in them the ideal loveliness to which he aspires, without which he cannot live; to whom all is clear and congenial, all lifts his soul out of the dust of life; who in them gathers up again the scattered fragments of his happiness! Happy is he whom good and pious parents have brought in childhood to the house of God, teaching him to pray among the people, and to celebrate its festivals with it! They have built him a sanctuary for life, they have taught him to love the people and to live in communion with it, making the church for him his parents' house, a place of pure and true communion with the people.

*   *   *

REVIEW QUESTIONS

1. For what reasons does Pobedonostsev reject democracy?
2. To what extent may his remarks be read as a defense of the existing Russian political system?

3. Why does Pobedonostsev reject the Catholic mass as "un-Russian"?

4. What, in his eyes, characterizes the Russian religious experience?

VLADIMIR LENIN

FROM *Our Programme*

The extreme conservatism of government officials such as Pobedonostsev found its answer in the revolutionary aspirations of late-nineteenth-century Russian political activists. While populists—the narodniki—*sought to mobilize the Russian peasantry as a revolutionary force, the emergence of an industrial working class convinced Marxist socialists that the urban proletariat would spearhead a revolution against the capitalist development being fostered by the tsarist state itself.*

Vladimir Ilich Ulyanov, better known as Lenin (1870–1924), was drawn into the Russian opposition movement after his brother was executed in 1887 for conspiring to assassinate Tsar Alexander III. In subsequent years, Lenin became one of the leading theorists of the Russian Social Democratic Workers' Party. In 1899, at the end of a period of exile in Siberia, he wrote the following statement of revolutionary principles, affirming his adherence to revolutionary Marxism and rejecting "reformist" tendencies within the international socialist movement. Four years prior to the historic schism between the Social Democratic Party's revolutionary Bolsheviks and reformist Mensheviks, it is clear that Lenin had already begun to reject worker cooperation with the liberal bourgeoisie and that he was becoming committed to the idea that a "vanguard" of professional revolutionaries must lead the workers' revolution.

From *Our Programme*, Vladimir Lenin, The Marxism-Leninism Project Website, <http://www.idbsu.edu/surveyrc/Staff/jaynes/marxism/lenin/programe.htm>.

International social democracy is at present going through a period of theoretical vacillations. Up to the present the doctrines of Marx and Engels were regarded as a firm foundation of revolutionary theory—nowadays voices are raised everywhere declaring these doctrines to be inadequate and antiquated. Anyone calling himself a social-democrat and having the intention to publish a social-democratic organ, must take up a definite attitude as regards this question, which by no means concerns German social-democrats alone.

We base our faith entirely on Marx's theory; it was the first to transform socialism from a Utopia into a science, to give this science a firm foundation and to indicate the path which must be trodden in order further to develop this science and to elaborate it in all its details. It discovered the nature of present-day capitalist economy and explained the way in which the employment of workers—the purchase of labour power—the enslavement of millions of those possessing no property by a handful of capitalists, by the owners of the land, the factories, the mines, etc., is concealed. It has shown how the whole development of modern capitalism is advancing towards the large producer ousting the small one, and is creating the prerequisites which make a socialist order of society possible and necessary. It has taught us to see, under the disguise of ossified habits, political intrigues, intricate laws, cunning theories, the class struggle, the struggle between, on the one hand, the various species of the possessing classes, and, on the other hand, the mass possessing no property, the proletariat, which leads all those who possess nothing. It has made clear what is the real task of a revolutionary socialist party—not to set up projects for the transformation of society, not to preach sermons to the capitalists and their admirers about improving the position of the workers, not the instigation of conspiracies, but the organisation of the class struggle of the proletariat and the carrying on of this struggle, the final aim of which is the seizure of political power by the proletariat and the organisation of a socialist society.

We now ask: What new elements have the touting "renovators" introduced into this theory, they who have attracted so much notice in our day and have grouped themselves round the German socialist Bernstein? Nothing, nothing at all; they have not advanced by a single step the science which Marx and Engels adjured us to develop; they have not taught the proletariat any new methods of fighting; they are only marching backwards in that they adopt the fragments of antiquated theories and are preaching to the proletariat not the theory of struggle but the theory of submissiveness—submissiveness to the bitterest enemies of the proletariat, to the governments and bourgeois parties who never tire of finding new methods of persecuting socialists. Plekhanov, one of the founders and leaders of Russian social-democracy, was perfectly right when he subjected to merciless criticism the latest "Criticism" of Bernstein, whose views have now been rejected even by the representatives of the German workers at the Party Congress in Hanover [1899].

We know that on account of these words we

shall be drenched with a flood of accusations; they will cry out that we want to turn the Socialist Party into a holy order of the "orthodox," who persecute the "heretics" for their aberrations from the "true dogma," for any independent opinion, etc. We know all these nonsensical phrases which have become the fashion nowadays. Yet there is no shadow of truth in them, no iota of sense. There can be no strong socialist party without a revolutionary theory which unites all socialists, from which the socialists draw their whole conviction, which they apply in their methods of fighting and working. To defend a theory of this kind, of the truth of which one is completely convinced, against unfounded attacks and against attempts to debase it, does not mean being an enemy of criticism in general. We by no means regard the theory of Marx as perfect and inviolable; on the contrary, we are convinced that this theory has only laid the foundation stones of that science on which the socialists must continue to build in every direction, unless they wish to be left behind by life. We believe that it is particularly necessary for Russian socialists to work out the Marxist theory independently, for this theory only gives general precepts, the details of which must be applied in England otherwise than in France, in France otherwise than in Germany, and in Germany otherwise than in Russia. * * *

What are the main questions which arise in applying the common programme of all social-democrats to Russia?

We have already said that the essence of this programme consists in the organisation of the class struggle of the proletariat and in carrying on this struggle, the final aim of which is the seizure of political power by the proletariat and the construction of a socialist society. The class struggle of the proletariat is divided into: the economic fight (the fight against [the] individual capitalist, or against the individual groups of capitalists by the improvement of the position of the workers) and the political fight (the fight against the Government for the extension of the rights of the people, i.e., for democracy, and for the expansion of the political power of the proletariat). Some Russian social-democrats * * * regard the economic fight as incomparably more important and almost go so far as to postpone the political fight to a more or less distant future. This standpoint is quite wrong. All social-democrats are unanimous in believing that it is necessary to carry on an agitation among the workers on this basis, i.e., to help the workers in their daily fight against the employers, to direct their attention to all kinds and all cases of chicanery, and in this way to make clear to them the necessity of unity. To forget the political for the economic fight would, however, mean a digression from the most important principle of international social-democracy; it would mean forgetting what the whole history of the Labour movement has taught us. Fanatical adherents of the bourgeoisie and of the government which serves it, have indeed repeatedly tried to organise purely economic unions of workers and thus to deflect them from the "politics" of socialism. It is quite possible that the Russian Government will also be clever enough to do something of the kind, as it has always endeavored to throw some largesse or other sham presents to the people in order to prevent them becoming conscious that they are oppressed and are without rights.

No economic fight can give the workers a permanent improvement of their situation, it cannot, indeed, be carried on on a large scale unless the workers have the free right to call meetings, to join in unions, to have their own newspapers and to send their representatives to the National Assembly as do the workers in Germany and all European countries (with the exception of Turkey and Russia). In order, however, to obtain these rights, a political fight must be carried on. In Russia, not only the workers but all the citizens are deprived of political rights. Russia is an absolute monarchy. The Tsar alone promulgates laws, nominates officials and controls them. For this reason it seems as though in Russia the Tsar and the Tsarist Government were dependent on no class and cared for all equally. In reality, however, all the officials are chosen exclusively from the possessing class, and all are subject to the influence of the large

capitalists who obtain whatever they want—the Ministers dance to the tune the large capitalists play. The Russian worker is bowed under a double yoke; he is robbed and plundered by the capitalists and the landowners, and, lest he should fight against them, he is bound hand and foot by the police, his mouth is gagged and any attempt to defend the rights of the people is followed by persecution. Any strike against a capitalist results in the military and police being let loose on the workers. Every economic fight of necessity turns into a political fight, and social-democracy must indissolubly combine the economic with the political fight into a united class struggle of the proletariat.

The first and chief aim of such a fight must be the conquest of political rights, the conquest of political freedom. Since the workers of St. Petersburg alone have succeeded, in spite of the inadequate support given them by the socialists, in obtaining concessions from the Government within a short time—the passing of a law for shortening the hours of work—the whole working class, led by a united "Russian Social-Democratic Labour Party," will be able, through obstinate fighting, to obtain incomparably more important concessions.

The Russian working class will see its way to carrying on an economic and political fight alone, even if no other class comes to its help. The workers are not alone, however, in the political fight. The fact that the people is absolutely without rights and the unbridled arbitrary rule of the officials rouses the indignation of all who have any pretensions to honesty and educations, who cannot reconcile themselves with the persecution of all free speech and all free thought; it rouses the indignation of the persecuted Poles, Finns, Jews, Russian sects, it rouses the indignation of small traders, of the industrialists, the peasants, of all who can nowhere find protection against the chicanery of the officials and the police. All these groups of the population are incapable of carrying on an obstinate political fight alone; if, however, the working class raises the banner of a fight of this kind it will be supported on all sides. Russian social-democracy will place itself at the head of all fights for the rights of the people, of all fights for democracy, and then it will be invincible.

*   *   *

REVIEW QUESTIONS

1. What tendencies within the socialist movement does Lenin reject here? Why?
2. Why, according to Lenin, must workers combine the fight for economic rights with the fight for political rights?
3. Compare and contrast the ideological positions of Pobedonostsev and Lenin.

Entangling Alliances: Great Power Treaties, 1870–1914

After Germany's decisive defeat of France in 1871, Chancellor Otto von Bismarck (1815–1898) sought reliable allies for the newly unified German nation, using careful diplomacy to counter the threat of encirclement. Bismarck believed that German interests were best served by peace, and he therefore worked to isolate France, which was still stinging from the loss of Alsace and Lorraine. Emphasizing the ideological compatibility of Austria-Hungary, Germany, and Russia, Bismarck negotiated a "Three Emperors' League" (1873), a strategic alliance between the three eastern European autocracies. When this alliance collapsed, Bismarck entered the Dual Alliance with Austria-Hungary (1879), later reinforced by the inclusion of Italy (the Triple Alliance, 1882). The Three Emperors' League was revived in 1881, but Germany's ties with Russia were broken after Wilhelm II dismissed Bismarck in 1890 and began to pursue a more adventurous foreign policy. Between 1890 and 1914, Germany remained bound to the Austro-Hungarian empire, which was increasingly troubled by nationalist unrest within its borders and in the Balkans.

In 1894, France and Russia entered a diplomatic marriage of convenience: the two nations shared few common interests other than the desire to escape diplomatic isolation, but their alliance proved surprisingly durable. When Britain settled its outstanding differences with France and Russia (in 1904 and 1907, respectively), the resulting Triple Entente realized Bismarck's worst nightmare: bound to a weak and unstable Austria-Hungary and an unreliable Italy, Germany faced the threat of a two-front war on the continent and British naval superiority on the world's waters.

The following treaties document the formation of the network of "entangling alliances" that divided the European Great Powers into two opposed and increasingly hostile power blocs in the years leading up to the outbreak of war in 1914.

The Dual Alliance Between Austria-Hungary and Germany (October 7, 1879)

ARTICLE 1. Should, contrary to their hope, and against the loyal desire of the two High Contracting Parties, one of the two Empires be attacked by Russia the High Contracting Parties are bound to come to the assistance one of the other with the whole war strength of their Empires, and accordingly only to conclude peace together and upon mutual agreement.

ARTICLE 2. Should one of the High Contracting Parties be attacked by another Power, the other High Contracting Party binds itself hereby, not only not to support the aggressor against its high Ally, but to observe at least a benevolent neutral attitude towards its fellow Contracting Party.

Should, however, the attacking party in such a case be supported by Russia, either by an active cooperation or by military measures which constitute a menace to the Party attacked, then the obligation stipulated in Article 1 of this Treaty, for reciprocal assistance with the whole fighting force, becomes equally operative, and the conduct of the war by the two High Contracting Parties shall in this case also be in common until the conclusion of a common peace.

ARTICLE 3. The duration of this Treaty shall be provisionally fixed at five years from the day of ratification * * *

ARTICLE 4. This Treaty shall, in conformity with its peaceful character, and to avoid any misinterpretation, be kept secret by the two High Contracting Parties * * *

From *The Dual Alliance Between Austria-Hungary and Germany (October 7, 1879)*, The World War I Document Archive Website, <http://www.lib.byu.edu/~rdh/wwi/1914m/allyahg.html>.

The Three Emperors' League (June 18, 1881)

The Courts of Austria-Hungary, of Germany, and of Russia, animated by an equal desire to consolidate the general peace by an understanding intended to assure the defensive position of their respective States, have come into agreement on certain questions * * *

ARTICLE 1. In case one of the High Contracting Parties should find itself at war with a fourth Great Power, the two others shall maintain towards it a benevolent neutrality and shall devote their efforts to the localization of the conflict.

This stipulation shall apply likewise to a war between one of the three Powers and Turkey, but only in the case where a previous agreement shall have been reached between the three Courts as to the results of this war.

*   *   *

ARTICLE 2. Russia, in agreement with Germany, declares her firm resolution to respect the interests arising from the new position assured to Austria-Hungary by the Treaty of Berlin.

The three Courts, desirous of avoiding all discord between them, engage to take account of their respective interests in the Balkan Peninsula. They further promise one another that any new modifications in the territorial status quo of Turkey in Europe can be accomplished only in virtue of a common agreement between them.

*   *   *

ARTICLE 3. The three Courts recognize the European and mutually obligatory character of the principle of the closing of the Straits of the Bosporus and of the Dardanelles * * *

They will take care in common that Turkey shall make no exception to this rule in favor of

From *Renewal of the Three Emperors' League (June 18, 1881), ibid.*, <http://www.lib.byu.edu/~rdh/wwi/1914m/liga3.html>.

the interests of any Government whatsoever, by lending to warlike operations of a belligerent Power the portion of its Empire constituted by the Straits.

*   *   *

ARTICLE 4. The present Treaty shall be in force during a period of three years, dating from the day of the exchange of ratifications.

*   *   *

Separate Protocol * * *

1. Bosnia and Herzegovina. Austria-Hungary reserves the right to annex these provinces at whatever moment she shall deem opportune.

*   *   *

3. Eastern Rumelia. The three Powers agree in regarding the eventuality of an occupation either of Eastern Rumelia or of the Balkans as full of perils for the general peace. In case this should occur, they will employ their efforts to dissuade the Porte [Ottoman Empire] from such an enterprise, it being well understood that Bulgaria and Eastern Rumelia on their part are to abstain from provoking the Porte by attacks emanating from their territories against the other provinces of the Ottoman Empire.

*   *   *

The Triple Alliance Between Austria-Hungary, Germany, and Italy (May 20, 1882)

ARTICLE 1. The High Contracting Parties mutually promise peace and friendship, and will enter into no alliance or engagement directed against any one of their States.

From *The Triple Alliance Between Austria-Hungary, Germany, and Italy (May 20, 1882)*, The World War I Document Archive Website, <http://www.lib.byu.edu/~rdh/wwi/1914m/tripally.html>.

They engage to proceed to an exchange of ideas on political and economic questions of a general nature which may arise, and they further promise one another mutual support within the limits of their own interests.

ARTICLE 2. In case Italy, without direct provocation on her part, should be attacked by France for any reason whatsoever, the two other Contracting Parties shall be bound to lend help and assistance with all their forces to the Party attacked.

This same obligation shall devolve upon Italy in case of any aggression without direct provocation by France against Germany.

ARTICLE 3. If one, or two, of the High Contracting Parties, without direct provocation on their part, should chance to be attacked and to be engaged in a war with two or more Great Powers non-signatory to the present Treaty, the *casus foederis* [event activating the alliance] will arise simultaneously for all the High Contracting Parties.

ARTICLE 4. In case a Great Power non-signatory to the present Treaty should threaten the security of the states of one of the High Contracting Parties, and the threatened Party should find itself forced on that account to make war against it, the two others bind themselves to observe towards their Ally a benevolent neutrality. Each of them reserves to itself, in this case, the right to take part in the war, if it should see fit, to make common cause with its Ally.

ARTICLE 5. * * *

They engage henceforward, in all cases of common participation in a war, to conclude neither armistice, nor peace, nor treaty, except by common agreement among themselves.

ARTICLE 6. The High Contracting Parties mutually promise secrecy as to the contents and existence of the present Treaty.

ARTICLE 7. The present Treaty shall remain in force during the space of five years, dating from the day of the exchange of ratifications.

The Reinsurance Treaty Between Germany and Russia (18 June 1887)

The Imperial Courts of Germany and of Russia, animated by an equal desire to strengthen the general peace by an understanding destined to assure the defensive position of their respective States, have resolved to confirm the agreement established between them by a special arrangement, in view of the expiration on June 15/27, 1887, of the validity of the secret Treaty and Protocol, signed in 1881 and renewed in 1884 by the three courts of Germany Russia, and Austria-Hungary.

ARTICLE 1. In case one of the High Contracting Parties should find itself at war with a third Great Power, the other would maintain a benevolent neutrality towards it, and would devote its efforts to the localization of the conflict. This provision would not apply to a war against Austria or France in case this war should result from an attack directed against one of these two latter Powers by one of the High Contracting Parties.

ARTICLE 2. Germany recognizes the rights historically acquired by Russia in the Balkan Peninsula, and particularly the legitimacy of her preponderant and decisive influence in Bulgaria and in Eastern Rumelia. The two Courts engage to admit no modification of the territorial status quo of the said peninsula without a previous agreement between them, and to oppose, as occasion arises, every attempt to disturb this status quo or to modify it without their consent.

ARTICLE 3. The two Courts recognize the European and mutually obligatory character of the principle of the closing of the Straits of the Bosporus and of the Dardanelles * * *

They will take care in common that Turkey shall make no exception to this rule * * *

Additional Protocol * * *

*   *   *

1. Germany, as in the past, will lend her assistance to Russia in order to reestablish a regular and legal government in Bulgaria * * *

2. In case His Majesty the Emperor of Russia should find himself under the necessity of assuming the task of defending the entrance of the Black Sea in order to safeguard the interests of Russia, Germany engages to accord her benevolent neutrality and her moral and diplomatic support to the measures which His Majesty may deem it necessary to take to guard the key of His Empire.

*   *   *

The Franco-Russian Alliance Military Convention (18 August 1892)

France and Russia, being animated by a common desire to preserve peace, and having no other object than to meet the necessities of a defensive war, provoked by an attack of the forces of the Triple Alliance against either of them, have agreed upon the following provisions:

1. If France is attacked by Germany, or by Italy supported by Germany, Russia shall employ all her available forces to attack Germany.

If Russia is attacked by Germany, or by Austria supported by Germany, France shall employ all her available forces to attack Germany.

2. In case the forces of the Triple Alliance, or of any one of the Powers belonging to it, should be mobilized, France and Russia, at the first news of this event and without previous agreement being necessary, shall mobilize immediately and simultaneously the whole of their forces, and shall

transport them as far as possible to their frontiers.

3. The available forces to be employed against Germany shall be, on the part of France, 1,300,000 men, on the part of Russia, 700,000 or 800,000 men.

These forces shall engage to the full with such speed that Germany will have to fight simultaneously on the East and on the West.

4. The General Staffs of the Armies of the two countries shall cooperate with each other at all times in the preparation and facilitation of the execution of the measures mentioned above.

*   *   *

5. France and Russia shall not conclude peace separately.

6. The present Convention shall have the same duration as the Triple Alliance.

*   *   *

Declaration between the United Kingdom and France Respecting Egypt and Morocco (8 April, 1904)

ARTICLE 1. His Britannic Majesty's Government declare that they have no intention of altering the political status of Egypt.

The Government of the French Republic, for their part, declare that they will not obstruct the action of Great Britain in that country * * *

*   *   *

ARTICLE 2. The Government of the French Republic declare that they have no intention of altering the political status of Morocco.

His Britannic Majesty's Government, for their part, recognise that it appertains to France, more

particularly as a Power whose dominions are conterminous for a great distance with those of Morocco, to preserve order in that country * * *

*   *   *

ARTICLE 6. In order to ensure the free passage of the Suez Canal, His Britannic Majesty's Government declare that they adhere to the treaty of the 29th October, 1888, and that they agree to their being put in force. * * *

ARTICLE 7. In order to secure the free passage of the Straits of Gibraltar, the two Governments agree not to permit the erection of any fortifications or strategic works on that portion of the coast of Morocco comprised between, but not including, Melilla and the heights which command the right bank of the River Sebou.

*   *   *

ARTICLE 9. The two Governments agree to afford to one another their diplomatic support, in order to obtain the execution of the clauses of the present Declaration regarding Egypt and Morocco.

Secret Articles

ARTICLE 1. In the event of either Government finding themselves constrained, by the force of circumstances, to modify their policy in respect to Egypt or Morocco, the engagements which they have undertaken towards each other by Articles 4, 6, and 7 of the Declaration of today's date would remain intact.

ARTICLE 2. His Britannic Majesty's Government have no present intention of proposing to the Powers any changes in the system of the Capitulations, or in the judicial organisation of Egypt.

In the event of their considering it desirable to introduce in Egypt reforms tending to assimilate the Egyptian legislative system to that in force in other civilised Countries, the Government of the French Republic will not refuse to entertain any such proposals, on the understanding that His Britannic Majesty's Government will agree to entertain the suggestions that the Government of the

From *Declaration Between the United Kingdom and France Respecting Egypt and Morocco (8 April, 1904)*, The World War I Document Archive Website, <http://www.lib.byu.edu/~rdh/wwi/1914m/entecord.html>.

French Republic may have to make to them with a view of introducing similar reforms in Morocco.

* * *

The Anglo-Russian Entente (1907)

The Governments of Great Britain and Russia having mutually engaged to respect the integrity and independence of Persia, and sincerely desiring the preservation of order throughout that country and its peaceful development, as well as the permanent establishment of equal advantages for the trade and industry of all other nations;

Considering that each of them has, for geographical and economic reasons, a special interest in the maintenance of peace and order in certain provinces of Persia adjoining, or in the neighborhood of, the Russian frontier on the one hand, and the frontiers of Afghanistan and Baluchistan on the other hand; and being desirous of avoiding all cause of conflict between their respective interests in the above-mentioned provinces of Persia;

Have agreed on the following terms:—

I. Great Britain engages not to seek for herself, and not to support in favour of British subjects, or in favour of the subjects of third Powers, any Concessions of a political or commercial nature— such as Concessions for railways, banks, telegraphs, roads, transport, insurance, etc.—beyond a line starting from Kasr-i-Shirin, passing through Isfahan, Yezd, Kakhk, and ending at a point on the Persian frontier at the intersection of the Russian and Afghan frontiers, and not to oppose, directly or indirectly, demands for similar Concessions in this region which are supported by the Russian Government. It is understood that the

above-mentioned places are included in the region in which Great Britain engages not to seek the Concessions referred to.

II. Russia, on her part, engages not to seek for herself and not to support, in favour of Russian subjects, or in favour of the subjects of third Powers, any Concessions of a political or commercial nature—such as Concessions for railways, banks, telegraphs, roads, transport, insurance, etc.—beyond a line going from the Afghan frontier by way of Gazik, Birjand, Kerman, and ending at Bunder Abbas, and not to oppose, directly or indirectly, demands for similar Concessions in this region which are supported by the British Government. It is understood that the above-mentioned places are included in the region in which Russia engages not to seek the Concessions referred to.

III. Russia, on her part, engages not to oppose, without previous arrangement with Great Britain, the grant of any Concessions whatever to British subjects in the regions of Persia situated between the lines mentioned in Articles I and II. Great Britain undertakes a similar engagement as regards the grant of Concessions to Russian subjects in the same regions of Persia.

* * *

REVIEW QUESTIONS

1. What advantages did each of the Great Powers expect to derive from the signing of these treaties?
2. What responsibilities did they accept in exchange for these advantages?
3. Why were these treaties kept secret?
4. What impact do you think this secrecy had on international relations in the years prior to 1914?
5. What role did the desire for territorial expansion—whether in Europe or elsewhere—play in the framing of these treaties?
6. How did colonial issues affect relations between the Great Powers?

From *The Anglo-Russian Entente (1907)*, The World War I Document Archive Website, <http://www.lib.byu.edu/~rdh/wwi/1914m/anglruss.html>.

FRIEDRICH VON BERNHARDI

FROM *Germany and the Next War*

The goal of the diplomats who met at the Congress of Vienna in 1814 and 1815 was to create a "Concert of Europe," a system by which international conflicts might be settled through peaceful arbitration and a harmonious "balance of power" maintained. After a long generation of Napoleonic warfare, most Europeans were convinced that peace was preferable to war. However, in the years following the Franco-Prussian War of 1870–1871, new cultural attitudes toward warfare emerged, incited by international competition for colonies and by increasingly tense relations between the European Great Powers. Social Darwinists (see Chapter 24) promoted the idea that war was a natural form of "race hygiene" acting to weed out unfit nations in the international struggle for survival.

In 1913, Friedrich von Bernhardi (1849–1930), a career military officer and former member of the German General Staff, published Germany and the Next War, *the second of a two volume series on modern warfare. Bernhardi rejected pacifism as outdated and unscientific, and criticized the German authorities for failing to maximize Germany's military preparedness, both in anticipation of an attack by another great power or for the purposes of territorial expansion. The book was enthusiastically received by German nationalists, but it was also widely read in translation throughout Europe. While Bernhardi's enthusiasm for war took an extreme form—and was not broadly representative of attitudes among the German officer corps or political leadership—it gave expression to a current of militant nationalism pervading broad sectors of European society.*

From *Germany and the Next War*, General Friedrich von Bernhardi, translated by Allen H. Powles, Longman's, 1914.

Chapter 1
The Right to Make War

* * * Long periods of war, far from convincing men of the necessity of war, have, on the contrary, always revived the wish to exclude war, where possible, from the political intercourse of nations.

This wish and this hope are widely disseminated even today. The maintenance of peace is lauded as the only goal at which statesmanship should aim. This unqualified desire for peace has obtained in our days a quite peculiar power over men's spirits. This aspiration finds its public expression in peace leagues and peace congresses; the Press of every country and of every party opens its columns to it. The current in this direction is, indeed, so strong that the majority of Governments profess—outwardly, at any rate—that the necessity of maintaining peace is the real aim of their policy; while when a war breaks out the aggressor is universally stigmatized, and all Governments exert themselves, partly in reality, partly in pretense, to extinguish the conflagration.

*   *   *

This desire for peace has rendered most civilized nations anemic, and marks a decay of spirit and political courage* * *

Everyone will, within certain limits, admit that the endeavors to diminish the dangers of war and to mitigate the sufferings which war entails are justifiable. It is an incontestable fact that war temporarily disturbs industrial life, interrupts quiet economic development, brings widespread misery with it, and emphasizes the primitive brutality of man. It is therefore a most desirable consummation if wars for trivial reasons should be rendered impossible, and if efforts are made to restrict the evils which follow necessarily in the train of war, so far as is compatible with the essential nature of war. * * * But it is quite another matter if the object is to abolish war entirely, and to deny its necessary place in historical development.

This aspiration is directly antagonistic to the great universal laws which rule all life. War is a biological necessity of the first importance, a regulative element in the life of mankind which cannot be dispensed with, since without it an unhealthy development will follow, which excludes every advancement of the race, and therefore all real civilization. "War is the father of all things." (Heraclitus) The sages of antiquity long before Darwin recognized this.

The struggle for existence is, in the life of Nature, the basis of all healthy development. All existing things show themselves to be the result of contesting forces. So in the life of man the struggle is not merely the destructive, but the life-giving principle. "To supplant or to be supplanted is the essence of life," says Goethe, and the strong life gains the upper hand. The law of the stronger holds good everywhere. Those forms survive which are able to procure themselves the most favorable conditions of life, and to assert themselves in the universal economy of Nature. The weaker succumb. This struggle is regulated and restrained by the unconscious sway of biological laws and by the interplay of opposite forces. In the plant world and the animal world this process is worked out in unconscious tragedy. In the human race it is consciously carried out, and regulated by social ordinances. The man of strong will and strong intellect tries by every means to assert himself, the ambitious strive to rise, and in this effort the individual is far from being guided merely by the consciousness of right. The life-work and the life-struggle of many men are determined, doubtless, by unselfish and ideal motives, but to a far greater extent the less noble passions—craving for possessions, enjoyment and honor, envy and the thirst for revenge—determine men's actions. Still more often, perhaps, it is the need to live which brings down even natures of a higher mold into the universal struggle for existence and enjoyment.

There can be no doubt on this point. The nation is made up of individuals, the state of communities. The motive which influences each member is prominent in the whole body. It is a persistent struggle for possessions, power, and sovereignty, which primarily governs the relations of one nation to another, and right is respected so far only as it is compatible with advantage. So long as there are men who have human feelings and aspirations, so long as there are nations who strive for an enlarged sphere of activity, so long will conflicting interests come into being and occasions for making war arise.

*   *   *

Strong, healthy, and flourishing nations increase in numbers. From a given moment they require a continual expansion of their frontiers, they require new territory for the accommodation of their surplus population. Since almost every part of the globe is inhabited, new territory must, as a rule be obtained at the cost of its possessors —that is today, by conquest, which thus becomes a law of necessity.

*   *   *

Chapter 5
World Power or Downfall

* * * We see the European Great Powers divided into two great camps. * * * on the continent of Europe the power of the Central European Triple Alliance and that of the states united against it by alliance and agreement balance each other, provided that Italy belongs to the league. If we take into calculation the imponderabilia, whose weight can only be guessed at, the scale is inclined slightly in favor of the Triple Alliance. On the other hand, England indisputably rules the sea. In consequence of her crushing naval superiority when allied with France, and of the geographical conditions, she may cause the greatest damage to Germany by cutting off her maritime trade. There is also a not inconsiderable army available for a continental war. When all considerations are taken into account, our opponents have a political superiority not to be underestimated. If France succeeds in strengthening her army by large colonial levies and a strong English landing-force, this superiority would be asserted on land also. If Italy really withdraws from the Triple Alliance, very distinctly superior forces will be united against Germany and Austria.

Under these conditions the position of Germany is extraordinarily difficult. We not only require for the full material development of our nation, on a scale corresponding to its intellectual importance, an extended political basis, but * * * we are compelled to obtain space for our increasing population and markets for our growing industries. But at every step which we take in this direction England will resolutely oppose us. English policy may not yet have made the definite decision to attack us; but it doubtless wishes, by all and every means, even the most extreme, to hinder every further expansion of German international influence and of German maritime power. The recognized political aims of England and the attitude of the English Government leave no doubt on this point. But if we were involved in a struggle with England, we can be quite sure that France would not neglect the opportunity of attacking our flank. Italy, with her extensive coast line, even if still a member of the Triple Alliance, will have to devote large forces to the defense of the coast to keep off the attacks of the Anglo-French Mediterranean Fleet, and would thus be only able to employ weaker forces against France. Austria would be paralyzed by Russia; against the latter we should have to leave forces in the East. We should thus have to fight out the struggle against France and England practically alone with a part of our army, perhaps with some support from Italy. It is in this double menace by sea and on the mainland of Europe that the grave danger to our political position lies, since all freedom of action is taken from us and all expansion barred.

*   *   *

We have fought in the last great wars for our national union and our position among the Powers of Europe; we now must decide whether we wish to develop into and maintain a World Empire, and procure for German spirit and German ideas that fit recognition which has been hitherto withheld from them.

Have we the energy to aspire to that great goal? Are we prepared to make the sacrifices which such an effort will doubtless cost us? or are we willing to recoil before the hostile forces, and sink step by step lower in our economic, political, and national importance? That is what is involved in our decision.

*   *   *

Chapter 9
The Crucial Question

*   *   *

France has at present day a population of some 40,000,000; Russia in Europe, with Poland and the Caucasus, has a population of 140,000,000. Contrasted with this, Germany has only 65,000,000 inhabitants. But since the Russian military forces are, to a great extent, hampered by very various causes and cannot be employed at any one time or place, and are also deficient in military value, a German army which corresponded to the population would be certainly in a position to defend itself successfully against its two enemies, if it operated resolutely on the inner line, even though England took part in the war.

Disastrously for ourselves, we have become disloyal to the idea of universal military service, and have apparently definitely discontinued to carry it out effectively. The country where universal service exists is now France. With us, indeed, it is still talked about, but it is only kept up in pretense, for in reality 50 per cent., perhaps, of the able-bodied are called up for training. In particular, very little use has been made of the larger towns as recruiting-grounds for the army.

*   *   *

In a future European war "masses" will be employed to an extent unprecedented in any previous one. Weapons will be used whose deadliness will exceed all previous experience. More effective and varied means of communication will be available than were know in earlier wars. These three momentous factors will make the war of the future.

"Masses" signify in themselves an increase of strength, but they contain elements of weakness as well. The larger they are and the less they can be commanded by professional soldiers, the more their tactical efficiency diminishes. The less they are able to live on the country during war time, especially when concentrated, and the more they are therefore dependent on the daily renewal of food supplies, the slower and less mobile they become. Owing to the great space which they require for their deployment, it is extraordinarily difficult to bring them into effective action simultaneously. They are also far more accessible to morally depressing influences than compacted bodies of troops, and may prove dangerous to the strategy of their own leaders, if supplies run short, if discipline breaks down, and the commander loses his authority over the masses which he can only rule under regulated conditions.

The increased effectiveness of weapons does not merely imply a longer range, but a greater deadliness, and therefore makes more exacting claims on the morale of the soldier. The danger zone begins sooner than formerly; the space which must be crossed in an attack has become far wider; it must be passed by the attacking party creeping or running. The soldier must often use the spade in defensive operations, during which he is exposed to a far hotter fire than formerly; while under all circumstances he must shoot more than in bygone days. The quick firing which the troops encounter increases the losses at every incautious movement. All branches of arms have to suffer under these circumstances. Shelter and supplies will be more scanty than ever before. In short, while the troops on the average have diminished in value, the demands made on them have become considerably greater.

Improved means of communication, finally, facilitate the handling and feeding of large masses, but tie them down to railway systems and main roads, and must, if they fail or break down in the course of a campaign, aggravate the difficulties, because the troops were accustomed to their use, and the commanders counted upon them.

The direct conclusion to be drawn from these reflections is that a great superiority must rest with the troops whose fighting capabilities and tactical efficiency are greater than those of their antagonists.

The commander who can carry out all operations quicker than the enemy, and can concentrate and employ greater masses in a narrow space than they can, will always be in a position to collect a numerically superior force in the decisive direction; if he controls the more effective troops, he will gain decisive successes against one part of the hostile army, and will be able to exploit them against other divisions of it before the enemy can gain equivalent advantages in other parts of the field.

Since the tactical efficiency and the morale of the troops are chiefly shown in the offensive, and are then most needful, the necessary conclusion is that safety only lies in offensive warfare.

*   *   *

We arrive, then, at the conclusion that, in order to secure the superiority in a war of the future under otherwise equal conditions, it is incumbent upon us: First, during the period of preparation to raise the tactical value and capabilities of the troops as much as possible, and especially to develop the means of concealing the attacking movements and damaging the enemy's tactical powers; secondly, in the war itself to act on the offensive and strike the first blow, and to exploit the maneuvering capacity of the troops as much as possible, in order to be superior in the decisive directions. Above all, a state which has objects to attain that cannot be relinquished, and is exposed to attacks by enemies more powerful than itself, is bound to act in this sense. It must, before all things, develop the attacking powers of its army, since a strategic defensive must often adopt offensive methods.* * *

everywhere in the wars of today, more than in any other ages, personality dominates all else. The effect of mass tactics has abolished all close formations of infantry, and the individual is left to himself.* * *

It has often been said that one man is as good as another; that personality is nothing, the type is everything; but this assertion is erroneous. In time of peace, when sham reputations flourish and no real struggle winnows the chaff from the wheat, mediocrity in performance is enough. But in war, personality turns the scale. Responsibility and danger bring out personality, and show its real worth, as surely as a chemical test separates the pure metal from the dross.

REVIEW QUESTIONS

1. Why, according to Bernhardi, is war necessary to the progress of nation-states?
2. Why must Germany prepare for war?
3. Based on Bernhardi's discussion of military strategy, what might one expect the "next war" to look like?

FROM The Constitution of the Black Hand

Pervasive militarism and a complex web of alliance treaties both served to produce a cultural and diplomatic climate conducive to the outbreak of international warfare. But the immediate cause of the First World War, the spark that lit the powder keg, was the assassination of Archduke Franz Ferdinand by Gavrilo Princip, a young Bosnian Serb linked to "Unification or Death," a secret nationalist organization.

Better known by the name the "Black Hand," Unification or Death was founded in 1911 by Dragutin Dimitrijevic (1876–1917), an army officer and military academy professor. Its ambition was to create a Greater Serbia, an ethnic-based state made up of all Balkan territories containing Serbian populations, a goal which necessarily set the Black Hand at odds with both the Austro-Hungarian and Ottoman empires. A powerful force within the Serbian military, the Black Hand used propaganda and terrorism to further its ends. Its constitution demonstrates the means by which Dimitrijevic and his co-conspirators sought to create a disciplined secret organization made up of Serbian patriots fiercely committed to the nationalist cause.

From *The Constitution of the Ujedinjenje ili Smrt: Unification or Death*, The World War I Document Archive Website, <http://www.lib.byu.edu/~rdh/wwi/1914m/blk-cons.html>.

The Constitution of Unification or Death

I. Purpose and Name

Article 1. For the purpose of realising the national ideals—the Unification of Serbdom—an organization is hereby created, whose members may be any Serbian irrespective of sex, religion, place or birth, as well as anybody else who will sincerely serve this idea.

Article 2. The organisation gives priority to the revolutionary struggle rather than relies on cultural striving, therefore its institution is an absolutely secret one for wider circles.

Article 3. The organization bears the name: "*Ujedinjenje ili Smrt*" ("Unification or Death").

Article 4. In order to carry into effect its task the organization will do the following things:

*   *   *

(2) It will carry out a revolutionary organisation in all the territories where Serbians are living:

(3) Beyond the frontiers, it will fight with all means against all enemies of this idea:

(4) It will maintain friendly relations with all the States, nations, organisations, and individual persons who sympathise with Serbia and the Serbian race:

(5) It will give every assistance to those nations and organisations who are fighting for their own national liberation and unification.

II. Official Departments of the Organisation

*   *   *

Article 7. The Supreme Central Directorate shall include, in addition to the members from the Kingdom of Serbia, one accredited delegate from each of the organisations of all the Serbian regions: (1) Bosnia and Herzegovina, (2) Montenegro, (3) Old Serbia and Macedonia, (4) Croatia, Slovenia and Symria (Srem), (5) Voyvodina, (6) Sea-coasts.

Article 8. It will be the task of the Supreme Central Directorate to carry out the principles of the organisation within the territory of the Kingdom of Serbia.

*   *   *

III. The Members of the Organisation

Article 23. The following rule, as a principle, shall govern all the detailed transactions of the organisation: All communications and conversations to be conducted only through specially appointed and authorised persons.

Article 24. It shall be the duty of every member to recruit new members, but it shall be understood that every introducing member shall vouch with his own life for all those whom he introduces into the organisation.

Article 25. The members of the organisation as amongst themselves shall not be known to one another. Only the members of Directorates shall be known personally to one another.

Article 26. In the organisation the members shall be registered and known by their respective numbers. But the Supreme Central Directorate must know them also by their respective names.

Article 27. The members of the organisation must unconditionally obey all the commands given by their respective Directorates, as also all the Directorates must obey unconditionally the commands which they receive direct from their superior Directorate.

Article 28. Every member shall be obliged to impart officially to the organisation whatever comes to his knowledge, either in his private life or in the discharge of his official duties, in as far as it may be of interest to the organisation.

Article 29. The interest of the organisation shall stand above all other interests.

Article 30. On entering into the organisation, every member must know that by joining the organisation he loses his own personality; he must not expect any glory for himself, nor any personal benefit, material or moral. Consequently the member who should dare to try to exploit the organisation for his personal, or class, or party interests shall be punished by death.

Article 31. Whosoever has once entered into the organisation can never by any means leave it, nor shall anybody have the authority to accept the resignation of a member.

Article 32. Every member shall support the organisation by his weekly contributions. The organisations, however, shall have the authority to procure money, if need be, by coercion. The permission to resort to these means may be given only by Supreme Central Directorate within the country, or by the regional Directorates within their respective region.

Article 33. In administering capital punishment the sole responsibility of the Supreme Central Directorate shall be to see that such punishment is safely and unfailingly carried into effect without any regard for the ways and means to be employed in the execution.

IV. The Seal and the Oath of Allegiance

Article 34. The Organisation's official seal is thus composed: In the centre of the seal there is a powerful arm holding in its hand an unfurled flag on which—as a coat of arms—there is a skull with crossed bones; by the side of the flag, a knife, a bomb and a phial of poison. Around, in a circle, there is the following inscription, reading from left to right: "Unification or Death", and in the base: "The Supreme Central Directorate".

Article 35. On entering into the organisation the joining member must pronounce the following oath of allegiance:

"I (the Christian name and surname of the joining member), by entering into the organisation "Unification or Death", do hereby swear by the Sun which shineth upon me, by the Earth which feedeth me, by God, by the blood of my forefathers, by my honour and by my life, that from this moment onward and until my death, I shall faithfully serve the task of this organisation and that I shall at all times be prepared to bear for it any sacrifice. I further swear by God, by my honour and by my life, that I shall unconditionally carry into effect all its orders and commands. I further swear by my God, by my honour and by my life, that I shall keep within myself all the secrets of this organisation and carry them with me into my grave. May God and my comrades in this organisation be my judges if at any time I should wittingly fail or break this oath!"

*   *   *

Done at Belgrade this 9th day of May, 1911 A.D.

*   *   *

REVIEW QUESTIONS

1. Why was the Black Hand a secret organization?
2. What means did its organizers use to insure that this secrecy be preserved?
3. On the basis of this document, what sort of actions would you expect members of the Black Hand to perform in pursuit of their nationalist objectives?

26 ⮂ THE FIRST WORLD WAR

The assassination of Archduke Franz Ferdinand in Sarajevo in 1914 unleashed a cataclysm of unparalleled magnitude. For four years the European combatants and their allies confronted one another in a war of global dimensions. By 1918 millions of soldiers had been killed on the battlefront, and the lives of civilians living behind the lines on the home front had been unalterably disrupted.

Europeans initially responded to the outbreak of war with jubilation and enthusiasm. Young men rushed to enlist, worried that the war—which everyone expected to be over by Christmas—would end before they could reach the front lines. But soldiers who had yearned for high drama and the chance to prove what one poet-soldier called their "untested manhood" soon discovered the sullen face of modern warfare. The ideal of personal heroism wilted as soldiers alternated between long drab days spent huddling in the trenches and brief but murderous bouts of combat. The new technologies of war, especially the machine gun and heavy artillery, reduced the individual soldier to insignificance, making a mockery of his bravery and leading him to fear not only the clean death brought by bullets, but the utter annihilation of being blown to bits or the long, drawn out agony of gas poisoning. For those who survived this ordeal, the "Great War" was a fundamental experience, forever separating them from the pre-war world—and from non-combatants—and leaving deep physical and psychological scars.

Although civilians were protected from the worst horrors of the trenches, they too were deeply affected by the war. The lines between the home front and the battlefront blurred as production of armaments and munitions made civilian workers crucial to the military effort and as government-sponsored propaganda campaigns encouraged noncombatants to do their part for the war effort. While the war brought hardships to civilians, it also brought new opportunities and even adventure, especially to young women who were suddenly freed from the restraints of pre-war society.

When the war ended, Europeans were eager to believe that they had, in fact, fought "the war to end all wars." But the end of hostilities did not bring an end to the trauma and dislocation occasioned by the war. The peace settlement itself, promoted by its framers as a new, more hopeful beginning, was widely condemned as an inadequate guarantee of international security and stability.

The Trench Poets of World War I

The outbreak of World War I inspired a spate of poetry; one historian estimates that more than one million poems were written in 1914 alone. Like Rupert Brooke (1887–1915), many poets initially greeted the war as a release from the dreariness of civilian life. Educated at Cambridge, Brooke's finely crafted and idealistic wartime poems, especially the sonnet series "1914," earned him lasting fame. However, as the war dragged on, soldier-poets' initial enthusiasm gave way to resignation. The stately verse of Alan Seeger (1888–1916), an American educated at Harvard, reflects the new acceptance of the tragic inevitability of death.

Some poets eventually expressed their outrage at the cost of the war. British poet Wilfred Owen (1893–1918), a graduate of the University of London, condemned the older generation that had allowed the war to happen and that was now refusing to end the slaughter of "half the seed of Europe, one by one." Owen's "Dulce et Decorum est," perhaps the most famous of all World War I poems, is noteworthy not only for its antiwar sentiments, but also for its stylistic innovation. The same disenchantment and modernist tone is found in "Trench Poets," written by a lesser known British author, John Edgell Rickword (1898–1982). Of the four poets whose verse is reproduced here, only Rickword survived the war.

From *The Collected Poems*, Rupert Brooke, edited by George E. Woodbury, John Lane Co., 1916.

Rupert Brooke
FROM "1914"

I. PEACE

Now, God be thanked Who has matched us with
    His hour,
  And caught our youth, and wakened us from
    sleeping,

With hand made sure, clear eye, and sharpened
    power,
  To turn, as swimmers into cleanness leaping,
Glad from a world grown old and cold and
    weary,
  Leave the sick hearts that honour could not
    move,
And half-men, and their dirty songs and dreary,
  And all the little emptiness of love!

Oh! we, who have known shame, we have found
   release there,
    Where there's no ill, no grief, but sleep has
     mending,
      Naught broken save this body, lost but
      breath;
Nothing to shake the laughing heart's long peace
   there
    But only agony, and that has ending;
     And the worst friend and enemy is but
     Death.

*   *   *

V. THE SOLDIER

If I should die, think only this of me:
   That there's some corner of a foreign field
That is for ever England. There shall be
   In that rich earth a richer dust concealed;
A dust whom England bore, shaped, made
    aware,
   Gave, once, her flowers to love, her ways to
    roam,
A body of England's, breathing English air,
   Washed by the rivers, blest by suns of home.

And think, this heart, all evil shed away,
   A pulse in the eternal mind, no less
    Gives somewhere back the thoughts by
    England given;
Her sights and sounds; dreams happy as her day;
   And laughter, learnt of friends; and gentleness,
    In hearts at peace, under an English heaven.

*   *   *

Alan Seeger
"Rendezvous"

I have a rendezvous with Death
At some disputed barricade,
I have a rendezvous with Death

At some disputed barricade,
When Spring comes back with rustling shade
And apple-blossoms fill the air—
I have a rendezvous with Death
When Spring brings back blue days and fair.

It may be he shall take my hand
And lead me into his dark land
And close my eyes and quench my breath—
It may be I shall pass him still.
I have a rendezvous with Death
On some scarred slope of battered hill,
When Spring comes round again this year
And the first meadow-flowers appear.

God knows 'twere better to be deep
Pillowed in silk and scented down,
Where love throbs out in blissful sleep,
Pulse nigh to pulse, and breath to breath,
Where hushed awakenings are dear . . .
But I've a rendezvous with Death
At midnight in some flaming town,
When Spring trips north again this year,
And I to my pledged word am true,
I shall not fail that rendezvous.

Wilfred Owen
"Dulce et decorum est"

Bent double, like old beggars under sacks,
Knock-kneed, coughing like hags, we cursed
    through sludge,
Till on the haunting flares we turned our backs
And towards our distant rest began to trudge.
Men marched asleep. Many had lost their boots
But limped on, blood-shod. All went lame; all
    blind;
Drunk with fatigue; deaf even to the hoots
Of tired, outstripped Five-Nines that dropped
    behind.

Gas! GAS! Quick, boys!

From *Poems*, Alan Seeger, Scribner's, 1916.

From *Poems*, Wilfred Owen, B. W. Huebsch, 1921.

An ecstasy of fumbling,
Fitting the clumsy helmets just in time;
But someone still was yelling out and stumbling,
And flound'ring like a man in fire or lime . . .
Dim, through the misty panes and thick green
    light,
As under a green sea, I saw him drowning.
In all my dreams, before my helpless sight,
He plunges at me, guttering, choking, drowning.
If in some smothering dreams you too could
    pace
Behind the wagon that we flung him in,
And watch the white eyes writhing in his face,
His hanging face, like a devil's sick of sin;
If you could hear, at every jolt, the blood
Come gargling from the froth-corrupted lungs,
Obscene as cancer, bitter as the cud
Of vile, incurable sores on innocent tongues,
My friend, you would not tell with such high
    zest
To children ardent for some desperate glory,
The old Lie: *Dulce et decorum est*
Pro patria mori[1]

Edgell Rickword
"Trench Poets"

I knew a man, he was my chum,
but he grew blacker every day,
and would not brush the flies away,
nor blanch however fierce the hum
of passing shells; I used to read,
to rouse him, random things from Donne[2]—

___

[1] "It is sweet and fitting to die for one's country." A line
   taken from the *Odes* of Horace (65–8 B.C.E.).
From *Behind the Eyes*, Edgell Rickword, Sidgwick and
Jackson, 1921.

[2] John Donne (1572–1631), an English poet of the late
   Renaissance. The citations in this poem are taken from
   Donne's works.

like "Get with child a mandrake-root."
But you can tell he was far gone,
for he lay gaping, mackerel-eyed,
and stiff, and senseless as a post
even when that old poet cried
"I long to talk with some old lover's ghost."

I tried the Elegies one day,
but he, because he heard me say:
"What needst thou have more covering than a
    man?"
grinned nastily, and so I knew
the worms had got his brains at last.
There was one thing that I might do
to starve the worms; I racked my head
for healthy things and quoted Maud.
His grin got worse and I could see
he sneered at passion's purity.
He stank so badly, though we were great chums
I had to leave him; then rats ate his thumbs.

Review Questions

1. Why does Rupert Brooke welcome war?
2. What virtues does he find in death on the
   battlefield?
3. How does this compare with Seeger's attitude
   toward his own impending "rendezvous with
   Death"?
4. How does Wilfred Owen's perception of warfare differ from Brooke's?
5. How do Owen's and Brooke's attitudes about
   patriotism differ?
6. What point about western culture is Edgell
   Rickword trying to make in "Trench Poets"?

HENRI BARBUSSE

FROM *Under Fire: The Story of a Squad*

French author Henri Barbusse (1873–1935) enlisted voluntarily in 1914, but was discharged as a result of battlefield injuries in 1917. Already a successful poet when the war began, Barbusse published Under Fire: The Story of a Squad, *a fictionalized account of his wartime experiences, in 1916. The novel won the Prix Goncourt, the highest French literary honor. Barbusse's antiwar sentiments, evident in the bitter sarcasm of* Under Fire, *inspired him to become a pacifist and to join the Communist Party after the war. He was living in the Soviet Union at the time of his death.*

Under Fire documents the life of the poilu, *the "hairy" French World War I soldier, through a group portrait of a squadron of men drawn from all walks of life. In the following excerpt from the opening of the novel, Barbusse introduces the soldiers and reveals their single, overwhelming preoccupation—the quality of their grub.*

From *Under Fire: The Story of a Squad*, H. Barbusse, translated by Fitzwater Wray, E. P. Dutton, 1917.

*   *   *

Mesnil Joseph drowses; Blaire yawns; Marthereau smokes, "eyes front." Lamuse scratches himself like a gorilla, and Eudore like a marmoset. Volpatte coughs, and says, "I'm kicking the bucket." Mesnil André has got out his mirror and comb and is tending his fine chestnut beard as though it were a rare plant. The monotonous calm is disturbed here and there by the outbreaks of ferocious resentment provoked by the presence of parasites—endemic, chronic, and contagious.

Barque, who is an observant man, sends an itinerant glance around, takes his pipe from his mouth, spits, winks, and says—

"I say, we don't resemble each other much."

"Why should we?" says Lamuse. "It would be a miracle if we did."

*   *   *

Our ages? We are of all ages. Ours is a regiment in reserve which successive reinforcements have renewed partly with fighting units and partly with Territorials. In our half-section there are reservists of the Territorial Army, new recruits, and *demi-poils.* Fouillade is forty; Blaire might be the father of Biquet, who is a gosling of Class 1913. The corporal calls Marthereau "Grandpa" or "Old Rubbish-heap," according as in jest or in earnest. Mesnil Joseph would be at the barracks if there were no war. It is a comical effect when we are in charge of Sergeant Vigile, a nice little boy, with a dab on his lip by way of mustache. When we were in quarters the other day, he played at skipping-rope with the kiddies. In our ill-assorted flock, in this family without kindred, this home without a hearth at which we gather, there are three generations side by side, living, waiting, standing still, like unfinished statues, like posts.

Our races? We are of all races; we come from everywhere. I look at the two men beside me. Poterloo, the miner from the Calonne pit, is pink; his eyebrows are the color of straw, his eyes flax-blue. His great golden head involved a long search in the stores to find the vast steel-blue tureen that bonnets him. Fouillade, the boatman from Cette, rolls his wicked eyes in the long, lean face of a musketeer, with sunken cheeks and his skin the color of a violin. In good sooth, my two neighbors are as unlike as day and night.

Cocon, no less, a slight and desiccated person in spectacles, whose tint tells of corrosion in the chemical vapors of great towns, contrasts with Biquet, a Breton in the rough, whose skin is gray and his jaw like a paving-stone; and Mesnil André, the comfortable chemist from a country town in Normandy, who has such a handsome and silky beard and who talks so much and so well—he has little in common with Lamuse, the fat peasant of Poitou, whose cheeks and neck are like underdone beef. The suburban accent of Barque, whose long legs have scoured the streets of Paris in all directions, alternates with the semi-Belgian cadence of those Northerners who came from the 8th Territorial; with the sonorous speech, rolling on the syllables as if over cobblestone, that the 144th pours out upon us; with the dialect blown from those ant-like clusters that the Auvergnats so obstinately form among the rest. I remember the first words of that wag, Tirette, when he arrived—"I, *mes enfants*, I am from Clichy-la-Garenne! Can any one beat that?"—and the first grievance that Paradis brought to me, "They don't give a damn for me, because I'm from Morvan!"

*   *   *

Our callings? A little of all—in the lump. In those departed days when we had a social status, before we came to immure our destiny in the molehills that we must always build up again as fast as rain and scrap-iron beat them down, what were we? Sons of the soil and artisans mostly. Lamuse was a farm-servant, Paradis a carter. Cadilhac, whose helmet rides loosely on his pointed head, though it is a juvenile size—like a dome on a steeple, says Tirette—owns land. Papa Blaire was a small farmer in La Brie. Barque, porter and mes-

senger, performed acrobatic tricks with his carrier-tricycle among the trams and taxis of Paris, with solemn abuse (so they say) for the pedestrians, fleeing like bewildered hens across the big streets and squares. Corporal Bertrand, who keeps himself always a little aloof, correct, erect, and silent, with a strong and handsome face and forth-right gaze, was foreman in a case-factory. Tirloir daubed carts with paint—and without grumbling, they say. Tulacque was barman at the Throne Tavern in the suburbs; and Eudore of the pale and pleasant face kept a roadside café not very far from the front lines. It has been ill-used by the shells—naturally, for we all know that Eudore has no luck. Mesnil André, who still retains a trace of well-kept distinction, sold bicarbonate and infallible remedies at his pharmacy in a *Grande Place*. His brother Joseph was selling papers and illustrated story-books in a station on the State Railways at the same time that, in far-off Lyons, Cocon, the man of spectacles and statistics, dressed in a black smock, busied himself behind the counters of an ironmongery, his hands glittering with plumbago; while the lamps of Bécuwe Adolphe and Poterloo, risen with the dawn, trailed about the coalpits of the North like weakling Will-o'-th'-wisps.

And there are others amongst us whose occupations one can never recall, whom one confuses with one another; and the rural non-descripts who peddled ten trades at once in their packs, without counting the dubious Pépin, who can have had none at all. (While at the depot after sick leave, three months ago, they say, he got married—to secure the separation allowance.)

The liberal professions are not represented among those around me. Some teachers are subalterns in the company or Red Cross men. In the regiment a Marist Brother is sergeant in the *Service de Santé*; a professional tenor is cyclist dispatch-rider to the Major; a "gentleman of independent means" is mess corporal to the C.H.R. But here there is nothing of all that. We are fighting men, we others, and we include hardly any intellectuals, or men of the arts or of wealth, who during this war will have risked their faces only at the loop-holes, unless in passing by, or under gold-laced caps.

Yes, we are truly and deeply different from each other. But we are alike all the same. In spite of this diversity of age, of country, of education, of position, of everything possible, in spite of the former gulfs that kept us apart, we are in the main alike. Under the same uncouth outlines we conceal and reveal the same ways and habits, the same simple nature of men who have reverted to the state primeval.

The same language, compounded of dialect and the slang of workshop and barracks, seasoned with the latest inventions, blends us in the sauce of speech with the massed multitudes of men who (for seasons now) have emptied France and crowded together in the North-East.

Here, too, linked by a fate from which there is no escape, swept willy-nilly by the vast adventure into one rank, we have no choice but to go as the weeks and months go—alike. The terrible narrowness of the common life binds us close, adapts us, merges us one in the other. It is a sort of fatal contagion. Nor need you, to see how alike we soldiers are, be afar off—at that distance, say, when we are only specks of the dust-clouds that roll across the plain.

We are waiting. Weary of sitting, we get up, our joints creaking like warping wood or old hinges. Damp rusts men as it rusts rifles; more slowly, but deeper. And we begin again, but not in the same way, to wait. In a state of war, one is always waiting. We have become waiting-machines. For the moment it is food we are waiting for. Then it will be the post. But each in its turn. When we have done with dinner we will think about the letters. After that, we shall set ourselves to wait for something else.

Hunger and thirst are urgent instincts which formidably excite the temper of my companions. As the meal gets later they become grumblesome and angry. Their need of food and drink snarls from their lips—

"That's eight o'clock. Now, why the hell doesn't it come?"

*   *   *

"There's the grub!" announces a poilu who was on the look-out at the corner.

"Time, too!"

And the storm of revilings ceases as if by magic. Wrath is changed into sudden contentment.

Three breathless fatigue men, their faces streaming with tears of sweat, put down on the ground some large tins, a paraffin can, two canvas buckets, and a file of loaves, skewered on a stick. Leaning against the wall of the trench, they mop their faces with their handkerchiefs or sleeves. And I see Cocon go up to Pépère with a smile, and forgetful of the abuse he had been heaping on the other's reputation, he stretches out a cordial hand towards one of the cans in the collection that swells the circumference of Pépère after the manner of a life-belt.

"What is there to eat?"

"It's there," is the evasive reply of the second fatigue man, whom experience has taught that a proclamation of the menu always evokes the bitterness of disillusion. So they set themselves to panting abuse of the length and the difficulties of the trip they have just accomplished: "Some crowds about, everywhere! It's a tough job to get along—got to disguise yourself as a cigarette paper, sometimes."—"And there are people who say they're shirkers in the kitchens!" As for *him*, he would a hundred thousand times rather be with the company in the trenches, to mount guard and dig, than earn his keep by *such* a job, twice a day during the night!

Paradis, having lifted the lids of the jars, surveys the recipients and announces, "Kidney beans in oil, bully, pudding, and coffee—that's all."

"*Nom de Dieu!*" bawls Tulacque. "And wine?" He summons the crowd: "Come and look here, all of you! That—that's the limit! We're done out of our wine!"

Athirst and grimacing, they hurry up; and from the profoundest depths of their being wells up the chorus of despair and disappointment, "Oh, Hell!"

"Then what's that in there?" says the fatigue man, still ruddily sweating, and using his foot to point at a bucket.

"Yes," says Paradis, "my mistake, there *is* some."

The fatigue man shrugs his shoulders, and hurls at Paradis a look of unspeakable scorn—"Now you're beginning! Get your gig-lamps on, if your sight's bad." He adds, "One cup each—rather less perhaps—some chucklehead bumped against me, coming through the Boyau du Bois, and a drop got spilled. "Ah!" he hastens to add, raising his voice, "if I hadn't been loaded up, talk about the boot-toe he'd have got in the rump! But he hopped it on his top gear, the brute!"

In spite of this confident assurance, the fatigue man makes off himself, curses overtaking him as he goes, maledictions charged with offensive reflections on his honesty and temperance, imprecations inspired by this revelation of a ration reduced.

All the same, they throw themselves on the food, and eat it standing, squatting, kneeling, sitting on tins, or on haversacks pulled out of the holes where they sleep—or even prone, their backs on the ground, disturbed by passers-by, cursed at and cursing. Apart from these fleeting insults and jests, they say nothing, the primary and universal interest being but to swallow, with their mouths and the circumference thereof as greasy as a rifle-breech. Contentment is theirs.

*   *   *

REVIEW QUESTIONS

1. How different from one another are the soldiers in this squad?
2. What social characteristics do they share?
3. How "democratic" was World War I, according to Barbusse?
4. Why is food so important to these men?
5. What point is Barbusse trying to make about the military experience in this passage?

ERNST JÜNGER

FROM *The Storm of Steel*

German author Ernst Jünger (born 1895) was so eager for adventure that he ran away from home and joined the French Foreign Legion at the age of eighteen. Still only nineteen when World War I was declared, Jünger volunteered immediately and served with considerable distinction as an officer. The Storm of Steel, Jünger's autobiographical account of his life in the trenches, was published in 1920 and is still recognized as one of the great wartime memoirs.

The following excerpt from Storm of Steel *provides a description of the German soldier's experience during the futile but extremely deadly First Battle of the Somme in 1916. In an attempt to relieve the French line during the German assault on Verdun, British and French troops first bombarded the German line north of the Somme River with heavy artillery and then launched an all-out assault. In the course of this battle six-hundred and fifty thousand Germans were killed or wounded; French and British casualties totaled one-hundred and ninety-five thousand and four-hundred and twenty thousand, respectively.*

Ernst Jünger, Basil Creighton, trans., *The Storm of Steel: From the Diary of a German Storm-Troop Officer on the Western Front*. Chatto & Windus, 1929. Reprinted with permission of the publisher.

*   *   *

In the evening we sat up a long while drinking coffee that two Frenchwomen made for us in a neighboring house. It was the strongest drink we could procure. We knew that we were on the verge this time of a battle such as the world had never seen. Soon our excited talk rose to a pitch that would have rejoiced the hearts of any freebooters, or of Frederick's Grenadiers. A few days later there were very few of that party still alive.

Guillemont

On the 23d of August we were transported in lorries to Le Mesnil. Our spirits were excellent, though we knew we were going to be put in where the battle of the Somme was at its worst. Chaff and laughter went from lorry to lorry. We marched from Le Mesnil at dusk to Sailly-Saillisel, and here the battalion dumped packs in a large meadow and paraded in battle order.

Artillery fire of a hitherto unimagined intensity rolled and thundered on our front. Thousands of twitching flashes turned the western horizon into a sea of flowers. All the while the wounded came trailing back with white, dejected faces, huddled into the ditches by the gun and ammunition columns that rattled past.

A man in a steel helmet reported to me as guide to conduct my platoon to the renowned Combles, where for the time we were to be in reserve. Sitting with him at the side of the road, I asked him, naturally enough, what it was like in the line. In reply I heard a monotonous tale of crouching all day in shell holes with no one on either flank and no trenches communicating with the rear, of unceasing attacks, of dead bodies littering the ground, of maddening thirst, of wounded and dying, and of a lot besides. The face half-framed by the steel rim of the helmet was unmoved; the voice accompanied by the sound of battle droned on, and the impression they made on me was one of unearthly solemnity. One could see that the man had been through horror to the limit of despair and there had learned to despise it. Nothing was left but supreme and superhuman indifference.

"Where you fall, there you lie. No one can help you. No one knows whether he will come back alive. They attack every day, but they can't get through. Everybody knows it is life and death."

One can fight such with fellows. We marched on along a broad paved road that showed up in the moonlight as a white band on the dark fields. In front of us the artillery fire rose to a higher and higher pitch. *Lasciate ogni speranza!*[1]

Soon we had the first shells on one side of the road and the other. Talk died down and at last ceased. Everyone listened—with that peculiar intentness that concentrates all thought and sensation in the ear—for the long-drawn howl of the approaching shell. Our nerves had a particularly severe test passing Frégicourt, a little hamlet near Combles cemetery, under continuous fire.

As far as we could see in the darkness, Combles was utterly shot to bits. The damage seemed to be recent, judging from the amount of timber among the ruins and the contents of the houses slung over the road. We climbed over numerous heaps of débris—rather hurriedly, owing to a few shrapnel shells—and reached our quarters. They

---

[1] "Abandon all hope!" These words are written on the gate of Hell in Dante Alighieri's *Inferno*.

were in a large, shot-riddled house. Here I established myself with three sections. The other two occupied the cellar of a ruin opposite.

At 4 A.M. we were aroused from our rest on the fragments of bed we had collected, in order to receive steel helmets. It was also the occasion of discovering a sack of coffee beans in a corner of the cellar; whereupon there followed a great brewing of coffee.

After breakfast I went out to have a look round. Heavy artillery had turned a peaceful little billeting town into a scene of desolation in the course of a day or two. Whole houses had been flattened by single direct hits or blown up so that the interiors of the rooms hung over the chaos like the scenes on a stage. A sickly scent of dead bodies rose from many of the ruins, for many civilians had been caught in the bombardment and buried beneath the wreckage of their homes. A little girl lay dead in a pool of blood on the threshold of one of the doorways.

*   *   *

In the course of the afternoon the firing increased to such a degree that single explosions were no longer audible. There was nothing but one terrific tornado of noise. From seven onward the square and the houses round were shelled at intervals of half a minute with fifteen-centimeter shells. There were many duds among them, which all the same made the houses rock. We sat all this while in our cellar, round a table, on armchairs covered in silk, with our heads propped on our hands, and counted the seconds between the explosions. Our jests became less frequent, till at last the foolhardiest of us fell silent, and at eight o'clock two direct hits brought down the next house.

From nine to ten the shelling was frantic. The earth rocked and the sky boiled like a gigantic cauldron.

Hundreds of heavy batteries were concentrated on and round Combles. Innumerable shells came howling and hurtling over us. Thick smoke, ominously lit up by Very lights, veiled everything. Head and ears ached violently, and we could only

make ourselves understood by shouting a word at a time. The power of logical thought and the force of gravity seemed alike to be suspended. One had the sense of something as unescapable and as unconditionally fated as a catastrophe of nature. An N. C. O. of No. 3 platoon went mad.

At ten this carnival of hell gradually calmed down and passed into a steady drum fire. It was still certainly impossible to distinguish one shell from another.

*   *   *

At last we reached the front line. It was held by men cowering close in the shell holes, and their dead voices trembled with joy when they heard that we were the relief. A Bavarian sergeant major briefly handed over the sector and the Very-light pistol.

My platoon front formed the right wing of the position held by the regiment. It consisted of a shallow sunken road which had been pounded by shells. It was a few hundred meters left of Guillemont and a rather shorter distance right of Bois-de-Trônes. We were parted from the troops on our right, the Seventy-sixth Regiment of Infantry, by a space about five hundred meters wide. This space was shelled so violently that no troops could maintain themselves there.

The Bavarian sergeant major had vanished of a sudden, and I stood alone, the Very-light pistol in my hand, in the midst of an uncanny sea of shell holes over which lay a white mist whose swaths gave it an even more oppressive and mysterious appearance. A persistent, unpleasant smell came from behind. I was left in no doubt that it came from a gigantic corpse far gone in decay. * * *

When day dawned we were astonished to see, by degrees, what a sight surrounded us.

The sunken road now appeared as nothing but a series of enormous shell holes filled with pieces of uniform, weapons, and dead bodies. The ground all round, as far as the eye could see, was plowed by shells. You could search in vain for one wretched blade of grass. This churned-up battlefield was ghastly. Among the living lay the dead.

As we dug ourselves in we found them in layers stacked one upon the top of another. One company after another had been shoved into the drum fire and steadily annihilated. The corpses were covered with the masses of soil turned up by the shells, and the next company advanced in the place of the fallen.

The sunken road and the ground behind were full of German dead; the ground in front, of English. Arms, legs, and heads stuck out stark above the lips of the craters. In front of our miserable defenses there were torn-off limbs and corpses over many of which cloaks and ground sheets had been thrown to hide the fixed stare of their distorted features. In spite of the heat no one thought for a moment of covering them with soil.

The village of Guillemont was distinguished from the landscape around it only because the shell holes there were of a whiter color by reason of the houses which had been ground to powder. Guillemont railway station lay in front of us. It was smashed to bits like a child's plaything. Delville Wood, reduced to matchwood, was farther behind.

*   *   *

It was the days at Guillemont that first made me aware of the overwhelming effects on the war of material. We had to adapt ourselves to an entirely new phase of war. The communications between the troops and the staff, between the artillery and the liaison officers, were utterly crippled by the terrific fire. Dispatch carriers failed to get through the hail of metal, and telephone wires were no sooner laid than they were shot into pieces. Even light-signaling was put out of action by the clouds of smoke and dust that hung over the field of battle. There was a zone of a kilometer behind the front line where explosives held absolute sway.

Even the regimental staff only knew exactly where we had been and how the line ran when we came back after three days and told them. Under such circumstances accuracy of artillery fire was out of the question. We were also entirely in the dark about the English line, though often, without our knowing it, it was only a few meters from us. Sometimes a Tommy, feeling his way from one shell hole to another like an ant along a track in the sand, landed in one that we occupied, and *vice versa*, for our front line consisted merely of isolated and unconnected bits that were easily mistaken.

Once seen, the landscape is an unforgettable one. In this neighborhood of villages, meadows, woods, and fields there was literally not a bush or a tiniest blade of grass to be seen. Every hand's-breadth of ground had been churned up again and again; trees had been uprooted, smashed, and ground to touchwood, the houses blown to bits and turned to dust; hills had been leveled and the arable land made a desert.

And yet the strangest thing of all was not the horror of the landscape in itself, but the fact that these scenes, such as the world had never known before, were fashioned by men who intended them to be a decisive end to the war. Thus all the frightfulness that the mind of man could devise was brought into the field; and there, where lately had been the idyllic picture of rural peace, there was as faithful a picture of the soul of scientific war. In earlier wars, certainly, towns and villages had been burned, but what was that compared with this sea of craters dug out by machines? For even in this fantastic desert there was the sameness of the machine-made article. A shell hole strewn with bully tins, broken weapons, fragments of uniform, and dud shells, with one or two dead bodies on its edge—this was the never-changing scene that surrounded each one of all these hundreds of thousands of men. And it seemed that man, on this landscape he had himself created, became different, more mysterious and hardy and callous than in any previous battle. The spirit and the tempo of the fighting altered, and after the battle of the Somme the war had its own peculiar impress that distinguished it from all other wars. After this battle the German soldier wore the steel helmet, and in his features there were chiseled the lines of an energy stretched to the utmost pitch, lines that future generations will perhaps find as fascinating and imposing as those of many heads of classical or Renaissance times.

For I cannot too often repeat, a battle was no longer an episode that spent itself in blood and fire; it was a condition of things that dug itself in remorselessly week after week and even month after month. What was a man's life in this wilderness whose vapor was laden with the stench of thousands upon thousands of decaying bodies? Death lay in ambush for each one in every shell hole, merciless, and making one merciless in turn. Chivalry here took a final farewell. It had to yield to the heightened intensity of war, just as all fine and personal feeling has to yield when machinery gets the upper hand. The Europe of to-day ap-

peared here for the first time on the field of battle. . . .

* * *

REVIEW QUESTIONS

1. What impact did the British bombardment have on the battle zone described by Jünger?
2. What affect does the bombardment seem to have had on the psyche of individual soldiers?
3. How does the kind of warfare described here differ from that of the past?
4. In what sense is this warfare a product of "the Europe of to-day"?

R. SCOTLAND LIDDELL

FROM *On the Russian Front*

British journalist R. Scotland Liddell (dates unknown) served on the eastern front as a medic for the 7th Group of Polish Red Cross Volunteers. Liddell witnessed first-hand both the bravery of the Russian troops and the woeful inadequacy of their arms and provisions. On the Russian Front, his report on the military campaign in the East, was published in 1916 with the intention of bolstering the Western Allies' sympathy for their Russian partners and convincing the British public that the tsar's army remained firmly committed to the Allied effort.

In May of 1915, Liddell was stationed at a Red Cross camp in Russian Poland, near the ongoing German offensive in western Galicia. His account provides a rare glimpse at the distinctive difficulties of warfare on the eastern front and the hardships being suffered by Russian soldiers less than two years prior to the collapse of the tsarist regime.

From *On the Russian Front*, R. Scotland Liddell, Simpkin, Marshall, 1916.

Staro-Radziwillow
Broken Rifles

Somewhere in Poland there was a smiling plain fringed by dark woods from which the roar of guns was heard by day and night.

*   *   *

At the edge of the wood there was a Red Cross camp where wounded men were brought from hour to hour. Two hundred yards across the field, behind a little grove, stood a cottage where broken rifles were repaired. The broken men came to be patched that they might go to fight again. The broken rifles were mended that once more they might be levelled against the invading foe. Some men— some rifles—were beyond repair. . . .

To the little cottage arsenal amongst the trees were brought six thousand rifles in a dozen weeks. Perhaps three thousand rifles were made good. Sometimes three broken guns were needed for the production of one serviceable weapon. One rifle, for instance, would have all its parts complete except the cartridge magazine and the firing bolt. Two other rifles would be wholly smashed except those needed parts. From three—one.

In the cottage itself, the kitchen had become a grimy foundry. The fire was now a tiny furnace. The pans of Polish *zur* and *kluski* had given way to pots of molten metal and bars of red-hot iron. Outside the kitchen window, the workmen sat on rough benches in the open air. The cottage folk stood idly by. Half of their house was still unoccupied by soldiers. An old man, undressed on head and neck and feet, apathetically watched the work. His poor old brain could scarcely understand it all. A wagon stood in the dusty yard, its clumsy wheels rusty from disuse. By the straw-strewn door of the cottage stable an old dog growled fiercely at each stranger's arrival. The working men hummed simple tunes and sang to the accompaniment of hammer and rasp. The boom of cannon seemed to shake the air.

There was a shed at one end of the yard—a wooden shed with many ragged gaps. The mended guns stood in it piled in neat stacks. Heaps of the various parts were all around. Here, a box of tiny screws; there, a pile of bayonets; and again, a heaped-up mass of firing bolts and other units of the gun. Each mended rifle was tested before it left the arsenal. When I was there I aimed one rifle at a small, fleecy cloud and fired a bullet up into the sky.

Across the field—the broken men. Across the woods—the broken land. And here—the broken rifles with their histories of varying tragedy.

*   *   *

This turning of the cottage into a workshop was significant of one of the greatest difficulties that Russia had to contend with—distance. The nearest town in which the rifles could have been repaired was too far away from the firing line to be convenient. The means of communication, moreover, were not sufficiently good. And yet again, there was a shortage of rifles. The broken ones had to be repaired with all speed. Hence the cottage arsenal, within sound of the rifle fire itself, within range of the German guns.

In England, it's a long, long way to Tipperary. On the Eastern front, it's a longer way to anywhere at all. New roads had to be cut through virgin forest—great straight roads that ran for miles without a turn. Little tramways were laid across the fields for the easier transport of guns and ammunition and wounded men. Later on, when we had retreated out of Poland into Lithuania, there were great stretches of country with no roads except mere rough tracks. For many versts there were no villages. It was possible to ride for hours across bleak country without encountering a single house.

Russia's lack of good routes was almost as bad as another enemy. I was told, when we were still west of Warsaw, that there were seventeen railway routes from Berlin to the Eastern front. This means of communication was almost as good as an ally for Germany.

*   *   *

One night, May 30, the firing was very heavy. Big guns boomed all the time, making the rifle volleys almost unheard. I stood on the top of the reserve trench embankment and thought of all the scenes beyond the wood. Then I went to my tent to sleep. Tired as I was, I could not. The noise of the battle was too great. It was the heaviest bombardment I had heard. * * *

Grey morning came and with the coming of the light we saw a wagon rumbling on the little tram-way over the fields towards us. There were six soldiers hanging over the sides, coughing and gasping for breath. The enemy had attacked with gas shells and the men were poisoned. Their lungs were terribly burned. We put the men on stretchers in the open sandy space between our sleeping tent and that in which the wounded men were placed. A doctor hurried to attend to them. To see these men choking was an awful sight. Three died in agony. It was very terrible to watch them, but it was nothing to what we were to witness that day.

More wagons came, and then an almost constant stream. Many of the poisoned men were dead before they arrived at our camp. In one wagon three dead lay on three dying. Before an hour had passed we had five hundred men, but hundreds more arrived. In all, that day, we had two thousand one hundred poisoned men, and many others who were wounded. One hundred and forty-three men died in our camp. Nearly five hundred died after we had sent them off to Zyrardow and Warsaw.

* * *

It was really almost impossible to do anything for the worst cases. We tried artificial respiration, but without much success. As the men choked for life they grew purple in the face—their tongues grew almost black. They died most painfully. I myself saw sixty-seven men die. I helped to carry their bodies to the large tent that we used as a mortuary. We found that not only had the brass parts of the men's equipment been turned green with the gas, but their clips of bullets were also all coated with a green film. Later on it was discovered that the gas used was a mixture of chloride and sulphur. The effect on the lungs was terrible. Doctor Sklodowski, a brother of Madame Curie of Radium fame, told

me that he feared that even should the men live, most of them would have tuberculosis. Very few poisoned men would escape the disease.

* * *

We dug graves for the men next day. One very large one and another. In the former were buried one hundred and eight men, and in the latter, thirty-five. Such graves are called "fraternal." The men were buried in their clothes—just as they had died. But first we took their belongings from their pockets, in order, if possible, to send them to their relatives. They were pathetically interesting. Almost every man had a purse, but very little money. The whole number had not a hundred roubles amongst them. There were watches of all sizes and metals. Silver rings—the favourite ones were fashioned in the form of a skull with green and red stones in the place of eyes. One man had only a brass button and a soiled piece of loaf sugar in his pocket. Another had a faded photograph of a woman, wrapped in a piece of coloured cloth. Some had pocket-books with letters in them and photographs of their folks and of themselves. These latter were of fine, brave, clean-looking men, moustaches well waxed and faces looking very proudly from out of the glossy card. The difference was striking—the men as they had been and as they now were. There were little trinkets, too, and nails and pieces of string and all manner of odds and ends. The heap of articles might have been treasure trove from schoolboys' pockets.

* * *

REVIEW QUESTIONS

1. What does Liddell's account suggest about Russian military preparedness?
2. How did conditions on the eastern front differ from those on the western front?
3. What special problems confronted the Russian military?
4. How do Liddell and Wilfred Owen describe the effects of poison gas on soldiers?

FROM Madame Lucie Gets Married

World War I produced a dramatic break in the continuity of soldiers' lives, but its effects on civilian populations were often less immediate, especially in the early stages of the war. Those living in close proximity to the battlefront suffered substantial loss of life and property, but those living safely behind the lines experienced the hardships of war in a less-direct manner, in the form of food rationing, long hours of work in armaments factories, or the dreaded telegram announcing the death of a loved one. Madame Lucie (1896–1981), an elderly Parisian interviewed by American historian Bonnie Smith in the 1970s, remembered the war less as a major "historical" event than as an important element in her developing personal life. When the war broke out in 1914, Madame Lucie and her mother were running a small hat shop in the garrison city of Lisieux in northwestern France. Madame Lucie was eighteen years old and, despite her mother's scolding, eager to flirt with the young soldiers who had been stationed in the town prior to their departure for the front.

From *Confessions of a Concierge: Madame Lucie's History of Twentieth Century France,* Bonnie Smith, Yale University Press, 1985. Reprinted with permission of the publisher.

*   *   *

* * * right under Maman's eyes, I met soldiers. They talked to me while I brought our waste to the doorstop. In those days, it was natural to say a little *bonjour* to one's neighbor while holding a chamber pot, whose contents would soon be fertilizing Norman fields. As I opened the shutters or watered the flowers in the windowboxes, a passing soldier might stop for a second, and I was polite. Often the young men quartered on the second floor of the house facing ours waved to me. How could one avoid soldiers in a city like this?

On my excursions to fetch water, I tried to see as much as I could, especially the pilgrims, and also the goods in shop windows. One day, rather preoccupied with the sights and with the water jar, I saw two soldiers approaching. Not alert enough to the situation, we met at a point where the sidewalk was narrow, bounded by a building on one side and a horsehitch on the other. The first soldier leaned politely toward the building while I navigated past the horsehitch, my water jar not making things easier. Suddenly we were bottle-

necked, for my skirt had caught in the hitch. I remained its prisoner, spilling water in my effort to move, until the soldier released me. The soldier was Philippe, friend of the young men across the street. Later, he said he had vowed to marry me at that very moment he saw me blushing and discomfited by our unexpected brush together.

From that time on Philippe passed by our boutique whenever possible, and I arranged to be at the counter, or even better, out watering the plants when I thought he might be passing. I looked for him and thought of him almost continually. Maman did not help matters any by singing her romantic songs, like the "Polka à Moustache," while we worked. I knew it was wrong to be thinking of soldiers, to meet a beau in this way, but there was no help for me. After weeks of this, one day I came into the store, having talked to Philippe while I (slowly, very slowly) closed the shutters.

"Who was that young man with you out there?" Maman asked sternly.

"Just a passing soldier, Maman," I replied.

"Enough of these stories. You are not to leave

this building, and above all you are not to talk to that soldier again."

There was nothing to say. One didn't argue with parents in those days. But that evening I wrote a note to Philippe explaining our problem. Next morning, the apprentice, sent to do my usual errands, took the note to a café where Philippe had told me he could be found in emergencies. She returned and, when Maman left the workroom, reported that he had indeed been in the café but had said nothing after reading the note.

My heart began to break. A dream of Philippe had taken over my life, and I couldn't accept that this, too, would have to end. I was sitting, desperate at the possibility, when a letter arrived for my parents. Maman took a long time reading it, then tucked it away. When Papa came home she handed it to him. Somehow I knew it was from Philippe, so much had Maman looked at me that day. Finally, they told me that he might visit me at home. Philippe had explained himself so finely that Maman called him "honorable."

In those visits, while we all sat and talked together, Philippe won my parents over, and before I knew it we were engaged to be married. What a time! How improbable! Philippe was an orphan, a soldier, a stranger to all of us. Yet we were going to get married. Maman and I started sewing, and the first thing we made was a new dress and hat for me to wear on an engagement trip to my grandmother's in Caen. Philippe wore his best uniform and met us at the train station with a white bouquet and a tiny ring for me. I have never been so happy and will always remember the day —July 14, the *fête nationale*, 1914. Three weeks later Philippe went off to war.

I did something unusual for our family by writing letters every day for three months until, in October, Philippe was killed. Some time later we held a family reunion and had our picture taken: Papa and his brother with their joking smiles; Maman in mourning out of respect and love for my fiancé; I, in mourning also, having vowed never to marry.

The death of Philippe made this war the most important and least significant event of my life.

That moment—his death—lasted forever; and then nothing else about wartime touched me. Besides, compared to the regions north and east of us we hardly suffered. Battles weren't fought on our fields; we weren't occupied; neither combatants nor wounded, nor ambulances nor munitions crossed our paths. Maman and I continued making hats, but our ingenuity was tested as luxury fabrics became scarce. We sewed with felt instead of silk, and especially we made mourning hats until, after a couple of years, every woman in Lisieux and the countryside had one. So you can see that while many people would thereafter be obsessed by the story of the war, for me it would always and only mean the death of Philippe.

*　　*　　*

But I was young, and one day in 1916 I met another soldier, with whom, as the expression goes, I fell in love at first sight. Entering our boutique to find corporal's stripes, Pierre was handsome in his uniform and his curled moustache.

*　　*　　*

We had only one problem: Pierre was married.

At any other time, I wouldn't have thought of looking at a married man, but war was different. Besides, being spoiled and headstrong, I felt that I should have the person I loved no matter what. From the first Pierre had explained his situation. Before the war he had worked for the Pathé brothers, our great film makers. He had set up their theaters around France, and while doing this work in Nancy had met a woman with whom he eloped. But war came, and when he went home on his first leave, his wife had left without a trace. Pierre was now in the process of getting a divorce, and even though it was not his fault, as one would say, still the whole business was scandalous.

My parents were astonished when we finally told them. Maman looked grim, even though Pierre was so obviously upset at having to talk of his own humiliation over the divorce procedure. Seeing my determination, Papa did nothing more than give his assent, but after Pierre left, he fumed.

"Oh, it's unfortunate to have an only daughter, and her about to marry a divorced man."

In spite of everything I was happy.

* * *

Then, right in the middle of it all, the war took Pierre to Salonika on the Balkan front—even though he was unfit, so the army decreed, for active service.

* * *

Suddenly the war ended, and my fiancé was on his way home.

* * *

Pierre returned, and together we waited for his divorce to be settled. Meanwhile, news of my impending marriage traveled the neighborhood, though we tried to keep it secret because of the circumstances. Our priest stopped me one day to offer his congratulations.

"This will be a fine marriage for the parish, Mlle Brun."

"I'm afraid not, Father. My fiancé is divorced." I explained the desertion by Pierre's wife, but that didn't soften his stern look.

"Well, Mademoiselle, I'm going to have to excommunicate you. Come back after the wedding and we'll see what it takes to straighten things out. I'll be waiting for you."

With that he turned back to the church, probably to start filling the forms and counting the costs for my reinstatement. I can assure you, he's still waiting for me.

We were married July 22, 1919, in a small and quiet ceremony because of this new scandal.

* * *

For three days the family celebrated. Pierre, now my excellent husband, and I spent our wedding night at my parents'. It was a shock, I can tell you, because except for my few months as an apprentice, I had never heard much about sex.

But we had good customs in Normandy. People sang all the time in those days. * * *

that night after my husband and I had gone to our room, after things began to seem strange to me, suddenly clanging and singing broke out, my father's voice louder than all the rest:

Said the mattress to the sheets
I have never seen such feats.
Said the pillow to the case
We've been shaken to the base.

Pierre and I giggled, holding one another until we went to sleep.

* * *

REVIEW QUESTIONS

1. How was Madame Lucie affected by the war?
2. What do her experiences tell you about the relationship between the homefront and the battlefront?
3. To what extent were traditions regulating marriage and the family transformed by the war?
4. What benefits might young women like Madame Lucie have derived from the social changes brought by the war?

VERA BRITTAIN

FROM *Testament of Youth*

Despite an eminently respectable "provincial young ladyhood," British author Vera Brittain (1893–1970) rebelled early against the constraints imposed by age, class, and sex. Brittain insisted upon pursuing her education, despite her parents' protests, and attended Sommerville, a college for women affiliated with Oxford. She experienced the outbreak of World War I as "an infuriating personal interruption rather than a world-wide catastrophe," but this attitude changed dramatically after her fiancé, brother, and best male friends enlisted and then died, one by one. Frustrated by her inability to become a soldier and share the hardships of her male peers, she chose the nearest thing: service as a Voluntary Aid Detachment nurse. After a period of training in England, she attended wounded soldiers on the island of Malta and the western front. The following excerpts from Brittain's widely read memoir, Testament of Youth, *demonstrate the various ways in which the lives of ordinary individuals were disrupted and transformed during the course of the war.*

The excerpts from *Testament of Youth: An Autobiographical Study of the Years 1900–1925,* by Vera Brittain are included with the permission of her literary executors.

*   *   *

NURSE'S TRAINING

On Sunday morning, June 27th, 1915, I began my nursing at the Devonshire Hospital. * * *

From our house above the town I ran eagerly downhill to my first morning's work, not knowing, fortunately for myself, that my servitude would last for nearly four years. The hospital had originally been used as a riding-school, but a certain Duke of Devonshire, with exemplary concern for the welfare of the sick but none whatever for the feet of the nursing staff, had caused it to be converted to its present charitable purpose. The main part of the building consisted of a huge dome, with two stone corridors running one above the other round its quarter-mile circumference. The nurses were not allowed to cross its diameter, which contained an inner circle reserved for convalescent patients, so that everything forgotten or newly required meant a run round the circumference. * * *

My hours there ran from 7.45 a.m. until 1 p.m., and again from 5.0 p.m. until 9.15 p.m.—a longer day, as I afterwards discovered, than that normally required in many Army hospitals. No doubt the staff was not unwilling to make the utmost use of so enthusiastic and unsophisticated a probationer. Meals, for all of which I was expected to go home, were not included in these hours. As our house was nearly half a mile from the hospital on the slope of a steep hill, I never completely overcame the aching of my back and the soreness of my feet throughout the time that I worked there, and felt perpetually as if I had just returned from a series of long route marches.

I never minded these aches and pains, which appeared to me solely as satisfactory tributes to my love for Roland. What did profoundly trouble and humiliate me was my colossal ignorance of the simplest domestic operations. Among other "facts of life," my expensive education had omitted to teach me the prosaic but important essentials of egg-boiling, and the Oxford cookery classes had triumphantly failed to repair the omission. I imagined that I had to bring the saucepan to the boil, then turn off the gas and allow the egg to lie for three minutes in the cooling water. The remarks of a lance-corporal to whom I presented an egg "boiled" in this fashion led me to make shamefaced inquiries of my superiors, from whom I learnt, in those first few days, how numerous and devastating were the errors that it was possible to commit in carrying out the most ordinary functions of everyday life. To me, for whom meals had hitherto appeared as though by clockwork and the routine of a house had seemed to be worked by some invisible mechanism, the complications of sheer existence were nothing short of a revelation.

Despite my culinary shortcomings, the men appeared to like me; none of them were very ill, and no doubt my youth, my naïve eagerness and the clean freshness of my new uniform meant more to them than any amount of common sense and efficiency. Perhaps, too, the warm and profoundly surprising comfort that I derived from their presence produced a tenderness which was able to communicate back to them, in turn, something of their own rich consolation.

Throughout my two decades of life, I had never looked upon the nude body of an adult male; I had never even seen a naked boy-child since the nursery days when, at the age of four or five, I used to share my evening baths with Edward. I had therefore expected, when I first started nursing, to be overcome with nervousness and embarrassment, but, to my infinite relief, I was conscious of neither. Towards the men I came to feel an almost adoring gratitude for their simple and natural acceptance of my ministrations. Short of actually going to bed with them, there was hardly an intimate service that I did not perform for one or another in the course of four years, and I still have reason to be thankful for the knowledge of masculine functioning which the care of them

gave me, and for my early release from the sex-inhibitions that even to-day—thanks to the Victorian tradition which up to 1914 dictated that a young woman should know nothing of men but their faces and their clothes until marriage pitchforked her into an incompletely visualised and highly disconcerting intimacy—beset many of my female contemporaries, both married and single.

In the early days of the War the majority of soldier patients belonged to a first-rate physical type which neither wounds nor sickness, unless mortal, could permanently impair, and from the constant handling of their lean, muscular bodies, I came to understand the essential cleanliness, the innate nobility, of sexual love on its physical side. Although there was much to shock in Army hospital service, much to terrify, much, even, to disgust, this day-by-day contact with male anatomy was never part of the shame. Since it was always Roland whom I was nursing by proxy, my attitude towards him imperceptibly changed; it became less romantic and more realistic, and thus a new depth was added to my love.

In addition to the patients, I managed to extract approval from most of the nurses—no doubt because, my one desire being to emulate Roland's endurance, I seized with avidity upon all the unpleasant tasks of which they were only too glad to be relieved, and took a masochistic delight in emptying bed-pans, washing greasy cups and spoons, and disposing of odoriferous dressings in the sink-room. The Matron described as "a slave-driver" by one of the elegant lady V.A.D.s who intermittently trotted in to "help" in the evenings after the bulk of the work was done—treated me with especial kindness, and often let me out through her private gate in order to save me a few yards of the inter-minable miles upon my feet.

My particular brand of enthusiasm, the nurses told me later, was rare among the local V.A.D.s, most of whom came to the hospital expecting to hold the patients' hands and smooth their pillows while the regular nurses fetched and carried everything that looked or smelt disagreeable. Probably this was true, for my diary records of one Buxton girl a month later: "Nancy thinks she would like to take up Red Cross work but does not want to go where she would have to dust wards and clean up as she does not think she would like that."

*   *   *

AT THE WESTERN FRONT

Only a day or two afterwards I was leaving quarters to go back to my ward, when I had to wait to let a large contingent of troops march past me along the main road that ran through our camp. They were swinging rapidly towards Camiers, and though the sight of soldiers marching was now too familiar to arouse curiosity, an unusual quality of bold vigour in their swift stride caused me to stare at them with puzzled interest.

They looked larger than ordinary men; their tall, straight figures were in vivid contrast to the under-sized armies of pale recruits to which we had grown accustomed. At first I thought their spruce, clean uniforms were those of officers, yet obviously they could not be officers, for there were too many of them; they seemed, as it were, Tommies in heaven. Had yet another regiment been conjured out of our depleted Dominions? I wondered, watching them move with such rhythm, such dignity, such serene consciousness of self-respect. But I knew the colonial troops so well, and these were different; they were assured where the Australians were aggressive, self-possessed where the New Zealanders were turbulent.

Then I heard an excited exclamation from a group of Sisters behind me.

"Look! Look! Here are the Americans!"

I pressed forward with the others to watch the United States physically entering the War, so god-like, so magnificent, so splendidly unimpaired in comparison with the tired, nerve-racked men of the British Army. So these were our deliverers at last, marching up the road to Camiers in the spring sunshine! There seemed to be hundreds of them, and in the fearless swagger of their proud strength they looked a formidable bulwark against the peril looming from Amiens.

Somehow the necessity of packing up in a hurry, the ignominious flight to the coast so long imagined, seemed to move further away. An uncontrollable emotion seized me—as such emotions often seized us in those days of insufficient sleep; my eyeballs pricked, my throat ached, and a mist swam over the confident Americans going to the front. The coming of relief made me realise all at once how long and how intolerable had been the tension, and with the knowledge that we were not, after all, defeated, I found myself beginning to cry.

*   *   *

WAR'S END

When the sound of victorious guns burst over London at 11 a.m. on November 11th, 1918, the men and women who looked incredulously into each other's faces did not cry jubilantly: "We've won the War!" They only said "The War is over."

From Millbank I heard the maroons crash with terrifying clearness, and, like a sleeper who is determined to go on dreaming after being told to wake up, I went on auto-matically washing the dressing bowls in the annex outside my hut. Deeply buried beneath my consciousness there stirred the vague memory of a letter that I had written Roland in those legendary days when I was still at Oxford and could spend my Sundays in thinking of him while the organ echoed grandly through New College Chapel. It had been a warm May evening, when all the city was sweet with the scent of wallflowers and lilac, and I had walked back to Micklem Hall after hearing an Occasional Oratorio by Handel, which described the mustering of troops for battle, the lament for the fallen and the triumphant return of the victors.

"As I listened," I told him, "to the organ swelling forth into a final triumphant burst in the song of victory, after the solemn and mournful dirge over the dead, I thought with what mockery and irony the jubilant celebrations which we hail the coming of peace will fall upon the ears of those to whom their best will never return, upon whose sorrow victory is built, who have paid with their mourning for the others' joy. I wonder if I shall be one of those who take happy part in the triumph—or if I shall listen to the merriment with a heart that breaks and ears that try to keep out the mirthful sounds."

And as I dried the bowls, I thought: "It's come too late for me. Somehow I knew, even at Oxford, that it would. Why couldn't it have ended rationally, as it might have ended, in 1916, instead of all that trumpet-blowing against a negotiated peace, and the ferocious talk of secure civilians about marching to Berlin? It's come five months too late—or is it three years? It might have ended last June, and let Edward, at least, be saved! Only five months—it's such a little time, when Roland died nearly three years ago."

But on Armistice Day not even a lonely survivor drowning in black waves of memory could be left alone with her thoughts. A moment after the guns had subsided into sudden, palpitating silence, the other V.A.D. from my ward dashed excitedly into the annex.

"Brittain! Brittain! Did you hear the maroons? It's over—it's all over! Do let's come out and see what's happening!" Mechanically, I followed her into the road, as I stood there, stupidly rigid, long after the triumphant explosions from Westminster had turned into a distant crescendo of shouting, I saw a taxicab turn swiftly in from the Embankment toward the hospital. The next moment there was a cry for doctors and nurses from passers-by, for in rounding the corner the taxi had knocked down a small elderly woman who in listening, like myself, to the wild noise of a world released from nightmare, had failed to observe its approach.

As I hurried to her side I realised that she was all but dead and already past speech. Like Victor in the mortuary chapel, she seemed to have shrunk to the dimensions of a child with the sharp features of age, but on the tiny chalk-white face an expression of shocked surprise still lingered, and she stared hard at me as Geoffrey had stared at his orderly in those last moments of conscious

silence beside the Scarpe. Had she been thinking, I wondered, when the taxi struck her, of her sons at the front, now safe? The next moment a medical officer and some orderlies came up, and I went back to my ward.

But I remembered her at intervals throughout that afternoon, during which, with a half-masochistic notion of "seeing the sights," I made a circular tour to Kensington by way of the intoxicated West End. With aching persistence my thoughts went back to the dead and the strange irony of their fates—to Roland, gifted, ardent, ambitious, who had died without glory in the conscientious performance of a routine job; to Victor and Geoffrey, gentle and diffident, who, conquering nature by resolution, had each gone down bravely in a big "show"; and finally to Edward, musical, serene, a lover of peace, who had fought courageously through so many battles and at last had been killed while leading a vital counter-attack in one of the few decisive actions of the War. As I struggled through the waving, shrieking crowds in Piccadilly and Regent Street on the overloaded top of a 'bus, some witty enthusiast for contemporary history symbolically turned upside down the sign-board "Seven Kings."

Late that evening, when supper was over, a group of elated V.A.D.s who were anxious to walk through Westminster and Whitehall to Buckingham Palace prevailed upon me to join them. Outside the Admiralty a crazy group of convalescent Tommies were collecting specimens of different uniforms and bundling their wearers into flag-strewn taxis; with a shout they seized two of my companions and disappeared into the clamorous crowd, waving flags and shaking rattles. Wherever we went a burst of enthusiastic cheering greeted our Red Cross uniform, and complete strangers adorned with wound stripes rushed up and shook me warmly by the hand. After the long, long blackness, it seemed like a fairy-tale to see the street lamps shining through the chill November gloom.

I detached myself from the others and walked slowly up Whitehall, with my heart sinking in a sudden cold dismay. Already this was a different world from the one that I had known during four life-long years, a world in which people would be light-hearted and forgetful, in which themselves and their careers and their amusements would blot out political ideals and great national issues. And in that brightly lit, alien world I should have no part. All those with whom I had really been intimate were gone; not one remained to share with me the heights and the depths of my memories. As the years went by and youth departed and remembrance grew dim, a deeper and ever deeper darkness would cover the young men who were once my contemporaries.

For the first time I realised, with all that full realisation meant, how completely everything that had hitherto made up my life had vanished with Edward and Roland, with Victor and Geoffrey.

The War was over; a new age was beginning; but the dead were dead and would never return.

REVIEW QUESTIONS

1. How did Brittain's experiences as a nurse change her attitude toward human sexuality?
2. Why did she so willingly accept the hard and sometimes unpleasant work nursing entailed?
3. How does Brittain describe the newly arrived American troops?
4. In a letter to her fiancé, Brittain expressed the fear that the war would put "a barrier of indescribable experience between men and the women whom they loved."
5. Do you think this concern was valid?

FROM **The Versailles Treaty**

Toward the end of the war, American president Woodrow Wilson began to lobby for a "peace without victory" and proposed a set of Fourteen Points as the basis for eventual peace negotiations. Wilson envisioned a just settlement that would permanently eradicate recourse to armed conflict by striking at the root causes of all wars and not simply at the incidental factors that had precipitated this particular war. He called for an end to the arms races and secret diplomacy of the pre-war era, and he proposed that the new international order be based on the principles of democracy, international free trade, and the right of ethnic minorities to self-determination, all of which would be guaranteed by a league of nations. When the new German government sued for peace in late 1918, it did so in the hopes that the peace settlement would be negotiated on the basis of Wilson's proposals. However, Germany was not allowed to send representatives to the Versailles Conference, and the representatives of the European Allies—Clemenceau for France, Lloyd George for Britain, and Orlando for Italy—produced a rather different treaty than that suggested by the Fourteen Points. Despite Wilson's very active role in the framing of the settlement, the Versailles Treaty was not ratified by the American congress, and the United States never joined Wilson's cherished League of Nations.

From *The Versailles Treaty*, The World War I Document Archive Webpage, <http://www.lib.byu.edu/ rdh/wwi/versailles.html>.

Peace Treaty of Versailles (1919)

THE COVENANT OF THE LEAGUE OF NATIONS.

THE HIGH CONTRACTING PARTIES, In order to promote international cooperation and to achieve international peace and security

by the acceptance of obligations not to resort to war by the prescription of open, just and honourable relations between nations

by the firm establishment of the understandings of international law as the actual rule of conduct among Governments, and

by the maintenance of justice and a scrupulous respect for all treaty obligations in the dealings of organised peoples with one another

Agree to this Covenant of the League of Nations.

*   *   *

ARTICLE 8.

The Members of the League recognise that the maintenance of peace requires the reduction of national armaments to the lowest point consistent with national safety and the enforcement by common action of international obligations. The Council, taking account of the geographical situation and circumstances of each State, shall formulate plans for such reduction for the consideration and action of the several Governments. Such plans shall be subject to reconsideration and revision at least every ten years.

*   *   *

ARTICLE 10.

The Members of the League undertake to respect and preserve as against external aggression the territorial integrity and existing political independence of all Members of the League. * * *

ARTICLE 11.

Any war or threat of war, whether immediately affecting any of the Members of the League or not, is hereby declared a matter of concern to the whole League, and the League shall take any action that may be deemed wise and effectual to safeguard the peace of nations. * * *

ARTICLE 12.

The Members of the League agree that if there should arise between them any dispute likely to lead to a rupture, they will submit the matter either to arbitration or to inquiry by the Council, and they agree in no case to resort to war until three months after the award by the arbitrators or the report by the Council.

*   *   *

ARTICLE 16.

Should any Member of the League resort to war in disregard of its covenants * * *, it shall ipso facto be deemed to have committed an act of war against all other Members of the League, which hereby undertake immediately to subject it to the severance of all trade or financial relations, the prohibition of all intercourse between their nations and the nationals of the covenant-breaking State, and the prevention of all financial, commercial, or personal intercourse between the nationals of the covenant-breaking State and the nationals of any other State, whether a Member of the League or not. * * * Any Member of the League which has violated any covenant of the League may be declared to be no longer a Member of the League by a vote of the Council concurred in by the Representatives of all the other Members of the League represented thereon.

*   *   *

ARTICLE 18.

Every treaty or international engagement entered into hereafter by any Member of the League shall be forthwith registered with the Secretariat and shall as soon as possible be published by it. No such treaty or international engagement shall be binding until so registered.

*   *   *

ARTICLE 22.

To those colonies and territories which as a consequence of the late war have ceased to be under the sovereignty of the States which formerly

governed them and which are inhabited by peoples not yet able to stand by themselves under the strenuous conditions of the modern world, there should be applied the principle that the well-being and development of such peoples form a sacred trust of civilisation and that securities for the performance of this trust should be embodied in this Covenant. The best method of giving practical effect to this principle is that the tutelage of such peoples should be entrusted to advanced nations who by reason of their resources, their experience or their geographical position can best undertake this responsibility, and who are willing to accept it, and that this tutelage should be exercised by them as Mandatories on behalf of the League. The character of the mandate must differ according to the stage of the development of the people, the geographical situation of the territory, its economic conditions, and other similar circumstances. Certain communities formerly belonging to the Turkish Empire have reached a stage of development where their existence as independent nations can be provisionally recognised subject to the rendering of administrative advice and assistance by a Mandatory until such time as they are able to stand alone. The wishes of these communities must be a principal consideration in the selection of the Mandatory. Other peoples, especially those of Central Africa, are at such a stage that the Mandatory must be responsible for the administration of the territory under conditions which will guarantee freedom of conscience and religion, subject only to the maintenance of public order and morals, the prohibition of abuses such as the slave trade, the arms traffic, and the liquor traffic, and the prevention of the establishment of fortifications or military and naval bases and of military training of the natives for other than police purposes and the defence of territory, and will also secure equal opportunities for the trade and commerce of other Members of the League. There are territories, such as South-West Africa and certain of the South Pacific Islands, which, owing to the sparseness of their population, or their small size, or their remoteness from the centres of civilisation, or their geographical contiguity to the territory of the Mandatory, and other circumstances, can be best administered under the laws of the Mandatory as integral portions of its territory, subject to the safeguards above mentioned in the interests of the indigenous population. In every case of mandate, the Mandatory shall render to the Council an annual report in reference to the territory committed to its charge. * * *
ARTICLE 23.

* * * the Members of the League: (a) will endeavour to secure and maintain fair and humane conditions of labour for men, women, and children, both in their own countries and in all countries to which their commercial and industrial relations extend, and for that purpose will establish and maintain the necessary international organisations; (b) undertake to secure just treatment of the native inhabitants of territories under their control; (c) will entrust the League with the general supervision over the execution of agreements with regard to the traffic in women and children, and the traffic in opium and other dangerous drugs; (d) will entrust the League with the general supervision of the trade in arms and ammunition with the countries in which the control of this traffic is necessary in the common interest; (e) will make provision to secure and maintain freedom of communications and of transit and equitable treatment for the commerce of all Members of the League. In this connection, the special necessities of the regions devastated during the war of 1914–1918 shall be borne in mind; (f) will endeavour to take steps in matters of international concern for the prevention and control of disease.

*   *   *

ARTICLE 25.

The Members of the League agree to encourage and promote the establishment and co-operation of duly authorised voluntary national Red Cross organisations having as purposes the improvement of health, the prevention of disease, and the mitigation of suffering throughout the world.

*   *   *

ARTICLE 42.

Germany is forbidden to maintain or construct any fortifications either on the left bank of the Rhine or on the right bank to the west of a line drawn 50 kilometres to the East of the Rhine.

ARTICLE 43.

In the area defined above the maintenance and the assembly of armed forces, either permanently or temporarily, and military maneuvers of any kind, as well as the upkeep of all permanent works for mobilization, are in the same way forbidden.

ARTICLE 44.

In case Germany violates in any manner whatever the provisions of Articles 42 and 43, she shall be regarded as committing a hostile act against the Powers signatory of the present Treaty and as calculated to disturb the peace of the world.

ARTICLE 45.

As compensation for the destruction of the coalmines in the north of France and as part payment towards the total reparation due from Germany for the damage resulting from the war, Germany cedes to France in full and absolute possession, with exclusive rights of exploitation, unencumbered and free from all debts and charges of any kind, the coalmines situated in the Saar Basin * * *

*   *   *

ARTICLE 49.

* * * At the end of fifteen years from the coming into force of the present Treaty the inhabitants of the [Saar Basin] shall be called upon to indicate the sovereignty under which they desire to be placed.

*   *   *

ARTICLE 51.

The territories [of Alsace and Lorraine] which were ceded to Germany in accordance with the Preliminaries of Peace signed at Versailles on February 26, 1871, and the Treaty of Frankfort of May 10, 1871, are restored to French sovereignty as from the date of the Armistice of November 11, 1918. * * *

*   *   *

ARTICLE 80.

Germany acknowledges and will respect strictly the independence of Austria * * *; she agrees that this independence shall be inalienable, except with the consent of the Council of the League of Nations.

ARTICLE 81.

Germany * * * recognises the complete independence of the Czecho-Slovak State * * *.

*   *   *

ARTICLE 84.

German nationals habitually resident in any of the territories recognised as forming part of the Czecho-Slovak State will obtain Czecho-Slovak nationality ipso facto and lose their German nationality.

*   *   *

ARTICLE 87.

Germany, in conformity with the action already taken by the Allied and Associated Powers, recognises the complete independence of Poland * * *

*   *   *

ARTICLE 102.

The Principal Allied and Associated Powers undertake to establish the town of Danzig, together with the rest of the territory described in Article 100, as a Free City. It will be placed under the protection of the League of Nations.

*   *   *

ARTICLE 116.

Germany acknowledges and agrees to respect as permanent and inalienable the independence of all the territories which were part of the former Russian Empire on August 1, 1914.

* * * Germany accepts definitely the abrogation of the Brest-Litovsk Treaties and of all other treaties, conventions, and agreements entered into by her with the Maximalist Government in Russia.

The Allied and Associated Powers formally reserve the rights of Russia to obtain from Germany restitution and reparation based on the principles of the present Treaty.

*　　*　　*

ARTICLE 119.

Germany renounces in favour of the Principal Allied and Associated Powers all her rights and titles over her oversea possessions.

*　　*　　*

ARTICLE 160.

* * * the total number of effectives in the Army of the States constituting Germany must not exceed one hundred thousand men, including officers and establishments of depots. The Army shall be devoted exclusively to the maintenance of order within the territory and to the control of the frontiers.

The total effective strength of officers, including the personnel of staffs, whatever their composition, must not exceed four thousand. * * *

*　　*　　*

ARTICLE 168.

The manufacture of arms, munitions, or any war material, shall only be carried out in factories or works the location of which shall be communicated to and approved by the Governments of the Principal Allied and Associated Powers, and the number of which they retain the right to restrict. * * *

*　　*　　*

ARTICLE 173.

Universal compulsory military service shall be abolished in Germany.

The German Army may only be constituted and recruited by means of voluntary enlistment.

*　　*　　*

ARTICLE 176.

On the expiration of two months from the coming into force of the present Treaty there must only exist in Germany the number of military schools which is absolutely indispensable for the recruitment of the officers of the units allowed. * * *

*　　*　　*

ARTICLE 181.

* * * the German naval forces in commission must not exceed:

6 battleships of the Deutschland or Lothringen type, 6 light cruisers, 12 destroyers, 12 torpedo boats * * *.

No submarines are to be included.

All other warships, except where there is provision to the contrary in the present Treaty, must be placed in reserve or devoted to commercial purposes.

*　　*　　*

ARTICLE 198.

The armed forces of Germany must not include any military or naval air forces. * * *

*　　*　　*

ARTICLE 227.

The Allied and Associated Powers publicly arraign William II of Hohenzollern, formerly German Emperor, for a supreme offence against international morality and the sanctity of treaties. * * *

*　　*　　*

ARTICLE 231.

The Allied and Associated Governments affirm and Germany accepts the responsibility of Germany and her allies for causing all the loss and damage to which the Allied and Associated Governments and their nationals have been subjected as a consequence of the war imposed upon them by the aggression of Germany and her allies. * * *

ARTICLE 232.

The Allied and Associated Governments recognise that the resources of Germany are not adequate, after taking into account permanent diminutions of such resources which will result from other provisions of the present Treaty, to make complete reparation for all such loss and damage.

The Allied and Associated Governments, however, require, and Germany undertakes, that she will make compensation for all damage done to the civilian population of the Allied and Associated Powers and to their property during the period of the belligerency of each as an Allied or Associated Power against Germany * * *

ARTICLE 233.

The amount of the above damage for which compensation is to be made by Germany shall be determined by an Inter-Allied Commission * * *

*   *   *

ORGANISATION OF LABOUR.

Whereas the League of Nations has for its object the establishment of universal peace, and such a peace can be established only if it is based upon social justice;

And whereas conditions of labour exist involving such injustice, hardship, and privation to large numbers of people as to produce unrest so great that the peace and harmony of the world are imperilled; and an improvement of those conditions is urgently required * * *;

Whereas also the failure of any nation to adopt humane conditions of labour is an obstacle in the way of other nations which desire to improve the conditions in their own countries;

The HIGH CONTRACTING PARTIES, moved by sentiments of justice and humanity as well as by the desire to secure the permanent peace of the world, agree to the following:

ARTICLE 387.

A permanent organisation is hereby established for the promotion of the objects set forth in the Preamble. * * *

*   *   *

ARTICLE 427.

[The High Contracting Parties] recognise that differences of climate, habits, and customs, of economic opportunity and industrial tradition, make strict uniformity in the conditions of labour difficult of immediate attainment. But, holding as they do, that labour should not be regarded merely as an article of commerce, they think that there are methods and principles for regulating labour conditions which all industrial communities should endeavour to apply, so far as their special circumstances will permit.

Among these methods and principles, the following seem to the High Contracting Parties to be of special and urgent importance:

First.—The guiding principle above enunciated that labour should not be regarded merely as a commodity or article of commerce.

Second.—The right of association for all lawful purposes by the employed as well as by the employers.

Third.—The payment to the employed of a wage adequate to maintain a reasonable standard of life as this is understood in their time and country.

Fourth.—The adoption of an eight hours day or a forty-eight hours week as the standard to be aimed at where it has not already been attained.

Fifth.—The adoption of a weekly rest of at least twenty-four hours, which should include Sunday wherever practicable.

Sixth.—The abolition of child labour and the imposition of such limitations on the labour of young persons as shall permit the continuation of their education and assure their proper physical development.

Seventh.—The principle that men and women should receive equal remuneration for work of equal value.

Eighth.—The standard set by law in each country with respect to the conditions of labour should have due regard to the equitable economic treatment of all workers lawfully resident therein.

Ninth.—Each State should make provision for a system of inspection in which women should take part, in order to ensure the enforcement of the laws and regulations for the protection of the employed. * * *

ARTICLE 428.

As a guarantee for the execution of the present Treaty by Germany, the German territory situated to the west of the Rhine, together with the bridgeheads, will be occupied by Allied and Associated troops for a period of fifteen years from the coming into force of the present Treaty.

*   *   *

ARTICLE 430.

In case either during the occupation or after the expiration of the fifteen years referred to above the Reparation Commission finds that Germany refuses to observe the whole or part of her obligations under the present Treaty with regard to reparation, the whole or part of the areas specified in Article 429 will be reoccupied immediately by the Allied and Associated forces.

ARTICLE 431.

If before the expiration of the period of fifteen years Germany complies with all the undertakings resulting from the present Treaty, the occupying forces will be withdrawn immediately.

*   *   *

ARTICLE 434.

Germany undertakes to recognise the full force of the Treaties of Peace and Additional Conventions which may be concluded by the Allied and Associated Powers with the Powers who fought on the side of Germany and to recognise whatever dispositions nay be made concerning the territories of the former Austro-Hungarian Monarchy, of the Kingdom of Bulgaria and of the Ottoman Empire, and to recognise the new States within their frontiers as there laid down.

REVIEW QUESTIONS

1. What guarantees of permanent international peace are incorporated into this treaty?
2. Assuming that all of the clauses in this treaty were to be enforced, does it provide the basis for a lasting peace?
3. Is this a "peace without victors"?
4. How do you think Germans responded to this treaty?
5. To what extent are the rights and liberties of disenfranchised minorities—whether ethnic minorities in eastern Europe, colonial subjects, or the world's laborers—guaranteed by this treaty?

JOHN MAYNARD KEYNES

FROM *The Economic Consequences of the Peace*

Criticism of the Versailles Treaty began almost immediately after it was signed. German outrage at this "dictated" peace was predictable, but objections were also voiced on the Allied side. One of the most stinging indictments came from British economist John Maynard Keynes (1883–1946), who believed that the economic clauses of the treaty had laid shaky foundations for a lasting peace. Keynes served as an economic adviser to Lloyd George at the Versailles Conference, but he abandoned this post in despair over the terms being imposed upon Germany, and then quickly made public his concerns in the highly influential book, The Economic Consequences of the Peace *(1919). Keynes was especially critical of the reparations settlement, arguing that punishing Germany by seriously weakening its economy would only serve to destabilize the European economy as a whole. After dissecting the characters and motives of the chief negotiators, he offered his own solutions to the economic crisis produced by the war, arguing that these remedies would benefit not only Europe, but also the United States, which would enjoy increased international trade with healthy trading partners.*

From *The Economic Consequences of the Peace*, John Maynard Keynes, Harcourt, Brace and Howe, 1920.

THE CONFERENCE

* * * the lead was taken by the French, in the sense that it was generally they who made in the first instance the most definite and the most extreme proposals. This was partly a matter of tactics. When the final result is expected to be a compromise, it is often prudent to start from an extreme position; and the French anticipated at the outset—like most other persons—a double process of compromise, first of all to suit the ideas of their allies and associates, and secondly in the course of the Peace Conference proper with the Germans themselves. These tactics were justified by the event.

*　　*　　*

Clemenceau was by far the most eminent member of the Council of Four, and he had taken the measure of his colleagues. He alone both had an idea and had considered it in all its consequences. His age, his character, his wit, and his appearance joined to give him objectivity and a defined outline in an environment of confusion. One could not despise Clemenceau or dislike him, but only take a different view as to the nature of civilized man, or indulge, at least, a different hope.

*　　*　　*

His principles for the peace can be expressed simply. In the first place, he was a foremost believer in the view of German psychology that the German understands and can understand nothing but intimidation, that he is without generosity or remorse in negotiation, that there is no advantage he will not take of you, and no extent to which he will not demean himself for profit, that he is without honor, pride, or mercy. Therefore you must never negotiate with a German or conciliate him; you must dictate to him. On no other terms will he respect you, or will you prevent him from cheating you. But it is doubtful how far he thought these characteristics peculiar to Germany, or whether his candid view of some other nations was fundamentally different. His philosophy had, therefore, no place for "sentimentality" in international relations. Nations are real things, of whom you love one and feel for the rest indifference—or hatred. The glory of the nation you love is a desirable end,—but generally to be obtained at your neighbor's expense. The politics of power are inevitable, and there is nothing very new to learn about this war or the end it was fought for; England had destroyed, as in each preceding century, a trade rival; a mighty chapter had been closed in the secular struggle between the glories of Germany and of France. Prudence required some measure of lip service to the "ideals" of foolish Americans and hypocritical Englishmen; but it would be stupid to believe that there is much room in the world, as it really is, for such affairs as the League of Nations, or any sense in the principle of self-determination except as an ingenious formula for rearranging the balance of power in one's own interests.

*　　*　　*

* * * [President Wilson] was like a Nonconformist minister, perhaps a Presbyterian. His thought and his temperament were essentially theological not intellectual, with all the strength and the weakness of that manner of thought, feeling, and expression.

*　　*　　*

The President's program for the World, as set forth in his speeches and his Notes, had displayed a spirit and a purpose so admirable that the last desire of his sympathizers was to criticize details, —the details, they felt, were quite rightly not filled in at present, but would be in due course. It was commonly believed at the commencement of the Paris Conference that the President had thought out, with the aid of a large body of advisers, a comprehensive scheme not only for the League of Nations, but for the embodiment of the Fourteen Points in an actual Treaty of Peace. But in fact the President had thought out nothing; when it came to practice his ideas were nebulous and incomplete. He had no plan, no scheme, no constructive ideas whatever for clothing with the flesh of life the commandments which he had thundered from the White House. He could have preached a sermon on any of them or have addressed a stately prayer to the Almighty for their fulfilment; but he could not frame their concrete application to the actual state of Europe.

He not only had no proposals in detail, but he was in many respects, perhaps inevitably, ill-informed as to European conditions. And not only was he ill-informed—that was true of Mr. Lloyd George also—but his mind was slow and unadaptable.

*   *   *

After a display of much principle and dignity in the early days of the Council of Ten, he discovered that there were certain very important points in the program of his French, British, or Italian colleague, as the case might be, of which he was incapable of securing the surrender by the methods of secret diplomacy. What then was he to do in the last resort?

*   *   *

Having decided that some concessions were unavoidable, he might have sought by firmness and address and the use of the financial power of the United States to secure as much as he could of the substance, even at some sacrifice of the letter. But the President was not capable of so clear an understanding with himself as this implied. He was too conscientious. Although compromises were now necessary, he remained a man of prin-

ciple and the Fourteen Points a contract absolutely binding upon him. He would do nothing that was not honorable; he would do nothing that was not just and right; he would do nothing that was contrary to his great profession of faith. Thus, without any abatement of the verbal inspiration of the Fourteen Points, they became a document for gloss and interpretation and for all the intellectual apparatus of self-deception,

*   *   *

The subtlest sophisters and most hypocritical draftsmen were set to work, and produced many ingenious exercises which might have deceived for more than an hour a cleverer man than the President.

Thus instead of saying that German-Austria is prohibited from uniting with Germany except by leave of France (which would be inconsistent with the principle of self-determination), the Treaty, with delicate draftsmanship, states that "Germany acknowledges and will respect strictly the independence of Austria, within the frontiers which may be fixed in a Treaty between that State and the Principal Allied and Associated Powers; she agrees that this independence shall be inalienable, except with the consent of the Council of the League of Nations," which sounds, but is not, quite different. And who knows but that the President forgot that another part of the Treaty provides that for this purpose the Council of the League must be *unanimous.*

*   *   *

Such instances could be multiplied. The honest and intelligible purpose of French policy, to limit the population of Germany and weaken her economic system, is clothed, for the President's sake, in the august language of freedom and international equality.

*   *   *

REMEDIES

*   *   *

By fixing the Reparation payments well within Germany's capacity to pay, we make possible the renewal of hope and enterprise within her territory, we avoid the perpetual friction and opportunity of improper pressure arising out of Treaty clauses which are impossible of fulfilment, and we render unnecessary the intolerable powers of the Reparation Commission.

*   *   *

It would be objected, I suppose, by some critics that such an arrangement might go some way in effect towards realizing the former German dream of Mittel-Europa.

*   *   *

If we take the view that for at least a generation to come Germany cannot be trusted with even a modicum of prosperity, that while all our recent Allies are angels of light, all our recent enemies, Germans, Austrians, Hungarians, and the rest, are children of the devil, that year by year Germany must be kept impoverished and her children starved and crippled, and that she must be ringed round by enemies; then we shall reject all the proposals of this chapter, and particularly those which may assist Germany to regain a part of her former material prosperity and find a means of livelihood for the industrial population of her towns. But if this view of nations and of their relation to one another is adopted by the democracies of Western Europe, and is financed by the United States, heaven help us all.

*   *   *

The Settlement of Inter-Ally Indebtedness

In proposing a modification of the Reparation terms, I have considered them so far only in relation to Germany. But fairness requires that so great a reduction in the amount should be accompanied by a readjustment of its apportionment between the Allies themselves.

*   *   *

I suggest, therefore, that we should by our acts prove ourselves sincere and trustworthy, and that accordingly Great Britain should waive altogether her claims for cash payment in favor of Belgium, Serbia, and France. The whole of the payments made by Germany would then be subject to the prior charge of repairing the material injury done to those countries and provinces which suffered actual invasion by the enemy * * *

*   *   *

With the Reparation problem thus cleared up it would be possible to bring forward with a better grace and more hope of success two other financial proposals, each of which involves an appeal to the generosity of the United States.

The first is for the entire cancellation of Inter-Ally indebtedness (that is to say, indebtedness between the Governments of the Allied and Associated countries) incurred for the purposes of the war.

*   *   *

On the one hand, Europe must depend in the long run on her own daily labor and not on the largesse of America; but, on the other hand, she will not pinch herself in order that the fruit of her daily labor may go elsewhere. In short, I do not believe that any of these tributes will continue to be paid, at the best, for more than a very few years. They do not square with human nature or agree with the spirit of the age.

*   *   *

An International Loan

I pass to a second financial proposal. The requirements of Europe are *immediate*. The prospect of being relieved of oppressive interest payments to England and America over the whole life of the next two generations (and of receiving from Germany some assistance year by year to the costs of restoration) would free the future from excessive anxiety. But it would not meet the ills of the immediate present,—the excess of Europe's imports over her exports, the adverse exchange, and the disorder of the currency. It will be very difficult for European production to get started again without a temporary measure of external assistance. I am therefore a supporter of an international loan in some shape or form, such as has been advocated in many quarters in France, Germany, and England, and also in the United States. In whatever way the ultimate responsibility for repayment is distributed, the burden of finding the immediate resources must inevitably fall in major part upon the United States.

*   *   *

But if America recalls for a moment what Europe has meant to her and still means to her, what Europe, the mother of art and of knowledge, in spite of everything, still is and still will be, will she not reject these counsels of indifference and isolation, and interest herself in what may prove decisive issues for the progress and civilization of all mankind?

*   *   *

REVIEW QUESTIONS

1. How did the characters and motives of Clemenceau and Wilson differ?
2. What problems were produced by the incompatability of their attitudes toward the peace settlement, according to Keynes?
3. How would Keynes revise the economic clauses of the treaty?
4. What benefit does he believe Britain would derive from sacrificing its demand for reparations payments?
5. What benefit would the United States derive from sacrificing its demand for repayment of wartime loans?

27 ☙ TURMOIL BETWEEN THE WARS

The Great War was not only physically devastating, but it also did considerable psychological and spiritual damage. During the war, the trauma of trench warfare sometimes pushed soldiers over the edge of sanity into madness, a condition euphemistically known as "shell shock." In the aftermath of the war, it almost seemed as if European society as a whole was suffering from a nervous breakdown of monumental proportions. Peace, so long desired, did not bring the security and prosperity for which so many yearned. Instead, the European nations lurched from one crisis to the next during the 1920s and 1930s, and another episode of international warfare erupted at the end of these two short decades of uneasy peace.

The crisis of "total" war produced conditions conducive to the rise of totalitarianism, a distinctively modern form of authoritarian government. In Russia, the initial stages of the Soviet Revolution generated hopes for the creation of a modern communist utopia, hopes shared both by Russian revolutionaries and by many progressives outside of Russia. However, Stalin's rise to power and his imposition of a Communist Party dictatorship put an end to this dream. Stalin's authoritarianism of the left was paralleled by fascist movements in eastern and central Europe. Mussolini's fascism and Hitler's Nazism shared many elements of traditional right-wing ideology, but they also sought to incorporate elements of left-wing theory and practice, producing a revolutionism of the right. Many Europeans, disillusioned with liberalism and democracy, greeted charismatic dictatorship as a new and attractive political option.

The tendency to look to extremist political movements for solutions to social problems was greatly reinforced by the economic crisis brought on by the Great Depression of the 1930s. Throughout Europe, the Depression caused a dramatic polarization of the political spectrum and a realignment of political allegiances. The greatest losers were the centrist parties still committed to liberalism and parliamentary democracy.

In response to the dislocations of the era, many intellectuals subjected traditional orthodoxies to ruthless scrutiny. Philosophers, scientists, and artists all puzzled over the purpose of human existence in a cosmos that seemed bereft of transcendent meaning, and many wondered whether God was dead, or at least unwilling to intervene in human affairs. The pointless carnage of the war had crushed the optimism of Belle Époque culture. That Europeans had allowed such a cataclysm to occur at all suggested that irrational impulses played an important role in human behavior and that progress was not as inevitable as nineteenth-century positivists had thought. Technological and scientific advances, while impressive, brought new dangers—including devastating increases in the destructiveness of military weapons—and they did not provide answers to human beings' deepest yearnings for spiritual knowledge and sustenance.

JOHN REED

FROM *Ten Days That Shook the World*

Despite his upper-class origins, the American John Reed (1887–1920) was drawn to the socialist and labor movements of the pre-war era. After graduating from Harvard in 1910, he traveled extensively as a reporter, covering the Mexican Revolution, worker protests in the United States, and the battlefronts of World War I. After the February Revolution in Russia, Reed set off for Petrograd, arriving in time to personally witness the Bolshevik takeover in late 1917. On the basis of his experiences, and using documents collected during his stay in Russia, Reed wrote Ten Days That Shook the World, *one of the best-known accounts of the Soviet Revolution, first published in 1919. For all its historical value,* Ten Days That Shook the World *is an intensely personal account of the revolutionary events of 1917, what Reed himself called a "slice of intensified history—history as I saw it." Recreating the swirling drama of unfolding events, Reed's book provides a blow-by-blow account of the key events of the revolution.*

On 8 November 1917, the day after the successful Bolshevik overthrow of the liberal provisional government, Lenin—who had only returned to Russia from exile two weeks before—gave a critically important speech to the All-Russia Congress of Soviets. In an attempt to rally support for the fledgling Communist regime, Lenin offered Russian soldiers, peasants, and workers what they most wanted: an end to the war and a redistribution of land.

From *Ten Days That Shook the World,* John Reed, Boni and Liveright, 1919.

*   *   *

It was just 8.40 when a thundering wave of cheers announced the entrance of the presidium, with Lenin—great Lenin—among them. A short, stocky figure, with a big head set down in his shoulders, bald and bulging. Little eyes, a snubbish nose, wide, generous mouth, and heavy chin; clean-shaven now, but already beginning to bristle with the well-known beard of his past and future. Dressed in shabby clothes, his trousers much too long for him. Unimpressive, to be the idol of a mob, loved and revered as perhaps few leaders in history have been. A strange popular leader—a leader purely by virtue of intellect; colourless, humourless, uncompromising and detached, without picturesque idiosyncrasies—but with the power of explaining profound ideas in simple terms, of analysing a concrete situation. And combined with shrewdness, the greatest intellectual audacity.

*   *   *

Now Lenin, gripping the edge of the reading stand, letting his little winking eyes travel over the crowd as he stood there waiting, apparently oblivious to the long-rolling ovation, which lasted several minutes. When it finished, he said simply, "We shall now proceed to construct the Socialist order!" Again that overwhelming human roar.

"The first thing is the adoption of practical measures to realise peace. . . . We shall offer peace to the peoples of all the belligerent countries upon the basis of the Soviet terms—no annexations, no indemnities, and the right of self-determination of peoples. At the same time, according to our promise, we shall publish and repudiate the secret treaties. . . . The question of War and Peace is so clear that I think that I may, without preamble, read the project of a Proclamation to the Peoples of All the Belligerent Countries. . . ."

His great mouth, seeming to smile, opened wide as he spoke; his voice was hoarse—not unpleasantly so, but as if it had hardened that way after years and years of speaking—and went on monotonously, with the effect of being able to go

on forever. . . . For emphasis he bent forward slightly. No gestures. And before him, a thousand simple faces looking up in intent adoration.

PROCLAMATION TO THE PEOPLES AND GOVERN-
MENTS OF ALL THE BELLIGERENT NATIONS.

The Workers' and Peasants' Government, created by the revolution of November 6th and 7th and based on the Soviets of Workers', Soldiers' and Peasants' Deputies, proposes to all the belligerent peoples and to their Governments to begin immediately negotiations for a just and democratic peace.

The Government means by a just and democratic peace, which is desired by the immense majority of the workers and the labouring classes, exhausted and depleted by the war—that peace which the Russian workers and peasants, after having struck down the Tsarist monarchy, have not ceased to demand categorically—immediate peace without annexations (that is to say, without conquest of foreign territory, without forcible annexation of other nationalities), and without indemnities.

*   *   *

To continue this war in order to permit the strong and rich nations to divide among themselves the weak and conquered nationalities is considered by the Government the greatest possible crime against humanity; and the Government solemnly proclaims its decision to sign a treaty of peace which will put an end to this war upon the above conditions, equally fair for all nationalities without exception.

*   *   *

In addressing this offer of peace to the Governments and to the peoples of all the belligerent countries, the Provisional Workers' and Peasants' Government of Russia addresses equally and in particular the conscious workers of the three nations most devoted to humanity and the three most important nations among those taking part in the present war—England, France, and Germany. The workers of these countries have rendered the greatest services to the cause of progress and of Socialism. The splendid examples of the Chartist movement in England, the series of revolutions, of world-wide historical significance, accomplished by the French proletariat—and finally, in Germany, the historic struggle against the Laws of Exception, an example for the workers of the whole world of prolonged and stubborn action, and the creation of the formidable organisations of German proletarians—all these models of proletarian heroism, these monuments of history, are for us a sure guarantee that the workers of these countries will understand the duty imposed upon them to liberate humanity from the horrors and consequences of war; and that these workers, by decisive, energetic and continued action, will help us to bring to a successful conclusion the cause of peace—and at the same time, the cause of the liberation of the exploited working masses from all slavery and all exploitation.

When the grave thunder of applause had died away, Lenin spoke again:

"We propose to the Congress to ratify this declaration. We address ourselves to the Governments as well as to the peoples, for a declaration which would be addressed only to the peoples of the belligerent countries might delay the conclusion of peace. The conditions of peace, drawn up during the armistice, will be ratified by the Constituent Assembly. In fixing the duration of the armistice at three months, we desire to give to the peoples as long a rest as possible after this bloody extermination, and ample time for them to elect their representatives. This proposal of peace will meet with resistance on the part of the imperialist governments—we don't fool ourselves on that score. But we hope that revolution will soon break out in all the belligerent countries; that is why we address ourselves especially to the workers of France, England and Germany. . . .

"The revolution of November 6th and 7th," he ended, "has opened the era of the Social Revolution. . . . The labour movement, in the name of peace and Socialism, shall win, and fulfil its destiny. . . ."

There was something quiet and powerful in all this, which stirred the souls of men. It was understandable why people believed when Lenin spoke. . . .

*　　*　　*

"We want a just peace, but we are not afraid of a revolutionary war. . . . Probably the imperialist Governments will not answer our appeal—but we shall not issue an ultimatum to which it will be easy to say no. . . . If the German proletariat realises that we are ready to consider all offers of peace, that will perhaps be the last drop which overflows the bowl—revolution will break out in Germany. . . .

"We consent to examine all conditions of peace, but that doesn't mean that we shall accept them. . . . For some of our terms we shall fight to the end—but possibly for others will find it impossible to continue the war. . . . Above all, we want to finish the war. . . ."

It was exactly 10:35 when Kameniev asked all in favour of the proclamation to hold up their cards. One delegate dared to raise his hand against, but the sudden sharp outburst around him brought it swiftly down. . . . Unanimous.

Suddenly, by common impulse, we found ourselves on our feet, mumbling together into the smooth lifting unison of the *Internationale*. A grizzled old soldier was sobbing like a child. Alexandra Kollontai rapidly winked the tears back. The immense sound rolled through the hall, burst windows and doors and seared into the quiet sky. "The war is ended! The war is ended!" said a young workman near me, his face shining. And when it was over, as we stood there in a kind of awkward hush, some one in the back of the room shouted, "Comrades! Let us remember those who have died for liberty!" So we began to sing the Funeral March, that slow, melancholy and yet-triumphant chant, so Russian and so moving. The *Internationale* is an alien air, after all. The Funeral March seemed the very soul of those dark masses whose delegates sat in this hall, building from their obscure visions a new Russia—and perhaps more.

You fell in the fatal fight
For the liberty of the people, for the honour of the people . . .

You gave up your lives and everything dear to you,
You suffered in horrible prisons,
You went to exile in chains. . . .

Without a word you carried your chains because you could not ignore your suffering brothers,
Because you believed that justice is stronger than the sword. . . .
The time will come when your surrendered life will count.
That time is near; when tyranny falls the people will rise, great and free!
Farewell, brothers, you chose a noble path,
You are followed by the new and fresh army ready to die and to suffer. . . .

Farewell, brothers, you chose a noble path,
At your grave we swear to fight, to work for freedom and the people's happiness. . . .

For this did they lie there, the martyrs of March, in their cold Brotherhood Grave on Mars Field; for this thousands and tens of thousands had died in the prisons, in exile, in Siberian mines. It had not come as they expected it would come, nor as the *intelligentzia* desired it; but it had come—rough, strong, impatient of formulas, contemptuous of sentimentalism; *real*. . . .

Lenin was reading the Decree on Land:

(1.) All private ownership of land is abolished immediately without compensation.

(2.) All land-owners' estates, and all lands belonging to the Crown, to monasteries, church lands with all their live stock and inventoried property, buildings and all appurtenances, are transferred to the disposition of the township Land Committees and the district Soviets of Peasants' Deputies until the Constituent Assembly meets.

(3.) Any damage whatever done to the confiscated property which from now on belongs to the whole People, is regarded as a serious crime, punishable by the revolutionary tribunals. The district Soviets of Peasants' Deputies shall take all necessary measures for the observance of the strictest order during the taking over of the land-owners' estates, for the determination of the dimensions of the plots of land and which of them are subject to confiscation, for the drawing up of an inventory of the entire confiscated property, and for the strictest revolutionary protection of all the farming property on the land, with all buildings, implements, cattle, supplies of products, etc., passing into the hands of the People.

(4.) * * * The lands of peasants and of Cossacks serving in the Army shall not be confiscated.

"This is not," explained Lenin, "the project of former Minister Tchernov, who spoke of 'erecting a frame-work' and tried to realise reforms from above. From below, on the spot, will be decided the questions of division of the land. The amount of land received by each peasant will vary according to the locality. . . .

*　*　*

REVIEW QUESTIONS

1. What kind of peace does Lenin propose?
2. How do you think the other governments of the belligerent nations would have responded to this proposal?
3. What policies were instituted by the "Decree on Land"? Why?
4. What does this document tell you about the aspirations of the Bolshevik revolutionaries?

ALEXANDRA KOLLONTAI

FROM *The Autobiography of a Sexually Emancipated Communist Woman*

Alexandra Kollontai (1872–1952) grew up in an educated, affluent, and fairly liberal Russian family. She married young, but left her husband and son to study political economy in Switzerland, where she became actively involved in socialist organizing. Originally a Menshevik, Kollontai became a Bolshevik in 1915, largely because of the Bolshevik opposition to the war, and entered into a friendly correspondence with Lenin.

After the October Revolution, Kollontai was named People's Commissar of Social Welfare, becoming the only woman to hold a cabinet post in the new Bolshevik government. As director of the Women's Bureau (Zhenotdel) she agitated in favor of economic liberty for working women and state welfare benefits for mothers. Her advocacy of women's rights and free love was not universally popular, and in the years following the revolution she found herself increasingly at odds with the Communist Party leadership. In 1922, Kollontai was assigned a diplomatic post in Norway—a gentle form of exile—and she spent much of the rest of her life outside of Russia. In memoirs written in 1926, she recounted the heady early days of the revolution, when a total transformation of Russian society still seemed possible.

From *The Autobiography of a Sexually Emancipated Communist Woman*, Alexandra Kollontai, translated by Salvator Attanasio, Herder and Herder, 1971.

*   *   *

When one recalls the first months of the Workers' Government, months which were so rich in *magnificent illusions*,[1] plans, ardent initiatives to improve life, to organize the world anew, months of the real romanticism of the Revolution, one would in fact like to write about all else save about one's self. I occupied the post of Minister of Social Welfare from October of 1917 *to March of 1918*. It was not without opposition that I was received by the former officials of the Ministry. Most of them sabotaged us openly and simply did not show up for work. But precisely this office could not interrupt its work, come what may, since in itself it was an extraordinarily complicated operation. It included the whole welfare program for the war-disabled, hence for hundreds of thousands of crippled soldiers and officers, the pension system in general, foundling homes, homes for the aged, orphanages, hospitals for the needy, the work-shops making artificial limbs, the administration of playing-card factories (the manufacture of playing cards was a State monopoly), *the educational system*, clinical hospitals for women. In addition a whole series of educational institutes for young girls were also under the direction of this Ministry.

---

[1] By 1926, it was already necessary to be cautious about how one described one's involvement in the revolution, and Kollontai censored her own writing. Italics indicate passages in the original manuscript that were not included in the published version of her memoirs.

One can easily imagine the enormous demands these tasks made upon a small group of people who, at the same time, were novices in State administration. In a clear awareness of these difficulties *I formed*, immediately, an auxiliary council in which experts such as physicians, jurists, pedagogues were represented alongside the workers and the minor officials of the Ministry. The sacrifice, the energy with which the minor employees bore the burden of this difficult task was truly exemplary. It was not only a matter of keeping the work of the Ministry going, but also of initiating reforms and improvements. New, fresh forces replaced the sabotaging officers of the old regime. A new life stirred in the offices of the formerly highly conservative Ministry. Days of grueling work! And at night the sessions of the councils of the People's Commissar (of the cabinet) under Lenin's chairmanship. A small, modest room and only one secretary who recorded the resolutions which changed Russia's life to its bottommost foundations.

*   *   *

My main work as People's Commissar consisted in the following: by decree to improve the situation of the war-disabled, to abolish religious instruction in the schools for young girls which were under the Ministry (this was still before the general separation of Church and State), and to transfer priests to the civil service, to introduce the right of self-administration for pupils in the schools for girls, to reorganize the former orphanages into government Children's Homes *(no distinction was to be made between orphaned children and those who still had fathers and mothers)*, to set up the first hostels for the needy and street-urchins, to convene a committee, composed *only* of doctors, which was to be commissioned *to elaborate* the free public health system for the whole country. In my opinion the most important accomplishment of the People's Commissariat, however, was the legal foundation of a Central Office for Maternity and Infant Welfare. The draft of the bill relating to this Central Office was signed by me in January of 1918. A second decree followed in which *I* changed all maternity hospitals into free Homes for Maternity and Infant Care, in order thereby to set the groundwork for a comprehensive government system of pre-natal care. I was greatly assisted in coping with these tasks by Dr. Korolef. We also planned a "Pre-Natal Care Palace," a model home with an exhibition room in which courses for mothers would be held *and, among many other things*, model day nurseries were also to be established. We were just about completing preparations for such a facility in the building of a girls' boarding school at which formerly young girls of the nobility had been educated and which was still under the direction of a countess, when a fire destroyed our work, which had barely begun! Had the fire been set deliberately? . . . I was dragged out of bed in the middle of the night. I rushed to the scene of the fire; the beautiful exhibition room was totally ruined, as were all the other rooms. Only the huge nameplate "Pre-Natal Care Palace" still hung over the entrance door.

My efforts to nationalize maternity and infant care set off a new wave of insane attacks against me. All kinds of lies were related about the "nationalization of women," *about my legislative proposals which assertedly ordained that little girls of 12 were to become mothers*. A special fury gripped the religious followers of the old regime when, *on my own authority (the cabinet later criticized me for this action)*, I transformed the famous Alexander Nevsky monastery into a home for war-invalids. The monks resisted and a shooting fray ensued. The press again raised a loud hue and cry against *me*. The Church organized street demonstrations *against my action* and also pronounced "anathema" against me . . .

I received countless threatening letters, but I never requested military protection. I always went out alone, unarmed and without any kind of a bodyguard. In fact I never gave a thought to any kind of danger, being all too engrossed in matters of an utterly different character. In February of 1918 a first State delegation of the Soviets was sent to Sweden in order to clarify different economic and political questions. As Peoples' Commissar I headed this delegation. But our vessel was shipwrecked; we were saved by landing on the Aland Islands which belonged to Finland. At this very time the struggle between the Whites and the Reds in the country had reached its most crucial moment and the German Army was also making ready to wage war against Finland.

*   *   *

Now began a *dark time* of my life which I cannot treat of here since the events are still too fresh in my mind. *But the day will also come when I will give an account of them.*

There were differences of opinion in the Party. I resigned from my post as People's Commissar *on the ground of total disagreement with the current policy. Little by little I was also relieved of all my other tasks. I again gave lectures and espoused my ideas on "the new woman" and "the new morality."* The Revolution was in full swing. The struggle was becoming increasingly irreconcilable and bloodier, *much of what was happening did not fit in with my outlook.* But after all there was still the unfinished task, women's liberation. Women, of course, had received all rights but in practice, of course, they still lived under the old yoke: without authority in family life, enslaved by a thousand menial household chores, bearing the whole burden of maternity, even the material cares, because many women now found life alone as a result of the war and other circumstances.

*   *   *

A flood of new work was waiting for me. The question now was one of drawing women into the people's kitchens and of educating them to devote their energies to children's homes and day-care centers, the school system, household reforms, and still many other pressing matters. The main thrust of all this activity was to implement, in fact, equal rights for women as a labor unit in the national economy and as a citizen in the political sphere and, of course, with the special proviso: maternity was to be appraised as a social function and therefore protected and provided for by the State.

*   *   *

A serious illness tore me away from the exciting work for months. Hardly having recovered—at that time I was in Moscow—I took over the direction of the Coordinating Office for Work among Women and again a new period of intensive, grueling work began. A communist women's *newspaper* was founded, conferences and congresses of women workers were convoked. The foundation was laid for work with the women of the East (Mohammedans). Two world conferences of communist women took place in Moscow. The law liberalizing abortion was put through and a number of regulations of benefit to women were introduced by our Coordinating Office and legally confirmed. *At this time I had to do more writing and speaking than ever before* . . . Our work received wholehearted support from Lenin. And Trotsky, although he was overburdened with military tasks, unfailingly and gladly appeared at our conferences. Energetic, gifted women, two of whom are no longer alive, sacrificially devoted all their energies to the work of the Coordinating Office.

At the eighth Soviet Congress, as a member of the Soviet executive *(now there were already several women on this body),* I proposed a motion that the Soviets in all areas contribute to the creation of a consciousness of the struggle for equal rights for women and, accordingly, to involve them in State and communal work. I managed to push the motion through and to get it accepted but not without resistance. It was a great, an enduring victory.

A heated debate flared up when I published my thesis on the new morality. *For our Soviet marriage law, separated from the Church to be sure, is not essentially more progressive than the same laws that after all exist in other progressive democratic countries.* * * * [A]lthough the illegitimate child *was* placed on a legal par with the legitimate child, in practice a great deal of hypocrisy and injustice still exists in this area. When one speaks of the "immorality" which the Bolsheviks purportedly propagated, it suffices to submit our marriage laws to a close scrutiny to note that in the divorce question we are on a par with North America whereas in the question of the illegitimate child we have *not yet even* progressed as far as the Norwegians.

The most radical wing of the Party was formed around this question. My theses, my *sexual and moral* views, were bitterly fought *by many Party comrades of both sexes: as were still other differences of opinion in the Party regarding political guiding principles.* Personal and family cares were added thereto and thus months in 1922 went by without fruitful work. Then in the autumn of 1922 came my official appointment to the legation of the Russian Soviet representation in Norway. I really believed that this appointment would be purely formal and that therefore in Norway I would find time to devote to myself, to my literary activity.

Things turned out quite differently. With the day of my entry into office in Norway I also entered upon a wholly new course of work in my life which drew upon all my energies to the highest degree.

*   *   *

Review Questions

1. What kind of work did Kollontai do as People's Commissar of Social Welfare?
2. What does her work tell you about the social welfare policies of the revolutionary government?
3. Who opposed Kollontai's efforts in favor of women's liberation? Why?

Nadezhda Mandelstam

FROM *Hope Against Hope*

The Soviet revolution also generated considerable excitement about revitalizing the arts in Russia. In the early 1920s a vibrant and sometimes contentious artistic culture emerged, a culture typified by experimentation and considerable optimism about the future of the new workers' state. However, as Stalin consolidated his grip on power, artists and writers were forced to either produce works that supported Stalinist orthodoxy or to retreat into silence. By the 1930s, any expression of resistance to the regime was firmly suppressed and the avant-gardism of the early revolution gave way to state-imposed socialist realism. During the great purges, many artists and intellectuals were imprisoned or executed.

Osip Mandelstam (1891–1938?), widely recognized as one of the greatest Russian poets of the twentieth century, was already an established author in 1917. As a poet, Mandelstam tended to be apolitical, but in 1934 he read a poem about Stalin to a private gathering, describing the Soviet dictator as having "cockroach whiskers" and "fingers . . . as fat as grubs." In retaliation, Stalin had Mandelstam and his wife, Nadezhda, exiled to the provinces. In 1938 Mandelstam was arrested and sent east to a prison camp, where he soon died. In the 1970s, Nadezhda Mandelstam

(1899–1980) wrote two volumes of memoirs about her life with and without Osip. In Hope Against Hope, *she documented the circumstances surrounding her husband's death, basing her account on scraps of evidence she carefully gathered in the years following the event.*

The Date of Death

At the end of December 1938 or in January 1939, according to some journalists from *Pravda*, who mentioned it to Shklovski, someone in the Central Committee said in their hearing that it now appeared that there had been no case against Mandelstam at all. This was shortly after the dismissal of Yezhov and was meant to serve as an illustration of his misdeeds. . . . The conclusion I drew was that M. must be dead.

Not long afterward I was sent a notice asking me to go to the post office at Nikita Gate. Here I was handed back the parcel I had sent to M. in the camp. "The addressee is dead," the young lady behind the counter informed me. It would be easy enough to establish the date on which the parcel was returned to me—it was the same day on which the newspapers published the long list of Government awards—the first ever—to Soviet writers.

My brother Evgeni went that same day to tell the Shklovskis in the writers' apartment building on Lavrushinski Street. They went to call Victor from the apartment downstairs—Katayev's, I think it was—where Fadeyev and other "Fellow Travelers" were drinking on the occasion of the honor done them by the State. It was now that Fadeyev shed a drunken tear for M.: "We have done away with a great poet!" The celebration of the awards took on something of the flavor of a surreptitious wake for the dead. I am not clear, however, as to who there (apart from Shklovski) really understood what M.'s destruction meant. Most of them, after all, belonged to the generation which had changed its values in favor of the "new." It was they who had prepared the way for the strong man, the dictator who was empowered to kill or spare people at his own discretion, to establish goals and choose whatever means he saw fit for their fulfillment.

In June 1940, M.'s brother Alexander was summoned to the Registry Office of the Bauman district and handed M.'s death certificate with instructions to pass it on to me. M.'s age was given as forty-seven, and the date of his death as December 27, 1938. The cause was given as "heart failure." This is as much as to say that he died because he died: what is death but heart failure? There was also something about arteriosclerosis.

The issue of a death certificate was not the rule but the exception. To all intents and purposes, as far as his civil status was concerned, a person could be considered dead from the moment he was sent to a camp, or, indeed, from the moment of his arrest, which was automatically followed by his conviction and sentence to imprisonment in a camp. This meant he vanished so completely that it was regarded as tantamount to physical death. Nobody bothered to tell a man's relatives when he died in camp or prison: you regarded yourself as a widow or orphan from the moment of his arrest. When a woman was told in the Prosecutor's office that her husband had been given ten years, the official sometimes added: "You can remarry." Nobody ever raised the awkward question as to how this gracious "permission" to remarry could be squared with the official sentence, which was technically by no means a death sentence. As I have said already, I do not know why they showed such exceptional consideration to me by issuing a death certificate. I wonder what was behind it.

In the circumstances, death was the only possible deliverance. When I heard that M. had died, I stopped having my nightmares about him. Later on, Kazarnovski said to me: "Osip Emilievich did well to die: otherwise he would have gone to Kolyma." Kazarnovski had himself served his sentence in Kolyma, and when he was released in 1944 he turned up in Tashkent. He lived there without a permit or ration cards, hiding from the police, terrified of everybody and drinking very heavily. He had no proper shoes, and I gave him some tiny galoshes that had belonged to my mother. They fitted him very well because he had no toes on his feet—they had become frozen in the camp and he had chopped them off with an ax to prevent gangrene. Whenever they were all taken to the baths, their clothes froze in the damp air of the changing room and rattled like sheets of tin.

Recently I heard an argument as to who was more likely to survive the camps: the people who worked, or those who managed not to. Those who worked died of exhaustion, and those who didn't starved to death. This much was clear to me, though I had neither arguments nor personal observations of my own to support either side in the discussion. The few people who survived were exceptions who proved the rule. In fact, the whole argument reminded me of the Russian folk ballad about the hero at the crossroads: whichever way he goes, he will perish. The main feature of Russian history, something that never changes, is that every road always brings disaster—and not only to heroes. Survival is a matter of pure chance. It is not this that surprises me so much as the fact that a few people, for all their frailty, came through the whole ordeal like heroes, not only living to tell the tale, but preserving the keenness of mind and memory that enables them to do so. I know people like this, but the time has not yet come to name them—apart from the one whom we all know: Solzhenitsyn.

Kazarnovski had come through only with his life and a few disjointed recollections. He had arrived at the camp in Kolyma in the winter and remembered that it was an utter wilderness which was only just being opened up to receive the enormous influx of people being sent to do forced labor. Not a single building or barracks existed yet. They lived in tents and had to put up the prison buildings themselves.

I have heard that prisoners were sent from Vladivostok to Kolyma only by sea, which freezes over in winter—though quite late in the year. I am puzzled, therefore, as to how Kazarnovski could have arrived at Kolyma in winter, after the sea route was no longer navigable. Could it be that he was first sent to another camp, somewhere in the neighborhood of Vladivostok, because of overcrowding in the "transit" camp? At this period the Vladivostok transit camp, where prisoners were held temporarily before being sent on to Kolyma, can hardly have coped with the prison trains arriving all the time. Everything was too confused in Kazarnovski's disordered brain, and I could not clear this point up, though in trying to establish the date of M.'s death it was very important to know at exactly what moment Kazarnovski left the transit camp.

Kazarnovski was the first more or less authentic emissary I had met from the "other world." Before he actually turned up, I had already heard about him from other people and knew that he had really been with M. in the transit camp and had apparently even helped him in some way. They had occupied bunks in the same barracks, almost next to each other. This was the reason I hid Kazarnovski from the police for three months while I slowly extracted from him all the information he had brought to Tashkent. His memory was like a huge, rancid pancake in which fact and fancy from his prison days had been mixed up together and baked into an inseparable mass.

I already knew that this kind of affliction of the memory was not peculiar to the wretched Kazarnovski or a result of drinking too much vodka. It was a feature of almost all the former camp inmates I have met immediately after their release—they had no memory for dates or the passage of time and it was difficult for them to distinguish between things they had actually experienced themselves and stories they had heard from others. Places, names, events and their sequence were all jumbled up in the minds of these broken people, and it was never possible to disentangle them. Most accounts of life in the camps appeared on first hearing to be a disconnected series of stories about the critical moments when the narrator nearly died but then miraculously managed to save himself. The whole of camp life was reduced to these highlights, which were intended to show that although it was almost impossible to survive, man's will to live was such that he came through nevertheless. Listening to these accounts, I was horrified at the thought that there might be nobody who could ever properly bear witness to the past. Whether inside or outside the camps, we had all lost our memories. But it later turned out that there were people who had made it their aim from the beginning not only to save themselves, but to survive as witnesses. These relentless keepers of the truth, merging with all the other prisoners, had bided their time—there were probably more such people in the camps than outside, where it was all too common to succumb to the temptation to make terms with reality and live out one's life in peace. Of course those witnesses who have kept a clear memory of the past are few in number, but their very survival is the best proof that good, not evil, will prevail in the end.

*   *   *

One Final Account

*   *   *

There is nowhere I can make inquiries and nobody who will tell me anything. Who is likely to search through those grisly archives just for the sake of Mandelstam, when they won't even publish a volume of his work?* * *

All I can do, therefore, is to gather what meager evidence there is and speculate about the date of his death. As I constantly tell myself: the sooner he died, the better. There is nothing worse than a slow death. I hate to think that at the moment when my mind was set at rest on being told in the post office that he was dead, he may actually have been still alive and on his way to Kolyma. The date of death has not been established. And it is beyond my power to do anything more to establish it.

*   *   *

REVIEW QUESTIONS

1. Why do you think it was so important to Nadezhda Mandelstam that she reconstruct the exact details of her husband's death?
2. Why do you think Nadezhda Mandelstam wrote her memoirs?
3. Why is she so concerned with remembering and documenting the past?
4. What does this document tell you about conditions in Stalin's prison camps?

BENITO MUSSOLINI

FROM Born of a Need for Action

Fascism emerged during the 1920s as a response to the unsettled political, economic, and social climate of the postwar period. While it was a global phenomenon, it enjoyed its greatest successes in Germany and Italy.

As the first fascist head of state, Benito Mussolini (1883–1945) was an inspiration to other would-be dictators throughout the 1920s. Mussolini began his political career as a socialist journalist, but his ardent support for Italian participation in World War I caused him to be expelled from the Socialist Party. In the chaos of the immediate postwar years in Italy, Mussolini created his own Fascist Party, encouraging his followers to silence political opponents through the use of violence. The Italian ruling elite, confronted with widespread strike activity and the threat of a communist takeover, handed over the reins of government to Mussolini in 1922, after he demonstrated the strength of the fascist movement through a "March on Rome." Many Italians welcomed this development, seeing Mussolini as a great leader—"Duce"—whose forceful rule would bring order, prosperity, and a renewal of national strength and pride. In 1932, ten years after his seizure of power, Mussolini wrote an article on fascism for an Italian encyclopedia, setting down in writing for the first time the ideological premises of the movement.

From *The Estate of Benito Mussolini*, Jane Soames, trans. Hogarth Press, 1933. Reprinted with permission of the publisher.

*   *   *

Fascism was not the nursling of a doctrine worked out beforehand with detailed elaboration; it was born of the need for action and it was itself from the beginning practical rather than theoretical; it was not merely another political party but, even in the first two years, in opposition to all political parties as such, and itself a living movement.

*   *   *

The years which preceded the march to Rome were years of great difficulty, during which the necessity for action did not permit of research or any complete elaboration of doctrine. The battle had to be fought in the towns and villages. There was much discussion, but—what was more important

and more sacred—men died. They knew how to die. Doctrine, beautifully defined and carefully elucidated, with headlines and paragraphs, might be lacking; but there was to take its place something more decisive—Faith.

*   *   *

Fascism is now a completely individual thing, not only as a regime but as a doctrine. And this means that to-day Fascism, exercising its critical sense upon itself and upon others, has formed its own distinct and peculiar point of view, to which it can refer and upon which, therefore, it can act in the face of all problems, practical or intellectual, which confront the world.

And above all, Fascism, the more it considers and observes the future and the development of humanity quite apart from political considerations of the moment, believes neither in the possibility nor the utility of perpetual peace. It thus repudiates the doctrine of Pacifism—born of a renunciation of the struggle and an act of cowardice in the face of sacrifice. War alone brings up to its highest tension all human energy and puts the stamp of nobility upon the peoples who have the courage to meet it. All other trials are substitutes, which never really put men into the position where they have to make the great decision—the alternative of life or death. Thus a doctrine which is founded upon this harmful postulate of peace is hostile to Fascism.

*   *   *

* * *Fascism [is] the complete opposite of * * * so-called scientific and Marxian Socialism, the materialist conception of history; according to which the history of human civilization can be explained simply through the conflict of interests among the various social groups and by the change and development in the means and instruments of production. That the changes in the economic field—new discoveries of raw materials, new methods of working them, and the inventions of science—have their importance no one can deny; but that these factors are sufficient to explain the history of humanity excluding all others is an absurd delusion. Fascism, now and always, believes in holiness and in heroism; that is to say, in actions influenced by no economic motive, direct or indirect.

*   *   *

* * *Fascism repudiates the conception of "economic" happiness, to be realized by Socialism and, as it were, at a given moment in economic evolution to assure to everyone the maximum of well-being. Fascism denies the materialist conception of happiness as a possibility,* * *: that is to say, Fascism denies the validity of the equation, well-being-happiness, which would reduce men to the level of animals, caring for one thing only—to be fat and well-fed—and would thus degrade humanity to a purely physical existence.

After Socialism, Fascism combats the whole complex system of democratic ideology, and repudiates it, whether in its theoretical premises or in its practical application. Fascism denies that the majority, by the simple fact that it is a majority, can direct human society; it denies that numbers alone can govern by means of a periodical consultation, and it affirms the immutable, beneficial and fruitful inequality of mankind, which can never be permanently levelled through the mere operation of a mechanical process such as universal suffrage.

*   *   *

* * *Fascism denies, in democracy, the absurd conventional untruth of political equality dressed out in the garb of collective irresponsibility, and the myth of "happiness" and indefinite progress. But, if democracy may be conceived in diverse forms—that is to say, taking democracy to mean a state of society in which the populace are not reduced to impotence in the State—Fascism may write itself down as "an organized, centralized and authoritative democracy."

*   *   *

A party which entirely governs a nation is a fact entirely new to history, there are no possible references or parallels. Fascism uses in its construction whatever elements in the Liberal, Social or Democratic doctrines still have a living value* * *

*   *   *

* * *if the nineteenth century was a century of individualism (Liberalism always signifying individualism) it may be expected that this will be the century of collectivism, and hence the century of the State.

*   *   *

The foundation of Fascism is the conception of the State, its character, its duty, and its aim. Fascism conceives of the State as an absolute, in comparison with which all individuals or groups are relative, only to be conceived of in their relation to the State.* * * In 1929, at the first five-yearly assembly of the Fascist regime, I said:

"For us Fascists, the State is not merely a guardian, preoccupied solely with the duty of assuring the personal safety of the citizens; nor is it an organization with purely material aims, such as to guarantee a certain level of well-being and peaceful conditions of life; for a mere council of administration would be sufficient to realize such objects. Nor is it a purely political creation, divorced from all contact with the complex material reality which makes up the life of the individual and the life of the people as a whole. The State, as conceived of and as created by Fascism, is a spiritual and moral fact in itself, since its political, juridical and economic organization of the nation is a concrete thing: and such an organization must be in its origins and development a manifestation of the spirit. The State is the guarantor of security both internal and external, but it is also the custodian and transmitter of the spirit of the people, as it has grown up through the centuries in language, in customs and in faith. And the State is not only a living reality of the present, it is also linked with the past and above all with the future, and thus transcending the brief limits of individual life, it represents the immanent spirit of the nation. The forms in which States express themselves may change, but the necessity for such forms is eternal. It is the State which educates its citizens in civic virtue, gives them a consciousness of their mission and welds them into unity; harmonizing their various interests through justice, and transmitting to future generations the mental conquests of science, of art, of law and the solidarity of humanity. It leads men from primitive tribal life to that highest expression of human power which is Empire: it links up through the centuries the names of those of its members who have died for its existence and in obedience to its laws, it holds up the memory of the leaders who have increased its territory and the geniuses who have illumined it with glory as an example to be followed by future generations. When the conception of the State declines, and disunifying and centrifugal tendencies prevail, whether of individuals or of particular groups, the nations where such phenomena appear are in their decline."

* * *

* * *the Fascist State is unique, and an original creation. It is not reactionary, but revolutionary, in that it anticipates the solution of the universal political problems which elsewhere have to be settled in the political field by the rivalry of parties, the excessive power of the Parliamentary regime and the irresponsibility of political assemblies; while it meets the problems of the economic field by a system of syndicalism which is continually increasing in importance, as much in the sphere of labour as of industry: and in the moral field enforces order, discipline, and obedience to that which is the determined moral code of the country. Fascism desires the State to be a strong and organic body, at the same time reposing upon broad and popular support. The Fascist State has drawn into itself even the economic activities of the nation, and, through the corporative social and educational institutions created by it, its influence reaches every aspect of the national life and includes, framed in their respective organizations, all the political, economic and spiritual forces of the nation. A State which reposes upon the support of millions of individuals who recognize its authority, are continually conscious of its power and are ready at once to serve it, is not the old tyrannical State of the medieval lord nor has it anything in common with the absolute governments either before or after 1789. The individual in the Fascist State is not annulled but rather multiplied, just in the same way that a soldier in a regiment is not diminished but rather increased by the number of his comrades. The Fascist State organizes the nation, but leaves a sufficient margin of liberty to the individual; the latter is deprived of all useless and possibly harmful freedom, but retains what is essential; the deciding power in this question cannot be the individual, but the State alone.

* * *

REVIEW QUESTIONS

1. Why does Mussolini reject pacifism?
2. What implications do his comments about war have for the policies of the fascist state?
2. Which aspects of socialism and democracy does Mussolini reject? Which does he retain?
4. What exactly does Mussolini mean when he defines the fascist state as "an organized, centralized and authoritative democracy"?
5. What role does the individual play in this state?

ADOLF HITLER

FROM *Mein Kampf*

German Nazism shared many of the tenets of Italian fascism. Like Mussolini, Adolf Hitler (1889–1945) rejected democracy as bankrupt and promoted an authoritarian politics based on the "leadership principle." Hitler was also an ardent militarist who believed that war was a crucial test of a nation's vigor. Germany's defeat in 1918 was not the result of military failure, he insisted, but rather the product of the diseased condition of German society in general. This corruption and weakness was caused by the diabolical machinations of the Jewish people, whom Hitler portrayed as a degenerate "race" engaged in an international conspiracy designed to destroy the "national principle" binding the German people together as a "master race." In response to this threat, Hitler offered himself as the leader—"Führer"—of a revitalized, militantly nationalist Germany purged of all those who would weaken or diminish the racial purity of the German people.

Hitler was jailed for nine months after a failed coup d'état, the Beer Hall Putsch of 1923. During his imprisonment, he wrote Mein Kampf (My Struggle), *a massive, rambling political memoir detailing the political agenda of the Nazi Party. Many of the political arguments presented in* Mein Kampf *parallel those underpinning Italian fascism. What distinguishes Hitler's thought is his obsessive preoccupation with racial "hygiene" as the basis of national strength.*

*   *   *

What we have to fight for is the security of the existence and the increase of our race and our people, the nourishment of its children and the preservation of the purity of the blood, the freedom and independence of the fatherland in order to enable our people to mature for the fulfillment of the mission which the Creator of the universe has allotted also to them.

*   *   *

A further example for the half-heartedness and the weakness of the leading authority in pre-War

Germany in the most important vital questions of the nation can be the following: Parallel with the political and moral infection of the people went a no less terrible poisoning of the health of the national body. Syphilis began to spread more and more, especially in the great cities,* * *

*   *   *

The cause* * * lies primarily in our prostitution of love. Even if the result of this were not this terrible disease, yet it would still be of deepest danger for the people, for the moral devastation which this depravity brings with it are sufficient to destroy a people slowly but surely. The Judaization of our spiritual life and the mammonization of our mating impulse sooner or later befouls our entire new generation, for instead of vigorous children of natural feeling, only the miserable specimens of financial expedience come forth. For this becomes more and more the basis and the only prerequisite for our marriages. Love, however, finds an outlet somewhere else.

Naturally, one can also here mock Nature for a certain time, but the revenge will not fail to appear, it only will appear later, or rather, it is often recognized too late by the people.

*   *   *

The sin against the blood and the degradation of the race are the hereditary sin of this world and the end of a mankind surrendering to them.

*   *   *

Prostitution is a disgrace to mankind, but one cannot abolish it by moral lectures, pious intentions, etc., but its limitation and its final elimination warrant the abolition of quite a number of preliminary conditions. But the first is and remains the creation of the possibility of early marriage, according to human nature, above all for the man; because the woman is here only the passive part, anyhow.

*   *   *

Marriage also cannot be an end in itself, but has to serve the one greater aim, the propagation

and preservation of the species and the race. Only this is its meaning and its task.

*   *   *

* * *education and training have to eliminate quite a series of evils about which one hardly cares at all today. Above all, in our present-day education a balance between intellectual instruction and physical training has to take place. What today calls itself a *gymnasium* is an insult to the Greek example. With our education one has entirely forgotten that in the long run a healthy mind is able to dwell only in a healthy body. Especially when, with a few exceptions, one looks at the great masses of the people, this principle receives absolute validity.

In pre-War Germany there was a time when one no longer cared for this truth. One simply went on sinning against the body, and one thought that in the one-sided training of the 'mind' one possessed a safe guaranty for the greatness of the nation. A mistake which began to avenge itself much sooner than one thought. It is no accident that the bolshevistic wave found nowhere a better ground than in those places where a population, degenerated by hunger and constant undernourishment, lives: in Central Germany, Saxony, and the Ruhr district. In all these districts, however, a serious resistance on the part of the so-called 'intelligentsia' to this Jewish disease hardly takes place any longer for the simple reason that the intelligentsia itself is physically completely degenerated, though less by reasons of distress than by reasons of education. The exclusively intellectual attitude of our education of the higher classes makes them unable—in a time where not the mind but the fist decides—even to preserve themselves, let alone to hold their ground. In physical deficiencies there lies not infrequently the first cause of personal cowardice.

The exceeding stress on a purely intellectual training and the neglect of physical training favor also in much too early youth the formation of sexual conceptions. The boy who, by sports and gymnastics, is brought to an ironlike inurement succumbs less to the need of sensual gratification than the stay-at-home who is fed exclusively on intellectual food. A reasonable education, however, must take this into consideration. Further, it must not forget that on the part of the healthy young man the expectations of the woman will be different than on the part of a prematurely corrupted weakling.

Thus the entire education has to be directed towards employing the free time of the boy for the useful training of his body. He has no right to loaf about idly in these years, to make streets and movie theaters insecure, but after his daily work he has to steel and harden his young body so that life will not find him too soft some day. To get this under way and also to carry it out, to guide and to lead is the task of the education of youth, and not the exclusive infiltration of so-called wisdom. It has also to do away with the conception that the treatment of the body were the concern of each individual. There is no liberty to sin at the expense of posterity and, with it, of the race.

*   *   *

It is a half measure to allow incurably ill people the permanent possibility of contaminating the other healthy ones. But this corresponds entirely to a humaneness which, in order not to hurt one individual, lets hundreds of others perish. The demand that for defective people the propagation of an equally defective offspring be made impossible is a demand of clearest reason and in its planful execution it means the most humane act of mankind. It will spare undeserved suffering to millions of unfortunates, but in the future it will lead to an increasing improvement of health on the whole. The determination to proceed in this direction will also put up a dam against the further spreading of venereal diseases. For here, if necessary, one will have to proceed to the pitiless isolation of incurably diseased people; a barbaric measure for one who was unfortunate enough to be stricken with it, but a blessing for the contemporaries and for posterity. The temporary pain of a century may and will redeem millenniums from suffering.

*   *   *

Any crossing between two beings of not quite the same high standard produces a medium between the standards of the parents. That means: the young one will probably be on a higher level than the racially lower parent, but not as high as the higher one. Consequently, it will succumb later on in the fight against the higher level. But such a mating contradicts Nature's will to breed life as a whole towards a higher level.

*   *   *

Just as little as Nature desires a mating between weaker individuals and stronger ones, far less she desires the mixing of a higher race with a lower one, as in this case her entire work of higher breeding, which has perhaps taken hundreds of thousands of years, would tumble at one blow.

Historical experience offers countless proofs of this. It shows with terrible clarity that with any mixing of the blood of the Aryan with lower races the result was the end of the culture-bearer. North America, the population of which consists for the greatest part of Germanic elements—which mix only very little with the lower, colored races—displays a humanity and a culture different from those of Central and South America, where chiefly the Romanic immigrants have sometimes mixed with the aborigines on a large scale. By this example alone one may clearly and distinctly recognize the influence of the race mixture. The Germanic of the North American continent, who has remained pure and less intermixed, has become the master of that continent, he will remain so until he, too, falls victim to the shame of blood-mixing.

*   *   *

Everything that today we admire on this earth—science and art, technique and inventions—is only the creative product of a few peoples and perhaps originally of *one* race. On them now depends also the existence of this entire culture. If they perish, then the beauty of this earth sinks into the grave with them.

* * *

All great cultures of the past perished only because the originally creative race died off through blood-poisoning.

* * *

He who wants to live should fight, therefore, and he who does not want to battle in this world of eternal struggle does not deserve to be alive.

* * *

What we see before us of human culture today, the results of art, science, and techniques, is almost exclusively the creative product of the Aryan.

* * *

If one were to divide mankind into three groups: culture-founders, culture-bearers, and culture-destroyers, then, as representative of the first kind, only the Aryan would come in question. It is from him that the foundation and the walls of all human creations originate, and only the external form and color depend on the characteristics of the various peoples involved. He furnishes the gigantic building-stones and also the plans for all human progress, and only the execution corresponds to the character of the people and races in the various instances.

* * *

But if it is ascertained that a people receives, takes in, and works over the essential basic elements of its culture from other races, and if then, when a further external influence is lacking, it stiffens again and again, then one can perhaps call such a race a 'culture-bearing' one but never a 'culture-creating' one.

* * *

The Jew forms the strongest contrast to the Aryan. Hardly in any people of the world is the instinct of self-preservation more strongly developed than in the so-called 'chosen people.' The fact of the existence of this race alone may be looked upon as the best proof of this. Where is the people that in the past two thousand years has been exposed to so small changes of the inner disposition, of character, etc., as the Jewish people? Which people finally has experienced greater changes than this one—and yet has always come forth the same from the most colossal catastrophes of mankind? What an infinitely persistent will for life, for preserving the race do these facts disclose!

Also the intellectual abilities were schooled in the course of centuries. Today the Jew is looked upon as 'clever,' and in a certain sense he has been so at all times. But his reason is not the result of his own development, but that of object lessons from without.

* * *

As now the Jew (for reasons which will immediately become evident from the following) was never in the possession of a culture of his own, the bases for his spiritual activity have always been furnished by others. At all times his intellect has developed through the culture that surrounds him.

* * *

In the Jewish people, the will to sacrifice oneself does not go beyond the bare instinct of self-preservation of the individual. The seemingly great feeling of belonging together is rooted in a very primitive herd instinct, as it shows itself in a similar way in many other living beings in this world. Thereby the fact is remarkable that in all these cases a common herd instinct leads to mutual support only as long as a common danger makes this seem useful or unavoidable. The same pack of wolves that jointly falls upon its booty dissolves when its hunger abates.

* * *

The Jew remains united only if forced by a common danger or is attracted by a common booty; if both reasons are no longer evident, then the qualities of the crassest egoism come into their own, and, in a moment, the united people becomes a horde of rats, fighting bloodily among themselves.

If the Jews were alone in this world, they would suffocate as much in dirt and filth, as they would carry on a detestable struggle to cheat and to ruin each other, although the complete lack of the will to sacrifice, expressed in their cowardice, would also in this instance make the fight a comedy.

Thus it is fundamentally wrong to conclude, merely from the fact of their standing together in a fight, or, more rightly expressed, in their exploiting their fellow human beings, that the Jews have a certain idealistic will to sacrifice themselves.

* * *

* * *the Jewish people, with all its apparent intellectual qualities, is nevertheless without any true culture, especially without a culture of its own. For the sham culture which the Jew possesses today is the property of other peoples, and is mostly spoiled in his hands.

* * *

No, the Jew possesses no culture-creating energy whatsoever, as the idealism, without which there can never exist a genuine development of man towards a higher level, does not and never did exist in him. His intellect, therefore, will never have a constructive effect, but only a destructive one* * *

* * *

The Jews were always a people with definite racial qualities and never a religion, only their progress made them probably look very early for a means which could divert disagreeable attention from their person. But what would have been more useful and at the same time more harmless than the 'purloining' of the appearance of being a religious community? For here, too, everything is purloined, or rather, stolen. But resulting from his own original nature the Jew cannot possess a re-ligious institution for the very reason that he lacks all idealism in any form and that he also does not recognize any belief in the hereafter.

* * *

The State is a means to an end. Its end is the preservation and the promotion of a community of physically and psychically equal living beings. This very preservation comprises first the racial stock and thereby it permits the free development of all the forces slumbering in this race. Again and again a part of them will primarily serve the preservation of the physical life and only another part will serve the promotion of a further mental development. But actually the one always creates the presumption for the other.

States that do not serve this purpose are faulty specimens, even miscarriages.

* * *

Thus the highest purpose of the folkish State is the care for the preservation of those racial primal elements which, supplying culture, create the beauty and dignity of a higher humanity. We, as Aryans, are therefore able to imagine a State only to be the living organism of a nationality which not only safeguards the preservation of that nationality, but which, by a further training of its spiritual and ideal abilities, leads it to the highest freedom.

* * *

REVIEW QUESTIONS

1. What are the greatest threats to the racial purity of Germans, according to Hitler?
2. What solutions does he propose?
3. What are the fundamental goals of education in the Nazi state?
4. In what sense do Jews pose a threat to Aryans?
5. Upon what evidence does Hitler base his arguments?

GEORGE ORWELL

FROM *The Road to Wigan Pier*

Europeans had hoped that the end of the war would signal a renewed prosperity: instead they experienced one economic crisis after another in the 1920s and 1930s. A feverish period of economic revival began in 1925, but it was brought to a precipitous halt by the crash of the American stock market in 1929. While the global economy was gradually stabilized during the middle to late 1930s, the Depression did not truly come to an end until a new world war—and a tremendous increase in the production of armaments—kicked the economies of the industrialized nations back into high gear.

The United States and Germany endured the greatest hardships during the Depression, but all of the industrialized nations of western Europe suffered from high rates of unemployment and the demoralization caused by economic collapse. In the mid-1930s, George Orwell (pseudonym of Eric Arthur Blair, 1903–1950), was asked by the Left Book Club to travel through northern England and write a report on workers' conditions for the book club's members. Already known to progressive readers as the author of Down and Out in Paris and London *(1933), a sympathetic account of life among the transient poor, Orwell was an unorthodox socialist whose perceptions of workers were strongly shaped by his rejection of the prejudices of the "shabby-genteel" lower middle class into which he had been born. In* The Road to Wigan Pier *(1937), Orwell describes the lives of unemployed workers living "on the dole," the welfare benefits provided by the British government.*

*   *   *

When you see the unemployment figures quoted at two millions, it is fatally easy to take this as meaning that two million people are out of work and the rest of the population is comparatively comfortable. I admit that till recently I was in the habit of doing so myself. I used to calculate that if you put the registered unemployed at round about two millions and threw in the destitute and those who for one reason and another were not registered, you might take the number of underfed people in England (for *everyone* on the dole or thereabouts is underfed) as being, at the very most, five millions.

This is an enormous under-estimate, because, in the first place, the only people shown on unemployment figures are those actually drawing the dole—that is, in general, heads of families. An unemployed man's dependants do not figure on the list unless they too are drawing a separate allowance. A Labour Exchange officer told me that to get at the real number of people *living on* (not drawing) the dole, you have got to multiply the official figures by something over three. This alone brings the number of unemployed to round about six millions. But in addition there are great numbers of people who are in work but who, from a financial point of view, might equally well be unemployed, because they are not drawing anything that can be described as a living wage. Allow for these and their dependants, throw in as before the old-age pensioners, the destitute and other nondescripts, and you get an *underfed* population of well over ten millions.* * *

Take the figures for Wigan, which is typical enough of the industrial and mining districts. The number of insured workers is round about 36,000 (26,000 men and 10,000 women). Of these, the number unemployed at the beginning of 1936 was about 10,000. But this was in winter when the mines are working full time; in summer it would probably be 12,000. Multiply by three, as above, and you get 30,000 or 36,000. The total population of Wigan is a little under 87,000; so that at any moment more than one person in three out of the whole population—not merely the registered workers—is either drawing or living on the dole. Those ten or twelve thousand unemployed contain a steady core of from four to five thousand miners who have been continuously unemployed for the past seven years. And Wigan is not especially badly off as industrial towns go. Even in Sheffield, which has been doing well for the last year or so because of wars and rumours of war, the proportion of unemployment is about the same—one in three of registered workers unemployed.

* * *

Nevertheless, in spite of the frightful extent of unemployment, it is a fact that poverty—extreme poverty—is less in evidence in the industrial North than it is in London. Everything is poorer and shabbier, there are fewer motor-cars and fewer well-dressed people; but also there are fewer people who are obviously destitute. Even in a town the size of Liverpool or Manchester you are struck by the fewness of the beggars. London is a sort of whirlpool which draws derelict people towards it, and it is so vast that life there is solitary and anon-

ymous. Until you break the law nobody will take any notice of you, and you can go to pieces as you could not possibly do in a place where you had neighbours who knew you. But in the industrial towns the old communal way of life has not yet broken up, tradition is still strong and almost everyone has a family—potentially, therefore, a home. In a town of 50,000 or 100,000 inhabitants there is no casual and as it were unaccounted-for population; nobody sleeping in the streets, for instance. Moreover, there is just this to be said for the unemployment regulations, that they do not discourage people from marrying. A man and wife on twenty-three shillings a week are not far from the starvation line, but they can make a home of sorts; they are vastly better off than a single man on fifteen shillings.

* * *

But there is no doubt about the deadening, debilitating effect of unemployment upon everybody, married or single, and upon men more than upon women.

* * *

Take a miner, for instance, who has worked in the pit since childhood and has been trained to be a miner and nothing else. How the devil is he to fill up the empty days? It is absurd to say that he ought to be looking for work. There is no work to look for, and everybody knows it. You can't go on looking for work every day for seven years.

* * *

I first became aware of the unemployment problem in 1928. * * *at that time nobody cared to admit that unemployment was inevitable, because this meant admitting that it would probably continue. The middle classes were still talking about "lazy idle loafers on the dole" and saying that "these men could all find work if they wanted to," and naturally these opinions percolated to the working class themselves. I remember the shock of astonishment it gave me, when I first mingled with tramps and beggars, to find that a fair proportion, perhaps a quarter, of these beings whom I had been taught to regard as cynical parasites, were decent young miners and cotton-workers gazing at their destiny with the same sort of dumb amazement as an animal in a trap. They simply could not understand what was happening to them. They had been brought up to work, and behold! it seemed as if they were never going to have the chance of working again. In their circumstances it was inevitable, at first, that they should be haunted by a feeling of personal degradation. That was the attitude towards unemployment in those days: it was a disaster which happened to *you* as an individual and for which *you* were to blame.

When a quarter of a million miners are unemployed, it is part of the order of things that Alf Smith, a miner living in the back streets of Newcastle, should be out of work. Alf Smith is merely one of the quarter million, a statistical unit.

*   *   *

When people live on the dole for years at a time they grow used to it, and drawing the dole, though it remains unpleasant, ceases to be shameful.* * * The people have at any rate grasped that unemployment is a thing they cannot help. It is not only Alf Smith who is out of work now; Bert Jones is out of work as well, and both of them have been "out" for years. It makes a great deal of difference when things are the same for everybody.

*   *   *

But they don't necessarily lower their standards by cutting out luxuries and concentrating on necessities; more often it is the other way about—the more natural way, if you come to think of it. Hence the fact that in a decade of unparalleled depression, the consumption of all cheap luxuries has increased. The two things that have probably made the greatest difference of all are the movies and the mass-production of cheap smart clothes since the war. The youth who leaves school at fourteen and gets a blind-alley job is out

of work at twenty, probably for life; but for two pounds ten on the hire-purchase system he can buy himself a suit which, for a little while and at a little distance, looks as though it had been tailored in Savile Row. The girl can look like a fashion plate at an even lower price. You may have three halfpence in your pocket and not a prospect in the world, and only the corner of a leaky bedroom to go home to; but in your new clothes you can stand on the street corner, indulging in a private daydream of yourself as Clark Gable or Greta Garbo, which compensates you for a great deal. And even at home there is generally a cup of tea going—a "nice cup of tea"—and Father, who has been out of work since 1929, is temporarily happy because he has a sure tip for the Cesarewitch.

Trade since the war has had to adjust itself to meet the demands of underpaid, underfed people, with the result that a luxury is nowadays almost always cheaper than a necessity. One pair of plain solid shoes costs as much as two ultra-smart pairs. For the price of one square meal you can get two pounds of cheap sweets. You can't get much meat for threepence, but you can get a lot of fish-and-chips. Milk costs threepence a pint and even "mild" beer costs fourpence, but aspirins are seven a penny and you can wring forty cups of tea out of a quarter-pound packet. And above all there is gambling, the cheapest of all luxuries. Even people on the verge of starvation can buy a few days' hope ("Something to live for," as they call it) by having a penny on a sweepstake.

*   *   *

Of course the post-war development of cheap luxuries has been a very fortunate thing for our rulers. It is quite likely that fish and chips, art-silk stockings, tinned salmon, cut-price chocolate (five two-ounce bars for sixpence), the movies, the radio, strong tea and the Football Pools have between them averted revolution. Therefore we are sometimes told that the whole thing is an astute manœuvre by the governing class—a sort of "bread and circuses" business—to hold the unemployed down. What I have seen of our governing class does not convince me that they have that much intelligence. The thing has happened, but by an unconscious process—the quite natural interaction between the manufacturer's need for a market and the need of half-starved people for cheap palliatives.

*   *   *

1. Why, according to Orwell, was "extreme poverty" less common in the north of England than in the south?
2. What impact did long-term unemployment have on workers in northern England?
3. Why were the poor addicted to "cheap luxuries"?

SIGMUND FREUD

FROM *Civilization and Its Discontents*

The interwar years witnessed a generalized collapse of confidence in the values and practices promoted by nineteenth-century liberalism. Many Europeans rejected the principles of parliamentary democracy, individualism, and reason in favor of authoritarianism, collectivism, and the reign of instinct. Writing in the late 1920s, Sigmund Freud asked himself, "How has it happened that so many people have come to take up this strange attitude of hostility to civilization?" Freud was puzzled and disturbed by the rise of irrationalist political movements, and he sought psychological explanations for the seething discontent with civilized society expressed by so many Europeans during this period. While Freud's earlier writings had focused on the expression—and repression—of the sexual instinct, Civilization and its Discontents (1930), dealt with what Freud identified as a countervailing aggressive instinct.

Freud's own perspective on civilization revealed a deep pessimism about human nature. While he conceived of modern European society as marking a high point in human cultural development, he argued that Western "Civilization" could only be realized and maintained through the painful repression of the individual's instinctual sexual and aggressive drives. When instinct was successfully "sublimated"—redirected into socially beneficial ends—it produced art, literature, science, industry, and stable government. On the other hand, no amount of human progress could ever compensate the individual for the loss of the spontaneous expression of these primordial impulses.

From *Civilization and Its Discontents* by Sigmund Freud, translated by James Strachey. Translation copyright © 1961 by James Strachey, renewed 1989 by Alix Strachey. Reprinted by permission of W. W. Norton and Company.

* * *

* * *sexual love is a relationship between two individuals in which a third can only be superfluous or disturbing, whereas civilization depends on relationships between a considerable number of individuals. When a love-relationship is at its height there is no room left for any interest in the environment; a pair of lovers are sufficient to themselves, and do not even need the child they have in common to make them happy.* * *

So far, we can quite well imagine a cultural community consisting of double individuals like this, who, libidinally satisfied in themselves, are connected with one another through the bonds of common work and common interests. If this were so, civilization would not have to withdraw any energy from sexuality. But this desirable state of things does not, and never did, exist. Reality shows us that civilization is not content with the ties we have so far allowed it. It aims at binding the members of the community together in a libidinal way as well and employs every means to that end. It favours every path by which strong identifications can be established between the members of the community, and it summons up aim-inhibited libido on the largest scale so as to strengthen the communal bond by relations of friendship. In order for these aims to be fulfilled, a restriction upon sexual life is unavoidable. But we are unable to understand what the necessity is which forces civilization along this path and which causes its antagonism to sexuality. There must be some disturbing factor which we have not yet discovered.

The clue may be supplied by one of the ideal demands, as we have called them, of civilized society. It runs: 'Thou shalt love thy neighbour as thyself.' It is known throughout the world and is undoubtedly older than Christianity, which puts it forward as its proudest claim. Yet it is certainly not very old; even in historical times it was still strange to mankind. Let us adopt a naïve attitude towards it, as though we were hearing it for the first time; we shall be unable then to suppress a feeling of surprise and bewilderment. Why should

we do it? What good will it do us? But, above all, how shall we achieve it? How can it be possible? My love is something valuable to me which I ought not to throw away without reflection. It imposes duties on me for whose fulfilment I must be ready to make sacrifices. If I love someone, he must deserve it in some way. (I leave out of account the use he may be to me, and also his possible significance for me as a sexual object, for neither of these two kinds of relationship comes into question where the precept to love my neighbour is concerned.) He deserves it if he is so like me in important ways that I can love myself in him; and he deserves it if he is so much more perfect than myself that I can love my ideal of my own self in him. Again, I have to love him if he is my friend's son, since the pain my friend would feel if any harm came to him would be my pain too—I should have to share it. But if he is a stranger to me and if he cannot attract me by any worth of his own or any significance that he may already have acquired for my emotional life, it will be hard for me to love him. Indeed, I should be wrong to do so, for my love is valued by all my own people as a sign of my preferring them, and it is an injustice to them if I put a stranger on a par with them. But if I am to love him (with this universal love) merely because he, too, is an inhabitant of this earth, like an insect, an earthworm or a grass-snake, then I fear that only a small modicum of my love will fall to his share—not by any possibility as much as, by the judgement of my reason, I am entitled to retain for myself. What is the point of a precept enunciated with so much solemnity if its fulfilment cannot be recommended as reasonable?

On closer inspection, I find still further difficulties. Not merely is this stranger in general unworthy of my love; I must honestly confess that he has more claim to my hostility and even my hatred. He seems not to have the least trace of love for me and shows me not the slightest consideration. If it will do him any good he has no hesitation in injuring me, nor does he ask himself whether the amount of advantage he gains bears any proportion to the extent of the harm he does to me. Indeed, he need not even obtain an advantage; if he can satisfy any sort of desire by it, he thinks nothing of jeering at me, insulting me, slandering me and showing his superior power; and the more secure he feels and the more helpless I am, the more certainly I can expect him to behave like this to me. If he behaves differently, if he shows me consideration and forbearance as a stranger, I am ready to treat him in the same way, in any case and quite apart from any precept. Indeed, if this grandiose commandment had run 'Love thy neighbour as thy neighbour loves thee', I should not take exception to it. And there is a second commandment, which seems to me even more incomprehensible and arouses still stronger opposition in me. It is 'Love thine enemies'. If I think it over, however, I see that I am wrong in treating it as a greater imposition. At bottom it is the same thing.

I think I can now hear a dignified voice admonishing me: 'It is precisely because your neighbour is not worthy of love, and is on the contrary your enemy, that you should love him as yourself.'* * *

Now it is very probable that my neighbour, when he is enjoined to love me as himself, will answer exactly as I have done and will repel me for the same reasons. I hope he will not have the same objective grounds for doing so, but he will have the same idea as I have.

*   *   *

The element of truth behind all this, which people are so ready to disavow, is that men are not gentle creatures who want to be loved, and who at the most can defend themselves if they are attacked; they are, on the contrary, creatures among whose instinctual endowments is to be reckoned a powerful share of aggressiveness. As a result, their neighbour is for them not only a potential helper or sexual object, but also someone who tempts them to satisfy their aggressiveness on him, to exploit his capacity for work without compensation, to use him sexually without his consent, to seize his possessions, to humiliate him, to cause him pain, to torture and to kill him. *Homo homini lupus*.[1] Who, in the face of all his experience of life and of history, will have the courage to dispute this assertion? As a rule this cruel aggressiveness waits for some provocation or puts itself at the service of some other purpose, whose goal might also have been reached by milder measures. In circumstances that are favourable to it, when the mental counter-forces which ordinarily inhibit it are out of action, it also manifests itself spontaneously and reveals man as a savage beast to whom consideration towards his own kind is something alien. Anyone who calls to mind the atrocities committed during the racial migrations or the invasions of the Huns, or by the people known as Mongols under Jenghiz Khan and Tamerlane, or at the capture of Jerusalem by the pious Crusaders, or even, indeed, the horrors of the recent World War—anyone who calls these things to mind will have to bow humbly before the truth of this view.

The existence of this inclination to aggression, which we can detect in ourselves and justly assume to be present in others, is the factor which disturbs our relations with our neighbour and which forces civilization into such a high expenditure [of energy]. In consequence of this primary mutual hostility of human beings, civilized society is perpetually threatened with disintegration. The interest of work in common would not hold it together; instinctual passions are stronger than reasonable interests. Civilization has to use its utmost efforts in order to set limits to man's aggressive instincts and to hold the manifestations of them in check by psychical reaction-formations. Hence, therefore, the use of methods intended to incite people into identifications and aim-inhibited relationships of love, hence the restriction upon sexual life, and hence too the ideal's commandment to love one's neighbour as oneself—a commandment which is really justified by the fact that nothing else runs so strongly counter to the original nature of man. In spite of every

---

[1] 'Man is a wolf to man.'

effort, these endeavours of civilization have not so far achieved very much. It hopes to prevent the crudest excesses of brutal violence by itself assuming the right to use violence against criminals, but the law is not able to lay hold of the more cautious and refined manifestations of human aggressiveness. The time comes when each one of us has to give up as illusions the expectations which, in his youth, he pinned upon his fellow-men, and when he may learn how much difficulty and pain has been added to his life by their ill-will.

*   *   *

REVIEW QUESTIONS

1. Why is it so difficult to love one's neighbor as oneself?
2. Why is this commandment a necessary requirement of civilized society?
3. What is human nature like, according to Freud?
4. What specific historical events and developments might be explained by Freud's theory of aggression?

ALBERT EINSTEIN

FROM *Science and Religion*

Soon after the publication of Civilization and Its Discontents, *Freud and German physicist Albert Einstein (1879–1955) exchanged letters commenting on the origins of war (published as* Why War? *in 1932). Both Freud and Einstein agreed that war was perhaps an inevitable, if undesirable, expression of instinctual aggression. When Hitler became chancellor of Germany in 1933, Einstein relocated to the United States and began teaching at Princeton. When Hitler sent troops into Austria in 1938, Freud, aging and very ill, was forced to flee Vienna and settle in London. As Jews and as purveyors of disturbingly modern scientific and psychological theories, neither of these great thinkers were welcome in Nazi-controlled territories.*

Perhaps the most famous scientist of the twentieth century, Einstein revolutionized physics in 1905 when he published a series of papers that forced a fundamental rethinking of the basic laws governing the properties of space, time, light, and motion. The best known of his discoveries was the special theory of relativity, according to which both time and motion are not absolutes, but relative to the observer. Einstein's passionate commitment to science was matched by an equally passionate commitment to the international peace movement and to spiritual growth. While Freud was an atheist who studied the psychology of religion from a strictly secular perspective, Einstein saw no incompatibility between religious faith and a scientific understanding of the cosmos. He rejected traditional revealed religion, but continued to believe in a "clockmaker" God "who reveals himself in the harmony of what exists."

From *Science and Religion*, Albert Einstein, Bonanza Books, 1954.

*   *   *

It would not be difficult to come to an agreement as to what we understand by science. Science is the century-old endeavor to bring together by means of systematic thought the perceptible phenomena of this world into as thorough-going an association as possible. To put it boldly, it is the attempt at the posterior reconstruction of existence by the process of conceptualization. But when asking myself what religion is I cannot think of the answer so easily. And even after finding an answer which may satisfy me at this particular moment, I still remain convinced that I can never under any circumstances bring together, even to a slight extent, the thoughts of all those who have given this question serious consideration.

At first, then, instead of asking what religion is I should prefer to ask what characterizes the aspirations of a person who gives me the impression of being religious: a person who is religiously enlightened appears to me to be one who has, to the best of his ability, liberated himself from the fetters of his selfish desires and is preoccupied with thoughts, feelings, and aspirations to which he clings because of their superpersonal value. It seems to me that what is important is the force of this superpersonal content and the depth of the conviction concerning its overpowering meaningfulness, regardless of whether any attempt is made to unite this content with a divine Being, for otherwise it would not be possible to count Buddha and Spinoza as religious personalities. Accordingly, a religious person is devout in the sense that he has no doubt of the significance and loftiness of those superpersonal objects and goals which neither require nor are capable of rational foundation. They exist with the same necessity and matter-of-factness as he himself. In this sense religion is the age-old endeavor of mankind to become clearly and completely conscious of these values and goals and constantly to strengthen and extend their effect. If one conceives of religion and science according to these definitions then a conflict between them appears impossible. For science can only ascertain what *is*, but not what *should be*,

and outside of its domain value judgments of all kinds remain necessary. Religion, on the other hand, deals only with evaluations of human thought and action: it cannot justifiably speak of facts and relationships between facts. According to this interpretation the well-known conflicts between religion and science in the past must all be ascribed to a misapprehension of the situation which has been described.

For example, a conflict arises when a religious community insists on the absolute truthfulness of all statements recorded in the Bible. This means an intervention on the part of religion into the sphere of science; this is where the struggle of the Church against the doctrines of Galileo and Darwin belongs. On the other hand, representatives of science have often made an attempt to arrive at fundamental judgments with respect to values and ends on the basis of scientific method, and in this way have set themselves in opposition to religion. These conflicts have all sprung from fatal errors.

Now, even though the realms of religion and science in themselves are clearly marked off from each other, nevertheless there exist between the two strong reciprocal relationships and dependencies. Though religion may be that which determines the goal, it has, nevertheless, learned from science, in the broadest sense, what means will contribute to the attainment of the goals it has set up. But science can only be created by those who are thoroughly imbued with the aspiration toward truth and understanding. This source of feeling, however, springs from the sphere of religion. To this there also belongs the faith in the possibility that the regulations valid for the world of existence are rational, that is, comprehensible to reason. I cannot conceive of a genuine scientist without that profound faith. The situation may be expressed by an image: science without religion is lame, religion without science is blind.

Though I have asserted above that in truth a legitimate conflict between religion and science cannot exist, I must nevertheless qualify this assertion once again on an essential point, with reference to the actual content of historical religions.

This qualification has to do with the concept of God. During the youthful period of mankind's spiritual evolution human fantasy created gods in man's own image, who, by the operations of their will were supposed to determine, or at any rate to influence, the phenomenal world. Man sought to alter the disposition of these gods in his own favor by means of magic and prayer. The idea of God in the religions taught at present is a sublimation of that old concept of the gods. Its anthropomorphic character is shown, for instance, by the fact that men appeal to the Divine Being in prayers and plead for the fulfillment of their wishes.

Nobody, certainly, will deny that the idea of the existence of an omnipotent, just, and omni-beneficent personal God is able to accord man solace, help, and guidance; also, by virtue of its simplicity it is accessible to the most undeveloped mind. But, on the other hand, there are decisive weaknesses attached to this idea in itself, which have been painfully felt since the beginning of history. That is, if this being is omnipotent, then every occurrence, including every human action, every human thought, and every human feeling and aspiration is also His work; how is it possible to think of holding men responsible for their deeds and thoughts before such an almighty Being? In giving out punishment and rewards He would to a certain extent be passing judgment on Himself. How can this be combined with the goodness and righteousness ascribed to Him?

The main source of the present-day conflicts between the spheres of religion and of science lies in this concept of a personal God. It is the aim of science to establish general rules which determine the reciprocal connection of objects and events in time and space. For these rules, or laws of nature, absolutely general validity is required—not proven. It is mainly a program, and faith in the possibility of its accomplishment in principle is only founded on partial successes. But hardly anyone could be found who would deny these partial successes and ascribe them to human self-deception. The fact that on the basis of such laws we are able to predict the temporal behavior of phenomena in certain domains with great preci-

sion and certainty is deeply embedded in the consciousness of the modern man, even though he may have grasped very little of the contents of those laws. He need only consider that planetary courses within the solar system may be calculated in advance with great exactitude on the basis of a limited number of simple laws. In a similar way, though not with the same precision, it is possible to calculate in advance the mode of operation of an electric motor, a transmission system, or of a wireless apparatus, even when dealing with a novel development.

To be sure, when the number of factors coming into play in a phenomenological complex is too large, scientific method in most cases fails us. One need only think of the weather, in which case prediction even for a few days ahead is impossible. Nevertheless no one doubts that we are confronted with a causal connection whose causal components are in the main known to us. Occurrences in this domain are beyond the reach of exact prediction because of the variety of factors in operation, not because of any lack of order in nature.

We have penetrated far less deeply into the regularities obtaining within the realm of living things, but deeply enough nevertheless to sense at least the rule of fixed necessity. One need only think of the systematic order in heredity, and in the effect of poisons, as for instance alcohol, on the behavior of organic beings. What is still lacking here is a grasp of connections of profound generality, but not a knowledge of order in itself.

The more a man is imbued with the ordered regularity of all events the firmer becomes his conviction that there is no room left by the side of this ordered regularity for causes of a different nature. For him neither the rule of human nor the rule of divine will exists as an independent cause of natural events. To be sure, the doctrine of a personal God interfering with natural events could never be *refuted*, in the real sense, by science, for this doctrine can always take refuge in those domains in which scientific knowledge has not yet been able to set foot.

But I am persuaded that such behavior on the

part of the representatives of religion would not only be unworthy but also fatal. For a doctrine which is able to maintain itself not in clear light but only in the dark, will of necessity lose its effect on mankind, with incalculable harm to human progress. In their struggle for the ethical good, teachers of religion must have the stature to give up the doctrine of a personal God, that is, give up that source of fear and hope which in the past placed such vast power in the hands of priests. In their labors they will have to avail themselves of those forces which are capable of cultivating the Good, the True, and the Beautiful in humanity itself. This is, to be sure, a more difficult but an incomparably more worthy task. After religious teachers accomplish the refining process indicated they will surely recognize with joy that true religion has been ennobled and made more profound by scientific knowledge.

If it is one of the goals of religion to liberate mankind as far as possible from the bondage of egocentric cravings, desires, and fears, scientific reasoning can aid religion in yet another sense. Although it is true that it is the goal of science to discover rules which permit the association and foretelling of facts, this is not its only aim. It also seeks to reduce the connections discovered to the smallest possible number of mutually independent conceptual elements. It is in this striving after the rational unification of the manifold that it encounters its greatest successes, even though it is precisely this attempt which causes it to run the greatest risk of falling a prey to illusions. But whoever has undergone the intense experience of successful advances made in this domain is moved by profound reverence for the rationality made man-ifest in existence. By way of the understanding he achieves a far-reaching emancipation from the shackles of personal hopes and desires, and thereby attains that humble attitude of mind toward the grandeur of reason incarnate in existence, and which, in its profoundest depths, is inaccessible to man. This attitude, however, appears to me to be religious, in the highest sense of the word. And so it seems to me that science not only purifies the religious impulse of the dross of its anthropomorphism but also contributes to a religious spiritualization of our understanding of life.

The further the spiritual evolution of mankind advances, the more certain it seems to me that the path to genuine religiosity does not lie through the fear of life, and the fear of death, and blind faith, but through striving after rational knowledge. In this sense I believe that the priest must become a teacher if he wishes to do justice to his lofty educational mission.

*   *   *

REVIEW QUESTIONS

1. Why, according to Einstein, are religion and science not mutually incompatible?
2. What sort of God does Einstein believe in?
3. How acceptable would this conception of God be to traditional Jews, Christians, or Muslims?
4. To what extent do you think Einstein's arguments are a product of his specific historical experience?

T. S. ELIOT

The Love Song of J. Alfred Prufrock

Freud and Einstein expressed their concerns about interwar culture in the form of tightly reasoned essays, but many artists and writers were drawn to new forms of expression that attempted to convey the nonlinearity and irrationality of lived experience. T. S. Eliot (1888–1965), one of the most prominent exponents of the modernist style, produced several collections of poetry, including The Waste Land *(1922) and* Four Quartets *(1943), that had a profound impact on both the form and content of interwar literature. Eliot, like John Reed (see first reading, this chapter), had been born into an affluent American family and attended Harvard, graduating one year before Reed in 1909. Eliot moved to Europe just prior to World War I, and spent most of the rest of his life in Britain.*

Eliot's first major work, "The Love Song of J. Alfred Prufrock," first published in 1915, is one of the great masterpieces of modernist poetry. Eliot's verse is steeped in the traditions of European high art culture—"Prufrock" contains numerous references to the works of other poets, including Hesiod, Dante, Andrew Marvell, and Shakespeare—but it also seeks to apply this literary tradition to the description of everyday life, uniting the heroic and the prosaic, the transcendent and the mundane, solemn drama and tawdry melodrama. In this poem, Eliot's skillful use of language lends a certain tragic grandeur to the thoughts and turns of phrase of a very ordinary and unromantic protagonist. It is the tortured complexity of J. Alfred Prufrock's mental processes, his agonized self-consciousness and even self-deprecation, that make him such an apt representative of the complex and tortured interwar years.

From *Prufrock and Other Observations*, T. S. Eliot, The Egoist Ltd., 1917.

S'io credesse che mia risposta fosse
A persona che mai tornasse al mondo,
Questa fiamma staria senza piu scosse.
Ma perciocche giammai di questo fondo
Non torno vivo alcun, s'i'odo il vero,
Senza tema d'infamia ti rispondo[1]

---

[1] "If I thought that my reply would be to one who would ever return to the world, this flame would stay without further movement; but since none has ever returned alive from this depth, if what I hear is true, I answer you without fear of infamy" (Dante, *Inferno* 27.61–66).

Let us go then, you and I,
When the evening is spread out against the sky
Like a patient etherized upon a table;
Let us go, through certain half-deserted streets,
The muttering retreats
Of restless nights in one-night cheap hotels
And sawdust restaurants with oyster shells:
Streets that follow like a tedious argument
Of insidious intent
To lead you to an overwhelming question . . .
Oh, do not ask, "What is it?"
Let us go and make our visit.

In the room the women come and go
Talking of Michelangelo.

The yellow fog that rubs its back upon the
    windowpanes,
The yellow smoke that rubs its muzzle on the
    windowpanes
Licked its tongue into the corners of the
    evening,
Lingered upon the pools that stand in drains,
Let fall upon its back the soot that falls from
    chimneys,
Slipped by the terrace, made a sudden leap,
And seeing that it was a soft October night,
Curled once about the house, and fell asleep.

And indeed there will be time
For the yellow smoke that slides along the street,
Rubbing its back upon the windowpanes;
There will be time, there will be time
To prepare a face to meet the faces that you
    meet;
There will be time to murder and create,
And time for all the works and days of hands
That lift and drop a question on your plate;
Time for you and time for me,
And time yet for a hundred indecisions,
And for a hundred visions and revisions,
Before the taking of a toast and tea.

In the room the women come and go
Talking of Michelangelo.

And indeed there will be time
To wonder, "Do I dare?" and, "Do I dare?"
Time to turn back and descend the stair,
With a bald spot in the middle of my hair—
(They will say: "How his hair is growing thin!")
My morning coat, my collar mounting firmly to
    the chin,
My necktie rich and modest, but asserted by a
    simple pin—
(They will say: "But how his arms and legs are
    thin!")
Do I dare
Disturb the universe?

In a minute there is time
For decisions and revisions which a minute will
    reverse.

For I have known them all already, known
    them all—
Have known the evenings, mornings, afternoons,
I have measured out my life with coffee spoons;
I know the voices dying with a dying fall
Beneath the music from a farther room.
  So how should I presume?

And I have known the eyes already, known
    them all—
The eyes that fix you in a formulated phrase,
And when I am formulated, sprawling on a pin,
When I am pinned and wriggling on the wall,
Then how should I begin
To spit out all the butt-ends of my days and
    ways?
  And how should I presume?

And I have known the arms already, known
    them all—
Arms that are braceleted and white and bare
(But in the lamplight, downed with light brown
    hair!)
Is it perfume from a dress
That makes me so digress?
Arms that lie along a table, or wrap about a
    shawl.
  And should I then presume?
  And how should I begin?

          • • •

Shall I say, I have gone at dusk through
    narrow streets
And watched the smoke that rises from the pipes
Of lonely men in shirt-sleeves, leaning out of
    windows? . . .

I should have been a pair of ragged claws
Scuttling across the floors of silent seas

          • • •

And the afternoon, the evening, sleeps so
    peacefully!
Smoothed by long fingers,

Asleep . . . tired . . . or it malingers,
Stretched on the floor, here beside you and me.
Should I, after tea and cakes and ices,
Have the strength to force the moment to its
    crisis?
But though I have wept and fasted, wept and
    prayed,
Though I have seen my head (grown slightly
    bald) brought in upon a platter,
I am no prophet—and here's no great matter;
I have seen the moment of my greatness flicker,
And I have seen the eternal Footman hold my
    coat, and snicker,
And in short, I was afraid.

    And would it have been worth it, after all,
After the cups, the marmalade, the tea,
Among the porcelain, among some talk of you
    and me,
Would it have been worth while,
To have bitten off the matter with a smile,
To have squeezed the universe into a ball
To roll it toward some overwhelming question,
To say: "I am Lazarus, come from the dead,
Come back to tell you all, I shall tell you all"—
If one, settling a pillow by her head,
    Should say: "That is not what I meant at all.
    That is not it, at all."

    And would it have been worth it, after all,
Would it have been worth while,
After the sunsets and the dooryards and the
    sprinkled streets,
After the novels, after the teacups, after the skirts
    that trail along the floor—
And this, and so much more?—
It is impossible to say just what I mean!
But as if a magic lantern threw the nerves in
    patterns on a screen:
Would it have been worth while
If one, settling a pillow or throwing off a shawl,
And turning toward the window, should say:
"That is not it at all,
That is not what I meant, at all."

• • •

No! I am not Prince Hamlet, nor was meant
    to be;
Am an attendant lord, one that will do
To swell a progress, start a scene or two,
Advise the prince; no doubt, an easy tool,
Deferential, glad to be of use,
Politic, cautious, and meticulous;
Full of high sentence, but a bit obtuse;
At times, indeed, almost ridiculous—
Almost, at times, the Fool.

    I grow old . . . I grow old . . .
I shall wear the bottoms of my trousers rolled.

    Shall I part my hair behind? Do I dare to eat
        a peach?
I shall wear white flannel trousers, and walk
    upon the beach.
I have heard the mermaids singing, each to each.

I do not think that they will sing to me.

I have seen them riding seaward on the waves
Combing the white hair of the waves blown back
When the wind blows the water white and black.

We have lingered in the chambers of the sea
By sea-girls wreathed with seaweed red and
    brown
Till human voices wake us, and we drown.

REVIEW QUESTIONS

1. Who are the "you and I" introduced in the first
   line of the poem?
2. Where are they going and why?
3. What exactly is it that Prufrock is afraid to
   "presume" to do?
4. What might Freud have to say about Prufrock's
   neurotic anxieties?

28   THE SECOND WORLD WAR

The Great War had been disastrous, but its outbreak could be blamed on the errors of political leaders and military planners who had allowed diplomatic arrangements and mobilization timetables to take on a life of their own. That a second World War could occur so soon after the first suggested that periodic outbreaks of global warfare were perhaps essential elements in the functioning of modern industrial societies. Similarly, that the nations of the world had again failed to avoid armed conflict suggested that human beings were incapable of controlling their innate aggressivity and learning from their past mistakes. World War II was a total war, and its worst horrors—the Holocaust and the bombing of major urban areas—resulted in the slaughter of civilians on a scale hitherto unimagined. Once again, the war made painfully clear the astounding degree of devastation that might occur when humans directed the technologies of industry toward destructive ends.

Yet, if World War II was dishearteningly destructive it was not as absurd as World War I had been. In 1914, the outbreak of war seemed almost arbitrary, and even the War Guilt Clause of the Versailles Treaty could not dispel the postwar conviction that the war had been the fault of no one and everyone. In 1939, on the other hand, the outbreak of war took the form of an overt act of aggression on the part of Germany. Many attempts had been made to appease Hitler, but all diplomatic negotiations had failed in the face of his determination to go to war. During the Great War, the military leadership's adoption of a strategy of attrition had served to strip the individual soldier's death of meaning, depriving military service of all heroism. During World War II, the German army's lightning war strategy returned the elements of speed and mobility to warfare. Military engagements once again reached decisive conclusions, producing clear winners and losers.

However, from the start, World War II was most clearly distinguished from World War I by its ideological component. To both soldiers and civilians, this *new conflict presented itself as a struggle not merely between competing nations, but between two fundamentally opposed political and social philosophies, between fascism and anti-fascism. On the level of the individual, this meant that the war presented clear choices, even if these choices often took the form of extremely difficult ethical decisions. On both sides, government propaganda fanned the flames of political passions, producing a strong sense of conviction among fascists and anti-fascists alike. At the same time, the increasingly manifest viciousness and brutality of the fascist regime generated intense opposition both within Germany and Italy and in the territories the two states occupied. Participants in resistance movements experienced an acute sense of human agency: having committed themselves to the anti-fascist cause, they engaged in actions that exposed them to the risk of imprisonment, torture, and execution.*

The defeat of the Axis powers seemed like a triumph for the principles of democracy, tolerance, and individual liberty. After the war, the world's nations renewed their commitment to international governance through the creation of the United Nations, but many people continued to fear that the twentieth century was doomed to experience yet another global cataclysm, especially as growing tensions between the Soviet Union and the United States developed into an ominously tense "Cold War." Any optimism generated by the return of peace was quickly overshadowed by the emergence of a "bi-polar" system of international relations: the world's two superpowers, armed to the teeth with devastating weapons of destruction, insisted that the rest of the world choose sides.

CONSTANCIA DE LA MORA

FROM *In Place of Splendor: The Autobiography of a Spanish Woman*

Spain suddenly became the subject of considerable international attention in 1936, after civil war broke out between the Republican Popular Front government and conservative nationalists under the leadership of General Francisco Franco. France and Britain failed to intervene in support of the Spanish republic, abiding by the terms of an international non-intervention agreement, but Germany and Italy eagerly supplied the nationalist uprising with troops, tanks, and airplanes. The Soviet Union sent some armaments to the loyalists, but this aid was inadequate and often served only to reinforce divisions between Communists and other political factions within the ranks of the republicans. European and American leftists viewed the Spanish Civil War as a first opportunity to take a strong stand against the rise of fascism, and many of them fought on the loyalist side as volunteers in international brigades.

Constancia de la Mora (1906–1950) was born into an aristocratic family with a long history of service to the Spanish crown. As a young woman she broke with her family, both by divorcing her first husband and by becoming an ardent supporter of the republican government. In 1933, she married an air force officer, Ignacio Hidalgo de Cisneros, an aristocrat who had also gone over to the republican side. During the Spanish Civil War, Constancia served the loyalist cause by running an orphanage, while her husband desperately tried to scrape together an air force to protect the republic from attack by Italian and German bombers.

---

*   *   *

It never occurred to us that the legal, democratically elected, recognized Government of Spain would have any difficulty buying the arms and supplies it needed to crush the remaining Rebel forces. We felt that the revolt was nearly over— the Spanish generals had no popular support whatsoever. The people were solidly behind the Government. It was a matter of buying rifles, artillery, supplies, and the like—then the Rebels would probably surrender and the whole thing would be over, with the minimum amount of loss of life.

On July 27, the news broke like a bomb in Madrid. The French Government has refused to sell us arms!

Why? We couldn't understand. We knew the British and the French reactionaries had put pressure on the Popular Front Government of France, but that a Socialist premier should deny a legal, recognized Government the right to buy arms to crush a fascist rebellion! It was monstrous! Worse, it was mad. What were the French thinking of?

On July 31, Ignacio brought me more terrible news: the Italians are invading Spain! Italian airplanes had been sighted flying to Rebel territory, some had been forced down in French Morocco, having lost the way. The orders found on them were dated July 16—the day before the rebellion

broke out. Mussolini promptly denied this news, just as Hitler denied he was sending arms, men, and guns. After the war was over, both dictators boasted that they helped prepare the plot and sent supplies and all kinds of aid, from troops to bandages, airplanes to trucks, the moment the traitor generals moved.

But in the early August days, Spaniards tried to convince the world—and especially France, England, and the United States—that our country was being invaded by fascists. The democracies turned a deaf ear to our pleas while the fascists strangled democracy in Spain.

When André Malraux arrived with a group of Frenchmen and some planes too old to be used by the French Air Force, we imagined that France was ready to sell us the planes that we so badly needed. It was common knowledge that Italy had sent and was sending Savoias, Capronis, and Fiats—four Savoias crashed in French Moroccan territory on their way to the Rebels—and that Germany's pocket battleships prevented bombardments of Rebel towns in Spanish Morocco by our Navy. On August 3, for instance, the *Deutschland* together with another German destroyer steamed slowly up and down the harbor of Ceuta, making it impossible for the *Jaime I* and other units of the Spanish Fleet to fire on their objectives.

German bombers and pursuit planes—Junkers 52 and Heinkels manned by German pilots—had already landed in Seville and Cadiz. They were helping to carry officers and troops of the Foreign Legion to the Peninsula, speeding the human cargo of Moors and white mercenaries coming across in great numbers every day.

But we were very innocent in those days. We thought France had realized her own danger and was willing to sell us the things we needed to defend ourselves. We did not know then that certain powerful people in France and England had made up their minds, even before the war had started.

*   *   *

Only one country in the world printed the truth about Spain, from the beginning and until the end—the Soviet Union. Spaniards who had never heard of the Soviet Union before suddenly awoke in those days in August, when we were being betrayed everywhere else in the world, to realize that at least one nation had not abandoned us in our struggle for democracy. Every Spanish newspaper carried the news in great headlines that the Soviet workers had levied a one per cent tax on their salaries and collected 14,000,000 rubles for the Spanish people within the first month of the rebellion.

The news helped us to bear the loss of Badajoz, a little town on the Portugal frontier. For Badajoz fell on August 13, with the "honor" of being the first Spanish town to be bombarded by Italian and German planes. The people of Badajoz will bear the distinction in history of being the first Spaniards to have been blown to eternity by the conquering bombs of foreign fascists. We grew more accustomed to stories of horror later on in the war—but at that time we could hardly bear to read the eyewitness accounts and see the few photographs of the terrible massacre the Moors and foreign legionnaires had committed in this peaceful town when they entered after the bombardment. The slaughter in the bull ring at Badajoz horrified the whole world.

*   *   *

I turned on the radio for the Government news reports.

And then I first heard the voice of Dolores Ibarruri, "La Pasionaria." This woman of the people, this living symbol of Spanish courage, spoke to the people of Spain at the grave moment when Madrid faced the enemy at its very gates.

The children at my home gathered around the radio. The cook came in from the kitchen. Paco came from the garage. We clustered around the little wireless set.

"They shall not pass! No pasarán!" Her beautiful voice, vibrant, strong, filled the room. We straightened up. After the long day of panic and fear, after the weeks of tense waiting which had weighed on even the children, this stirring voice called us all back to our faith in Spain, to our faith in ourselves.

"The fascists will not pass! They will not pass because we are not alone!"

I glanced at our cook. She had clasped her hands together in that beautiful, unconscious gesture which is native to all women of Spain. She was leaning toward the radio, her lips moving a little, repeating without sound, the words of "La Pasionaria."

"We must not conceal the fact that Madrid is in danger! The removal of this danger depends on the people of Madrid, and on them alone. . . . All the people of Madrid, men and women, must learn the use of arms."

Paco was nearly in tears. His hand covered his mouth. I saw him gulping hard.

The strong voice, powerful and sure, went on, growing more vibrant, more electric. *"The lives and future of our children are at stake! This is not the time for hesitation; this is not the time for timidity. We women must demand that our men be courageous. We must inspire them with the thought that a man must know how to die worthily. Preferimos ser viudas de héroes antes que esposas de cobardes!"*

"We prefer to be the widows of heroes rather than wives of cowards!"

November 5, 1936.

In Alicante we did not know that this day Madrid fought for its life. I had the use of a car and a holiday at long last. I had not seen Ignacio for almost two months. He was stationed at Albacete, the new air base the Government had built slightly away from Madrid. I started early in the afternoon, before the radio began to broadcast the news of the attack on Madrid. The drive took four hours and when we reached Albacete, the parched ugly little town was almost dark. Ignacio was not in when I went to the Central Hotel but the porter led me to his room. I was just inspecting the dreary, dusty metal furniture, the taps marked hot and cold from which only cold water and very little of that ever came, when the door opened and Ignacio came in.

I turned to face him with a lump in my throat. Two months. We had never even been separated for two weeks until the war came.

His hair had turned from premature gray to white. That was the first thing I noticed. His face had grown thinner. His eyes mirrored a heavy worry.

For a moment, while he stood still, I was afraid he was ill. Then when he spoke, his voice was full of energy. He had just been promoted from major to lieutenant-colonel, but he still wore his old overalls with a sweater sticking out under his collar and his old major's insignias.

I think we were so happy to see each other that for a minute or so, we actually forgot the war.

At last, Ignacio said, "I must work tonight, but now we can have dinner, alone, and we will talk."

We had our coffee in the lobby. The place had the air of a family encampment. The wives of the Air Force officers sat in rocking chairs, knitting. The children played on the floor. Foreign correspondents sat at little tables, drinking and talking. French, German, Italian, English rose from corner tables all around the room—conversation of the international volunteers, exiles from fascist countries, young doctors, lawyers, workers, from the democratic countries, men who had come hundreds and thousands of miles to fight for democracy in Spain.

Next day, Ignacio, who could spare no time from his work, sent me to visit the hospitals newly moved to Albacete. I found conditions very bad.

The town had a very poor water supply and almost no plumbing. The doctors and nurses were struggling with inadequate buildings and supplies. Ignacio had asked me to visit the wounded of the Air Force, and that night I said thoughtfully to him, "We need some sort of a convalescent home for the pilots. Some place where they could grow strong after the first weeks at a regular hospital."

Ignacio grinned. "I wouldn't want to ask you, darling. . . ." I had the plans made in my mind for a convalescent home that first day in Albacete.

And then, for forty-eight hours, everyone in Albacete forgot everything else but Madrid.

Madrid!

The Moors and the "blond Moors," as Franco called his German troops, and the Italians were at the very gates of the city. Fascists fought at the barricades the people of Madrid had built. The whole city rose. Every man, every woman, leaped to the defense of their native Madrid.

And then, in this critical hour, on November 6, 1936, as the fascist planes rose over the city, defenseless from the air, a miracle (or so it seemed to all of Spain) happened.

For flying with impossible speed, swift, deadly, fierce, came a squadron of new planes, planes of the Spanish Government. While all Madrid looked on choking with excitement, the Government planes fought off the fascists.

Ignacio told me about it first. His face shone like a child's. "Connie! One country at least understands our fight. They sold us planes!"

I could hardly believe his story. The planes Spain had bought from Russia arrived at Cartagena on November 2—in parts of course. The mechanics, working almost without stop for four solid days, had assembled a whole squadron of pursuit planes, enough to save the capital from the merciless bombing Franco planned to synchronize with his attack on the gates of the city.

"The people call them *Chatos*, the pug noses," Ignacio said, grinning.

And that night, November 7, I had dinner with the young Russian pilots who had just arrived. The Spanish aviators were almost delirious with joy. Planes! At last! Ignacio had been trying to build an Air Force out of thin air, trying to train men with no planes to fly with. Now there were planes to save Madrid from bombing, pilots to teach ours how to operate the new planes, mechanics to school our mechanics and help us in our factories.

The dinner started off with a joke. One of the Spanish aviators turned to me with great pride and said, "I have already learned a Russian word. Listen!" Then, carefully setting his lips, he said, "Propeller!"

He was most crestfallen when I explained that the word was English. Probably some early American engineer had taught it to the Russians.

But although we laughed, our dinner was not hilarious but very solemn. Ignacio made a little speech, only saying that the people of Madrid were dying tonight, dying with the words, *"No pasarán"* on their lips. He did not need, he said, to ask his men to make the same great sacrifice. He knew that they were always willing to give their lives for freedom. But now, more than ever, the Republic faced danger. The Russian pilots who had come as volunteers to help the people of Madrid were an heroic example.

"Viva la República!" Ignacio said quietly. *"No pasarán."*

"No pasarán," the men at the table answered solemnly.

Then everyone went back to the air field.

*   *   *

REVIEW QUESTIONS

1. What problems confronted the loyalist military effort?
2. To what extent was the Spanish Civil War shaped by international factors?
3. What role did the Soviet Union play in the civil war?
4. How did de la Mora respond to the military aid provided by the Soviet government?
5. How did Dolores Ibarruri attempt to rally Spaniards to the republican cause in her radio speech?

FROM Treaty of Non-Aggression Between Germany and the Soviet Union (August 23, 1939)

In early 1939, Germany absorbed the western half of Czechoslovakia and Hitler then prepared to proceed with the conquest of additional lebensraum ("living space") in eastern Europe. Bismarck and his generals had been plagued by the dilemma of Germany's encirclement and its vulnerability to a two-front war with France and Russia. In an attempt to solve this problem of military strategy, Hitler began negotiations with Stalin.

Hitler and Stalin were ideological enemies, but they were also opportunists willing to cooperate, if only temporarily, in the interest of their own nation's power. Stalin's great purges of 1936 and 1937 had seriously weakened the Red Army, depriving it of much of its officer corps, and Stalin was eager to buy time to rebuild the strength of the Soviet military. At the same time, Stalin's expressions of interest

*in an alliance with France and Britain had gone largely unheeded, and he contin-
ued to distrust the western democracies almost as much as Nazi Germany.*

*Late in August of 1939 the international community was shocked to learn that
Joachim von Ribbentropp and Vyacheslav Molotov, respectively the German and Soviet foreign ministers, had signed a nonaggression pact between their two governments. One week later, Hitler invaded Poland.*

From *German-Soviet Non-Aggression Pact*, Documents Relating to the Nazi-Soviet Nonaggression Pact and Partition of Poland Webpage, <http://omni.cc.purdue.edu/~pha/policy/pact.html>. Originally published in *Nazi-Soviet Relations 1939–1941. Documents from the Archives of the German Foreign Office*, Washington, D.C., 1948.

The Government of the German Reich and the Government of the Union of Soviet Socialist Republics desirous of strengthening the cause of peace between Germany and the U.S.S.R., and proceeding from the fundamental provisions of the Neutrality Agreement concluded in April 1926 between Germany and the U.S.S.R., have reached the following agreement:

ARTICLE I

Both High Contracting Parties obligate themselves to desist from any act of violence, any aggressive action, and any attack on each other, either individually or jointly with other powers.

ARTICLE II

Should one of the High Contracting Parties become the object of belligerent action by a third power, the other High Contracting Party shall in no manner lend its support to this third power.

ARTICLE III

The Governments of the two High Contracting Parties shall in the future maintain continual contact with one another for the purpose of consultation in order to exchange information on problems affecting their common interests.

ARTICLE IV

Neither of the two High Contracting Parties shall participate in any grouping of powers whatsoever that is directly or indirectly aimed at the other party.

ARTICLE V

Should disputes or conflicts arise between the High Contracting Parties over problems of one kind or another, both parties shall settle these disputes or conflicts exclusively through friendly exchange of opinion or, if necessary, through the establishment of arbitration commissions.

ARTICLE VI

The present treaty is concluded for a period of ten years, with the proviso that, in so far as one of the High Contracting Parties does not denounce it one year prior to the expiration of this period, the validity of this treaty shall automatically be extended for another five years.

ARTICLE VII

The present treaty shall be ratified within the shortest possible time. The ratifications shall be exchanged in Berlin. The agreement shall enter into force as soon as it is signed.

*   *   *

Secret Additional Protocol

On the occasion of the signature of the Non-aggression Pact between the German Reich and the Union of Socialist Soviet Republics the undersigned plenipotentiaries of each of the two parties discussed in strictly confidential conversations the question of the boundary of their respective spheres of influence in Eastern Europe. These conversations led to the following conclusions:

1. In the event of a territorial and political rearrangement in the areas belonging to the Baltic States (Finland, Estonia, Latvia, Lithuania), the northern boundary of Lithuania shall represent the boundary of the spheres of influence of Germany and the U.S.S.R. In this connection the in-

terest of Lithuania in the Vilna area is recognized by each party.

2. In the event of a territorial and political re-arrangement of the areas belonging to the Polish state the spheres of influence of Germany and the U.S.S.R. shall be bounded approximately by the line of the rivers Narew, Vistula, and San.

The question of whether the interests of both parties make desirable the maintenance of an independent Polish state and how such a state should be bounded can only be definitely determined in the course of further political developments.

In any event both Governments will resolve this question by means of a friendly agreement.

3. With regard to Southeastern Europe attention is called by the Soviet side to its interest in Bessarabia. The German side declares its complete political disinterestedness in these areas.

4. This protocol shall be treated by both parties as strictly secret.

*   *   *

REVIEW QUESTIONS

1. To what terms does this treaty bind Germany and the Soviet Union?
2. Who do you think derived the most advantage from the treaty? Why?
3. Using a map of eastern Europe, locate the various spheres of influence designated by the secret protocol.
4. What territories in eastern Europe did Hitler and Stalin expect to gain as a result of this agreement?

MARC BLOCH

FROM *Strange Defeat, A Statement of Evidence Written in 1940*

After an extended period of inactivity on the west front—known to the French as the drôle de guerre *("funny war")—Hitler's armies attacked France on 10 May 1940. The defeat of the combined French and British forces was astoundingly rapid, and France signed its surrender on June 22. French generals had expected a long war of attrition along the lines of the First World War. Instead, they discovered that Hitler and his strategists had formulated a new offensive strategy:* Blitzkrieg *("lightning war"). Quickly moving massed tank formations, supported by aerial bombardment, were used to overwhelm enemy troops and smash through their lines. While this approach relied on an intensive deployment of troops and weapons, it was not intended to annihilate opponents, but rather to immobilize them in the face of a swift and crushing assault.*

In the immediate aftermath of the French military collapse, historian Marc Bloch (1886–1944), wrote an extended essay on this "strange defeat," combining an account of his personal experience as a captain in charge of fuel supplies with a more general analysis of French military preparedness. Bloch had served with distinction in World War I and then worked as a university professor during the inter-war years, publishing several extremely influential studies of medieval society. In 1939, at the age of 53, he enlisted once again, serving until the French surrender in 1940. As a Jew and as an ardent patriot, he soon became active in the French resistance movement. In 1944 he was captured by the Germans and executed before a firing squad.

*   *   *

We have just suffered such a defeat as no one would have believed possible. On whom or on what should the blame be laid?

*   *   *

What drove our armies to disaster was the cumulative effect of a great number of different mistakes. One glaring characteristic is, however, common to all of them. Our leaders, or those who acted for them, were incapable of thinking in terms of a *new* war. In other words, the German triumph was, essentially, a triumph of intellect—and it is that which makes it so peculiarly serious.

*   *   *

The ruling idea of the Germans in the conduct of this war was speed. We, on the other hand, did our thinking in terms of yesterday or the day before. Worse still: faced by the undisputed evidence of Germany's new tactics, we ignored, or wholly failed to understand, the quickened rhythm of the times. So true is this, that it was as though the two opposed forces belonged, each of them, to an entirely different period of human history. We interpreted war in terms of assagai *versus* rifle made familiar to us by long years of colonial expansion. But this time it was we who were cast for the rôle of the savage!

*   *   *

Did we ever, really, in the whole course of the campaign know the precise location of the enemy at any given time? That our commanders should have had a very imperfect idea of his intentions, and, worse still, of his material resources, can easily be explained by the faulty organization of our Intelligence Service. But the fact that we were never quite certain of his movements was due mainly to a persistent failure ever to judge distances correctly. Our own rate of progress was too slow and our minds were too inelastic for us ever to admit the possibility that the enemy might move with the speed which he actually achieved. When we left Lens on 22 June, H.Q. was split into two sections—an 'advanced' group at Estaires, with a less mobile organization at Merville, where it was thought that it would be at a safe distance from the theatre of operations. What was our surprise when it was borne in upon us that, in fact, the so-called 'rear' H.Q. was a great deal closer to the line than its advanced brother! When the Germans crashed through the Meuse defences, we were compelled to improvise at short notice alternative rail-heads for the division which we were preparing to rush into the lion's mouth in the hope of blocking egress from the pocket.

*   *   *

It can be seen from what I have said that the war was a constant succession of surprises. The effect of this on morale seems to have been very serious. And here I must touch on a delicate subject. I have no right to do more than record impressions which are those only of a looker-on. But there are some things that must be said, even at the risk of hurting a good many feelings. Men are so made that they will face expected dangers in expected places a great deal more easily than the sudden appearance of deadly peril from behind a turn in the road which they have been led to suppose is perfectly safe. Years ago, shortly after the Battle of the Marne, I saw men who the day before had gone into the line under murderous fire without turning a hair, run like rabbits just because three shells fell quite harmlessly on a road where they had piled arms in order to furnish a water-fatigue. 'We cleared out because the Germans came.' Again and again I heard that said in the course of last May and June. Analysed, the words mean no more than this: 'Because the Germans turned up where we didn't expect them and where we had never been told we ought to expect them.' Consequently, certain breakdowns, which cannot, I fear, be denied, occurred mainly because men had been trained to use their brains too slowly. Our soldiers were defeated and, to some extent, let themselves be too easily defeated, principally because their minds functioned far too sluggishly.

Not only did we meet the enemy too often in unexpected places, but for the most part, especially, and with increasing frequency, *in a way* which neither the High Command nor, as a result, the rank and file had anticipated. We should have been perfectly prepared to spend whole days potting at one another from entrenched positions, even if the lines had been only a few yards apart as they were in the Argonne during the last war. It would have seemed to us the most natural thing in the world to carry out raids on occupied saps. It would have been well within our capacity to stand firm in face of an assault through a curtain of wire more or less cut by 'Minenwerfer', or to have gone over the top courageously in an attempt to rush a position that had already been flattened—though, as a rule, not very completely—by artillery fire. In short, we could have played our part without difficulty in operations beautifully planned by our own staff and the enemy's, if only they had been in accordance with the well-digested lessons learned at peace-time manœuvres. It was much more terrifying to find ourselves suddenly at grips with a section of tanks in open country. The Germans took no account of roads. They were everywhere. They felt their way forward, stopping whenever they ran up against serious resistance. Where, however, the resistance was not serious and they could find a 'soft spot', they drove ahead, exploiting their gains, and using them as a basis from which to develop the appropriate tactical movement or, rather, as it seemed, to take their choice of a number of alternative possibilities already envisaged in accordance with that methodical opportunism which was so characteristic of Hitler's methods. They relied on action and on improvisation. We, on the other hand, believed in doing nothing and in behaving as we always had behaved.

*   *   *

Is it true to say that by then—the precise moment at which Pétain announced that he had asked for an armistice—all hope of resistance had become impossible? Several officers thought not, especially the younger officers, for, with the quickened pace of events, a wider gulf began to show between the generations. Unfortunately, our leaders were not drawn from among those who suffered least from a hardening of the arteries. I am still strongly of the opinion to-day that what we called, in 1918, our 'last-ditchers' were right. They dreamed of a modern type of warfare waged by guerrillas against tanks and motorized detachments. Some of them, if I am not wrong, had drawn up plans for such a war, plans which will never now see the light of day. The motorcyclists, of whom the enemy made such extensive and such excellent use, could move rapidly, and without too many accidents, only on metalled roads. Even vehicles equipped with caterpillar treads proceed less slowly on macadamized highways than across open country, and mobile guns and tractors of the normal type must have a good hard surface on which to manœuvre. That is why the Germans, true to their doctrine of speed, tended more and more to move their shock elements along the main arteries. It was, therefore, absolutely unnecessary to cover our front with a line extending for hundreds of kilometres, almost impossible to man, and terribly easy to pierce. On the other hand, the invader might have been badly mauled by a few islands of resistance well sited along the main roads, adequately camouflaged, sufficiently mobile, and armed with a few machine-guns and anti-tank artillery, or even with the humble 75!

*   *   *

The story goes that Hitler, before drawing up his final plans for the campaign, summoned a number of psychologists to his headquarters and asked their advice. I cannot vouch for the truth of this, but it does not seem to be altogether beyond the bounds of probability. However that may be, the air offensive, conducted with such dash by the Germans, does seem to prove that they had gone very deeply into the whole question of nerves and the best way of breaking them. Nobody who has ever heard the whistling scream made by dive-bombers before releasing their load is ever likely to forget the experience. It is not only that the strident din made by the machines terrifies the victim by awakening in his mind associated images of death and destruction. In itself, and by reason of what I may call its strictly acoustic qualities, it can so work upon the nerves that they become wrought to a pitch of intolerable tension whence it is a very short step to panic.

*   *   *

I am going to relate one small experience of my own, and without mincing words. I underwent my baptism of fire in 1940 (my earlier baptism of 1914 took place at the Marne) on 22 May on a road in Flanders—for I do not count the bombing of Douai and of the environs of Lens, in neither of which was I closely concerned. On the morning of the day in question, the convoy of which my car formed part was first machine-gunned from the air and then bombed. The machine-gunning, though it killed a man quite close to me, left me more or less unmoved. Of course, it is never very pleasant to be within touching-distance of death, and I do not mind admitting that I was a good deal relieved when the

storm of bullets passed. But all through that particular episode my uneasiness had been much more a matter of intellect than of instinct. It was a sort of *cold* fear, with nothing in it of the quality of genuine *terror*. The bombing attack, so far as I am aware, killed no one, or no one who was anywhere near me. Nevertheless, it left me profoundly shaken, and when I crept out of the ditch where I had been crouching I was trembling pretty badly. During the latter part of the campaign I came under a number of artillery bombardments. I have known worse, and should be the last to exaggerate their violence. Still, they were quite nasty enough. But I stood up to them without much difficulty, and I think I can say that they never made me lose my presence of mind. But under air bombing I was never able to retain anything like the same calmness except by making a very considerable effort of will.

*   *   *

* * *our war, up to the very end, was a war of old men, or of theorists who were bogged down in errors engendered by the faulty teaching of history. It was saturated by the smell of decay rising from the Staff College, the offices of a peace-time General Staff, and the barrack-square. The world belongs to those who are in love with the new. That is why our High Command, finding itself face to face with novelty, and being quite incapable of seizing its opportunities, not only experienced defeat, but, like boxers who have run to fat and are thrown off their balance by the first unexpected blow, accepted it.

*   *   *

REVIEW QUESTIONS

1. According to Bloch, what specific failings of French military leaders contributed to the French defeat?
2. What made Hitler's Blitzkrieg strategy so successful?

3. How might the French military have fended off the German assault, according to Bloch?
4. What did Bloch's personal experience of aerial

bombardment teach him about Hitler's military strategy?

WINSTON CHURCHILL

FROM *Wars Are Not Won by Evacuation*

Having defeated France, Hitler turned his attention to Britain. Before the amphibious landing of German troops, known as Operation Sea-Lion, could proceed, it was necessary for the German air force to establish control of the airways above the English Channel. Beginning in June 1940, the German Luftwaffe began a series of bombing raids on air fields and other strategic military targets. However, following a retaliatory British bombing raid on Berlin, Hitler called for the bombing of civilian targets, against the advice of many of his military advisors. Beginning in September, the city of London was bombed for almost two months, and tens of thousands of Londoners were killed. Hitler expected this blitz to break civilian morale, but it only served to rally support to the wartime effort. Unable to dominate the British skies, Hitler turned his attention to the invasion of the Soviet Union, planned for mid-1941.

The British victory was at least in part the result of the forceful leadership provided by Winston Churchill (1874–1965). Churchill, long an opponent of Neville Chamberlain's policy of appeasement, had become prime minister in May 1940, and then led Britain in its struggle against the German assault. In June, after the collapse of the combined British and French counter-offensive on the western front, Churchill readied the British people for the coming battle, calling on them to prepare to stand alone against the German onslaught. Just after every available seaworthy vessel had been drafted into service to ferry the more than three hundred thousand British and French troops trapped at Dunkirk back to Britain, Churchill gave a rousing speech to Parliament, announcing his firm resolve to resist German occupation of his island nation.

From *Wars Are Not Won By Evacuation* vol. 6, edited by R. R. James, Chelsea House Publishers. Reprinted with permission of the publisher.

*   *   *

When, a week ago today, I asked the House to fix this afternoon as the occasion for a statement, I feared it would be my hard lot to announce the greatest military disaster in our long history. I thought—and some good judges agreed with me —that perhaps 20,000 or 30,000 men might be re-embarked. But it certainly seemed that the whole of the French First Army and the whole of the

British Expeditionary Force north of the Amiens-Abbeville gap would be broken up in the open field or else would have to capitulate for lack of food and ammunition. These were the hard and heavy tidings for which I called upon the House and the nation to prepare themselves a week ago.

*   *   *

* * *the Royal Navy, with the willing help of countless merchant seamen, strained every nerve to embark the British and Allied troops; 220 light warships and 650 other vessels were engaged. They had to operate upon the difficult coast, often in adverse weather, under an almost ceaseless hail of bombs and an increasing concentration of artillery fire. Nor were the seas, as I have said, themselves free from mines and torpedoes. It was in conditions such as these that our men carried on, with little or no rest, for days and nights on end, making trip after trip across the dangerous waters, bringing with them always men whom they had rescued. The numbers they have brought back are the measure of their devotion and their courage. The hospital ships, which brought off many thousands of British and French wounded, being so plainly marked were a special target for Nazi bombs; but the men and women on board them never faltered in their duty.

*   *   *

* * *the Navy, using nearly 1,000 ships of all kinds, carried over 335,000 men, French and British, out of the jaws of death and shame, to their native land and to the tasks which lie immediately ahead. We must be very careful not to assign to this deliverance the attributes of a victory. Wars are not won by evacuations.* * * Can you conceive a greater objective for the Germans in the air than to make evacuation from these beaches impossible, and to sink all these ships which were displayed, almost to the extent of thousands? Could there have been an objective of greater military importance and significance for the whole purpose of the war than this? They tried hard, and they were beaten back; they were frustrated in their task. We got the Army away; and they have paid

fourfold for any losses which they have inflicted. Very large formations of German aeroplanes—and we know that they are a very brave race—have turned on several occasions from the attack of one-quarter of their number of the Royal Air Force, and have dispersed in different directions. Twelve aeroplanes have been hunted by two. One aeroplane was driven into the water and cast away by the mere charge of a British aeroplane, which had no more ammunition. All of our types—the Hurricane, the Spitfire and the new Defiant—and all our pilots have been vindicated as superior to what they have at present to face.

When we consider how much greater would be our advantage in defending the air above this Island against an overseas attack, I must say that I find in these facts a sure basis upon which practical and reassuring thoughts may rest. I will pay my tribute to these young airmen. The great French Army was very largely, for the time being, cast back and disturbed by the onrush of a few thousands of armored vehicles. May it not also be that the cause of civilization itself will be defended by the skill and devotion of a few thousand airmen? There never has been, I suppose, in all the world, in all the history of war, such an opportunity for youth.* * *

I return to the Army. In the long series of very fierce battles, now on this front, now on that, fighting on three fronts at once, battles fought by two or three divisions against an equal or somewhat larger number of the enemy, and fought fiercely on some of the old grounds that so many of us knew so well—in these battles our losses in men have exceeded 30,000 killed, wounded and missing. I take occasion to express the sympathy of the House to all who have suffered bereavement or who are still anxious.

*   *   *

* * * our losses in material are enormous. We have perhaps lost one-third of the men we lost in the opening days of the battle of 21st March, 1918, but we have lost nearly as many guns—nearly one thousand—and all our transport, all the armored vehicles that were with the Army in the north

* * * An effort the like of which has never been seen in our records is now being made. Work is proceeding everywhere, night and day, Sundays and week days. Capital and Labor have cast aside their interests, rights, and customs and put them into the common stock. Already the flow of munitions has leaped forward. There is no reason why we should not in a few months overtake the sudden and serious loss that has come upon us, without retarding the development of our general program.

Nevertheless, our thankfulness at the escape of our Army and so many men, whose loved ones have passed through an agonizing week, must not blind us to the fact that what has happened in France and Belgium is a colossal military disaster. * * * The whole of the Channel ports are in his hands, with all the tragic consequences that follow from that, and we must expect another blow to be struck almost immediately at us or at France. We are told that Herr Hitler has a plan for invading the British Isles. This has often been thought of before. When Napoleon lay at Boulogne for a year with his flat-bottomed boats and his Grand Army, he was told by someone. "There are bitter weeds in England." There are certainly a great many more of them since the British Expeditionary Force returned.

The whole question of home defense against invasion is, of course, powerfully affected by the fact that we have for the time being in this Island incomparably more powerful military forces than we have ever had at any moment in this war or the last. But this will not continue. We shall not be content with a defensive war. We have our duty to our Ally. We have to reconstitute and build up the British Expeditionary Force once again, under its gallant Commander-in-Chief, Lord Gort. All this is in train; but in the interval we must put our defenses in this Island into such a high state of organization that the fewest possible numbers will be required to give effective security and that the largest possible potential of offensive effort may be realized. On this we are now engaged.* * *

We have found it necessary to take measures of increasing stringency, not only against enemy aliens and suspicious characters of other nationalities, but also against British subjects who may become a danger or a nuisance should the war be transported to the United Kingdom. I know there are a great many people affected by the orders which we have made who are the passionate enemies of Nazi Germany. I am very sorry for them, but we cannot, at the present time and under the present stress, draw all the distinctions which we should like to do.* * *

Turning once again, and this time more generally, to the question of invasion, I would observe that there has never been a period in all these long centuries of which we boast when an absolute guarantee against invasion, still less against serious raids, could have been given to our people. In the days of Napoleon the same wind which would have carried his transports across the Channel might have driven away the blockading fleet. There was always the chance, and it is that chance which has excited and befooled the imaginations of many Continental tyrants. Many are the tales that are told. We are assured that novel methods will be adopted, and when we see the originality of malice, the ingenuity of aggression, which our enemy displays, we may certainly prepare ourselves for every kind of novel stratagem and every kind of brutal and treacherous maneuver. I think that no idea is so outlandish that it should not be considered and viewed with a searching, but at the same time, I hope, with a steady eye. We must never forget the solid assurances of sea power and those which belong to air power if it can be locally exercised.

I have, myself, full confidence that if all do their duty, if nothing is neglected, and if the best arrangements are made, as they are being made, we shall prove ourselves once again able to defend our Island home, to ride out the storm of war, and to outlive the menace of tyranny, if necessary for years, if necessary alone. At any rate, that is what we are going to try to do. That is the resolve of His Majesty's Government—every man of them. That is the will of Parliament and the nation. The British Empire and the French Republic, linked together in their cause and in their need, will defend to the death their native soil, aiding each other like good comrades to the utmost of their strength. Even though large tracts of Europe and many old and famous States have fallen or may fall into the grip of the Gestapo and all the odious apparatus of Nazi rule, we shall not flag or fail. We shall go on to the end, we shall fight in France, we shall fight on the seas and oceans, we shall fight with growing confidence and growing strength in the air, we shall defend our Island, whatever the cost may be, we shall fight on the beaches, we shall fight on the landing grounds, we shall fight in the fields and in the streets, we shall fight in the hills; we shall never surrender, and even if, which I do not for a moment believe, this Island or a large part of it were subjugated and starving, then our Empire beyond the seas, armed and guarded by the British Fleet, would carry on the struggle, until, in God's good time, the New World, with all its power and might, steps forth to the rescue and the liberation of the old.

REVIEW QUESTIONS

1. According to Churchill, what problems confront Britain in its approaching battle with Germany?
2. What advantages does Britain enjoy?
3. What is the purpose of Churchill's speech?
4. What message is he attempting to convey to both parliament and the British people?

HILDE MARCHANT

FROM *Women and Children Last: A Woman Reporter's Account of the Battle of Britain*

Initial bombing raids on London targeted armaments factories and other strategically sensitive sites, most of which were concentrated in the poorer East End. London's working class resented the fact that even in war the rich seemed to escape from hardship. However, the bombing of Buckingham Palace, the royal residence, brought an end to any hard feelings. Princess Elizabeth commented, "I'm glad we've been bombed. It makes me feel I can look the East End in the face."

Having grown up in northern England, young journalist Hilde Marchant (dates unknown) admitted that she did not feel at home in London prior to the war. However, her experience covering the blitz gradually changed her opinion of the city and its people. With an eye toward encouraging Americans to come to the aid of the British war effort, Marchant published Women and Children Last: A Woman Reporter's Account of the Battle of Britain *in 1941. It contains a lively account of Londoners' stoicism in the face of devastating bombing raids and of the quiet heroism of ordinary people in extraordinary circumstances.*

From *Women and Children Last: A Woman Reporter's Account of the Battle of Britain*, Hilde Marchant, V. Gollancz, 1941.

*   *   *

Mr. Smith is not a big man, not a handsome man, not a strong man. Mr. Smith is a little man. He is rather narrow across the chest, his face is deflated of its youth, his hair is as thin as the grass in a London park. First of all, Mr. Smith would describe himself as a Cockney, and secondly he would describe himself as a Londoner. For his affection and civic patriotism is for those tightly packed miles of wavering roof tops that make a shabby border for the South side of the river Thames. He has lived there all his life and when he goes West for a Saturday night treat with his wife he is like a provincial on the loose. And Mr. Smith would tell you that he loved every one of those narrow, suppurating streets that miraculously bulge with life. Though looking at the blackened mortar, and ruptured walls you might wonder why.

So just before the war Mr. Smith decided to express his fervent love for these homes and people who dwell there and became one of the war's new soldiers—a warden of Stepney. His uniform is a pair of blue overalls, a tin hat and a gasmask and he is a veteran member of the civilian defence force that has defended and saved the citizens of London. Mr. Smith would not regard himself as a particularly brave man, because in his peace time life there was never any occasion to be brave. It was just a routine, unnoticed fight, to survive such things as unemployment, rent and a fourth child.

At first Smith was very uncomfortable about his chosen job as nursemaid to the streets. Khaki broke the everyday street scene and he had to take a lot of unpleasant remarks about dodging the army and taking £3 5s. 0d. for sitting by a telephone that never rang and polishing a whistle that never played a tune. He was either a comedian or a coward. Until one day in September when he fell flat on his face in a road. He was covered with bricks and dust.

From that day it was Smith's war. From that day Mr. Smith was the hero of the streets to everybody but Mr. Smith. He regards himself as a

"trained officer of incidents"—that delightful piece of under-statement that so fits his character. For an "incident" can mean climbing into fires, burrowing under crushed homes, or comforting a broken spirit.

But perhaps the greatest battle of all in those early days was a personal one. Smith had to adjust his warm, sentimental, domestic nature to the grim agonising sights of the night. He loves humanity, in all its virtue and vice, and it was a shock for him to see the pain and distortion of life around him. Yet he corseted his sentimentality with the months of training he had had and became the handyman of the blitz.

Smith's post is in a basement on the corner of a street in Stepney. He was resting—not sleeping —when I met him. He can only sleep in the daytime now.

There were half a dozen other men at the post who, apart from their names, were no more distinctive than Smith. There was a tailor, a food porter, a driver, a fishmonger, men who until the September days had not been able to express their desire for action.

Smith began to tell me about that first night, the night he fell in the road and broke his glasses. A bomb just a few yards from him had hit a block of buildings, and there were eleven people trapped on the ground floor.

"It was a noisy night, but every time we bent low we could hear the groans of the people underneath. I thought I'd be sick. I held a man's hand that was clear. It took us nine hours to get him out. An hour later we got a woman out. They were in a bad way. There was dirt and blood caked on the woman's face. We wiped it off. She must have been about thirty. They both died. We were all a bit quiet. It was the first we'd seen. We couldn't have got them out quicker—we'd torn our hands up dragging the stones away. But it was awful seeing them take the last gasps as they lifted them into the ambulance."

Smith was quiet, even retelling the story, and one of the men said:

"It was the first, you see."

Then Smith told me about the next night—the night when he was really "blooded". Incendiaries had started a fire in one of the smaller streets and high explosives began to fall into the fire. Smith approached the houses from the back and got through to the kitchen of one of the houses.

"I fell over something. I picked it up and it was a leg. I stood there with it in my hand wondering what I should do with it. I knew it was a woman's leg. I put it down and went to look for the ambulance. They had got the fire out at the front. The ambulance men brought a stretcher and I showed them the leg. Then we looked farther in and there were pieces all over. All they said was they didn't need a stretcher."

As Smith sat thinking, his whole body seemed to pause . . .

"Funny, I don't seem to remember what I thought that night. Surprising how you forget things."

It would be slighting Smith's imagination to say that the sight in the kitchen did not affect him. It did.

"You see, how we look at things now is like this. If they're alive you work like the devil to keep 'em alive and get 'em out. We listen to their groans and know they have breath in them. If they're dead there's nothing we can do. Getting upset hampers your work."

So Smith learned not to over-indulge his sensitivity on seeing death, or torn limb and flesh. His job was with the spark of life that survived.

*   *   *

The next day he took me round his streets in a baby car, showing me the damage. Damage has been described over and over again, but I still like Smith's own description of a house:

"Cut in two like a slice of cheese, showing all the little holes where the maggots crawled in and out."

It has a touch of that high-flown philosophising that the Cockney is so fond of twisting into his own flamboyant phrases.

The house was neatly cut. It was the usual scene—the waxed flowers still on the mantelpiece, the portrait of Grandma still hanging from the bedroom wall, the clock still ticking on the wall. Yet in every house strange things remain intact. In this one there was a mirror hanging in a shattered hall and the glass had not broken, china cups hanging over the kitchen sink were still whole, the beer glasses on the sideboard were covered with plaster, but unbroken. I pointed this out to Smith.

"Same as the 'umans. Some of the skinniest get through all right and some of the big ones come off worst."

*   *   *

As we wandered through these broken streets people called out to Smith.

"Any more bombs?" or "When do we get the roof mended?" They all knew Mr. Smith the Warden. He walked through the streets like the squire of a village, smiling and chatting to the people standing at their doors.

*   *   *

A woman came out of the huddle round the canteen.

"We looked for you on Wednesday and couldn't find you. My husband wants to say thank you and buy you a pint," she said.

Smith told me that story as we went back to his post. They had discovered a D.A. bomb in a garden. They knew there were people in the house, so they went round knocking at the door, telling them to get out. At the end of the street a small high explosive had broken one house. They thought the house was empty until they were moving the others. Then one of the men said he had heard a sound from the back of the garden. With the delayed action bomb only a few yards away, the wardens began to investigate. They found that a huge piece of the wall had locked a man and wife in the Anderson. For two hours they worked, wondering all the time if the delayed action was going up. They got the man and wife out and then ran down the street. And an hour later the bomb exploded.

"Lucky to be alive," said Smith casually. Smith is a little man but only in his size.

We had a cup of tea at the post and Smith went over to a box marked "Biscuits". He shook it. There was no sound, so he cursed.

"If there's one thing I like it's a chocolate biscuit with my tea."

*   *   *

REVIEW QUESTIONS

1. What are the duties of a warden? What impact did the blitz have on Mr. Smith's ward?
2. How did it affect Mr. Smith himself?
3. What point is Marchant trying to make through her pencil-portrait of this "little man"?
4. To what extent does her reporting support the sentiments expressed in Churchill's speech?

VASSILY GROSSMAN

FROM In the Line of the Main Attack

By mid-1942, the Germans had advanced deep into the Soviet Union. To the north, the Red Army fought desperately to hold Moscow; to the southeast, Soviet troops took their stand at Stalingrad, an industrial city and a significant source of armaments for the Russian war effort, standing between the German army and the rich oil fields of the Caucasus. In some of the fiercest fighting of the war, Red Army troops successfully defended Stalingrad, despite intense bombardment by the Germans. During the battle, which marked a decisive turning point in the war on the eastern front, as many as eight-hundred thousand combined Axis troops and as many as one-million Soviet troops died.

Vassily Grossman (1905–1964) was a wartime correspondent for the Soviet periodical Krasnaya Zvezda. In late 1942 he wrote a report on the battle of Stalingrad, documenting the valiant efforts of a division of Siberian troops under the command of Coloniel Gurtiev. Like all wartime reporting, including Hilde Marchant's stories of the blitz, Grossman's account was shaped by its propagandistic aims. In this particular case, the Siberian troops are described in much the same manner as the "heroes of labor" whose astounding acts of industrial production were celebrated during the 1930s. However, Grossman's eyewitness testimony also provides a lively and sympathetic portrait of the Red Army, conveying the dogged determination and loyalty of the many soldiers who died defending Russia—if not necessarily Stalinism—from the ferocious Nazi onslaught.

From "In the Line of the Main Attack," Vassily Grossman, in *Moscow-Stalingrad, 1941–1942: Recollections, Stories, Reports,* compiled by Vladimir Sevruk, translated from the Russian, Progress Publishers, 1970.

*   *   *

Colonel Gurtiev is a lean man of fifty. When the First World War broke out in 1914 he left the St. Petersburg Polytechnic where he was studying in his second year to volunteer for the army, and fought as a gunner at Warsaw, Baranovichi and Chartoriisk.

Gurtiev has been in the army for twenty-eight years, seeing active service and training officers. His two sons went off to the front as lieutenants. He has left his wife and daughter behind in far-away Omsk. On this terrible and solemn day he thought of his lieutenant sons, his daughter and his wife, and the many young officers he had trained, and his whole long, hard, Spartan life. The time has come when all the principles of military science, morale and duty which he taught his sons, his pupils and fellow soldiers will be put to the test, and he looked anxiously at the faces of the Siberians—the men from Omsk, Novosibirsk, Krasnoyarsk and Barnaul—the men with whom it was his destiny to repel the enemy onslaught.

The Siberians came to the Volga well-prepared. The Division had been well-trained before being sent to the front. Colonel Guttiev had trained his men thoroughly and wisely, had never stood for any nonsense and if anything had been over-exacting. He knew that however hard military training might be—the night practice raids, the lying in trenches and slits being "ironed" by tanks, the long forced marches—the real thing was far grimmer. He had faith in the fortitude and stamina of his Siberians. He had tested it on the way to the front, when throughout the whole long journey there had been only one incident: one of the soldiers had dropped his rifle from the moving train, and had leapt down, picked it up and run three kilometres to the next station to rejoin his regiment. He had tested their stamina in the Stalingrad steppes, where his men had had their baptism of fire and calmly repelled a surprise attack of thirty German tanks. He had tested their endurance during the last leg of the march to Stalingrad, when they had covered two hundred kilometres in forty-eight hours. Yet he still looked anxiously at the faces of the men, now that they were there on the front line, where they would be bearing the brunt of the main attack.

*   *   *

Hardly had the division had time to entrench itself in the stony ground of Stalingrad, hardly had the command post moved into a deep gallery cut in the sandy escarpment above the Volga, the communications lines been laid and the transmitters begun to tap out their messages to the artillery positions on the other side of the river, hardly had the first pale light of dawn pierced the darkness, than the Germans opened fire. For eight hours solid the German Junkers dive-bombed the Division's positions, for eight hours, without a moment's pause, wave after wave of German planes passed over, for eight hours the sirens wailed, the bombs whistled through the air, the earth trembled and what was left of the brick buildings crashed to the ground. For eight hours the air was dark with smoke and dust and deadly splinters zipped everywhere. Anyone who has heard the whine of the air rent by falling bomb, anyone who has experienced an intense ten-minute bombing raid by the Luftwaffe will understand what eight hours of solid aerial bombardment by dive-bombers means. For eight hours the Siberians kept up a constant barrage of fire at the enemy aircraft, and the Germans doubtless felt something like despair as the whole area of the plant, burning and shrouded in a black cloud of dust and smoke, crackled with rifle shots, rattled with machine-gun fire, the short thuds of anti-tank rifles and the regular, angry fire of ack-ack guns. It would seem that everything living must be broken, annihilated; yet there were the Siberian Division, dug into the ground, uncowed and unbroken, keeping up a continuous deadly barrage of fire. The Germans had thrown in their heavy mortars and artillery. The monotonous hiss of mines and the crash of shells merged with the whine of sirens and the roar of exploding bombs. So it continued until nightfall. Then in solemn silence the Red Army men buried their dead comrades. That was the first day, the "house-warming". The German mortar-batteries kept up their racket all night, and few of the men got any sleep.

*   *   *

In the course of a month the enemy launched one hundred and seventeen attacks against the Siberian Division.

There was one terrible day when the German tanks and infantry attacked twenty-three times. And all twenty-three attacks were repulsed. Every day except three for a month, the Luftwaffe was in the air over the Division's positions for ten to twelve hours—three hundred and twenty hours in the whole month. The operations department counted up the astronomical number of bombs dropped on the Division. It ran into tens of thousands; so did the number of Luftwaffe sorties. All this on a front little over a mile long! The roar of explosions was enough to deafen the whole of mankind, the fire and metal was enough to wipe a whole country off the map. The Germans thought they were breaking the morale of the Siberians. They thought they had exceeded the limits of human endurance, the power of human hearts and nerves to stand up to such punishment. But, amazingly, the men had not crumpled, had not gone insane, had not lost control of their hearts and nerves, but had instead become stronger and calmer. The sturdy, tight-lipped Siberians had become even sterner, even more tight-lipped; their cheeks had become hollow, and their eyes more determined. Here where the brunt of the German attack was borne there was no singing, no accordions, no light conversation in the short lulls in the fighting. Here men were undergoing a superhuman strain. There were times when no one slept for three or four days and nights, and talking with his men Gurtiev was pained to hear a soldier say quietly:

"We've got everything, Comrade Colonel; nine hundred grammes of bread, and hot meals in thermoses twice a day without fail—but we're just not hungry."

Gurtiev loved and respected his men, and he knew that when a soldier is "not hungry", he's really finding the going hard. But now Gurtiev's mind was at ease. He realised that there was no power on earth that could shake his Siberians.

*   *   *

After almost twenty days the Germans launched a "decisive" attack on the plant. Never in history had an assault been preceded by such massive preparation. The Luftwaffe and the heavy mortars and artillery showered the Division with bombs and shells for eighty hours solid: three days and nights that were a chaos of smoke, fire and thunder. The whistle of falling bombs, the scream of mortar shells from the six-barrel "goofies", the thunder of heavy shells and the protracted wail of the sirens was alone enough to deafen people— but they were only the prelude to the thunder of explosions. Jagged tongues of flame spurted up and the air was rent by the howl of tormented metal. For eighty hours it went on, then the preparation finished suddenly at five in the morning and immediately German tanks and infantry advanced to the attack. The Germans managed to penetrate into the plant workshops, their tanks roared at its very walls, they broke through our defences and cut off the command posts from the forward lines. It would have seemed that deprived of their commanders, further resistance by the troops would have been impossible, and that the command posts, under direct enemy attack, would be wiped out. But an extraordinary thing happened: every trench, every dugout, every firing-point and every fortified ruin became a separate, isolated fortress with its own command, its own communications. Sergeants and rank-and-file soldiers assumed command, and skilfully repulsed all attacks. And in this bitter, critical hour, the commanders and HQ staff turned the command posts into fortified strong-points, and fought like rank-and-file soldiers to repulse the enemy attacks. Chamov beat off ten attacks. A giant, red-haired tank commander defending Chamov's command post used up all his grenades and ammunition and then took to hurling stones at the advancing Germans. Chamov himself manned a mortar.

The golden boy of the Division, Mikhalyev, was killed by a direct bomb hit on the command post. "They've killed our father," said the men. Major Kushnaryov, who replaced Mikhalyev, transferred his command post to a concrete pipe that passed beneath the workshops. Along with his Chief-of-Staff, Dyatlenko, and six other staff officers he successfully defended the entrance to the pipe for several hours with a few boxes of grenades, repulsing numerous German attacks.

This battle, unequalled in its cruelty and ferocity, lasted for several days and nights uninterrupted. It was fought for every step of a staircase, for every corner in a dark passage, for every machine and the space between them, for every gas pipe. No one took a step back in this battle. And if the Germans gained some ground it meant that there was nobody left alive to defend it. Everyone fought like the giant red-haired tankman, whose name Chamov was never to learn; like the sapper Kosichenko, who, his left arm broken, took to removing the pin of his grenades with his teeth. It was as if the fallen were giving added strength to the living, and there were moments when ten men held a line that had been defended by a whole battalion. The workshops changed hands many times in the course of the battle. The Germans succeeded in occupying several buildings and workshops. It was in this battle that the German offensive reached its climax. This was the high-water mark of their main attack. As if they had lifted a weight that was too heavy for them, they overstrained some inner spring that had set their battering-ram in motion.

The German onslaught began to falter. They had three divisions, the 94th, the 305th and the 389th, fighting the Siberians. Their hundred and seventeen infantry attacks cost 5,000 German lives. The Siberians withstood this superhuman pressure. Two thousand tons of scrap metal from enemy tanks littered the ground in front of the plant. Thousands of tons of bombs, mines and shells had fallen on the factory yard and on the workshops, but still the Division held out. The troops faced death, without ever once looking back, for they knew that behind them lay the Volga and the fate of Russia.

One cannot help wondering how this tremendous strength was forged. It was partly the national character, the tremendous sense of responsibility, and that stolid Siberian stubbornness, excellent military and political training and strict discipline. But there was something else I should like to mention as having played no mean role in this great, tragic epic—and that was the amazingly fine morale and the strong bond of love that united all the men of the Siberian Division. A spirit of Spartan simplicity was characteristic of the whole staff. It was reflected in ordinary, everyday details, in the refusal to accept the rationed hundred grammes of vodka that was theirs by right throughout the whole long Stalingrad battle, and in their sensible, calm, business-like manner. I saw the love that united the men of the Division, in the deep distress with which they mourned the loss of their fallen comrades.

I saw it in the moving meeting between the grey-haired Colonel Gurtiev and the battalion nurse, Zoya Kalganova, when she returned to duty after her second wound. "Hello, my dear child," Gurtiev said quietly, and quickly went forward with outstretched hands to greet the thin girl with close-cropped hair—just like a father greeting his own daughter.

This love and faith in one another was what helped the soldiers in the heat of battle to take the place of their commander and the commanders and staff to take up machine-guns, hand-grenades, and incendiary bottles to repulse the German tanks approaching the command post.

The wives and children of these men will never forget their husbands and fathers who fell in the great battle on the Volga. They cannot be forgotten, these fine, true men. There is only one worthy way in which our Red Army can honour the sacred memory of the men who bore the brunt of the enemy's main attack—and that is by an unlimited, liberating offensive. We believe that the hour of this offensive is at hand.

*   *   *

REVIEW QUESTIONS

1. How does the warfare described by Grossman differ from that described by World War I soldiers Henri Barbusse and Ernst Jünger?

2. How does it differ from Marc Bloch's description of the western front engagements of 1940?
3. On the basis of this account, why do you think that the Soviet troops were able to hold Stalingrad?

ANNY LATOUR

FROM *The Jewish Resistance in France, 1940–1944*

Despite the brutal treatment that the Nazi government meted out to its opponents, organized resistance to Hitler's regime began almost immediately after he seized power in 1933, and it developed into an important component of the military effort during World War II. Resistance took many forms, including espionage, sabotage, the smuggling of refugees, and armed assaults on occupying forces. Resisters were drawn from all walks of life, but active resistance to Nazism tended to flourish among those with strong preexisting political, ideological, or religious allegiances. Armed resistance was most successful in regions whose terrain was conducive to guerrilla warfare, from the rugged maquis *of southern France to the mountains of Yugoslavia.*

European Jews had strong incentives for joining resistance movements, for they were the first to be targeted for imprisonment and deportation when German troops occupied a country or region. On the other hand, Jews were also subject to heavy surveillance and were often deported or imprisoned immediately after German occupation, making overt acts of resistance difficult and very dangerous. Despite these obstacles, many Jews joined the resistance, often at great personal cost. In 1970, Anny Latour, a historian and a former resister, published a study of the Jewish resistance in France, based on the testimony of survivors and on her own experiences as a resister. In the following excerpt from this study, Latour describes some of the tactics of the Groupes Francs, *the assault units of the armed Jewish resistance.*

From *The Jewish Resistance in France, 1940–1944*, Anny Latour, translated by Irene R. Ilton, Schocken Books, 1981.

*   *   *

The more the networks of the Jewish Resistance developed, the harder the Gestapo tried to destroy them. Arrests became more and more frequent.

But didn't the Jews have excellent false papers?

The Gestapo relied on another weapon: treacherous informers. They are paid 5,000 francs for each Jew they denounce—a handsome sum for that time.

These who are something of "physiognomists" are particularly valuable to the Germans, and are placed on their payroll; these individuals are talented at distinguishing Jews from non-Jews, and are sent to roam the streets and mingle in crowds—until they pounce upon their prey!

Another method—though it only works on men—is conducting "undressing sessions," as we referred to them; men would be stopped in the middle of the street, and told to pull down their pants, so as to be examined for circumcision.

Means of self-defense were needed. The Jewish Army forms its own Groupes Francs in all the great urban centers.

Unmask the traitors—strike them down without pity!

The "specialty" of the commandos is surprise attack. Targets range from the traitors themselves, to German military installations.

Today, conversing with men and women who seem incapable of hurting a fly, I am dumbfounded as I listen to their exploits: former killers they certainly were; and yet, striking down men whose actions were a threat to so many, clearly seems an act of legitimate self-defense. Blowing up German munition dumps, removing bolts from the rail tracks so as to delay German trains bound for the front after D-Day—all these were acts of patriotism.

But executing traitors, sabotaging ammunition dumps and fighting in the maquis—these all required bombs and weapons.

The Groupes Francs had their own suppliers, particularly in Marseille. The real problem was of transport: baggage was subject to inspection; officials were often on the lookout for black marketeers—what if, instead of a nice cut of ham, or chunk of butter, they found a few guns . . .

Moreover, police informers are posted at all the outskirts of the stations keeping an alert eye out for suspects. Just the way in which a traveler holds his suitcase, can give him away—and a heavy-looking bag he's having trouble with, could be stuffed with arms.

Women were less often the target than men, so it was they who were assigned the job of arms transport. There are "specialists" in the field: Reine Roman; Betty Knout (daughter of Ariane Knout), who is just sixteen, Evelyne Gottlieb, and Nina Jefroykin, to name but a few.

Tommy-guns and rifles for the maquis groups; revolvers and incendiary bombs for executing the traitors—they were conveyed in suitcases, bicycle "saddlebags" and even the huge housings of radios.

Reine, in particular, is extremely daring. Radiantly beautiful, she sails shamelessly through all obstacles. It seems miraculous that she survived— I recall one particularly dramatic plan we devised. At the time, she was carrying a revolver of her own: "I don't surrender without a fight," she liked to say.

Brazen it out—it was the only way to emerge unscathed. Tony Gryn tells a story about Betty Knout:

> It was shortly before the Liberation. The railroad bridge crossing the Loire had been blown up. To get to Paris, then, we had to get off the train, cross the river on foot via another bridge, and get back on a different train north of the river.—No easy matter when you're loaded down with a suitcase of arms!
>
> A German officer spies this cute young thing with a roguish look to her, and sees her laboring with the large suitcases.
>
> 'Need some help, mademoiselle?' Then: 'These weigh a ton! What have you got here—butter? cheese? some ham?'
>
> Betty adopts a knowing look: "Shh! I've got weapons in there!—tommy guns, and revolvers!'
>
> The officer breaks out into a hearty laugh.
>
> Allow me!' He lifts both suitcases and carries them all the way to the new train, even going so far as to help Betty get comfortably settled. . . .

*   *   *

REVIEW QUESTIONS

1. How did the German occupying forces identify Jewish resisters?
2. How did Jews respond to the threat of discovery?
3. How did Jewish resisters procure guns?
4. What special advantages did women have as gunrunners?

TADEUSZ BOROWSKI

FROM *This Way for the Gas, Ladies and Gentlemen*

In the years following World War II, the resistance movement inspired a certain optimism about the fundamental goodness of human nature. On the other hand, the unparalleled brutality of the Nazi's "Final Solution"—the systematic extermination of European Jews—provided crushing evidence of the depths of depravity to which "civilized" societies might sink. While some explained away the mechanized genocide of the concentration camps as the result of German barbarism, others rejected this approach, analyzing the Holocaust as the product of social pathologies to which all human beings might succumb, given the proper circumstances.

Polish author Tadeusz Borowski (1922–1951) was born in the Soviet Ukraine and both of his parents were imprisoned in Siberia during the Stalinist terror of the 1930s. The family was reunited in Poland before World War II, and Borowski began his literary career in Warsaw. He was arrested as a political dissident in 1943 and was interned in the concentration camps of Dachau and Auschwitz until 1945. Because he was young, healthy, and not a Jew, Borowski managed to survive in the camps, performing services that facilitated the extermination of Jewish prisoners. After the war he was haunted by this coerced collaboration and published several collections of fictionalized stories about his camp experiences. Not long after he returned to Warsaw, now under the control of a pro-Soviet communist regime, Borowski committed suicide, at least in part out of a deep despair over what he perceived as the survival of the concentration camp mentality in Cold War Poland. In the short story, "This Way for the Gas, Ladies and Gentleman," Borowski describes unloading the cattle cars that brought Jews to Auschwitz.

*   *   *

'Want to come with us on the ramp?'

'Sure, why not?'

'Come along then, grab your coat! We're short of a few men. I've already told the Kapo,' and he shoves me out of the barracks door.

We line up. Someone has marked down our numbers, someone up ahead yells, 'March, march,' and now we are running towards the gate, accompanied by the shouts of a multilingual throng that is already being pushed back to the barracks. Not everybody is lucky enough to be going on the ramp. We have almost reached the gate. *Links, zwei, drei, vier! Mützen ab!* Erect, arms stretched stiffly along our hips, we march past the gate briskly, smartly, almost gracefully. A sleepy S.S. man with a large pad in his hand checks us off, waving us ahead in groups of five.

'*Hundert!*' he calls after we have all passed.

'*Stimmt!*' comes a hoarse answer from out front.

We march fast, almost at a run. There are guards all around, young men with automatics. We pass camp II B, then some deserted barracks and a clump of unfamiliar green—apple and pear trees. We cross the circle of watchtowers and, running, burst on to the highway. We have arrived. Just a few more yards. There, surrounded by trees, is the ramp.

A cheerful little station, very much like any other provincial railway stop: a small square framed by tall chestnuts and paved with yellow gravel. Not far off, beside the road, squats a tiny wooden shed, uglier and more flimsy then the ugliest and flimsiest railway shack; farther along lie stacks of old rails, heaps of wooden beams, barracks parts, bricks, paving stones. This is where they load freight for Birkenau: supplies for the construction of the camp, and people for the gas chambers. Trucks drive around, load up lumber, cement, people—a regular daily routine.

And now the guards are being posted along the rails, across the beams, in the green shade of the Silesian chestnuts, to form a tight circle around the ramp. They wipe the sweat from their faces and sip out of their canteens. It is unbearably hot; the sun stands motionless at its zenith.

"Fall out."

We sit down in the narrow streaks of shade along the stacked rails. The hungry Greeks (several of them managed to come along, God only knows how) rummage underneath the rails. One of them finds some pieces of mildewed bread, another a few half-rotten sardines. They eat.

'*Schweinedreck,*' spits a young, tall guard with corn-coloured hair and dreamy blue eyes. 'For God's sake, any minute you'll have so much food to stuff down your guts, you'll bust!' He adjusts his gun, wipes his face with a handkerchief.

'Hey you fatso!' His boot lightly touches Henri's shoulder. '*Pass mal auf,* want a drink?'

'Sure, but I haven't got any marks,' replies the Frenchman with a professional air.

'*Schade,* too bad.'

'Come, come, Herr Posten, isn't my word good enough any more? Haven't we done business before? How much?'

'One hundred. *Gemacht?*'

'*Gemacht.*'

We drink the water, lukewarm and tasteless. It will be paid for by the people who have not yet arrived.

'Now you be careful,' says Henri, turning to me. He tosses away the empty bottle. It strikes the rails and bursts into tiny fragments. 'Don't take any money, they might be checking. Anyway, who the hell needs money? You've got enough to eat. Don't take suits, either, or they'll think you're planning to escape. Just get a shirt, silk only, with a collar. And a vest. And if you find something to drink, don't bother calling me. I know how to shift for myself, but you watch your step or they'll let you have it.'

'Do they beat you up here?'

'Naturally. You've got to have eyes in your ass. *Arschaugen.*'

Around us sit the Greeks, their jaws working greedily, like huge human insects. They munch on stale lumps of bread. They are restless, wondering what will happen next. The sight of the large beams and the stacks of rails has them worried. They dislike carrying heavy loads.

'*Was wir arbeiten?*' they ask.

'*Niks. Transport kommen, alles Krematorium, compris?*'

'*Alles verstehen,*' they answer in crematorium Esperanto. All is well—they will not have to move the heavy rails or carry the beams.

In the meantime, the ramp has become increasingly alive with activity, increasingly noisy. The crews are being divided into those who will open and unload the arriving cattle cars and those who will be posted by the wooden steps. They receive instructions on how to proceed most efficiently. Motor cycles drive up, delivering S.S. officers, bemedalled, glittering with brass, beefy men with highly polished boots and shiny, brutal faces. Some have brought their briefcases, others hold thin, flexible whips. This gives them an air of military readiness and agility. They walk in and out of the commissary—for the miserable little shack by the road serves as their commissary, where in the summertime they drink mineral water, *Studentenquelle*, and where in winter they can warm up with a glass of hot wine. They greet each other in the state-approved way, raising an arm Roman fashion, then shake hands cordially, exchange warm smiles, discuss mail from home, their children, their families. Some stroll majestically on the ramp. The silver squares on their collars glitter, the gravel crunches under their boots, their bamboo whips snap impatiently.

We lie against the rails in the narrow streaks of shade, breathe unevenly, occasionally exchange a few words in our various tongues, and gaze listlessly at the majestic men in green uniforms, at the green trees, and at the church steeple of a distant village.

'The transport is coming,' somebody says. We spring to our feet, all eyes turn in one direction. Around the bend, one after another, the cattle cars begin rolling in. The train backs into the station, a conductor leans out, waves his hand, blows a whistle. The locomotive whistles back with a shrieking noise, puffs, the train rolls slowly alongside the ramp. In the tiny barred windows appear pale, wilted, exhausted human faces, terror-stricken women with tangled hair, unshaven men. They gaze at the station in silence. And then, suddenly, there is a stir inside the cars and a pounding against the wooden boards.

'Water! Air!'—weary, desperate cries.

Heads push through the windows, mouths gasp frantically for air. They draw a few breaths, then disappear; others come in their place, then also disappear. The cries and moans grow louder.

A man in a green uniform covered with more glitter than any of the others jerks his head impatiently, his lips twist in annoyance. He inhales deeply, then with a rapid gesture throws his cigarette away and signals to the guard. The guard removes the automatic from his shoulder, aims, sends a series of shots along the train. All is quiet now. Meanwhile, the trucks have arrived, steps are

being drawn up, and the Canada men[1] stand ready at their posts by the train doors. The S.S. officer with the briefcase raises his hand.

'Whoever takes gold, or anything at all besides food, will be shot for stealing Reich property. Understand? *Verstanden?*'

'*Jawohl!*' we answer eagerly.

'*Also los!* Begin!'

The bolts crack, the doors fall open. A wave of fresh air rushes inside the train. People . . . inhumanly crammed, buried under incredible heaps of luggage, suitcases, trunks, packages, crates, bundles of every description (everything that had been their past and was to start their future). Monstrously squeezed together, they have fainted from heat, suffocated, crushed one another. Now they push towards the opened doors, breathing like fish cast out on the sand.

'Attention! Out, and take your luggage with you! Take out everything. Pile all your stuff near the exits. Yes, your coats too. It is summer. March to the left. Understand?'

'Sir, what's going to happen to us?' They jump from the train on to the gravel, anxious, worn-out.

'Where are you people from?'

'Sosnowiec-Będzin. Sir, what's going to happen to us?' They repeat the question stubbornly, gazing into our tired eyes.

'I don't know, I don't understand Polish.'

It is the camp law: people going to their death must be deceived to the very end. This is the only permissible form of charity. The heat is tremendous. The sun hangs directly over our heads, the white, hot sky quivers, the air vibrates, an occasional breeze feels like a sizzling blast from a furnace. Our lips are parched, the mouth fills with the salty taste of blood, the body is weak and heavy from lying in the sun. Water!

---

[1] Canada men were those prisoners fortunate enough to be assigned to transport duty. Canada, to which many Europeans had immigrated prior to the war, was imagined by camp inmates as an ideal land of peace and plenty.

A huge, multicoloured wave of people loaded down with luggage pours from the train like a blind, mad river trying to find a new bed. But before they have a chance to recover, before they can draw a breath of fresh air and look at the sky, bundles are snatched from their hands, coats ripped off their backs, their purses and umbrellas taken away.

'But please, sir, it's for the sun, I cannot . . .'

'*Verboten!*' one of us barks through clenched teeth. There is an S.S. man standing behind your back, calm, efficient, watchful.

'*Meine Herrschaften*, this way, ladies and gentlemen, try not to throw your things around, please. Show some goodwill,' he says courteously, his restless hands playing with the slender whip.

'Of course, of course,' they answer as they pass, and now they walk alongside the train somewhat more cheerfully. A woman reaches down quickly to pick up her handbag. The whip flies, the woman screams, stumbles, and falls under the feet of the surging crowd. Behind her, a child cries in a thin little voice 'Mamele!'—a very small girl with tangled black curls.

The heaps grow. Suitcases, bundles, blankets, coats, handbags that open as they fall, spilling coins, gold, watches; mountains of bread pile up at the exits, heaps of marmalade, jams, masses of meat, sausages; sugar spills on the gravel. Trucks, loaded with people, start up with a deafening roar and drive off amidst the wailing and screaming of the women separated from their children, and the stupefied silence of the men left behind. They are the ones who had been ordered to step to the right—the healthy and the young who will go to the camp. In the end, they too will not escape death, but first they must work.

Trucks leave and return, without interruption, as on a monstrous conveyor belt. A Red Cross van drives back and forth, back and forth, incessantly: it transports the gas that will kill these people. The enormous cross on the hood, red as blood, seems to dissolve in the sun.

The Canada men at the trucks cannot stop for a single moment, even to catch their breath. They shove the people up the steps, pack them in tightly, sixty per truck, more or less. Near by stands a young, cleanshaven 'gentleman', an S.S. officer with a notebook in his hand. For each departing truck he enters a mark; sixteen gone means one thousand people, more or less. The gentleman is calm, precise. No truck can leave without a signal from him, or a mark in his notebook: *Ordnung muss sein*. The marks swell into thousands, the thousands into whole transports, which afterwards we shall simply call 'from Salonica', 'from Strasbourg', 'from Rotterdam'. This one will be called 'Sosnowiec-Będzin'. The new prisoners from Sosnowiec-Będzin will receive serial numbers 131–2—thousand, of course, though afterwards we shall simply say 131–2, for short.

The transports swell into weeks, months, years. When the war is over, they will count up the marks in their notebooks—all four and a half million of them. The bloodiest battle of the war, the greatest victory of the strong, united Germany. *Ein Reich, ein Volk, ein Führer*—and four crematoria.

* * *

REVIEW QUESTIONS

1. Why does the narrator consider himself "lucky" to be doing this work?
2. What are the benefits of unloading the cattle cars?
3. What will happen to the people in the Sosnowiec-Będzin transport?
4. Why won't the camp inmates unloading the trains explain what is going to happen to these new arrivals?
5. Compare Borowski's depictions of the unloading crew ("the Canada men"), the camp administrators, and the Jews arriving in Auschwitz.
6. What message is conveyed by Borowski's portrayal of these distinct concentration camp subpopulations?

FROM The Nuremberg Trials

Borowski's detached, even clinical, descriptions of life in the concentration camps offered little solace to a world desperate for a renewed sense of decency and justice. While many postwar philosophers emphasized the moral ambiguities of human action and the relativism of all moral and ethical systems, these "post-modern" approaches were counter-balanced by a desire to reaffirm the existence of clear lines between good and evil, right and wrong. Survivors sought to ensure that all of humanity would know about the murder of millions of concentration camp inmates, and they called for a judgment upon those who had committed crimes against humanity.

Beginning in 1945, many surviving members of the Nazi leadership were put on trial in the city of Nuremberg. The "doctors' trial," which began in December 1946, involved the prosecution of twenty-three German doctors and administrators who had used concentration camp inmates as unwilling volunteers in a variety of gruesome and often pointless experiments, including intentional infection with contagious diseases like malaria and spotted fever, experimental surgery, and exposure to extreme cold, mustard gas, and various poisons. On 6 December 1946, Brigadier General Telford Taylor presented the opening statement for the prosecution, detailing both the specific crimes committed by the defendants and the broader significance of their trial.

From *Opening Statement of the Prosecution by Brigadier General Telford Taylor, 9 December 1946*, United States Holocaust Memorial Museum Webpage, <http://www.ushmm.org/research/doctors/telfptx.htm>. Originally published in *Trials of War Criminals before the Nuremberg Military Tribunals under Control Council Law No. 10. Nuremberg, October 1946–April 1949*, U.S. Government Printing Office, 1949–1953.

Opening Statement of the Prosecution by Brigadier General Telford Taylor, 9 December 1946

The defendants in this case are charged with murders, tortures, and other atrocities committed in the name of medical science. The victims of these crimes are numbered in the hundreds of thousands. A handful only are still alive; a few of the survivors will appear in this courtroom. But most of these miserable victims were slaughtered outright or died in the course of the tortures to which they were subjected.

For the most part they are nameless dead. To their murderers, these wretched people were not individuals at all. They came in wholesale lots and were treated worse than animals. They were 200 Jews in good physical condition, 50 gypsies, 500 tubercular Poles, or 1,000 Russians. The victims of these crimes are numbered among the anonymous millions who met death at the hands of the Nazis and whose fate is a hideous blot on the page of modern history.

*   *   *

The mere punishment of the defendants, or even of thousands of others equally guilty, can never redress the terrible injuries which the Nazis visited on these unfortunate peoples. For them it is far more important that these incredible events be established by clear and public proof, so that no one can ever doubt that they were fact and not fable; and that this Court, as the agent of the United States and as the voice of humanity, stamp these acts, and the ideas which engendered them, as barbarous and criminal.

We have still other responsibilities here. The defendants in the dock are charged with murder, but this is no mere murder trial. We cannot rest content when we have shown that crimes were committed and that certain persons committed them. To kill, to maim, and to torture is criminal under all modern systems of law. These defendants did not kill in hot blood, nor for personal enrichment. Some of them may be sadists who killed and tortured for sport, but they are not all perverts. They are not ignorant men. Most of them are trained physicians and some of them are distinguished scientists. Yet these defendants, all of whom were fully able to comprehend the nature of their acts, and most of whom were exceptionally qualified to form a moral and professional judgment in this respect, are responsible for wholesale murder and unspeakably cruel tortures. It is our deep obligation to all peoples of the world to show why and how these things happened. It is incumbent upon us to set forth with conspicuous clarity the ideas and motives which moved these defendants to treat their fellow men as less than beasts.

* * *

To the German people we owe a special responsibility in these proceedings. Under the leadership of the Nazis and their war lords, the German nation spread death and devastation throughout Europe. This the Germans now know. So, too, do they know the consequences to Germany: defeat, ruin, prostration, and utter demoralization. Most German children will never, as long as they live, see an undamaged German city.

* * *

This case, and others which will be tried in this building, offer a signal opportunity to lay before the German people the true cause of their present misery. The walls and towers and churches of Nuremberg were, indeed, reduced to rubble by Allied bombs, but in a deeper sense Nuremberg had been destroyed a decade earlier, when it became the seat of the annual Nazi Party rallies, a focal point for the moral disintegration in Germany * * *

* * *

That murder should be punished goes without the saying, but the full performance of our task requires more than the just sentencing of these defendants. Their crimes were the inevitable result of the sinister doctrines which they espoused, and these same doctrines sealed the fate of Germany, shattered Europe, and left the world in ferment. Wherever those doctrines may emerge and prevail, the same terrible consequences will follow. That is why a bold and lucid consummation of these proceedings is of vital importance to all nations. That is why the United States has constituted this Tribunal.

* * *

Before taking up these experiments one by one, let us look at them as a whole. Are they a heterogeneous list of horrors, or is there a common denominator for the whole group?

A sort of rough pattern is apparent on the face of the indictment. Experiments concerning high altitude, the effect of cold, and the potability of processed sea water have an obvious relation to aeronautical and naval combat and rescue problems. The mustard gas and phosphorous burn experiments, as well as those relating to the healing value of sulfanilamide for wounds, can be related to air raid and battlefield medical problems. It is well known that malaria, epidemic jaundice, and typhus were among the principal diseases which had to be combated by the German Armed Forces and by German authorities in occupied territories.

To some degree, the therapeutic pattern outlined above is undoubtedly a valid one, and explains why the Wehrmacht, and especially the German Air Force, participated in these experiments. Fanatically bent upon conquest, utterly ruthless as to the means or instruments to be used in achieving victory, and callous to the sufferings of people whom they regarded as inferior, the German militarists were willing to gather whatever scientific fruit these experiments might yield.

But our proof will show that a quite different and even more sinister objective runs like a red thread through these hideous researches. We will show that in some instances the true object of these experiments was not how to rescue or to cure, but how to destroy and kill. The sterilization experiments were, it is clear, purely destructive in purpose. The prisoners at Buchenwald who were shot with poisoned bullets were not guinea pigs to test an antidote for the poison; their murderers really wanted to know how quickly the poison would kill.

*   *   *

The 20 physicians in the dock range from leaders of German scientific medicine, with excellent international reputations, down to the dregs of the German medical profession. All of them have in common a callous lack of consideration and human regard for, and an unprincipled willingness to abuse their power over the poor, unfortunate, defenseless creatures who had been deprived of their rights by a ruthless and criminal government. All of them violated the Hippocratic commandments which they had solemnly sworn to uphold and abide by, including the fundamental principles never to do harm* * *

*   *   *

I intend to pass very briefly over matters of medical ethics, such as the conditions under which a physician may lawfully perform a medical experiment upon a person who has voluntarily subjected himself to it, or whether experiments may lawfully be performed upon criminals who have been condemned to death. This case does not present such problems. No refined questions confront us here.

None of the victims of the atrocities perpetrated by these defendants were volunteers, and this is true regardless of what these unfortunate

people may have said or signed before their tortures began. Most of the victims had not been condemned to death, and those who had been were not criminals, unless it be a crime to be a Jew, or a Pole, or a gypsy, or a Russian prisoner of war.

Whatever book or treatise on medical ethics we may examine, and whatever expert on forensic medicine we may question, will say that it is a fundamental and inescapable obligation of every physician under any known system of law not to perform a dangerous experiment without the subject's consent. In the tyranny that was Nazi Germany, no one could give such a consent to the medical agents of the State; everyone lived in fear and acted under duress. I fervently hope that none of us here in the courtroom will have to suffer in silence while it is said on the part of these defendants that the wretched and helpless people whom they froze and drowned and burned and poisoned were volunteers.

*   *   *

This case is one of the simplest and clearest of those that will be tried in this building. It is also one of the most important. It is true that the defendants in the box were not among the highest leaders of the Third Reich. They are not the war lords who assembled and drove the German military machine, nor the industrial barons who made the parts, nor the Nazi politicians who debased and brutalized the minds of the German people. But this case, perhaps more than any other we will try, epitomizes Nazi thought and the Nazi way of life, because these defendants pursue the savage promises of Nazi thought so far. The things that these defendants did, like so many other things that happened under the Third Reich, were the result of the noxious merger of German militarism and Nazi racial objectives.

*   *   *

Germany surrendered herself to this foul conjunction of evil forces. The nation fell victim to the Nazi scourge because its leaders lacked the wisdom to foresee the consequences and the courage to stand firm in the face of threats. Their failure was the inevitable outcome of that sinister undercurrent of German philosophy which preaches the supreme importance of the state and the complete subordination of the individual. A nation in which the individual means nothing will find few leaders courageous and able enough to serve its best interests.

*   *   *

The Nazis have, to a certain extent, succeeded in convincing the peoples of the world that the Nazi system, although ruthless, was absolutely efficient; that although savage, it was completely scientific; that although entirely devoid of humanity, it was highly systematic—that "it got things done." The evidence which this Tribunal will hear will explode this myth. The Nazi methods of investigation were inefficient and unscientific, and their techniques of research were unsystematic.

These experiments revealed nothing which civilized medicine can use. It was, indeed, ascertained that phenol or gasoline injected intravenously will kill a man inexpensively and within 60 seconds. * * * There is no doubt that a number of these new methods may be useful to criminals everywhere and there is no doubt that they may be useful to a criminal state.

*   *   *

Apart from these deadly fruits, the experiments were not only criminal but a scientific failure. * * * The moral shortcomings of the defendants and the precipitous ease with which they decided to commit murder in quest of "scientific results," dulled also that scientific hesitancy, that thorough thinking-through, that responsible weighing of every single step which alone can insure scientifically valid results. Even if they had merely been forced to pay as little as two dollars for human experimental subjects, such as American investigators may have to pay for a cat, they might have thought twice before wasting unnecessary numbers, and thought of simpler and better ways to solve their problems. The fact that

these investigators had free and unrestricted access to human beings to be experimented upon misled them to the dangerous and fallacious conclusion that the results would thus be better and more quickly obtainable than if they had gone through the labor of preparation, thinking, and meticulous preinvestigation.

*   *   *

In short, this conspiracy was a ghastly failure as well as a hideous crime. The creeping paralysis of Nazi superstition spread through the German medical profession and, just as it destroyed character and morals, it dulled the mind.

Guilt for the oppressions and crimes of the Third Reich is widespread, but it is the guilt of the leaders that is deepest and most culpable. Who could German medicine look to to keep the profession true to its traditions and protect it from the ravaging inroads of Nazi pseudo-science? This was the supreme responsibility of the leaders of German medicine* * * That is why their guilt is greater than that of any of the other defendants in the dock. They are the men who utterly failed their country and their profession, who showed neither courage nor wisdom nor the vestiges of moral character. It is their failure, together with the failure of the leaders of Germany in other walks of life, that debauched Germany and led to her defeat. It is because of them and others like them that we all live in a stricken world.

REVIEW QUESTIONS

1. Why, according to General Taylor, is it so important that the defendants be tried for their crimes?
2. Other then punishing specific guilty individuals, what purpose is being served by these trials?
3. To what extent is Taylor's statement an indictment of Nazi science in general?
4. How does Taylor's perspective on Nazi atrocities differ from Borowski's?
5. What can account for this difference?

TADATAKA KURIBAYASHI

FROM *A Child's Experience: My Experience of the Atomic Bomb*

On 6 August 1945, an atomic bomb was dropped on the Japanese city of Hiroshima, killing sixty-six thousand people outright. On 9 August another bomb was dropped on Nagasaki, killing thirty-nine thousand. In the following weeks and months, many more died as a result of radiation exposure and of injuries sustained at the time of the explosions.

The decision to drop the newly developed atomic bomb on Japan continues to generate heated debate among philosophers, historians, and the general public. Those who defend this particular deployment of nuclear weapons argue that it brought a more rapid end to the war, thereby saving the lives of countless American soldiers and Japanese civilians. Others counter that the Japanese government was already on the verge of surrender, and that the targeting of civilian populations for military ends is, in any case, indefensible. Evaluation of this event is further complicated by the fact that the decision to use the atomic bomb was made in the context of emerging Cold War hostilities. Truman was eager to end the war with Japan and keep the Soviet Union out of the Asian theater, and he may also have wished to provide Stalin with a graphic demonstration of the enhanced military might of the United States.

During the war years, Allied propaganda supplied Americans and Europeans with highly stereotyped and racist caricatures of the Japanese. In the postwar period, this dehumanized image was challenged by movies and books documenting the tragic consequences of the use of nuclear weapons. In the 1960s, Tadataka Kuribayashi recounted his own experience of the bombing of Hiroshima. In early 1945, Kuribayashi had been attending school in Hiroshima. In April of that year he was evacuated to the nearby peasant village of Tsutsuga, along with eighteen other children.

From *A Child's Experience: My Experience of the Atomic Bomb*, Tadataka Kuribayashi, A-Bomb WWW Page, <http://www.csi.ad.jp/ABOMB/RERF/setb-4.html>.

The Fatal Day (6 August)

The weather was fine in the village on the morning of the 6 August, which was more than one month after the parents-visiting day. In the precincts of a shrine adjacent to the school, we boys in the 6th grade were undergoing training in the Morse signals. Cool breeze blew under ginkgo trees, and the cicadas seemed to be singing the joys of summer. Suddenly I felt something warm on my left cheek and turned back. It seemed like a strong reflection from a mirror. Then a roaring sound shook the whole village. While I was wondering what had happened, a column of clouds appeared above the mountains in the south. That was not an ordinary cloud but of a superb pink color. Gradually it assumed the shape of a mushroom and rose to the sky.

When I returned to the temple, the matron said she had felt a strong tremor even in the temple. As time passed, the fine sky gradually became dark, and in the late afternoon, a lot of cinders of paper and other things fell down from the sky. First a rumor said that an arsenal had exploded, but I later heard that a fire engine from an adjacent village had gone to Hiroshima City for rescue, but because of the strong fire, could not go beyond Yokogawa and returned. Thus, though I was small, I felt something unusual had happened. However, I didn't even imagine that the big city of Hiroshima had instantaneously become a sheet of fire.

Soon I heard that many people with severe burns had returned to the village. All of these people were from the village and were working in Hiroshima. Since then, there was no communication from the parents. After more than a week, a teacher told us that there had been an important announcement and that Japan had lost the war, but now I cannot remember sorrow or anxiety at that time. We might have been too young to have any direct emotion about the big change for the nation. Even though the war ended, we couldn't do anything. No one came to fetch us, and everyone lived anxiously from day to day.

At the beginning of September, I received a wrinkled-up postcard. Though my mother's name was mentioned, the handwriting with a pencil, some parts of which were blurred, was not my mother's. The card simply said, "I am in the reception center in Miyajima. Come here immediately." and a simple map of the place was shown. I wondered why my mother had not written it herself, but was glad to know where she was. However, the date on the card showed that many days had passed since it had been written. Next day, I, accompanied by Mr. Yamakawa, left for Miyajima. That was the 2 September.

I looked at the town of Hiroshima while I proceeded from Yokogawa to Koi. It was a field of charred ruins. The city streetcar which just began to run between Koami-cho and Koi had numerous flies on the ceiling. It was a strange sight. We took a boat from Miyajima-guchi. I saw the old big torii (Shinto shrine archway) and the beautiful Itsukushima Shrine, but they just looked a faded landscape painting to me. I wanted to go to the reception center and see the face of my mother as soon as possible. I was so eager to see her that I felt the boat was extremely slow. Soon we arrived at the center, which was a big building to the north of the shrine. When I stood at the entrance, I felt some kind of anxiety, which was an emotion difficult to express.

Attending on Mother

I looked for Mother with my teacher. It was a big room with tens of tatami mats, and the spaces between A-bomb survivors lying on futon (bedclothes) produced a forlorn atmosphere. We took one round, but couldn't find her. While I took the second round, looking into the face of each person, I was astonished to find Mother, lying on her face and exhausted. She was a small person, but she looked even smaller. Suppressing the tremor of my voice, I called her quietly. There was no answer. I called her again. Then she noticed and slightly raised her head. She saw the teacher behind me, and took out some bills to give to him. He refused to receive them, and left there after a short while saying that he had business at the school.

When Mother told me about the death of Father, I was not so surprised. I might have been somewhat ready to hear the news. Deprived of a flush of hope, I imagined my father being burnt to death in agony. My heart was wrung. We didn't know if my elder brother, who had gone abroad to war was dead or alive. I naturally had a dark prospect about our future, but resolved firmly to continue to live with my mother no matter how poor we would be. Mother told me to take the cloth off her back. I found brown burns all over her back. Because of the burns, she couldn't lie on her back. Why does my mother, as innocent as a person could be, have to be tortured like this? I could not suppress the anger I felt. From that day, I took care of her for 2 nights and 3 days. However, the only medicine provided was mercurochrome. We were even short of cresol. When Mother arrived at the center, she was fine and even washed other people's clothes, but when I got there she couldn't even move her body.

She was engaged in building-demolition work near the Tsurumi Bridge when she was exposed to the flash. She couldn't do anything for Mrs. Takai, who was immediately burned to death in front of her, and climbed the Hijiyama Hill in a hurry with her back burned. From the hill, she looked at the city, which was a hell on earth. With other people, she was first accommodated in the reception center in Ninoshima, and moved to Miyajima. The terrible gas which entered to the depth of her body gradually damaged her bones and organs. She had completely lost her appetite.

Remorse

No one had disposed of my mother's urine, so her lower body gave out a stench. Her stool was not like that of a human being. Its color and smell were like those of internal organs that had been melted and had become a sticky liquid. I felt that the only way to give humaneness back to her was to clean the chamber pot often. Though I was eager to care for her, I became negligent once. On the second night at the center, I heard Mother's small voice calling me, but I was so sleepy that I pretended as though I didn't hear her. She called me twice, but didn't say anything more. Whenever I remember this, there is a sharp pain in my heart.

At the camp, simple food such as salty soup with one dumpling was served three times. No boiled rice was served. We were allowed to drink as many cups of soup as we liked, and I had three or four more cups of soup. My mother smiled wryly. At that time, she was too weak to speak. I saw the front of a big torii, gateway to a Shinto shrine, from the window of the lavatory. Looking

at the B-29 bomber which sometimes came flying, I shouted to myself "Idiot!" It was all the resistance I, as a boy, could offer. And I sometimes cried secretly in the lavatory.

Death of Mother

At lunch-time on 4 September, the third day, Mother started to writhe in pain. Her unusual action completely upset me. All I could do was to absentmindedly look at my suffering Mother. After suffering for 30 minutes, she regained her calmness. However, it was the last calmness, the sign of the end of life. I continued calling her name, clinging to her body. Tears welled up in the eyes of my speechless mother and tears rolled down her cheek. I wondered if the tears were from the sorrow of eternal parting between mother and child or from an anxiety about my future. I shall never forget the tears of my Mother I saw on that day.

I continued crying even after a white cloth was placed over Mother's face. Some irritated people reproached me, saying "Be quiet!" Shouldn't I feel sorry for the death of my most precious mother? My tears seemed to have forgotten to stop until evening.

Return to Tsutsuga Village

There was a middle-aged man who happened to come to the camp as an attendant. He was kind enough to offer to take charge of me, probably in pity of me who had been left an orphan. I answered I would decide after consulting with my teacher at the Saihoji Temple where I had been evacuated. He decided to take me there. Wrapping my mother's personal belongings, I had rice ball made for lunch. The man and I left Miyajima Island, leaving what had to be done including the burial of my dead mother to the officials at the camp.

Arriving at the Miyajima-guchi streetcar station, I found a streetcar already there. The streetcar was about to leave the station. I had a return ticket but the man did not have one and bought his own ticket. He hurried to the platform after he had his ticket punched. I tried to follow him, but a man at the gate told me that the ticket I had was for a train, not for a streetcar and showed me the way to the railway station. I started walking toward the station at once, never thinking of anything. There is no way of knowing if the man left for Hiroshima by streetcar or returned to Miyajima. The fact that the one ticket I had served as the turning point of my fate still makes me think of the mysteriousness of fate.

The train I got on took me close to Tsutsuga Village; from Miyajima-guchi to Yokogawa and from Yokogawa to Kabe to Aki-imuro. I felt relieved when I was picked up by a truck driver at Aki-imuro who took me to Kake. An old man who shared the ride had a water bottle and gave me some water. The water tasted so good and I felt the water coursing down through my bowels. The old man was returning to Tsutsuga Village and I asked him to take me there.

It was very far from Kake to Tsutsuga. The road along a river seemed to be endless. I tottered after several persons while half sleeping late at night. When I reached Tsutsuga Village, I noticed there were no other people except the old man who had given me water. We walked for another 40 minutes and finally reached the front of the Saihoji Temple at dawn. At that time I felt undescribably happy. I expressed my thanks and said farewell to the old man. I entered the main hall of the temple. I thought I had to report to my teacher that I had returned, but I decided to do so later in the morning because I did not want to wake him up. I stole into a mosquito net, under which some children were sleeping, carrying my bedclothes and lay down. In the morning, my teacher was very surprised to learn that I had returned. I had never experienced such a long trip.

Left Alone

I resumed my life at the temple. An increasing number of children were leaving the temple together with their parent or sibling or relative who came there to take them home. However, traffic was completely paralyzed due to a heavy flood caused by an unprecedented typhoon which hit the prefecture. So, there was no choice but to walk all the way to Hiroshima.

Children who had homes to return to were happy. Most of the children had lost either a parent or other family members. It was only I that had lost both parents and had no relatives. I had nowhere to go except an orphanage where I was taken care of. In spite of sheer unhappiness, I, as a child, did not think so seriously of it.

In the end, only three children including myself stayed behind at the temple. The temple was too big for the three of us. I heard that the relatives of Yoshihiro Inoue and Yoko Minematsu would come to the temple later for some reason. Then, it was decided that children including those living in neighboring villages who had no home to return would be accommodated in a temple at Togouchi adjacent to Tsutsuga. I was hurriedly crossing a mountain pass when it began to get dark on 3 October. There was no one to be seen and everything was ominously still and silent.

I, an 11-year-old boy, only thought of running out of the weird trees, not being afraid of my future life which would bring me loneliness and starvation. Frequently frightened at the sound of my footsteps, I kept running, only wishing I could reach the village as soon as possible.

*   *   *

REVIEW QUESTIONS

1. What does this account tell you about the Japanese experience of World War II?
2. How does Kuribayashi's ordeal compare with

Mr. Smith's experience of the London blitz, for example?

3. To what extent might the testimony of survivors like Kuribayashi influence historical interpretations of the use of atomic weapons?

4. How should historians approach the analysis of events heavily charged with moral significance, such as the Holocaust and the deployment of nuclear weapons?

5. How do the bombings of Hiroshima and Nagasaki differ from the Holocaust?

FROM The United Nations Charter

Before the atomic bomb brought the war in the Pacific to a dramatic close, a new international peacekeeping organization was already being organized to replace the League of Nations. On 26 June 1945, the United Nations was established by a formal charter drawn up at an international congress held in San Francisco. Vested with the authority to maintain and deploy peacekeeping forces, the United Nations was intended to be a more effective agency for world peace than its predecessor had been. And, while the United Nations was not able to solve the many problems generated by the Cold War, it nevertheless served as an important arena for the negotiation of conflicts between member nations. The preamble and first chapter of the United Nations Charter sets out the primary goals of the organization.

From *Charter of the United Nations*, University of Minnesota Human Rights Library Website, <http://www.umn.edu/humanrts/instree/aunchart.htm>.

Preamble to the Charter of the United Nations

WE THE PEOPLES OF THE UNITED NATIONS DETERMINED

to save succeeding generations from the scourge of war, which twice in our lifetime has brought untold sorrow to mankind, and

to reaffirm faith in fundamental human rights, in the dignity and worth of the human person, in the equal rights of men and women and of nations large and small, and

to establish conditions under which justice and respect for the obligations arising from treaties and other sources of international law can be maintained, and

to promote social progress and better standards of life in larger freedom,

AND FOR THESE ENDS

to practice tolerance and live together in peace with one another as good neighbours, and

to unite our strength to maintain international peace and security, and

to ensure, by the acceptance of principles and the institution of methods, that armed force shall not be used, save in the common interest, and

to employ international machinery for the promotion of the economic and social advancement of all peoples,

HAVE RESOLVED TO COMBINE OUR EFFORTS TO ACCOMPLISH THESE AIMS

Accordingly, our respective Governments,

through representatives assembled in the city of San Francisco, who have exhibited their full powers found to be in good and due form, have agreed to the present Charter of the United Nations and do hereby establish an international organization to be known as the United Nations.

Article 1

The Purposes of the United Nations are:

1. To maintain international peace and security, and to that end: to take effective collective measures for the prevention and removal of threats to the peace, and for the suppression of acts of aggression or other breaches of the peace, and to bring about by peaceful means, and in conformity with the principles of justice and international law, adjustment or settlement of international disputes or situations which might lead to a breach of the peace;

2. To develop friendly relations among nations based on respect for the principle of equal rights and self-determination of peoples, and to take other appropriate measures to strengthen universal peace;

3. To achieve international co-operation in solving international problems of an economic, social, cultural, or humanitarian character, and in promoting and encouraging respect for human rights and for fundamental freedoms for all without distinction as to race, sex, language, or religion; and

4. To be a centre for harmonizing the actions of nations in the attainment of these common ends.

Article 2

The Organization and its Members, in pursuit of the Purposes stated in Article 1, shall act in accordance with the following Principles.

1. The Organization is based on the principle of the sovereign equality of all its Members.

2. All Members, in order to ensure to all of them the rights and benefits resulting from membership, shall fulfill in good faith the obligations assumed by them in accordance with the present Charter.

3. All Members shall settle their international disputes by peaceful means in such a manner that international peace and security, and justice, are not endangered.

4. All Members shall refrain in their international relations from the threat or use of force against the territorial integrity or political independence of any state, or in any other manner inconsistent with the Purposes of the United Nations.

*   *   *

REVIEW QUESTIONS

1. How does this preamble compare with the covenant of the League of Nations (see Chapter 26)?

2. To what extent was this statement of goals formulated as a response to the World War II experience?

29 ∽ NEW POWER RELATIONSHIPS AND THE NEW EUROPE

*At the beginning of the twentieth century, the European Great Powers domi-
nated the world, both materially and—at least in the opinion of Europeans—
culturally. Even after World War I, European power seemed only slightly diminished, especially when the newest contender for world power status, the United
States, chose to retreat again into isolationism after the war.*

*After World War II, the world was a dramatically different place. A second
great cataclysm had left much of Europe in ruins, and the former great powers
found themselves confronted with the enormous task of reconstructing what they
themselves had destroyed. The new "bi-polar" balance of world power, pitting
the United States against the Soviet Union, decreased the global power and pres-
tige of individual European nations, drawing them into the orbits of the two
competing superpowers. Europe was divided in two by an "iron curtain," and
the cultures, economies, and political systems of the two Europes were deeply
marked by the new realities of the Cold War.*

*European dominance had ended, but the western European nations soon
rallied, achieving general levels of prosperity, technological sophistication, and
democratic participation never before experienced in their histories. American economic aid reinvigorated western European economies, greatly increasing the
material well-being of ordinary people. Cradle-to-grave social welfare programs
provided education, medical care, and guarantees that no citizen would be deprived of the minimum necessities of life. The appurtenances of consumer
culture—radios, cars, televisions, dishwashers, seaside vacations—became available to the majority of western Europeans.*

*The economic "miracle" did not come to eastern Europe. Always underde-
veloped by western standards, eastern Europe's poverty and technological backwardness were only reinforced by the domination of the powerful Soviet Union.
Communist regimes throughout eastern Europe retained their hold on power not*

through popular support but through the threat of Soviet invasion. Communist heads of state were forced to follow the dictates of economic and military planners in Moscow, often to the detriment of their own citizens. The death of Stalin in 1953 brought some easing of repression, and standards of living did improve, if more gradually and less opulently than in the West. But Stalin's successors continued to rule eastern Europe with a firm hand, stifling dissent and emphasizing heavy industrial and military production at the expense of consumer goods. When the Soviet bloc collapsed in the late 1980s, bringing a surprisingly sudden end to the Cold War, eastern Europe remained burdened with the bitter legacy of economic underdevelopment and political immaturity.

In both the East and the West, post-war culture was unsettled and complex. The war had demonstrated the moral bankruptcy of fascism (even if nostalgia for militarism, nationalism, and racial cleansing lingered in the hearts of many), but no other alternative ideologies won unqualified support. For many, the simple joys of life were enough. After the hardships of the war, consumerism and leisure culture offered a welcome respite from ideology. On the other hand, intellectuals struggled to come to terms with the implications of wartime genocide, economic and political globalization, and the "Americanization" of European culture. While the Cold War left many feeling powerless in the face of impersonal forces such as superpower politics and the threat of nuclear annihilation, others drew renewed hope from the anti-colonial struggles of third-world peoples and the protests of civil rights activists around the world.

WINSTON CHURCHILL

FROM The Sinews of Peace

During World War II, long-standing tensions between the Soviet Union and the other Allied states were set aside in favor of a unified war effort. However, even before the war had ended, mutual suspicions were revived, especially as Allied leaders began to negotiate post-war territorial settlements. The United States and Great Britain promoted the creation of capitalist democracies throughout Europe, while Stalin sought to establish communist satellite states in the East.

One of the defining moments of the emerging Cold War came on 5 March 1946, when Winston Churchill (1874–1965), who had been voted out of office as prime minister by war-weary Britons that year, gave a speech at Westminster College in Fulton, Missouri, attended by American President Harry S. Truman. In this speech, entitled "Sinews of Peace," Churchill called on Americans and western Europeans to maintain a unified front against the Soviet threat.

From *The Sinews of Peace,* vol. 7, edited by R. R. James, Chelsea House Publishers. Reprinted with permission of the publisher.

*   *   *

A shadow has fallen upon the scenes so lately lighted by the Allied victory. Nobody knows what Soviet Russia and its Communist international organisation intends to do in the immediate future, or what are the limits, if any, to their expansive and proselytising tendencies. I have a strong admiration and regard for the valiant Russian people and for my wartime comrade, Marshal Stalin. There is deep sympathy and goodwill in Britain—and I doubt not here also—towards the peoples of all the Russias and a resolve to persevere through many differences and rebuffs in establishing lasting friendships. We understand the Russian need to be secure on her western frontiers by the removal of all possibility of German aggression. We welcome Russia to her rightful place among the leading nations of the world. We welcome her flag upon the seas. Above all, we welcome constant, frequent and growing contacts between the Russian people and our own people on both sides of the Atlantic. It is my duty however, for I am sure you would wish me to state the facts as I see them to you, to place before you certain facts about the present position in Europe.

From Stettin in the Baltic to Trieste in the Adriatic, an iron curtain has descended across the Continent. Behind that line lie all the capitals of the ancient states of Central and Eastern Europe. Warsaw, Berlin, Prague, Vienna, Budapest, Belgrade, Bucharest and Sofia, all these famous cities and the populations around them lie in what I must call the Soviet sphere, and all are subject in one form or another, not only to Soviet influence but to a very high and, in many cases, increasing measure of control from Moscow. Athens alone—Greece with its immortal glories—is free to decide its future at an election under British, American and French observation. The Russian-dominated Polish Government has been encouraged to make enormous and wrongful inroads upon Germany, and mass expulsions of millions of Germans on a scale grievous and undreamed-of are now taking place. The Communist parties, which were very small in all these Eastern States of Europe, have been raised to pre-eminence and power far beyond their numbers and are seeking everywhere to obtain totalitarian control. Police governments are prevailing in nearly every case, and so far, except in Czechoslovakia, there is no true democracy.

*   *   *

The safety of the world requires a new unity in Europe, from which no nation should be permanently outcast. It is from the quarrels of the strong parent races in Europe that the world wars we have witnessed, or which occurred in former times, have sprung. Twice in our own lifetime we have seen the United States, against their wishes and their traditions, against arguments, the force of which it is impossible not to comprehend, drawn by irresistible forces, into these wars in time to secure the victory of the good cause, but only after frightful slaughter and devastation had occurred. Twice the United States has had to send several millions of its young men across the Atlantic to find the war; but now war can find any nation, wherever it may dwell between dusk and dawn. Surely we should work with conscious purpose for a grand pacification of Europe, within the structure of the United Nations and in accordance with its Charter. That I feel is an open cause of policy of very great importance.

*   *   *

From what I have seen of our Russian friends and Allies during the war, I am convinced that there is nothing they admire so much as strength, and there is nothing for which they have less respect than for weakness, especially military weakness. For that reason the old doctrine of a balance of power is unsound. We cannot afford, if we can help it, to work on narrow margins, offering temptations to a trial of strength. If the Western Democracies stand together in strict adherence to the principles of the United Nations Charter, their influence for furthering those principles will be immense and no one is likely to molest them. If however they become divided or falter in their duty and if these all-important years are allowed to slip away then indeed catastrophe may overwhelm us all.

*   *   *

REVIEW QUESTIONS

1. What is the "iron curtain"? Where is it?
2. What policies is Churchill promoting in this speech?
3. What specific response do you think he hoped to elicit from his American audience?
4. To what extent are Churchill's remarks shaped by the existence of nuclear weapons?
5. By the American tradition of isolationism?

GEORGE C. MARSHALL

FROM The Marshall Plan

Following World War II, the United States broke decisively with its pre-1945 foreign policy, rejecting the isolationism that had typified American international relations throughout the first half of the twentieth century. In the military arena, this was demonstrated through American participation in the North Atlantic Treaty Organization (NATO). But the United States did not limit its active engagement in international affairs to a purely military role. Amid anxiety about the appeal of communist parties to the population of devastated postwar Europe, many American policy makers called for the United States government to provide economic aid to the European states. Healthy democracies with viable economies, they argued, would serve as bulwarks against further Soviet expansion and would also be rewarding trading partners for American businesses.

In a speech given at Harvard University in 1947, U.S. Secretary of State George C. Marshall (1880–1959) signaled the Truman administration's readiness to engage in a massive "European Recovery Program," which came to be known as the Marshall Plan. Between 1948 and 1951, the United States proceeded to distribute almost $13,000,000,000 to seventeen European nations, greatly stimulating the economies of western and southern Europe.

From *The Marshall Plan Speech*, George C. Marshall, Marshall Plan Website, <http://www.usis.usemb.se/topical/pol/marshall/mp-toc.htm>.

*   *   *

I need not tell you that the world situation is very serious. That must be apparent to all intelligent people. I think one difficulty is that the problem is one of such enormous complexity that the very mass of facts presented to the public by press and radio make it exceedingly difficult for the man in the street to reach a clear appraisement of the situation. Furthermore, the people of this country are distant from the troubled areas of the earth and it is hard for them to comprehend the plight and consequent reactions of the long-suffering peoples, and the effect of those reactions on their governments in connection with our efforts to promote peace in the world.

In considering the requirements for the rehabilitation of Europe, the physical loss of life, the visible destruction of cities, factories, mines, and railroads was correctly estimated, but it has become obvious during recent months that this visible destruction was probably less serious than the dislocation of the entire fabric of European economy. For the past ten years conditions have been abnormal. The feverish preparation for war and the more feverish maintenance of the war effort engulfed all aspects of national economies. Machinery has fallen into disrepair or is entirely obsolete. Under the arbitrary and destructive Nazi rule, virtually every possible enterprise was geared into the German war machine. Long-standing commercial ties, private institutions, banks, insurance companies, and shipping companies disappeared through loss of capital, absorption through nationalization, or by simple destruction. In many countries, confidence in the local currency has been severely shaken. The breakdown of the business structure of Europe during the war was complete. Recovery has been seriously retarded by the fact that two years after the close of hostilities a peace settlement with Germany and Austria has not been agreed upon. But even given a more prompt solution of these difficult problems, the rehabilitation of the economic structure of Europe quite evidently will require a much longer time and greater effort than has been foreseen.

There is a phase of this matter which is both interesting and serious. The farmer has always produced the foodstuffs to exchange with the city dweller for the other necessities of life. This division of labor is the basis of modern civilization. At the present time it is threatened with breakdown. The town and city industries are not producing adequate goods to exchange with the food-producing farmer. Raw materials and fuel are in short supply. Machinery is lacking or worn out. The farmer or the peasant cannot find the goods for sale which he desires to purchase. So the sale of his farm produce for money which he cannot use seems to him an unprofitable transaction. He, therefore, has withdrawn many fields from crop cultivation and is using them for grazing. He feeds more grain to stock and finds for himself and his family an ample supply of food, however short he may be on clothing and the other ordinary gadgets of civilization. Meanwhile, people in the cities are short of food and fuel, and in some places approaching the starvation levels. So the governments are forced to use their foreign money and credits to procure these necessities abroad. This process exhausts funds which are urgently needed for reconstruction. Thus a very serious situation is rapidly developing which bodes no good for the world. The modern system of the division of labor upon which the exchange of products is based is in danger of breaking down.

The truth of the matter is that Europe's requirements for the next three or four years of foreign food and other essential products—principally from America—are so much greater than her present ability to pay that she must have substantial additional help or face economic, social, and political deterioration of a very grave character.

The remedy lies in breaking the vicious circle and restoring the confidence of the European people in the economic future of their own countries and of Europe as a whole. The manufacturer and the farmer throughout wide areas must be able and willing to exchange their product for currencies, the continuing value of which is not open to question.

Aside from the demoralizing effect on the world at large and the possibilities of disturbances arising as a result of the desperation of the people concerned, the consequences to the economy of the United States should be apparent to all. It is logical that the United States should do whatever it is able to do to assist in the return of normal economic health in the world, without which there can be no political stability and no assured peace. Our policy is directed not against any country or doctrine but against hunger, poverty, desperation, and chaos. Its purpose should be the revival of a working economy in the world so as to permit the emergence of political and social conditions in which free institutions can exist. Such assistance, I am convinced, must not be on a piecemeal basis as various crises develop. Any assistance that this Government may render in the future should provide a cure rather than a mere palliative. Any government that is willing to assist in the task of recovery will find full cooperation, I am sure, on the part of the United States Government. Any government which maneuvers to block the recovery of other countries cannot expect help from us. Furthermore, governments, political parties, or groups which seek to perpetuate human misery in order to profit therefrom politically or otherwise will encounter the opposition of the United States.

It is already evident that, before the United States Government can proceed much further in its efforts to alleviate the situation and help start the European world on its way to recovery, there must be some agreement among the countries of Europe as to the requirements of the situation and the part those countries themselves will take in order to give proper effect to whatever action might be undertaken by this Government. It would be neither fitting nor efficacious for this Government to undertake to draw up unilaterally a program designed to place Europe on its feet economically. This is the business of the Europeans. The initiative, I think, must come from Europe. The role of this country should consist of friendly aid in the drafting of a European program and of later support of such a program so far as it may be practical for us to do so. The program

should be a joint one, agreed to by a number, if not all, European nations.

An essential part of any successful action on the part of the United States is an understanding on the part of the people of America of the character of the problem and the remedies to be applied. Political passion and prejudice should have no part. With foresight, and a willingness on the part of our people to face up to the vast responsibility which history has clearly placed upon our country the difficulties I have outlined can and will be overcome.

I am sorry that on each occasion I have said something publicly in regard to our international situation, I've been forced by the necessities of the case to enter into rather technical discussions. But to my mind, it is of vast importance that our people reach some general understanding of what the complications really are, rather than react from a passion or a prejudice or an emotion of the moment. As I said more formally a moment ago, we are remote from the scene of these troubles. It is virtually impossible at this distance merely by reading, or listening, or even seeing photographs or motion pictures, to grasp at all the real significance of the situation. And yet the whole world of the future hangs on a proper judgment. It hangs, I think, to a large extent on the realization of the American people, of just what are the various dominant factors. What are the reactions of the people? What are the justifications of those reactions? What are the sufferings? What is needed? What can best be done? What must be done?

REVIEW QUESTIONS

1. Why, according to Marshall, should the United States offer economic aid to Europe?
2. What advantages will the United States derive from this aid?
3. What are the risks of not providing aid? To what extent is this speech marked by Cold War concerns?
4. How does Marshall's speech compare with Churchill's?

NIKITA KHRUSHCHEV

FROM On the Cult of Personality and Its Consequences

Stalin's death in 1953 was followed by an intense struggle for power within the Soviet leadership. At midnight on the night of 25 February 1956, the victor of this contest, first secretary Nikita Khrushchev (1894–1971), gave a "secret speech" to the twentieth congress of the Communist Party. In blunt language, Khrushchev denounced Stalin's authoritarianism as a deviation from the Marxist-Leninist principles of the Bolshevik revolution. Later that year, Khrushchev reestablished friendly relations with Yugoslavia's independent communist leader, Tito, demonstrating a new willingness on the part of the Soviet state to tolerate "different roads to Socialism." When he became premier in 1958, Khrushchev rejected the inevitability of war with non-Communist states, cultivating a foreign policy based on "peaceful coexistence."

As a loyal communist, Khrushchev remained committed to single-party rule, the planned economy, and state censorship, but his de-Stalinization campaign produced a notable "thaw" within the Soviet Union. Many political prisoners were released, and many of those who had died or been imprisoned during Stalin's reign of terror were exonerated of any crimes. Greater intellectual freedom was granted to artists, while ordinary Soviet citizens, who had long suffered as a result of Stalin's single-minded focus on the development of heavy industry, benefited from a redirection of the economy toward greater production of consumer goods.

From *The Stalin Dictatorship: Khrushchev's "Secret Speech" and Other Documents*, edited by T. H. Rigby, Sydney University Press, 1968. Reprinted with permission of the publisher.

Comrades! In the report of the Central Committee of the party at the 20th Congress, in a number of speeches by delegates to the Congress, as well as before this during plenary sessions of the CPSU Central Committee, quite a lot has been said about the cult of the individual and about its harmful consequences.

After Stalin's death the Central Committee of the party began to implement a policy of explaining concisely and consistently that it is impermissible and foreign to the spirit of Marxism-Leninism to elevate one person, to transform him into a superman possessing supernatural characteristics akin to those of a god. Such a man supposedly knows everything, sees everything, thinks for everyone, can do anything, and is infallible in his behaviour.

This kind of belief about a man, namely about Stalin, was cultivated among us for many years.

*   *   *

The great modesty of the genius of the revolution, Vladimir Ilyich Lenin, is known. Lenin always stressed the role of the people as the creator of history, the directing and organizational role of the party as a living and creative organism, and also the role of the Central Committee.

Marxism does not negate the role of the leaders of the workers' class in directing the revolutionary liberation movement.

While ascribing great importance to the role of the leaders and organizers of the masses, Lenin at the same time mercilessly stigmatized every manifestation of the cult of the individual, inexorably combated views which are foreign to Marxism, about the 'hero' and the 'crowd', and countered all efforts to oppose the 'hero' to the masses and to the people.

*   *   *

In addition to the great accomplishments of V. I. Lenin for the victory of the working class and of the working peasants, for the victory of our party and for the application of the ideas of scientific communism to life, his acute mind expressed itself also, in the fact that he detected in Stalin in time those negative characteristics which resulted later in grave consequences.

*   *   *

Stalin acted not through persuasion, explanation, and patient co-operation with people, but by imposing his concepts and demanding absolute submission to his opinion. Whoever opposed this concept or tried to prove his viewpoint, and the correctness of his position, was doomed to removal from the leading collective and to subsequent moral and physical annihilation. This was especially true during the period following the 17th Party Congress [in 1934], when many prominent party leaders and rank-and-file party workers, honest and dedicated to the cause of communism, fell victim to Stalin's despotism.

*   *   *

It was precisely during this period (1935–1937–1938) that the practice of mass repression through the government apparatus was born, first against the enemies of Leninism—Trotskyites,

Zinovievites, Bukharinites, long since politically defeated by the party, and subsequently also against many honest communists, against those party cadres who had borne the heavy load of the Civil War and the first and most difficult years of industrialization and collectivization, who actively fought against the Trotskyites and the rightists for the Leninist party line.

Stalin originated the concept 'enemy of the people'. This term automatically rendered it unnecessary that the ideological errors of a man or men engaged in a controversy be proven; this term made possible the employment of the most cruel repression, violating all norms of revolutionary legality, against anyone who in any way disagreed with Stalin, against those who were only suspected of hostile intent, against those who had bad reputations. This concept, 'enemy of the people', actually eliminated the possibility of any kind of ideological struggle or the making of one's views known on this or that issue, even those of a practical character. In the main, and in actuality, the only proof of guilt used, against all norms of current legal science, was the 'confession' of the accused himself; and, as subsequent probing proved, 'confessions' were acquired through physical pressures against the accused.

*   *   *

[Stalin] discarded the Leninist method of convincing and educating; he abandoned the method of ideological struggle for that of administrative violence, mass repressions, and terror. He acted on an increasingly larger scale and more stubbornly through punitive organs, at the same time often violating all existing norms of morality and of Soviet laws.

Arbitrary behavior by one person encouraged and permitted arbitrariness in others. Mass arrests and deportations of many thousands of people, execution without trial and without normal investigation created conditions of insecurity, fear and even desperation.

This, of course, did not contribute toward unity of the party ranks and of all strata of working people, but on the contrary brought about the annihilation and expulsion from the party of workers who were loyal but inconvenient to Stalin.

*   *   *

Were our party's sacred Leninist principles observed after the death of Vladimir Ilyich?

Whereas during the first few years after Lenin's death party congresses and Central Committee plenums took place more or less regularly, later, when Stalin began increasingly to abuse his power, these principles were crudely violated. This was especially evident during the last 15 years of his life. Was it a normal situation when over 13 years elapsed between the 18th and 19th Party Congresses, years during which our party and our country experienced so many important events? These events demanded categorically that the party pass resolutions pertaining to the country's defense during the Patriotic War and to peacetime construction after the war. Even after the end of the war a congress was not convened for over 7 years.

*   *   *

In practice Stalin ignored the norms of party life and trampled on the Leninist principle of collective party leadership.

Stalin's arbitrariness *vis-à-vis* the party and its Central Committee became fully evident after the 17th Party Congress which took place in 1934.

*   *   *

It has been established that of the 139 members and candidates of the Party's Central Committee who were elected at the 17th Congress, 98 persons, i.e. 70 percent, were arrested and shot (mostly in 1937–1938). *(Indignation in the hall.)*

*   *   *

The power accumulated in the hands of one person, Stalin, led to serious consequences during the Great Patriotic War.

When we look at many of our novels, films and historical 'scientific studies', the role of Stalin in the Patriotic War appears to be entirely im-

probable. Stalin had foreseen everything. The Soviet Army, on the basis of a strategic plan prepared by Stalin long before, used the tactics of so-called 'active defense', i.e., tactics which, as we know, allowed the Germans to come up to Moscow and Stalingrad. Using such tactics the Soviet Army, supposedly thanks only to Stalin's genius, turned to the offensive and subdued the enemy. The epic victory gained through the armed might of the Land of the Soviets, through our heroic people is ascribed in this type of novel, film and 'scientific study' as being completely due to the strategic genius of Stalin.

*   *   *

During the war and after the war Stalin put forward the thesis that the tragedy which our nation experienced in the first part of the war was the result of the 'unexpected' attack of the Germans against the Soviet Union. But, Comrades, this is completely untrue. As soon as Hitler came to power in Germany he assigned himself the task of liquidating communism. The fascists were saying this openly; they did not hide their plans. In order to attain this aggressive end all sorts of pacts and blocs were created, such as the famous Berlin-Rome-Tokyo axis. Many facts from the pre-war period clearly showed that Hitler was going all out to begin a war against the Soviet state and that he had concentrated large armed units, together with armored units, near the Soviet borders.

Documents which have now been published show that by April 3, 1941, Churchill, through his ambassador to the U.S.S.R., Cripps, personally warned Stalin that the Germans had begun regrouping their armed units with the intent of attacking the Soviet Union. It is self-evident that Churchill did not do this at all because of his friendly feeling toward the Soviet nation. He had in this his own imperialistic goals—to bring Germany and the U.S.S.R. into a bloody war and thereby to strengthen the position of the British Empire. Just the same, Churchill affirmed in his writings that he sought to 'warn Stalin and call his attention to the danger which threatened him'. Churchill stressed this repeatedly in his dispatches of April 18 and in the following days. However, Stalin took no heed of these warnings. What is more, Stalin ordered that no credence be given to information of this sort, in order not to provoke the initiation of military operations.

*   *   *

When there developed an exceptionally serious situation for our army in 1942 in the Kharkov region, we correctly decided to drop an operation whose objective had been to encircle Kharkov, because the real situation at that time would have threatened our army with fatal consequences if this operation had been proceeded with.

We communicated this to Stalin, stating that the situation demanded changes in operational plans in order to prevent the enemy from liquidating a sizable concentration of our army.

Contrary to common sense, Stalin rejected our suggestion and issued the order to continue the operation aimed at the encirclement of Kharkov, despite the fact that at this time many army concentrations were themselves actually threatened with encirclement and liquidation.

*   *   *

And what was the result of this? The worst that we had expected. The Germans surrounded our army concentrations and consequently we lost hundreds of thousands of our soldiers. This is Stalin's military 'genius'; this what it cost us. (*Movement in the hall.*)

*   *   *

In the same vein, let us take, for instance, our historical and military films and some works of literature; they make us feel sick. Their true objective is the propagation of the theme of praising Stalin as a military genius. Let us recall the film, 'The Fall of Berlin'. Here only Stalin acts; he issues orders in the hall in which there are many empty chairs and only one man approaches him and reports something to him—that is Poskrebyshev, his loyal shieldbearer. (*Laughter in the hall.*)

And where is the military command? Where is the Political Bureau? Where is the Government? What are they doing and with what are they engaged? There is nothing about them in the film. Stalin acts for everybody; he does not reckon with anyone, he asks no one for advice. Everything is shown to the nation in this false light. Why? In order to surround Stalin with glory, contrary to the facts and contrary to historical truth.

*   *   *

Not Stalin, but the party as a whole, the Soviet Government, our heroic army, its talented leaders and brave soldiers, the whole Soviet nation—these are the ones who assured the victory in the Great Patriotic War. (*Tempestuous and prolonged applause.*)

*   *   *

Comrades, let us reach for some other facts. The Soviet Union is justly considered as a model of a multi-national state because we have in practice assured the equality and friendship of all nations which live in our great fatherland.

All the more monstrous are the acts whose initiator was Stalin and which represent crude violations of the basic Leninist principles of the nationality policy of the Soviet state. We refer to the mass deportations from their native places of whole nations, together with all communists and komsomol members without any exception; this deportation action was not dictated by any military considerations.

Thus, as early as the end of 1943, when there occurred a permanent breakthrough at the fronts of the Great Patriotic War benefiting the Soviet Union, a decision was taken and carried out concerning the deportation of all the Karachai from the lands on which they lived. In the same period, at the end of December 1943, the same lot befell the whole population of the Kalmyk Autonomous Republic. In March 1944 all the Chechen and Ingush peoples were deported and the Chechen-Ingush Autonomous Republic was liquidated. In April 1944, all Balkars were deported to faraway places from the territory of the Kabardino-Balkar Autonomous Republic and the Republic itself was renamed the Karbardin Autonomous Republic.

The Ukrainians avoided meeting this fate only because there were too many of them and there was no place to which to deport them. Otherwise, he would have deported them also. *(Laughter and animation in the hall.)*

* * *

The willfulness of Stalin showed itself not only in decisions concerning the internal life of the country but also in the international relations of the Soviet Union.

The July plenary session of the Central Committee studied in detail the reasons for the development of conflict with Yugoslavia. It was a shameful role which Stalin played here. The 'Yugoslav affair' contained no problems which could not have been solved through party discussions among comrades. There was no significant basis for the development of this 'affair'; it was completely possible to have prevented the rupture of relations with that country. This does not mean, however, that the Yugoslav leaders did not make mistakes or did not have shortcomings. But these mistakes and shortcomings were magnified in a monstrous manner by Stalin, which resulted in a break of relations with a friendly country.

* * *

Comrades! The 20th Congress of the Communist Party of the Soviet Union has manifested with a new strength the unshakable unity of our party, its cohesiveness around the Central Committee, its resolute will to accomplish the great task of building communism. *(Tumultuous applause.)* And the fact that we present in all their ramifications the basic problems of overcoming the cult of the individual which is alien to Marxism-Leninism, as well as the problem of liquidating its burdensome consequences, is evidence of the great moral and political strength of our party. *(Prolonged applause.)*

We are absolutely certain that our party, armed with the historical resolutions of the 20th Congress, will lead the Soviet people along the Leninist path to new successes, to new victories. *(Tumultuous, prolonged applause.)*

Long live the victorious banner of our party —Leninism! *(Tumultuous, prolonged applause ending in ovation. All rise.)*

REVIEW QUESTIONS

1. What is the "cult of personality"?
2. In what sense did Stalin's style of rule represent a violation of Marxist-Leninist theory, according to Khrushchev?
3. What specific errors is Stalin accused of in this speech?
4. What do these accusations tell you about Khrushchev's intentions as the new leader of the Soviet Union?
5. How do you think Lenin would have responded to this speech? Nadezhda and Osip Mandelstam? Winston Churchill?

French Students and Workers Unite in Protest

In the Soviet bloc, the brief easing in state repression initiated by Khrushchev came to an end with his abrupt fall from power in 1964. Under Leonid Brezhnev the Soviet political leadership returned to more traditional policies, although Stalinism was not revived. When the Czechoslovakian leadership sought to loosen its ties to the Soviet Union in 1968, tanks and Soviet troops soon put an end to the "Prague Spring."

During this same period, the centrist governments and "white collar" bureau-crats of western Europe cooperated to produce unprecedentedly prosperous econo-mies. Yet affluence and political stability generated their own frustrations: young people, especially, rejected the stodgy conformity of their elders, calling for a radical recasting of social, political, and economic relations. De-Stalinization in the East had stimulated the revival of socialist and communist parties in the West, and this inspired a new generation of radical activists operating outside of the established left-wing parties. In 1968, French students in Paris followed the lead of their Czechoslovakian counterparts, engaging in violent protests against the stifling tradi-tionalism of the universities and against the conservatism of Charles de Gaulle's government. They were eventually joined by as many as ten million striking work-ers, bringing France to a virtual standstill in mid-1968.

Your Struggle is Our Struggle!

We are occupying the faculties, you are occu-pying the factories. Aren't we fighting for the same thing? Higher education only contains 10 per cent workers' children. Are we fighting so that there will be more of them, for a democratic university reform? That would be a good thing, but it's not the most important. These workers' children would just become like other students. We are not aiming for a worker's son to be a manager. We want to wipe out segregation between workers and management.

There are students who are unable to find jobs on leaving university. Are we fighting so that they'll find jobs, for a decent graduate employ-ment policy? It would be a good thing, but it is not vital. Psychology or sociology graduates will become the selectors, the planners and psycho-technicians who will try to organise your working conditions; mathematics graduates will become engineers, perfecting maximum-productivity ma-chines to make your life even more unbearable. Why are we, students who are products of a middle-class life, criticising capitalist society? The son of a worker who becomes a student leaves his own class. For the son of a middle-class family, it could be his opportunity to see his class in its true

light, to question the role he is destined for in society and the organisation of our society. We refuse to become scholars who are out of touch with real life. We refuse to be used for the benefit of the ruling class. We want to destroy the sepa-ration that exists between those who organise and think and those who execute their decisions. We want to form a classless society; your cause is the same as ours.

You are asking for a minimum wage of 1,000 francs in the Paris area, retirement at sixty, a 40-hour week for 48 hours' pay.

These are long-standing and just demands: nevertheless, they seem to be out of context with our aims. Yet you have gone on to occupy facto-ries, take your managers as hostages, strike with-out warning. These forms of struggle have been made possible by perseverence and lengthy action in various enterprises, and because of the recent student battles.

These struggles are even more radical than our official aims, because they go further than simply seeking improvements for the worker within the capitalist system, they imply the destruction of the system. They are political in the true sense of the word: you are fighting not to change the Prime Minister, but so that your boss no longer retains his power in business or society. The form that your struggle has taken offers us students the model for true socialist activity: the appropriation of the means of production and of the decision-making power by the workers.

Our struggles converge. We must destroy everything that seeks to alienate us (everyday habits, the press, etc.). We must combine our occupations in the faculties and factories.

Long live the unification of our struggles!

The Workers' Red Flag is Flying over Renault: Down with the Anti-Popular Gaullist Régime

For ten years the working class has gradually fought to gain unity in each factory; to defend in each company its working conditions, which are systematically attacked by the big capitalists. Workers' fights have succeeded in containing the bosses' offensive, but the division of the workers' forces and the policy of class collaboration which has become the rule *even at the level of the confederate leadership of the CGT*[1] have prevented the mass struggles from bringing about the downfall of the anti-popular régime of unemployment and poverty.

For a month now the progressive students who reject the bourgeois university, who want to be on the side of the people struggling against the bosses' régime, have put their full strength into the battle. *By their tenacity, their resolution, their desire to link their struggle with that of the working class, which is the main force in the struggle against the big capitalist bosses and the government*, the mass of progressive students has been able to strike a resounding blow against Gaullism. The workers have understood this: the progressive current in the student movement reflects the desire of the people to fight, its desire to get rid of Gaullism. The progressive students' determination has reminded the workers that only forceful action pays off. The class-collaborating unions which have en-

couraged the workers to demonstrate peacefully and with dignity only in order to receive alms, the unions which have sabotaged the mass struggles at Caen, at La Rhodia in Lyon, at Schwarz-Haumont, at Alluvac, at Alès in the ceramics industry, at Dassault, at Renault, *can today no longer resist the drive of the working masses.*

The battle flag has passed into the hands of the proletariat. The leaders of the CGT have first of all attacked the students' progressive movement in a disgusting way, using the same phrases as the government is using. Then, when the workers demonstrated their desire to intervene in force to take the lead in the battle against capitalism and its régime, the CGT and PCF[2] leaderships called for a strike with petty-bourgeois, academic slogans. But the workers understood, and put all their strength into the battle.

The government wishes to quell the revolt; Pompidou has just said so. The government is panic-stricken. The repression of the workers and the progressive students, the repression of the real communists who are fighting for popular victory, will change nothing. People's hatred of the class enemy will increase tenfold. A tremendous force is rising today. *The people will win!*

Against unemployment, starvation wages, fiendish work rates. Against police and bosses' repression. Freedom for the people!

REVIEW QUESTIONS

1. In what sense is the workers' struggle also the students' struggle?
2. What specific reforms were students and workers seeking?
3. What were their broader goals?
4. Why did radical workers at Renault reject the leadership of the General Confederation of Labor and the French Communist Party?
5. Why did they seek to ally their movement with that of the student protesters?

---

[1] *Confédération Générale du Travail* ("General Confederation of Labor"), a communist labor union.

[2] *Parti Communiste Français* ("French Communist Party").

MARGARET THATCHER

FROM Speech to the Conservative Party Conference (10 October, 1975)

The international financial crisis precipitated by the Arab oil embargo of 1973 served to revitalize conservative movements in the mid- to late-1970s. In the face of tightened economic circumstances, the right wing in America and much of western Europe sought to dismantle the social welfare systems created by post-war govern- ments. In the United States, this trend resulted in the election of Ronald Reagan (born 1911), who served as president from 1980 to 1988. In Britain, it brought the conservative Tories to power from 1979 to 1997.

In 1975, Margaret Thatcher (born 1925) was chosen as the new leader of the British Conservative Party. The first women ever to be elected Prime Minister in a European nation, she served in this position for three consecutive terms, from 1979 to 1990. Thatcher was a "new" conservative, committed to breaking with the "tax- and-spend" policies of previous governments, whether right or left. A fierce opponent of trade unions, she drew her support largely from the upper and upper-middle classes, although a critical minority of Tory workers gave Conservatives an edge in elections. During her tenure in office, Thatcher limited state intervention in the British economy, privatized many state-owned industries, and reduced taxes by sub- stantially decreasing government spending, especially for social services and welfare. Unemployment increased substantially during her years in power, but many mem- bers of her upper-class constituency benefited from lower taxes and the government's pro-business policies. The following speech, her first as head of the Conservative Party, provides a blueprint for the "Thatcher Revolution," and demonstrates the of- ten biting wit of the "Iron Lady."

From *The Revival of Britain: Speeches on Home and European Affairs, 1975–1988*, Margaret Thatcher, edited by Alastair Cooke, Aurum, 1989. Reprinted with permission of the publisher.

*   *   *

Our Leaders have been different men with dif- ferent qualities and different styles, but they all had one thing in common: each met the challenge of his time.

Now, what is the challenge of our time? I be- lieve there are two: to overcome the country's economic and financial problems, and to regain our confidence in Britain and ourselves.

*   *   *

Whatever could I say about Britain that is half as damaging as what this Labour Government has done to our country? Let us look at the record. It is the Labour Government that has caused prices to rise at a record rate of 26 per cent a year. They told us the Social Contract would solve everything, but now everyone can see that the so-called Contract was a fraud—a fraud for which the people of this country have had to pay a very high price. It is the Labour Government whose past policies are forcing unemployment higher than it need ever have been. Thousands more men and women are losing their jobs every day, and there are going to be men and women, many of them youngsters straight out of school, who will be without a job this winter because Socialist Ministers spent last year attacking us instead of attacking inflation.

It is the Labour Government that brought the level of production below that of the three-day week in 1974. We have really got a three-day week now, only it takes five days to do it. It is the Labour Government that has brought us record peace-time taxation. They have the usual Socialist disease: they have run out of other people's money. It is the Labour Government that has pushed public spending to record levels. How have they done it? By borrowing and borrowing. Never in the field of human credit has so much been owed.

Serious as the economic challenge is, the political and moral challenge is just as grave and perhaps even more so, because economic problems never start with economics. They have much deeper roots in human nature and roots in politics, and they do not finish at economics either. Labour's failure to cope, to look at the nation's problems from the viewpoint of the whole nation, and not just one section of it, has led to a loss of confidence, and to a sense of helplessness; and with it goes a feeling that Parliament, which ought to be in charge, is not in charge, and that the actions and decisions are taken elsewhere.

It goes even deeper than that, to the voices that seem anxious not to overcome our economic difficulties, but to exploit them, to destroy the free enterprise society and put a Marxist system in its place. Today those voices form a sizeable chorus in the parliamentary Labour Party, a chorus which, aided and abetted by the many constituency Labour Parties, seems to be growing in numbers.

*   *   *

I sometimes think the Labour Party is like a pub where the mild is running out. If someone does not do something soon all that is left will be bitter, and all that is bitter will be Left.

Whenever I visit Communist countries their politicians never hesitate to boast about their achievements. They know them all by heart; they reel off the facts and figures, claiming this is the rich harvest of the Communist system. Yet they are not prosperous as we in the West are prosperous, and they are not free as we in the West are free.

Our capitalist system produces a far higher standard of prosperity and happiness because it believes in incentive and opportunity, and because it is founded on human dignity and freedom. Even the Russians have to go to a capitalist country—America—to buy enough wheat to feed their people—and that after more than fifty years of a State-controlled economy. Yet they boast incessantly, while we, who have so much more to boast about, for ever criticize and decry. Is it not time we spoke up for our way of life? After all, no Western nation has to build a wall round itself to keep its people in.

So let us have no truck with those who say the free enterprise system has failed. What we face today is not a crisis of capitalism but of Socialism. No country can flourish if its economic and social life is dominated by nationalization and State control.

The cause of our shortcomings does not, therefore, lie in private enterprise. Our problem is not that we have too little Socialism. It is that we have too much. If only the Labour Party in this country would act like Social Democrats in West Germany. If only they would stop trying to prove their Socialist virility by relentlessly nationalizing one industry after another.

Of course, a halt to further State control will not on its own restore our belief in ourselves, because something else is happening to this country. We are witnessing a deliberate attack on our values, a deliberate attack on those who wish to promote merit and excellence, a deliberate attack on our heritage and our great past, and there are those who gnaw away at our national self-respect, rewriting British history as centuries of unrelieved gloom, oppression and failure—as days of hopelessness, not days of hope. And others, under the shelter of our education system, are ruthlessly attacking the minds of the young. Everyone who believes in freedom must be appalled at the tactics employed by the far Left in the systematic destruction of the North London Polytechnic—blatant tactics of intimidation designed to undermine the fundamental beliefs and values of every student, tactics pursued by people who are the first to insist on their own civil rights while seeking to deny them to the rest of us.

We must not be bullied or brainwashed out of our beliefs. No wonder so many of our people, some of the best and the brightest, are depressed and talking of emigrating. Even so, I think they are wrong. They are giving up too soon. Many of the things we hold dear are threatened as never before, but none has yet been lost, so stay here, stay and help us defeat Socialism so that the Britain you have known may be the Britain your children will know.

These are the two great challenges of our time—the moral and political challenge, and the economic challenge. They have to be faced together and we have to master them both.

What are our chances of success? It depends on what kind of people we are. What kind of people are we? We are the people that in the past made Great Britain the workshop of the world, the people who persuaded others to buy British, not by begging them to do so but because it was best.

*   *   *

We export more of what we produce than either West Germany, France, Japan or the United States, and well over 90 per cent of these exports come from private enterprise. It is a triumph for the private sector and all who work in it, and let us say so loud and clear.

With achievements like that who can doubt that Britain can have a great future, and what our friends abroad want to know is whether that future is going to happen.

Well, how can we Conservatives make it happen? Many of the details have already been dealt with in the Conference debates. But policies and programmes should not just be a list of unrelated items. They are part of a total vision of the kind of life we want for our country and our children. Let me give you my vision: a man's right to work as he will, to spend what he earns, to own property, to have the State as servant and not as master—these are the British inheritance. They are the essence of a free country and on that freedom all our other freedoms depend.

But we want a free economy, not only because it guarantees our liberties, but also because it is the best way of creating wealth and prosperity for the whole country, and it is this prosperity alone which can give us the resources for better services for the community, better services for those in need.

By their attack on private enterprise, this Labour Government has made certain that there will be next to nothing available for improvements in our social services over the next few years. We must get private enterprise back on the road to recovery, not merely to give people more of their own money to spend as they choose, but to have more money to help the old and the sick and the handicapped. And the way to recovery is through profits, good profits today leading to high investment, leading to well-paid jobs, leading to a better standard of living tomorrow. No profits mean no investment and that means a dying industry geared to yesterday's world, and that means fewer jobs tomorrow. Other nations have recognized that for years now, and because they have recognized it they are going ahead faster than we are; and the gap between us will continue to increase unless we change our ways. The trouble here is that for years the Labour Party has made people feel that profits are guilty unless proved innocent.

When I visit factories and companies I do not find that those who actually work in them are against profits; on the contrary, they want to work for a prosperous concern, a concern with a future—their future.

Governments must learn to leave these companies with enough of their own profits to produce the goods and jobs for tomorrow. If the Socialists will not, or cannot, there will be no profit-making industry left to support the losses caused by fresh bouts of nationalization. If anyone should murmur that I am preaching *laissez-faire*, let me say I am not arguing, and have never argued, that all we have to do is to let the economy run by itself. I believe that, just as each of us has an obligation to make the best of his talents, so Governments have an obligation to create the framework within which we can do so—not only individual people, but individual firms and particularly small firms. If they concentrated on doing that, they would do a lot better than they are doing now. Some of the small firms will stay small, but others will expand and become the great companies of the future. The Labour Government has pursued a disastrous vendetta against small businesses and the self-employed. We will reverse its damaging policies.

*   *   *

So today what is the picture? Depressed profits, low investment, no incentive, and, overshadowing everything, Government spending, spending, spending far beyond the taxpayers' means.

To recover, to get from where we are to where we want to be—and I admit we would rather not be here—will take time. 'Economic policy,' wrote Maynard Keynes, 'should not be a matter of tearing up by the roots but of slowly training a plant to grow in a different direction.'

It will take time to reduce public spending, to rebuild profits and incentives, and to benefit from the investments which must be made. But the sooner that time starts, the better it will be for Britain's unemployed and for Britain as a whole.

One of the reasons why this Labour Government has incurred more unemployment than any Conservative Government since the war is because they have concentrated too much on distributing what we have and too little on seeing that we have more.

We Conservatives hate unemployment. We hate the idea of men and women not being able to use their abilities. We deplore the waste of natural resources and the deep affront to people's dignity from being out of work through no fault of their own. It is ironic that we should be accused of wanting unemployment to solve our economic problems by the very Government which has produced a record post-war unemployment and is expecting more.

*   *   *

Now let me turn to something I spoke about in America. Some Socialists seem to believe that people should be numbers in a State computer. We believe they should be individuals. We are all unequal. No one, thank heavens, is quite like anyone else, however much the Socialists may pretend otherwise. We believe that everyone has the right to be unequal. But to us, every human being is equally important. Engineers, miners, manual workers, shop assistants, farmworkers, postmen, housewives—these are the essential foundations of our society, and without them there would be no nation. But there are others with special gifts who should also have their chance, because if the adventurers who strike out in new directions in science, technology, medicine, commerce and industry are hobbled, there can be no advance. The spirit of envy can destroy; it can never build. Everyone must be allowed to develop the abilities he knows he has within him, and she knows she has within her, in the way they choose.

Freedom to choose is something we take for granted until it is in danger of being taken away. Socialist Governments set out perpetually to restrict the area of choice, and Conservative Governments to increase it. We believe that you become a responsible citizen by making decisions for yourself, not by having them made for you. But they are made for you by Labour all right!

*   *   *

When the next Conservative Government comes to power many trade unionists will have put it there. Millions of them vote for us at every election. I want to say this to them and to all of our supporters in industry: go out and join in the work of your unions; go to their meetings and stay to the end, and learn the union rules as well as the far Left knows them. Remember that if parliamentary democracy dies, free trade unions die with it.

*   *   *

There is one part of this country where, tragically, defiance of the law is costing life day after day. In Northern Ireland our troops have the dangerous and thankless task of trying to keep the peace and hold a balance. We are proud of the way they have discharged their duty. This party is pledged to support the unity of the United Kingdom, to preserve that unity and to protect the people, Catholic and Protestant alike. We believe our Armed Forces must remain until a genuine peace is made. Our thoughts are with them and our pride is with them, too.

I have spoken of the challenges which face us here in Britain—the challenge to recover economically and the challenge to recover our belief in ourselves—and I have shown our potential for recovery. I have dealt with some aspects of our strength and approach and I have tried to tell you something of my personal vision and my belief in the standards on which this nation was greatly built, on which it greatly thrived and from which in recent years it has greatly fallen away. I believe we are coming to yet another turning point in our long history. We can go on as we have been going and continue down, or we can stop and with a decisive act of will say 'Enough'.

Let all of us here today, and others far beyond this hall who believe in our cause, make that act of will. Let us proclaim our faith in a new and better future for our party and our people; let us resolve to heal the wounds of a divided nation, and let that act of healing be the prelude to a lasting victory.

REVIEW QUESTIONS

1. In what ways, according to Thatcher, has Labour Party rule undermined the British economy?
2. In what ways has it undermined British confidence?
3. On the basis of this speech, what specific policies would Thatcher be likely to pursue once elected as Prime Minister?
4. To what extent might Thatcher's conservatism be considered a product of the general economic malaise of the 1970s?

JEAN-YVES POTEL

FROM *The Promise of Solidarity: Inside the Polish Workers' Struggle, 1980–82*

While conservatives in the West lashed out at organized labor, in Poland a revitalized and independent workers' movement pitted itself against the entrenched communist authorities. Poland's weak and backward economy produced simmering unrest among workers. When the government announced food price increases in 1970, a wave of strikes broke out; force was used to end these protests, resulting in the deaths of one-hundred workers. A second wave of strikes in 1976, again sparked by food costs, was also firmly repressed, but this time without bloodshed.

In August 1980, scattered strikes broke out across industrialized Poland, again in response to increased food prices. In mid-August, seventeen-thousand workers at the Lenin Shipyards in Gdansk went out on strike, at first demanding increased wages, but eventually expanding their demands to include greater political liberties and the right to organize independent trade unions. Under the leadership of Lech Walesa, a shipyard electrician who had been fired for his participation in the worker protests of 1976, the strikers won concessions from management on bread and butter issues, but then decided to continue their protest in "solidarity" with other Polish workers. French journalist Jean-Yves Potel, who witnessed these events, provided the following report on the early stages of the Gdansk strike.

From *The Promise of Solidarity: Inside the Polish Worker's Struggle, 1980–82,* Jean-Yves Potel, translated by Phil Markham. Copyright © 1982, Praeger Publishers. Reproduced with permission of Greenwood Publishing Group Inc., Westport, CT.

*   *   *

The strike that had broken out on the shores of the Baltic Sea one day in August 1980 was an event capable of reviving abandoned hopes. Like an unexpected breeze, it breathed life into them. It set them buzzing. It confounded the sceptics, and worried the strategists. Because this was a most unusual strike. It was innovative, capable of astounding and transforming. It was strong and unified. It shook up a system many had thought immovable. It revived prospects and desires that people had almost forgotten. The march of history was set in motion again.

Such was Poland in the summer of 1980. A Poland where the strike arrived, quietly, and spread, gathering strength, and consuming all around it. Calmly and peacefully.

For the third time, the trigger seemed clear enough. As in the two preceding times food prices were to go up.

*   *   *

Andrzej stood there with seven posters rolled under his arm. It was 5.00 am at the *Lenin* shipyard, Thursday 14 August. He was waiting for Bogdan. Kazik arrived—whom he had also arranged to

meet the previous evening. Kazik worked in the W3 section. They went over to the section. A few minutes later, workers changing in that section's locker room saw a poster stuck up under the clock which read: "We demand a 1,000 zloty wage rise, a cost-of-living bonus, and news on the sacking of Anna Walentynowicz!" Groups of workers gathered and asked for more detailed information.

*   *   *

In the central square there were by now several thousand men and women, cheerfully waiting there. Neither Andrzej and Kazik, nor Jurek and Bogdan, who eventually arrived with the workers from their department, imagined that this spot would give birth to the most important strike in the history of 'people's' Poland.

*   *   *

The procession set off again, with the banner at its head. It was a fine morning. They strolled along, whistling, singing, and calling out those who were still in their sections. At the far end of the shipyard, Wojcik, the yard's director, or at least, the man who thought he was still director of the yard, waited. His first words were:

"What's all this about?"

"It's a strike," they all chorused.

"Why?"

"Because you've sacked Anna Walentynowicz."

"Anna Walentynowicz?" replied the director, with feigned surprise.

Somebody refreshed his memory: "She's been sacked without warning. It's disgraceful, somebody like her . . . A woman who's been decorated with three Orders of Merit—bronze, silver and gold. She's got 30 years of work behind her, and only five months to go before she retires." The director made as if to protest. "We don't want to talk with you now!" shouted Bogdan in his direction. And the crowd set off again, leaving the director to his own thoughts.

The workers began to organise. Some people remained on the canal bridge, to make sure this route was not cut off. Then they all went to Gate No. 2, where, in 1970, four workers had fallen to police gunfire, and a minute's silence was observed to honour their memory. Before long, thousands of workers of all ages were gathered in the square, around the mechanical excavator. Somebody climbed up and made the first speech: "We must elect a strike committee. We need trusted people from each squad . . ." At that moment the director appeared, with his entourage. They set him up on the excavator, and for a few moments he was able to speak: "What more do you want? You get 9,000 zloty per month—isn't that enough?" He was unable to say much more. From the crowd came a great roar of protest, whistling and people speaking all at the same time. Was the director really so unaware of the huge disparities in rates of pay?!

It was at this point that Lech Walesa came out of the ranks. He had got into the shipyard by shinning over one of the gates. "Do you recognise me? I worked here for ten years. You sacked me in 1976 for being involved in a strike. But I still consider myself a dockworker. I have everyone's trust!" The crowd roared its approval. A number of workers hoisted him on their shoulders, and he said: "We are going on strike and occupying the plant!" The director could not get another word

in—he was drowned out by the 'Hurrah! Hurrah!' which rose from the crowd. They demanded that the loudspeakers of the yard's internal broadcast system be connected up, so that everybody could hear what was said.

Somebody shouted: "We must go and find Anna Walentynowicz." Another chimed in: "With the manager's car . . ." The manager protested, but the strikers were determined, and the driver had to do what they said.

They still had to negotiate the rest of their demands, so they needed to elect delegates and draw up a list of priority demands. They decided to go back into their sections. There were more than a hundred sections in that enormous shipyard. Each section elected one or two delegates, mandated on a set of precise demands, and at the start of the afternoon they got up one after another, perched on the excavator, to present their section's case to the crowd. People cheered and sang, in a kind of relaxed party atmosphere. Then the 200 delegates assembled in the conference hall next to the canteen. This general assembly laid out 11 basic demands, which were far more radical than those of the July strikes. They were both political and economic demands with the former taking priority. They took as their starting point the advanced demand of the Lublin workers for the dissolution of the (official) trade union factory council. Other demands already pointed to the Gdansk strikers' role as leading the whole of the Polish working class. They demanded the release of political prisoners; the reinstatement of all those sacked; family allowance parity with the militia; and the erection of a monument in front of the shipyard gates to the memory of the martyrs of 1970.

The delegates also set up a 'negotiating committee' of about 20 workers, headed by Lech Walesa. Anna Walentynowicz was also on it. She had just arrived, and visibly moved by this first victory, she spoke to the strikers: "We are firmly resolved to carry forward our movement until our demands are satisfied," she concluded. A workers' militia was set up to make sure that everything went smoothly in each section, and to prevent provocations. Stewards were stationed at the entrances to the shipyard. The 1970 massacres were still fresh in everyone's minds: the shipyard was to be occupied, but they were not venturing out into the streets.

At the start of the afternoon, negotiations began in the conference hall, under the dull gaze of a statue of Lenin erected by the authorities. Facing the workers' delegates sat the yard's manager, accompanied by Tadeusz Fiszbach, First Secretary of the Party in Gdansk. The discussions were stormy, and continued till daybreak. Management gave way very fast on the question of reinstating those sacked, and on the construction of a monument in memory of the victims of 1970. They also undertook that there would be no reprisals against the strike committee, and that family allowances would be brought in line with those of the militia. On the other demands they suggested a fresh meeting two or three weeks later.

This was unacceptable: "If we are going to negotiate, we do it here and now!" said one delegate. The manager would have none of it. He would only agree to a 1,200 zloty wage rise (the workers were demanding 2,000), and said that he was not authorised to negotiate on the other points. Talks were broken off. Management agreed to return at five in the morning. They never came back. The workers were already settling in for their first night in the shipyard.

In Gdansk itself the news of a strike at the *Lenin* shipyard—already the symbol of so many important struggles—spread like wildfire. By four in the morning tram drivers were stopping work in sympathy. Only the electric train serving the Three Towns continued to run. As usual, it unloaded thousands of workers in front of their factory gates. That Friday morning, everybody knew that they would be discussing strike action. For example, the morning shift at the *Paris Commune* yard in Gdynia: from the moment they arrived there was an air of expectancy, and nobody really started working. They talked among themselves. At around 7.30 am, groups of workers gathered in the two largest departments, the K2 and K3 hull-construction sections. A group of them came out and marched towards the management office. Almost immediately the other departments emptied, with workers downing tools and following the demonstration.

Andrzej Kolodziej, a young 20-year old worker, was at the head of the march. He didn't work at the Gdynia yard, but had just spent the night at the *Lenin* shipyard, from which he had been sacked in January 1980. Everyone knew him from his earlier activities. They listened to him and they trusted him. The demonstration marched towards the management building. "This is too soon," Kolodziej explained. "We are not ready. They may organise a provocation to divide us." He led the crowd towards the central square, next to the main gate. This spot was to become the venue for all meetings in the weeks to come. The workers needed to get organised, to decide on their objectives. They elected a 20-person strike committee, of which Andrzej Kolodziej was naturally elected President, and before negotiating they decided to get in touch with the Gdansk workers. *Act together*—that was their main principle.

*   *   *

At the *Lenin* shipyard, negotiations resumed at seven o'clock on Saturday morning, but proved fruitless. Once again, talks were broken off. They began again at 11 o'clock. This time management offered a 1,500 zloty wage rise plus a cost of living bonus. Outside, the workers, who were following every word of the negotiations, began to shout: "Two thousand! Two thousand!" The negotiator asked for a delegate vote. The majority of delegates accepted the compromise offered by the management, but first it had to be put into writing. After a brief withdrawal, the management returned with a document. It was signed. At 3.00 pm, in line with the majority vote, Lech Walesa announced that the occupation of the shipyard had ended.

At this point the movement entered a critical phase. The decision to end the occupation was not accepted. People wanted to continue.

*   *   *

Delegations from other factories arrived at the yard. They were alarmed: 'If you return to work,' explained a representative from a bus depot, 'nobody else will win anything.' He was applauded. Walesa stood up to speak, and in a quiet voice this 40-year old man turned the situation on its head: 'We must respect democracy,' he said, 'and therefore accept the compromise, even if it is not brilliant; but we do not have the right to abandon others. We must continue the strike, out of solidarity, until everyone has won.'

*   *   *

It was at this moment that the name 'Solidarity' was born. Leszek said: 'We will continue, in solidarity with all workers in Poland.' The gates were closed again, and the strike began anew."

This was a historic moment. Effectively the strike was no longer a simple collective protest, a defence against rising prices. That phase, which had begun at the start of July had now come to an end. In its place came a political offensive by the whole of the Polish working class, an offensive that was better organised and more resolute than ever before.

*   *   *

REVIEW QUESTIONS

1. Why did the workers at Gdansk go out on strike?
2. What were their initial demands? What new demands did they make after winning concessions from the shipyard's managers?
3. What is the significance of the name "Solidarity"?

MIKHAIL GORBACHEV

FROM On Restructuring the Party's Personnel Policy

The Polish reform movement's eventual triumph in the late 1980s would have been unimaginable if it had not been for the dramatic changes taking place in the Soviet Union. After the ouster of Khrushchev in 1964, the aging Soviet political bureaucracy had returned to business as usual, under the leadership of Leonid Brezhnev. This ended when Mikhail Gorbachev (born 1931), the youngest member of the Politburo, was elected general secretary of the Communist Party in 1985, a position he held until the collapse of the Soviet Union in 1991. Beginning in 1987, Gorbachev initiated an extensive reform campaign, intended to revitalize the Soviet economy through increased democracy, greater "openness" (glasnost) and a substantial "restructuring" (perestroika) of the political and economic institutions of the Soviet state. At the same time, he encouraged reform movements within other eastern European states, allowing organizations such as Solidarity and Civic Forum in Czechoslovakia to emerge as powerful and influential forces for change.

Although Gorbachev embraced democratization and economic modernization, he was not ready to relinquish state control over the Soviet economy. "Restructuring" introduced limited free-market mechanisms, but it also upheld the fundamental premise of the state-planned economy. In an important speech given to the Communist Party Central Committee in January 1987, Gorbachev laid out his critiques of the existing Soviet system and his plans for reforming that system.

From *Speeches and Writings*, Mikhail Gorbachev, Pergamon, 1986.

Restructuring is an Objective Necessity

Our Plenary Meeting is taking place in the year of the 70th anniversary of the Great October Socialist Revolution. Almost seven decades ago the Leninist Party raised over the country the victorious banner of Socialist revolution, of struggle for Socialism, freedom, equality, social justice and progress and against oppression and exploitation, poverty and the subjugation of minority nationalities.

For the first time in world history, the working man and his interests and needs were made the focal point of state policy. The Soviet Union achieved truly epoch-making successes in political, economic, social, cultural and intellectual development as it built Socialist society. Under the leadership of the Party, the Soviet people built Socialism, won the victory over Nazism in the Great Patriotic War, rehabilitated and strengthened the national economy and made their homeland a mighty power.

Our achievements are immense and indubitable and the Soviet people rightfully take pride in their successes. They constitute a firm base for the fulfilment of our current programmes and our plans for the future. But the Party must see life in its entirety and complexity. No accomplishments, not even the most impressive, should obscure either contradictions in societal development or our mistakes and failings.

*   *   *

A need for change was coming to a head in the economy and other fields—but it was not realized through the political and practical work of the Party and the State.

What was the reason for that complex and controversial situation?

The main cause—and the Politburo considers it necessary to say so with utmost frankness at the Plenary Meeting—was that the CPSU Central Committee and the leadership of the country failed, primarily for subjective reasons, to see in time and in full the need for change and the danger of the intensification of crisis phenomena in society, and to formulate a clear policy for overcoming them and making better use of the opportunities intrinsic to the Socialist system.

*   *   *

In fact, a whole system of weakening the economic tools of government emerged and a mechanism of retarding socio-economic development and hindering progressive change developed, which made it possible to tap and use the advantages of Socialism. That retarding process was rooted in serious shortcomings in the functioning of the institutions of Socialist democracy, outdated political and theoretical concepts, that often did not correspond to reality, and conservative managerial machinery.

All this adversely affected development in many spheres in the life of society. Take material production: the growth rates of the national income in the past three five-year plan periods dropped by more than half. Most plan targets have not been met since the early 1970s. The economy as a whole became cumbersome and relatively unreceptive to innovation. The quality of a considerable part of the output no longer met current requirements, and imbalances in production became aggravated.

*   *   *

Having successfully resolved the question of employment and provided basic social guarantees, at the same time we failed to realize in full the potential of Socialism to improve housing conditions, food supply, transport, health care and education, and to solve a number of other vital problems.

There were violations of the most important principle of Socialism—distribution according to work. Efforts to control unearned income were indecisive. The policy of material and moral incentive to work efficiently was inconsistent. Large, unjustified bonuses and various additional incentives were paid and figure-padding for profit was allowed to take place. Parasitic sentiments grew stronger and the mentality of "wage levelling" began to take hold, and that hit workers who could work better and wanted to work better, while making life easier for the idle.

The violation of the organic relationship between the measure of work and measure of consumption not only perverts the attitude to work, holding back the growth of productivity, but leads to distortion of the principle of social justice—and that is a question of great political importance.

Elements of social corrosion that emerged in the past few years had a negative effect on society's morale and inconspicuously eroded the lofty moral values which have always been characteristic of our people and of which we are proud—ideological dedication, labour enthusiasm and Soviet patriotism.

As an inevitable consequence of all this, interest in the affairs of society slackened, manifestations of callousness and scepticism appeared and the role of moral incentive to work declined. The stratum of people, some of them young people, whose ultimate goal in life was material wellbeing and gain by any means, grew wider. Their cynical stand acquired more and more aggressive forms, poisoning the mentality of those around them and triggering a wave of consumerism. The spread of alcohol and drug abuse and a rise in crime became indicators of the decline of social mores.

Disregard for laws, report-padding, bribe-taking and the encouragement of toadyism and sycophancy had a deleterious influence on the moral atmosphere in society.

Real care for people, for the conditions of their life and work and for social wellbeing were often replaced with political flirtation—the mass distribution of awards, titles and prizes. An atmosphere of permissiveness was taking shape, and exactingness, discipline and responsibility were declining.

Serious shortcomings in ideological and political education were in many cases disguised with ostentatious activities and campaigns and celebrations of numerous jubilees at the centre and in the provinces. The world of day-to-day realities and that of make-believe wellbeing were increasingly parting ways.

The ideology and mentality of stagnation had their effect on culture, literature and the arts. Criteria in appraising artistic creative work were debased. As a consequence, quite a few mediocre, faceless works appeared, which did not give anything to the mind or the heart, along with works which raised serious social and moral problems and reflected true to life conflicts. Stereotypes from capitalist mass culture, with its propagation of vulgarity, primitive tastes and spiritual callousness, began to infiltrate Soviet society to a larger extent.

*   *   *

The situation in the Party was also influenced by the fact that in a number of cases the Party bodies did not attach proper attention to strict compliance with the Leninist principles and norms of Party life. This made itself especially manifest, perhaps, in breaches of the principle of collective leadership. What I mean is the weakening of the role of Party meetings and elective bodies, which denied Communists the opportunity to contribute energetically to the discussion of vital issues and, in the analysis, actually to influence the atmosphere in work collectives and in society as a whole.

The principle of equality between Communists was often violated. Many Party members in senior executive positions were beyond control or criticism, which resulted in failures in work and serious breaches of Party ethics.

We cannot overlook the just indignation of working people at the conduct of senior officials in whom trust and authority had been vested and who were called upon to stand guard over the interests of the state and its citizens, and who themselves abused their authority, suppressed criticism and sought personal gain, some even becoming accomplices in—if not organizers of—criminal activities.

*   *   *

It was in this situation that the question of accelerating the socio-economic development of the country—the question of restructuring—was raised. The case in point is actually a radical turn, comprising measures of a revolutionary character. When we talk about restructuring and associated processes of profound democratization, we mean truly revolutionary and comprehensive transformations in society.

We need to make this decisive turn because we simply do not have the choice of any other way. We must not retreat and do not have anywhere to retreat to.

*   *   *

The main purport of our strategy is to combine the achievements of the scientific and technological revolution with a plan-based economy and set the entire potential of Socialism going again.

Restructuring is reliance on the creative endeavour of the masses, all-round extension of democracy and Socialist self-government, encouragement of initiative and self-organized activities, better discipline and order, greater openness, criticism and self-criticism in all fields of public life, and high respect for the value and dignity of the individual.

Restructuring means the ever greater role of intensive growth factors in Soviet economic development, reinstatement and enhancement of Leninist principles of democratic centralism in the management of the national economy, employment of cost benefit methods of management everywhere, renunciation of the domineering style of management and administration by decree, conversion of all units of the economy to the principles of full-scale economic accountability and new forms of organizing labour and production, and every kind of incentive for innovation and Socialist enterprise.

Restructuring means a decisive turn to science, the businesslike partnership of science and practice for the sake of the highest possible end-results, the ability to ground any undertaking on sound scientific basis, readiness and keen desire on the part of scientists to assist the Party's policy of revitalizing society, and concern for the development of science and research personnel and for their active engagement in the process of change.

Restructuring means the priority development of the social sphere, increasingly satisfying the Soviet people's requirements for adequate working and living conditions, recreational facilities, education and medical services. It means unfailing concern for raising the intellectual and cultural standards of every person and of society as a whole: it is the ability to combine decision making on the major, cardinal problems of public life with that on the current issues of immediate interest to the people.

Restructuring means vigorously ridding society of any deviations from Socialist morals, consistently enforcing the principles of social justice, harmony between words and deeds, indivisibility of rights and duties, promotion of conscientious, high quality work, and overcoming pay-levelling and consumerism.

The final aim of the restructuring effort is, I believe, clear: it is to effect a thorough going change in all aspects of public life, to give Socialism the most advanced forms of social organization, and to bring out the humane nature of our system in all decisive aspects—economic, social, political and moral—to the fullest possible degree.

This is, comrades, the task we have in motion. The restructuring effort is unfolding along the entire front. It is acquiring a new quality, not only gaining in scope but also penetrating the deepest fibres of life.

*   *   *

To Deepen Socialist Democratism and Develop Self-government by the People

We now understand better than ever before the profundity of Lenin's thought about the vital, inner link between Socialism and democracy.

The entire historical experience of our country has convincingly demonstrated that the Socialist System has in practice ensured citizens' political and socio-economic rights and personal freedoms, demonstrated the advantages of Soviet democracy and given each person confidence in the morrow.

But in conditions of restructuring, when the task of intensifying the human factor has become so urgent, we must return once again to Lenin's approach to the question of the maximum democratism of the Socialist system under which people feel that they are their own masters and creators.

"We must be guided by experience, we must allow complete freedom to the creative faculties of the masses", Vladimir Lenin said.

Indeed, democracy, the essence of which is the power of the man of labour, is the form of realizing his extensive political and civil rights, his interest in transformations and practical participation in their implementation.

A simple and lucid thought is becoming increasingly entrenched in social consciousness: a house can be put in order only by a person who feels that he owns this house. This truth is correct not only in the wordly sense but also in the sociopolitical one.

This truth must be undeviatingly applied in practice. I repeat, in practice. Otherwise the human factor will be ineffectual.

It is only through the consistent development of the democratic forms inherent in Socialism, through a broadening of self-government, that our advancement in production, science and technology, literature, culture and the arts, in all areas of social life, is possible. It is only this way that ensures conscientious discipline. The restructuring itself is possible only through democracy and due to democracy. It is only this way that is is possible to give scope to Socialism's most powerful creative force—free labour and free thought in a free country.

Therefore the further democratization of Soviet society is becoming the Party's urgent task. Herein, properly speaking, lies the essence of the course of the April Plenum, of the 27th Congress of the CPSU for deepening Socialist self-government by the people. The point at issue is, certainly, not any break up of our political system. We should make use of all its potentialities with maximum effectiveness, fill the work of the Party, the Soviets and the government bodies, public organizations and work collectives with deep democratic contents, breathe new life into all cells of the social organism.

This process is already under way in the country. The life of the Party organizations is becoming more full-blooded. Criticism and self-criticism are broadening. The mass media have begun working more actively. The Soviet people can sense the salutary effect of openness, which is becoming a norm of society's life.

The congresses of the creative unions proceeded in an atmosphere of principledness and criticism. New public organizations are being set up. The All-Union Organization of War and Labour Veterans has come into being. The Soviet Cultural Fund has been set up. Work is under way to set up women's councils. All these facts indicate the growing participation of the working people in social affairs and in the administration of the country.

*   *   *

We wish to turn our country into a model of a highly developed state, into a society with the most advanced economy, the broadest democracy, the most humane and lofty ethics, where the working man will feel that he is master, will enjoy all the benefits of material and spiritual culture, where the future of his children will be secure, where he will have everything that is necessary for a full and interesting life. And even sceptics would be forced to say: yes, the Bolsheviks can accomplish anything. Yes, truth is on their side. Yes, Socialism is a system serving man, working for his benefit, in his social and economic interests, for his spiritual elevation.

REVIEW QUESTIONS

1. Why, according to Gorbachev, is restructuring an "objective necessity"?
2. What social, political, and economic forms will this restructuring take?
3. Why is it crucial that social, political, and economic reform go hand in hand?
4. What elements of free-market capitalism are included in Gorbachev's economic restructuring?
5. In what ways does Gorbachev remain a traditional communist in his economic thinking?

FROM Treaty on European Union (as amended on 7 February 1992)

In the late nineteenth century, French author Victor Hugo expressed the hoped that the twentieth century would witness the birth of a "United States of Europe," followed by a "United States of the World." In fact, the history of twentieth-century Europe has been shaped more by the hostilities generated by aggressive nationalism than by Hugo's internationalist utopianism. Yet, despite the battles that have raged, and continue to rage, in Europe, the desire for peaceful cooperation has lingered. After 1945, Europe was divided between East and West, but regional cooperation (or, in the case of the Soviet bloc, regional exploitation) flourished. Cooperative agreements created competing regional economic associations (the European Community and the European Free Trade Association in the West; the Council for Mutual Economic Assistance in the East) and defense alliances (the North Atlantic Treaty Organization; the Warsaw Pact).

Interest in integrating the European economy has been greatly stimulated in recent years by both economic globalization and the end of the Cold War. In an effort to make Europe more competitive in the world economy, the twelve members of the European Community—Belgium, Denmark, France, Germany, Greece, Ireland, Italy, Luxembourg, The Netherlands, Portugal, Spain, and the United Kingdom— signed a treaty establishing the European Union in the Dutch city of Maastricht in December 1991. While the future of the European Union is still very much in doubt, it is designed to create a single free trade zone, the European Economic Area, sharing a common currency (the "ecu"), to grant shared citizenship to residents of participating nations, and to coordinate the member states' common trade, defense, justice, and financial needs.

From *Treaty on European Union*, Europa Website, <http://europa.eu.int/en/record/mt/top.html>.

The signatory heads of state:]
Resolved to mark a new stage in the process of European integration undertaken with the establishment of the European Communities,

Recalling the historic importance of the ending of the division of the European continent and the need to create firm bases for the construction of the future Europe,

Confirming their attachment to the principles of liberty, democracy and respect for human rights and fundamental freedoms and of the rule of law,

Desiring to deepen the solidarity between their peoples while respecting their history, their culture and their traditions,

Desiring to enhance further the democratic and efficient functioning of the institutions so as to enable them better to carry out, within a single institutional framework, the tasks entrusted to them,

Resolved to achieve the strengthening and the convergence of their economies and to establish an economic and monetary union including, in accordance with the provisions of this Treaty, a single and stable currency,

Determined to promote economic and social progress for their peoples, within the context of the accomplishment of the internal market and of reinforced cohesion and environmental protection, and to implement policies ensuring that advances in economic integration are accompanied by parallel progress in other fields,

Resolved to establish a citizenship common to the nationals of their countries,

Resolved to implement a common foreign and security policy including the eventual framing of a common defense policy, which might in time lead to a common defense, thereby reinforcing the European identity and its independence in order to promote peace, security and progress in Europe and in the world,

Reaffirming their objective to facilitate the free movement of persons while ensuring the safety and security of their peoples, by including provisions on justice and home affairs in this Treaty,

Resolved to continue the process of creating an ever closer union among the peoples of Europe, in which decisions are taken as closely as possible to the citizen in accordance with the principle of subsidiarity,

In view of further steps to be taken in order to advance European integration,

Have decided to establish a European Union* * *

*   *   *

Title V: Provisions on a Common Foreign and Security Policy
ARTICLE J
A common foreign and security policy is hereby established which shall be governed by the following provisions.
ARTICLE J.1
1. The union and its Member States shall define and implement a common foreign and security policy, governed by the provisions of the Title and covering all areas of foreign and security policy.

2. The objectives of the common foreign and security policy shall be:

to safeguard the common values, fundamental interests and independence of the Union;

to strengthen the security of the Union and its Member States in all ways;

to preserve peace and strengthen international security, in accordance with the principles of the United Nations Charter as well as the principles of the Helsinki Final Act and the objectives of the Paris Charter;

to promote international cooperation;

to develop and consolidate democracy and the rule of law, and respect for human rights and fundamental freedoms.

3. The Union shall pursue these objectives;

by establishing systematic cooperation between Member States in the conduct of policy* * *;

by gradually implementing * * * joint action in the areas in which the Member States have important interests in common.

4. The Member States shall support the Union's external and security policy actively and unreservedly in a spirit of loyalty and mutual solidarity. They shall refrain from any action which is contrary to the interests of the Union or likely to impair its effectiveness as a cohesive force in international relations. The Council shall ensure that these principles are complied with.

*   *   *

Provisions on Cooperation in the Fields of Justice and Home Affairs
ARTICLE K
Cooperation in the fields of justice and home affairs shall be governed by the following provisions.
ARTICLE K.1
For the purposes of achieving the objectives of the Union, in particular the free movement of persons, and without prejudice to the powers of the European Community, Member States shall regard the following areas as matters of common interest:

1. asylum policy;

2. rules governing the crossing by persons of the external borders of the Member States and the exercise of controls thereon;

3. immigration policy and policy regarding nationals of third countries;

(a) conditions of entry and movement by nationals of third countries on the territory of Member States;

(b) conditions of residence by nationals of third countries on the territory of Member States, including family reunion and access to employment;

(c) combating unauthorized immigration, residence and work by nationals of third countries on the territory of Member States;

4. combating drug addiction in so far as this is not covered by 7 to 9;

5. combating fraud on an international scale in so far as this is not covered by 7 to 9;

6. judicial cooperation in civil matters;

7. judicial cooperation in criminal matters;

8. customs cooperation;

9. police cooperation for the purposes of preventing and combating terrorism, unlawful drug trafficking and other serious forms of international crime, including if necessary certain aspects of customs cooperation, in connection with the organization of a Union-wide system for exchanging information within a European Police Office (Europol).

REVIEW QUESTIONS

1. Based on your reading of this treaty, why do you think the European Union was created?
2. What advantages will it provide to member states?
3. What disadvantages might there be to participation?
4. Does the treaty create a *fully* integrated Europe?
5. To what extent does it maintain the individual sovereignty of participating nations?
6. Why might the inclusion of former Soviet bloc states in the European Union be problematic?

SIMONE DE BEAUVOIR

FROM *The Second Sex*

During the twentieth century, the traditional divisions between the experiences of men and women started to blur. New technologies decreased the premium once placed on men's greater physical strength, making it possible for women to do jobs once reserved only for men. At the same time, female fertility decreased substantially: as improved health conditions allowed more children to survive to adulthood, couples increasingly sought to have fewer children and new birth-control technologies made this increasingly easy. Whereas reproductive and child-rearing duties had once played a predominant role in most women's adult lives, motherhood now became only one aspect of a more varied lifetime experience.

However, if the material conditions of women's lives had changed significantly, attitudes toward women had not. If anything, the immediate post-war period saw a resurrection of "traditional" models of femininity and masculinity. On the other hand, the popularization of Existentialist philosophy, which argued that every individual has responsibility to be an active agent, to create the self through "engagement" with other human beings, helped to fuel a growing resistance to "objectification"—entrapment in the limiting conceptual categories of outside society —whether on the basis of race, gender, or class. In 1949 the French novelist and existential philosopher Simone de Beauvoir (1908–1986) published The Second Sex, *an extended philosophical essay that called on women to reject socially imposed models of appropriate feminine identity and to become authentic individuals in their own right.* The Second Sex *was initially greeted with outrage and howls of derision, but the revival of feminism in the 1960s brought de Beauvoir a new, more sympathetic audience, and her arguments exercised a strong influence over the American and European women's movements.*

If being female is not a sufficient definition of woman, if we also refuse to explain her through "the eternal feminine," and if we nevertheless admit (if only provisionally), that there are women on this planet, then we are forced to ask ourselves the question: what is a woman?

Simply stating the problem suggests one immediate response. It is significant that I ask this question. A man would never think of writing a book about the peculiar position that males oc- cupy in the ranks of humanity. If I want to define myself, I am first obligated to declare: "I am a woman." That truth constitutes the foundation upon which all other affirmations will be based. A man never begins by declaring himself an individual of a certain sex: that he is a man goes without saying. It is only as a formality that "male" and "female" appear as symmetrical terms in town hall records and identification papers. The relationship between the sexes is not that of two electrical poles: the man represents both the positive and the neutral to such an extent that in French one says *"les hommes"* ("men") to designate all human beings* * *Woman is so strongly associated with the negative that her every trait is imputed to her as a limitation, without reciprocity. It annoys me when, during the course of an abstract discussion, a man says: "You think such and such a thing because you are a woman." I know that my only defense is to reply: "I believe it because it is true," eliminating in that manner my own subjectivity. It's out of the question to answer: "And you think the contrary because you are a man," because it is understood that the fact of being a man is not a peculiarity. A man is in the right in being a man; it is the woman who is in the wrong. In practice, just as the ancients identified an absolute vertical against which the oblique was defined, there is an absolute human type that is masculine. Woman has ovaries, a uterus; these are the peculiarities that enclose her in her subjectivity. It is often said that she thinks with her glands. Man arrogantly forgets that his own anatomy also includes hormones, testicles. He experiences his body as being in a direct and normal relationship with the world, which he believes he apprehends objectively, whereas he considers the body of a woman to be weighted down by all of its specificities: an obstacle, a prison.* * * Humanity is male and man defines woman not in and of herself but relative to him; she is not considered an autonomous being. * * * And she is nothing other than what man decides; thus she is called "the sex," meaning that she appears to the male, in essence, as a sexuated being. For him, she is sex, and therefore she is so absolutely. She is defined and differentiated in relation to man and not he in relation to her; she is the inessential as compared with the essential. He is the Subject, he is the Absolute: she is the Other.

The category of the *Other* is as old as consciousness itself. * * * No collectivity ever defines itself as the One without immediately positing an Other in opposition to it. If three travelers happen to be gathered together by chance in the same cabin, that is enough to make all other travelers vaguely hostile "others." For the villager, all of the

people who do not belong to his village are suspect "others"; for the native of one country, the inhabitants of other countries are "foreigners." Jews are "others" to the antisemite; Blacks are "others" to American racists; indigenous peoples are "others" to the colonizers; proletarians are "others" to the propertied classes. * * *

But the other consciousness opposes to this claim a reciprocal claim: when he travels, the native is shocked to discover that the natives of neighboring countries regard him in his turn as a foreigner. Between villages, clans, nations, and classes there are wars, potlatches, markets, treaties, and conflicts that deprive the idea of the Other of its absolute sense and reveal its relativity. Willingly or not, individuals and groups are forced to recognize the reciprocity of their relations. How then has it happened that between the sexes that reciprocity has not been admitted, that one of the terms has affirmed itself as the only essential one, denying all relativity in relation to its corollary, defining it as pure otherness? Why don't women contest male sovereignty? No subject spontaneously admits, from the first, that it is the inessential. It is not the Other who by defining himself as Other defines the One: he is posited as Other by the One posing himself as One. But in order for the return from Other to One not to happen, it is necessary that he submit to this foreign point of view. Where does woman's submission come from?

*   *   *

* * *the parallel established by Bebel between women and the proletariat is the most apt: like women, proletarians are not a minority and they have never constituted a separate collectivity. Nevertheless, in the absence of a *single* event, it is a historical development that explains their existence as a class and which accounts for the distribution of *these* individuals in that class. There have not always been proletarians; there have always been women. Women are women through their physiology. However far one goes back into history, women have always been subordinated to man. Their dependency is not the consequence of

an event or a development; it did not *happen*. It is in part because otherness escapes the accidental character of a historical fact in this case that it appears here as an absolute. Something that happened over time can be undone at another time. The Blacks of Haiti, among others, have proved this. On the other hand, it would appear that a natural condition defies change. In truth, nature is no more an immutable given than historical reality. If woman reveals herself as the inessential that never returns to the essential, it is because she herself does not set that reversal into motion. Proletarians say "We." Blacks too. Positing themselves as subjects they change the bourgeoisie and Whites into "others." * * * Women do not say "we." Men say "women" and women use this word to designate themselves, but they do not posit themselves authentically as Subject. Proletarians made a revolution in Russia, the Blacks in Haiti, the Indochinese are fighting in Indochina. Women's action has never been anything more than a symbolic disturbance. They have won only what men were willing to concede to them. They have taken nothing: they have merely received.

*   *   *

There are deep analogies between the situation of women and that of Blacks. Today both are emancipating themselves from the same paternalism and the former master class wishes to keep them in "their place," that is to say, the place it has chosen for them. In both cases, that master class lavishes more or less sincere praise on the virtues of the "good Black," childish, happy-go-lucky, his soul slumbering, and on "the real woman," who is frivolous, puerile, irresponsible, submissive to man. In both cases, it derives its argument from the situation it has in fact created. George Bernard Shaw's witticism is well known: "The white American," he said, in essence, "relegates the Black to the rank of shoeshine boy and he concludes from this that the Black is good for nothing but shining shoes." This vicious circle is found in all analogous circumstances; when an in-

dividual, or a group of individuals, is held in a situation of inferiority, the fact is that he *is* inferior. But we must be clear about what we mean by *to be*. It is in bad faith to give it a substantial meaning, when it should be read in the dynamic, Hegelian sense: *to be* is to have become, it is to have been made that which one appears to be. Yes, as a whole women today *are* inferior to men, which is to say that their situation is offered them fewer opportunities. The problem is determining whether or not this state of affairs should continue.

Many men hope that it will; not all of them have disarmed themselves yet. The conservative bourgeoisie continues to see women's emancipation as a menace to its morality and its interests. Certain males fear feminine competition. Just the other day, a male student declared in the *Hebdo-Latin*: "Every female student who takes a position as a doctor or a lawyer *steals* a place from us." He certainly doesn't have any questions about his rights over this world. But it is not only economic concerns that are at play here. One of the benefits that oppression guarantees to the oppressors is that the humblest among them feels himself *superior*: a "poor White" in the Southern United States consoles himself by saying that he is not a "dirty Negro," and more affluent Whites skillfully exploit this pride. In the same way, the most mediocre of males believes himself a demigod compared with women.

REVIEW QUESTIONS

1. What *is* a woman, according to de Beauvoir?
2. How has woman become an "Other"?
3. How can she become a "Self"?
4. In what ways are the conditions of blacks, Jews, workers, and women similar? In what ways are they different?
5. Why do you think de Beauvoir chose to make these particular comparisons?

REINHOLD WAGNLEITNER

FROM *Coca-Colonization and the Cold War*

Western Europeans greatly appreciated the influx of Marshall Plan money after World War II, but they were far more ambivalent about the cultural "Americanization" that seemed to accompany this aid. As European domination of the globe receded in the face of superpower conflict and as the great European empires crumbled in the face of Third World independence movements, many Europeans, in both the East and the West, continued to cling to a belief in the enduring supremacy of European cultural traditions. Yet even in this area, the European cultural elite soon found itself powerless to influence a general public more interested in dancing to the rock and roll of Elvis Presley than the waltzes of Strauss.

On one level, ordinary Europeans welcomed the brash vibrancy of American pop culture as a relief from the horrors of World War II. In the immediate post-war period, American movies and radio programs filled the void left by the collapse of the European entertainment industry, offering a diversion from the hardships of the reconstruction era. On a deeper level, the appeal of American culture lay also in its mythic qualities. Especially for young people, "America" represented an idealized embodiment of democracy in stark contrast to the authoritarian fascism that had been accepted, or at least tolerated, by their parents' generation. In his recent historical study of American cultural policies in occupied Austria, Reinhold Wagnleitner begins with an account of the ways in which his own childhood was affected by the "coca-colonization" of European culture.

When I was born in Upper Austria in 1949, Mauerkirchen was a small, sleepy market town—but it was also situated in the American occupation zone of Austria. Although during the period of occupation, 1945–55, the U.S. Army was barely visible in our part of the woods, we children religiously waited for the best action of the year: the annual U.S. Army maneuvers and our rations of chewing gum.

For us, the horrors of the Second World War were in the distant past, but still they were everywhere. Our everyday experience included quite a few mutilated men, and for the nicer ones we picked up cigarette butts from the streets. It seemed absolutely normal that most men and many women looked old and tired—and not only because we were children and they wore dark clothes. But what a contrast when we saw pictures of GIs or, even better, met "the real thing." Somehow, they clashed with our images of soldiers. They looked young and healthy. Contrasted to our poverty, they seemed incredibly rich, and many were generous to us kids. Of course, their casualness and loudness were proverbial—but we admired them precisely for that.

Although most families with a Nazi past repressed and hid this past from the children, the war remained everywhere—and we did not need a war memorial to be reminded of the many ghosts roaming our streets. Unspoken Nazi-past or not, it was clear that most adults objected to those crass boys from across the Atlantic. "We" had indeed lost the war, but look at those uncultured American guys who chewed gum and put their feet on the table. (This, it seemed, was the utmost crime!) How could an army manned by such unmilitaristic, childish, and undisciplined boys (even blacks!) win a war, especially one against Germany! A few of us children, however, secretly suspected that an army advancing to the rhythm of swing music *deserved* to win the war. It did not help our elders to warn us that if we chewed gum we would look like Americans: that was exactly what we wanted to look like!

In my family, I was spared this routine of Austrian cultural superiority versus American cultural inferiority mostly for two reasons. First, my parents and grandparents had not been Nazis, and my mother loved American music, while my father enjoyed American action movies, which had returned to Mauerkirchen's little cinema in the wake of the U.S. Army. Second, a traumatic incident in my father's childhood—he had lost one foot in a car accident at age thirteen—spared him the fate of having to fight in the Second World War. It was rather rare, indeed, to grow up in Austria during the 1950s with parents like that. (Of course, for most of my teenage friends, American pop culture became *the* major vehicle of protest against their parents.)

While our household was uncharacteristically open to what parents of my friends despised as "American trash," I was far from being the vanguard of American popular culture in our family. It is my only brother, Günter, born in 1940, who has to take the main responsibility for my un-Austrian behavior. Günter is extremely musical.

He started to take piano lessons at age four and passed the entrance exam to the Vienna Boys Choir at age six—we still possess a 78 shellac recording of Günter's voice, which my father had ordered for this occasion. But in the end, my parents decided against sending him to Vienna. They did not want to hand over their six-year-old boy to a boarding school, especially to a boarding school in Vienna, which was surrounded by the Soviet occupation zone. (After all, we lived in the *Goldenen Westen* of Austria.)

Yet, my parents had no idea that they built the perfect stage for American music for their still-unborn second child. Günter, who had a voracious appetite for any kind of good music, did more than simply improve his playing of Mozart and Beethoven, Bach and Brahms, Schubert and Strauss; he also discovered Frank Sinatra and Ray Charles, Dizzy Gillespie and Miles Davis. And when he discovered rock 'n' roll in the middle of the 1950s, nothing remained the same. While he worked the piano and made our living room rock like a jailhouse, I would work the matchboxes and pretend I was something like a rock 'n' roll drum machine. Many were the sighs of my poor parents—not because we played American music, but because we didn't do *anything else*. And then one day Günter really became the King. A friend of my mother gave him the absolutely most yearned for article of clothing imaginable: the first and only pair of Levi's in Mauerkirchen, which she had received as a present from an American officer.

While my brother was lost for good to any "respectable profession" and became a musician in dance bands, I finished *Gymnasium* (high school), although I had been playing in amateur dance bands since the age of fourteen. After copying my major role model's rock 'n' roll, however, I had my second awakening in 1963 when the British beat bands confronted us—just as they simultaneously confronted white American teenagers, to the annoyance of *their* parents—with the Liverpool, Birmingham, and London version of American blues and rhythm and blues.

So it happened that shortly before entering

university, I already had a sort of final graduation: my brother picked me as the bass player for his band. Hardly a weekend passed during my teenage years when our living room was not transformed into a rehearsal room for a band of screaming and strumming kids. Still, I will always be grateful for the proud look on my parents' faces when they saw their sons on stage together for the first time.

Of course, I had no money to buy records, and the Austrian radio stations still pretended that we lived in an age before "Roll Over Beethoven." My major source of musical information about British and American groups consisted of the daily fix of three hours of rock programs that were aired by Radio Free Europe every weekday afternoon. The political messages of Radio Svobodna Evropa (ten minutes of news to fifty minutes of music for three hours) were directed at Czechoslovakian listeners and, as bait, had far and away the best music program of any European station. It really worked like a commercially sponsored program, only here the commercials were the news and the political commentaries. As their reactions showed, the Czechoslovak and other Eastern European governments had not the least inkling of what was really going on. Otherwise they would have jammed the music, not the news.

Contemporary parallels must not be overlooked; the present transformations in Eastern Europe should remind us of the developments in Western Europe after the Second World War. It is of the utmost political significance that practically the whole East German population chose to emigrate to the West every night via television. The effects of such a temporary electronic emigration, the impact of thus becoming quasi-Americans by tuning in to modern mass media, should not be underrated. The Iron Curtain—is not its name already symbolic for an outdated industrial sector, largely connoting the nineteenth century?—in the end was no match for the messages produced by the electronic-consciousness industry in the West, the real heavy industry of the twentieth century (in the apt words of Hans Magnus Enzensberger). Or what does it really mean that during the weekend of February 19–21, 1993, only 6 Russian movies were shown in the cinemas of Moscow compared with 111 American films?

During my student days, I soon learned that there was another side to the United States. Just like many of my peer group on American campuses, I objected to American involvement in Indochina and other foreign policy adventures as well as the repression of minorities in the United States. Yet, we demonstrated in blue jeans and T-shirts and attended sit-ins and teach-ins. What's more, quite a few of us understood what it meant to be able to demonstrate against a war in wartime without being court-martialed. Some of us were also aware that we had learned our peaceful tactics of democratic protest and opposition from the American civil rights movement and the anti-nuclear-armament movement. After all, we did not intone the "Internationale" but instead sang "We Shall Overcome."

*   *   *

REVIEW QUESTIONS

1. Why did so many Austrian adults dislike American culture?
2. Why did this same American culture appeal so strongly to Austrian children and teenagers?
3. What specific aspects of American culture appealed to young Europeans?
4. What sorts of values did these cultural expressions seem to embody?
5. Why do you think "youth culture" became such an important phenomenon after World War II?

30 &ce; PROBLEMS OF WORLD CIVILIZATION

At the beginning of recorded human history, the entire population of the world probably consisted of fewer than ten million people. Ten thousand years later, the world population is rapidly approaching six billion. Human ingenuity has made possible the production of enough food and material goods to sustain this enormous population, but this achievement puts serious strains on the environment and creates intense competition for limited resources.

Innovations in transportation and communication have made it possible for people around the world to have far more intimate and informed relations with one another than ever before. The earth's surface remains subdivided by national boundaries, but the problems confronting humanity are, increasingly, international problems that can only be solved through global cooperation. From a historical perspective, it is already clear that human history has become world history and that even the most isolated regions are no longer insulated from the general trend toward global integration.

One of the most important factors in the emerging history of the contemporary world is the deep divide separating "developed" and "developing" nations. Most of the inhabitants of affluent and technologically advanced regions such as Japan, the United States, and western Europe enjoy extremely high standards of living and can expect to live long and healthy lives. The four-fifths of the earth's people who live in the less-developed regions regularly suffer from a lack of basic necessities, including adequate food, clean drinking water, and a bare minimum of health care.

The reasons for this dramatic disparity in the distribution of wealth are complex, but they are closely linked to the historical processes of colonization and decolonization. During the late nineteenth century, imperialist powers acquired colonies in the hopes of procuring raw materials, cheap labor, and national grandeur. The builders of empire were largely uninterested in modernizing the economies or political systems of their colonies, and they often destroyed in-

digenous industries and governments at the same time that they crushed expressions of cultural resistance. After World War II, most of these colonies regained their independence, either as a result of more or less voluntary withdrawal on the part of the colonizers or as a result of violent conflict.

The newly independent nations of Africa and Asia faced substantial challenges, not the least of which were the international tensions generated by the Cold War. When the Soviet Union and the United States sought allies in the Third World, both superpowers tended to support dictators friendly to their strategic aims, thereby discouraging the emergence of independent democracies. In addition, most former colonies were strongly disadvantaged in the economic arena by technological backwardness, a legacy of colonial rule. The developed nations have been slow to come to the aid of struggling Third World nations, and the political instability produced by desperate poverty and often-violent competition for land and resources continues to threaten global peace and prosperity.

As underdeveloped regions struggle to come to terms with the legacies of colonialism and superpower conflict, they are also called upon to share in the project of forging global solutions to global problems. Uncontrolled population growth, the exploitation and mismanagement of natural resources, and unregulated industrial and commercial development pose serious dangers to the survival of all humanity. Similarly, the international transfer of people, capital, consumer goods, and land, air, and water pollution can no longer be contained within national boundaries. While individual identity remains deeply rooted in local cultural traditions, the future history of humanity may hinge on our ability to develop a model of global citizenship that balances the rights of the individual with the responsibilities of all human beings to both the local and the global community.

MAHATMA GANDHI

FROM The Doctrine of the Sword and FROM On Non-Violence

The Indian struggle for independence from Great Britain can be traced back to the early nineteenth century, but it first became a mass movement after World War I. Indian nationalists supported India's participation in the war on the Allied side, but they were angered by Britain's failure to reward this service with a greater degree of self-government. Under the charismatic leadership of Mahatma ("Great Soul")

Gandhi (1869–1948), the Indian independence movement became a model for other colonial independence struggles.

Having trained as a lawyer in Britain, the young Mohandas Gandhi worked for many years among the East Indian community of South Africa, where he experienced the effects of racial discrimination in the acute form of apartheid. As he struggled to maintain his human dignity in a system that looked on him as nothing more than a "coolie," he drew sustenance from the Hindu religious traditions of India, building his "soul force" through a commitment to truth, love, and ascetic practices (such as vegetarianism, sexual abstinence, and manual labor). When he returned to India in 1913, Gandhi became active in the Indian National Congress and directed the fledgling independence movement toward adopting a strategy of peaceful non-cooperation. At the same time, he also lobbied for economic self-sufficiency. Taking as his symbol the spinning wheel, he argued that the spiritual and material poverty of the Indian masses could be alleviated through the revival of indigenous traditions of small-scale, low-tech textile production.

From *The Essential Writings of Mahatma Gandhi*, Mahatma Gandhi, edited by Raghavan Iyer, Oxford University Press, 1991. Reprinted with permission of Navajivan Trust.

The Doctrine of the Sword

In this age of the rule of brute force, it is almost impossible for anyone to believe that anyone else could possibly reject the law of the final supremacy of brute force. And so I receive anonymous letters advising me that I must not interfere with the progress of non-co-operation even though popular violence may break out. Others come to me and assuming that secretly I must be plotting violence, inquire when the happy moment for declaring open violence will arrive. They assure me that the English will never yield to anything but violence secret or open. Yet others, I am informed, believe that I am the most rascally person living in India because I never give out my real intention and that they have not a shadow of a doubt that I believe in violence just as much as most people do.

Such being the hold that the doctrine of the sword has on the majority of mankind, and as success of non-co-operation depends principally on absence of violence during its pendency and as my views in this matter affect the conduct of a large number of people, I am anxious to state them as clearly as possible.

I do believe that where there is only a choice between cowardice and violence I would advise violence. Thus when my eldest son asked me what he should have done, had he been present when I was almost fatally assaulted in 1908, whether he should have run away and seen me killed or whether he should have used his physical force which he could and wanted to use, and defended me, I told him that it was his duty to defend me even by using violence. Hence it was that I took part in the Boer War, the so-called Zulu rebellion and the late War. Hence also do I advocate training in arms for those who believe in the method of violence. I would rather have India resort to arms in order to defend her honour than that she should in a cowardly manner become or remain a helpless witness to her own dishonour.

But I believe that non-violence is infinitely superior to violence, forgiveness is more manly than punishment. *Kshama virasya bhushanam.* 'Forgiveness adorns a soldier.' But abstinence is forgiveness only when there is the power to punish; it is meaningless when it pretends to proceed from a helpless creature. A mouse hardly forgives a cat when it allows itself to be torn to pieces by her. I, therefore, appreciate the sentiment of those who cry out for the condign punishment of General Dyer and his ilk. They would tear him to pieces if they could. But I do not believe India to be helpless. I do not believe myself to be a helpless creature. Only I want to use India's and my strength for a better purpose.

Let me not be misunderstood. Strength does not come from physical capacity. It comes from an indomitable will. An average Zulu is any way more than a match for an average Englishman in bodily capacity. But he flees from an English boy, because he fears the boy's revolver or those who will use it for him. He fears death and is nerveless in spite of his burly figure. We in India may in a moment realize that one hundred thousand Englishmen need not frighten three hundred million human beings. A definite forgiveness would therefore mean a definite recognition of our strength. With enlightened forgiveness must come a mighty wave of strength in us, which would make it impossible for a Dyer and a Frank Johnson to heap affront upon India's devoted head. It matters little to me that for the moment I do not drive my point home. We feel too downtrodden not to be angry and revengeful. But I must not refrain from saying that India can gain more by waiving the right of punishment. We have better work to do, a better mission to deliver to the world.

I am not a visionary. I claim to be a practical idealist. The religion of non-violence is not meant merely for the * * * saints. It is meant for the common people as well. Non-violence is the law of our species as violence is the law of the brute. The spirit lies dormant in the brute and he knows no law but that of physical might. The dignity of man requires obedience to a higher law—to the strength of the spirit.

I have therefore ventured to place before India the ancient law of self-sacrifice.* * *

Non-violence in its dynamic condition means conscious suffering. It does not mean meek submission to the will of the evil-doer, but it means the putting of one's whole soul against the will of the tyrant. Working under this law of our being, it is possible for a single individual to defy the whole might of an unjust empire to save his honour, his religion, his soul and lay the foundation for that empire's fall or its regeneration.

And so I am not pleading for India to practise non-violence because it is weak. I want her to practise non-violence being conscious of her strength and power. No training in arms is required for realization of her strength. We seem to need it because we seem to think that we are but a lump of flesh. I want India to recognize that she has a soul that cannot perish and that can rise triumphant above every physical weakness and defy the physical combination of a whole world. What is the meaning of Rama, a mere human being, with his host of monkeys, pitting himself against the insolent strength of ten-headed Ravana surrounded in supposed safety by the raging waters on all sides of Lanka? Does it not mean the conquest of physical might by spiritual strength? However, being a practical man, I do not wait till India recognizes the practicability of the spiritual life in the political world. India considers herself to be powerless and paralysed before the machine-guns, the tanks and the aeroplanes of the English. And she takes up non-co-operation out of her weakness. It must still serve the same purpose, namely, bring her delivery from the crushing weight of British injustice if a sufficient number of people practise it.

* * *I invite even the school of violence to give this peaceful non-co-operation a trial. It will not fail through its inherent weakness. It may fail because of poverty of response. Then will be the time for real danger. The high-souled men, who are unable to suffer national humiliation any longer, will want to vent their wrath. They will take to violence. So far as I know, they must perish without delivering themselves or their country from the wrong. If India takes up the doctrine of the sword, she may gain momentary victory. Then India will cease to be the pride of my heart. I am wedded to India because I owe my all to her. I believe absolutely that she has a mission for the world. She is not to copy Europe blindly. India's acceptance of the doctrine of the sword will be the hour of

my trial. I hope I shall not be found wanting. My religion has no geographical limits. If I have a living faith in it, it will transcend my love for India herself. My life is dedicated to service of India through the religion of non-violence which I believe to be the root of Hinduism.

Meanwhile I urge those who distrust me, not to disturb the even working of the struggle that has just commenced, by inciting to violence in the belief that I want violence. I detest secrecy as a sin. Let them give non-violent non-co-operation a trial and they will find that I had no mental reservation whatsoever.

Non-Violence — The Greatest Force

*   *   *

The cry for peace will be a cry in the wilderness, so long as the spirit of non-violence does not dominate millions of men and women.

An armed conflict between nations horrifies us. But the economic war is no better than an armed conflict. This is like a surgical operation. An economic war is prolonged torture. And its ravages are no less terrible than those depicted in the literature on war properly so called. We think nothing of the other because we are used to its deadly effects.

Many of us in India shudder to see blood spilled. Many of us resent cow-slaughter, but we think nothing of the slow torture through which by our greed we put our people and cattle. But because we are used to this lingering death, we think no more about it.

The movement against war is sound. I pray for its success. But I cannot help the gnawing fear that the movement will fail, if it does not touch the root of all evil—man's greed.

Will America, England and the other great nations of the West continue to exploit the so-called weaker or uncivilized races and hope to attain peace that the whole world is pining for? Or will Americans continue to prey upon one another, have commercial rivalries and yet expect to dictate peace to the world?

Not till the spirit is changed can the form be altered. The form is merely an expression of the spirit within. We may succeed in seemingly altering the form but the alteration will be a mere make-believe if the spirit within remains unalterable. A whited sepulchre still conceals beneath it the rotting flesh and bone.

Far be it from me to discount or under-rate the great effort that is being made in the West to kill the war-spirit. Mine is merely a word of caution as from a fellow-seeker who has been striving in his own humble manner after the same thing, maybe in a different way, no doubt on a much smaller scale. But if the experiment demonstrably succeeds on the smaller field and, if those who are working on the larger field have not overtaken me, it will at least pave the way for a similar experiment on a large field.

I observe in the limited field in which I find myself, that unless I can reach the hearts of men and women, I am able to do nothing. I observe further that so long as the spirit of hate persists in some shape or other, it is impossible to establish peace or to gain our freedom by peaceful effort. We cannot love one another, if we hate Englishmen. We cannot love the Japanese and hate Englishmen. We must either let the Law of Love rule us through and through or not at all. Love among ourselves based on hatred of others breaks down under the slightest pressure. The fact is such love is never real love. It is an armed peace. And so it will be in this great movement in the West against war. War will only be stopped when the conscience of mankind has become sufficiently elevated to recognize the undisputed supremacy of the Law of Love in all the walks of life. Some say this will never come to pass. I shall retain the faith till the end of my earthly existence that it shall come to pass.

REVIEW QUESTIONS

1. Why must the strategy of non-violence proceed from a position of strength, according to Gandhi?
2. In what ways are Indians strong?
3. What does Gandhi mean by "economic war"?
4. How can human beings bring an end to *all* wars?
5. Why do you think the strategy of "passive resistance" to oppression was so popular among many participants in the independence and civil rights movements of the mid-twentieth century?

FRANTZ FANON

FROM *The Wretched of the Earth*

Gandhi's strategy of peaceful resistance had a profound impact on other twentieth-century movements for social change. Yet many independence activists rejected this approach, arguing that the imperial powers would never relinquish their control over colonial holdings without violence. Instead, these activists looked for inspiration to the armed struggles led by Ho Chi Minh in Vietnam and Fidel Castro in Cuba. Militant anti-imperialists recognized that resistance movements could never outgun the colonizers, but they were convinced that sustained guerilla warfare would eventually convince the imperial powers that the costs of maintaining control over a colony were simply too high.

For Frantz Fanon (1925–1961), violence was not simply a tactic in anti-imperial conflicts: it also served an important role in the psychological decolonization of subject peoples. Born in the French colony of Martinique, Fanon trained as a psychiatrist in Martinique and France before becoming an active participant in the Algerian independence movement of the 1950s. Fanon argued that the physical and psychological violence of the colonial system had traumatized colonized peoples, generating individual and communal mental illness. Violent resistance to imperialism would permit subject peoples to purge this trauma and to build a new and independent community based on this shared experience of retaliation. In The Wretched of the Earth, *published in 1961 shortly before his untimely death from cancer, Fanon analyzed anti-imperial violence as a pathological response to a pathological system and as a necessary therapy for the social maladies generated by colonialism.*

*   *   *

The existence of an armed struggle shows that the people are decided to trust to violent methods only. He of whom *they* have never stopped saying that the only language he understands is that of force, decides to give utterance by force. In fact, as always, the settler has shown him the way he should take if he is to become free. The argument the native chooses has been furnished by the settler, and by an ironic turning of the tables it is the native who now affirms that the colonialist understands nothing but force. The colonial regime owes its legitimacy to force and at no time tries to hide this aspect of things. Every statue, whether of Faidherbe or of Lyautey, of Bugeaud or of Sergeant Blandan—all these conquistadors perched on colonial soil do not cease from proclaiming one and the same thing: "We are here by the force of bayonets. . . ."

*   *   *

The violence of the colonial regime and the counter-violence of the native balance each other and respond to each other in an extraordinary reciprocal homogeneity. This reign of violence will be the more terrible in proportion to the size of the implantation from the mother country. The development of violence among the colonized people will be proportionate to the violence exercised by the threatened colonial regime. In the first phase of this insurrectional period, the home governments are the slaves of the settlers, and these settlers seek to intimidate the natives and their home governments at one and the same time. They use the same methods against both of them. The assassination of the Mayor of Evian, in its method and motivation, is identifiable with the assassination of Ali Boumendjel. For the settlers, the alternative is not between *Algérie algérienne* and *Algérie française* but between an independent Algeria and a colonial Algeria, and anything else is mere talk or attempts at treason. The settler's logic is implacable and one is only staggered by the counter-logic visible in the behavior of the native insofar as one has not clearly understood be-

forehand the mechanisms of the settler's ideas. From the moment that the native has chosen the methods of counter-violence, police reprisals automatically call forth reprisals on the side of the nationalists. However, the results are not equivalent, for machine-gunning from airplanes and bombardments from the fleet go far beyond in horror and magnitude any answer the natives can make. This recurring terror de-mystifies once and for all the most estranged members of the colonized race. They find out on the spot that all the piles of speeches on the equality of human beings do not hide the commonplace fact that the seven Frenchmen killed or wounded at the Col de Sakamody kindles the indignation of all civilized consciences, whereas the sack of the douars of Guergour and of the dechras of Djerah and the massacre of whole populations—which had merely called forth the Sakamody ambush as a reprisal—all this is of not the slightest importance. Terror, counter-terror, violence, counter-violence: that is what observers bitterly record when they describe the circle of hate, which is so tenacious and so evident in Algeria.

In all armed struggles, there exists what we might call the point of no return. Almost always it is marked off by a huge and all-inclusive repression which engulfs all sectors of the colonized people. This point was reached in Algeria in 1955 with the 12,000 victims of Phillippeville* * *

*   *   *

Then it became clear to everybody, including even the settlers, that "things couldn't go on as before." Yet the colonized people do not chalk up the reckoning. They record the huge gaps made in their ranks as a sort of necessary evil. Since they have decided to reply by violence, they therefore are ready to take all its consequences. They only insist in return that no reckoning should be kept, either, for the others. To the saying "All natives are the same" the colonized person replies, "All settlers are the same."

*   *   *

The appearance of the settler has meant in the terms of syncretism the death of the aboriginal society, cultural lethargy, and the petrification of individuals. For the native, life can only spring up again out of the rotting corpse of the settler. This then is the correspondence, term by term, between the two trains of reasoning.

But it so happens that for the colonized people this violence, because it constitutes their only work, invests their characters with positive and creative qualities. The practice of violence binds them together as a whole, since each individual forms a violent link in the great chain, a part of the great organism of violence which has surged upward in reaction to the settler's violence in the beginning. The groups recognize each other and the future nation is already indivisible. The armed struggle mobilizes the people; that is to say, it throws them in one way and in one direction.

The mobilization of the masses, when it arises out of the war of liberation, introduces into each man's consciousness the ideas of a common cause, of a national destiny, and of a collective history. In the same way the second phase, that of the building-up of the nation, is helped on by the existence of this cement which has been mixed with blood and anger. Thus we come to a fuller appreciation of the originality of the words used in these underdeveloped countries. During the colonial period the people are called upon to fight against oppression; after national liberation, they are called upon to fight against poverty, illiteracy, and underdevelopment. The struggle, they say, goes on. The people realize that life is an unending contest.

We have said that the native's violence unifies the people. By its very structure, colonialism is separatist and regionalist. Colonialism does not simply state the existence of tribes; it also reinforces it and separates them. The colonial system encourages chieftaincies and keeps alive the old Marabout confraternities. Violence is in action all-inclusive and national. It follows that it is closely involved in the liquidation of regionalism and of tribalism. Thus the national parties show no pity at all toward the caids and the customary chiefs.

Their destruction is the preliminary to the unification of the people.

At the level of individuals, violence is a cleansing force. It frees the native from his inferiority complex and from his despair and inaction; it makes him fearless and restores his self-respect. Even if the armed struggle has been symbolic and the nation is demobilized through a rapid movement of decolonization, the people have the time to see that the liberation has been the business of each and all and that the leader has no special merit.

*   *   *

Today, national independence and the growth of national feeling in underdeveloped regions take on totally new aspects. In these regions, with the exception of certain spectacular advances, the different countries show the same absence of infrastructure. The mass of the people struggle against the same poverty, flounder about making the same gestures and with their shrunken bellies outline what has been called the geography of hunger. It is an underdeveloped world, a world inhuman in its poverty; but also it is a world without doctors, without engineers, and without administrators. Confronting this world, the European nations sprawl, ostentatiously opulent. This European opulence is literally scandalous, for it has been founded on slavery, it has been nourished with the blood of slaves and it comes directly from the soil and from the subsoil of that underdeveloped world. The well-being and the progress of Europe have been built up with the sweat and the dead bodies of Negroes, Arabs, Indians, and the yellow races. We have decided not to overlook this any longer. When a colonialist country, embarrassed by the claims for independence made by a colony, proclaims to the nationalist leaders: "If you wish for independence, take it, and go back to the Middle Ages," the newly independent people tend to acquiesce and to accept the challenge; in fact you may see colonialism withdrawing its capital and its technicians and setting up around the young State the apparatus of economic pressure. The apotheosis of independence is transformed into the curse of independence, and the colonial power through its immense resources of coercion condemns the young nation to regression. In plain words, the colonial power says: "Since you want independence, take it and starve." The nationalist leaders have no other choice but to turn to their people and ask from them a gigantic effort. A regime of austerity is imposed on these starving men; a disproportionate amount of work is required from their atrophied muscles. An autarkic regime is set up and each state, with the miserable resources it has in hand, tries to find an answer to the nation's great hunger and poverty. We see the mobilization of a people which toils to exhaustion in front of a suspicious and bloated Europe.

*   *   *

* * *the imperialist states would make a great mistake and commit an unspeakable injustice if they contented themselves with withdrawing from our soil the military cohorts, and the administrative and managerial services whose function it was to discover the wealth of the country, to extract it and to send it off to the mother countries. We are not blinded by the moral reparation of national independence; nor are we fed by it. The wealth of the imperial countries is our wealth too. On the universal plane this affirmation, you may be sure, should on no account be taken to signify that we feel ourselves affected by the creations of Western arts or techniques. For in a very concrete way Europe has stuffed herself inordinately with the gold and raw materials of the colonial countries: LatinAmerica, China, and Africa. From all these continents, under whose eyes Europe today raises up her tower of opulence, there has flowed out for centuries toward that same Europe diamonds and oil, silk and cotton, wood and exotic products. Europe is literally the creation of the Third World. The wealth which smothers her is that which was stolen from the underdeveloped peoples. The ports of Holland, the docks of Bordeaux and Liverpool were specialized in the Negro slave trade, and owe their renown to millions of deported slaves. So when we hear the head of a European state declare with his hand on his heart that he must come to the aid of the poor underdeveloped peoples, we do not tremble with gratitude. Quite the contrary; we say to ourselves: "It's a just reparation which will be paid to us."

*   *   *

REVIEW QUESTIONS

1. In what ways do colonial regimes breed violence?
2. What are the positive benefits of anti-imperial violence for the community? For the individual?
3. According to Fanon, how does Europe compare with its former colonies?
4. In what sense is the wealth of Europe the "creation of the Third World"?

RUHOLLAH KHOMEINI

FROM *Islamic Government*

Throughout his lifetime, Mahatma Gandhi sought to universalize traditional Hindu religious concepts in the interest of uniting Indians of diverse religious backgrounds in a non-violent independence movement. Iranian nationalist leader Ruhollah Khomeini (1900?–1989) took a radically different approach, formulating a narrow and highly conservative Islamic fundamentalism intended to unite Iranian Moslems in violent opposition to the western-supported government of the Shah of Iran and against western culture in general. While Khomeini's version of Islam is not representative of more liberal mainstream traditions in the Moslem world, it has had a powerful influence on those Moslems seeking an alternative to western cultural, political, and economic hegemony.

Born into a family of Shi'ite Moslem religious leaders, Khomeini was recognized as the leading Iranian religious authority—the "Grand Ayatollah"—in the 1950s. Forced out of Iran in the early 1960s, Khomeini continued to voice his opposition to the Iranian government from exile. After the Shah was expelled from Iran in early 1979, Khomeini returned to his homeland and served as both religious and political head of state until his death in 1989. In Islamic Government, *written in the early 1970s, Khomeini had already outlined his own model of theocratic government based in a rigid, anti-modern reading of Islamic political and legal doctrines.*

From *Islamic Government*, Ruhollah Khomeini, translated by Joint Publications Research Service, Manor Books, 1979.

The Islamic government is not similar to the well-known systems of government. It is not a despotic government in which the head of state dictates his opinion and tampers with the lives and property of the people. The prophet, may God's prayers be upon him, and 'Ali, the amir of the faithful, and the other imams had no power to tamper with people's property or with their lives.[1] The Islamic government is not despotic but constitutional. However, it is not constitutional in the well-known sense of the word, which is represented in the parliamentary system or in the people's councils. It is constitutional in the sense that those in charge of affairs observe a number of conditions and rules underlined in the Koran and in the Sunna and represented in the necessity of observing the system and of applying the dictates and laws of Islam.[2] This is why the Islamic government is the government of the divine law. The difference between the Islamic government and the constitutional governments, both monarchic and republican, lies in the fact that the people's representatives or the king's representatives are the ones who codify and legislate, whereas the power of legislation is confined to God, may He be praised, and nobody else has the right to legislate and nobody may rule by that which has not been given power by God. This is why Islam replaces the legislative council by a planning council that works to run the affairs and work of the ministries so that they may offer their services in all spheres.

All that is mentioned in the book (Koran) and in the Sunna is acceptable and obeyed in the view of the Moslems. This obedience facilitates the state's responsibilities, however when the majorities in the constitutional monarchic or republican governments legislate something, the government has to later exert efforts to compel people to obey, even if such obedience requires the use of force.

The Islamic government is the government of the law and God alone is the ruler and the legislator. God's rule is effective among all the people and in the state itself. All individuals—the prophet, his

---

[1] "The prophet" refers to Muhammed; 'Ali was Muhammed's son-in-law and, according to the Shi'ite tradition, his legitimate heir; an amir is a high military official; and an imam, in the Shi'ite tradition, is an important spiritual leader with sole power to make decisions about doctrine.

[2] The Koran is the book of the holy scriptures of Islam; the Sunna is the body of customary Islamic law second only to the Koran in authority.

successors and other people—follow what Islam, which descended through revelation and which God has explained through the Koran and through the words of His prophet, has legislated for them.

*   *   *

Yes, government in Islam means obeying the law and making it the judge. The powers given to the prophet, may God's peace and prayers be upon him, and to the legitimate rulers after him are powers derived from God. God ordered that the prophet and the rulers after him be obeyed: "Obey the prophet and those in charge among you." There is no place for opinions and whims in the government of Islam. The prophet, the imams and the people obey God's will and Shari'a.[3]

The government of Islam is not monarchic,* * * and not an empire, because Islam is above squandering and unjustly undermining the lives and property of people. This is why the government of Islam does not have the many big palaces, the servants, the royal courts, the crown prince courts and other trivial requirements that consume half or most of the country's resources and that the sultans and the emperors have. The life of the great prophet was a life of utter simplicity, even though the prophet was the head of the state, who ran and ruled it by himself.* * * Had this course continued until the present, people would have known the taste of happiness and the country's treasury would not have been plundered to be spent on fornication, abomination and the court's costs and expenditures. You know that most of the corrupt aspects of our society are due to the corruption of the ruling dynasty and the royal family. What is the legitimacy of these rulers who build houses of entertainment, corruption, fornication and abomination and who destroy houses which God ordered be raised and in which His name is mentioned? Were it not for what the court wastes and what it embezzles, the country's budget would not experience any deficit that forces the state to

borrow from America and England, with all the humiliation and insult that accompany such borrowing. Has our oil decreased or have our minerals that are stored under this good earth run out? We possess everything and we would not need the help of America or of others if it were not for the costs of the court and for its wasteful use of the people's money. This is on the one hand. On the other hand, there are state agencies that are not needed and that consume money, resources, paper and equipment. This is a waste banned by our religion because such waste escalates the people's problems, wastes their time and effort and consumes monies of which they are in the direct need. In Islam, when Islam was the ruler, justice was dispensed, restrictions established and disputes settled with utter simplicity. The qadi (judge) saw to it that all this was done by a handful of persons with some pencils and a little ink and paper. Behind all this, the qadi directed people to work for an honorable and virtuous life. But now, only God knows the number of the justice departments, bureaus and employees—all of which are futile and do the people no good, not to mention the hardship, difficulties, waste of time and monies, and, consequently, the loss of justice and rights that they cause the people.

Qualifications of Ruler

The qualifications that must be available to the ruler emanate from the nature of the Islamic government. Regardless of the general qualifications, such as intelligence, maturity and a good sense of management, there are two important qualifications:

1. Knowledge of Islamic Law

2. Justice

A. In view of the fact that the Islamic government is a government of law, it is a must that the ruler of the Moslems be knowledgeable in the law,* * * Knowledge of the law and of justice are among

---

[3] Shari'a is Islamic law as a whole, including the Koran and the Sunna.

the most important mainstays of the imamate. If a person knows a lot about nature and its secrets and masters many arts but is ignorant of the law, then his knowledge does not qualify him for the caliphate and does not put him ahead of those who know the law and deal with justice. It is an acknowledged fact among the Moslems since the first days and until our present day that the ruler or the caliph must know the law and possess the faculty of justice with a sound faith and good ethics. This is what sound reason requires, especially since we know that the Islamic government is an actual embodiment of the law and not a matter of whims.

* * *

B. The ruler must have the highest degree of faith in the creed, good ethics, the sense of justice and freedom from sins, because whoever undertakes to set the strictures, to achieve the rights, and to organize the revenues and expenditures of the treasury house must not be unjust. God says in his precious book: "The unjust shall not have my support." Thus, if the ruler is not just, he cannot be trusted not to betray the trust and not to favor himself, his family and his relatives over the people.

* * *

REVIEW QUESTIONS

1. What prevents Islamic government from becoming despotic, according to Khomeini?
2. In what sense is Islamic government "constitutional"?
3. Why is there no legislative branch in Islamic government?
4. What is the role of the executive and the judiciary in this form of government?
5. What qualifications must a Moslem ruler have?
6. How will his method of governing differ from that of a traditional monarch?

TOMÁS BORGE

FROM The New Education in the New Nicaragua

The small nations of Central America gained their independence in the early nine-teenth century, but were subject to the informal economic and political imperialism of the United States well into the late twentieth century. Saddled with weak, single-commodity economies vulnerable to the fluctuations of the international market, these "banana republics" remained poor and underdeveloped. For the most part, they were ruled by dictators whose expressions of anti-communism and subservience to United States foreign policy objectives won them the money and weapons they needed to suppress internal dissent.

In 1979, Nicaragua's Sandinista National Liberation Front (FSLN) overthrew the dictatorial regime of Anastasio Somoza, replacing it with a hybrid synthesis of political democracy, an economy combining elements of socialism and capitalism, and a Christian radicalism based in Catholic liberation theology. Despite fierce opposition on the part of the Reagan administration, the Sandinista's struggled throughout the 1980s to solidify their claim to power through improving the basic living conditions of ordinary Nicaraguans. But as Tomás Borge, one of the original founders of the FSLN, argued, the transformation of Nicaragua was to be not only material, but also intellectual. In 1983, Borge addressed the National Association of Nicaraguan Educators and called on them to apply their skills in support of the revolution.

From "The New Education in the New Nicaragua," Tomás Borge, in *Nicaragua: The Sandinista People's Revolution, Speeches by Sandinista Leaders*, edited by Bruce Marcus. Copyright © 1985 Pathfinder Press. Reprinted by permission.

*   *   *

It is not at all unusual that teachers who yesterday fought the *somocista* dictatorship today defend the revolution they helped make, that they do not stand apart from the heroic struggle of the peoples of Central America. In February 1979 Nicaraguan teachers did not struggle, could not struggle, for a new system of education. They had to fight to create the conditions of struggle for a new education.

Right now that struggle is the order of the day. A new philosophy, a new structure, a new strategy of education constitute the most important task of this revolutionary process, a task that belongs to the entire society but whose fundamental responsibility lies with the teachers.

Of course, when we speak of the new education, we are not only referring to academic programs or to the social priorities of this great challenge. We are referring to the quest for the new man, to the transformation of man through education. We are referring to the unpostponable task of converting our people into a nation of students and teachers—that is, a country where the students learn to be teachers and the teachers learn to be students.

One of the most important challenges is to create in teachers the consciousness that they too must be students. To be capable of teaching others, the teacher must learn to be his own instructor as well.

*   *   *

But how can teachers raise the cultural level of their students if they haven't mastered new teaching techniques; if they lack culture adequate to the level that should be imparted in their teaching? How can teachers form patriotic and revolutionary consciousness in their students if they lack the basic elements for projecting this capacity as architects or sculptors of consciousness?

How can teachers explain the politics of the revolution to their students if they have no basis on which to form an opinion, if they themselves don't know what the revolution is? How can teachers explain to their students the essence of exploitation, exploitation that has stripped part of their own hides, if they don't know how to explain exploitation conceptually? How can they create profoundly anti-imperialist consciousness if they are ignorant of the essence of imperialism?

How can they speak to their students of the perspectives of the new society if they don't know what pillars the new society must be built on? How can they involve their students in conceiving a strategy of education if they don't have the remotest idea of what the new education is?

To answer all these problems we must understand their roots. Before speaking about what the new education means, it's essential that we understand what the role of education has been in the social process. It's necessary for us to define education in the full sense in order to later place it in the context of the revolutionary process.

Education is the process through which society reproduces the ideas, values, moral and ethical principles, and behavioral habits of the successive generations. All social organization is a function of the class interests that hold state power. Education is a process of forming individuals in ideology, in a complex system of values and ideas that justifies the interests of the class that wields state power.

*   *   *

In Nicaragua, at the time it was incorporated into the capitalist world market, at the end of the last century when massive coffee production began, the oligarchy's vehicle of ideological domination was fundamentally the church. The great masses of urban and rural workers, the so-called marginal sectors, and the great mass of the peasantry were denied access to education at any level.

This paved the way for an almost bloodcurdling illiteracy in our country. It was the rich coffee growers and landlords, the political sectors that controlled the government, and the rich merchants who sent their sons to the national and foreign universities.

*   *   *

After victory in the war of liberation against all the material means of domination, all our people and you teachers in particular opened up a second battle, just as important, in the field of ideological liberation. I am referring to the National Literacy Crusade.

However, other battles remain to be opened, perhaps some of the most difficult battles and confrontations, battles in the sphere of ideological formation. And you, teachers, you who can carry in your knapsacks the reproduction of ideology, science, and culture should be part of the vanguard in this battle for the new education and the formation of the new man.

This battle is going to complete the liberation of Nicaragua. It will open the way for the formation of a society where man can unleash all his physical, spiritual, scientific, and artistic faculties, that is, a society that develops man's freedom to create, construct, and fabricate beauty and culture, to master science.

*   *   *

* * *you should teach all those who enter your area of influence to be patriots, revolutionaries, exemplars of solidarity, dedicated to the interests of the workers and peasants and of all the toiling masses. You should teach them to be anti-imperialist, to fight discrimination and oppression, and encourage love for justice, liberty, and defense of the homeland.

You should help create a new man who is responsible, disciplined, creative, cooperative, an efficient worker, with high moral, civic, and spiritual principles, endowed with a critical and self-critical capacity, and with a scientific view of the world and society.

Teachers should help to create a new man who will know how to appreciate beauty and who will recognize and value the dignity of sweat and daily labor, to create a new man who is profoundly humanitarian, reliable, and selfless, a man ready to fight in the quest for the great joining together of individual and collective interests.

*   *   *

At this point the importance of the links between education and work is perhaps all too obvious. One time we put it this way: We should create a society where all students work and all workers study.

*   *   *

To create a new education we must create a new teacher. What should this new teacher be like? The teacher should:

1. Be revolutionary—that is, master of the new morality, archetype of the new man.

2. Have a high degree of commitment.

3. Identify with the interests of the workers.

4. Be a bearer of critical and self-critical attitudes.

5. Be capable of teaching and capable of learning.

6. Give each student the same love as would be given to his or her own children.

7. Be responsible and disciplined.

8. Be a teacher in the classroom and in the community.

9. Participate in defense of the homeland.

10. Participate in and bring participation from the community into all decision making.

These are principles that cannot be negotiated. Sovereignty of the homeland cannot be negotiated. The arms that defend this sovereignty are not negotiable.

And what are these arms? The cannons, the tanks, the rifles. We don't ever want to use them, and it is to be hoped that we won't have to. The violent fire of these arms will be used only to defend ourselves. We are sure that one day, when the ferocious fangs of imperialism have been pulled, we are not going to need these arms any more.

But there are other arms, ideological arms, that also defend the sovereignty of our homeland. The main ideological arm our people possess is the new education. This is an arm that cannot be laid down. The imperialists can shout all they want. Even if they shout their heads off we will hold tight to our ideological arms with the same tenacity that we hang on to our rifles.

*　　*　　*

REVIEW QUESTIONS

1. Why is education critical to the revolutionary project, according to Borge?
2. Based on Borge's remarks, what kind of society were the Sandinistas hoping to build?
3. What would the "new man" of the post-revolutionary period be like?
4. How would the "new teacher" help to create this "new man"?
5. How does the "new" education differ from the old?

CHAI LING

FROM I Am Still Alive

The growing liberalization of Soviet policies in the late 1980s generated new hopes for political reform and increased civil liberties in Communist China. After the death of Mao Zedong in 1976, the new Chinese leadership under Deng Xiaoping (1904–1997) had begun to introduce limited economic reforms, including a greater willingness to condone small-scale private industry, and had ended the Cultural Revolution, permitting somewhat greater freedom of cultural expression. Many hoped that the aging Chinese leadership would follow the lead of the Soviet "gerontocracy" and move to institute a more democratic system of government.

In the spring of 1989, the seventieth anniversary of the 4 May 1919 student movement sparked pro-democracy protests in Beijing. At the height of the demonstrations, China's capital was occupied by as many as one-million protesters. In Tiananmen Square, long a focal point for political protests, one-hundred thousand demonstrators gathered, led by students who served as leaders of the protest movement. Despite strong international pressure to deal gently with the protesters, Deng Xiaoping declared martial law on 20 May. Trustworthy troops recruited from the countryside were called in and on 4 June they put an end to the demonstrations by firing on the protesters, killing hundreds and arresting thousands. A few days later, Chai Ling, one of the student leaders, wrote a description of the massacre in the hopes of stirring international indignation over this incident.

From Chai Ling, "I Am Still Alive," in *Voices From Tiananmen Square: Beijing Spring and the Democracy Movement.* Mok Chiu Yu and J. Frank Harrison, eds. (Montreal: Black Rose Books, 1990). Reprinted with permission.

Today is June 8th, 1989. It is now 4:00 p.m. I am Chai Ling, Commander-in-Chief in Tiananmen Square. I am still alive.

I believe I am the best qualified witness to the situation in the Square during the period from June 2nd to 4th June, and I also have the responsibility to tell that truth to everyone, every single countryman, every single citizen.

At about 10 p.m. on the night of June 2nd, the first warning of what was to come was given when a police car knocked down four innocent persons, three of whom died. The second signal immediately followed when soldiers abandoned whole truckloads of armaments, military uniforms and other equipment, leaving them behind for the people and my college mates who had blocked their way. We were very suspicious of this act; so we immediately collected together everything that had been abandoned and sent them to the Public Security Bureau, retaining a receipt as proof. The third signal occurred at 2:10 p.m. on June 3rd, when large numbers of military police beat up students and citizens at Xinhuamen. At that time, the students were standing on top of cars, using microphones to cry out to the police: "The people's police love the people," "The people's police won't beat people up." Instantly, a soldier rushed towards a student, kicked him in the stomach, and scoffed: "Who loves you?" He then gave him another bash in the head and the student collapsed.

*   *   *

At 9:00 p.m. sharp, all of the students in the Square stood up and with their right hands raised, declared: "I vow that, for the promotion of our nation's process of democratization, for the true prosperity of our nation, for our great nation, for defense against a handful of schemers, for the salvation of our 1.1 billion countrymen from White Terror, that I will give up my young life to protect Tiananmen Square, to protect the Republic. Heads can fall, blood can run, but the people's Square can never be abandoned. We are willing to sacrifice our young lives in a fight to the death of the very last person."

At 10:00 p.m. sharp, the Democratic University was formally established in the Square, with vice-commander Jiang Deli becoming the principal, and people from all sides celebrated the occasion enthusiastically. At that time, the commanding unit was receiving many urgent warnings, as the situation became very tense. On one hand, there was the thunderous applause for the establishment of our Democratic University in the northern part of the Square near the Statue of the Goddess of Liberty; whereas along the Boulevard of Eternal Peace at the eastern edge of the Square, there was a river of blood. Murderers, those soldiers of the 27th Battalion, used tanks, heavy machine guns, bayonets (tear gas being already outdated) on people who did no more than utter a slogan, or throw a stone. They chased after the people, shooting with their machine guns. All the corpses along the Boulevard of Eternal Peace bled heavily from their chests; and all the students who ran to us were bleeding in the arms, chests and legs. They did this to their own countrymen, taking their life's blood. The students were very angry and held their dead friends in their arms.

After 10:00 p.m. we, the commanding unit,

made a request based upon the principle that our Patriotic-Democratic Movement, as both a Student Movement and People's Movement, had always been to demonstrate peacefully. In opposition, therefore, to the many students and citizens who angrily declared that it was time to use weapons, we proposed the supreme principle of peace and sacrifice.

In this way, hands joined together, shoulder to shoulder, singing "The International," we slowly came out from our tents. Hands joined, we came to the western, northern and the southern sides of the Monument of the People's Heroes, and sat there quietly, with serenity in our eyes, waiting for the attack by murderers. What we were involved in was a battle between love and hate, not one between violence and military force. We all knew that if we used things like clubs, gasoline bottles and the like (which are hardly weapons) against those soldiers, who were holding machine guns or riding in tanks, and who were out of their minds, then this would have been the greatest tragedy for our Democracy Movement.

So the students sat there silently, waiting to give up their lives. There were loudspeakers next to the commanding unit's tent playing "The Descendants of the Dragon." We sang along with it, with tears in our eyes. We embraced each other, shook hands, because we knew that the last moment of our lives, the moment to give up our lives for our nation, had arrived.

There was this student called Wang Li, who was fifteen. He had written his will. I have forgotten the exact wording, but I remember him saying: "Life is strange. The difference between life and death is just a split second. If you see an insect crawling toward you, all you have to do is to think about killing it and the insect will instantly stop crawling." He was only fifteen, and yet he was thinking about death. People of the Republic, you must not forget the children who fought for you.

*   *   *

I chatted with the students and told them the old story that goes: "There were these 1.1 billion

ants living on a mountain top. One day, the mountain was ablaze. To survive, the ants had to get down the mountain. They gathered themselves into a giant ball and rolled down the mountain. The ants on the outside were burnt to death. But the lives of many more were saved. My fellow students, we at the Square are the outermost layer, because in our hearts we understand that only by dying can we ensure the survival of the Republic."* * * The hunger strikers went to negotiate with the soldiers, with the so-called Martial Law Command Post, to tell them we were leaving. It was hoped that they would ensure the students' safety and peaceful retreat. Our headquarters consulted students on whether to leave or to stay. We decided to leave.

But the executioners didn't keep their word. As students were leaving, armed troops charged up to the third level of the Monument.* * * We only found out later, that some students still had hope in the Government and they thought that, at worst, they would be removed.

Then the tanks made "mincemeat" of them. Some say more than 200 students died. Some say more than 4000 died in the Square alone. I don't know the total. But the members of the Independent Workers' Union were on the outside. They stood their ground and they're all dead. There were twenty to thirty of them. I heard that, after the students left, tanks and armoured personnel carriers flattened tents with bodies inside. They poured gasoline over them and burned them. Then they washed away the traces with water. Our movement's symbol, the Goddess of Democracy, was crushed to bits.

*   *   *

The radio kept saying that the troops had come to Beijing to deal with riotous elements and to maintain order in the capital. I think I'm most qualified to say that we students are not riotous elements. Anyone with a conscience should put his hand on his chest and think of children, arm in arm, shoulder to shoulder, sitting quietly under the Monument, their eyes awaiting the executioner's blade. Can they be riotous elements? If they were riotous elements, would they sit there quietly? How far have the fascists gone? They can turn their backs on their conscience and tell the biggest lie under the sky. If you say soldiers who kill innocent people with their rifles are animals, what do you call those who sit in front of the camera and lie?

As we left the Square, arm in arm, as we walked along Changan Avenue, a tank charged at us and fired tear gas at the students. Then the tank rolled toward us, rolled over the students' heads, and legs. We couldn't find any of our classmates' bodies intact. Who's the riotous element? In spite of this, we in the front continued on our way. Students put on masks because the tear gas hurt their throats. What can we do to bring back those students who were sacrificed? Their souls will always remain on Changan Avenue. We who walked away from Tiananmen Square, arrived at Beijing University, still alive. Many students from other universities, students from out of town, had prepared beds to welcome us. But we were very, very sad. We were alive. Many more were left in the Square, and on Changan Avenue. They'll never come back. Some of them were very young. They will never come back.

As we entered Beijing University, our hunger strike turned sit-in, our peaceful protest, came to an end. Later we heard that Li Peng, at 10 p.m. on June 3rd, had handed down three orders: First, troops can open fire. Second, military vehicles must go forward without stopping. They must take back the Square by June 4th. Third, the leaders and organizers of the Movement must be killed.

My compatriots, this is the frenzied, puppet government that initiated a slaughter and is still commanding troops and ruling China. But my compatriots, even at the darkest moment, dawn will still break. Even with the frenzied, fascist crackdown, a true people's democratic republic will be born. The critical moment has come. My compatriots, all Chinese nationals with a conscience, all Chinese people, wake up! The ultimate victory must be the people's! Yang Shangkun, Li Peng, Wang Zhen and Bo Yibo, the final hour of your puppet regime is near!

Down with Fascism!
Down with Military Rule!
Long Live the Republic!

REVIEW QUESTIONS

1. According to Chai Ling, what were the goals of the student protesters?
2. How does Chai Ling characterize the actions of the political leadership and the troops sent in to put down the protests?
3. Why were Chinese students willing to die for their cause?
4. To what extent did the Chinese student protesters accept Gandhi's principles of non-violent resistance?
5. Why do you think that strategy failed in this particular case?

THE UNITED NATIONS

FROM *Global Outlook 2000*

Whereas population growth rates were once largely controlled by local conditions such as the fertility of the soil, the availability of natural resources, and local weather conditions, the globalization of production and distribution have created a situation in which a region's population growth rate is directly affected by the operation of the international market. Better distribution of food surpluses now makes it possible for local famines to be averted, while the transfer of medical technologies can have a dramatic impact on decreasing the number of deaths caused by disease and accidents. On the other hand, political instability and weak infrastructures can interfere with the distribution of available resources to threatened populations. In this sense, the global outlook for the world's population is determined as much by politics as by the productive capacity of humankind.

As the following excerpts from a recent United Nations report demonstrate, the demographic history of late twentieth-century human populations is strongly shaped by continuing economic disparities between the developed and undeveloped regions of the world.

From *Global Outlook 2000: An Economic, Social and Environmental Perspective*, United Nations, 1990. The United Nations is the author of the original material. Reprinted with permission.

*   *   *

DEMOGRAPHIC TRENDS are fairly predictable and provide a good basis for the analysis of structural economic change and the associated economic and social policy issues of the next decade. Against a background of generally slower population growth, which will result in a world population of 6 billion just before the turn of the century, there will be considerable regional diversity. The fastest growth (an annual rate of 3 per cent) will occur in Africa, where the task of economic recovery and restoration of self-sustained growth will be particularly difficult. There will be less dispersion, however, in labour force growth rates in the developing world. The rate will average 2.5 to 3 per cent. In contrast, labour force growth rates in developed countries will be less than 1 per cent. Employment is likely to grow more slowly than the labour force in most countries, and unemployment will be a concern for all groups of countries.

For the world as a whole, the dependency ratio is expected to fall, but this is the result of opposing trends in major world regions. In the developing countries, the total dependency ratio should fall as fertility declines. In the developed countries it is expected to rise, mainly as a result of the increase in the elderly population. This increase will raise the level of the real and financial resources needed for health care and other support of the elderly.

The pressure for international migration should accelerate in the 1990s as income differentials increase and the cost of transportation declines relative to incomes. Urban population will continue to grow faster than rural population in all regions of the world, due principally to rural-urban migration, and the number and size of "megacities" is expected to increase rapidly in developing countries.

*   *   *

The world's population surpassed 5 billion in the middle of 1987 and is projected to grow to 6 billion just before the turn of the century. In the previous 13 years, it grew from 4 to 5 billion. The quarter century from 1975 to 2000 will have witnessed the greatest absolute expansion of the global population in such a short time. From 1980 to 1985 the annual rate of population growth was 1.7 per cent, compared with the peak rate of 2.0 per cent in the period from 1965 to 1970. It is expected to continue to decline slowly in the future. Only in the next century, however, will there be a significant decline in the size of the net annual increments to the world total.

There was a clear dichotomy in the 1960s between slow growth of population in the developed countries (the average annual rate was 1.1 per cent) and rapid growth in the developing countries (the average annual rate was about 2.5 per cent). The major developing regions showed little diversity, ranging from 2.4 per cent in Asia (excluding Japan) to 2.7 per cent in Latin America (see table 9.1). Since the 1960s, however, the rates of population increase have become more diverse among the developing regions and their constituent countries, and the divergence is expected to increase in the 1990s. Population growth in Africa began to accelerate in the 1950s and continued to do so through the 1980s, while in most of the other developing regions it began to decelerate in the 1970s. The drop in the growth rate was particularly notable in China and the Asian planned economies; the drop is expected to continue in the 1990s, falling to little more than half the rate of the 1960s. Projected population growth rates for the 1990s are now about 3 per cent in Africa and Western Asia, 2 per cent in South and East Asia (excluding Japan and the Asian planned economies), 1.9 per cent in Latin America, and 1.3 per cent in China together with the Asian planned economies. The growth rate in the developed countries as a whole has fallen to 0.6 per cent in

the 1980s and is projected to be only 0.5 per cent in the 1990s (0.8 per cent or less in North America and Eastern Europe and 0.3 to 0.5 per cent in the European market economies and Japan). These differential growth rates will result in quite different age structures that, in turn, will affect many aspects of development.

The shift in the regional shares of global population is dominated by the growth of developing Africa and West Asia. Their combined share was 10 per cent in 1960 and 12 per cent in 1980. It is projected to reach 16 per cent in 2000. In contrast, the proportion of world population accounted for by the developed countries declined from 31.4 per cent in 1960 to 25.8 per cent in 1980, and is projected to be only 20.6 per cent in 2000.

Population growth in the least developed countries has accelerated from an average rate of 2.4 per cent in the 1960s to 2.6 per cent in the 1980s. This is in contrast to a dramatic drop in China together with the Asian planned economies, from 2.4 per cent to 1.3 per cent, and a slight decline in the other developing countries as a whole. The difference is expected to be even greater in the 1990s—2.9 per cent in the least developed countries versus 1.3 per cent in China and the Asian planned economies and 2.3 per cent in the developing countries as a whole.

*   *   *

Population growth rates are affected by trends in mortality and fertility. Mortality has declined unevenly in most countries during recent decades. Although it remains high in most of the developing countries, the mortality rate has declined very rapidly in some and has reached levels as low, or nearly as low, as those in developed countries. In the past decade, there have been decreases in infant mortality rates in nearly all countries, but more than one quarter, representing 29 per cent of world population, still have rates above 100 per 1,000 live births. Between 1985 and 1990, the average in the least developed countries is estimated at 123 per 1,000. In Africa as a whole it is 106, while the average in the developed countries (excluding South Africa) is about 15.

Mortality levels and trends are influenced by many social, economic, and cultural factors, including policies and programmes outside the health sector. Economic development is usually associated with mortality decline, since improved economic conditions imply higher living standards and increased financial resources for health services. But low mortality levels have also been achieved in some low-income countries where Governments are committed to reducing mortality; China, Cuba, Sri Lanka, and the state of Kerala in India are well-known examples, as is Costa Rica among middle-income countries.

Deaths of young children in developing countries constitute a large share of all deaths, and children are considered the major target in efforts to reduce overall mortality. The factors having the greatest effect on the mortality of children are those related to parental education, especially of mothers. Analysis of data from the World Fertility Surveys show that infant and child mortality generally decreases as the average number of years of the mother's education increases. Survey results suggest that the effect of parental education may be greater than that of income-related factors and access to health facilities combined.

One of the most important findings from the World Fertility Surveys concerns the exceptionally high mortality among children born after a short birth interval. This suggests that family planning programmes aimed at spacing births and avoiding high-risk pregnancies could help to reduce infant, child, and also maternal mortality. Other interventions that can lower mortality in developing countries include efforts to improve the nutritional level of the population, immunization programmes, and other health measures.

*   *   *

In the developed countries, life expectancy at birth has increased from 66 years in the early 1950s to 73 years in the late 1980s, while in the developing countries as a whole (including China), it has increased from 41 to 60. There was a dramatic increase in China, from 41 years in the early 1950s to 69 in the late 1980s; in Africa, it

increased from 35 years to 49. The average life expectancy in the least developed countries in the period from 1985 to 1990 is also about 49 years. The low life expectancy and high infant mortality in the least developed countries reflect their unfavourable living conditions and imply that their population may increase even more rapidly in the future if mortality conditions improve and fertility remains unchanged.

Life expectancy at birth is generally several years longer for women than for men, especially in the developed countries: 77 years for women versus 70 years for men in the late 1980s. In the developing countries (including China), it is about 61 years for women and 59 years for men. The region where average expectancy for women is the same as for men is South Asia, although improvements in female life expectancy in Sri Lanka in the past two decades have resulted in a more normal pattern in that country. By the year 2000, the difference is projected to increase to three years in the developing countries as a whole, and to remain constant in the developed countries.

*   *   *

The most rapid fertility declines have occurred in developing countries with a combination of profound improvements in child survival, increases in educational levels, and strong family planning programmes. Since the late 1950s, total fertility rates have declined by 2 to 3 children per woman in China, the Republic of Korea, Thailand, Malaysia, Sri Lanka, Brazil, Mexico, and Colombia. The proportion of married women of childbearing age currently using contraception in all these countries grew rapidly since at least the mid-1960s, gaining 2 to 3 percentage points a year. In the 1980s, it reached levels of 50 to 70 per cent. Simultaneously, under-five mortality (i.e., the combined mortality of infants and children under age 5) declined in China from 240 per thousand to 55, and from a range of 120 to 190 per thousand in the other seven countries to a range of 40 to 90. Gross enrolment ratios of females for the second level of education rose from less than 15 per cent in all these countries to between 30 and

35 per cent in Thailand, Brazil, and China. It rose to about 50 per cent in Sri Lanka, Malaysia, Mexico, and Colombia and to 90 per cent in the Republic of Korea.

Conversely, low rates of child survival, low levels of education, and insufficient access to birth control methods impede the transformation to lower fertility in most countries of sub-Saharan Africa, as well as in such Asian countries as Pakistan, Bangladesh, Nepal, and Afghanistan. Total fertility rates in many of these countries average 6 or 7 children per woman. They show few signs of decline despite significant government initiatives in immunization and family planning. Under-five mortality is still well above 150 per 1000 in most of them and often exceeds 250; the female gross enrolment ratio for the second level of education and the proportion of married women currently using contraception are typically below 10 per cent and rarely above 20 per cent.

*   *   *

REVIEW QUESTIONS

1. What general trends can the world population be expected to follow in coming years?
2. What are the most important differences between the demographic trends of the developed and undeveloped regions of the globe?
3. Why are population growth rates higher in undeveloped regions than in developed regions?
4. How do the population profiles of undeveloped and developed regions differ?
5. What role does infant mortality play in the demographic patterns of developed and undeveloped regions?
6. Why is a decrease in infant mortality usually associated with economic development?
7. What is the relationship between family planning and infant mortality?

NIGEL HARRIS

FROM *The New Untouchables: Immigration and the New World Worker*

The geographic distribution of the human population is increasingly determined by economic trends favoring the transfer of substantial numbers of people from one region to another. Immigration has always played an important role in human experience—the history of the United States is, in its very essence, a history of migration—but greatly enhanced opportunities for long-distance travel make migration an especially significant factor in the late twentieth century.

Labor migration has long been a highly contentious social and political issue. When shortages of workers threaten to limit the economic development of a nation or region, as they did in western Europe during the 1950s and 1960s, for example, skilled and unskilled workers are often recruited and encouraged to relocate to host countries. However, when an economic downturn occurs, as happened around the world in the 1970s, native workers often come to resent immigrants, even when those immigrants hold jobs that native workers do not want. At the same time, cultural differences between natives and immigrants may breed hostility, especially when the language, religion, or ethnicity of immigrants sets them apart from the native majority. Yet, as Nigel Harris argues in a recent study of labor migration, legislation intended to stem the influx of migrant workers runs counter to processes of global economic integration which tend to break down existing national boundaries and blur the lines separating citizens from non-citizens.

From *The New Untouchables: Immigration and the New World Worker*, Nigel Harris, I. B. Tauris & Company, Ltd., 1995. Reprinted with permission of the publisher.

*   *   *

In the case of Britain, workers had been recruited from the West Indies, Asia and Africa during the Second World War (the restrictions on their entry to Britain were removed in 1942). In the immediate postwar years, while emigration continued to be encouraged, the government made significant efforts to recruit displaced—but white—persons in Europe (for example, 170,000 Poles and Italians were brought in). However, from 1948, the spontaneous arrival of West Indian workers began a process that expanded to include those from the Indian subcontinent, parts of Africa, Cyprus, and so on, and continued up to the ending of the automatic right of entry for Empire subjects in 1962. Up to that time, immigrants from the Empire were automatically citizens with the same rights as those born in Britain (including the right to vote and stand for public office).

The 1962 measure by no means settled the issue, since many groups in the former Empire retained the status of British nationality, and it was thus necessary to remove from this status any right to enter Britain. Through successive crises, leading to the flight of British passport holders—particularly those of Indian origin living in Kenya, Uganda, Malawi and, later, Chinese from Hong Kong—two types of British passport were created: one carrying the right to enter and live in Britain, one without it. The unfortunates who gained the

second type were thus unilaterally deprived of their former rights. For the first time, a specific British nationality was invented, based upon a quasi-ethnic origin or 'patriality', turning upon the nationality of a parent or grandparent.

*   *   *

If the British, at least in theory, accepted Empire or Commonwealth citizens resident in Britain as British, and then sought to identify newcomers as foreigners (other than those entering for family reunification), France identified those with French identity cards (including, for example, the inhabitants of the four main cities of Senegal) as having the right to settle in the country. Furthermore, the efforts to incorporate Algeria into France led in 1947 to the recognition of Muslim Algerians as French citizens. Yet severe conflicts of interest remained: the French Algerian authorities at various stages discouraged migration to protect the local labour supply; however, as the movement for an independent Algeria developed, they began to encourage movement to France as a safety valve, while Paris shifted from seeking labour to trying to discourage the spread of sedition to metropolitan France. Later, under the Evian Agreements (1962) which ended the war in Algeria, Paris agreed to the free movement of labour to France in return for Algerian protection of French interests and population in Algeria, and in particular, French oil and gas installations; in the event, the Algerian government nationalized these assets in 1971. Only two years after the Evian Agreements, Paris tried to restrict the movement in a new bilateral agreement with Algiers—an annual quota of 35,000 was laid down as from 1968 (under separate agreements with the relevant governments, France agreed to accept 150,000 workers from Morocco and 100,000 from Tunisia). In practice, the Algerian government saw the outflow of workers, particularly the skilled, as deleterious to Algeria's economic development, and eventually suspended the arrangement just ahead of a decision by Paris to do so.

For Germany,* * * under the federal constitution, workers drawn in by the extraordinary growth of the economy remained temporary or 'guest workers' (Gastarbeiter). Political and economic status, citizen and worker, remained distinct. While by 1960 possibly a quarter of West Germany's population had been born abroad, by 1990 there were some 5 million 'immigrants' (including those born in Germany of non-German parents). The initial movement had been started and regulated by bilateral government agreements. The rush of agreements came after the main supply of labour, from East Germany, ended with the building of the Berlin Wall in 1961. However, once established, direct relationships between employers and source areas tended to take over—up to 35 per cent of the migration of Turkish workers to Germany took place outside the bilateral agreements, and two-fifths of these were requested by companies rather than being recruited by German government agents* * * The agreements, however, restricted the freedom of the government to act unilaterally on the flows.

What had been created by government action tended to be sustained by employers, even after the government had reversed its position. As we have seen, as controls tightened, so the exceptions increased, particularly for seasonal workers in construction and agriculture from Poland and the Czech and Slovak Republics. Companies also recruited workers from Albania, Bulgaria, Poland and Hungary. It was still insufficient and reputedly the numbers of illegal entrants continued to rise.

In Europe generally, from the early 1970s and shortly before the onset of the largest recession since the Second World War, increasing attempts were made to end immigration, deter the arrival of newcomers with a right of entry, and encourage immigrants to leave. Britain was among the first to seek to suspend the process with the 1962 Commonwealth Immigration Act; Denmark temporarily suspended new arrivals in 1970; Norway increased the restrictions on the issue of work permits in 1971; West Germany ended the right of foreign tourists to apply for work permits in 1972, with other disincentives to those with the right to enter Germany under family reunification privileges; the Netherlands restricted entries from 1973, France from 1974. Thus, within a very short space of time, the desperate search for workers was replaced by a no less desperate struggle to exclude them. In December 1978, the French government suspended the granting of extensions to ten-year residents' permits which were due to expire in 1979, affecting some half a million North Africans; in the spring of the following year, Paris eased the provisions to expel immigrants without judicial appeal (the same innovation took place in Britain), and tried to introduce summary detention (a measure subsequently defeated in the Assembly). Governments tried also—unsuccessfully—to pressurize governments in source countries to restrict emigration (without an increase in foreign aid to compensate for the loss in emigrant remittances). Some also penalized the carriers, forcing airline officials to implement immigration legislation, and thus avoided the legal complexities of expelling landed immigrants (the US Coastguards, for similar reasons, arrested suspected immigrants on the high seas and expelled them—acts that might be construed as acts of piracy). As we have seen, employers were also used to help implement immigration law by making them liable to charges for hiring illegal immigrants.

Governments also, as we have seen, tried to encourage existing immigrants to give up voluntarily their residential rights and leave. Britain made provision for this under the 1971 Act, but, as has been frequently noted, those who utilized the provisions usually intended to leave the country in any case. Similarly under the West German regulations of 1984–85, most of the 180,000 immigrants who left seemed to have decided to do so independently of any incentives offered. In 1977–78, the French government offered financial help to encourage unemployed immigrants and their families to leave; out of the targeted 100,000, some 45,000—mainly Portuguese and Spaniards—responded, but again, it was thought the beneficiaries had already decided to leave.

The context of increased control, in conditions of world recession from 1973, ensured that the question of immigration was interwoven with increased economic insecurity among the population at large. If this were not enough, in almost all European countries there were political leaders to urge on the process, to seek to stimulate sudden waves of panic at the 'foreign invasion' (the words used by former President of France, Giscard d'Estaing). Former British cabinet minister Enoch Powell spoke in 1968 of British decline in terms of the fall of the Roman Empire, overwhelmed by barbarians. Edith Cresson, prime minister of France, promised the mass expulsion of illegal immigrants. Some British borough councils refused to implement their legal obligation to rehouse the homeless if they were foreign-born; French local authorities also refused the citizens of French overseas territories the right to public housing.

Having established the context of the public debate, governments feel obliged to proclaim, at one- or two-year intervals, a complete end to immigration, knowing full well that the promise cannot be fulfilled. In the jostling for a political edge, the lies are traded without a flicker of shame. French minister Charles Pasqua in mid-1993, preparing for the presidential elections of 1995, announced the government's target as 'zero immigration' and promised legislation to legalize random identity checks and introduce an accelerated expulsion procedure; such measures were necessary because illegal immigrants were responsible for crime and drug dealing.

This verbal froth may have been effective in directing public attention to some of the more defenceless members of society, but it had little impact on the number of arrivals. According to one of the better estimates, the entries for residence of non-Europeans into the European Union increased from 1 million per year in 1985 to 3 million in 1992—with legal immigration increasing from 700,000 to 1 million; the number applying for asylum from 170,000 to 690,000; citizens of former Yugoslavia with temporary protected status from 100,000 to 300,000; the entry of 'ethnic' Germans (nationals of countries other than Germany but claiming German descent) from 100,000 to 300,000; and illegals from 50,000 to 400,000* * * Of course, figures for arrivals say nothing about the stock of foreign residents, since the numbers leaving were also rising; by 1990, there were only about 8 million resident aliens, or just over 2 for every 100 of the population of the European Union.

The numbers of illegal entrants seemed to be rising and, as in the case of Canada and the United States, governments in Europe were periodically obliged to regularize their status in order that they could be brought into the area of public supervision. Regularization was a recognition of the failure of immigration regulation to control the labour market.

* * *

REVIEW QUESTIONS

1. Why did European governments allow immigration after World War II?
2. Why have they sought to discourage it since the 1970s?
3. Where did immigrants to Britain, France, and Germany come from?
4. What factors influenced non-European workers' decisions about where to relocate?
5. Why is it difficult for European governments to enforce "zero immigration" policies?

KATHRYN KOPINAK

FROM *Desert Capitalism: Maquiladoras in North America's Western Industrial Corridor*

*In recent years, many manufacturers have also become "migrants," having trans-
ferred production facilities from their home country to other regions. Seeking large
pools of low-cost workers and freedom from government labor and environmental
regulations, these corporations have broken their ties to a single nation or region,
taking a "transnational" approach to doing business. American, European, or Japanese consumers benefit from this system because manufactured goods made in
China, the Philippines, or Honduras tend to be cheaper; corporate shareholders benefit from increased profits. On the other hand, workers in developed regions suffer
from a loss of jobs, while workers in the developing world suffer from low pay, long
hours, and dangerous or abusive conditions.*

*In the mid-1960s, the Mexican government passed legislation allowing foreign-
owned companies to establish duty-free production facilities—known as
maquiladoras—on the United States–Mexico border. Car parts manufactured in the
United States, for example, might be transported across the border to be assembled
by unskilled or semi-skilled Mexican laborers, and then be returned for sale in the
United States. Japanese and United States corporations would be able to take advantage of the low cost of hiring Mexican workers, and Mexican peasants would
benefit from access to new, better-paid jobs in the industrial sector. In theory, a
"dual-technology transfer" would occur: maquiladoras would provide not only unskilled jobs, but also some highly paid and highly skilled managerial and technical
positions. However, as Kathryn Kopinak demonstrates in her recent study of No-
gales-area maquiladoras, the migration of production facilities does not necessarily
result in the creation of an affluent consumer economy in Mexico, although it could
create incentives for migrant laborers to remain within their country of origin.*

From *Desert Capitalism: Maquiladoras in North America's Western Industrial Corridor*, Kathryn Kopinak, University of Arizona Press, 1996. Reprinted with permission of the publisher.

*   *   *

Biological reproduction and migration are alternative ways of constituting a labor force, and the
household is an important structure facilitating either option. While Mexico as a country has no
difficulty in biologically reproducing itself, the economic restructuring of the eighties—which cul-
minated in NAFTA—meant that for many
Mexicans, employment was available at home less
often than it used to be. Journalists* * * have observed that the media have been used by the state
as vehicles "for convincing people to change their
reproductive behavior, to control or encourage
migration—like migration toward the northern
border—and it has been those media . . . which

propagate the idea that it would be a better life with a small family, without questioning what women or couples want."

* * *the individuals who get the Nogales and Imuris transport-equipment jobs advertised in the newspaper actively organize their lives outside of work to take the most advantage of whatever opportunity maquila employment offers. Many have left their families and traveled from Nayarit, Sinaloa, and from locations within Sonora to work at the border. Most of them come from within the western industrial corridor, rather than outside of it. Even though most were not employed before their first maquila job, or worked marginally in agriculture, they now comprise an industrial labor force that this corridor internally generates. (The central corridor also generates its own maquila labor force, but the Pacific corridor does not.)

Workers organize themselves into households which attempt to mediate some of the sharpest difficulties of the economy. The household is especially important in this attempted mediation due to the absence* * * of effective trade-union organizations that might help defend workers' rights and represent their interests. The others with whom workers undertake the active organization of their lives are in most cases members of their families.

Given Mexico's economic crisis in the eighties, and the concomitant drop in real wages, the average maquiladora worker's household must be seen as an organization promoting family survival, rather than one whose goal is to accumulate consumer goods. The goal of subsistence is accomplished better by some maquila households than others, and the optimum form seems to be a household with both men and women wage earners, as opposed to a household with only male wage earners or only female wage earners. Households with both male and female wage earners had the highest total household and per capita incomes, the least dependence on the income of any one worker, and the lowest proportion of economically active members working in maquilas. They were also larger than households that had only male or only female workers, indicating that

the slogan used by family-planning promoters that "between fewer burros, there are more cobs of corn" is not necessarily a valid assumption.* * *

While Nogales has one of the lowest proportions of women in its maquila labor force of any maquiladora center, the wages of women transport-equipment workers were found to be about the same as anyone else's wages in their households. Women workers who identified themselves as wives or daughters of the head of the household in which they lived were definitely not supplementary wage earners, as is often assumed. Women workers also headed their own households, and sometimes could not count on any income brought home by men. Households without any economic support from men probably provide for the most precarious existence.

Perhaps if maquiladoras paid workers higher wages, there would be more reason for workers to separate their work life from their family life* * * however, such a wage increase would have to be quite substantial to make up for the drop in real wages that occurred in the eighties. Even if wages did increase to a level that could provide the material possibility for living independently from family, Mexicans might very well not choose such a lifestyle, since there is strong cultural support for family economies. * * *at present, this question is not dependent on culture, as many managers indicated, but on the material basis that would make it a possibility. Maquiladoras do not pay workers enough for them to put work before family even if they valued their work more highly than their families, which, in general, they do not.

While household organization enhances the well-being of the family group as a unit, it may also create and maintain inequalities structured internally on the basis of age and gender. Other authors have argued that women maquila workers are subordinated by their families. Although redistribution of income within the household was not specifically investigated in this study, I think there is no doubt that the household is one site of women's subordination. The fact that some men said they had migrated because of curiosity or for excitement, whereas women never gave such a reason for migrating, is an indication of the greater choices available to men for acting outside of family structures. The household, however, is not the only source of women's subordination.* * *

Even those households with both men and women wage earners, the best type of household for pooling income, often failed to meet basic standards set by Mexicans for decent living. Evidence for this is the finding that the average maquila household in Nogales, including all wage earners, only brought together enough income to be considered "absolutely poor" by prevailing standards. Moreover, many of the households evaluated as having achieved an effective structure for group survival share housing that is overcrowded, built of inadequate materials, and poorly serviced by utilities like water and electricity.

In general, employment in Nogales transport-equipment maquilas does not serve workers very well. If the dual-technology thesis were becoming a reality, more workers would be expected to live in households that were accumulating consumer goods rather than merely surviving. Also, more workers would be expected to have better housing due to an increase in skilled jobs, which should be better rewarded.

The existence of the border to stop migration means that maquila workers' main cross-border travel is for shopping to take advantage of lower prices, greater variety, and better quality in the United States. Most Nogales workers buy their groceries and other basic supplies in the United States in dollar-denominated values* * * With little to spend, they are limited to stores in the immediate Nogales area. They may, however, consider more permanent trips farther into the United States if maquila employment provides them with enough resources. On the other hand, higher wages might help Mexicans establish a better standard of living south of the border and root them there.

*   *   *

REVIEW QUESTIONS

1. Where do maquiladora workers come from?
2. Why have they migrated to Nogales?
3. How do maquiladora workers organize their lives once they arrive in Nogales?
4. What sort of family structure allows these workers to maximize their standard of living?
5. Why do these workers remain "absolutely poor"?

THE UNITED NATION'S FOURTH WORLD CONFERENCE ON WOMEN

FROM Platform for Action

In September 1995, women representing one-hundred and eighty-five of the world's nations gathered in Beijing to attend the United Nations' Fourth World Conference on Women. Delegates to the conference adopted a "platform for action" that outlined the various problems confronting women around the world, established a set of strategic objectives, and listed the specific actions to be taken to achieve these objectives. Working from a general consensus in favor of women's empowerment, partici-

pants discussed the ways in which women are affected by poverty, violence, armed conflict, human rights violations, pollution, and differing access to medical treatment, education, economic advancement, and political power.

Certain issues addressed by the conference were highly controversial, and drew formal reservations from the governments of participating nations. Language intended to guarantee access to abortion and contraceptive technologies or to protect the rights of lesbians, for example, was rejected by many who attended the conference. Representatives of Islamic nations also refused to accept clauses that were seen as violating Muslim practice in the area of marriage, female sexuality, and inheritance. On the other hand, few reservations were expressed about one of the key issues addressed by the conference: the fact that women (and children) are disproportionately represented among the world's poor.

From *Report of the Fourth World Conference on Women (Beijing, 4–15 September 1995)*, United Nations Website, <http://www.undp.org/fwcw/daw1.htm>.

*   *   *

A. WOMEN AND POVERTY

47. More than 1 billion people in the world today, the great majority of whom are women, live in unacceptable conditions of poverty, mostly in the developing countries.* * *

48. In the past decade the number of women living in poverty has increased disproportionately to the number of men, particularly in the developing countries. The feminization of poverty has also recently become a significant problem in the countries with economies in transition as a short-term consequence of the process of political, economic and social transformation. In addition to economic factors, the rigidity of socially ascribed gender roles and women's limited access to power, education, training and productive resources as well as other emerging factors that may lead to insecurity for families are also responsible. The failure to adequately mainstream a gender perspective in all economic analysis and planning and to address the structural causes of poverty is also a contributing factor.

49. Women contribute to the economy and to combating poverty through both remunerated and unremunerated work at home, in the community and in the workplace. The empowerment of women is a critical factor in the eradication of poverty.

50. While poverty affects households as a whole, because of the gender division of labour and responsibilities for household welfare, women bear a disproportionate burden, attempting to manage household consumption and production under conditions of increasing scarcity. Poverty is particularly acute for women living in rural households.

51. Women's poverty is directly related to the absence of economic opportunities and autonomy, lack of access to economic resources, including credit, land ownership and inheritance, lack of access to education and support services and their minimal participation in the decision-making process. Poverty can also force women into situations in which they are vulnerable to sexual exploitation.

52. In too many countries, social welfare systems do not take sufficient account of the specific conditions of women living in poverty, and there is a tendency to scale back the services provided by such systems. The risk of falling into poverty is greater for women than for men, particularly in old age, where social security systems are based on the principle of continuous remunerated employ-

ment. In some cases, women do not fulfil this requirement because of interruptions in their work, due to the unbalanced distribution of remunerated and unremunerated work. Moreover, older women also face greater obstacles to labour-market re-entry.

53. In many developed countries, where the level of general education and professional training of women and men are similar and where systems of protection against discrimination are available, in some sectors the economic transformations of the past decade have strongly increased either the unemployment of women or the precarious nature of their employment. The proportion of women among the poor has consequently increased. In countries with a high level of school enrolment of girls, those who leave the educational system the earliest, without any qualification, are among the most vulnerable in the labour market.

*   *   *

55. Particularly in developing countries, the productive capacity of women should be increased through access to capital, resources, credit, land, technology, information, technical assistance and training so as to raise their income and improve nutrition, education, health care and status within the household. The release of women's productive potential is pivotal to breaking the cycle of poverty so that women can share fully in the benefits of development and in the products of their own labour.

56. Sustainable development and economic growth that is both sustained and sustainable are possible only through improving the economic, social, political, legal and cultural status of women. Equitable social development that recognizes empowering the poor, particularly women, to utilize environmental resources sustainably is a necessary foundation for sustainable development.

*   *   *

F. WOMEN AND THE ECONOMY

150. There are considerable differences in women's and men's access to and opportunities to exert power over economic structures in their societies. In most parts of the world, women are virtually absent from or are poorly represented in economic decision-making, including the formulation of financial, monetary, commercial and other economic policies, as well as tax systems and rules governing pay.* * *

151. In many regions, women's participation in remunerated work in the formal and non-formal labour market has increased significantly and has changed during the past decade. While women continue to work in agriculture and fisheries, they have also become increasingly involved in micro, small and medium-sized enterprises and, in some cases, have become more dominant in the expanding informal sector. Due to, inter alia, difficult economic situations and a lack of bargaining power resulting from gender inequality, many women have been forced to accept low pay and poor working conditions and thus have often become preferred workers. On the other hand, women have entered the workforce increasingly by choice when they have become aware of and demanded their rights. Some have succeeded in entering and advancing in the workplace and improving their pay and working conditions. However, women have been particularly affected by the economic situation and restructuring processes, which have changed the nature of employment and, in some cases, have led to a loss of jobs, even for professional and skilled women. In addition, many women have entered the informal sector owing to the lack of other opportunities. Women's participation and gender concerns are still largely absent from and should be integrated in the policy formulation process of the multilateral institutions that define the terms and, in co-

operation with Governments, set the goals of structural adjustment programmes, loans and grants.

152. Discrimination in education and training, hiring and remuneration, promotion and horizontal mobility practices, as well as inflexible working conditions, lack of access to productive resources and inadequate sharing of family responsibilities, combined with a lack of or insufficient services such as child care, continue to restrict employment, economic, professional and other opportunities and mobility for women and make their involvement stressful. Moreover, attitudinal obstacles inhibit women's participation in developing economic policy and in some regions restrict the access of women and girls to education and training for economic management.

153. Women's share in the labour force continues to rise and almost everywhere women are working more outside the household, although there has not been a parallel lightening of responsibility for unremunerated work in the household and community. Women's income is becoming increasingly necessary to households of all types. In some regions, there has been a growth in women's entrepreneurship and other self-reliant activities, particularly in the informal sector. In many countries, women are the majority of workers in nonstandard work, such as temporary, casual, multiple part-time, contract and home-based employment.

154. Women migrant workers, including domestic workers, contribute to the economy of the sending country through their remittances and also to the economy of the receiving country through their participation in the labour force. However, in many receiving countries, migrant women experience higher levels of unemployment compared with both non-migrant workers and male migrant workers.

*   *   *

156. * * *Women contribute to development not only through remunerated work but also through a great deal of unremunerated work. On the one hand, women participate in the production of goods and services for the market and household consumption, in agriculture, food production or family enterprises.* * *this unremunerated work —particularly that related to agriculture—is often undervalued and underrecorded. On the other hand, women still also perform the great majority of unremunerated domestic work and community work, such as caring for children and older persons, preparing food for the family, protecting the environment and providing voluntary assistance to vulnerable and disadvantaged individuals and groups. This work is often not measured in quantitative terms and is not valued in national accounts. Women's contribution to development is seriously underestimated, and thus its social recognition is limited. The full visibility of the type, extent and distribution of this unremunerated work will also contribute to a better sharing of responsibilities.

157. Although some new employment opportunities have been created for women as a result of the globalization of the economy, there are also trends that have exacerbated inequalities between women and men. At the same time, globalization, including economic integration, can create pressures on the employment situation of women to adjust to new circumstances and to find new sources of employment as patterns of trade change. More analysis needs to be done of the impact of globalization on women's economic status.

158. These trends have been characterized by low wages, little or no labour standards protection, poor working conditions, particularly with regard to women's occupational health and safety, low skill levels, and a lack of job security and social security, in both the formal and informal sectors. Women's unemployment is a serious and increasing problem in many countries and sectors. Young workers in the informal and rural sectors and migrant female workers remain the least protected by labour and immigration laws. Women, particularly those who are heads of households with young children, are limited in their employment opportunities for reasons that include inflexible working conditions and inadequate sharing, by men and by society, of family responsibilities.

159. In countries that are undergoing fundamental political, economic and social transformation, the skills of women, if better utilized, could constitute a major contribution to the economic life of their respective countries. Their input should continue to be developed and supported and their potential further realized.

160. Lack of employment in the private sector and reductions in public services and public service jobs have affected women disproportionately. In some countries, women take on more unpaid work, such as the care of children and those who are ill or elderly, compensating for lost household income, particularly when public services are not available. In many cases, employment creation strategies have not paid sufficient attention to occupations and sectors where women predominate; nor have they adequately promoted the access of women to those occupations and sectors that are traditionally male.

161. For those women in paid work, many experience obstacles that prevent them from achieving their potential. While some are increasingly found in lower levels of management, attitudinal discrimination often prevents them from being promoted further. The experience of sexual harassment is an affront to a worker's dignity and prevents women from making a contribution commensurate with their abilities. The lack of a family-friendly work environment, including a lack of appropriate and affordable child care, and inflexible working hours further prevent women from achieving their full potential.

162. In the private sector, including transnational and national enterprises, women are largely absent from management and policy levels, denoting discriminatory hiring and promotion policies and practices. The unfavourable work environment as well as the limited number of employment opportunities available have led many women to seek alternatives. Women have increasingly become self-employed and owners and managers of micro, small and medium-scale enterprises. The expansion of the informal sector, in many countries, and of self-organized and independent enterprises is in large part due to women, whose collaborative, self-help and traditional practices and initiatives in production and trade represent a vital economic resource. When they gain access to and control over capital, credit and other resources, technology and training, women can increase production, marketing and income for sustainable development.

163. * * *To realize fully equality between women and men in their contribution to the economy, active efforts are required for equal recognition and appreciation of the influence that the work, experience, knowledge and values of both women and men have in society.

164. In addressing the economic potential and independence of women, Governments and other actors should promote an active and visible policy of mainstreaming a gender perspective in all policies and programmes so that before decisions are taken, an analysis is made of the effects on women and men, respectively.

REVIEW QUESTIONS

1. Why are women more likely to be poor than men?
2. What role does the increasing integration of the global economy play in female poverty?
3. What specific types of difficulties do women confront as workers?
4. Which of the problems addressed in this document are more likely to be confronted by women in undeveloped regions?
5. Which are specific to developed regions?

LYUBOV SIROTA

FROM Chernobyl Poems

On the night of 25 April 1986, one of the reactors at the Chernobyl nuclear power station in the Soviet Ukraine exploded during a poorly implemented experiment, releasing a substantial amount of radiation and resulting in a partial meltdown of the reactor's core. The Soviet government initially attempted to keep news of this disaster from the public, but was later forced to acknowledge the magnitude of the incident. While the long-term effects of this serious nuclear accident remain to be seen, those living in the immediate vicinity of Chernobyl were exposed to substantial levels of radiation. Thirty-two people died immediately from massive radiation exposure, but many others in the general vicinity suffered from a variety of radiation-related illnesses. Thyroid cancer rates among the children in the region, for example, are abnormally high.

The thirty-thousand residents of Pripyat, the town closest to the Chernobyl plant, were not evacuated immediately, resulting in exposure to radiation and lingering illness. Lyubov Sirota, an employee of the Chernobyl Atomic Energy Station, was one of the few who actually saw the explosion on that April night. Both she and her son were eventually evacuated to Kiev, but they continue to suffer from the aftereffects of radiation exposure. The following poems by Sirota, from a collection of her poems on the Chernobyl accident, entitled Burden, *serves as a farewell to her home town.*

From "Chernobyl Poems" in *Burden,* Lyubov Sirota, translated by Leonid Levin and Elisavietta Ritchie, Chernobyl Poems Website, <http://www.wsu.edu:8080/˷brians/chernobyl_poems/chernobyl_poems.html>.

To Pripyat

1.

We can neither expiate nor rectify
the mistakes and misery of that April.
The bowed shoulders of a conscience awakened
must bear the burden of torment for life.
It's impossible, believe me,
to overpower
or overhaul
our pain for the lost home.
Pain will endure in the beating hearts
stamped by the memory of fear.
There,

surrounded by prickly bitterness,
our puzzled town asks:
since it loves us
and forgives everything,
why was it abandoned forever?

2.

At night, of course, our town
though emptied forever, comes to life.
There, our dreams wander like clouds,
illuminate windows with moonlight.
live by unwavering memories,
remember the touch of hands.
How bitter for them to know

there will be no one for their shade
to protect from the scorching heat!
At night their branches quietly rock
our inflamed dreams.
Stars thrust down
onto the pavement,
to stand guard until morning . . .
But the hour will pass . . .
Abandoned by dreams,
the orphaned houses
whose windows
have gone insane
will freeze and bid us farewell! . . .

3.
We've stood over our ashes;
now what do we take on our long journey?
The secret fear that wherever we go
we are superfluous?
The sense of loss
that revealed the essence
of a strange and sudden kinlessness,
showed that our calamity is not
shared by those who might, one day,
themselves face annihilation?
. . . We are doomed to be left behind by the
         flock
in the harshest of winters . . .
You, fly away!
But when you fly off
don't forget us, grounded in the field!
And no matter to what joyful faraway lands
your happy wings bear you,
may our charred wings
protect you from carelessness.

At the Crossing

A century of universal decay.
In cyclotrons nuclei are split;
souls are split,
sounds are split
insanely.

While behind a quiet fence
on a bench in someone's garden
Doom weighs
a century of separation
on the scales.

And her eyes are ancient,
and her palms are taut with nerves,
and her words clutch
in her throat . . .

Nearby and cynical, death
brandishes a hasty spade.
Here, whispers are worse than curses,
offer no consolation.

Yet out on the festive streets
the mixed chorus
of pedestrians and cars
never stops.
The stoplight
winks with greed,
gobbles the fates of those it meets
in the underground passageways
of eternity.

How long
the bureaucrats
babbled on
like crows
about universal good . . .
Yet somehow
that universal good
irreversibly
seeps away.
Have we slipped up?

In the suburbs, choke-cherries
came out with white flowers
like gamma fluorescence.
What is this—a plot by mysterious powers?
Are these intrigues?
We have slipped up!

Choke-cherries are minor.
They are not vegetables . . .

Here, tomatoes ripened too early:
someone just ate one—the ambulance
had to be called in a rush.
We have slipped up.

We came to the sea—
the eternal source of healing . . .
And—we were stunned.
The sea is an enormous waste dump.
What happened?
Have we slipped up?

How masterfully
the blind promoters
of gigantic plans
manipulated us so far!
Now the bitter payment
for what we so easily
overlooked yesterday.

Has day died?
Or is this the end of the world?
Morbid dew on pallid leaves.
By now it's unimportant
whose the fault,
what the reason,
the sky is boiling only with crows . . .
And now—no sounds, no smells.

And no more peace in this world.
Here, we loved . . .
Now, eternal separation
reigns on the burnt out Earth . . .

These dreams are dreamed
ever more often.
Ever more often I am sad for no reason,
when flocks of crows
circle over the city
in skies, smoky, alarmed . . .

REVIEW QUESTIONS

1. What do Lyubov Sirota's poems tell you about individual reactions to this sort of nuclear accident?
2. Why do you think Sirota chose to write about this experience in the form of poetry?
3. On the basis of your reading of these poems, how has the relationship between human beings and nature been transformed by Chernobyl and other ecological disasters?
4. What shared concerns appear in these poems and Mikhail Gorbachev's "restructuring" speech (chapter 29)?
5. In what ways might Sirota's poems be read as a critique of the Soviet system?

HOWARD H. FREDERICK

FROM Computer Networks and the Emergence of Global Civil Society: The Case of the Association for Progressive Communications

As the Chernobyl disaster demonstrates, the benefits of new technologies are some-times offset by substantial local and global risks. However, certain recent advances in communication technologies promise to greatly enhance the quality of human in-teraction, making it possible for the world's people to enter into far more intimate and informed relationships with one another than ever before. Dramatic increases in the ease and rapidity of information transfer—through the use of satellite transmis-sion and the "internet," an international computer network—now make it possible for people almost anywhere in the world to communicate freely with one another.

Certain autocratic regimes have sought to impose strict regulations on access to these new forms of communications, fearful that their citizens will be able to use fax machines and modems to circumvent the state's monopoly over the media. Even nations with a traditionally strong allegiance to the freedom of speech and the free-dom of the press have sought to place some restrictions on the free flow of informa-tion. In the United States, for example, the Computer Decency Act—recently overturned by the U.S. Supreme Court—was passed into law with the intent of limiting children's exposure to pornography. However, the potential benefits of the "information superhighway" are readily apparent, even to those who believe that it must be subject to a certain degree of government control. In 1992, Howard H. Frederick, of the Institute for Global Communications, presented a paper to the An-nual Conference of the Peace Studies Association, arguing that modern communica-tions technologies may have an important role to play in maintaining world peace.

From "Computer Networks and the Emergence of Global Civil Society: The Case of the Association for Progressive Communications (APC)," Howard H. Frederick, in *Globalizing Networks: Computers and International Communication*, edited by Linda Harasim and Jan Walls, Oxford University Press, 1997. Electronic Frontier Foundation Website, <http://www.eff.org/pub/Net culture/Global village/global civil soc networks.paper>.

*   *   *

What we call "community" used to be limited to face-to-face dialogue among people in the same physical space, a dialogue that reflected mutual concerns and a common culture. For thousands of years, people had little need for long-distance communication because they lived very close to one another. The medieval peasant's entire life was spent within a radius of no more than twenty-five miles from the place of birth. Even at the begin-ning of our century, the average person still lived in the countryside and knew of the world only through travelers' tales.

Today, of course, communications technologies have woven parts of the world together into an electronic web. No longer is community or dialogue restricted to a geographical place. With the advent of the fax machine, telephones, international publications, and computers, personal and professional relationships can be maintained irrespective of time and place. Communication relationships are no longer restricted to place, but are distributed through space. Today we are all members of many global "non-place" communities.

In the last decade there has emerged a new kind of global community, one that has increasingly become a force in international relations. We speak of the emergence of a global civil society, that part of our collective lives that is neither market nor government but is so often inundated by them. Still somewhat inarticulate and flexing its muscles, global civil society is best represented in the global "NGO Movement," nongovernmental organizations and citizens advocacy groups uniting to fight planetary problems whose scale confound local or even national solutions. Previously isolated from one another, nongovernmental organizations (NGOs) are flexing their muscles at the United Nations and other world forums as their power and capacity to communicate increase.

The concept of civil society arose with John Locke, the English philosopher and political theorist. It implied a defense of human society at the national level against the power of the state and the inequalities of the marketplace. For Locke, civil society was that part of civilization—from the family and the church to cultural life and education—that was outside of the control of government or market but was increasingly marginalized by them. Locke saw the importance of social movements to protect the public sphere from these commercial and governmental interests.

From the industrial age to the present, mercantilist and power-political interests pushed civil society to the edge. In most countries, civil society even lacked its own channels of media communication. It was speechless and powerless, isolated behind the artifice of national boundaries, rarely able to reach out and gain strength in contact with counterparts around the world. What we now call the "NGO Movement" began in the middle of the last century with a trickle of organizations and has now become a flood of activity. Nongovernmental organizations (NGOs) today encompass private citizens and national interest groups from all spheres of human endeavor. Their huge increase in number and power is due in no small measure to the development of globe-girdling communications technologies.

As Dutch social theorist Cees J. Hamelink has written, we are seeing a new phenomenon emerging on the world scene—global civil society, best articulated by the NGO movement. New communications technologies now facilitate communication among and between the world's national civil societies, especially within the fields of human rights, consumer protection, peace, gender equality, racial justice, and environmental protection.

* * *

The continued growth and influence of global civil society face two fundamental problems: increasing monopolization of global information and communication by transnational corporations; and the increasing disparities between the world's info-rich and info-poor populations. Global computer networking makes an electronic "end-run" around the first problem and provides an appropriate technological solution to overcome the second.

Hamelink observed that the very powers that obstructed civil society at the national level—markets and governments—also controlled most of the communication flows at the global level. Government monopolies still control a huge share of the world's air waves and telecommunications flows. Even worse, a handful of immense corporations now dominate the world's mass media. If present trends continue, [Ben] Bagdikian predicted, by the turn of the century "five to ten corporate giants will control most of the world's important newspapers, magazines, books, broadcast stations, movies, recordings and videocassettes." Telecommunications infrastructures and data networks must also be included in this gloomy account. Today's "lords of the global village" are huge corporations that "exert a homogenizing power over ideas, culture and commerce that affects populations larger than any in history. Neither Caesar nor Hitler, Franklin Roosevelt nor any Pope, has commanded as much power to shape the information on which so many people depend to make decisions about everything from whom to vote for to what to eat."

Why is this happening? The most fundamental reason is that fully integrated corporate control of media production and dissemination reaps vast profits and creates huge corporate empires. Already more than two-thirds of the U.S. work force is now engaged in information-related jobs. * * * While there are more than one hundred news agencies around the world, only five—Associated Press, United Press International, Reuters, Agence France Presse, and TASS—control about ninety-six percent of the world's news flows.* * *

In addition to transnational control of information, global civil society and the NGO movements confront the increasing gap between the world's info-rich and info-poor populations. In virtually every medium, the disparities are dramatic.

Ninety-five percent of all computers are in the developed countries.

While developing countries have three-quarters the world's population, they can manage only thirty percent of the world's newspaper output.

*   *   *

Only seventeen countries in the world had a Gross National Product larger than total U.S. advertising expenditures.

*   *   *

Ten developed countries, with 20 percent of the world's population, accounted for almost three-quarters of all telephone lines.* * *

Even within the United States we have the info-rich and the info-poor. From the streets of Manhattan to the barrios of Los Angeles, from the homeless to the immigrant populations, from Appalachia to the inner cities, there are millions upon millions of our fellow Americans who cannot read or type, do not have access to computers, do not consume newsprint, cannot afford a book.

*   *   *

To counter these twin trends that threaten to engulf civil society with a highly controlled form of commercialization, there has arisen a worldwide metanetwork of highly decentralized technologies—computers, fax machines, amateur radio, packet data satellites, VCRs, video cameras and the like. They are "decentralized" in the sense that they democratize information flow, break down hierarchies of power, and make communication from top and bottom just as easy as from horizon to horizon. For the first time in history, the forces of peace and environmental preservation have acquired the communication tools and intelligence gathering technologies previously the province of the military, government and transnational corporations.

*   *   *

[Association for Progressive Communication] members are fond of saying that they "dial locally and act globally."* * *

The APC Networks can now set up complete electronic mail and conferencing systems on small, inexpensive appropriate-technology microcomputers* * * Individual users typically make a local phone call to connect to their host machine, which stores up mail and conference postings until contacted by a partner computer in the network, typically about every two hours. Aside from its low cost, this technological configuration is appropriate for countries whose telecommunications infrastructure is still poor.

*   *   *

One user, let's say a peace researcher in Finland, uses her computer to dial into a local data network (analogous to the telephone network but for data traffic instead of voice). She either types in a message or "uploads" a prepared text, into her host computer, in this case, NordNet in Stockholm. Within a short time that message is transferred via high-speed modems through the telephone lines to the host system of her correspondent, a university peace studies professor in Hawaii. His host system is the PeaceNet computer in California. At his convenience, he connects to his host and "downloads" the message. This miraculous feat, near instantaneous communication across half the globe, costs each user only the price of a local phone call plus a small transmission charge.

Unlike systems used by the large commercial services, the APC Networks are highly decentralized and preserve local autonomy. One microcomputer serves a geographical region and is in turn connected with other "nodes."

*   *   *

The first large-scale impact of these decentralizing technologies on international politics happened in 1989. When the Chinese government massacred its citizens near Tianamen Square, Chinese students transmitted the most detailed, vivid reports instantly by fax, telephone and computer networks to activists throughout the world. They organized protests[,] meetings, fundraising, speaking tours and political appeals. Their impact was so immense and immediate that the Chinese government tried to cut telephone links to the exterior and started to monitor the Usenet computer conferences where much of this was taking place.

Another example is the 1991 Gulf War, where computer networks such as PeaceNet and its partner networks in the APC exploded with activity. While mainstream channels of communication were blocked by Pentagon censorship, the APC Networks were carrying accurate reports of the effects of the Gulf War on the Third World, Israel and the Arab countries and the worldwide antiwar movement.

*   *   *

During the attempted coup in the Soviet Union in August 1990, the APC partners used telephone circuits to circumvent official control. Normally, the outdated Russian telephone system requires hordes of operators to connect international calls by hand, and callers must compete fiercely for phone lines. But the APC partner networks found other routes for data flow.

*   *   *

Around the globe, other APC networks are working on issues of peace, social justice, and environmental protection. In Australia, the members of the Pegasus network are working to hook up the affluent 18 percent of the electorate that votes Green, which would make the party more powerful. Back in the United States, EcoNet is helping high school students monitor water quality in local rivers. One such experiment involved 50 students along the Rouge River in Michigan. When in 1991 neo-Nazi skinheads ransacked a Dresden neighborhood populated by foreigners, users of the German partner network ComLink posted news of the event. Soon Dresden newspapers were flooded with faxes from around the world deploring the action. All in all, tens of thousands of messages a day pass back and forth within the "APC village," and the number grows every day.

*   *   *

The partner networks of the Association for Progressive Communications have built a truly global network dedicated to the free and balanced flow of information. The APC Charter mandates its partners to serve people working toward "peace, the prevention of warfare, elimination of militarism, protection of the environment, furtherance of human rights and the rights of peoples, achievement of social and economic justice, elimination of poverty, promotion of sustainable and equitable development, advancement of participatory democracy, and nonviolent conflict resolution."

The APC Networks are trying to make an "end-run" around the information monopolies and to construct a truly alternative information infrastructure for the challenges that lie ahead. By providing a low-cost, appropriate solution for nongovernmental organizations and poor countries, they are attempting to civilize and democratize cyberspace.

We are moving into a "new world order." The age of democracy may have had its beginnings in the French and the American revolutions, but only today is it finally reaching the hearts and minds of sympathetic populations around the world. This "preferred" world order of democratic change depends heavily on the efficiency of communication systems.

*   *   *

REVIEW QUESTIONS

1. What is a "global civil society"?
2. How is it being created, according to Howard Frederick?
3. What might threaten its continued expansion and development?
4. In what ways does access to computer technologies reflect existing disparities between rich and poor nations?
5. How might the existence of a global information infrastructure undercut this division?
6. In what ways do new information and communications technologies lessen the importance of existing national borders?
7. What might be the benefits of the emergence of a global culture?
8. What dangers are there to an ever-increasing integration of the cultures of the world?